Communications in Computer and Information Science 827

More information about this series at http://www.springer.com/series/7899

Pushpak Bhattacharyya · Hanumat G. Sastry
Venkatadri Marriboyina · Rashmi Sharma (Eds.)

Smart and Innovative Trends in Next Generation Computing Technologies

Third International Conference, NGCT 2017
Dehradun, India, October 30–31, 2017
Revised Selected Papers, Part I

Editors
Pushpak Bhattacharyya
Indian Institute of Technology Patna
Patna, Bihar
India

Hanumat G. Sastry
University of Petroleum and Energy Studies
Dehradun
India

Venkatadri Marriboyina
University of Petroleum and Energy Studies
Dehradun
India

Rashmi Sharma
University of Petroleum and Energy Studies
Dehradun
India

ISSN 1865-0929 ISSN 1865-0937 (electronic)
Communications in Computer and Information Science
ISBN 978-981-10-8656-4 ISBN 978-981-10-8657-1 (eBook)
https://doi.org/10.1007/978-981-10-8657-1

Library of Congress Control Number: 2018944386

Printed on acid-free paper

This Springer imprint is published by the registered company Springer Nature Singapore Pte Ltd.
part of Springer Nature
The registered company address is: 152 Beach Road, #21-01/04 Gateway East, Singapore 189721, Singapore

Preface

These proceedings comprise the best research papers presented at the Third International Conference on Next-Generation Computing Technologies (NGCT 2017) organized by the School of Computer Science at the University of Petroleum and Energy Studies, Dehradun, India during October 30–31, 2017. The conference theme was "Smart and Innovative Trends for Next-Generation Computing" and all the tracks and sub-tracks focused on contemporary research in computing and information technology. NGCG 2017 offered a platform to researchers, experts, academics, and industry fellows to share and discuss their research findings with the aim of offering humans better daily living with the help of next-generation computing technologies. NGCT 2017 followed a strict peer-review process, with 135 top-quality papers being selected and presented out 948 submissions from various parts of the globe.

The present proceedings contain five parts, namely, "Smart and Innovative Trends in Computational Intelligence and Data Science," "Smart and Innovative Trends in Communication Protocols and Standards," "Smart and Innovative Trends in Image Processing and Machine Vision," "Smart and Innovative Trends in Security and Privacy," and "Smart and Innovative Trends in Natural Language Processing for Indian Languages."

We express our thanks to the university leaders, advisory and technical board members, keynote speakers, and Organizing Committee members. We extend our thanks to the conference sponsors IBM India, SERB-DST, DRDO, Springer, CSI, and IUPRAI.

April 2018

Pushpak Bhattacharyya
Hanumat G. Sastry
Venkatadri M.
Rashmi Sharma

Organization

Steering Committee

Chief Patron

S. J. Chopra	UPES, Dehradun, India

Patron(s)

Utpal Ghosh	UPES, Dehradun, India
Deependra Kumar Jha	UPES, Dehradun, India

Co-patron(s)

Kamal Bansal	UPES, Dehradun, India
Manish Prateek	UPES, Dehradun, India

General Chair

Pushpak Bhattacharyya	IIT, Patna, India

Honorary Chair(s)

Ajoy Kumar Ray	IIEST, Shibpur, India
Valentina E. Balas	Aurel Vlaicu University of Arad, Romania

Conference Chair

Hanumat G. Sastry	UPES, Dehradun, India

Conference Secretary

Venkatadri M.	UPES, Dehradun, India

Advisory Committee

William Stallings	Independent Consultant, USA
Sartaj Sahni	University of Florida, USA
Margaret Burnett	Oregon State University, USA
Luciana Salgado	Universidade Federal Fluminense, Brazil
Cristian Rodriguez Rivero	Universidad Nacional de Córdoba, Argentina
Ramachandran Venkatesan	Memorial University of Newfoundland, Canada
Vincenzo Piuri	The University of Milan, Italy
N. Subba Reddy	Gyeongsang National University, South Korea
Mohammed A. Aseeri	National Centre for Sensors and Defense Systems Technologies (NCSDST), Saudi Arabia

Ankur Mani	University of Minnesota, USA
Ajith Abraham	Machine Intelligence Research Labs (MIR Labs), Washington, USA
Ravi Muttineni	E2E INC, USA
Amit Cohen	Huawei Technologies, Israel
Kei Eguchi	Fukuoka Institute of Technology, Japan
Hussein A. Abbass	University of New South Wales, Australia
B. V. Babu	Graphic Era University, Dehradun, India
Vijay K. Vaishnavi	Georgia State University, USA
Arun K. Somani	Iowa State University, USA
Subramaniam Ganesan	Oakland University, USA
Jonathan Reichental	City of Palo Alto, USA
Kiran Thatikonda	Accenture, Houston, USA
Jerry Luftman	Global Institute for IT Management, USA
Dennis K. Peters	Memorial University, Canada
Durg Singh Chauhan	GLA University, Mathura, India
Paruchuri Gangadhar Rao	University of Science and Technology, Baridua, India
M. N. Hoda	BVICAM, New Delhi, India
C. V. D. Ramprasad	STPI, Hyderabad, India
Rajaneesh Aggarwal	STPI, Noida, India
C. S. R. Prabhu	NIC, Hyderabad, India
Prabir Kumar Das	STPI, Assam, India
Manisha Mohan	Tata Interactive, Mumbai, India
Sanjeev Asthana	I-Farm Venture Advisors Pvt. Ltd., Gurgaon, India
K. R. Murali Mohan	National Resources Data Management Systems, New Delhi, India
Pranay Chaudhuri	Heritage Institute of Technology, Kolkata, India
Nitin	JIIT, Noida, India
Niladri Chatterjee	IIT, New Delhi, India
Hemanatha Kumar	University of Mysore, India
Rajani Parthasarathy	Anna University, Chennai, India
Awadesh Kumar Singh	NIT, Kurukshetra, India
Himani Bansal	Jaypee Institute of Institute Technology, Noida, India
Suresh Gupta	Panipat Institute of Engineering and Technology, India
Vijayakumari Gunta	Jawaharlal Nehru Technological University, Hyderabad, India
Sipra Das Bit	IIEST Shibpur, Howrah, India
Jaya Sil	IIEST Shibpur, Howrah, India
K. Chandrasekaran	NIT, Surathkal, India
S. Sampath	Madras University, Chennai, India
Lokanatha C. Reddy	Dravidian University, Kuppam, India
M. L. Saikumar	Institute of Public Enterprise, Medchal, India
K. K. Shukla	I.I.T., Varanasi, India
Umapada Pal	Indian Statistical Institute, Calcutta, India
S. Muthukumar	Indian Institute of Information Technology, Srirangam, India

Pabitra Pal Choudhury	Indian Statistical Institute, Kolkata, India
Anirban Basu	CSI, India Council, Bangalore, India
Shekhar Sahasrabudh	ACM, India Council, Bangalore, India
Preeti Bajaj	IEEE, India Council, India
Akshaya Nayak	CSI, India Council, India
Sandhya Chintala	NASSCOM, Noida, India
Prosenjit Pal	Prophecy Sensorlytics, LLC, Bangalore, India
Hari Seetha	VIT University, Vellore, India
Jimson Mathew	IIT, Patna, India
R. Rajendra Prasath	Indian Institute of Information Technology, Chittoor, India
C. A. S. Murthy	C-DAC, Hyderabad, India
Kunwar Singh Vaisla	Uttarakhand Technical University, Dehradun, India
Vikram Bali	Panipat Institute of Engineering and Technology, Panipat, India
Jayraj Ugarkar	Infosys, Bangalore, India
Rajesh Khambayat	NITTR, Bhopal, India
Sanjay Sood	C-DAC, Mohali, India
Nikhil R. Pal	Indian Statistical Institute, Calcutta, India
Karunesh Arora	C-DAC, Noida, India
Sapna Poti	Kyungpook National University, NSDC, New Delhi, India
C. Rama Krishna	NITTTR, Chandigarh, India
Suman Bhattacharya	TCS, Bhubaneswar, India
V. S. K. Reddy	Malla Reddy College of Engineering and Technology, Medchal, India
Rathna G. N.	IISc, Bangalore, India
Rajesh Siddavatam	REVA University, Bangalore, India
Bhabatosh Chanda	Indian Statistical Institute, Kolkata, India
D. Vasumathi	Jawaharlal Nehru Technological University, Hyderabad, India
Vithal Madyalkar	IBM Innovation Center for Education, India
Ganesh Venkatesan	Elsevier, Chennai, India
Gopi Krishna Durbhaka	TCS Innovation and Transformation Group, Pune, India
Hema Gopal	TCS, India
E. Balagurusamy	EBG Foundation, Coimbatore, India
Yashavant P. Kanetkar	KICIT and KSIT, Nagpur, India
Ujjwal Maulik	Jadavpur University, India
Arindam Biswas	NSHM Knowledge Campus, Durgapur, India
Arindam Biswas	IIEST, Shibpur, India

Keynote Speakers

Pushpak Bhattacharyya	IIT Patna, India
Rajkumar Buyya	University of Melbourne, Australia
Valentina E. Balas	University 'AurelVlaicu', Arad, Romania
R. K. Shyamasundar	IIT Bombay, India

Technical Program Committee

Technical Program Chair(s)

Rashmi Sharma	UPES, Dehradun, India
Kamal Kumar	UPES, Dehradun, India
Sriparna Saha	IIT, Patna, India
Vinay Avasthi	UPES, Dehradun, India
Nitin	JIIIT, Noida, India

Editor(s)

Pushpak Bhattacharyya	IIT, Patna, India
Hanumat G. Sastry	UPES, Dehradun, India
Venkatadri M.	UPES, Dehradun, India
Rashmi Sharma	UPES, Dehradun, India

Members

William Stallings	Independent Consultant, USA
Sartaj Sahni	University of Florida, USA
Margaret Burnett	Oregon State University, USA
Luciana Salgado	Universidade Federal Fluminense, Brazil
Cristian Rodriguez Rivero	Universidad Nacional de Córdoba, Argentina
Ramachandran Venkatesan	Memorial University of Newfoundland, Canada
Vincenzo Piuri	The University of Milan, Italy
N. Subba Reddy	Gyeongsang National University, South Korea
Mohammed A. Aseeri	National Centre for Sensors and Defense Systems Technologies (NCSDST), Saudi Arabia
Ankur Mani	University of Minnesota, USA
Ajith Abraham	Machine Intelligence Research Labs (MIR Labs), Washington, USA
Ravi Muttineni	E2E INC, USA
Amit Cohen	Huawei Technologies, Israel
Kei Eguchi	Fukuoka Institute of Technology, Japan
Hussein A. Abbass	University of New South Wales, Australia
Vijay K. Vaishnavi	Georgia State University, USA
Arun K. Somani	Iowa State University, USA
Subramaniam Ganesan	Oakland University, USA
Jonathan Reichental	City of Palo Alto, USA
Kiran Thatikonda	Accenture, Houston, USA

Nikhil R. Pal	Indian Statistical Institute, Calcutta, India
Karunesh Arora	C-DAC, Noida, India
Sapna Poti	Kyungpook National University, NSDC, New Delhi, India
Suman Bhattacharya	TCS, Bhubaneswar, India
V. S. K. Reddy	Malla Reddy College of Engineering and Technology, Medchal, India
Rathna G. N.	IISc, Bangalore, India
Rajesh Siddavatam	REVA University, Bangalore, India
Bhabatosh Chanda	Indian Statistical Institute, Kolkata, India
D. Vasumathi	Jawaharlal Nehru Technological University, Hyderabad, India
Ganesh Venkatesan	Elsevier, Chennai, India
Gopi Krishna Durbhaka	TCS Innovation and Transformation Group, Pune, India
Hema Gopal	TCS, India
Brojo Kishore Mishra	C.V. Raman College of Engineering, Bhubaneswar, India
Souvik Pal	Elitte College of Engineering, Kolkata, India
Pooja Kamat	Symbiosis International University, Pune, India
Preeti Mulay	Symbiosis International University, Pune, India
Yogita Gigras	The Northcap University, Gurugram, India
Sudan Jha	Nepal Engineering College, Changunarayan, Nepal
Manjula Sanjay Koti	Dayananda Sagar Academy of Technology and Management Technical Campus, Bangalore, India
Bautu Elena	Ovidius University, Romania
K. Shashi Prabh	Shiv Nadar University, Dadri, India
Sunil Tekale	R&D Glenmark Generics Ltd., Mumbai, India
G. Sridevi	KL University, Guntur, India
Kiran Ravulakollu	Sharda University, Greater Noida, India
Zarinah Mohd Kasirun	University of Malaya, Malaysia
Akshaye Dhawan	Ursinus College, USA
M. S. Aswal	Gurukul Kangri University, Haridwar, India
Dilip Singh Sosodia	National Institute of Technology, Raipur, India
Atul Garg	Maharishi Markandeshwar University, Ambala, India
B. Surendiran	National Institute of Technology, Puducherry, India
Charu	Jaypee Institute of Information Technology, Noida, India
Vinay Nassa	South Point Technical Campus, Sonipat, India
Neeta Singh	Gautam Buddha University, Greater Noida, India
Sapna Gambhir	Maharishi Dayanand University, Rohtak, India
Deepti Mehrotra	Amity University, Noida, India
R. K. Yadav	JRE Group of Institution, Greater Noida, India

Gurpreet Singh	Giani Zail Singh Campus College of Engineering and Technology, Maharaja Ranjit Singh Punjab Technical University, Bathinda, India
Mangal Sain	Dongseo University, South Korea
Girish Kumar Sharma	Indraprastha University, New Delhi, India
Emmanuel Pilli	Malaviya National Institute of Technology, Jaipur, India
Himanshu Agarwal	Punjabi University, Patiala, India
Sarika Jain	Amity University, Noida, India
S. R. Balasundaram	National Institute of Technology, Trichy, India
Manu Sood	Himachal Pradesh University, Shimla, India
Sharad Saxena	Thapar University, Patiala, India
Anil Verma	Thapar University, Patiala, India
Asif Anwar Alig	Northern Border University, Arar, Saudi Arabia
Subodh Wairya	Uttar Pradesh Technical University, Lucknow, India
S. Mini	National Institute of Technology, Goa, India
Rabindra Jena	Institute of Management Technology, Nagpur, India
Ashutosh Gupta	MJP Rohilkhand University, Bareilly, India
Subodh Srivastava	Indian Institute of Technology, Varanasi, India
Shashidhar G. Koolagudi	National Institute of Technology, Surathkal, India
Shyamal Tanna	L. J. Institute of Engineering and Technology, Ahmedabad, India
Rambir Singh	Indraprastha Engineering College, Ghaziabad, India
Vinay Chavan	Seth Kesarimal Porwal College, Nagpur, India
Sujata Pandey	Amity University, Noida, India
Sridhar Vaithianathan	Institute of Management Technology, Hyderabad, India
Raman Chadha	Chandigarh Group of Colleges, Chandigarh, India
Rajeev Kumar	Jaypee University of Information Technology, Solan, India
Satish Chandra	Jaypee Institute of Information Technology, Noida, India
Zubair Ahmad Khattak	Iqra National University, Peshawar, Pakistan
Saru Dhir	Amity University, Noida, India
Kalpana Tiwari	Amity University, Noida, India
Paresh Virparia	S. P. University, Anand, India
Arputha Rathina	B. S. Abdur Rahman University, Vandalur, India
Promod Joshi	Amrapali Group of Institutes, Haldwani, India
Haribabu	BITS, Pilani, India
Rohit Khokher	Vidya College of Engineering, Meerut, India
Satish Chhokar	Rajkumar Garg Institute of Technology, Ghaziabad, India
Vinay Rishiwal	MJP Rohilkhand University, Bareilly, India
Inderjeet Kaur	Ajay Kumar Garg Engg College, Ghaziabad, India
Yashwant Singh	Jaypee University of Information Technology, Solan, India
M. Sandhya	B. S. Abdur Rahman University, Chennai, India

Tarun Gupta	Radha Govind Engineering College, Meerut, India
Satyanarayana Reddy	Cambridge Institute of Technology, Bangalore, India
Anil Kumar Dubey	Govt. Engineering College, Ajmer, India
Punyaban Patel	Mala Reddy Institute of Technology, Hyderabad, India
Hemant Sahu	Geetanjali Institute of Technical Studies, Udaipur, India
K. Ammulu	Dravidian University, Kuppam, India
Rajesh Mehta	Amity School of Engineering and Technology, New Delhi, India
B. V. Kiranmayee	VJIT, Nizampet, India
Manju Kaushik	JECRC University, Jaipur, India
Surendra Kumar Yadav	JECRC University, Jaipur, India
Naveen Hemrajani	JECRC University, Jaipur, India
Narendra Singh Yadav	JECRC University, Jaipur, India
S. Arvind	CMR Institute of Technology, Kundalahalli, India
T. Venu Gopal	JNTUH, Medak, India
D. Murali	MRCET, Hyderabad, India
Bhabatosh Chanda	ISI, Kolkata, India
Luciana Salgado	Universidade Federal Fluminense, Niterói, Brazil
Visvasuresh Victor Govindaswamy	Concordia University, Montréal, Canada
Phalguni Gupta	Indian Institute of Technology, Kanpur, India
Bimal Kumar Misra	BIT, Mesra, India
Hemraj Saini	Jaypee University of Information Technology, Waknaghat, India
Praveen Srivastava	Indian Institute of Management, Rohtak, India
Deepak Garg	Bennett University, Greater Noida, India
V. Singh Vr.	National Physical Laboratory, New Delhi, India
Mario Dantas	Universidade Federal De Santa Catarina, Trindade, Brazil
Maninder Singh	Thapar University, Patiala, India
Sunil Bhooshan	Jaypee University of Information Technology, Waknaghat, India
Prashant Deshmukh	Sipna College of Engineering and Technology, Amravati, India
Manoj Diwakar	Babasaheb Bhimrao Ambedkar University, Lucknow, India
Ashish Ghosh	ISI, Kolkata, India
Gagandeep Jagdev	Punjabi University, Damdama Sahib, India
Prasanta Jana	Indian Institute of Technology, Dhanbad, India
Brijendra Joshi	Military College of Telecommunication Engineering, Indore, India
Rajib Kar	National Institute of Technology, Durgapur, India
Rajeev Kumar	Teerthanker Mahaveer University, Moradabad, India
Durbadal Mandal	National Institute of Technology, Durgapur, India
Manas Patra	Berhampur University, Brahmapur, India

Jasbir Saini	DCR University of Science and Technology, Murthal, India
Abdus Samad	Aligarh Muslim University, Aligarh, India
Baldev Singh	VIT, Vellore, India
Harikesh Singh	Jaypee University of Engineering and Technology, Guna, India
Tarachand Amgoth	IDM, Dhanbad, India
Pallav Kumar Baruah	Sri Sathya Sai Institute of Higher Learning, Puttaparthi, India
Nagarajan Kathiresan	SIDRA Medical and Research Center, Qatar
Rajiv Pandey	Amity University, Lucknow, India
Fereshteh-Azadi Parand	Allameh Tabatabae'i University, Iran
Kanchana Rajaram	Anna University, Guindy, India
Diptendu Sinha Roy	National Institute Technology, Meghalaya, India
Shrikant Tiwari	Chhattisgarh Swami Vivekananda Technical University, Bhilai, India
Priyanka Tripathi	NITTTR, Bhopal, India
Ajay Pratap	Indian Institute of Technology, Patna, India
Xiao Zhang	Syracuse University, USA
Shashank Joshi	Bharti Vidyapeeth College of Engineering, Pune, India
Meenakshi Sood	Jaypee University of Information Technology, Solan, India
Rajeev Sharma	National Institute of Technology, Kurukshetra, India
Hiren Deva Sarma	Sikkim Manipal Institute of Technology, Rangpo, India
Satya Ghrera	Jaypee University of Information Technology, Solan, India
Arjun Singh	Manipal University, Jaipur, India
Sumit Srivastava	Manipal University, Jaipur, India
Manik Lal Das	DA-IICT, Gandhinagar, India
Sandeep Chaurasia	Manipal University, Jaipur, India
Vishnu Srivastava	CSIR CEERI, Chennai, India
Jyotirmoy Karjee	TCS Research and Innovation Lab, India
Arun Somani	Iowa State University, Iowa, USA
Chittaranjan Pradhan	Kiit University, Bhubaneswar, India
Bimal Roy	Indian Statistical Institute, Kolkata, India
Sangram Ray	National Institute of Technology, Sikkim, India
Vijay Bhasker Semwal	IIIT, Dharwad, India
Arun Mishra	Defence Institute of Advanced Technology, DRDO, Pune, India
Chhagan	University of Padova, Italy
Kharmega Sundararaj G.	PSN College of Engineering and Technology, Tirunelveli, India
Abhijit Das	CDAC, Silchar, India
Rajesh Bhat	IIIT Delhi, New Delhi, India
Preeti Gera	SGI, Gurgaon, India
Arvind Jain	RJIT, Tekanpur, India

Mantosh Biswas	National Institute of Technology, Kurukshetra, India
Srikanth	CDAC, Hyderabad, India
Shamanth Rai	Sahyadri College of Engineering and Management, Mangalore, India
Divya Rishi Sahu	SIRT, Bhopal, India
Raju Baraskar	RGPV, Bhopal, India
Rajeev Kumar Gupta	SISTec, Bhopal, India
Abhineet Anand	Galgotias University, Grater Noida, India
Indu Bhusan Lal	L. N. Mishra College of Business Management, Bihar, India
Manish Kumar	Vidya Vihar Institute of Technology, Bihar, India
Manish Saini	DCRUST, Haryana, India
Hitender Tyagi	Kurukshetra University, Kurukshetra, India
Seng Loke	Melbourne Burwood Campus, Deakin University, Burwood, Australia
Gang Li	Melbourne Burwood Campus, Deakin University, Australia
Ashok Kumar Saxena	Indian Institute of Technology, Roorkee, India
Rajdeep Chakraborty	Netaji Subhash Engineering College, Kolkata, India
Mahesh Kumar Porwal	Sree Chaitanya College of Engineering, Hyderabad, India
Gopalakrishnan T.	Bannari Amman Institute of Technology, Erode, India
J. Bhuvana	King Khalid University, Kingdom of Saudi Arabia
Shuchi Dave	Poornima College of Engineering, Jaipur, India
Harish Mittal	B.M. Institute of Engineering and Technology, Sonipat, India
Sonal Purohit	FMS-WISDOM Banasthali University, Banasthali, India
Nupur Srivastava	Poornima College of Engineering, Jaipur, India
Nidhi Mishra	Poornima College of Engineering, Jaipur, India
J. K. Deegwal	Government Engineering College, Ajmer, India
Ghanshyam Singh	Malaviya National Institute of Technology, Jaipur, India
Vipul H. Chudasama	Nirma University, Ahmedabad, India
Sathiyamoorthi	Sona College of Technology, Salem, India
Vrijendra Singh	Indian Institute of Information Technology, Allahabad, India
Rakesh Kumar Bansal	Maharaja Ranjit Singh Punjab Technical University, Bathinda, India
Savina Bansal	Maharaja Ranjit Singh Punjab Technical University, Bathinda, India
Saurabh Mukherjee	Banasthali Vidyapith, Jaipur, India
Arun Kumar Verma	MNIT, Jaipur, India
N. Narayanan Prasanth	National College of Engineering, Maruthakulam, India
Arvind Rehalia	Bharti Vidyapeeth, New Delhi, India

N. V. Ganapathi Raju	Gokaraju Rangaraju Institute of Engineering and Technology, Hyderabad, India
Anuradha Sharma	IIT, Delhi, India
J. A. Laxminarayana	Goa College of Engineering, India
Arun Kumar	Doon University, Dehradun, India
Arun Sharma	Indira Gandhi Delhi Technical University for Women, New Delhi, India
Chitra Ganesh Desai	Mit, Aurangabad, India
Sathyanarayana S. V.	JNN College of Engineering, Shimoga, India
H. N. Suresh	Bangalore Institute of Technology, India
Rinkle Rani	Thapar University, Patiala, India
Rashid Ali	Aligarh Muslim University, India
Angelina Geetha	B. S. Abdur Rahman University, Chennai, India
Natarajan Meghanathan	Jackson State University, USA
Sanjay Misra	Federal University of Technology, Nigeria
Majid Bakhtiari	University Technology Malaysia, Malaysia
Vigna Kumaran	Universiti Tenaga Nasional, Malaysia
K. Anitha Kumari	PSG College of Technology, Coimbatore, India
B. K. Sarkar	B.I.T., Mesra, India
T. Amudha	Bharathiar University, Coimbatore, India
Amandeep Singh Sappal	Punjabi University, Patiala, India
A. K. Mohapatra	Indira Gandhi Delhi Technical University for Women, New Delhi, India
Y. J. Nagendra Kumar	Gokaraju Rangaraju Institute of Engineering and Technology, Hyderabad, India
Om Prakash Sharma	Poornima College of Engineering, Jaipur, India
Rajesh Bodade	Military College of Telecommunication Engineering, Mhow, India
Lokesh Kumar Bansal	Skyline Institute of Engineering and Technology, Greater Noida, India
A. K. Verma	Thapar University, Patiala, India
Rahila Sheikh	Rajiv Gandhi College of Engineering Research and Technology, Chandrapur, India
Sarat Kr. Chettri	Assam Don Bosco University, Guwahati, India
Sagar Gulati	Technology Education and Research Integrated Institutions, Kurukshetra, India
Geeta Patil	Army Institute of Technology, Pune, India
P. M. Jat	DA-IICT, Gandhinagar, India
Anil Rajput	CSA Govt. PG Nodal College, Sehore, India
Gang Wang	Hefei University of Technology, China
Bharati Ainapure	MITCOE, Pune, India
Priyanka Sharma	Nirma University, Ahmedabad, India
Devendra Kumar Sharma	Meerut Institute of Engineering and Technology, Meerut, India
Geetali Banerji	Institute of Innovation in Technology and Management, New Delhi, India

Sanjeev Dewra	Shaheed Bhagat Singh State Technical Campus, Ferozepur, India
Hazman Yusoff	University Technology Mara Shah Alam, Selangor, Malaysia
Adel Alyan Fahmy	Nuclear Research Center, Atomic Energy Authority, Cairo, Egypt
Piyush Kumar Shukla	Rajiv Gandhi Technological University, Bhopal, India
Noor Elaiza Binti Abdul Khalid	University Technology Mara Shah Alam, Selangor, Malaysia
Rajni	Shaheed Bhagat Singh State Technical Campus, Ferozepur, India
Daya Gupta	Delhi Technological University, Delhi, India
Vandana Niranjan	IGDTUW, New Delhi, India
Jyotirmay Patel	MIET, Meerut, India
Soumen Bag	Indian Institute of Technology (Indian School of Mines), Dhanbad, India
Prabhat Verma	Harcourt Butler Technical University, Kanpur, India
Vitor Hugo Mendes Costa Carvalho	Polytechnic Institute of Cávado and Ave, Portugal
Pradeep Kumar	Maulana Azad National Urdu University, Gachibowli, India
Manoj Kumar Majumder	International Institute of Information Technology, Naya Raipur, India
Ram Shringar Rao	Indira Gandhi National Tribal University, Amarkantak, India
Surya Prakash	Indian Institute of Technology, Indore, India
Chandresh Kumar Chhatlani	Janardan Rai Nagar Rajasthan Vidyapeeth University, Udaipur, India
Satish Kumar Singh	Indian Institute of Information Technology, Allahabad, India
Ravi M Gulati	Veer Narmad South Gujarat University, Surat, India
Ajay Parikh	Gujarat Vidyapith, Ahmedabad, India
Vivek Jaglan	Amity University, Manesar, India
Jayant Umale	Pimpri Chinchwad College of Engineering, Pune, India
Shrivishal Tripathi	Indian Institute of Technology, Jodhpur, India
S. Ghosh	Galgotias University, Greater Noida, India
Manoj Kumar Gupta	KIET, Ghaziabad, India
Sajai Vir Singh	Jaypee Institute of Information Technology, Noida, India
Manoj Kumar Panda	G. B. Pant Engineering College, Garhwal, India
Dhaval R. Kathiriya	Anand Agricultural University, India
Nanhay Singh	Ambedkar Institute of Advanced Communication Technologies and Research, New Delhi, India
Pankaj Kumar	NIT, Rourkela, India
Vishal Nagar	Pranveer Singh Institute of Technology, Kanpur, India
Ashutosh Kumar Bhatt	Birla Institute of Applied Sciences, Nainital, India

Rajan Patel	Sankalchand Patel College of Engineering, Visnagar, India
Ankit Mundra	Manipal University, Jaipur, India
Raghvendra Kumar	LNCT Group of College, Jabalpur, India
Vithal Madyalkar	IBM Innovation Center for Education, India
Anita Sahoo	JSS Academy of Technical Education, Noida, India
Rama Challa	NITTTR, Chandigarh, India
Abishi Chowdhury	NITTTR, Bhopal, India
Shibendu Debbarma	Tripura University, Agartala, India
Suchi Johari	Jaypee University of Information Technology, Waknaghat, India
Sanjay Kumar	Pandit Ravishankar Shukla University, Raipur, India
Hari Mewara	Government Engineering College, Ajmer, India
Samaresh Mishra	KIIT University, Patia, India
Atul Sharma	Kurukshetra University, Kurukshetra, India
Vijander Singh	Amity University, Jaipur, India
Ankur Bist	KIET, Ghaziabad, India
Nguyen Cuong	Quang Nam University, Vietnam
Surinder Khurana	Central University of Punjab, Bathinda, India
Sanjaya Kumar Panda	Veer Surendra Sai University of Technology, Burla, India
Ashutosh Tripathi	Amity University, Jaipur, India
Mithun Mukherjee	Guangdong University of Petrochemical Technology, China
Vandita Singh	JEMTEC, G. Noida, India
Bhupendra Singh	CDAC, Noida, India
Pratiyush Guleria	NIELIT, DOEACC Society, India
Saiyedul Islam	BITS, Pilani, India
Rajat Saxena	Indian Institute of Technology, Indore, India
Debi Prasad Mishra	College of Engineering and Technology, Bhubaneswar, India
Suket Arora	Amritsar College of Engineering and Technology, Amritsar, India
Mohit Dua	National Institute of Technology, Kurukshetra, India
Ankit Jain	National Institute of Technology, Kurukshetra, India
Vijay Verma	National Institute of Technology, Kurukshetra, India
Sumit Yadav	Indira Gandhi Delhi Technical University for Women, New Delhi, India
Kaushlendra Pandey	Cental Institute of Technology, Kokrajhar, India
Bhawna Ahuja	Amity School of Engineering and Technology, New Delhi, India
Shaveta Tatwani	Amity School of Engineering and Technology, New Delhi, India
Gautam Kumar	Galgotias University, Grater Noida, India
Vishnu Pratap Patel	DRDO, Hyderabad, India
Priyank Jain	AVP, Barclays, Mumbai, India

Ashok Yadav	Amity School of Engineering and Technology, New Delhi, India
Mukul Kumar Yadav	DEITY, New Delhi, India
Neelam Choudhary	Suresh Gyan Vihar University, Jaipur, India
Deepak Agarwal	Poornima College of Engineering, Jaipur, India
Mayank Sharma	Poornima College of Engineering, Jaipur, India
Shakti Arora	Panipat Institute of Engineering and Technology, India
Rahul Hada	Criterion Networks, Bangalore, India
Neha Mathur	Poornima College of Engineering, Jaipur, India
Ashish Sharma	Maharaja Agrasen Institute of Technology, New Delhi, India
Anuj Aggarwal	KITM, Kurukshetra, India
Lalit B. Damahe	Yeshwantrao Chavan College of Engineering, Nagpur, India
Prashant Modi	U. V. Patel College of Engineering, Mehsana, India
Mukesh Kalla	SPSU, Udaipur, India
Debabrata Chowdhury	Kalyani Govt. Engineering College, Nadia, India
Nikita Chavan	G. H. Raisoni College of Engineering, Nagpur, India
Gurmeet Singh	KITM, Kurukshetra, India
Arun Malik	Lovely Professional University, Jalandhar, India
Kanwar Pal	G.L. Bajaj Institute of Technology and Management, Noida, India
Arvind Dhingra	Guru Nanak Dev Engineering College, Ludhiana, India
Arun Kumar M. V.	Bapuji Polytechnic, Davangere, India
Rajat Singh	Theem College of Engineering, Thane, India
Umesh L. Kulkarni	VIT Wadala, Vellore, India
Suhas Bhagate	D.K.T.E Society's Textile and Engineering Institute, Kolhapur, India
Aparajita Pandey	B.I.T., Mesra, India
Sanjeev Yadav	Govt. Women Engineering College, Ajmer, India
A. Sajeevram	VELS University, Chennai, India
Ashok Kumar	Govt. Women Engineering College, Ajmer, India
Supriya M.	Amrita School of Engineering, Bengaluru, India
G. Yogarajan	Mepco Schlenk Engineering College, Sivakasi, India
Swagata Paul	Techno India College of Technology, Kolkata, India
Rakesh Sharma	CRM Jat College, Hissar, India
Ashim Saha	National Institute of Technology, Agartala, India
Ashok Kumar	Ambala College of Engineering and Applied Research, Ambala, India
Arunvinodh C.	Al-Ameen Engineering College, Shoranur, India
Deepak Kumar	Panipat Institute of Engineering and Technology, India
Sandeep Singh Bindra	Panipat Institute of Engineering and Technology, India
Arun Rana	Panipat Institute of Engineering and Technology, India
Ashish Upadhyay	Alstom India, Bangalore, India
Ramkrishna Vadali	Pimpri Chinchwad College of Engineering, Pune, India
Ripon Patgiri	National Institute of Technology, Silchar, India

Neha Bajpai	CDAC, Noida, India
C. Radha Charan	JNT University, Hyderabad, India
Trupti Kodinariya	Government Engineering College, Rajkot, India
Deepa Abin	Pimpri Chinchwad College of Engineering, Pune, India
Dharmendra Gupta	Chameli Devi Group of Institution, Indore, India
Ashish Vashishth	KITM, Kurukshetra, India
Nihar Ranjan Roy	GD Goenka University, Gurgaon, India
Nandini Sharma	SRCEM, Palwal, India
Girish Paliwal	Amity University, Jaipur, India
Shrikant Ardhapurkar	Yeshwantrao Chavan College of Engineering, Nagpur, India
P. S. Bogawar	Priyadarshini College of Engineering, Nagpur, India
Nilesh Patel	JUET, Guna, India
Aditya Dev Mishra	Galgotias University, Greater Noida, India
Purnima Sharma	Mody University of Science and Technology, Lakshmangarh, India
Rohini G. Pise	Pimpri Chinchwad College of Engineering, Pune, India
Kalyani Pendke	Rajiv Gandhi College of Engineering, Nagpur, India
Chaitra D. Desai	REVA University, Bengaluru, India
Anita Thengade	MITCOE, Pune, India
Ahmed Mateen Buttar	University of Agriculture, Faisalabad, Pakistan
Archana Kadam	Pimpri Chinchwad College of Engineering, Pune, India
Rashmi Thakur	Thakur College of Engg and Technology, Mumbai, India
Vikram Singh	National Institute of Technology, Kurukshetra, India
Madhuri Sachin Wakode	Pune Institute of Computer Technology, Pune, India
Sumitra Purushottam Pundlik	MITCOE, Pune, India
Deepali Javale	MITCOE, Pune, India
H. R. Mhaske	Pimpri Chinchwad College of Engineering, Pune, India
Kranti Dive	MITCOE, Pune, India
Vimal Gupta	JSS Academy of Technical Education, Noida, India
S. Prakash	M.M.M. University of Technology, Gorakhpur, India
Manoj Kumar	Shri Mata Vaishno Devi University, Katra, India
Anagha Chaudhari	Pimpri Chinchwad College of Engineering, Pune, India
Sameer Saxena	Amity University, Jaipur, India
Xavier Arputha Rathina	B. S. Abdur Rahman University, Chennai, India
Ashok Kumar Sahoo	Sharda University, Greater Noida, India
Sangeetha B	PSG College of Technology, Coimbatore, India
Suman Saurabh	Sapient, New Delhi, India
I. Joe Louis Paul	SSN College of Engineering, Kalavakkam, India
Emmanuel Shubhakar Pilli	MNIT, Jaipur, India
Mahendra P. Dhore	Rashtrasant Tukadoji Maharaj Nagpur University Campus, India
R. V. Bidwe	PICT, Pune, India
Poulami Dutta	Techno India University, Kolkata, India

Anand Singh Gadwal	SIRT, Indore, India
Sirisha Velampalli	JNTU-K, Kakinada, India
Milan Goyal	Jaipur, India
Amit Andre	Vinsy, New Jersey, USA
Manisha Saini	G.D. Goenka University, Gurgaon, India
Manik Sharma	DAV University, Jalandhar, India
G. Suseendran	VELS University, Chennai, India
Tanupriya Choudhury	Amity University, Noida, India
Kamal Kumar Ranga	Delhi University, New Delhi, India
Aditya Patel	Relicmail Software Solution, Jabalpur, India
T. R. V. Anandharajan	Einstein College of Engineering, Tirunelveli, India
Navnish Goel	S. D. College of Engineering and Technology, Muzaffarnagar, India
Krishan Kant Singh Gautam	Shivaji College, Delhi, India
Sudhanshu Kumar Jha	National Institute of Technology Jamshedpur, Jamshedpur, India
Hariharan Ravi	St. Joseph's College of Commerce, Bangalore, India
Gopi Krishna Durbhaka	TCS, Pune, India
Kusum Yadav	University of Hail, Kingdom of Saudi Arabia
S. Balan	Government Arts College, Coimbatore, India
Jeevan Das Koli	Scientific Analysis Group, DRDO, New Delhi, India
Abdul Jabbar Shaikh Azad	Kasturi Shikshan Santha's Arts, Commerce and Science College, Pune, India
Rajarshi Bhatraju	IBM, Hyderabad, India
Hemant Gupta	Seven N India Pvt Ltd., Gurgaon, India
Rashmi Agrawal	Manav Rachna International University, Faridabad, India
Nisha Thakur	Armacell Pvt Ltd., Pune, India
Charu Sharma	IMS, Ghaziabad, India
Nilam Choudhary	VIT (East), Jaipur, India
Syed Abudhagir Umar	B. V. Raju Institute of Technology, Hyderabad, India
Shruti Mathur	JERC University, Jaipur, India
Shakti Ranjan	Emoksha, Chandigarh, India
Praveen Gupta	VIT East, Jaipur, India
K. M. Mehata	Hindustan University, Chennai, India
Chitra A. Dhawale	P. R. Pote College of Engineering and Management, Amravati, India
Anwesa Das	NFET, NSHM Knowledge Campus, Durgapur, India
Ajay Prasad	University of Petroleum and Energy Studies, Dehradun, India
Abhijit Kumar	University of Petroleum and Energy Studies, Dehradun, India
Inder Singh	University of Petroleum and Energy Studies, Dehradun, India
Kingshuk Srivastava	University of Petroleum and Energy Studies, Dehradun, India

Hitesh Kumar Sharma	University of Petroleum and Energy Studies, Dehradun, India
Madhushi Verma	University of Petroleum and Energy Studies, Dehradun, India
J. C. Patni	University of Petroleum and Energy Studies, Dehradun, India
Ankur Dumka	University of Petroleum and Energy Studies, Dehradun, India
Ved Prakash	University of Petroleum and Energy Studies, Dehradun, India
Monit Kapoor	University of Petroleum and Energy Studies, Dehradun, India
Rajeev Tiwari	University of Petroleum and Energy Studies, Dehradun, India
Neeraj Chugh	University of Petroleum and Energy Studies, Dehradun, India
Amitava Choudhury	University of Petroleum and Energy Studies, Dehradun, India
Susheela Dahiya	University of Petroleum and Energy Studies, Dehradun, India
B. Surekha	K.S. Institute of Technology, Bangalore, India
Neha Gulati	University Business School, Panjab University, Chandigarh, India
Pooja Jain	S.V.V.V. University, Indore, India
Bright Keswani	Suresh Gyan Vihar University, Jaipur, India
Sumitra Pundlik	M.I.T.COE, Pune, India
Amit Banerjee	Innovative Photonics Evolution Research Center, Shizuoka, Japan
S. Palaniyappan	TRP Engineering College, Tiruchirappalli, India
Neetu Mishra	IIIT, Allahabad, India
Akhilesh Kumar Sharma	Manipal University, Jaipur, India
Mohd Vasim Ahamad	University Women's Polytechnic, Aligarh, India
Atul M. Gonsai	Saurashtra University, Rajkot, India
Siddharth S. Rautaray	KIIT University, Bhubaneswar, India
Praveen Kumar	Amity School of Engineering and Technology, Noida, India
Manisha Rathee	NIT, New Delhi, India
Venkatesh Gauri Shankar	Manipal University, Jaipur, India
Ujjwal Maulik	Jadavpur University, India
Arvind Kumar	Government College, Solan, India
Swati Gupta	Panipat Institute of Engineering and Technology, Panipat, India
Narendra Kohli	Harcourt Butler Technical University, Kanpur, India
Ambika Annavarapu	Kakatiya Institute of Institute and Sciences, Warangal, India
Prachi Gupta	ICFAI University, Dehradun, India

Nitish Mittal	Noon.com, Dubai, UAE
Kannimuthu	Karpagam College of Engineering, Coimbatore, India
Pranjal Bogawar	R.T.M. Nagpur University, Nagpur, India
Wenjun Hu	Palo Alto Networks, Santa Clara, USA
Kalavathi P.	Gandhigram Rural Institute - Deemed University, Dindigul, India
Ashutosh Kumar Bhatt	Birla Institute of Applied Sciences, Bhimtal, India
Furkan Ahmad	AMU, Aligarh, India
Rajeev Gupta	Maharishi Markandeshwar University, Mullana (Ambala), India
Krishna Kumar Singh	RGUKT Nuzvid, India
E. Golden Julie	Anna University Tirunelveli, India
Chandra Kanta Samal	Delhi University, New Delhi, India
Neha Verma	VIPS, Affiliated to Guru Gobind Singh Indraprastha University, Delhi, India
Varsha Garg	Jaypee Institute of Information Technology, Noida, India
Mala Kalra	NITTTR, Chandigarh, India
Kumar Anurupam	Rgukt-Iiit, Nuzvid, India
Arputha Rathina	B. S. Abdur Rahman Crescent University, Chennai, India
R. China Appala Naidu	St. Martin's Engineering College, Hyderabad, India

Organizing Committee

Convener(s)

Hanumat G. Sastry	UPES, Dehradun, India
Venkatadri M.	UPES, Dehradun, India

Publication Chair(s)

Neelu Jyoti Ahuja	UPES, Dehradun, India
Raghvendra Kumar	LNCT Group, India
Hitesh Kumar Sharma	UPES, Dehradun, India

Web Master

Ravi Tomar	UPES, Dehradun, India

Joint Secretary(s)

Sunil Kumar	UPES, Dehradun, India
Ankit Khare	UPES, Dehradun, India

Technical Program Sub-Committee

Sumit Kumar	UPES, Dehradun, India
P. Srikanth	UPES, Dehradun, India
Aradhana Singh	UPES, Dehradun, India
Amitava Chowdary	UPES, Dehradun, India
Sunil Kumar	UPES, Dehradun, India
Ankit Khare	UPES, Dehradun, India

Members

Anurag Jain	UPES, Dehradun, India
J. C. Patni	UPES, Dehradun, India
Kingshuk Srivastava	UPES, Dehradun, India
Nilima Salankar Fulmare	UPES, Dehradun, India
Rajeev Tiwari	UPES, Dehradun, India
Shamik Tiwari	UPES, Dehradun, India
Susheela Dahiya	UPES, Dehradun, India
Tanmay Bhowmik	UPES, Dehradun, India
Abhijeet Kumar	UPES, Dehradun, India
Abhijit Kumar	UPES, Dehradun, India
Alok Jhaldiyal	UPES, Dehradun, India
Amitava Chaudhary	UPES, Dehradun, India
Ankit Vishanoi	UPES, Dehradun, India
Bhagwant Singh	UPES, Dehradun, India
Deepak Sharma	UPES, Dehradun, India
Gagan Deep Singh	UPES, Dehradun, India
Harvinder Singh	UPES, Dehradun, India
Neeraj Chugh	UPES, Dehradun, India
Nitin Arora	UPES, Dehradun, India
P. Srikant	UPES, Dehradun, India
Prashant Rawat	UPES, Dehradun, India
Sandeep Partap	UPES, Dehradun, India
Sandip Kumar Chaurasiya	UPES, Dehradun, India
Saurabh Jain	UPES, Dehradun, India
Saurabh Shanu	UPES, Dehradun, India
Vishwas Rathi	UPES, Dehradun, India
Varun Sapra	UPES, Dehradun, India
Ambika Agarwal	UPES, Dehradun, India
Anushree	UPES, Dehradun, India
Apurva Gupta	UPES, Dehradun, India
Aradhana Singh	UPES, Dehradun, India
Kalpana Rangra	UPES, Dehradun, India
Niharika Singh	UPES, Dehradun, India
Prerna Pandey	UPES, Dehradun, India
Richa Chaudhary	UPES, Dehradun, India

Roohi Sille	UPES, Dehradun, India
Ruchika Saini	UPES, Dehradun, India
Sachi Chaudhary	UPES, Dehradun, India
Shahina Anwarul	UPES, Dehradun, India
Sheetal Bisht	UPES, Dehradun, India
Shelly	UPES, Dehradun, India
Dhiviya Rose	UPES, Dehradun, India

Contents – Part I

Smart and Innovative Trends in Computational Intelligence and Data Science

Recommender System Based on Fuzzy C-Means 3
Priya Gupta, Aradhya Neeraj Mathur, Kriti Kathuria, Rishabh Chandak, and Satyam Sangal

A Noval Approach to Measure the Semantic Similarity for Information Retrieval 19
Shelly and Mamta Kathuria

Comparative Analysis of Metaheuristics Based Load Balancing Optimization in Cloud Environment 30
Amanpreet Kaur, Bikrampal Kaur, and Dheerendra Singh

Twitter Recommendation and Interest of User Using Convolutional Neural Network 47
Baljeet Kaur Nagra, Bharti Chhabra, and Amit Verma

Classification of Hyperspectral Imagery Using Random Forest 66
Diwaker Mourya and Ashutosh Bhatt

A Model for Resource Constraint Project Scheduling Problem Using Quantum Inspired PSO 75
Reya Sharma, Rashika Bangroo, Manoj Kumar, and Neetesh Kumar

Detection and Estimation of 2-D Brain Tumor Size Using Fuzzy C-Means Clustering 88
Rahul Chauhan, Surbhi Negi, and Subhi Jain

A Computational Approach for Designing Tiger Corridors in India 97
Saurabh Shanu and Sudeepto Bhattacharya

Enhanced Task Scheduling Algorithm Using Multi-objective Function for Cloud Computing Framework 110
Abhikriti Narwal and Sunita Dhingra

Descriptive, Dynamic and Hybrid Classification Algorithm to Classify Engineering Students' Sentiments 122
Mitali Desai and Mayuri A. Mehta

Comparison of Runtime Performance Optimization Using Template-Metaprogramming 139
Vivek Patel, Piyush Mishra, J. C. Patni, and Parul Mittal

Comparative Performance Analysis of PMSM Drive Using ANFIS and MPSO Techniques 148
Deepti Yadav and Arunima Verma

Developing the Hybrid Multi Criteria Decision Making Approach for Green Supplier Evaluation. 162
Muhammad Nouman Shafique

A Quadratic Model for the Kurtosis of Decay Centrality 176
Natarajan Meghanathan

Development of an Automated Water Quality Classification Model for the River Ganga. 190
Anil Kumar Bisht, Ravendra Singh, Ashutosh Bhatt, and Rakesh Bhutiani

A Data Mining Approach Towards HealthCare Recommender System. 199
Mugdha Sharma and Laxmi Ahuja

Root Table: Dynamic Indexing Scheme for Access Protection in e-Healthcare Cloud 211
M. B. Smithamol and Rajeswari Sridhar

Efficient Artificial Bee Colony Optimization. 228
Ankita Rajawat, Nirmala Sharma, and Harish Sharma

Gaussian Scale Factor Based Differential Evolution. 246
Rashmi Agarwal, Harish Sharma, and Nirmala Sharma

An Efficient Parallel Approach for Mapping Finite Binomial Series (Special Cases) on Bi Swapped Network Mesh. 263
Ashish Gupta and Bikash Kanti Sarkar

Parallel Multiplication of Big Integer on GPU 276
Jitendra V. Tembhurne

Multi Objective Task Scheduling Algorithm for Cloud Computing Using Whale Optimization Technique 286
G. Narendrababu Reddy and S. Phani Kumar

Multilayered Feedforward Neural Network (MLFNN) Architecture as Bidirectional Associative Memory (BAM) for Pattern Storage and Recall. . . . 298
Manisha Singh and Thipendra Pal Singh

Critical Success Factors and Critical Barriers for Application of Information Technology to Knowledge Management/Experience Management for Software Process Improvement – Findings from Literary Studies 310
Mitali Chugh and Nitin

Traffic Prediction Using Viterbi Algorithm in Machine Learning Approach . . . 323
D. Suvitha, M. Vijayalakshmi, and P. M. Mohideen Sameer

Application of Grey Wolf Optimizer for Optimization of Fractional Order Controllers for a Non-monotonic Phase System 334
Santosh Kumar Verma and Shyam Krishna Nagar

Forecasting Hydrogen Fuel Requirement for Highly Populated Countries Using NARnet 349
Srikanta Kumar Mohapatra, Tripti Swarnkar, Sushanta Kumar Kamilla, and Susanta Kumar Mohapatra

Automatic Diagnosis of Dental Diseases 363
Punal M. Arabi, T. S. Naveen, N. Vamsha Deepa, and Deepak Samanta

Ensemble Algorithms for Islanding Detection in Smart Grids 376
Rubi Pandey and Damanjeet Kaur

An Analytical Approach for the Determination of Chemotherapeutic Drug Application Trade-Offs in Leukemia 390
Probir Kumar Dhar, Tarun Kanti Naskar, and Durjoy Majumder

Term Co-occurrence Based Feature Selection for Sentiment Classification . . . 405
Sudarshan S. Sonawane and Satish R. Kolhe

A Classification Approach for Monitoring and Locating Leakages in a Smart Water Distribution Framework 418
Shailesh Porwal, Mahak Vijay, S. C. Jain, and B. A. Botre

Chlorine Decay Modelling in Water Distribution System Case Study: CEERI Network 430
Mahak Vijay, Shailesh Porwal, S. C. Jain, and B. A. Botre

Estimation of Link Margin for Performance Analysis of FSO Network 444
Kappala Vinod Kiran, Vikram Kumar, Ashok Kumar Turuk, and Santos Kumar Das

Web Documents Prioritization Using Iterative Improvement 459
Kamika Chaudhary, Neena Gupta, and Santosh Kumar

On Lagrangian Twin Parametric-Margin Support Vector Machine 474
Parashjyoti Borah and Deepak Gupta

Artificial Neural Network and Response Surface Methodology Modelling of Surface Tension of 1-Butyl-3-methylimidazolium Bromide Solution 488
Divya P. Soman, P. Kalaichelvi, and T. K. Radhakrishnan

Optimized Food Recognition System for Diabetic Patients 504
B. Anusha, S. Sabena, and L. Sairamesh

Distributional Semantic Phrase Clustering and Conceptualization Using Probabilistic Knowledgebase 526
V. S. Anoop and S. Asharaf

Pong Game Optimization Using Policy Gradient Algorithm 535
Aditya Singh and Vishal Gupta

Forensics Data Analysis for Behavioral Pattern with Cognitive Predictive Task 549
S. Mahaboob Hussain, Prathyusha Kanakam, D. Suryanarayana, and Sumit Gupta

Enhancing Personalized Learning with Interactive Note Taking on Video Lectures–An Analysis of Effective HCI Design on Learning Outcome 558
Suman Deb and Paritosh Bhattacharya

Intelligent Data Placement in Heterogeneous Hadoop Cluster 568
Subhendu Sekhar Paik, Rajat Subhra Goswami, D. S. Roy, and K. Hemant Reddy

Effective Heuristics for the Bi-objective Euclidean Bounded Diameter Minimum Spanning Tree Problem 580
V. Prem Prakash, C. Patvardhan, and Anand Srivastav

Analysis of Least Mean Square and Recursive Least Squared Adaptive Filter Algorithm for Speech Enhancement Application 590
Mrinal Bachute and R. D. Kharadkar

A Novel Statistical Pre-processing Based Spatial Anomaly Detection Model on Cyclone Dataset 605
Lakshmi Prasanthi Malyala and Nandam Sambasiva Rao

Mathematical Modeling of Economic Order Quantity in a Fuzzy Inventory Problem Under Shortages 617
P. K. De, A. C. Paul, and Mitali Debnath

Dynamic Processing and Analysis of Continuous Streaming Stock Market Data Using MBCQ Tree Approach 623
M. Ananthi and M. R. Sumalatha

Energy Consumption Forecast Using Demographic Data Approach with Canaanland as Case Study 641
Oluwaseun Aderemi, Sanjay Misra, and Ravin Ahuja

A Cloud-Based Intelligent Toll Collection System for Smart Cities 653
Segun I. Popoola, Oluwafunso A. Popoola, Adeniran I. Oluwaranti, Aderemi A. Atayero, Joke A. Badejo, and Sanjay Misra

An Announcer Based Bully Election Leader Algorithm in Distributed Environment 664
Minhaj Khan, Neha Agarwal, Saurabh Jaiswal, and Jeeshan Ahmad Khan

Deep Learning Based Adaptive Linear Collaborative Discriminant Regression Classification for Face Recognition 675
K. Shailaja and B. Anuradha

A Novel Clustering Algorithm for Leveraging Data Quality in Wireless Sensor Network 687
B. Prathiba, K. Jaya Sankar, and V. Sumalatha

Smart and Innovative Trends in Natural Language Processing

Development of a Micro Hindi Opinion WordNet and Aligning with Hown Ontology for Automatic Recognition of Opinion Words from Hindi Documents 697
D. Teja Santosh, Vikram Sunil Bajaj, and Varun Sunil Bajaj

Evaluation and Analysis of Word Embedding Vectors of English Text Using Deep Learning Technique 709
Jaspreet Singh, Gurvinder Singh, Rajinder Singh, and Prithvipal Singh

POS Tagging of Hindi Language Using Hybrid Approach 723
Nidhi Mishra and Simpal Jain

Prosody Detection from Text Using Aggregative Linguistic Features 736
Vaibhavi Rajendran and G. Bharadwaja Kumar

Deep Neural Network Based Recognition and Classification of Bengali Phonemes: A Case Study of Bengali Unconstrained Speech 750
Tanmay Bhowmik, Amitava Choudhury, and Shyamal Kumar Das Mandal

Do Heavy and Superheavy Syllables Always Bear Prominence in Hindi? 761
Somnath Roy and Bimrisha Mali

Design and Development of a Dictionary Based Stemmer for Marathi Language 769
Harshali B. Patil, Neelima T. Mhaske, and Ajay S. Patil

Deep Convolutional Neural Network for Handwritten Tamil Character Recognition Using Principal Component Analysis 778
M. Sornam and C. Vishnu Priya

Neural Machine Translation System for Indic Languages Using Deep Neural Architecture 788
Parth Shah, Vishvajit Bakarola, and Supriya Pati

Author Index 797

Contents – Part II

Smart and Innovative Trends in Communication Protocols and Standards

IEEMARP: Improvised Energy Efficient Multipath Ant Colony Optimization (ACO) Routing Protocol for Wireless Sensor Networks 3
Anand Nayyar and Rajeshwar Singh

Locating Real Time Faults in Modern Metro Train Tracks Using Wireless Sensor Network 25
Nitya Komalan and Aarti Chauhan

A Sugeno-Mamdani Fuzzy System Based Soft Computing Approach Towards Sensor Node Localization with Optimization 40
Abhishek Kumar and Bhawana Saini

Interference Aware Adaptive Transmission Power Control Algorithm for Zigbee Wireless Networks 56
K. Vikram and Sarat Kumar Sahoo

Controlled Replication Based Bubble Rap Routing Algorithm in Delay Tolerant Network 70
Sweta Jain and Pavan Yadav

Plasmonics for THz Applications: Design of Graphene Square Patch Antenna Tested with Different Substrates for THz Applications 88
Manisha Khulbe, Malay Ranjan Tripathy, and Harish Parthasarathy

Sparse Channel Estimation Based on Compressive Sensing with Overcomplete Dictionaries in OFDM Communication Systems 99
Yi Zhang, Ramachandran Venkatesan, Octavia A. Dobre, and Cheng Li

Gesture Supporting Smart Notice Board Using Augmented Reality 112
P. Selvi Rajendran

Non-live Task Migration Approach for Scheduling in Cloud Based Applications 124
Neelam Panwar, Sarita Negi, and Man Mohan Singh Rauthan

Enhanced Secure Transmission of Data in Wireless Body Area Network for Health Care Applications 138
Sumit Kumar, Anurag Singh Tomar, and Sandip K. Chaurasiya

Reliable Vertical Handoff Technique Based on Probabilistic Classification Model 146
C. S. Jayasheela and Gowrishankar

Optical Wireless Systems with DPSK and Manchester Coding 155
Jagana Bihari Padhy and Bijayananda Patnaik

CAMQU: A Cloudlet Allocation Strategy Using Multilevel Queue and User Factor 168
Vinayak Bajoria and Avita Katal

Performance Analysis of Hybrid CPU Scheduling Algorithm in Multi-tasking Environment 183
Harvinder Singh, Sachin Kumar Sarin, Arushi Patel, and Supriya Sen

Location and Energy Based Hierarchical Dynamic Key Management Protocol for Wireless Sensor Networks 198
S. Christalin Nelson and J. Dhiviya Rose

Performance Evaluation of RPL Routing Protocol for IoT Based Power Distribution Network 212
Rijo Jackson Tom and Suresh Sankaranarayanan

Throughput and Energy Efficiency Analysis of the IEEE 802.11ah Restricted Access Window Mechanism 227
Miriyala Mahesh and V. P. Harigovindan

Underwater Navigation Systems for Autonomous Underwater Vehicle 238
Sachi Choudhary, Rashmi Sharma, Amit Kumar Mondal, and Vindhya Devalla

Fast and Efficient Data Acquisition in Radiation Affected Large WSN by Predicting Transfaulty Nodes. 246
Manish Pandey, Sachin Dhanoriya, and Amit Bhagat

An Energy Efficient Clustering Algorithm for Increasing Lifespan of Heterogeneous Wireless Sensor Networks 263
Manish Pandey, Lalit Kumar Vishwakarma, and Amit Bhagat

Analysis of Heterogeneity Characteristics for Heterogeneous WSNs 278
Sukhwinder Sharma, Rakesh Kumar Bansal, and Savina Bansal

Performance Evaluation of Adaptive Telemetry Acoustic Modem for Underwater Wireless Sensor Networks 291
Hareesh Kumar, Y. N. Nirmala, and M. N. Sreerangaraju

Chain Assisted Tree Based Self-healing Protocol for Topology Managed WSNs 305
Shivangi Katiyar and Devendra Prasad

Smart and Innovative Trends in Security and Privacy

Isotropic Pore Detection Algorithm for Level 3 Feature Extraction 323
Subiya Zaidi, Shrish Kumar Singh, and Sandhya Tarar

An SQL Injection Defensive Mechanism Using Reverse Insertion Technique 335
Shaji N. Raj and Elizabeth Sherly

Study and Proposal of Probabilistic Model for SIP Server Overload Control 347
Atul Mishra

A Novel Approach to Detect and Mitigate Cache Side Channel Attack in Cloud Environment 361
Bharati S. Ainapure, Deven Shah, and A. Ananda Rao

Normalized Scores for Routes in MANET to Analyze and Detect Collaborative Blackhole Attack 371
Abhishek Bajpai and Shivangi Nigam

Light Weight Two-Factor Authentication Using Hybrid PUF and FSM for SOC FPGA 381
J. Kokila, Manjith Baby Chellam, Arjun Murali Das, and N. Ramasubramanian

A Simple, Secure and Time Efficient Multi-way Rotational Permutation and Diffusion Based Image Encryption by Using Multiple 1-D Chaotic Maps 396
K. Abhimanyu Kumar Patro, Ayushi Banerjee, and Bibhudendra Acharya

Design and Development of a Cloud Assisted Robot 419
Rajesh Singh, Anita Gehlot, Mamta Mittal, Rohit Samkaria, Devendra Singh, and Prakash Chandra

Adaptive Dynamic Partial Reconfigurable Security System 430
B. C. Manjith, J. Kokila, and Ramasubramanian Natarajan

Fuzzy Entropy Based Feature Selection for Website User Classification in EDoS Defense 440
Sukhada Bhingarkar and Deven Shah

Spark Based ANFIS Approach for Anomaly Detection Using Big Data 450
Thakur Santosh and Dharavath Ramesh

Data Privacy in Hadoop Using Anonymization and T-Closeness 459
Praveen Kaushik and Varsha Dipak Tayde

An Eagle-Eye View of Recent Digital Image Forgery Detection Methods. . . . 469
Savita Walia and Krishan Kumar

Quantum IDS for Mitigation of DDoS Attacks by Mirai Botnets. 488
Yagnesh Balasubramanian, Durga Shankar Baggam, Swaminathan Venkatraman, and V. Ramaswamy

Smishing-Classifier: A Novel Framework for Detection of Smishing Attack in Mobile Environment 502
Diksha Goel and Ankit Kumar Jain

Cluster Based Mechanism for Avoidance of Duplicate Tag Data in RFID Networks. 513
S. Bagirathi, Sharmila Sankar, and Sandhya

A Secure and Flexible One Way Hash Function for Data Integrity Verification in Cloud Computing Environment 526
Meena Kumari and Rajender Nath

Analyzing Threats of IoT Networks Using SDN Based Intrusion Detection System (SDIoT-IDS) 536
Azka Wani and S. Revathi

An Enhanced and Secured RSA Public Key Cryptosystem Algorithm Using Chinese Remainder Theorem. 543
Vinod Kumar, Rajendra Kumar, and S. K. Pandey

A Comparative Analysis of Various Segmentation Techniques on Dental Images 555
Prerna Singh and Priti Sehgal

Inferring Trust from Message Features Using Linear Regression and Support Vector Machines. 577
Shifaa Basharat and Manzoor Ahmad

Smart and Innovative Trends in Image Processing and Machine Vision

Improved Reversible Data Embedding in Medical Images Using I-IWT and Pairwise Pixel Difference Expansion 601
R. Geetha and S. Geetha

Fusion Based Image Retrieval Using Local and Global Descriptor 612
Akshata V. Shendre, Lalit B. Damahe, and Nileshsingh V. Thakur

V-HOG: Towards Modified Query Based Image Retrieval 628
Ruchi D. Sharma, Lalit B. Damahe, and Nileshsingh V. Thakur

A Hybrid Feature Extraction Approach for Finding Local Discriminative Coordinates for Face Recognition 640
Abhisek Gour

Vision-Based Gender Recognition Using Hybrid Background Subtraction Technique 651
Gourav Takhar, Chandra Prakash, Namita Mittal, and Rajesh Kumar

Content Based Medical Image Retrieval System (CBMIRS) to Diagnose Hepatobiliary Images 663
Manoj Kumar and Kh. Manglem Singh

Robust Global Gradient Thresholds Estimation in Anisotropic Diffusion for Image Restoration Using DE 677
Nagaraj Bhat, U. Eranna, and Manoj Kumar Singh

An AHP Based Automated Approach for Pole-like Objects Detection Using Three Dimensional Terrestrial Laser Scanner Data 692
Arshad Husain and R. C. Vaishya

Human Identification by Gait Using Fourier Descriptor and Angle-Based Pseudo Anatomical Landmark Model 704
Mridul Ghosh and Debotosh Bhattacharjee

Acute Myeloid Leukemia Detection in WBC Cell Based on ICA Feature Extraction 722
Jasvir Kaur, Isha Vats, and Amit Verma

Optimizing Rice Plant Diseases Recognition in Image Processing and Decision Tree Based Model 733
Toran Verma and Sipi Dubey

Real Time Hand Gesture Recognition Using Histogram of Oriented Gradient with Support Vector Machine 752
Saurav Dhakad, Jayesh Gangrade, Jyoti Bharti, and Antriksha Somani

A New Objective Function Based Multi-Level Image Segmentation Using Differential Evolution 761
Rupak Chakraborty, Rama Sushil, and M. L. Garg

Target Tracking in WSN Using Dynamic Neural Network Techniques. 771
Moxanki A. Bhavsar, Jayesh H. Munjani, and Maulin Joshi

Color Image Segmentation of Disease Infected Plant Images Captured in an Uncontrolled Environment 790
Toran Verma, Sipi Dubey, and Hiteshwari Sabrol

Intelligent Vulnerability Analyzer – A Novel Dynamic Vulnerability Analysis Framework for Mobile Based Online Applications 805
D. Jeya Mala, M. Eswaran, and N. Deepika Malar

Detection of Leukemia in Human Blood Samples Through Image Processing 824
Ravi Raj Choudhary, Savita Sharma, and Gaurav Meena

Automatic Screening Method for Bone Health Diagnosis 835
Punal M. Arabi, Gayatri Joshi, Tejaswi Bhat, and Varini Chinnabhandar

Robust Face Recognition Using Sparse and Dense Hybrid Representation with Local Correlation. 844
M. A. Sahla Habeeba, Philomina Simon, and R. Prajith

CIELch Color Space Based Satellite Image Segmentation Using Soft Computing Techniques 854
P. Ganesan, B. S. Sathish, L. M. I. Leo Joseph, and V. Kalist

Despeckling Filter Evaluation Using Image Quality Metrics and Coefficient of Variation 862
R. J. Hemalatha and V. Vijayabaskar

Not Too Deep CNN for Face Detection in Real Life Scenario 870
Sanjoy Chowdhury, Parthasarathi Mukherjee, and Ujjwal Bhattacharya

Feasibility Study of NIR, DSLR Imaging Techniques for Automatic Diabetic Foot Screening. 887
Punal M. Arabi, T. P. Prathibha, and Surekha Nigudgi

Feature Extraction and Classification of X-Ray Lung Images Using Haralick Texture Features. 899
N. Vamsha Deepa, Nanditha Krishna, and G. Hemanth Kumar

Human Activity Recognition Using Local Motion Histogram 908
Awadhesh Kumar Srivastava and K. K. Biswas

Feature Based Multiple Vehicle License Plate Detection and Video Based Traffic Counting 918
P. L. Chithra and B. Prashanthi

Automated Detection of Epileptic Seizure Using Histogram of Oriented Gradients for Analysing Time Frequency Images of EEG Signals 932
N. J. Sairamya, S. Thomas George, D. Narain Ponraj, and M. S. P. Subathra

Detection of Lung Cancer with the Fusion of Computed Tomography and Positron Emission Tomography. 944
Jaspreet Kaur, Sidharth Pancholi, and Amit M. Joshi

Multi Minimum Product Spanning Tree Based Indexing Approach for Content Based Retrieval of Bio Images. 956
Meenakshi Srivastava, Sanjay Kumar Singh, and S. Q. Abbas

Author Index 965

Smart and Innovative Trends in Computational Intelligence and Data Science

Recommender System Based on Fuzzy C-Means

Priya Gupta(✉), Aradhya Neeraj Mathur, Kriti Kathuria, Rishabh Chandak, and Satyam Sangal

Department of Computer Science, Maharaja Agrasen College, University of Delhi, New Delhi, India
pgupta1902@gmail.com

Abstract. Modern E-Commerce sites require a concrete method of retaining their user base besides keeping a wide variety of items. In order to maintain user interest, it is necessary to suggest users the items that would help them to retain and increase their attraction towards products. This not only means showing items that would interest the users but also help the e-commerce companies to get profits out of sales. Thus, recommender systems come into picture. These systems are designed to help ecommerce companies help retain their user base. The recommender systems deploy a variety of different algorithms to study user preferences and make smart suggestions. Modern recommender engines are able to address only a single issue at a time. It is a trade-off between response time and accurate results that take into account variety of factors. This paper talks about the techniques that are used to build reliable and fast recommender systems as well as it discusses their working techniques.

Keywords: Collaborative · Recommender systems · Scalability Ontology · Fuzzy

1 Introduction

Artificial intelligence and machine learning are changing the way humans could think about machines. The machines are not only becoming much faster and capable computationally but also providing humans a better and newer insight. In 1950s, the research began to study Artificial Intelligence in earnest, even though the idea of thought capable artificial beings has very popular in the storytelling world. Artificial Intelligence, in essence, is an ideal "intelligent" machine and flexible rational agent that perceives its environment and takes actions that maximize its chance of success at some goal [10]. Colloquially, the term "artificial intelligence" is applied when a machine mimics "cognitive" functions that humans associate with other human minds, such as "learning" and "problem solving" [15]. A part of this was the ability of a machine to learn from its environment and experiences and use those experiences while making decisions. Hence, the revolution of machine learning came about. In the simplest terms, it is the ability of a machine to learn, without being explicitly programmed. It came

P. Bhattacharyya et al. (Eds.): NGCT 2017, CCIS 827, pp. 3–18, 2018.
https://doi.org/10.1007/978-981-10-8657-1_1

about from the study of pattern recognition and computational learning in artificial intelligence, and it explores the avenues, which may be employed to make the machine learn from the data provided to it, and make deductions and predictions, based on that. Essentially, it requires a machine to learn from its environment and experiences, and employ the knowledge gained in future unprecedented scenarios and make decisions; much like a human. With the advent of computers with more computational power, and their proliferation, and the result boom in data has made the ground very fertile to further the ways data can aid us decision-making, and widening our horizons. One such area is the filtering relevant information from the exponentially increasing amount of data being generated every day, which is estimated at the 2.7 ZB, today 90% of data generated by 2012 was generated in years 2010–2012, and the data generated by 2003 is equal to the data generated in 2 days in 2014 [11].

The internet continues to grow at an exponential rate, and consequently the amount of information available for consumption. As a result, finding relevant information is becoming a complex and time consuming task [13]. Building personalized websites aids the average surfer by showing content that match their interests. This is usually by asking the user to select items or topics of interest from a predefined list. However, this method is cumbersome as users are not always self-knowledgeable and with time their interests may shift, requiring them to change their selection frequently [13].

Therefore, recommender systems provide personalized information to any user by learning the user's preference from past interactions. Recommendation systems are a subclass of information filtering systems, which seek to predict the rating or the preference that a user will have for an item. From the boundless and unlimited number of options available to the user, the recommendation engine aims to find the option most suited to the user, based on some sort of evaluation parameter. We see recommender systems all around us, these days. Google uses them to filter our search results, on basis of our past activity, so that the results maybe best suited for our needs. A recommender system performs recommendation in multiple ways. Consider, for example, a website selling books. It builds a user profile, based primarily on the types of books the user likes to read. This could be decided based upon which books are bought, and which books are put into the bucket labelled "wish-list" and "already read". It could also take into account the books that are never browsed. From this, an idea of the user's preference is generated and books of similar genre, author, word count, illustrations, etc. are suggested to the user. The pitfall of this would be that no new recommendations will be made to the user, and the suggestions to the user will remain limited to the pool of the things the user usually prefers. This happens because the profile is built on the activity of the user, hence limiting the scope of the recommendations. The fact that this method does not require much to start making suggestions, make this preferable in the very beginning of the recommendation process. There can be rating system, for users to rate the items based on their experience and usefulness of the item. The click rates can be recorded and the time spent on any particular website.

2 About Recommender Systems

2.1 Collaborative Filtering Based Recommender Systems

Collaborative filtering, also called social filtering, filters information based on the histories of other people. The idea behind this type of filtering is that the people who agreed on the evaluation criteria of certain items are likely to agree in the future too. For example, a person looking to watch movies is more likely to trust the suggestion of his friends who have similar taste than the suggestion of a stranger [13].

Collaborative Filtering (CF) algorithms provide item recommendations by finding similar users based on their preferences [4]. Opinions are gathered using explicit methods or implicit methods. In CF algorithm the main 2 vector spaces are formed by the users and the items, where each item in item vector has some rating by a user. These ratings are used to calculate the likelihood for preference of an object.

Collaborative Filtering (CF) algorithms provide item recommendations by finding similar users based on their preferences [4]. Opinions are gathered using explicit methods or implicit methods. In CF algorithm the main 2 vector spaces are formed by the users and the items, where each item in item vector has some rating by a user. These ratings are used to calculate the likelihood for preference of an object.

CF is of several types

(a) **Item Based Collaborative filtering**:- In item based similarity takes into user rated items. It tries to find the items x similar to an item y depending on the previous rating of x. The similarity is computed using the item characteristics for example in movie recommender system a movie has different characteristics such as the director, the cast, the producer, genre etc. that could be used to map other movies of the similar kind [4]. A simple cosine similarity can be used to find the similar items in this case where we check the distance of the two feature vectors of a movie. Correlation based similarity can be used by using Pearson Correlation on two feature vectors of the movies liked by the person. Today most of the recommender systems use item based collaborative filtering because of its ability to overcome the following challenges.

- Quality of Recommendations
- Performing large number of recommendations in a given timeframe
- Performing recommendations on a large dataset
- High coverage when data is sparse are searched.

(b) **Memory Based Collaborative filtering** [4] algorithm utilise entire dataset of user and item. It statistically finds the neighbours that have previously share similar preferences and gives recommendations based on those users. These techniques are also called nearest neighbour or user-based collaborative filtering.

(c) **Model Based Collaborative** filtering algorithms use probabilistic modelling to provide item recommendation. This model makes the use of different algorithms such as rule based, clustering and Bayesian network.

(d) **User Based Collaborative Filtering** is done by mapping item preferences by users. Clusters of similar items to a target person and recommended. Scalability is a major issue for searching the number of potential neighbours. The amount of information for a particular user too creates problems as it can slow down the algorithms as the number of data points for a user increase. In addition, the recommendations with higher probability of liking by the potential customer need to be determined accurately. User based Collaborative filtering focuses on potential neighbours to a user, which are a large user population whereas item-item collaborative filtering helps to prevent this bottleneck by finding relations between the items before the users.

Since the properties of the items do not change rapidly, they provide easier computation. Bayesian networks [4] provide advantage that they help in prediction of changing preferences over time and can adapt to it however cannot handle rapidly changing preferences. Clustering produce, more average recommendations than the other algorithms since it forms by identifying similar user groups and gives the recommendation based on the average preferences of the users. However, the quality of the result may not be good for the users that are far from the centre of the cluster. User Collaborative filtering uses two primary techniques for prediction - weighted sum and regression In live environments things are different. They cater to millions of users, have to be scalable and fault tolerant. In addition, the recommendations have to keep up with speed and accuracy.

The lack of user rated data also affects the predictions. The quality of predictions is also adversely affected by noise that is present in both training and testing dataset. The data sparseness also further deteriorates the quality of prediction. To overcome these problems Netflix announced a competition the Netflix Prize Problem [6] where a group of participants came up with the idea of Alternating-Least-Squares with Weighted-Regularisation (ALS-WR), which was developed as a parallel algorithm for large scale collaborative filtering. It provided a 5% improvement over Netflix's CineMatch System. It focuses on the application of reduction of empirical loss function and uses Tikhonov Regularization [6].

2.2 Ontology Based Recommendation Systems

One of the techniques used in filtering is knowledge based filtering. This is where ontology comes in.

Usually, recommendations are done on the basis of mapping between what the user wants and what product can get the work done, and do not take into account the reviews of the product done by other users of that particular product. Ontology is naming entities that exist for a domain, and defining types, properties and relationships associated with them. It determines the variables that will be needed for a set of computations and establishes the relationship between them. (User spatial, user characteristics can also be used to augment the recommendation procedure to make accurate predictions). The need for ontology is so that we can make user profiles, and eventually be able to map requirements of users, characteristics of users and product specifications [4].

In order to perform ontology based recommendation a knowledge base needs to be created. Knowledge base basically means all the features that the recommendation system can acquire about what products meet the user's requirement. This system helps to navigate among a wide range of products based on the knowledge of product domain [6].

The essential elements for building a knowledge base:

(1) Information about product: specification, prices, brand, features, etc.
(2) Information about product features along with sentiments associated with different features: this is correlation is calculated for each of the three components. E.g.: correlation of the keywords typed in the search bar and keywords used in previous queries. In case of filters and features, the results with the filters and features common with the filters and features with the search query, are used.
(3) The sentiments about a product are extracted from reviews. Review can be converted to XML for this purpose. The result is a sentence dictionary, which is further processed using RIKTEXT [4] (a predictive text mining tool) to gain sentiments. Therefore, we get product features along with their sentiments.
(4) Information about mapping user requirements with product features. We need info from domain experts for assigning weights to product depending on mappings from requirements to features.

Text mining is done to classify sentiments of a product, or approach Latent Class Regression Model (LCRM) (Fig. 1).

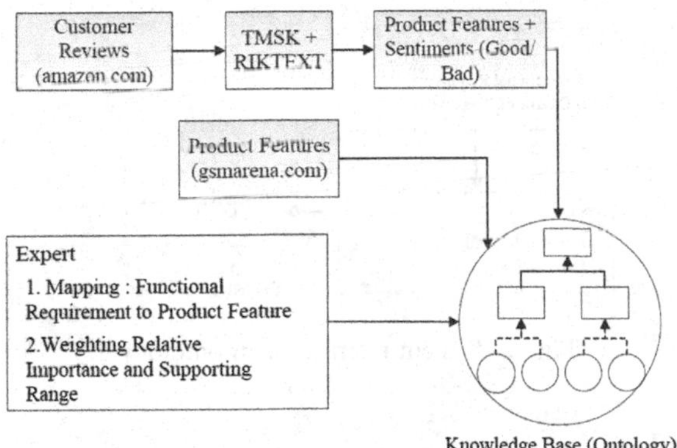

Fig. 1. Structure of knowledge base

LCRM [4] is a clustering technique, which identifies sub communities on a network, where each community belongs to a review cluster. This technique does not take into account the requirements that a user has.

There are two models considered most popular, for the use of ontology in recommender systems:

(1) Ontology structure developed by Hendratmo and Baizals (what the user needs), specifications (details about the product), product (product in domain).

(2) Blanco and Fernandez used semantic reasoning (tracing relations) to address the problem of over specialization. However, does not elaborate product review for rec purposes.

Technology Acceptance Model (TAM) [4] can be used to evaluate and interpret user's perception of the new system.

User System Interaction in ontology based recommender system.

As given in the model used in the paper:

(1) User chooses his requirements, from a list of predefined requirements aggregated from all the possible products from which recommendation has to made from.
(2) User assigns as DOI (degree of interest) for each of the requirements. The values are 0 and 1 (This could be extended into a multi-level system, and incorporated into our own recommender system).
(3) The recommendation is based on the value of the degree at which the product matched the user's needs (MAUT, multi attribute utility theory used here) recommendations are obtained by tracing nodes and relationships in ontology using semantic reasoning.
(4) For each recommendation, there is an explanation for that recommendation; this is accomplished using backtracking to trace the nodes that were passed based on user requirements (Fig. 2).

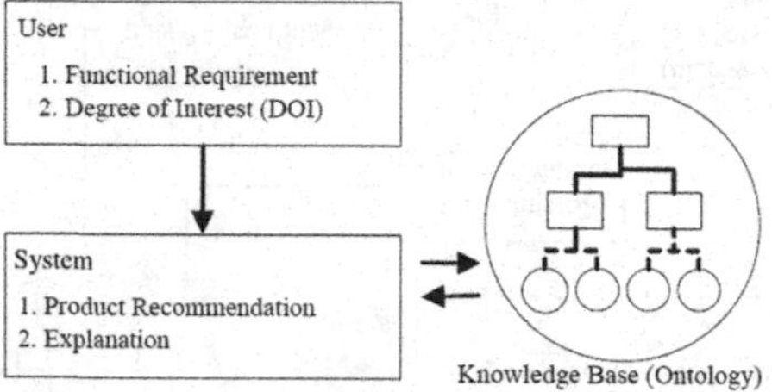

Fig. 2. System interaction in ontology

Structure of Ontology

In the field of computer science, ontology is specifying a vocabulary to define classes, relationships, functions, etc. to represent objects in a domain. Techniques based on ontology can potentially reduce the problems that content based recommender systems suffer from.

The class specification has a depth of 2, i.e., it will be having two levels. First of them will give them the generalized version of specifications (e.g. for a phone, battery, chipset, camera). These are called specification types.

Each individual in the class will have three values associated with them: supporting range value, opinion range value, relative importance value.

The second level will further be divided into sub-classes appropriate. Like (good camera, poor camera. This well encompasses cameras of all the phone brands available to the recommender engine to choose from).

Here the supporting range is calculated.

Opinion grade is grade of opinion of the specifications of a particular product. These are derived from the reviews, and looked up in the sentence dictionary.

Similarly, opinion range is calculated by normalizing the opinion grades for different features.

Relative importance indicates how much the specification suits the requirements of the user. Having the base values, a final rank is calculated which is used to rank the recommended products. The analysis told us that the mapping of functional requirement with the reviews lead to better result.

The recommendations are primarily classified into two categories depending on their use case. The first one depends on user and item interactions i.e. collaborative filtering whereas the latter is the content based whereby user and item profiling is done. Thus the above two discuss both of these methods.

3 Practical Implementation of Item Based Collaborative Filtering

In order to conduct research in recommender systems a road-map was created. The road-map focuses on two key areas of our work (Fig. 3).

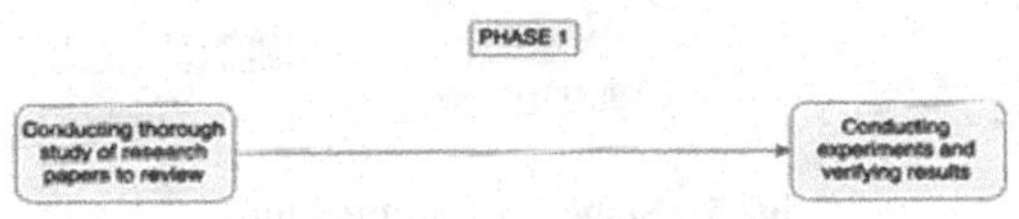

Fig. 3. Phase of study

Stage 1

Firstly, the road-map focuses on developing a thorough knowledge of the recommender systems and the algorithms used by them. In order to be able to give an insight first is the step of knowledge acquisition which is done by doing a thorough literature survey which is done by referring to research papers, online journals, websites etc. which help to get the requisite data on the recommender systems. Once we have the necessary data, it is further ordered and different algorithms of the recommender systems are studied. The study not only includes the theoretical and conceptual applications but also the underlying core mathematics, which would further help us in devising our own methodology later (Fig. 4).

Stage 2

Second stage includes the run-time evaluations of different algorithms. Learning the programming implementations of the algorithms studied in stage 1. Setting up the run-time environment necessary for different libraries such as Apache Spark, which has multiple dependencies for its run-time.

Installing Java-ML library for running different tests. Understand the documentation of the libraries that would be used in the process and improving on the methodology required to program in future (Fig. 5).

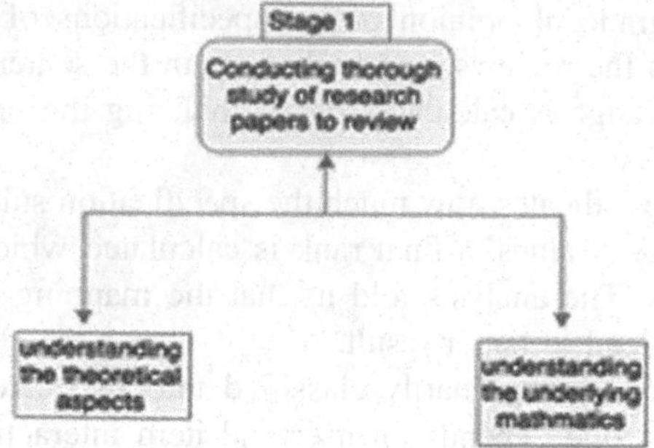

Fig. 4. Stage 1 of architecture

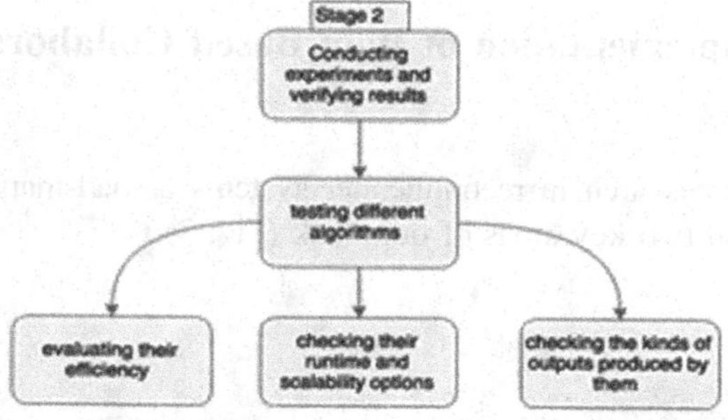

Fig. 5. Stage 2 of architecture

System Requirement
Hardware Used: Intel Dual Core, 2 GB RAM, 2.40 GHz.

Initial Setup
In order to test the algorithms initially standard java machine-learning library (javaml-0.1.7 [12]) was used in NetBeans IDE. The Spark Ecosystem was also set up in the system with a single node cluster to conduct test on the dataset on a single system.

Implementing
As discussed in [8] the user based collaborative filtering is similar to the item based collaborative filtering but instead of checking similarity among items it focuses on finding the similarity among the users. User based collaborative filtering uses the following formula to compute the similarity among users u and v where P is the prediction and s is similarity (Fig. 6).

$$P_{u,i} = \frac{\sum_v (r_{v,i} * s_{u,v})}{\sum_v s_{u,v}}$$

Fig. 6. Formula to compute similarity

It also uses a correlation based similarity by calculating weighted sum of different ratings on item i [8].

(1) In order to see the difference in the recommendations we performed clustering based on items in order to demonstrate item based collaborative filtering on the Netflix Movie dataset.
We first performed an item based clustering using java-ml library and performed cross validation to improve the accuracy. The chosen dataset had various entries of form {UserID, ProductID, Rating} (Fig. 7).

```
Total number of users : 30
Total number of products :100
Total Ratings : 1501
USERS :[0, 1, 2, 3, 4, 5, 6, 7, 8, 9, 10, 11, 12, 13, 14, 15, 16, 17, 18, 19, 20, 21, 22, 23, 24, 25, 26, 27, 28, 29]
PRODUCTS :[0, 1, 2, 3, 4, 5, 6, 7, 8, 9, 10, 11, 12, 13, 14, 15, 16, 17, 18, 19, 20, 21, 22, 23, 24, 25, 26, 27, 28, 29, 30, 31, 32, 33, 34, 35, 36, 37, 38, 39, 40, 41, 42, 43, 44,
45, 46, 47, 48, 49, 50, 51, 52, 53, 54, 55, 56, 57, 58, 59, 60, 61, 62, 63, 64, 65, 66, 67, 68, 69, 70, 71, 72, 73, 74, 75, 76, 77, 78, 79, 80, 81, 82, 83, 84, 85, 86, 87, 88, 89,
90, 91, 92, 93, 94, 95, 96, 97, 98, 99]
```

Fig. 7. Dataset

(2) Now after performing K-means Classification product-wise we get (Figs. 8 and 9):

```
EVALUATE PRODUCT CLASSFICIATION USING K-Means
Product ID : 88, Accuracy: 0.9880079946702198 Error Rate:0.011992005329780146
Product ID : 89, Accuracy: 0.9926715522984677 Error Rate:0.007328447701532311
Product ID : 90, Accuracy: 0.9893404397068621 Error Rate:0.010659560293137908
Product ID : 91, Accuracy: 0.9906728847435043 Error Rate:0.009327115256495669
Product ID : 92, Accuracy: 0.9906728847435043 Error Rate:0.009327115256495669
Product ID : 93, Accuracy: 0.9933377748167888 Error Rate:0.006662225183211193
Product ID : 94, Accuracy: 0.894070619586942 Error Rate:0.10592938041305797
Product ID : 95, Accuracy: 0.988674217188541 Error Rate:0.01132578281145902
Product ID : 96, Accuracy: 0.9900066622251832 Error Rate:0.009993337774816789
Product ID : 97, Accuracy: 0.9900066622251832 Error Rate:0.009993337774816789
Product ID : 10, Accuracy: 0.9900066622251832 Error Rate:0.009993337774816789
Product ID : 98, Accuracy: 0.988674217188541 Error Rate:0.01132578281145902
Product ID : 11, Accuracy: 0.9920053297801465 Error Rate:0.007994670219853431
Product ID : 99, Accuracy: 0.9913391072618255 Error Rate:0.008660892738174551
Product ID : 12, Accuracy: 0.988674217188541 Error Rate:0.011325782811459028
Product ID : 13, Accuracy: 0.9893404397068621 Error Rate:0.010659560293137908
Product ID : 14, Accuracy: 0.9880079946702198 Error Rate:0.011992005329780146
Product ID : 15, Accuracy: 0.9873417721518988 Error Rate:0.012658227848101266
Product ID : 16, Accuracy: 0.9926715522984677 Error Rate:0.007328447701532311
Product ID : 17, Accuracy: 0.9913391072618255 Error Rate:0.008660892738174551
Product ID : 18, Accuracy: 0.8914057295136576 Error Rate:0.10859427048634245
Product ID : 19. Accuracy: 0.988674217188541 Error Rate:0.011325782811459028
```

Fig. 8. Product wise K-means classification

Similarly using K-means User wise:

(3) Now based on the technique of finding K-Nearest Neighbours, for every input where a User Rates a Product, a set was formed the members of which contains either all similar rated product or those users who used that particular product (Fig. 10).
For item-item classification, it was noted that the root mean square error was observed as 0.069892.

(4) Using Alternating Least Square Method on Apache Spark Using apache Spark [4], parallel processing was added along with its own machine library tools. One of the most studied techniques is Alternating Least Square (ALS) method where the users (A) and products (B) make two different matrices. We have to find a matrix C = A * B. If we keep A constant and vary B, C gives our most likely

```
EVALUATE CLASSIFICATION USING K-Means
User ID : 22, Accuracy: 0.9626915389740173 Error Rate:0.03730846102598267
User ID : 23, Accuracy: 0.9653564290473018 Error Rate:0.03464357095269820
User ID : 24, Accuracy: 0.9653564290473018 Error Rate:0.03464357095269820
User ID : 25, Accuracy: 0.9693537641572285 Error Rate:0.03064623584277148
User ID : 26, Accuracy: 0.9673550966022652 Error Rate:0.0326449033977348
User ID : 27, Accuracy: 0.9693537641572285 Error Rate:0.03064623584277148
User ID : 28, Accuracy: 0.966688874083944 Error Rate:0.0333111259160559
User ID : 29, Accuracy: 0.9693537641572285 Error Rate:0.03064623584277148
User ID : 10, Accuracy: 0.9706862091938707 Error Rate:0.02931379080612924
User ID : 11, Accuracy: 0.9626915389740173 Error Rate:0.03730846102598267
User ID : 12, Accuracy: 0.9633577614923384 Error Rate:0.0366422385076615
User ID : 13, Accuracy: 0.9680213191205863 Error Rate:0.03197868087941372
User ID : 14, Accuracy: 0.9620253164556962 Error Rate:0.037974683544303
User ID : 15, Accuracy: 0.9680213191205863 Error Rate:0.03197868087941372
User ID : 16, Accuracy: 0.9700199866755497 Error Rate:0.02998001332445036
User ID : 17, Accuracy: 0.9693537641572285 Error Rate:0.03064623584277148
User ID : 18, Accuracy: 0.9653564290473018 Error Rate:0.03464357095269820
User ID : 19, Accuracy: 0.9673550966022652 Error Rate:0.0326449033977348
User ID : 0, Accuracy: 0.03264490339773484 Error Rate:0.967355096602265
User ID : 1, Accuracy: 0.9673550966022652 Error Rate:0.0326449033977348
```

Fig. 9. Classification using K-means

```
Enter USER ID :0

Enter PRODUCT ID :0

Enter the Rating :4

([0.0, 4.0]:0)k nearest :(([4.0, 1.0]:0), ([16.0, 4.0]:12), ([85.0, 4.0]:11), ([14.0, 4.0]:4), ([69.0, 4.0]:11), ([86.0, 4.0]:3), ([10.0, 4.0]:28), ([70.0, 4.0]:28), ([34.0, 4.0]:2
2), ([8.0, 4.0]:2), ([0.0, 1.0]:3), ([4.0, 2.0]:7), ([87.0, 4.0]:5), ([29.0, 4.0]:24), ([71.0, 4.0]:7), ([51.0, 4.0]:11), ([25.0, 4.0]:11), ([43.0, 4.0]:0), ([35.0, 4.0]:35), ([17.
0, 4.0]:2), ([64.0, 4.0]:4), ([81.0, 4.0]:11), ([56.0, 4.0]:2), ([90.0, 4.0]:20), ([65.0, 4.0]:26), ([40.0, 4.0]:9), ([99.0, 4.0]:9), ([66.0, 4.0]:21), ([83.0, 4.0]:4), ([57.0, 4.0
]:6), ([49.0, 4.0]:26), ([41.0, 4.0]:2), ([20.0, 4.0]:18), ([33.0, 4.0]:1], ([62.0, 4.0]:1), ([15.0, 4.0]:23), ([77.0, 4.0]:17), ([54.0, 4.0]:25), ([94.0, 4.0]:5), ([46.0, 4.0]:14)
, ([79.0, 4.0]:3), ([63.0, 4.0]:24), ([31.0, 4.0]:23), ([79.0, 4.0]:17), ([55.0, 4.0]:24), ([27.0, 4.0]:26), ([47.0, 4.0]:19), ([23.0, 4.0]:7), ([19.0, 4.0]:4), ([0.0, 2.0]:1), ([4
.0, 4.0]:18), ([89.0, 4.0]:15), ([60.0, 4.0]:6), ([75.0, 4.0]:3), ([0.0, 3.0]:0), ([3.0, 4.0]:0), ([44.0, 4.0]:12), ([74.0, 4.0]:13), ([36.0, 4.0]:14), ([53.0, 4.0]:12), ([45.0, 4.
0]:8), ([37.0, 4.0]:20))
```

Fig. 10. After applying KNN

products for a user, and keeping B constant and varying A, we get most likely users for a product. While Singular Value Decomposition is used for approximating A and B, for missing elements in matrix standard SVD algorithms [6] do not work well. Therefore, alternating least squares is used for solving the problem of factorisation. Using 4 threads, and Spark inbuilt library org.apache.spark.mllib [8] on the same dataset but this time with 1500 entries, the results were very much surprising (Fig. 11).

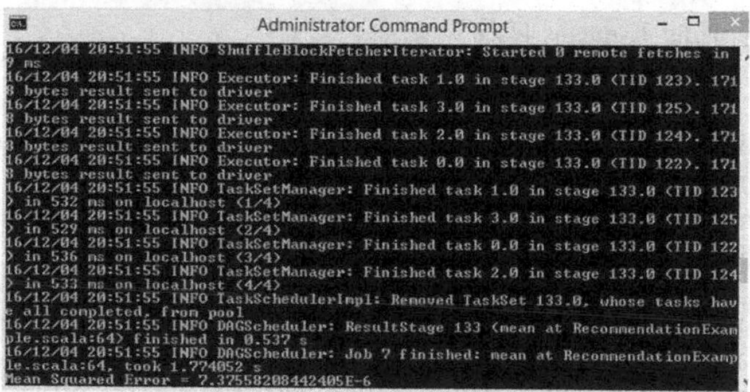

Fig. 11. Calculating RMS using ALS

The time it took was 2.311105 s. The Root Mean Squared Error was roughly $7 * 10^{-6}$, which means a very high accuracy. It is observed that big difference is made by using a BIG DATA processing framework on the same hardware. Another factor is memory used. In one conventional method memory was required only for process life. In second method, Hadoop File System permanently stores the mapped model because every query needs to revisit those mapping again and again. Its needed only to use the training Dataset once and then keep updating the saved model.

Thus from the above experiments we observed that item to item RMS error is 0.068 and for ALS it is 7.375 and has been summarized in Table 1.

Table 1. Comparison of KNN and ALS

Algorithm	Platform	RMS (error)
KNN-classifier	JAVA-ML	0.06892809265393839
ALS	Spark	7.37558200442405E-6

4 Proposed Model

Fuzzy Clustering Based Recommender System
The above recommender systems use crisp data. Our proposed model makes use of fuzzy sets to recommend movies to users.

Fuzzy partitions and fuzzy clustering as explained in [12] as a system in which data points do not fully belong to any one group or cluster, but to multiple groups or clusters to some degree. With clustering, we split the data points into groups based on the similarities between the said data points, and looks to find patterns and similarity between the items in a set [17]. Hence, items in a cluster share similarity with other items in the cluster, and are different from items in the other clusters [9].

The term "hard clustering" has been coined, to mean that a data point may belong to only one cluster. On the other hand, "soft" or fuzzy clustering allows a data point to belong to multiple clusters at the same time [17]. Fuzzy clustering used the least squares solution to find the various degrees that a particular data point belongs to a cluster [16].

Narrowing Down Recommendations Using Fuzzy Clusters
In order to have better recommendations to the users, the dataset of the movies can further be reduced by creating fuzzy partitions based on average ratings of movies by users. In order to demonstrate fuzzy partitions we have used 100k movielens dataset (Fig. 12).

Fuzzy clustering helps to create fuzzy dataset from crisp dataset and create fuzzy partitions. Scikit-fuzzy was used for implementing the fuzzy c-means.

Algorithm for fuzzy partition generation using FCM

```
read fuzziness parameter m
for each qp ∈ QA (p = 1, 2,…, r)
    FPp = apply_FCM(qp)
    for each partition t ∈ FPi
        label t appropriately

function apply_FCM(q)
    read k (number of clusters)
    until max{|μij (k + 1) - μij (k)|} < δ
        for each xi ∈ D (i = 1, 2,…, N)
            for each cluster j (j = 1, 2,…, C)
                calculate μij as per Eq. 1

    FP = set of fuzzy clusters (partitions) after completion of above
    iteration

    return FP
```

Fig. 12. Algorithm for fuzzy partitioning

Figure 13 shows the clustering of movies into two fuzzy partitions. However, the above partitioning still has the drawback since the movie ratings with low mean ratings have been classified with the movies with average ratings (Table 2).

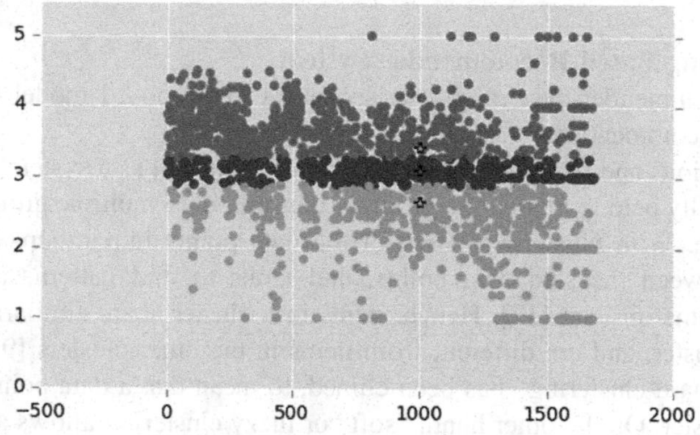

Fig. 13. Clustering into 3 partition

Table 2. Comparison of partitioning

Number of partitions	Time (in sec)	Max Iter parameter
2	.492	1000
3	.508	1000
5	.550	1000

In order to resolve that problem we can increase the number of partitions as shown in Figs. 14 and 15. In these figures the number of partitions have be increased. The average rating as shown by the Y-Axis shows 3 fuzzy partitions. The movies with good average ratings, movies with average ratings and movies with less liking by their users.

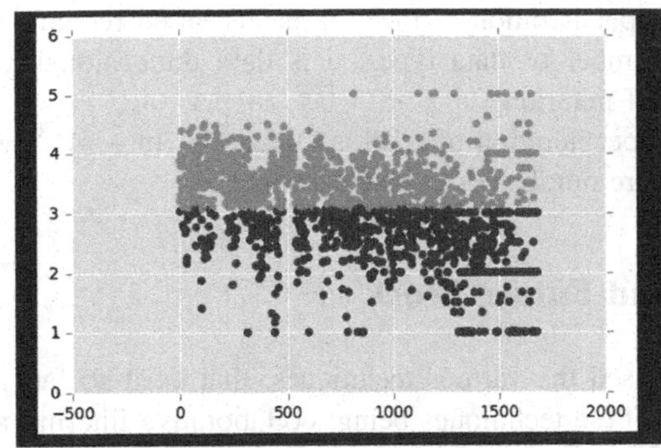

Fig. 14. Clustering into two partition

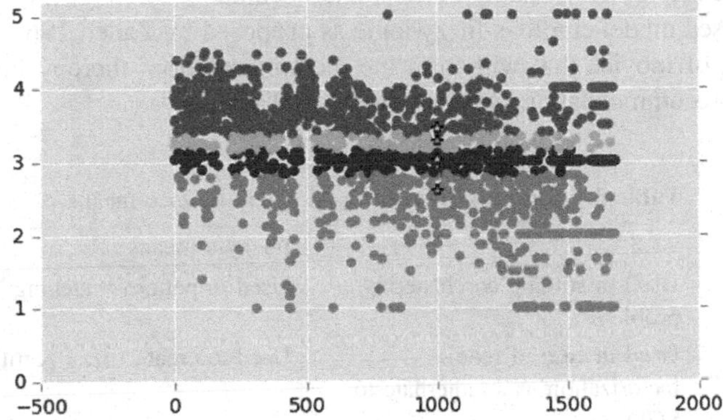

Fig. 15. Clustering into 4 partition

The stars have marked the ratings of the partitions in the above figure.

How Fuzziness Helps

Creating fuzzy partitions on the movies with ratings helps to reduce the target movies for suggestions. Before finding the movies similar to the movies liked by user, the movie dataset can be reduced by partitioning it into fuzzy partitions based on ratings. Then movies with higher average rating can be picked to create user suggestions thus helping to improve the quality of recommendations and creating much filtered results. Figure 13 shows the clustering of movies into two fuzzy partitions. However, the above partitioning still has the drawback since the movie ratings with low mean ratings have been classified with the movies with average ratings.

Runtime Metrics

With reference to the above movie dataset fuzzy clustering could help obtain better partitions to classify movies as instead of getting not only highly rated movies it would help assign other movies to the group unlike hard partitioning where the partition boundaries would be much more rigid thus reducing the number of movies that could be recommended to the user by being biased only to the higher rating ones.

Time complexity per iteration of fuzzy c-means based recommender system is O (ndc^2) where n is number of data types, d is data dimensionality, c is number of clusters, and i is no of iteration.

Time complexity per iteration of ALS is $O(|\Omega|k^2 + (m + n)k^3)$ where k is rank of matrix and m and n are number of user and items.

5 Conclusion and Future Work

This paper has discussed the various techniques, that exist so far, to implement recommender systems. These techniques being: collaborative filtering and content based filtering. This paper shows a comparitive analusis of the ALS and the KNN implementation for recommender systems. The main purpose of this work was to compare and comprehensively study the various approaches, and the algorithms developed to build recommender systems that are robust and accurate.

The proposed model employs fuzzy logic as proposed by Zadeh 1965. This helped reduce the set of movies that will form the recommendation, thereby improving the quality of the recommendation. As it is shown in Table 3.

Table 3. Comparison between ALS and fuzzy c-means

Property	ALS	Fuzzy c-means
Used with	Used in solving co clustering problems	Used in pattern matching
Method use case	Used in case of matrix factorization as an alternate to SGD	Used to create fuzzy partitions of data
Complexity	$O(\|\Omega\|k^2 + (m+n)k^3)$	$O(ndc^2)$
Parallelization capabilities	Can be parallelized using distributed matrices ideal for distributed computing	Can be parallelized however involves a greater overhead since the cluster centers need to be communicated after each iteration

This paper is a study of ontology and how it gives further refinement by considering product specifications and needs of the user, with the reviews that have been given to a product.

Fuzzy based recommender systems are best suited for overlapped data set and are comparatively better then k-means based recommender systems. In fuzzy based clustering data point can be assigned membership to more than one cluster index which results in data point belonging to more than one cluster which gives better recommendation (Table 4).

Table 4. Comparison of different recommendation techniques

	Features	Use case	Drawbacks	Advantage
KNN	Determine the rating of User u on Product m, we can find other Products that are similar to Product m, and based on User u's ratings on those similar Products we infer his rating on Product m	Used when product are semantically similar, when there is little or no prior knowledge about the distribution of the data	We need to specify the number of clusters in which to divide data. Computational cost is very high as we need to calculate the distance of each data point to centroids determined by training samples	Simple to implement and use, Robust to noisy data by averaging k-nearest neighbour.x
ALS	From the ratings that users have given movies, an estimate of ratings is made for those movies without any rating, let this be called X. then an estimate is made for what rating a user will give a previously unwatched movie, let this be called Y. X is used to estimate Y in one iteration, and Y is used to estimate X in the next. This alternation continues till X and Y converge	Used when of a small subset of users' preference is known. The features of the items targeted, may be unknown	Since the recommendations depend on the use history, there will a Cold Start problem. Sparsity and scalability will be issues when implemented on large scale	The features of the items, or the history of the user are not basis for recommendations. Recommendations are performed based on the collective history of all the users. This maintains accuracy and relevance of the recommendation across the board, even in case of change of preference of the user
Proposed	Fuzzy c-means for recommendations, by partitioning the data based on fuzzy sets	Where partitioning/classification is required	Can be computationally expensive	Can be applied to non-crisp data thus better generalization opportunity. It also helps in narrowing down the suggestions and improving the quality of it
Ontology	This study utilizes product features and product reviews for recommending products based on product functional requirements desired by user	When product features and reviews are available	Product features and reviews are must to algorithm to work and produce accurate results	It increases the perceived usefulness and ease of use

References

1. Baizal, Z.K.A., Iskandar, A., Nasution, E.: Ontology-based recommendation involving consumer product reviews. In: 2016 4th International Conference on Information and Communication Technology (ICoICT). IEEE (2016)
2. Burke, R.: Integrating knowledge-based and collaborative-filtering recommender systems. In: Proceedings of the Workshop on AI and Electronic Commerce (1999)
3. Mangalampalli, A., Pudi, V.: Fuzzy logic-based pre-processing for fuzzy association rule mining. Centre for Data Engineering International Institute of Information Technology (2008)
4. Sarwar, B., et al.: Item-based collaborative filtering recommendation algorithms. In: Proceedings of the 10th International Conference on World Wide Web. ACM (2001)
5. Yao, G., Cai, L.: User-based and item-based collaborative filtering recommendation algorithms design
6. Zhou, Y., Wilkinson, D., Schreiber, R., Pan, R.: Large-scale parallel collaborative filtering for the netflix prize. In: Fleischer, R., Xu, J. (eds.) AAIM 2008. LNCS, vol. 5034, pp. 337–348. Springer, Heidelberg (2008). https://doi.org/10.1007/978-3-540-68880-8_32
7. Zuzuarregui, M., et al.: PRISENIT–a probabilistic search recommendation algorithm to improve search efficiency for network intelligence and troubleshooting. In: Proceedings of the 2015 17th UKSIM-AMSS International Conference on Modelling and Simulation. IEEE Computer Society (2015)
8. https://github.com/apache/spark. Accessed 23 Nov 2016
9. https://home.deib.polimi.it/matteucc/Clustering/tutorial_html/cmeans.html. Accessed 18 Jan 2017
10. http://introtonewmedia.mynmi.net/bots-ai-artificial-intelligence/. Accessed 9 Dec 2016
11. https://www.itu.int/en/ITU-D/Statistics/Documents/publications/mis2012/MIS2012_without_Annex_4.pdf. Accessed 10 Jan 2017
12. http://java-ml.sourceforge.net/. Accessed 17 Nov 2016
13. https://www.mapr.com/blog/parallel-and-iterative-processing-machine-learning-recommendations-spark. Accessed 29 Spet 2016
14. http://opentopic.com/what-is-artificial-intelligence/. Accessed 9 Dec 2016
15. http://recommender-systems.org/. Accessed 9 Dec 2016
16. http://reference.wolfram.com/legacy/applications/fuzzylogic/Manual/12.html. Accessed 23 Jan 2017
17. http://www.statisticshowto.com/fuzzy-clustering/. Accessed 23 Jan 2017

A Noval Approach to Measure the Semantic Similarity for Information Retrieval

Shelly[1(✉)] and Mamta Kathuria[2]

[1] University of Petroleum and Energy Studies Bidholi Campus, Dehradun, India
shelly@ddn.upes.ac.in

[2] YMCA University of Science and Technology, Faridabad, India
Mamtakathuria7@rediffmail.com

Abstract. In this fast paced multitasking world, internet users are increasing day by day so is our database is increasing and manually maintaining similarity between words of database is a troublesome task. Maintaining semantic similitude between words is substantial chore in chromatic areas such as Natural Language processing tasks like Word sense disambiguation, query expansion as well as web chore such as document bunching, community excavating and automatic metadata breeding. With its wide area applications and usage, in a document still it is very tough to calculate the measure for any two words or entities. We propound a formula using Google, computing semantic similarity employing page count (retrieved by Google only) as a metric. The bounced method outperforms or contribute almost same results to chromatic base lines and compared with the previously proposed web-based semantic similarity methods. The results obtained compared with various online tools like UMBC, SEMILAR etc. Moreover, proposed method has less computation complexity as well as significantly improves the exactitude and efficiency of calculating semantic similarity between two words.

Keywords: Database · Page count · Text extraction · Similarity Web mining

1 Introduction

Co-occurrence-based semantic similarity techniques often known as semantic similarity measures, is a drill of evaluating similarity between words or terms in any given dataset (MC, MeSH or Word Net). This concept is pragmatic in information retrieval, also many concepts of web mining such as entity disambiguation, community mining, relation detection, need the capability for precise measurement of similarity between entities and chromatic natural language procedure chore such as speech understanding, word sense disambiguation, spoken dialogue system, grammar induction, language modeling [1]. For example by doing query expansion (a process of adding semantically parallel words to any query), it is presumably to increase the materiality of recaptured documents.

Improving term coverage continues to be an open research area as new words added day by day and use and update of resources like dataset or thesauri, is a tiresome

P. Bhattacharyya et al. (Eds.): NGCT 2017, CCIS 827, pp. 19–29, 2018.
https://doi.org/10.1007/978-981-10-8657-1_2

as well as time consuming and costly task. Previously many formulas proposed to scan semantic similarity between frequently occurring words.

Words acquire meaning according to their usage in society, nowadays numerous data is available and the escalated elaborative correspondence of web, makes it time absorbing to anatomize document divergently. Web search engine provides an appropriate interface to hither wide facts. Web search engines generally produces two information i.e. Page Count and Snippets [1]. When anyone performs search via web search engine, obtains a metric containing the number of fetched pages called page count [1]. It is necessary that page count will be equal to frequency of words as words may repeat quite voluminous times during a single search [1]. We always fire two queries, say P and Q, where queries takes into account the Page Count metric for both of them stating degree of co-occurrence for the two queries P, Q [1]. Likewise Page Count of query proposed by user "coast" AND "hill" on Google is 24,20,00,000 whereas Page Count of another query i.e. "coast" AND "forest" is 27,90,00,000 makes it 10 times more numerous page counts indicating that forest is more semantically similar to coast than is hill.

We proposed an automatic method, which takes input as page count and tells the similarity between two words. The words, which are highly similar, considered in output results whenever user fires query. In addition, this helps in improving thesaurus where indication of similarity index are done to show how much similar words they are on a scale of 0 to 1. The following are the contribution of this work:

1. New similarity method is proposed and computed over wide collection of downloaded parchments.
2. The metric proposed deemed on Charles-Miller dataset containing noun pairs of broad-brush use, with their congruency in aspect of semantic similarity defined by 38 human subjects to investigate word parallelism.
3. The results obtained compared with formulas already proposed as well as online tools available on web search engines.
4. Improves the efficiency in query expansion where user query word replaced by the synonym obtained after checking similarity score to improve search efficiency.

The odds and ends of this work is clocklike in the following manner: In Sect. 2, the work which has been already done and related with this work is acquainted. Section 3 contains the method showing a basic outline and architecture of work. Section 4 contains the proposed work in detail with all prone and cone related to our work. Sections 5 and 6 summarizes the paper and tells further work that can be done in nearby future.

2 Related Work

Various methods has been deployed so far to compute semantic similarity for any query on a web search engine, few of the work we will discuss here as this concept can be used on a good scale in area of NLP and its various application as suggested in the abstract of this paper [1]. One method to improve the efficiency of search is to suggest user similar query, which is been previously searched as a suggestion related to current query or used by search engine for internal modification, deployed by many search engines now days.

A modest method to analyze semantic similarity is by taking two words and considering Path Length, by calculating the shortest path which connects the taken two words in dataset [6]. What if any word is having more than one meaning, then multiple paths will going to be exist between those two words. As we take into account only the shortest path then the solution to such a case is to consider only shortest path between those words. This solution also results into a major disadvantage that it consider all links are situated in taxonomy at even distance.

Resnik proposed method based on Information Content. The value calculation takes into account the information content(IC) of Least Common Subsume (LCS) or Subsume that is at supreme informative [4]. In addition, the value gained will be hither zero or greater-than that and difference will come depending on the mass of the work chosen to decide information content estimate [4]. Being subtle, the higher bound of the value obtained has to be natural logarithm of total number of words enclosed in the corpus [4]. He calculated information content using Brown corpus and WordNet as taxonomy [4].

Cilibrasi and Vitanyi propound a method based on page count, metric obtained from web search engine often called normalized Google Distance (NGD) [3]. Which defined follows:

$$NGD(X,Y) = \frac{\max\{\log H(X), \log H(Y)\} - \log H(X,Y)}{\log N - \min\{\log(H(X), \log H(Y)\}} \quad (1)$$

NGD uses two words as query i.e. X and Y on which above formula is applied. Page Count for individual query demonstrated as H(X) and for both the queries together i.e. X and Y demonstrated as H(X, Y). NGD is well-defined using Kolmogorov complexity, also by not consider the framework of words co-occurrence.

Lin [6] defined likeliness of two concepts by using the information, which is common to the information in the individual concepts. The results obtained by Lin in form of number is equal to

$$\frac{2 * IC(lcs)}{IC(synset1) + IC(synset2)} \quad (2)$$

Where IC(y) is information content for that word defined in the bracket. Here also value lies between 0 and 1.

After applying the formula, if in any case result obtained is zero for any two synsets, it has counted as an output but it also symbolizes to the fact that the lack of data is there. This scenario happens only when synset used is the root node.

Sahami and Heilman uses the other concept discussed in the abstract i.e. Snippets, which also retrieved from search engine only [1]. Snippet in this scenario represented as TF-IDF weighted term vector. In this method, to calculate the desired value firstly we need to calculate centroid of the vectors, for which the Vector L_2 normalized and then set of vectors gained and by doing inner product of those centroid vectors we can gain our value [1].

Chen et al. suggested a model known as Co-occurrence Double Checking (CODC) method using double-checking as a concept based on text snippets [1] [2]. After collecting the snippets of given two words say P and Q of query given by user, and then snippets counting procedure done in the opposite word i.e. for P, snippets of word Q will be taken into account and same procedure will be performed in vice versa manner. Thus to compute the final similarity, the values obtained are combined non-linearly.

$$CODC(P,Q)=\begin{cases}0 & \text{if } f(P@Q)=0,\\ \exp\left(\log\left[\dfrac{f(P@Q)}{H(P)}\times\dfrac{f(P@Q)}{H(Q)}\right]^{\alpha}\right) & \text{otherwise}\end{cases} \quad (3)$$

H(P) is same page count metric discussed so far and in engine by taking top ranking snippets gained for Q we find the integer of co-occurrences for P, and here α is a constant and experimentally value set as 0.15. The major basis of this method is ranking algorithm used by search engine.

3 Method

A. Outline:

To model the problem of semantic similarity, we use any given two words say P and Q, we proposed a formula that takes two word as query and taking page count as our metric which is retrieved from Google search engine we define similarity by applying those metric into that formula and this procedure returns score between 0 and 1. Higher the correspondence value tends to come close to 1 whereas, as much as words are poles apart value tends to bend towards 0.

B. Proposed Architecture:

Query proposed by a user is taken as an input and another word is extracted through a large database having numerous files or datasets e.g. Charles-Miller, MeSh etc. and afterwards the word-pair is taken on which our formula is applied i.e. semantic similarity is calculated and results are stored. Here we have considered only general word dataset i.e. Charles-Miller one for considering the word pair combinations. This work can also be proved for other datasets in near future (Fig. 1).

After getting the semantic similarity through the formula, same word-pair taken as an input for various web tools available like UMBC, Semilar etc. The results obtained through online tools compared with the results gained by Formula and compared thoroughly and a final list is prepared which shows that this word is very much similar, less similar or not at all similar on a scale of 0 to 1. If any value crosses the 1 then it is taken to be as threshold and those words will be synonym or fall into the category of very much similar. Similarly, if some results are going less than 0 then they will fall

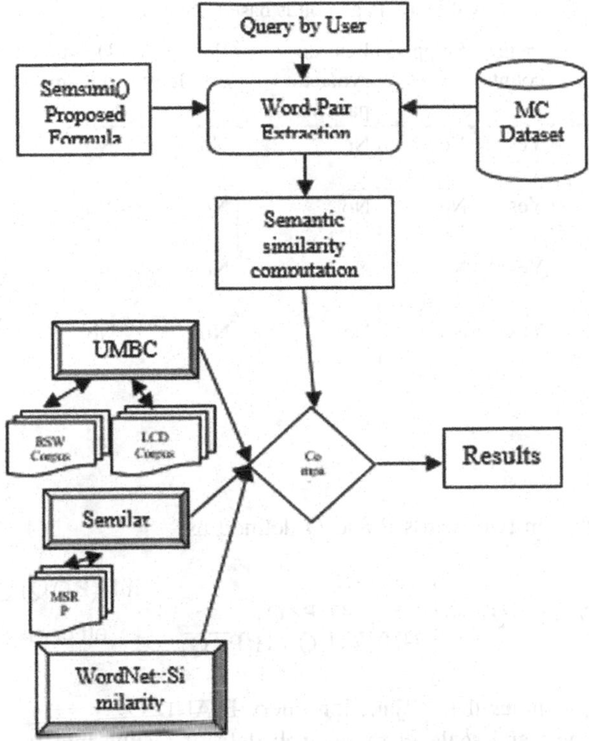

Fig. 1. Outline of proposed method

into category of not at all similar or antonym. Before discussing that work, we would like to show you a glimpse of work that has already been done in this field.

C. Page Count-Based Co-occurrence Measures:

To consider an approximate value of co-occurrence of given two words on network, a metric need to be consider called Page count. On the other hand it is necessary to consider the individual page counts of any word as the page count of the query C AND D alone can't demonstrate the similarity score accurately as response for page count of "car" AND "automobile" by Google: 16,70,00,000 whereas the same for "car" AND "apple" is 22,80,00,000 [1]. Although we all know automobile is more semantically similar to car as compared to apple still page count of "car" AND "apple" is more. To calculate semantic similarity more efficiently we need to consider individual page counts.

There are four main co-occurrence measures: Jaccard, Dice, Overlap (Simpson), and Pointwise Mutual information (PMI), to compute semantic similarity based page counts [1] (Table 1).

Table 1. Page count based measures

Metric	WWW search engine	Page counts	Snippets	Lexi co-syntactic patterns	WordNet ontology	Download documents	Need of external knowledge
Jaccard (J)	Yes	Yes	No	No	No	No	No
Dice (C)	Yes	Yes	No	No	No	No	No
Mutual info. (I)	Yes	Yes	No	No	No	No	No
Google (G')	Yes	Yes	No	No	No	No	No

- Web Jaccard:

Similarity between two words P and Q defined as:

$$WebJacc(P,Q) = \begin{cases} 0 & \text{if } \mathrm{H(P \cap Q)} \le \mathrm{c}, \\ \frac{\mathrm{H(P \cap Q)}}{\mathrm{H(P) + H(Q) - H(P \cap Q)}}, & \text{otherwise} \end{cases} \quad (4)$$

Where P ∩Q denotes the conjunction query P AND Q.

Because of noise and scale factor in web data, it results into occurrence of two words on same page despite of no relationship between them. If page count for the query P AND Q is less than threshold, web jaccard coefficient is set to zero to minimize the effects of such co-occurrences [1].

- Web Dice:

It is a variation of Dice coefficient and defined as

$$WebDice(P,Q) = \begin{cases} 0 & \text{if } \mathrm{H(P \cap Q)} \le \mathrm{c}, \\ \frac{\mathrm{2H(P \cap Q)}}{\mathrm{H(P) + H(Q)}}, & \text{otherwise} \end{cases} \quad (5)$$

- Web Overlap:

A natural modification to the Overlap (Simpson) coefficient and defined as follows

$$WebOverlap(P,Q) = \begin{cases} 0 & \text{if } \mathrm{H(P \cap Q)} \le \mathrm{c}, \\ \frac{\mathrm{H(P \cap Q)}}{\mathrm{min(H(P),H(Q))}}, & \text{otherwise} \end{cases} \quad (6)$$

- Pointwise Mutual Information (PMI):

It is a measure that derived from information theory; it deliberated to reflect the dependency of two probabilistic events. Defined as:

$$WebPMI(P,Q) = \begin{cases} 0 & \textit{if } H(P \cap Q) \leq c, \\ \log \frac{\frac{H(P \cap Q)}{N}}{\frac{H(P)H(Q)}{NN}} & \text{otherwise} \end{cases} \quad (7)$$

Number of documents indexed by Google represented by N and to compute PMI must know N. Although estimating the number of documents indexed is an interesting task and when searching on Google it accounts that Google uses 9,20,000 servers with 10^8 GB data and pages indexed are $3 * 10^{13}$ pages are indexed so far. We all know that page counts are mere approximations but still they have effectively used to develop a variety of dialectal modeling.

4 Proposed Work

To calculate semantic similarity more efficiently using page count as a metric we propose a formula which take input any two word page counts individually and conjunctively gained from Google followed for query P, P AND Q.

A. Benchmark Data Set:

Followed by the work that has already been done, we take a dataset popularly called Miller-Charles which contains noun pairs used in day to day life and also graded according to their similarity by 38 human subjects. The output similarity ranges between 0 (not alike) and 1 (perfect synonym).

B. Online Tools:

We compare our results with the various online tools available on Google search engine which uses various measures and compute similarity score with the formula proposed.

(1) *UMBC* [10]:

Tool computes concept of similarity between.

Simple words such as noun, verb, adjective, adverbs etc., and no proper nouns added except of country names. It uses hybrid of two approaches to compute either similarity between words using a thesaurus (e.g. WordNet) or statistics obtained from a large corpus. Statistical methods based on latent Semantic Analysis (LSA) and distributional similarity. The results obtained further complimented with semantic relations extracted from WordNet. It is an automatic process and can be trained using different corpora. This tool has a word co-occurrence models based on a predefined vocabulary of having more than 20,000 common English words as well as noun phrases also. Addition of 20,000 verb phrases done which extracted from WordNet. It contains two datasets one is Refined Stanford WebBase corpus and other is LCD English Gigawords Corpus [10].

(2) *SEMILAR* [9]:

In this online tool, demo version is used which compute semantic similarity between two words which are given by Latent Semantic Analysis (LSA) model which is constructed over whole Wikipedia (spring 2013 version). This tool proposes a protocol that maps existing word similarity metrics onto qualitative verdict of similarity. The qualitative judgments are [9, 11]:

- CLOSE: shows without any uncertainty words are matching e.g. student and learner.
- RELATED: relationship exists between words despite of being less similar e.g. boxing and fight.
- CONTEXT: matching of words is done in the interior of context of text need to be accessed e.g. totaling and volume.
- KNOWLEDGE: necessitates the domain knowledge e.g. retailer and WalMart.

It uses Microsoft Research Paraphrase Corpus (MSRP) [11].

(3) *WordNet* [5]:

A database that contains the definition or context of any word or concept. It is an online tool available comprising various measures to compute similarity between words. Out of them, we choose these two measures:

- Gloss vectors:
  It is inspired by 2nd order sense discrimination approach which is then related to LSA. Words belongs to same corpus can be represented as a vector. Afterwards cosine of angle calculated between their gloss vectors to compute the similarity. Forms a super gloss by combining the adjacent glosses and then forms a vector equivalent to "super-glosses". Still according to studies regular gloss vector are better than pair-wise gloss vectors in terms of performance [6].
- Gloss vectors pair-wise:
  It is like regular gloss vector, except that it augments the glosses with adjacent glosses. It creates different gloss for every adjacent glosses (no super glosses formed). This measure then form cosine of the corresponding gloss vectors and take their sum [6].
- *C. Computing Semantic Similarity and Algorithm:*

Formula proposed SemSimi (P,Q) to compute semantic similarity efficiently is:

$$SemSimi(P,Q) = \begin{cases} 0 & \text{if } \mathrm{H}(\mathrm{P} \cap \mathrm{Q}) \leq \mathrm{c}, \\ \frac{\ln(\mathrm{H}(\mathrm{P} \cap \mathrm{Q}))}{\ln|\mathrm{H}(\mathrm{P}) - \mathrm{H}(\mathrm{Q})|}, & \text{Otherwise} \end{cases} \tag{8}$$

To simplify the calculation, natural logarithm is used. Also, individual page counts are taken into account stating H(P) denotes for first word and H(Q) denotes for second word and H(P $\cap$Q) denotes for query P AND Q.

Table 2 denotes the output on MC Dataset work out for the proposed formula; previously proposed work i.e. page count-based metrics with NGD. All the similarity

Table 2. Semantic similarity scores

Word pair	Web Jaccard	Web dice	PMI	Normalized Google distance	UMBC	Semilar	Word::Net (gloss vector)	Word::Net (gloss vector-pair wise)	Proposed formula (with ln)
Automobile-car	.05	.09	.25	.94	1.0	.84	1	.68	.88
Journey-voyage	.04	.07	.61	.87	1.0	.52	.80	.33	.89
Gem-jewel	.04	.07	1.6	.70	0.7	.82	1	.5	.88
Boy-lad	.02	.04	.92	.85	0.5	.67	.74	.18	.81
Coast-shore	.24	.39	3.2	.37	1.0	.69	.64	.25	.95
Asylum-madhouse	.00	.01	4.5	.63	0.0	.42	.77	.02	.83
Magician-wizard	.00	.00	.4	1.1	.37	.81	1	.5	.71
Midday-noon	.02	.04	3.1	.62	1.0	.89	1	.17	.76
Furnace-stove	.05	.10	3.2	.52	.7	.64	.58	.02	.92
Food-fruit	.01	.02	2.3	1.6	.37	.65	.30	.01	.91
Bird-cock	.02	.03	1.0	.84	.125	.39	.66	.03	.80
Bird-crane	.03	.05	.8	.86	.32	.64	.36	.03	.84
Implement-tool	.12	.22	2.4	.55	.09	.71	.36	.19	.90
Brother-monk	.01	.01	.5	1.1	.39	.33	.43	.16	.81
Brother-lad	.02	.04	.8	.86	.39	.40	.42	.24	.81
Car-journey	.08	.14	.5	.88	.00	.23	.39	.03	.90
Monk-oracle	.00	.00	1.8	1.3	.23	.32	.13	.04	.71
Food-roaster	.00	.00	3.4	1.5	.00	.49	.12	.01	.68
Coast-hill	.20	.34	1.7	.51	.40	.27	.23	19	.98
Forest-graveyard	.00	.00	1.9	1.2	.11	.26	.09	.03	.66
Monk-slave	.00	.00	1.8	1.3	.23	.28	25	.01	.71
Coast-forest	.15	.26	3.4	1.3	.08	.22	.16	.02	1.1
Lad-wizard	.00	.00	1.7	1.3	.19	.55	.05	.01	.74
Cord-smile	.01	.01	1.9	1.3	.00	.33	.19	.02	.77
Glass-magician	.00	.00	1.8	1.0	.00	.29	.07	.01	.65
Rooster-voyage	.00	.00	1.6	.19	.00	.11	.03	.00	.66
Noon-string	.01	.03	1.9	.11	.00	.16	.09	.00	.82

scores are normalized between [0, 1] for comparison ease. We used few online tools available like UMBC, which tells top N similar words, as well as calculate phrase similarity between words using distribution similarity and latent semantic analysis. In addition, we use Semilar tool, its demo is available online and it works on LSA made over Wikipedia. In addition, the results compared with tool i.e. WordNet::Similarity where Gloss vector measure considered which finds out the similarity score based on cosine angle between the vectors (Fig. 2).

This graph depicts the similarity between word pairs Correlation metric corresponding to their page counts retrieved through Google. The evaluated results compared with one of the online tool to show the results. According to graph, we can clearly see that our formula is much more efficient as compared to one of the online tool. These whole results obtained on MC General Word dataset.

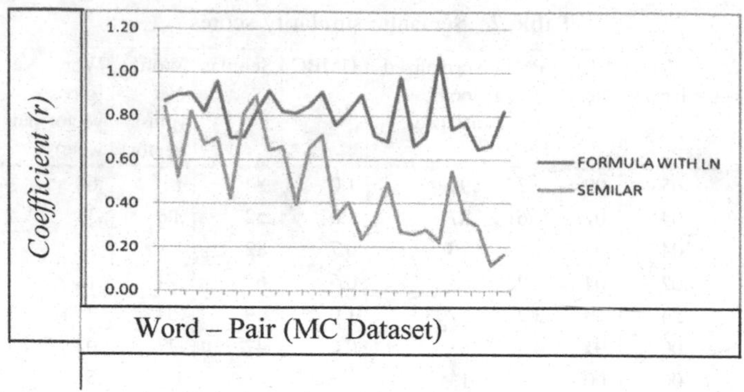

Fig. 2. Correlation vs page count metric

MC Dataset contains polysemous words such as oracle (priest versus database system), simple noun word pairs whose page counts considered from Google web search engine. Likewise, on MC Dataset, our proposed method outperforms all other previously proposed method or results are almost close in few cases showing a high correlation between the query words. Regardless of the fact that projected method does not require any manually generated resources like fixed corpora still results obtained from anticipated method are very much analogous to the approaches that use such resources. One of the mesmerizing facts about finding semantic similarity is non-dependency on dictionaries.

To find out semantic similarity here is sequence of steps known as algorithm.

SemSimi(P,Q) Algorithm:
Step 1: Take a lexical resource, S (here Charles-Miller[1]).
Step 2: Choose a word pair for semantic similarity, say w_1 *and w2.*
Step 3: Make a list of all word pairs, say one word pair is (w_1, w_2).
Step 4: For each w_1 □*S,* Compute P, Page Count of first word using Google.
Step 5: For each w_2 □*S,* Compute Q, Page Count of second word using Google.
Step 6: Compute *P* □*Q*, Page Count of Query "P AND Q" using Google.
Step 7: Compute similarity index between w_1 and w_2, using co-occurrence measure discussed in related work.
Step 8: Compute similarity index between w_1 and w_2 using proposed method

$$\text{SemSimi}(P,Q)= \ln⁡ [(P∩Q)] / \ln⁡ [|A-B|]$$

Step 9: Choose an appropriate index and check its range lies between [0, 1].
Step 10: if value lies in [0, 1] is considered to be as similar, if value is higher than 1 comes out to be highly similar and if less than 0 fall into category of not similar.
Step 11: Compare with tools available using web search engine.
Step 12: Stop.

5 Conclusion

Based on page count metric, we are trying to present procedure that is more effective for computing semantic similarity for relevant information retrieval so far. This paper has focused on different approaches for reckoning of semantic similarity between the concepts or words in a domain. Semantic similarity is a computational method that quantifies the similarity among concepts belonging to single dataset or multiple datasets. Therefore, this paper presents a method that uses a matric of page count to match words efficiently and having less computational complexity as compared to all other formulas. This work will be mainly useful in very important area of information retrieval i.e. query expansion where the word input in a query by any user can be replaced with the most similar words and results can be shown along with original query results to increase the efficiency and materiality in day to day usage. Moreover, proposed method almost outperforms or gives almost same results when compared with the online tools available as well as previous work, which makes it helpful in actual tasks, which take in name entities sheltered by manually fashioned resources.

6 Futurescope

The work presented is contemptible on similarity between words but this can be further extended to similarity between multiple entities, sentences and then between complete documents. Also we have done analysis on the Charles-Miller dataset but we can analyze the same work on various other big datasets which is beyond the scope of this work, still various datasets available are like biomedical i.e. MeSh or Rubenstein-Goodenough (RG: 65 pairs, 36 annotators) or WordSimilarity-353 (353 pairs, 13 annotators).

References

1. Bollegala, D., Matsuo, Y., Ishizuka, M.: A web search engine-based approach to measure semantic similarity between words. IEEE Trans. Knowl. Data Eng. **23**(7), 977–990 (2011)
2. Iosif, E., Potamianos, A.: Unsupervised semantic similarity computation between terms using web documents. IEEE Trans. Knowl. Data Eng. **22**(11), 1637–1647 (2010)
3. NGD: IEEE Trans. Knowl. Data Eng. **19**, 370–383 (2010)
4. Resnik, P.: J. Artif. Intell. Res. 95–130 (1999). https://www.jair.org/media/514/live-514-1722-jair.pdf
5. WordNet:: Similarity. http://maraca.d.umn.edu/similarity.html
6. WordNet:: Similarity. http://maraca.d.umn.edu/similarity/measures.html
7. WordNet. http://www.d.umn.edu/~tpederse/Pubs/AAAI04PedersenT.pdf
8. WordNet, Gloss Vector Measure. http://www.aclweb.org/anthology/S12-1070
9. SEMILAR. http://www.semanticsimilarity.org/
10. UMBC. http://swoogle.umbc.edu/SimService/
11. Rus, V., Lintean, M., Moldovan, C., Baggett, W., Niraula, N., Morgan, B.: The SIMILAR corpus: a resource to foster the qualitative understanding of semantic similarity of texts
12. Han, L., Kashyap, A., Finin, T., Mayfield, J., Weese, J.: UMBC EBIQUITY-CORE: semantic textual similarity system. In: Proceedings of the Second Joint Conference on Lexical and Computational Semantics, vol 1, pp. 44–52

Comparative Analysis of Metaheuristics Based Load Balancing Optimization in Cloud Environment

Amanpreet Kaur[1(✉)], Bikrampal Kaur[2], and Dheerendra Singh[3]

[1] IK Gujral Punjab Technical University, Jalandhar, Punjab, India
Er.amanpreet14@gmail.com

[2] Chandigarh Engineering College, Landran, Mohali, Punjab, India
mca.bikrampal@gmail.com

[3] Chandigarh College of Engineering and Technology, Chandigarh, India
professordsingh@gmail.com

Abstract. Cloud Computing Technology provides computing resources as a utility service. The objective is to achieve maximum resource utilization with minimum service delivery time and cost. The main challenge is to balance the virtual machines (VM) load in cloud environment and it requires distributing the load between many virtual machines while avoiding underflow and overflow conditions, which depend on capacity of VMs. In this paper, load balancing of VMs have been done based on Ant Colony Optimization (ACO) and Bat algorithm for underflow and overflow VM identifications respectively. As cloud applications involve huge computations and are highly dynamic in nature, so Directed Acyclic Graph (DAG) files of various scientific workflows have been used as input data during implementation of the proposed methodology. Workflows used for experiments are Cybershake, Genome, Ligo, Montage, Sipht and VMs vary from 2 to 20 on a single host configuration. Initially, the workflows are parsed through Predict earliest Finish time (PEFT) heuristic which initializes the metaheuristics rather than using random initialization. Thus, metaheuristics are providing optimal initial parameters which further optimize the VM utilization by balancing their load. The performance of metaheuristics on the basis of makespan and cost metrics has been evaluate, analyzed and compared with the Particle Swarm Optimization (PSO) approach used for load balancing.

Keywords: Ant Colony Optimization (ACO) · BAT algorithm
Particle Swarm Optimization (PSO) · Predict Earliest Finish Time (PEFT)
Performance analysis · Makespan · Cost

1 Introduction

Cloud computing is today's emerging paradigm providing services to scientific, engineering and business applications built for both cloud service provider and service consumer. Load balancing is an important facet of cloud computing which is necessary for uniform load distribution among resources like nodes or virtual machines (VMs)

P. Bhattacharyya et al. (Eds.): NGCT 2017, CCIS 827, pp. 30–46, 2018.
https://doi.org/10.1007/978-981-10-8657-1_3

hosted on physical servers [1]. The heterogeneous cloud resources are distributed across different geographical locations across the globe in various datacenters, so it requires load distribution among available resources to improve their utilization (maximize throughput), fault tolerance while minimizing makespan, migration time, and cost of utilizing the resources. This results in improving the overall performance cloud computing technology while reducing energy consumption, cost and response time [1, 2]. The dynamic load of incoming cloud tasks are handled by Virtualization technology is used to map tasks to cloud resources available in the form of VMs [3].

Before Load balancing, the tasks are allocated to suitable resources available in datacenters; this process is called resource provisioning which is followed by task scheduling. Task scheduling is an important phase before load balancing. A single resource is capable of handling multiple tasks so the order in which tasks will be executed by the resource (CPU/VM) is determined by the scheduling algorithm. A number of task scheduling algorithms are available in literature for executing dynamic tasks using distributed cloud resources and the resources are allocated in such a manner that the scheduling and load balancing algorithms must ensure minimum resource wastage while avoiding overloading/underloading of resources [4].

In this paper, a metaheuristic based framework for load balancing in cloud environment has been implemented for workflow applications. The performance evaluation has been done on the basis of two important metrics-Makespan and cost. The results are compared for three metaheuristics- Ant Colony Optimization (ACO), Bat optimization and Particle Swarm Optimization (PSO).

2 Related Work

Literature shows that many complex and NP-hard engineering problems can be optimally solved by metaheuristic algorithms. A variety of heuristic and metaheuristics including swarm intelligence and evolutionary techniques are based on physical or nature's biological behaviours. Ant Colony Optimization (ACO), particle swarm optimization (PSO), Bat optimization, harmony search, firefly algorithms are some examples of metaheuristics. To achieve fast convergence of these metaheuristic algorithms, they are hybridized with heuristics like heterogeneous Earliest Finish Time (HEFT) [5], Min-Min, Max-Min [6], Divisible Load Theory (DLT) and Predict Earliest Finish Time (PEFT). The analysis done by Arabnejad in [7] show that the results of PEFT algorithm are better than state-of-the-art list based algorithms. Verma and Kaushal [8] presented a scheduling technique Hybrid Genetic Algorithm to minimize execution cost of workflow applications based on Deadline Constrained Heuristic based Genetic Algorithms. Mehmood [1] and Ghomi et al. [2] presented a comparative study of various load balancing techniques and analyzed them on the basis of various metrics. Authors in [4] presented adaptive load balancing algorithms for heavy workload conditions. Bhaskar [3] proposed and implemented VM load balancing algorithm Amazon EC2 Cloud computing environment, resulted in decreased response time. Mishra [9] proposed ACO based load distribution approach and proved that pheromone updation as an effective mechanism for load balancing. Author in [10] described the origin, basics applications and hybridization of ACO for optimization of frameworks. In [11], researchers has applied Bat algorithm to solve various engineering problems and achieved efficient results better than genetic algorithm and PSO. The application of bat algorithm to dynamic optimization problems such as load balancing in cloud environment is mentioned to be future extension of this algorithm. Modified Bat algorithm is used for data de-duplication in [12] and authors claimed to achieve better results than genetic programming. Masdari et al. [13] presented existing PSO-based scheduling techniques in cloud computing environment and analyzed the improvements of PSO in these scheduling schemes and compared them on the basis of cost, makespan and load balancing. Authors in [14] minimized the cost of execution of scientific workflows in cloud environments. A modified min-min algorithm, namely, Load Balance Improved Min-min (LBIMM) algorithm has been proposed in [16] for the makespan minimization and utilization of resource improvement. In [17], a mathematical model based on heuristic for initializing ACO and GA was proposed to reduce the imbalance among the parallel machines during scheduling. Their results show that heuristic based ACO perform better than GA. Problem of Effective resource utilization with load balancing in heterogeneous Grid environment has been discussed in [18] and authors proposed a hybrid threshold based solution to perform load balancing. In their work, a random selection policy has been used which will select processes on overloaded nodes and transfer them to under-loaded nodes. Kaur et al. [19] discussed different techniques for optimizing scheduling and load balancing and further the comparisons among discussed techniques have been done on the basis of time, cost, SLA and energy efficiency parameters. Authors of [20] proposed a framework based on fat-tree topology for controlling the switching elements and hence, communication among VMs in data centers. The framework organizes the VMs such that VMs involving high communication are localized onto single host machine. A multi-tenant private cloud is generated by the framework which allows multiple VMs to communicate in parallel. The evaluation and analysis results of framework show good performance and achieve global load balancing of tasks across VMs.

3 The Methodology

In this paper, PEFT heuristic is used to provide initial seed to ACO, BAT and PSO. The three metaheuristic approaches are used for load balancing and their performance is evaluated and compared on the basis of makespan and cost metrics.

3.1 Seeding of Metaheuristics Based on Predict Earliest Finish Time (PEFT) Heuristic

The workflow tasks are highly dynamic in nature as their computation requirements vary significantly due to dependencies. PEFT is a list based scheduling approach which is well suited for scheduling dynamic tasks in heterogeneous computing systems. PEFT predict the VM which is best for the completing a particular task with minimum cost of execution and smallest task finish time on selected VM. In comparison with other list based scheduling algorithms like Heterogeneous Earliest Finish Time (HEFT), Mapping Heuristic (MH) and Dynamic Level Scheduling (DLS) algorithms, the results of

PEFT on the basis of schedule length and efficiency are far better [7]. The tasks workflow applications are represented as a direct acyclic graph (DAG) G(T, E) where 'T' is the set of n tasks $\{t_1, t_2, \ldots t_n\}$ to be executed on a same VM and 'E' is the set of edges depicting the dependencies among them [15]. An edge $e_{i,j} = (t_i, t_j) \in E$ represent dependency among tasks t_i, and t_j with a precedence constraint indicating that the execution of the task t_i should be completed before the start t_j. Further, an entry task t_{entry} in DAG is without any parent and an exit task t_{exit} is without any child nodes. The execution time from/to these tasks is zero.

Figure 1 shows the seeding algorithm for ACO, BAT and PSO initial to generate initial schedule based on PEFT approach. $C(t_k, t_l)$ is the weight or the average communication cost for scheduling two dependent tasks t_k and t_l such that $C(t_k, t_l)$ = zero if scheduled on the common VM. $Cost_{computation}(t_k, v_m)$ is the cost of executing t_k on VM $v_{m.}$

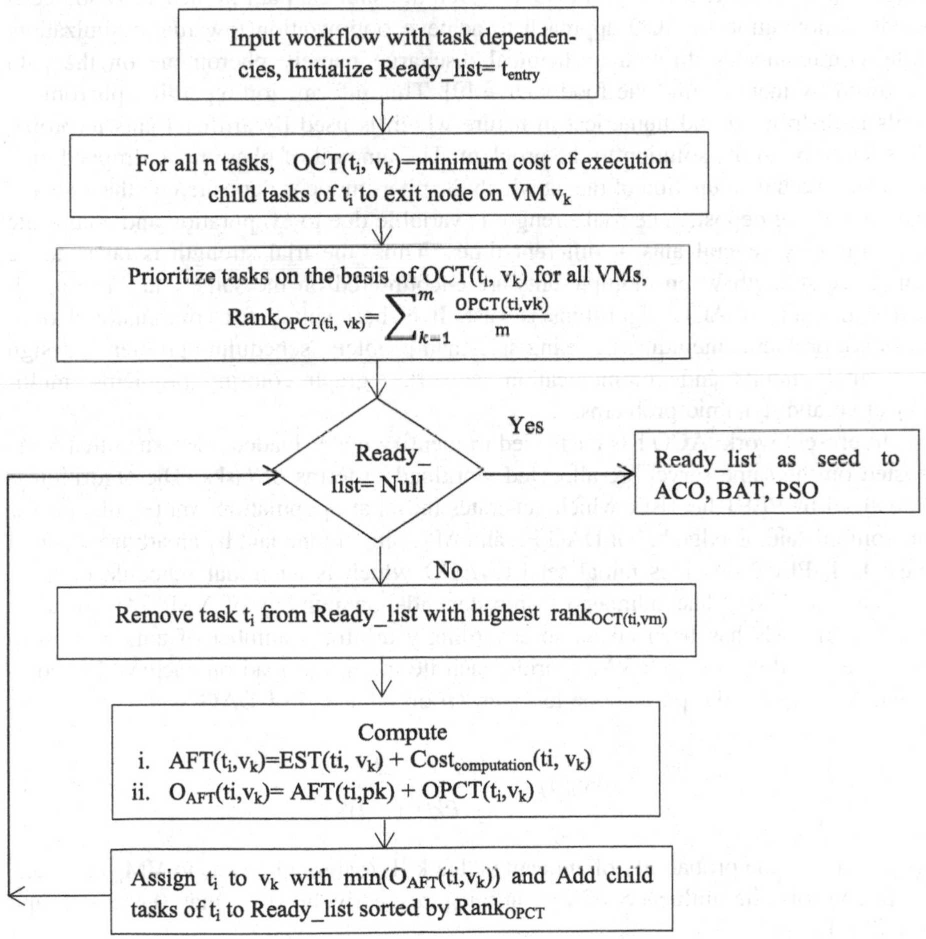

Fig. 1. PEFT approach for seeding ACO, BAT and PSO algorithms

EST(t_k, v_m) is the earliest time when v_m is available to execute t_k AFT(t_k, v_m) Actual finish time of task t_k on VM v_m. OPCT(t_k, v_m) Optimal cost of executing t_k on v_m $rank_{OPCT(tk,vm)}$ refers to priority of task t_k assigned to v_m (see Fig. 1).

3.2 Ant Colony Optimization Based VM Load Balancing

Ant Colony Optimization (ACO) is a swarm optimization based metaheuristic technique proposed by Marco Dorigo in 1992. It is used to solve optimization problems especially hard combinatorial problems [10]. ACO is based on the biological ant behavior which is a random and unsophisticated species when act individually due to their limited memory. However, their collective and cooperative behavior is significant to perform complex tasks with more reliability and uniformity. The social behavior of ants is used by researchers to develop algorithms to get solution for complex combinatorial problems. The ability of ants to search the shortest path to their food source is used as motivation to ACO approach to achieve optimization towards minimization. Ants communicates through a chemical discharge namely pheromone on the path followed by them to find the food source [9]. This information regarding pheromone trails is distributed and numerical in nature which is used by artificial ants to probabilistically build the solution to the problem. The amount of pheromone dropped on a particular path is a function of rate at which the pheromone is deposited on the path and the quantity of deposit. The trial strength is variable due to evaporation and composite deposition by several ants at different times. Thus, the trial strength is taken to be collective strength when multiple ants are encountered on the same path. The application domain of ACO algorithms is vast. It is best suited for combinatorial optimization problems including traveling salesman problem, scheduling problems, design of digital circuits and communication networks, graph coloring problems, multi-objective and dynamic problems.

In present work, ACO has been used to identify under loaded VMs such that VMs hosted on the same server are allocated workload in terms of tasks. The algorithm is initialized by PEFT heuristic which generates initial ant population Ant population A_p, pheromone laid on edge k, l of DAG P_{kl} and ΔP_{kl} pheromone laid by an arbitrary ant on edge k, l. PEFT provides initial seed to ACO which is an initial schedule of tasks allocated to VMs. The number of ants depends on number of VMs. As dynamic number of VMs has been taken, so accordingly arbitrary number of ants is used to generate schedule for each VM. During each iteration, the load on each VM is computed accordingly the pheromone level $Pr_{kl}(i)$ on edge k, l of DAG as:

$$Pr_{kl}(i) = \frac{(Pkl)^{\alpha}(\mu kl)^{\beta}}{\sum (Pkl)^{\alpha}(\mu kl)^{\beta}} \quad (1)$$

where 'μkl' is the probability of choosing edge k, l; assigning task t_k to VM_l, constants α, β controls the influence of P_{kl} and μ_{kl} respectively such that $0 < \alpha < 1$ and $0 < \beta < 1$.

As the tasks undergo execution, the load on VMs also decreases, this is similar to evaporation of pheromone on edge k, l, so the intensity of pheromone changes (decreases) according to following equation:

$$P_{kl} = (1 - \rho)P_{kl}(t) + \sum_{i=1}^{Np} \Delta T_{ij}^{k} \quad (2)$$

where 'ρ' is pheromone evaporation rate, which depends on capacity of VM, higher if VM computation power is higher.

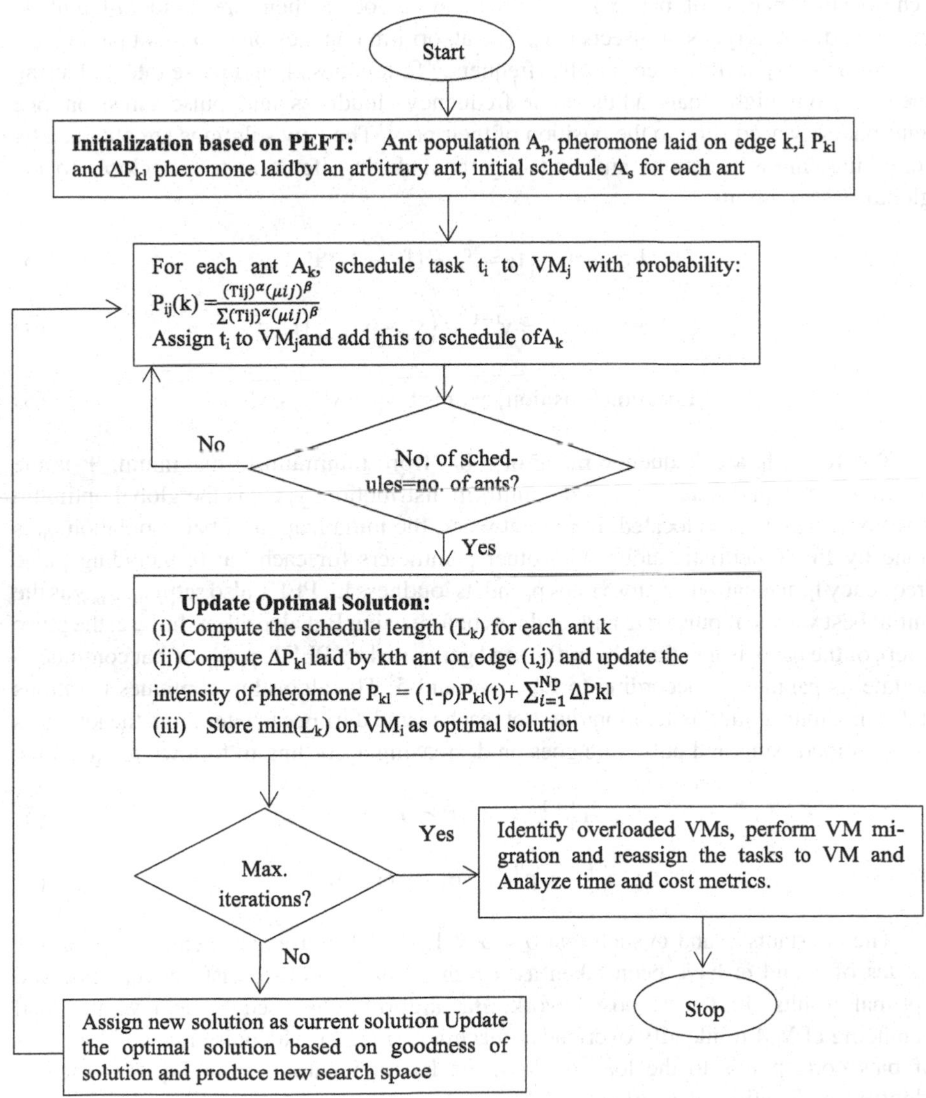

Fig. 2. Load balancing approach based on ACO

The load is distributed on the basis of minimum threshold. This threshold value is set according to the computing capacity of the VM. If the load on the VM is less than the calculated threshold, then artificial ant of ACO finds an under loaded VM among the neighbor of the current VM to transfer its load to the current under loaded machine. This is done after checking the updated foraging pheromone value. The flowchart in Fig. 2 shows the underutilization management based on ACO.

3.3 BAT Algorithm for VM Load Balancing

Bat Algorithm (BA) is a promising and new metaheuristic which depends on echolocation nature of bats which help them to locate their prey and differentiate between different types of insects [11]. The algorithm depends on important parameters like velocity (v_i) with which bats fly, frequency f_i, loudness l_i and pulse rate p_i. During their random flight, bats adjust their frequency, loudness and pulse emission rate automatically according to the position of their prey. The new solutions are obtained by following fitness functions and updating them during iteration to get closer to the global best solutions:

$$\text{Frequency}, f_i = f_a + (f_b - f_a)\Psi, \tag{3}$$

$$\text{Velocity}, v_i = v_i^{t-1} + \left(y_i^t - y_{gbest}\right) f_i, \tag{4}$$

$$\text{Location (position) at time t}, y_i^t = y_i^{t-1} + v_i^t \tag{5}$$

Where, f_a, f_b are frequency range of a bat from minimum to maximum, Ψ is the random vector in domain [0, 1] from uniform distribution, y_{gbest} is the global optimum position where prey is located. In present work, the initialization of bat population b_p is done by PEFT heuristic along with other parameters for each bat b_i including pulse frequency f_i, at location y_i, pulse rates p_i and its loudness L_i. PEFT also setp_{peft}, L_{peft} as the initial best values of pulse rate and loudness before using Bat algorithm. In case, the pulse ratep_i of the bat b_i is less than the initial seed generated by PEFT, $p_{peft,}$ the bat continue to update its parameters according to Eqs. 3, 4 and 5. The algorithm continues iterations until maximum count of iterations has not reached and during each iteration, the loudness goes on increasing and pulse rate goes on decreasing according to following equations.

$$L_i^{t+1} = \alpha L_i, 0 < \alpha < 1 \tag{6}$$

$$p_i^{t+1} = p_i^0[1 - e^{-\omega t}], \omega > 0 \tag{7}$$

The constants α and ω such that $0 < \alpha < 1$, $\omega > 0$. For experimental purpose, the values of α and ω have been taken as $\alpha = \omega = 0.9$ to achieve fast convergence and optimal results. In the proposed work, Bat algorithm is used to achieve the load balancing of VM to identify overloaded machines (Fig. 2). The pulse rate and loudness of bats corresponds to the load on VM, the location parameter in Eq. 5 is used to identify the location of overloaded VM (see Fig. 3).

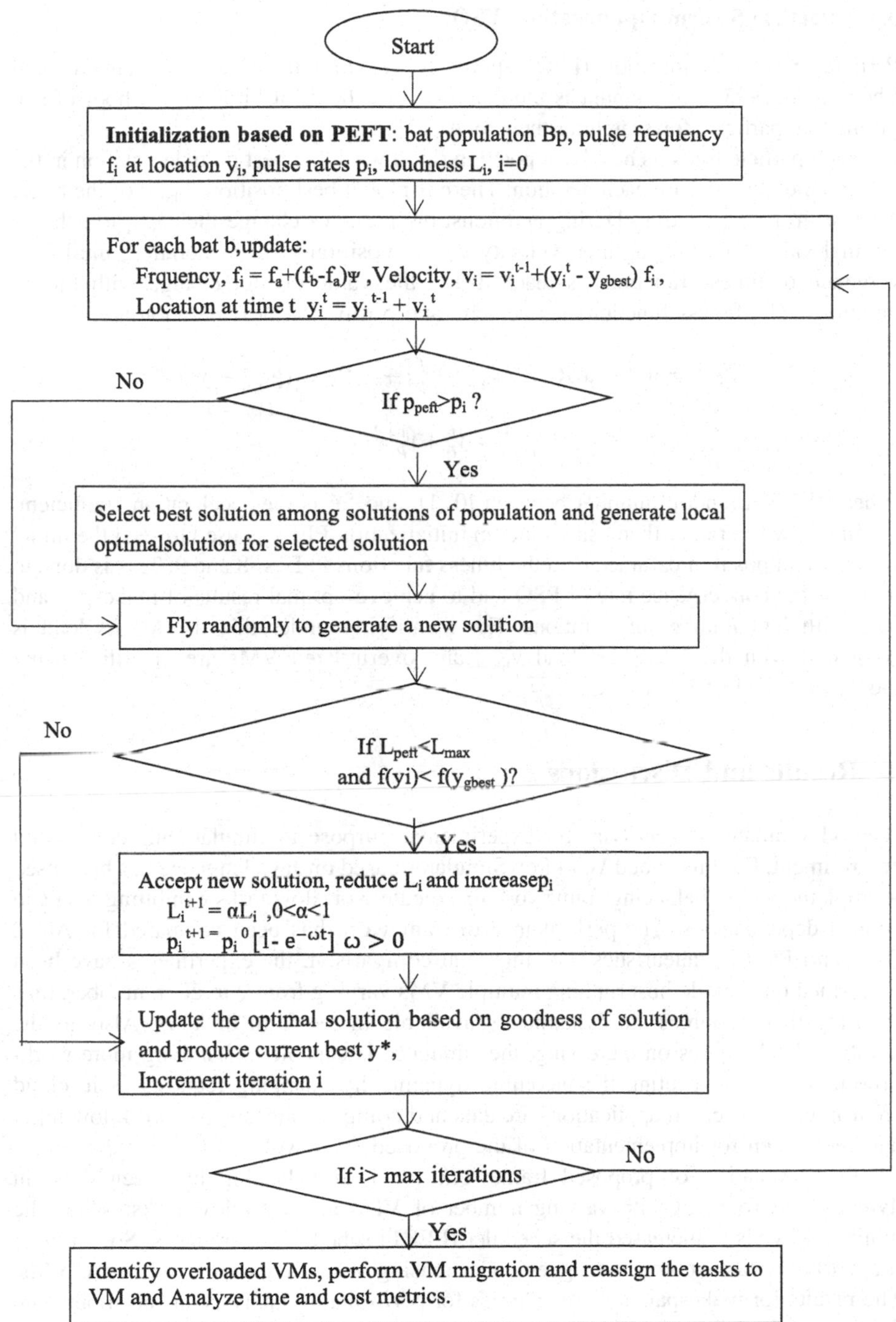

Fig. 3. VM load balancing using BAT algorithm

3.4 Particle Swarm Optimization (PSO)

Particle swarm optimization (PSO) approach was initially given by Kennedy and Eberhart in 1995 which emulates the behavior of a flock of birds or a school of fish (termed as particle) for searching their food [13].

Each particle finds its best local position (l_{best}) w.r.t. the best particle position in the entire population during each iteration. There is global best position (g_{best}) of the fittest particle in the population. During iterations, the particles change their l_{best} to achieve optimal value by adjusting their velocity v_p and position y_p at i^{th} iteration, until convergence of fitness functions is reached and the value do not change with further iterations. The fitness functions for velocity and position at next iteration are:

$$v_p^{i+1} = wv_p^i + a_1R_1 \times (l_{bestp}^i - y_p^i) + a_1R_2 \times (g_{best} - y_p^i), \tag{8}$$

$$y_p^{i+1} = y_p^i + v_p^{i+1} \tag{9}$$

Where 'R' is a random number between [0, 1], and 'a' is the acceleration coefficient.

In this work, rather than using random initialization PEFT is used to seed the initial velocity and position parameters in the fitness functions in Eqs. 8 and 9. This is done to improve the convergence rate of PSO and to achieve optimal results of makespan and cost with less number of iterations. For identifying underutilized VM, its load is compared with the local best load v_{lbest} and overutilized VMs are identified using global best load of VMs v_{gbest}.

4 Results and Discussions

A good simulator is necessary for experimental purpose to simulate an actual cloud environment. For this, cloud WorkflowSimulator based on Java language has been used to implement load balancing framework to execute workflow tasks exhibiting data and control dependencies. The performance of framework has been compared for ACO, BAT and PSO metaheuristics. For impartial comparison, the experiments have been performed on a single host running multiple VMs varying from 2 to 20 in number, thus ensuring that resources are dynamically available in the form of VMs. Also, as the number of VMs goes on increasing, the simulator is capable of handling more workflow tasks, thus executing the incoming dynamically changing requests as in cloud environment. As cloud applications are data and compute intensive, so workflow input has been taken for implementation of the proposed framework.

The simulation of proposed framework for load balancing has been done in dynamic environment with varying number of VMs and workflow tasks. When the number of VMs is increased the scheduler (PEFT) schedules more tasks. So, the time for workflow tasks completion goes on increasing with increase of number of VMs. The results for makespan and cost metrics for performance analysis has been obtained for 6 workflows among which five are scientific workflows- Cybershake, Genome, Ligo, Montage and Sipht and for validation of results, one Proposed workflow has been generated using Pegasus tool. These workflow tasks have been executed on multiple

Table 1. Total time results for Cybershake, Genome and Ligo workflow tasks

No. of VMs	Cybershake			Genome			Ligo		
	ACO	BAT	PSO	ACO	BAT	PSO	ACO	BAT	PSO
2	0	0	0	1.30E+4	6.43E+3	1.45E+4	1.04E+2	7.71E+2	1.02E+2
4	3.22E+2	1.28E+2	4.26E+2	2.62E+4	1.92E+4	3.12E+4	2.87E+3	1.41E+3	2.24E+3
6	6.96E+2	2.96E+2	7.00E+2	3.78E+4	2.47E+4	4.51E+4	4.13E+3	2.12E+3	4.25E+3
8	9.15E+2	5.25E+2	9.42E+2	6.66E+4	3.39E+4	6.89E+4	5.60E+3	2.57E+3	5.58E+3
10	1.25E+3	6.72E+2	1.30E+3	8.38E+4	4.30E+4	7.74E+4	6.64E+3	3.35E+3	6.71E+3
12	1.58E+3	7.90E+2	1.49E+3	9.94E+4	4.75E+4	8.96E+4	7.95E+3	3.98E+3	8.03E+3
14	1.62E+3	7.43E+2	1.57E+3	1.01E+5	5.71E+4	1.16E+5	9.13E+3	4.69E+3	9.17E+3
16	1.73E+3	1.03E+3	2.06E+3	1.27E+5	6.18E+4	1.35E+5	1.06E+4	5.24E+3	1.05E+4
18	1.95E+3	9.57E+2	1.81E+3	1.58E+5	7.02E+4	1.49E+5	1.18E+4	5.82E+3	1.14E+4
20	2.14E+3	8.68E+2	2.20E+3	1.71E+5	8.16E+4	1.48E+5	1.28E+4	6.43E+3	1.32E+4

Table 2. Makespan results for Montage, Sipht and Proposed workflow tasks

No. of VMs	Montage			Sipht			Proposed		
	ACO	BAT	PSO	ACO	BAT	PSO	ACO	BAT	PSO
2	1.15E+2	0	0	5.40E+3	2.34E+3	4.25E+3	0	2.13E+2	4.86E+2
4	3.08E+2	5.95E+1	5.00E+2	1.01E+4	5.12E+3	9.48E+3	2.71E+2	3.66E+2	1.65E+3
6	5.28E+2	3.51E+2	4.51E+2	1.16E+4	6.28E+3	1.29E+4	1.29E+3	4.86E+2	1.54E+3
8	5.39E+2	2.95E+2	5.59E+2	1.64E+4	8.30E+3	1.62E+4	9.08E+2	1.45E+3	3.32E+3
10	6.27E+2	6.39E+2	7.55E+2	1.84E+4	1.07E+4	2.08E+4	3.51E+3	2.86E+3	3.02E+3
12	7.36E+2	3.69E+2	1.15E+3	2.63E+4	1.18E+4	2.47E+4	5.39E+3	2.12E+3	5.54E+3
14	9.31E+2	6.27E+2	1.46E+3	2.80E+4	1.41E+4	2.96E+4	3.40E+3	1.35E+3	No-ex
16	1.35E+3	6.12E+2	1.07E+3	3.08E+4	1.59E+4	3.26E+4	No-ex	2.23E+3	No-ex
18	1.26E+3	5.96E+2	1.09E+3	No-ex	No-ex	No-ex	No-ex	4.77E+3	No-ex
20	1.77E+3	7.84E+2	1.10E+3	No-ex	No-ex	No-ex	No-ex	No-ex	No-ex

VMs on single host. The VM load balancing is done using three metaheuristics-ACO, Bat and PSO separately and their results for makespan and cost have been compared. The initial population of these metaheuristics has been seeded by PEFT heuristic rather than random seeding to improve the rate of convergence. Tables 1 and 2 shows the makespan of different workflows used as input to the proposed framework for scheduling and load balancing. The average makespan of ACO and PSO for these workflows are found to be overlapping at 19.68 ms while the average results for Bat algorithm shows much improved to 10.05 ms.

Figure 4 shows the results for makespan for workflows. The varying number of VMs from 2 to 20 is taken on X-axis and Y-axis shows the makespan (in millisec) for workflow execution completion. The makespan results of Cybershake, Genome, Ligo and Sipht workflows based on ACO and PSO are overlapping with increasing the number of VMs while in case of Montage and Proposed workflows, ACO performs

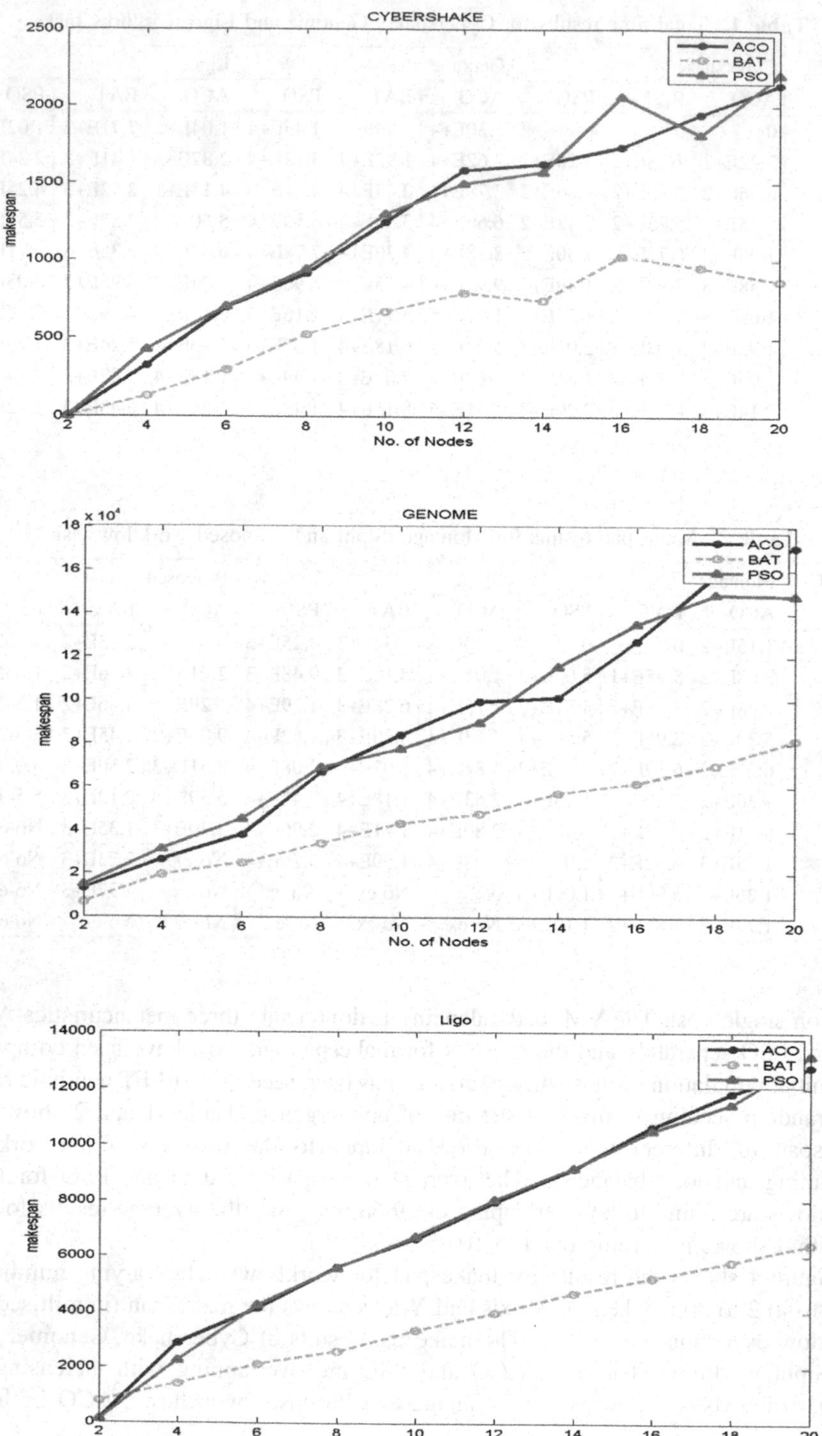

Fig. 4. Makespan analysis for ACO, BAT and PSO for different workflows

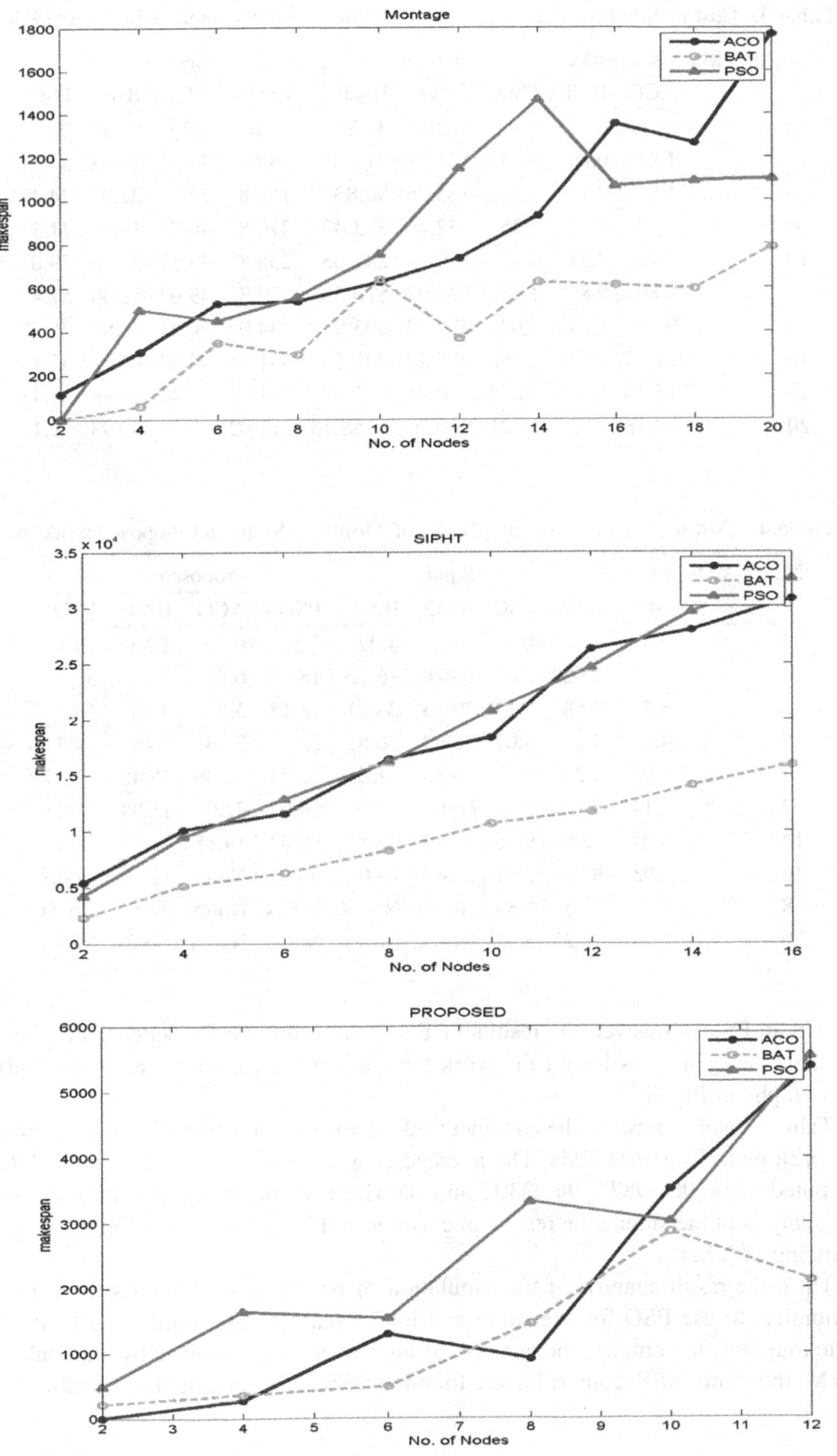

Fig. 4. *(continued)*

Table 3. Cost incurred for executing tasks of Cybershake, Genome and Ligo workflow

No. of VMs	Cybershake			Genome			Ligo		
	ACO	BAT	PSO	ACO	BAT	PSO	ACO	BAT	PSO
2	0	0	0	56.84	31.72	43.8	0.29	9.51	0.3
4	1.21	0.86	1.95	126.23	71.66	48.6	17.5	19.38	5.4
6	4.71	2.1	2.12	185.25	90.83	158.87	27	21.97	24.47
8	3.82	6.33	3.35	332.46	373.42	270.84	40.98	15.2	71.31
10	4.71	8.57	6.11	359.5	285.63	238.89	43.57	36.88	29.02
12	9.89	9.8	10.52	597.97	570.53	520.76	49.67	52.44	57.47
14	9.07	10.35	7.62	421.73	693.04	744.06	60.31	83.9	76.39
16	11.53	11.28	12.66	755.28	706.34	831.55	89.14	85.7	55.19
18	15.43	13.55	15.24	950.75	543.68	591.62	79.41	85.96	67.41
20	20.18	13.37	16.21	960.29	1158.13	611.02	92.76	89.93	79.1

Table 4. Cost incurred for executing tasks of Montage, Sipht and Proposed workflows

No. of VMs	Montage			Sipht			Proposed		
	ACO	BAT	PSO	ACO	BAT	PSO	ACO	BAT	PSO
2	0.57	0	0	4.42	4.02	3.52	0	1.36	1.61
4	1.9	0.62	2.67	16.78	16.75	18.19	0.88	3	5
6	3.53	4.68	2.34	20.13	24.91	18.18	5.5	4.16	5.87
8	4.25	4.2	3.02	28.69	30.83	22	3.18	9.46	14.4
10	5.02	8.26	5.13	19.33	41.65	26.54	11.46	15.42	12.89
12	5.14	5.14	9.32	66.68	35.01	50.07	22.91	13.94	26.33
14	6.94	7.69	9.36	39.67	47.81	88.07	14.15	12.77	No-ex
16	8.93	8.77	9.33	52.87	79.06	66.21	No-ex	18.66	No-ex
18	8.01	9.85	8.83	No-ex	No-ex	No-ex	No-ex	37.16	No-ex
20	12.47	11.25	8.99	No-ex	No-ex	No-ex	No-ex	No-ex	No-ex

better than PSO. However, the results of BAT algorithm are far better than other two optimization techniques for all the workflows taken for experimentation as analyzed from graphs in Fig. 4.

Tables 3 and 4 presents the cost incurred for execution followed by load balancing of workflow tasks across VMs. The average cost results for ACO, BAT and PSO are computed to be 96.29873, 94.02302 and 85.61636 respectively. Figure 5 shows the cost analysis of the simulation results of execution of input workflows followed by load balancing of VMs.

Thus, the result analysis of the simulation of proposed work shows the it is more economical to use PSO for execution and load balancing of workflow tasks on VMs while total time to complete the last task of input workflow followed by load balancing of VM, the results of Bat algorithm are found to be better than other two metaheuristics.

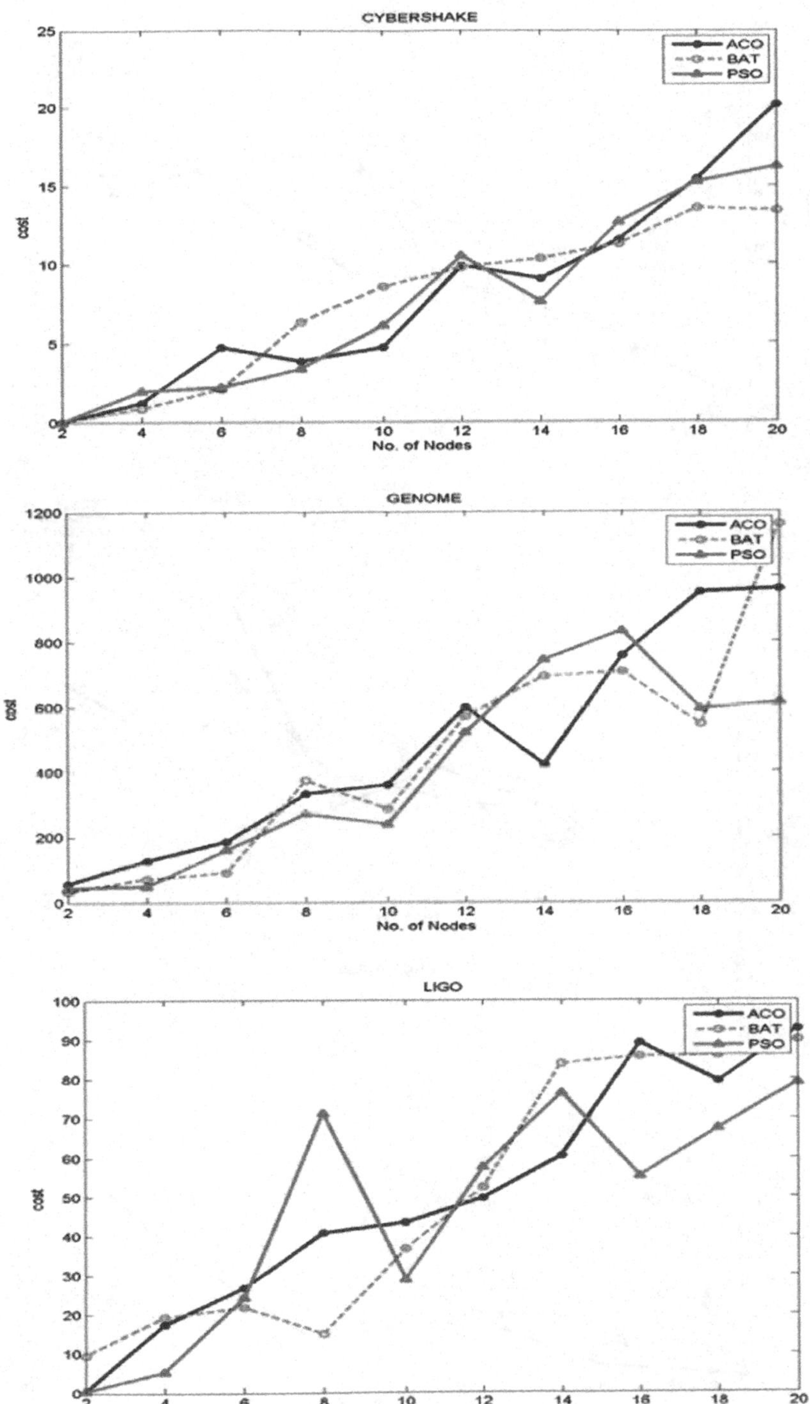

Fig. 5. Cost analysis for ACO, BAT and PSO for different workflows

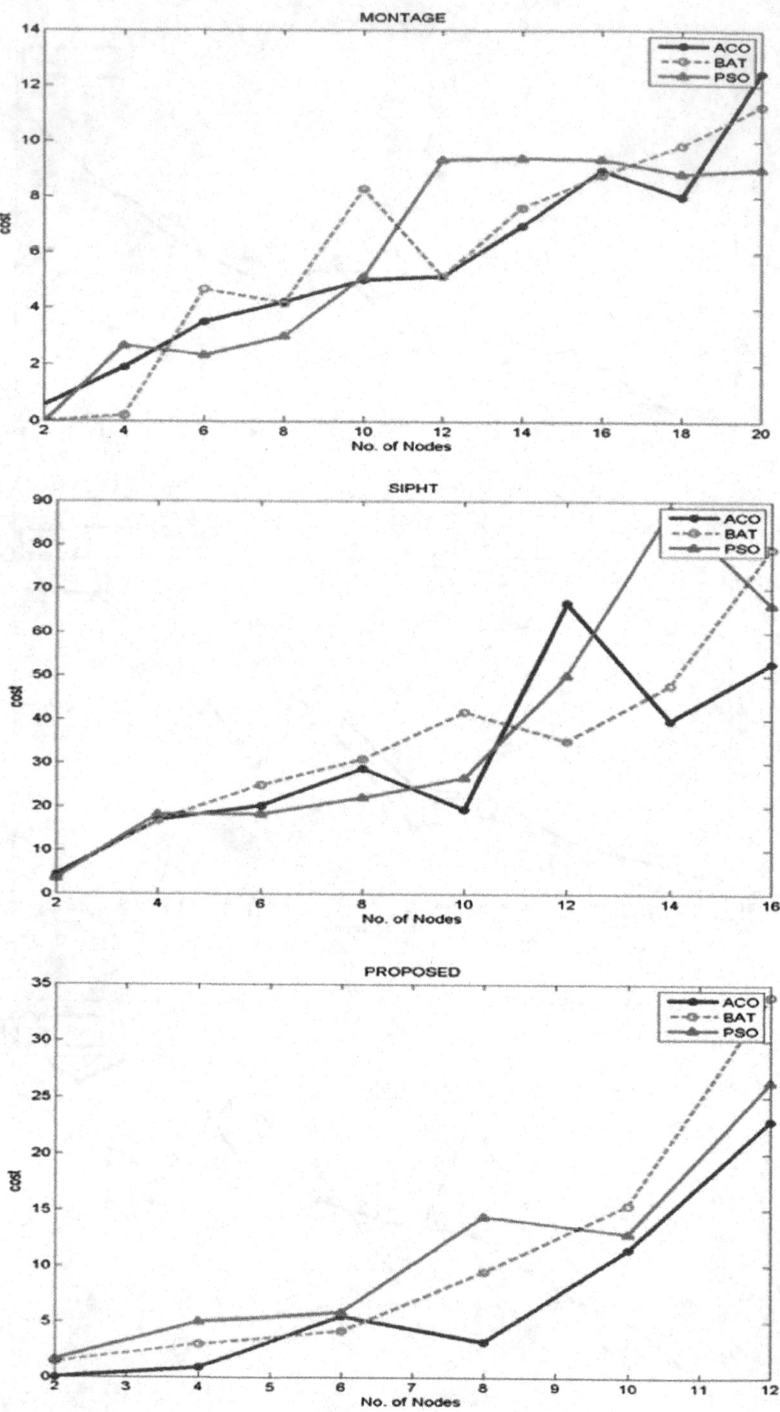

Fig. 5. *(continued)*

5 Conclusion

In this paper, ACO, BAT and PSO algorithms are used for load balancing in cloud environment using Java based CloudWorkflowSim. PEFT heuristic is used to provide initial seed to these metaheuristics. Their performance is evaluated on the basis of makespan and cost metrics. Experiments have been performed on DAG files of scientific workflows and a proposed workflow generated by Pegasus tool. The analysis of results of simulation shows that it is more economical to use PSO for execution and load balancing of workflow tasks on VMs, on the other hand, the results of Bat algorithm for total time to complete the last task of input workflow and VM optimization for load balancing are found to be better than other two metaheuristics.

References

1. Mehmood, M.: Load balancing approach in cloud computing. J. Inf. Technol. Soft. Eng. **05** (03), 1–5 (2015)
2. Ghomi, E.J., Rahmani, A.M., Qader, N.N.: Load-balancing algorithms in cloud computing: a survey. J. Netw. Comput. Appl. **88**, 50–71 (2017)
3. Bhaskar, R.: Dynamic allocation method for efficient load balancing in virtual machines for cloud computing environment. Adv. Comput.: Int. J. **3**(5), 53–61 (2012)
4. Kaur, P., Kaur, P.D.: Efficient and enhanced load balancing algorithms in cloud computing. Int. J. Grid Distrib. Comput. **8**(2), 9–14 (2015)
5. Ahmad, S.G., Liew, C.S., Munir, E.U., Ang, T.F., Khan, S.U.: A hybrid genetic algorithm for optimization of scheduling workflow applications in heterogeneous computing systems. J. Parallel Distrib. Comput. **87**, 80–90 (2016)
6. Rahman, M., Hassan, R., Ranjan, R., Buyya, R.: Adaptive workflow scheduling for dynamic grid and cloud computing environment. Concurr. Comput.: Pract. Exp. **25**(13), 1816–1842 (2013)
7. Arabnejad, H., Barbosa, J.G.: List scheduling algorithm for heterogeneous systems by an optimistic cost table. IEEE Trans. Parallel Distrib. Syst. **25**(3), 682–694 (2014)
8. Verma, A., Kaushal, S.: Deadline constraint heuristic-based genetic algorithm for workflow scheduling in cloud. Int. J. Grid Util. Comput. **5**(2), 96–106 (2014)
9. Mishra, R.: Ant colony optimization: a solution of load balancing in cloud. Int. J. Web Semant. Technol. **3**(2), 33–50 (2012)
10. Blum, C.: Ant colony optimization: introduction and recent trends. Phys. Life Rev. **2**(4), 353–373 (2005)
11. Yang, X.S., Hossein Gandomi, A.: Bat algorithm: a novel approach for global engineering optimization. Eng. Comput. **29**(5), 464–468 (2012)
12. Faritha Banu, A., Chandrasekar, C.: An optimized approach of modified BAT algorithm to record deduplication. Int. J. Comput. Appl. **62**(1), 10–15 (2013)
13. Masdari, M., Salehi, F., Jalali, M., Bidaki, M.: A survey of PSO-based scheduling algorithms in cloud computing. J. Netw. Syst. Manag. **25**(1), 122–158 (2016)
14. Pandey, S., Wu, L., Guru, S.M., Buyya, R.: A particle swarm optimization-based heuristic for scheduling workflow applications in cloud computing environments. In: 2010 24th IEEE International Conference on Advanced Information Networking and Applications, pp. 400–407 (2010)

15. Maheshwari, K., Jung, E., Meng, J., Morozov, V., Vishwanath, V., Kettimuthu, R.: Workflow performance improvement using model-based scheduling over multiple clusters and clouds. Future Gener. Comput. Syst. **54**, 206–218 (2016)
16. Chen, H., Wang, F., Helian, N., Akanmu, G.: User-priority guided Min-Min scheduling algorithm for load balancing in cloud computing. In: 2013 National Conference on Parallel Computing Technologies (PARCOMPTECH), pp. 1–8 (2013)
17. Keskinturk, T., Yildirim, M.B., Barut, M.: An ant colony optimization algorithm for load balancing in parallel machines with sequence-dependent setup times. Comput. Oper. Res. **39** (6), 1225–1235 (2012)
18. Roman, M., Ashraf, J., Habib, A., Ali, G.: Load balancing in partner-based scheduling algorithm for grid workflow. Int. J. Adv. Comput. Sci. Appl. **7**(5), 444–453 (2016)
19. Kaur, A., Kaur, B., Singh, D.: Optimization techniques for resource provisioning and load balancing in cloud environment: a review. Int. J. Inf. Eng. Electron. Bus. **9**(1), 28–35 (2017)
20. Duan, J., Yang, Y.A.: Load balancing and multi-tenancy oriented data center virtualization framework. IEEE Trans. Parallel Distrib. Syst. **28**(8), 2131–2144 (2017)

Twitter Recommendation and Interest of User Using Convolutional Neural Network

Baljeet Kaur Nagra(✉), Bharti Chhabra, and Amit Verma

Department of Computer Science, Chandigarh Group of Colleges, Landran, Mohali, Punjab, India
baljeetkaur.nagral26@gmail.com, cecm.cse.bharti@gmail.com, dramitverma.cu@gmail.com

Abstract. There is a tremendous growth in the area of social networking in the last couple of years. It is a way of having a huge amount of information where users can see other users' opinions, which are further divided into various recommender Classes, that are growing fast as a main component in decision making in recommender system's. In this paper, we took one popular micro blog called Twitter. The tweets are taken from twitter gives opinion and interests about different subjects. A Recommender System is basically made up of different software tools and techniques related to deep machine learning which gives meaningful information's about those tweets which are tweeted. Recommender system is very popular in every field like research, commercial fields and industrial areas. A lot of methods have been proposed for classifications in recommendations. Certainly, recommendation systems have various unique characteristics that its needs to experiences the different user such as users 'preference, prediction accuracy, confidence, trust, etc. In our work, we proposed an algorithm and work is done on feature set by reducing the sparseness of feature by phrase features and classified high non linear dataset by deep learning because deep learning use different pattern layer all possibility of existing pattern in feature set.

Keywords: Classifier · Feature set · Micro blogging
Recommendation system

1 Introduction

By the passing of time and improvement in the latest version of Web 2.0, users registers on social sites and creates a huge numbers of online information like reviews, blogs, tweets, etc. This lot of information contains users' reviews, opinions about events, people and trending. It gives various opportunities for inaugurated of companies and to understand their users and improvement in the product quality as well as enhancement of their competitiveness.

Social networking sites like face book, twitter and instagram contains textual information and images. Textual information consists of various tweets characters. Text

P. Bhattacharyya et al. (Eds.): NGCT 2017, CCIS 827, pp. 47–65, 2018.
https://doi.org/10.1007/978-981-10-8657-1_4

mining information supports various sort of interest. These types of groups of companies are interested in users' interests whether it is of any subject's weather it's of advertisement of a tweet post. For example today's tech oriented world, everybody wants to know in brief. So people need short but exact reviews or rating of hotel at any palace for vacations booking for vacations. A try is done by politicians to find out the estimation of next presidential election (Table 1).

Table 1. List of various sort of bugs and solutions of recommendation system for bug analyzer

Type of bugs	Solutions
Data reduction for bug triage	Binary classifier for prediction of applying part selection and feature selection
Design of bug fixes	Based on qualitative research of different programmer
Graphical models for text processing	Concept of distance graph representations using SVM
Minimum consistent subset: by the use concept of consistency constrained optimization problem	A tabu search approach to the condensed nearest neighbor rule[7]
For unsupervised learning, efficient greedy feature selection	Novel method for unsupervised feature selection
Information needs in bug reports	Cooperation improvement between users and developers
By the use of explicit-state model checking and dynamic test generation, to find the bugs in web applications	For the domain of dynamic web applications solved by the use of dynamic test generation technique
Error of any learning algorithm	Boosting—algorithm called AdaBoost
Duplicate bug reports accurate retrieval	Using retrieval function to measure the duplicity between two bug reports

2 Related Work

In this technical world, researchers have developed many different tools for recommendation system which automatically detect the bugs. Research work is done by the researchers is presented here.

Collobert et al. (2011) the author focuses on CNNs to model sentences. To make a sentence representation in sentimental analysis, one convolution layer is used by the researchers which are followed by a max pooling layer. We also used same method by integrating supplementary attribute focused on the duality classification task in recommendation system.

Kalchbrenner et al. (2014), in this paper author showed that a Convolutional neural network for modeling sentences. It has an ability to acquire competitive results in polarity classification. To provide length, researchers introduced a dynamic k-max pooling method that adapts max pooling. By taking idea of their work we used a simpler architecture of the Convolutional neural network in twitter recommendation based on their tweets, we also used max-pooling, because of this max pooling method there is a ease in research work.

Moreover, to reduce the parameters, basically filter is used by us for every dimension whereas their adopted model uses a various sort of filter per dimension. We used Convolutional Neural Network model and SVM model for comparing the performance with one another classifier to produce the optimum results. Using the CNN and SVM for classification is a common approach. Classification systems are used bag-of-words features and Support vector Machine to classify the classes (Movie, politics, games, computer science, and science).

Pang et al. (2002) in this Paper, author focused on the classification system took features like bag of words and a classifier named support vector machine which basically classify movie related reviews.

SemEval et al. (2013, 2014), an SVM with many different features is used in their work. We also got result after implementation of their most helpful features with the help of SVM & CNN, which are the bag-of-words and summed the CNN & SVM output to get the final result.

3 Basic Concepts

This section describes the basic concepts of Recommender system, Data description, Data pre processing and Neural Network convolution neural algorithm, SVM algorithm.

3.1 Recommender System

Recommendation System is very popular information filtering technology which plays a very important role in aiding the users' internet systems to discover the appropriate

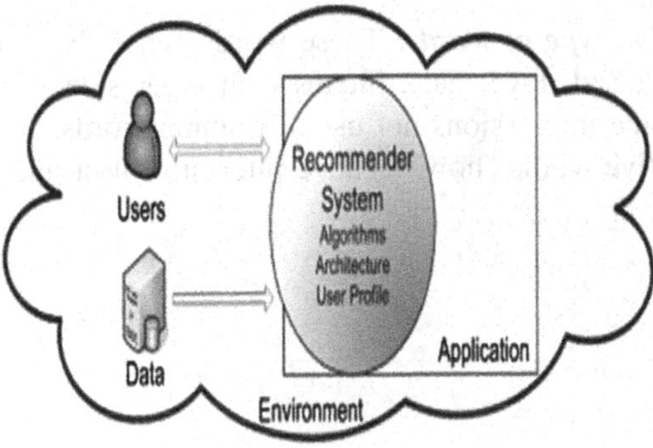

Fig. 1. Recommendation system.

data by providing the hints of relevant information of potential interest and search behaviour to the users'. Because of the possible outcomes of social correlation in SRS, social SRSs have gathered a lot of attention lately.

3.2 Data Description

Twitter is a social networking site or micro blogging site which lets its users to write and read real time posts and messages in the term of post and tweets,. Tweets have various types of unique characteristics. Twitter has 600 million accounts s and users post millions of messages every day, it has now turned into a gold mine for large organizations to keep eye on their image in the market and their brands values by analyzing the sentiment behind that post, tweets, retweets posted by the users about their remarks, markets, and other contenders and then provide recommendations on the basis of their interest or behavior. Performing recommendation on the basis of twitter posts, Twitter is hard to understand than doing it for large reviews. We acquire 15000 tweets of three distinct categories i.e. computer science, science, news, games and movie (5000 tweets for each categories). Then we performed 2nd stage named pre-processing on tweets.

3.3 Data Pre-processing

Twitter textual data has become very stimulating because of short character length up to 140 characters; twitter's user uses abbreviations and acronyms to complete their twitter post. Due to this, out of vocabulary rate goes high and makes tasks like tokenizing, stop word removal, stemming, Part-of-speech tagging, and lexicon search gets more and more tough so before going classification pre-processing happens. In tokenization all the words divides into tokens to save the memory. After tokenization, stop word removal and stemming data goes to index for storage. After then TF/ITF calculation is done. There are some Terms related to be given below:

- ***Terms Frequency and Inverse term frequency:*** These types of features generally are the single words or n-grams words with term frequency. It either uses term frequency weights or gives binary weighting to the words.
- ***Parts of speech:*** To find out the descriptive-words from given content, those give opinion indications.
- ***Phrases & Opinion type of words:*** These words generally applied to find out the interest like good, bad, love, hate, interests on other side if we see some of the phrases shows some impressions not use of opinion words.
- ***Negations:*** Negative words show negative interest of user and change the opinion of the user.

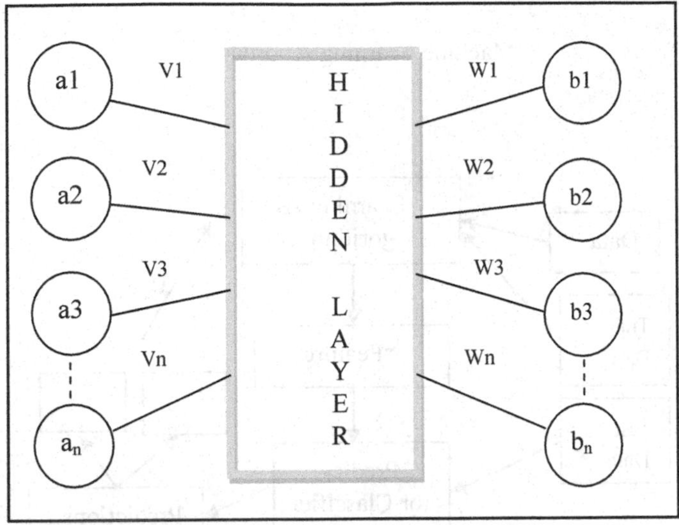

Fig. 2. Basic model of neural network

3.4 Neural Network Back Propagation Neural Network NN-CNN

Convolutional Neural Network which like to all others they have learnable weights and biases. CNN are made-up large no of neurons. An input is provided to the neurons which perform dot products of those inputs non-linearly. Entire network gives differentiable score function in which raw input is at one place and output score is on other hand. At the last layer, it has a loss function like SVM/Softmax (Fig. 2).

Here, a_1, a_2, a_3 … a_n are the inputs, H_L is Hidden layer, b_1, b_2, b_3 … b_n are the outputs to the given inputs.

4 Approach

4.1 Deep Machine Learning Approach

Deep Learning is a part of machine learning agitated with algorithms which is inspired by the structure and function of the brain known as artificial neural networks. The textual classification techniques by the use of deep learning approach are divided into two learning methods. First one is supervised and other one is unsupervised learning methods. Generally, deep learning approach is best suited to sentiment analysis and now these days to recommendation system because it mostly belongs to supervised classification and text classification techniques particularly.

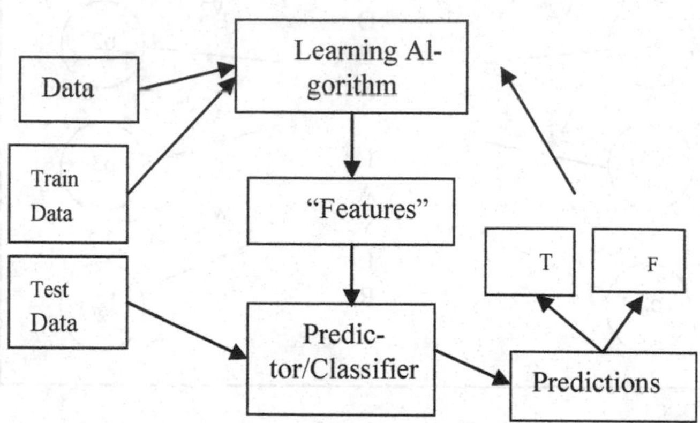

Thus, this method is known as "supervised learning". Couple of documents sets is required in deep learning based classification i.e. training and a testing set. A Classifier uses training set to learn the different types of tweets dataset's characteristics and a test set is use to ratify that classifier's performance. Different types of deep learning methods have been adapted for the classification of different type of classes. Deep machine learning techniques like Support vector machine (SVM), maximum entropy etc. has made huge triumph in textual classification field.

Basic Approach

Basic approach has become a popular approach which we have adapted in recommender system for product ranking. The predicted ratings which are notified by system are ranked from high to low.

$$Rank(p) = R \times (s, p) - 1 \tag{1.1}$$

Where R × (s, p) is predicted rating of the system. Products with have a highest predicted ratings which are recommended to all the users of twitter are who those who those have a power of minus one. This implemented approach only enhances accuracy but not diversity.

5 Model

5.1 Supervised Learning

Supervised learning process is basically applied to our project work. Here in the work, firstly training the classifiers is done by the help of selected features and labeled tweets (Fig. 3).

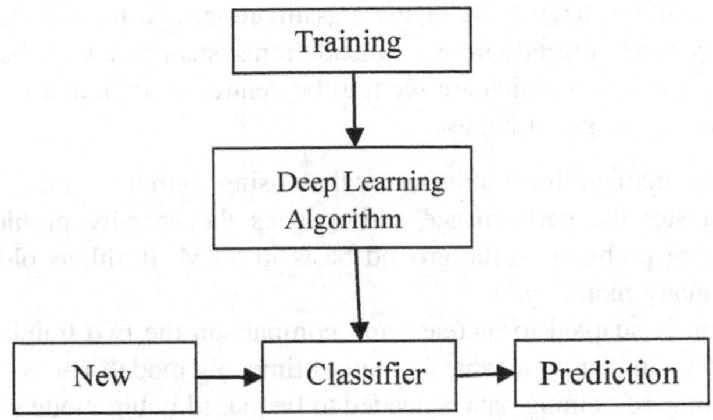

Fig. 3. Supervised learning

Then prediction of the new tweet is defined by help of trained classifier and extracted feature is then united with the labels to get the training dataset. The whole training set is then used to make the classifier. Then used the train classifier to classify the testing data.

6 Classifiers

The system architecture consists of three main components. The first components a CNN (right side in the figure), in which use of the sequential words in a tweet is made. 2nd bit is a Support Vector Machine (left side of the figure) classifier which uses several linguistic features.

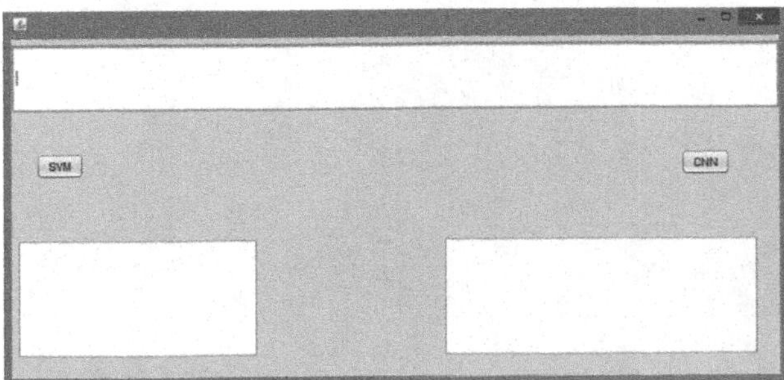

Finally, to predict the tweets on the basis of classes (movies, games, science, politics, and computer science), we used CNN and the SVM classifiers separately to compare their parameters (accuracy, precision, recall). Then we use comparison SVM & CNN classifiers (SVM_CNN) to compare performance.

6.1 Convolution Neural Networks

Two classifiers are used in this paper, first is CNN and second one is SVM. To improve the state of art of every field, Convolutional neural networks have recently been adapt like speech recognition, large-scale image classification, and textual information like sentimental analysis and recently in recommendation system by a large bases. There are basically three components which are seem to be central of attraction in the victory of this approach, those are given below:

- We have used rectified linear units rather than using sigmoid nonlinearities because it leads to faster the performance and reduces the sparsity problem (which is basically facing problem on the ground basis in SVM. It afflicts old l neural networks with many more layers.
- Parallelization is adapted to increase and comparison the two training and testing results, so that within a reasonable amount of time, big models can be easily trained.
- A heavy volume of training data is needed to be placed in big models like CNN and SVM with three parameters (Accuracy, Precision, and Recal). This Network mainly consists of enough quantity of training data to be able to train those large models effectively.

Convolution neural networks are especially made for predicting and estimating latent factor and textual information from classes which are here (Movies, Games, Politics, Science & Computer science).

Softmax

In the final layer of Convolutional neural network Softmax classifier is used. By giving a non-linear variant of multinomial logistic regression, training of such types of networks is done under a log loss regime, Convolutional Neural Network output and pooling layers X is move to Relu layer. After then computation of probability distribution over labels is done (Fig. 4).

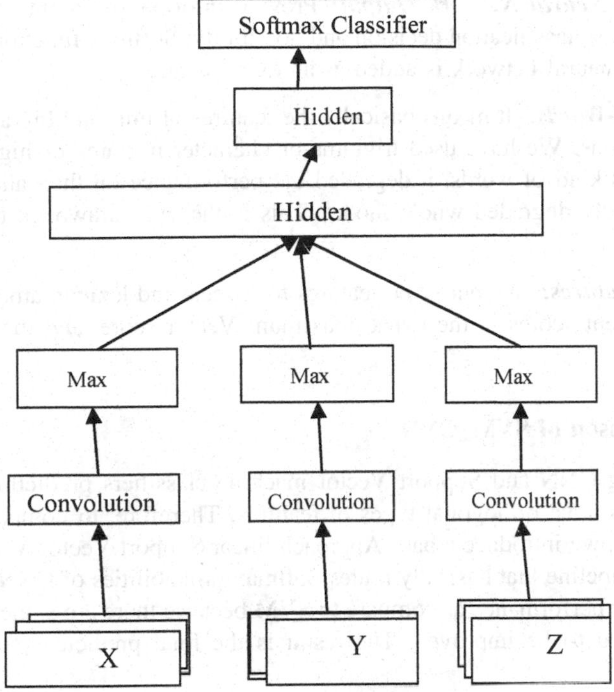

Fig. 4. Softmax function

6.2 Support Vector Machine (SVM)

Textual data information's are perfectly suited for SVM classification due to textual data's sparse nature, in which some features are unconnected and peripheral; it has a tendency of correlation. SVM can make a nonlinear decision surface is made by support vector machine in the original feature space. It is done by mapping the data instances non-linearly to an inner product space. It is that place where actually the classes can be linearly separated.

Since training the CNN for many epochs because Convolutional Neural Network is run over the whole dataset, always forward to outdated, so second classifier is added for a comparison, called SVM. Although CNN Proved itself as better classifier for Twitter Textual Recommendation. Some terms which we used in our work that are given below:

Convolutional Neural Network Output: Provide information about output of CNN about the CNN's classification decision and possibility; Softmax function output of the Convolutional neural network is added as an extra feature:

Binary Bag-of-Words: It means basically the features of uni- and bigrams, as well as character trigrams. We have used trigrams or character n-grams of higher order, but because of this kind of words, it degraded the performance on the validation set and that automatically degraded whole model. This is the only drawback to work for as future scope.

Characters Features: We put some features for tweets and lexicon amount of tokens, total of sentiment scores in the tweet, maximum Vector score, and the max score of classes.

6.3 Comparison of SVM_CNN

After analyzing CNN and Support Vector machine classifiers predictions, we got to know that both have orthogonal types of features. Therefore, to compare the performance of CNN, we introduce a base Approach linear Support Vector Machine into the classification pipeline that basically unites Softmax probabilities of CNN that says that CNN has better performance as compare to SVM because there are some bugs in SVM which is needed to be improved. The result is the final predicted polarity label of system.

7 Problem Formulation

Basic problem in classification of recommendation is features and select the model of classifier. Problem with features is it is highly sparse so computation of processing is without using any Information so feature should be less sparse. Second problem is selection of classifier, which is depending on dataset which is highly non- linear and when use more than two classes this problem, will increase exponentially.

7.1 Problem Statement

In this research, work is done on feature set by reducing the sparseness of feature by phrase features and classified high non linear dataset by deep learning because deep learning use different pattern layer all possibility of existing pattern in feature set.

8 Proposed Work

Algorithm

Step 1: Streaming the API tweets.

Step 2: For the pre-processing of text, tweets text are input.

Step 3: TF-IDF of pre-processed Data text is generated & Bi-gram, tri-gram features are extracted.

Step 4: The generated feature set is clustered and labeled in accordance to their hash tag scores. Cluster input that every input vector belongs uniquely to extract features.

$c=j=1_n c_n$ with $c_i \Pi c_j = \phi \forall j=i$

Step 5: Learning CNN with several layered approach having random weight value.

$$F_i(u) = \sum_{j=1}^{D} w_j^{0,i} H_j^k(u) + a^{0,i}, i = 1, 2, \ldots \ldots c$$

Where $w^0 \leftarrow$ random weight value

Step 6: Training classifier of training model

$$\sum_{i=1}^{n} L(F(u_i), O)$$

$$+ \lambda(\sum_{i,j=1}^{m+x} l(F(u_i).F(u_j), W(i,j))$$

Step 7: Training model instances are tested and calculating the accuracy, precision and recall.

$$\xi_{m:y} \leftarrow \sqrt{\frac{2}{\Pi} \sum_{x\epsilon\Omega_{m-1}} e^{A_m^{-\frac{1}{2}\|m-y\|^2}} - \xi_{m-1}(x)}$$

Flow Chart

In the Fig. 1, the flowchart of the proposed work is defined (Fig. 5):

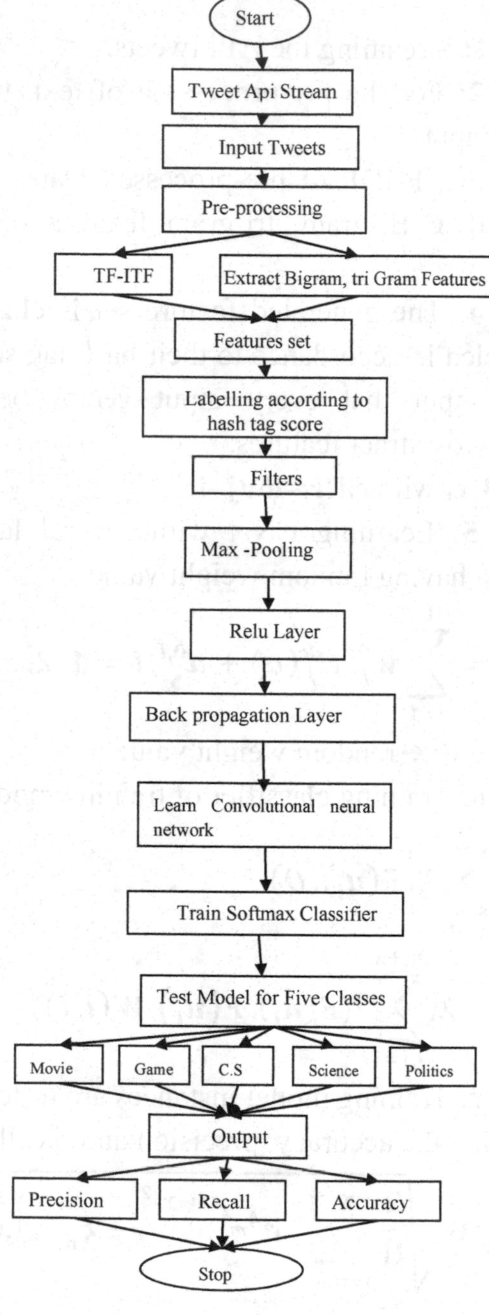

Fig. 5. Proposed flowchart

8.1 System Description

In the proposed system, we have a Graphic user interface. This system has two modules. One is the graphic user interface module in which when you run a task bar open, user can find out input belonging class. After classifying, user also find the Accuracy, Precision, Recall by two networks SVM as well as CNN Separately. And another is the user module is SVM_CNN in which user can directly determine the class belong to that input.

9 Experimental Results and Discussion

Twitter has its own service terms that do not provides tweets as textual information. Researchers of SEM Eval 2015 task those who had to get the tweets by downloading using a list of people registration and tweeter application identity documents. But now, Twitter' tweets are obtainable offline as a dataset collected from twitter. So getting tweets, user will have to register through twitter4j.

The java tool (NET BEAN) is basically used to figure out the better performance of recommender system. Windows 8 based system with 4 GB of RAM, 500 GB of hard disk, an Intel(R) Core(TM) i5 CPU, is used for our project purpose. Java based platform, Net Beans IDE 8.1 extension is used for implementing this work. For overall evaluation of implemented concept, parameters of precision, recall and Accuracy are considered (Fig. 6).

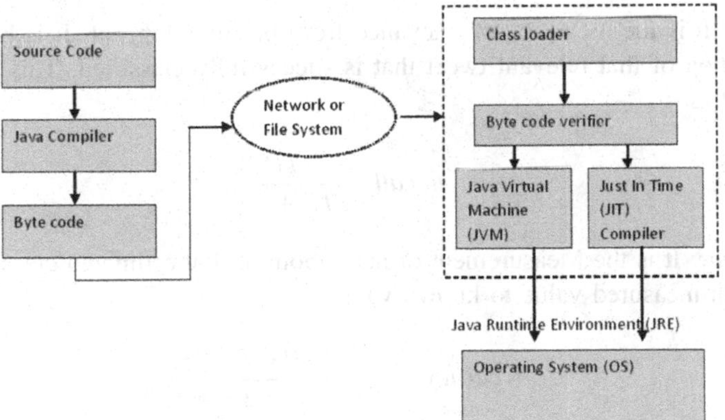

Fig. 6. Architecture of java tool

The NET BEAN is the technology introduced by sun micro system which is now subsidiary of oracle, on which all other technologies will be depending on in the future. It is a major technology change; to latch the market from the Java System use matrix based approach to manage all the entries on server side. Once all the entries uploaded to the server for processing it forward the control to the next module for data extraction and verification of data entries.

9.1 Evaluation Parameters

For evolution of various sort of techniques, different sort of matrices can be used. In our research work, for measuring performance, three parameters named Precision, Recall and Accuracy parameters is used.

To find out the Precision, Recall and Accuracy, some terms which are given below:

- TP (True Positive): is basically number of commodity accurately labeled as belonging to positive class.
- FN (False Negative is basically is the incorrect rejection of true null hypotheses.
- TN (True Negative): is basically number of commodity accurately labeled as belonging to negative class.
- FP (False Positive): is the failure to reject false null hypotheses.

Precision, Recall and Accuracy are evaluated by the bases of some measures which are given above. Descriptions and formulas of these parameters are given below:

(1) *Precision:* It basically measures how much positivity is in that concept. It is the proportion of the classified tweets which are relevant to that query or not. This can be calculated as:

$$Precision = \frac{TP}{TP + FP} \tag{1.2}$$

(2) *Recall:* It is the measures of relevance from positive concept. It is basically the proportion of that relevant tweet that is successfully classified. This can be calculated as:

$$Recall = \frac{TP}{TP + FN} \tag{1.3}$$

(3) *Accuracy:* It is the Measurement of near about of that estimated classified tweets or result measured value to known value.

$$Accuracy = \frac{TP + TN}{TP + TN + FP + FN} \tag{1.4}$$

In this proposed approach, java tool NET BEAN has been tested for different twitter based projects. Output varies every run time because every time tweet score would be different. The evaluated results of different classifiers for 5 classes with parameters of precision, recall and Accuracy values are shown in table.

After getting results, it can be easily seen and figure out that various sort of projects have different sort of result value with different type of algorithm and classifiers. Precision value of tweets (movie, games, computer science, politics and science) inconsistency will vary every time.

System used Vector matrix based approach to manage all the input entries. Once input is uploaded, input tweets goes for Pre-processing. After pre-processing, it forwards the control to the next module named filtering in which all tweets filters as random data. After that, Max polling is done. Max polling is basically the activation function on that layer is max. A vector matrix id formed.

A vector matrix is done under the product rule with max score of five classes file (movie, computer science, science, politics, and games) and this comes under the Relu Layer with a formula given below:

$$\tan h = \frac{\mathrm{e}^{\mathrm{x}} - \mathrm{e}^{-\mathrm{x}}}{\mathrm{e}^{\mathrm{x}} + \mathrm{e}^{-\mathrm{x}}}$$

After that it goes for back propagation network through Softmax classifier, it classifies the input tweets and mention the class in which it belongs to and also gives the Precision, Recall, Accuracy.

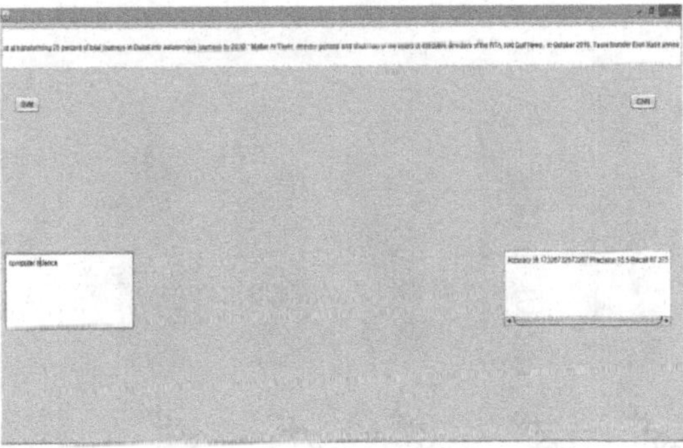

We have also included a base Approach named SVM for compare the Proposed Approach. After Comparing We got to know that CNN work better than SVM and has better result and performance.

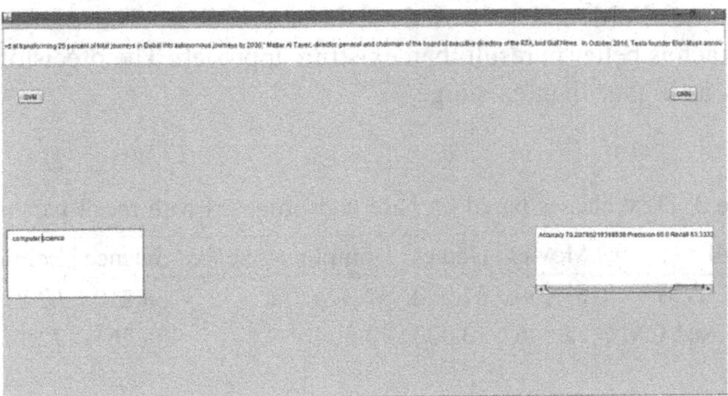

In Table 2: Other parameters are also calculated in this module to check the performance of the proposed approach. The high rate of precision recall and Accuracy are shows high performance of a system. Here it proves the working of the proposed approach gives better results than Existing Approach in the term of precision.

Table 2. Test case with precision, based upon based and proposed

Precision	Movies	Games	Computer science	Science	Politics
Base SVM	74.521	76.391	75.513	76.321	73.640
Proposed CNN	81.143	80.123	80.126	78.126	79.168

The above given table compares the various test classes for existing SVM based Approach and proposed CNN based approach in terms of precision. The performance of the proposed approach is higher if compare to existing one.

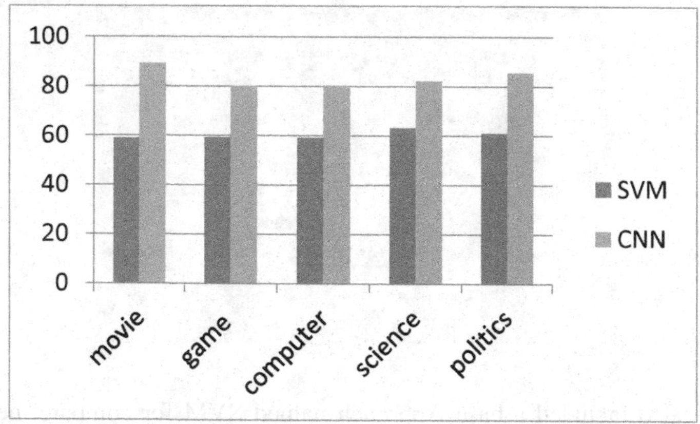

In given graph with the help of two different Approaches, Precision is calculated in both existing base SVM and proposed CNN approaches. The performance of the proposed approach is better in result than existing approach. The precision rate is stable in all the cases as higher than existing.

Table 3. Test classes based on base and proposed with recall parameter

Recall	Movies	Games	Computer science	Science	Politics
Base SVM	67.250	67.222	67.375	68.210	62.810
Proposed CNN	72.846	73.333	73.564	75.261	72.112

The Table 3 compares the various test cases for SVM based approach and proposed CNN based approach in terms of recall. The performance of the proposed approach is higher as compare to other test cases of existing.

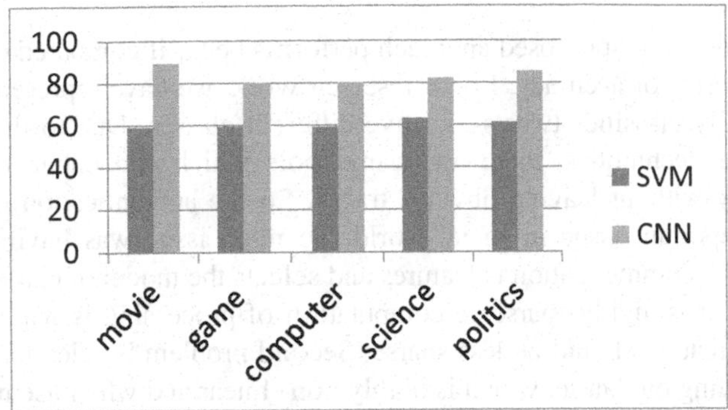

In given graph with the help of two different Approaches, Recall is calculated in both existing base SVM and proposed CNN approaches. The performance of the proposed approach is better in result and performance wise than existing approach. The recall rate is higher in proposed than existing.

Table 4. Test case in recall based on base and proposed work with accuracy

Accuracy	Movies	Games	Computer science	Science	Politics
Base SVM	58.906	59.323	59.177	63.181	61.121
Proposed CNN	89.287	80.207	80.257	82.123	85.457

The Table 4 compares different classes for existing SVM based and proposed CNN based approach in terms of accuracy. The performance of the proposed approach is higher as compare to other test cases of existing.

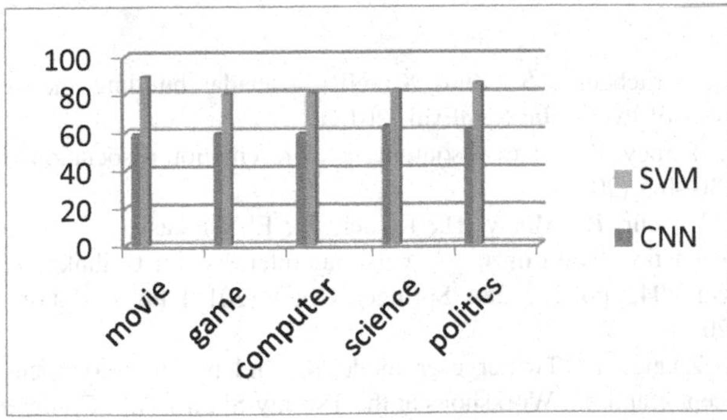

In given graph with the help of two different Approaches, Accuracy is calculated in both existing base SVM and proposed CNN approaches. The performance of the proposed approach is better in result than existing approach. The accuracy rate higher in proposed than existing.

10 Conclusion

As in the conclusion the proposed approach performs better if compared to SVM based approaches in terms of accuracy. In our research work, we have represented a method that automatically classifies tweets into five different classes. Due to the advances in recommendation techniques, there are many tools which can enhance the existing algorithm easily without leaving obvious traces. So the authentication of recommendation is an important issue in social world. Te main issue was having problem in classification of recommendation is features and selects the model of classifier. Problem with features is it is highly sparse so computation of processing is without using any information so feature should be less sparse. Second problem is selection of classifier, which is depending on dataset which is highly non- linear and when use more than two classes this problem, will increase exponentially. So, In this research, work is done on feature set by reducing the sparseness of feature by phrase features and classified high non linear dataset by deep learning because deep learning use different pattern layer all possibility of existing pattern in feature set. The proposed work can be extended in two aspects as follows: We can add parameters for better performance of classifier. For measuring performance of any classifier, different measures e.g. train time, test time, precision, recall, f-measure, Accuracy, Density and error rate. Second, we can further improve this algorithm to get better result with less time taken. Third, we can work on resource problem and can work on real social interest and can recommend positive and highly rated topics.

Acknowledgement. First of all, I would like to thank my thesis guide Bharti Chhabra, Assistant professor, Department of Computer Science and Engineering, CEC Landran, for giving me a chance to work on this project under her guidance. She has given her precious time, advice and resources during different stages of project.

References

Mohammad, S.M., Kiritchenko, S., Zhu, X.: NRC-Canada: building the state-of-the-art in sentiment analysis of tweets. In: SemEval (2013)

Mohammad, S.M., Turney, P.D.: Crowdsourcing a word-emotion association lexicon. Comput. Intell. **29**(3), 436–465 (2013)

Elmongui, H.G., Mansour, R., Morsy, H., Khater, S., El-Sharkasy, A., Ibrahim, R.: TRUPI: twitter recommendation based on users' personal interests. In: Gelbukh, A. (ed.) CICLing 2015. LNCS, vol. 9042, pp. 272–284. Springer, Cham (2015). https://doi.org/10.1007/978-3-319-18117-2_20

Lu, C., Lam, W., Zhang, Y.: Twitter user modeling and tweets recommendation based on Wikipedia concept graph. In: Workshops at the Twenty-Sixth AAAI Conference on Artificial Intelligence (2012)

Aher, S.B., Lobo, L.M.R.J.: Combination of machine learning algorithms for recommendation of courses in E-learning system based on historical data. Knowl.-Based Syst. **51**, 1–14 (2013)

Collobert, R., Weston, J., Bottou, L., Karlen, M., Kavukcuoglu, K., Kuksa, P.: Natural language processing (almost) from scratch. JMLR **12**, 2493–2537 (2011)

Kalchbrenner, N., Grefenstette, E., Blunsom, P.: A convolutional neural network for modelling sentences. In: ACL (2014)

Hu, M., Liu, B.: Mining and summarizing customer reviews. In: KDD (2004)

Otsuka, E., Wallace, S.A., Chiu, D.: Design and evaluation of a witter hash tag recommendation system. In: Proceedings of the 18th International Database Engineering & Applications Symposium. ACM (2014)

Liang, P.-W., Dai, B.-R.: Opinion mining on social media data. In: 2013 IEEE 14th International Conference on Mobile Data Management, pp. 91–96 (2013)

Classification of Hyperspectral Imagery Using Random Forest

Diwaker Mourya[1(✉)] and Ashutosh Bhatt[2]

[1] Uttarakhand Technical University, Dehradun, India
dkmourya01@gmail.com

[2] Birla Institute of Applied Sciences, Bhimtal, India
ashutoshbhatt74@gmail.com

Abstract. In this paper the classification of hyperspectral images is investigated by using a supervised approach. The spectral feature are extracted with well known decision boundary feature extraction (DBFE) and non-parametric weighted feature extraction (NWFE) techniques. The most informative features are fed to random forest (RF) classifier to perform pixel-wise classification. The experiments are carried out on two benchmark hyperspectral images. The results show that RF classifier generates good classification accuracies for hyperspectral image with smaller execution time. Among feature extraction techniques, DBFE has produced better results than NWFE.

Keywords: Hyperspectral image · DBFE · NWFE · Random forest

1 Introduction

In present scenario the huge archive generated by hypespectral remote sensors is becoming very important source of information. This helps in analyzing the spectral response of various earth surface elements by interpretation of land use and land cover evolution [1]. Spectral signature provides a large archive of reflectance values over electromagnetic spectrum [2]. Classification of hyperspectral imagery helps in many areas such as disaster management, environmental studies, crop growth monitoring and urban planning etc. The spectral signatures obtained from hyperspectral data provides significant information for physical analysis of hyperspectral images in a detailed manner [3]. However high dimensionality of images and availability of few training samples poses some challenges called "Hughes phenomenon" [4], in case of supervised classification.

Usually some feature extraction techniques like Decision Boundary Feature extraction (DBFE) [5], Principal Component Analysis (PCA) [6], and maximum noise fraction [7], etc. are used to map high dimensional data into lower dimensional space. These techniques are used as preprocessing step before classification to remove noise and redundant information to improve classification accuracy [8]. The spectral analysis involves determining information from pixels of image. The major approaches in this field are based on PCA, Nonparametric Weighted Feature Extraction (NWFE), Discriminative Analysis Feature Extraction (DAFE) etc.

P. Bhattacharyya et al. (Eds.): NGCT 2017, CCIS 827, pp. 66–74, 2018.
https://doi.org/10.1007/978-981-10-8657-1_5

In this research work first DBFE and NWFE are used to extract spectral features from hyperspectral images. Obtained features are then used for supervised classification of the image using most widely used classification technique random forest. The rest of this paper is organized as follows. Section 2 describes some techniques for feature extraction, Sect. 3 describes the proposed methodology, in Sect. 4 experimental results are presented, and Sect. 5 finally concludes the work.

2 Decision Boundary Feature Extraction

2.1 Decision Boundary Feature Extraction

This technique is based on Baye's decision rule for minimum error. It uses decision boundary feature matrix in order to extract discriminately redundant features and discriminately informative features from the decision boundary [5, 9]. The procedure of DBFE [10] is given as follows:

Step 1: Obtain classified training data.
Step 2: Obtain the closest sample accurately classified as class w2, corresponding to every ample accurately classified as class w1. Iterate the similar procedure for other samples.
Step 3: Obtain pairs of samples from step2 and connect them.
Step 4: Obtain the normal unit vector N_i at every point of step 3.
Step 5: Using normal vectors, Obtain the decision boundary feature matrix.
Step 6: Using decision boundary feature matrix obtain eigenvectors as novel feature vector.

2.2 Nonparametric Weighted Feature Extraction

Kuo and Landgrebe [11], have proposed a new feature extraction technique NWFE to overcome the limitations of DBFE, Since DBFE does not perform well with limited training set. This technique is based on Linear Discriminative Analysis. Here Matrices like between the class and within-class are calculated in a nonparametric way, to obtain local means. Hence unlike DBFE the NWFE requires features that maximize class separability. Plenty of experiments exposed the effectiveness of these approaches in classification of hyperspectral data [11]. This technique is applicable to the spectral data, but Benediktsson and their co-workers have effectively applied them to the Extended Morphological Profile (EMP) [12], also.

2.3 Random Forest

RF is a group classification technique that combines a group of treelike classifiers. This classifier uses a voting process that combine the results obtained after training many classifiers. RF find the most popular class through majority voting on a huge number of individual decision voting on trees [14]. This classifier poses two main characteristics: first is relatively high accuracy and the second one is speed of processing. Finally, majority votes performs classification on all trees, and uses nearly two third of training data for this purpose. The rest of the data is used for accuracy evaluation [15].

3 Proposed Methodology

The flow chart in Fig. 1 shows the proposed spectral image classification scheme. Here to reduce the computational cost, redundancy, and to ensure training samples to scale well with number of features, feature extraction is performed as preprocessing step before actual classification is performed on hyperspectral data. Feature extraction can be performed using either supervised or unsupervised classification techniques.

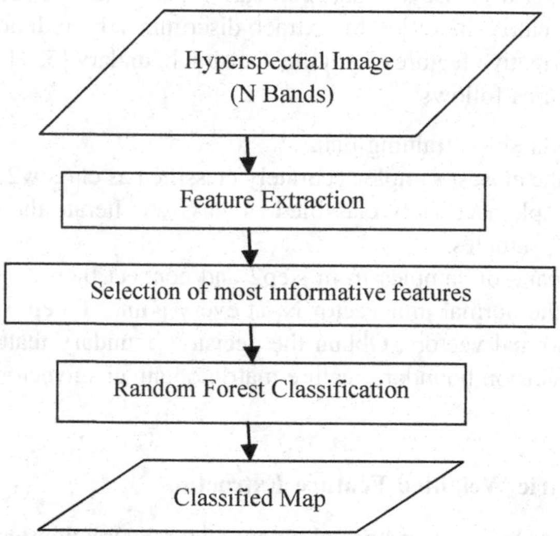

Fig. 1. Flow chart for proposed methodology

Many such techniques like Independent Component Analysis (ICA) [16], Discrete Wavelet Transform (DWT) [17, 18], DBFE, and PCA have been efficiently used for hyperspectral data. These techniques selects most informative features, with reduced feature set, and then pixel wise classification is performed using probabilistic classifier RF to obtain classified map.

4 Results and Discussion

The experiments are performed on two airborne hyperspectral images namely Pavia Centre (PC) and Pavia University (PU). PC image was obtained using DIAS sensor with spatial resolution of 1.3 m in the spectral region from 0.43–12.3 μm over Pavia City, Italy. This image is an urban image having 80 bands. It consists of nine information classes, whose false color composite (FCC) and Ground reference map is shown in Fig. 2.

The other dataset PU was acquired using ROSIS sensor with spatial resolution of 1.3 m in the spectral region from 0.43–8.6 μm over Pavia City, Italy. It consists of 115 bands from which 12 noisy bands have been removed. It also consists of nine information classes including some manmade and some natural structures. The (FCC) and ground reference map of PU is given in Fig. 3.

In the proposed work DBFE and NWFE are used to reduce the size of feature vector. Then classification is performed using RF classifier to obtain classified maps shown in Figs. 4 and 5. The RF classifier is implemented using MATLAB. The class wise test and training samples along with classification results for PC and PU are reported in Tables 1 and 2 respectively. The number of training samples obtained directly from ground reference using random selection and rest of the ground reference pixels are taken as test samples.

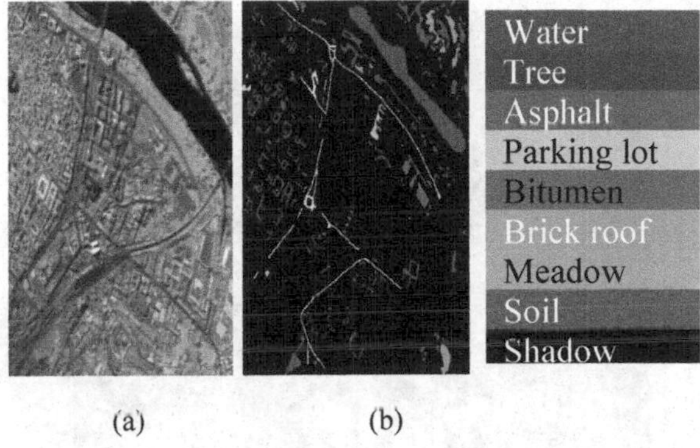

Fig. 2. PC image: (a) FCC (b) Ground reference

For both the images all experiments are performed ten times, and average is reported as final result. These experiments are performed with spectral features only, then classification results for DBFE and NWFE are compared.

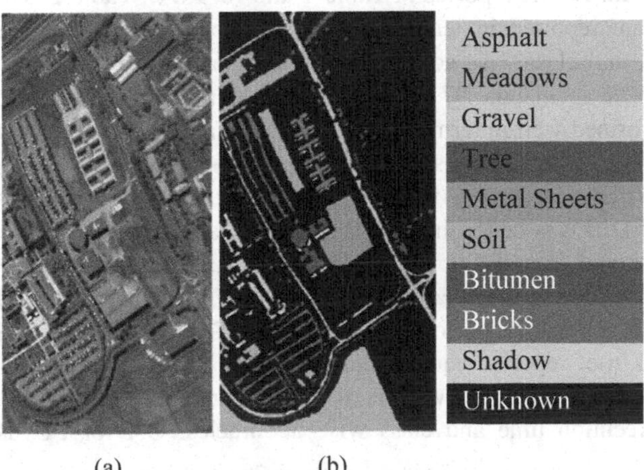

Fig. 3. PU image: (a) FCC (b) Ground reference

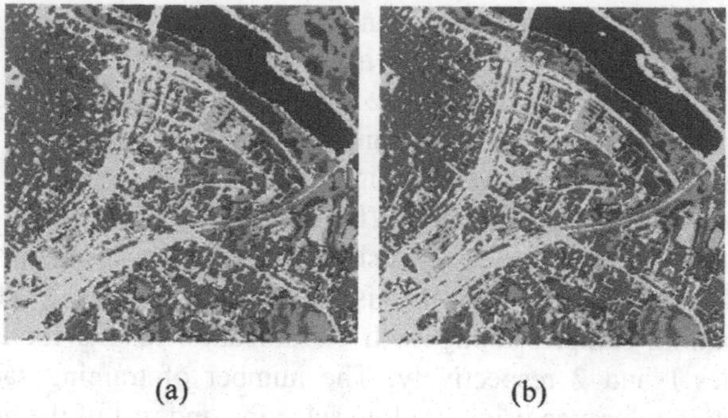

(a) (b)

Fig. 4. Classified maps for PC image: (a) DBFE (b) NWFE

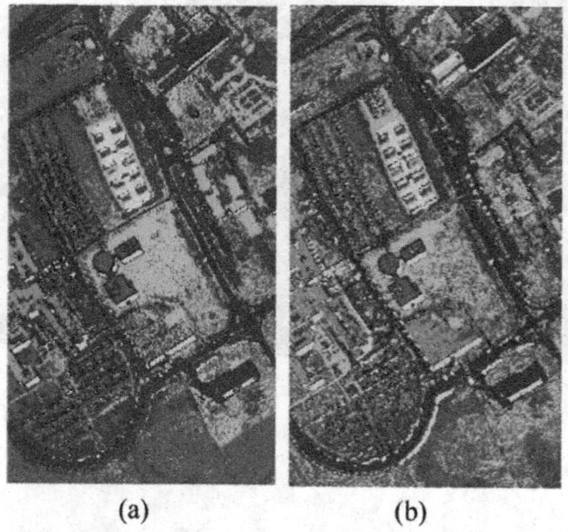

(a) (b)

Fig. 5. Classified maps for PU image: (a) DBFE (b) NWFE

Here results for PC are reported in Table 1 and for PU in Table 2. The performance of algorithms are reported in terms of Overall accuracy (OA), Overall Kappa (κ), execution time, and class wise accuracy. The OA for PC using DBFE is reported in Table 1 as 97.52% against the 97.50% for NWFE, it means both the feature extraction techniques performed well in terms of OA. The (κ) value for DBFE is 96.93% against 96.92% for NWFE, which again shows better performance. Further execution time for DBFE and NWFE is reported as 10.87 s and 10.61 s respectively. Although Overall performance of DBFE is better than NWFE, but in terms of execution time NWFE is better. It is observed from Table 1 that class wise accuracy for classes like Bitumen, Meadows and Shadow performed better with NWFE against classes Tree, Asphalt, Parking lot, and soil which performed better with DBFE, while two classes namely water and Brick roof reported equal accuracies.

Similar to Table 1 here observations of Table 2 are analyzed and reported in terms of OA, (κ), execution time and class wise accuracies. OA for PU using DBFE is

Table 1. Information classes, training and test samples, class wise and overall classification accuracies for PAVIA CENTER

Class		No. of samples		Class wise accuracy in (κ)%	
No.	Name	Test	Training	DBFE (35)	NWFE (35)
1	Water	4084	203	99.95	99.95
2	Tree	2301	206	**94.39**	93.84
3	Asphalt	1135	205	**98.03**	97.14
4	Parking lot cover	1300	206	**93.25**	93.21
5	Bitumen	1632	203	95.34	**96.41**
6	Brick roof	130	200	97.13	97.13
7	Meadow	2040	313	98.29	**98.70**
8	Soil	492	201	**95.46**	94.88
9	Shadow	161	120	97.45	**97.53**
Overall Accuracy (OA)				**97.52**	97.50
Kappa (κ)				**96.93**	96.92
Execution time				10.87	**10.61**

Table 2. Information classes, training and test samples, class wise and overall classification accuracies for PAVIA UNIVERSITY

Class		No. of samples		Class wise accuracy in (κ)%	
No.	Name	Test	Training	DBFE (40)	NWFE (40)
1	Asphalt	6083	548	90.80	77.29
2	Meadows	18109	540	85.54	68.50
3	Gravel	1707	392	82.57	69.42
4	Tree	2540	524	95.90	88.25
5	Metal sheets	1080	265	99.77	98.78
6	Soil	4497	532	92.43	72.92
7	Bitumen	955	375	91.15	87.36
8	bricks	3168	514	88.71	75.73
9	Shadow	716	231	99.93	99.20
Overall Accuracy (OA)				**92.17**	81.40
Kappa (κ)				**89.47**	75.45
Execution time				22.45	**21.60**

92.17% against 81.40% for NWFE, it means DBFE performed well in terms of OA. The (κ) value for DBFE is 89.47% against 75.45% for NWFE reported in Table 2. Further execution time for DBFE and NWFE is reported as 22.45 s and 21.60 s respectively. Although Overall performance of DBFE is better than NWFE, but in terms of execution time NWFE is better. It is observed from Table 2 that class wise accuracy for classes like Bitumen, Meadows and Shadow performed better with NWFE

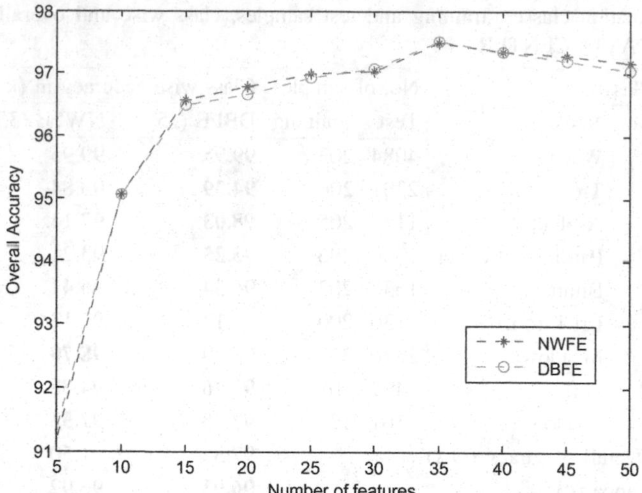

Fig. 6. Relationship between classification accuracy and number of features for PC image using random forest(Color figure online)

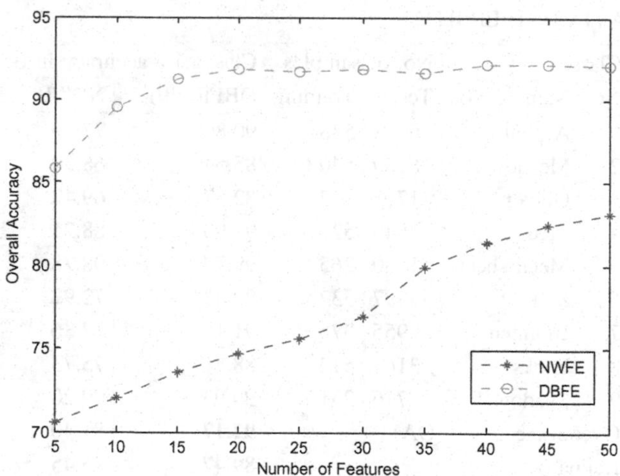

Fig. 7. Relationship between classification accuracy and number of features for PU image using random forest (Color figure online)

against classes Tree, Asphalt, Parking lot, and soil which performed better with DBFE, while two classes namely water and Brick roof reported equal accuracies.

The Comparative analysis of both the feature extraction techniques are also reported with the help of graphs. The graph for PC image is shown in Fig. 6 while that of PU image is shown in Fig. 7. These graphs are plotted as number of features vs. overall accuracy, and in both figures DBFE is represented using red line while NWFE using blue line. It is observed from reported results in Tables 1 and 2 as well as from graphs shown in Figs. 6 and 7 that DBFE is better feature extraction technique for hyperspectral images.

5 Conclusions

In this research work, we have performed spectral analysis on two different datasets using well known feature extraction techniques DBFE and NWFE. It is observed from the results that DBFE is better feature extraction techniques for hyperspectral images. It is also observed from the experimental results that only a subset of features are sufficient for good classification accuracy. If number of features is increased beyond a certain limit, the classification accuracy drops. The future work includes the analysis of spectral as well as spatial features using most widely used feature extraction techniques for dimensionality reduction followed by various classification techniques on different data sets.

Acknowledgement. Authors are very thankful to Dr. David Landgrebe, Purdue University, for providing Multispec tool and Dr. Paolo Gamba, Professor at PU, Italy, for providing Hyperspectral dataset used in this research work.

References

1. Camps-Valls, G., Gomez-Chova, L., Munoz-Mari, J., Rojo-Alvarez, J., Martinez-Ramon, M.: Kernel-based framework for multitemporal and multisource remote sensing data classification and change detection. IEEE Trans. Geosci. Remote Sens. **46**(6), 1822–1835 (2008)
2. Heinz, D., Davidson, C., Ben-David, A.: Temporal-spectral detection in long-wave IR hyperspectral imagery. IEEE Sens. J. **10**(3), 509–517 (2010)
3. Kumar, B., Dikshit, O.: Spectral contextual classification of hyperspectral imagery with probabilistic relaxation labeling. IEEE Trans. Cybern. **47**, 4380–4391 (2017). https://doi.org/10.1109/tcyb.2016.2609882
4. Diwaker, Chaudhary, M.K., Tripathi, P., Bhatt, A., Saxena, A.: A comparative performance analysis of feature extraction techniques for hyperspectral image classification. Int. J. Softw. Eng. Appl. **10**(12), 179–188 (2016)
5. Lee, C., Landgrebe, D.A.: Feature extraction based on decision boundaries. IEEE Trans. Pattern Anal. Mach. Intell. **15**(4), 388–400 (1993)
6. Jolliffe, I.: Principal Component Analysis. Springer, New York (2002). https://doi.org/10.1007/b98835
7. Chang, C.-I., Du, Q.: Interference and noise adjusted principal components analysis. IEEE Trans. Geosci. Remote Sens. **37**(5), 2387–2396 (1999)
8. Kumar, B., Dikshit, O.: Spectral-spatial classification of hyperspectral imagery based on moment invriants. IEEE J. Sel. Topics Appl. Earth Observ. Remote Sens. **8**(6), 2457–2463 (2015)
9. Chang, C.: Hyperspectral Imaging: Techniques for Spectral Detection and Classification. Kluwer, Norwell (2003)
10. Lee, C., Landgrebe, D.A.: Decision boundary feature extraction for non-parametric classification. https://doi.org/10.1109/21.229456

11. Landgrebe, D.A.: Signal Theory Methods in Multispectral Remote Sensing. Wiley, Hoboken (2003)
12. Kendall, M.G.: A Course in the Geometry of n-Dimensions. Dover, New York (1961)
13. Comon, P.: Independent component analysis, a new concept? Signal Process. **36**(3), 287–314 (1994)
14. Bhatt, A.K., Pant, D., Singh, R.: An analysis of the performance of artificial neural network technique for apple classification. AI Soc. **29**, 103–111 (2014)
15. Quesada-Barriuso, P., Argüello, F., Heras, D.B.: Spectral-spatial classification of hyper-spectral images using wavelets and extended morphological profiles. IEEE J. Sel. Topics Appl. Earth Observ. Remote Sens. **7**(4), 1177–1185 (2014)
16. Bhatt, A.K., Pant, D.: Automatic apple grading model development based on back propagation neural network and machine vision, and its performance evaluation. AI Soc. **30**, 45–56 (2015)
17. Bhatt A.K., Saxena, A., Datt, G.: An Investigation of artificial neural network based prediction systems in rain forecasting. Int. J. Recent Innov. Trends Comput. Commun. **3**(8) (2015). (ISSN 2321-8169)
18. Diwaker, Dutta, M.: Assessment of feature extraction techniques for classification of hyperspectrral imagery. In: IEEE International Conference on Advances in Computer Engineering and Applications (ICACEA), 978-1-4673-6911 (2015)

A Model for Resource Constraint Project Scheduling Problem Using Quantum Inspired PSO

Reya Sharma[1(✉)], Rashika Bangroo[1], Manoj Kumar[1], and Neetesh Kumar[2]

[1] Shri Mata Vaishno Devi University, Katra, Jammu and Kashmir, India
sharmareya327@gmail.com
[2] Atal Bihari Vajpayee Indian Institute of Information Technology and Management, Gwalior, Gwalior, Madhya Pradesh, India

Abstract. Resource Constrained Project Scheduling Problem (RCPSP) is a NP-hard project planning scheduling problem. It has been widely applied in real life industrial scenarios to optimize the project makespan with the limitation of the resources. In order to solve RCPSP, this paper suggests a Quantum inspired Particle Swarm Optimization (Q-PSO) probabilistic optimization technique. A classical PSO is very hard to map to the RCPSP because of its solution lies in continuous values position vector. To overcome this, Sequence Position Vector (SPV) rule is incorporated into PSO. Since, the activities of the project follows dependency constrains, due to updation in position vector, the dependency constrains are violated. To handle this situation, Valid Particle Generator (VPG) is used. With an assembling of these operators, a Q-PSO is introduced to solve RCPSP effectively. The effectiveness of the QPSO is verified on a standard dataset of PSPLIB for J30. Results show that Q-PSO has significant improvement in the performance over number of state of the arts. Since it uses probabilistic particle representation in terms of quantum bits (Q-bits) and thus replaces the inertia weight tuning and velocity update method in classical PSO.

Keywords: Resource constrained project scheduling problem
Particle swarm optimization · Quantum computing · Q-bit

1 Introduction

Resource Constrained Project Scheduling Problem (RCPSP) is a significant but NP-hard combinatorial optimization problem in project scheduling [1]. Several methods have been developed over the past in order to solve the RCPSP including branch-and-bound, heuristics, meta-heuristics and exact ones. However these methods often take considerable amount of time for convergence leading to poor results. Now a days researchers have augmented their focus approaching to optimal solution for RCPSP adopting advanced heuristics and metaheuristics [2].

P. Bhattacharyya et al. (Eds.): NGCT 2017, CCIS 827, pp. 75–87, 2018.
https://doi.org/10.1007/978-981-10-8657-1_6

Particle swarm optimization is a meta-heuristic optimization technique firstly improvised by Kennedy and Eberhart in 1995 [3]. It is derived from swarm intelligence, and set up on flock of birds and shoal of fishes. It has been exercised on number of optimization problems in order to find optimist solution due to its inherent advantages [4] like (1) easy and simple execution, (2) robustness to oversee parameters, (3) greater optimization ability due to simple calculation, (4) fast researching based on speed of particle, (5) number of parameters are confined, (6) relatively rapid convergence to optimal solution, (7) little reliance on initial particles, (8) solution is of good quality.

Zhang et al. firstly discovered PSO in order to solve RCPSP which make use of permutation based and priority based representation and found out that permutation based schedule had better performance [5]. They proposed a general schema of PSO and also gave an oversight for using PSO in solving RCPSP for future research. Afterwards, Jarboui et al. suggested combinatorial PSO having several execution approaches to resolve the RCPSP [6]. Each activity has assigned a mode in their scheme and in order to better prioritize the arrangement of corresponding activities they used local search optimization. Combinatorial PSO has better performance as compare to SA but very close to the one suggested by Zhang et al. [5]. Chen et al. [7] proposed PSO using bi-directional scheduling and delay local search [8] to solve RCPSP. An improved PSO has been proposed in [9] to solve RCPSP using double justification operator, priority based representation, move operator and also greedy search. Results revealed that improved PSO has better performance than other contemporary PSO techniques. However, the above model is time consuming because it uses additional operators (such as move operator, double justification operator) along with basic PSO approach for the betterment of results. Besides, it also uses inertia weight selection which requires additional preprocessing time. The models of PSO and its variants that we discussed above usually lack performance in terms of computation time and convergence to optimal solution. However, it provides an oversight for further exploring PSO in order to obtain refined technique for solving RCPSP with faster convergence and better solution.

This paper proposes a variant of PSO, called Quantum inspired Particle Swarm Optimization (Q-PSO) based on the concept and idea of quantum computing which is derived from Quantum Physics. Quantum Computing uses Quantum bit (Q-bit) which is the smallest unit of information and superposition of states to improve the performance of contemporary PSO approaches [10–12]. The proposed Q-PSO eliminates the need of velocity vector updating by using Q-bit for representing probability of the particle. In Q-PSO, inertia weight tuning is also eliminated and thus only a single factor is involved for updating the particles position and this factor is the rotation angle. The rotation angle is greatly responsible for speedy convergence of Q-PSO. Efficiency of solution is examined on the basis of makespan by assigning RCPSP to utmost processing unit at the instant. The Q-PSO is applied to standard data sets of J30 from the popular Project Scheduling Problem Library (PSPLIB) (http://www.omdb.wi.tum.de/psplib/data.html) [13] in order to check the fitness of model.

The layout of this paper has following sections. Section 2 illustrate the RCPSP problem, Sect. 3 depicts the overview of standard PSO, Sect. 4 describes the proposed Q-PSO in detail, in Sect. 5 experimental results for the proposed model together with comparative experimental analysis are described, Sect. 6 gives the conclusion about the model.

2 RCPSP Problem Description

A RCPSP consists of several renewable resources [14,15]. It constitutes a set A of n + 2 activities from 0 to n + 1 and K renewable resources for the execution of these activities. Each activity a_i in the set A has a duration $d_i \geq 0$, however the starting activity (source) a_0 and the ending activity (sink) a_{n+1} are called the dummy activities because the durations d_0 and $d_{n+1} = 0$. Each renewable resource type $k \in K$ has an availability of $R_k \geq 0$ units. The numbers of units required by an activity a_i are $r_{ik} \geq 0$ units of k resource types; the resource requirements of dummy activities are zero i.e. r_{0k} and $r_{(n+1)k} = 0$. Suppose FT_i be the finish time of activity a_i and finish time various activities constituting the schedule S is given by $FT_1, FT_2, FT_3, \ldots, FT_N$. The objective function of the RCPSP is to minimize the project makespan by finding a feasible schedule subjected to precedence, resource and decision variable constraints [16]. Precedence constraint among the activities ensures that no activity starts execution until all its predecessor or parent activities are executed completely. Resource limitation constraint indicates that sum of resources required per period cannot exceed the availability of renewable resources. Decision variable constraint indicates that the completion time of an activity is always positive.

Mathematically, the RCPSP problem can be represented as follows [17,18]:

$$Minimize\ FT_{N+1} \tag{1}$$

Subjected to:

$$FT_i \leq FT_j - d_j\ for\ i = 1, 2, \ldots, N+1; j \in parent_i, \tag{2}$$

$$\sum_{i \in A(t)} r_{ik} \leq R_k\ for\ k = 1, 2, \ldots, K;\ t \geq 0, \tag{3}$$

$$FT_i \geq 0\ for\ i = 1, 2, \ldots, N+1. \tag{4}$$

The objective function in Eq. 1 represents the minimization of completion time of the schedule. Equation 2 ensures precedence relationship constraint among activities. Equation 3 indicates that total number of resources required cannot exceed the available resources. Equation 4 depicts that completion time of an activity is positive.

Figure 1 illustrates an example of RCPSP problem consisting of 9 activities where activities 0 and 8 are dummy activities. The number of renewable resource types available to schedule the activities is one with 5 units i.e. K = 1 and $R_k = 5$. Figure 2 shows one of the feasible schedules for activities in Fig. 1.

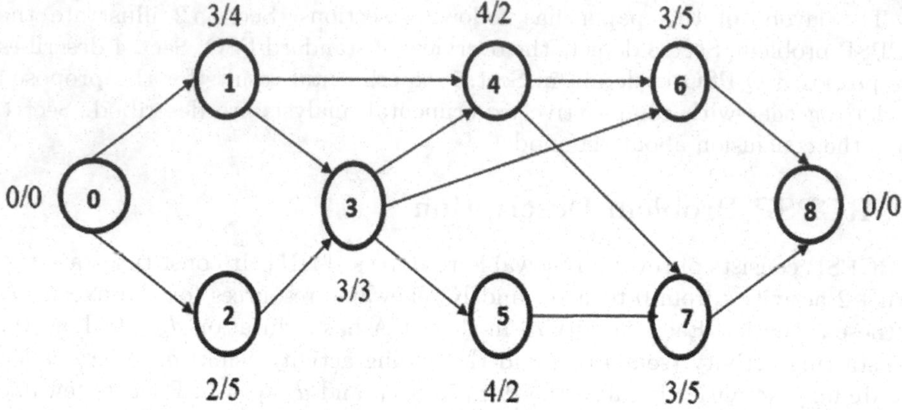

Fig. 1. A RCPSP example

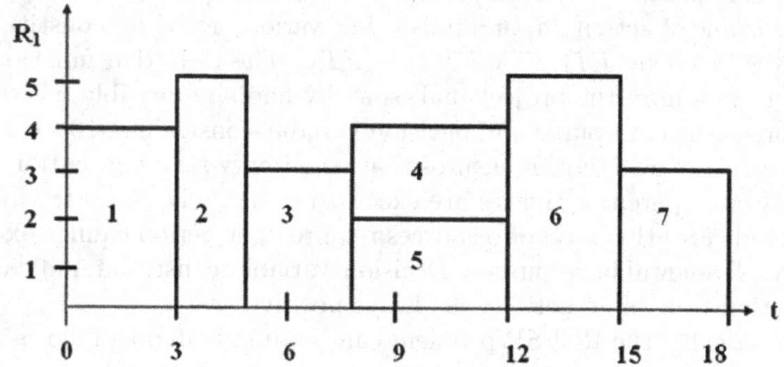

Fig. 2. A feasible schedule corresponding to the problem in Fig. 1

3 Overview of Particle Swarm Optimization

Particle Swarm Optimization is a population based global optimization technique suggested by Kennedy and Eberhart. PSO is derived from swarm intelligence and based on the behaviour of bird swam and fish flock movement. The particles shares and transmits the information among them in the group and thereby leading to increased efficiency [19]. While searching for the food in multidimensional space two factors are important one is the position and other is the velocity. Because the information is being transmitted among the particles therefore a particle attracts others if it discovers better location where it can find the food. On the basis of fitness the optimum solution is evaluated. The personal best (p-best) of the particles and global best (g-best) of the swarm are updated leading all particles towards same position that represents the optimal solution.

The position vector of nth particle with k dimension can be represented as $X_n = \{x_{n1}, x_{n2}, \ldots, x_{nk}\}$ and velocity vector as $V_n = \{v_{n1}, v_{n2}, \ldots, v_{nk}\}$.

Suppose p-best of nth particle be P-$best_n = \{x^P_{n1}, x^P_{n2}, \cdots, x^P_{nk}\}$ and g-best of the swarm be G-$best = \{x^G_1, x^G_2, \ldots, x^G_k\}$. The velocity and position of nth particle at i^{th} iteration can be updated as follows:

$$V_n^{i+1} = \omega * V_n^i + c_1 r_1 * (P - best_n^i - X_n^i) + c_2 r_2 * (G - best^i - X_n^i)$$

$$X_n^{i+1} = X_n^i + V_n^{i+1}$$

where ω stands for inertia weight, c_1 and c_2 are speeding constants, r_1 and r_2 represents random numbers lying between 0 and 1, X_n^i represents the position of nth particle at i^{th} iteration and V_n^i represents the velocity of nth particle at i^{th} iteration.

The classical PSO as discussed in [20,21] is shown below:

```
Classical PSO
{
 Initialize position and velocity vector of the particles
 Assign initial values to personal best and global best
 For n = 1 to population size
{
   Calculate the fitness
   Update the personal best of nth particle
}
 Update the global best of the swarm
 While the termination criteria are not satisfied do
{
 For n = 1 to population size
   Modify velocity and position
   Calculate the fitness
   Update personal best of nth particle if it is superior to prior one
}
 Update global best of the swarm if it is superior to previous one
}
```

4 Quantum Inspired PSO for RCPSP

4.1 Quantum Computing

The concept of Quantum Computing (QC) is derived from the Quantum Physics and it is essentially a new paradigm of computer science. Quantum Bit (Q-bit) is a basic unit for representing information in quantum computer [11]. Unlike traditional computing in which a bit may hold either state 0 or state 1, a Q-bit may exist in state 0, state 1 or superposition two states. The capability of being in more than two states allows QC to provide the better exploration and exploitation of search space. Hence, the algorithms based on QC are more efficient.

A Q-bit is represented by pair of complex numbers (α, β) where $|\alpha|^2$ and $|\beta|^2$ gives the probability of occurrence of Q-bit in state 0 and state 1 respectively such that $|\alpha|^2 + |\beta|^2 = 1$. A quantum individual with n dimensions is represented by sequence of Q-bits:

$$\begin{bmatrix} \alpha_1 \, \alpha_2 \, \alpha_3 \ldots \alpha_n \\ \\ \beta_1 \, \beta_2 \, \beta_3 \ldots \beta_n \end{bmatrix}$$

where $|\alpha_k|^2 + |\beta_k|^2 = 1$, K = 1, 2, . . . , n.

Quantum individual is updated using rotation operator and the rotation matrix for updating quantum population is given below:

$$\cup(\Delta\theta) = \begin{bmatrix} \cos \Delta\theta & -\sin \Delta\theta \\ \\ \sin \Delta\theta & \cos \Delta\theta \end{bmatrix}$$

where $\Delta\theta$ determines the angle of rotation which provides information about direction of rotation. Appropriate selection of $\Delta\theta$ is highly essential as it determines the degree convergence of solution. On the basis of problem $\Delta\theta$ value is set up through experimental tests by tuning experiments.

Then the updated values of quantum individual are obtained by:

$$\begin{bmatrix} \alpha(n+1) \\ \\ \beta(n+1) \end{bmatrix} = \cup(\Delta\theta) \begin{bmatrix} \alpha(n) \\ \\ \beta(n) \end{bmatrix}$$

4.2 Quantum Inspired Particle Swarm Optimization (QPSO)

(1) The Proposed Model: In the proposed Q-PSO, Q-bit is introduced that uses $|\alpha|^2$ and $|\beta|^2$ for representing probability of each individual in the particle to be in state 0 and state 1. This procedure replaces the need of velocity vector update process in the conventional PSO. Therefore, in the proposed Q-PSO inertia weight (ω) and two acceleration constants (c_1 and c_2) are also removed and an angle of rotation $(\Delta\phi)$ is added.

The proposed model is commenced by randomly initializing the position of particles, Q-bit individual and by setting initial personal best and global best. Then the fitness is evaluated and termination conditions are checked in order to verify whether the termination criterion is met or not. If the termination criterion is not met then firstly the rotation angle is updated using coordinate rotation approach and then the Q-bit is updated using a rotation operator matrix. After this the position of nth particle $X_n = \{x_{n1}, x_{n2}, \ldots, x_{nk}\}$ is modified by using probability $|\beta|^2$ present in n^{th} Q-bit. In order to obtain discrete value position vector from the continuous position values a smallest position value (SPV) method is applied. Sometimes obtained discrete sequence may correspond to an invalid discrete sequence. A valid particle generator (VPG) rule is used that transforms an invalid sequence into valid one. Now the fitness function is used in order to evaluate the fitness of the particles. Depending upon the value of fitness p-best of the particles and g-best of the group are updated. This procedure is repeated until the termination standards are satisfied. The flowchart corresponding to the proposed model is shown in Fig. 3:

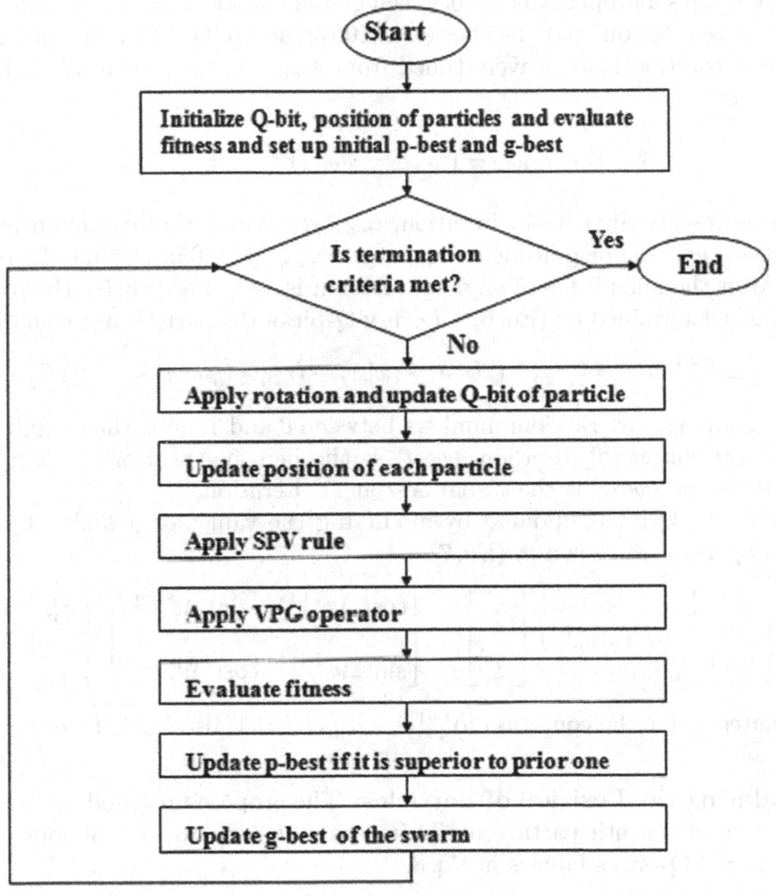

Fig. 3. The flowchart of Q-PSO model

(2) Initializing Q-Bit and Position of the Particles: Initially, random numbers of particles are created by assigning initial Q-bit value and position for every particle. The Q-bit individual is initialized by setting α and β values as $\frac{1}{\sqrt{2}}$ which indicates linear superposition of all states with equal probability. The initial position of particles is set as uniformly distributed random numbers between 0 and 1 by using a random function. The initial p-best value of each particle is set as corresponding initial position of respective particle. The p-best with minimum makespan is assigned as initial g-best.

(3) Updating the Q-Bit Individual of Particles: Q-PSO uses rotation operator for updating the Q-bit individual. The rotation operator uses a rotation angle ϕ. The magnitude of angle of rotation plays a significant role in speed of convergence and determines the solution quality. Therefore with a proper selection of ϕ we can find the optimal solution in lesser number of iterations and it also maintains a proper balance between global and local search. In general the magnitude of rotation angle lies between 0.001π and 0.05π [11]. The magnitude of angle of rotation is adaptively tuned from ϕ_{max} to ϕ_{min} using (Eq. 5) along the iteration.

$$\phi = \phi_{max} - (\phi_{max} - \phi_{min}) * \frac{i}{i_{max}} \tag{5}$$

where i represents the current iteration, i_{max} represents the maximum number of iterations and the magnitude of ϕ_{max} and ϕ_{min} are 0.05π and 0.001π respectively. After the magnitude of angle of rotation is set using (Eq. 5), the rotation angle $\Delta\phi$ is determined by (Eq. 6) for every Q-bit of the particle as given in [12].

$$\Delta\phi_n^{i+1} = \phi^i * ((r_{1n} * (pbest_n^i - x_n^i)) + (r_{2n} * (gbest^i - x_n^i))) \tag{6}$$

where r_{1n} and r_{2n} are random numbers between 0 and 1, ϕ^i is the magnitude of angle of rotation at i^{th} iteration, $pbest_n^i$ is the personal best of nth particle at i^{th} iteration and $gbest^i$ is the global best at i^{th} iteration.

Finally the Q-bit is updated by modifying the values of α and β by using rotation operator as shown in (Eq. 7).

$$\begin{bmatrix} \alpha_n^{i+1} \\ \\ \beta_n^{i+1} \end{bmatrix} = \cup(\Delta\phi_n^{i+1}) \begin{bmatrix} \alpha_n^i \\ \\ \beta_n^i \end{bmatrix} = \begin{bmatrix} \cos(\Delta\phi_n^{i+1}) & -\sin(\Delta\phi_n^{i+1}) \\ \\ \sin(\Delta\phi_n^{i+1}) & \cos(\Delta\theta_n^{i+1}) \end{bmatrix} \begin{bmatrix} \alpha_n^i \\ \\ \beta_n^i \end{bmatrix} \tag{7}$$

For updated Q-bit the condition $|\alpha_n^{i+1}|^2 + |\beta_n^{i+1}|^2 = 1$ also holds true.

(4) Updating the Position of Particles: The proposed method for updating the position of the nth particle at i^{th} iteration (i.e. x_n^i) uses probability $|\beta_n|^2$ present in n^{th} Q-bit as follows in Eq. 8.

$$x_n^{i+1} = mod((\beta_n^{i+1} + x_n^i), 1) \tag{8}$$

(5) Apply Smallest Position Value: Tasgetiren et al. proposed the heuristics Smallest Position Value rule which transforms continuous position values vector into discrete value vector [22]. SPV heuristic rule gives discrete sequence S as a result of sorting the continuous position value vector X in ascending order. SPV rule is illustrated in Table 1 [22,23].

In Table 1, S_n^i represents the discrete position values vector of nth particle at i^{th} iteration corresponding to X_n^i continuous position values vector. S_n^i is obtained by firstly sorting the position values X_n^i in ascending order and then enumerating the sequence vector S_n^i with discrete values of dimension corresponding to the respective position values.

Table 1. SPV rule representation

Dim	1	6	4	3	5	2	7
X_n^i	2.12	0.54	1.56	2.42	0.94	0.34	3.30
S_n^i	6	2	5	3	1	4	7

(6) Apply Valid Particle Generator: A valid particle generator (VPG) is a technique that transforms an invalid sequence into a valid one. RCPSP problems are subjected to various constraints like precedence relation constraints and therefore the activities of the problem are dependent on one another. Due to this dependency there exists a possibility that after updation the particles may become invalid. In order to deal with invalid particles a large number of iterations and huge computations are required. It leads to the wastage of computational energy and it may take a lot of time in order to reach a valid particle. A VPG operator is used in order to deal with this problem. It converts invalid particle into valid one by suspecting and swapping those activities of particle that results in generation of invalid particle.

(7) Evaluating Fitness and Update p-Best and g-Best: After passing through valid particle generator the particle is approved to be valid. This validation allows us to apply fitness function in order to evaluate fitness of the schedule. Hence the fitness function is used for evaluating the fitness of the particles and obtaining the schedule with minimum makespan.

If position of nth particle at (i + 1) iteration X_n^{i+1} has better fitness value than $pbest_n^i$, then the $pbest_n^{i+1}$ is set to X_n^{i+1} otherwise $pbest_n^{i+1}$ will remain same as $pbest_n^i$.

The $gbest^{i+1}$ is set as $pbest_n^{i+1}$ with the best evaluated fitness value.

(8) Termination Criteria: The termination criterion for the proposed Q-PSO model is when the iteration reaches to a specified maximum iteration.

5 Experimental Analysis

The proposed Q-PSO model is verified on standard dataset of PSPLIB for J30 created by standard problem generator [13]. The datasets of J30 have 480 instances with each instance having 30 jobs. These datasets are available publicly at PSPLIB library [13] along with their best or optimum solutions obtained over the years by various researchers.

The solution quality of the model is measured by the performance parameter called average deviation (A_dev). The average deviation indicated the deviation that appears between the solution computed by this work and the best solution obtained. The equation for evaluating average deviation is given below:

$$A\_dev = \frac{\sum instances\,(\frac{obtained-best}{best} * 100)}{instances} \tag{9}$$

Table 2. Results of algorithms corresponding to the J30 case study

Algorithm	References	Avg_dev
Q-PSO	Present work	.47
PSO	Jia and Seo [9]	.49
BSO	Ziaratia et al. [24]	.65
PSO	Ziaratia et al. [24]	.69
AS	Kolisch and Hartmann [15]	1.44
PSO-bidirectional	Chen et al. [7]	.84
ABC	Ziaratia et al. [24]	.98
BA	Ziaratia et al. [24]	.63
GA	Hartmann [25]	.54
PSO	Chen et al. [7]	1.33
PSO+	Chen et al. [7]	.54
AS	Schirmer [26]	.65
PSO-delay	Chen et al. [7]	1.03
GA	Hartmann [25]	1.38
PSO	Zhang et al. [8]	.98
ACO	Chen et al. [7]	1.57

5.1 Parameter Initialization

The proposed model begins with randomly initializing position of the particles with random values between 0 and 1. The magnitude of angle of rotation ϕ is tuned by using (Eq. 5), with ϕ_{max} and ϕ_{min} having magnitude 0.05π and 0.001π, respectively [11]. The proper selection of magnitude of angle of rotation is required so that we can find the optimal solution in lesser number of iterations and it also maintains a proper balance between global and local search. Therefore, the magnitude of angle of rotation is adaptively modified at each iteration using self adaptive rotation angle approach. The α and β values of Q-bit are initialized with $\frac{1}{\sqrt{2}}$, since the sum of squares of α and β are one i.e. $|\alpha|^2 + |\beta|^2 = 1$ [11]. The number of particles that are being generated are 90 particles and the total number of iterations being used are 12.

5.2 Experimental Results

The results are evaluated on the basis of comparative analysis of the result obtained in this work with the other meta-heuristics and heuristics. The heuristics that are used for the comparative analysis of the result obtained in this work are Genetic Algorithm (GA), Particle Swarm Optimization (PSO), Artificial Bee Colony (ABC), Bees Algorithm (BA), Ant Colony Optimization (ACO) etc.

Table 2 displays the average deviation percentage with respect to the optimal makespan for instances of J30 dataset, the average deviation for the PSPLIB J30 dataset in the proposed work is computed to be 0.47. Table 2 clearly indicates that this model performs better or gives better results than other meta heuristics and heuristics models.

6 Conclusion

The proposed work gives a variant of PSO called Quantum inspired Particle Swarm Optimization (QPSO). Q-PSO algorithm has been applied to RCPS problem. The proposed Q-PSO eliminates the need of velocity vector updating by using Q-bit for representing probability of the particle. In Q-PSO, inertia weight tuning and two accelerating constants are also eliminated and thus only a single factor called rotation angle is involved for updating the position of the particle. The rotation angle is greatly responsible for speedy convergence of Q-PSO and it also has an effect on the solution quality. Therefore, with a proper selection of ϕ we can find the optimal solution in lesser number of iterations and it also maintains a proper balance between global and local search.

The performance of proposed model has been studied by simulating it on the J30 instance of RCPSP problem. The results are evaluated on the basis of comparative analysis of the results obtained in this work with the other meta-heuristics and heuristics. A comparative analysis is done on the basis of average deviation. The results indicate that this model performs better and gives competitive results, with an average deviation of 0.47. The proposed model also gives better results than several other existing meta-heuristics and heuristics models for J30 instance of PSPLIB dataset. The proposed model has an advantage of faster convergence and it can also be used efficiently for solving various other combinatorial optimization problems.

References

1. Blazewicz, J., Lenstra, J.K., Rinnooy Kan, A.H.G.: Scheduling subject to resource constraints: classification and complexity. Discret. Appl. Math. **5**(1), 11–24 (1983)
2. Valls, V., Ballestín, F., Quintanilla, S.: Justification and RCPSP: a technique that pays. Eur. J. Oper. Res. **165**(2), 375–386 (2005)
3. Kennedy, J., Eberhart, R.: Particle swarm optimization. In: IEEE International Conference on Neural Networks, Proceedings, vol. 4, pp. 1942–1948. IEEE (1995)
4. Kumar, N., Vidyarthi, D.P.: A model for resource-constrained project scheduling using adaptive PSO. Soft. Comput. **20**(4), 1565–1580 (2016)
5. Zhang, H., Li, H., Tam, C.M.: Particle swarm optimization for resource-constrained project scheduling. Int. J. Proj. Manag. **24**(1), 83–92 (2006)
6. Jarboui, B., Damak, N., Siarry, P., Rebai, A.: A combinatorial particle swarm optimization for solving multi-mode resource-constrained project scheduling problems. Appl. Math. Comput. **195**(1), 299–308 (2008)

7. Chen, R.-M., Wu, C.-L., Wang, C.-M., Lo, S.-T.: Using novel particle swarm optimization scheme to solve resource-constrained scheduling problem in PSPLIB. Expert Syst. Appl. **37**(3), 1899–1910 (2010)
8. Zhang, H., Li, X., Li, H., Huang, F.: Particle swarm optimization-based schemes for resource-constrained project scheduling. Autom. Constr. **14**(3), 393–404 (2005)
9. Jia, Q., Seo, Y.: Solving resource-constrained project scheduling problems: conceptual validation of FLP formulation and efficient permutation-based ABC computation. Comput. Oper. Res. **40**(8), 2037–2050 (2013)
10. Moore, M., Narayanan, A.: Quantum-inspired computing. Department of Computer Science, University of Exeter, Exeter, UK (1995)
11. Han, K.-H., Kim, J.-H.: Quantum-inspired evolutionary algorithm for a class of combinatorial optimization. IEEE Trans. Evol. Comput. **6**(6), 580–593 (2002)
12. Jeong, Y.-W., Park, J.-B., Jang, S.-H., Lee, K.Y.: A new quantum-inspired binary PSO: application to unit commitment problems for power systems. IEEE Trans. Power Syst. **25**(3), 1486–1495 (2010)
13. Kolisch, R., Sprecher, A.: PSPLIB-a project scheduling problem library: OR software-ORSEP operations research software exchange program. Eur. J. Oper. Res. **96**(1), 205–216 (1997)
14. Kolisch, R., Hartmann, S.: Heuristic algorithms for solving the resource-constrained project scheduling problem: classification and computational analysis. Technical report, Manuskripte aus den Instituten für Betriebswirtschaftslehre der Universität Kiel (1998)
15. Kolisch, R., Hartmann, S.: Experimental investigation of heuristics for resource-constrained project scheduling: an update. Eur. J. Oper. Res. **174**(1), 23–37 (2006)
16. Schirmer, A.: Case-based reasoning and improved adaptive search for project scheduling. Technical report, Manuskripte aus den Instituten für Betriebswirtschaftslehre der Universität Kiel (1998)
17. Christofides, N., Alvarez-Valdés, R., Tamarit, J.M.: Project scheduling with resource constraints: a branch and bound approach. Eur. J. Oper. Res. **29**(3), 262–273 (1987)
18. Alba, E., Chicano, J.F.: Software project management with gas. Inf. Sci. **177**(11), 2380–2401 (2007)
19. Kumar, N., Vidyarthi, D.P.: A novel hybrid PSO-GA meta-heuristic for scheduling of DAG with communication on multiprocessor systems. Eng. Comput. **32**(1), 35–47 (2016)
20. Şevkli, Z., Sevilgen, F.E., Keleş, Ö.: Particle swarm optimization for the orienteering problem. In: Proceedings of International Symposium on Innovation in Intelligent Systems and Application, Istanbul, Turkey, pp. 185–190, June 2007
21. Mendes, R., Kennedy, J., Neves, J.: The fully informed particle swarm: simpler, maybe better. IEEE Trans. Evol. Comput. **8**(3), 204–210 (2004)
22. Tasgetiren, M.F., Sevkli, M., Liang, Y.-C., Gencyilmaz, G.: Particle swarm optimization algorithm for single machine total weighted tardiness problem. In: Congress on Evolutionary Computation, CEC 2004, vol. 2, pp. 1412–1419. IEEE (2004)
23. Al Badawi, A., Shatnawi, A.: Static scheduling of directed acyclic data flow graphs onto multiprocessors using particle swarm optimization. Comput. Oper. Res. **40**(10), 2322–2328 (2013)
24. Ziarati, K., Akbari, R., Zeighami, V.: On the performance of bee algorithms for resource-constrained project scheduling problem. Appl. Soft Comput. **11**(4), 3720–3733 (2011)

25. Hartmann, S.: A competitive genetic algorithm for resource-constrained project scheduling. Nav. Res. Logist. **45**(7), 733–750 (1988)
26. Schirmer, A.: Case-based reasoning and improved adaptive search for project scheduling. Nav. Res. Logist. **47**(3), 201–222 (2000)

Detection and Estimation of 2-D Brain Tumor Size Using Fuzzy C-Means Clustering

Rahul Chauhan[1(✉)], Surbhi Negi[1], and Subhi Jain[2]

[1] Electronics and Communication Department, Graphic Era Hill University, Dehradun, India
chauhan14853@gmail.com, sur.negi1191@gmail.com
[2] Computer Science and Engineering Department, Graphic Era Hill University, Dehradun, India
2510shubhijain@gmail.com

Abstract. Brain tumor is the main cause of mortality among children and adults which cause the abnormal growth of mass of tissues. So exact segmentation of this tissue mass is required for the exact diagnosis of tumor. This paper presents a technique for brain tumor segmentation and detection in magnetic resonance image (MRI) using a hybrid approach of fuzzy c-means clustering followed by mathematical morphology. Further length & width is calculated based on Euclidean distance measure and an approach is applied based on calculating the height and width of tumor to approximately detect the size of tumor in 1D and 2D for estimating the cancer stages.

Keywords: Segmentation · Tumor · MRI · Fuzzy c-means · Morphology Euclidean

1 Introduction

The unusual growth of cells in the brain is called brain tumor. The cancerous cells grow in the brain from blood vessels, brain cells and even the nerves in the brain. Cancerous cells also damage healthy brain cells by exercising pressure, swelling and spreading to healthy cells [1]. One of the leading causes of rising mortality rate among adults and children is brain cancer. The tumors can be classified into two major parts depending on the malignancy and the area in which they start and grow. The tumors that begin in the brain due to abnormal growth of cells within the brain are called primary tumors. The tumor that develops as a result of primary tumors in another part of the body that spreads to the brain, is called a metastasis tumor or secondary tumor. Another classification of tumors is benign and malignant. A benign tumor is a non cancerous tumor which can be removed, but it poses a threat to be cancerous as it is a precancerous tumor. A malignant tumor is a cancerous tumor which can spread to its neighboring cells. The increase in number of people dying from brain tumor has increased up to 300 in the last few decades. Magnetic Resonance Imaging (MRI) is a technology that uses radiology and generates pictures of the human anatomy and the physiological processes of the body [2–4]. The technology of MRI provides valuable information about the analysis of the tumor in the brain, which assists in efficient supervision and treatment of

P. Bhattacharyya et al. (Eds.): NGCT 2017, CCIS 827, pp. 88–96, 2018.
https://doi.org/10.1007/978-981-10-8657-1_7

tumor. The techniques of MRI have been reduced and made efficient to determine and monitor the changes in anatomic features, abnormality in volume etc. of primary and metastasis brain tumors [5].

The present diagnosis is a standard diagnosis method which uses human domain knowledge for explaining and deducing the results from an MRI-scan for tumor identification, this increases the chance of false judgment and identification of brain tumor. In contrast to this, the digital image processing techniques give a more accurate result in tumor identification [6]. The segmentation process is a widely used technique to extricate information from an intricate medical image which has various applications in medical [4, 7]. The central idea behind image segmentation is to divide the digital image into set of pixels or smaller segments which may change the overall representation of the image which is easier to scan. Image segmentation helps in detecting the objects and its boundaries. There are various criterion for homogeneity values, some of them are color, intensity, range, surface normals and curvatures [16]. The various image segmentation techniques are listed below:

- Thresholding technique
- Clustering techniques
- Supervised and unsupervised classification methods
- Histogram based techniques etc.

Various techniques have been presented previously for brain tumor segmentation. For example:

Sindhushree et al. [8] presented a brain tumor segmentation technique and used 2-D MRI data for proving segmentation and representation in 3-D of the identified tumor. Tumors were identified using techniques like thresholding. Histogram equalization, High pass filtering etc. The 2-D images extricated were rebuilt into 3-D data to calculate the volume of tumor. Another approach is K Means clustering using a marker controlled watershed segmentation to identify brain tumor and adds up fuzzy means clustering in it for medical segmentation [9].

This paper integrates modified fuzzy clustering with morphological filtering to segment the brain tumor in brain MRI. Further an approach is presented which approximately identifies and calculate the tumor size (1D, 2D) based on the area and width of tumor.

1.1 Fuzzy C-Means Clustering (FCM)

Clustering is technique of grouping information into sets where data showing similar properties are grouped into a set called a cluster. There are two types of clustering techniques: crisp clustering and fuzzy clustering. Crisp clustering is good technique for clusters that have clearly defined boundaries but in many real cases boundaries cannot be clearly defined and hence it is difficult to identify that the data point belongs to which cluster. Fuzzy clustering is an unsupervised clustering approach for better identification approach and is useful in real-time as it groups datasets into K clusters where every data points belongs to every cluster to a certain level. This technique is widely used in data mining, classification, image segmentation and medical data analysis etc. The task of representation of segmentation of objects which have an uncommon color composition is difficult due to illumination and threshold selection for objects and its color composition [12]. Fuzzy C means clustering segments the image using a membership criteria to a cluster. The data points in soft clustering or fuzzy clustering can belong to more than one cluster and be associated with elements to be a members of a cluster. FCM allocates the data points with certain membership levels and uses then uses them to allot elements to clusters [10, 11].

The Fuzzy C Means clustering algorithm chooses clusters and allocates it coefficients for being members of clusters. The centroid is calculated for each cluster and for each data point coefficients are calculated to determine its clusters. The steps are repeated till the algorithm converges. The FCM algorithm segments a finite group of 'n' data elements. It is represented as D = $\{d_1, d_2, d_3 \ldots d_n\}$. These elements are segmented into 'c' clusters, which are fuzzy clusters made according to some criteria. Consider the finite group of 'n' data elements as 'D', c is the set of cluster centers returned by the algorithm represented as C = $\{c_1, c_2, \ldots c_n\}$ along with a partition matrix 'W' represented as W = $w_{i,j}$, where, $w_{i,j} \in [0, 1]$ and I ranges from 1 to c, j ranges from 1 to n. Each element of the partition matrix ($W_{i,j}$), gives the degree to which the data element d_i belongs to the cluster C_j. 'm' is the weight which defines the effect of partial cluster members on the clustering result in degrees. The main task of FCM is to minimize the objective function 'obj'. Fuzzy c-means is similar to hard c-means in the respect that both try to search of an efficient partition or segment for prototypes 'y_i' to minimize 'obj'.

$$obj = \sum_{j=1}^{n} \sum_{i=1}^{c} wij^m \|dj - yi\|^2 \tag{1}$$

Where,

W_{ij} = shows the belonging of image pixel x_j in i^{th} cluster,
M = 2 (constant, to check the fuzziness of partitioned clusters),
y_i = cluster centre,
D = data set $(d_1, d_2 \ldots d_n)$,
n = no. of pixels.

$$wij = \frac{1}{\sum_{k=1}^{c} \left(\frac{|dj-yi|^2}{|dj-yk|^2}\right)^{\frac{1}{m-1}}} \tag{2}$$

Where, C = number of clusters $(c_1, c_2, \ldots c_k)$.

$$yi = \frac{\sum_{j=1}^{n} wij^m dj}{\sum_{j=1}^{n} wij^m} \tag{3}$$

1.2 Steps to Implement FCM Algorithm

Step 1. Input image $\rightarrow$ data set $(d_1, d_2 \ldots d_n)$.
Step 2. Initialize cluster centers $(y_i = y_1, y_2, \ldots y_c)$.

Step 3. Compute the membership function (w_{ij}) using Eq. (2).
Step 4. Update cluster centers (y_i) using Eq. (3).
Step 5. Calculate the objective function (obj) until it converges to a certain pre-defined value using Eq. (1).

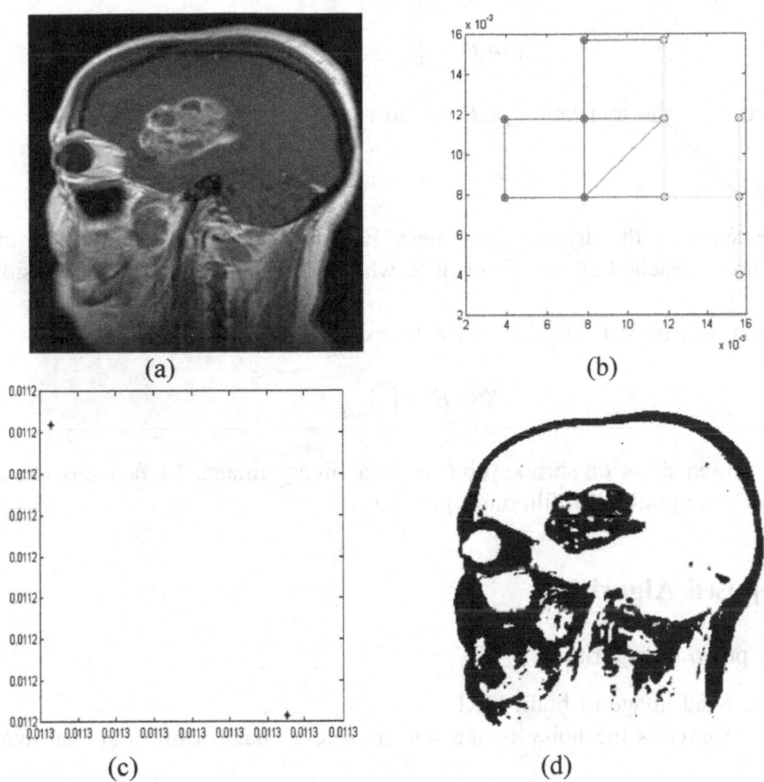

Fig. 1. (a) Brain MRI image [27] (b) cluster formation (no. of clusters = 5) (c) cluster centers (d) fuzzy segmented image

1.3 Mathematical Morphology

MM or Mathematical morphology [14] is a branch of signal processing, which is the study of shapes and geometrical structures based on implementation of set theory, graph theory concepts on image analysis. It is non linear and has filters or operators which are non linear transformations, that alter the image and its geometric features. Structuring elements are the images of certain shapes and sizes which are used along with the filters or operators, in iteration, to change the original image. Some of the operators are dilation, erosion, opening, closing and other derived transforms [15].

1.4 Erosion

Erosion is a binary morphology. The image is seen as a subset of an integer grid 'Z^b' or Euclidean space 'R^d', for a dimension 'd'. The main concept of binary morphology is to investigate a simple image with pre-defined shape. Let 'S' be the Euclidean space or integer grid, and 'X' is a binary image in 'S'. The erosion with respect to structuring element 'E' of the binary image 'X' id defined as:

$$X \ominus E = \{Z \in S | E_z \in X\} \tag{4}$$

Where, E_z is the translation of E by the vector 'z',

$$E_z = \{y + z | y \in E\}, \forall_z \in S \tag{5}$$

If the center for the structuring element 'E' is located on the origin of 'S', then the locus of points reached by the center of E, when E moves inside X is the erosion of X by E.

Erosion of X by E is also given by the expression

$$X \ominus E = \bigcap\nolimits_{y \in E} X_{-y} \tag{6}$$

The erosion thins or shrinks objects in a binary image. In fact erosion can be viewed as a morphological filtering operation.

2 Proposed Algorithm

Steps for proposed algorithm:

Step 1: Read image of brain MRI.

Step 2: Converts the noisy image into noiseless image using a spatial averaging filter.

Step 3: The preprocessed image is segmented using fuzzy c-means clustering algorithm as shown above.

Step 4: Morphological filtering (erosion with SE (disk of radius 2)) is applied over fuzzy segmented image to detect the boundary of tumor.

Step 5: Brain tumor is detected. Region containing tumor is for the further processing.

Step 6: Length and width of tumor is calculated based on (Euclidean distance) [13].

$$D = \sqrt{(X_2 - X_1)^2 + (Y_2 - Y_1)^2} \tag{7}$$

Step 7: Size in 1D is calculated by taking the average of all the lengths and size in 2D is calculated from the area of tumor.

3 Result Analysis

MATLAB is used to perform the proposed hybrid image segmentation algorithm discussed in Sect. 2, and the code was tested on brain MRI images. Input image is first segmented using hybrid approach of fuzzy c-means clustering and morphological filtering to get very accurate segmented image so that tumor can be easily detected as shown in (Fig. 1b and c). Due to irregular shape of tumor it is difficult to accurately calculate the size of the tumor and as well as there are large number of points between two boundaries of tumor.

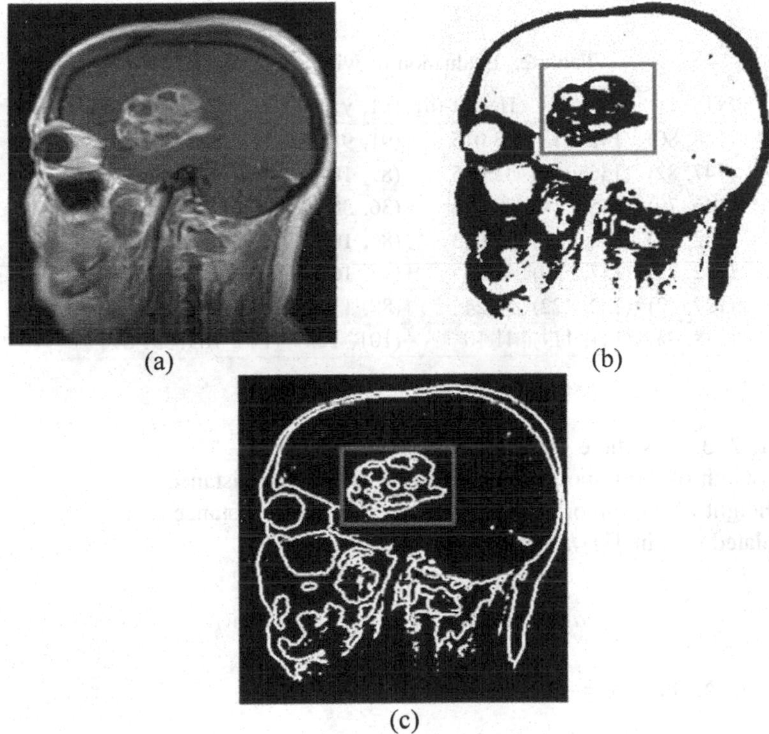

Fig. 2. (a) Brain MR image (b) fuzzy segmented image (c) morphological filtered image

So for the ease of simplification Euclidean distance formula is used. The algorithm approximately calculates the size of tumor Pixel coordinates of region containing tumor (Fig. 2c) are observed and distance between two boundaries is calculated. The simulation results show that integrating fuzzy c-means and mathematical morphology can detect the segments of the image with a high degree of accuracy. As well as the algorithm is suitable to calculate the size (1D, 2D) of tumor. The result of proposed algorithm is compared with the standard statistical methods [16, 17] as shown in Tables 1 and 2.

Table 1. Measurement of tumor sizes in 1-D, 2-D, 3-D

Size	1D (mm)	2D (mm^2)	3D (mm^3)	1D → 2D (mm^2)	1D → 3D (mm^3)	2D → 3D (mm^3)
Minimum	2.8	22.5	53.5	6.2	11.6	80.3
Maximum	206.6	22645.4	131387.4	33501.7	4613963.1	2564157.0
Mean	78.6	4240.2	34416.5	5922.4	454253.8	253035.7

**Size in 1D* (mm); *Size in 2D* (mm^2)

$$\text{average height}\,(h_{av}) = \frac{1}{N}\sum\nolimits_{k=1}^{N} h_k \tag{8}$$

Table 2. Evaluation of width and height

(x1, y1)	(x2, y2)	Height (h)	(x1, y1)	(x2, y2)	Width (w)
(148, 80)	(147, 113)	33.015	(91, 98)	(151, 87)	40.804
(147, 82)	(146, 114)	32.015	(89, 102)	(150, 89)	61
(146, 79)	(145, 114)	35.014	(36, 30)	(264, 36)	62.369
(142, 75)	(143, 113)	38.013	(86, 106)	(151, 96)	65.764
(132, 73)	(137, 120)	47.26	(87, 108)	(150, 97)	63.953
(127, 72)	(132, 122)	50.24	(88, 117)	(148, 100)	62.361
(138, 73)	(141, 114)	41.10	(101, 125)	(148, 103)	51.894

Where,

k = 1, 2, 3…, N (here N = 10)
W = width of the tumor calculated using Euclidean distance
h = height of the tumor calculated using Euclidean distance
calculated size in 1D, h_{av} = 47.484 mm.

$$\textit{average width}\,(w_{av}) = \frac{1}{N}\sum\nolimits_{k=1}^{N} w_k \tag{9}$$

k = 1, 2, 3…N (here N = 8)

$$w_{av} = 58.622\,\text{mm}$$

Using Eq. (8),

$$h_{av} = 40.648$$

The tumor area is calculated based on the approximate calculation

$$\textit{area}\,(\textit{in}\,\text{mm}^2) = h_{av} * w_{av} \tag{10}$$

Calculated size in 2D, area = 2375.56 mm^2.

The size of tumor can help to monitor the extent of tumor and its stages. The stages of the tumor are given below (Table 3).

Table 3. Stages of cancer

Stage 0	Tumor is detected in the place where it started and it has not yet spread to healthy neighboring tissues
Stage I	The tumor has not spread deeply in neighboring tissues
Stage II and III	The tumor is larger and has spread to neighboring tissues
Stage IV	The cancer has spread to organs and other parts of body

4 Conclusion

The results calculated by the algorithm are compared with previously proposed algorithms. The integration of fuzzy means clustering with the morphological filters produces more exact results and reduces the measurement complexity of the tumor size. Future scope can involve the 3-D assessment of brain images using MATLAB with 3-D slicers.

Acknowledgement. Author would like to pay thanks to Rafael C. Gonzalez & Richard E. Woods for valuable resource of information & image database and BITE database for provide free access of MRI images for this research work.

References

1. Logeswari, T., Karnan, M.: An improved implementation of brain tumor detection using segmentation based on soft computing. J. Cancer Res. Exp. Oncol. **2**, 006–014 (2010)
2. Selvakumar, J., Lakshmi, A., Arivoli, T.: Brain tumor segmentation and its area calculation in brain MR images using K-mean clustering and fuzzy C-mean algorithm. In: International Conference on Advances in Engineering, Science and Management, ICAESM. IEEE (2012)
3. Rimner, A., Holodny, A.I., Hochberg, F.H.: Perfusion magnetic resonance imaging to assess brain tumor responses to new therapies. US Neurol. Dis. **1**, 1–6 (2006)
4. Parra, C.A., Iftekharuddin, K., Kozma, R.: Automated brain tumor segmentation and pattern recognition using ANN. In: Computational Intelligence Robotics and Autonomous Systems (2003)
5. Dahab, D.A., Ghoniemy, S.S.A., Selim, G.M.: Automated brain tumor detection and identification using image processing and probabilistic neural network techniques. Int. J. Image Process. Vis. Commun. **1**, 1–8 (2012)
6. Nagalkar, V.J., Asole, S.S.: Brain tumor detection using digital image processing based on soft computing. J. Signal Image Process. **3**, 102–105 (2012)
7. Alirezaie, J., Jernigan, M.E., Nahmias, C.: Neural network based segmentation of magnetic resonance images of the brain. IEEE Trans. Nucl. Sci. **18**(2), 7–30 (2002)

8. Sindhushree, K.S., Manjula, T.R., Ramesha, K.: Detection and 3D reconstruction of brain tumor from brain MRI images. Int. J. Eng. Res. Technol. IJERT **2**, 528–534 (2013)
9. Ananda, R.S., Thomas, T.: Automatic segmentation framework for primary tumors from brain MRIs using morphological filtering techniques. In: 5th International Conference on Biomedical Engineering and Informatics. IEEE (2012)
10. Kumar, S., Ray, S.K., Tewari, P.: A hybrid approach for image segmentation using fuzzy clustering and level set method. Int. J. Image Graph. Signal Process. **4**, 1 (2012)
11. Sasikala, M., Kumaravel, N., Ravikumar, S.: Segmentation of brain MR images using genetically guided clustering. In: Proceedings of the 28th IEEE, MBS Annual International Conference, New York City, USA, 30 August–3 September (2006)
12. El Abbadi, N., Al Saadi, E.: Blood vessel diameter measurement on retinal image. J. Comput. Sci. **10**, 879–883 (2014)
13. Pesaresi, M., Benediktsson, J.A.: A new approach for the morphological segmentation of high-resolution satellite imagery. IEEE Trans. Geosci. Remote Sens. **39**, 309–320 (2001)
14. Dempsey, M.F., Condon, B.R., Hadley, D.M.: Measurement of tumor size in recurrent malignant glioma: 1D, 2D, or 3D. AJNR **26**, 770–776 (2005)
15. Bland, M.: An Introduction to Medical Statistics. Oxford University Press, Oxford (2000)
16. Kabade, R.S., Gaikwad, M.S.: Segmentation of brain tumour and its area calculation in brain MR images using K-mean clustering and fuzzy C-mean algorithm. Int. J. Comput. Sci. Eng. Technol. IJCSET (2013)
17. BITE database. www.bic.mni.mcgill.ca/Services/ServicesBIT

A Computational Approach for Designing Tiger Corridors in India

Saurabh Shanu[1(✉)] and Sudeepto Bhattacharya[2]

[1] Department of Virtualization, School of Computer Science and Engineering, University of Petroleum and Energy Studies, Dehradun 248007, Uttarakhand, India
sshanu@ddn.upes.ac.in

[2] Department of Mathematics, School of Natural Sciences, Shiv Nadar University, P.O. Shiv Nadar University, Greater Noida, Gautam Buddha Nagar 201 314, Uttar Pradesh, India

Abstract. Wildlife corridors are components of landscapes, which facilitate the movement of organisms and processes between intact habitat areas, and thus provide connectivity between the habitats within the landscapes. Corridors are thus regions within a given landscape that connect fragmented habitat patches within the landscape. The major concern of designing corridors as a conservation strategy is primarily to counter, and to the extent possible, mitigate the effects of habitat fragmentation and loss on the biodiversity of the landscape, as well as support continuance of land use for essential local and global economic activities in the region of reference.

In this paper, we use game theory, graph theory, membership functions and chain code algorithm to model and design a set of wildlife corridors with tiger (*Panthera tigris tigris*) as the focal species. We identify the parameters which would affect the tiger population in a landscape complex and using the presence of these identified parameters construct a graph using the habitat patches supporting tiger presence in the landscape complex as vertices and the possible paths between them as edges. The passage of tigers through the possible paths has been designed using an Assurance game, with tigers as an individual player. The game is recursively played as the tiger passes through each grid considered for the model. The iteration causes the tiger to choose the most suitable path signifying the emergence of adaptability.

As a nominal explanation of the game, we design this model through the interaction of tiger with the parameters as deterministic finite automata, for which the transition function is obtained by the game payoff.

Keywords: Landscape complex · Corridor · Assurance game
Graph theory · Chain code algorithm · Finite deterministic automata

1 Introduction

Landscape linkage can be defined as the extent to which the landscape permits movement among resource habitat patches [40, 41]. We also define a corridor as a patch, usually linearly, enclosed in a matrix within a landscape, that joins two or bigger

P. Bhattacharyya et al. (Eds.): NGCT 2017, CCIS 827, pp. 97–109, 2018.
https://doi.org/10.1007/978-981-10-8657-1_8

habitat patches, thereby providing linkage between the habitats and that is designed for conservation on the basis that it will improve or maintain the passage as well as existence of focal wildlife populations in the concerned habitat patches. Further, we define a strategy for selection of path as traversal via a corridor by individuals of the focal species from one habitat patch to another [6].

Wildlife corridors, as implied from the definition above, are integral components of ecological landscapes. The objective of wildlife corridors is to facilitate the movement of processes and organisms between considered areas in the landscape. Corridors are thus regions within a considered landscape that generally comprise native vegetation, and link otherwise disconnected and fragmented wildlife habitat patches in the given landscape [6, 11].

Corridors, being integral components of landscapes, are characterized by two distinct categories of components, namely, pattern and process components [11]. The structural corridor and the functional corridors present the categories of wildlife corridors. The structural categorization refers to the geographical existence of the landscape between the focal patches and the functional corridor is a resultant of both – species and landscape. Hence, a functional wildlife corridor refers to both, species - as well as landscape-specific concept. Corridors thus, may be considered as evolving phenomena, caused by the interaction between process and pattern attributes of the area. The essential function and utility of wildlife corridors is thus to link at least two key habitat patches of biological significance, and thus ensure gene flow between spatially separate populations of species, fragmented due to landscape modifications, by supporting the movements of both biotic and abiotic processes [5, 6, 11, 13].

Researchers have demonstrated that presence of species-specific wildlife corridors within a given landscape to be instrumental in increasing gene flow and population sizes of the species [6, 17–20].

The above discussions imply that any realistic modelling to design wildlife corridor has to be a species – specific task, with a proper selection of habitat for the concerned focal species. In the present paper, we present a computational procedure for designing corridor for the Indian Royal Bengal Tiger (*Panthera Tigris Tigris*) in the Indian landscape. For a country biogeographically as diverse and vast as India, relative spatial location of national reserves in reference to each other turn out to be an important factor to consider for taking optimized decisions on resource allocations, and thus either protecting existing tiger corridors, or even in some instances, creating proper wildlife corridors in. An important concern in such a decision support model therefore must be to select the critical tiger habitats (CTH) in a manner that their spatial configuration guarantees a high degree of interconnectivity within the intensely human-dominated landscapes, over a long term land use scenario.

One means to achieve the above objective would be to design the interconnectivity among the existing (or even potential) habitats or CTH using a network model. In such a network, each tiger habitat would be treated as a vertex, and the tiger corridors between these vertices would be the edges.

The major focus of this paper is to provide a basic computational architecture for understanding a viable corridor network design within the focal landscape complex for tigers. In this paper, all arguments and observations are focused on the basic definition of connectivity, where the existence and viability of a corridor is required to be understood and determined entirely by the landscape features and structure.

We describe the problem of tiger corridor planning and designing within the landscape as a connection subgraph problem [6]. We next incorporate the conflict of interest between the traversing tiger and the landscape features resultant of primarily anthropogenic modifications, through an Assurance game. Finally, informed about the possible costs, we provide an optimized path and thus use these optimized paths to design a Deterministic Finite Automata to obtain the grammar for designing corridors, which we claim, could serve as a rule base for corridor design.

Although the present work makes reference to a landscape map of the focal complex, it is essentially semi-empirical and schematic in nature. Since the work focuses on the presence or absence of corridors linking various tiger habitats in the complex, the distances involved, and the ease of movement for the tiger through these corridors, we are, however, of the opinion that the work could serve as a schema for an informed decision-making by conservationists and wildlife managers in designing real-world corridors.

Section 2 contains the essentials of the mathematical concepts that have been used in this paper. Sections 3 and 4 describe the modelling and the conclusion of the work, respectively.

2 Background for Modelling

In the present work, we shall describe a modelling of a feasible wildlife corridor for the tiger using few specific concerned areas of computational frameworks. In this section, we shall provide the key concept of these areas, in order to make the work self-contained.

We apply game theory to model the effect of presence or absence of identified parameters in a grid leading to selection for movement by tigers. The choice of tigers for movement happens to be random but computationally what must be preferable according to the behavioral pattern of tigers has been modelled here, which could act as an active strategy for designing the corridors. The results are basically the implications of the major non-linear computational interactions between the parameters and the focal species.

Assurance game, best represents the present scenario. While modelling the present interactions, we suppose that set of parameters and the focal species are players of the game, thus accrue a series of pay-offs focusing on the co-player's as well as its own strategies. The game is recursively repeated over discrete time-steps to produce the complex dependencies of parameters affecting the focal species.

Moreover, in Assurance game, always a minimal cost is contributed by all the interacting players if they are to obtain any advantage from their own chosen strategy. Thus, Assurance game would best capture the flavor of coordinated, evolutionary games as such games properly describe the behaviors especially with reference to the biological communities [31, 32, 38].

To create a feasible interactions model for consequent tiger movements, we suppose that the game on every iteration proceeds by sharing of processed data between the players. Each interacting tiger obtains a countable number of data as an input from the contributing factor at each discrete time step at a particular state, and makes a transition to an unambiguously determined next state at the successive time step. Proceeding with this assumption, we construct a finite deterministic automaton to model the movement of the focal species [18, 19, 23]. We propose that the functional characterization of corridors, exchange information can be understood using a regular grammar, which is derived via the automata.

Proceeding with the above discussions, we design our research problem as: What are the finite deterministic automaton and the transition rule/grammar that model the designing of wildlife corridors in the Indian Landscape?

Let $G(\Theta, \Sigma, \Pi)$ be a normal form, strategic game where $\forall i \in I = \{1, \ldots, n\} \subset \aleph, n \geq 2$,

(i) $\Theta = \{\Theta_i\}$ is the set of interacting agents or players;
(ii) $\Sigma_i \neq \{\}$ is the set of strategies for the player Θ_i. $\Sigma = \Sigma_1 \times \ldots \times \Sigma_n$ is the space of strategies, with $\sigma = (\sigma_1, \ldots, \sigma_n) \in \Sigma$ being a strategy profile of the game G;
(iii) $\Pi_i : \Sigma \rightarrow \Re$ is the payoff function, which assigns to each strategy profile σ a real number $\Pi_i(\sigma)$, the payoff earned by the player Θ_i when σ is played in G. $\Pi = \Pi_1 \times \ldots \times \Pi_n$ is the space of payoff functions in the game.

Let an n-player Assurance game be represented by $G(\Theta, \Sigma, \Pi)$, where $\Theta = \{\Theta_i\}$ is the set of players, with $i \in \Im = \{1, 2, \ldots, n\}$ a finite index set and $n \geq 2$. $\Sigma = \{\Sigma_i\}$ where Σ_i is the pure strategy set for each player Θ_i, with $\sigma = \{\sigma_1, \sigma_2, \ldots, \sigma_n\}$ where $\sigma_i \in \Sigma_i$ for $i \in \Im$ is a pure strategy profile of the game and $\Pi = \{\Pi_i\}$, the set of pay-off functions $\Pi_i : S \rightarrow \Re \, \forall i \in \Im$ where S is the set of strategy profiles, give the player's von Neumann-Morgenstern utility $\Pi_i(\sigma)$ for every profile.

To understand the interactions between the parameters and tiger that lead to the designing of corridors in a landscape, we next study the Assurance game. For the purpose of analyzing this n-player Assurance game, we use the pay-off matrix adopted from [4]:

The matrix represents the pay-offs obtained by each player who cooperate and interact. As could be observed from the payoff matrix, the payoff from strategies for a player depends on the ratio with which players play C or play D in the entire population. It can be noticed that the pay-offs for the players playing C varies monotonically with the number of co-operators in the parameters. On the other hand, the scores obtained by the game player using the strategy of Defection remain constant irrespective of the count of players choosing to defect.

A membership function (MF) is a degree value curve that describes the factor by which each parameter in the input space is mapped to a membership value (or degree of membership) between 0 and 1. For the present modeling the input space is the total grid area which would considered for the landscape.

Chain code [12] is used to represent an edge by a connected sequence of pixels. Typically this representation is based on 4 (or) 8 connectivity of the segments (as shown in Fig. 1a and b). The direction of each segment is coded by using a numbering scheme.

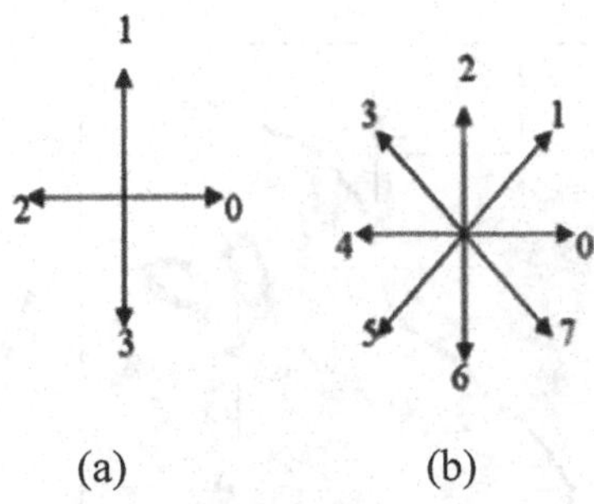

Fig. 1. Neighbour directions of chain code

3 Modelling

For the purpose of the present work, we assume that the tiger habitat patches in India constitute the vertices and the collection of connections within this complex that connect any two of the habitats constitute the edges, comprising the focal landscape complex as a graph $\Gamma(V, E, \psi_\Gamma)$. The existence of an edge between any two vertices represents some ecological flux, such as animal movement, between the adjacent vertices.

To model the possible paths to serve as passages for tigers from one habitat patch to another habitat patch within any considered landscape complex, we first identify a set landscape factors or parameters, which may be natural or anthropogenic, and each of which may either constrain or support the passage of the tiger through the focal landscape matrix to various degrees, and hence become the major determinants in the structural connections becoming a corridor. For describing the present model, we consider five parameters *a, b, c, d* and *e*.

We assume that tigers in the landscape (Θ_1) and the set of above mentioned parameters of the landscape (Θ_2) constitute the two rational agents that play the Assurance game *G* iterated over a number of generations. The players may use a number of strategies in the game in order to optimize their payoff. These payoffs are the costs incurred by the tiger population (called tiger henceforth in the paper) in using the landscape matrix for movement between habitats.

Next we code the different tiger habitats included in the focal landscape complex, by the following Table 2:

In order to explain the model we create a random landscape image as shown in Fig. 2.

Table 1 and the map in Fig. 2 lead to an adjacency matrix $A = [a_{ij}]$, $i = 1, 2, \ldots, n; j = 1, 2, \ldots, n$, where n = 4 for tiger habitat patches, which can be seen in Table 3 and visualized through Fig. 3.

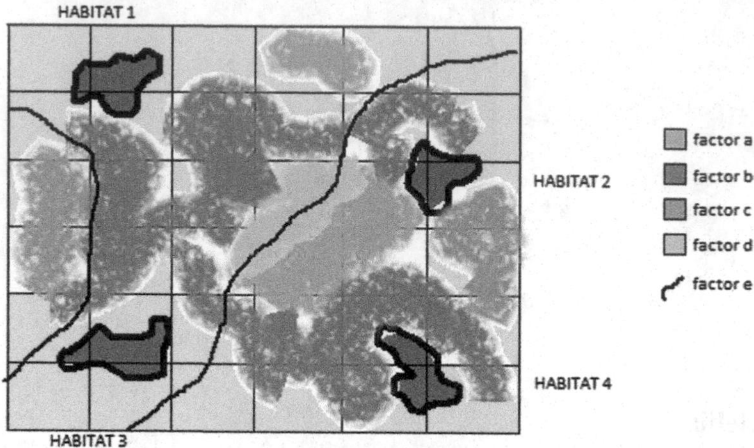

Fig. 2. Sample landscape complex

Table 1. n-Player Assurance payoff matrix

	Proportion of cooperators in the group					
	100%	80%	60%	40%	20%	0%
C	20	14	8	1	−8	−15
D	6	6	6	6	6	6

Table 2. Coding for the tiger habitats in the complex

S. No	Tiger habitat	Code
1.	Habitat 1	1
2.	Habitat 2	2
3.	Habitat 3	3
4.	Habitat 4	4

Table 3. Adjacency matrix A = $[a_{ij}]$ for tiger habitats in the sample landscape complex

	Habitat 1	Habitat 2	Habitat 3	Habitat 4
Habitat 1	0	1	1	1
Habitat 2	1	0	1	1
Habitat 3	1	1	0	1
Habitat 4	1	1	1	0

From the obtained adjacency matrix we can check that there exists connectivity between every patch but the basic question lies in finding the most feasible connection of the entire set of connections that would facilitate the passage of tigers with minimal loss. In order to find out such path, we next compute the costs incurred on tigers in

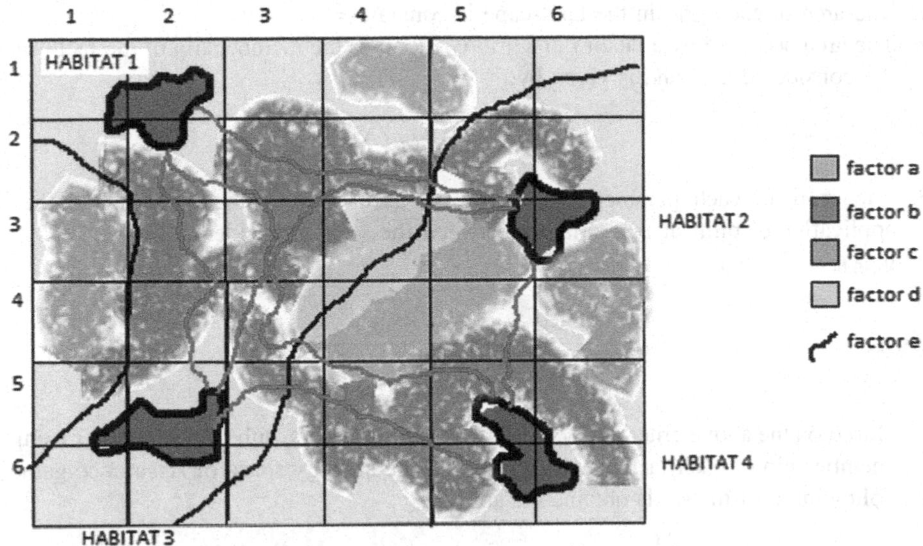

Fig. 3. Sample landscape complex with connectivity.

using the connections between different habitat patches in the given landscape complex.

$$c : E \rightarrow \aleph$$
$$\ni \; e \mapsto c(e) = r \in \aleph, \forall e \in E, \aleph = \{0, 1, \ldots\}.$$

In computing the cost matrix, we further create the Assurance game model using the contribution of each factor in the grid. Each factor of the landscape, due to its presence or absence contributes towards the cost matrix. For the present model, we consider 5 factors and categorize them as shown in Table 4.

Table 4. Factor categorization and score contribution

Factor	Nature (assumed)	Membership contribution						*Example*
		1	0.8	0.6	0.4	0.2	0	
a	Cooperative	20	14	8	1	−8	−15	Water body
b	Cooperative	20	14	8	1	−8	−15	Forest cover
c	Defecting	6	6	6	6	6	6	Agriculture land
d	Cooperative	20	14	8	1	−8	−15	Prey base
e	Defecting	6	6	6	6	6	6	Highways

For the purpose of scoring, we make few assumptions for our model, which can be perfectly calculated once worked on with the Remote Sensing and GIS data. The assumptions made are:

1. The area of each grid in the landscape is constant = A.
2. The area occupied by a factor f in a grid G_{ij} denotes the membership of the factor in the considered grid and is given by:

$$\mu_{f/Gij} = A_{f/Gij}/A$$

3. The score of each parameter in a grid is based on its categorization and then application of bilinear interpolation between the values considered. For e.g. if $\mu_{a/G14} = .7$, then

$$\pi_{a/G14} = \frac{14(.7-.6)+8(.8-.7)}{(.7-.6)+(.8-.7)} = 11.$$

Based on the above criteria of scoring, the various factors with respect to tiger using the membership of each factor in each grid and the strategy space of Assurance game the following cost matrix is obtained (Table 5):

Table 5. Cost matrixes of the tiger for using existing corridors between different habitat patches in the complex

	Habitat 1	Habitat 2	Habitat 3	Habitat 4
Habitat 1	8	S12	S13	S14
Habitat 2	S21	8	S23	S24
Habitat 3	S31	S32	8	S34
Habitat 4	S41	S42	S43	8

For the present theoretical modelling we assume the following order of the scores, which can be correctly obtained using the presence, absence and abundance data of Remote Sensing and GIS:

$$S13 = S31 < S12 = S21 < S34 = S43 < S23 = S32 < S24 = S42 < S14 = S41$$

Using the above scores, we can rank the grids using the chain code algorithm which can be seen as (Fig. 4):

Let the DFA that models the corridor designing and improving the landscape conditions for supporting movement of tigers be $M(Q, \Sigma, q, \delta, h)$. We list the objects comprising M in the following paragraphs:

Q comprises the following set of states, representing the different states of grids that the tiger encounters while moving through it:

- Initial state (I)
- Not favourable state (NFS)
- Fairly favourable state (FFS)
- Moderately favourable state (MFS)
- favourable state (FS)

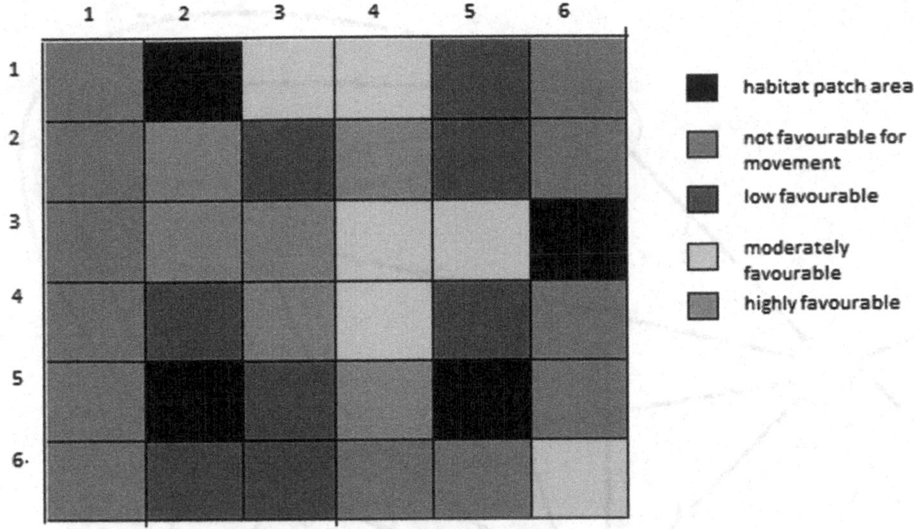

Fig. 4. Ranked grids using the cost matrix

The set of symbols also termed as alphabet Σ = {a, b, c, d, e} includes the letters (inputs for the automata), that happen to be the parameters present in the grid to play G.

I is the initial state, describing the initial state of a grid which appears as the tigers move out from the territorial region. The transition function δ is explained by the following matrix (Table 6):

Table 6. Transitions of Δ to various states

State	Letter				
	a	b	c	d	e
I	MFS	FS	NFS	FFS	NFS
NFS	FFS	FS	NFS	FFS	NFS
FFS	MFS	FS	NFS	MFS	NFS
MFS	FS	FS	FFS	FS	NFS
FS	FS	FS	FFS	FS	NFS

There exist two states which may be included in the state of final states which are:

- NFS: Not favourable for movement of tigers and thus cannot be supported or converted to corridor due to massive interferences from inhibitory sources.
- FS: favourable State for movement, as it supports the movement of tigers through them with highest priority (Fig. 5).

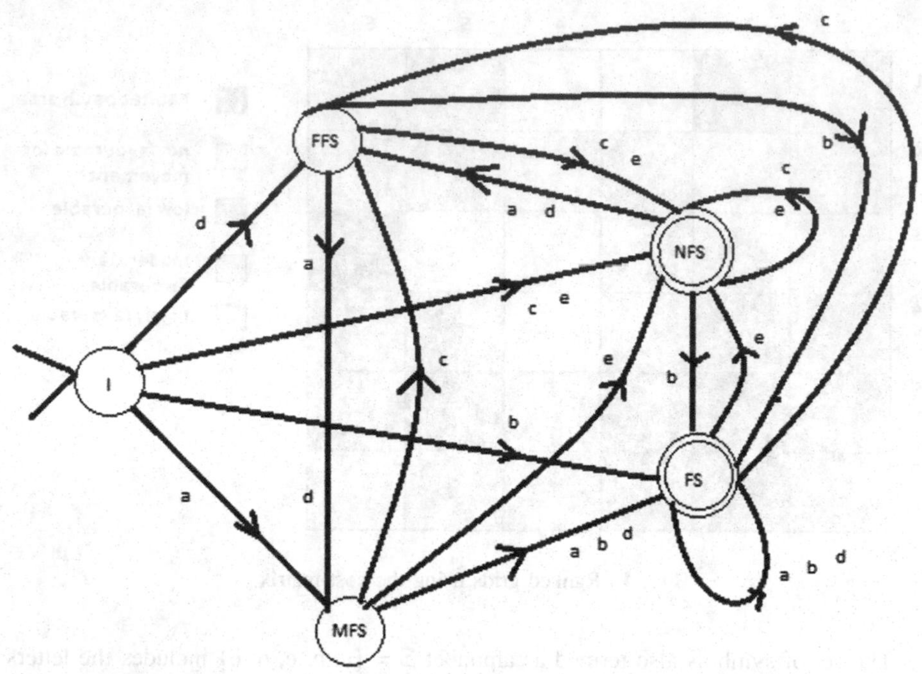

Fig. 5. DFA for grid state transitions to model wildlife corridors.

The above Automaton would generate a regular grammar (CFG), which would, in essence, be obtained by the transition function δ. Let the non-terminals in the DFA are denoted by Y. Y comprises the following states:

- I: Initial state (I)
- J: Not favourable state (NFS)
- K: Fairly favourable state (FFS)
- L: Moderately favourable state (MFS)
- M: favourable state (FS)

Corresponding to such a set of non-terminal states, the context free grammar (CFG) could be written as

→ I → cJ|aK|cL|Dm|eK
∗J → cJ|aK|cL|dM|eK
K → cJ|aK|cL|dM|eK
L → cJ|aK|cL|dM|eK
∗M → cJ|aK|cL|dM|eK

J, M is the final state of the automata, which, for the sake of identification, is prefixed by an asterisk sign.

4 Conclusion

The present work has been developed with objectives to (i) obtain a rule set to design a feasible tiger corridor network, connecting the habitat patches for the tiger in the landscape complex using a replicable computational procedure and (ii) identify the most important habitat patches, along with their underlying community structure so as to focus efforts towards conserving them.

In this paper, we have used Deterministic Finite Automaton to obtain a grammar that could serve as a model framework for a real-world tiger corridor designing in the Indian landscape.

A limitation in the modelling described in the paper is that the corridor designing is based entirely on the structural definition of connectivity, and thus does not take into account some critically vital landscape features such as the biotic factors of availability of prey base and water, in computing the cost matrix. The work is, by choice, kept rudimentary so as to provide a basic computational architecture for perceiving a viable structural corridor network design in the focal landscape complex for tigers. We may justify this absence of path redundancy consideration due to two reasons: first, our priority in the paper was to focus on the path efficiency over repetitions, and second, the work focuses on estimation of optimal strategies for connecting the CTHs, rather than inclusion of alternative paths [55]. We are aware that such a simplification is more often not in consonance with the real-world corridor scenario. We however hope that our present effort would make available a computational template for tiger corridor designing, which could certainly be improved upon by incorporating field data from realistic considerations.

References

1. Axelrod, R., Hamilton, W.D.: The evolution of cooperation. Science **211**, 1390–1396 (1981)
2. Axelrod, R.: The Evolution of Cooperation. Basic Books Inc., New York (1984)
3. Baum, K.A., Haynes, K.J., Dillemuth, F.P., Cronin, J.T.: The matrix enhances the effectiveness of corridors and stepping stones. Ecology **85**(10), 2671–2676 (2004)
4. Baland, J.M., Platteau, J.P.: Halting Degradation of Natural Resources. Oxford University Press, Oxford (1996)
5. Beier, P., Loe, S.: A checklist for evaluating impacts to wildlife movement corridors. Wildl. Soc. Bull. **20**, 434–440 (1992)
6. Beier, P., Noss, R.F.: Do habitat corridors provide connectivity? Conserv. Biol. **12**(6), 1241–1252 (1998)
7. Bonacich, P.: Factoring and weighting approaches to status scores and clique identification. J. Math. Sociol. **2**(1), 113–120 (1972)
8. Bondy, J., Murty, U.S.R.: Graph Theory. Springer, New Delhi (2008)
9. Bunn, A.G., Urban, D.L., Keitt, T.H.: Landscape connectivity: a conservation application of graph theory. J. Environ. Manag. **59**, 265–278 (2000)
10. Cantwell, M.D., Forman, R.T.T.: Landscape graphs; ecological modelling with graph-theory to detect configurations common to diverse landscapes. Landsc. Ecol. **8**, 239–255 (1993)
11. Chetkiewicz, B.C.-L., St. Clair, C.C., Boyce, M.S.: Corridors for conservation: integrating pattern and process. Annu. Rev. Ecol. Evol. Syst. **37**, 317–342 (2006)

12. Dunne, J.A., Williams, R.J., Martinez, N.D.: Network structure and biodiversity loss in food webs: robustness increases with connectance. Ecol. Lett. **5**, 558–567 (2002)
13. Dutta, T., Sharma, S., Maldonado, J.E., Wood, T.C., Panwar, H.S., Seidensticker, J.: Gene flow and evolutionary history of leopards (*panthera pardus*) in central Indian highlands. Evol. Appl. (2013). https://doi.org/10.1111/eva12078
14. Gonzalez, R.C., Woods, R.E.: Digital Image Processing, 2nd edn. Pearson Publications, London (2012)
15. Fall, A., Fortin, M.-J., Manseau, M., O'Brien, D.: Spatial graphs: principles and applications for habitat connectivity. Ecosystems **10**, 448–461 (2007)
16. Gopal, R., Qureshi, Q., Bhardwaj, M., Singh, R.K.J., Jhala, Y.V.: Evaluating the status of the endangered tiger *Panthera tigris* and its prey in Panna Tiger Reserve, Madhya Pradesh, India. Oryx **44**, 383–398 (2010)
17. Hanski, I.: Metapopulation dynamics. Nature **396**, 41–49 (1998)
18. Hanski, I., Gilpin, M.: Metapopulation dynamics – brief-history and conceptual domain. Biol. J. Linn. Soc. **42**, 3–16 (1991)
19. Hanski, I., Ovaskainen, O.: The metapopulation capacity of a fragmented landscape. Nature **404**, 755–758 (2000)
20. Harris, L.D., Gallagher, P.B.: New initiatives for wildlife conservation: the need for movement corridors. In: Mackintosh, G. (ed.) Preserving Communities and Corridors, p. 96. Defenders of Wildlife, Washington, D.C. (1989)
21. Hofstadter, D.R.: Godel, Escher, Bach: An Eternal Golden Braid. Penguin, London (2000)
22. Hopcroft, J.E., Motwani, R., Ullman, J.D.: Introduction to Automata Theory, Languages and Computation. Addison Wesley, Boston (2006)
23. Hofbauer, J., Sigmund, K.: Evolutionary Games and Population Dynamics. Cambridge University Press, Cambridge (1998)
24. Jhala, Y.V., Gopal, R., Qureshi, Q. (eds.): Status of Tigers, Co-predators and Prey in India, p. 151. National Tiger Conservation Authority, Govt. of India, New Delhi, and Wildlife Institute of India, Dehradun. TR08/001 (2008)
25. Jhala, Y.V., Qureshi, Q., Gopal, R., Sinha, P.R. (eds.): Status of Tigers, Co-predators and Prey in India, 2010, p. 302. National Tiger Conservation Authority, Govt. of India, New Delhi, and Wildlife Institute of India, Dehradun. TR2011/003 (2011)
26. Levett, W.J.M.: An Introduction to the Theory of Formal Languages and Automata. John Benjamins, Amsterdam (2008)
27. Jordan, F., Liu, W.C., Davis, A.J.: Topological keystone species: measures of positional importance in food webs. Oikos **112**, 535–546 (2006)
28. Keitt, T.H.: Network theory: an evolving approach to landscape conservation. In: Dale, V.H. (ed.) Ecological Modelling for Resource Management. Springer, New York (2003). https://doi.org/10.1007/0-387-21563-8_7
29. Kruskal Jr., J.B.: On the shortest spanning subtree of a graph and the travelling salesman problem. Proc. Am. Math. Soc. **7**(1), 48–50 (1956)
30. Nowak, M.A., Sigmund, K.: A strategy of win-stay, lose-shift that outperforms tit-for-tat in the Prisoner's Dilemma game. Nature **364**, 56–58 (1993)
31. Nowak, M.A., Sigmund, K.: Chaos and the evolution of cooperation. Proc. Natl. Acad. Sci. USA **90**, 5091–5094 (1993)
32. Nowak, M.A., Bonhoeffer, S., May, R.M.: Spatial games and maintenance of cooperation. Proc. Natl. Acad. Sci. USA **91**, 4877–4881 (1994)
33. Minor, E.S., Urban, D.L.: A graph-theory framework for evaluating landscape connectivity and conservation planning. Conserv. Biol. **22**(2), 297–307 (2008)
34. Opdam, P., Verboom, J., Powels, R.: Landscape cohesion: an index for the conservation potential of landscapes for biodiversity. Landsc. Ecol. **18**, 113–126 (2003)

35. Opdam, P., Steingrover, E., van Rooij, S.: Ecological networks: a spatial concept for multi-actor planning of sustainable landscapes. Landsc. Urban Plann. **75**, 322–332 (2006)
36. Ozgur, A., Vu, T., Erkan, G., Radev, D.R.: Identifying gene-disease associations using centrality on a literature mined gene-interaction network. Bioinformatics **24**(13), i277–i285 (2008)
37. Santos, M., Szathmary, E.: The evolution of cooperation. Treballs de la SCB **60**, 213–229 (2009). https://doi.org/10.2436/20.1501.02.87
38. Pulliam, H.R.: Sources, sinks and population regulation. Am. Nat. **132**, 652–661 (1988)
39. Rayfield, B., Fortin, M.-J., Fall, A.: Connectivity for conservation: a framework to classify network measures. Ecology **92**(4), 847–858 (2011)
40. Taylor, P.D., Fahrig, L., Henein, K., Merriam, G.: Connectivity is a vital element of landscape structure. Oikos **68**, 571–573 (1993)
41. Taylor, P.D., Fahrig, L., With, K.A.: Landscape connectivity: a return to the basics. In: Crooks, K.R., Sanjayan, M. (eds.) Connectivity Conservation, pp. 29–43. Cambridge University Press, Cambridge (2006)
42. Urban, D.L., Keitt, T.H.: Landscape connectivity: a graph-theoretic perspective. Ecology **82**, 1205–1218 (2001)
43. Urban, D.L., Minor, E.S., Treml, E.A., Schick, R.S.: Graph models of habitat mosaics. Ecol. Lett. **12**, 260–273 (2009)
44. Webb, J.N.: Game Theory: Decisions, Interactions and Evolution. Springer, New Delhi (2007). https://doi.org/10.1007/978-1-84628-636-0
45. Wikramanayake, E.D., Dinerstein, E., Robinson, J.G., Karanth, U., Rabinowitz, A., Olson, D., Mathew, T., Hedao, P., Conner, M., Hemley, G., Bolze, D.: An ecology based method for defining priorities for large mammal conservation: the tiger as case study. Conserv. Biol. **12**(4), 865–878 (1998)
46. Wikramanayake, E., McKnight, M., Dinerstein, E., Joshi, A., Gurung, B., Smith, D.: Designing a conservation landscape for tiger in human-dominated environments. Conserv. Biol. **18**(3), 839–844 (2004)
47. Yumnam, B., Jhala, Y.D., Qureshi, Q., Maldonado, J.E., Gopal, R., Saini, S., Srinivas, Y., Fleischer, R.C.: Prioritizing tiger conservation through landscape genetics and habitat linkages. PLoS ONE **9**(11), e111207 (2014)

Enhanced Task Scheduling Algorithm Using Multi-objective Function for Cloud Computing Framework

Abhikriti Narwal(✉) and Sunita Dhingra

Department of Computer Science and Engineering,
University Institute of Engineering and Technology,
Maharshi Dayanand University, Rohtak, Haryana, India
abhikritiin@gmail.com

Abstract. Cloud computing era refers to a dynamic, scalable and pay-per-use distributed computing model empowering designers to convey applications amid task designation and storage distribution. The cloud computing mainly aims to give proficient access to remote and geographically distributed resources. The essential advantage of moving to Clouds is application versatility. It is exceptionally advantageous for the applications which are sharing their assets on various hubs. The cloud computing for the most part plans to give capable access to remote and geographically distributed resources. As cloud innovation is advancing step by step and confronts various difficulties, one of them being revealed is scheduling. To accomplish distinctive objectives and high performance of cloud computing framework, it is expected to configure, create, and propose a scheduling algorithm that outperforms the appropriate allocation of tasks with different factors. Algorithms are vital to schedule the tasks for execution. Task scheduling algorithms believed to be the most hypothetical problems in the cloud computing domain. This paper proposed a multi-objective task scheduling algorithm that considers wide variety of attributes in cloud environment and uses non-dominate sorting for prioritizing the tasks. The proposed algorithm considers three parameters i.e. Total processing cost, total processing time and average waiting time. The main objective of this paper is to enhance the performance and evaluate the performance with FCFS, SJF and previously implemented multi-objective task scheduling algorithm.

Keywords: Cloud computing · Scheduling · Task scheduling
Quality of service (QoS) · Resource allocation · Virtual machine (VM)

1 Introduction

Cloud computing is the growing innovation that conveys numerous kinds of resources as services, for the most part over the internet. The latest advancements in cloud computing are building our business applications fundamentally more versatile like the most of the community and business applications in the cloud are going in that course only.

P. Bhattacharyya et al. (Eds.): NGCT 2017, CCIS 827, pp. 110–121, 2018.
https://doi.org/10.1007/978-981-10-8657-1_9

Cloud computing is the early development which depends on pay-per-use basis. The goal of the cloud organization providers is to utilize the resources effectively and accomplish the most extreme benefits [2]. This new advancing perfect model of cloud computing is appealing a lot of vendors and various associations by understanding the profits of putting their applications and data onto the cloud. This makes cheaper and efficient utilization of available resources and easier handling of larger computational problems. In cloud, consumers can evade capital payments on hardware, software, and services. Computation done in cloud depends on services with the aim to achieve maximum resource utilization and 24/7 availability at minimized cost. According to the type of services given to its customers, cloud computing is described into three service models – (SaaS) Software as a Service, (PaaS) Platform as a Service and (IaaS) Infrastructure as a Service [8]. A large variety of applications can be initiated and utilized dynamically using cloud services. The Infrastructure as a Service model consists of the outsourcing of the resources needed to carry on operations, consisting of storage, hardware, servers and networking components. The equipment is owned by the service provider and is in charge for running, housing and maintaining it. The consumer need not control or manage the underlying cloud infrastructure directly and typically pays according to per-use basis. In Platform as a Service (PaaS) model virtualized servers, specific cloud environment and associated services are given to user on rent basis for running existing applications and developing or testing new ones. PaaS has several benefits as it provides users with an abstraction layer that allows them to focus on developing their applications without worried about the fundamental infrastructure. With SaaS, a provider gives access of an application to its customers either as an utility which is named as 'pay-as-you-go' model, or at no charge.

As a immense number of customers share cloud resources and dispatch their tasks to the cloud, it has become a challenge to schedule these tasks. Subsequently, task scheduling is a necessary topic in distributed and cloud computing. Task scheduling in a cloud environment is one of the NP- problems, which deals with the optimal assignment of a task [12]. The scheduling stages of any task scheduling algorithms run in a virtualized environment of cloud computing [2]. The scheduling algorithms belonging to distributed systems mainly aim to partition the load and assign sub loads to processors to achieve their maximum utilization while minimizing the total load execution time. As cloud computing is highly dynamic and to cope up with the fluctuating demands of customers it becomes severely necessary to address the resource allocation problems. However, it is a big challenge in itself to achieve an efficient scheduling algorithm design and implement in cloud computing. Scheduling in cloud is generally comprised of three stages: Resource discovery and filtering- resources in system and their related status data are gathered. Resource choice- target resource is picked based on different parameters. Job submission- job is submitted to the picked resource [8]. Since Scheduling is a challenging subject in cloud computing, it can be handled by numerous heuristic methods which provide the solution for the problem within restriction [11].

In this paper, we talk about scheduling in cloud framework. The prologue to proposed work zone is incorporated into Sect. 1. Related work is shown in Segment 2. Section 3 shows the problem formulation and approach is clarified in Sect. 4. Section 5 includes result and discussions. Finally, Sect. 6 concludes the paper.

2 Related Work

In Past, an extensive number of studies have been done with respect to the scheduling in cloud computing. In [1], authors exhibit the First Come First Serve alias First in First out algorithm in which the jobs are organized into the structure with respect to the request of their arriving time. The FCFS algorithm may additionally breed the convoy impact which usually takes place when huge amount of workload tasks is there in the task queue. In this situation, all the tasks that are at the end of the list will have to wait for the large task to get finish then the resource is allocated to that task. In [3] authors illustrate the Shortest Job First (SJF) or Shortest Job Next (SJN). This picks up the task with the least execution time. Highest priority is assigned to the jobs with minimum execution time and placed first in queue while the lowest priority is assigned to the job with the maximum execution time. It can be either pre-emptive or non-preemptive. SJF algorithm with pre-emptive nature will stop the execution of the process which is currently in execution, whereas SJF algorithm with a non-pre-emptive nature will let the process that is currently working to complete. In [4], authors present the paper which included the Round Robin algorithm. It is considered as one of the least difficult, ordinary and most utilized scheduling algorithm which works extraordinarily better to timesharing frameworks. It distributes the load equally to all the resources. It works in a very similar way in cloud computing as it does in process scheduling. The working includes a circular queue and a fixed time unit called quantum. Every individual job's execution happens just inside this quantum. In the event that if the job does not accomplish in one allocated quantum, it comes back to the list of queue and have to wait for the following round. The massive benefit is that the task are in sequential form of execution i.e. turn wise and it is necessary for the job to wait for the exiting in execution job to get completed. Consequently, there is no starvation issue. But the dark side is that if the workload is heavy and queue is fully loaded, large amount of time has been used by all the jobs and moreover, a perfectly specific time slot is hard to choose. In [5] authors illustrate the Min-Min scheduling algorithm. The working concept in the Min-Min algorithm is to map each task to the resources such that they can accomplish the task in the minimum possible time. It estimates the execution and completion time of each job on each available resources. There are two phase in the Min-Min algorithm. In the first phase it calculates the least execution time of all tasks. Further in second phase, the task with the least execution time among all the tasks is picked up. The Max-min algorithm works very similar to the Min-min algorithm [5]. The differentiating feature is as per the name as the word "minimum" is replaced by "maximum" similarly, here the task having the maximum earliest completion time is allocated to the corresponding resource. Here, larger tasks are given priority over the smaller tasks. In [6] authors demonstrated the Resource Aware Scheduling Algorithm. RASA is a hybrid scheduling algorithm composed of two traditional techniques i.e. Min-min and Max-min. Min-Min technique is utilized to execute little tasks before huge tasks and Max-Min procedure is applied to avoid the delays in vast tasks execution. Both the methodologies are utilized alternatively for tasks and exchange results in successive execution of a little and a huge task on diverse resources thus overlooking the small tasks waiting time in Max-min calculation and analysing the large allocations waiting time in Min-min calculation. In [7], an author shows the Priority Scheduling Algorithm. Priority scheduling algorithm is pre-emptive in nature where each procedure in the framework depends on the need and need is allowed to run. The most elevated need job can run first whereas lower priority job can be made to wait. Equal-Priority processes are scheduled in FCFS order. The drawback of this algorithm is starvation of a process. In [9, 10] authors illustrate the Honey Bee Scheduling. This algorithm is also inspired by social agents and simulates the foraging manner of honey bees for finding the best possible solution. The food source here is the flower patches with more nectar and pollens. The particular class "scout bees" forage for food sources. After successfully finding the food source, they come back to the hive and start to dance. The principle reason behind this move is to publicize about the quality or amount of food furthermore its area. In bee house society, Forager honey bees then take after the Scout Bees to the food location and afterward start to procure it. They then come back to the beehive and do a waggle move to other basic honey bees in the hive giving a thought of the left food. This prompts more investigation of the way.

3 Problem Formulation

Scheduling is always been a testing area in the field of cloud computing, which can be resolved by using various heuristic techniques that gives the answer for the issue inside the confinements. After the accommodation of the accumulation of assignments to the cloud, the most critical stride is planning of scheduling and to screen the execution of the task. Cloud task scheduling is performed by picking the most ideal asset accessible for execution of assignments keeping in mind the end goal to limit the finish time. As a rule, in scheduling strategies a list of tasks is structured by assigning a priority to the tasks following any parameter. Tasks are additionally picked up by their needs and are allotted to the accessible assets to meet the pre-characterized aims.

A huge segment of the task scheduling approaches in cloud computing is single-targeted which does not describe beneficial resource use. These targets, for example, diminish the time, cost, and expanding execution and so on. Rather than looking for a solitary optimal solution based on the single unity objective, multiobjective optimization [13] aims at finding for the set that is known to be as Pareto-optimal solutions set. In this way, it is basic to convey multicriteria to enhance the system execution and grow resource utilization. There are numerous criteria like execution time, cost, and data transfer capacity for communication, due date, makespan and so on. An enhanced multi-objective task scheduling algorithm (EMOSA) has been proposed considering three basic criteria's i.e. processing time, average waiting time and processing cost. The proposed approach additionally incorporated with non-dominated sorting for requesting of undertakings.

The various formulae's that has been used for implementing the EMOSA algorithm are defined below:

Processing Time of any tasks can be calculated as:

$$\boldsymbol{Processing_{time} = cloudlet_{length} / VM_{MIPS*no\_pf\ PES}}$$

Where PES is processing elements defined in terms of Million Instructions per second.

Processing Cost is defined as:

$$\boldsymbol{Processing_{cost} = Datacenter_{costpermemory} * VM_{Ram}}$$

Average Waiting Time for the tasks will be calculated as:

$$\boldsymbol{Waiting_{time} = \sum_{i=1}^{\text{no. of cloudlets}} cloudlet_{i}.waitingtime()}$$

4 Approach

The cloud computing framework design comprises of the cloud broker, the VM chief, the scheduling algorithm, servers and VMs. Cloud includes a few server farms which contain a system of virtual services encouraging the user to get to and convey applications from anyplace in the world on demand at competitive costs depending on their QoS requirements. Each VMs have particular capacity to execute diverse QoS's assignments that is looked up by the customers. In cloud framework, the scheduling of the tasks is a very essential and challenging job. For the enhancement and also for good services the modification of scheduling is necessary. The Fig. 1 depicts the way the task scheduling is been done in cloud network. The users submit the tasks, then the datacentre broker acts as a medium between the tasks and VM. Datacentre broker finds out the most appropriate VM for the task and then assign the particular task to the VM. Task scheduling can be seen from two bearings from the cloud resources client view where client need to recognize which cloud computing resources can meet their task QoS requirements for processing and how much extra add up to be paid for the cloud.

Scheduling includes the mapping of the tasks to the assets. The essential thought is to tie the arrangement of assignments got by the specialists to the accessible VMs; with

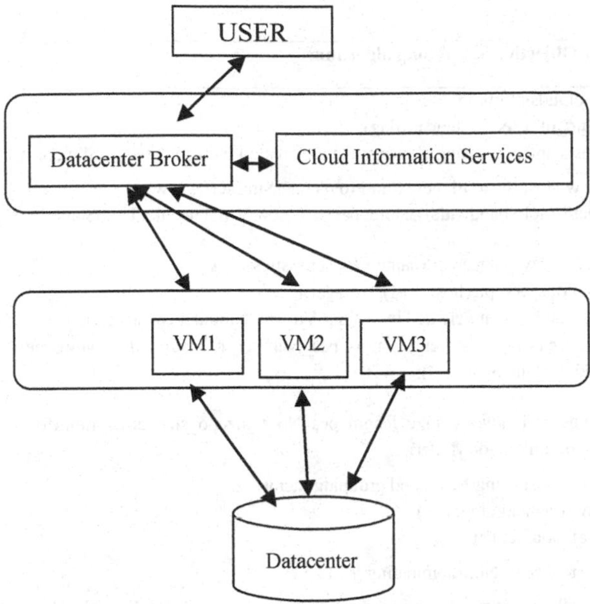

Fig. 1. Task scheduling in cloud computing framework

an objective to decrease the execution time of the tasks and the operational cost. These existing approaches have some disadvantages of coming about into more execution time and diminished throughput. The improved scheduling of the individual task in cloud is as yet an issue to get it. Since cloud involves various unmistakable assets and cost of performing assignments in cloud additionally fluctuates so the scheduling of undertakings in cloud is altogether different from the existing approaches of scheduling.

EMOSA considers the QoS parameter for appointing the need to the tasks. Low QoS worth is designated to a High QoS task and the other way around. In this way, the task with less QoS factor worth is a high need and the task with high QoS factor worth is a low need. The QoS parameters for task are specified in Service level agreement (SLA). Here, the cloud broker sends the task request to the Cloud service provider (CSP) for utilizing the VMs created in the hosts of datacenters. In the way of getting the list in response from Cloud Service Provider, cloud representative assigns QoS to the VMs utilizing Millions of guidelines for every second (MIPS) of a VM and the granularity size. The proposed scheduling strategy is including Non-dominated sorting which focuses on the multi-objective issues considering numerous criteria [12]. In the proposed work, the primary goal is to minimize the processing time of task. The principle focus is expert by choosing an task from the sorted list and assigning the best optimized machine to it. The pseudocode for the proposed algorithm is given below:

Enhanced Multi-Objective Scheduling algorithm

```
1. Initializing the cloudsim library.
2. CloudSim.init(no_of_users, calendar, flag);
3. Datacenters, hosts and processing elements list are created by using the specific constructors
   Host host= new Host (host_Id, new RamProvisionerSimple(r), new
   BwProvisionerSimple(bandwidth), store, pes_list, new VmSchedulerTimeShared(pes_list))

   DataCenter dc = new Datacenter (name, characteristics, new
   VmAllocationPolicySimple(host_List), storageList
4. Virtual machines and task are created by calling Vm and Cloudlet constructor.
   Vm v1 = new Vm (vm_id, broker_Id, mips, pes_Number, r, bandwidth, s, vmm, new
   CloudletSchedulerTimeShared ());

   Cloudlet c1 = new Cloudlet (c_id, c_length, pes_No, f_size, o_size, utilizationModel,
   utilizationModel, utilizationModel);
5. Sort the created vm list using MIPS and grouping factor
6. Non-dominating_List.add(cloudlets)
7. for k=1 to size of cloudlet list
       for all l=0 to size of Non-dominating_List
           if cloudlet (l) dominates cloudlet (k) on the basis of cloudet_length, filesize, fileoutputsize
               Put cloudlet (l) into Non-dominating_List
           Else if cloudlet (k) dominates cloudlet (l)then
               Put cloudlet (k) into Non-dominating_List
           Else
               Put cloudlet (k) and cloudlet (l) into Non-dominating_List
           end if
     end for
   end for.
8. Submit Non-dominating_List and sorted VMList to Broker.
9. Cloudsim.startSimulation()
10. for v=1 to size of sorted VMList
       for all c=0 to size of Non-dominating_List
           Mapping of cloudlet to the vm is done sendNow(getVmsToDatacentersMap().
           get(vm.getId()), CloudSimTags.CLOUDLET_SUBMIT, cloudlet);
       End for
    End for
11. Analyse the parameters for each cloudlet processing on vm.
12. Cloudsim.stopSimulation()
13. Received the processed cloudlet List and analyse the performance parameters.
```

The scheduling of these huge number of tasks is an extremely fundamental and testing work for cloud. The fundamental thought process of task scheduling is to accomplish better cloud execution of tasks as far as better throughput, load balancing, QoS, economic feasibility and the optimal operation time.

5 Results and Discussions

This section exhibits the simulation results of the proposed technique (EMOSA) utilized with the help of CloudSim 3.0 test system on windows 7 OS. NetBeans IDE 8.0 is used to run CloudSim. The proposed procedure is executed by taking diverse datasets of machines and assignments. The execution of the proposed algorithm is evaluated with existing algorithms, for example, FCFS, SJF algorithm and previously existing multi-objective task scheduling algorithm (MOSA) [13]. An arrangement of experiments are conducted to measure parameters like Processing time, Average waiting time of tasks and the Processing Cost. The parameters used for analysis of results are depicted in Table 1:

Table 1. List of parameters for analysis of results

Cloudsim entities	Input parameters	Value
Task (cloudlet)	Task_Length	100–2000
	No._of_Tasks	50–1000
Virtual machine	No._of_Vms	60
	MIPS of machines	250–1000
	Ram of machines	1024–2048
	Bandwidth of machines	50–1000
	Scheduler for cloudlets	Space shared and time shared
	Num_of_Pes	1–4
Datacenter	Num_of_Datacenter	10
	Num of Host	2–6
	Scheduler for Virtual machine	Space shared and time shared

Table 2. Simulation results of MOSA (parameters with MIPS).

========== OUTPUT ==========

Cloudlet ID	STATUS	Data center ID	VM ID	Time	Start Time	Finish Time
0	SUCCESS	2	0	59.99	0.1	60.09
1	SUCCESS	2	0	263.62	0.1	263.72
2	SUCCESS	2	0	368.54	0.1	368.64
3	SUCCESS	2	1	946.83	0.1	946.93
4	SUCCESS	2	1	1141.97	0.1	1142.07
5	SUCCESS	2	1	1226.26	0.1	1226.36
6	SUCCESS	2	2	1762.01	0.1	1762.11
7	SUCCESS	2	2	1972.68	0.1	1972.78
8	SUCCESS	2	2	2072.72	0.1	2072.82

From the Table 2 the total processing time for the tasks obtained is 3667.549, total processing cost obtained is 226.869 and average waiting time obtained is 0.3689 under the scenario of 3 VMs and 9 cloudlets.

Table 3. Simulation results of EMOSA (parameters with MIPS and granularity size).

```
========== OUTPUT ==========
Cloudlet ID   STATUS    Data center ID   VM ID   Time      Start Time   Finish Time
  0          SUCCESS        2             0      59.99       0.1        60.09
  1          SUCCESS        2             0      257.54      0.1        257.64
  2          SUCCESS        2             0      355.49      0.1        355.59
  3          SUCCESS        2             1      920.38      0.1        920.48
  4          SUCCESS        2             1      1092.27     0.1        1092.37
  5          SUCCESS        2             1      1182.61     0.1        1182.71
  6          SUCCESS        2             2      1700.63     0.1        1700.73
  7          SUCCESS        2             2      1902.82     0.1        1902.92
  8          SUCCESS        2             2      1993.66     0.1        1993.76
```

From the Table 3 the total processing time for the tasks obtained is 3538.16, total processing cost calculated is 115.19 and the average waiting time is 0.353. So from the Tables 2 and 3 observations we can conclude that EMOSA outperforms the MOSA algorithm.

Table 4. Simulation results in terms of average waiting time

Workload	Virtual machine	Cloudlets	FCFS	SJF	MOSA	EMOSO
Workload1	3	9	0.5126	0.4536	0.3689	0.353
Workload2	3	50	0.6091	0.5696	0.4047	0.3907
Workload3	30	200	1.95296	0.819	0.526	0.4827
Workload4	40	300	1.523041	0.8459	0.5897	0.495
Workload5	60	500	1.568611	0.8964	0.5676	0.5009

Figure 2 and Table 4, compare the results obtained for Average waiting time of EMOSA with FCFS, SJF and MOSA [13]. It is clear that proposed EMOSA technique is outperforming others. For workload 1 the obtained average time for EMOSA is 0.353 while for MOSA is 0.3689, SJF is 0.4536 and FCFS is 0.5126. Likewise for workload 2, 3, 4, 5 EMOSA outperforms the other algorithms.

Figure 3 and Table 5, compare the results obtained for Processing Cost of EMOSA with FCFS, SJF and MOSA [13]. It is clear that proposed EMOSA technique is outperforming others. For workload 1 the obtained processing cost for EMOSA is 115.19 while for MOSA is 226.28, SJF is 301.36 and FCFS is 312.6. Likewise for workload 2, 3, 4, 5 EMOSA outperforms the other algorithms.

Figure 4 and Table 6, compare the results obtained for processing time of EMOSA with FCFS, SJF and MOSA [13]. For workload 1 the obtained processing time for EMOSA is 3538.16 while for MOSA is 3667.54, SJF is 3991.69 and FCFS is 3999.96. It is clear that proposed EMOSA technique is outperforming others. Likewise for workload 2, 3, 4, 5 EMOSA outperforms the other algorithms.

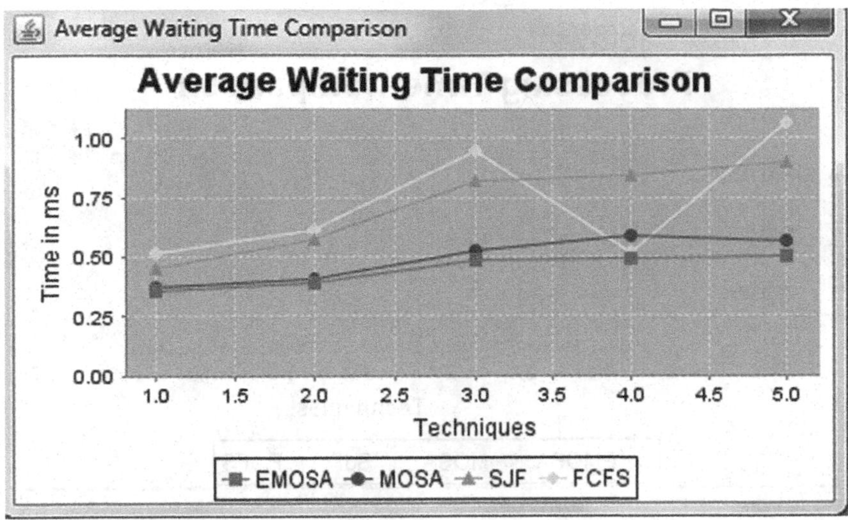

Fig. 2. Comparison of average waiting time of EMOSA with SJF, FCFS and MOSA [13].

Table 5. Simulation results in terms of processing cost

Workload	Virtual machine	Cloudlets	FCFS	SJF	MOSA	EMOSA
Workload1	3	9	312.6	301.36	226.28	115.19
Workload2	3	50	603.65	550.36	528	308
Workload3	30	200	8896.69	6984	6568.699	6233.69
Workload4	40	300	15032.05	10213.05	9803.05	9740
Workload5	60	500	39101.75	20500.56	19869.55	18584.55

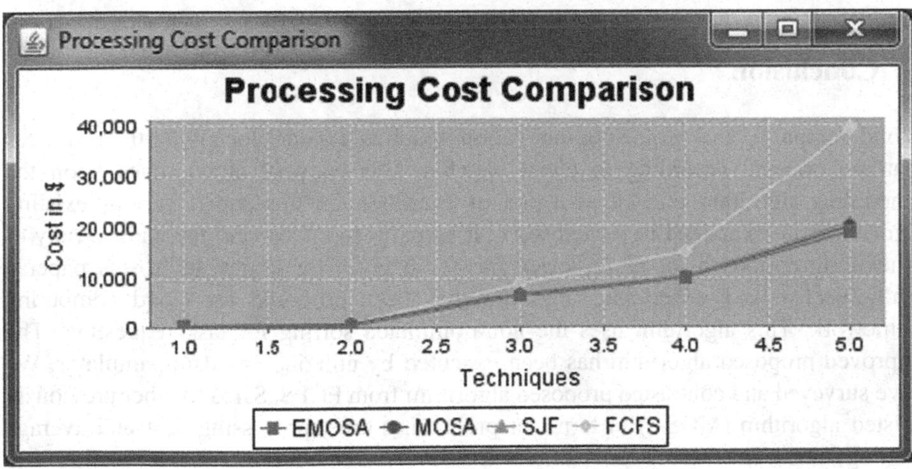

Fig. 3. Comparison of processing cost of EMOSA scheduling algorithm with SJF, FCFS and previously MOSA algorithm [13].

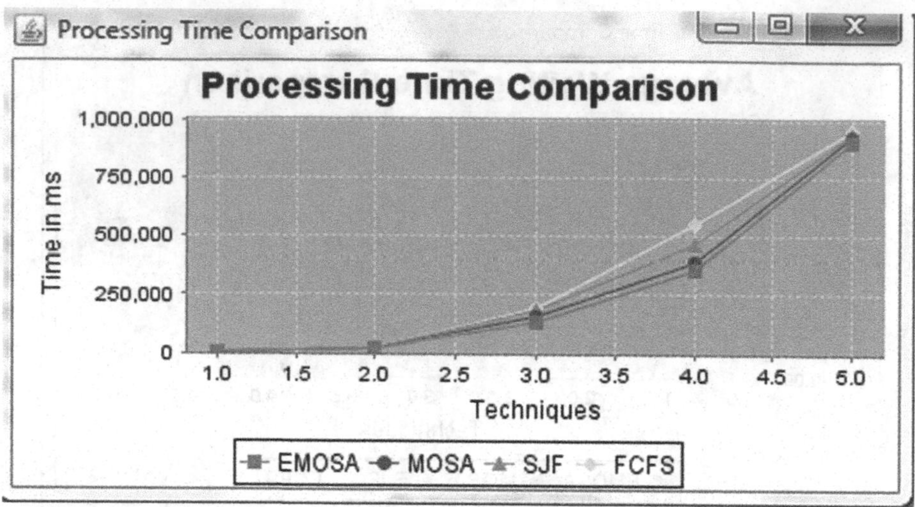

Fig. 4. Comparison of processing time of EMOSA scheduling algorithm with SJF, FCFS and MOSA algorithm [13].

Table 6. Simulation results in term of processing time

Workload	Virtual machine	Cloudlets	FCFS	SJF	MOSA	EMOSA
Workload1	3	9	3999.96	3991.69	3667.54	3538.16
Workload2	3	50	24667.61	22956.54	20758.91	20237.26
Workload3	30	200	193562.2	183562.2	161747.7	130290.7
Workload4	40	300	553923.1	469123.4	393071.8	359123.4
Workload5	60	500	955701	937016	9.26E + 05	906072.8

6 Conclusion

Cloud computing is a promising innovation which is a model for giving the resources that are oriented according to client benefits. Efficiency of cloud relies upon the scheduling algorithm utilized as a part of condition. In this paper, various existing algorithms are examined in related work. It helps us to understand the wide variety of scheduling options in order to select one for a given environment. In this paper a multiobjective task scheduling algorithm has been proposed for cloud computing framework. This algorithm uses the non-dominated sorting for task requesting. The improved proposed algorithm has been executed by utilizing cloudsim simulator. We have surveyed and contrasted proposed algorithm from FCFS, SJF and other previously existed algorithm (MOSA) in terms of processing time, processing cost and average waiting time. The perception exhibits that the proposed technique is beating and upgrades the execution. As cloud computing works in real time and single criteria based algorithm may not be the one for task scheduling. So this algorithm can perform far superior if the tasks can be scheduled utilizing different QoS parameters and thus further the outcomes can be enhanced and better scheduling with enhanced parameters can be accomplished on Cloud. It can further be converged with energy aware task scheduling technique.

References

1. Narwal, A., Dhingra, S.: A systematic review of scheduling in cloud computing framework. Int. J. Adv. Stud. Comput. Sci. Eng. **5**(7), 1–9 (2016)
2. Chawla, Y., Bhonsle, M.: A study on scheduling methods in cloud computing. Int. J. Emerg. Trends Technol. Comput. Sci. (IJETTCS) **1**(3), 12–17 (2011)
3. Kansal, N.J., Chana, I.: Cloud load balancing techniques: a step towards green computing. Int. J. Comput. Sci. Issues **9**(1), 238–246 (2012)
4. Kumar, L., Verma, A.: Workflow scheduling algorithms in cloud environment - a survey. In: Proceedings of RAECS, pp. 1–4. UIET Panjab University, Chandigarh (2014). 978-1-4799-2291-8/14
5. Devipriya, S., Ramesh, C.: Improved Max-min heuristic model for task scheduling in cloud. In: International Conference on Green Computing, Communication and Conservation of Energy, ICGCE, pp. 883–888 (2013)
6. Parsa, S., Entezari-Maleki, R.: RASA: a new task scheduling algorithm in grid environment. World Appl. Sci. J. **7**(special issue), 778–785 (2009)
7. Shamsollah, G., Othman, M.: A priority based job scheduling algorithm in cloud computing. Proc. Eng. **50**, 778–785 (2012)
8. Karthick, A.V., Ramaraj, E., Subramanian, R.G.: An efficient multi queue job scheduling for cloud computing. In: Proceedings of International Conference on Green Computing, Communication and Conservation of Energy, ICGCE. IEEE (2014)
9. Kumar, P., Gopal, K., Gupta, J.P.: Fault aware honey bee scheduling algorithm for cloud infrastructure. In: Proceedings of 4th International Conference Confluence 2013: The Next Generation Information Technology Summit, p. 3.03. IET (2013)
10. Garg, A., RamaKrishna, C.: An improved honey bees life scheduling algorithm for a public cloud. In: International Conference on Contemporary Computing and Informatics, pp. 1140–1147 (2014)
11. Narwal, A., Dhingra, S.: Task scheduling algorithm using multi-objective functions for cloud computing environment. Int. J. Control Theory Appl. **10**(14), 227–238 (2017)
12. Kaur, G.: A DAG based task scheduling algorithms for multiprocessor system - a survey. Int. J. Grid Distrib. Comput. **9**(9), 103–114 (2016)
13. Lakra, A.V., Yadav, D.K.: Multi-objective tasks scheduling algorithm for cloud computing throughput optimisation. In: International Conference on Intelligent Computing, Communication & Convergence, pp. 107–115. Procedia Computer Science, Elsevier (2015)

Descriptive, Dynamic and Hybrid Classification Algorithm to Classify Engineering Students' Sentiments

Mitali Desai(✉) and Mayuri A. Mehta

Computer Engineering Department,
Sarvajanik College of Engineering and Technology, Surat, India
mitalidesai17@gmail.com, mayuri.mehta@scet.ac.in

Abstract. The social networking sites have brought a novel horizon for students to share their views about the learning process. Such casually shared information has a great venue in decision making. However, the growing scale of data needs automatic classification method. Sentiment analysis is one of the automated methods to classify huge data. The existing sentiment analysis methods are extremely used to classify online reviews to provide business intelligence. However, they are not useful to draw conclusions on education system as they classify the sentiments into merely three pre-set categories: positive, negative and neutral. Moreover, classifying students' sentiments into positive or negative category does not provide concealed vision into their problems and perks. Unlike traditional predictive algorithms, our Hybrid Classification Algorithm (HCA), makes the sentiment analysis process descriptive. The descriptive process helps future students and education system in decision making. In this paper, we present the performance evaluation of HCA under four datasets collected by different methods, different time spans, different data dimensions and different vocabulary and grammar. The experimental results show that the hybrid, dynamic and descriptive algorithm potentially outperforms the traditional static and predictive methods.

Keywords: Sentiment analysis · Machine learning · Opinion mining
Educational data mining · Twitter

1 Introduction

Social media platforms are extremely useful for people as an easy and personalized conversation medium to share their emotions, inner thoughts and views in an informal manner [1–3]. The data generated by engineering students on social media platforms can be a prospective source for the analysis of sentiments and thoughts. Such analysis or mining is highly useful to draw conclusions on education system. The abundance of data generated on social media platforms needs some automatic mining techniques [2, 4–7]. Sentiment analysis relates to the problem of mining the sentiments from online available data and categorizing them into pre-set categories. [3, 7–28].

Numerous sentiment analysis techniques have been applied in the fields such as disaster relief and humanitarian assistance, marketing and trade predictions, checking

P. Bhattacharyya et al. (Eds.): NGCT 2017, CCIS 827, pp. 122–138, 2018.
https://doi.org/10.1007/978-981-10-8657-1_10

political polls, advertising market, scientific surveys, checking customer loyalty, finding job opportunities, population health care and understanding students' learning experiences [1–7]. Apart from these applications, sentiment analysis has a great importance in educational system [7, 28]. The students' informal discussion on social media platforms reveals their present or past learning experiences. Mining of such data extracts useful patterns from a large volume of students' generated raw data to support decision making in education system. However, this process increases the complications in gaining the concealed emotions.

The existing techniques use predictive sentiment analysis to classify the students' data into merely three pre-set categories: positive, negative and neutral [8–27]. Classifying students' data into just positive and negative categories do not provide satisfactory knowledge of their actual problems related to learning process. Moreover, it is essential to get deeper understanding of their problems and their perks. The sentiment analysis of students' data is an emerging field and it needs a descriptive analysis technique to provide deeper insight into their sentiments.

Our Hybrid Classification Algorithm (HCA) [28] makes the traditional predictive sentiment analysis process descriptive by incorporating qualitative analysis along with data mining technique. The descriptive process classifies the engineering students' data into several problems and perks categories rather than just positive and negative content identification. In addition, the HCA makes the process of category generation dynamic. This dynamic process eliminates the need to change the algorithm each time when the new data is added. The dynamic category generation makes the HCA applicable to datasets of different domains by generating a suitable category corpus with a minimal overhead. We make our classification algorithm hybrid by combining knowledge based method and supervised machine learning method that increases the accuracy of the classifier.

In this paper, we present the performance analysis of HCA considering four datasets that vary with respect to the following properties: data collection method, time span, data dimension, involved vocabulary and grammar. The datasets are developed collecting data from Twitter as recently Twitter has witnessed a tremendous growth in the number of users [28]. The experimental results show that the HCA descriptively identifies engineering students' problems along with perks shared on Twitter and provides in-depth insight into engineering students' sentiments. Moreover, it works more accurately than the traditional static and predictive methods.

The remaining sections of the paper are organized as follows: In Sect. 2, we describe the HCA. The analysis of HCA is presented in Sect. 3. Finally, the conclusion and future directions are specified in Sect. 4.

2 The Hybrid Classification Algorithm

In Table 1, we define the notations that are used throughout the paper.

Our hybrid classification algorithm makes the traditional static and predictive sentiment analysis process descriptive and dynamic. Moreover, its hybrid nature increases the accuracy of the classifier.

The descriptive HCA classifies students' problems along with their perks into various categories rather than merely positive and negative categories. The descriptive categories help the future students in their selection of educational stream and ease the decision making in the education system. To make the process descriptive, we integrate subjective analysis as well as data mining technique.

The dynamic HCA eliminates the requirement of changing the algorithm for newly added data and hence, it is applicable on dataset of any domain with the construction of corpus with a minimal overhead.

We make our classification algorithm hybrid combining knowledge based method and supervised machine learning method [28]. The knowledge based method is used to create the corpus and supervised machine learning method is used to classify the data into several problems and perks categories. Knowledge based method and supervised machine learning method are two distinct methods applied in data mining process. From our literature [9, 10, 12, 28], it is found that the hybrid approach increases the accuracy of a classifier for predictive sentiment analysis. Thus, we combined both knowledge based method and supervised machine learning method in our descriptive approach. It is evident from the results that the hybrid approach increases the accuracy of the built classifier for descriptive sentiment analysis also.

Table 1. List of notations

Notation	Description
N	Total no. of Tweets in the set
M	Total no. of generated class categories
T	Set of n Tweets
C	Set of m class categories
T_p	Set of pre-processed Tweets
T′	Set of classified Tweets
RTN	Remove Twitter Notations function
RE	Remove Emoticons function
RH	Remove URLs
RSTP	Remove Stop Words
CELNG	Compress Elongated Words
DSLNG	Decompress Slang Words
t_i Where $1 \leq i \leq n$	i^{th} Tweet
c_i	i^{th} class category
t_{rtni}	i^{th} Tweet after removing twitter notations
t_{rei}	i^{th} Tweet after removing emoticons
t_{rhi}	i^{th} Tweet after removing URLs
t_{stpi}	i^{th} Tweet after removing stop words
t_{dslngi}	i^{th} Tweet after decompressing slangs
t_{celngi}	i^{th} Tweet after compressing elongated words
t_{pi}	i^{th} Tweet after cleansing process
t'_i	i^{th} Tweet with the belonging class label

In Fig. 1, we show the pseudo code of the HCA.

```
Input: Set T = {t1, t2, t3, ......., tn} //n Tweets that consist of #engineeringProblems and
#engineeringPerks hashtags
Output: Set T' = {t'1, t'2, t'3, ......., t'n } //n Tweets with the belonging class labels

HCA (T)

  BEGIN
    1.  T' = Φ
    2.  Extended_Preprocessing (T)
    3.  Generate descriptive m class categories c1, c2, ..., cm using lexicon method
    4.  T' = Classifier (T)
  END
```

Fig. 1. Hybrid classification algorithm

As shown in Fig. 1, firstly n Tweets of Engineering students consisting of #engineeringProblems and #engineeringPerks hashtags are collected. Subsequently, the Tweets are pre-processed using the extended preprocessing algorithm shown in Figs. 2 and 3. Next the corpus is generated from the pre-processed data. Finally, the supervised machine learning classifier is applied to classify the n Tweets into their belonging m categories.

HCA includes two major steps: Preprocessing and Classification.

2.1 Preprocessing

We have added the following two new steps in existing preprocessing algorithm [7]: removal of emoticons and decompression of slangs. The extended preprocessing algorithm is presented in Figs. 2 and 3.

As our focus is on textual data, it is necessary to take away non letter data and symbols from the Tweets. Hence, firstly we remove the Twitter notations such as hashtags (#), account Id (@), and retweets (RT). Secondly, the emoji or emoticons are removed from the Tweets. Thirdly, the URLs and hyperlinks are removed.

The stop words do not emphasis on any emotions. Moreover, removal of stop words reduces the size of dataset. Hence, fourthly the stop words (such as is, are, am, the, there) are eliminated from the Tweets.

Typically, the Tweets contain the slangs and elongated words. The slang words are abbreviated adjectives or nouns that enclose the hidden sentiments. Hence, it is essential to decompress the slangs such as g8 into great. The elongated words are stretched words to show the extreme level of sentiments. Hence, it is necessary to compress the elongated words such as happyyy into happy.

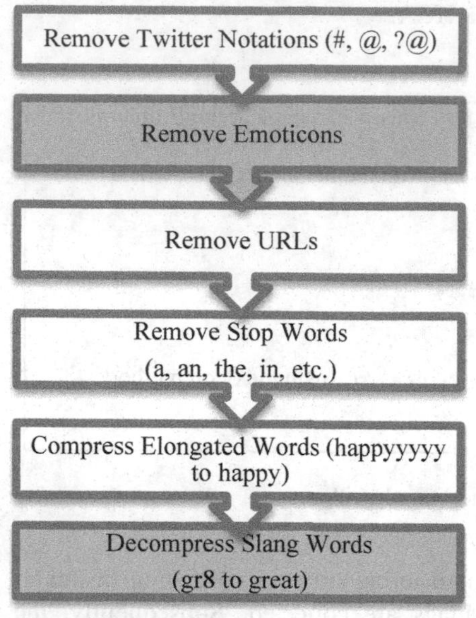

Fig. 2. Processing steps of extended pre-processing algorithm

Input: Set $T = \{t_1, t_2, t_3, \ldots\ldots, t_n\}$

Output: Set $T_p = \{t_{p1}, t_{p2}, t_{p3}, \ldots\ldots, t_{pn}\}$ //Pre-processed n Tweets

Extended_Preprocessing (T)

BEGIN

$T_p = \Phi$
for i = 1 to n Tweets
$t_{rtni} = RTN(t_i)$
$t_{rei} = RE(t_{rtni})$
$t_{rhi} = RH(t_{rei})$
$t_{rstpi} = RSTP(t_{rhi})$
$t_{celngi} = CELNG(tr_{stpi})$
$t_{dslngi} = DSLNG(t_{celngi})$
$t_{pi} = t_{dslngi}$
$T_p = T_p \cup t_{pi}$

END

Fig. 3. Extended pre-processing algorithm

2.2 Classification

To make the classification process hybrid, the following two steps are carried out.

- Generate corpus using knowledge based method
- Apply supervised machine learning algorithm

The corpus consists of the class categories with their associated keywords. The class categories and associated keywords are developed by conducting the qualitative analysis on dataset. For any Tweet ti, if the match is found between the Tweet words and the associated keywords of class category, then ti is assigned category label ci.

The corpus makes the traditional static category generation process dynamic. The dynamic category generation process has two benefits: (1) it eliminates the requirement of changing the algorithm for newly added data. For newly added data, we can dynamically add the suitable class category into corpus without any additional overhead. (2) The algorithm will be applicable on dataset of any domain. For new dataset, the corpus can be constructed with a minimal overhead.

We make the category generation process dynamic using the following three steps: manage categories, manage category words, find and assign categories to Tweets. The first two steps allow us to add the suitable categories and associated words dynamically in the corpus. The last step assigns the suitable categories to each Tweet in the dataset.

- Manage categories

We can dynamically add the suitable categories. If the category is not present in the corpus, we can successfully add the category else the error message is generated.

- Manage category words

We can dynamically add the associated keywords for each category. If the word is not present in the corpus, we can successfully add the word in the corresponding category else the error message is generated.

- Find and assign categories to Tweets

For any Tweet, if any Tweet word is matched with the associated keyword, then the corresponding category label is allotted to the Tweet.

Table 2 shows the developed class categories and the corresponding associated keywords.

Table 2. Categories and the associated keywords

Category name	Associated keywords
Heavy study load	Hour, homework, exam, day, class, work, problem, study, week, too much, all, lab, still, out, time, page, library, spend, today, long, school, college, due, engineering, already
Lack of social engagement	Friday, homework, out, study, work, weekend, life, class, exam, engineer, break, drink, saturday, sunday, people, social, lab, spend, tonight, watch, game, miss, party
Negative emotions	FML, sad, bad, day, feel, tired, damn, death, hard, hate, f***, fuck, shit, week, hell, sucks
Sleep problems	Sleep, hour, night, bed, all night, exam, homework, nap, coffee, dream, class, late, work, more, long, morning, wake, awake, no sleep, insomnia, insomniac
Diversity issues	Girl, class, only, guy, engineer, speak, English, professor, kid, female, male, foreign, white, teach, black
Good things	Degree, depth, flexible, power, society, repair, mind, professional, tool, success, idea, life, good, helpful, path, strength, careers, job, service, incredible, fast, perfect, nice, happy, clean, free, peace, win, best
Knowledge	Direction, knowledge, brain, intelligence, intelligent, powerful, project, expert, development, technology, science, research

3 Results and Analysis

Based on our in-depth study on the existing data collection methods [28], we have selected Twitter Search API and Topsy to collect the data. We have chosen Weka as classification tool studying several existing classification tools [7, 15, 17]. The results of HCA are compared with the classification algorithm proposed in [7]. To evaluate the performance of HCA, we have prepared four different datasets collecting Tweets from Twitter.

The details of the datasets are shown in Table 3. They have the following properties.

- Every dataset consists of t_1, t_2, t_3, …, tn Tweets. The HCA classifies n Tweets into dynamically generated m class categories c_1, c_2, c_3, …, c_m.

- Each t_i consists of only two hashtags namely #engineeringProblems and #engineeringPerks. Focusing on these two precise hashtags helps in collecting the accurate Tweets related to engineering students' problems and perks and thereby decreases the amount of noisy Tweets.
- We assume that no dataset contains any spam Tweets and any Tweet from any dataset can fall under more than one class category.
- Tweets that do not belong to any of the generated class categories are eliminated. We consider such Tweets as outliers and remove them.

Table 3. Summary of datasets

Dataset	Dimension (No. of Tweets)	Time span	Data collection method
Dataset1	120	1st July 2015 to 31st August 2015	Topsy tool
Dataset2	93	1st July 2015 to 31st August 2015	Twitter search API
Dataset3	264	1st September 2015 to 31st October 2015	Topsy tool
Dataset4	400	1st November 2015 to 31st December 2015	Topsy tool

The datasets vary with respect to the following parameters:

- data collection method
- time span
- data dimension
- grammar and vocabulary

All four datasets have the constant time span of two months. However, the two months are different for each dataset to analyze students' sentiments over different phases of their single academic term. This is necessary to avoid the situational biasness towards any sentiments or opinions.

Dataset1 and Dataset2 have the same time span and collected by two different methods - Twitter Search API and Topsy. Twitter Search API has a constraint to allow limited access of the posted Tweets for any period of time and hence, the number of Tweets collected using Twitter Search API is less than the number of Tweets collected using Topsy for the same time span July–August, 2015. Moreover, the Tweets collected using Twitter Search API are the subsets of the Tweets collected using Topsy. This was observed for other two time spans - September–October, 2015 and November–December, 2015. Hence, in our further experiments, we considered the datasets collected using Topsy.

Following are the observations from the datasets shown in Table 3.

1. At the beginning of the semester (1st July 2015 to 31st August 2015), number of Tweets is less.
2. At the mid of the semester (1st September 2015 to 31st October 2015), the number of Tweets increases as the academic term progresses.
3. At the end of the semester (1st November 2015 to 31st December 2015), due to exams and vacations, the number of Tweets is high.

3.1 Existing and Extended Pre-processing Algorithm

We have analysed the performance of our extended pre-processing algorithm for all four datasets mentioned in Table 3 and compared the results with exiting pre-processing algorithm [7].

We have tested the performance for following two scenarios.

- Scenario1: Two datasets collected by two different methods, namely Topsy and Twitter Search API, over the same time span.
- Scenario2: Three datasets collected by Topsy over three different time spans.

The processing time of the existing preprocessing algorithm and the extended preprocessing algorithm under scenario1 and scenario2 is shown in Figs. 4 and 5 respectively. Exis. shows the time to implement the existing pre-processing algorithm and Extd. shows the time to implement the extended pre-processing algorithm.

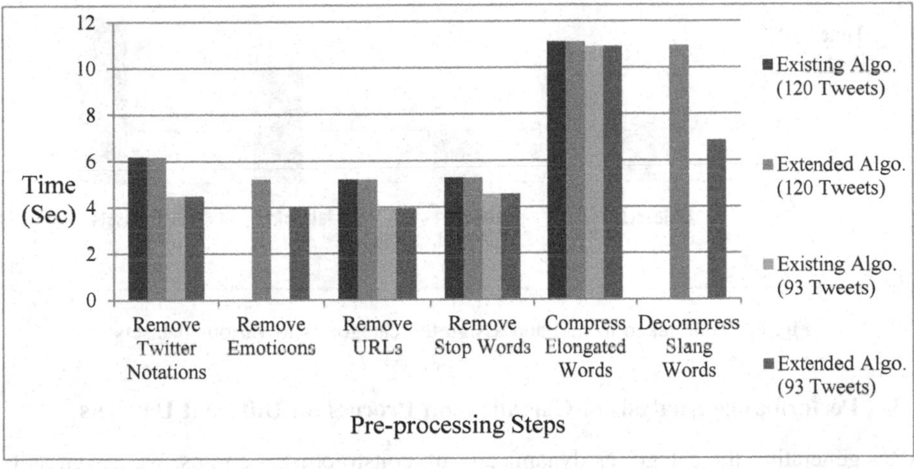

Fig. 4. Processing time for the existing and extended pre-processing algorithms

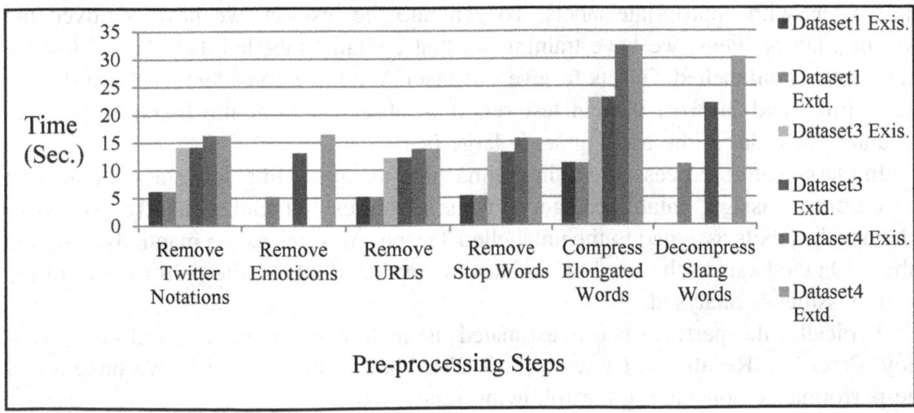

Fig. 5. Processing time for the existing and extended pre-processing algorithms of the datasets collected by Topsy

The experimental results show that the total time of the extended pre-processing algorithm is marginally higher than the existing algorithm because two additional steps are incorporated. However, with two additional steps, we are getting cleaner output of pre-processing. Moreover, it is said in literature that the accuracy will be high if the pre-processing is exhaustive [7, 13, 18, 27, 28].

3.2 Label Assigning Process for Different Datasets

Figure 6 shows the time taken to find and assign the suitable category labels to all the Tweets in each dataset. It is observed that the training time increases as the size of the dataset increases.

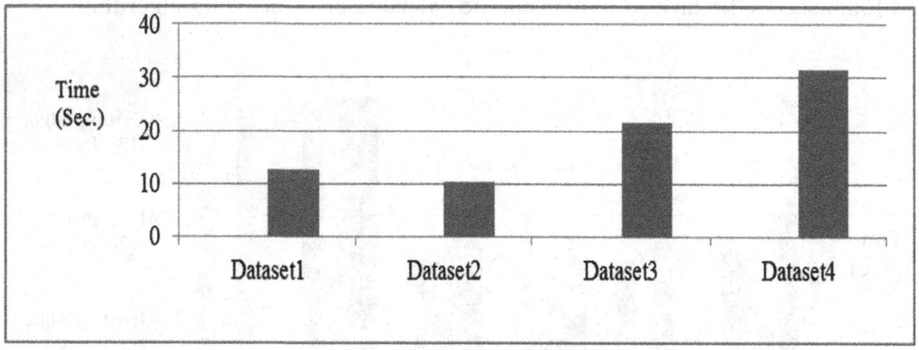

Fig. 6. Time taken to find and assign the categories to various datasets

3.3 Performance Analysis of Classification Process on Different Datasets

After generating the categories dynamically by constructing a corpus, we assign suitable category labels to every Tweet in each dataset. To carry out classification step, the datasets are partitioned into two parts: training set and test set. Training set contains all the Tweets with appropriate labels. To generate the test set, we have removed the assigned labels. Thus, we have training set that contains labelled Tweets and test set that contains unlabelled Tweets for every dataset. We have considered 70% of data in the training and 30% of data in test set. It is observed from the literature that the accuracy increases if the training set is large [7].

In classification process, we train the machine using training set data and construct the corpus to assign suitable category labels to the test set. Subsequently, we verify whether the labels assigned to the unlabelled Tweets are same as the manually assigned labels. On the basis of the level of similarity in assigned labels, the performance of the built classifier is analysed.

Typically, the performance is estimated using four parameters as follows: Accuracy, Precision, Recall and F1-score [3, 7–27]. For complete analysis, we have tested the performance considering the following scenarios.

- Scenario1: Two datasets collected by two different methods, namely Topsy and Twitter Search API, over the same time span.
- Scenario2: Three datasets collected by Topsy over three different time spans.
- Scenario3: Apply widly used learning based classifiers on all four datasets.

The performance is evaluated considering two hashtags: #engineeringProblems and #engineeringPerks.

We have applied the multi label classification that allows any Tweet to fall under more than one class category. It is necessary to use multi label classification because for one Tweet, multiple different associated words corresponding to different class categories may be found. For example, for Tweet: "Submissions going on…lots of work and no sleep", two kinds of emotions are shared that can be partitioned in two constructed categories: Heavy Study Load and Sleep Problems.

The results of the first scenario are displayed shown in Fig. 7. #ePbms denotes the hashtags #engineeringProblems and #ePrks denotes the hashtag #engineeringPerks.

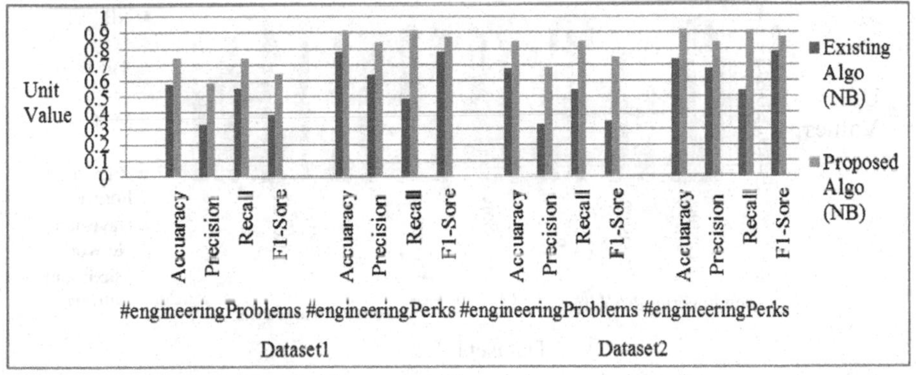

Fig. 7. Performance indices for the HCA and existing algorithm

Naïve Bayes (NB) approach is applied for classification in existing technique as well as in HCA. The results show that the accuracy, precision, recall and F1-score of the HCA are higher than the existing algorithm for hashtags #engineeringProblems as well as #engineeringPerks due to the following reasons: (1) we have carried out thorough pre-processing and have obtained highly cleansed Tweets and (2) we have prepared the category corpus using dynamic method that improves the overall performance.

In the second scenario, the evaluation is carried out considering Datset1, Dataset3 and Dataset4 and the results are shown in Fig. 8.

In third scenario, we have applied various and widely used other supervised machine learning based classifiers on all four datasets and measured the performance. To determine the suitable classifier in terms of accuracy, we have tested our HCA with six classifiers [21–27]: Naïve Bayes (NB), Support Vector Machine (SVM), Multi Class Classifier (MCC), Random Forest, Bayesian Network and Maximum Entropy [21–27]. The experimental results are shown in Figs. 9, 10, 11 and 12 of scenario 3.

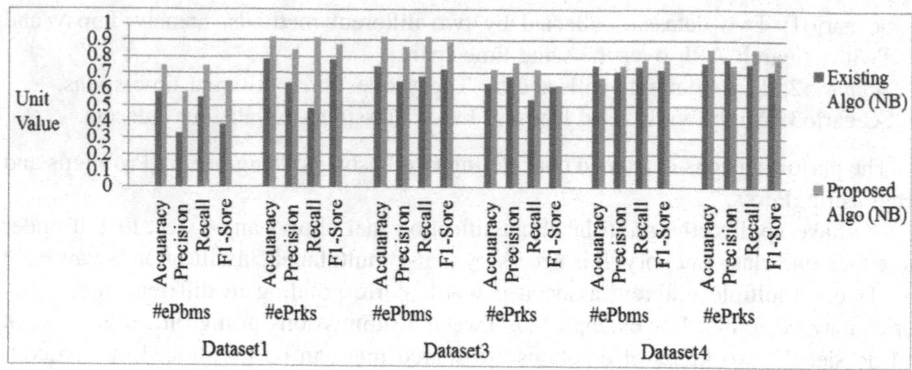

Fig. 8. Performance indices for the HCA and existing and algorithm on datasets collected by Topsy

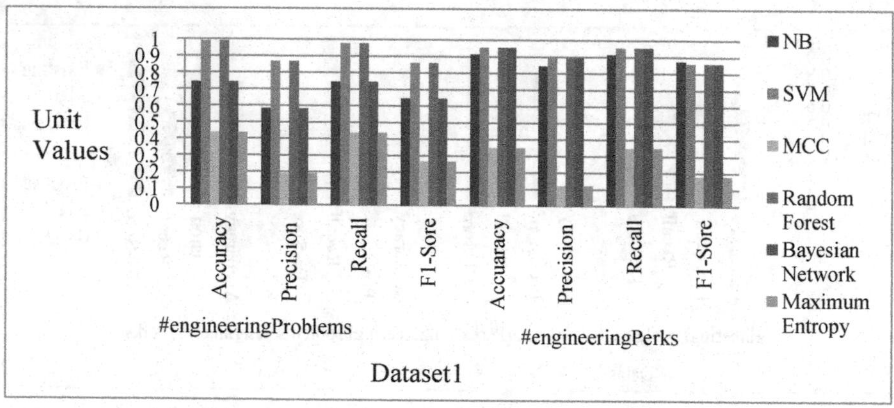

Fig. 9. Performance of the various machine learning algorithms on Dataset1.

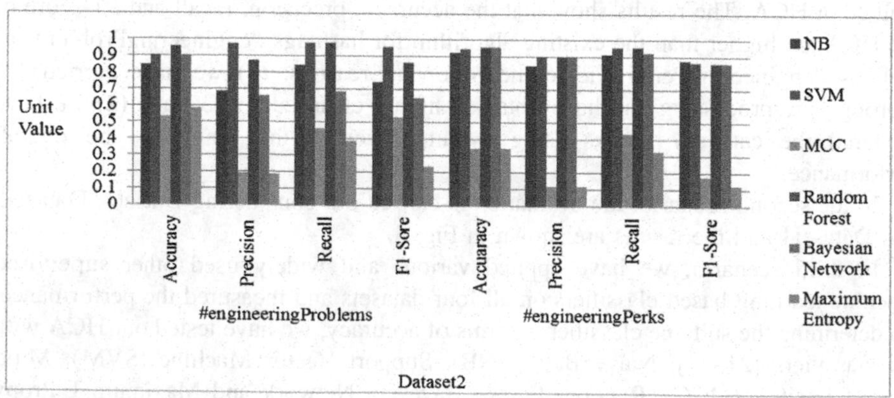

Fig. 10. Performance of the various machine learning algorithms on Dataset2

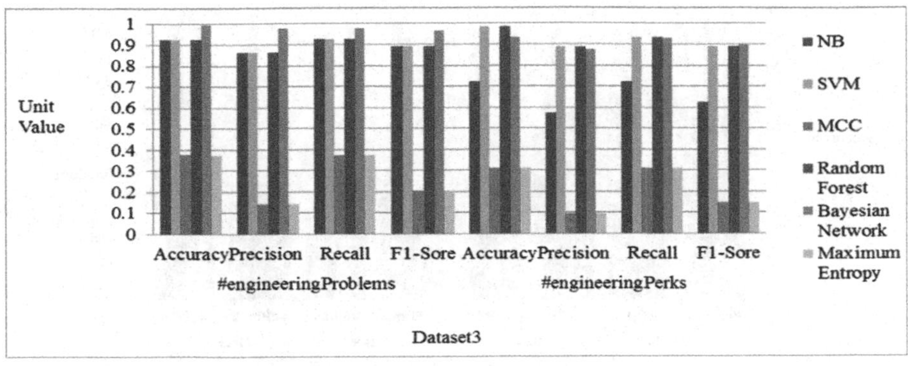

Fig. 11. Performance of the various machine learning algorithms on Dataset3.

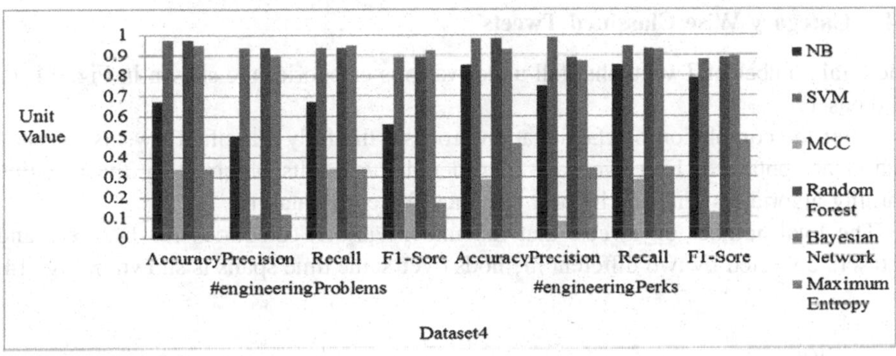

Fig. 12. Performance comparison of the various machine learning algorithms on dataset

We have observed that the understanding complexity of Naïve Bayes algorithm is less compared to Support Vector Machine and Maximum Entropy. However, it suffers from lower accuracy due to its simple Bayesian probability assumption. Whereas Support Vector Machine provides the better accuracy however, it does not support automatic learning of features. Maximum Entropy provides the moderated accuracy but supports the automatic learning of features. Random Forest is based on decision tree method, which gives high accuracy with automatic feature learning. Bayesian Network gives average accuracy. Whereas MCC giver lower accuracy.

From the results of the scenario three, the following observations are apprehended.

- SVM and Random Forest give higher accuracy on all datasets.
- SVM and Random Forest give similar accuracy on majority of datasets.
- Bayesian Network and NB give the moderate accuracy.
- MCC and Maximum Entropy give the low accuracy for majority of datasets.

Figure 13 shows the accuracy (%) of all the six discussed machine learning algorithms.

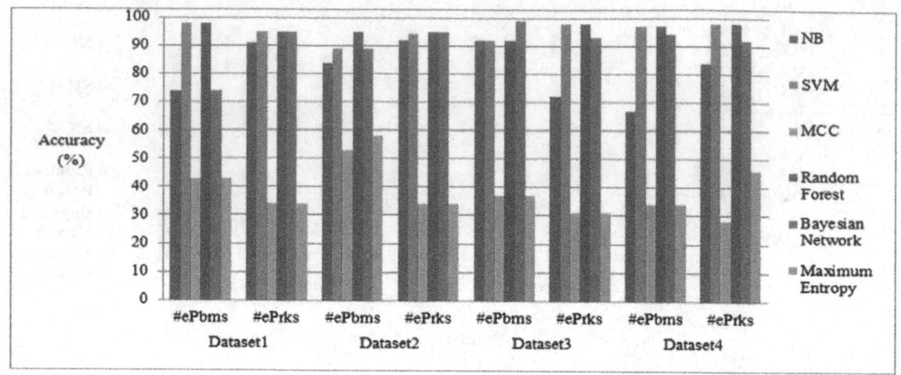

Fig. 13. Accuracy of various machine learning algorithms on collected datasets

3.4 Category Wise Classified Tweets

The total number of Tweets that fall under various categories are shown in Fig. 14 for all datasets.

After the completion of classification process, the fully classified Tweets for each dataset are obtained. Here we have considered the results obtained by the machine learning algorithms with the highest accuracy for each dataset.

The total number of Tweets that fall under various categories for Dataset1 and Dataset2 collected by two different methods over same time spans is shown in Fig. 14.

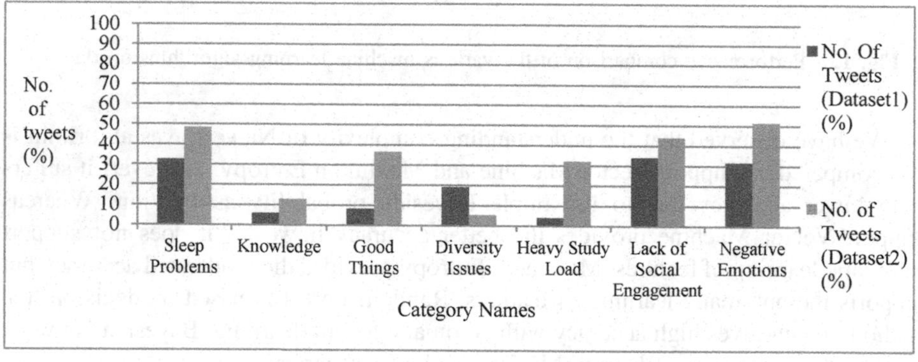

Fig. 14. Category wise no. of Tweets for Dataset1 and Dataset2

Finally calculate the total no. of Tweets that fall under problem tag and perk tag. The problem tag consists of the category labels as follows: Sleep Problems, Diversity Issues, Heavy Study Load, Lack of Social Engagement and Negative Emotions. Whereas the perk tag consist of class categories as follows: Knowledge and Good Things.

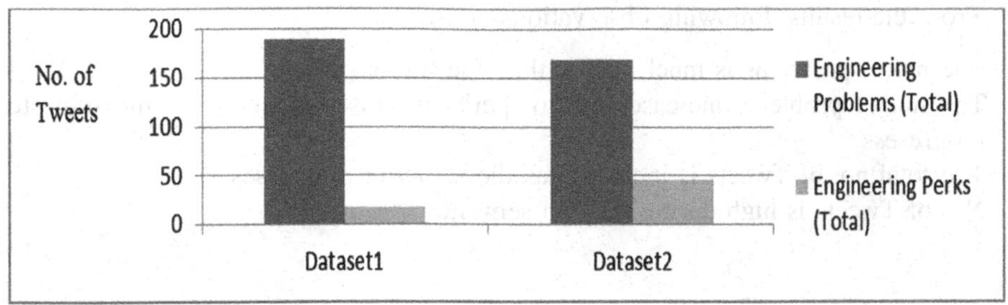

Fig. 15. Total no. of problems and perks Tweets in Dataset1 and Dataset2

From Fig. 15, the followings interpretations are derived.

- As the number of Tweets increase, the identified problems and perks also increase.
- No. of identified problems and perks differs with different data collection method.

The total number of Tweets that fall under various categories for Dataset1, Dataset3 and Dataset4 collected by a single method over different time spans is shown in Fig. 16.

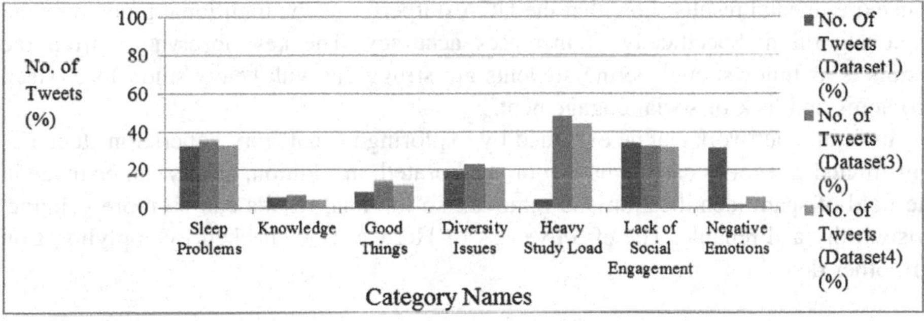

Fig. 16. Category wise no. of Tweets for datasets collected by Topsy

The total no. of Tweets that fall under problem tag and perk tag for Datset1 Dataset3 and Dataset4 is shown in Fig. 17.

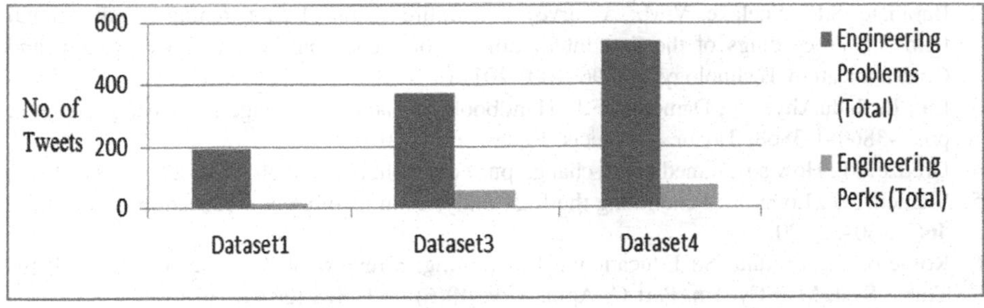

Fig. 17. Total no. of problems and perks Tweets in various datasets collected Topsy

From the results, following observations are made.

- The no. of problems is much higher than the no. of perks
- The no. of problems increases, no. of perks increases gradually as the semester progresess
- The total no. of Tweets is increased as the semester progresses
- No. of Tweets is high during the end semester

4 Conclusion and Future Work

Our Hybrid Classification Algorithm (HCA) makes the traditional predictive sentiment analysis process descriptive. The descriptively generated categories help future students in their selection of educational stream. Moreover, it helps to enhance the quality of education system. The dynamic category generation eliminates the need to change the algorithm for newly added data. Furthermore, it makes HCA applicable on data of any other domain. The hybrid approach increases the accuracy of the classifier. It gives the accuracy of 97% to 98% for all four datasets.

We have evaluated the performance of HCA on four datasets that vary with respect to data collection method, time span, data dimension, and vocabulary and grammar. The experimental results show that the HCA outperforms the traditional predictive and static algorithm. Specifically, it increases accuracy. The key observation from the results is as follows: engineering students are struggling with heavy study load, sleep problems and lack of social engagement.

In future, our work can be extended by exploring the category generation step. The constructed categories can be made more elaborated. In addition, efforts can be made in the field of spam identification and removal, so the final results can be more genuine, trustworthy and reliable. The effectiveness of HCA can be checked by applying it on any other domain data.

References

1. King, I., Li, j., Chan, K.T.: A brief survey of computational approaches in social computing. In: Proceedings of the International Joint Conference on Neural Network, pp. 2699–2706 (2009)
2. Barahate, S.R., Shelake, V.M.: A survey and future vision of data mining in educational field. In: Proceedings of the 2nd International Conference on Advanced Computing and Communication Technology, pp. 96–100 (2012)
3. Liu, B., Indurkhya, N., Damerau, F.J.: Handbook of Natural Language Processing. 2nd edn, pp. 1-3860–1-3868. Taylor & Francis, Boca Raton (2010)
4. Dredze, M.: How social media will change public health. IEEE Intell. Syst. **27**, 81–84 (2012)
5. Siemens, G., Long, P.: Penetrating the fog: analytics in learning and education. Educ. Rev. **46**(5), 30–32 (2011)
6. Romero, C., Ventura, S.: Educational data mining: a review of the state of the art. IEEE Trans. Syst. Man Cybern. Part C: Appl. Rev. **40**(6), 601–618 (2010)

7. Chen, X., Vorvoreanu, M., Madhavan, K.: Mining social media data to understand students' learning experiences. IEEE Trans. Learn. Technol. **7**(3), 246–259 (2014)
8. Kasture, N., Bhilare, P.: An approach for sentiment analysis on social networking sites. In: Computing Communication Control and Automation (ICCUBEA), pp. 390–395 (2015)
9. Bhuta, S., Doshi, A., Doshi U., Narvekar, M.: A review of techniques for sentiment analysis of Twitter data. In: Issues and Challenges in Intelligent Computing Techniques (ICICT), pp. 583–591 (2014)
10. Neethu, M.S., Rajasree, R.: Sentiment analysis in Twitter using machine learning techniques. In: 4th International Conference on Computing, Communications and Networking Technologies (ICCCNT), pp. 1–5 (2013)
11. Bahrainian, S., Dangel, A.: Sentiment analysis using sentiment features. In: International Joint Conference of Web Intelligence and Intelligent Agent Technologies, pp. 26–29 (2013)
12. Gautam G., Yadav, D.: Sentiment analysis of Twitter data using machine learning approaches and semantic analysis. In: 7th International Conference on Contemporary Computing, pp. 437–442 (2014)
13. Gokulakrishnan, B., Plavnathan, P., Thiruchittampalam, R., Perera, A., Prasath, N.: Opinion mining and sentiment analysis on a Twitter data stream. In: International Conference on Advances in ICT for Engineering Regions, pp. 182–188 (2012)
14. Celikyilmaz, A., Hakkani-Tur, D., Feng J.: Probabilistic model-based sentiment analysis of Twitter messages. In: IEEE Spoken Language Technology Workshop (SLT), pp. 79–84 (2010)
15. Sehgal, V., Song, C.: SOPS: stock prediction using web sentiment. In: 7th IEEE International Conference on Data Mining Workshop, pp. 21–26 (2007)
16. Kechaou, Z., Ammar, B.M., Alimi, A.M.: Improving e-learning with sentiment analysis of users' opinions. In: Global Engineering Education Conference (EDUCON), pp. 1032–1038 (2011)
17. Lima, A.C.E.S., Castro L.N.: Automatic sentiment analysis of Twitter messages. In: 4th International Conference on Computational Aspects of Social Networks (CASoN), pp. 52–57 (2012)
18. Batool, R., Khattak, A.M., Maqbool, J., Lee, S.: Precise tweet classification and sentiment analysis. In: 12th International Conference on Computer and Information Science (ICIS), pp. 461–466 (2013)
19. Altrabsheh, N., Cocea M., Fallahkhair, S.: Sentiment analysis: towards a tool for analysing real-time students feedback. In: 26th International Conference on Tools with Artificial Intelligence, pp. 420–423 (2014)
20. Wang, Z., Tong, V.J.C., Xin, X., Chin, H.C.: Anomaly detection through enhanced sentiment analysis on social media data. In: 6th International Conference on Cloud Computing Technology and Science, pp. 918–922 (2014)
21. Singh, V., Dubey, S.K.: Opinion mining and analysis: a literature review. In: 5th International Conference on Confluence: The Next Generation Information Technology Summit (Confluence), pp. 232–239 (2014)
22. Khan, K., Baharudin, B., Khan, A., Malik, F.: Mining Opinion from Text Documents: A Survey. In: Digital Ecosystems and Technologies, pp. 217–222 (2009)
23. Ghag, K., Shah, K.: Comparative analysis of the techniques for sentiment analysis. In: International Conference on Advances in Technology and Engineering, pp. 1–7 (2013)
24. Medhat, W., Hassan, A., Korashy, H.: Sentiment analysis algorithms and applications: a survey. Ain Shams Eng. J. **5**(4), 1093–1113 (2014)
25. Khairnar, J., Kinikar, M.: Machine learning algorithms for opinion mining and sentiment classification. Int. J. Sci. Res. Publ. **3**(6), 1–6 (2013)

26. Sarlan, A., Nadam C., Basri, S.: Twitter sentiment analysis. In: International Conference on Information Technology and Multimedia, pp. 213–216 (2014)
27. Saloun, P., Hruzik, M., Zelinka, I.: Sentiment analysis – e-business and e-learning common issue. In: 11th IEEE International Conference on Emerging eLearning Technologies and Applications, pp. 339–34 (2013)
28. Desai, M., Mehta, M.A.: A hybrid classification algorithm to classify engineering students' problems and perks. Int. J. Data Min. Knowl. Manag. Process (IJDKP) **6**(2), 73–81 (2016)

Comparison of Runtime Performance Optimization Using Template-Metaprogramming

Vivek Patel, Piyush Mishra(✉), J. C. Patni, and Parul Mittal

University of Petroleum and Energy Studies, Dehradun 248007, India
vivek.p96@gmail.com, suyashmishra96@gmail.com

Abstract. Programs capable of generating code are known as meta-programs and the technique of writing these programs is known as meta programming Meta programming is supported by various programming languages such as C#, where reflection is used; Ruby allows defining classes and methods at runtime using meta-programming; the first language to introduce the concept of meta-programming was LISP. The meta-programs written using these languages are generally parsers, theorem proofs and interpreters. In this paper, we'll be demonstrating the use of meta-programming in C++ through template meta-programming (TMP). We pick up common mathematical operations, creating a run time code of them along with a compile time based equivalent code done through TMP. The two set of codes are then benchmarked on the basis of their execution time and a bar-graph is generated to compare the TMP and non-TMP programs.

Keywords: Meta-programming · Runtime-performance
Compile-time constants · Benchmarking

1 Introduction

Metaprograms are temporary programs that take another program as input and modify it. Some examples of these are gcc, YACC and Scheme. Metaprogramming in the host language defines the language as a subset of the expressible forms of the underlying language. Template Metaprogramming is defined as the way to use C++ template system to perform the computations at compile-time when the code is compiled for execution. It can also be considered as "programming with types" which has "values" that the metaprogramming works with are specific C++ types. TMP uses these types as the basic objects for computation [1,2].

TMP is inter-related to functional programming because "variables" are immutable, that is, it is necessary to use recursion rather than the iteration to process elements of a set. Though the syntax in template metaprogramming is generally different from the programming language where it is used, there

P. Bhattacharyya et al. (Eds.): NGCT 2017, CCIS 827, pp. 139–147, 2018.
https://doi.org/10.1007/978-981-10-8657-1_11

are some practical uses. Many reasons to use templates are that it is used to implement generic programming (that is, avoiding sections of the code that are similar) or it can be used to perform automatic compile-time optimization, that is, performing operations once at compile time rather than performing every time the program is run. Generic programming paradigm and template metaprogramming are the two techniques that work on C++ STL, which is heavily used in modern professional programs [2]. In template-metaprogramming, compiler is utilized to generate transient metaprograms according to template definitions which are executed at compile-time and output is merged with existing source code and then compiled. This can be leveraged to shift computations to compile time provided that they don't require any runtime information.

Also, template-metaprogramming is a Turing-complete subset of C++. This means that in theory it can be used to express any computational algorithm, which in turn facilitates a powerful native language metaprogramming. Moreover, the execution time takes into consideration the various constants that get hidden while approximating the time complexities [3]. Also, actual performance depends highly on the input datasets [3,4]. Hence, if the sorting algorithms are compared on the basis of their execution time while operating on the above-mentioned input data set of 50 random elements, the result will be evident without any ambiguity.

2 Previous Work

The execution of a C++ program involves four stages using different compilation and execution tools, which are set of programs that help to complete the C++ program's execution process.

1. Preprocessor
2. Compiler
3. Linker
4. Loader

These tools make the program running. Erwin Unruh did the first work on template meta-programming, in which he wrote program to compute prime numbers, although it did not actually finish compiling and the list of prime numbers was a part of an error message. TMP has advanced considerably now, and is used as a practical tool for library developers in C++ [7]. In the existing system, compiler is utilized to generate transient metaprograms according to template definitions that are executed at compile-time and output is merged with existing source code and then compiled. Thus, it increases the runtime and complexity by performing computation at runtime [4]. This can be leveraged to shift computations to compile time provided that they don't require any runtime information. The template metaprogramming in C++ uses the system of templates in generating types, and does coding in the process described: The types are generated using templates, and used to computations or in generating the desired code [5].

3 Proposed Algorithmic Tool

The software tool has been defined for cross platforms, thus enabling it to be run on windows operating system as well as on various flavors of Linux. A graphical user interface (GUI) which has been created using GIMP Toolkit (GTK). For the purpose of Graph display, OpenGL is used to plot the graph. The GUI prompts the user to select from two options: Injector and Benchmark. At present, the application supports the following mathematical operations: exponent, LCM, GCD, number of divisors, sum of divisors, factorial, primality test, Co-primality test, and number of primes, floor and ceiling.

In order to analyze a predefined file that comes along with the lication, the user chooses Benchmark option [5,7]. There are 2 predefined files, one which contains the usual function definitions for the mathematical operations and the other which has the equivalent code of the operations written using templates. Both the files, now on referred to as Non-TMP and TMP respectively, are then run to record their execution time. The two times generated are then plotted against the order of input (n). In order to test the user-defined file, the user chooses Inject option. Thereafter, he is prompted with three options: Choose .cpp file, inject now and Perform Benchmarks. The user first locates his input file by choosing it through the file chooser dialog box. Upon clicking Inject now! He is asked to select the mathematical operation he wishes to execute from the drop-down box and then provide his function declaration's name for the same mathematical operation. For example, if he chooses 'findGCD' from the drop down and his function name for calculating GCD is 'xyz', then he enters xyz in the text box. The working of custom user input is done using regex. Using regular expressions, the function declarations in the user file are identified and upon match with the options selected in the drop-down box, the function definition is replaced with the TMP code for the corresponding operation (Fig. 1).

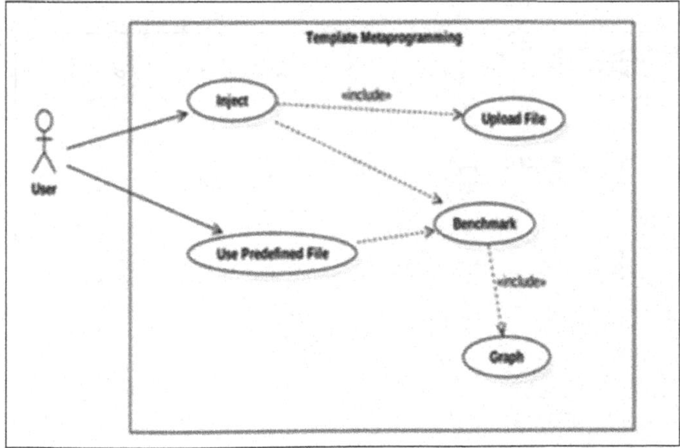

Fig. 1. Use-case diagram

As seen from the class diagram below, there are five main classes: GUI, Benchmark, Charter, Inject and TMP. The GUI class displays the front end of the application. The Inject class holds the function that uses regular expressions to modify the user file. Benchmark class fetches the execution time of the TMP and Non-TMP file and generates the statistics. These statistics are passed on to the Charter class that presents the results using bar graph. All the mathematical functions are defined in the TMP class (Fig. 2).

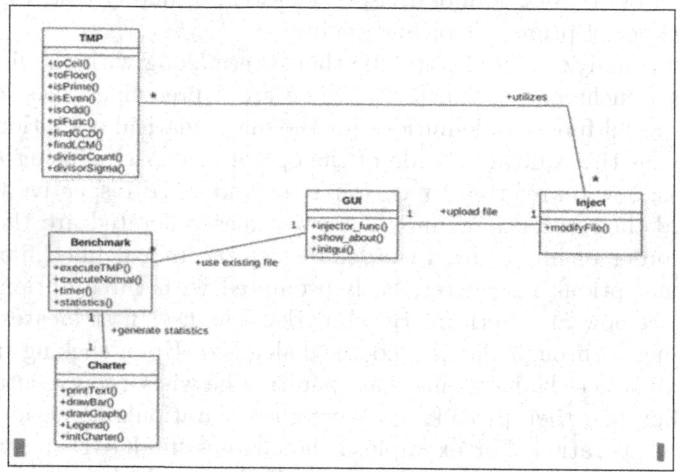

Fig. 2. Class diagram

The sequence diagram below shows the two possible paths of execution in the program (Figs. 3, 4 and 5).

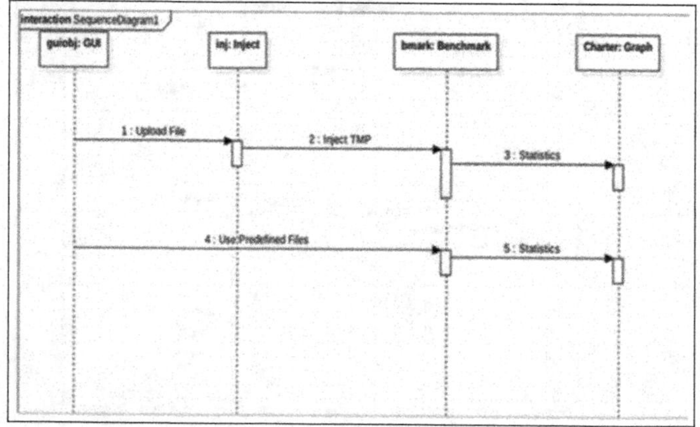

Fig. 3. Sequence diagram

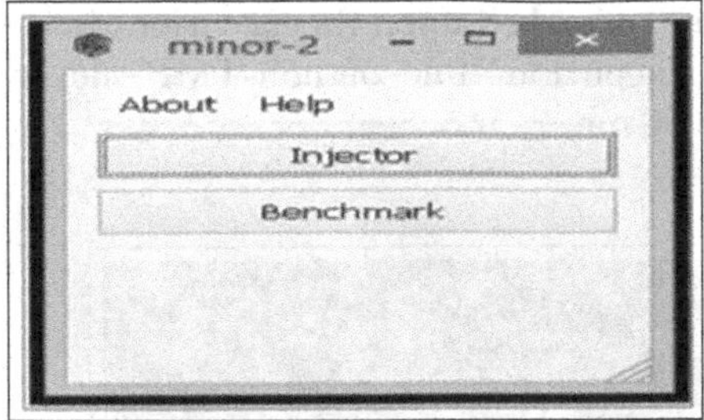

Fig. 4. Main menu

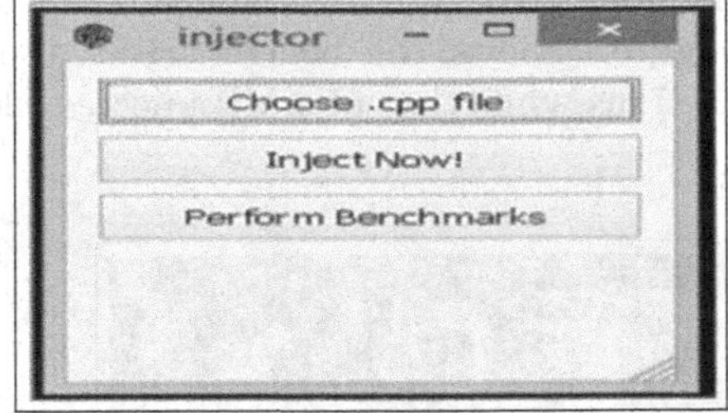

Fig. 5. Injection menu

4 Software Requirements

The following requirements ensure the smooth running of the application:

- OS: Linux or Windows
- Code Blocks IDE (software tested on Code Blocks 16)
- Gimp Toolkit (GTK), preferably GTK+2

5 Results

In this particular provided result set we have selected the following function to be injected out of the total supported function by TMP libraries, (as shown in Fig. 6)

- Exponent
- LCM
- GCD
- Factorial
- Count of primes
- Count of divisors
- Sum of divisors
- Coprimality check
- Primality check
- Floor and Ceil

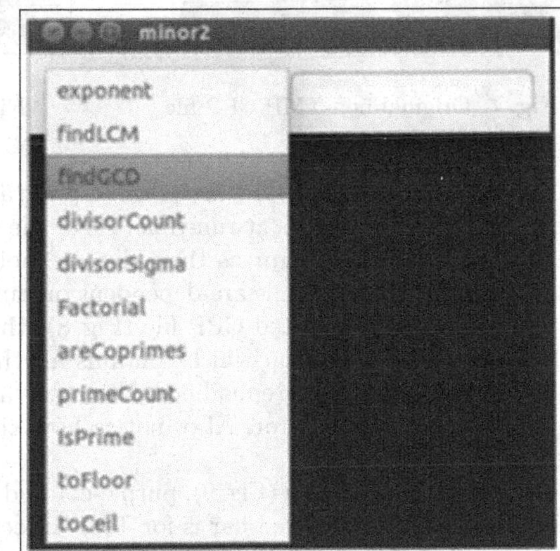

Fig. 6. Supported functions

Corresponding function names in the uploaded C++ program file are given for each functionality mentioned above. Then, the file is analyzed for compile-time constant function invokes and injected appropriately. Figure 7 shows the original program file and Fig. 8 shows the injected file that includes TMP. Finally, these two files are benchmarked upon its execution time. Figure 8 shows the benchmarked results. Execution time of non-TMP file is 1087 ms while that of TMP injected file is 690 ms.

```
#include <iostream>
#include <cstdio>
#include <cmath>
using namespace std;

int fact(int n);                          //***************
int divCount(int s, int n);               //
int divSigma(int s, int n);               //
bool primeCheck(int n);                   // User Defined
int myprimecount(int n);                  //   Functions
int mygcd(int a,int b);                   //
int mylcm(int a,int b);                   //
bool mycoprime(int a, int b);             //***************

int main()
{
    freopen("ex1input.txt","r",stdin);
    int arr[divCount(100,9244)];
    int arr2[mygcd(4425,6610)];

    cout<<ceil(234.6234)<<"\n";
    cout<<floor(234.6234)<<"\n";
    cout<<primeCheck(9231)<<endl;
    cout<<myprimecount(100)<<endl;
    cout<<mycoprime(661,662)<<endl;
    cout<<fact(10)<<endl;
    cout<<divSigma(1,4566)<<endl;
    cout<<divCount(100,9244)<<endl;
    cout<<mygcd(6234,8791)<<endl;
    cout<<mylcm(6234,8792)<<endl;
    cout<<pow(2,16)<<endl;
    cout<<fact(8) + divCount(1,6566)<<endl;

    int f, s, n;
    cin>>f;
    cin>>s;
    cin>>n;
    cout<<divCount(s,n)<<endl;
    cout<<fact(f)<<endl;
    cout<<mygcd(s,n)<<endl;

    return 0;
```

Fig. 7. Original non-TMP CPP file

```
#include <tmp.hpp>
#include <iostream>
#include <cstdio>
#include <cmath>
using namespace std;

int fact(int n);                          //***************
int divCount(int s, int n);               //
int divSigma(int s, int n);               //
bool primeCheck(int n);                   // User-Defined
int myprimecount(int n);                  //   Functions
int mygcd(int a,int b);                   //
int mylcm(int a,int b);                   //
bool mycoprime(int a, int b);             //***************

int main()
{
    freopen("ex1input.txt","r",stdin);
    int arr[divisorCount <100,9244>::value];
    int arr2[findGCD <4425,6610>::value];

    cout<<toCeil <float>::value(234.6234)<<"\n
    cout<<floor(234.6234)<<"\n";
    cout<<primeCheck(9231)<<endl;
    cout<<primeCount <100>::value<<endl;
    cout<<mycoprime(661,662)<<endl;
    cout<<Factorial <10>::value<<endl;
    cout<<divSigma(1,4566)<<endl;
    cout<<divisorCount <100,9244>::value<<endl
    cout<<findGCD <6234,8791>::value<<endl;
    cout<<mylcm(6234,8792)<<endl;
    cout<<exponent <2,16>::value<<endl;
    cout<<Factorial <8>::value + divisorCount <

    int f, s, n;
    cin>>f;
    cin>>s;
    cin>>n;
    cout<<divCount(s,n)<<endl;
    cout<<fact(f)<<endl;
    cout<<mygcd(s,n)<<endl;
```

Fig. 8. TMP-injected CPP file

In original non-TMP CPP file (Fig. 7), program utilizes user-defined functions to perform computations at run-time. Also, the 'arr' and 'arr2' declarations will result in compilation error as their size are not compile-time constant. Notice that last few function calls are dependent on run-time info.

While in TMP-injected CPP file (Fig. 8), the developed tool's TMP header file is included at the top which contains all the function templates. Only the selected functionalities are modified. Now, the 'arr' and 'arr2' declarations won't result in compilation error. Also, notice how the run-time dependent function calls aren't modified.

In benchmark results (Fig. 9), purple-colored bar is for non-TMP file's execution time and pink-colored bar is for TMP-injected file's execution time. 'Order of N' on X-axis, and time (ms) on Y-axis. Non-TMP file takes 1087 ms to perform computations while TMP-injected file takes only 690 ms as desired run-time independent info has already been computed at compile-time.

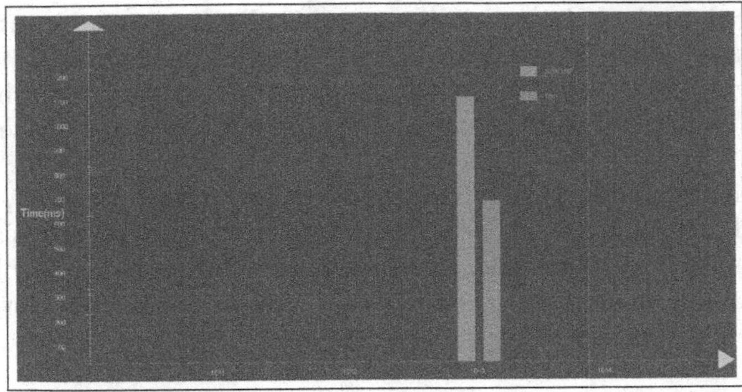

Fig. 9. Execution time benchmark results (Color figure online)

Thus, there is a considerable amount of computations that has been shifted from run-time to compile-time using template metaprogramming that results in this execution-time difference.

6 Limitations and Future Work

6.1 Limitations

- **Support basic mathematical operations:** Right now, the application only provides support for the above-mentioned basic mathematical operations. More complex operations such as Strassen matrix multiplication, string hashing, Bezier curves, etc. need to be included.
- **Not applicable for all types of programs:** Template metaprogramming is applicable for algorithms and other mathematical procedures that are independent of run-time information and can be implemented as a recursive function. Other programs that don't suffice above given criteria can't be implemented using template metaprogramming.
- **Dependence on stack size:** Any program will have the recursive function call limit. The limit depends on the operating system and hardware configuration [1]. It depends on the stack limit. The template programs are recursive in nature. The program will stop executing if the stack limit exceeds.
- **GUI needs more robustness:** The GUI performs only searching and sorting operations. Additional functionality should be added to the interface so that it can be over for multiple purposes. The GUI should have more features that will make it robust. The GUI can have other functionality such as file handling, more operations, etc.
- **Chronometer module for Windows OS has lesser precision in measuring execution time:** The chronometer module on windows has lesser precision as compared to Linux. It can create problem in analysis and graph precision. Analysis on value having minor difference will be tough on windows.

- **Statistical analysis being shown graphically may not be intuitive to some users:** Some users might not be interested in the graphical analysis. They might just be concerned about the execution time. Many technical analysts just need the statistical values. They are not concerned of the graphical analysis.
- **Compilation time:** As per the compile time runtime trade-off, when the runtime decreases, the compile time increases. As the computations are shifted from compile time to runtime, the compile time increases [6]. For large data sets containing numbers, the compile time can be considerable low that can affect the performance of the program.

6.2 Future Enhancements

- **Improving GUI robustness:** This would involve adding more functionality to the GUI and adding more ways for analysis. GUI can be made more robust by adding more features to the GUI. GUI should be made more users friendly. The GUI should also include more features other than searching and sorting. It should be made more and more attractive so that the users use it for educational purposes. The GUI should also add functionality of storing files and other file handling operations. This would help in more robustness of the GUI.
- **Improving chronometer module for Windows OS:** The chronometer for windows does not show precise values in the analysis. It should be improved so that proper graph based on analysis can be made. As most of the people use windows operating system, the chronometer should be made more precise so that people use the analysis tool for educational purposes.
- **Making the graphical analysis more intuitive:** The graph should be made more intuitive to the users who might not be interested in graphical analysis. Some technicians may just want comparison of values. So, the analysis should be made more intuitive in such a way so that everyone uses it.
- **Extending support for more operations:** The current GUI deals with searching and sorting operations. The functionality for adding more operations such as string matching and inbuilt functions should be added. This would make the GUI robust also. The tool can be used for educational purposes.
- **Adding various other graphs for improved understanding and insight:** Adding more types of graph such as line graphs, etc. should be added so that proper analysis can be done. Adding other graphs will also help in making GUI more attractive.

7 Conclusion

Though the syntax in template metaprogramming is generally different from the programming language where it is used, there are some practical uses. Many reasons to use templates are that it is used to implement generic programming (that is, avoiding sections of the code that are similar) or it can be used to perform automatic compile-time optimization, that is, performing operations once at compile time rather than performing every time the program is run [1].

Generic programming paradigm and template metaprogramming are the two techniques that work on C++ STL that is heavily used in modern professional programs [2, 5]. In template-metaprogramming, compiler is utilized to generate transient metaprograms according to template definitions which are executed at compile-time and output is merged with existing source code and then compiled. This can be leveraged to shift computations to compile time provided that they don't require any runtime information [4].

Our system has been developed as an educational tool by building software library of functions and data structures empowered with C++ template-metaprogramming to further optimize the runtime and augment its ease of use in other software development by graphically conveying how runtime is reduced when computations are shifted to compiler time [6]. It also provides dynamic benchmarking against other available libraries to manifest the compile-time tradeoff that it creates against traditional runtime programs.

According to the statistical analysis shown through the graph, we can analyze that the runtime is reduced when the computations are shifted from runtime to compile time. This helps in program optimization and better maintenance [5]. The project is compatible to both Windows and Linux. The implementation is shown on the both of the systems. The project also provided a developed user-friendly graphical user interface to perform operations and show the runtime optimization through template metaprogramming [6]. The project can be used for educational and research purposes. The research can be further extended to more complex functions and show how runtime is affected in complex scenarios.

References

1. Abrahams, D., Gurtovoy, A.: C++ Template Metaprogramming: Concepts, Tools, and Techniques from Boost and Beyond, Portable Documents. Pearson Education, London (2004)
2. Czarnecki, K., Eisenecker, U.W.: Generative Programming: Methods, Tools and Applications. Addison-Wesley, Boston (2000)
3. Porkoláb, Z., Mihalicza, J., Sipos, Á.: Debugging C++ template metaprograms. In: Proceedings of the 5th International Conference on Generative Programming and Component Engineering (2006)
4. Teodorescu, L.R., Dumitrel, V., Potolea, R.: Moving computations from run-time to compile-time: hyper-metaprogramming in practice. In: Proceedings of the 11th ACM Conference on Computing Frontiers. ACM (2014)
5. Vandevoorde, D., Josuttis, N.M.: C++ Templates: The Complete Guide. Addison-Wesley, Boston (2003)
6. Sorting Algorithms Animation showing efficiency of different algorithms on different types of data sets (n.d.). https://www.toptal.com/developers/sorting-algorithms
7. Isensee, P.: Fast math using template metaprogramming. In: Game Programming Gems, pp. 20–34. Charles River Media Inc. (2003)

Comparative Performance Analysis of PMSM Drive Using ANFIS and MPSO Techniques

Deepti Yadav(✉) and Arunima Verma

Electrical Engineering Department, IET, Lucknow 226021, India
deepti.yadav00@gmail.com, arunima_eed@ietlucknow.edu

Abstract. The major problem in permanent Magnet Synchronous Motor (PMSM) drive systems are the nonlinear behavior which arises mainly from motor dynamics and load characteristics. So, the speed control technique should be adaptive and robust for successful industrial applications. The conventional proportional integral derivative (PID) controllers used to control speed of the drive are tuned mainly using Ziegler-Nichols' (Z-N) tuning technique. Since, PID controller works well under linear operating condition and underperforms when nonlinearity arises. So Artificial Intelligence (AI) techniques are being implemented to achieve better performance i.e. Adaptive Neuro Fuzzy Inference System (ANFIS), Modified Particle Swarm Optimization (MPSO). This paper proposes novel design of ANFIS and MPSO- AI techniques based PID speed controller which has been incorporated in PMSM drive to improve its dynamic performance. A model of PMSM drive is simulated under various operating conditions to analyze its performance in terms of transient response specification such as rise time, settling time, peak overshoot and peak time. The results obtained give much better performance as compared to conventionally used Z-N technique.

Keywords: Permanent Magnet Synchronous Motor (PMSM)
Proportional integral derivative controller (PID) · Ziegler-Nichols (Z-N)
Adaptive neuro fuzzy inference system (ANFIS)
Modified Particle Swarm Optimization (MPSO)

1 Introduction

PMSM drives have emerged as efficient variable speed drive systems in the recent trend of industrial applications giving stiff competition to the classical brushed DC and induction motor (IM) drives in the low to medium power range. The replacement of electrically excited field windings by constant flux producing permanent magnets in PMSMs have led to elimination of brushes, slip rings and rotor copper losses resulting in higher efficiencies. Although PMSMs are more expensive as compared to IMs but with high-energy magnet material (Nd-Fe-B), offer higher efficiency, higher torque to inertia ratio, higher power density reduced size and high performance in wide range of speed. Owing to these advantages PMSMs are being widely used in electric vehicles, audio equipment, household appliances, medical instruments, robotics, textiles and chemical industries [1, 2]. Due to the presence of non-linearity in the system the

P. Bhattacharyya et al. (Eds.): NGCT 2017, CCIS 827, pp. 148–161, 2018.
https://doi.org/10.1007/978-981-10-8657-1_12

conventional approach of PID tuning is not very efficient with the dynamic conditions of a system because of varying parameters and complicated environmental applications [3]. The Zeigler and Nichols (Z-N) tuning method is one of the most widely used method for tuning of PID controller [4]. ANFIS based speed controller is a good tool to deal with complicated, non-linear and ill-defined systems [5]. Another evolutionary computation technique [PSO] was first presented by Kennedy and Eberhart in 1995 [6] for optimize the gain of PID controller. PSO has some demerits as the rate of convergence, problem of local extreme, premature and halt condition in searching process. In order to overcome these defects MPSO have been incorporated [7–12]. The objective of this paper is to use the MPSO algorithm in order to obtain optimal values of gains for PID speed controller for improved performance of PMSM drive. By incorporating AI techniques such as ANFIS and MPSO for tuning the conventionally used PID speed controller, an improvement in the performance of PMSM in terms of transient response under various operating conditions has been presented in this paper.

2 Design of ANFIS Based Speed Controller

The FIS to be used in ANFIS based speed controller consists of input block, output block and their respective membership functions. Figure 1 explains the development of fuzzy inference system using ANFIS edit GUI toolbox [13].

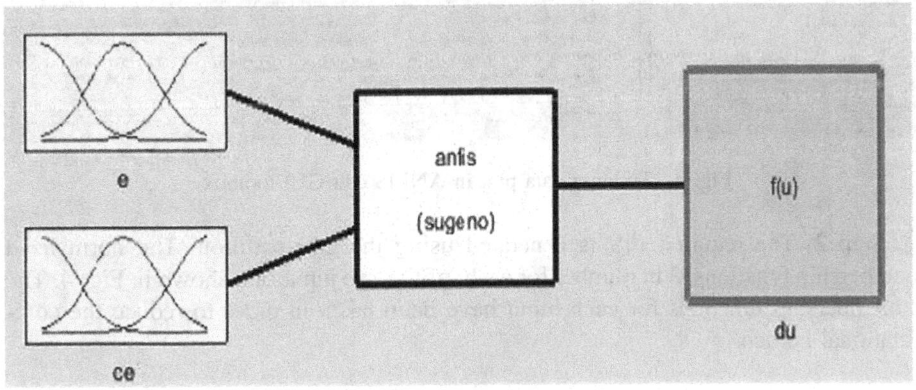

Fig. 1. Design of adaptive neural-fuzzy inference system

In this PMSM motor drive, there are two inputs and one output. The inputs are the speed error (e) and change in speed error (ce) and the value of du is taken as output from the ANFIS based speed controller. Algorithm of ANFIS based Speed Controller. The block diagram representing the ANFIS based controller for the speed control of the PMSM is shown in Fig. 2 [5].

Basically, the ANFIS controller includes four processes as.

(a) Fuzzification (b) Knowledge base (c) Neural network (d) Defuzzification.

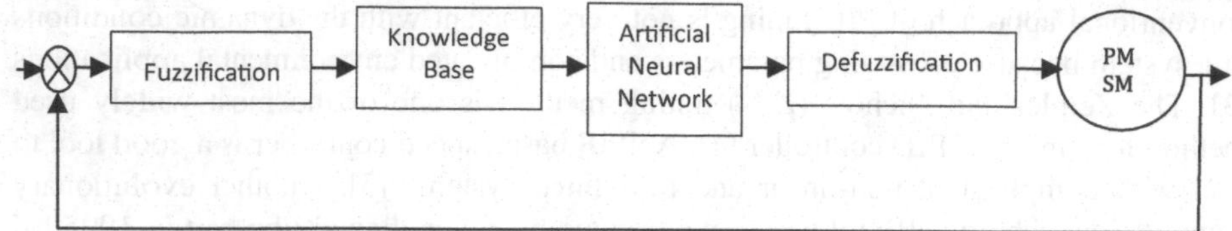

Fig. 2. ANFIS speed control of the PMSM

The process of designing ANFIS based speed controller involves the following steps as.

Step 1: The data of the two inputs e, ce and the output du are collected and fed as a loading data to the ANFIS edit GUI toolbox. The training data obtained is shown in Fig. 3.

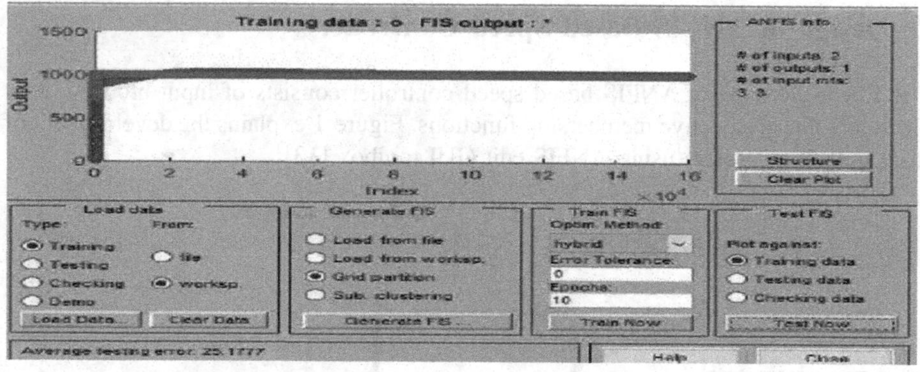

Fig. 3. Training data plot in ANFIS edit GUI toolbox

Step 2: The required FIS is generated using the grid partition. The normalized membership functions, 3 in number for each, of the two inputs are shown in Fig. 4. The 3 membership functions for each input have been taken in order to reduce the computational burden.

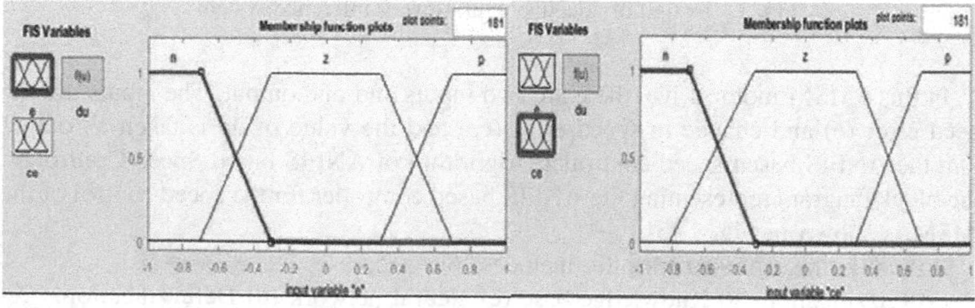

Fig. 4. Normalized membership functions of the two inputs variables

Step 3: The control of the speed is done by the ANFIS based speed controller; the following rules are used and summarized in Table 1. The structure of ANFIS developed with all the 5 layers is shown in Fig. 5.

Table 1. Control expression of ANFIS based speed controller

e	ce		
	NB	Z	PB
NB	NB	NB	Z
Z	NB	Z	PB
PB	Z	PB	PB

The abbreviations in Table are as follows.
NB - Negative Big, PB - Positive Big, Z - zero.

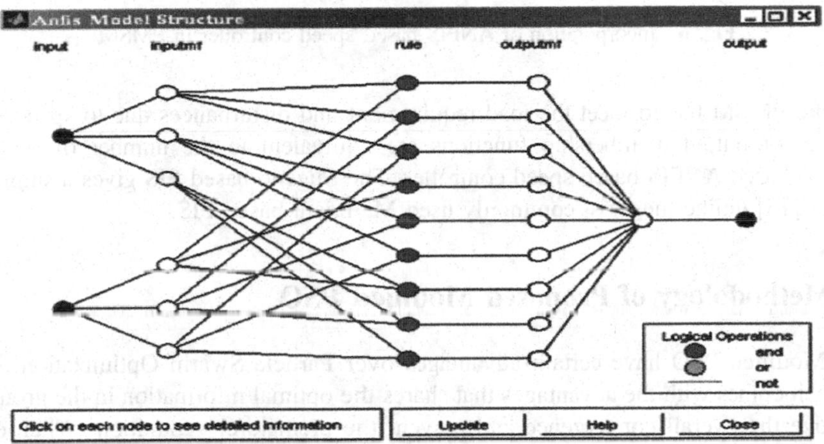

Fig. 5. ANFIS model structure with 2 inputs & 1 output

Step 4: The loaded training data with the generated FIS is trained using the hybrid method with the following parameters given in Table 2.

Table 2. ANFIS based speed controller training parameters [13]

Variables	Value
AND	prod
OR	probOR
Fuzzification	Sugeno [2, 31–32, 53, 158]
Defuzzification	Wtaver
Optimization method	Hybrid
No. of epochs	40
Type of membership function	Constant Gaussian function

2.1 Incorporation of ANFIS Based Speed Controller in PMSM

The ANFIS based speed controller is obtained using the algorithm of ANFIS. It is incorporated in the PMSM drives. As shown in Fig. 6 the conventional PID speed controllers in the drives have been replaced by this ANFIS based speed controller.

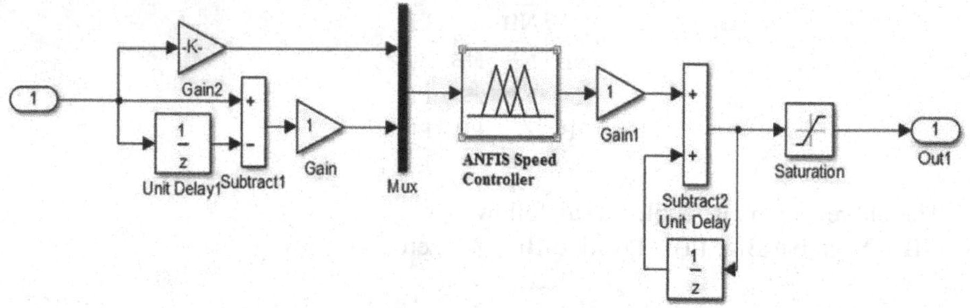

Fig. 6. Incorporation of ANFIS based speed controller in PMSM

The PMSM has to meet the load requirement and disturbances due to speed. The number of output membership functions are equivalent to the number of rules in Sugeno based ANFIS based speed controller. The Sugeno based FIS gives a singleton output [13] unlike the most commonly used Mamdani based FIS.

3 Methodology of Proposed Modified PSO

The Modified PSO have certain advantages over Particle Swarm Optimization technique, it comes with the advantages that shares the optimal information in the group to improve the overall convergence and prevent the prematurely condition. When each group is divided, the group which has maximum population at the center is preferred. It shows a particle subgroup as a central subgroup, and the other subgroups are neighborhoods to the central subgroups, it can communicate with other subgroup near to it and other subgroups cannot share the information with each other. By using MPSO technique the information can transmit faster and improving efficiency of the algorithm. Accordingly, the distance of two vectors was obtained by the space position of each particle. The L_{max} denoted as the maximum distance of any two particles. Meanwhile $||X_i(k) - X_i(k)||/L_{max}$ was also calculated. Each particle updates its status according to Eqs. (1, 2) as follows

$$V_i(k+1) = w(k)\, V_i(k) + c_1(k)\, r_1(P_i - X_i(k)) + c_2(k)\, r_2\big(P_g - X_i(k)\big) \tag{1}$$

$$X_i(k+1) = X_i(k) + V_i(k+1) \tag{2}$$

Fitness function is used to evaluate every new position. In MPSO technique, the value of weight w adjust the properly, which prevent algorithm from getting into a local optimization. In this algorithm, a quasi-linear speed-weights way is used in the iterative process. This way used is illustrated as follows:

$$w(k) = w_{initial} + (w_{initial} - w_{final})(1 - k/K) \tag{3}$$

$$c_1(k) = c_{1initial} + (c_{1initial} - c_{1final})(1 - k/K) \tag{4}$$

$$c_2(k) = c_{2initial} + (c_{2initial} - c_{2final})(1 - k/K) \tag{5}$$

k denotes current iterate time; K denotes max iterate time.

The searching procedure of the implemented MPSO-PID controller is described in flowchart given in Fig. 7.

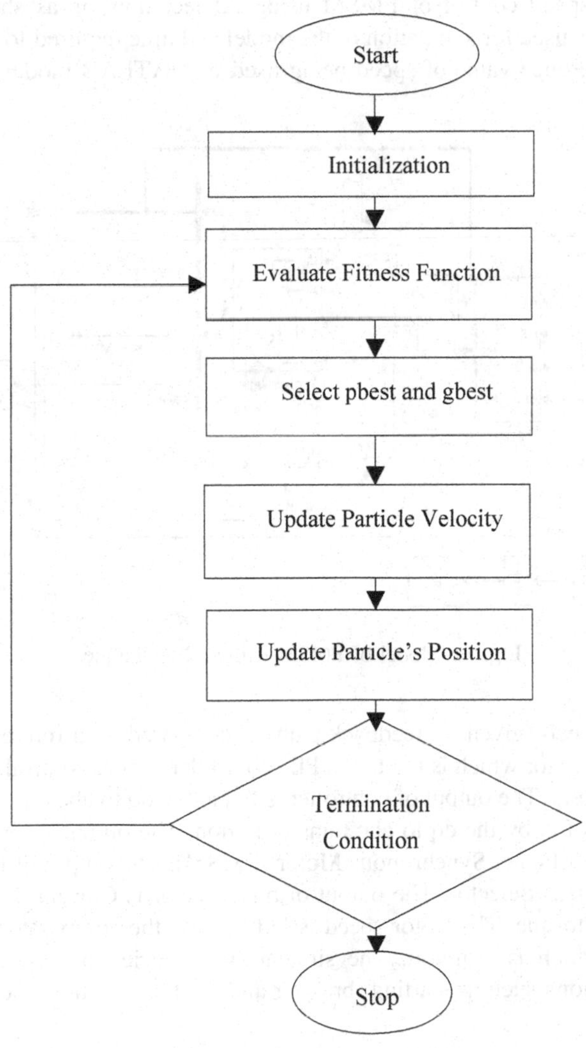

Fig. 7. Flowchart of MPSO PID controller

The optimized values of PID controller gains are shown in Table 3.

Table 3. Values of K_p, K_i and K_d obtained from MPSO method

K_p, K_i and K_d using Z-N method are	K_p, K_i and K_d using MPSO technique are
K_p: 0.34584	K_p: 2
K_i: 3.460165	K_i: 3
K_d: 0.008641591	K_d: 0.008

4 Model of PMSM and Results

The model for speed control of PMSM using AI technique is as shown in Fig. 8. Matlab R2013a is used for simulation of the model and time required for the simulation is 0.5 s. The reference value of speed being used in MATLAB model is 1000 r.p.m.

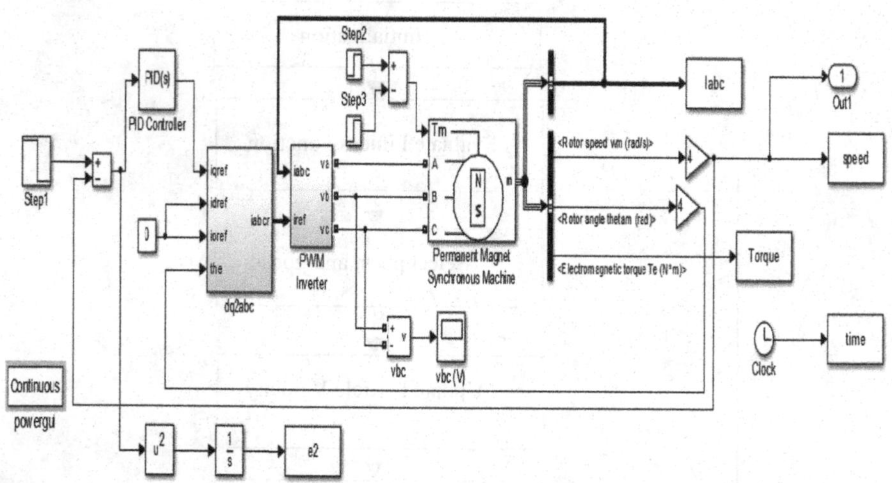

Fig. 8. Model of PMSM using AI technique

The motor speed (given by feedback path) is compared with reference speed with the help of comparator which is fed to the PID controller. These controllers improve the transient parameters. The output of controller is fed to the dq to abc transformation. The inverter circuit is fed by the dq to abc transformation. The output of inverter circuit is fed to Permanent Magnet Synchronous Motor (PMSM). The output of PMSM is taken with the help of Bus Selector. The output of bus selector is Current, Rotor Speed and Electromagnetic torque. The Rotor speed is fed back to the comparator to achieve the desired speed which is required. The simulation is carried out under the different operating conditions such as starting, braking and load application and removal.

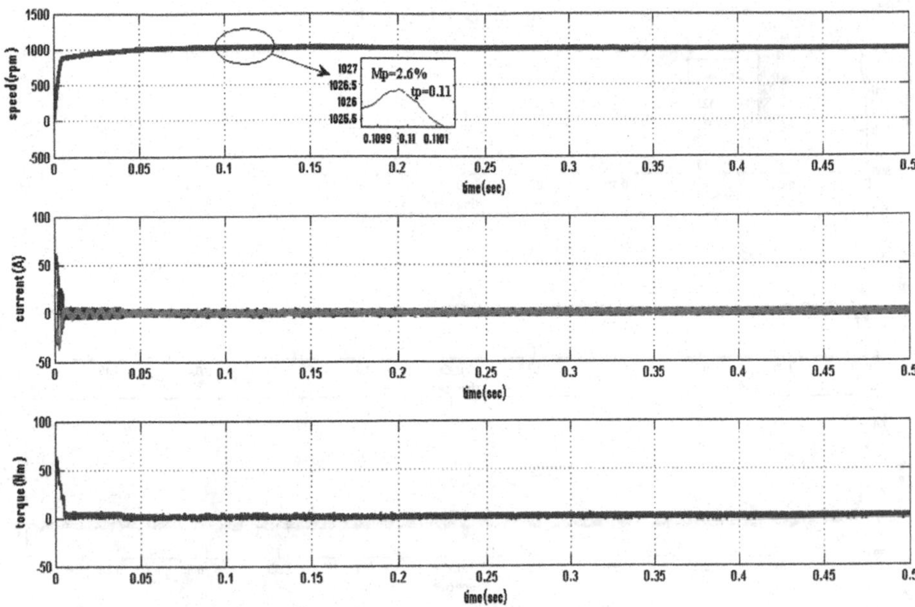

Fig. 9. Starting dynamics of PMSM drive using Z-N method

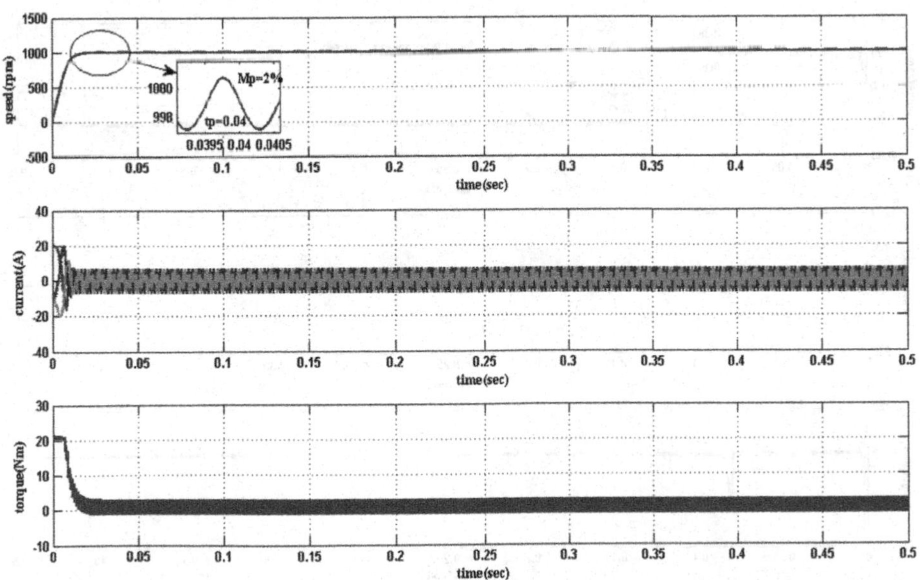

Fig. 10. Starting dynamics of PMSM drive using ANFIS method

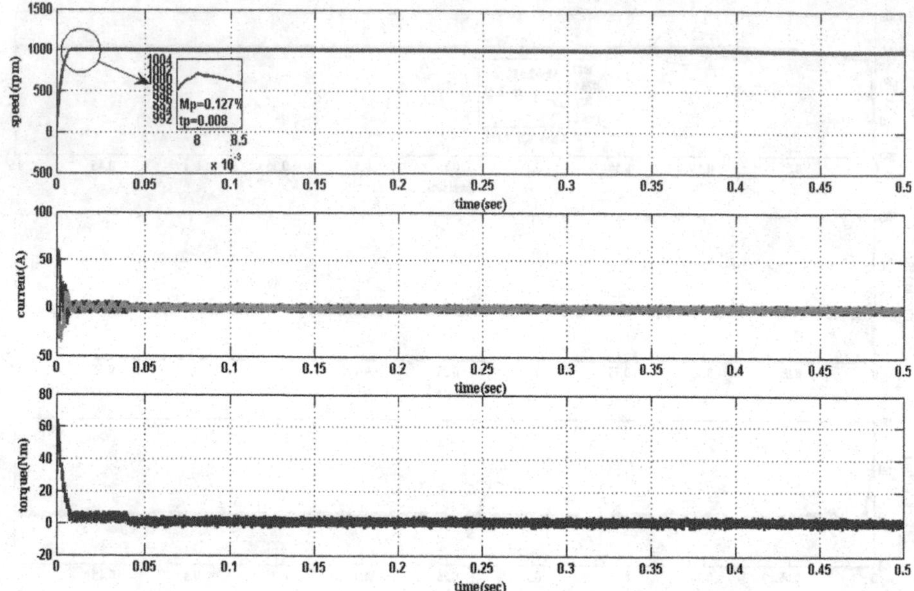

Fig. 11. Starting dynamics of PMSM drive using MPSO method

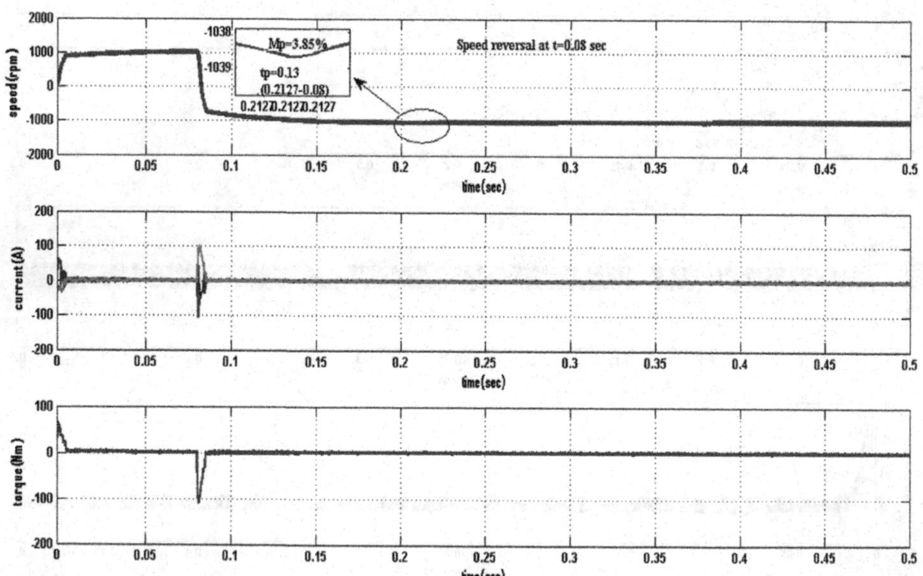

Fig. 12. Speed reversal characteristics of PSMM drive using Z-N

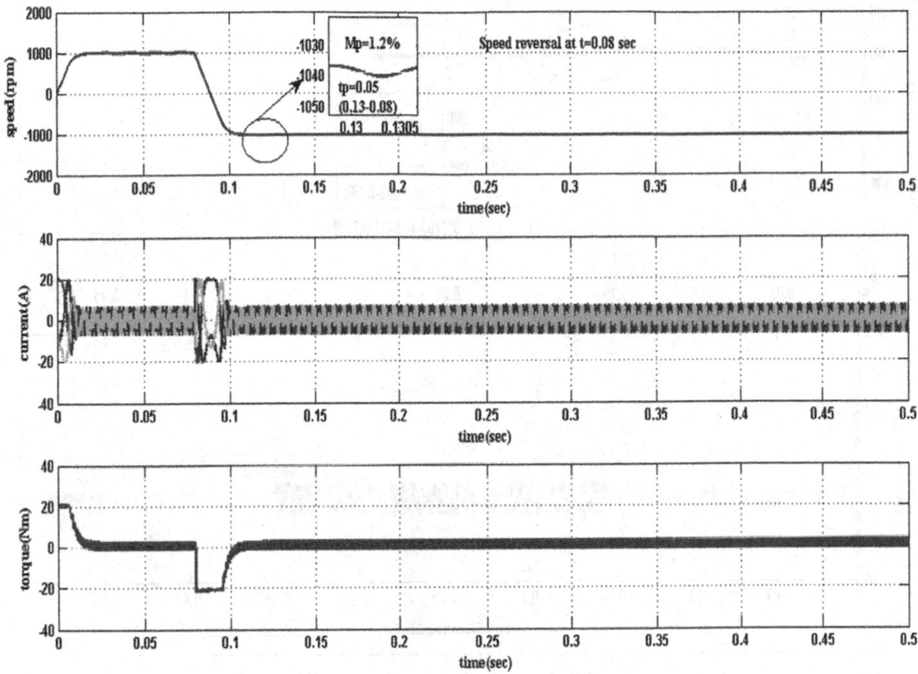

Fig. 13. Speed reversal characteristics of PSMM drive using ANFIS

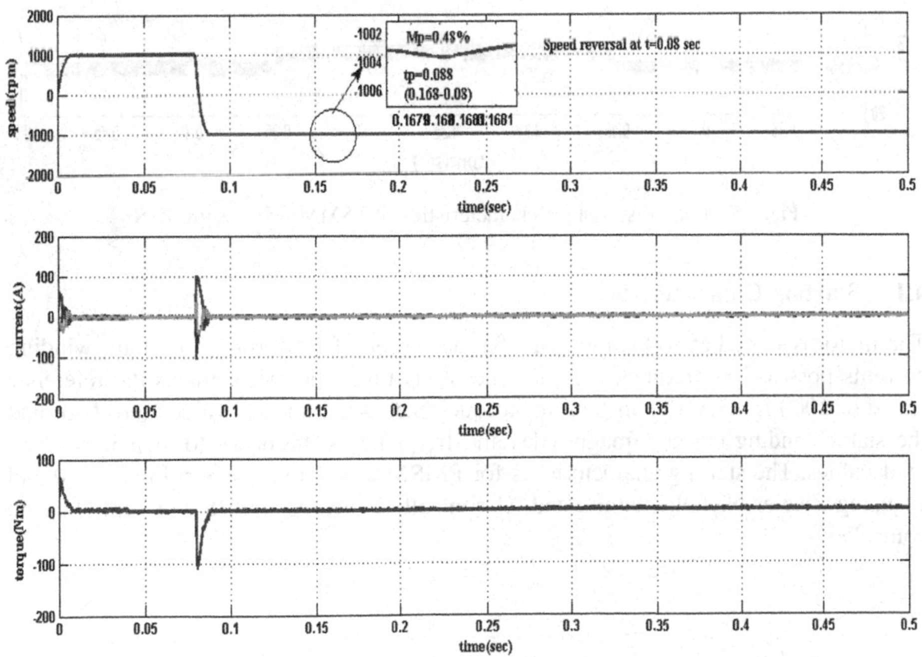

Fig. 14. Speed reversal characteristics of PSMM drive using MPSO

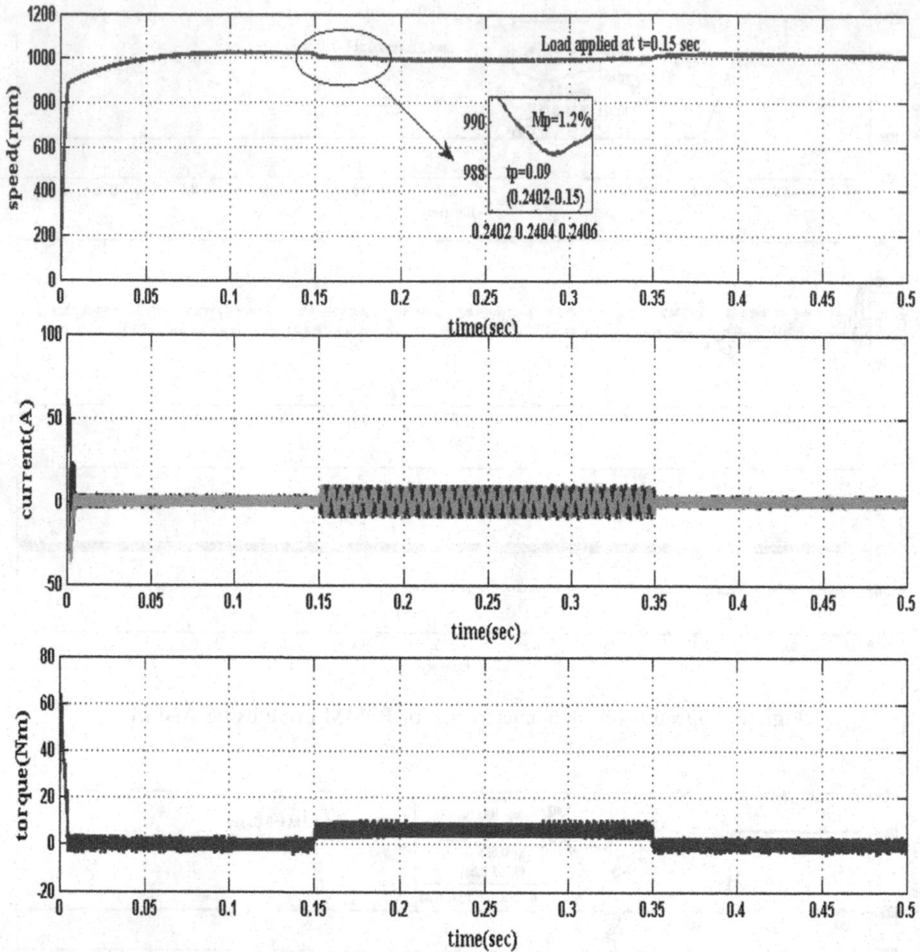

Fig. 15. Load disturbance characteristics of PSMM drive using Z-N

4.1 Starting Characteristics

The motor is started at no load with a reference speed of 1000 rpm. The stator winding currents possess low frequency at the time of starting. The motor tracks the reference speed of 1000 rpm. At this instant, the torque reaches it's no load value (zero Nm) and the stator winding currents magnitudes and frequency settle down to their normal no load values. The starting characteristics for PMSM drive are shown in Figs. 9, 10 and 11 using Ziegler-Nichols method and AI controllers such as ANFIS and MPSO speed controller.

4.2 Speed Reversal Characteristics

The reference speed is reversed at t = 0.08 s to −1000 rpm. The rotor speed follows and tries to attain the reference value as seen from Figs. 12, 13 and 14.

The torque T_{em} also reduces, the speed settles down to its new reference value of −1000 rpm and the torque reverts to the no load value of zero Nm.

4.3 Load Application and Load Removal

Load application and removal of load are shown in Figs. 15, 16 and 17. When the sudden load is applied at t = 0.15 s. The developed torque follows the value of load torque. The rotor speed ω_m decreases when the load is applied and increases, try to attain the reference value when the load is removed at t = 0.35 s.

The values of the transient response specifications under starting, speed reversal and load disturbance conditions obtained from the AI techniques and Z-N method of PMSM tuned PID speed controller as shown in Table 4.

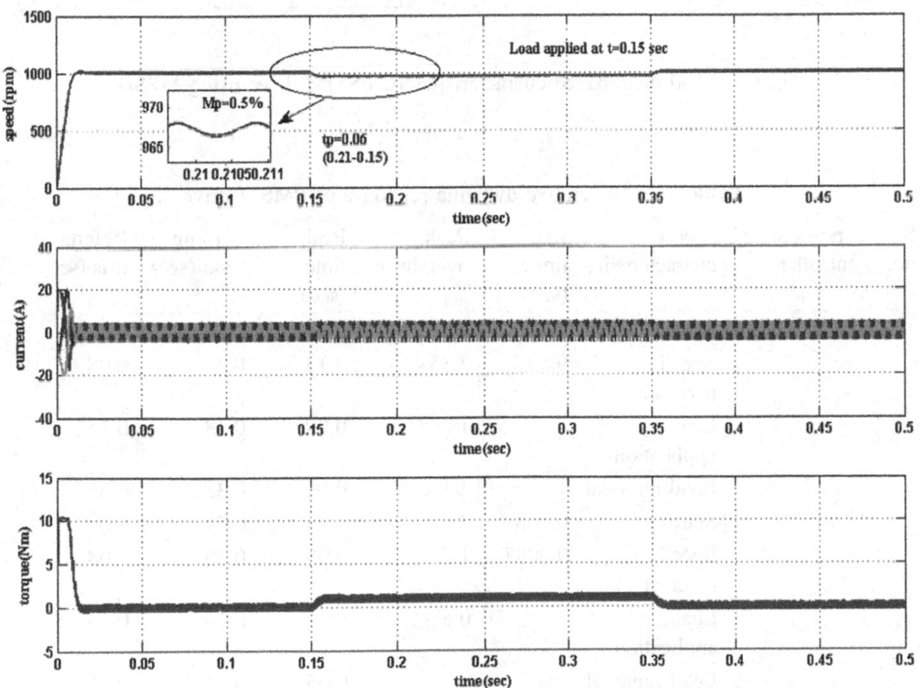

Fig. 16. Load disturbance characteristics of PSMM drive using ANFIS

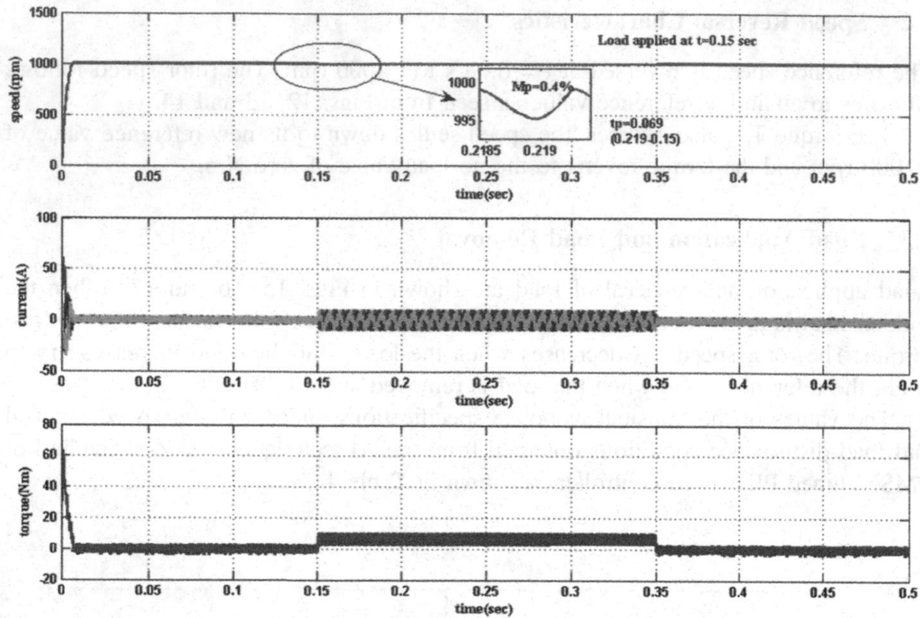

Fig. 17. Load disturbance characteristics of PSMM drive using MPSO

Table 4. Comparative dynamic response of PMSM drive

S. no.	Type of speed controller	Motor characteristics	Rise time (sec)	Peak overshoot (%)	Peak time (sec)	Settling time (sec)	Reference time(sec)
1	Z-N	Starting	0.010	2.6	0.118	0.44	0.0
		Speed reversal	0.03	3.85	0.13	0.4	0.08
		Load application	-	1.2	0.09	0.18	0.15
		Load removal	-	2.1	0.06	0.38	0.35
2	ANFIS	Starting	0.008	2	0.04	0.41	0.0
		Speed reversal	0.0087	1.2	0.05	0.39	0.08
		Load application	-	0.5	0.06	0.15	0.15
		Load removal	-	2	0.055	0.35	0.35
3	MPSO	Starting	0.007	0.127	0.008	0.0088	0.0
		Speed reversal	0.087	0.48	0.088	0.44	0.08
		Load application	-	0.4	0.069	0.12	0.15
		Load removal	-	1.8	0.02	0.28	0.35

5 Conclusion

The performance of the PMSM motor is improved by tuning PID parameters effectively along with AI technique i.e. ANFIS and MPSO. Further, these results are compared with those of Z-N method. The proposed controller has significantly improved the transient response of the drive by optimizing gains of PID controller as compared to Z-N tuned method. Further, the proposed method incorporated in PMSM motor is robust, efficient and easy to implement. In this paper, the performance of PID speed controller with and without AI tuning has been compared and the obtained results clearly demonstrate the difference between the two waveforms obtained from simulation of PMSM model. Under various operating conditions, the analysis and comparison between the improved static and dynamic characteristics in terms of rise time, peak overshoot and settling time are demonstrated which are helpful in selection of PMSM drive for particular industrial applications.

References

1. Krishnan, R.: Permanent Magnet Synchronous and Brushless DC Motor Drives. CRC Press/Taylor & Francis Group, Boca Raton/Milton Park (2010)
2. Bose, B.K.: Modern Power Electronic and Drives. The University of Tennessee, Knoxville (2001)
3. Pan, T.-H., Li, S.-Y.: Adaptive PID control for nonlinear systems based on lazy learning. Control Theory Appl. (2009)
4. Ogata, K.: Modern Control Engineering, 4th edn. Prentice Hall of India, New Delhi (2002)
5. Jain, L.C., Martin, N.M.: Fusion of Neural Networks, Fuzzy Systems and Genetic Algorithms: Industrial Applications. CRC Press, Boca Raton (1998)
6. Kennedy, J., Eberhart, R.: Particle swarm optimization. In: Proceedings of the IEEE International Conference on Neural Networks, vol. 4, pp. 1942–1948 (1995)
7. Jeong, S., Hasegawa, S., Shimoyama, K., Obayashi, S.: Development and investigation of efficient GA/MPSO-hybrid algorithm applicable to real-world design optimization. IEEE Comput. Intell. Mag. 777–784 (2009)
8. Shayeghi, H., Mahdavi, M., Bagheri, A.: Discrete MPSO algorithm based optimization of transmission lines loading in TNEP problem. Energy Convers. Manag. **51**, 112–121 (2010)
9. Duan, Z., Zhang, C., Hu, Z., Ding, T.: Design for multi-machine power system damping controller via particle swarm optimization approach. In: International Conference, SUPERGEN 2009 (2009)
10. Shoorehdeli, M.A., Teshnehlab, M., Sedigh, A.K.: Training ANFIS as an identifier with intelligent hybrid stable learning algorithm based on particle swarm optimization and extended Kalman filter. Fuzzy Sets Syst. **160**, 922–948 (2009)
11. Karakuzu, C.: Fuzzy controller training using particle swarm optimization for nonlinear system control. ISA Trans. **47**, 229–239 (2008)
12. Catalão, J.P.S., Pousinho, H.M.I., Mendes, V.M.F.: Hybrid wavelet-MPSO-ANFIS approach for short-term wind power forecasting in Portugal. IEEE Trans. Sustain. Energy **2**, 50–59 (2011)
13. ANFIS and ANFIS editor GUI - User's Guide. The MathWorks. www.mathworks.com

Developing the Hybrid Multi Criteria Decision Making Approach for Green Supplier Evaluation

Muhammad Nouman Shafique(✉)

Dongbei University of Finance and Economics, Dalian 116000, China
shafique.nouman@gmail.com

Abstract. Environment-friendly policies have developed the awareness to protect the environment from hazardous effects. ISO 9000 certification, legal laws and public demands enhance the green corporate social responsibilities. Organizational traditional processes changed into green concepts. A dramatic shift from supplier selection to green supplier selection has been adopted in organizations to reduce the product impact on environment. Supplier selection is the most important organizational strategic decision to design, produce and distribute green. This paper is focused to develop the criteria for green supplier selection. This decision is based on both quantitative and qualitative methods. So, Multi Criteria Decision Making (MCDM) has been used to take the rational decisions. In this study, a hybrid multi criteria decision making approach based on Decision Making Trial and Evaluation Laboratory Model (DEMATEL), the Analytical Network Process (ANP), and Technique for Order Performance by Similarity to Ideal Solution (TOPSIS) in fuzzy environment have been used to take the ideal decisions. This study will focus on the development of hybrid MCDM model for green supplier selection.

Keywords: Green supply chain management · Green supplier Supplier selection · MCDM · Fuzzy ANP · Fuzzy DEMATEL Fuzzy TOPSIS

1 Introduction

Global marketing, legislation and competitor's pressures brings the dramatic changes from conventional supply-chain management processes to green supply-chain management practices to protect the environment. The proper information management, components, processes and money can design the good traditional supply-chain management system, but they cannot protect the environment. Today, due to globalization and awareness customers, societies and nations got concerned about the environmental protection and made some laws to protect it. So, without implementing environmental friendly activities organizations cannot survive in the global market. The objective of green supply-chain management (GSCM) is to enhance corporate social responsibility, market share and profit through the effectively implementation of environment-friendly activities (Van Hoek 1999).

P. Bhattacharyya et al. (Eds.): NGCT 2017, CCIS 827, pp. 162–175, 2018.
https://doi.org/10.1007/978-981-10-8657-1_13

The success of GSCM is the integration of all supply-chain management (SCM) members with each other to gain maximum environmental benefits (Lee et al. 2009). Considering that it is the supplier social responsibility to legal and fair use of natural resources. Moreover, organizations should consider only green supplier for social, economic and environmental benefits because environmental practices will reduce cost, time and wastages. So, the purpose of this study is to develop and validate the model for the selection and judgement of best green supplier to enhance social, environmental and economic benefits.

Green supplier can be evaluated through different multi criteria decision making techniques. Some of the previous studies have focused on the analytical hierarchy process (AHP) to evaluate the green supplier (Sevkli et al. 2007). Furthermore, some studies focused on the fuzzy analytical hierarchy process (AHP) (Lee et al. 2009). On the other hand, some studies have focused on fuzzy analytic network process (ANP) to evaluate the green supplier (Lin 2009). Data envelopment analysis (DEA) is also based on MCDM is also used to evaluate green supplier (Wu 2009). Moreover, some studies have also focused on heuristics (He et al. 2009) and one more important fuzzy goal programing techniques programming (Tsai and Hung 2009).

Green supplier evaluation is a complex decision based on both qualitative and quantitative techniques. To identify and set the criteria is qualitative techniques while the numerical salutations through different method and matrix are the quantitative techniques. So, it is the combination of both techniques that's why MCDM technique is appropriate for the selection of green supplier. ANP technique is suitable to develop the effective relationship between study factors (Saaty 1996). Considering that ANP develops a dependence relationship among factors systematically.

Decision Making Trial and Evaluation Laboratory (DEMATEL) technique are also used to develop and strengthen the mutual relationship between interdependence factors (Gabus and Fontela 1972). Moreover, Technique for Order Performance by Similarity to Ideal Solution (TOPSIS) is used to select the ideal alternative solution. The purpose of these techniques is to choose the best green supplier for organization. Furthermore, fuzzy logic techniques also used to reduce the ambiguity and uncertainty of human decision. All these techniques have been used in this study to reach at ideal solution of selecting the green supplier through MCDM hybrid method.

Complex decision problems can be resolved through the fuzzy TOPSIS (Iç and Yurdakul 2010), fuzzy ANP (Yüksel and Dağdeviren 2010) and fuzzy DEMATEL (Tseng 2009) techniques. A huge literature support to these techniques which shows how to make a rationale decision in complex environment. In previous studies, only single techniques are used to analyze the problem. According to author best knowledge only one study is focused on these three techniques in fuzzy environment (Büyüközkan and Çifçi 2012). In this study, the hybrid MCDM approach will be developed and validated the previous study. Furthermore, a general hybrid MCDM model focused on green supplier selection criteria will be developed, it can be implemented in other fields of studies, which will enable to reach the idealist and rational solution for complex problems. So, the purpose of this study is to develop a general hybrid model MCDM approach focused on green supplier selection criteria.

2 Literature Review

Globalization prosperous the human progress, concepts changed very rapidly. The shift towards the mass industrial production did a negative effect on natural resources, especially human life and environment. Environmental issues becoming more concerned for organizations, policy makers and researchers in last few years. Organizations change their traditional processes to sustainable activities. Most of the organizations shift from supply-chain management to green supply-chain management. This shift also changed the selection of the supplier to green supplier to enhance organizational performance (Simpson and Power 2005). Moreover, green suppliers enhance the quality and reduce costs to improve the human-resource practices, social and economic performance (Theyel 2006).

Excellent strategy can be failed due to weak management and practices. So, if organizations have good environmental performance strategies but their implementation and management are poor, then it will be failed. So, green supplier selection is the most important decision for organizations to go green. If organizations choose a good green supplier, then their practices will be green, which will results to save cost through the reduction in wastages, which will results to enhance economic performance (Handfield et al. 2002). So, the selection and evaluation of green supplier are a very critical decision in green supply-chain management practices.

The environmental principles have been implemented in management since last few years. Environmental principles are based on the multi objective decision support system. Government, organizational, NGO's and environmental regulations push organizations to focus on environment protection. The major criteria for material determination are solid, liquid and gaseous residue and use of energy was measured through AHP technique in the previous study (Lu et al. 2007). In another study multi objective criteria for supplier evaluation is based on two phases. The first is supplier evaluation and second is order allocation, which is based on the responsiveness, reliability, delivery, flexibility, assets and costs (Önüt et al. 2008).

Hybrid fuzzy multi criteria decision making approach for supplier evaluation has been studied in the previous study which is the combination of Fuzzy Preference Ranking Organization Method for Enrichment Evaluations (PROMETHEE) and fuzzy ANP techniques. This study has been focused on the legislative management, green process management, green image, environmental cost, green production and pollution control as major determinants to evaluate green supplier (Tuzkaya et al. 2009).

The combination of TOPSIS and fuzzy AHP techniques of multi criteria decision making was used to find out the transportation hazardous waste. The main determinants of this study are service time, environmental protection, problem-solving ability, economic factors, owned vehicle fleet, complementary service and the quality related to services were focused in the previous study (Gumus 2009). In another study, high-technology industry was focused to evaluate green supplier. In this study environment management, green image, pollution control, green competency, technology capability and green product are the major determinants to evaluate green supplier (Lee et al. 2009).

Rough set theory method is also used for green supplier development, analysis and evaluation in the previous study. This study has interlinked different attributes of decisions with performance in the broad sense based on business, joint and environmental performance (Bai and Sarkis 2010). In another hybrid multi criteria decision making study is based on ANP and DAE methods interlinked with artificial neural network (ANN). This mixture of different methodologies aimed to select best green supplier who can fulfill corporate social responsibilities through green supply-chain management practices (Kuo et al. 2010).

A combination of fuzzy logic and structure equation modeling has been focused to be analyzed and evaluate supplier because it is the strategic decision for organizations. The main criterion for this study is to focus on technical capability, cost, delivery, environmental concerns, management, service, financial position and safety (Punniyamoorthy et al. 2011). In another study, fuzzy TOPSIS method is used for evaluation of environmental performance of the supplier. The major criteria for this study are partnership with green organization, staff training, environmental certification, green market share, lean process planning, pollution-control initiatives, environmental friendly material, technologies and policies in green projects (Awasthi et al. 2010).

3 Framework

The framework of this study is divided into two parts. First part is to identify methodological techniques, which are fuzzy DEMATEL, fuzzy ANP and fuzzy TOPSIS. Second, the identification of green supplier evaluation criteria.

3.1 Methodologies

In this study, hybrid MCDM methodologies were used. Details have mentioned in the following subsection.

Fuzzy DEMATEL

DEMATEL method is a programmatic method which is used to building models and visualize the casual relationship of complicated factors and their structures. It was originated from Geneva Research Centre of the Battelle Memorial Institute (Gabus and Fontela 1973). Previous literature also supports that DEMATEL is used to see the casual effect during the measurement of complex problems (Chen-Yi et al. 2007). In this method, the relationship between integrated elements should have shown, and the numeric values will show the strengthen of determinants or factor those are participating in study. DEMATEL method is good for crisp values but in real-world uncertainty, level should be found. The probability of uncertainty can be reduced through fuzzy theory. It is very hard to predict human behavior. So, it is impossible to judge human behavior on the exact number. Fuzzy theory will reduce uncertainty of human preferences a lot of literature support fuzzy DEMATEL approach (Tseng 2009).

Fuzzy ANP

Analytical hierarchy process (AHP) is a technique is used to develop the interrelationship among different attributes of the decision-making process. This method shows the unidirectional relationship in the hierarchy among different decision levels. This method was introduced by Saaty (1996). On the other hand, ANP is the advance form of AHP because it is two directional relationship. In this method relationship, feedback is also included in the dependence relationship between different criteria (Saaty 1996). ANP has not been hard-and-fast rules for hierarchy. This system measures the relationship among factors on ratio scale for the pair comparisons. This feature created the difference between AHP and ANP. Furthermore, ANP shows the direct and indirect both relationships among the feedback features. It also shows the different levels of dominant and dominated determinant criteria with their decision attributes. All these features showed the structural differences between hierarchy and network.

ANP method enables to develop the super matrix on the basis of composite weights of different interdependence elements. The structure of ANP network is based on node, lines and loop. Node shows the composite variable or element; lines show the interaction between elements and loop show's dependence of elements. So, if "Goal" is the component which depends on another component of "Criteria," then it makes the relationship Goal to Criteria, which shows in the super matrix. Fuzzy ANP method is used to reduce the human factor uncertainty. The previous literature supported the ANP fuzzy method in different fields (Vinodh et al. 2011).

Fuzzy TOPSIS

In multi criteria decision making technique, TOPSIS method is used to identify different solutions from current available alternatives. This method was introduced by Chen and Hwang (1992). The purpose of this method is to identify and differentiate between the most positive and negative solutions. So, the perfect solution must be too near to ideal positive solution and must be far away distance from ideal negative solution, which will result from the ideal solution for any problem (Chen and Hwang 1992).

There is also fuzzy TOPSIS is used to reduce the human uncertainty from solutions. The fuzzy TOPSIS method is based on some criteria based on the important weights assign to each criterion. The weighted criteria should be represented with w_j. The weighted values can be measured through fuzzy DEMATEL and fuzzy ANP methods. There are different studies, those participate in the good literature review on fuzzy TOPSIS such as supplier selection (Roghanian et al. 2010), clean agent selection (Aiello et al. 2009), personnel selection (Kelemenis and Askounis 2010), evaluation of competitive advantage of shopping websites (Sun and Lin 2009), and many other studies in different fields (Iç and Yurdakul 2010).

Mixed Methods

There are different studies those focused in the combined methods of DEMATEL, ANP and TOPSIS of multi criteria decision making approach. One important study was held in Taiwan for their higher education. This study was focused to develop the innovation support system based on combined fuzzy ANP, TOPSIS and DEMATEL methodology of multi criteria decision making method (Chen and Chen 2010). In another study, ANP, DEMATEL and TOPSIS, technique was used to evaluate the vehicle telemetric system (Lin et al. 2010).

Recently, trends have gone for combined novelty method of the decision support system. However, the number of these studies are very least, according to best knowledge of author. Only one study has been done on the combined method of ANP, TOPSIS and DEMATEL in fuzzy environment. That study was held in Turkey focused on green supplier evaluation for vehicle industry (Büyüközkan and Çifçi 2012). The purpose of current study validates this study and developed the general framework for combined methodology focused on green supplier selection criteria. It can be implemented in other fields of studies.

3.2 Green Supplier Evaluation Criteria

Green supplier evaluation criteria are based on the following elements. The foundation and dimensions of green supplier is based on strong literature support.

Green Logistics
Supply chain provides the base for green logistics. Supply chain can manage the external and internal activities of organizations. The major dimensions for green logistics are green production, procurement, green packaging, reverse logistics and distribution of products. These dimensions have been observed in a number of studies (Punniyamoorthy et al. 2011). The selection of material and product design plays the more important role on the impacting the environment. Previous study shows that the design phase of product cycle effect around 80% on environment. If organization has green product design, their products will also environment friendly. So, for green design, green material is required through green supplier (Goosey 2004).

Green supply-chain management started from the selecting of green supplier and then green procurement. If organization chose green supplier, subsequently they are able to adopt green process to produce green products. This cycle is also interlinked with other concepts of value added contribution, total quality environment management and de-manufacturing and other functional areas (Sarkis et al. 2004). The ideal product should not use the hazardous materials during the manufacturing of products, which will reduce the environmental effect. It also reduced the wastages of material during the production (Jabbour and Jabbour 2009).

Environmental effects can be reduced through the distribution. The distribution concept is not a single concept. It is interlinked with the selection of vehicle, fuel, transportation type, distance between organization and customer and frequency of distribution. If organizations go towards green distribution, then their green supply-chain management practices should be increased automatically. Another factor is reverse logistics, it the reuse and recycle the products and materials. Organizations collect material from customers through the forward supply-chain management concept. The reverse logistic is the key factor to gain economic and environmental benefits (Srivastava 2007).

Packaging is the most important factor for green logistics. Organizations should consider the packaging material, packaging size and shape. Because if organizations have good packaging material with considering the size, then they can deliver more products at the same time. Furthermore, it will increase the space in warehouse and trucks and make the logistics channel more convenient. Attractive packaging also developed good relationship between supplier and customers. Packaging also effect on the price of product and it also put a direct effect on environment (Büyüközkan and Çifçi 2012).

Green Organizational Activities
Green organizational activities played a major role in remanufacturing, reduce, disposal, reuse and recycle have been supported through a number of studies (Awasthi et al. 2010). Organizations should be involved in the proactive and in process activities in green supply-chain management. The reduction is the major dimension of organizational activity, which involved in proactive and in process activities. So, reduction is related at process and reduction in material at every stage.

Reuse is the most important component for achieving the economic and environmental benefits. Reuse may be the reuse of products over the whole like second hand computers and cars, or it may be in the shape of reuse of production material to produce same goods. While the remanufacturing of products is the re-engineering related to products. The purpose of remanufacturing is to increase the quality of old, used or manufacturing substandard product to high-quality products like the new product (Büyüközkan and Çifçi 2012).

Recycling is a complete process in supply-chain management. In recycling process the organizations want to reuse the products instead to dispose of products. The reuse of products should be continued until the products are economical and environmental friendly after that products should be burned or refill in the land to reduce the negative environmental effects of products (Büyüközkan and Çifçi 2012).

Organizational Performance
Organizational performance can be achieved through green supply-chain management. Organizational performance can be measured through four major dimensions. These are flexibility, quality, cost and delivery (Punniyamoorthy et al. 2011). There are many other studies have also supported the organizational performance The organizational performance is not directly measured in terms of environment but through the environmental activities, the overall of business perspectives will be increased (Ketchen and Hult 2007). Organizational performance is dynamic. It can be measured at the stage of the product life cycle. Time and flexibility are the most important factors as compared to cost at introduction stage but in mature stage, cost plays the most important role. So, all organizational performance factors are dynamics.

4 Development, Validation and Output

4.1 Computational Steps

Step 1: Model determination and evaluation. The expert committee should evaluate the model and choose the best one from alternatives based on some decision-making techniques, criteria and goals. Criteria for green supplier evaluation have already formulated, further om the basis of green supplier criteria the diagrammatical model has been developed. Evaluation criterion is mentioned in Sect. 3.2.

Step 2: Fuzzy linguistic terms, values and scale have been evaluated. In this step, the consensus of expert opinions has been developed the relationship within and among the attributes. The fuzzy linguistic terms and scale have been mentioned in Fig. 1.

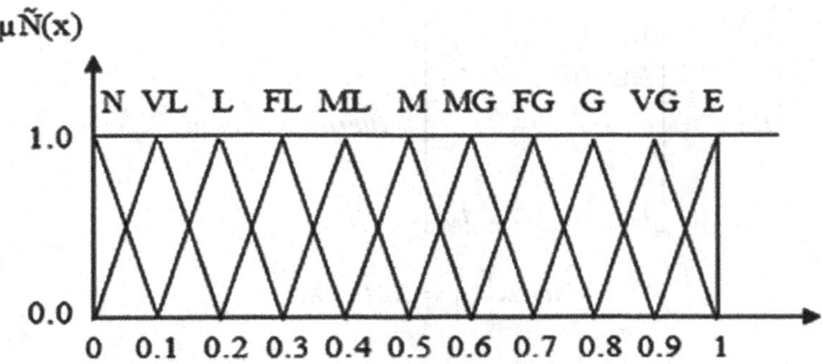

Fig. 1. Fuzzy membership function for linguistic value

Step 3: Fuzzy DEMATEL method has been used to develop the casual relationship.
Step 3.1: Fuzzy direct relationship matrix should be developed on the basis of pair wise comparison and direction. The influence comparison and direction of attributes should make the matrix $\tilde{A} = n \times n$. In this matrix $\tilde{a}_{ij} = (l_{ij}, m_{ij}, u_{ij})$. In this matrix criteria i will effect on criteria j.
Step 3.2: Normalized the fuzzy direct relationship matrix. DEMATEL method is used in the normalization of fuzzy direct – direct relationship. The direct relationship matrix $\tilde{A}$ is normalized to matrix $\tilde{X}$ through Eq. 1 and details are mentioned in Eq. 2.

$$\tilde{X} = S \times \tilde{A}. \tag{1}$$

$$While\ \tilde{a}_{ij} = (l_{ij}, m_{ij}, u_{ij})\ and\ s = \frac{1}{max_{1 \leq i \leq n} \sum_{j=1}^{n} u_{ij}} \tag{2}$$

Step 3.3: Develop total fuzzy relationship matrix based on the direct relationship matrix $\tilde{X}$. The total relationship matrix $\tilde{T}$ can be calculated from the following formula.

$\tilde{X}_{ij} = (l_{ij}, m_{ij}, u_{ij})$ while l shows the identical matrix. The values of $\tilde{X}_{ij}$ matrix can be calculated from the following matrix. Same matrix can use for the calculation of m_{ij} and u_{ij} matrix as mentioned in Eq. 3.

$$X_1 = \begin{bmatrix} 0 & l_{12} & \cdots & l_{1n} \\ l_{21} & 0 & \cdots & l_{2n} \\ \cdot & \cdot & \cdot & \cdot \\ \cdot & \cdot & \cdot & \cdot \\ \cdot & \cdot & \cdot & \cdot \\ l_{n1} & l_{n2} & \cdots & 0 \end{bmatrix} \tag{3}$$

Total relation fuzzy matrix can be obtained from the following formula mentioned in Eq. 4 while details are mentioned in Eqs. 5 and 6.

$$\tilde{T} = \tilde{X}\left(1 - \tilde{X}\right)^{-1} \tag{4}$$

$$Let\,\tilde{T} = \begin{bmatrix} \tilde{t}_{11} & \tilde{t}_{12} & \cdots & \tilde{t}_{1n} \\ \tilde{t}_{21} & \tilde{t}_{22} & \cdots & \tilde{t}_{2n} \\ . & . & . & . \\ . & . & . & . \\ . & . & . & . \\ \tilde{t}_{n1} & \tilde{t}_{n2} & \cdots & \tilde{t}_{nn} \end{bmatrix}, \, where\, \tilde{t}_{ij} = \left(\acute{l}_{ij}, \acute{m}_{ij}, \acute{u}_{ij}\right)\, then \tag{5}$$

$$Matrix\left[\acute{l}_{ij}\right] = X_l(I - X_l)^{-1} \tag{6}$$

Step 3.4: Develop the inner dependence matrix. It can be obtained through the defuzzification of matrix $\tilde{T}$ by using Eq. 6. The normalization method is applied on total relation matrix, in this method sum of each column became 1. The unweighted values of this matrix will be used in ANP.

Step 4: Determine and establish the remaining values and relations of fuzzy ANP. The relative importance of each criterion can be evaluated because it is the pair wise the comparison. The relative strength of each element with its preferences can be evaluated. The fuzzy judgmental matrix is given below in Eq. 7.

$$\tilde{A} = \begin{bmatrix} \tilde{a}_{11} & \tilde{a}_{12} & \cdots & \tilde{a}_{1n} \\ \tilde{a}_{21} & \tilde{a}_{22} & \cdots & \tilde{a}_{2n} \\ \vdots & \vdots & \vdots & \vdots \\ . & . & . & . \\ \tilde{a}_{n1} & \acute{a}_{n2} & \cdots & \tilde{a}_{nn} \end{bmatrix} \tag{7}$$

The values of $\tilde{a}_{ij} = \left(\acute{l}_{ij}, \acute{m}_{ij}, \acute{u}_{ij}\right)$ shows the comparative criteria of $i = j = 1, 2, 3, \ldots..., n$.

Step 4.1: In this step importance weights should be calculated through pair wise comparison based on fuzzy priorities through $\tilde{w}_k$ where $k = 1, 2, 3, \ldots, n$. The logarithm least square method is used to calculate weights mentioned in Eq. 8 (Önüt et al. 2009; Ramik 2006; Tuzkaya et al. 2009; Tuzkaya and Önüt 2008).

$$\tilde{w}_k = \left(w_l k, w_k^m, w_k^u\right)\; k = 1, 2, \ldots, n\, where, \tag{8}$$

Step 4.2: In this step defuzzification weights should be calculated. Furthermore, fuzzy weights can be used to dufuzzification. In the same way w_k^m and w_k^u can be calculated.

Step 5: ANP is used to find the interdependence within and between the clusters.

Step 5.1: In this step, super matrix should be solved. It can be solved in two steps. In first step, each column should be normalized by dividing each weight with the sum of

column. In second step priority ranking of elements should be considered. The overall priorities should be obtained through the limited power of the normalized super matrix.
Step 6: The next procedure is the evaluation of alternatives through fuzzy TOPSIS technique adapted from the previous study (Chen and Hwang 1992). Fuzzy TOPSIS technique is based on the following steps.
Step 6.1: Green supplier can be evaluated through the fuzzy decision matrix based on m alternatives and n criteria. On the basis of alternatives and criteria, fuzzy MCDM problem can be interpreted as follows mentioned in Eq. 9.

$$\tilde{D} = \begin{matrix} A_1 \\ A_2 \\ A_3 \\ A_4 \\ \end{matrix} \overset{\begin{matrix} C_1 & C_2 & \cdots & C_n \end{matrix}}{\begin{bmatrix} \tilde{x}_{11} & \tilde{x}_{12} & \cdots & \tilde{x}_{1n} \\ \vdots & \ddots & & \vdots \\ \vdots & & \ddots & \vdots \\ \tilde{x}_{m1} & \tilde{x}_{m2} & \cdots & \tilde{x}_{mn} \end{bmatrix}} \tag{9}$$

The above fuzzy decision matrix $\tilde{D}$ shows the criteria with C and alternative A.
Step 6.2: In this step, fuzzy decision matrix should be normalized through matrix $\tilde{R}$ calculated in Eqs. 10 and 11.

$$\tilde{R} = [\tilde{r}_{ij}]_{m*n}, i = 1, 2\ldots, m; j = 1, 2\ldots n, \tag{10}$$

$$\tilde{r}_{ij} = \left(\frac{a_{ij}}{C_j^+}, \frac{b_{ij}}{C_j^+}, \frac{c_{ij}}{C_j^+} \right), where\ C_j^+ = max_i C_{ij} \tag{11}$$

TOPSIS method for normalization is very complex. The comparable linear scale will be used to transform various criteria scales (Chen 2000). Furthermore, other studies also suggest linear transformation of scales Kuo et al. (2007) and Celik et al. (2009). $C_{ij} = 1$ shows the normalized matrix.
Step 6.3: Normalized matrix should be weighted in the decision matrix. The weighted decision matrix should be calculated through Eq. 12.

$$\tilde{v}_{ij} = \tilde{r}_{ij} \otimes \tilde{w}_j, \qquad where\ \tilde{v} = [\tilde{v}_{ij}]_{m*n}, i = 1, 2, \ldots, m; j = 1, 2, \ldots, n. \tag{12}$$

Step 6.4: Now the positive and negative distances should be calculated. FPRIP and FNIRP can be used to calculate the positive and negative distances while the (0, 1) are the ranges of the fuzzy matrix mentioned in Eq. 13.

$$A^+ = \{\tilde{v}_1^+, \tilde{v}_2^+, \ldots, \tilde{v}_n^+\}, A^- = \{\tilde{v}_1^-, \tilde{v}_2^-, \ldots, \tilde{v}_n^-\} \tag{13}$$

$$where\ \tilde{v}_j^+ = (1, 1, 1), \tilde{v}_1^- = (0, 0, 0)$$

Step 6.5: FPIRP and FNIRP can be used to measure the positive and negative distances. So, it can be considered as the reference point through Eqs. 14, 15 and 16.

$$d_i^+ = \sum\nolimits_{j=1}^{n} d\left(\tilde{v}_{ij}^+, \tilde{v}_j^+\right), i = 1, 2, \ldots, m; j = 1, 2, \ldots, n, \tag{14}$$

$$d_i^- = \sum\nolimits_{j=1}^{n} d\left(\tilde{v}_{ij}^-, \tilde{v}_j^-\right), i = 1, 2, \ldots, m; j = 1, 2, \ldots, n, \tag{15}$$

$$d(A, B) = \sqrt{\frac{1}{3}\left[(a_1 - b_1)^2 + (a_2 - b_2)^2 + (a_3 - b_3)^2\right]} \tag{16}$$

Step 6.6: The last step is to rank the alternatives. In ranking alternative sorting on descending basis can be done, which will show the best alternative on top and then other alternative according to their preferences. So, through this hybrid methodology its rationale to choose the best alternative.

4.2 Output by Using Software

The basic purpose of this study is to find the best supplier. The selection of supplier is not so easy. The rational decision can be taken on the basis of MCDM. Some special software has also design for MCDM. The purpose of these software is to make the rational decision. One software "Make It Rational" was co-founded by European Union Regional Development Fund Innovation Economy Operational Programme. The purpose of this software is to take a rational decision through MCDM techniques. The latest version of this software is "Transparent Choice." It is web based software and limited version is free available (Programme 2017).

Transparent Choice is working on MCDM approach. In Transparent Choice special software applications has been designed for special purpose. They have design special software named vendor (Supplier) selection. The vendor selection application give output on the basis of four steps. In first step software require the list of vendors. The second step, software requires to build some vendor selection criteria. It requires multi criteria list. On third step, software requires to conduct the survey and compare each criterion with other. Only two criteria will compare each time. In the fourth and last step, software evaluates each criterion with each vendor. When the evaluation is completed then it gives the output in graph (Programme 2017). The output of MCDM is mentioned in Fig. 2. Organizations can use this output for the rational decision of their supplier selection.

The dummy results show that supplier 5 is the best green supplier option among all suppliers. Because this supplier is 78% practicing the green logistic, 17 green organizational activities and 4% organizational performance, these are green supplier evaluation criteria results during that time. Those are the highest score among all competitors. So, the rational choice for organization is to choose supplier 5.

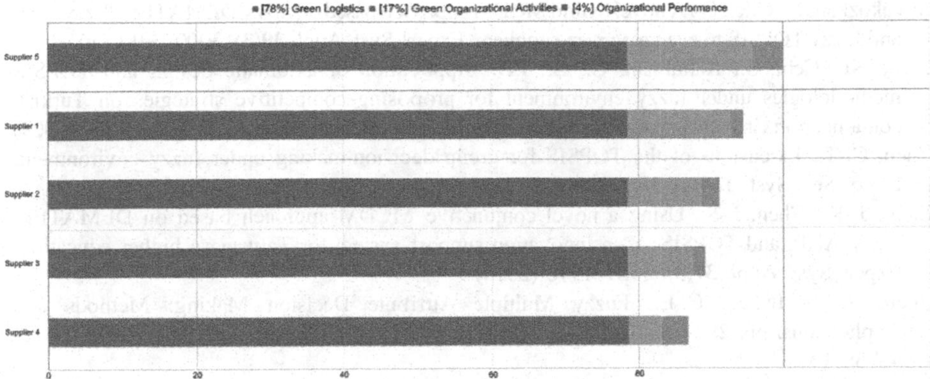

Fig. 2. Green supplier selection output

5 Conclusion

In this study MCDM combined approach is focused to analyze the green supplier. Mixed MCDM approach enabled organizations to choose the optimal green supplier among all available suppliers based on scientific method, which will reduce the error of supplier selection. Because the selection of best green supplier will enhance the effectiveness of green supply-chain management practices in organizations.

Fuzzy ANP and fuzzy DEMATEL approaches give a lot support to take accurate decisions. Considering that both approaches used to design and select different criteria based on interdependent relationships among different attributes. Moreover, in this study fuzzy TOPSIS approach is also used to enhance the effectiveness of decision up to ideal stage to solve the problems.

In this study, the general hybrid MCDM model focused on green supplier selection criteria was developed. This general model can be used to implement different fields of studies to solve complex problems. This study also validates the previous study with the help of in-depth literature review and opinion of industrial experts (Büyüközkan and Çifçi 2012). Because no data has been collected during this study. Because the scope of this study is limited to only the development of general model focused on green supplier selection criteria. So, data collection is out of scope for this study but in future studies, data can be collected and interpreted in tables to resolve the specific problem.

References

Aiello, G., Enea, M., Galante, G., La Scalia, G.: Clean agent selection approached by fuzzy TOPSIS decision-making method. Fire Technol. **45**(4), 405 (2009)

Awasthi, A., Chauhan, S.S., Goyal, S.K.: A fuzzy multicriteria approach for evaluating environmental performance of suppliers. Int. J. Prod. Econ. **126**(2), 370–378 (2010)

Bai, C., Sarkis, J.: Green supplier development: analytical evaluation using rough set theory. J. Clean. Prod. **18**(12), 1200–1210 (2010)

Büyüközkan, G., Çifçi, G.: A novel hybrid MCDM approach based on fuzzy DEMATEL, fuzzy ANP and fuzzy TOPSIS to evaluate green suppliers. Expert Syst. Appl. **39**(3), 3000–3011 (2012)
Celik, M., Cebi, S., Kahraman, C., Er, I.D.: Application of axiomatic design and TOPSIS methodologies under fuzzy environment for proposing competitive strategies on Turkish container ports in maritime transportation network. Expert Syst. Appl. **36**(3), 4541–4557 (2009)
Chen, C.-T.: Extensions of the TOPSIS for group decision-making under fuzzy environment. Fuzzy Sets Syst. **114**(1), 1–9 (2000)
Chen, J.-K., Chen, I.-S.: Using a novel conjunctive MCDM approach based on DEMATEL, fuzzy ANP, and TOPSIS as an innovation support system for Taiwanese higher education. Expert Syst. Appl. **37**(3), 1981–1990 (2010)
Chen, S.-J., Hwang, C.-L.: Fuzzy Multiple Attribute Decision Making: Methods and Applications, pp. 289–486. Springer, Heidelberg (1992). https://doi.org/10.1007/978-3-642-46768-4
Chen-Yi, H., Ke-Ting, C., Gwo-Hshiung, T.: FMCDM with fuzzy DEMATEL approach for customers' choice behavior model. Int. J. Fuzzy Syst. **9**(4) (2007)
Gabus, A., Fontela, E.: World problems, an invitation to further thought within the framework of DEMATEL. Battelle Geneva Research Center, Geneva, Switzerland (1972)
Gabus, A., Fontela, E.: Perceptions of the world problematique: communication procedure, communicating with those bearing collective responsibility. Battelle Geneva Research Centre, Geneva, Switzerland (1973)
Goosey, M.: End-of-life electronics legislation–an industry perspective. Circ. World **30**(2), 41–45 (2004)
Gumus, A.T.: Evaluation of hazardous waste transportation firms by using a two step fuzzy-AHP and TOPSIS methodology. Expert Syst. Appl. **36**(2), 4067–4074 (2009)
Handfield, R., Walton, S.V., Sroufe, R., Melnyk, S.A.: Applying environmental criteria to supplier assessment: a study in the application of the Analytical Hierarchy Process. Eur. J. Oper. Res. **141**(1), 70–87 (2002)
He, S., Chaudhry, S.S., Lei, Z., Baohua, W.: Stochastic vendor selection problem: chance-constrained model and genetic algorithms. Ann. Oper. Res. **168**(1), 169–179 (2009)
Iç, Y.T., Yurdakul, M.: Development of a quick credibility scoring decision support system using fuzzy TOPSIS. Expert Syst. Appl. **37**(1), 567–574 (2010)
Jabbour, A.B.L., Jabbour, C.J.: Are supplier selection criteria going green? Case studies of companies in Brazil. Ind. Manag. Data Syst. **109**(4), 477–495 (2009)
Kelemenis, A., Askounis, D.: A new TOPSIS-based multi-criteria approach to personnel selection. Expert Syst. Appl. **37**(7), 4999–5008 (2010)
Ketchen, D.J., Hult, G.T.M.: Bridging organization theory and supply chain management: the case of best value supply chains. J. Oper. Manag. **25**(2), 573–580 (2007)
Kuo, M.-S., Tzeng, G.-H., Huang, W.-C.: Group decision-making based on concepts of ideal and anti-ideal points in a fuzzy environment. Math. Comput. Model. **45**(3–4), 324–339 (2007)
Kuo, R.J., Wang, Y.C., Tien, F.C.: Integration of artificial neural network and MADA methods for green supplier selection. J. Clean. Prod. **18**(12), 1161–1170 (2010)
Lee, A.H., Kang, H.-Y., Hsu, C.-F., Hung, H.-C.: A green supplier selection model for high-tech industry. Expert Syst. Appl. **36**(4), 7917–7927 (2009)
Lin, R.-H.: An integrated FANP–MOLP for supplier evaluation and order allocation. Applied Mathematical Modelling **33**(6), 2730–2736 (2009)
Lin, C.-L., Hsieh, M.-S., Tzeng, G.-H.: Evaluating vehicle telematics system by using a novel MCDM techniques with dependence and feedback. Expert Syst. Appl. **37**(10), 6723–6736 (2010)
Lu, L.Y., Wu, C., Kuo, T.-C.: Environmental principles applicable to green supplier evaluation by using multi-objective decision analysis. Int. J. Prod. Res. **45**(18–19), 4317–4331 (2007)

Önüt, S., Gülsün, B., Tuzkaya, U.R., Tuzkaya, G.: A two-phase possibilistic linear programming methodology for multi-objective supplier evaluation and order allocation problems. Inf. Sci. **178**(2), 485–500 (2008)

Önüt, S., Kara, S.S., Işik, E.: Long term supplier selection using a combined fuzzy MCDM approach: a case study for a telecommunication company. Expert Syst. Appl. **36**(2), 3887–3895 (2009)

Programme E.U.R.D.F.I.E.O. (2017). Transparent Choice: https://www.transparentchoice.com/

Punniyamoorthy, M., Mathiyalagan, P., Parthiban, P.: A strategic model using structural equation modeling and fuzzy logic in supplier selection. Expert Syst. Appl. **38**(1), 458–474 (2011)

Ramik, J.: A decision system using ANP and fuzzy inputs. Paper Presented at the 12th International Conference on the Foundations and Applications of Utility, Risk and Decision Theory, Roma (2006)

Roghanian, E., Rahimi, J., Ansari, A.: Comparison of first aggregation and last aggregation in fuzzy group TOPSIS. Appl. Math. Model. **34**(12), 3754–3766 (2010)

Saaty, T.L.: The Analytic Network Process: Decision Making with Dependence and Feedback; the Organization and Prioritization of Complexity. RWS Publications (1996)

Sarkis, J., Meade, L.M., Talluri, S.: E-logistics and the natural environment. Supply Chain Manag.: Int. J. **9**(4), 303–312 (2004)

Sevkli, M., Lenny Koh, S., Zaim, S., Demirbag, M., Tatoglu, E.: An application of data envelopment analytic hierarchy process for supplier selection: a case study of BEKO in Turkey. Int. J. Prod. Res. **45**(9), 1973–2003 (2007)

Simpson, D.F., Power, D.J.: Use the supply relationship to develop lean and green suppliers. Supply Chain Manag.: Int. J. **10**(1), 60–68 (2005)

Srivastava, S.K.: Green supply-chain management: a state-of-the-art literature review. Int. J. Manag. Rev. **9**(1), 53–80 (2007)

Sun, C.-C., Lin, G.T.: Using fuzzy TOPSIS method for evaluating the competitive advantages of shopping websites. Expert Syst. Appl. **36**(9), 11764–11771 (2009)

Theyel, G.: Customer and supplier relations for environmental performance. In: Sarkis, J. (ed.) Greening the Supply Chain, pp. 139–150. Springer, London (2006). https://doi.org/10.1007/1-84628-299-3_8

Tsai, W.-H., Hung, S.-J.: A fuzzy goal programming approach for green supply chain optimisation under activity-based costing and performance evaluation with a value-chain structure. Int. J. Prod. Res. **47**(18), 4991–5017 (2009)

Tseng, M.-L.: Using the extension of DEMATEL to integrate hotel service quality perceptions into a cause–effect model in uncertainty. Expert Syst. Appl. **36**(5), 9015–9023 (2009)

Tuzkaya, G., Ozgen, A., Ozgen, D., Tuzkaya, U.R.: Environmental performance evaluation of suppliers: a hybrid fuzzy multi-criteria decision approach. Int. J. Environ. Sci. Technol. **6**(3), 477–490 (2009)

Tuzkaya, U.R., Önüt, S.: A fuzzy analytic network process based approach to transportation-mode selection between Turkey and Germany: a case study. Inf. Sci. **178**(15), 3133–3146 (2008)

Van Hoek, R.I.: From reversed logistics to green supply chains. Supply Chain Manag.: Int. J. **4** (3), 129–135 (1999)

Vinodh, S., Ramiya, R.A., Gautham, S.: Application of fuzzy analytic network process for supplier selection in a manufacturing organisation. Expert Syst. Appl. **38**(1), 272–280 (2011)

Wu, D.: Supplier selection: a hybrid model using DEA, decision tree and neural network. Expert Syst. Appl. **36**(5), 9105–9112 (2009)

Yüksel, İ., Dağdeviren, M.: Using the fuzzy analytic network process (ANP) for Balanced Scorecard (BSC): a case study for a manufacturing firm. Expert Syst. Appl. **37**(2), 1270–1278 (2010)

A Quadratic Model for the Kurtosis of Decay Centrality

Natarajan Meghanathan(✉)

Computer Science, Jackson State University, Mailbox 18839, Jackson, MS, USA
natarajan.meghanathan@jsums.edu

Abstract. Decay centrality (DEC) is a measure of the closeness of a node to the rest of the nodes in the network, with the importance given to the distance weighted on the basis of a decay parameter, δ ($0 < \delta < 1$). Kurtosis has been traditionally used to evaluate the extent of fat-tailedness of the degree distribution of the vertices in a complex network. In this paper, we compute the Kurtosis of the decay centrality of the vertices in real-world networks for the entire range of δ values and observe the Kurtosis(DEC_δ)/Kurtosis(DEG) ratio to be simply a quadratic function of δ (of the form: $a * \delta^2 + b * \delta + c$, with $a > 0$, $b < 0$ and c in the vicinity of 1.0). We estimate the coefficients a, b and c of the quadratic models for a suite of 70 real-world networks of diverse degree distributions, with R^2 values of at least 0.99. Using the coefficients a, b and c of the quadratic model for a real-world network, we could estimate the $\delta_{critical}$ value (given by: $-b/2a$) for which the Kurtosis($DEC_{\delta critical}$)/Kurtosis(DEG) ratio is the lowest (given by: $c - b^2/4a$) for the real-world network.

Keywords: Decay centrality · Quadratic model · Kurtosis · Degree centrality
Complex networks

1 Introduction

The decay centrality (DEC) metric [1] is a measure of the closeness of a vertex to the rest of the vertices in the network, with the distance weighed with respect to a decay parameter, δ ($0 < \delta < 1$). The DEC metric for a vertex v_i is computed as [1]: $DEC_\delta(v_i) = \sum_{v_i \neq v_j} \delta^{d(v_i, v_j)}$ where $d(v_i, v_j)$ is the distance between nodes v_i and v_j. Unlike the commonly studied centrality metrics (such as degree, eigenvector, closeness and betweenness centralities), the decay centrality metric is a parameter-driven centrality metric and the extent of importance given to the distance (in the form of the decay parameter δ) could affect the distribution of the decay centrality values of the vertices.

In the context of complex network analysis, Kurtosis [2] has been traditionally used to quantify the extent of fat-tailedness in the degree distribution of the vertices. In this paper, we apply the Kurtosis measure to quantify the extent of fat-tailedness in the distribution of the decay centrality values of the vertices for the entire range of δ values (varied from 0.01 to 0.99) for a suite of 70 real-world networks of diverse degree distributions. We make use of the results from recent studies [3] that the decay centrality metric exhibits a very strong correlation with degree centrality (DEG) for δ

P. Bhattacharyya et al. (Eds.): NGCT 2017, CCIS 827, pp. 176–189, 2018.
https://doi.org/10.1007/978-981-10-8657-1_14

values closer to 0 and attempt to model the Kurtosis(DEC$_\delta$)/Kurtosis(DEG) ratio for the entire range of δ values for each of the 70 real-world networks. We observe the Kurtosis(DEC$_\delta$)/Kurtosis(DEG) ratio to be a quadratic function (modeled as: $a * \delta^2 + b * \delta + c$) of the decay parameter δ, and the modeling accuracy in the form of the R^2 value is at least 0.99 for each real-world network. We observe the values of the coefficients 'a' and 'b' (of the quadratic model) to be greater than 0 and less than 0 respectively for any real-world network. The positive values for the coefficient 'a' indicate that the Kurtosis(DEC$_\delta$)/Kurtosis(DEG) ratio values tend to first decrease (with increase in δ from 0.01 to $\delta_{critical} \leq 0.99$) and then possibly increase (with increase in δ from $\delta_{critical}$ onwards) for each of the 70 real-world networks. Such an "open up" quadratic model for the Kurtosis(DEC$_\delta$)/Kurtosis(DEG) ratio indicates that the inclusion of distance values greater than 1.0 (in the decay centrality computation) indeed contributes to a decrease in the extent of fat-tailedness in the decay centrality values of the vertices vis-a-vis degree centrality. Depending on the real-world network, the decrease in the Kurtosis(DEC$_\delta$)/Kurtosis(DEG) ratio values may last for the entire range of δ values or be only up to a certain δ value (referred to as $\delta_{critical}$).

Using the coefficients a, b and c quadratic model ($a * \delta^2 + b * \delta + c$) for the Kurtosis (DEC$_\delta$)/Kurtosis(DEG) ratio for a real-world network, we could estimate the critical value of the decay parameter δ (computed as: $\delta_{critical} = -b/2a$) until which the Kurtosis (DEC$_\delta$)/Kurtosis(DEG) ratio decreases and above which the Kurtosis(DEC$_\delta$)/Kurtosis (DEG) ratio increases as well as the maximum Kurtosis reduction ratio, which we define as one minus the lowest possible value for the Kurtosis(DEC$_\delta$)/Kurtosis(DEG) ratio $\{1 - (c - b^2/4a)\}$. The maximum Kurtosis reduction ratio is a measure of the contribution of the path lengths (especially, the path lengths that are greater than one) towards lowering the fat-tailedness of the decay centrality distribution vis-a-vis the degree centrality distribution. Note that one could obtain the above estimates for a real-world network with just the empirical quadratic model listed for the real-world network and there is no need to compute either the decay centrality metric or the degree centrality metric.

The rest of the paper is organized as follows: Sect. 2 illustrates the computation of the decay centrality of the vertices in an example graph for a particular δ value and the corresponding Kurtosis value. Section 3 presents the modeling of the Kurtosis(DEC$_\delta$)/ Kurtosis(DEG) ratio for the example graph of Sect. 2 as a quadratic function of δ. Section 4 presents the 70 real-world networks chosen for the analysis and presents the quadratic model for each of them as well as compares the estimates of the measures listed above with their actual values. Section 5 discusses related work on the use of Kurtosis for centrality metrics. Section 6 concludes the paper. Throughout the paper, the terms 'node' and 'vertex', 'link' and 'edge', 'network' and 'graph' are used interchangeably. They mean the same.

2 Decay Centrality and Kurtosis

In this section, we use an example graph (see Fig. 1) to first illustrate the computation of the decay centrality of the vertices (see Fig. 1) for different values of δ and then show the computation of the Kurtosis (see Fig. 2) of the decay centralities obtained for a particular δ value.

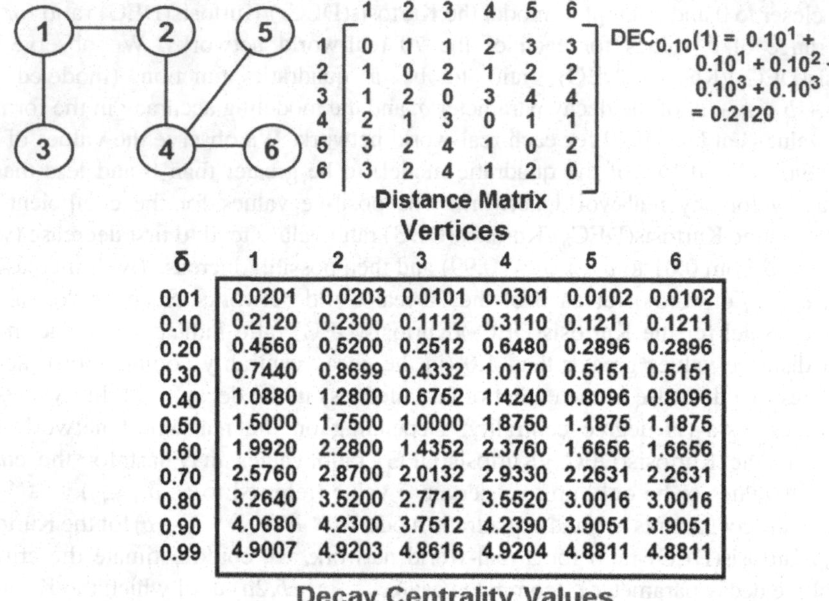

	1	2	3	4	5	6
1	0	1	1	2	3	3
2	1	0	2	1	2	2
3	1	2	0	3	4	4
4	2	1	3	0	1	1
5	3	2	4	1	0	2
6	3	2	4	1	2	0

δ	1	2	3	4	5	6
0.01	0.0201	0.0203	0.0101	0.0301	0.0102	0.0102
0.10	0.2120	0.2300	0.1112	0.3110	0.1211	0.1211
0.20	0.4560	0.5200	0.2512	0.6480	0.2896	0.2896
0.30	0.7440	0.8699	0.4332	1.0170	0.5151	0.5151
0.40	1.0880	1.2800	0.6752	1.4240	0.8096	0.8096
0.50	1.5000	1.7500	1.0000	1.8750	1.1875	1.1875
0.60	1.9920	2.2800	1.4352	2.3760	1.6656	1.6656
0.70	2.5760	2.8700	2.0132	2.9330	2.2631	2.2631
0.80	3.2640	3.5200	2.7712	3.5520	3.0016	3.0016
0.90	4.0680	4.2300	3.7512	4.2390	3.9051	3.9051
0.99	4.9007	4.9203	4.8616	4.9204	4.8811	4.8811

Fig. 1. An example to compute the decay centrality of the vertices

The decay centrality of a vertex v_i for a particular value of the decay parameter δ is computed as [1]: $\mathrm{DEC}_\delta(v_i) = \sum_{v_i \neq v_j} \delta^{d(v_i,v_j)}$ where d(v_i, v_j) is the distance (typically, the minimum number of hops on the shortest path, as is also used in this paper) from node v_i to node v_j. The importance given to the distance from node v_i to each of the other nodes is controlled by the decay parameter δ ($0 < \delta < 1$). The larger the value for δ, the larger the importance given to nodes that are farther away from the node for which the decay centrality is computed. Nodes with higher decay centrality are considered to have several neighbors as well as be closer to the rest of the nodes in the network [4].

Figure 1 presents an example graph of six vertices and the distance matrix (indicating the minimum number of hops on the shortest path between any two vertices). We show the application of the decay centrality formulation to compute the decay centrality for vertex 1 with respect to δ = 0.10. Finally, we present the decay centrality values for all the six vertices with respect to δ values ranging from 0.10 to 0.90, in increments of 0.10, as well as for the extreme δ values of 0.01 and 0.99.

The formulation (Eq. 1) to compute the Kurtosis values for a centrality metric is explained as follows: Let *C*(*i*) be the value of the centrality metric for vertex *i*, where $1 \leq i \leq N$, and *N* is the number of vertices in the network. We denote μ_C to be the average of the centrality values of the vertices. The notation E(…) denotes the average of the entries considered. Figure 2 presents the calculation of the Kurtosis values for the decay centrality metric (*C* = *DEC*) of the vertices in the example graph of Fig. 1 with respect to δ = 0.20.

$$Kurtosis(C) = \frac{E\left[\left(\underset{1 \le i \le N}{C[i]} - \mu_C\right)^4\right]}{\left(E\left[\left(\underset{1 \le i \le N}{C[i]} - \mu_C\right)^2\right]\right)^2} \quad (1)$$

Vertex	DEC $_{\delta=0.20}$	$(DEC_{\delta=0.20} - \mu_{DEC})^2$	$(DEC_{\delta=0.20} - \mu_{DEC})^4$
1	0.4560	0.002200	0.000005
2	0.5200	0.012299	0.000151
3	0.2512	0.024932	0.000622
4	0.6480	0.057073	0.003257
5	0.2896	0.014280	0.000204
6	0.2896	0.014280	0.000204
Avg.	0.4091 μ_{DEC}	0.020844	0.000740

$$Kurtosis(DEC_{\delta=0.20}) = \frac{E[(DEC_{\delta=0.20} - \mu_{DEC})^4]}{(E[(DEC_{\delta=0.20} - \mu_{DEC})^2])^2} = \frac{0.000740}{(0.020844)^2} = 1.7032$$

Fig. 2. Sample illustration to compute the Kurtosis of the decay centrality of the vertices in the example graph of Fig. 1

3 Quadratic Model for the Kurtosis of Decay Centrality

Based on results of the empirical modeling of the Kurtosis values of the decay centrality (DEC) of the vertices for the entire range of $\delta \in (0, 1)$ values for a suite of 70 real-world networks, we hypothesize that the Kurtosis(DEC_δ) of the vertices is a quadratic function of the decay parameter δ. More specifically, we show that for any real-world network, Kurtosis(DEC_δ)/Kurtosis(DEG) = $a * \delta^2 + b * \delta + c$, where Kurtosis(DEG) is a constant for a particular real-world network (i.e., does not depend on the value of δ) and the coefficients a, b and c decide the contour of the quadratic curve for the real-world network. In this section, we illustrate the development of the quadratic model for the example graph of Fig. 1 and introduce the critical estimates one could arrive at about the decay parameter, Kurtosis measure and the contribution of the path lengths. In Sect. 4, we do the same for a suite of 70 real-world networks of diverse degree distributions.

Figure 3 lists the Kurtosis values for the entire range δ = {0.01, 0.10, 0.20, …, 0.90, 0.99} values shown in Fig. 1. Note that we also list the value of the ratio Kurtosis (DEC$_\delta$)/Kurtosis(DEG) for the above eleven δ values, wherein Kurtosis(DEG) = 2.04. The Kurtosis(DEC$_\delta$)/Kurtosis(DEG) ratio starts with a value closer to 1.0 (attributed to the very strong positive correlation [3] between degree centrality and decay centrality of the vertices computed for δ values closer to 0) and then decreases with increase in δ. After a critical value of δ ($\delta_{critical}$; observed to be in the vicinity of 0.50 … 0.70 for the graph in Fig. 1), the Kurtosis(DEC$_\delta$)/Kurtosis(DEG) ratio values display a trend of increase with further increase in δ. This is the typical nature of the δ vs. Kurtosis(DEC$_\delta$)/Kurtosis(DEG) ratio distribution observed for the real-world networks in this paper.

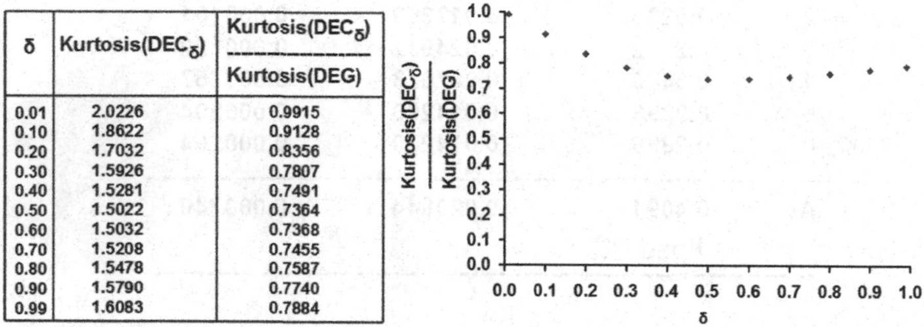

δ	Kurtosis(DEC$_\delta$)	Kurtosis(DEC$_\delta$) / Kurtosis(DEG)
0.01	2.0226	0.9915
0.10	1.8622	0.9128
0.20	1.7032	0.8356
0.30	1.5926	0.7807
0.40	1.5281	0.7491
0.50	1.5022	0.7364
0.60	1.5032	0.7368
0.70	1.5208	0.7455
0.80	1.5478	0.7587
0.90	1.5790	0.7740
0.99	1.6083	0.7884

Fig. 3. Distribution of the δ vs. Kurtosis(DEC$_\delta$)/Kurtosis(DEG) ratio values for the example graph of Fig. 1

We now describe the two estimates that could be obtained with just the coefficients '*a*', '*b*' and '*c*' of the quadratic model for the Kurtosis of the decay centrality metric for a real-world network:

(i) Critical δ Value: For every real-world network analyzed, the values of the coefficients '*a*' and '*b*' of the quadratic model are positive and negative respectively. This indicates the quadratic curve is of the "open up" type and there exists a critical δ value ($\delta_{critical}$) until which the Kurtosis(DEC$_\delta$)/Kurtosis(DEG) ratio value decreases (as δ increases past 0.0) and beyond which the Kurtosis(DEC$_\delta$)/ Kurtosis(DEG) ratio value either almost remains the same or shows an appreciable trend to increase (as δ increases towards 1.0). The value of $\delta_{critical}$ could be obtained by setting the derivative of the quadratic function of δ to zero and solving for δ. That is, we set $\frac{d}{d\delta}\left(a\delta^2 + b\delta + c\right) = 0$ to obtain $\delta_{critical} = \frac{-b}{2a}$.

(ii) Maximum Kurtosis Reduction Ratio: The Kurtosis(DEC$_\delta$)/Kurtosis(DEG) ratio will be the lowest at $\delta = \delta_{critical}$. Hence, we can set $\delta = -b/2a$ in the quadratic model $a * \delta^2 + b * \delta + c$ to obtain Kurtosis(DEC$_{\delta critical}$) = Kurtosis(DEG) * $(c - b^2/4a)$. The maximum Kurtosis reduction ratio is defined as: 1 − Kurtosis (DEC$_{\delta critical}$)/Kurtosis(DEG) = $1 - (c - b^2/4a)$. The lower the value for the

Kurtosis($DEC_{\delta critical}$)/Kurtosis(DEG) ratio, the larger the value for the maximum Kurtosis reduction ratio. The magnitude of the maximum Kurtosis reduction ratio could also be construed as a quantitative measure of the effectiveness of the path lengths (especially, those greater than one) incorporated in the decay centrality formulation towards reducing the fat-tailedness of the decay centrality distribution vis-a-vis the degree centrality distribution.

We fit the δ vs. Kurtosis(DEC_{δ})/Kurtosis(DEG) ratio values as a quadratic curve of the form: $a * \delta^2 + b * \delta + c$. The R^2 values for all the fits developed in this paper are above 0.99. Note that for illustration purposes, we use only δ values of 0.01, 0.10, 0.20, …, 0.90, 0.99 (i.e., a total of eleven δ values) and the corresponding Kurtosis (DEC_{δ})/Kurtosis(DEG) ratios to fit the quadratic curve. Though the accuracy of the model is expected to increase with the number of δ values (dependent on the increment in the δ values) and their corresponding Kurtosis(DEC_{δ})/Kurtosis(DEG) ratios, we notice from Table 1 that for the example graph of Fig. 1: if we target a precision of two decimal digits for the R^2 value as well as for the estimates of $\delta_{critical}$ and the maximum Kurtosis reduction ratio, an increment of 0.01 for the δ values is sufficient. For the real-world networks analyzed in Sect. 4, we use the entire range of δ values from: 0.01, 0.02, …, 0.99 (i.e., in increments of 0.01) and the corresponding Kurtosis(DEC_{δ})/ Kurtosis(DEG) ratios to fit the quadratic model.

Table 1. Impact of the increment in δ value on the coefficients of the quadratic model and estimates of the $\delta_{critical}$ and maximum Kurtosis reduction ratio

Increment in δ value	'a'	'b'	'c'	R^2 value	Estimate of $\delta_{critical}$	Estimate of maximum Kurtosis reduction ratio
0.10000	0.98982	−0.86749	0.71288	0.99648	0.51000	0.27409
0.01000	0.98106	−0.81586	0.65568	0.99829	0.54000	0.27273
0.00100	0.97983	−0.70934	0.64889	0.99970	0.54400	0.27254
0.00010	0.97969	−0.70860	0.64812	0.99998	0.54369	0.27251
0.00001	0.97969	−0.70860	0.64813	0.99999	0.54369	0.27251

4 Real-World Networks and Their Analysis

In this section, we use a suite of 70 real-world networks of diverse degree distributions (whose spectral radius ratio for node degree ranges from 1 to 25) [5] to conduct the Kurtosis analysis and present the empirical quadratic model to estimate the Kurtosis of the decay centrality metric as a function of the decay parameter δ. The types of the networks analyzed range from social networks to biological networks. For a more detailed description of the different networks, the interested reader is referred to [13]. Table 2 lists the number of nodes and edges for the real-world networks.

Table 2. Fundamental information about the real-world networks used in the Kurtosis analysis

#	Net.	#nodes	#edges	#	Net.	#nodes	#edges
1	TEN	22	39	36	CGD	259	640
2	KCN	34	78	37	APN	332	2126
3	DLN	37	81	38	ERD	433	1314
4	MPN	35	117	39	MSJ	475	625
5	SWC	35	118	40	HIV	1005	1189
6	FHT	33	91	41	ROG	1022	3648
7	MMN	30	61	42	MTN	1130	2403
8	KFP	37	85	43	RVU	1133	10903
9	WSB	43	336	44	ERN	1174	1417
10	FTC	48	170	45	PGI	1203	1205
11	TWF	47	77	46	YIN	1278	1809
12	DON	62	159	47	YPN	1407	4083
13	PFN	67	142	48	NDN	1421	7710
14	MTB	64	295	49	PBL	1490	16715
15	GLN	67	118	50	LCI	1536	2925
16	HCN	76	302	51	JDN	1538	8032
17	SJN	75	155	52	ETN	1552	3123
18	LMN	77	254	53	NSC	1589	2742
19	UKF	83	578	54	DMN	1781	8911
20	CFN	89	407	55	HTR	1837	6896
21	SPR	92	477	56	TCS	1882	1740
22	PBN	105	441	57	WEN	1976	17235
23	ADJ	112	425	58	IUI	2288	2969
24	FON	115	613	59	YPI	2361	6646
25	CLN	118	613	60	RGI	2640	3263
26	AKN	140	494	61	CND	2749	13578
27	MUN	167	301	62	ODL	2909	16377
28	GD96	180	228	63	WAJ	3177	8300
29	JBN	198	2742	64	CGI	3879	4554
30	FMH	147	202	65	SGI	4092	10160
31	RHF	217	1839	66	TND	4275	7874
32	SDI	230	359	67	YTN	4441	12873
33	CEN	297	2148	68	AIN	4866	11373
34	DRN	212	284	69	ARX	5242	28980
35	ISP	309	1924	70	MGI	7747	10375

Table 3. Coefficients of the quadratic model, the R^2 value and the estimates

#	Net.	‘a’	‘b’	‘c’	R^2 value	Estimate of $\delta_{critical}$	Estimate of max. Kurtosis reduction ratio
1	TEN	0.8143	−1.0660	0.9730	0.9985	0.6546	0.3759
2	KCN	1.2799	−1.7630	1.0040	0.9996	0.6887	0.6031
3	DLN	1.5345	−0.7860	0.9353	0.9998	0.2561	0.1654
4	MPN	0.3530	−0.7537	1.0178	1.0000	0.9677	0.3845
5	SWC	0.9298	−0.9450	0.9678	0.9983	0.5082	0.2723
6	FHT	3.8412	−1.3262	0.8830	0.9976	0.1726	0.2314
7	MMN	1.0932	−1.2091	0.8413	0.9917	0.5530	0.4930
8	KFP	3.7189	−2.7371	1.0870	0.9998	0.3680	0.4167
9	WSB	0.1557	−0.1400	0.9995	0.9999	0.4495	0.0319
10	FTC	0.6694	−0.3224	0.9467	0.9990	0.2408	0.0921
11	TWF	1.5491	−0.4917	1.0053	0.9954	0.1587	0.0338
12	DON	1.7559	−0.9711	1.0237	0.9998	0.2765	0.1106
13	PFN	1.4423	−1.1955	0.9567	0.9996	0.4144	0.2910
14	MTB	3.6837	−2.3678	0.9844	0.9967	0.3214	0.3961
15	GLN	1.8489	−2.2320	0.8985	0.9957	0.6036	0.7751
16	HCN	2.1779	−2.1698	0.8401	0.9917	0.4982	0.7003
17	SJN	0.8152	−1.4396	1.1187	1.0000	0.8829	0.5169
18	LMN	1.0994	−1.6942	0.9736	0.9996	0.7705	0.6791
19	UKF	0.6353	−0.8178	0.9588	0.9985	0.6436	0.3043
20	CFN	0.3970	−1.0463	1.0457	0.9999	0.9177	0.6436
21	SPR	1.2156	−1.2351	0.8637	0.9965	0.5080	0.4501
22	PBN	0.9047	−1.1535	0.9752	0.9984	0.6375	0.3925
23	ADJ	1.4417	−1.8957	0.7869	0.9978	0.6575	0.8363
24	FON	0.7541	−0.8159	0.6964	0.9940	0.5410	0.5243
25	CLN	2.2853	−1.8794	0.7805	0.9909	0.4112	0.6059
26	AKN	1.6821	−2.0664	0.9150	0.9991	0.6142	0.7196
27	MUN	1.8456	−2.7943	1.1471	0.9996	0.7570	0.9106
28	GD96	1.6597	−2.3729	0.9126	0.9988	0.7149	0.9356
29	JBN	3.0738	−1.3130	0.9343	1.0000	0.2136	0.2059
30	FMH	1.1401	−1.9599	1.0045	0.9999	0.8595	0.8377
31	RHF	1.0581	−1.1483	0.8147	0.9965	0.5426	0.4968
32	SDI	2.5572	−2.7598	1.1870	1.0000	0.5396	0.5576
33	CEN	1.5674	−2.0406	0.7428	0.9972	0.6510	0.9214
34	DRN	1.3853	−2.2724	1.0609	0.9999	0.8202	0.8711
35	ISP	2.1780	−1.8997	0.9528	0.9998	0.4361	0.4615
36	CGD	1.8097	−1.8932	0.9667	0.9944	0.5231	0.5285
37	APN	1.6461	−1.9673	0.8203	0.9980	0.5976	0.7676
38	ERD	2.9381	−2.8641	0.9571	0.9977	0.4874	0.7408
39	MSJ	0.6253	−1.4524	1.0387	1.0000	0.9613	0.8046
40	HIV	1.7473	−2.2444	0.6474	0.9963	0.6422	0.9267

(*continued*)

Table 3. (*continued*)

#	Net.	'*a*'	'*b*'	'*c*'	R^2 value	Estimate of $\delta_{critical}$	Estimate of max. Kurtosis reduction ratio
41	ROG	16.5540	−10.570	1.8448	1.0000	0.3193	0.8426
42	MTN	4.4263	−3.8916	0.7495	0.9907	0.4396	0.8941
43	RVU	1.3326	−1.6052	0.8301	0.9982	0.6023	0.6533
44	ERN	1.3708	−2.0633	1.1471	0.9908	0.7526	0.6293
45	PGI	1.3339	−2.2104	1.1076	0.9999	0.8285	0.8081
46	YIN	1.7462	−2.2709	0.6823	0.9967	0.6502	0.9440
47	YPN	11.6093	−9.3313	1.3774	0.9939	0.4019	0.5023
48	NDN	1.3508	−2.2726	1.0456	0.9999	0.8412	0.9103
49	PBL	1.2185	−1.4038	0.4973	0.9937	0.5761	0.9070
50	LCI	1.8707	−2.6971	1.0540	0.9995	0.7209	0.9182
51	JDN	1.0407	−1.2875	0.3504	0.9963	0.6186	0.9523
52	ETN	1.2494	−1.5083	0.4013	0.9961	0.6036	0.9461
53	NSC	0.8005	−1.7068	1.0610	1.0000	0.9661	0.8489
54	DMN	1.1205	−1.1818	0.2728	1.0000	0.5274	0.9612
55	HTR	3.2879	−2.9147	0.5765	0.9976	0.4432	0.9305
56	TCS	1.9126	−2.6660	0.8931	0.9981	0.6970	0.9640
57	WEN	1.3630	−1.4011	0.3982	0.9926	0.5140	0.9618
58	IUI	1.4975	−2.4369	1.0733	0.9997	0.8136	0.9181
59	YPI	3.0378	−2.7695	0.7828	0.9971	0.4558	0.8484
60	RGI	1.2950	−1.6109	0.4366	0.9961	0.6219	0.9357
61	CND	1.1090	−1.3782	0.3726	0.9963	0.6213	0.9444
62	ODL	3.1345	−2.7373	0.4997	0.9931	0.4366	0.9020
63	WAJ	0.7449	−0.9097	0.2453	0.9966	0.6106	0.9675
64	CGI	0.9979	−1.2274	0.3250	0.9965	0.6150	0.9476
65	SGI	1.5022	−1.8917	0.5253	0.9960	0.6296	0.9297
66	TND	2.4555	−2.8112	0.8503	0.9980	0.5724	0.9543
67	YTN	1.0591	−1.3332	0.4006	0.9965	0.6294	0.9811
68	AIN	1.3108	−1.5667	0.4280	0.9960	0.5976	0.9599
69	ARX	2.0885	−2.9222	1.0781	0.9989	0.6996	0.9440
70	MGI	0.8698	−1.0655	0.2797	0.9968	0.6125	0.9535

Table 3 provides details the about quadratic model as a function of the decay parameter δ (in the form of: $a * \delta^2 + b * \delta + c$) for each of the 70 real-world networks as well as the R^2 value for the model and the presents estimates for the $\delta_{critical}$ and the maximum Kurtosis reduction ratio. The δ increment used to develop the dataset for the models is 0.01, with the δ values ranging from 0.01 to 0.99. We notice the values of coefficients '*a*' and '*b*' to be positive and negative respectively for all the 70 real-world networks, indicating the quadratic curve to be of "open up" nature and the presence of a critical δ value until which the Kurtosis($DEC_{\delta critical}$)/Kurtosis(DEG) ratio decreases and above which the ratio either remains almost the same or appreciably increases.

Figure 4 presents the distribution of the δ vs. the observed and estimated Kurtosis (DEC_δ)/Kurtosis(DEG) ratio values for selected real-world networks (covering the entire range of estimated $\delta_{critical}$ values). We observe the real-world networks to more likely incur an appreciable increase in the Kurtosis(DEC_δ)/Kurtosis(DEG) ratio after the $\delta_{critical}$ values if they have $\delta_{critical}$ values that are less than 0.50. For real-world networks with $\delta_{critical}$ values between 0.50 and 0.70, the Kurtosis(DEC_δ)/Kurtosis (DEG) ratio values do not incur a significant decrease until the $\delta_{critical}$ value as well as do not incur a significant increase beyond $\delta_{critical}$ and continue to remain the same almost throughout the entire range of δ values. For real-world networks with $\delta_{critical}$ values above 0.70, the Kurtosis(DEC_δ)/Kurtosis(DEG) ratio values decrease appreciably until the $\delta_{critical}$ value and remain about the same beyond the $\delta_{critical}$ value.

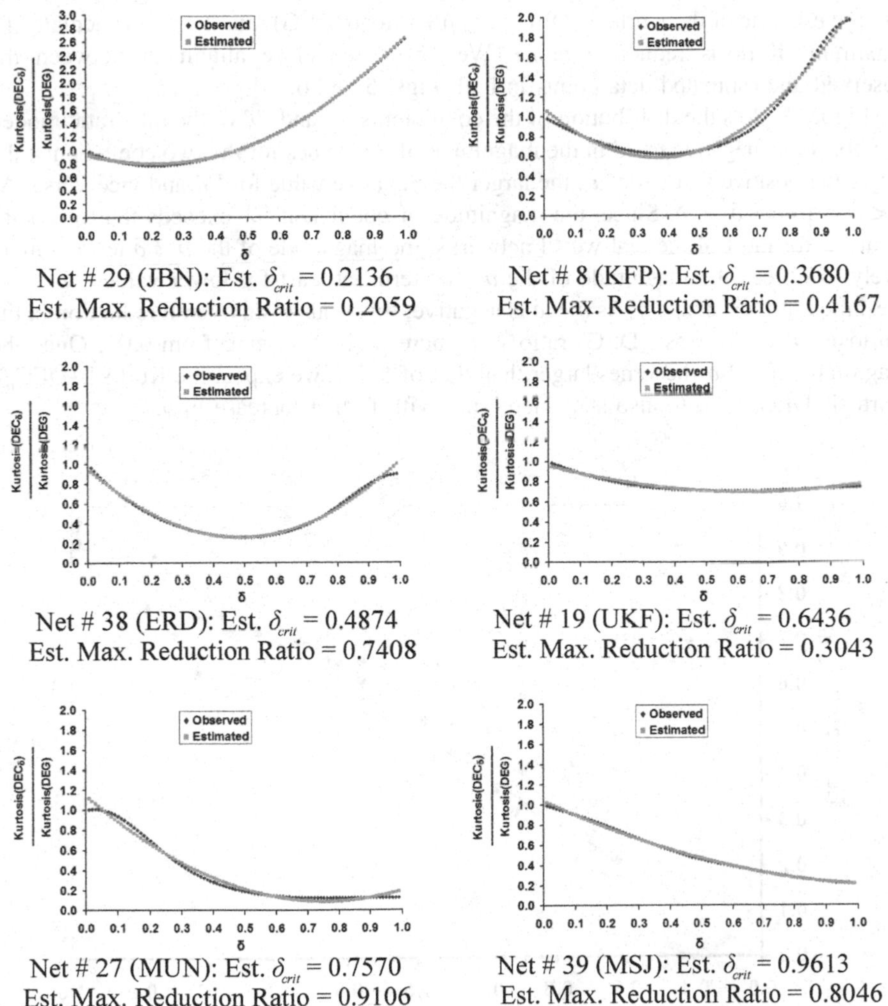

Fig. 4. Distribution of the δ vs. observed and estimated Kurtosis(DEC_δ)/Kurtosis(DEG) ratios for selected real-world networks (covering the entire range of estimated $\delta_{critical}$ values)

With regards to the estimated maximum Kurtosis reduction ratio, we observe the real-world networks to incur a lower reduction ratio for $\delta_{critical}$ values less than 0.30 and incur an appreciably larger reduction ratio for $\delta_{critical}$ values between 0.30 and 0.50. For real-world networks that do not go through a significant variation in the Kurtosis(DEC$_{\delta}$) values (those networks that have $\delta_{critical}$ between 0.5 and 0.7) below as well as above $\delta_{critical}$, the estimated maximum Kurtosis reduction ratio is also only moderate. As real-world networks with larger $\delta_{critical}$ values exhibit a larger reduction in the Kurtosis(DEC$_{\delta}$) values (at least until the $\delta_{critical}$ value), the estimated maximum Kurtosis reduction ratio is also larger for such networks.

Figure 5 compares the $\delta_{critical}$ value observed based on the dataset and the estimate of the $\delta_{critical}$ value obtained with the quadratic model. Figure 6 compares the lowest value for the Kurtosis(DEC$_{\delta critical}$)/Kurtosis(DEG) ratio observed based on the dataset and the estimate of the Kurtosis(DEC$_{\delta critical}$)/Kurtosis(DEG) ratio (which is actually 1 - maximum Kurtosis reduction ratio). We observe a close alignment between the observed and estimated data points in both Figs. 5 and 6.

Figure 7 plots the distribution of the coefficients '*a*' and '*b*' of the quadratic model. We observe a negative trend in the magnitude of the values for the two coefficients: the larger the positive value for '*a*', the larger the negative value for '*b*' and vice-versa. As $0 < \delta < 1 ==> \delta^2 < \delta$. Since, the magnitude of coefficient '*b*' exceeds that of coefficient '*a*' for most of the real-world networks, the magnitude of the $b * \delta$ term is more likely to exceed the magnitude of the $a * \delta^2$ term, at least for lower values of δ (we presume until $\delta = \delta_{critical}$). As $b * \delta$ is negative, this leads to an overall reduction in the Kurtosis(DEC$_{\delta}$)/Kurtosis(DEG) ratio with increase in δ starting from 0.01. Once the magnitude of $a * \delta^2$ becomes larger than that of $b * \delta$, we expect the Kurtosis(DEC$_{\delta}$)/Kurtosis(DEG) ratio to also start increasing with further increase in δ.

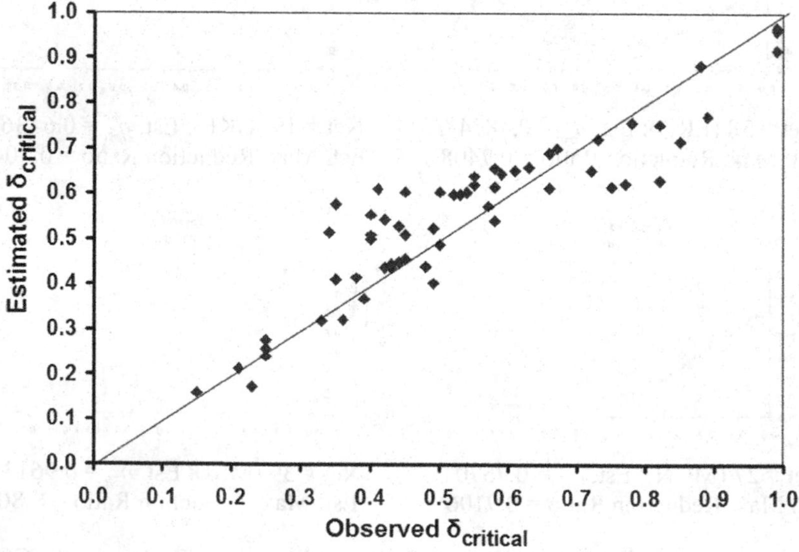

Fig. 5. Distribution of the observed $\delta_{critical}$ vs. estimated $\delta_{critical}$ values for real-world networks

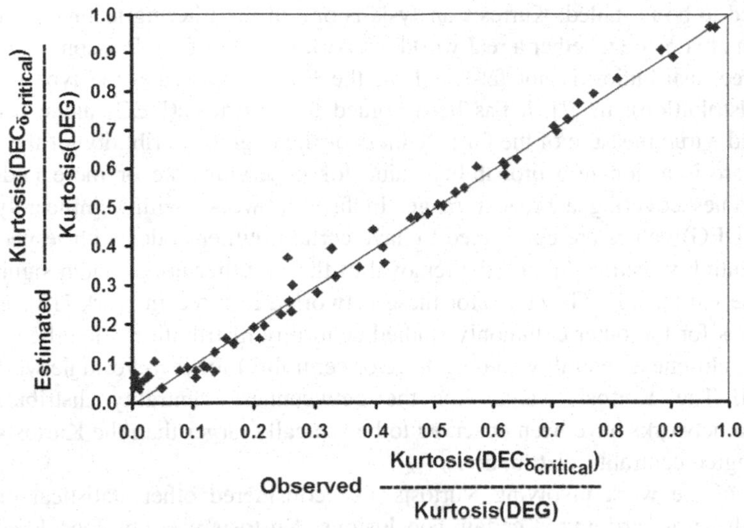

Fig. 6. Distribution of the observed Kurtosis(DEC$_{\delta critical}$)/Kurtosis(DEG) ratio vs. estimated Kurtosis(DEC$_{\delta critical}$)/Kurtosis(DEG) ratio for the real-world networks

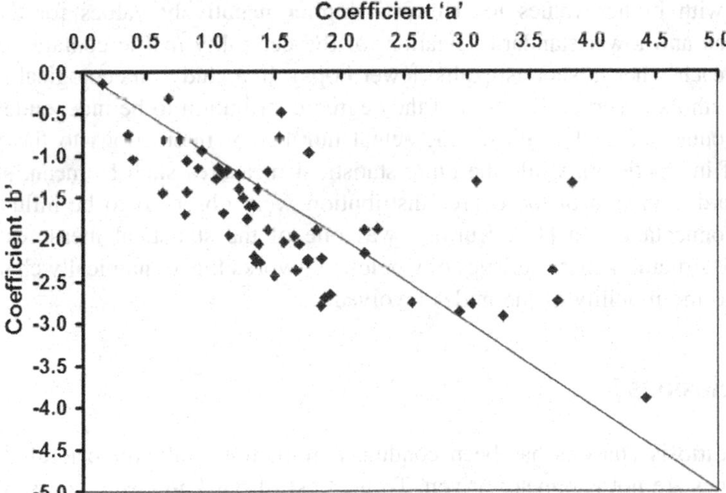

Fig. 7. Quadratic model ($a * \delta^2 + b * \delta + c$) for the Kurtosis of decay centrality metric for real-world networks: comparison of coefficients '*a*' and '*b*'

5 Related Work

In the context of complex network analysis, Kurtosis has been typically used to quantify the extent of fat-tailedness in the degree distribution of the vertices [2, 6]. In the context of degree centrality, networks with Kurtosis(DEG) values greater than 3 are considered to be fat-tailed. Kurtosis analysis is one of the filtering techniques used by researchers to decide whether a real-world network is more of the Poisson random type (the degree distribution is not fat-tailed) or the Power-law scale-free type (fat-tailed degree distribution). In [7], it has been argued that Kurtosis(DEG) alone cannot be considered a true measure of the fat-tailedness of the degree distribution of the vertices unless there is a non-zero probability value for observing one or more nodes with degree values covering a broader range. In fact, networks with significantly larger Kurtosis(DEG) values are considered to have certain outlier nodes with respect to the degree centrality metric [6], and the removal of these outlier nodes could significantly reduce the Kurtosis(DEG) values for these networks. In a recent work [12], the Kurtosis values for the other commonly studied centrality distributions (like betweenness centrality, closeness centrality and eigenvector centrality) for real-world networks were measured. The Kurtosis values for the betweenness centrality distributions in real-world networks have been observed to be typically larger than the Kurtosis values for the degree centrality distributions.

Most of the work involving Kurtosis also considered other statistical measures along with before arriving at certain conclusions. Kurtosis was not considered as the only statistical measure for any topological analysis. In [8], the Kurtosis of the clustering coefficient metric was used along with other statistical measures (such as mean, standard deviation and skewness) to quantify the extent of clumpiness of a real-world network. In [9], with respect to the closeness centrality metric, it was observed that networks with higher values for Kurtosis, higher negatively values for Skewness, higher mean and lower standard deviation for the centrality metric contain nodes that can reach each other in shortest paths (fewer hops). In a study on ecological networks [10], the authors observed Kurtosis of the degree distribution to be independent of the network connectance (the ratio of the actual number of interactions to the potential number of interactions), while the other statistical measures such as mean, skewness and standard deviation of the degree distribution were observed to be influenced by network connectance. In [11], Kurtosis was one of the statistical measures used to analyze the structural characteristics of wireless networks that dynamically change with time due to the mobility of the nodes involved.

6 Conclusions

Overall, Kurtosis analysis has been conducted until now only for centrality metrics whose values are not parameter-driven. To the best of our knowledge, ours is the first work to evaluate the Kurtosis values for the distribution of a parameter-driven centrality metric (in our case, the decay centrality metric) for real-world networks. The high-level contribution of our work is that we empirically demonstrate a quadratic relationship between the Kurtosis of the decay centrality metric and the decay parameter, δ for 70 real-world networks of diverse degree distributions. We also observe the quadratic model to be of "open up" type and there exists a $\delta_{critical}$ value until which the Kurtosis(DEC_δ) values decrease and beyond which the Kurtosis(DEC_δ) values either remain about the same or increase. We also show that it is sufficient to use δ values of 0.01, 0.02, …, 0.99 (with an increment of 0.01) and the corresponding

Kurtosis(DEC$_\delta$)/Kurtosis(DEG) ratio values to develop the quadratic model for a real-world network with R^2 values above 0.99. Once we know the quadratic model for the Kurtosis(DEC$_\delta$)/Kurtosis(DEG) ratio and the Kurtosis(DEG) value for a real-world network, the lowest value for Kurtosis(DEC$_\delta$) and the corresponding $\delta_{critical}$ value for a real-world network could be estimated using the coefficients '*a*', '*b*' and '*c*' of the quadratic model and there is no need to determine the actual values of the decay centrality of the vertices for one or more δ values in a trial-and-error manner.

References

1. Jackson, M.O.: Social and Economic Networks, 1st edn. Princeton University Press, Princeton (2010)
2. Kolaczyk, E.D.: Statistical Analysis of Network Data, 1st edn. Springer, Berlin (2009). https://doi.org/10.1007/978-0-387-88146-1
3. Meghanathan, N.: Correlation analysis of decay centrality. In: Silhavy, R., Senkerik, R., Kominkova Oplatkova, Z., Prokopova, Z., Silhavy, P. (eds.) CSOC 2017. AISC, vol. 574, pp. 407–418. Springer, Cham (2017). https://doi.org/10.1007/978-3-319-57264-2_41
4. Tsakas, N.: On decay centrality, arXiv:1604.05582, April 2016
5. Meghanathan, N.: Spectral radius as a measure of variation in node degree for complex network graphs. In: Proceedings of the 3rd International Conference on Digital Contents and Applications, Hainan, China, 20–23 December 2014, pp. 30–33 (2014)
6. Barabasi, A.L.: Network Science, 1st edn. Cambridge University Press, Cambridge (2016)
7. Meghanathan, N.: Kurtosis: is it an appropriate measure to compare the extent of fat-tailedness of the degree distribution for any two real-world networks? In: Proceedings of the Fifth International Conference on Foundations of Computer Science and Technology, Sydney, Australia, 24–25 June 2017, pp. 89–99 (2017)
8. Sloan, L., Quan-Haase, A.: The SAGE Handbook of Social Media Research Methods, 1st edn. SAGE Publications, Thousand Oaks (2017)
9. Kock, N.: Interdisciplinary Applications of Electronic Collaboration Approaches and Technologies, 1st edn. IGI Global, Hershey (2012)
10. Poisot, T., Gravel, D.: When is an ecological network complex? Connectance drives degree distribution and emerging network properties. PeerJ **2**, e251 (2014)
11. Hossmann, T., Spyropoulos, T., Legendre, F.: A complex network analysis of human mobility. In: Proceedings of the Workshop on Network Science for Communication Networks, Shanghai, China, pp. 876–881, April 2011
12. Meghanathan, N.: An analysis of the fat-tailedness of the centrality distributions of real-world networks. Int. J. Comput. Netw. Commun. **9**(5), 1–13 (2017)
13. Meghanathan, N.: Randomness index for complex network analysis. Soc. Netw. Anal. Min. **7**(25), 1–15 (2017)

Development of an Automated Water Quality Classification Model for the River Ganga

Anil Kumar Bisht[1(✉)], Ravendra Singh[1], Ashutosh Bhatt[2], and Rakesh Bhutiani[3]

[1] Department of CS & IT, MJP Rohilkhand University, Bareilly, UP, India
anilbisht_20@yahoo.com, r.singh@mjpru.ac.in
[2] Department of CSE, BIAS, Bhimtal, UK, India
ashutoshbhatt123@gmail.com
[3] Department of Zoology and Environmental Science, Gurukul Kangri University, Haridwar, UK, India
rbhutani@gmail.com

Abstract. Recently, Water Quality (WQ) comes out to be the central point of concern all around the globe. The purpose of this work is to develop an automated procedure that can be used to classify the water quality of the River Ganga proficiently in the stretch from Devprayag to Roorkee Uttarakhand, India. The monthly data sets of five water quality parameters temperature, pH, dissolved oxygen (DO), biochemical oxygen demand (BOD) and total coliform (TC) for the time period from 2001 to 2015 is used for this research work. The proposed method involves developing various water quality classification models using one of the concept of data mining called decision tree (DT) for evaluating the WQ classes. The experiments are conducted using Weka data mining tool. Models first developed using (60–40)% data division approach and then using (80–20)% approach of data division. Five different decision tree models are developed named J48 (C4.5), Random Forest, Random Tree, LMT (logistic model tree) and Hoeffding Tree. These classifiers were analyzed to determine the most accurate classifier model for the present dataset by evaluating their performance via measures like Accuracy, Kappa Statistics, Recall, Precision, F-Measure, Mean absolute error and Root mean squared error. The results concluded that the random forest model outperforms all other classifiers with a great accuracy rate of 100% in both approaches and least error rate when developed using the second approach. Such a highly acceptable and attractive results may be helpful for the decision makers in water management and planning.

Keywords: Decision tree (DT) · Logistic model tree (LMT) Mean absolute error (MAE) · Root mean square error (RMSE) Water quality (WQ)

1 Introduction

Water is the most precious gift given by the nature to the mankind. It is the necessity for human as well as for the wild and marine spices. Whether the water is suitable for its designated use or not that is to be identified by its water quality. The biological,

P. Bhattacharyya et al. (Eds.): NGCT 2017, CCIS 827, pp. 190–198, 2018.
https://doi.org/10.1007/978-981-10-8657-1_15

chemical and physical features are used to define the quality of water. As we know rivers are the most important source of water which can be utilized for drinking, bathing, irrigation and cooling purpose in the industries. But, recently, a gradual deterioration in the water quality of rivers have been reported. The causes behind such kind of water pollution are alarming rate of increase in population, dense industrialization, urbanization as well as human deeds. The Ganga River is the largest river basin in India covering 26.2% of India's total geographical area and recently the court had granted the living entity status to this river highlighting its importance for us. The Ganga is not only considered as Holy River in India but also it is acting as one of the pillar for the economic growth of India. But, the river Ganga is no more carrying the pure water because of severe degradation in its water quality as well which has been reported in various surveys. The Government of India had initiated so many programs for improving quality of the Ganga River and also putting efforts till today. The water management authorities requires efficient and technical solutions for dealing with this problem of water [1]. A Classification model is the need of time that will classify the water efficiently as per the water quality standards so that it will be used accordingly for WQ prediction or forecasting and become useful for the water resource planning and management [2]. Classification is one of the important type of machine learning method. The goal of classification is to perform mapping of data items into their respective predefined known classes.

This paper makes use of one of the popular machine learning method i.e. decision tree as classifier. Five different decision tree models are developed named J48 (C4.5), Random Forest, Random Tree, LMT (logistic model tree) and Hoeffding Tree. The experiments are conducted using Weka data mining tool. Each classifier model is developed using the two different approaches of data division. First one is based on (60–40)% and the second one is (80–20)%. These classifiers were analyzed to determine the most accurate classifier model for the present dataset by evaluating their performance via measures like Accuracy, Kappa Statistics, Recall, Precision, F-Measure, Mean absolute error and Root mean squared error.

The rest of the paper is organized in five sections. Section 2 presents the literature survey. Section 3 illustrates the study region and the data undertaken. The research methodology explained in the Sect. 4. Results are determined and discussed in the Sect. 5. Finally Sect. 6 concludes this paper.

2 Literature Survey

Data mining is the process of discovering or uncovering the hidden patterns in the huge datasets. Decision tree is one of the most popular data mining technique used for classification and prediction [3]. Decision tree is simple to understand as it explains the process graphically. In the field of data mining classification is the significant task for the purpose of machine learning [4]. Assignment of each input data to a class from a set of predefined classes is the ultimate target of any classifier. Any classification model can be applied for predicting the label of class of any unknown data sets. There exist various types of classification techniques i.e. classifiers like neural networks, decision trees, support vector machines, naive Bayes classifier etc. Each of these classifier involves a learning scheme for finding a model that maps well the relationship between the characteristic set of the problem and its corresponding class.

Development of a classifier involves a systematic process in order to solve a classification problem. First of all relevant data is extracted from the available data, than the classification technique to be applied is selected, prepare the training set that contains records with known classes, start training the chosen classifier by selecting best structure and parameters utilizing the training set, once the trained model or classifier is developed validate it by applying it onto the data sets with unknown class contained in the test set not belonging to the training set. Finally the performance of the developed classifier is to be determined in terms of its accuracy in classifying or predicting the data cases correctly with respect to the total number of data cases.

A vast of literature is available regarding the role of decision tree in solving classification problem. A model has been developed in weka by the author [4] using the concept of decision tree for weather forecasting problem where the model predict various events like fog, rain and thunder on the basis of temperature, humidity and pressure. An improved decision tree based learning method was suggested by the authors [5] for forecasting the water quality of Chao lake. The results were found to be satisfactory with higher accuracy. Authors in [3] applied three different decision tree methods in order to develop a model for predicting the food demands in public food courts. Authors have got the prediction accuracies upto 0.83. Therefore, they concluded that the decision tree based prediction method is suitable for prediction of the food consumption. Authors in [6] applied the decision tree approach for finding the significant predictors for the demands of the health meteorological information. They concluded that their developed model can be helpful for the policy makers in the field of health. The authors [7] make use of both decision trees as well as artificial neural network in building the water quality assessment forecast model. Authors in [8] accomplished a review of papers which were based on the concept of ANN as a tool used for performing the classification. Their study concludes that the Back Propagation Neural Network (BPNN) can be used as an efficient tool for the data classification with proper combination of various training parameters. Authors in [9] compared three different neural network models for analyzing their performance in solving the classification problem. The authors in [10] explained the concept of decision tree with its application in the real observations. They have given the general decision tree algorithm which involves the following three basis steps:

- Start at the root node
- To each element apply the split condition
- Is the stopping criteria is reached stop else apply step second to each further sub node.

It is concluded from the literature survey that decision tree is one of the simplest and popular technique used for classification purpose. Apart from this technique, several other classification techniques are existing like artificial neural networks, support vector machines, naive Bayes classifier etc. As far as our paper is concern, we have applied the decision tree method for developing various classification models at the initial stage. Later on, we will expand our work by adopting above said techniques as an extension to this research work.

3 Study Region and Data Used for Water Quality

The Ganga River which is also the largest river basin in India has been taken as the study region. It is the national river of India that comprises of 26.3% of the country's land mass (8, 61,404 km^2). The Ganga River is supporting about 43% of its population (448.3 million as per 2001 census). River Ganga formed at Devprayag with the joining of the River Bhagirathi with river Alaknanda initiating in Garhwal Himalayas. This river lies between East longitudes 73°30 and 89°0 and North latitudes of 22°30 and 31°30, covering an area of 1,086,000 km^2. About 79% area of Ganga basin is in India and remaining area lying in Nepal and Bangladesh. [11].

The river crosses a total length of 2525 km originated from the Uttarakhand state towards the Uttar Pradesh, Bihar, Jharkhand and West Bengal, and finally falls into the Bay of Bengal. Various cities like Haridwar, Kannauj, Kanpur, Allahabad, Varanasi, Patna and Kolkata are located on the banks of river Ganga [12]. The view of Ganga River basin in India is presented in Fig. 1 [13]. Five sampling stations along this river were selected. The monthly data sets from 2001 to 2015, comprising of five water quality parameters temperature, pH, dissolved oxygen (DO), biochemical oxygen demand (BOD) and total coliform (TC) is used for the this research work, analyzed by Limnology & Ecological Modelling Laboratory, department of Zoology and Environment Science, Gurukul Kangri Vishwavidhyalaya, Haridwar, Uttarakhand, India.

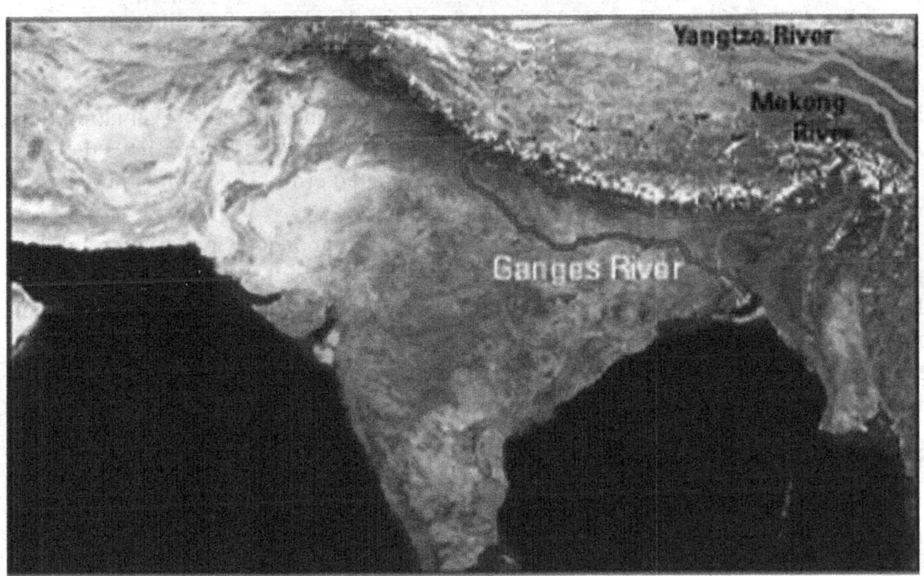

Fig. 1. The Ganga river basin [13]

4 Methodology

In the present research work, our objective is to develop various water quality classification models using one of the concept of data mining called decision tree (DT) for evaluating the WQ classes. The experiments are conducted using a data mining tool called WEKA 3.8 [14]. Now a days weka tool is getting more popular among the academicians [15]. WEKA stands for Waikato Environment for Knowledge Learning which was developed by the University of Waikato, New Zealand. It is an open source software available for supporting various data mining tasks like pre-processing, classification, clustering, visualization etc.

The classification of water quality is based on the standards prescribed by Central pollution control board (CPCB) which has classified the water resources of the country as per their uses. Five different decision tree models are developed named J48 (C4.5), Random Forest, Random Tree, LMT (logistic model tree) and Hoeffding Tree.

5 Experiments, Results and Discussion

5.1 First Approach of Data Division (60–40)%

For conducting the experiments the available dataset of size 900 is divided with the policy of (60–40)% into two sets: 60% of data is used for the training purpose and the remaining 40% for the testing. Weka tool is used for developing five different types of classifier. Once the model is trained and tested using the specified data the performance of the developed classifiers is to be evaluated. These classifiers were analyzed to determine the most accurate classifier model for the present dataset by evaluating their performance via measures like Accuracy, Kappa Statistics, Recall, Precision, F-Measure, Mean absolute error and Root mean squared error. The confusion matrix is used to represent the accuracy of different classifiers.

The Classification performance of various classifier models w.r.t. different performance measures is as shown in the Table 1. After analyzing the results it is concluded that the random forest method based classifier comes out to be the best among all others. Its classification accuracy is found to be 100% with minimum root mean square error (RMSE) of 0.027. Among all the undertaken classifiers the classification summary of the best model i.e. the random forest based classifier is as follows:

Summary for the Best Model (Random Forest)

Correctly Classified Instances	360	100%
Incorrectly Classified Instances	0	0%

The confusion matrix for the best model is presented in the Table 2. It is clearly highlighted by this matrix that there are total 17 instances of class ‘A’ which are correctly classified in class ‘A’. Similarly there are 210 instances of class ‘B’ and 133 instances of class ‘D’ and all these are again classified correctly by the developed model. It can be seen that there is no such instance which was classified incorrectly.

Hence the results indicate that the random forest based decision tree model perform with a very high classification accuracy of 100%.

Table 1. The classification performance of various classifier models w.r.t. different performance measures adopting (60–40)% data division approach

Models Performance parameter	J48	Random forest	Random tree	LMT	Hoeffding tree
Accuracy	99.17%	100%	99.44%	98.89%	96.11%
Cohen's Kappa	0.984	1	0.989	0.978	0.924
Recall	0.992	1.000	0.994	0.989	0.961
Precision	0.992	1.000	0.994	0.989	0.962
F-Measure	0.991	1.000	0.994	0.989	0.961
Mean absolute error	0.006	0.006	0.003	0.023	0.028
Root mean squared error	0.064	0.027	0.053	0.082	0.126

Table 2. Confusion matrix for the best model (Random Forest):

A	B	C	D		→ classified as
17	0	0	0	|	A = 1
0	210	0	0	|	B = 2
0	0	0	0	|	C = 3
0	0	0	133	|	D = 4

5.2 Second Approach of Data Division (80–20)%

In this second approach, for conducting the experiments the available dataset of size 900 is divided with the policy of (80–20)% into two sets: 80% of data is used for the training purpose and the remaining 20% for the testing. After applying the same methodology as in the first approach the classification performance of various classifier models w.r.t. different performance measures is as shown in the Table 3. It can be seen from the result that the random forest method based classifier again comes out to be the best among all others. Its classification accuracy is found to be 100% with minimum root mean square error (RMSE) of 0.023. Among all the undertaken classifiers the classification summary of the best model i.e. the random forest based classifier is as follows:

Summary for the Best Model (Random Forest)

Correctly Classified Instances	180	100%
Incorrectly Classified Instances	0	0%

Table 3. The classification performance of various classifier models w.r.t. different performance measures adopting (80–20)% data division approach

Models Performance parameter	J48	Random forest	Random tree	LMT	Hoeffding tree
Accuracy	99.44%	100%	99.44%	99.44%	95.56%
Cohen's Kappa	0.989	1	0.989	0.9892	0.910
Recall	0.994	1.000	0.994	0.994	0.956
Precision	0.994	1.000	0.995	0.994	0.920
F-Measure	0.994	1.000	0.994	0.994	0.937
Mean absolute error	0.004	0.003	0.003	0.004	0.054
Root mean squared error	0.053	0.023	0.053	0.054	0.146

The confusion matrix for the best model is presented in the Table 4. It is understood by this matrix that there are total 7 instances of class 'A' which are correctly classified in class 'A'. Similarly there are 104 instances of class 'B' and 69 instances of class 'D' and all these are again classified correctly by the developed model. It can also be seen that no instance was misclassified. Hence the results indicate that the random forest based decision tree model again outperforms other models and provides a very high classification accuracy of 100% even when we have adopted the 80%–20% data division policy.

Table 4. Confusion matrix for the best model (Random Forest):

A	**B**	**C**	**D**	**→ classified as**
7	0	0	0	A = 1
0	104	0	0	B = 2
0	0	0	0	C = 3
0	0	0	69	D = 4

5.3 Comparison Among Two Different Data Division Approaches

In order to compare the performance of developed decision tree based different water quality classifiers we have analyzed their overall results. This can easily be seen from the Tables 1 and 3 that the random forest based water quality classifier proved to be the best one by achieving a very high accuracy of 100% in both the approaches (60–40)% as well as in (80–20)%. However this classifier can be able to classify the data with least error when it was developed using the second approach where the mean absolute error is 0.003 and root mean square error is 0.023 as compared to the error in the first approach where the MAE is 0.006 and RMSE is 0.027.

Furthermore, among all five water quality classifiers except the Hoeffding tree based classifier all other achieves a greater percentage of accuracy when developed using the second approach of data division. The Hoeffding tree based classifier comes out to be the worst one having least percentage accuracy. While the Random forest based classifier outperforms all other classifiers.

6 Conclusion and Future Scope

In this present work, we have developed an automated water quality classification model for the river Ganga in the stretch from Devprayag to Roorkee Uttarakhand, India using the most popular data mining approach known as decision trees. The monthly data sets from 2001–2015 consisting of five water quality parameters temperature, pH, dissolved oxygen (DO), biochemical oxygen demand (BOD) and total coliform (TC) is used for this research work. The experiments are conducted using Weka tool: an open source software that supports various data mining tasks like pre-processing, classification, clustering, visualization etc. Models first developed using (60–40)% data division approach and then using (80–20)% approach of data division. Five different decision tree based water quality classifier models are developed named J48 (C4.5), Random Forest, Random Tree, LMT (logistic model tree) and Hoeffding Tree.

When these WQ classifier models are developed using the second approach of data division except the Hoeffding tree based classifier, all other classifiers achieves an increased percentage of accuracy. This concludes that in general on increasing the training set size the performance of the developed model is also improved. The Hoeffding tree based classifier comes out to be the worst one having least percentage accuracy. While the Random forest based classifier outperforms all other classifiers.

Finally, this study concluded that water quality classification models developed using the approach of decision tree are proved to be the efficient one. These models are capable of achieving a higher classification percentage of accuracy with least error rate or no misclassification. In this paper, we have applied the decision tree method for developing various classification models at the initial stage. Later on, we will expand our work by adopting another classification techniques like artificial neural networks, support vector machines, naive Bayes classifier etc. as an extension to this research work. To conclude we can say, development of such an automated water quality classification model with a highly acceptable and efficient classification results may be helpful for the decision makers in water management and planning.

References

1. Technology Mission: Winning, Augmentation and Renovation. Technology Mission: WAR for Water, Plan Document Prepared by Union Ministry of Science and Technology Government of India, on the directive of Supreme Court of India Order on Writ Petition (C) No. 230 of 2001 Dated 28th April (2009)

2. Heydari, M., Olyaie, E., Mohebzadeh, H., Kisi, O.: Development of a neural network technique for prediction of water quality parameters in the Delaware river Pennsylvania. Middle-East J. Sci. Res. **13**(10), 1367–1376 (2013)
3. Bozkir, A.-S., Sezer, E.-A.: Predicting food demand in food courts by decision tree approaches. Procedia Comput. Sci. **3**, 759–763 (2010)
4. Kumar, R.: Decision tree for the weather forecasting. Int. J. Comput. Appl. **76**(2), 31–34 (2013)
5. Liao, H., Sun, W.: Forecasting and evaluating water quality of chao lake based on an improved decision tree method. In: International Society for Environmental Information Sciences 2010 Annual Conference (ISEIS). Elsevier (2010)
6. Oh, J., Kim, B.: Prediction model for demands of the health meteorological information using a decision tree method. Asian Nurs. Res. **4**(3), 151–162 (2010)
7. Liu, B.-X., Wan, X., Wu, X.-D., Li, Y.-X., Zhu, H.-Q.: Application of decision tree and neural network algorithm in water quality assessment forecast. In: International Conference on Material Science and Application, ICMSA 2015. Atlantis Press (2015)
8. Saravanan, K., Sasithra, S.: Review on classification based on artificial neural network. Int. J. Ambient Syst. Appl. (IJASA) **2**(4) (2014). https://doi.org/10.5121/ijasa.2014.2402
9. Daoud, E.-L.: A comparison between three different neural network models for classification problems. J. Artif. Intell. **2**(2), 56–64 (2009)
10. Lytvynenko, T.-I.: Problems of data analysis and forecasting using decision tree methods. In: Proceedings of the 10th International Conference of Programming UkrPROG', Kyiv, Ukraine (2016)
11. Status Paper on River Ganga. State of Environment and Water Quality. National River Conservation Directorate Ministry of Environment and Forests Government of India, August 2009
12. Pollution Assessment: River Ganga, Central Pollution Control Board (Ministry of Environment and Forests, Govt. of India), July 2013
13. http://www.all-about-india.com/Route-of-Ganges-River.html
14. http://www.cs.waikato.ac.nz/ml/weka
15. Rosly, R., Makhtar, M., Awang, M.-K., Rahman, M.-N.-A., Deris, M.-M.: The study on the accuracy of classifiers for water quality application. Int. J. u-, e-Serv. Sci. Technol. **8**(3), 145–154 (2015)

A Data Mining Approach Towards HealthCare Recommender System

Mugdha Sharma[1(✉)] and Laxmi Ahuja[2]

[1] Amity School of Engineering and Technology, Amity University, Noida, UP 201313, India
mugdha.sharma145@gmail.com
[2] Amity Institute of Information Technology, Amity University, Noida, UP 201313, India
lahuja@amity.edu

Abstract. Healthcare recommender systems are meant to provide accurate and relevant predictions to the patients. It is very difficult for people to explore various online sources to find some useful recommendations as per their medical conditions. So the proposed approach is an effort to provide accurate recommendations to the patients on the basis of their current medical condition as well as their medical history and constraints. First of all, patients are categorized into different groups based on their profiles and then rules predicting the medical condition of each group are mined. The proposed approach is unique in the way that it provides accurate treatments to the patients in the form of recommendations based on content based matching. It also considers the preferences of the patient, which are stored in the system as mined rules or estimated from the medical history of patient. The results of experimental setup also demonstrate that the proposed system provides more accurate outcomes over other healthcare recommendation systems.

Keywords: Data mining · Healthcare · Feature selection · Decision trees Classification rules

1 Introduction

Healthcare has become one of leading sectors in India. And digitalization plays an important role in this growth. According to Deloitte, with increased digital adoption, the Indian healthcare market is expected to grow at a CAGR of 23% from US$ 100 billion (2016), to US$ 280 billion by 2020. Enormous amounts of clinical data have been collected at various hospitals and medical Institutes in the form of patient's medical reports, laboratory results, treatment plans, etc. However, a lot of information is available online for the patients to understand those medical documents but is often spread across different sources online, like informational blogs, sites, etc. So, patients often get confused and feel unsure while investigating on their treatments [1]. So, Recommender systems can be used in health care industry to provide better health services to patients.

P. Bhattacharyya et al. (Eds.): NGCT 2017, CCIS 827, pp. 199–210, 2018.
https://doi.org/10.1007/978-981-10-8657-1_16

In today's digital world, one of the major challenging task is to get the relevant information from the huge amount of data that is available on the internet. Same is the case with information related to health care industry and therefore, people needs more intelligent and efficient system for this category. When people searches for any particular disease or its treatments, they usually have their own constraints and restrictions. So there is need for a user friendly system for health care recommendation which can provide accurate treatments to the patients based on their medical conditions.

So, a health care recommendation system has been proposed in this paper, which will provide the relevant information regarding the different treatments as per the patient's needs and constraints. This framework will understand the medical condition of the patient and will provide right treatment associated to patient's profile. It will also use the patient's profile for categorization into different groups so that they can get relevant information regarding various treatments available for particular symptoms.

2 Related Work

Various researchers have done a lot of research in the domain of recommender systems for healthcare industry. Plenty of healthcare recommendation systems are already present in the market which implies different approaches to provide recommendations by exploring various aspects of the information [1, 2].

Davis et al. proposed a unique recommender system - The Collaborative and Recommendation Engine (CARE). They used collaborative filtering to analyze the medical condition of patients and predict the future disease risks [3]. They categorized the patients into different clusters having information of patients with similar profiles and then applied collaborative filtering to predict the future disease risks of patient. Feldman and Chawla proposed an iterative method of this algorithm i.e., ICARE in which they repeated the process many times to test the patient. Each iteration utilized a different basis to prepare the cluster. A group was formed by combining all these clusters together. Finally, ICARE system provides a list of diseases with their ranking on the basis of estimated future risk [4].

Kulev et al. proposed a collaborative filtering approach to recommend exercises for improving the overall person's health and fitness. Collaborative Health Care System Model (COHESY) analyses the current medical condition and previous medical history of the patient and recommends exercises to improve the patient's health by modifying the value of any health parameter against which the algorithm is being tested [5]. Exercises which are recommended by this approach like jogging, cycling, etc. help in simply improving certain health parameters of the patient.

A hierarchical approach, Hierarchical Association Rule Mining Model (HARM), was proposed by McCormick et al. This method uses the concept of associative rule mining through which it can predict the patient's future symptoms by analyzing patient's present or the previous symptoms. This algorithm generates a set of association rules through which it recommends a list of future symptoms with ranking [6].

Pheng and Husain proposed an intelligent wellness recommender system, I-Wellness, which analyzes patient's current medical condition and recommends appropriate wellness treatment for them. They followed a knowledge based approach which has ability to store knowledge from medical experts so that it can provides more reliable recommendations with accuracy. Patients' current wellness problems are resolved with the help of solutions available in the database for same or similar situation [7].

Weider et al. proposed a Big-data approach towards health care recommendation systems which provides recommendations after comparing the data generated by patients with that of data which is cleansed by the system with the help of Apache Spark and IBM Watson services [8]. It is a self-learning method which auto-upgrades itself with the inflow of data. This system provides a user-friendly platform for patients to monitor their symptoms, learn more about the symptoms on the basis of recommendations provided by machine learning algorithm.

Every Doctor has a specialty or expertise in some particular domain. That's why they are known as experts in their field. And there are various hybrid approaches which have been suggested to find the right experts [9–11]. Such as, Balog et al. proposed a combined language modeling approach to find an expert [9], and Deng et al. suggested a topic-based model and a hybrid approach to improve the performance of the system over the basic language model [10]. Macdonald and Ounis also proposed a new combined approach with the help of a voting model to find the right expert [11].

The relevance of the healthcare recommendations is well justified in the literature review mentioned above. However, the quality recommendations to the patients are not yet carried out. So, a novel data mining technique has been proposed in this paper, to recommend the relevant treatments to the patients. Benefits of the proposed approach over the other approaches, which are covered in this section, are also highlighted in the paper.

3 Proposed Recommender System Design

3.1 Feature Selection

The features were categorized for 2 important entities in the proposed approach: Patient and Treatment. To judge the medical condition of the patient, the features that were considered for a Patient are: Age, Gender, Weight, Symptoms, Annual Income, Insurance, Lifestyle and Medical History (if any). And the features relating to the treatment are: Symptoms specific Medication, Treatment duration, Special Hospitals, Medical field, and Treatment Cost.

3.2 Data Categorization

The whole proposed approach revolves around two main data sets – Patient data and Treatment data. The primary objective was to discover the criteria which would be considered by the patients to go ahead for a particular treatment. So, the complete categorization was done on the basis of patient's demographic information and other characteristics such as, gender, age, symptoms, annual income, etc. Few generalized groups were formed for the patient data as well as treatment data both, to study the relationship between the two. Four different parameter were decided to check the patient's belonging to a particular group for deciding the right treatment: Hospitals group level, Medical Field, Treatment Duration and Treatment Cost. The categorization of the above mentioned features to study the medical condition of a patient, is shown below:

Patient's Data:

- Age: 6 generalized groups for the Age- 10–20, 21–30, 31–40, 41–50, 51–60, >60.
- Gender: 2 groups- Male or Female.
- Weight: 3 groups- Under Weight (UW), Over Weight (OW) or Equal Weight (EW).
- Annual Income: 4 Groups - Level A (>50 Lakh Rupees), Level B (30–50 Lakh Rupees), Level C (10–30 Lakh Rupees) and Level D (0–10 Lakh Rupees).
- Lifestyle: 3 groups- Non Drinkers (ND), Drinkers (D) and Drinkers & Smokers both (DS).
- Symptoms: This field was not considered for grouping. This particular feature acts as a catalyst in patient's validation for a particular treatment.
- Insurance: 2 groups- Yes or No.
- Medical History: This was not considered for grouping. Instead, this feature helps in deciding the better treatment for a particular patient. So, only the keywords are considered. Here it is considered that patient's medical history is already there in patient's records and can be used to represent as vector space model.

Treatment's Data:

- Hospitals: 4 types of hospitals as per their ranking: Group 1 (top 25%), Group 2, Group 3, Group 4 (lowest ranked).
- Medical Field: 4 Groups: Cardiology (C), Gynecology (G), Orthopedics (O), Physician Medicines (P).
- Treatment Duration: 3 Groups: High (H) (>1 month), Medium (M) (2 weeks–1 month), Low (L) (1 week–2 weeks).
- Treatment Cost: 4 Groups: Level A (0–10000 Rupees), Level B (10000–50000 Rupees), Level C (50000–2 Lakh Rupees) and Level D (>2 Lakh Rupees).

One of the most crucial parameter for the proposed approach is the domain Knowledge regarding various medical fields, such as knowledge of different treatments for specific symptoms of a patient. So, the domain knowledge is being stored in the proposed system, to get the accurate treatment for the mentioned symptoms.

3.3 Decision Tree Classification

There are various decision tree algorithms present for classification. But, C4.5 Algorithm has been used in the proposed approach because this technique uses the normalized information gain for the splitting criteria. This algorithm recursively chooses the attributes, that split the set of samples into subsets enriched in one class or another.

For patients, categorization was done based on their features as mentioned in the previous section. But for treatments, 20 different significant categories were formed, each having distinctive combinations in terms of hospital category, medical field, treatment duration and cost. The data for each treatment category was collected and examined separately. All the rules were exhaustively explored, that can help in determining the patient's choice for the corresponding treatment category.

Three major evaluation criterion – Lift, Confidence and Sample Size were considered to determine the strength of these rules [12]. Importance of a particular rule is determined by "Lift" and reliability of a rule is determined by "Confidence". Both the parameters are obtained as follows:

$$\text{Lift X(Rule a)} = \text{P(target class X| subset a)/P(target class X| population)} \quad (1)$$

$$\text{Confidence X(Rule a)} = \text{P(class X| subset data by Rule a)} \quad (2)$$

For proposed system, the value of lift more than 1 and confidence percentage of more than 80% is taken into consideration. For sample size, a threshold value was defined. Any rule with significant lift and confidence value but not sufficient value for sample size, is not considered for the proposed approach. After that, redundancy was checked for all the generated rules that passed the defined criteria. Then, a common matrix was formed which represents preferences of all the treatment categories, against all the generated rules. If there is any particular rule that fits for a particular treatment, then that particular treatment category is mentioned as 1 otherwise 0. This matrix representation for the generated rules and different treatment categories is shown in Table 1.

$$\begin{aligned} \text{Matrix[i, j]} &= 1 \text{ (if ith rule is fit for jth Treatment)} \\ &= 0 \text{ (otherwise zero)} \end{aligned} \quad (3)$$

Table 1. Matrix representation of the mined rules against different treatment categories.

Age	10–20	21–30	31–40	41–50	51–60
Gender	–	–	M	F	F
Weight	EW	OW	–	UW	–
Annual income	C	–	D	A	–
Lifestyle	–	D	DS	ND	–
Insurance	–	–	N	Y	N
T1	1	0	0	1	0
T2	1	0	0	0	0
T3	0	0	0	0	0
T4	0	0	0	0	0
T5	1	0	1	0	0
T6	1	1	0	0	0
T7	0	1	0	1	1
T8	0	1	0	0	0
T9	0	0	1	0	0
T10	0	0	1	1	1
T11	0	1	1	1	1
T12	0	1	1	0	0

There are 5 rules and 12 treatment categories that are shown in the Table 1. For example, 2nd rule depicts that the patients which belongs to age category of 21–30 and who are overweight (OW), having lifestyle = Drinkers (D), tends to select the treatments of category T6, T7, T8, T11 and T12.

After this step, four preference matrix were created. Each matrix further authenticates the rules which are generated. And the corresponding probabilities for choosing a particular field are saved in the system. Probability is calculated by dividing the weights assigned by the total available instances for the treatment.

For example, treatment duration matrix keeps data for its 3 different kind of duration's preference. First position for high duration required for treatments, 2nd for Medium, and Low duration preference for 3rd as: [PH PM PL].

Now consider the last rule which is mentioned in Table 1. A Female with Age Group = 51–60, and having No Insurance. The four preference matrices are:

1. Matrix for Hospital: [0 2/3 1/3 0]
2. Matrix for Medical Field: [0 1/3 2/3 0]
3. Matrix for Treatment Duration: [1/3 2/3 0]
4. Matrix for Treatment Cost: [0 1/1 0 0].

3.4 Generating Recommendations

Let's understand the whole recommendation generation process with an example. Suppose there is a patient with the following data:

{47, M, 98 Kgs, (tightness in the chest, pain in neck, back and arms, fatigue, light-headedness, abnormal heartbeat, anxiety), has Insurance Policy, Level C Income, Drinker, and we have the following 10 treatments which are available in the system, shown in Table 2.

Table 2. Sample treatments available in the system.

Treatments	Medical field	Medication	Duration
T1	Orthopedics	Body pain treatment with the help of medical devices such as transcutaneous electrical nerve stimulation	1 month
T2	Physician medicines	ACE inhibitors treatment	3 weeks
T3	Physician medicines	Aldosterone inhibitors treatment	3 weeks
T4	Cardiology	Angioplasty & stent	2 months
T5	Gynecology	Immunizations and injections for infections	1 week
T6	Cardiology	Stent operation	1 month
T7	Orthopedics	Acupuncture treatment for body pain	2 weeks
T8	Cardiology	Cardioversion	1 month
T9	Cardiology	Heart bypass surgery	3 months
T10	Gynecology	Cystectomy treatment	2 weeks

Step 1: The treatments are shortlisted which are currently best fit for the patient, on the basis of symptoms and medical history of the patient. So, treatments T3, T5, T9 and T10 get excluded from the above mentioned 10 treatments. Hence now only 6 treatments are left for prioritization: {T1, T2, T4, T6, T7 and T8}. Redundancy in the treatments is also removed in this step, if there is any.

Step 2: Now the Content Based Similarity is calculated for the selected treatments according to the patient's symptoms. This is calculated by comparing the general symptoms for those medical treatments and the symptoms possessed by patient. Here cosine similarity is used for obtaining the similarity index:

$$\text{Cosine similarity } (x, y) = (x.y)/(|x|\,|y|) \quad (4)$$

First of all, preference matrix vector is generated for symptoms and then accordingly patient's vector is generated [2]. Now suppose, if the impact for any particular symptom is very high, then a higher weight value can be assigned to that particular vector. For instance, if the impact of "chest pain" is considered high as 4 out of 5 scale, then weight can be assigned as 4 in the symptom vector. Now, if there is an exact match exists between 2 symptoms or they are inter-related and belong to same medical field, then weight 1 is allotted else a 0 is allotted as demonstrated in Table 3.

Table 3. Sample calculations of cosine similarity.

Treatment	Symptoms	Symptom vector	Patient vector	Cosine similarity
T1	High fever, headache, pain in neck, pain in back and arms	[1, 1, 1, 1]	[0, 0, 1, 1]	0.707
T2	High fever, headache, anxiety, stomach pain	[1, 1, 1, 1]	[0, 0, 1, 0]	0.5
T4	Tightness in the chest, high fever, pain in back and arms, abnormal heartbeat, cold	[1, 1, 1, 1, 1]	[1, 0, 1, 1, 0]	0.774
T6	Tightness in the chest, pain in back and arms, abnormal heartbeat, anxiety	[1, 1, 1, 1]	[1, 1, 1, 1]	1
T7	Pain in neck, pain in back and arms, fatigue, anxiety	[1, 1, 1, 1]	[1, 1, 1, 1]	1
T8	Tightness in the chest, high fever, cold, abnormal heartbeat, anxiety	[1, 1, 1, 1, 1]	[1, 0, 0, 1, 1]	0.774

Step 3: Now, the Induction Rules generated by Decision Tree are applied for the patient's group to which they belong. First of all, the basic treatment categorization is carried out. Then, these categories are compared as per the preference matrices of the generated rules and then preference weights are assigned accordingly. Now, consider the patient mentioned in our case: {41–50, M, OW, C, D, Y}. The preference matrices

for this patient are: Hospitals [0, 1/5, 2/5, 2/5], Treatment Duration [1/5, 3/5, 1/5] and Treatment Cost [0, 2/5, 1/5, 2/5]. Now, the exact weights are calculated for the corresponding treatments, in the form of normalized rule's weight:

$$\text{Normalized Weight} = (W_i - W_{min})/(W_{max} - W_{min}) \quad (5)$$

Where W_i is the weight of the rule allotted to the corresponding ith treatment and W_{min} & W_{max} are the minimum and maximum of all the weights together.

Step 4: In this step, final weight score is calculated by adding up the cosine similarity value and rules weight as demonstrated below:

$$\text{Final Weight Score}(i) = w1.\,cosin_i + w2.\,rlw_i \quad (6)$$

Where i signifies ith treatment which is shortlisted, $cosin_i$ signifies cosine similarity for ith treatment, rlw_i is the rules weight allotted to the ith treatment, w1 and w2 signifies the weights allotted to cosine similarity and rules weight respectively, which are used to maintain their significance. In the proposed approach, both the values (w1 & W2) are taken as 0.5.

Step 5: The final step of the proposed approach is sorting the treatments in descending order as per the final weight score. So, the final recommendations suggested to the patient (as per our example) are {T6, T8, T1, T4, T7, T2} as shown in Table 4.

Table 4. Final calculation for obtaining treatment's ranking.

Treatment	T1	T2	T4	T6	T7	T8
Cosine similarity	0.707	0.5	0.774	1	1	0.774
Hospital	B	B	D	C	D	C
Treatment duration	M	M	H	M	L	M
Treatment cost	B	A	D	C	A	C
Weight for the rules	{1/5 + 3/5 + 2/5} = 1.2	{1/5 + 3/5 + 0} = 0.8	{2/5 + 1/5 + 2/5} = 1	{2/5 + 3/5 + 1/5} = 1.2	{2/5 + 1/5 + 0} = 0.6	{2/5 + 3/5 + 1/5} = 1.2
Normalized weight for the rules	1	0.34	0.67	1	0	1
Final weight score	0.8535	0.42	0.722	1	0.5	0.887
Final ranking	3	6	4	1	5	2

4 Results and Discussions

In the research dataset, there were 500 patients and 150 treatments. Twenty different significant treatment's categories were formed and all the treatments were categorized into these categories. Python was used to implement the proposed approach and orange library [13] was used for data mining purpose. Some significant rules were obtained after data mining corresponding to each treatment category and stored in the system as knowledge base to generate further recommendations.

To measure the performance and significance of recommendations generated by the proposed approach, prediction accuracy was used as a performance metric [14]. The following graph compares the prediction accuracies of three systems - Content based recommendation system, Collaborative filtering recommendation systems, and the Proposed Recommendation System, shown in Fig. 1, for Top N Recommendations suggested to the patients. An accuracy of about 72% was achieved by the proposed recommender system, against the lower performance of traditional recommendation approaches.

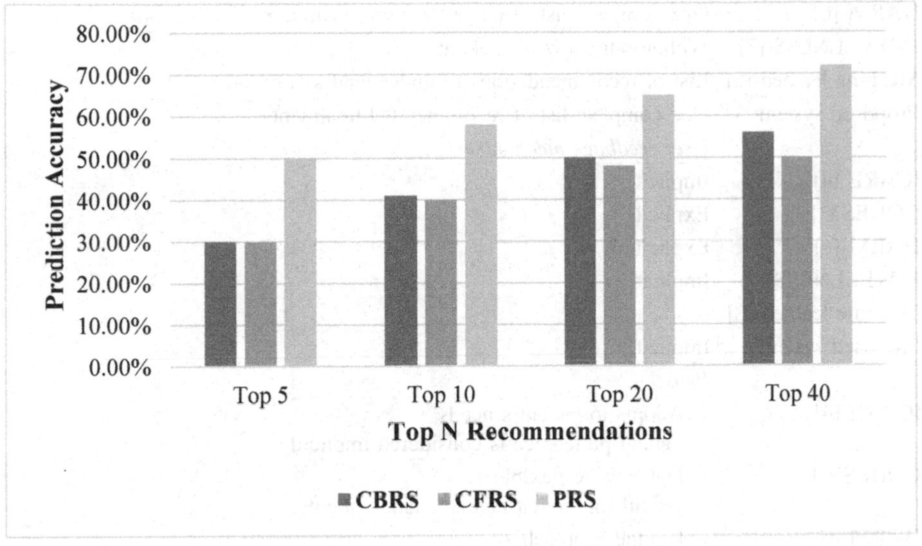

Fig. 1. Prediction accuracy comparison.

Table 5 represents the comparison among various healthcare recommender systems with that of the proposed approach.

Table 5. Comparison between various HealthCare recommendation approaches.

	Input for user profile
ICARE [4]	Patient information
COHESY [5]	Patient information and historical data
HARM [6]	Patient's current and past symptoms
I -WELLNESS [7]	Patient information
Machine learned [8]	Patient information and symptoms
Proposed system	Patient information and symptoms
	Recommendation strategy
ICARE [4]	Memory based & cluster based collaborative filtering recommender system
COHESY [5]	Collaborative filtering & knowledge based recommender system

(*continued*)

Table 5. (*continued*)

HARM [6]	Association rule mining
I -WELLNESS [7]	Hybrid content based & knowledge based recommender system
Machine learned [8]	Big data, apache spark and IBM Watson services
Proposed system	Content based & collaborative filtering recommender system
	Output of recommendation
ICARE [4]	A list of diseases
COHESY [5]	One complete list of physical activities
HARM [6]	One complete list of patient's future symptoms
I -WELLNESS [7]	Wellness therapy for patient
Machine learned [8]	List of recommendations to understand symptoms
Proposed system	One complete list of recommended treatments
	User feedback mechanism
ICARE [4]	Implicit
COHESY [5]	Explicit
HARM [6]	Explicit
I -WELLNESS [7]	Implicit
Machine learned [8]	–
Proposed system	Implicit
	Pros
ICARE [4]	1. Adopts to patient's needs 2. Patient preference is considered implicitly
COHESY [5]	1. Dynamic & flexible 2. Useful for similar characteristic patients
HARM [6]	1. Unique approach
I -WELLNESS [7]	1. Reliable 2. Less error prone
Machine learned [8]	1. Patients can monitor their symptoms. 2. Visual dashboards
Proposed system	1. Patient preference is considered implicitly 2. Adopts to patient's needs 3. Different recommendations for different patient's categories
	Cons
ICARE [4]	1. Patient profile not proper accurate 2. 1 way recommendations
COHESY [5]	1. 1 Way recommendations 2. Explicit feedback required
HARM [6]	1. Feedback is required explicitly 2. No standard methods are defined
I -WELLNESS [7]	1. 1 Way recommendations 2. Problem of data sparsity
Machine learned [8]	1. 1 Way recommendations 2. Problem of data sparsity
Proposed system	1. 1 Way recommendations 2. Problem of data sparsity at initial level

5 Conclusion and Future Scope

In this paper, a unique approach has been proposed in which the preferences of patients and their medical condition are considered to recommend accurate treatments to them with the help of content based profile matching. As the general group preferences are imposed in the proposed system, it also solved the general issue of the patients that they are often confused regarding appropriate treatments as per their medical condition. Prediction accuracy is used as the performance measure metric, as discussed in previous section. The prediction accuracy of the proposed approach came out to be better and efficient as compared to the other traditional recommender systems such as content based and collaborative filtering based recommender system.

In future, we would like to include more medical fields in the database for the treatment to cater broad categories of patients. Also, we would like to improve the performance of the proposed approach by considering the impact of patient's allergies and other characteristics to provide better and accurate recommendations.

References

1. Al-Nazer, A., Helmy, T., Al-Mulhem, M.: User's profile ontology-based semantic framework for personalized food and nutrition recommendation. Procedia Comput. Sci. **32**, 101–108 (2014)
2. Bhat, S., Aishwarya, K.: Item-based hybrid recommender system for newly marketed pharmaceutical drugs. In: International Proceedings on Advances in Computing, Communications and Informatics, pp. 2107–2111. IEEE, Mysore (2013)
3. Davis, D.A., Chawla, N.V., Blumm, N., Christakis, N., Barabasi, A.-L.: Predicting individual disease risk based on medical history. In: 17th International Proceedings on Information and knowledge management, pp. 769–778. ACM, New York (2008)
4. Feldman, K., Davis, D., Chawla, N.V.: Scaling and contextualizing personalized healthcare. J. Biomed. Inf. **57**(c), 377–385 (2015)
5. Kulev, I., Vlahu-Gjorgievska, E., Trajkovik, V., Koceski, S.: Recommendation algorithm based on collaborative filtering and its application in health care. In: 10th International Proceedings on Informatics and Information Technology, pp. 34–38. Faculty of Computer Science & Engineering, Skopje, Bitola (2013)
6. McCormick, T., Rudin, C., Madigan, D.: A hierarchical model for association rule mining of sequential events: an approach to automated medical symptom prediction. Ann. Appl. Stat. (2011)
7. Pheng, L.T., Husain, W.: I-Wellness: a hybrid case-based framework for personalized wellness therapy. In: International Proceedings on Information Technology, pp. 1193–1198. IEEE, Kuala Lumpur (2010)
8. Weider, D.Y., Gill, J.S., Dalal, M., Jha, P., Shah, S.: Big data approach in healthcare used for intelligent design—Software as a service. In: International Proceedings on Big Data, pp. 3443–3449. IEEE, Washington, DC (2016)
9. Balog, K., Azzopardi, L., Rijke, M.D.: A language modeling framework for expert finding. Inf. Process. Manag. **45**(1), 1–19 (2009)
10. Deng, H., Han, J., Lyu, M.R., King, I.: Modeling and exploiting heterogeneous bibliographic networks for expertise ranking. In: Proceedings of the 12th ACM/IEEE-CS Joint Conference on Digital Libraries, pp. 71–80. ACM, Washington, DC (2012)

11. Macdonald, C., Ounis, I.: Voting techniques for expert search. Knowl. Inf. Syst. **16**(3), 259–280 (2008)
12. Chien, C.F., Chen, L.F.: Data mining to improve personnel selection and enhance human capital: a case study in high-technology industry. Expert Syst. Appl. **34**(1), 280–290 (2008)
13. Demšar, J., Zupan, B.: Orange: data mining fruitful and fun – a historical perspective. Informatica Slovenia **37**(1), 55–60 (2013)
14. Del Olmo, F.H., Gaudioso, E.: Evaluation of recommender systems: a new approach. Expert Syst. Appl. **35**(3), 790–804 (2008)

Root Table: Dynamic Indexing Scheme for Access Protection in e-Healthcare Cloud

M. B. Smithamol(✉) and Rajeswari Sridhar

Department of Computer Science and Engineering, Anna University, Chennai 600025, India
smithamolm@acm.org, rajisridhar@gmail.com

Abstract. The popularity and large-scale adoption of cloud computing have accelerated the development of e-healthcare systems. Outsourcing electronic health records (EHRs) demands the assurance of search privacy, given that data and its access are not in control of the EHR owner. Here, we adopted a different approach to the problem of access privacy in EHRs by addressing the problem of information leakage based on revealing access patterns in semi-trusted cloud servers. In this paper, we proposed a dynamic data structure called a Root table (R-table) to create a storage index, which ensures access privacy while querying the outsourced database. The objective of R-table is to hide access pattern from a honest-but-curious server. R-table is an adaptation of dynamic arrays and randomized binary search trees, which randomly shuffle locations of data blocks following each access. This model provides access privacy with minimum communication and storage overhead and enables the EHR owner to perform a private read or write without revealing the type of operation and target data fragment processed. The results of our experiments showed limited performance overhead, indicating that R-table is suitable for practical use.

Keywords: Cloud computing · Root table (R-table) · Access pattern
Electronic health record (EHR) · Data outsourcing

1 Introduction

Cloud computing has evolved as a successful paradigm with hypothetically unlimited storage and computation capacity, and advantages of the cloud model are prompting many health providers to find more innovative and cost-effective solutions to the problem of outsourcing electronic health records (EHRs) [1]. An EHR system provides stable and secure storage for large volumes of health data, including patient medical histories, laboratory results, and billing records [2,3]. Most medical applications require secure, efficient, reliable, and scalable access to the medical records, and these requirements demand the use of secured storage services [4–6]. Consequently, use of the cloud for e-health services magnifies the need for access privacy.

P. Bhattacharyya et al. (Eds.): NGCT 2017, CCIS 827, pp. 211–227, 2018.
https://doi.org/10.1007/978-981-10-8657-1_17

Access and pattern confidentiality require hiding the information involved in one or more requests involving a specific EHR. Semi-trusted cloud data service providers (CDSPs) and unauthorized users are capable of observing access patterns to obtain information regarding sensitive records in the database [7]. Additionally, access privacy is a significant requirement during the integration of different medical databases from various healthcare providers [8,9]. Compared to content protection, relatively little research has focused on the problem of access privacy in the cloud-assisted healthcare system.

State-of-the-art solutions for access protection include private information retrieval [10,11], oblivious random access memory (ORAM) [12,13], and dynamically allocated data structures [14,15]. However, these schemes are not practically used by cloud-assisted healthcare systems due to their high computational complexity. Therefore, there remains a large demand for simple and efficient access-protection systems to enhance EHR security.

Here, we introduced a dynamic data structure called a Root table (R-table) that performs indexing of the outsourced database to ensure access privacy by adapting well-known data structures, such as the dynamic array and randomized binary search tree (RBST) [16]. The main advantage of R-table is that it provides access privacy with minimum communication and storage overhead. We subsequently performed an extensive evaluation to confirm the efficiency of R-table. The major contributions are summarized as follows:

1. Proposed and implemented dynamic indexing structure R-table which effectively hides access pattern from the eye of a honest-but-curious data server.
2. Proposed and implemented novel retrieval algorithm using R-table which hides the type of operation from the server.
3. Validated the performance of R-table with the publicly available dataset.

The organization of the paper is as follows. Section 2 provides an overview of related works. Section 3 illustrates the proposed R-table and associated algorithms necessary to perform dynamic indexing to achieve access privacy. Section 4 gives the details of access protection ensured by the R-table. Sections 5 and 6 focus on experimental analysis and verification of R-table efficiency. Finally, Sect. 7 summarizes our findings and offers valuable insight into potential future improvements.

2 Related Works

Cloud computing provides scalable infrastructure and offers the availability of internet-based health-information services [3,17]. Additionally, cloud-assisted e-healthcare systems offer quality services at the expense of complex data management and privacy issues. EHR-data privacy in the healthcare cloud requires balanced security solutions capable of managing both data and access privacy [3].

The ORAM methodology mixes data fragments with identically sized dummy items and stores them on the remote host, with alterations in physical location following each access [13]. The independence between the data and its physical location, therefore, hides the access pattern. Williams et al. analyzed a practical ORAM scheme involving a shuffle operation to introduce multiple changes in data-block location, which represents the primary bottleneck preventing the use of ORAM in practical scenarios [18]. A lightweight solution that preserves access patterns over multiple changes was subsequently proposed by Yang et al. [19]. A write-only ORAM protecting write pattern is proposed in [20]. To process user requests concurrently, Sahin et al. proposed a tree-based ORAM methodology to protect access pattern [21].

A previous study [22] discussed a hybrid protocol enabling medical-data sharing in the cloud. To assist healthcare systems, Guo et al. implemented an attribute-level access-control scheme to perform a search operation on an outsourced database [23]. Additionally, Drozdowicz et al. proposed an access-control method for health records that incorporates semantics included in health documents, which is based on the well-known and widely used eXtensible Access Control Markup Language, and uses an ontology approach [24]. Furthermore, Lin et al. suggested a cloud-assisted privacy preserving a mobile health-monitoring system that provides privacy to both users and data [25], and Chen et al. presented a secured index to promote keyword-searchable encryption over encrypted EHRs [26]. The dynamic tree-based data structure for indexing is proposed in [27], which provides access privacy.

Most of the previous research works concentrated only on access-control policies and query execution over encrypted EHRs. Given that EHRs contain highly sensitive and private information, it is important to ensure access protection for outsourced information. The proposed index structure R-table effectively hides information related to an access request or a sequence of requests that aimed at a specific EHR.

3 Proposed Indexing Scheme R-table

An initial level of protection is offered by the storage organization of R-table. The basic construction of R-table adapts both a dynamic array and an RBST. The database is divided into equal-sized data fragments which are then mapped into partitions. Each partition is organized as a RBST to support efficient access without exposing index information.

We considered a data owner who wishes to outsource the database to a semi-trusted CDSP while preserving privacy. The objective of R-table is to hide data-access patterns from semi-trusted CDSPs. We assume that the data outsourced is fragmented into small units of information (equal to disk block) and is indexed by a unique key. To support efficient retrieval, the storage construction organizes the data using the proposed indexing structure R-table. The data fragments are grouped into partitions using random mapping function, which is then indexed using an RBST. The partition process enables to limit the height of the underlying RBST and therefore the length of the search path. Index values are randomly mapped into a partition index in a non-order preserving way which protects the relationship between a fragment index and partition index. Every fragment has the same size and if not then padded with dummy bits. All the fragments are well distributed among the partitions. The number of partition is fixed in advance as $\log n$, where n is the total number of fragments. If any partition has less than $n/\log n$, then that partition is added with dummy fragments. Figure 1 shows the storage organization R-table in detail.

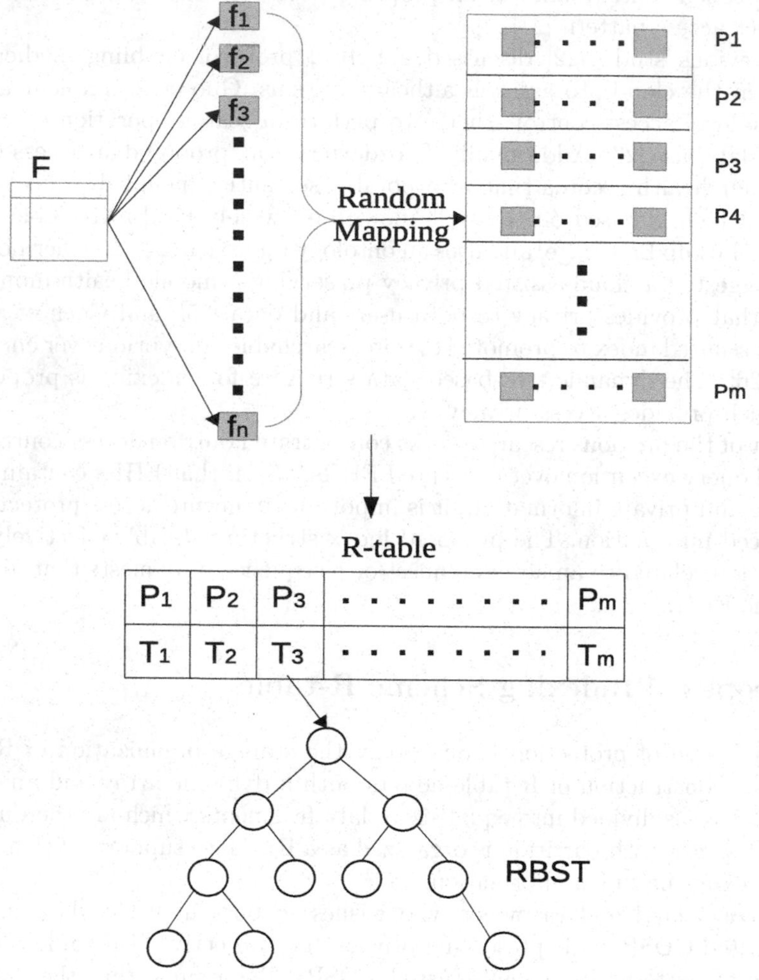

Fig. 1. Storage organization of R-table

To provide content confidentiality, the data owner encrypts each fragment before uploading to the cloud. In the proposed model, we have used Advanced Encryption Standard (AES-256) [28] encryption algorithm. Also, the model employs MAC (Message Authentication Code) to achieve message integrity and authenticity. Therefore, the data owner maintains two secret keys namely SK

for encryption and K_M for MAC function. Formally, a node content is created as $node = CT||Ticket$ where $CT = E(f_{ID}, SK)$ and $Ticket = MAC(id||CT, K_M)$.

3.1 Index Creation

The database is divided into n fragments $\{f_1, f_2, \ldots, f_n\}$ of δ-sized bits. For efficient physical access, we assumed that δ is a multiple of the disk-block size [15], and each fragment, f_i, is identified by an index value for the search. Assuming that n is a power of 2, $\log n$ bits are needed to represent a fragment identifier (f_{id}). Let $I = \{i_1, i_2, \ldots, i_n\}$ represent the entire index space. Each index, i_k, is mapped into an equivalence table using the modulus operator ($mod \quad m$), where m is a design parameter, and we assume that $m = \log n$. Here the index space I is partitioned as, $I = p_0 \cup p_1 \cup p_2 \cup \ldots \cup p_{m-1}$ and $p_j \cap p_k = \phi$ where $j \neq k$. R-table creation is given in Algorithm 1.

A two-level logical-storage structure is proposed that prevents the CDSP from learning access-pattern information. First-level indexing stores partitions, with the second-level storing indexing information associated with the data fragments in a given partition. Each partition holds $\lfloor n/m \rfloor$ elements, which limits the height of the BST, given that the BST is organized as an RBST. To support index-based retrieval, R-table requires both the partition and file identifiers. Implementation of R-table assumes that the RBST node and file identifiers are the same. Additionally, R-table indexing comprises a combination of partition and fragment identifiers called a slot index (Definition 1).

Definition 1. *Slot index is defined as,* $I = \langle P_{id}, n_{id} \rangle$ *which represents a slot in the R-table where* P_{id} *is the partition identifier and* n_{id} *is the node in the respective RBST.*

The server organizes data in the R-table as distinct, but connected, RBSTs. Note that only first mapping uses the equivalence function and that subsequent access to a data item will always randomly map to a new slot index. The calculation of the slot index is shown in Fig. 2.

Map-table H stores the information associated with the random mapping for each partition. A single map table requires O(log(n/m)) bits, as each partition holds $\lfloor n/m \rfloor$ elements. To retrieve a file from the CDSP, a user issues a request with the file identifier, and map-table H_i representing the map value of the requested file is retrieved. Using the file identifier allows the current slot index to be determined, and enables the CDSP to locate the intended partition and node identifier according to the slot index calculation shown in Fig. 2.

R-table Read and Write. R-table uses masking requests to hide the access to a particular index location, with the number of masking requests varying from [3... m] (<3 introduces very low entropy; Figs. 3 and 4). Irrespective of the type of operation (read or write), proposed algorithm follows the same sequence of actions, search-splay-remove-insert. The requested data fragment is searched on a tree and is then splayed to the root node. Splaying is essential as it creates new parent-child relationships with rotations in the BST. The root node now holds

Algorithm 1. Root Table Creation

Input: Data file fragments $F = \{f_1, f_2, \ldots, f_n\}$
Output: Storage Index R-table

Initialize CU map tables $H_0, H_1, H_2, \ldots, H_{m-1} \longleftarrow$ NULL;
Initialize partition tables of RT $p_0, p_1, \ldots, p_{m-1} \longleftarrow$ NULL ;
foreach $(f_i \; in \; F)$ **do**
  Partition id $id \leftarrow f_i(mod \quad M)$;
  Assign map value, $bv_i \leftarrow id$;
  Add f_i to the respective partition Class;
  $H_{id} \leftarrow H_{id} \cup (f_i, bv)$;
  $p_{id} \leftarrow p_{id} \cup f_i$;
end
foreach $(p_i, i \in [0..m-1])$ **do**
  $root \leftarrow createRBST\,(p_i)$;
  $RT[i][0] \leftarrow i$;
  $RT[i][1] \leftarrow root$;
end
Return R-table, RT.

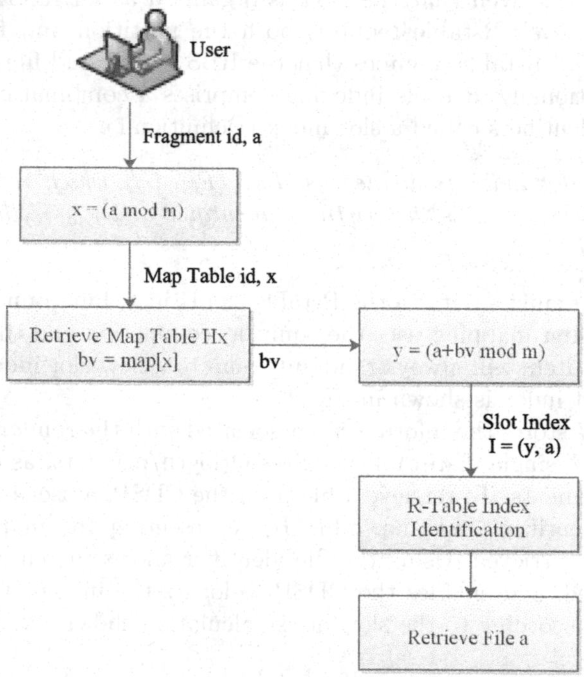

Fig. 2. Calculation of slot index, I

the target fragment which is deleted and send to the data user. Then, either the left child or right child is made as the new root. The selection of new root element is performed in such a way that it avoids degeneration.

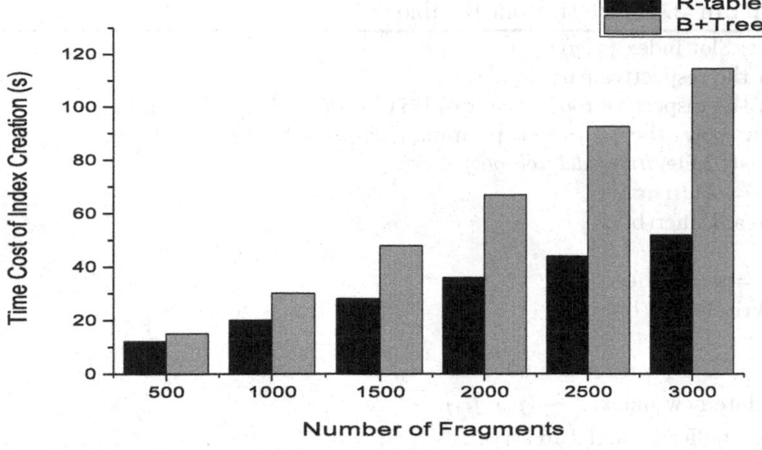

Fig. 3. Time cost of index creation

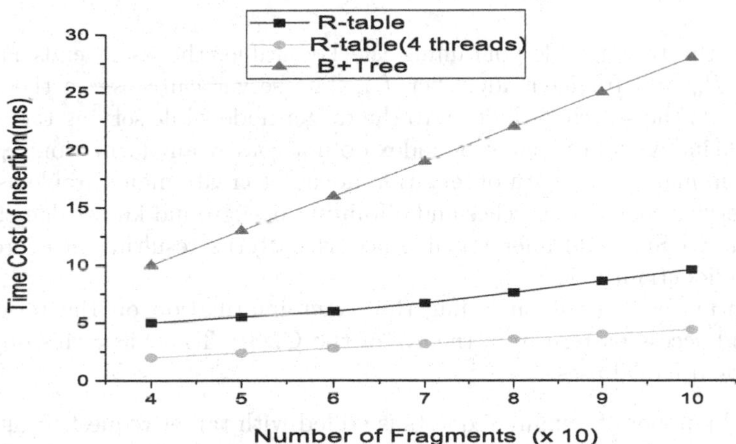

Fig. 4. Time cost of insertion

The retrieval process is shown in Algorithm 2. Retrieval removes the target file irrespective of the type of operation (read or write), thereby hiding the access operation from the observer. The ReadBuffer subroutine decrypts the file before reading, and WriteBuffer decrypts and modifies the file. Later, the file is randomly mapped to a different slot index, with the random mapping destroying the static relationship between fragments and the index location.

Algorithm 2. Retrieval from R-table

Input: Slot index (x, y),operation op
Fetch the respective partition, x;
Fetch the respective root pointer of BST, $root \leftarrow R - table(y)$;
Search splays the f_{id} to root position, $Search - Splay(root, f_{id})$;
Requested file, $bf \leftarrow delete(root)$;
if $op = read$ **then**
    ReadBuffer(bf);
end
if $op = write$ **then**
    WriteBuffer(bf);
end
$bv_{new} \leftarrow UniformRandom[0 \ldots m - 1]$;
Calculate new index, $\hat{I} \leftarrow (\grave{p}_{id}, f_{id})$;
Upload buffer bf and $\hat{I}$ to server;

4 Access Protection

To access the target node containing the key value, the user sends partition identifier P_{id} and fragment identifier f_{id}. The server can observe the specific partition and the search path down to the target node while serving the request. Since node index and the partition index do not convey any formation regarding the random mapping, a path observation does not create many problems. However, observing multiple searches and obtaining background knowledge of target nodes, the CDSP could infer possible access patterns resulting in a breach in access confidentiality.

The primary focus is on hiding the exact information on the target of a search and access pattern from the eye of the CDSP. To achieve this objective, the proposed model uses:

- A fixed number of dummy requests is added with target request to introduce more entropy regarding the exact target node.
- Each requested node (containing the target fragment) is splayed to the root node. Splaying introduces random repositioning of a fraction of nodes in the BST.
- Each operation (read or write) follows the same sequence of operations, search-splay-remove-insert, which hides the type of access operation from the CDSP.

Accessing always a constant number of partitions regardless of where the target is located makes all accesses look alike from the view of a CDSP. The use of height balanced tree creates computational overhead during insertion and deletion. To have an optimal tree giving freedom in height balancing, we use RBST. During insertion, RBST behaves as ordinary BST. However, during the search, the target node is splayed to the root and is removed. The splaying property of Splay trees is used here. Therefore, the RBST used in the proposed model imparts dual behavior to introduce more entropy. The use of RBST avoids the situation of degeneration (maximum tree height).

The use of masking requests are chosen in such a way that they initiate a search in different partitions. Each request is serviced in the same manner as the target request. The search begins with the intended partition, and it follows a path in the BST from the root node to target node. Then, the target node is splayed to the root, and it is removed and send to the data user. The removed node is then inserted into another partition different from the original which ensures that almost every partition is randomly accessed. The random accessing of partitions prevents the server from making a statistical analysis on frequently accessed partitions. Moreover, splaying the target node to the root introduces rotation on subtrees which swaps the parent-child nodes. This makes the server not to identify repeated search strings. Since the accessed fragments are inserted into a different partition, the proposed storage structure induces a dynamic indexing structure. Hence, the uncertainty in finding the indexing relationship is high in the proposed storage model R-table. The random re-allocation in partitions prevents the server from accumulating information on the indexing structure. A subsequent access visiting the same partition may follow a different path and will target a different fragment. This prevents the server from determining whether two repeated visits in the same partition and same tree node is for the same fragment.

5 Security Analysis

We analyzed the security of the R-table by considering a sequence of requests, $x_1 = ((f_1, op), (f_2, op), \ldots, (f_m, op))$, and $x_2 = ((f_1, op), (f_2, op), \ldots, (f_m, op))$. Both request strings x_1 and x_2 denote the same request pattern; however, execution of x_1 followed by x_2 or x_2 followed by x_1 results in different index-access patterns according to the retrieval algorithm. The proposed algorithm ensures minimal correlation between the access patterns of slot indexes, because each access results in a new map value. Following each access request, the intended file is randomly remapped randomly to a new slot index in the R-table to ensure maximum entropy while effectively hiding the access pattern, thereby preserving access-order privacy.

Considering a situation where the CDSP has identified the slot index of a particular data fragment via other means and attempts to track future access of this data fragment. Each time the access information is divided over m partitions and n/m nodes in the RBST, dynamic remapping destroys the relationship between the data fragments and the slot index. Although the R-table cannot achieve a zero probability of accessing information, given that it contains only a finite number of partitions, random mapping allows for a reduced probability of obtaining the access information.

Repeated requests for a file in the R-table are mapped to different partition tables and RBSTs, thereby making it difficult to establish relationships between the slot index and the file. Simultaneously, repeated partition access does not point to the same file in the R-table. For example, access of data fragment d_i from partition p_j results in a probability of accessing d_i from the same partition, p_j, in the next request of zero. The results of our security analysis indicated the effectiveness of R-table in providing access privacy for EHRs outsourced to the cloud.

5.1 Communication and Storage Overhead

To process an access request (read or write), the following operations are performed:

- Retrieve the map table, H_i, corresponding to the request.
- Compute the slot index, I.
- Send the request, $R(I)$, along with r masking requests, where $r \in [1 \ldots m-1]$.
- The server identifies the respective partitions, removes those data fragments from the respective RBSTs, and sends the results to the user.
- The CU decrypts the received data fragments, remaps the data fragments to new slot indexes, and sends the data back to the CDSP.
- The CDSP identifies the respective partitions and inserts them into the RBSTs.

Assume that the data-fragment size is δ bytes, and that the number of partitions is $m = \log n$. For r requests, r map tables will be retrieved, where each H_i needs $O(\log m)$ bits to store the binding information. Therefore, the total number of bytes transferred to and from the server per single-access request is:

$$\Delta = r * O(\log n . \log m) + r * \delta + r * \delta + r * O(\log n . \log m) \quad (1)$$

where $\log m$ is $\log \log n$.

The server needs to store mapping tables in addition to the R-table, which induces a storage overhead of $O(n \log n)$ bits. Additionally, to process read and write requests, the client is required to store only partition identifiers from the R-table, which introduces $O(\log (n/m))$ bits of storage overhead.

In Table 1, we compared the overhead of the R-table with that of a lightweight protocol (LWP) [19] and access scheme for an untrusted-storage server [18].

Table 1. Comparison of overhead incurred in access protection schemes

	Comm. overhead	Storage overhead (Server)	Storage overhead (Client)
R-table(r = 4)	$O(\log n \log \log n + \delta)$	$O(n . \log n)$	$O(\log (n/m))$
LWP (m = 4) [19]	$O((\log n)^2 + \delta)$	$O(n.max(\log n, \delta))$	$O(max(\log n, \delta))$
ORAM based [18]	$O(\log n \log \log n.\delta)$	$O(n.\delta)$	$O(\sqrt{n}.\delta)$

The improved communication and storage overhead facilitates the use of the R-table on thin clients. The LWP suggested by Yang et al. [19] uses previous access-history files, and the storage organization proposed by Williams et al. [18] is ORAM-based and uses oblivious scrambling and fake data bits to achieve access privacy. However, R-table achieves better performance with masking requests without using fake data bits or previous access-history files.

6 Experimental Analysis

We implemented the proposed R-table in Java and used the datasets from the University of California, Irvine [29] to validate the performance of R-table. To evaluate the effectiveness of providing access privacy via R-table, we used breast cancer and thyroid-disease datasets containing basic information regarding disease characteristics and symptoms. The design of R-table claims that:

1. Dummy mask requests and dynamic remapping effectively reduced CDSP knowledge regarding correspondence between nodes and data fragments.
2. Similarities between data-fragment-access profiles was indistinguishable by the CDSP.

We evaluated the time cost of R-table index creation against the number of records. Since, the dataset had only 1500 records, we have duplicated the records with varying some field data. The performance is compared with the well known state-of-art index creation data structure B+Tree. Since R-table uses simple random mapping function to partition the entire database records, it takes less than linear time to do the partition job. Then, the RBST tree creation can be performed in parallel using multiple threads and the time cost is at the most $\log \log n$. Therefore, index creation cost of R-table is almost linear and is better compared to that of B+Tree as shown in Fig. 3.

Each access operation irrespective or read or write follows the same sequence of actions, search-splay-remove-insert, in the proposed model permitting R-table to hide the type of operation. Therefore, insertion and deletion are frequent operations in the proposed retrieval algorithm. Hence, the time cost of both insertion and deletion is measured against the number of fragments. Since each partition can be handled independently, the implementation used multiple threads to achieve optimal performance. Insertion is a simple operation as per the retrieval algorithm and the time complexity to perform a single insertion operation in partition is $\log \log n$. Find a suitable leaf node for insertion in a partition RBST and the number of elements present in tree is $\log n$. Compared to B+Tree, R-table achieves better performance since insertion in a B+Tree includes the cost of node splitting and rearranging the key values and the result is shown in Fig. 4.

The deletion cost is slightly more in R-table compared to that of B+Tree. In the case of B+Tree, deletion involves search and sometimes node merging, whereas in R-table deletion follows binary search then splaying (which involves rotation) and removing the root node. However, better performance can be achieved by multiple threads in parallel and the results are shown in Fig. 5.

The probability of determining the location of a fragment, f_i, is divided into the probabilities associated with determining the partition and the corresponding RBST node inside of the partition. Assuming that the CDSP knows both

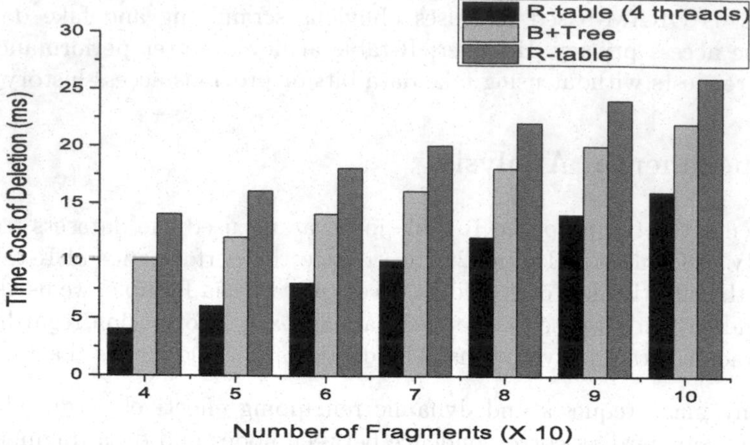

Fig. 5. Time cost of deletion

the partition and node location in the RBST $p(f_i, L_i) = 1$, where L_i denotes the location of the ith fragment, following the first access, this probability is divided over m partitions and n/m nodes in the RBST, which is equal to $(1/m \times 1/n/m) = 1/n > 0$. A probability of $1/n$ introduces maximum randomness, thereby increasing entropy, and subsequent accesses will destroy the relationship between the fragment identifier and the slot index. The selection of a partition identifier is random, with each location having an equal probability of being selected.

The access pattern of the primary location distribution for repeated request strings $d_{22}, d_5, d_{39}, d_{23}, d_{41}$ is shown in Table 2, where d_i refers to the ith data block. Let us assume that there exists 4096 data blocks in total and 12 partitions ($\log 4096 = 12$). As shown in Fig. 2, d_{22} is initially mapped onto partition $p_{10}, (22 \ \ mod 12 = 10)$ with a binding value of 10. For subsequent access, d_{22} is retrieved from partition p_{10}, but remapped onto another partition $[rand(1 \ldots 12)]$, resulting in an entirely different location and verifying that the R-table introduces maximum entropy and effectively hides the access pattern.

Table 2. Primary location distribution for repeated access request

Request	Initial P_{id}	Remapped P_{id}	Repeating request	Retrieved P_{id}	Remapped P_{id}
d_{22}	p_{10}	p_2	d_{22}	p_2	p_7
d_5	p_5	p_{10}	d_5	p_{10}	p_1
d_{39}	p_3	p_8	d_{39}	p_8	p_{11}
d_{23}	p_{11}	p_6	d_{23}	p_6	p_{12}
d_{41}	p_5	p_9	d_{41}	p_9	p_3

Maximum entropy is achieved when all index locations are accessed with equal probability. For a total of 4096 data blocks, the maximum entropy will be

$$H_R^{max} = -4096 \times 1/4096 \quad log(1/4096) = 12 \tag{2}$$

We evaluated how the entropy of user-access frequency changes as the number of masking requests increases. Figure 6 shows that average entropy increases at a higher rate with the increase in the number of masking requests. R-table achieves 50% entropy with the number of masking requests equal to three. Therefore, the proposed model fixes the lower bound of masking requests as three. The results show that maximum entropy is achieved with masking requests 11 and 12, where 12 is the maximum number of partitions. However, more number of masking requests incurs overhead in computation and communication cost.

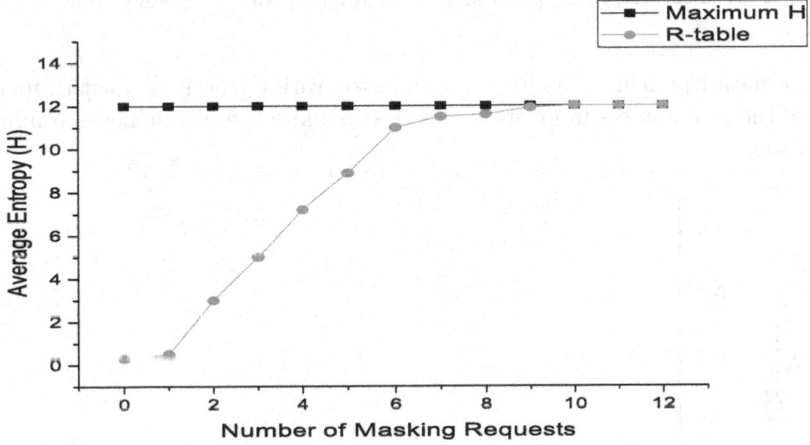

Fig. 6. Change in average entropy as the number of masking request increases

Average entropy of slot index location for frequently accessed data items is shown in Fig. 7. The uncertainty in location similarity is measured for various masking requests. After a few rounds of execution, the maximum entropy is achieved due to random mapping of partition and splaying in the BST. More number of masking requests enables R-table to converge fast towards the maximum entropy. Therefore, the experiments have used $r = 4$ as the number of masking request to achieve optimal performance with minimum communication and computation cost.

Similar Access Profile. Initially, we have measured the correlation between location accesses for the same input request string and the result is shown in Fig. 8. Due to the random mapping of partition and splaying, though the request is

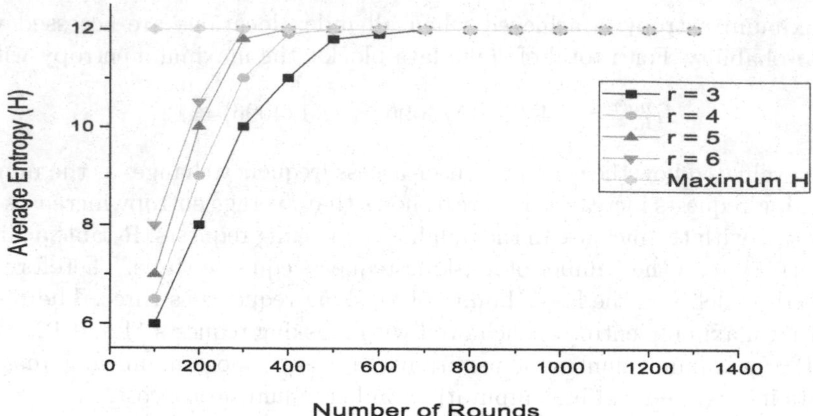

Fig. 7. Average entropy of slot index for frequently accessed items

for same data fragments, the location accessed varies greatly. As with repeated accesses the randomness in location accessed is more thereby achieves minimum correlation.

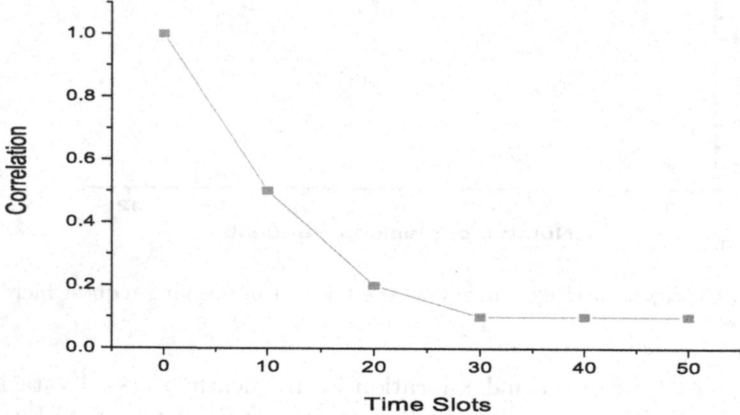

Fig. 8. Correlation between accessed index location for the same input request string.

Sequence of slot indexes following normal distribution is artificially generated to measure the correlation between similar access profiles. Four request distributions are created with varying levels of similarity and the correlation between successive location accesses are measured. Figure 9 shows that the R-table achieved the minimum correlation.

Experimental and security analysis shows that the proposed indexing structure R-table efficiently provides user-access privacy for querying the outsourced medical database. This performance can be further improved by adding access-control policies for sharing information in EHRs.

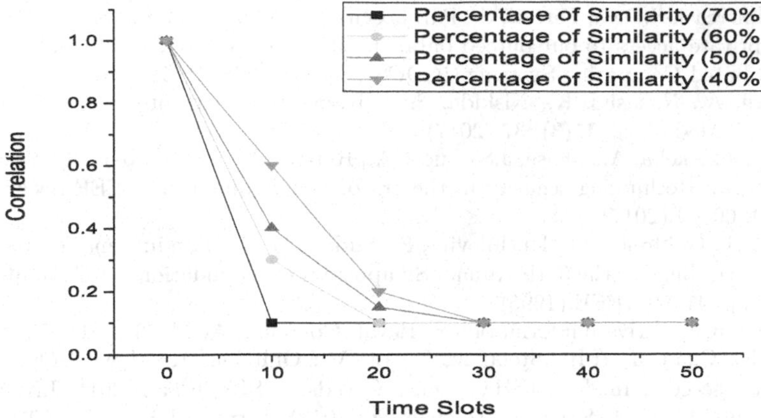

Fig. 9. Correlation between access profiles

7 Conclusion and Future Work

In this study, we implemented a novel, dynamically allocating data structure called R-table that preserves access privacy to EHRs outsourced to the cloud. The data structure R-table focuses on storage organization, which provides dynamic remapping of data fragments, thereby destroying static relationships between data fragments and indexes. R-table ensures access privacy with minimal overhead and costs as compared with other prominent previously proposed schemes. Additionally, R-table indexing can be used for thin client, such as mobile users.

Future work in this area will involve modification of R-table to support range queries. Also, we look into the real-world deployment of R-table in healthcare systems to integrate efficient encryption and access-control schemes, thereby providing a complete cloud-based security solution.

References

1. Mell, P., Grance, T.: The NIST definition of cloud computing (2011)
2. Fernández-Alemán, J.L., Señor, I.C., Lozoya, P.Á.O., Toval, A.: Security and privacy in electronic health records: a systematic literature review. J. Biomed. Inform. **46**(3), 541–562 (2013)
3. Sajid, A., Abbas, H.: Data privacy in cloud-assisted healthcare systems: state of the art and future challenges. J. Med. Syst. **40**(6), 1–16 (2016)
4. Latif, R., Abbas, H., Latif, S., Masood, A.: Distributed denial of service attack source detection using efficient traceback technique (ETT) in cloud-assisted healthcare environment. J. Med. Syst. **40**(7), 1–13 (2016)
5. Sultan, N.: Making use of cloud computing for healthcare provision: opportunities and challenges. Int. J. Inf. Manag. **34**(2), 177–184 (2014)
6. Zhou, J., Cao, Z., Dong, X., Vasilakos, A.V.: Security and privacy for cloud-based IoT: challenges. IEEE Commun. Mag. **55**(1), 26–33 (2017)

7. di Vimercati, S.D.C., Foresti, S., Paraboschi, S., Pelosi, G., Samarati, P.: Efficient and private access to outsourced data. In: 2011 31st International Conference on Distributed Computing Systems (ICDCS), pp. 710–719. IEEE (2011)
8. Miyaji, A., Nakasho, K., Nishida, S.: Privacy-preserving integration of medical data. J. Med. Syst. **41**(3), 37 (2017)
9. Aikat, J., Akella, A., Chase, J.S., Juels, A., Reiter, M.K., Ristenpart, T., Sekar, V., Swift, M.: Rethinking security in the era of cloud computing. IEEE Secur. Priv. **15**(3), 60–69 (2017)
10. Chor, B., Goldreich, O., Kushilevitz, E., Sudan, M.: Private information retrieval. In: Proceedings of the 36th Annual Symposium on Foundations of Computer Science, pp. 41–50. IEEE (1995)
11. Yekhanin, S.: Private information retrieval. Commun. ACM **53**(4), 68–73 (2010)
12. Shi, E., Chan, T.-H.H., Stefanov, E., Li, M.: Oblivious RAM with $O((\log N)^3)$ worst-case cost. In: Lee, D.H., Wang, X. (eds.) ASIACRYPT 2011. LNCS, vol. 7073, pp. 197–214. Springer, Heidelberg (2011). https://doi.org/10.1007/978-3-642-25385-0_11
13. Goodrich, M.T., Mitzenmacher, M., Ohrimenko, O., Tamassia, R.: Privacy-preserving group data access via stateless oblivious RAM simulation. In: Proceedings of the Twenty-Third Annual ACM-SIAM Symposium on Discrete Algorithms, pp. 157–167. Society for Industrial and Applied Mathematics (2012)
14. Tang, J., Cui, Y., Li, Q., Ren, K., Liu, J., Buyya, R.: Ensuring security and privacy preservation for cloud data services. ACM Comput. Surv. (CSUR) **49**(1), 13 (2016)
15. di Vimercati, S.D.C., Foresti, S., Paraboschi, S., Pelosi, G., Samarati, P.: Shuffle index: efficient and private access to outsourced data. ACM Trans. Storage (TOS) **11**(4), 19 (2015)
16. Martínez, C., Roura, S.: Randomized binary search trees. J. ACM (JACM) **45**(2), 288–323 (1998)
17. AbuKhousa, E., Mohamed, N., Al-Jaroodi, J.: e-Health cloud: opportunities and challenges. Future Internet **4**(3), 621–645 (2012)
18. Williams, P., Sion, R., Carbunar, B.: Building castles out of mud: practical access pattern privacy and correctness on untrusted storage. In: Proceedings of the 15th ACM conference on Computer and communications security, pp. 139–148. ACM (2008)
19. Yang, K., Zhang, J., Zhang, W., Qiao, D.: A light-weight solution to preservation of access pattern privacy in un-trusted clouds. In: Atluri, V., Diaz, C. (eds.) ESORICS 2011. LNCS, vol. 6879, pp. 528–547. Springer, Heidelberg (2011). https://doi.org/10.1007/978-3-642-23822-2_29
20. Li, L., Datta, A.: Write-only oblivious RAM-based privacy-preserved access of outsourced data. Int. J. Inf. Secur. **16**(1), 23–42 (2017)
21. Sahin, C., Magat, A., Zakhary, V., El Abbadi, A., Lin, H.R., Tessaro, S.: Understanding the security challenges of oblivious cloud storage with asynchronous accesses. In: 2017 IEEE 33rd International Conference on Data Engineering (ICDE), pp. 1377–1378. IEEE (2017)
22. Yang, J.-J., Li, J.-Q., Niu, Y.: A hybrid solution for privacy preserving medical data sharing in the cloud environment. Future Gener. Comput. Syst. **43**, 74–86 (2015)
23. Guo, C., Zhuang, R., Jie, Y., Ren, Y., Wu, T., Choo, K.-K.R.: Fine-grained database field search using attribute-based encryption for e-Healthcare clouds. J. Med. Syst. **40**(11), 235 (2016)
24. Drozdowicz, M., Ganzha, M., Paprzycki, M.: Semantically enriched data access policies in ehealth. J. Med. Syst. **40**(11), 238 (2016)

25. Lin, H., Shao, J., Zhang, C., Fang, Y.: CAM: cloud-assisted privacy preserving mobile health monitoring. IEEE Trans. Inf. Forensics Secur. **8**(6), 985–997 (2013)
26. Chen, Y.-C., Horng, G., Lin, Y.-J., Chen, K.-C.: Privacy preserving index for encrypted electronic medical records. J. Med. Syst. **37**(6), 9992 (2013)
27. di Vimercati, S.D.C., Foresti, S., Moretti, R., Paraboschi, S., Pelosi, G., Samarati, P.: A dynamic tree-based data structure for access privacy in the cloud (2016)
28. Chen, Y., Sion, R.: On securing untrusted clouds with cryptography. In: Proceedings of the 9th Annual ACM Workshop on Privacy in the Electronic Society, pp. 109–114. ACM (2010)
29. Lichman, M.: UCI machine learning repository (2013)

Efficient Artificial Bee Colony Optimization

Ankita Rajawat(✉), Nirmala Sharma, and Harish Sharma

Rajasthan Technical University, Kota, India
ankitarajawat2@gmail.com, nsharma@rtu.ac.in, harish.sharma0107@gmail.com

Abstract. Artificial bee colony (ABC) algorithm is one of the proficient meta-heuristic technique in the field of nature inspired algorithms to solve the optimization problems. ABC has been proven itself as better candidate in the field of nature inspired algorithms. But, still it shows some limitations like improper balance betwixt exploration and exploitation, premature convergence and stagnation problem. To overcome these limitations, a new variant of ABC algorithm named as Efficient Artificial Bee Colony Optimization (EABC) algorithm. In the proposed EABC, three new strategies are incorporated named as Self-Adaptive Strategy, Self-Adaptive Mutual Learning Strategy, and Exploring Strategy. The Self-Adaptive Strategy is incorporated in the employed bee phase and it help to improve the balance betwixt exploration and exploitation. The Self-Adaptive Mutual Learning Strategy is applied on onlooker phase and it help remove premature convergence. And last Exploring Strategy is applied on scout bee phase to remove stagnation and improve the optimal searching ability. The EABC is compared over 21 test benchmark functions and there results are compared with basic version of ABC, its significant variants namely, Best So Far ABC (BSFABC), Modified ABC (MABC), Black Hole ABC (BHABC), Memetic ABC (MeABC) and one recent swarm intelligence based Spider Monkey Optimization (SMO). The examination of the outcomes demonstrates that the proposed EABC Algorithm is a competitive variant of ABC.

Keywords: Optimization techniques
Artificial bee colony algorithm · Nature inspired algorithm

1 Introduction

With the advent of computational intelligence, swarm intelligence came into attention in nature inspired methods for solving a real-world optimization problems. In past decade, swarm intelligence based algorithms mimic the collective behavior of animals, insects, and birds which live in groups. An animal, insects, and birds use the social learning ability to solve the complex problems. Many researchers working on the social behavior of creatures and developed many algorithms like particle swarm optimization (PSO) [13], ant colony optimization

P. Bhattacharyya et al. (Eds.): NGCT 2017, CCIS 827, pp. 228–245, 2018.
https://doi.org/10.1007/978-981-10-8657-1_18

(ACO) [17], spider monkey optimization (SMO) [7], artificial bee colony (ABC) [14], grey wolf Optimizer (GWO) [20], etc. for solving the nonlinear, non-convex, and discrete optimization problem. According to the previous research, swarm intelligent algorithm has a high potential to find the optimum solution for real world problem.

Swarm intelligence based artificial bee colony algorithm which is developed by Karaboga in [14]. ABC mimic the social behavior of honey bees for finding the quality food source. Honey bee contains two types of bee one is employed bee and other one un-employee bee. In ABC there are three different stages are employed bee stage, onlooker bee stage, and scout bee stage. Employed bee goes first and finds the food in the search area. Then according to the fitness of food source onlooker bee went for the solution search. Therefore, if food source has lost its food, then that particular bee became scout bee and searched food randomly in the search area. In ABC employed bee and onlooker bee, responsible for the position update in the search space and scout bee for finding food source randomly. ABC is very effective, efficient, simple and populace based stochastic algorithm. But there are some drawbacks in ABC like premature convergence, stagnation problem, poor convergence rate and bad at exploration ability. So researcher continuous working [4,6,8,23] towards its drawbacks and developed many variants. Zhu and Kwong in [25] introduce a new variant to improve the exploitation of ABC by using global best information in position update equation. Karaboga and Akay in [15] developed new variant to improve its efficiency by incorporating Deb's rules with three heuristic rules and a probabilistic selection scheme. Banharnsakun et al. in [3] developed a new variant to improve slow convergence by modifying the position update equation by incorporating best so far position information and it also introduces an adjustable radius in scout bee phase. Tsai in (2009) introduces gravitational approach in ABC to enhance the exploration ability. Pan in [21] developed a discrete approach in ABC to improve local search ability. Lei in [16] improve the precision and efficiency of ABC by using inertia weight which balances the local and global search. In 2013 Bansal and Sharma [5] developed new variant which balance diversification and intensification by incorporating a new phase. Sharma in [24] also introduce a new concept of black hole in ABC to improve exploration capability while maintaining the exploitation ability.

Therefore, in this paper, another variation of ABC introduced names as EABC algorithm is proposed to balance the exploitation and exploration abilities of ABC algorithm. This variant is tested on 21 well-known optimization problem. Through measurable examinations, it is asserted that the EABC is competitive variant of ABC for solving consistent optimization problems.

Rest of the paper is sorted as: Sect. 2 portrays brief outline of the artificial bee colony algorithm. Efficient Artificial Bee Colony Optimization (EABC) is proposed and tried in Sect. 3. In Sect. 4, execution of the proposed methodology is broke down. At last, in the last Sect. 5, paper is summarized.

2 Overview of Artificial Bee Colony (ABC) Algorithm

ABC algorithm is swarm based meta-heuristic iterative search method which is used to solve the optimization problems. ABC imitate the behavior of food searching of bees, and its process mainly separated into four steps which are initialization stage, employed bee stage, onlooker bee stage, and scout bee stage. Each of the steps explained below:

Initialization: In first step food source m_i ($i = 1, 2, \ldots;$ SN) randomly initialized in search area with D-dimension vector among the uniformly scattered food source SN and D is the number of a variable present in the optimization problem.

$$m_{ij} = m_{lowj} + rand[0,1](m_{uppj} - m_{lowj}) \tag{1}$$

Where, m_{lowj} and m_{uppj} are represent the lower (low) and upper (upp) bounds of m_i in j^{th} direction and the uniformly scattered the population in the range $[0, 1]$.

After initial stage of population, ABC move to the next steps which named as employed bee stage, onlooker bee stage, and scout bee stage to be executed.

2.1 Employed Bee Stage

In this stage, i^{th} candidate update its position by using neighboring search and the fitness value of the new solutions, if it is higher than current solution then update the new solution otherwise remain current position. The solution update equation is given below:

$$u_{ij} = m_{ij} + \phi_{ij}(m_{ij} - m_{kj}) \tag{2}$$

Here, $k \in \{1, 2, \ldots, SN\}$ and $j \in \{1, 2, \ldots, D\}$ are chosen randomly $k \neq i$. The random number $\phi_{ij} \in [-1, 1]$.

Probability Calculation: After updating the position of solution in employee bee stage, bee return to its hive and share information of nectar to the onlooker bee by dancing. Now, onlooker bee apply roulette wheel selection to select the food source according to the nectar information provided by employed bee. Therefore probability of selecting food source i as shown:

$$prob_i = \frac{0.9 \times fit_i}{maxfit} + 0.1 \tag{3}$$

Where, fit_i represent fitness of ith solution. Now, fit_i is calculated by:

$$fit_i = \begin{cases} \frac{1}{1+f_i} & \text{if } f_i \geq 0, \\ 1 + |(f_i)| & \text{if } f_i \leq 0. \end{cases} \tag{4}$$

where, f_i is objective function value.

2.2 Onlooker Bee Stage

In this stage according to the probability calculation, each of the onlooker bee chooses a food source to search its nearby area further. The position update equation of onlooker bee is same as employed bee Eq. 2.

2.3 Scout Bee Stage

When a food source cannot be improved after some limit then this food source considered as abandoned food source. Then the employed bee of that abandoned food source became scout bee and randomly search for a new food source in search area by using Eq. 1.

3 Efficient Artificial Bee Colony Optimization

In this section, to overcome the premature convergence and to prevent the situation of avoiding the true solution due to the unpredicted long jumps, a new variant of ABC algorithm is proposed namely Efficient artificial bee colony (EABC) optimization algorithm.

It is evident from the position update condition 2 of the ABC that the new sustenance position is produced by coordinating the old one towards an arbitrarily choose sustenance position's from the swarm. In this way, there is equal opportunity to avoid the global optima, to get a good food solution or to get a terrible one. Advance, the solution update condition is altogether ruled by a coefficient ϕ_{ij} which is a uniform random number generator in the range $[-1, 1]$. This way, the ϕ_{ij} enhances the diversification at the cost of exploitation. In order to make the ABC better at both exploration and exploitation or to balance these two properties, in the proposed EABC algorithm, a self-adaptive step size mechanisms are applied in the employed as well as onlooker bee phase as well as to improve the diversification, the initialization process of scout be phase is updated as follows: The main aim of this modification to remove it drawback by incorporating three strategies in this paper as follow:

1. **Self Adaptive Position Update Strategy in Employed Bee Phase:** In optimization algorithms, an algorithm is considered as an efficient algorithm that explores the search area in early iterations while exploits in the later iteration. The existing position update equation in employed bee phase (refer 2) always depends on random difference vector and the random component (ϕ) and that may lead to skipping the best solution due to large step size or make the convergence process slow.
   Therefore, a self adaptive position update process is incorporated in employed bee phase as shown in Eq. 5. The proposed process is inspired from DE [9].

$$u_{ij} = \begin{cases} m_{ij} + \phi_{ij}(m_{ij} - m_{kj}) & \text{if } (r < 1 - (t/T_m)^2), \\ m_{ij} + \phi_{ij}(Gm_j - m_{kj}) & \text{Otherwise.} \end{cases} \quad (5)$$

In Eq. 5, t is current iteration, T_m is maximum number of iterations, Gm_j is the best solution in the swarm, and r is a uniform random number between $[0, 1]$. This solution search process in divided into two parts based on the condition $(r < 1-(t/T_m)^2)$. If the condition is true, then the normal solution search process takes place i.e. the proposed algorithm will explore the search area while when the condition is false, the global best-guided solution search process starts which helps in an exploitation of the search area. Further, it is clear that the chance of getting true of condition $(r < 1 - (t/T_m)^2)$ will be high in early iteration due to the low value of t and vice-versa. So in early iterations, the proposed solution search process will explore while in later iterations, it will exploit the search area.

2. **Self Adaptive Mutual Learning in Onlooker Bee Phase:** In this phase, a self-adaptive mutual learning strategy is incorporated in onlooker bee phase as shown in Eq. 6.

$$u_{ij} = \begin{cases} \text{if } (r < 1 - (t/T_m)^2 \text{ and } fitm_i > fitm_k) \\ m_{ij} + \phi_{ij}(Gm_i - m_{kj}) * W + \phi_{ij}(m_{ij} - m_{kj}) * W \\ \text{else} \\ m_{ij} + \phi_{ij}(Gm_i - m_{kj}) * W + \phi_{ij}(m_{kj} - m_{ij}) * W \end{cases} \tag{6}$$

Here, $W = 0.5 + r/2$ is a weighted factor [11], $fitm_i$ and $fitm_k$ are fitness of m_i and m_k solutions. It is clear from the third component of the Eq. 6 that the condition $(fitm_i > fitm_k)$ shows that the ith solution is at better position than the kth solution, hence the kth solution will be attracted towards the ith solution whereas if the fitness of kth solution is higher than the fitness of ith solution then the solution move towards the kth solution. This mechanism shows a mutual learning between the neighboring solution and the current solution and the current solution will update while taking a step towards the better solutions. Here, W is used to avoid the situation of premature convergence while maintaining a minimum step size during the position update process.

3. **Exploring Strategy in Scout Bee Phase:** In above optimization search process, the solutions converge to an optimum location (locally or globally) and to avoid stagnation, and scout bee phase plays an important role while randomly initializing the stagnated solutions. As it is clear that the inter-solution differences are reduced as per the iterations during the solution search process and this affects the step size (as the step size of a solution is depends on the vector difference with the neighboring solution) of the solution. So, in later iterations, the solutions in the search area may be too close to each other that the step size or movement of the solutions may become insignificant. Therefore, the position update process of scout bee phase is updated as shown in Eq. 7.

$$m_{ij} = \begin{cases} \text{if } (t > (T_m/2) \text{ and } r < P) \\ m_{ij} = m_{lowj} + rand[0,1](m_{uppj} - m_{lowj}) * W \\ \text{else} \\ m_{ij} = m_{lowj} + rand[0,1](m_{uppj} - m_{lowj}) \end{cases} \tag{7}$$

Here, W and r are same as mentioned in Eq. 6, P represents the a constant. The larger value of P disrupt the searching trajectory of all bees which lead to poor convergence and small value of P will lead to insufficient randomization. So, a median value of P is advisable. According to the Eq. 7 the W is used for maintaining the minimum step size in later iterations of the solution search process and improves the diversification ability of the algorithm.

So, overall, we can say that the above three strategies will help the ABC to balance the exploration and exploitation abilities and improve the optimal searching ability. This is stated experimentally in the subsequent sections. A flow chart in Fig. 1 discusses the entire working of EABC.

4 Outcomes and Discussions

4.1 Test Functions Under Contemplation

To demonstrate the effectiveness of intended EABC, it is applied on 21 distinctive global optimization dilemma here (f_1 to f_{17}) from [2], (f_{18}) from [22], (f_{19}) from [10], f_{20} from [12], and (f_{21}) from [19] as demonstrate in Table 1.

4.2 Experimental Setting

To determine the accomplishment of the suggested algorithm EABC, an analogous analysis is derived out among EABC, ABC, GABC, BSFABC, MABC, BHABC, SMO, and MeABC. To standardized EABC over ABC, GABC, BSFABC, MABC, BHABC, SMO, and MeABC over the deliberate problems, following empirical setting is adopted:

- Run = 100,
- Colony size ($NP = 50$),
- Number of food sources ($SN = NP/2$),
- $P = 0.5$
- $\phi_{ij} = rand[-1, 1]$,
- limit = $D \times SN$ [1] here D = Dimension,
- Parameter setting for the algorithms ABC, GABC, BSFABC, MABC, BHABC, SMO, and MeABC are same as their legitimate research paper.

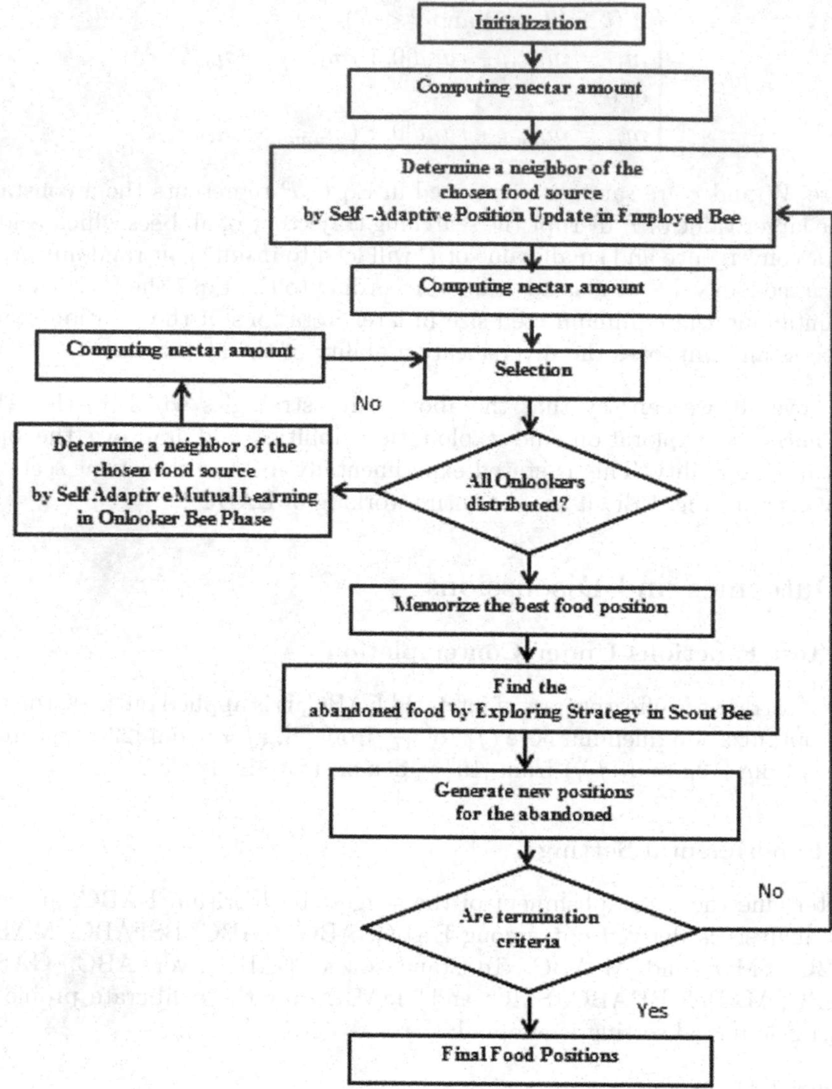

Fig. 1. EABC flowchart

4.3 Results Comparison

The research out-turn over deliberate algorithms are presented in Table 2. The result shown in Table 2 is an estimation over standard-deviation (SD), mean-error (ME), average number of function evaluations (AFE), and success-rate (SR). Results in Table 2 emulate that EABC dominate most of the times in terms of reliability, efficiency, and accuracy as assessed with the ABC, GABC, BSFABC, MABC, BHABC, SMO, and MeABC.

Table 1. Test problems

Test problem	Objective function	Search range	Optimum value	D	Acceptable error
Griewank	$f_1(m) = 1 + \frac{1}{4000}\sum_{i=1}^{D} m_i^2 - \prod_{i=1}^{D}\cos(\frac{m_i}{\sqrt{i}})$	$[-600, 600]$	$f(0) = 0$	30	1.0E−5
Rosenbrock	$f_2(m) = \sum_{i=1}^{D}(100(m_{i+1} - m^2)^2 + (m_i - 1)^2)$	$[-30, 30]$	$f(0) = 0$	30	1.0E−1
Ackley	$f_3(m) = -20 + e + exp(-\frac{0.2}{D}\sqrt{\sum_{i=1}^{D} m_i{}^3}) - exp(\frac{1}{D}\sum_{i=1}^{D}\cos\,(2\pi x_i)m_i)$	$[-11]$	$f(\mathbf{0}) = 0$	30	1.0E−05
Alpine	$f_4(m) = \sum_{i=1}^{n} \lvert m_i \sin\, m_i + 0.1 m_i\rvert$	[-10 10]			
Michalewicz	$f_5(m) = -\sum_{i=1}^{D}\sin\, m_i(\sin\,(\frac{i m_i{}^2}{\pi})^{20})$	$[0, \pi]$	$f_{min} = -9.66015$	10	1.0E−05
Cosine mixture	$f_6(m) = \sum_{i=1}^{D} m_i{}^2 - 0.1(\sum_{i=1}^{D}\cos\, 5\pi m_i) + 0.1D$	$[-11]$	$f(\mathbf{0}) = -D \times 0.1$	30	1.0E−05
Salomon problem (SAL)	$f_7(m) = 1 - cos(2\pi\sqrt{\sum_{i=1}^{D} m_i^2}) + 0.1(\sqrt{\sum_{i=1}^{D} m_i^2})$	$[-100, 100]$	$f(0) = 0$	30	1.0E+0
Step function	$f_8(m) = \sum_{i=1}^{D}(\lfloor m_i + 0.5\rfloor)^2$	$[-100, 100]$	$f(-0.5 \leq m \leq 0.5) = 0$	30	1.0E−06
Beale function	$f_9(m) = [1.5 - m_1(1 - m_2)]^2 + [2.25 - m_1(1 - m_2^2)]^2 + [2.625 - m_1(1 - m_2^3)]^2$	$[-4.5, 4.5]$	$f(3, 0.5) = 0$	2	1.0E−05
Branin function	$f_{10}(m) = a(m_2 - bm_1^2 + cm_1 - d)^2 + e(1 - f)\cos m_1 + e$	$m_1 = [-5, 10]$, $m_2[0, 15]$	$f(-\pi, 12.275) = 0.3979$	2	1.0E−05
Goldstein-Price	$f_{11}(m) = (1 + (m_1 + m_2 + 1)^2 \cdot (19 - 14m_1 + 3m_1^2 - 14m_2 + 6_1 m_2 + 3m_2^2)) \cdot (30 + (2m_1 - 3m_2)^2 \cdot (18 - 32m_1 + 12m_1^2 + 48m2 - 36m_1 m_2 + 27m_2^2))$	$[-2, 2]$	$f(0, -1) = 3$	2	1.0E−14
Six-hump camel back	$f_{12}(m) = (4 - 2.1m_1^2 + m_1^4/3)m_1^2 + m_1 m_2 + (-4 + 4m_2^2)m_2^2$	$[-5, 5]$	$f(-0.0898, 0.7126) = -1.0316$	2	1.0E−05
Easom's function	$f_{13}(m) = -\cos m_1 \cos m_2\, e^{((-(m_1 - \Pi)^2 - (m_2 - \Pi)^2))}$	[-10,10]	$f(\pi, \pi) = -1$	2	1.0E−13
Dekkers and Aarts	$f_{14}(m) = 10^5 m_1^2 + m_2^2 - (m_1^2 + m_2^2)^2 + 10^{-5}(m_1^2 + m_2^2)^4$	$[-20, 20]$	$f(0, 15) = f(0, -15) = -24777$	2	5.0E−01

(*continued*)

Table 1. (*continued*)

Test problem	Objective function	Search range	Optimum value	D	Acceptable error
Hosaki problem	$f_{15}(m) =$ $(1 - 8m_1 + 7m_1^2 - 7/3m_1^3 + 1/4m_1^4)m_2^2 \exp(-m_2)$, subject to $0 \leq m_1 \leq 5, 0 \leq m_2 \leq 6$	$[0, 5]$, $[0, 6]$	−2.3458	2	1.0e−6
McCormick	$f_{16}(m) = \sin(m_1+m_2)+(m_1-m_2)^2-\frac{3}{2}m_1+\frac{5}{2}m_2+1$	$-1.5 \leq x_1 \leq 4, -3 \leq x_2 \leq 3$	$f(-0.547, -1.547) = -1.9133$	30	1.0E−04
Sinusoidal	$f_{17}(m) =$ $-[A\prod_{i=1}^{D}\sin(m_i - z) + \prod_{i=1}^{D} sin(B(m_i - z))]$, $A = 2.5, B = 5, z = 30$	$[0, 180]$	$f(\mathbf{90} + z) = -(A + 1)$	10	1.00E−02
Moved axis parallel hyper-ellipsoid	$f_{18}(m) = \sum_{i=1}^{D} 5i \times m_i^2$	$[-5.12, 5.12]$	$f(m) = 0; m(i) = 5 \times i, i = 1 : D$	30	1.0E−15
Lennard jones	$f_{19}(m) = \sum_{i=1}^{D-1}\sum_{j=i+1}^{D}(r_{ij}^{-12} - 2r_{ij}^{-6})$	$[-2, 2]$	$f(\mathbf{0}) = -9.103852$	3*nAtoms	1.0E−3
Welded beam design optimization problem	$f_{20}(m) =$ $1.10471*m_1*m_1*m_2+0.04811*m_3*m_4(14.0+m_2)$	$0.125 \leq m_1 \geq 5, 0.1 \leq m_2 \geq 10, 0.1 \leq m_3 \geq 10, 0.1 \leq m_4 \geq 5$	$f(m) = 1.724852$	4	1.0e−1
Constraint problem 3	$f_{21}(m) = 5\sum_{i=1}^{4} m_i - 5\sum_{i=1}^{4} m_i^2 - \sum_{i=5}^{13} m_i$	$m_i[0, 1]$, $m_i[0, 100]$, $m_{13}[0, 1]$	$f(\mathbf{0}) = -15$	13	1.0E−1

Table 2. Assessment of the outcomes of test problems, TP: Test Problem

TP	Algorithm	SD	ME	AFE	SR
f_1	EABC	2.87E−06	6.74E−06	35042.580	100
	ABC	1.26E−03	2.28E−04	45942.820	97
	GBEST	2.99E−06	6.33E−06	33334.580	99
	BSFABC	2.79E−06	5.96E−06	63314.450	100
	MABC	5.42E−07	9.24E−06	44038.500	100
	BHABC	2.59E−03	6.30E−04	46515.200	94
	SMO	6.09E−03	4.24E−03	96340.610	61
	MeABC	1.42E−03	2.04E−04	42456.940	98
f_2	EABC	2.77E+00	1.47E+00	168344.78	33
	ABC	3.08E+00	1.60E+00	172861.00	28
	GBEST	1.15E+01	4.66E+00	181878.68	20
	BSFABC	3.31E+00	1.97E+00	190595.00	20
	MABC	2.49E+01	3.77E+01	200007.42	0
	BHABC	1.51E+01	9.11E+00	188088.91	17
	SMO	4.12E+01	4.27E+01	200056.23	0
	MeABC	6.78E+00	1.75E+00	134255.03	69
f_3	EABC	1.13E−06	8.74E−06	36334.500	100
	ABC	1.56E−06	8.28E−06	49107.000	100
	GBEST	1.37E−06	8.56E−06	30579.500	100
	BSFABC	1.67E−06	8.11E 06	72879.000	100
	MABC	4.23E−07	9.53E−06	43630.000	100
	BHABC	1.99E−06	8.05E−06	105493.04	100
	SMO	9.27E−02	9.32E−03	29669.970	99
	MeABC	1.20E−06	8.93E−06	34998.510	100
f_4	EABC	1.55E−06	8.53E−06	63779.500	100
	ABC	2.27E−06	8.21E−06	77527.000	100
	GBEST	2.09E−06	8.23E−06	58457.540	100
	BSFABC	3.82E−06	7.43E−06	142411.50	98
	MABC	9.69E−04	1.07E−03	199760.11	1
	BHABC	1.63E−06	8.62E−06	60825.960	100
	SMO	2.85E−05	1.28E−05	76779.090	97
	MeABC	1.85E−05	1.02E−05	89005.540	97
f_5	EABC	3.79E−06	5.02E−06	21852.910	100
	ABC	3.74E−06	3.66E−06	27213.730	100
	GBEST	3.56E−06	4.53E−06	22200.130	100
	BSFABC	3.76E−06	3.63E−06	46436.860	100

(*continued*)

Table 2. (*continued*)

TP	Algorithm	SD	ME	AFE	SR
	MABC	2.76E−06	6.80E−06	35180.490	100
	BHABC	3.63E−06	4.43E−06	27594.860	100
	SMO	7.12E−03	1.26E−03	53268.860	97
	MeABC	3.55E−06	5.14E−06	24806.930	100
f_6	EABC	2.27E−06	7.61E−06	17699.500	100
	ABC	2.63E−06	7.22E−06	23015.500	100
	GBEST	1.89E−06	8.17E−06	15346.000	100
	BSFABC	2.25E−06	7.01E−06	31788.500	100
	MABC	6.17E−07	9.18E−06	22791.000	100
	BHABC	2.41E−06	7.55E−06	35515.180	100
	SMO	6.63E−02	2.51E−02	48494.250	86
	MeABC	1.98E−06	7.86E−06	17611.150	100
f_7	EABC	4.64E−02	9.24E−01	78140.280	100
	ABC	6.61E−02	9.77E−01	158845.77	60
	GBEST	3.39E−02	9.40E−01	84554.500	96
	BSFABC	7.68E−02	9.60E−01	188482.20	62
	MABC	3.54E−02	9.29E−01	27680.500	100
	BHABC	3.56E−02	9.39E−01	94735.030	95
	SMO	3.33E−02	1.87E−01	190767.47	12
	MeABC	3.37E−02	9.35E−01	86155.500	95
f_8	EABC	0.00E+00	0.00E+00	10221.000	100
	ABC	0.00E+00	0.00E+00	11501.020	100
	GBEST	0.00E+00	0.00E+00	9034.0000	100
	BSFABC	0.00E+00	0.00E+00	37060.600	100
	MABC	0.00E+00	0.00E+00	15824.500	100
	BHABC	0.00E+00	0.00E+00	8835.5600	100
	SMO	1.40E−01	2.00E−02	17762.420	98
	MeABC	0.00E+00	0.00E+00	10154.680	100
f_9	EABC	1.89E−06	8.60E−06	16198.700	100
	ABC	1.88E−06	8.56E−06	16289.570	100
	GBEST	2.88E−06	5.35E−06	9492.8400	100
	BSFABC	7.59E−05	2.54E−05	57019.120	90
	MABC	2.94E−06	5.47E−06	9369.3500	100
	BHABC	3.03E−06	5.63E−06	6934.6300	100
	SMO	2.95E−06	4.71E−06	1570.1400	100
	MeABC	3.08E−06	7.02E−06	5578.3500	100
f_{10}	EABC	6.72E−06	5.93E−06	1419.6600	100
	ABC	6.33E−06	5.46E−06	2042.7400	100

(*continued*)

Table 2. (*continued*)

TP	Algorithm	SD	ME	AFE	SR
	GBEST	6.80E−06	5.96E−06	1025.8300	100
	BSFABC	6.59E−06	5.74E−06	21587.170	90
	MABC	6.73E−06	5.97E−06	22809.080	90
	BHABC	6.67E−06	5.86E−06	1527.6400	100
	SMO	6.73E−06	6.51E−06	31056.100	85
	MeABC	7.45E−06	6.62E−06	18869.760	91
f_{11}	EABC	1.67E−14	1.88E−14	5629.5000	100
	ABC	2.68E−06	5.65E−07	102725.42	65
	GBEST	1.00E−02	9.34E−03	185547.63	13
	BSFABC	6.14E−03	2.91E−02	197487.95	2
	MABC	7.03E−03	4.80E−03	173165.47	27
	BHABC	1.78E−14	1.63E−14	32021.900	100
	SMO	4.74E−14	5.77E−14	117435.15	42
	MeABC	4.87E−14	5.13E−14	104153.48	49
f_{12}	EABC	1.18E−05	1.21E−05	741.00000	100
	ABC	1.07E−05	1.12E−05	1044.5200	100
	GBEST	1.80E−14	1.77E−14	3802.1100	100
	BSFABC	4.66E−14	3.73E−14	78238.270	65
	MABC	4.43E−15	5.40E−15	14370.250	100
	BHABC	1.04E−05	1.08E−05	682.43000	100
	SMO	1.48E−05	1.82E−05	112397.00	44
	MeABC	1.57E−05	1.44E−05	76372.890	62
f_{13}	EABC	2.85E-14	4.43E-14	8484.7600	100
	ABC	1.02E−04	3.24E−05	185404.17	15
	GBEST	1.20E−05	1.29E−05	580.50000	100
	BSFABC	1.46E−05	2.01E−05	128302.64	36
	MABC	1.49E−05	1.58E−05	94866.770	53
	BHABC	2.98E−14	4.85E−14	85060.200	100
	SMO	2.70E−14	4.26E−14	12020.770	100
	MeABC	2.99E−14	5.41E−14	29790.100	100
f_{14}	EABC	5.24E−03	4.90E−01	998.50000	100
	ABC	5.26E−03	4.90E−01	1435.0600	100
	GBEST	2.09E−11	2.15E−12	52995.070	98
	BSFABC	3.11E−14	4.01E−14	4546.4400	100
	MABC	1.29E−03	9.18E−04	197778.97	2
	BHABC	5.28E−03	4.90E−01	912.37000	100
	SMO	5.12E−03	4.90E−01	1266.2100	100
	MeABC	5.65E−03	4.91E−01	762.33000	100

(*continued*)

Table 2. (*continued*)

TP	Algorithm	SD	ME	AFE	SR
f_{15}	EABC	6.51E−06	5.95E−06	459.00000	100
	ABC	6.06E−06	5.65E−06	645.00000	100
	GBEST	5.33E−03	4.89E−01	800.00000	100
	BSFABC	5.32E−03	4.91E−01	2805.7300	100
	MABC	5.46E−03	4.91E−01	2347.1900	100
	BHABC	6.13E−06	5.63E−06	323.76000	100
	SMO	3.39E−06	1.05E−05	180100.34	10
	MeABC	6.38E−06	6.04E−06	22349.620	89
f_{16}	EABC	6.54E−06	8.91E−05	732.00000	100
	ABC	6.67E−06	8.90E−05	1222.0400	100
	GBEST	5.70E−06	5.41E−06	363.00000	100
	BSFABC	6.40E−06	5.86E−06	16628.280	92
	MABC	6.10E−06	5.33E−06	12957.850	94
	BHABC	6.64E−06	8.90E−05	716.66000	100
	SMO	6.52E−06	8.67E−05	731.61000	100
	MeABC	6.91E−06	9.14E−05	612.70000	100
f_{17}	EABC	1.77E−03	8.00E−03	44011.790	100
	ABC	2.21E−03	7.44E−03	55538.420	100
	GBEST	5.52E−06	4.79E−06	2451.3700	100
	BSFABC	5.21E−06	4.44E−06	8951.5700	100
	MABC	5.37E−06	4.65E−06	26573.930	100
	BHABC	1.70E−03	8.08E−03	44281.200	99
	SMO	7.19E−03	1.15E−02	155677.93	66
	MeABC	1.52E−03	8.41E−03	23863.570	100
f_{18}	EABC	7.42E−17	9.29E−16	48228.500	100
	ABC	6.40E−17	9.37E−16	62789.500	100
	GBEST	2.18E−03	7.75E−03	49648.100	99
	BSFABC	2.23E−03	7.49E−03	61941.190	100
	MABC	1.02E−01	6.03E−01	200036.98	0
	BHABC	1.93E−11	1.29E−11	200025.97	0
	SMO	7.51E−17	9.15E−16	34074.810	100
	MeABC	7.59E−17	9.22E−16	45550.190	100
f_{19}	EABC	1.21E−04	8.47E−04	57806.870	100
	ABC	1.53E−04	8.72E−04	70814.640	100
	GBEST	3.32E+00	6.67E+00	200024.95	0
	BSFABC	1.97E+01	2.23E+01	200035.91	0
	MABC	8.74E+00	1.51E+01	200027.20	0

(*continued*)

Table 2. (*continued*)

TP	Algorithm	SD	ME	AFE	SR
	BHABC	1.90E−04	8.91E−04	93156.710	96
	SMO	1.28E−03	1.55E−03	165103.39	57
	MeABC	9.71E−05	8.98E−04	22726.220	100
f_{20}	EABC	4.92E−03	9.57E−02	40600.090	99
	ABC	9.08E−02	2.50E-01	198121.11	1
	GBEST	4.98E+00	3.55E+00	180636.87	18
	BSFABC	4.74E+00	9.51E+00	200032.16	0
	MABC	2.54E+00	2.38E+00	200022.10	0
	BHABC	8.61E−03	9.71E−02	96187.490	86
	SMO	5.16E−03	9.38E−02	4573.9800	100
	MeABC	6.33E−03	9.74E−02	46432.230	96
f_{21}	EABC	4.99E+04	4.60E+04	131995.82	54
	ABC	3.00E+04	9.00E+04	190486.69	10
	GBEST	2.28E+00	5.63E+00	200027.46	0
	BSFABC	1.45E+00	4.80E+00	200034.29	0
	MABC	4.48E−01	1.16E+00	137174.58	58
	BHABC	4.00E+04	8.00E+04	182556.91	20
	SMO	1.49E+01	5.04E+01	185157.28	8
	MeABC	3.36E+04	8.70E+04	198642.66	1

Afar from these upshots, boxplots evaluation of AFE is derived out. The boxplots for EABC, ABC, GABC, BSFABC, MABC, BHABC, SMO, and MeABC are as shown in Fig. 2. The evaluation reveals that the interquartile range and the median of EABC are quite low.

Further, Table 3 display the Mann-Whitney U rank sum (MWURS) test [18] in which result depend on average function evaluations on 100 simulations using. In Mann-Whitney U rank sum (MWURS) test, we check the notable dissimilarity in data sets that they are dissimilar to each other or not. If dissimilarity is not there then sign '=' and when a noteworthy dissimilitude notified, i.e., we decline the null then differentiate the average number of function evaluations. Here '+' and '−' sign appropriately signify the modified algorithm EABC take more or less average number of function evaluation. In Table 3, '+' and '−' sign signify that EABC is more desirable and deficient respectively. The Table 3 includes 147 total signs in which '+' signs are 113. Therefore, from results of EABC, it is more efficacious than ABC, GABC, BSFABC, MABC, BHABC, SMO, and MeABC over contemplate test problems.

Moreover, Using AFEs of the contemplate algorithm we differentiate the speed of congregation (convergence). If the value of AFEs is low, then the rate of a congregation is higher and if it is high, then the rate of a congregation low.

Table 3. Comparison based on MWURS test table

Test problems	ABC	GBEST	BSFABC	MABC	BHABC	SMO	MeABC
f_1	+	−	+	+	+	+	+
f_2	+	+	+	+	+	+	−
f_3	+	−	+	+	+	−	−
f_4	+	+	+	+	−	+	+
f_5	+	+	+	+	+	+	+
f_6	+	−	+	+	+	+	−
f_7	+	+	+	−	+	+	+
f_8	+	−	+	+	−	+	−
f_9	+	−	+	−	−	+	−
f_{10}	+	−	+	+	+	+	+
f_{11}	+	+	+	+	+	+	+
f_{12}	+	+	+	+	−	+	+
f_{13}	+	−	+	+	+	+	+
f_{14}	+	+	+	+	−	+	−
f_{15}	+	−	+	+	−	+	+
f_{16}	+	−	+	+	−	−	−
f_{17}	+	−	+	−	+	+	−
f_{18}	+	+	+	+	+	−	−
f_{19}	+	+	+	+	+	+	−
f_{20}	+	+	+	+	+	−	+
f_{21}	+	+	+	+	+	+	+
Total number of + sign	21	11	21	18	14	17	11

To reduce the effect of the stochastic nature of the algorithms, the considered function evaluated on each test problem by taken averaged over 100 runs. To compare convergence speeds, we take a test which is known as acceleration rate (AR) which is defined as follows:

$$AR = \frac{AFE_{ALGO}}{AFE_{EABC}}, \tag{8}$$

Here, ALGO $\in$ {ABC, GABC, BSFABC, MABC, BHABC, SMO, and MeABC} and if $AR > 1$ that means EABC much faster congregation then other considered algorithms. In order to compare the AR of the proposed algorithm with the considered algorithms, results of Table 4 are examine and AR is evaluate by Eq. (8). Table 4 shows a contradiction between EABC and ABC, EABC and GABC, EABC and BSFABC, EABC and MABC, EABC and BHABC, EABC and SMO, EABC and MeABC in terms of AR. It displays clearly from the

Table 4. Comparison based table (Average Function evaluation AFEs based)

Test problems	ABC	GBEST	BSFABC	MABC	BHABC	SMO	MeABC
f_1	1.311057006	0.951259297	1.806786201	1.256713975	1.327390849	2.749244205	1.211581453
f_2	1.026827205	1.080393939	1.132170537	1.188082102	1.117283886	1.188372042	0.797500404
f_3	1.35152541	0.84161059	2.005779631	1.200787131	2.903384937	0.816578458	0.963230814
f_4	1.215547315	0.916556887	2.232872631	3.132042584	0.95369139	1.20382082	1.395519563
f_5	1.245313782	1.015888959	2.124973745	1.609876671	1.26275448	2.437609453	1.13517742
f_6	1.300347467	0.867030142	1.796011187	1.287663493	2.006564027	2.739865533	0.995008334
f_7	2.032828267	1.082085961	2.412100392	0.354241116	1.212371264	2.441346128	1.102574754
f_8	1.125234321	0.883866549	3.625927013	1.548234028	0.864451619	1.737835828	0.993511398
f_9	1.005609709	0.586024804	3.519981233	0.578401353	0.428097934	0.096930001	0.344370227
f_{10}	1.43889382	0.722588507	15.20587324	16.06657932	1.076060465	21.87573081	13.29174591
f_{11}	18.24769873	32.95987743	35.08090417	30.76036415	5.688231637	20.86067146	18.50137312
f_{12}	1.409608637	5.131052632	105.5847099	19.39304993	0.920958165	151.682861	103.0673279
f_{13}	21.85143363	0.068416785	15.12154027	11.18084306	10.02505669	1.416748382	3.511012686
f_{14}	1.437215824	53.07468202	4.553269905	198.0760841	0.913740611	1.268112168	0.763475213
f_{15}	1.405228758	1.74291939	6.112701525	5.113703704	0.705359477	392.3754684	48.69198257
f_{16}	1.669453552	0.495901639	22.71622951	17.70198087	0.979043716	0.999467213	0.837021858
f_{17}	1.261898687	0.05569803	0.203390273	0.603791166	1.006121314	3.537186967	0.542208576
f_{18}	1.301916916	1.029434878	1.284327524	4.14769234	4.147464051	0.706528505	0.944466239
f_{19}	1.225021178	3.460227997	3.460417594	3.46026692	1.611516244	2.856120561	0.393140469
f_{20}	4.879819478	4.449174127	4.926889571	4.926641788	2.369144748	0.112659356	1.14364845
f_{21}	1.443126684	1.515407533	1.515459277	1.039234273	1.383050691	1.402751087	1.504916292

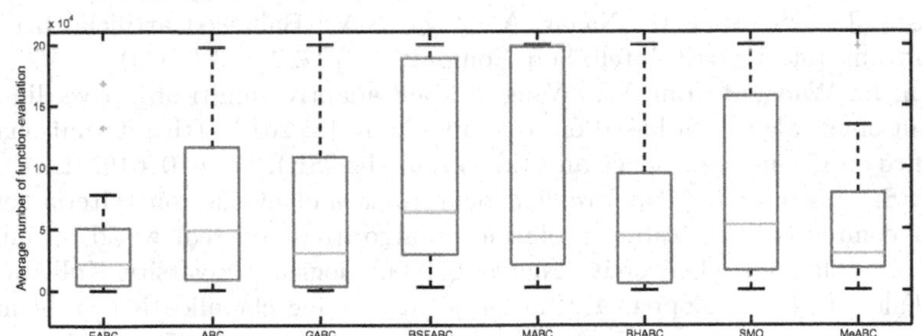

Fig. 2. Boxplots graphs for average function evaluation

Table 4 that speed of congregation (convergence) of EABC is better than contemplate algorithms for utmost of the functions.

5 Conclusion

To produce a better trade of in ABC, the balance between convergence and diversification abilities required in the search process. In this paper, a new variant is developed which is named as Efficient artificial bee colony optimization

(EABC) algorithm. In which we introduce a new concept contains three strategy named as Self-Adaptive, Self-Adaptive Mutual Learning, and Exploring Strategy. These strategies help in improving the optimal searching ability and keep balance between the exploration and exploitation of search space. To demonstrate the proposed algorithm, it is applied on 21 distinctive benchmark functions. After various statistical analysis, it is demonstrated that EABC shows comparatively better results in solving the continuous optimization problems.

References

1. Akay, B., Karaboga, D.: A modified artificial bee colony algorithm for real-parameter optimization. Inf. Sci. **192**, 120–142 (2012)
2. Ali, M.M., Khompatraporn, C., Zabinsky, Z.B.: A numerical evaluation of several stochastic algorithms on selected continuous global optimization test problems. J. Global Optim. **31**(4), 635–672 (2005)
3. Banharnsakun, A., Achalakul, T., Sirinaovakul, B.: The best-so-far selection in artificial bee colony algorithm. Appl. Soft Comput. **11**(2), 2888–2901 (2011)
4. Bansal, J.C., Sharma, H., Arya, K.V., Deep, K., Pant, M.: Self-adaptive artificial bee colony. Optimization **63**(10), 1513–1532 (2014)
5. Bansal, J.C., Sharma, H., Arya, K.V., Nagar, A.: Memetic search in artificial bee colony algorithm. Soft. Comput. **17**(10), 1911–1928 (2013)
6. Bansal, J.C., Sharma, H., Jadon, S.S.: Artificial bee colony algorithm: a survey. Int. J. Adv. Intell. Paradig. **5**(1), 123–159 (2013)
7. Bansal, J.C., Sharma, H., Jadon, S.S., Clerc, M.: Spider monkey optimization algorithm for numerical optimization. Memet. Comput. **6**(1), 31–47 (2014)
8. Bansal, J.C., Sharma, H., Nagar, A., Arya, K.V.: Balanced artificial bee colony algorithm. Int. J. Artif. Intell. Soft Comput. **3**(3), 222–243 (2013)
9. Chen, L., Wang, B., Liu, W., Wang, J.: Self-adaptive multi-objective differential evolutionary algorithm based on decomposition. In: 2016 11th International Conference on Computer Science and Education (ICCSE), pp. 610–616. IEEE (2016)
10. Das, S., Suganthan, P.N.: Problem definitions and evaluation criteria for CEC 2011 competition on testing evolutionary algorithms on real world optimization problems. Jadavpur University, Nanyang Technological University, Kolkata (2010)
11. De Falco, I., Della Cioppa, A., Tarantino, E.: Facing classification problems with particle swarm optimization. Appl. Soft Comput. **7**(3), 652–658 (2007)
12. Deb, K.: Optimal design of a welded beam via genetic algorithms. AIAA J. **29**(11), 2013–2015 (1991)
13. Jordehi, A.R.: Enhanced leader PSO (ELPSO): a new PSO variant for solving global optimisation problems. Appl. Soft Comput. **26**, 401–417 (2015)
14. Karaboga, D.: An idea based on honey bee swarm for numerical optimization. Technical report, Technical report-tr06, Erciyes University, Engineering Faculty, Computer Engineering Department (2005)
15. Karaboga, D., Akay, B.: A modified artificial bee colony (ABC) algorithm for constrained optimization problems. Appl. Soft Comput. **11**(3), 3021–3031 (2011)
16. Lei, X., Huang, X., Zhang, A.: Improved artificial bee colony algorithm and its application in data clustering. In: 2010 IEEE Fifth International Conference on Bio-Inspired Computing: Theories and Applications (BIC-TA), pp. 514–521. IEEE (2010)

17. Liao, T., Socha, K., de Oca, M.A.M., Stützle, T., Dorigo, M.: Ant colony optimization for mixed-variable optimization problems. IEEE Trans. Evol. Comput. **18**(4), 503–518 (2014)
18. Mann, H.B., Whitney, D.R.: On a test of whether one of two random variables is stochastically larger than the other. Ann. Math. Stat. **18**, 50–60 (1947)
19. Mezura-Montes, E., Miranda-Varela, M.E., del Carmen Gómez-Ramón, R.: Differential evolution in constrained numerical optimization: an empirical study. Inf. Sci. **180**(22), 4223–4262 (2010)
20. Mirjalili, S., Mirjalili, S.M., Lewis, A.: Grey wolf optimizer. Adv. Eng. Softw. **69**, 46–61 (2014)
21. Pan, Q.-K., Tasgetiren, M.F., Suganthan, P.N., Chua, T.J.: A discrete artificial bee colony algorithm for the lot-streaming flow shop scheduling problem. Inf. Sci. **181**(12), 2455–2468 (2011)
22. Pohlheim, H.: Examples of objective functions. Retrieved **4**(10), 2012 (2007)
23. Sharma, H., Bansal, J.C., Arya, K.V.: Opposition based lévy flight artificial bee colony. Memet. Comput. **5**(3), 213–227 (2013)
24. Sharma, N., Sharma, H., Sharma, A., Bansal, J.C.: Black hole artificial bee colony algorithm. In: Panigrahi, B.K., Suganthan, P.N., Das, S., Satapathy, S.C. (eds.) SEMCCO 2015. LNCS, vol. 9873, pp. 214–221. Springer, Cham (2016). https://doi.org/10.1007/978-3-319-48959-9_19
25. Zhu, G., Kwong, S.: Gbest-guided artificial bee colony algorithm for numerical function optimization. Appl. Math. Comput. **217**(7), 3166–3173 (2010)

Gaussian Scale Factor Based Differential Evolution

Rashmi Agarwal(✉), Harish Sharma, and Nirmala Sharma

Rajasthan Technical University, Kota, India
{rashmi.mtech17,nsharma}@rtu.ac.in, harish.sharma0107@gmail.com

Abstract. Differential Evolution (DE) is a easy and basic populace based probabilistic approach for global optimization. It has reportedly outperformed very well as compared to different nature inspired algorithms like Genetic algorithm (GA), Particle swarm optimization (PSO) when tested over both benchmark and real world problems. In DE algorithm there are crossover rate (CR), and scale factor (SF) are two control parameters, which play a crucial role to retain the proper equilibrium betwixt intensification and diversification abilities. But, DE, like other probabilistic optimization approaches, sometimes behave prematurely in convergence. Therefore, to retain the proper equilibrium betwixt exploitation and exploration capabilities, we introduce a modified SF in which the Gaussian distribution function and a flexible parameter (N) are introduced in mutation process of DE. The significant advantage of Gaussian distribution is full scale searching. The resulting algorithm is named as Gaussian scale factor based differential evolution $GSFDE$ algorithm. To prove the efficiency and efficacy of $GSFDE$, it is tested over 20 benchmark optimization problems and the results are compared with the basic DE and advanced variants of DE namely, Gbest-guided differential evolution (Gbest DE), L'evy Flight based Local Search in Differential Evolution (LFDE) and some swarm intelligence based algorithms like Modified artificial bee colony algorithm (MABC), Best-so-far ABC (BSFABC), Particle swarm optimization (PSO), and spider monkey optimization (SMO). The obtained results depict that $GSFDE$ is a competent in the field of optimization.

Keywords: Evolutionary · Optimization · Exploration Exploitation · Heuristics · Gaussian scale factor

1 Introduction

Evolutionary algorithms (EA's) are the subcategory of nature inspired algorithms, in which the agents evolve from the previous generation to ameliorate the features of a new generation. Differential Evolution (DE) [9] is a category of evolutionary algorithms (EA's), which was introduced by Storn and Price. DE algorithm is relatively fast and an easily understandable algorithm [19] for solving the real world optimization problems.

P. Bhattacharyya et al. (Eds.): NGCT 2017, CCIS 827, pp. 246–262, 2018.
https://doi.org/10.1007/978-981-10-8657-1_19

Like other EA's, DE repeats mutation, crossover and selection operators for taking the solution near or in the direction of the global optimum. There are two control parameters namely CR, and SF which affect the capability of DE such as rate of convergence, robustness and searching precision. Evolution of DE population is piloted using two fundamental process: First one is variation process, which explores the various fields of search area and another one is selection process that fortifies the exploitation of the antecedent experience [20]. This concept of DE is used in wide range of applications like recognition of patterns [16], power dispatch, and processing of signals [7], optimisation of fermentation of alcohol etc. and attain better results than most evolutionary approach including genetic algorithm (GA) etc. [11].

In any case, it has been demonstrated that DE may once in a while quit continuing towards the global optimum even though the populace has not converged to a local optimum [13]. Researchers are ongoing to enhancing the performance of DE. A few variations of DE with apt applications can be seen in [5]. Therefore for keeping a proper equilibrium betwixt exploitation and exploration, we introduce a approach named as Gaussian scale factor based DE (GSFDE). In which the Gaussian distribution function (normal distribution) is introduced in mutation equation with a flexible parameter (N). Gaussian distribution has a significant advantage of full-scale searching whereas flexible parameter N is diminishing iteration by iteration, that helps to keep proper equilibrium betwixt exploitation and exploration. The invented strategy tested by performing on 20 prominent test problems with the DE [19], Gbest-DE [14], LFDE [21], MABC [10], BSFABC [2], PSO [12], and SMO [3].

Rest of the paper is composed as follows:- DE quick overview is presented in segment (Sect. 2). Variants of DE are appeared in segment (Sect. 3). The proposed strategy (GSFDE) is proposed and built up in segment (Sect. 4). In Sect. 4 a comprehensive set of experimental results are provided. Finally, in segment (Sect. 5), paper is concluded.

2 Quick Overview of Differential Evolution Algorithm

Like other populace based search algorithms, in DE a populace of potential solutions (individuals) search the solution. In a y-D search area, an individual is denoted by a y-D vector $(k_{i_1}, k_{i_2}, \ldots, k_{i_y})$, $i = 1, 2, \ldots, NP$ where number of individuals denoted by NP.

In DE, three operators are used namely: mutation, selection and crossover. Initially, a populace is created arbitrary using uniform distribution then these three operators are applied to produce a new populace. Generation of trial vector is a crucial process in DE process. DE administrators are clarified quickly in subsequent subsections.

2.1 Mutation

In DE, mutation operator used for originating trial vector for each and every individual of the present populace. For producing the trial vector, a target vector is chosen from the populace than this target vector is multiplied with a weighted difference vector for generating trial vector. Generation of trial vector $b_i(l)$ from the parent vector $k_i(l)$ is as per the following:

- From the populace select a target vector $k_{i_1}(l)$, such that $i \neq i_1$.
- Again, two individuals pick arbitrary from populace, k_{i_2} and k_{i_3}, among the populace such that $i \neq i_1 \neq i_2 \neq i_3$.
- At that point the parent vector mutated for creating the trial vector as appeared:-

$$b_{ij}(l) = k_{i_1}(l) + \underbrace{SF \times \overbrace{(k_{i_2}(l) - k_{i_3}(l))}^{\text{Variation Component}}}_{\text{Step size}} \tag{1}$$

Here, trial vector is denoted by $b_{ij}(l)$ and scale factor $SF \in [0, 1]$ denotes the scale factor of mutation operation that is used for managing the amplification of the DE algorithm. Trial vector denoted by $b_{ij}(l)$.

2.2 Crossover

This operation is put to generate, offspring $k'_i(l)$ and it is done by deploying crossover betwixt both parent vector and trial vector respectively $k_{ij}(l)$, $b_{ij}(l)$ respectively shown as:

$$k'_{ij}(l) = \begin{cases} b_{ij}(l), & \text{if } m \in M \\ k_{ij}(l), & \text{otherwise.} \end{cases} \tag{2}$$

Here group of crossover points is denoted by M that will go under perturbation, $k_{ij}(l)$ is the $k_i(l)$ solution's j^{th} dimension. Exponential and Binomial crossover methods [8] are the two very famous methods that are mostly used. We use binomial crossover approach in this paper. Crossover points are arbitrarily picked from the set $\{1, 2, \ldots, y\}$. Here, y denotes the dimension of the problem. Algorithm 1 shows the series of steps of binomial crossover to generate crossover points. The parameter CR defines the probability that the considered crossover point will be choose, and $A(1, y)$ indicates uniformly distributed random number betwixt 1 and y, here y is the dimension of search area. The higher value of CR, defines that more crossover points will be included.Here, M is a group of crossover points.

2.3 Selection

In the selection process, the solution possessing lower cost is selected for the minimization problem.

$$k_i(l+1) = \begin{cases} k'_i(l), & \text{if } f(k'_i(l)) > f(k_i(l)). \\ k_i(l), & \text{otherwise.} \end{cases} \tag{3}$$

```
M = φ(empty set)
m* ~ G(1, f);
M ← A ∪ m*;
for each and every a ∈ 1...f do
  if G(0,1) < CR and a ≠ m* then
    M ← M ∪ m;
  end if
end for
```

Algorithm 1. Binomial Crossover

This shows that the population does not progressively worse (determinate). The working of differential Evolution algorithm is explained by Algorithm 2 as shown below:

```
Initialized Control parameters, SF and CR;
population initialize, H(0), of NP individuals;
while condition(s) of termination do
  for every individual, k_i(l) ∈ H(l) do
    Calculate the fitness, f(k_i(l));
    mutation is used to produce the trial vector, b_i(l) 1;
    Producing an offspring, k'_i(l), by deploying the crossover operator;
    if f(k'_i(l)) is better than f(k_i(l)) then
      Add k'_i(l) to k(l + 1);
    else
      Add k_i(l) to k(l + 1);
    end if
  end for
end while
Return the best solution found so far.
```

Algorithm 2. DE steps

Here, Scale factor is denoted by SF, the probability of crossover is denoted by CR and H is the vector of the population. SF and CR both are the control parameters of DE and the picking up the right value of these two parameter affects the performance of DE.

3 Quick Review on Variants of Differential Evolution

Remembering the true objective to get evacuate the hitch of the conventional DE, Researchers have improved DE in different styles. Storn and Price [19] have inspected that the value of SF should be in the range of [0.5, 1] and 0.5 is a good inceptive option. The value of NP should be in the range of $[5y, 10y]$, where y is introduce as the problem dimension.

There are various approaches in DE based on we select the target vector, the number of difference vectors and crossover type. Like DE/rand/2/bin approach. Rand symbolize that we randomly selected the target vector and bin indicates that there we deploy binomial crossover [21].

1. Hybridization of DE with other populace based probabilistic or deterministic algorithms
2. Introducing a new process for controlling the evolution, which may require new parameters and/or fine tuning of DE control parameters NP, F, CR.

Teaching and learning based self-adaptive differential evolution($TLBSaDE$) proposed by Biswas [4] using the concept of roulette wheel one of the strategies of mutation in DE for selection. It is based on the success rates of all the strategies over the last LP generation. The scale vector SF chosen between the range (0.5, 0.3) and from $X(CR_m 0.1)$ is taken. The mean of successful CR is termed as CR_m.

A new variant of DE Algorithm which is introduced by Yan et al. [25] called simulated annealing DE ($SADE$). In this approach, each single holds a set of SF values rather then a single value between [0.1, 1] range, the value of SF and CR are assigned to every single and the value of SF and CR are altered, based on τ_1 and τ_2 both are new factors of probability. SF is reintroduced with the τ_1 probability by a random value if not then it remains unaltered. With the probability τ_2 in the range [0, 1] CR also reintroduced. In an identical manner, CR is allocated to each single.

Sharma et al. introduce Dynamic scaling factor based differential evolution algorithm (DSFDE) [20], in this paper the idea of Dynamic scale factor (DSF) which progressively changes the step size with adjusted expulsion and attraction of the differential variety for producing trial vector. For this reason, at first we appoint DSF, arbitrary in the scope of $[-0.8, 0.8]$ and at that point it diminishes directly till $[-0.4, 0.4]$.

Omran et al. [17] presented a approach for scale factor F which is self-adaptive. They created the value of CR for every individual from an ordinary appropriation $N(0.5, 0.15)$. This approach (named as SDE) was tried on four benchmark functions and checked to be functioned superior to different variants of DE.

In addition, rather then setting of control parameters (F and CR), a few researchers additionally adjust the size of populace (NP) for enhancing the performance. Teo proposed a alternative of DE which is based on the idea of Self adapting populations (DESAP) [22].

Noman and Iba [15] proposed a crossover-based local search method for DE named as the Fittest individual refinement (FIR). An exploration capability of DE is hastened by the FIR scheme as it enhances DE's search capability in the neighborhood for the best solution in successive generations.

Das et al. [6] proposed an alternative of DE algorithm called ($DEGL$). The introduced approach uphold proper equilibrium betwixt the exploration and exploitation capabilities of DE. $DEGL$ defines four new control parameters: α, β, w, and the neighborhood radius k. In $DEGL$, w is the very important parameter as it upholds the balance betwixt the exploration and exploitation capabilities. It is define in the following equation.

$$V = w \times Global + (1 - w) \times Local$$

here, $w \in [0,1]$. little values of w support the local neighborhood component, thereby resulting in better exploration. On the other hand, large values support the global variant component, encouraging exploitation. Therefore, values of w near about 0.5 result the most balanced $DEGL$ version.

Weber et al. [23] proposed scale factor inheritance approach in distributed DE algorithm. In the proposed approach, the populace is circulated more than a few sub-populations assigned by a ring topology. Each sub-population having its own SF value. What's more, a perturbation component likewise presented which improves the exploration attribute of the calculation.

3.1 Gaussian Scale Factor Based Differential Evolution (GSFDE)

Exploration and exploitation are two vital qualities of any populace based optimization algorithms. In these optimization algorithms, the exploration shows the capacity to review the different obscure locales in the search area to locate the global optimum. While, the exploitation shows the capacity to execute the experience of past good solution for finding the better solution. The exploration and exploitation capabilities contradict with each other, however the both ought to be very much adjusted to accomplish better optimization performance. If, a populace based approach is fit for adjusting amongst exploration and exploitation of search area with least number of parameters, then the approach is viewed as an effective approach.

To improve the exploration and exploitation capabilities of the DE, a new strategy is used to calculate the Scale factor. Scale factor is a factor of mutation operation as explained in Eq. 1, which is used to decide the step-size to find the global optimum solution. But sometimes, that global optimum solution is skipped due to fast convergence speed. Hence a proper equilibrium is needed between divergence and convergence rates of the solutions in the search area.

In order to resolve this state, a modified scale factor (MSF) is introduced which is calculated through the following Eq. 4.

$$: MSF = (1.5 - randguass()) \times N \times (alea(0,1) - 0.5) \tag{4}$$

Here, N is calculated as Eq. 5

$$: N = (1 - (0.25 \times (iteration/max_iteartion))); \tag{5}$$

As per the Eq. 4, Gaussian distribution with a flexible parameter (N) is used in place of constant scale factor (SF). Gaussian distribution has a significant advantage of full-scale searching whereas flexible parameter N is diminishing iteration by iteration. During the initial iterations, the value of parameter (N) will be high. Hence the step length of the solution will be high and this will help in exploring the search area, after the lapse of few iterations, the value of parameter N will diminishing so now the solution will move using reduced step size and this will improve the exploitation capability of the algorithm. By using this strategy we are able to uphold proper equilibrium betwixt exploitation and exploration abilities of the algorithm. The behaviour of flexible parameter N shown in Fig. 1.

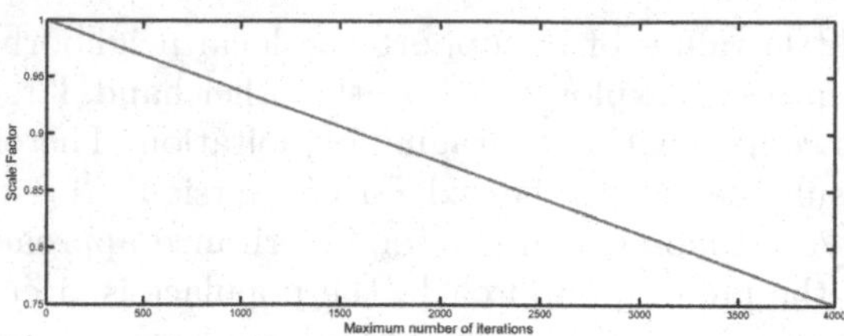

Fig. 1. Nature of flexible parameter N

The Pseudo-code for the $GSFDE$ algorithm is shown in Algorithm 3. In Algorithm 3 H denotes the vector of the population, and l denotes the generation.

4 Experimental Outcomes and Deliberation

4.1 Test Problems Under Consideration

To inspect the performance of $GSFDE$, 20 different well known optimization problems (f_1 to f_{20}) are taken. Here (f_2, f_5, f_6, f_7, f_{15}, f_{16}, f_{17}, f_{18}, f_{19}, f_{20}) are taken from [1] are shown in (Recorded in Table 1). These problems are minimization problems and have heterogeneous degree of convolution and multi-modality.

4.2 Experimental Setting

To test $GSFDE$ over test problems, following experimental setting is adopted:

- The scale factor SF is taken = 0.54,
- The crossover rate CR is set to = 0.9
- Population size NP is selected = 50,
- The number of simulations = 30,
- Parameters for the basic DE are $CR = 0.8, F = 0.5$ [18].

4.3 Results Comparison

The numerical results of the GSFDE and traditional DE/rand/1/bin and other algorithm Gbest DE, LFDE, MABC, BSFABC, PSO, SMO are shown in Table 2. The table showed the achievement in terms of four parameters such as, Mean error (ME), Average function evaluation (AFEs), Success rate (SR) and Standard deviation (SD). From the Table 2 it is clear that the proposed approach GSFDE performs superior to conventional DE, Gbest DE, LFDE, MABC, BSFDE, PSO, and SMO. Some more rigorous statistical examination based on t test, Acceleration rate (AR), Boxplot have been done for results of GSFDE, DE, Gbest DE, LFDE, PSO, and SMO.

Initialize the control parameters, SF, CR;
Initialize Generation counter $l = 1$;
Create and initialize the population, $H(0)$, of NP individuals;
while termination condition(s) **do**
  for each individual, $Q_i(l) \in k(l)$ **do**
    Calculate the fitness, $f(k_i(l))$;
    mutation is used to produce the trial vector, $b_i(l)$;
    For mutation process modified scale factor (MSF) calculated as:-

$$N = (1 - (0.25 \times (iteration/max_iteartion))); \quad (6)$$

$$MSF = (1.5 - randguass()) \times N \times (alea(0,1) - 0.5) \quad (7)$$

    if($alea(0,1) \leq randguass()$)
    then

$$trialvector = k_{i_1}(l) + \underbrace{MSF \times \overbrace{(k_{i_2}(l) - k_{i_3}(l))}^{\text{Variation Component}}}_{\text{Step size}}; \quad (8)$$

    else

$$trialvector = k_i(l) \times N; \quad (9)$$

    Generate an offspring, $k_i'(l)$, by using the crossover operator;
    if $f(k_i'(l))$ is better than $f(k_i(l))$ **then**
      Add $k_i'(l)$ to $H(l+1)$;
    else
      Add $k_i(l)$ to $H(l+1)$;
    end if
  end for
end while
Return the best individual;

Algorithm 3. Gaussian scale factor based Differential Evolution ($GSFDE$) algorithm

Statistical Analysis. The t-test is very well known amid scientists in the area of evolutionary computing. In Table 3 there '+' denotes the significant distinction (or the null hypothesis is rejected) at a 0.05 level of significance, '–' implies that there is no significant distinction. In Table 3, GSFDE is compared with the DE, Gbest DE, LFDE, MABC, BSFABC, PSO, and SMO. The last row of Table 3, establishes the superiority of GSFDE over DE, Gbest DE, LFDE, MABC, BSFABC, PSO, and SMO.

Further, an examination is made on the basis of convergence speed of the considered approches by measuring the average function evaluations (AFEs).

Table 1. Test problems

Test problem	Objective function	Search range	Optimum value	D	Acceptable error
De Jong	$f_1(k) = \sum_{i=1}^{y} i.(k_i)^4$	$[-5.12, 5.12]$	$f(\mathbf{0}) = 0$	30	$1.0E-05$
Griewank	$f_2(k) = 1 + \frac{1}{4000}\sum_{i=1}^{y} k_i^2 - \prod_{i=1}^{y}\cos(\frac{k_i}{\sqrt{i}})$	$[-600, 600]$	$f(\mathbf{0}) = 0$	30	$1.0E-05$
Rastrigin	$f_3(k) = 10y + \sum_{i=1}^{y}[k_i^2 - 10\cos(2\pi k_i)]$	$[-5.12, 5.12]$	$f(\mathbf{0}) = 0$	30	$1.0E-05$
Michalewicz	$f_4(k) = -\sum_{i=1}^{y} \sin\, k_i(\sin\,(\frac{i{k_i}^2}{\pi})^{20})$	$[0,\ \pi]$	$f_{min} = -9.66015$	10	$1.0E-05$
Cosine mixture	$f_5(k) = \sum_{i=1}^{y} {k_i}^2 - 0.1(\sum_{i=1}^{y} \cos\, 5\pi k_i) + 0.1y$	$[-1, 1]$	$f(\mathbf{0}) = -y \times 0.1$	30	$1.0E-05$
Step function	$f_6(k) = \sum_{i=1}^{y} (\lfloor k_i + 0.5 \rfloor)^2$	$[-100, 100]$	$f(-0.5 \leq k \leq 0.5) = 0$	30	$1.0E-05$
Inverted cosine wave	$f_7(k) = -\sum_{i=1}^{y-1}\left(\exp\left(\frac{-(k_i^2 + k_{i+1}^2 + 0.5k_i k_{i+1})}{8}\right) \times \mathrm{I}\right)$	$[-5, 5]$	$f(\mathbf{0}) = -y + 1$	10	$1.0E-05$
Braninss function	$f_8(k) = a(k_2 - bk_1^2 + ck_1 - y)^2 + e(1-f)\cos k_1 + e$	$k_1 \in [-5, 10]$, $k_2 \in [0, 15]$	$f(-\pi, 12.275) = 0.3979$	2	$1.0E-05$
Six-Hump-Camel-Back	$f_9(k) = (4 - 2.1k_1^2 + k_1^4/3)k_1^2 + k_1k_2 + (-4 + 4k_2^2)k_2^2$	$[-5, 5]$	$f(-0.0898, 0.7126) = -1.0316$	2	$1.0E-05$
Hosaki problem	$f_{10}(k) = (1 - 8k_1 + 7k_1^2 - 7/3k_1^3 + 1/4k_1^4)k_2^2\exp(-k_2)$	$k_1 \in [0, 5]$, $k_2 \in [0, 6]$	-2.3458	2	$1.0E-6$
Sinusoidal problem	$f_{11}(k) = -[A\prod_{i=1}^{y}\sin(k_i - z) + \prod_{i=1}^{y}\sin(B(k_i - z))]$, $A = 2.5, B = 5, z = 30$	$[0,\ 180]$	$f(\mathbf{90} + z) = -(A+1)$	10	$1.0E-02$
Moved axis parallel hyper-ellipsoid	$f_{12}(k) = \sum_{i=1}^{y} 5i \times k_i^2$	$[-5.12, 5.12]$	$f(k) = 0; k(i) = 5 \times i, i = 1 : y$	30	$1.0E-15$
Shifted Griewank	$f_{13}(k) = \sum_{i=1}^{y}\frac{z_i^2}{4000} - \prod_{i=1}^{y}\cos(\frac{z_i}{\sqrt{i}}) + 1 + f_{bias}$, $z = (k - o)$, $k = [k_1, k_2, \ldots k_y]$, $o = [o_1, o_2, \ldots o_y]$	$[-600, 600]$	$f(0) = f_{bias} = -180$	10	$1.0E-05$
Ellipsoidal	$f_{14}(k) = \sum_{i=1}^{y}(x_i - i)^2$	$[-30, 30]$	$f(1, 2, 3, \ldots, y) = 0$	30	$1.0E-05$
Schewel	$f_{15}(k) = \sum_{i=1}^{y}\lvert k_i\rvert + \prod_{i=1}^{y}\lvert k_i\rvert$	$[-10, 10]$	$f(\mathbf{0}) = 0$	30	$1.0E-05$
Cigar	$f_{16}(k) = {k_0}^2 + 100000\sum_{i=1}^{y}{k_i}^2$	$[-10, 10]$	$f(\mathbf{0}) = 4$	30	$1.0E-05$
Ackley	$f_{17}(k) = -20 + e + exp(-\frac{0.2}{y}\sqrt{\sum_{i=1}^{y}{k_i}^3})$	$[-1, 1]$	$f(\mathbf{0}) = 0$	30	$1.0E-05$
Sphere	$f_{18}(k) = \sum_{i=1}^{y} k_i^2$	$[-5.12, 5.12]$	$f(\mathbf{0}) = 0$	30	$1.0E-05$
Exponential	$f_{19}(k) = -(exp(-0.5\sum_{i=1}^{y}{k_i}^2)) + 1$	$[-1, 1]$	$f(\mathbf{0}) = -1$	30	$1.0E-05$
Rotated hyper-ellipsoid	$f_{20}(k) = \sum_{i=1}^{y}\sum_{j=1}^{i} k_j^2$	$[-65.536, 65.536]$	$f(\mathbf{0}) = 0$	30	$1.0E-05$

Table 2. Comparison of the results of *GSFDE*, *DE*, *GbestDE*, *LFDE*, MABC, BSFABC, PSO, and SMO problems

Test problem	Algorithm	SD	ME	AFE	SR
f_1	GSFDE	1.51E−06	8.42E−06	17613.33333	30
	DE	1.90E−02	3.55E−03	26075.00000	29
	Gbest DE	1.15E−06	8.43E−06	12616.66667	30
	LFDE	1.15E−06	8.52E−06	18032.33333	30
	MABC	9.75E−07	8.69E−06	22801.66667	30
	BSFABC	2.76E−06	4.79E−06	24035.00000	30
	PSO	7.36E−07	9.21E−06	33253.33333	30
	SMO	1.09E−06	8.56E−06	10672.20000	30
f_2	GSFDE	9.33E−07	8.81E−06	29158.33333	30
	DE	5.95E−03	2.63E−03	65393.33333	24
	Gbest DE	8.93E−07	8.97E−06	28013.33333	30
	LFDE	7.37E−07	9.14E−06	33914.00000	30
	MABC	4.69E−07	9.38E−06	43565.00000	30
	BSFABC	3.29E−06	5.58E−06	64375.10000	30
	PSO	7.37E−03	4.44E−03	102425.00000	21
	SMO	1.84E−03	5.20E−04	85981.60000	27
f_3	GSFDE	1.79E−01	3.32E−02	103070.00000	29
	DE	3.77E+00	1.34E+01	200000.00000	0
	Gbest DE	4.62E+00	1.72E+00	186586.66670	11
	LFDE	9.29E−07	9.14E−06	147962.00000	30
	MABC	7.88E+00	6.39E+01	200013.10000	0
	BSFABC	3.23E−06	5.48E−06	119508.33330	30
	PSO	1.62E+01	4.23E+01	200050.00000	0
	SMO	1.67E−06	8.17E−06	95626.06667	30
f_4	GSFDE	1.22E−03	3.34E−04	24706.66667	28
	DE	5.11E−02	4.96E−02	182670.00000	4
	Gbest DE	3.59E−06	5.75E−06	29823.33333	30
	LFDE	8.80E−04	1.72E−04	23095.30000	29
	MABC	3.30E−06	6.76E−06	35151.70000	30
	BSFABC	3.85E−06	4.08E−06	42067.50000	30
	PSO	2.11E−01	3.68E−01	200050.00000	0
	SMO	3.53E−06	5.67E−06	57600.83333	30
f_5	GSFDE	6.95E−07	8.94E−06	18910.00000	30
	DE	4.43E−02	1.48E−02	40745.00000	27
	Gbest DE	8.41E−07	9.15E−06	15496.66667	30
	LFDE	6.22E−07	9.24E−06	21674.00000	30
	MABC	1.06E−06	9.06E−06	22513.33333	30
	BSFABC	2.10E−06	7.27E−06	31711.66667	30
	PSO	6.53E−02	3.94E−02	83043.33333	22
	SMO	3.67E−06	6.17E−06	79025.40000	30

(*continued*)

Table 2. (*continued*)

Test problem	Algorithm	SD	ME	AFE	SR
f_6	GSFDE	0.00E+00	0.00E+00	13011.66667	30
	DE	2.49E−01	6.67E−02	27738.33333	28
	Gbest DE	0.00E+00	0.00E+00	10506.66667	30
	LFDE	0.00E+00	0.00E+00	14748.00000	30
	MABC	0.00E+00	0.00E+00	15571.66667	30
	BSFABC	0.00E+00	0.00E+00	36616.66667	30
	PSO	0.00E+00	0.00E+00	35410.00000	30
	SMO	0.00E+00	0.00E+00	23099.83333	30
f_7	GSFDE	1.51E−06	8.12E−06	43308.33333	30
	DE	5.98E−01	8.29E−01	171855.00000	6
	Gbest DE	1.70E−06	8.27E−06	51826.66667	29
	LFDE	1.76E−06	8.41E−06	55035.40000	30
	MABC	1.49E−06	8.43E−06	63654.80000	30
	BSFABC	2.31E−01	6.12E−02	120768.46670	26
	PSO	7.49E−01	1.58E+00	195055.00000	2
	SMO	1.72E−06	8.59E−06	68564.46667	30
f_8	GSFDE	6.39E−06	6.34E−06	23845.00000	27
	DE	6.28E−06	5.82E−06	35083.33333	25
	Gbest DE	3.01E−05	4.62E−05	2108.333333	30
	LFDE	7.03E−06	5.93E−06	28785.63333	26
	MABC	3.32E−05	4.38E−05	2325.533333	30
	BSFABC	2.82E−05	5.25E−05	1409.76666	30
	PSO	3.72E−06	5.14E−06	22480.00000	27
	SMO	7.25E−06	7.08E−06	56623.76667	26
f_9	GSFDE	1.49E−05	1.64E−05	94686.66667	16
	DE	1.44E−0	1.64E−05	100773.33330	15
	Gbest DE	1.57E−05	1.66E−05	100951.66670	15
	LFDE	1.42E−05	1.59E−05	94345.56667	16
	MABC	1.56E−05	1.75E−05	107421.40000	14
	BSFABC	1.53E−05	1.83E−05	113699.20000	13
	PSO	1.20E−05	1.82E−05	114803.33330	13
	SMO	1.27E−05	2.01E−05	264142.40000	11
f_{10}	GSFDE	6.11E−06	5.35E−06	14690.00000	28
	DE	6.35E−06	6.53E−06	40778.33333	24
	Gbest DE	6.16E−06	5.62E−06	20995.00000	27
	LFDE	6.51E−06	6.34E−06	21517.93000	27
	MABC	6.73E−06	6.33E−06	27578.80000	26
	BSFABC	5.83E−06	5.08E−06	7327.06666	29
	PSO	3.79E−06	1.01E−05	173570.00000	4
	SMO	3.80E−06	1.01E−05	361126.16670	4

(*continued*)

Table 2. (*continued*)

Test problem	Algorithm	SD	ME	AFE	SR
f_{11}	GSFDE	1.82E−03	7.66E−03	76720.00000	30
	DE	2.45E−01	5.03E−01	195111.66670	2
	Gbest DE	8.61E−03	1.33E−02	150891.66670	16
	LFDE	2.05E−03	7.49E−03	37247.23333	30
	MABC	1.06E−01	6.00E−01	200037.03330	0
	BSFABC	2.09E−03	6.68E−03	63575.73333	30
	PSO	2.66E−01	4.53E−01	183558.33330	5
	SMO	4.80E−03	9.11E−03	199230.63330	25
f_{12}	GSFDE	7.11E−17	9.10E−16	52463.33333	30
	DE	9.81E−17	8.89E−16	59130.00000	30
	Gbest DE	6.68E−17	9.29E−16	40545.00000	30
	LFDE	7.43E−17	9.09E−16	58792.00000	30
	MABC	6.35E−17	9.15E−16	59300.00000	30
	BSFABC	2.65E−16	7.20E−16	70638.33333	30
	PSO	6.02E−17	9.22E−16	104743.33330	30
	SMO	6.09E−17	9.01E−16	34009.80000	30
f_{13}	GSFDE	1.82E−06	8.09E−06	20171.66667	30
	DE	1.22E−02	1.11E−02	139011.66670	12
	Gbest DE	2.17E−03	5.82E−04	67145.00000	28
	LFDE	2.08E−06	8.03E−06	25377.96667	30
	MABC	3.00E−06	6.48E−06	65212.83333	30
	BSFABC	6.62E−03	5.42E−03	125819.30000	17
	PSO	3.22E−02	4.89E−02	197973.33330	1
	SMO	3.76E−05	1.31E−05	157870.86670	29
f_{14}	GFDE	8.16E−07	9.19E−06	23480.00000	30
	DE	1.14E−06	8.83E−06	27381.66667	30
	Gbest DE	6.20E−07	9.18E−06	17950.00000	30
	LFDE	8.75E−07	8.95E−06	26826.00000	30
	MABC	8.17E−07	9.05E−06	26635.00000	30
	BSFABC	2.26E−06	7.23E−06	41475.00000	30
	PSO	8.11E−07	9.01E−06	44593.33333	30
	SMO	8.28E−07	9.00E−06	15285.60000	30
f_{15}	GSFDE	4.15E−07	9.49E−06	31735.00000	30
	DE	3.24E−07	9.63E−06	45363.33333	30
	Gbest DE	6.34E−07	9.40E−06	26671.66667	30
	LFDE	4.17E−07	9.59E−06	38172.53333	30
	MABC	4.87E−07	9.31E−06	32973.33333	30
	BSFABC	1.37E−06	8.79E−06	53181.66667	30
	PSO	4.59E−07	9.64E−06	71468.33333	30
	SMO	4.94E−07	9.37E−06	22977.90000	30

(*continued*)

Table 2. (*continued*)

Test problem	Algorithm	SD	ME	AFE	SR
f_{16}	GSFDE	7.43E−07	9.07E−06	34896.66667	30
	DE	7.03E−07	9.08E−06	39768.33333	30
	Gbest DE	1.11E−06	9.07E−06	26950.00000	30
	LFDE	7.60E−07	9.03E−06	39078.00000	30
	MABC	7.95E−07	8.80E−06	40033.33333	30
	BSFABC	7.21E−06	7.21E−06	62496.66667	30
	PSO	7.13E−07	9.29E−06	69461.66667	30
	SMO	6.09E−07	8.86E−06	22723.80000	30
f_{17}	GSFDE	2.69E−07	9.62E−06	37183.33333	30
	DE	5.61E−07	9.27E−06	42663.33333	30
	Gbest DE	3.71E−07	9.51E−06	28888.33333	30
	LFDE	4.46E−07	9.32E−06	41988.00000	30
	MABC	2.13E−07	9.68E−06	43461.66667	30
	BSFABC	1.60E−06	8.17E−06	72865.00000	30
	PSO	3.52E−07	9.63E−06	77275.00000	30
	SMO	1.26E−06	9.33E−06	29664.80000	30
f_{18}	GSFDE	5.48E−07	9.24E−06	20003.33333	30
	DE	8.63E−07	9.15E−06	22300.00000	30
	Gbest DE	6.76E−07	9.26E−06	15303.33333	30
	LFDE	6.49E−07	9.18E−06	22514.00000	30
	MABC	9.09E−07	8.96E−06	22275.00000	30
	BSFABC	2.23E−06	6.88E−06	30320.00000	30
	PSO	6.64E−07	9.36E−06	38386.66667	30
	SMO	9.20E−07	8.76E−06	12563.10000	30
f_{19}	GSFDE	5.48E−07	9.24E−06	20003.33333	30
	DE	8.63E−07	9.15E−06	22300.00000	30
	Gbest DE	6.76E−07	9.26E−06	15303.33333	30
	LFDE	6.49E−07	9.18E−06	22514.00000	30
	MABC	9.09E−07	8.96E−06	22275.00000	30
	BSFABC	2.23E−06	6.88E−06	30320.00000	30
	PSO	6.64E−07	9.36E−06	38386.66667	30
	SMO	9.20E−07	8.76E−06	12563.10000	30
f_{20}	GSFDE	8.00E−07	9.11E−06	15180.00000	30
	DE	9.21E−07	8.79E−06	16905.00000	30
	Gbest DE	9.00E−07	9.11E−06	11705.00000	30
	LFDE	7.88E−07	9.15E−06	17100.33333	30
	MABC	5.69E−07	9.31E−06	16508.33333	30
	BSFABC	1.97E−06	7.35E−06	18413.33333	30
	PSO	7.78E−07	9.14E−06	28241.66667	30
	SMO	9.91E−07	8.84E−06	9718.50000	30

Table 3. Results of the student's t test

TP	GSFDE vs DE	GSFDE vs Gbest DE	GSFDE vs Levy DE	GDE vs MABC	GSFDE vs BSFABC	GSFDE vs PSO	GSFDE vs SMO
fn_1	+	−	+	+	+	+	−
fn_2	+	−	+	+	+	+	+
fn_3	+	+	+	+	+	+	−
fn_4	+	+	−	+	+	+	+
fn_5	+	−	+	+	+	+	+
fn_6	+	−	+	+	+	+	+
fn_7	+	+	+	+	+	+	+
fn_8	+	−	+	−	−	−	+
fn_9	+	+	−	+	+	+	+
fn_{10}	+	+	+	+	−	+	+
fn_{11}	+	+	−	+	−	+	+
fn_{12}	+	−	+	+	+	+	+
fn_{13}	+	+	+	+	+	+	+
fn_{14}	+	−	+	+	+	+	−
fn_{15}	+	−	+	+	+	+	−
fn_{16}	+	−	+	+	+	+	−
fn_{17}	+	−	+	+	+	+	−
fn_{18}	+	−	+	+	+	+	−
fn_{19}	+	−	+	+	+	+	−
fn_{20}	+	−	+	+	+	+	−

A littler AFEs implies excessive convergence speed. So as to limit the impact of the stochastic nature of the algorithms, the reported function evaluations for each test problem is the average over 30 runs. In order to compare convergence speeds, we use Acceleration Rate (AR) which is defined as follows, based on the AFEs for the two algorithms $ALGO$ and $GSFDE$:

$$AR = \frac{AFE_{ALGO}}{AFE_{GSFDE}}, \tag{10}$$

where, $ALGO \in \{DE, GbestDE, LFDE, MABC, BSFDE, PSO, SMO\}$ and $AR > 1$ means $GSFDE$ converges faster. Table 4 shows a clear comparison between $GSFDE$ - DE, $GSFDE$ - $GbestDE$, $GSFDE$ - $LFDE$, $GSFDE$ - $MABC$, $GSFDE$ - $BSFABC$, $GSFDE$ - PSO, and $GSFDE$ - SMO in terms of AR. It is clear from Table 4 that, for most of the test problems, convergence speed of $GSFDE$ is faster among all the considered algorithms. For the purpose of comparison in terms of consolidated performance, boxplot analyses have been

Table 4. Acceleration Rate (AR) of *GSFDE* compare to the basic *DE*, *GbestDE*, *LFDE*, *MABC*, *BSFABC*, *PSO*, and *SMO*

Test problems	DE	Gbest DE	LFDE	MABC	BSFABC	PSO	SMO
fn_1	1.480412566	0.716313399	1.023788796	1.294568509	1.364591219	1.887963664	0.605915973
fn_2	2.242697914	0.960731638	1.163098028	1.494084024	2.207777079	3.512717919	2.948783081
fn_3	1.940428835	1.810290741	1.435548656	1.940555933	1.15948708	1.940913942	0.927777886
fn_4	7.393550998	1.2070966	0.934780086	1.422761738	1.70267809	8.097004857	2.331388289
fn_5	2.154680063	0.819495858	1.14616605	1.190551736	1.676978671	4.391503613	4.17902697
fn_6	2.13180479	0.807480466	1.133444345	1.19674651	2.814141155	2.721403868	1.775317023
fn_7	3.968173947	1.196690398	1.270780835	1.469804887	2.788573408	4.503867616	1.583170291
fn_8	1.471307751	0.088418257	1.207197875	0.097527085	0.059122108	0.942755295	2.374659957
fn_9	1.064282194	1.066165599	0.996397592	1.134493417	1.200794198	1.212455115	2.789647258
fn_{10}	2.775924665	1.42920354	1.464801225	1.877385977	0.498779215	11.81552076	24.58312911
fn_{11}	2.543165624	1.966783976	0.485495742	2.607364877	0.828672228	2.39257473	2.596853928
fn_{12}	1.127072876	0.772825465	1.120630281	1.130313235	1.346432429	1.996505495	0.648258466
fn_{13}	6.891431876	3.32867884	1.258099645	3.232892671	6.237427084	9.814426174	7.826367016
fn_{14}	1.16616979	0.764480409	1.142504259	1.134369676	1.766396934	1.899204997	0.651005111
fn_{15}	1.429441731	0.840449556	1.202852791	1.03902106	1.675804842	2.252035082	0.724055459
fn_{16}	1.139602636	0.772280065	1.119820422	1.147196485	1.790906486	1.990495749	0.651173942
fn_{17}	1.147377857	0.776916181	1.129215598	1.16884805	1.959614523	2.078216047	0.797798297
fn_{18}	1.114814198	0.76503916	1.125512415	1.113564406	1.515747375	1.919013498	0.628050325
fn_{19}	1.113636364	0.771080369	1.126504172	1.08750549	1.212999561	1.86045235	0.640217391
fn_{20}	1.132713392	0.772171517	1.126783767	1.135296481	1.681705987	1.938694679	0.645224729

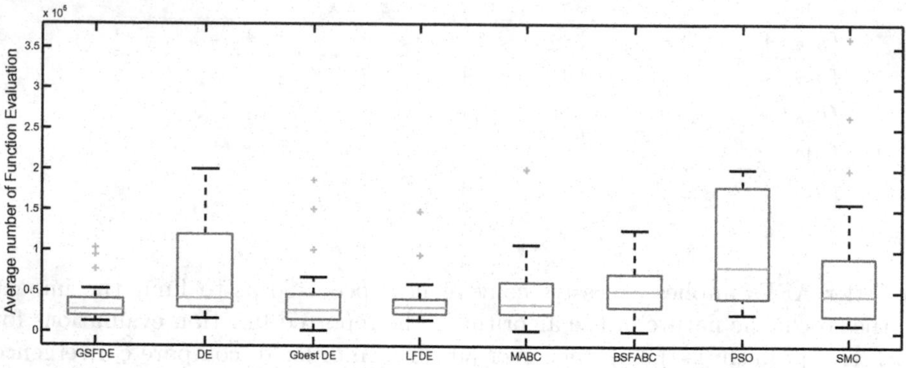

Fig. 2. Boxplot graph for average function evaluation: (1) *GSFDE* (2) *DE* (3) *GbestDE* (4) *LFDE* (5) *MABC* (6) *BSFABC* (7) *PSO* (8) *SMO*

carried out for all the considered algorithms. The empirical distribution of data is efficiently represented graphically by the boxplot analysis tool [24]. The boxplots for *GSFDE*, *DE*, *GbestDE*, *LFDE*, *MABC*, *BSFABC*, *PSO*, and *SMO* are shown in Fig. 2. It is clear from this figure that *GSFDE* is better than the considered algorithms as interquartile range and median are comparatively low.

5 Conclusion

In this paper, a new scale factor approach is proposed. This article proposed efficient Differential evolution algorithm based on a modified scale factor approach (MSF). It uses a Gaussian distribution function (GDF) with a flexible parameter (N). The GDE provides full scale searching while N is diminishing iteration by iteration. By using this strategy we are able to uphold proper equilibrium betwixt exploitation and exploration abilities of the algorithm. In the proposed approach the scale factor SF is removed and use a Gaussian distribution function with a flexible parameter N. The introduced algorithm is named as Gaussian scale factor based DE (GSFDE). Further, GSFDE is compared with DE, $GbestDE$, $LFDE$, $MABC$, $BSFABC$, PSO, and SMO and with the help of experiments over test problems, it is shown that the $GSFDE$ outperforms to the considered algorithms in terms of reliability, efficiency and accuracy.

References

1. Ali, M.M., Khompatraporn, C., Zabinsky, Z.B.: A numerical evaluation of several stochastic algorithms on selected continuous global optimization test problems. J. Global Optim. **31**(4), 635–672 (2005)
2. Banharnsakun, A., Achalakul, T., Sirinaovakul, B.: The best-so-far selection in artificial bee colony algorithm. Appl. Soft Comput. **11**(2), 2888–2901 (2011)
3. Bansal, J.C., Sharma, H., Jadon, S.S., Clerc, M.: Spider monkey optimization algorithm for numerical optimization. Memetic Comput. **6**(1), 31–47 (2014)
4. Biswas, S., Kundu, S., Das, S., Vasilakos, A.V.: Teaching and learning best differential evolution with self adaptation for real parameter optimization. In: 2013 IEEE Congress on Evolutionary Computation (CEC), pp. 1115–1122. IEEE (2013)
5. Chakraborty, U.K.: Advances in Differential Evolution. Springer, Heidelberg (2008). https://doi.org/10.1007/978-3-540-68830-3
6. Das, S., Abraham, A., Chakraborty, U.K., Konar, A.: Differential evolution using a neighborhood-based mutation operator. IEEE Trans. Evol. Comput. **13**(3), 526–553 (2009)
7. Das, S., Konar, A.: Two-dimensional IIR filter design with modern search heuristics: a comparative study. Int. J. Comput. Intell. Appl. **6**(03), 329–355 (2006)
8. Engelbrecht, A.P.: Computational Intelligence: An Introduction. Wiley, Hoboken (2007)
9. Fleetwood, K.: An introduction to differential evolution. In: Proceedings of Mathematics and Statistics of Complex Systems (MASCOS) One Day Symposium, 26th November, Brisbane, Australia (2004)
10. Gao, W., Liu, S.: A modified artificial bee colony algorithm. Comput. Oper. Res. **39**(3), 687–697 (2012)
11. Goldberg, D.E.: Genetic and evolutionary algorithms come of age. Commun. ACM **37**(3), 113–120 (1994)
12. Kenndy, J., Eberhart, R.C.: Particle swarm optimization. In: Proceedings of IEEE International Conference on Neural Networks, vol. 4, pp. 1942–1948. IEEE Press (1995)
13. Lampinen, J., Zelinka, I., et al.: On stagnation of the differential evolution algorithm. In: Proceedings of MENDEL, pp. 76–83 (2000)

14. Mokan, M., Sharma, K., Sharma, H., Verma, C.: Gbest guided differential evolution. In: 2014 9th International Conference on Industrial and Information Systems (ICIIS), pp. 1–6. IEEE (2014)
15. Noman, N., Iba, H.: Enhancing differential evolution performance with local search for high dimensional function optimization. In: Proceedings of the 7th Annual Conference on Genetic and Evolutionary Computation, pp. 967–974. ACM (2005)
16. Omran, M.G.H., Engelbrecht, A.P., Salman, A.: Differential evolution methods for unsupervised image classification. In: The 2005 IEEE Congress on Evolutionary Computation, vol. 2, pp. 966–973. IEEE (2005)
17. Omran, M.G.H., Salman, A., Engelbrecht, A.P.: Self-adaptive differential evolution. In: Hao, Y., Liu, J., Wang, Y., Cheung, Y., Yin, H., Jiao, L., Ma, J., Jiao, Y.-C. (eds.) CIS 2005. LNCS (LNAI), vol. 3801, pp. 192–199. Springer, Heidelberg (2005). https://doi.org/10.1007/11596448_28
18. Price, K.V.: Differential evolution: a fast and simple numerical optimizer. In: 1996 Biennial Conference of the North American, Fuzzy Information Processing Society, NAFIPS 1996, pp. 524–527. IEEE (1996)
19. Price, K.V., Storn, R.M., Lampinen, J.A.: The differential evolution algorithm. Diff. Evol.: Pract. Approach Glob. Optim. 37–134 (2005)
20. Sharma, H., Bansal, J.C., Arya, K.V.: Dynamic scaling factor based differential evolution algorithm. In: Deep, K., Nagar, A., Pant, M., Bansal, J. (eds.) SocProS 2011. AISC, vol. 130, pp. 73–85. Springer, India (2012). https://doi.org/10.1007/978-81-322-0487-9_8
21. Sharma, H., Jadon, S.S., Bansal, J.C., Arya, K.V.: Lèvy flight based local search in differential evolution. In: Panigrahi, B.K., Suganthan, P.N., Das, S., Dash, S.S. (eds.) SEMCCO 2013. LNCS, vol. 8297, pp. 248–259. Springer, Cham (2013). https://doi.org/10.1007/978-3-319-03753-0_23
22. Teo, J.: Exploring dynamic self-adaptive populations in differential evolution. Soft Comput. - Fusion Found. Methodol. Appl. **10**(8), 673–686 (2006)
23. Weber, M., Tirronen, V., Neri, F.: Scale factor inheritance mechanism in distributed differential evolution. Soft. Comput. **14**(11), 1187–1207 (2010)
24. Williamson, D.F., Parker, R.A., Kendrick, J.S.: The box plot: a simple visual method to interpret data. Ann. Intern. Med. **110**(11), 916–921 (1989)
25. Yan, J., Ling, Q., Sun, D.: A differential evolution with simulated annealing updating method. In: 2006 International Conference on Machine Learning and Cybernetics, pp. 2103–2106. IEEE (2006)

An Efficient Parallel Approach for Mapping Finite Binomial Series (Special Cases) on Bi Swapped Network Mesh

Ashish Gupta(✉) and Bikash Kanti Sarkar

Department of Computer Science and Engineering,
Birla Institute of Technology, Mesra, Ranchi, Jharkhand, India
ashish.parj@gmail.com, bk_sarkarbit@hotmail.com

Abstract. The efficient parallel mapping of numerical problems (over different parallel architectures) is necessary for fast execution of massive data. In fact, it is a challenging task and significant ongoing subject of research. The Bi Swapped Network (BSN) is recently reported 2-level hybrid and symmetrical optoelectronic network architecture, offer major improvements especially for drawbacks aroused due to the asymmetrical behavior of the well known swapped/OTIS network. In this paper, the efficient parallel mapping of binomial function (special cases: Taylor series and Negative Binomial Series) of $2n^4 + 1$ terms is presented on $n \times n$ Bi Swapped Network mesh in $2T + 24(n - 1)$ electronic and 8 optical moves, Here, we assume T is the time required to compute parallel prefix for each identical cluster (mesh).

Keywords: Bi Swapped Networks · Bi Swapped Network mesh
Parallel algorithm · Time complexity

1 Introduction

Over time, several important interconnection networks have been reported that plays the significant role in the efficient parallel execution of different numerical and non-numerical problems. Recently, Xiao [7, 17] addressed the issue of asymmetricity in the well known OTIS network and presented the more competitive and efficient 2-level symmetrical network named Bi-Swapped Networks, Recall the processor architecture of swapped/OTIS networks, where processors do not have optical connections when cluster number matches with the processor number. Thus, an issue of asymmetry arisen in the popular OTIS networks. It is important to note that, symmetry is a relevant property of Cayley graph and in fact an important benchmark for any interconnection network.

In Bi Swapped Networks (a two-level symmetrical network), each processor has an exactly single inter-part (optical) connection to connect their corresponding processor in their opposite part. Thus, it ensures vertex symmetry. However, Bi Swapped Networks also have certain *trade-offs*. For example, the single unit higher diameter than the Optical Transpose Interconnection Networks (OTIS). However, it has a very limited impact on the overall performance of network architecture.

P. Bhattacharyya et al. (Eds.): NGCT 2017, CCIS 827, pp. 263–275, 2018.
https://doi.org/10.1007/978-981-10-8657-1_20

Wei and Xiao [8, 11] presented some basic operations on biswapped network and also presented matrix multiplication for biswapped network mesh. Ye et al. [9] presented broadcasting for biswapped network hypercube. Wei and Xiao [10, 12] presented fault tolerant and parallel sorting in biswapped networks. Yu and Wei [13, 14] presented load balancing approaches for Bi-Swapped Networks. Wei [15] used un-safety vectors and presented fault-tolerant routing algorithm over BSN hypercube. Gupta [16] presented parallel algorithm for mapping binomial series (special cases) on mesh network. Wei et al. [18] presented parallel prefix algorithm on BSN mesh. Zhao [19] reported load balancing approach for Biswapped networks. Linc and Chen [20] presented node to set disjoint paths for biswapped network. Wei et al. [21] presented the variation of Bi-Swapped Networks named Bi Swapped Network mesh. They also showed the parallel mapping of some relevant numerical problems such as data sum, prefix sum, sorting etc. Sun and Tonc [22] presented basic operations on BSN hypercube such as data sum, prefix sum etc. Gupta and Sarkar [23] presented the improved parallel approach for mapping prefix sum on Bi Swapped Network mesh. Gupta and Sarkar [24] also presented the parallel mapping of LaGrange's interpolation on Bi Swapped Network mesh. We first explore, in this paper, the different cases (special cases) of binomial series (having finite terms), and thereafter perform their parallel mapping over 2-level optoelectronic Bi Swapped network mesh.

The essence of the binomial theorem is inevitable in various areas such as economic prediction, computing area, higher mathematics, etc. Binomial theorem is very useful in the automatic distribution of IP address. Further, It is heavily used in the probabilistic analysis. Prediction of future economic gain and loss is also an utmost relevant part for a nation's economy and the probabilistic analysis is helpful in it. Also, forecasting services such as disaster and the weather forecast are not possible without the use of the binomial theorem. Moreover, binomial theorem is also used in the construction services such as finding the cost of the construction by taking the estimation of the amount of material used by shape and area of infrastructure. Having such an importance in the real world, an efficient parallel mapping is demanding for the faster execution of it.

A brief introduction regarding the computational model and applications of binomial theorem has already been illustrated in the present section. For the rest of the present work, the organization of the paper is as follows. The network architecture of Bi Swapped Network mesh is shown to be thoroughly investigated in Sect. 2. Further, the methodology of Binomial Series (Special Cases) is shown in Sect. 3, and the proposed parallel implementation of them is shown to be implemented over Bi Swapped Network mesh in Sect. 4 followed by the conclusion in Sect. 5.

2 Computational Model

In this section, we investigate the horizontal and vertical intra-cluster (electronic) and inter-part (optical) links of Bi Swapped Network mesh. The intra-cluster (electronic) connections are entirely depends on the connectivity among the processors of each cluster or component graph. On the other hand, inter-part (optical) connections always remain similar irrespective of each clusters' intra-cluster processor connections. Assume P(c, p, P) represents the processor, where parameters c, p and P represents the cluster-number,

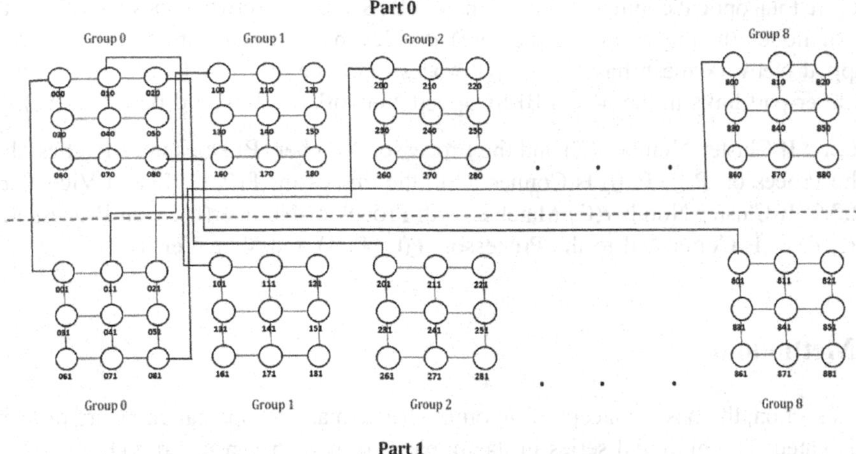

Fig. 1. 3×3 Bi Swapped Network mesh. All links are not shown. Inter part connectivity from group-0 is shown only.

processor-number and the part-number respectively. Note that, N is the size of cluster and n shows the row or column processors in a cluster. The detailed illustration of horizontal and vertical intra-cluster (electronic) and inter-part (optical) connections are shown in Subsects. 2.1, 2.2 and 2.3 respectively. For better understanding, the processor connectivity of 3×3 Bi Swapped network mesh is shown in Fig. 1.

2.1 Horizontal Intra-cluster (Electronic) Links

$\forall p$ and $\forall c$, in each row, processors: P(c, p, P) follows linear pattern starting from processor: P(c, $i \times n$, P), $0 \leq i \leq n - 1$. Hence, for $0 \leq i \leq n - 1$, $0 \leq j < n - 1$, processor: P(c, $i \times n + j$, P) is directly connected to processor: P(c, $i \times n + j + 1$, P). Note that, $n \times n$ Bi Swapped Network mesh has in total $n(n - 1)$ horizontal intra-cluster connections, since each cluster has n rows and each row has $n - 1$ connections.

2.2 Vertical Intra-cluster (Electronic) Links

$\forall P$ and $\forall c$, in each column, processors: P(c, p, P) follows a linear pattern starting from the processor: P(c, p, P), $0 \leq p \leq n - 1$. Hence, processor: P(c, $j + i \times n$, P) is directly connected to processors: P(c, $j + (i + 1)n$, P'), where $0 \leq i \leq n - 1$, $0 \leq j < n - 1$. Note that, $n \times n$ Bi Swapped Network mesh has in total $n(n - 1)$ vertical intra-cluster connections, since each cluster has n columns and each column has $n - 1$ connections.

2.3 Inter-part (Optical) Links

In $n \times n$ Bi Swapped Network mesh, each processor has a single optical connection, which connects them to their corresponding processors in the opposite part. Since all optical connections are bi-directional and each processor has a single optical connection, therefore total optical connections in the n × n Bi Swapped Network mesh would be the sum of nodes (in the entire architecture) divided by 2. Each part of the n × n Bi Swapped Network mesh has N^2 (or n^4) processors, where N equals to n × n. Hence, total inter-part links in the n × n Bi Swapped Network mesh would be N^2 (or n^4).

2.3.1. If Cluster-Number (C) and the Processor-Number (P) Does not Matches, then the Processor: P(C, P, 0) Is Connected to the Processor: P(P, C, 1) and Vice Versa
2.3.2. If Cluster-Number(C) Matches with Processor-Number(P), then Processor: P (C, P, 0) Is Connected to the Processor: P(C, P, 1) and Vice Versa

3 Methodology

In this section, the basic concept of binomial theorem and its special cases are properly investigated. The binomial series in its simplest form is shown in Eq. (1).

$$(x+a)^z = \sum_{k=0}^{\infty} \binom{z}{k} x^k a^{z-k} \tag{1}$$

Where, $\binom{z}{k}$ represents the binomial coefficient and z is a real number. The series converges for $z \geq 0$ and integer, or $\left|\frac{x}{a}\right| < 1$. In Eq. (1), the binomial series can expand in infinite terms. However, the implementation of binomial series over Bi Swapped Network mesh would require the finite number of terms, which entirely depends on the size of the network. In our case, the parallel mapping of finite binomial series would require $2N^2 + 1$ terms, since each cluster of Bi Swapped Network mesh has N (or n^2 processors). The general form of binomial series based on the network size of N node Bi Swapped Network mesh having finite terms ($2N^2 + 1$) is shown below in Eq. (2). Further, the expansion of special cases for binomial series is shown in Eqs. (3) and (4).

$$(x+a)^N = \sum_{k=0}^{2N^2} \binom{N}{k} x^k a^{N-k} \tag{2}$$

A. Binomial Series (special case-1): Taylor Series

Condition ($a = 1, |x| > 1$)

$$(1+x)^N = \sum_{k=0}^{2N^2} \frac{(-N)_K}{k!} (x^k)$$

//The expansion of taylor series//

$$(1+x)^N = 1 + (N)(x) + \frac{1}{2!}N(N-1)x^2 + \frac{1}{3!}N(N-1)(N-2)x^3 +,\ldots,+ \frac{1}{2N^2-1!}N(N-1)(N-2),\ldots,(N-2N^2-1)x^{2N^2} \tag{3}$$

B. Binomial Series (special case-2):
Negative Binomial Series

Condition (Negative integer $-v$, $a = 1$, $|x| < 1$)

$$(1-x)^{-N} = \sum_{k=0}^{2N^2} \frac{(N)_K}{k!} (x)^k$$

//The expansion of negative binomial series/

$$(1-x)^{-N} = 1 + (N)(x) + \frac{1}{2!}N(N+1)x^2 + \frac{1}{3!}N(N+1)(N+2)x^3 +,\ldots,+ \frac{1}{2N^2-1!}N(N+1)(N+2),\ldots,(N+2N^2-1)x^{2N^2} \tag{4}$$

Remarks 1. *The symbol* $(N)_k$ *represents pochhammer symbol.*

$(N)_k = \frac{\Gamma(N+x)}{\Gamma(N)}$ **//Pochhammer Symbol//**

//Expansion of pocchammer symbol//

$$(N)_k = N \times (N+1) \times (N+2) \times \ldots \times (N+k-1).$$

4 Parallel Algorithm

In performing parallel algorithm, assume, each processor would have nine registers namely: X(c, p, P), Y(c, p, P), Z(c, p, P), X_1(c, p, P), Y_1(c, p, P), Z_1(c, p, P), X_2(c, p, P), Y_2(c, p, P) and Z_2(c, p, P) (Table 1).

Table 1. Key notations with its significance

Key notations	Significance
#c	Copy data from source to destination processor
#b	Broadcast data from source processor
#s	Store data in destination processor
#i	Perform inter-part move and store the outcome in destination processor
$\#i^+$	Perform binary addition via inter-part move and store the outcome in destination processor
$\#i^*$	Perform binary multiplication via inter-Part move and store the outcome in destionation processor

The symbols, ⊕, ⊖, ⊠, ⊖ represents binary summation, binary subtraction, binary multiplication and binary divide respectively.

4.1 Parallel Algorithm

Regiter Initialization:

$$\begin{array}{lll} X(c,p,P) \leftarrow x; & Y(c,p,P) \leftarrow 1; & Z(c,p,P) \leftarrow 1; \\ X_1(c,p,P) \leftarrow N; & Y_1(c,p,P) \leftarrow 1; & Z_1(c,p,P) \leftarrow 1; \\ X_2(c,p,P) \leftarrow 1; & Y_2(c,p,P) \leftarrow 0; & Z_2(c,p,P) \leftarrow 0; \end{array}$$

STEP 1. Perform Step-A for performing (Taylors Series) and Step-B for performing (Negative Binomial Series).

A. $\forall$P, $\forall$c and $\forall$p, $X_1(c,p,P) \xleftarrow{\#S} X_1(c,p,P) \oplus X_2(c,p,P)$.

B. $\forall$P, $\forall$c and $\forall$p, $X_1(c,p,P) \xleftarrow{\#S} X_1(c,p,P) \ominus X_2(c,p,P)$.

Remarks 2. *Assume, T represents the time complexity for performing parallel prefix algorithm* [1–6] .

STEP 2. ∀P, ∀c and ∀p, Perform parallel prefix binary addition [1–6] using registers: $X_2(c, p, P)$ and $Y_2(c, p, P)$ in each cluster of each part, and store the result in their respective register: $Y_2(c, p, P)$.
STEP 3. ∀P and ∀c, $Y_2(c, N-1, P) \xleftarrow{\#c} X_2(c, N-1, P)$.
STEP 4. ∀P and ∀c, $\xrightarrow{\#b} Y_2(c, N-1, P)$. //Parallel broadcast in each cluster//
STEP 5. Perform Steps-A and B in parallel for the following inter-part moves.

A. $Z_2(c+k, c, 1) \xleftarrow{\#i} Y_2(c, c+k, 0), 0 \le c \le N-1, 0 \le k \le (N-1)-c.$

B. $Z_2(c+k, c, 0) \xleftarrow{\#i} Y_2(c, c+k, 1), 0 \le c \le N-1, 0 \le k \le (N-1)-c.$

STEP 6. *//Row wise parallel data summation//*

$$\forall P \text{ and } \forall c,\ Z_2(c, j+in+1, P) \xleftarrow{\#s} Z_2(c, j+in, P) \oplus Z_2(c, j+in+1, P), 0 \le i < n-1, 0 \le j < n-1$$

STEP 7. *//Last column parallel data summation //*

$$\forall P \text{ and } \forall c,\ Z_2(c, ((i+2)(n))-1, P) \xleftarrow{\#s} Z_2(c, ((i+1)(n))-1, P) \oplus Z_2(c, ((i+2)(n))-1, P), 0 \le i < n-1.$$

STEP 8. $\xrightarrow{\#b} Z_2(N-1, N-1, 1)$. //Broadcast//
STEP 9. $Z_2(p, N-1, 0) \xleftarrow{\#i^*} Z_2(N-1, p, 1), 0 \le p \le N-1.$
STEP 10. ∀P and ∀c, $\xrightarrow{\#b} Z_2(c, N-1, P)$. // Parallel broadcast//
STEP 11. ∀c, perform parallel steps-A and B in parallel for the inter part move.

A. $Y_2(c+1, c, 1) \xleftarrow{\#i} Z_2(c, c+1, 0), 0 \le c < N-1.$

B. $Y_2(c+1, c, 0) \xleftarrow{\#i} Z_2(c, c+1, 1), 0 \le c < N-1.$

STEP 12. ∀P and ∀c, $\xrightarrow{\#b} Y_2(c, c-1, P)$.
STEP 13. ∀P, ∀c and ∀p, $X_2(c, p, P) \xleftarrow{\#s} X_2(c, p, P) \oplus Y_2(c, p, P)$.
STEP 14. Perform step-A for Taylors Series and step-B for Negative Binomial Series.

A. $\forall P, \forall c \text{ and } \forall p, X_1(c,p,P) \overset{\#S}{\leftarrow} X_1(c,p,P) \ominus X_2(c,p,P)$.

B. $\forall P, \forall c \text{ and } \forall p, X_1(c,p,P) \overset{\#S}{\leftarrow} X_1(c,p,P) \oplus X_2(c,p,P)$.

STEP 15. Perform Step-A and B in parallel.

A. $\forall P, \forall c, \text{ and } \forall p, Y_2(c,p,P) \overset{\#C}{\leftarrow} Y_1(c,p,P)$.

B. $\forall P, \forall c, \text{ and } \forall p, Z_2(c,p,P) \overset{\#C}{\leftarrow} Z_1(c,p,P)$.

STEP 16. Perform Steps-A, B and C in parallel.

A. ∀P, ∀c and ∀p, perform parallel prefix binary multiplication [1–6] using registers: *X (c, p, P) and Y(c, p, P),* and store the result in their respective register: *X(c, p, P).*
B. ∀P, ∀c and ∀p, perform parallel prefix binary multiplication [1–6] using registers: $X_1(c, p, P)$ *and* $Y_1(c, p, P)$, *and* store the result in their respective register: $X_1(c, p, P)$.
C. ∀P, ∀c and ∀p, perform parallel prefix binary multiplication [1–6] using registers: $X_2(c, p, P)$ *and* $Y_2(c, p, P)$, and store the result in their respective register: $Y_2(c, p, P)$.

STEP 17. Perform Steps-A, B and C in parallel.

A. $\forall P \text{ and } \forall c, Y(c, N-1, P) \overset{\#C}{\leftarrow} X(c, N-1, P)$.

B. $\forall P \text{ and } \forall c, Y_1(c, N-1, P) \overset{\#C}{\leftarrow} X_1(c, N-1, P)$.

C. $\forall P \text{ and } \forall c, Y_2(c, N-1, P) \overset{\#C}{\leftarrow} X_2(c, N-1, P)$.

STEP 18. Perform steps-A, B and C for parallel cluster broadcasting of data.

A. $\forall P \text{ and } \forall c, \overset{\#b}{\rightarrow} Y(c, N-1, P)$.

B. $\forall P \text{ and } \forall c, \overset{\#b}{\rightarrow} Y_1(c, N-1, P)$.

C. $\forall P \text{ and } \forall c, \overset{\#b}{\rightarrow} Y_2(c, N-1, P)$.

STEP 19. Perform Step-I, Step-II and Step-III in parallel.

STEP-I. Perform parallel Steps-A and B for the following inter-part moves.

A. $Z(c + k, c, 1) \overset{\#i}{\longleftarrow} Y(c, c + k, 0),\ 0 \le c \le N - 1,\ 0 \le k \le (N - 1) - c.$

B. $Z(c + k, c, 0) \overset{\#i}{\longleftarrow} Y(c, c + k, 1),\ 0 \le c \le N - 1,\ 0 \le k \le (N - 1) - c.$

STEP-II. Perform parallel Steps-A and B for the following inter-part moves.

A. $Z_1(c + k, c, 1) \overset{\#i}{\longleftarrow} Y_1(c, c + k, 0),\ 0 \le c \le N - 1,\ 0 \le k \le (N - 1) - c.$

B. $Z_1(c + k, c, 0) \overset{\#i}{\longleftarrow} Y_1(c, c + k, 1),\ 0 \le c \le N - 1,\ 0 \le k \le (N - 1) - c.$

STEP-III. Perform Steps-A and B in parallel for the inter-part move.

A. $Z_2(c + k, c, 1) \overset{\#i}{\longleftarrow} Y_2(c, c + k, 0),\ 0 \le c \le N - 1,\ 0 \le k \le (N - 1) - c.$

B. $Z_2(c + k, c, 0) \overset{\#i}{\longleftarrow} Y_2(c, c + k, 1),\ 0 \le c \le N - 1,\ 0 \le k \le (N - 1) - c.$

STEP 20. Perform Steps-A, B and C in parallel.

A. $\forall P$ and $\forall c$, $Z(c, j + in, P)$
$\overset{\#S}{\longleftarrow} Z(c, j + in, P) \otimes Z(c, j + in + 1, P),\ 0 \le i \le n - 1,\ 0 \le j < n - 1.$

B. $\forall P$ and $\forall c$, $Z_1(c, j + in, P)$
$\overset{\#S}{\longleftarrow} Z_1(c, j + in, P) \otimes Z_1(c, j + in + 1, P), 0 \le i \le n - 1, 0 \le j < n - 1.$

C. $\forall P$ and $\forall c$, $Z_2(c, j + in, P)$
$\overset{\#S}{\longleftarrow} Z_2(c, j + in, P) \otimes Z_2(c, j + in + 1, P), 0 \le i \le n - 1, 0 \le j < n - 1.$

STEP 21. Perform Steps-A, B and C in parallel.

A. $\forall P$ and $\forall c$, $Z(c, (i+2)(n) - 1, P)$
$\overset{\#S}{\longleftarrow} Z(c, ((i + 1)(n)) - 1, P) \otimes Z(c, ((i + 2)(n)) - 1, P), 0 \le i \le n - 1.$

B. $\forall P$ and $\forall c$, $Z_1(c, ((i + 2)(n)) - 1, P) \overset{\#S}{\longleftarrow} Z_1(c, ((i + 1)(n)) - 1, P)$
$\otimes Z_1(c, ((i + 2)(n)) - 1, P), 0 \le i \le n - 1.$

C. $\forall P$ and $\forall c$, $Z_2(c, ((i + 2)(n)) - 1, P) \overset{\#S}{\longleftarrow} Z_2(c, ((i + 1)(n)) - 1, P)$
$\otimes Z_2(c, ((i + 2)(n)) - 1, P), 0 \le i \le n - 1.$

STEP 22. Perform Steps-A, B and C in parallel.

A. $\xrightarrow{\#b} Z(N-1, N-1, 1)$.

B. $\xrightarrow{\#b} Z_1(N-1, N-1, 1)$.

C. $\xrightarrow{\#b} Z_2(N-1, N-1, 1)$.

STEP 23. Perform parallel Steps-A, B and C for the following inter-part move addition.

A. $Z(p, N-1, 0) \xleftarrow{\#i^+} Z(N-1, p, 1), 0 \le p \le N-1$.

B. $Z_1(p, N-1, 0) \xleftarrow{\#i^+} Z_1(N-1, p, 1), 0 \le p \le N-1$.

C. $Z_2(p, N-1, 0) \xleftarrow{\#i^+} Z_2(N-1, p, 1), 0 \le p \le N-1$.

STEP 24. Perform Steps-A, B and C in parallel.

A. $\forall P$ and $\forall c \xrightarrow{\#b} Z(c, N-1, P)$.

B. $\forall P$ and $\forall c \xrightarrow{\#b} Z_1(c, N-1, P)$.

C. $\forall P$ and $\forall c \xrightarrow{\#b} Z_2(c, N-1, P)$.

STEP 25. Perform Steps-I, II and III in parallel.

STEP-I. $\forall c$, perform parallel Steps-A and B for following inter-part moves.

A. $Y(c+1, c, 1) \xleftarrow{\#i} Z(c, c+1, 0), 0 \le c < N-1$.

B. $Y(c+1, c, 0) \xleftarrow{\#i} Z(c, c+1, 1), 0 \le c < N-1$.

STEP-II. $\forall c$, perform parallel Steps-A and B for the following inter-part moves.

A. $Y_1(c+1, c, 1) \xleftarrow{\#i} Z_1(c, c+1, 0), 0 \le c < N-1$.

B. $Y_1(c+1, c, 0) \xleftarrow{\#i} Z_1(c, c+1, 1), 0 \le c < N-1$.

STEP-III. ∀c, perform parallel Steps-A and B for the following inter-part moves.

A. $Y_2(c+1, c, 1) \xleftarrow{\#i} Z_2(c, c+1, 0), 0 \le c < N-1.$

B. $Y_2(c+1, c, 0) \xleftarrow{\#i} Z_2(c, c+1, 1), 0 \le c < N-1.$

STEP 26. Perform Steps-A, B, and C in parallel.

A. $\forall P$ and $\forall c$, $\xrightarrow{\#b} Y(c, c-1, P).$

B. $\forall P$ and $\forall c$, $\xrightarrow{\#b} Y_1(c, c-1, P).$

C. $\forall P$ and $\forall c$, $\xrightarrow{\#b} Y_2(c, c-1, P).$

STEP 27. Perform Steps-A, B, and C in parallel.

A. $\forall P, \forall c$ and $\forall p, X(c, p, P) \xleftarrow{\#S} X(c, p, P) \otimes Y(c, p, P).$

B. $\forall P, \forall c$ and $\forall p, X_1(c, p, P) \xleftarrow{\#S} X_1(c, p, P) \otimes Y_1(c, p, P).$

C. $\forall P, \forall c$ and $\forall p, X_2(c, p, P) \xleftarrow{\#S} X_2(c, p, P) \otimes Y_2(c, p, P).$

STEP 28. $\forall P, \forall c$ and $\forall p, X(c, p, p) \xleftarrow{\#S} X(c, p, P) \otimes X_1(c, p, P)$.//Binary Miltiplication//

STEP 29. $\forall P, \forall c$ and $\forall p, X(c, p, p) \xleftarrow{\#S} X(c, p, P) \ominus X_2(c, p, P)$.//Binary Divide//

STEP 30. //Row wise parallel data summation//

$\forall P$ and $\forall c, X(c, j-1+i \times n, P)$
$\xleftarrow{\#S} X(c, j-1+i \times n, P) \oplus X(c, j+i \times n, P), 0 \le i \le n-1, n > j > 0.$

STEP 31. //First column parallel data summation//

$\forall P, \forall c, X(c, (i-1)n, p) \xleftarrow{\#S} X(c, (i-1)n, P) \oplus X(c, i \times n, P), n > i > 0.$

STEP 32. Perform Steps-A and B for inter-part optical moves as follows.

$$\text{A.}\quad \forall c, X(0,c,0) \xleftarrow{\#i} X(c,0,1).$$

$$\text{B.}\quad \forall c, X(0,c,1) \xleftarrow{\#i} X(c,0,0).$$

STEP 33. //Row wise parallel data summation//

$$\forall P, X(0, j-1+in, P) \xleftarrow{\#S} X(0, j-1+in, P) \oplus X(0, j+in, P), 0 \le i \le n-1, n > j > 0.$$

STEP 34. //First column parallel data summation//

$$\forall P, X(0,(i-1)n, p) \xleftarrow{\#S} X(0,(i-1)n, P) \oplus X(0, i \times n, P), n > i > 0.$$

STEP 35. Perform inter-part move binary addition, as follows.

$$X(0,0,0) \xleftarrow{\#i^{+}} X(0,0,1).$$

STEP 36. $X(0,0,0) \xleftarrow{\#S} X(0,0,0) \oplus X_2(0,0,0).$

Remarks 3. The Final outcome is obtained from the register: X(0, 0, 0).

4.2 Time Complexity Analysis

The following are the necessary steps for performing the parallel implementation of special cases of binomial series over the n×n Bi Swapped Network mesh. Each of the Steps-1, 3, 13, 14, 15, 17, 27, 28, 29 and 36 demands a constant move. Let assume, T is the time required to implement parallel prefix in each cluster (mesh)). Each of the Step-2 and 16 demands time T to compute prefix in each cluster parallely. Step-4 needs *2 (n − 1)* moves for parallel broadcasting of data in each cluster, whereas Step-6 and 7 need *n − 1* moves each. Step 8 requires *2(n − 1)* electronic moves for broadcasting. Further, Steps-5, 9, 11, 19, 23, 25, 32 and 35 requires one inter-part move each of inter-part communication. Each of the Steps-10, 12, 18, 22, 24 and 26 required *2(n − 1)* electronic moves each for performing cluster broadcast parallely. Step-20 and 21 need n − 1 steps each. At a later stage of the proposed algorithm, Steps-30, 31, 33 and 34 demands n − 1 steps each. Therefore, total $2T + 24(n-1)$ or$2T + 24\left(\sqrt{N}-1\right)$ electronic and *8* optical moves are required for mapping finite binomial series (special cases) over n × n Bi Swapped Network mesh (containing $2n^4 + 1$ terms).

5 Conclusions and Future Work

Binomial Series has a wide range of applications in the real world. Having such an importance, faster execution of it, is a desirable task. The two-level, symmetrical, modular and scalable behavior of Bi Swapped Networks with its larger network size, when compared to its counterpart OTIS Networks, enables to perform parallel mapping of numerical problems containing massive data for faster execution. In this paper, we show the parallel mapping of finite binomial series (special cases) over n × n Bi Swapped network mesh. The proposed parallel algorithm is shown to be mapped over n × n Bi Swapped Network mesh in total $2T + 24(n-1)$ or $2T + 24\ (\sqrt{N} - 1)$ electronic and *8* optical moves (assume *T* is the time required to implement parallel prefix in each cluster (mesh). From the future perspective, numerous other relevant numerical problems could be further investigated and implemented in parallel over the symmetrical optoelectronic Bi Swapped Network mesh for the faster execution.

References

1. Akl, S.G.: The Design and Analysis of Parallel Algorithms. Prentice-Hall, Englewood Cliffs (1989)
2. Ladner, R.E., Fischer, M.J.: Parallel prefix computation. J. Assoc. Comput. Mach. **27**(4), 831–838 (1980)
3. Horowitz, E., Sahnp, S., Rajasekaran, S.: Fundamentals of Computer Algorithms. Galgotia Publications Pvt. Ltd., Delhi (1998)
4. Parhami, B.: Introduction to Parallel Processing: Algorithms and Architectures, 1st edn. Springer, Heidelberg (1999). https://doi.org/10.1007/b116777
5. Grama, A., Karypis, G., Kumar, V., Gupta, A.: Introduction to Parallel Computinc, 2nd edn. Addison Wesley, Boston (2003)
6. Jha, S.K.: An improved parallel prefix computation on 2D mesh network. In: Interntional Conference of Computational Intelligence: Modelinc, Tehniques and Applications (CIMTA) (2013)
7. Xiao, W., Chen, W., He, M., Wei, W., Parhamp, B.: Biswapped network and their topological properties. In: Proceedings-Eighth ACIS International Conference on Software Engineering, Artificial Intelligence, Networking, and Parallel/Distributed Computing, pp. 193–198 (2007)
8. Wei, W., Xiao, W.: Matrix multiplication on the biswapped-mesh network. In: Proceedings Eighth ACIS International Conference on Software Engineering, Artificial Intelligence, Networking, and Parallel/Distributed Computing, pp. 211–215 (2007)
9. Ye, H., Xiao, W., Wu, J.: Broadcasting on the BSN-hypercube network. In: 2009 Second International Conference on Information and Computing Science, vol. 01, pp. 167–170 (2009)
10. Wei, W., Xiao, W.: Fault tolerance in the biswapped network. In: Bourgeois, A.G., Zheng, S.Q. (eds.) ICA3PP 2008. LNCS, vol. 5022, pp. 79–82. Springer, Heidelberg (2008). https://doi.org/10.1007/978-3-540-69501-1_10
11. Wei, W., Xiao, W.: Algorithms of basic communication operation on the biswapped network. In: Bubak, M., van Albada, G.D., Dongarra, J., Sloot, Peter M.A. (eds.) ICCS 2008. LNCS, vol. 5101, pp. 347–354. Springer, Heidelberg (2008). https://doi.org/10.1007/978-3-540-69384-0_40

12. Wei, W., Xiao, W.: Efficient parallel algorithm for sorting on the biswapped network. J. Comput. Infor. Syst. **4**(4), 1365–1370 (2008)
13. Yu, Y., Wei, W.: Load balancing on the biswapped network. In: Proceedings of the 2nd International Conference on Intelligent Networks and Intelligent Systems, pp. 146–149 (2009)
14. Wei, W., Li, Y.: Load balancing on heterogeneous biswapped network. In: 3rd International Symposium on Electronic Commerce and Security, IEEE CS, pp. 253–256 (2010)
15. Wei, W., Li, Y.: Fault-tolerant routing algorithm for BSN-hypercube using unsafety vectors. J. Comput. Inf. Syst. **1**(2), 623–630 (2011)
16. Gupta, A.: Parallel algorithm for binomial series (special cases) using mesh architecture. In: 2nd IEEE International Conference on Parallel, Distributed and Grid Computing (PDGC), Solan, pp. 153–157 (2012)
17. Xiao, W., Parhami, B., Chen, W., He, M., Wei, W.: Biswapped networks: a family of interconnection architectures with advantages over swapped or OTIS networks. Int. J. Comput. Math. **88**(13), 2669–2684 (2011)
18. Wei, W., Li, Q., Tao, M.: Parallel prefix algorithm on BSN-mesh. In: Fourth International Conference on Emerging Intelligent Data and Web Technologies, pp. 46–50 (2013)
19. Zhao, C.: Efficient load balancing on biswapped networks. Cluster Comput. **17**(2), 403–411 (2014)
20. Linc, S., Chen, W.: Node-to-set disjoint paths in bi-swapped networks. Comput. J. **57**(7), 953–967 (2014)
21. Wei, W., Li, Q., Tao, M.: BSN-mesh and its basic parallel algorithms. Int. J. Grid Util. Comput. **6**(¾), 213–220 (2015)
22. Sun, L., Tonc, C.: Basic operations on BSN-hypercube multiprocessors. J. Comput. Inf. Syst. **10**(12), 5211–5218 (2014)
23. Gupta, A., Sarkar, B.K.: A new parallel approach for prefix sum on Bi Swapped Network mesh. In: IEEE 2nd International Conference on Next Generation Computing Technologies, pp. 393–396 (2016)
24. Gupta, A., Sarkar, B.K.: Parallel algorithm for LaGrange's interpolation on BSN-mesh. In: Singh, R., Choudhury, S. (eds.) Proceeding of International Conference on Intelligent Communication, Control and Devices. Advances in Intelligent Systems and Computing, vol. 479, pp. 673–682. Springer, Singapore (2017). https://doi.org/10.1007/978-981-10-1708-7_77

Parallel Multiplication of Big Integer on GPU

Jitendra V. Tembhurne(✉)

St. Vincent Pallotti College of Engineering and Technology, Nagpur, Maharashtra, India
jtembhurne@stvincentngp.edu.in

Abstract. In this article, we present a method for implementation of FFT based big integer multiplication acceleration for RSA encryption and decryption. The DIF (Decimation-In-Frequency) based FFT was utilized to compute the multiplication operation for two big integers. The algorithm is implemented on Graphics Processing Units (GPUs) by utilizing the CUDA programming model. This DIF method is similar to divide-and-conquer approach. In addition, we have concentrated on the efficiency of our proposed method by dealing with the optimal time use, efficient memory utilization and the data transfer time between host (CPU) to device (GPU) which has an impact on the complete computation time on the GPU. We compare our implementation between GPU and CPU and present the performance results.

Keywords: FFT · Multiplication · CUDA · GPU

1 Introduction

Multiplication of two big integers applicable in various cryptographic algorithms such as Rivest *et al.* [1], Diffie-Hellman [2] and ECC [3], etc. These cryptographic algorithms are commonly used to secure the data over the internet, due to its high security and complex mathematical computational model. The main operation in RSA is the computation of big integer multiplication, which employed to compute the big integer exponentiation. The computation of big integer multiplication for the large key length such as 1024-bit or more, is a more time consuming process, and it affects the performance of an entire cryptographic system.

In the literature, various algorithms to compute the multiplication of two polynomials or two big integers have been proposed by researchers such as basic iterative [4], divide-and-conquer based [5–7] and Fast Fourier Transform (FFT) based multiplication [8] algorithms. To achieve the high speed of multiplication acceleration, we have employed the FFT based big integer multiplication method due to its optimal time complexity of $O(nlogn)$ as compared with [4–7]. In this paper, we target to speed up the cryptographic process by accelerating the big integer multiplication. However, FFT is the main operation in the computation of big integer multiplication using FFT, which has been used for the RSA implementation. The FFT [9] algorithm was used in many scientific applications ranging from signal processing to integer arithmetic. The different FFT implementations are already been reported in the literature such as [10–13]. In most of the GPU implementations, the main bottleneck is a small memory offered by

P. Bhattacharyya et al. (Eds.): NGCT 2017, CCIS 827, pp. 276–285, 2018.
https://doi.org/10.1007/978-981-10-8657-1_21

the GPU. This bottleneck restricts the large data size to be handled on the GPU. Hence, for the acceleration of RSA, the bottlenecks are long key-size and large message for encryption and decryption. This research work is an extension of our previous work carried in [14, 15] towards the proposed big integer multiplication using FFT.

The modular multiplication and exponentiation using Montgomery's multiplication has been proposed in Sutter *et al.* [16]. The LSB (Least Significant Bit) first and MSB (Most Significant Bit) first algorithms were proposed with an optimized version of the Montgomery algorithm on Xilinx Virtex 5. Exponentiation is the most time consuming operation in cryptography. The most efficient method to handle this problem is addressed in [17, 18]. The big integer multiplication is the active research area and this problem was also addressed by various researchers in the past to compute big integer multiplication on different hardware platforms and software technologies. An efficient multiplication of large integers in parallel is implemented in [19]. In this implementation a large integer is subsequently partitioned into small integers and their partial multiplications are computed, finally these multiplications are combined to produce the resultant multiplication. The Big-One representation of integer was proposed in Jahani *et al.* [20] for the computation of the multiplication and square of large integer for cryptographic applications. A finite field based software implementation techniques for multiplication on different hardware architectures such as 32-bit and 64-bit were proposed in [21] by using latest parallel technologies. The implementation of big integer and polynomial multiplication highlights the efficient parallel algorithm design and better performance on multi-core architecture systems which were addressed in [22–24].

The latest advancement in the parallel hardware design such as multi-core CPUs, many-core Graphics Processing Units (GPUs), GPU emerges with a power of the higher computing model, which is utilized to solve the wide range of compute intensive problems from bioinformatics to astrology. In addition, with the availability of GPUs, the researchers have started to port their applications on the GPUs for the performance measurement and to achieve the significantly higher performance compared to the CPU. The polynomial multiplication on the GPU was proposed in [25], the author developed a dense univariate polynomial multiplication on the GPU and achieved the speedup of 21x to 37x on the use of randomly generated large data set. The GPU based arithmetic cryptography library was implemented for the different memory coding techniques in [26] and comparison of modular arithmetic algorithms was carried with available arithmetic libraries. A new data structure based technique for the computation of large integer multiplication on the GPU was proposed in [27]. The GPU based results runs 12.8x and 71.4x faster than GMP library and NTL library respectively as compared to a single CPU. Emmart and Weems [28], presented the multiple size FFT computation model for the computation of high precision integer multiplication on the GPU and witnessed the 19x speedup over single core CPU implementation.

1.1 Big Integer Multiplication

The algorithm presented in [8] is a powerful computational method for the computation of multiplication of two big integers. The algorithm reported in [8] is similar to the convolution theorem of two signals in the frequency domain, where u, v are two signals which satisfy the Eqs. (1) and (2).

$$\Psi(u \times v) = \Psi(u)\,\Psi(v) \tag{1}$$

$$u \times v = \Psi^{-1}\{\Psi(u)\,\Psi(v)\} \tag{2}$$

where Ψ represents to be a Fourier transformation.

Here, the Fourier transformation is applied first on both the signal u and v with the signal size of N_u and N_v. Then point-to-point multiplication is performed and in the last step the inverse Fourier transformation is computed to get the final result [30]. Both the signals u and v are padded to the size of original signals to get the required result signal. The padding is usually done with the zeros. Hence, the size of resulting signal becomes the $N = N_u + N_v - 1$, which leads the time complexity of FFT computation as $O(NlogN)$ (for more details see [4, 29, 30]).

2 Method

2.1 FFT Based Big Integer Multiplication

The GPU based FFT big integer multiplication is discussed in this section. Easier and direct implementation of integer multiplication on the GPU has been demonstrated in Algorithm 1. The five major tasks have been performed: (1) Data transfer from CPU to GPU, (2) FFT computation, (3) Point-by-point multiplication, (4) Inverse FFT computation, and (5) Data transfer from GPU to CPU.

The point-by-point multiplication implementation on the GPU is very simple. Every data point is mapped to the respective GPU threads, which in turn provides memory access in a coalesced fashion. The parallel FFT computation on the GPU is provided by the NVIDIA in the form of cuFFT library [31], the fastest FFT computing library available on the GPU with all possible optimizations applied. The optimization issues considered in cuFFT are texture memory, shared memory utilization and memory coalescing, etc. While handling big integers and large message size for RSA implementation on the GPU, it makes computation impossible with the limited global memory present on the GPU. We have proposed a novel method for the parallel computation of FFT-based big integer multiplication using DIF (Decimation-In-Frequency). This method is based on the approach of divide-and-combine, where DIF is used to divide the data and prepare the FFT-based big integer multiplication process in small parts.

In the literature, several different methods were available to divide the FFT computation problem. The optimality of these methods depends upon the operation on every data point and transfer of data. We have chosen the DIF method instead of the Decimation-In-Time (DIT) method. The DIT method does not give the separate results of the sub-problems. Hence, the data transfers are redundant. The Algorithm 1 computes the big integer multiplication on the GPU using cuFFT library. First, data transfer is performed from the CPU side to GPU side for both big integers. Second, FFT is computed for big integers using cuFFT. Third, point-by-point multiplication is performed on the integers and normalization is performed, then inverse FFT is computed for the resultant and at last result data is transferred back to the CPU.

Algorithm 1: *GPUMultiplication(u, v, N, normal)*
1. CUDAMemoryCopy(*u_device, u*, HostToDevice)
2. CUDAMemoryCopy(*v_device, v*, HostToDevice)
3. *u_device* ← CUDAFFT(*u_device*) //in-place FFT
4. *v_device* ← CUDAFFT(*v_device*) //in-place FFT
5. *u_device* ← PointMul(*u_device, v_device, N, normal*)
6. *u_device* ← CUDAIFFT(*u_device*) //in-place inverse FFT
7. CUDAMemoryCopy(*u, u_device*, DeviceToHost)

2.2 Proposed Method for Big Integer Multiplication

In our proposed implementation of FFT-based big integer multiplication, to compute the FFT we have used the DIF method to divide the input data into different parts. We describe in this section how this method can be applied to compute 1D FFT. Let $F(q)$ is the Fourier transformation of $f(p)$, p, q ranges from 0 to $N-1$. The N is chosen to be the power of 2. The new function $g(n)$ and $h(n)$ with $0 \geq n > N/2$ can be expressed by

$$g(n) = f(n) + f(n + N/2) \tag{4}$$

$$h(n) = \{f(n) - f(n - N/2)\} \times \omega_N{}^n \tag{5}$$

where $\omega_N = e^{\frac{2\pi i}{N}}$. The inverse of Eqs. (4) and (5) can be expressed as follows;

$$f(n) = 1/2\{g(n) + h(n) \times \omega_N^n\} \tag{6}$$

$$f(n + N/2) = 1/2\{g(n) - h(n) \times \omega_N^n\} \tag{7}$$

Then the function $G(q')$ and $H(q')$ are the Fourier transformations for Eqs. (4) and (5), satisfies the following properties by G and H;

$$G(q') = F(2q') \tag{8}$$

$$H(q') = F(2q' + 1) \tag{9}$$

The function f is further divided into two equal parts as g and h. In frequency domain g and h are completely different parts than f. The DIF method is applied on the functions g and h recursively, which divides the original function f into four different parts and so on.

Here, we present a new algorithm for the computation of FFT on the GPU. This algorithm is used to compute the parallel multiplication of big integers on the CUDA architecture. The proposed algorithm employs the DIF to divide the data for the successive computation. The data is divided as per the data type is used for the implementation. The In-place computation is performed when complex data is used and out-of-place computation is performed when data is real. In this paper, we have used In-place computation for dividing input data into different sub-parts.

The general overview of the proposed algorithm is illustrated in the Fig. 1. The high level description of the same is demonstrated in Algorithm 2. We have chosen the size of input data is divisible by *D*. Before to compute the FFT, a zero padding of size *N* is applied on both signals (i.e. big integers) to provide the resultant multiplication of size $(2N - 1)$. The proposed algorithm uses the Eqs. (4), (5), (6) and (7) to implement the *Divide* and *Combine* operation for input data. The *Divide* and *Combine* strategy works to divide and combine data into two, four, eight or sixteen different parts. The divide operation is based on the Eqs. (4) and (5) and combine operation is based on the Eqs. (6) and (7) respectively. The implementation of *DIV4* and *COM4* is as follows; directly dividing the data into four different parts, performing the computation and combined back the divided parts for the resulting solution.

Algorithm 2: *GPUDivComMultiplication(u, v, N, D, normal)*
1. *u_device ← Divide(u, D)*
2. *v_device ← Divide(v, D)*
3. *for i ← 0 to D – 1*
   GPUMultiplication(u, v, N/D, normal)
4. *u ← Combine(u_device, D)*

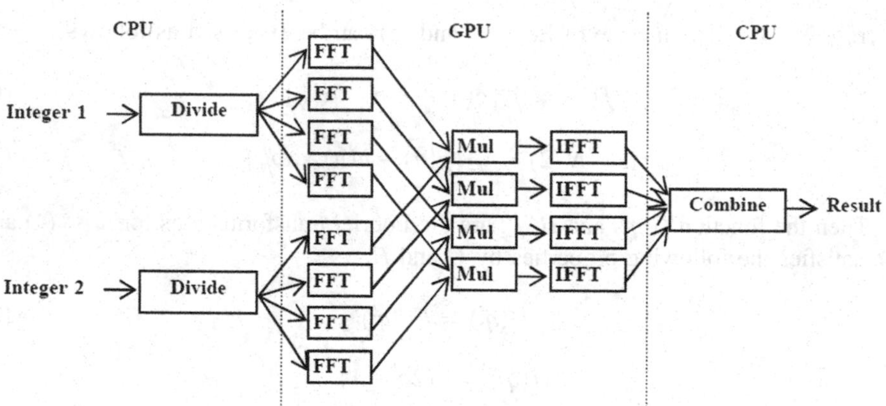

Fig. 1. Proposed method for big integer multiplication using DIF.

3 Result and Discussion

All the experimentation and results were obtained on the parallel hardware, Dell Precision Tower 7910 with Intel Xeon processor with 32 GB RAM and NVIDIA Quadro K5200 graphics card with 8 GB of global memory. On the CPU side, we have used the FFTW library [32] and on the GPU we have implemented the proposed algorithm. The divide and combine operations are to be performed on the CPU, hence these operations were implemented on the CPU. The fixed sized big integers were randomly generated to utilize in the experimentation and performance measurement on the CPU and GPU. The power-of-two big integer was used. The big integers are padded with zero initially, and then the memory requirement will increase to double the size of original big integers. The padding is applied from N to $(2N - 1)$, where N is the length of the big integer in digit.

In the computation of big integer multiplication, the division value D was so chosen as to fit into the GPU shared memory by the threads. Hence, if the integer was small then no division into sub part was performed; if the integer size is large then it is divided into subparts. The big integer pairs of the same size were randomly generated for the experimentation using random number generator routine on the CPU. The pair of big integer size in digits varies from 512 to 256K and the batch size of the big integer pair varies from 1K to 8K.

Figures from Figs. 2, 3, 4 and 5 shows the computation time and speedup achieved for the computation of FFT on the CPU using FFTW and own FFT implementation on the GPU with different length of big integers for the batch size of 1K. Figure 2 depicts the computation timing of FFT for single and double precision data values. Figures 3 and 4 demonstrate the GPU timings for single and double precision data with and without memory data transfer time respectively. Moreover, the speedup response determines for the single and double precision data on the GPU is highlighted in Fig. 5. Figures from Figs. 3, 4 and 5, the computation time for the FFT length 256K is not found due to the unavailability of memory on the GPU card. After performance analysis, we observed that the GPU implementation witnesses the high speedup as compared to CPU implementation. Table 1 illustrates the implementation of big integer multiplication on the CPU and GPU. The implementation results based on the GPU run 18x faster as compared with a single core CPU. The speedup not mentioned for some

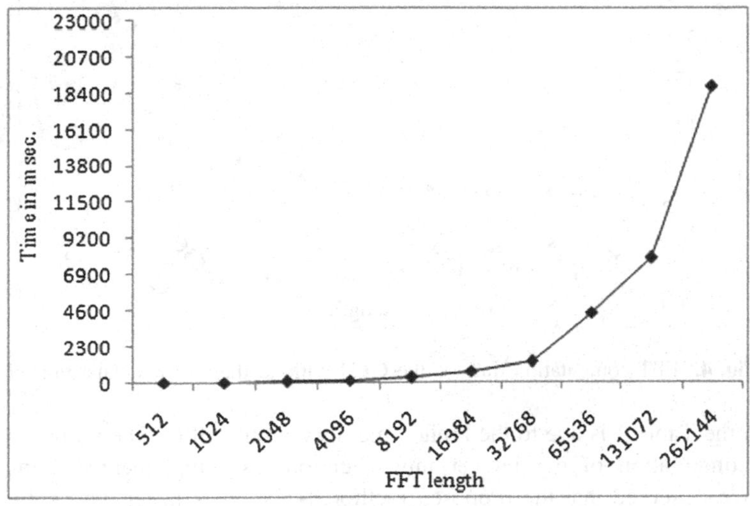

Fig. 2. FFT computation time on the CPU.

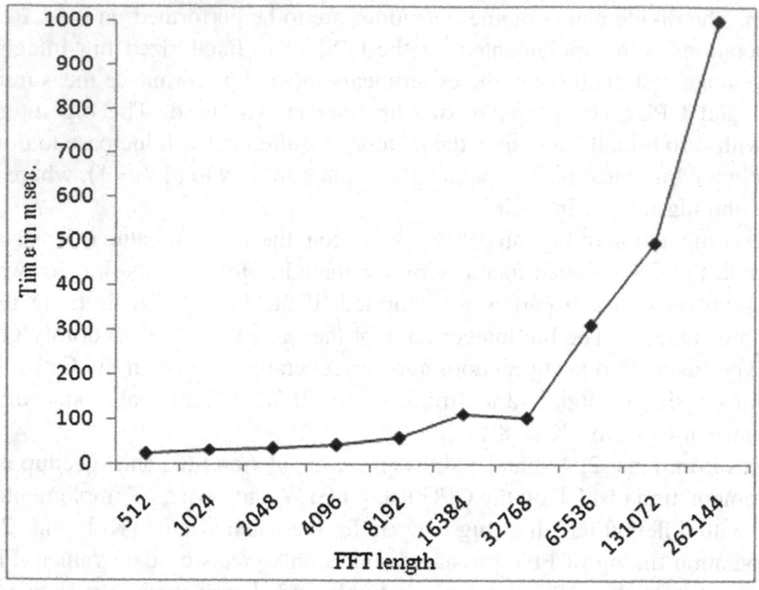

Fig. 3. FFT computation time on the GPU with the memory data transfer.

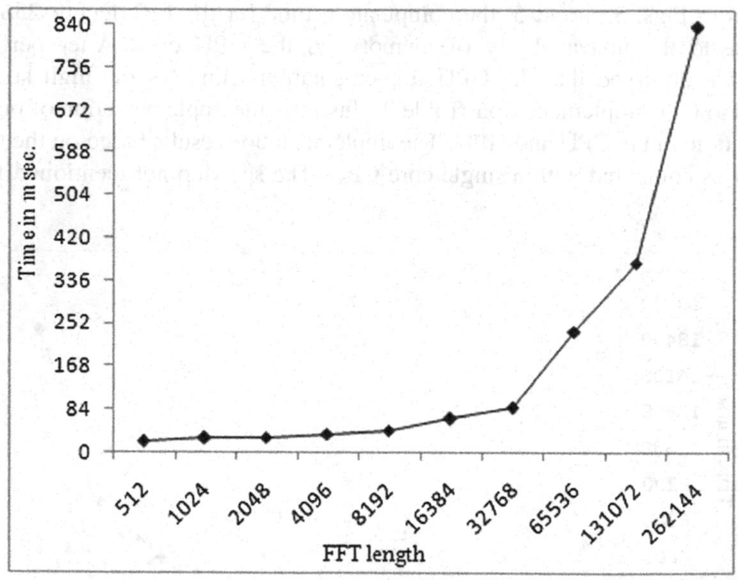

Fig. 4. FFT computation time on the GPU without the memory data transfer.

entries in the Table 1 is due to the limited memory on the GPU. The proposed method for the computation of big integer multiplication also implemented using cuFFT library. We observed that the proposed method is 7x times faster than cuFFT based implementation.

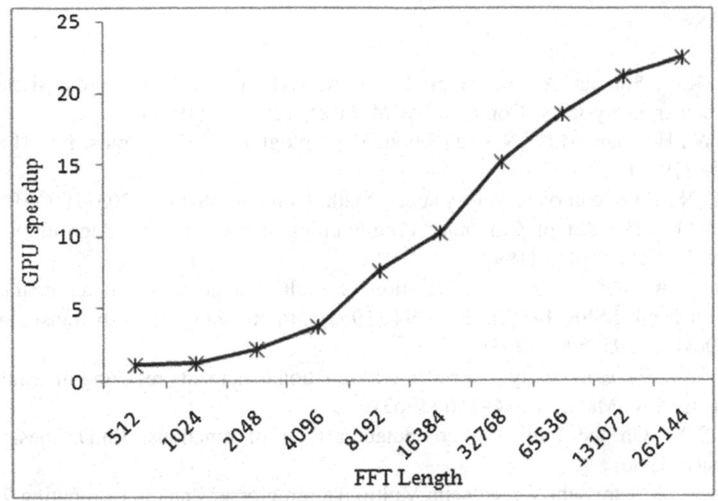

Fig. 5. GPU FFT speedup.

Table 1. Multiplication of big integer for different batch size.

Batch size	1024	2048	4096	8192
Digits (N × N)	*Speedup*			
512	1.09916	1.25468	1.56700	2.45698
1K	1.22865	1.45868	1.64569	3.62333
2K	2.16936	2.45700	2.73137	5.46785
4K	4.25672	4.25663	4.87156	7.42524
8K	6.24588	7.89520	8.76542	10.2340
16K	10.2740	11.2477	12.7592	***

4 Conclusion

In this paper, a novel approach for computing big integer multiplication using FFT was proposed. A divide-and-conquer based FFT big integer multiplication was implemented by utilizing the computing power of the GPU. In this method complex data type is utilized to store input data and the imaginary part is substituted with a zero value. The proposed results indicate that good speedup was achieved on the GPU. The proposed method divides the big integer into smaller subparts hence; this method turns out to be efficient for implementation. The proposed approach can also be implemented in parallel programming languages such as OpenCL, OpenACC etc. The other GPU cards as well as parallel hardware can be utilized for the proposed implementation. In addition, the same method can be utilized to handle the optimized use of real data for FFT computation.

References

1. Rivest, R.L., Shamir, A., Adleman, L.: A method for obtaining digital signatures and public-key cryptosystems. Commun. ACM **21**(2), 120–126 (1987)
2. Diffie, W., Hellman, M.E.: New directions in cryptography. IEEE Trans. Inf. Theor. IT **22**, 644–654 (1976)
3. Koblitz, N.: Elliptic curve cryptosystems. Math. Comput. **48**(177), 203–209 (1987)
4. Knuth, D.E.: The Art of Computer Programming: Seminumerical Algorithms, 3rd edn. Addison-Wesley, Boston (1997)
5. Karatsuba, A., Ofman, Y.: Multiplication of multidigit numbers on automata. Doklady Akademii Nauk SSSR **145**(2), 293–294 (1962). (in Russian). English translation in Sov. Phys.-Dokl. **7**, 595–596 (1963)
6. Toom, A.L.: The complexity of a scheme of functional elements realizing the multiplication of integers. Sov. Math. **3**, 714–716 (1963)
7. Cook, S.A.: On the minimum computation time of functions. Ph.D. thesis, Harvard University (1966)
8. Schönhage, A., Strassen, V.: Schnelle Multiplikation grosser Zahlen. Computing **7**, 281–292 (1971)
9. Cooley, J.W., Tukey, J.W.: An algorithm for the machine calculation of complex Fourier series. Math. Comput. **19**(90), 297–301 (1965)
10. Nukada, A., Ogata, Y., Endo, T., Matsuoka, S.: Bandwidth intensive 3-D FFT kernel for GPUs using CUDA. In: Proceedings of the ACM/IEEE Conference on Supercomputing (SC-2008), High Performance Computing, Networking, Storage and Analysis, pp. 1–11. ACM/IEEE (2008)
11. Nukada, A., Matsuoka, S.: Auto-tuning 3-D FFT library for CUDA GPUs. In: Proceedings of the ACM/IEEE Conference on Supercomputing (SC-2009), High Performance Computing, Networking, Storage and Analysis, pp. 1–10. ACM/IEEE (2009)
12. Govindaraju, N.K., Lloyd, B., Dotsenko, Y., Smith, B., Manferdelli, J.: High performance discrete Fourier transforms on graphics processors. In: Proceedings of the ACM/IEEE Conference on Supercomputing, pp. 1–12. ACM/IEEE (2009)
13. Volkov, V., Kazian, B.: Fitting FFT onto the G80 architecture (2008). www.cs.berkeley.edu/~kubitron/courses/cs258S08/projects/reports/project6_report.pdf
14. Tembhurne, J.V., Sathe, S.R.: Performance evaluation of long integer multiplication using OpenMP and MPI on shared memory architecture. In: Proceedings of the 7th International Conference on Contemporary Computing, pp. 283–288. IEEE (2014)
15. Tembhurne, J.V., Sathe, S.R.: High throughput long integer multiplication using fast Fourier transform on parallel workstation. In: Proceedings of the 11th Annual IEEE India Conference on (INDICON), pp. 1–6. IEEE (2014)
16. Sutter, G.D., Deschamps, J., Imana, J.L.: modular mutlitplicatio and exponentiation architecture for fast RSA cryptosyatem based on digit serial computation. IEEE Trans. Ind. Electron. **58**(7), 3101–3109 (2011)
17. Lou, D.C., Chang, C.C.: Fast exponentiation method obtained by folding the exponent in half. Electron. Lett. **32**(11), 984–985 (1996)
18. Comba, P.G.: Exponentiation cryptosystems on the IBM PC. IBM Syst. J. **29**(4), 526–538 (1990)
19. Bunimov, V., Schimmler, M.: Efficient parallel multiplication algorithm for large integers. In: Kosch, H., Böszörményi, L., Hellwagner, H. (eds.) Euro-Par 2003. LNCS, vol. 2790, pp. 923–928. Springer, Heidelberg (2003). https://doi.org/10.1007/978-3-540-45209-6_127

20. Jahani, S., Samsudin, A., Subramanian, K.G.: Efficient big integer multiplication and squaring algorithms for cryptographic applications. J. Appl. Math. **2014**, 9 (2014). Article ID 107109
21. Brumnik, R., Kovtun, V., Okhrimenko, A., Kavun, S.: Techniques for performance improvement of integer multiplication in cryptographic applications. Math. Prob. Eng. **2012**, 7 (2014). Article ID 863617
22. Baktir, S., Savas, E.: Highly-parallel montgomery multiplication for multi-core general-purpose microprocessors. In. Proceedings of the 27th International Symposium on Computer and Information Sciences, pp. 467–476 (2012)
23. Maza, M.M., Xie, Y.: Balanced dense polynomial multiplication on multi-cores. In: Proceedings of the International Conference on Parallel and Distributed Computing, Applications and Technologies, pp. 1–9 (2009)
24. Chmielowiec, A.: Fast, parallel algorithm for multiplying polynomials with integer coefficients. In: Proceedings of the World Congress on Engineering, WCE-2012, vol. II, pp. 1136–1140 (2012)
25. Maza, M.M., Pan, W.: Fast polynomial multiplication on a GPU, high performance computing symposium. J. Phys: Conf. Ser. **256**, 012009 (2010)
26. Giorgi, P., Izard, T., Tisserand, A.: Comparison of modular arithmetic algorithms on GPUs. In: Proceedings of the International Conference on Parallel Computing, pp. 315–322 (2009)
27. Kitano, K., Fujimoto, N.: Multiple precision integer multiplication on GPUs. In: Proceedings of the 2014 World Congress in Computer Science, Computer Engineering, and Applied Computing, PDPTA-2014 (2014)
28. Emmart, N., Weems, C.C.: High precision integer multiplication with a GPU using Strassen's algorithm with multiple FFT sizes. Parallel Process. Lett. **21**(3), 359–375 (2011)
29. Bracewell, R.: The Fourier Transform and Its Applications, 3rd edn. McGraw-Hill Science/Engineering/Math, New York City (1999)
30. Chu, E., George, A.: Inside the FFT Black Box: Serial and Parallel Fast Fourier Transform Algorithms (Computational Mathematics), 1st edn. CRC Press, Boca Raton (1999)
31. NVIDIA Corporation, CUDA cuFFT library 4.0 (2014). http://docs.nvidia.com/cuda/pdf/CUFFT_Library.pdf
32. FFTW3 Library. http://www.fftw.org/

Multi Objective Task Scheduling Algorithm for Cloud Computing Using Whale Optimization Technique

G. Narendrababu Reddy[1(✉)] and S. Phani Kumar[2]

[1] CSE Department, GNITS, Hyderabad, India
gnbreddy25@gmail.com
[2] CSE Department, GST, GITAM University, Hyderabad, India
phanikumar.s@gmail.com

Abstract. The new and emerging IT paradigm, Cloud computing provides different options to customers to compute the tasks' based on their choice and preference. Cloud systems provide services to customers as a utility. The customers are interested in the availability of service at low cost and minimization of task completion time. The performance of cloud systems depends on efficient scheduling of tasks. When cloud server receives multiple user requests, it is necessary for the service provider to schedule the tasks to the appropriate resources to realize the customer satisfaction. In this paper we propose Multi objective Whale Optimization Algorithm (WOA) to schedule tasks in cloud environment. WOA schedules the tasks based on a fitness parameter. The fitness parameter depends on three major constraints: resource utilization, quality of service and energy. The proposed WOA schedules the tasks based on above three parameters such that the task execution time and cost involved in the execution on virtual machines is minimal. The efficiency of the scheduling algorithm depends on minimum fitness parameter. The experimental results show that proposed WO scheduling algorithm provides superior results when compared with existing algorithms.

Keywords: Cloud computing · Virtual machines
Multi objective task scheduling · Whale optimization

1 Introduction

A disruptive computing model in which services are provided to customers over the internet on demand based on pay - as you consume is called as cloud computing [1]. Different types of resources like infrastructure, platform and software are provided by cloud service provider to different types of customers on demand as a service utility. It has a significant role of providing services to the customers to realize enough customer satisfaction. Cloud computing systems can assign, expand and withdraw its services dynamically at any point in time. Cloud environment leverages the virtualization features, and provide scalable resources and software services on demand over the internet to the customers [2]. Applications and files are thronged on a remote cloud which is a combination of multiple systems connected together and is accessible over

P. Bhattacharyya et al. (Eds.): NGCT 2017, CCIS 827, pp. 286–297, 2018.
https://doi.org/10.1007/978-981-10-8657-1_22

the internet in cloud computing. Cloud computing environment can provide adequate resources on demand to the users to process their tasks. In general, there is an inverse relation between the pricing of task computation time to its processing time [3]. Customers always look for the best service at least cost. Minimizing the make span of tasks in a workflow will increase the cost because more resources would be required to minimize the completion time.

Researchers tend to explore different techniques that efficiently perform workflow scheduling in the cloud environment. Scheduling is the process of permitting the processors to access the resources based on some order. Scheduling plays an important role in the cloud computing environment, which aligns all the tasks for executing them with all the restrictions imposed on them. The main aim of scheduling is to reduce the processing time of the task or to satisfy any other criteria regarding the task. Thus, scheduling is the process that is all about the resource allocation to perform specific task in the specific time [12].

Understanding the significance of scheduling in the cloud computing environment, researchers have contributed a lot in the advancement of a number of algorithms that aim at workflow scheduling [9]. Scientists propose novel techniques and make continuous effort to resolve the problems associated with workflow optimization in order to overcome the issues existing in the development process of the scientific applications [5].

This paper uses the proposed algorithm named as WOA for scheduling the task for the corresponding virtual machines. Initially, the physical machines in the cloud and the number of virtual machines are defined. The capacity and the energy of the virtual machine to run a task are evaluated. The solution is determined randomly and formulated to form a solution matrix. The fitness of the solution matrix is determined and the fitness function depends on the parameters like the QoS, energy, and the resource utilization. For an effective solution, the fitness value takes a minimum value and the optimized selection of the solution matrix depends on the WO algorithm. The WOA searches for the optimal position of the prey, which in other words, is the best solution indicating the execution of a task in the virtual machine.

The organization of the paper is: Sect. 1 introduces the paper; Sect. 2 presents the brief explanation of the existing methods. Section 3 explains the system model of the cloud environment, the contribution of the work with the proposed methodology is presented in Sects. 4 and 5 depicts the results and discussion of the proposed work and Sect. 6 concludes the paper.

2 Literature Survey

Lia *et al.* [3] proposed an algorithm named as security and cost aware scheduling (SCAS) algorithm for heterogeneous tasks of scientific workflow in clouds that is based on the meta-heuristic particle swarm optimization (PSO) technique. This method minimizes the total workflow execution cost. But full security is not ensured using this algorithm. The reduction in the cost of workflow was addressed by Rodriguez and Buyya in [4]. In [4], an algorithm based on the meta-heuristic Particle Swarm Optimization (PSO) technique was proposed for scientific workflows on Infrastructure as a

Service (IaaS) Clouds. It reduced the overall workflow execution cost and met the deadline constraints. But it failed to consider the data transfer cost between the data centers. Zuo *et al.* [5] proposed a multi-objective optimization scheduling method based on an improved ant colony algorithm. This approach considered the makespan and the user's budget costs as constraints of the optimization problem and achieved the optimal solution through the adjustment of the quality. In this method, the cost is bit high compared to the existing methods. Ahmada *et al.* [6] proposed Hybrid Genetic Algorithm (HGA) for optimizing the load balance and for enabling the maximum resource utilization. It enabled quality schedules with less makespans but unable to handle complex workflow with big data. Thus, Zhong *et al.* [7] proposed a Greedy Particle Swarm Optimization (G&PSO) based algorithm to solve the task scheduling problem. The performance was good and improved the efficiency of the virtual machine but this method did not consider the effects of bandwidth and data transmission. Netjinda *et al.* [8] proposed a variable neighbourhood search technique incorporated with the Particle swarm optimization that provided a better performance but Failed to consider the communication overhead in task scheduling.

3 Task Scheduling Problem

The main challenge in the cloud computing environment is to identify the trade-off between the user requirements and the resource utilization. Multiple users provide multiple tasks with different requirements including the computing time, memory space, data traffic, response time, and so on, posing the difficulty in modelling, analyzing and evaluating in cloud task scheduling [4].

Yet another important challenge of task scheduling relies on concerning the optimum assignment of the service request because it is required to provide the necessary information with a good Quality-of-Service [3] without violating any of the system constraints [11]. Also, the consideration of useful parameters for scheduling algorithms namely the execution time, cost of scheduling, and the energy of the scheduling are very important [5].

Another issues faced in the task scheduling involves that it took huge time in computing while dealing with huge number of user requests in the cloud environment [7]. So, optimization algorithms can be considered to reduce the computational burden.

3.1 System Model

Cloud environment consists of a number of service providers to provide services and infrastructure to the users as per their request. In the cloud environment, there are a number of physical machines and each physical machine possesses a number of virtual machines. When a multiple number of requests arrive at the cloud requesting for the same resource, there exists a shortage for the resources and the problem is regarding the allotment of the resource to the users. Each virtual machine possesses various configurations like CPU size, memory and cost for executing the tasks and so on. Therefore, allotting the perfect virtual machine that takes less time and cost for executing the task is the major issue. The scheduling technique orders the request for providing service to the users. The schedule is based on the capacity and energy required to run the task. Let us consider the cloud consists of q number of physical machines that are represented as,

$$P = \{p_1, p_2, \ldots, p_i, \ldots, p_q\} \tag{1}$$

where $p_1, p_2, \ldots, p_i, \ldots p_q$ are the individual physical machines, and p_i is the ith physical machine in the cloud. The total virtual machines corresponding to the ith physical machine is,

$$|V^i| = \left\{V_1^i, V_2^i, \ldots, V_j^i, \ldots, V_g^i\right\} \tag{2}$$

where, V^i represent the total virtual machines corresponding to the ith physical machine, g is the total number of virtual machines and V_g^i represents the g number of virtual machines corresponding to the ith physical machine. V_j^i is the jth virtual machine of the ith physical machine. The resource cost of the jth virtual machine present in the ith physical machine is denoted as R_j^i. The capacity of the jth virtual machine present in the ith physical machine is denoted as C_j^i. Let the total task is notated as T and the total number of tasks is given as,

$$T = \{t_1, t_2, \ldots, t_k, \ldots, t_n\} \tag{3}$$

where, T is the total tasks represents all the individual tasks for execution and n denotes the total number of tasks in the cloud. t_k denotes the kth task. Each task carries a number of sub-tasks and the subtasks in the kth task is represented as,

$$t_k = \{t_1^k, t_2^k, \ldots, t_l^k, \ldots, t_m^k\} \tag{4}$$

where, $t_1^k, t_2^k, \ldots, t_l^k, \ldots, t_m^k$ denote the subtasks of the kth task and m is the total number of subtasks in the kth task. The length of the task enables to decide the virtual machine for executing the task. The length of the task is denoted as L and the task length depends on the number of task waiting for execution. Another parameter that decides the virtual machine to execute the task is energy. Let the energy parameter is denoted as ε_{jk}, which is the energy required for executing the kth task in the jth virtual machine.

4 Proposed Method

In the cloud computing environment, a number of user request are fulfilled based on their requirements. In the cloud there are a plenty of resources but there is a lack of a proper scheduling. There are a lot of techniques for scheduling and the existing methods faced a lot of problems regarding the cost of resources, communication overheads, and cost of data transfer between the data centers and so on. All the issues mentioned above were tackled using the proposed method of workflow scheduling that depends on the WO algorithm. The execution time of the proposed method is low, execution cost is low, and it results in an effective task scheduling using the WO algorithm. The task schedule depends on three constraints, namely the QoS, energy required for executing the task in the individual virtual machine, and the resource utilization.

4.1 Multi-objective Scheduling

When the users request for the same resource at the same time, the need for the task scheduling occurs and the scheduling strategy depends on the fitness parameter of the solution matrix. An efficient solution is determined through the evaluation of the fitness that is based on the three parameters like energy, resource utilization, and energy. The solution matrix with the minimal value of fitness is chosen for executing the task in their corresponding fitness order of the virtual machines. The solution matrix is represented as w and w_{jk} is the solution value of the kth task executed in the jth virtual machine. The set matrix is determined from the solution matrix that is obtained through the division of the length of the task and the capacity of the machine. The set matrix is represented as S. Fitness evaluation is the key factor that determines the efficient virtual machine for running the task without affecting the performance of the system in task scheduling mechanism, the fitness function depends on three parameters, namely the resource utilization, energy, and the QoS. For an effective solution, the fitness function returns a minimum value.

$$\text{Fitness}\, F = \frac{1}{3} \times [(1 - R_U) + E + (1 - QoS)] \tag{4.1}$$

where, R_U is the resource utilization, E is the energy required to run a task in the virtual machines, and QoS is the quality of service. To highlight that the resource of utilization is maximum the term $(1 - R_U)$ is added in the formula and the term $(1 - QoS)$ highlights the maximum quality of service.

4.1.1 QoS

It is of key importance in the cloud computing environment and it is essential to schedule the virtual machines with the high quality. It mainly depends on two parameters, namely the time and the cost of executing the task in the virtual machine. The time and the cost constraints are minimum for enabling a good quality of service to the users. The terms $(1 - t)$ and $(1 - c)$ denotes that the scheduling time and cost are minimum.

$$QoS = \frac{1}{2}[(1 - t) + (1 - c)] \tag{5}$$

where, t is the execution time and c is the execution cost of executing the task in the virtual machine. The execution time of the task in the virtual machine depends on the solution matrix and the set matrix. The execution time is given as,

$$t = \max_{\substack{\forall \\ k \in m}} \left[w_{jk} \times S_{jk}\right] \tag{6}$$

where, w_{jk} is the solution of the kth task executed in the jth virtual machine and S_{jk} is the set value of the kth task executed in the jth virtual machine. The execution cost of the virtual machine is,

$$c = \frac{1}{N}\sum_{j=1}^{N} Y_{jk} \times \left[R_{jk}\right] \tag{7}$$

and,

$$Y_{jk} = w_{jk} \times S_{jk} \tag{8}$$

where, c is the execution cost of executing the task in the jth virtual machine, Y_{jk} is the product factor that is determined using the w_{jk} and S_{jk}, and R_{jk} is the resource cost of the jth virtual machine. Therefore, the parameters that ensure the maximum QoS are execution cost, execution time, and resource cost. These parameters should hold a minimum value for reaching the maximum value of quality, which improves the performance of the overall system.

4.1.2 Resource Utilization

The resource utilization of the virtual machine is another factor that should be essentially maximum to enhance the performance of the system. It depends on the solution matrix and the set matrix. It depends on the solution value and set value of the solution.

$$R_U = \frac{1}{m \times Q_1} \times \sum_{i=1}^{m} w_{jk} \times S_{jk};\ 1 \le j \le N;\ 1 \le k \le m \tag{9}$$

where,

$$Q_1 = \max(S) \tag{10}$$

where, S denotes the set matrix, m is the total number of tasks, w_{jk} is the solution of the kth task executed in the jth virtual machine and S_{jk} is the set value of the kth task executed in the jth virtual machine. The parameter Q_1 is determined based on the maximum value of the set matrix. N denotes the total number of virtual machines in the cloud.

4.1.3 Energy

The energy of the virtual machine for executing the task should be minimum for an effective model. The energy of the virtual machine depends on the solution value of the kth task executed in the jth virtual machine and the energy required for executing the kth task executed in the jth virtual machine.

$$E = \frac{1}{m \times Q_2} \sum_{k=1}^{m} w_{jk} \times \varepsilon_{jk} \tag{11}$$

$$Q_2 = \max(\varepsilon) \tag{12}$$

Where, m is the total number of tasks in the virtual machine, and Q_2 is the factor that is the maximum of all the energy values required to execute the task in the virtual machine.

4.2 Multi-objective Task Scheduling Using the WO Algorithm

This section presents the multi-objective task scheduling mechanism using the proposed WO algorithm. The tasks are scheduled to a particular virtual machine based on their cost of execution, execution time, and energy. For efficiently executing the task, the WO algorithm is used which attains faster convergence to the optimal position with the less time and it saves the cost of executing the task in the virtual machine. The reduction in the execution cost and the execution time improves the efficiency of the task scheduling mechanism. Upon the arrival of the multiple user requests, the WO algorithm allocated the task to the more efficient virtual machine and executes the task to yield the optimized results.

4.2.1 Solution Encoding

The solution encoding is represented in Fig. 1. The solution is chosen randomly and subjected to fitness evaluation. Initially, the randomly selected solution is sorted and the exact solution is determined using the operation $m \bmod (5) + 1$. The randomly selected solution is sorted and presented in Fig. 1. The task t_1 is executed in the V_5, task t_2 is executed in V_2, task t_3 is executed in V_1 and so on. The sorted solution w_s is subjected undergo an operation using $m \bmod (5) + 1$ and the obtained solution determines the exact virtual machine to run the corresponding task. Suppose let us consider there are two physical machines represented as $P = \{P_1, P_2\}$. Let us assign two virtual machines to P_1 and three physical machines to P_2. The total number of virtual machines is represented as $V = \{V_1, V_2, V_3, V_4, V_5\}$. Let us consider the randomly selected solution for evaluating the fitness as w_o. The random solution is sorted based on the capacity of the virtual machines and the sorted solution is represented as w_s. Then, the approximation is carried out using the formula $m \bmod (N) + 1$. The solution thus obtained as a result of performing $m \bmod (N) + 1$ is denoted as w_k. The solution w_k is converted into the matrix format represented as w. w_{jk} is the solution value of the kth task executing in the jth machine. The set matrix is calculated that depends on two parameters, namely the length of the task and the capacity of the virtual machine. The set matrix is denoted as S. Figure 1 shows the solution encoding that denotes that the virtual machines that execute the tasks $\{t_1, t_2, \ldots t_5\}$. Here, m is the total number of tasks and takes the value five in case of five tasks.

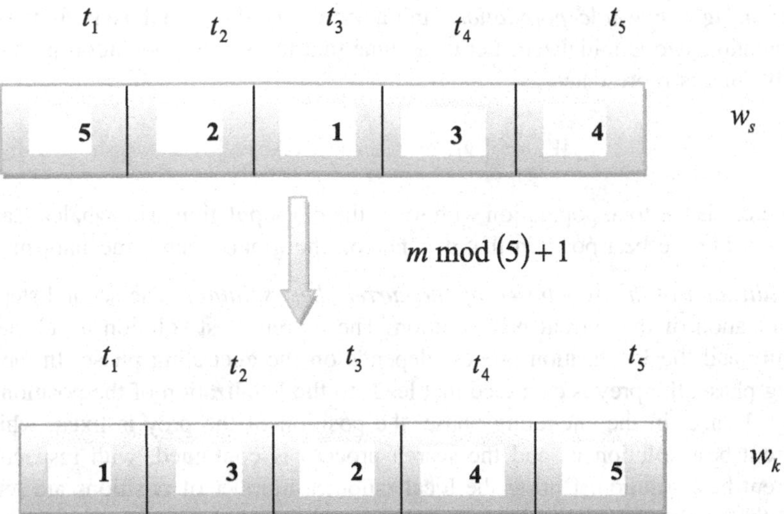

Fig. 1. Solution encoding

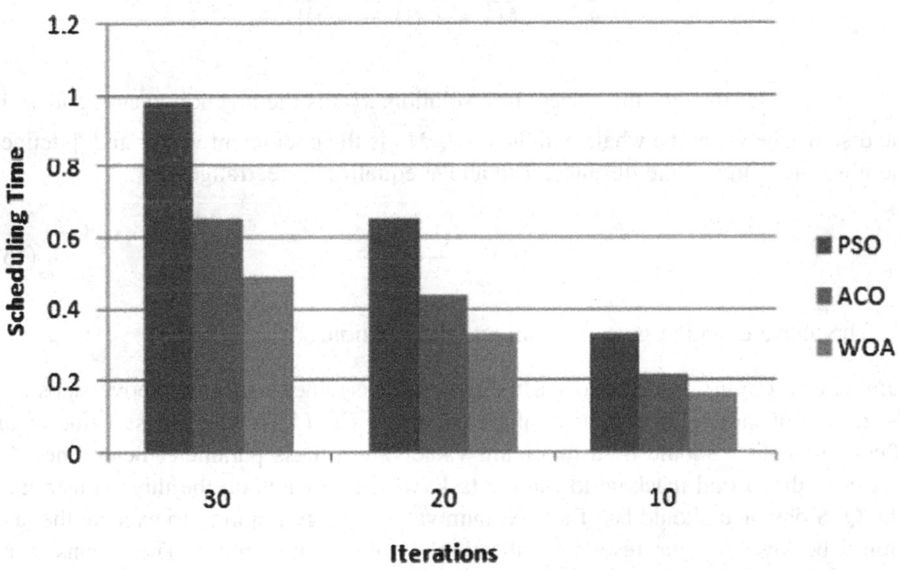

Fig. 2. Scheduling time

4.2.2 Whale Optimization

This section presents the proposed WO algorithm. Advantage of using the WOA [10] is that it determines the position based on global search and the cost of search is low. The convergence of the solution occurs at the global level.

1. *Initializing the whale population:* Initialization is the initial step in which the population size is initialized. Let us assume that the whale population is initialized as W_p that is represented as

$$W_p = \{w_1, w_2, \ldots, w_o, \ldots, w_r\} \tag{13}$$

Where, r is the total population with w_o as the oth population. The whales search for the prey using the best position that depends on the global search mechanism.

2. *Localization of the prey based on the current best solution:* The second step is the localization of the current best solution. The current best solution is selected randomly and the localization process depends on the encircling phase. In the encircling phase, the prey is encircled that leads to the localization of the position of the prey. Hence, in the encircling phase, the position of the prey is fixed, which the current best solution is, and the search process is continued, with respect to the current best solution. During the localization, a number of positions are retrieved and the best position with respect to the current best solution is updated using the following formula.

$$\vec{d} = \left| \overrightarrow{M} \bullet \overrightarrow{x^*(t)} - \overrightarrow{x(t)} \right| \tag{14}$$

Where, $\overrightarrow{x^*(t)}$ denotes the current best solution, $x(t)$ is the position vector, and $\vec{d}$ is the distance between the whale and the prey. $\overrightarrow{M}$ is the coefficient vector and || defines the absolute value of the distance. The above equation is rearranged as,

$$x^*(t) = \frac{\vec{d} + \vec{x}(t)}{\vec{M}} \tag{15}$$

The above equation gives the current best solution.

Fitness evaluation: The position of the prey is determined using the above steps and the fitness of the solution is determined using the Eq. (4.1). The fitness value of an effective solution should be a minimum value. The fitness parameter determines the fitness of the virtual machine to run the task, which depends on the three constraints. The QoS obtained should be of a maximum value, energy required to execute the task should be low, and the resource utilization should be maximum. These constraints determine the fitness value and the solution with the minimum value of the fitness is chosen to execute the task.

5 WO Algorithm

```
Input: W_p = {w_1, w_2,..., w_o,..., w_r}

Output: x(t)- Best position

Parameters: s, M, A, r, p
            Read
            Update the parameters
                       If (p<0.5)
                   And if (A<1)
              Update the position based on equation (15)
                      Else
                   Repeat update the parameters

          Compute the fitness parameter
      Return the best position, x(t)
   End
```

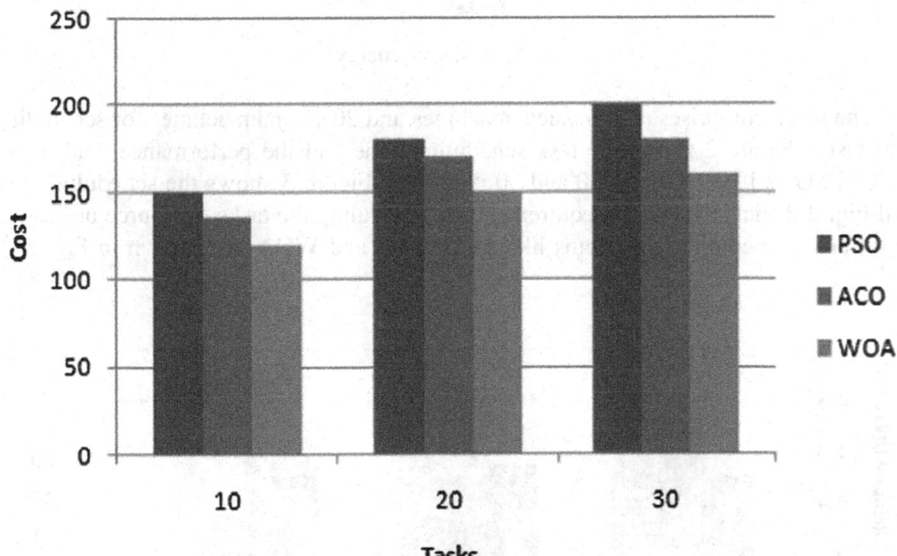

Fig. 3. Scheduling cost

6 Results and Discussions

The performance of the proposed WOA for scheduling the workflow is evaluated using the experiment. Experimentation is done in the personal computer with Intel Core i-3 processor 4 GB RAM and Windows 8 operating system. The experimentation is carried out using the cloudsim tool with JAVA. The result of the proposed method is compared with the existing methods like the ACO [2], PSO [8]. The comparison is made in terms of the evaluation metrics like the task scheduling time, the scheduling cost, energy, and the resource utilization.

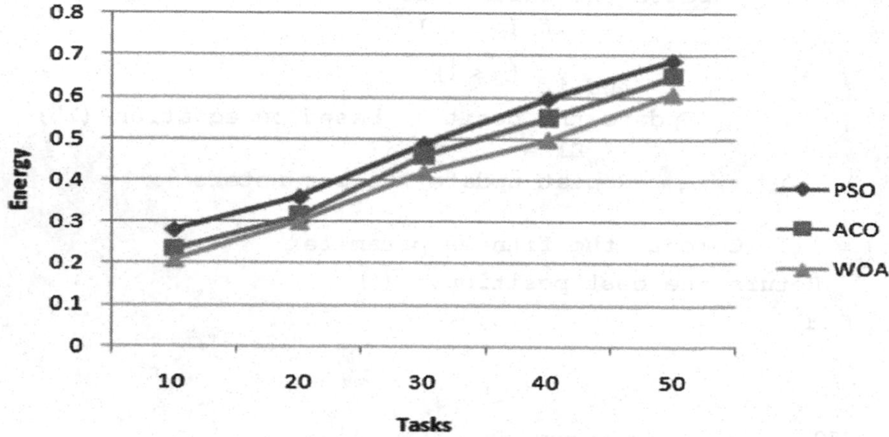

Fig. 4. Tasks vs energy

The setup comprises of 5 physical machines and 20 virtual machines for scheduling 100 tasks. Figure 2 shows the task scheduling time and the performance analysis of ACO, PSO and WOA at 10, 20 and 30 iterations. Figure 3 shows the scheduling cost and Fig. 4 depicts the energy requirement for scheduling the tasks. Resource utilization in different scheduling algorithms like ACO, PSO and WOA was shown in Fig. 5.

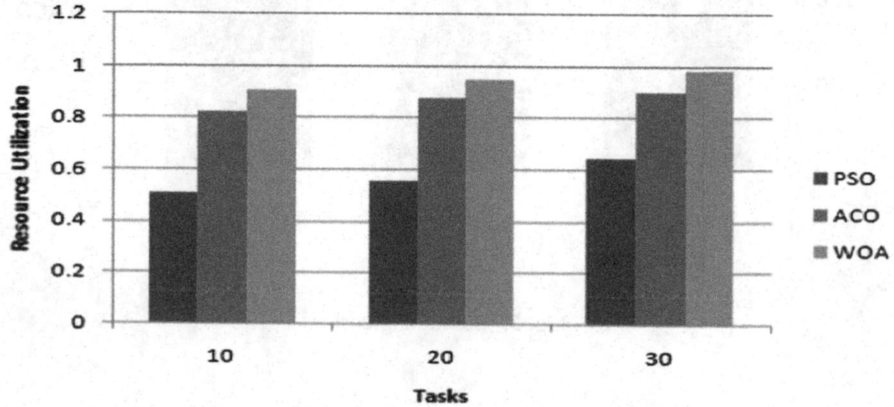

Fig. 5. Tasks vs resource utilization

7 Conclusion

Here we proposed WOA for performing the multi-objective task scheduling using a fitness parameter. The proposed WOA, which is a meta-heuristic optimization algorithm. This model enables the reduction in the execution cost and the execution time. The best optimization solution depends on the fitness parameter and the value of the fitness parameter should remain minimum to ensure the maximum utilization of the resources, minimum energy, and the good quality, and to achieve customer satisfaction. The better QoS improves the overall performance of the system and hence, ensures better scheduling order for executing the tasks. The performance analysis is carried out using the experimental setup with the comparative analysis of the proposed method with the existing methods like ACO and PSO.

References

1. Buyya, R., Pandey, S., Vecchiola, C.: Cloudbus toolkit for market-oriented cloud computing. In: Jaatun, M.G., Zhao, G., Rong, C. (eds.) CloudCom 2009. LNCS, vol. 5931, pp. 24–44. Springer, Heidelberg (2009). https://doi.org/10.1007/978-3-642-10665-1_4
2. Pandey, S., Wu, L., Guru,. S, Buyya, R.: Workflow engine for clouds. In: Buya, R., Broberg, J. (eds.) Cloud computing: Principles and Paradigms, pp. 321–344. Wiley Press, New York, February 2011. ISBN-13 978-0470887998
3. Lia, Z., Gea, J., Yangc, H., Huangd, L., Hue, H., Hua, H., Luoa, B.: A security and cost aware scheduling algorithm for heterogeneous tasks of scientific workflow in clouds. Future Gener. Comput. Syst. **65**, 140–152 (2016)
4. Rodriguez, M.A., Buyya, R.: Deadline based resource provisioning and scheduling algorithm for scientific workflows on clouds. IEEE Trans. Cloud Comput. **2**(2), 222–235 (2014)
5. Zuo, L., Shu, L., Dong, S., Zhu, C., Hara, T.: A multi-objective optimization scheduling method based on the ant colony algorithm in cloud computing. IEEE Access **3**, 2687–2699 (2015)
6. Ahmada, S.G., Liewa, C.S., Munirb, E.U., Anga, T.F., Khanc, S.U.: A hybrid genetic algorithm for optimization of scheduling workflow applications in heterogeneous computing systems. J. Parallel Distrib. Comput. **87**, 80–90 (2016)
7. Zhong, Z., Chen, K., Zhai, X., Zhou, S.: Virtual machine-based task scheduling algorithm in a cloud computing environment. Tsinghua Sci. Technol. **21**(6), 660–667 (2016)
8. Netjinda, N., Sirinaovakul, B., Achalakul, T.: Cost optimal scheduling in IaaS for dependent workload with particle swarm optimization. J. Supercomput. **68**(3), 1579–1603 (2014)
9. Ananth, A., Chandrasekaran, K.: Cooperative game theoretic approach for job scheduling in cloud computing. In: 2015 International Conference on Computing and Network Communications (CoCoNet), pp. 147–156, February 2016
10. Mirjalili, S., Lewis, A.: The whale optimization algorithm. Adv. Eng. Softw. **95**, 51–67 (2016)
11. Tareghian, S., Bornaee, Z.: Algorithm to improve job scheduling problem in cloud computing environment. In: 2nd International Conference on Knowledge-Based Engineering and Innovation (KBEI), pp. 684–688 (2015)
12. Tao, F., Li, C., Liao, T.W., Laili, Y.: BGM-BLA: a new algorithm for dynamic migration of virtual machines in cloud computing. IEEE Trans. Serv. Comput. **9**(6), 910–925 (2015)

Multilayered Feedforward Neural Network (MLFNN) Architecture as Bidirectional Associative Memory (BAM) for Pattern Storage and Recall

Manisha Singh[1,2] and Thipendra Pal Singh[2(✉)]

[1] AKTU, Lucknow, India
[2] School of Computer Science and Engineering, University of Petroleum and Energy Studies, Dehradun, Uttarakhand, India
thipendra@gmail.com

Abstract. Between two popular ANN architectures – feedforward and feedback, also known as recurrent – feedback architectures have been extensively used for memorization and recall task due to their feedback connections. Due to the inherent simpler dynamics of FNNs, these structures have been explored in the present work for association task. Variation of standard BP algorithm, two-phase BP algorithm has been proposed for training MLFNNs to behave as associative memory. The results thus collected show that with the proposed algorithm, MLFNN start behaving as associative memory and the recall capability for corrupted versions of the stored patterns is at par with BAM but with lesser time.

Keywords: Artificial neural networks (ANN) · Associative memory Pattern storage and recall

1 Introduction

Human brain is equipped with the inherent capability of memorizing the patterns for later recall of these while presented ditto or with some error. This capability makes human brain an intelligent machine, which is an objective of present day researchers to achieve the same in case of computers and make them a general-purpose machines. This is realized by establishing a mapping between the input and output patterns such that when prototype test pattern is presented, the best matching pattern of the generalized system is recalled. In intelligent systems researches this is named as problem of pattern association and recall. An artificial neural network (ANNs) is defined as a massive parallel architectures of neurons and has been very popular off late for pattern association and recall task. Through a training method, a neural network is expected to learn the system characteristics in their connection weights. If a trained ANN is expected to produce the same output which the system would have produced even in the case a new pattern is presented.

P. Bhattacharyya et al. (Eds.): NGCT 2017, CCIS 827, pp. 298–309, 2018.
https://doi.org/10.1007/978-981-10-8657-1_23

2 Related Work

Broadly, out of the two categories of ANNs – Feedforward NNs (FNNs) and Recurrent NNs (RNNs) – the later has been popularly used for pattern association and recall tasks. It is basically the design due to which FNNs with hidden layers have been greatly used for the classification purposes and hence when used for pattern mapping task, suffers the problem of generalization, sometimes referred as ill-posed problem [1]. On the other hand, various RNNs have been studied in the literature [2–13] for achieving pattern association and recall. Among all these, bidirectional associative memory (BAM) neural network proposed by Kosko [8] has been extensively studied due to its simplicity and similar working dynamics to that of human brain. BAM architectures are trained using Hebbian learning rule and thus suffers great limitations in terms of storage and recall capability. Literature is rich enough in which this limitation has been addressed [14–31]. In the high-order BAM [14], high-order nonlinearity is applied to forward and backward information flows to increase the memory capacity and improve error correction capability. The exponential BAM [15] employs an exponential scheme of information flow to exponentially enhance the similarity between an input pattern and it's nearest stored pattern. It improves the storage capacity and error correcting capability of the BAM, and has a good convergence property. In [16], a high capacity fuzzy associative memory (FAM) for multiple rule storage is described. A weighted-pattern learning algorithm for BAM is described in [17] by means of global minimization. As inspired by the perceptron-learning algorithm, an optimal learning scheme for a class of BAM is advanced [18], which has superior convergence and stability properties. In [19], the synthesis problem of bidirectional associative memories is formulated as a set of linear inequalities that can be solved using the perceptron training algorithm. A multilayer recursive neural network with symmetrical interconnections is introduced in [21] for improved recognition performance under noisy conditions and for increased storage capacity. In [22], a new bidirectional hetero-associative memory is defined which encompasses correlational, competitive and topological properties and capable of increasing its clustering capability. Other related work can be found in [23–26]. These approaches have mainly used addition of dummy neuron, higher number of layers or manipulating the interconnection among neurons in each layer. Training with some new algorithms [27–31] has also been proposed which improve the performance of original BAM.

In the high-order BAM [19], high-order nonlinearity is applied to forward and backward information flows to increase the memory capacity and improve error correction capability. The exponential BAM [20] employs an exponential scheme of information flow to exponentially enhance the similarity between an input pattern and it's nearest stored pattern. It improves the storage capacity and error correcting capability of the BAM, and has a good convergence property. In [21], a high capacity fuzzy associative memory (FAM) for multiple rule storage is described. A weighted-pattern learning algorithm for BAM is described in [22] by means of global minimization. As inspired by the perceptron-learning algorithm, an optimal learning scheme for a class of BAM is advanced [23], which has superior convergence and stability properties. In [24], the synthesis problem of bidirectional associative memories is formulated as a set of linear inequalities that can be solved using the perceptron training algorithm. A multilayer recursive neural network with symmetrical interconnections is introduced in [25] for improved recognition performance under noisy conditions and for increased storage capacity. In [27], a new bidirectional hetero-associative memory is defined which encompasses correlational, competitive and topological properties and capable of increasing its clustering capability. Other related work can be found in [28–31] in which either by adding dummy neuron, increasing in number of layers or manipulating the interconnection among neurons in each layer, the issue of performance improvement of BAM is addressed. Even some new learning algorithms were introduced to improve the performance of original BAM and can be found in detail in [32–36].

As has been said, the dynamics of multilayer feed-forward neural networks is simpler compared to recurrent neural networks and BAMs. To take advantage of this feature, in the present study the application of back propagation algorithm to MLFNN has been proposed in such a way that feed-forward architecture behaves like BAM. Thus created structure is applied to store some patterns and later the recall of porotype of these patterns with induced error.

Rest of the paper is organized as follows: Sect. 3 establishes the background of BAM and then discusses the proposed two-phase BP algorithm to train MLFNN so that it starts behaving as associative memory. Section 4 contains the simulation design and experimental setup while the results and discussions are included in Sect. 5. The paper concludes with the future scope of the work.

3 Background and Proposed Model

3.1 Structure of BAM

Kosko's original structure of BAM is fully connected two-layer neural network architecture. It stores bipolar pattern pairs $P = \{(X^{(k)}, Y^{(k)})\}, k = 1, \ldots q$ in a weight matrix, called *correlation matrix* **W**. Here $P^{(k)} = \left(p_1^{(k)}, \ldots p_N^{(k)}\right) \in \{-1, 1\}^N$, $Y^{(k)} = \left(y_1^{(k)}, \ldots y_N^{(k)}\right) \in \{-1, 1\}^M$. This correlation matrix **W**, which stores training pairs P is guided by Hebbian learning rule and is defined as follows [6]:

$$W = \sum\nolimits_{k=1}^{q} X^{(k)^T} Y^{(k)} \tag{1}$$

$$w_{ij} = \sum\nolimits_{k=1}^{q} x_i^k y_j^k \tag{2}$$

Here $\left\{x_i^k, y_j^k, i = 1, \ldots N, j = 1, \ldots M; k = 1, \ldots .q\right\}$ is a set of $'q'$ distinct pattern pairs to be stored, N and M are the number of neurons present in both layers.

For activation, a sigmoidal function is used for calculation of threshold value and defined as follows:

For forward direction

$$\beta_j^k = \sum_{i=1}^{N} w_{ij}\, x_i^k \tag{3}$$

$$y_j^k = sign\left(\alpha_j^k\right) = \begin{cases} 1 & if \;\; \beta_j^k > 0 \\ -1 & if \;\; \beta_j^k < 0 \\ y_j^{k-1} & if \;\; \beta_j^k = 0 \end{cases} \tag{4}$$

And for reverse direction

$$\alpha_i^{k+1} = \sum_{j=1}^{P} w_{ji}\, y_j^k \tag{5}$$

$$x_i^{k+1} = sign\left(\alpha_i^{k+1}\right) = \begin{cases} 1 & if \;\; \alpha_i^{k+1} > 0 \\ -1 & if \;\; \alpha_i^{k+1} < 0 \\ x_i^k & if \;\; \alpha_i^{k+1} = 0 \end{cases} \tag{6}$$

The requirement of correctly storing of all 'q' training pairs in a $N \times M$ BAM is that there should be one stable state associated with each stored pattern pair. This dynamics can be represented with the help of following Eqs. (7) and (8) for both the directions correspondingly:

$$x_i^{k+1} = x_i^k \tag{7}$$

$where\, i = 1, \ldots N\, and\, k - 1, \ldots q$

$$y_j^{k+1} = y_j^k \tag{8}$$

$where\, j = 1, \ldots M\, and\, k = 1, \ldots q$

After learning all the pattern pairs, the final correlation matrix of dimensions $N \times M$ is obtained.

To ensure the stability of the system, Kosko also defined an energy function or Lyapunov function as, for each pair (X,Y):

$$E = -X^T WY \tag{9}$$

The BAM converges to some stable point in energy landscape such that the corresponding energy for every training pair is at locally minimum.

3.2 Proposed Structure of BAM

Phase-I

The standard BP algorithm

- Initialize a **1-n-1** feed-forward network architecture (one input, **n** hidden units and one output).
- Set all the interconnection weights to small random values.

- Repeat until $(\mathbf{E_{avg}} = \sum_{k=1}^{Q} \mathbf{Ek} < \tau)$ where τ is the tolerance level of error

1. Input pattern $\mathbf{X_k}$ from training set and compute the corresponding output $\mathbf{S_y}$
2. For corresponding output, calculate the error as

$$\delta_o = \mathbf{S_y}(\mathbf{D} - \mathbf{S_y})(\mathbf{1} - \mathbf{S_y})$$

3. For each hidden unit **h**, calculate

$$\delta_h = \mathbf{S_h}(\mathbf{1} - \mathbf{S_h})\mathbf{W_{hj}}\delta_o$$

4. Update each network weight between hidden and output layer $\mathbf{W_{hj}}$ as follows:

$$\mathbf{W_{hj}} = \mathbf{W_{hj}} + \eta\Delta\mathbf{W_{hj}} + \alpha\Delta\mathbf{W_{hj}}\text{old}$$

where

$$\Delta\mathbf{W_{hj}} = \mathbf{S_h} * \delta_o \text{ and } \Delta\mathbf{W_{hj}}\text{old} = \Delta\mathbf{W_{hj}}$$

5. Update each network weight between input and hidden layer $\mathbf{W_{ih}}$ as follows:

$$\mathbf{W_{ih}} = \mathbf{W_{ih}} + \eta\Delta\mathbf{W_{ih}} + \alpha\Delta\mathbf{W_{ih}}\text{old}$$

where

$$\Delta\mathbf{W_{ih}} = \delta_h * \mathbf{X_k} \text{ and } \Delta\mathbf{W_{ih}}\text{old} = \Delta\mathbf{W_{ih}}$$

Phase-II

- Repeat until $(\mathbf{E_{avg}} = \sum_{k=1}^{Q} \mathbf{Ek} < \tau)$ where τ is the tolerance level of error

1. $\mathbf{W_{hi}} = \mathbf{W'_{ih}}$ and $\mathbf{W_{jh}} = \mathbf{W'_{hj}}$
2. Input pattern $\mathbf{D_k}$ for corresponding $\mathbf{X_k}$ and compute the corresponding output $\mathbf{S_u}$
3. For corresponding output $\mathbf{S_u}$, calculate the error as

$$\delta_i = \mathbf{S_u}(\mathbf{X} - \mathbf{S_u})(\mathbf{1} - \mathbf{S_u})$$

4. For each hidden unit **h**, calculate

$$\delta_h = \mathbf{S_h}(\mathbf{1} - \mathbf{S_h})\mathbf{W_{hi}}\delta_i$$

5. Update each network weight between hidden and input layer $\mathbf{W_{hi}}$ as follows:

$$\mathbf{W_{hi}} = \mathbf{W_{hi}} + \eta\Delta\mathbf{W_{hi}} + \alpha\Delta\mathbf{W_{hi}}\text{old}$$

where

$$\Delta \mathbf{W_{hi}} = \mathbf{S_h} * \delta_i \text{ and } \Delta \mathbf{W_{hi}}\text{old} = \Delta \mathbf{W_{hi}}$$

6. Update each network weight between output and hidden layer $\mathbf{W_{jh}}$ as follows:

$$\mathbf{W_{jh}} = \Delta \mathbf{W_{jh}} + \eta \Delta \mathbf{W_{jh}} + \alpha \Delta \mathbf{W_{jh}}\text{old}$$

where

$$\Delta \mathbf{W_{jh}} = \delta_i * \mathbf{D_k} \text{ and } \Delta \mathbf{W_{jh}}\text{old} = \Delta \mathbf{W_{jh}}$$

4 Simulation Design and Experiments

For the purpose of testing the developed model, pixel images of the English numerals 0..9 on a grid of 7 X 5 are taken (Fig. 1). Whereas a white pixel is representing '−1' and a black pixel is representing '1'. These pixel grids are converted to vectors of dimension 35 before input to the network. The network task was to associate these patterns to themselves (auto-association) and while the prototype of a pattern is produced, the corresponding same pattern is recalled.

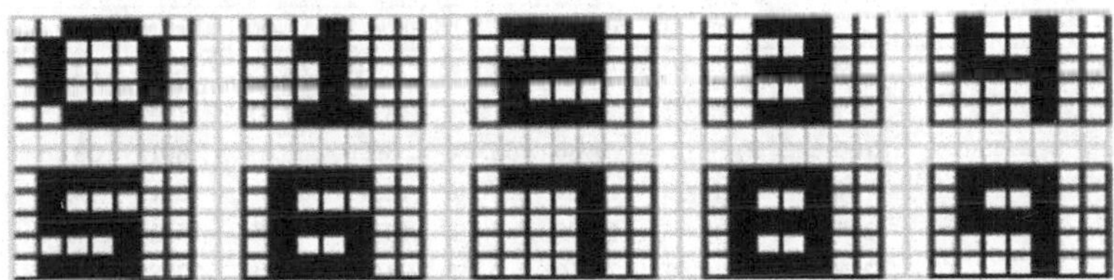

Fig. 1. The taken set of patterns for experimentation

The MLFNN architecture created in the present study contains one input layer, one hidden layer and one output layer. The number of neurons present in input and output layers are 35 (grid of 7 X 5 = 35), while different number of neurons (5/10/15/20/25) in hidden layer are taken for the experimentation. The various parameters are enlisted in Table 1.

During the experimentation, the taken set of patterns were stored in various MLFNN architectures and success rate was calculated when the presented pattern has different level of randomly induced noise in these patterns. The noise was induced by randomly changing a bit i.e. either from 1 to −1 or from −1 to 1. The number of bits thus changed correspond to 0 to 25% level of noise. The tabulation of the results is done and presented on a comparative basis.

Each experiment contained presenting the prototype pattern to the network 100 times and the noise was induced randomly 5 different times. This resulted 500 (5 X 100) runs for each prototype pattern. The average of successful recalls was reported for each architecture.

Table 1. List of various parameters

Parameter	Value
No. of neurons in input layer	35
No. of neurons in hidden layer	5…25
No. of patterns to be stored	10
Learning rate, η	0.7…1.0
Momentum, α	0.6
Tolerance, τ	0.0005

5 Results and Discussion

Table 2 contains the summary of the created MLFNN architecture performance for recall function while a noisy prototype of the already stored patterns is presented to the network. To note here, when both forward and backward phases run once for all

Table 2. Recalling success of MLFNN-as-BAM architecture with the different learning rates

Architecture (input-hidden-output)	Induced noise	Recalling success of MLFNN-as-BAM architecture with the different learning rates							
		η = 0.7	Epochs	η = 0.8	Epochs	η = 0.9	Epochs	η = 1.0	Epochs
35-5-35	0%	64.1%	7584	64.3%	6931	64.4%	6120	64.4%	5520
	5%	61.0%	9004	61.1%	8134	61.0%	7542	61.1%	7123
	10%	53.5%	9986	53.4%	8990	53.6%	8015	53.7%	7543
	15%	14.0%	13129	13.9%	12545	14.0%	12111	14.1%	11540
	20%	7.5%	17875	7.6%	16767	7.6%	15321	7.7%	15005
	25%	0.3%	25010	0.3%	24444	0.3%	22980	0.4%	22878
35-10-35	0%	88.1%	6748	88.1%	6132	88.4%	5740	88.7%	4438
	5%	85.0%	8110	85.1%	7787	85.3%	6398	85.3%	5790
	10%	55.0%	9701	55.2%	9120	55.1%	8555	55.2%	7895
	15%	17.0%	11343	17.1%	10877	17.3%	9810	17.3%	8888
	20%	8.9%	15569	9.1%	14487	9.3%	13881	9.4%	13002
	25%	0.3%	20103	0.6%	19980	0.7%	19320	0.7%	17333
35-15-35	0%	99.2%	5545	99.1%	4899	99.0%	3777	99.3%	3321
	5%	96.9%	5987	97.0%	5432	97.0%	4206	97.1%	3562
	10%	68.7%	8576	69.5%	7171	69.8%	6777	69.9%	4877
	15%	23.9%	9801	24.0%	9176	24.1%	8567	24.1%	7109
	20%	17.1%	12206	17.5%	11866	17.6%	11067	17.6%	10180
	25%	1.2%	17100	1.1%	15998	1.4%	15004	1.5%	14608
35-20-35	0%	89.0%	5944	99.2%	5287	99.1%	4935	99.2%	4244
	5%	96.8%	6300	96.9%	5897	97.0%	5419	97.0%	3999
	10%	68.6%	9194	69.5%	8579	69.7%	7005	69.9%	6107
	15%	23.8%	10001	24.0%	9677	24.2%	8999	24.2%	7911
	20%	17.0%	14095	17.4%	13988	17.6%	12108	17.5%	11981
	25%	1.0%	20154	1.2%	17444	1.4%	16321	1.5%	15814

Table 3. Comparison between the MLFNN and BAM in terms of recall success rate and time taken

Level of induced noise	Recall success when best MLFNN architecture used (35-15-35)	Time taken (mSec.)	Recall success BAM	Time taken (mSec.)
0%	99.3%	3055	99.2%	3012
5%	97.1%	3277	96.3%	3254
10%	69.9%	4487	70.1%	4456
15%	24.1%	6540	24.2%	6515
20%	17.6%	9366	17.2%	9361
25%	1.5%	13439	1.9%	13422

patterns, this will constitute one epoch. Four different architectures with varying numbers of neurons in hidden layer are created and trained using proposed two-phase BP algorithm, for each using four learning rates 0.7, 0.8, 0.9 and 1.0. The recall performance of these different network architectures was calculated for noisy prototypes. The results show that the performance is best for an architecture having 15 neurons at hidden layer (i.e. 35-15-35 architecture) with learning rate 1.0. Although the recall performance is almost similar on increased numbers of neurons at hidden layer but the number of epochs taken to converge and thus the time becomes higher. Therefore, we conclude that the most suitable MLFNN architecture for the studied set of patterns is 35-15-35.

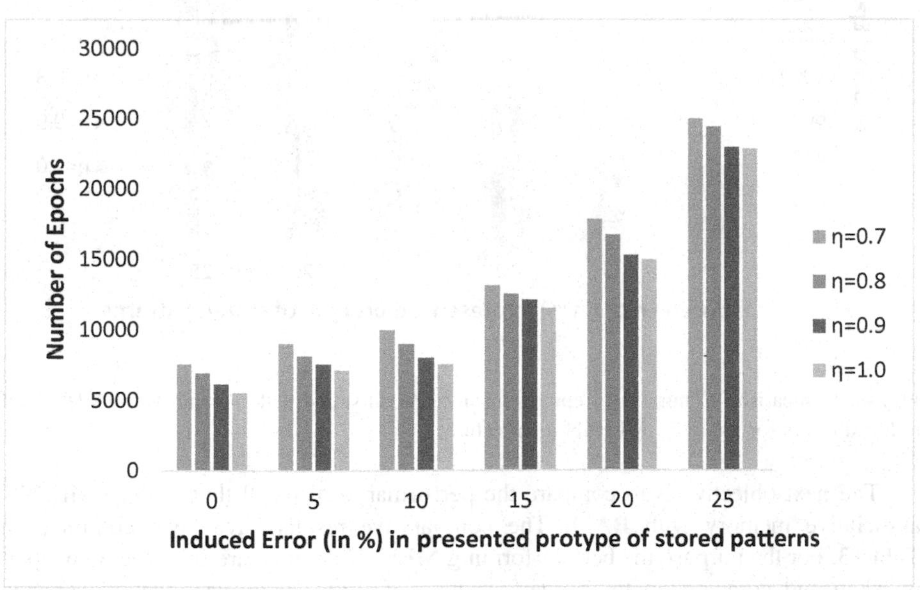

Fig. 2. Comparison of number of epochs taken to recall stored patterns with various levels of induced errors for 35-5-35 MLFNN architecture

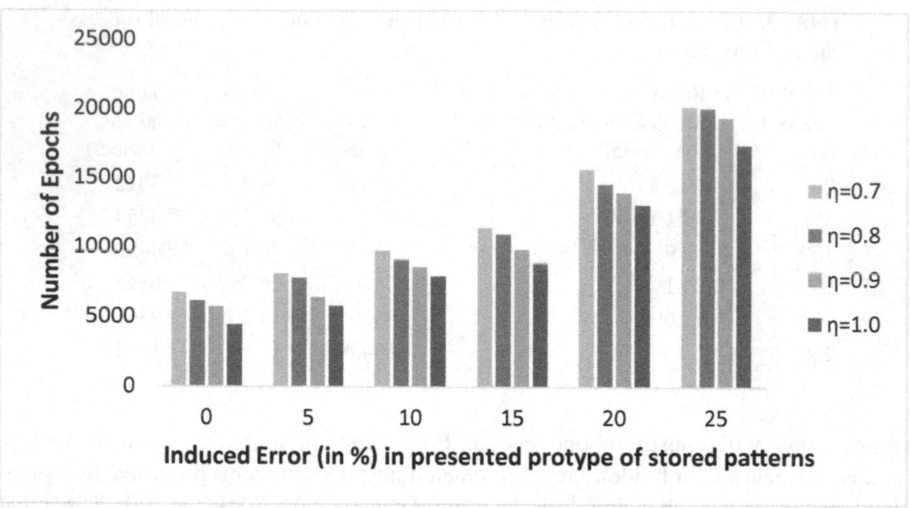

Fig. 3. Comparison of number of epochs taken to recall stored patterns with various levels of induced errors for 35-10-35 MLFNN architecture

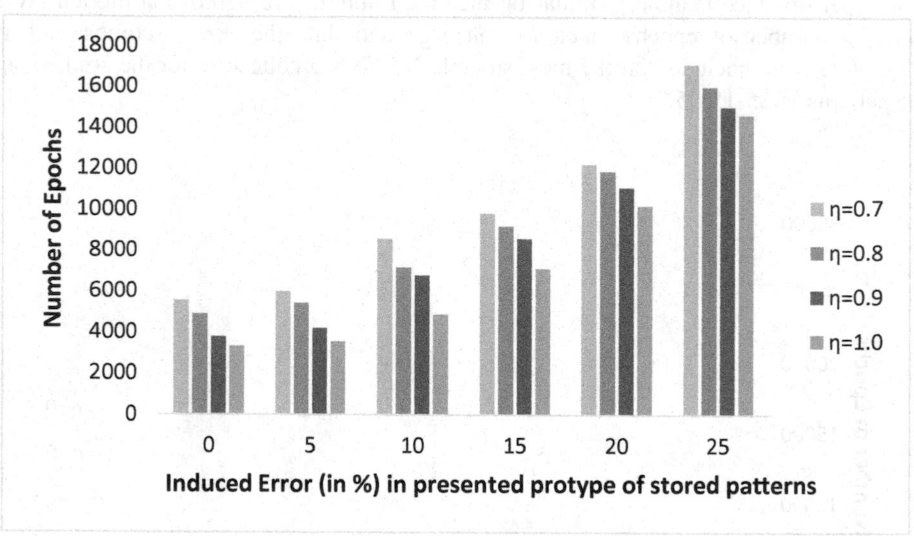

Fig. 4. Comparison of number of epochs taken to recall stored patterns with various levels of induced errors for 35-15-35 MLFNN architecture

The next objective is to compare the performance of recall thus created MLFNN associative memory with BAM. The comparative results have been compiled in Table 3. For the purpose the best performing MLFNN architecture from the above part is taken and compared with the performance of BAM. It is clear that the created MLFNN with the proposed two-phase BP algorithm works at par with BAM. Thus, we conclude that MLFNN can also work as associative memory (Figs. 2, 3, 4, 5 and 6).

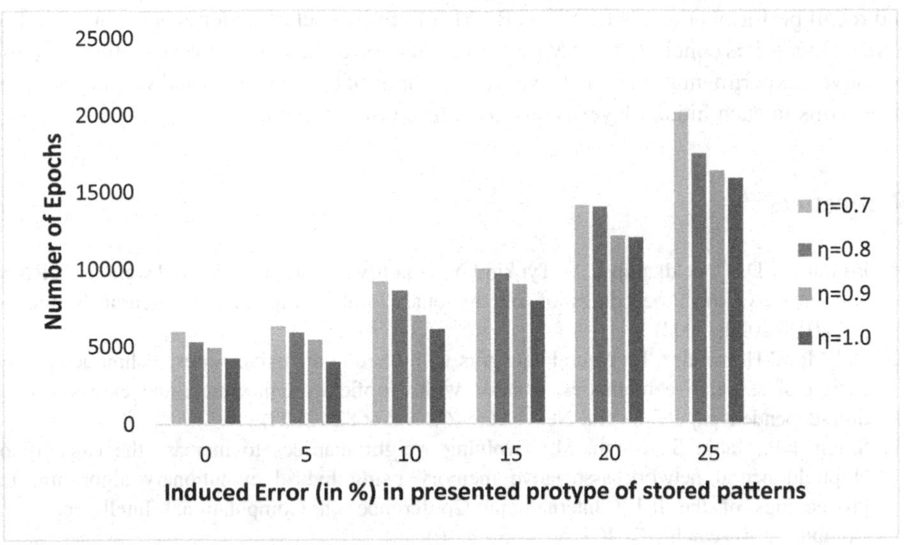

Fig. 5. Comparison of number of epochs taken to recall stored patterns with various levels of induced errors for 35-20-35 MLFNN architecture

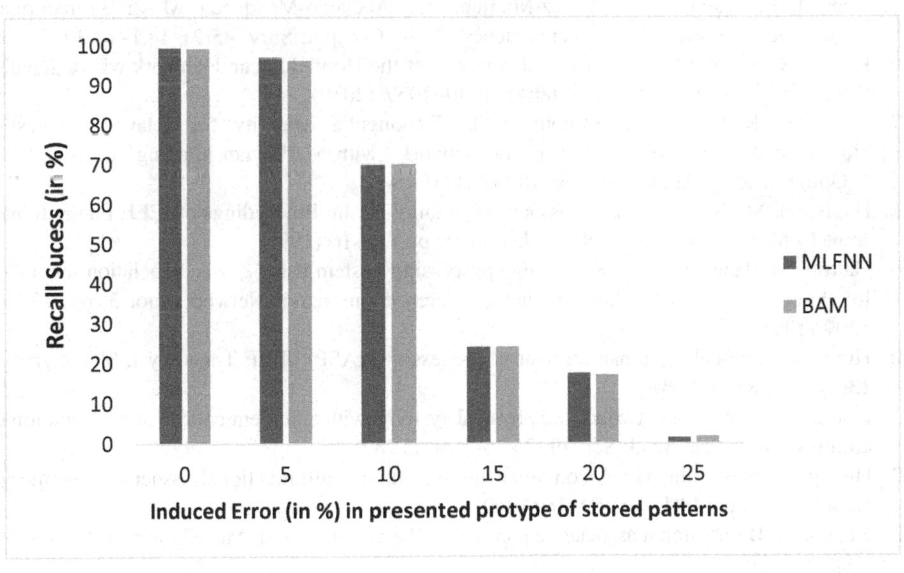

Fig. 6. Recall success: MLFNN vs BAM

6 Conclusion and Future Scope

If a multi-layered feed-forward neural network (MLFNN) is trained with the above proposed two-phase BP algorithm, this architecture develops the memorization capability and starts behaving as bidirectional associative memory (BAM). As discussed above, the store and recall performance of MLFNN as BAM for studied set of patterns is at par to that of BAM. Hence, it is concluded that MLFNN can also be used as associative memory. At the next level, experimentation with the varying number of hidden layers and varying number of neurons in each hidden layer is proposed to be undertaken.

References

1. Prokhorov D.V., Feldkamp L.A., Tyukin I.Y: Adaptive behavior with fixed weights in RNN: an overview. In: Proceedings of International Joint Conference on Neural Networks, pp. 2018–2022 (2002)
2. Del-Moral-Hernandez, E.: Neural networks with chaotic recursive nodes: techniques for the design of associative memories, contrast with Hopfield architectures, and extensions for time-dependent inputs. Neural Netw. **16**(5–6), 675–682 (2003)
3. Singh T.P., Jabin S., Singh, M.: Evolving weight matrices to increase the capacity of Hopfield neural network associative memory using hybrid evolutionary algorithm. In: Proceedings of the IEEE International Conference on Computational Intelligence and Computing Research (ICCIC), pp. 1–5 (2010)
4. Singh, T.P., Jabin, S.: Evolving connection weights for pattern storage and recall in Hopfield model of feedback neural network using genetic algorithm. Int. J. Soft Comput. **3**(2), 55–62 (2012)
5. Acevedo-Mosqueda, M.E., Yáñez-Márquez, C., Acevedo-Mosqueda, M.A.: Bidirectional associative memories: different approaches. ACM Comput. Surv. **45**(2), 18.1–18.30 (2013)
6. Kumar, S., Singh, M.P.: Pattern recall analysis of the Hopfield neural network with a genetic algorithm. Comput. Math Appl. **60**(4), 1049–1057 (2010)
7. Sakthivel, R., Raja, R., Anthoni, S.M.: Exponential stability for delayed stochastic bidirectional associative memory neural networks with Markovian jumping and impulses. J. Optim. Theory Appl. **150**, 166–187 (2011)
8. Hagiwara, M.: Multidirectional associative memories. In: Proceedings of IEEE International Joint Conference on Neural Networks, no. 1, pp. 15–16 (1990)
9. Hattori, M., Hagiwara, M.: Knowledge processing system using chaos association memory. In: Proceedings of IEEE International Conference on Neural Networks, no. 3, pp. 1304–1309 (1995)
10. Hirai, Y.: A model of human associative processor (HASP). IEEE Trans. Syst. Man Cybern. **13**(5), 851–857 (1983)
11. Hopfield, J.J.: Neural networks and physical systems with emergent collective computational abilities. Proc. Nat. Acad. Sci. **79**, 2554–2558 (1982)
12. Huang, J., Masafumi, H.: A combined multi-winner multidirectional associative memory. Neurocomputing **48**(1–4), 369–389 (2002)
13. Kosko, B.: Bidirectional associative memories. IEEE Trans. Syst. Man Cybern. **18**(1), 49–60 (1988)
14. Nakano, J.: Associatron - a model of associative memory. IEEE Trans. Syst. Man Cybern. **2** (3), 380–388 (1972)
15. Osana, Y., Hattori, M., Hagiwara, M.: Chaotic bidirectional associative memory. In: Proceedings of IEEE International Conference on Neural Networks, no. 2, pp. 816–821 (1996)
16. Osana, Y., Hattori, M., Hagiwara, M.: Chaotic multidirectional associative memory. In: Proceedings of IEEE International Conference on Neural Networks, no. 2, pp. 816–821 (1996)

17. Du, S., Chen, Z., Yuan, Z., Zhang, X.: Sensitivity to noise in bidirectional associative memory (BAM). IEEE Trans. Neural Netw. **16**(4), 887–898 (2005)
18. Gu, H., Jiang, H., Teng, Z.: Existence and globally exponential stability of periodic solution of BAM neural networks with impulses and recent-history distributed delays. Neurocomputing **71**(4–6), 813–822 (2008)
19. Tai, H.-M., Wu, C.-H., Jong, T.-L.: High-order bidirectional associative memory. Electron. Lett. **25**(21), 1424–1425 (1989)
20. Jeng, Y.-J., Yeh, C.-C., Chiueh, T.D.: Exponential bidirectional associative memories. Electron. Lett. **26**(11), 717–718 (1990)
21. Chung, F.L., Lee, T.: On fuzzy associative memory with multiple-rule storage capacity. IEEE Trans. Fuzzy Syst. **4**(3), 375–384 (1996)
22. Wang, T., Zhuang, X., Xing, X.: Weight learning of bidirectional associative memories by global minimization. IEEE Trans. Neural Netw. **3**(6), 1010–1018 (1992)
23. Shanmukh, K., Venkatesh, Y.V.: Generalized scheme for optimal learning in recurrent neural networks. IEEE Proc. Vis. Image Signal Process. **142**(2), 71–77 (1995)
24. Salih, I., Smith, S.H., Liu, D.: Design of bidirectional associative memories based on the perceptron training technique. In: Proceedings of IEEE International Symposium on Circuits and Systems, no. 5, pp. 355–358 (1999)
25. Kwan H.K, Tsang P.C.: Multi -layer recursive neural network. In: Proceedings of Canadian Conference on Electrical and Computer Engineering, Montreal, Canada, no. 1, pp. 428–431 (1989)
26. Widrow, B., Winter, R.: Neural nets for adaptive filtering and adaptive pattern recognition. IEEE Comput. Mag. **21**, 25–39 (1988)
27. Chartier, S., Giguere, G., Langlois, D.: A new bidirectional hetero-associative memory encompassing correlational, competitive and topological properties. Neural Netw. **22**, 568–578 (2009)
28. Wang, Y.F., Cruz, J.B., Mulligan, J.H.: Two coding strategies for bidirectional associative memory. IEEE Trans. Neural Netw. **1**(1), 81–92 (1990)
29. Wang, Y.F., Cruz, J.B., Mulligan, J.H.: Guaranteed recall of all training pairs for bidirectional associative memory. IEEE Trans. Neural Netw. **2**(6), 559–567 (1991)
30. Kang, H.: Multilayer associative neural network (MANN's): storage capacity versus perfect recall. IEEE Trans. Neural Netw. **5**, 812–822 (1994)
31. Wang, Z.: A bidirectional associative memory based on optimal linear associative memory. IEEE Trans. Neural Netw. **45**, 1171–1179 (1996)
32. Hassoun, M.H., Youssef, A.M.: A high performance recording algorithm for Hopfield model associative memories. Opt. Eng. **27**, 46–54 (1989)
33. Simpson, P.K.: Higher-ordered and interconnected bidirectional associative memories. IEEE Trans. Syst. Man. Cybern. **20**(3), 637–652 (1990)
34. Zhuang, X., Huang, Y., Chen, S.S.: Better learning for bidirectional associative memory. Neural Netw. **6**(8), 1131–1146 (1993)
35. Oh, H., Kothari, S.C.: Adaptation of the relaxation method for learning bidirectional associative memory. IEEE Trans. Neural Netw. **5**, 573–583 (1994)
36. Wang, C.C., Don, H.S.: An analysis of high-capacity discrete exponential BAM. IEEE Trans. Neural Netw. **6**(2), 492–496 (1995)

Critical Success Factors and Critical Barriers for Application of Information Technology to Knowledge Management/Experience Management for Software Process Improvement – Findings from Literary Studies

Mitali Chugh[1(✉)] and Nitin[2]

[1] UPES, Bidholi, Dehradun 248001, Uttarakhand, India
mchugh@upes.ac.in

[2] College of Engineering and Applied Science-Department of Electrical Engineering and Computer Science, University of Cincinnati, 2851 Woodside Drive, Cincinnati, OH 45221-0030, USA
nitinfu@ucmail.uc.edu

Abstract. Present-day Software Organizations are gradually changing into knowledge based organization as Knowledge Management (KM) is important for their viability. Regardless of this KM is considered as a challenging endeavor and its application is considered critical by the organizations. Studies in literature report KM Initiatives have not been successful in many cases. Thus in depth knowledge of the Critical Success Factors (CSFs) is prerequisite for successful KM implementation. A wide-ranging set of CSFs assist organizations to be aware of the important concerns that should be taken care of when designing and implementing a KM initiative for enhancing the Software quality.

Different models proposed by SEI exist which provide the insights and standards for the improvement of Software quality. However, Software Process Improvement is also evolving as an important area of study for the enhancement of software quality. There are various models suggested in literature for the application of knowledge based/Experience based SPI, there is lack of consent on factors that contribute for the success of SPI. This research paper explores the Critical Success Factors for the efficacious application of knowledge based SPI. Research methodology used is an extensive literature survey for identification of critical success factors. Identified CSFs are used to design a survey for Indian Software Engineering Organizations for Application of IT to experience based SPI.

Keywords: Software Process Improvement · Knowledge Management
Experience management · Critical success factors · Critical barriers
Indian Software Engineering Organizations

1 Introduction

Software Process Improvement can be constantly enhanced by gathering, structuring and managing software development experiences. Knowledge can exist in the form of Lessons learnt, Best Practices, processes data, project data, reusable software artifacts

P. Bhattacharyya et al. (Eds.): NGCT 2017, CCIS 827, pp. 310–322, 2018.
https://doi.org/10.1007/978-981-10-8657-1_24

etc. Knowledge reuse forms the basis of Software Process Improvement (Basili et al. 1994). SPI efforts are determined by the implicit knowledge of practitioners in the organization. Many Research works in literature report KM Initiatives have not been efficacious in a lot of cases (Storey and Barnett 2000). Knowledge for being exploited or reused has to be warehoused in a knowledge repository. These knowledge repositories are referred to as Experience bases. Experience Bases facilitate knowledge reuse by making knowledge/experiences available at the various organizational levels. Insights of knowledge and experience management are thus potentially beneficial in SPI efforts so as to support the creation, amendment, and collaboration of software processes knowledge in an organization. Quality of developed software is directly associated to the process of development of software. SPI helps to assess existing processes, find possibilities of improvements as well as to evaluate the effects of improvements (Florac et al. 2000).

The present study is centered on the notion that organization and storage of software engineers knowledge and experience aids in SPI. The study provides comprehensive set of CSFs using extensive literature survey as a methodology. CSFs can support organizations to address the significant concerns for Experience Based SPI.

2 Literature Survey

2.1 KM/EM in SE

Knowledge Management in SE is different from the conventional/comprehensive KM due to the fact that discussion for issues associated with KM and SE occurs merely at Software Engineering conferences (Edwards 2003).

Studies existing on Knowledge Management in Software Engineering have been found in the extensive literature review. Rus et al. (2001) gives a synopsis of KM in SE, centering on approaches and factors for KM implementations. Lindvall et al. (2001) presents in depth account of software tools for KM: document management tools, content management tools, collaboration tools and competence management tools.

Conradi and Dingsøyr (2000) present an overview of Knowledge Management Systems (KMS). They also list significant elements of success for implementing KMS in Software Organizations.

Dingsøyr et al. (2001) give an account of challenges encountered by small and medium sized organizations when KM techniques are used in SE. Rus and Lindvall (2002) also state KM supports existing SPI methods and facilitate Knowledge sharing for software developers with the help of KMS. Dingsøyr and Conradi (2002) based on exhaustive literature review of KM initiatives in SE found eight lessons learned report. These are descriptions of what kind of KM strategies were used and what are the effects and benefits of the strategies implementation. They categorize the study in two sets: technical enhancement for efficacious KM, and analysis of consequence of KM on an organization. They also provide an account of software tools that provide support for

KM in software development. Precisely, Experience Management System (Seaman et al. 1999), Case Based Reasoning (CBR) for recollecting and recovering experience (Althoff et al. 1998a), CBR for building learning software organizations (Althoff et al. 1998b) have been exhaustively discussed.

2.2 The Experience Factory Approach

The Experience Factory (Basili et al. 2001) approach is based upon the notion that knowledge and experience can be made explicit so that they can be stored in knowledge and experience bases. Numerous studies have elucidated the practice of KMS to support Software Process Improvement, such as Borges and Falbo (2002) and Markkula (1999). Borges and Falbo (2002) present the concept of construction of Experience repository for collecting experiences throughout the software process. Markkula (1999) has proposed a framework for the various phases (planning, design and coding) of software development and has given an outline to facilitate the capture, storage and collaboration of knowledge for the projects as well as for the entire organization.

Some other works have linked KM processes with software processes and the KM framework incorporates the software processes (Kess and Haapasalo 2002). Literature also has studies that show improvement in software process with suitable knowledge structure and planning activity (Aurum et al. 2003).

Seleim and Kalil (2007) have examined 38 Egyptian software firms and stressed that knowledge application effects organizational performance and Knowledge Management (Aurum et al. 2008). Johansson et al. (2000) has applied a variance of Experience Factory Approach to KM in SPI i.e. Experience Engine and also list the issues which are recognized with the EF approach- experimental nature, the reorganization it brings to the Software Organization as well as its dependence on an experience base having wide-ranging written records. Komi-Sirvio et al. 2002 examined a requirement based method for guiding KM in SE. Their primary results show failure of suggested methods such as Lessons Learned databases and Data Transfer Days. A different method applied by the organization studied was based on EF. This eleventh hour methodology is suggestive of the restraints positioned on software developers for being incompetent to dedicate significant amounts of time for packing experience to be used in future. Strohmaier et al. (2007) has mentioned that experience factory concept facilitates knowledge transfer in organizations. Boehm 2003 recommends the use of value based version of the Experience Factory at the Organizational Level for accomplishment of business goals. Rodrígue et al. 2008 have recognized the role of KM tools used in organizational processes and procedures play as knowledge flow facilitators.

Basili et al. (1994) and Schneider et al. (2002) talk over the methodologies to EM as Experience Factory approach. Procedures to gather experience in software engineering environments have been discussed by many researchers (Althoff et al. (1999) and Land et al. (2001)). Moreover, Houdek et al. (1998) and Lindvall et al. (2001) have given an account of the methods for structuring of Experiences. Many others have given an account of Tools and Techniques used in EM (Henninger and Schlabach (2001), Basili et al. (2001), and Mendonca et al. (2001)). Althoff et al. (1999a) has stated that an Organizational memory can facilitate the software engineering experience reuse and have proposed an architecture for SE experience reuse. An experience management system in software consultancy firm has been explained by Mendonca et al. (2001). Few studies have also discussed the outcomes of applications of EM. Brossler (1999); Dingsøyr and Royrvik (2003); Diaz and Sligo (1997). Ward and Aurum 2004 have studied the practices of KM in SE by EF approach and have also examined the activities of KM in Software Organizations. Ericsson Software Technology AB has implemented an Experience Engine approach which is a variation of Experience Factory. It focuses on the tacit human expertise and not on documented knowledge and experience (Johansson and Hall 2000). Rus and Lindvall 2002 has suggested a Methodology for Implementing an Experience Management System.

2.3 Analysis

In-depth literature study and analysis help to identify that few studies are present on the comprehensive use and structure of effective experience repositories in software organizations. It is concluded that these studies deal with the concerns associated to knowledge creation, storage, retrieval and sharing are significant for SPI initiatives.

3 Critical Success Factors and Critical Barriers

An extensive literature review and analyses for IT being a Critical Success factor for KM has been done. Several studies have proposed IT is a CSF for efficacious implementation of Knowledge Management. However there is a wide divergence in the literature about the role of Information Technology in KM projects for SPI. The successful implementation of IT for KM is subject to the Critical Success Factors which can be studied by exploring the literature for implementation of IT in KM initiatives in the Software Engineering Organizations. (Davenport et al. 1998b; Moffet et al. (2003); Davenport and Prusak (1998)) mention that though application of IT may not assure the success of Knowledge Management initiatives as such however it is a critical enabler for the KM processes. IT bridges the temporal and spatial distance between members of an organization, restructures the flow of knowledge and facilitates teamwork and association among organizational members.

Ruggles (1998) remarks that the success factors people, process and technology need to be balanced in a 50/25/25 relation. He also mentions that for the technology being used in KM, executives state "Should-Do" efforts as: (1) Mapping sources of internal expertise (Kankanhalli et al. 2003). (2) Forming Nets of Knowledge workers. (3) Establishing New Knowledge Roles.

Moffett et al. (2003) and Kankanhalli et al. (2003) consider that when culture of teamwork and trust are amalgamated with Information Technology aids in flow of knowledge rapidly. Alavi and Leinder (2001) in accordance with the same school of thought state that IT supports and strengthens the informal and casual links among the individuals in the organization; however the nonappearance of shared knowledge space can make the actual effect of IT on Knowledge interchange questionable. They also mention that Firm wide Knowledge management systems (KMS) involve intense cultural makeovers. In many organizations a major cultural shift may be prerequisite to change the organizational members' attitude so that they freely and constantly share their knowledge through the usage of IT. Top management support is considered essential for fruitful information technology (IT) and IS implementation and adoption. It plays an important role in evolving and supporting an idea for the implementation of IT infrastructure (Lee et al. (2016); Akkermans and Helden (2002); Law and Ngai 2007; Nah et al. 2003); Kim et al. (2005)).

Fairchild 2002 has stated that Information technology can support the development and the maintenance of organizational knowledge if it is taken into consideration that IT here is a facilitator; corporate culture and work practices are equally related and significant. Information technologies extremely suitable for this purpose should be specifically planned and designed with knowledge management and organizational capital.

Wei et al. (2002) insist that management support, amalgamation with prevailing technology organization, and an organizational culture that supports knowledge creation and sharing are critical success factors for KM system implementation. Incorporating a KM system with technology is principally significant, as it lessens learning time for the knowledge workers and facilitates system acceptance and use. A system's ease of use is important and critically depends on its interfaces with users. Milton et al. 1999 mentions the term Knowledge Technology and have proposed a framework for the same. Knowledge Technology refers to main activities that are supported by Knowledge Oriented Techniques and tools. According to them Knowledge Technology should have two important characteristics: (1) It should encompass a wide range of methods, (2) for most applications it should be usable by relative novices. In addition they have also considered training and evaluation of novices for learning the knowledge engineering practices as a CSF for implementation of Knowledge Technology (IT for KM initiatives).

Ngwenyama and Nielsen (2014) have revealed lack of formal power and influence over the organization targeted for change, weak support from top management and organizational memories of prior failures as barriers to implementation. According to Sedighi and Fardad (2012) implementation of new IT support in Software Organizations is a multifaceted and challenging task which profoundly alters the organizational culture (social structure, processes and conduct of employees). Top Management support is also considered an important enabler or CSF (Abrahamsson 2001; Börjesson and Mathiassen 2004; Sabherwal et al. 2006).

According to Markus and Benjamin (1996), the following three conditions are 'structurally incompatible' with IS implementation success: (1) the absenteeism of managerial power over the organization targeted for change; (2) negative perceptions of the change agents by organization members; and (3) weak top-management support for the IS change initiative. However, an empirical study by Ngwenyama and Nørbjerg (2010) states that the strategic use of associations can facilitate in overcoming these situations and can help to attain implementation success. Iversen et al. 1999; Nielsen and Ngwenyama 2002; Ngwenyama and Nørbjerg 2010 have cross-examined the design and deployment of synchronized organizational impact strategy intended at overcoming SPI implementation barriers in a software company.

Desouza (2003) has stated that IT is a way to facilitate KM in Software Engineering Organizations and has considered knowledge sharing as a CSF for implementation of IT and also mentions that an organization must boost knowledge sharing culture by clearly defining incentives. In the order of severity critical barriers mentioned by him are: (1) Confrontation to be recognized as an expert. (2) Necessary knowledge cannot be captured and categorized. (3) Fruitfulness of substitute knowledge interchange medium. He concludes as *"It is not enough just to store knowledge in repositories; one has to reap intended benefits by exploiting the knowledge."*

As stated by Heeseok and Byounggu (2003) many knowledge management projects practically concentrate on IT (Davenport and Prusak (1998); Gold et al. (2001); Swan and Robertson (2000)). However an organization may encounter problems in structuring its environment for creation of knowledge due to nonexistence of adequate culture although IT infrastructure in such organizations may be well developed (DeTienne and Jackson (2001); Lubit (2001)).

Stein and Zwass (1995) insisted the importance of organizational culture (organizational values) and the learning methods for successful information systems. (Davenport and Prusak (1998)). A key factor that should be considered in the development of a KM technological system is ease of technological interface, comfort of use, aptness to users' expectations, relevance and standardization of knowledge (Wong (2005)).

Furthermore, the IT infrastructure should support creation and retention of the network of experts and should provide a shared knowledge space for knowledge management within the firm (Chua and Lam (2005)). Moreover, the security and protection of knowledge have been recognized by firms as a critical factor for implementing KM systems as users want to know that what they share is secure (Plessis (2007)). The role of KM software in nurturing inter-functional cooperation and the coordination of knowledge hinge on the firm's capability to fit in procedures which maintain bidirectional knowledge flows between local and global knowledge (D'Adderio (2001)).

Table 1. Critical success factors/critical barriers for application of IT to KM initiatives: summary

S. No.	CSFs/CBs	References
1	Organizational culture (teamwork and trust, strengthening informal and casual contacts, organizational values)	Kankanhalli et al. (2003); Jennex and Olfman (2000); Moffet et al. (2003); Alavi and Leinder (2001); Sedighi and Fardad (2012); Stein and Zwass (1995); Davenport and Prusak (1998); Chua and Lam (2005)
2	Shared knowledge space	Alavi and Leinder (2001); Ruggles (1998); Wei et al. (2002)
3	Top management support	Akkermans and Helden (2002); Law and Ngai (2007); Nah et al. (2003); Kim et al. (2005), Lee et al. (2016); Wei et al. (2002); Ngwenyama and Nielsen (2014); Sedighi and Fardad (2012); Abrahamsson (2001); Borjesson and Mathiassen (2004); Sabherwal et al. (2006); Jennex and Olfman (2000)

(*continued*)

Table 1. (*continued*)

S. No.	CSFs/CBs	References
4	Mapping of technical infrastructure with internal expertise, organizational capital and procedures with two directional knowledge flows	Fairchild (2002); Ruggles (1998); Wei et al. (2002); D'Adderio (2001); Jennex and Olfman (2000); Kankanhalli et al. (2003)
5	Defining new knowledge roles	Ruggles (1998)
6	IT infrastructure and system's interface (ease or simplicity of use, comfort of use, appropriateness of user's desires)	Wei et al. (2002); Milton et al. (1999); Wong (2005); Jennex and Olfman (2000)
7	Relevance and standardization of knowledge	Wong (2005); Jennex and Olfman (2000)
8	Incorporating wide range of methods	Milton et al. (1999)
9	Training and evaluation of employees	Milton et al. (1999); Stein and Zwass (1995); Jennex and Olfman (2000)
10	Memories of prior failure	Ngwenyama and Nielsen (2014)
11	Lack of formal power and influence over organization targeted for change	Ngwenyama and Nielsen (2014); Markus and Benjamin (1996); Ngwenyama and Norbjerg (2010)
12	Negative perceptions of change agents by organizational members	Ngwenyama and Nielsen (2014); Markus and Benjamin (1996); Ngwenyama and Norbjerg (2010)
13	Knowledge sharing behavior of employees	Desouza (2003)
14	Fruitfulness of substitute knowledge exchange medium	Desouza (2003)
15	Required knowledge cannot be captured	Desouza (2003); Detienne and Jackson (2001); Lubit (2001)
16	Security and protection of knowledge	Chua and Lam (2005); Plessis (2007); Jennex and Olfman (2000)
17	Time required for capturing and search of knowledge	Rodríguez et al. (2008); Desouza (2003); Rus and Lindvall (2002)
18	Support for distributed KM	Rodríguez et al. (2008); Banerjee (2005); Bonifaci et al. (2002); Cruel (2003); van Elst et al. (2004)
19	Availability of automation at the stages of KM	Marwick (2001); van Elst et al. (2004); Rodríguez et al. (2008)

Jennex and Olfman (2000) studied three KM projects to identify design recommendations for building a successful KMS. These recommendations include: Well developed IT infrastructure, standardization of hardware and software across the organization, shared knowledge space (Enterprise-wide knowledge structure), senior management support, training and evaluation of users, security of KMS and + identifying organizational culture concerns that could inhibit KMS usage. An account of studies related to IT being a CSF for KM initiatives for Software Engineering Organizations has been given by Sharma et al. (2011).

Rodríguez (2008) have identified two enablers for the application of IT as: (1) Lessening of user's work by automation at certain stages of KM life cycle (Marwick (2001); van Elst et al. (2004). (2) Organization and Structuring of distributed knowledge (Banerjee (2005); Bonifaci et al. (2002); van Elst et al. (2004); Cruel(2003)).

Time required for Knowledge creation and Knowledge search is also an important factor for the use of IT in KM initiatives (Rodríguez et al. 2008; Desouza (2003); Rus and Lindvall (2002); Aurum et al. (2003)).

4 The Indian Scenario

In this study, two KM models were used to create a theoretical foundation for studying the KM process for SE. The first model was the SECI model developed by Nonaka and Takeuchi (1995). which has been recognized as a significant contribution to understanding the creation of diverse kinds of knowledge. The second model was the 'Experience Factory' (Basili et al. 1994) which is identical with KM in SE.

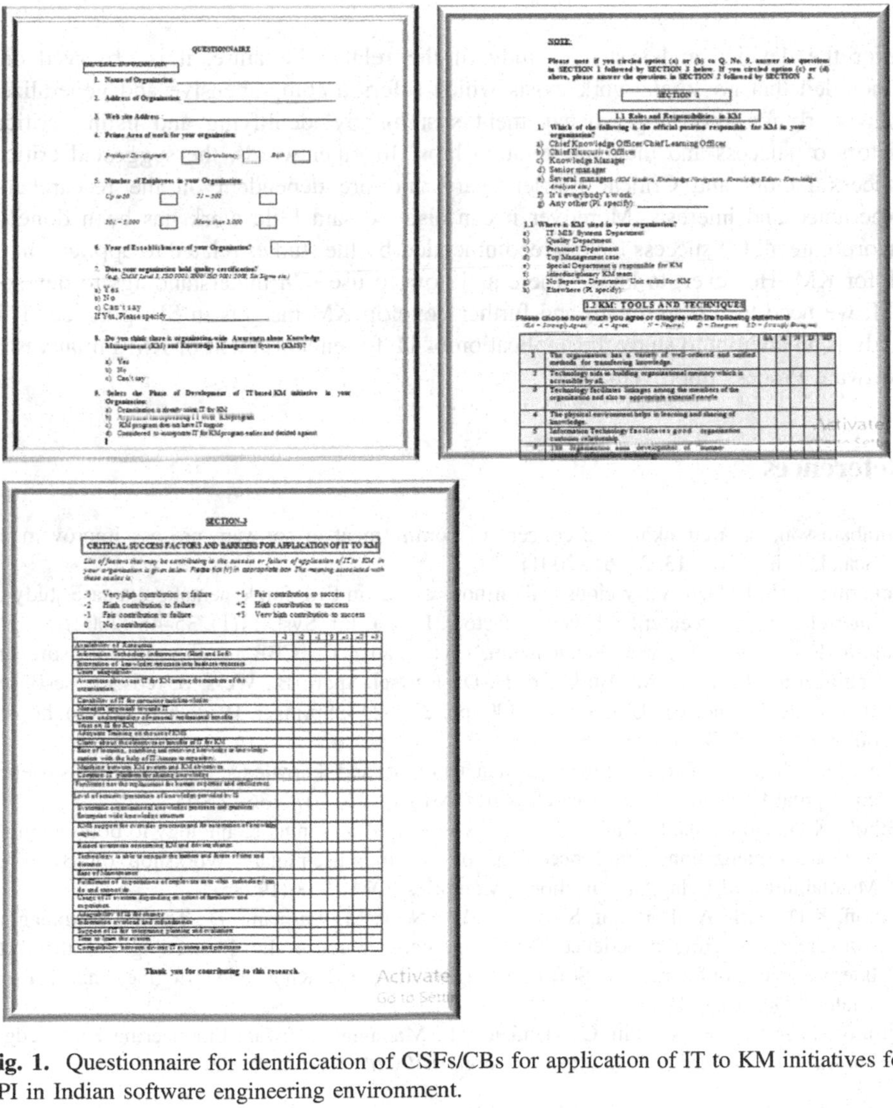

Fig. 1. Questionnaire for identification of CSFs/CBs for application of IT to KM initiatives for SPI in Indian software engineering environment.

After reviewing these well-known KM models, as well as existing literature, KM activities were developed. These process activities are: (1) knowledge Creation, (2) knowledge Storage and Retrieval, (3) knowledge Transfer, (4) knowledge application, (5) Application of IT to KM initiatives.

The questionnaire was grounded on components of prevailing KM models, as well as the KM activities mentioned above. The questionnaire integrated three main sections: (1) General information about each KM Organization, (2) activities performed in the KM process for SE and (3) Critical Success factors and Critical Barriers for application of IT to KM process.

5 Conclusion

After the detailed and systemic study of the related literature, it is observed and concluded that no single work exists which offers a comprehensive and generalized framework for knowledge management systems by identifying and listing critical factors of success and their interrelationships. In other words, the suggested critical success factors and Critical Barriers vary and are dependent on the researchers' experience and interests. Moreover it can also be said little work has been done to incorporate all the success factors recommended by the studies related to application of IT for KM. However, to know where and how to use KM understandings to develop SPI, we need to research with and further develop KM insights in SPI practice. This study is an attempt to study the application of IT for enhancement of KM initiatives in Software Process Improvement.

References

Abrahamsson, P.: Rethinking the concept of commitment in software process improvement. Scand. J. Inf. Syst. **13**, 37–61 (2001)

Akkermans, H., Helden, V.: Vicious and virtuous cycles in ERP implementation: a case study of interrelations between critical success factors. Eur. J. Inf. Syst. **11**(1), 35–46 (2002)

Althoff, K.-D., Birk, A., von Wangenheim, C.G., Tautz, C.: CBR for experimental software engineering. In: Lenz, M., Burkhard, H.-D., Bartsch-Spörl, B., Wess, S. (eds.) Case-Based Reasoning Technology. LNCS, vol. 1400, pp. 235–254. Springer, Heidelberg (1998). https://doi.org/10.1007/3-540-69351-3_9

Alavi, M., Leidner, D.E.: Knowledge management and knowledge management systems: conceptual foundations and research issues. MIS Q. **25**, 107–136 (2001)

Althoff, K.D., Bomarius, F., Tautz, C.: Using case-based reasoning technology to build learning software organizations. In: Proceedings of the Interdisciplinary Workshop on Building, Maintaining and Using Organizational Memories, OM 1998 (1998b)

Althoff, K.D., Birk, A., Hartkopf, S., Muller, W., Nick, M., Surmann, D., Tautz, C.: Managing software engineering experience for comprehensive reuse. In: Proceedings of the 11th International Conference on Software Engineering and Knowledge Engineering, Kaiserslautern, Germany (1999)

Aurum, A., Jeffery, R., Wohlin, C., Handzic, M.: Managing Software Engineering Knowledge. Springer, Heidelberg (2003). https://doi.org/10.1007/978-3-662-05129-0

Aurum, A., Farhad, D., James, W.: Investigating knowledge management practices in software development organisations–an australian experience. Inf. Softw. Technol. **50**(6), 511–533 (2008)

Banerjee, R.: A fool with a tool is still a fool. In: Rao, M. (ed.) KM Tools and Techniques, pp. 283–292. Elsevier, Amsterdam (2005)

Basili, V.R., Caldiera, G., Rombach, H.: The experience factory, Chap. X. In: Marciniak, J. (ed.) Encyclopedia of Software Engineering, vol. 1, pp. 468–476. Wiley, Hoboken (1994)

Basili, V.R., Lindvall, M., Costa, P.: Implementing the experience factory concepts as a set of experience bases. In: 13th International Conference on Software Engineering & Knowledge Engineering, Knowledge Systems Institute, pp. 102–109 (2001)

Boehm, B.: Value-based software engineering. ACM SIGSOFT Softw. Eng. Notes **2**(28), 3–15 (2003)

Bonifaci, M., Bouquet, P., Traverso, P.: Enabling distributed knowledge management: managerial and technological implications. Novatica Informatik/Informatique **3**, 23–29 (2002)

Borges, L.M.S., Falbo, R.A.: Managing software process knowledge. In: Proceeding of the CSITeA 2002 (2002)

Börjesson, G., Mathiassen, L.: Improving software organizations: agility challenges and implications. Inf. Technol. People **18**(4), 359–382 (2004)

Brössler, P.: Knowledge management at a software engineering company - an experience report. In: Workshop on Learning Software Organizations, LSO 1999, Kaiserslautern, Germany, pp. 163–170 (1999)

Chua, A., Lam, W.: Why KM projects fail: a multi-case analysis. J. Knowl. Manag. **9**, 6–17 (2005)

Conradi, R., Dingsøyr, T.: Software experience bases: a consolidated evaluation and status report. In: Bomarius, F., Oivo, M. (eds.) PROFES 2000. LNCS, vol. 1840, pp. 391–406. Springer, Heidelberg (2000). https://doi.org/10.1007/978-3-540-45051-1_33

Cruel, R.: A new methodology for distributed KM analysis. In: Proceedings for International Symposium on Knowledge Management, I-KNOW 2003, Graz, Austria, pp. 531–537 (2003)

D'Adderio, L.: Crafting the virtual prototype: how firms integrate knowledge and capabilities across organisational boundaries. Res. Policy **30**, 1409–1424 (2001)

Davenport, T.H., De Long, D., David, W., Beers, M.C.: Successful knowledge management projects. Sloan Manag. Rev. **39**(2), 43–57 (1998a)

Davenport, T.H., Prusak, L.: Working Knowledge: How Organizations Manage What They Know. Harvard Business School Press, Boston (1998b)

Desouza, K.C.: Barriers to effective use of knowledge management systems in software engineering. Commun. ACM **46**(1), 99–101 (2003)

DeTienne, K.B., Jackson, L.A.: Knowledge management: understanding theory and developing strategy. Compet. Rev. **11**(1), 1–11 (2001)

Diaz, M., Sligo, J.: How software process improvement helped Motorola. IEEE Softw. **14**, 75–81 (1997)

Dingsøyr, T., Moe, N.B., Nytrø, Ø.: Augmenting experience reports with lightweight postmortem reviews. In: Bomarius, F., Komi-Sirviö, S. (eds.) PROFES 2001. LNCS, vol. 2188, pp. 167–181. Springer, Heidelberg (2001). https://doi.org/10.1007/3-540-44813-6_17

Dingsøyr, T., Conradi, R.: A survey of case studies of the use of knowledge management in software engineering. Int. J. Software Eng. Knowl. Eng. **12**(4), 391–414 (2002)

Dingsøyr, T., Royrvik, E.: An empirical study of an informal knowledge repository in a medium-sized software consulting company. In: Proceedings of the 25th International Conference on Software Engineering (2003)

Edwards, J.S.: Managing software engineers and their knowledge. In: Aurum, A., Jeffrey, R., Wohlin, C., Handzic, M. (eds.) Managing Software Engineering Knowledge, pp. 5–27. Springer, Heidelberg (2003). https://doi.org/10.1007/978-3-662-05129-0_1

van Elst, L., Dignum, V., Abecker, A.: Towards agent-mediated knowledge management. In: van Elst, L., Dignum, V., Abecker, A. (eds.) AMKM 2003. LNCS, vol. 2926, pp. 1–30. Springer, Heidelberg (2004). https://doi.org/10.1007/978-3-540-24612-1_1

Fairchild, A.M.: Knowledge management metrics via a balanced scorecard methodology. In: Proceedings of the 35th Annual Hawaii International Conference on System Sciences, HICSS, pp. 3173–3180. IEEE (2002)

Florac, W.A., Carleton, A.D., Barnard, J.R.: Statistical process control: analyzing a space shuttle onboard software process. IEEE Softw. **17**(4), 97–106 (2000)

Gold, A.H., Malhotra, A., Segars, A.H.: Knowledge management: an organizational capabilities perspective. J. Manag. Inf. Syst. **18**(1), 185–214 (2001)

Heeseok, L., Byounggu, C.: Knowledge management enablers, processes, and organizational performance: an integrative view and empirical examination. J. Manag. Inf. Syst. **20**(1), 179–228 (2003)

Henninger, S., Schlabach, J.: A tool for managing software development knowledge. In: Bomarius, F., Komi-Sirviö, S. (eds.) PROFES 2001. LNCS, vol. 2188, pp. 182–195. Springer, Heidelberg (2001). https://doi.org/10.1007/3-540-44813-6_18

Houdek, F., Schneider, K., Wieser, E.: Establishing experience factories at Daimler-Benz: an experience report. In: Proceedings of the 20th International Conference on Software Engineering, pp. 443–447 (1998)

Iversen, J., Nielsen, P.A., Nørbjerg, J.: Situated assessments of problems in software development. Database Adv. Inf. Syst. **30**(2), 66–81 (1999)

Jennex, M.E., Olfman, L.: Development recommendations for knowledge management organizational memory systems. In: Information System Development Conference, pp. 209–222 (2000)

Johansson, C., Hall, P., Coquard, M.: "Talk to paula and peter—They are experienced" the experience engine in a nutshell. In: Ruhe, G., Bomarius, F. (eds.) SEKE 1999. LNCS, vol. 1756, pp. 171–185. Springer, Heidelberg (2000). https://doi.org/10.1007/BFb0101420

Kankanhalli, A., Tanudidjaja, F., Sutanto, J., Tan, B.C.Y.: The role of IT in successful knowledge management initiatives. Commun. ACM **46**, 69–73 (2003)

Kess, P., Haapasalo, H.: Knowledge creation through a project review process in software production. Int. J. Prod. Econ. **80**(1), 49–55 (2002)

Kim, Y., Lee, Z., Gosain, S.: Impediments to successful ERP implementation process. Bus. Process Manag. J. **11**(2), 158–170 (2005)

Komi-Sirvio, S., Mantyniemi, A., Seppanen, V.: Towards a practical solution for capturing knowledge for software projects. IEEE Softw. **19**(3), 60–62 (2002)

Land, L., Aurum, A., Handzic, M.: Capturing implicit software engineering knowledge. In: 2001 Australian Software Engineering Conference, pp. 108–114 (2001)

Law, C.C., Ngai, E.W.: ERP systems adoption: an exploratory study of the organizational factors and impacts of ERP success. Inf. Manag. **44**(4), 418–432 (2007)

Lee, J.C., Shiue, Y.C., Chen, C.Y.: Examining the impacts of organizational culture and top management support of knowledge sharing on the success of software process improvement. Comput. Hum. Behav. **54**, 462–474 (2016)

Lindvall, M., Rus, I., Jammalamadaka, R., Thakker, R.: Software tools for knowledge management. Technical report. DoD Data Analysis Center for Software, Rome (2001)

Lubit, R.: Tacit knowledge and knowledge management: the keys to sustainable competitive advantage. Org. Dyn. **29**(4), 164–178 (2001)

Markkula, M.: Knowledge management in software engineering projects. In: Proceedings of the 11th International Conference on Software Engineering and Knowledge Engineering, Kaiserslautern, Germany (1999)

Markus, M.L., Benjamin, R.I.: Change agentry – the next IS frontier. MIS Q. **20**(4), 385–407 (1996)

Marwick, A.D.: KM technology. IBM Syst. J. **40**, 814–830 (2001)

Mendonca, M.G., Seaman, C.B., Basili, V.R., Kim, Y.M.: A prototype experience management system for a software consulting organization. In: Proceedings of the 13th International Conference on Software Engineering and Knowledge Engineering, Buenos Aires, Argentina, pp. 29–36 (2001)

Milton, N., Shadbolt, N., Cottam, H., Hammersley, M.: Towards a knowledge technology for knowledge management. Int. J. Hum.-Comput. Stud. **51**(3), 615–641 (1999)

Moffett, S., McAdam, R., Parkinson, S.: An empirical analysis of knowledge management applications. J. Knowl. Manag. **7**(3), 6–26 (2003)

Nah, F.F.H., Zuckweiler, K.M., Lau, J.L.S.: ERP implementation: chief information officers' perceptions of critical success factors. Int. J. Hum.-Comput. Interact. **16**(1), 5–22 (2003)

Ngwenyama, O., Nielsen, P.A.: Using organizational influence processes to overcome IS implementation barriers: lessons from a longitudinal case study of SPI implementation. Eur. J. Inf. Syst. **23**(2), 205–222 (2014)

Ngwenyama, O., Nørbjerg, J.: Software process improvement with weak management support: an analysis of the dynamics of intra-organizational alliances in IS change initiatives. Eur. J. Inf. Syst. **19**(3), 303–319 (2010)

Nielsen, P.A., Ngwenyama, O.F.: Organizational influence processes in software process improvement. In: Proceedings of the Xth European Conference on Information Systems, ECIS 2002. University of Gdansk, Gdansk (2002)

Nonaka, I., Takeuchi, H.: The knowledge-Creating Company: How Japanese Companies Create the Dynamics of Innovation. Oxford University Press (1995)

Plessis, M.D.: Knowledge management: what makes complex implementations successful? J. Knowl. Manag. **11**, 91–101 (2007)

Rodríguez, E., Oscar, M., Ana, I., García, M., Vizcaíno, A., Favela, J., Piattini, J.: A framework to analyze information systems as knowledge flow facilitators. Inf. Softw. Technol. **50**(6), 481–498 (2008)

Ruggles, R.: The state of the notion: knowledge management in practice. Calif. Manag. Rev. **40** (3), 80–89 (1998)

Rus, I., Lindvall, M., Sinha, S.S.: Knowledge management in software engineering - A DACS state-of-the-art report. Fraunhofer Center for Experimental Software Engineering, The University of Maryland, Maryland (2001)

Rus, I., Lindvall, M.: Knowledge management in software engineering. IEEE Softw. **19**(3), 26–38 (2002)

Sabherwal, R., Jeyaraj, A., Chowa, C.: Information system success: individual and organizational determinants. Manag. Sci. **52**(12), 1849–1864 (2006)

Saleim, A., Kalil, O.: KM and organisational performance in the Egyptian software firms. Int. J. Knowl. Manag. **3**(4), 37–66 (2007)

Schneider, K., Hunnius, V.J.P., Basili, V.R.: Experience in implementing a learning software organization. IEEE Softw. **19**(3), 46–49 (2002)

Seaman, C., Mendonca, M., Basili, V.R., Kim, Y.M.: An experience management system for a software consulting organization. In: Proceedings of the 24th Annual NASA Software Engineering Workshop (1999)

Sedighi, M., Fardad, Z.: Knowledge management: review of the critical success factors and development of a conceptual classification model. In: 2012 10th International Conference on ICT and Knowledge Engineering, ICT & Knowledge Engineering. IEEE (2012)

Sharma, N., Singh, K., Goyal, D.P.: What makes or mars a knowledge based software process improvement initiative?-Prescriptions from the field. Int. J. Eng. Sci. **1**, 283–302 (2011)

Stein, E.W., Zwass, V.: Actualizing organizational memory with information systems. Inf. Syst. Res. **6**(2), 85–117 (1995)

Storey, J., Barnett, E.: Knowledge management initiatives: learning from failure. J. Knowl. Manag. **4**(2), 145–156 (2000)

Strohmaier, M., Eric, Y., Horkoff, J., Aranda, J., Easterbrook, S.: Analyzing knowledge transfer effectiveness-an agent-oriented approach. In: Proceedings of the 40th Hawaii International Conference on System Sciences (2007)

Swan, J., Newell, S., Robertson, M.: Limits of IT-driven knowledge management for interactive innovation processes: towards a community-based approach. In: Sprague Jr., R.H. (ed.) Proceedings of the Thirty-Third Hawaii International Conference on System Sciences, pp. 84–94. IEEE Computer Society Press, Los Alamitos (2000)

Ward, J., Aurum, A.: Knowledge management in software engineering-describing the process. In: Proceedings of the 2004 Australian Software Engineering Conference, ASWEC 2004, pp. 137–146. IEEE (2004)

Wei, C.P., Hu, P.J.H., Chen, H.H.: Design and evaluation of a knowledge management system. IEEE Softw. **19**(3), 56–59 (2002)

Wong, K.Y.: Critical success factors for implementing knowledge management in small and medium enterprises. Ind. Manag. Data Syst. **105**, 261–279 (2005)

Traffic Prediction Using Viterbi Algorithm in Machine Learning Approach

D. Suvitha(✉), M. Vijayalakshmi(✉), and P. M. Mohideen Sameer(✉)

Department of Information Science and Technology, Anna University, CEG Campus, Chennai, Tamil Nadu, India
suvitha19@gmail.com, mohideensam93@gmail.com, vijim@annauniv.edu

Abstract. Road traffic snarl-up is a major issue in metropolitan area of both developing and developed countries. In order to diminish this imperative, traffic congestion states of road systems are assessed, so that congested path can be avoided and flipside path can be chosen while traveling from one place to another. Information's are gathered by the GPS gadgets and offers new open doors for traffic and route prediction, particularly in urban city systems. The core purpose of this research work is to build up an Android application which gives a deliberate approach in providing the best route between a source and destination to the drivers so that driver will not be caught in the traffic. Android application uses Machine Learning algorithms. In this paper, Hidden Markov Model (HMM) is used for predicting traffic states which performs better and more robust than the other models. The best path from source to destination is predicted using Viterbi algorithm taking into the account of road traffic at the time and the driver will be directed to the best path. This application takes Json request as input to interface with the local server through Internet for predicting the traffic state and the best path. The output is returned back from the server as a Json response to the Android application.

Keywords: Hidden Markov Model (HMM) · Forward Trellis algorithm Viterbi · Android app

1 Introduction

A precise approach has been proposed for characterizing and foreseeing the overall city traffic conditions. The aim is to set up a traffic flow analysis model with the ultimate objective of predicting the future traffic speed based upon which the best path to the destination can be furnished to the drivers who are using GPS gadgets. The immense help of navigation devices in vehicles (route frameworks and advanced cell applications), has prompted a growing enthusiasm on utilizing GPS information for determining the traffic flow on the roads. A quantifiable approach is provided for predicting the road traffic that gives the inputs of future speeds on the differing road joins. In the first, it helps in going past traffic estimation to future traffic forecast, which in general requires more historical information and the traffic has been predicted using Hidden Markov Model (HMM).

P. Bhattacharyya et al. (Eds.): NGCT 2017, CCIS 827, pp. 323–333, 2018.
https://doi.org/10.1007/978-981-10-8657-1_25

Second is to provide the finest path to the destination based upon the predetermined future speed on the road junctions which is made by the Viterbi algorithm.

The user input is taken in Android device. It is sent as a Json request to the local server and the traffic state with highest probability is calculated using Forward Trellis approach in Hidden Markov Model (HMM) and is stored in the database. This traffic state is calculated for each and every link within the city. Based on the stored traffic state values, the best path from source to destination is determined using Viterbi algorithm and the output is returned back to the Android device as Json response.

The rest of the paper is organized as follows. In Sect. 2, related work is been discussed. Section 3 includes the proposed work architecture of the Traffic and Route Prediction Model using Forward Trellis and Viterbi algorithm in Hidden Markov Model. Section 4 deals with the Dataset Description. Section 5 includes Results and Discussion and finally, Sect. 6 includes the conclusion and future work of the paper.

2 Related Work

Advancement of Intelligent Transportation Systems (ITS) is one of the quick becoming urgent segments in the plan of future savvy urban communities given real necessity for authorizing super-effective route. Urban traffic prediction has huge impact on city management. Yugeng et al. [1] intended to characterize the key method of urban traffic movement and the prediction of the progress between various modes in light of Shanghai urban traffic speed information. Firstly, the citywide speed time series information was changed over into cluster number series utilizing clustering technique in a specific cycle period. Second, dynamic multi-models with various occasional succession numbers were assembled in view of Variable-Order Markov Model (VOMM), where weighted coefficients were prepared by handling an ideal issue through cross-validation. Lastly, the anticipated traffic modes evolution was displayed as a probabilistic suffix tree. Transportation frameworks may be intensely influenced by components, for example, road mishaps and climate. In particular, severe climate conditions may have uncommon effect on travel time and traffic stream. This examination has two targets: to start with, to explore a relationship between weather parameters and traffic stream, and to enhance traffic movement stream prediction by proposing a novel all-encompassing architecture. It incorporates deep belief networks for traffic and weather prediction and, decision-level data fusion scheme to upgrade prediction exactness utilizing climate conditions. Precise on-street vehicle speed prediction is vital for some intelligent vehicular and transportation applications. It's additionally testing in light of the fact that the individual vehicle speed is influenced by many elements, e.g., traffic speed, vehicle sort, and drivers conduct, in either deterministic or stochastic ways [3].

Yunsi et al. [4] proposed a novel vehicle speed prediction technique with regards to vehicular systems, where the real-time traffic information is available. Traffic speed Movement rates of following road sections are first anticipated by Neural Networks (NNs) in light of existing traffic information. Hidden Markov model (HMM) is trained by the Baum-Welch calculation with historical traffic movement and vehicle information to display the measurable connection between vehicle speed and traffic speed.

The forward backward algorithm is exercised on HMMs to extract vehicles speed on every road section along the driving course. Simulation is set upon the SUMO microscopic traffic simulator with the use of an actual Luxembourg highway network and traffic count data [5]. Multilayer perceptrons are utilized concurrently to predict number of vehicles going through various junctions situated in different places in Wroclaw. The proposed way of traffic prediction over significant city intersections is a new approach for preparing the Levenberg Marquardt calculation, which is an exceptionally proficient and stable gradient strategy. An early ceasing, which is a type of regularization, was connected with a specific end goal to maintain a strategic distance from over fitting and loss of speculation capacity. In addition, in-order to diminish errors and fundamentally enhance generalization properties, an ensemble technique with a populace of multilayer perceptrons was used.

Precise short term traffic speed forecast has been a standout amongst the most essential issues of Intelligent Traffic Systems [6]. They have utilized 122 speed sensors information from Istanbul that was gathered from first January to 31st December 2014. They extricated four distinctive capabilities for regression algorithms. At that point they clustered the sensors into various gatherings and prepared a model for each gathering. Prediction results are acquired by utilizing decision tree and KNN based regression algorithms. KNN algorithm which is used to determine the traffic state in the existing system could not able to predict more accurate values in the prediction. Regression model requires more computational power and more volume of data are needed for its prediction accuracy. Then again, incorporating climate information doesn't enhance the performance.

Some of the issues discussed in prediction models are as follows: ARIMA model does not provide more accurate results when the data generation process is not stable. Bayesian Network Model does not able to obtain a reliable prediction with changing traffic condition. Each algorithm can attain only a certain level of accuracy in predicting the traffic. The time taken for the algorithm to predict the traffic varies from one to another.

This study aims to establish traffic congestion states of user's desired source-destination and provides the estimated traffic result in the application. HMM is used for estimating the traffic condition states of these road network based on the provided historical traffic data of a city. The best path to the destination is provided to the user in the application by the Viterbi algorithm based on the estimated traffic condition states which prevent the user from being trapped in traffic.

3 The Proposed Framework

3.1 Traffic Prediction Architecture

This section gives an overview of how the user input from the application is taken to the local server, the process involved in traffic and route prediction model, returning the output to the application and the various function available to the user in the application. This is explained with the help of system architecture in Fig. 1.

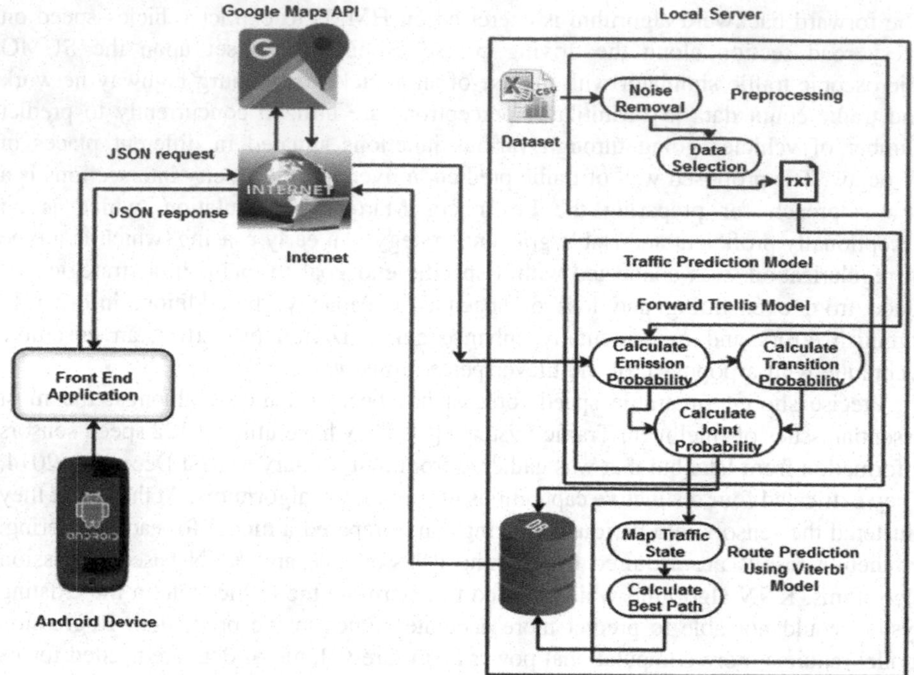

Fig. 1. Traffic route prediction architecture

Front-End Application

The Android application is used for getting the input and displaying the output to the user. The Android application contains a unique key through which the map UI is obtained over the Internet from the Google Maps API. It connects with the local server for predicting the traffic and route. The input and output to the application is sent as Json request and Json response.

Preprocessing

The dataset is been preprocessed to eliminate the null values and the missing values. From the dataset the required attributes are selected as an input for Traffic Prediction model.

Traffic Prediction Model

In this model the sequence of the average speed is collected from the dataset based on the user input from the Android application. Then the Hidden Markov Model using Forward Trellis is applied to find the joint probability based on the calculated emission and transition probability for the given sequence which gives the traffic state with highest probability as the output of this model.

Route Prediction

Based on the predicted traffic state for each link within a network, the best path to the destination is chosen by using Viterbi algorithm. The output of this model contains a series of geo-locations which will be mapped in the Android application.

3.2 Prediction Based on HMM

HMM Model

HMM model is depicted by the following characteristics:

- Hidden states $H = \{h_1, h_2, \ldots\}$
- Observations states $F = \{f_1, f_2, \ldots\}$
- λ = (X, Y, π): Hidden Markov Model
- X - State transition probability

$$x_{np} = P(h_{t+1} = p | h_t = n) \tag{1}$$

- Y - Observation probability

$$y_p(q) = P(f_t = q | h_t = p) \tag{2}$$

- $\pi = \{\pi_n\}$: initial state distribution

$$\pi_n = P(h_1) \tag{3}$$

HMM model can be depicted by the determination of H, F, X, Y and π. To start with, the initial distribution π indicates the initial state. By then, the new state can be gotten by the state transition likelihood distribution X. At long last, the observation value is offered by the observation likelihood distribution Y. This is illuminated with the assistance of HMM Formalism in Fig. 2.

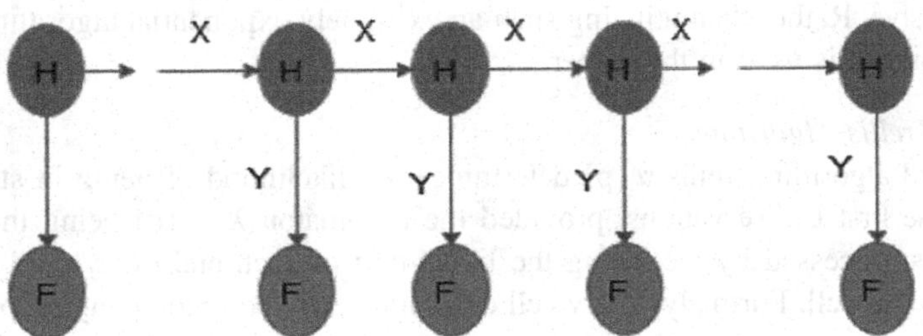

Fig. 2. HMM formalism

A first-order HMM divides into two streamlining assumptions. In the first, the likelihood of a specific state depends only on the past state:

$$\text{Markov Rule}: \ P(h_n | h_1 \ldots h_{n-1}) = P(h_n | h_{n-1}) \tag{4}$$

Second, the likelihood of an output observation f_n depends particularly on that state which gives the observation h_n:

$$\text{Output Independence}: \mathrm{P}(\mathrm{f_n}|\mathrm{h_1}.....\mathrm{h_n},\ldots.\mathrm{h_T}, \mathrm{f_1}.....\mathrm{f_n},\ldots.\mathrm{f_T}) = \mathrm{P}(\mathrm{f_n}|\mathrm{h_n}) \quad (5)$$

Definition 1. HMM λ = (X, Y) and observation sequence F is given, compute the probability P(F|λ).

Definition 2. Observation sequence F and HMM λ = (X, Y) is given, determine the finest possible hidden state sequence H.

Likelihood Computation: The Forward Algorithm

Every hidden state gives only one observation. Accordingly, the cycle of hidden states and the cycle of observations have similar length. Markov assumptions for a particular hidden state sequence $\mathrm{H} = \mathrm{h_0}, \mathrm{h_1}, \mathrm{h_2}, \ldots \mathrm{h_T}$ (slow, below average, average, above average, free) and an observation sequence $\mathrm{F} = \mathrm{f_1}, \mathrm{f_2}, \ldots \mathrm{f_T}$ (speed, time, id, day), the likelihood of the observation sequence is

$$\mathrm{P}(\mathrm{F}|\mathrm{H}) = \prod\nolimits_{n=1}^{\mathrm{T}} \mathrm{P}(\mathrm{f_n}|\mathrm{h_n}) \quad (6)$$

Joint Probability Distribution

To begin with, we figure the joint probability of sequence H and generating a specific sequence F. In general, this is

$$P(F, H) = P(F|H) * P(H) = \prod\nolimits_{n=1}^{l} P(f_n|h_n) * \prod\nolimits_{n=1}^{l} P(h_n|h_{n-1}) \quad (7)$$

Given HMM with L hidden states and an observation sequence of T observations, there are L^T conceivable hidden sequences. For actual undertakings, where L and T are both extensive, Rather than utilizing such an extremely exponential algorithm, forward trellis algorithm is used in this paper.

Forward Trellis Algorithm

Forward algorithm trellis $\alpha_t(p)$ determines the likelihood of being in state p after noticing the first t observations, provided the automaton λ. $\alpha_t(p)$ being the value of each cell is processed by reckoning the likelihood of each and every path that could takes us to this cell. Formally, every cell communicates the accompanying probability:

$$\alpha_t(p) = P(f_1, f_2, \ldots f_t, h_t = \mathrm{p}|\lambda) \quad (8)$$

Here, $\mathrm{h_t} = \mathrm{p}$ signifies "the $\mathrm{t^{th}}$ state in the sequence of states is state p". Probability $\alpha_t(\mathrm{p})$ is processed by adding over the extensions of every paths that prompt to the present cell. h_p being a given state at time t, the value $\alpha_t(\mathrm{j})$ is figured as,

$$\alpha_t(p) = \sum\nolimits_{n=1}^{L} \alpha_{t-1}(n) x_{np} y_p(f_t) \quad (9)$$

$\alpha_{t-1}(n)$ - Earlier forward path probability obtained from the earlier time step
x_{np} - Transition probability obtained from earlier state h_n to present state h_p

$y_p(f_t)$ - State observation likelihood of the observation symbol f_t with the present state *p*.

Thus the traffic state with highest probability is calculated with the given current traffic variables.

Decoding: Viterbi Algorithm

Viterbi is a unique technique that makes uses of a dynamic programming trellis. Its fundamental objective is to determine the single best state sequence. The single best state sequence especially alludes to increase the possibility $P(H|O, \lambda)$ using dynamic programming.

The estimation of each cell $\delta_t(p)$ is handled by recursively taking the probable path that could lead us to this cell. Formally, every cell communicates the probability.

$$\delta_t(p) = \max_{h_{0,h_1,h_{t-1}}} [P(h_1, h_2, \ldots h_{t-1}, f_1, f_2, \ldots f_t, h_t = p|\lambda)] \quad (10)$$

The most plausible path is represented by considering the maximum sequences over all conceivable earlier state sequences $\max\limits_{h_{0,h_1,h_{t-1}}}$. Other programming techniques like Viterbi, fills every cell recursively. Consider that we have just processed the probability of being in each state at time $t - 1$, Viterbi probability is computed by finding the best predicted route in traffic data. The value $\delta_t(p)$ is processed at given state h_p at time t as

$$\delta_t(p) = \max_{n=1}^{1} \delta_{t-1}(n) x_{np} y_p(f_t) \quad (11)$$

$\delta_{t-1}(n)$ - Earlier path probability of Viterbi obtained from the earlier time step

x_{np} - Transition probability obtained from earlier state h_n to present state h_p

$y_p(f_t)$ - State observation likelihood of the observation symbol f_t given the present state p.

4 Dataset Description

The traffic data were collected from the roads of 'Aarhus' city in Denmark. The traffic data contains all 450 links of the 'Aarhus' city. It contains the traffic information over a period of nine months taken for every 5 min in 2014. It consists of more than one million records. The dataset contains many attributes among which some of the important attributes used in the traffic and route prediction model are segment id, source latitude-longitude, destination latitude-longitude, average speed, and time-stamp.

4.1 Traffic Related Variables

There are many factors that influence Traffic congestion. Encountering such various mixtures of factors, user's psychological states vary and result in various decision-making thoughts. Traffic can be slow, below average, average, above average, free. Henceforth, these states are represented as hidden state variables and they can be computed by the observed variables in the view of observation probability distribution.

Hidden State Variables: {slow, below average, average, above average, free}
Observed Variables: {speed, time, id, day}.

5 Results and Discussion

In the proposed application Fig. 3. shows the user interface for the traffic prediction of the 'Aarhus' city. The user interface consists of three input fields with a button. The first input field is for the id which denotes a source with a destination, the second input field is for the day of the week and the third input field is for the time for which the traffic state has to be calculated. On clicking the button, the application sends the input as json request to the local server through internet and the traffic state prediction for the user input is calculated using Hidden Markov Model (HMM).

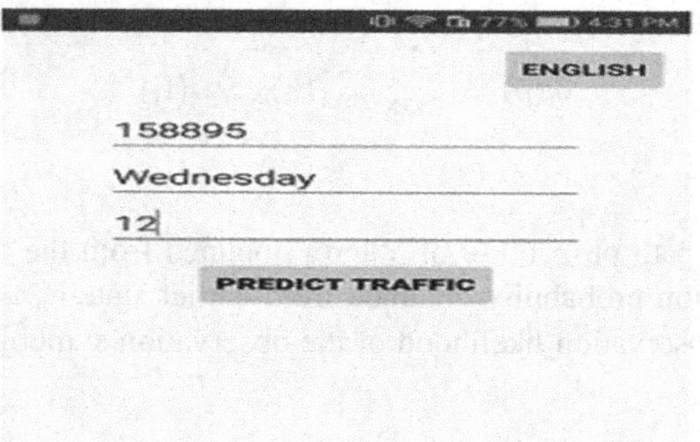

Fig. 3. Input from the user

The local server returns the geo-location for user input source and destination along with the traffic state in the form of Json response to the Android application. Based on the traffic state a line is drawn from source to destination with its geo-location.

The proposed application provides the user with two input fields and a button for finding the best path between the source and destination. The user gives the input locations from the dataset and on clicking the button, the user input is sent as Json request to the local server through internet. The best path for the user input is calculated using Viterbi algorithm based on the predicted traffic state and the output is returned back to the android application as Json response. The Json response consists of a series of geo-location which is mapped into the android application. The best path of predicted route is given in the above Fig. 4.

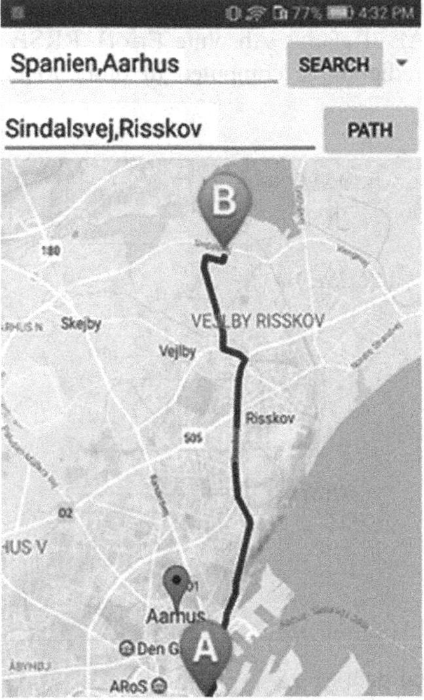

Fig. 4. Best path of predicted route

Figure 5 Portrays the information caught for average speed made from an information stream that has been gathered from a bustling street of the city of Aarhus. The sensitivity level is high (i.e. small standard deviation). This empowered it to catch a comparable shape to the actual data stream. Despite what might be expected, it couldn't execute also when there is a sensational change in the road. This can be plainly observed when one takes after the portrayal of the data at each peak points given in the graphs.

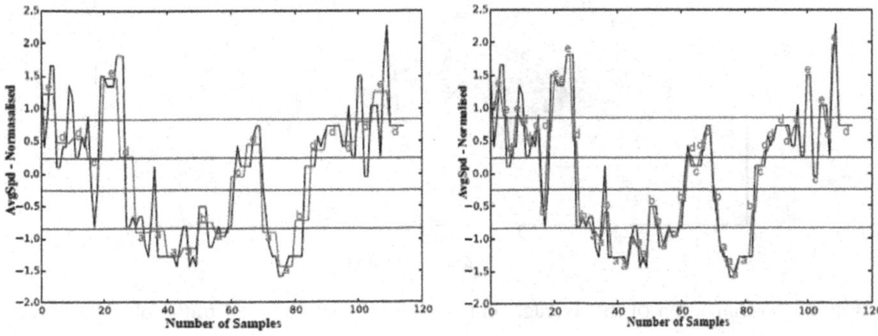

Fig. 5. Data aggregation using HMM model for average speed data of traffic stream.

To measure the traffic prediction error, MAE (Mean Absolute Error), RMSE (Root Mean Square Error), RAE (Relative Absolute Error), RRSE (Root Relative Squared Error) is used. Error prediction is computed in order to enhance the performance measure.

$$MAE = \frac{1}{N}\sum_{i=1}^{N} |f_i - y_i| \tag{12}$$

$$RMSE = \sqrt{\frac{1}{N}\sum_{i=1}^{N} (f_i - y_i)^2} \tag{13}$$

$$RAE = \frac{\sum_{i=1}^{N} |f_i - y_i|}{\sum_{i=1}^{N} |y - y_i|} \tag{14}$$

$$RRSE = \sqrt{\frac{\sum_{i=1}^{N} (f_i - y_i)^2}{\sum_{i=1}^{N} (y - y_i)^2}} \tag{15}$$

Where,
f_i = Real data
y_i = Predicted data
y = Mean value of real data
N = Number of data calculated.

Figure 6 Illustrates the graphical portrayal of the mean (i.e. x-axis) and standard deviation (i.e. y-axis) of the unprocessed average speed traffic data for 450 links.

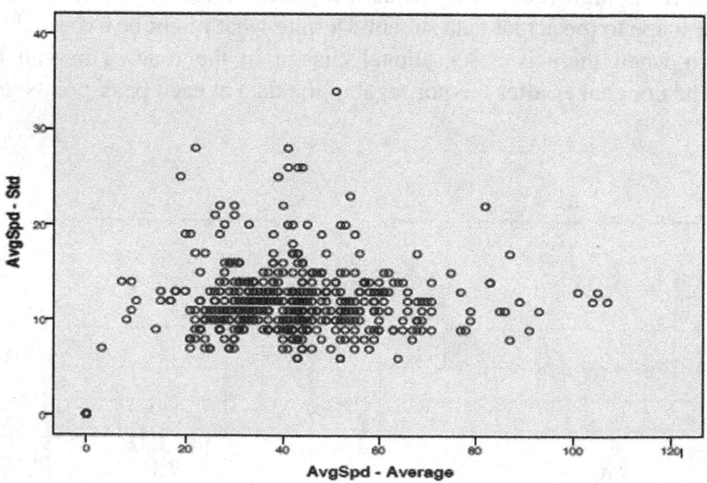

Fig. 6. Visualization of the average and standard deviation of all traffic observations.

6 Conclusion

An effective route prediction has been implemented which helps the drivers to get on time to the destination without being trapped in the traffic. The prediction of the traffic state is based on Hidden Markov Model which performs better and robust than the existing models. This provenance can be utilized to quantify the unwavering quality of the data. With this unwavering quality outcomes, the application designer or the client can foresee the best route. The best route to the destination is implemented in the system using Viterbi algorithm based on the Traffic state prediction. Future work can be implemented in the cloud which extends the user to access the system. If the size of the data increases to two or more cities, the response time of the application becomes slow. So this system with the spark framework technology for processing can highly improvise the response time of the system.

References

1. Yuan, C., Li, D., Xi, Y.: Short term urban traffic mode prediction based on VOMM. In: Chinese Control and Decision Conference, CCDC, pp. 4421–4426. IEEE (2016)
2. Necula, E.: Dynamic traffic flow prediction based on GPS Data. In: 26th International Conference on Tools with Artificial Intelligence, ICTAI, pp. 922–929. IEEE (2014)
3. Koesdwiady, A., Soua, R., Karray, F.: Improving traffic flow prediction with weather information in connected cars: a deep learning approach. IEEE Trans. Veh. Technol. **65**(12), 9508–9517 (2016)
4. Jiang, B., Fei, Y.: Traffic and vehicle speed prediction with neural network and hidden Markov model in vehicular networks. In: Intelligent Vehicles Symposium (IV), pp. 1082–1087. IEEE (2015)
5. Halawa, K., Bazan, M., Ciskowski, P., Janiczek, T., Kozaczewski, P., Rusiecki, A.: Road traffic predictions across major city intersections using multilayer perceptrons and data from multiple intersections located in various places. IET Intell. Transp. Syst. **10**(7), 469–475 (2016)
6. Gulaçar, H., Yaslan, Y., Oktuğ, S.F.: Short term traffic speed prediction using different feature sets and sensor clusters. In: Network Operations and Management Symposium, NOMS, pp. 1265–1268. IEEE/IFIP (2016)
7. Comert, G., Bezuglov, A., Cetin, M.: Adaptive traffic parameter prediction: effect of number of states and transferability of models. Transp. Res. Part C: Emerg. Technol. **72**, 202–224 (2016)
8. Faro, A., Giordano, D.: Algorithms to find shortest and alternative paths in free flow and congested traffic regimes. Transp. Res. Part C: Emerg. Technol. **73**, 1–29 (2016)
9. City Pulse Dataset of the City Aarhus in Denmark. http://iot.ee.surrey.ac.uk:8080/datasets.html#traffic

Application of Grey Wolf Optimizer for Optimization of Fractional Order Controllers for a Non-monotonic Phase System

Santosh Kumar Verma(✉) and Shyam Krishna Nagar(✉)

Department of Electrical Engineering, Indian Institute of Technology (BHU), Varanasi 221005, U.P., India
{santosh.rs.eee13,sknagar.eee}@iitbhu.ac.in

Abstract. In this paper, an optimized fractional order proportional-integral (FOPI), proportional-derivative (FOPD) and proportional-integral-derivative (FOPID) controllers are proposed for controlling the non-monotonic phase DC-buck regulator system. The parameters of controllers are optimized using a new meta-heuristic technique known as Grey Wolf Optimizer (GWO). Integral time absolute error (ITAE) has been taken as the fitness function for optimizing the parameters of the controller. Output response shows that the FOPI controller provides faster closed-loop performance and enhances the robustness of the system. Moreover, the FOPI controller also preserves the monotonic phase behavior of the system within the desired bandwidth. The results have validated by comparing the time domain as well as frequency domain characteristics of the system with another technique in the literature.

Keywords: Fractional order controller · Non-monotonic phase system
DC-buck regulator · Grey Wolf Optimizer · Integral time absolute error (ITAE)
Nelder's Mead Optimizer

1 Introduction

Fractional calculus was first introduced by the mathematicians in the middle of the ninetieth century [1]. Past decade is a witness of enhancement in research work related to fractional calculus and its applications to control theory. Improving or optimizing performance is the main task from an engineering point of view. Having two an extra degree of freedom, the fractional order controller successfully enhances the performance of any system. The fractional order PID controller ($PI^{\lambda}D^{\mu}$) has fractional power in its integral and derivative terms, which increases the complexity of the controller but make it more dominant than the conventional PID controllers [2–6]. It is also shown in [5] that the two additional tuning knobs present in FOPID controller are very helpful to maintain a balance between time-domain specifications of the system. The fractional order PID controller has already been used in many control application in the literature [4, 7–11]. Toolbars (like CRONE, NINTEGER and FOMCON, etc.) are also present in MATLAB for working with fractional order system and fractional controller design [12, 13]. Moreover, many optimization techniques have been installed in the toolboxes

P. Bhattacharyya et al. (Eds.): NGCT 2017, CCIS 827, pp. 334–348, 2018.
https://doi.org/10.1007/978-981-10-8657-1_26

for designing optimum controller. For example, Nelder's-Mead optimization (NMO) algorithm, Interior-point method, Sequential quadratic programming (SQP), and Active set based method are present in FOMCON toolbox for finding the best result of FOPID controller.

In classical feedback control design, the frequency response satisfaction of a continuous-time linear time-invariant (LTI) system is done by applying a negative feedback control system. In addition to this, the system having a zero in left half-plane situated next to the dominant-poles (i.e., minimum-phase system) shows non-monotonic phase actions within the bandwidth [14]. As we know that a closed loop system to be stable, both gain margin and phase margin must be positive. Also, the phase margin of a closed-loop system also estimates the robustness of the system and shows the variation in phase of the open-loop system while the closed-loop system remains stable [15]. DC-buck regulator taken for this work also shows the non-monotonic phase action within the bandwidth. Hence a controller is needed to overcome the non-monotonic phase action of the system and also to get the wider bandwidth, faster time response. A monotonic and non-monotonic phase analytical PID controller has been designed for DC-buck regulator system using frequency-domain specifications in [14], which offer attractive developments in comparison the classical monotonic design [16]. Further, an FOPI controller in the time domain had also be designed and implemented in [17] which gives better result in compared with the previous techniques discussed. Here the parameters of FOPI controller have been optimized using Nelder's-Mead (NM-FOPI) optimization technique.

In this brief, an optimized FOPI controller is presented. The FOPI parameters $\left(K_p\, and\, K_i\right)$ are firstly chosen by conventional Ziegler–Nichols (ZN) technique and then optimized using GWO. The key inspiration for using this particular algorithm is the performance of the algorithm shown in previous research articles [11, 18–21]. The fractional order terms of the controller are approximated using Oustaloup's approximation algorithm inside $\omega \in (10^{+3} - 10^{+8})\,\text{rad/s}$ [22, 23]. This range of frequency is selected according to the operational range of the DC-buck regulator system. This controller preserves the monotonic phase between the required bandwidth and improves the time domain as well as frequency domain performance of the system.

Rest of this paper has been arranged as follows: In Sect. 2 introduction of fractional calculus and the fractional controller has been given. Section 3 presents circuit diagram and non- monotonically decreasing phase behavior of DC-buck regulator system. Section 4 shows the simulation results and comparative study of FOPI and techniques present in the literature. Finally, the conclusion followed by the references.

2 Introduction of Fractional Calculus and Fractional Controller

History of fractional calculus is more than 300 years old. It was first introduced by two scientists Leibniz and L'Hôpital in terms of the half-order derivative in 1695 [1]. They generalized the representation of differentiation and integration as ${}_{\alpha}D_t^r$ where α and t are the limits of the operation.

2.1 The Definition of Integro-Differential Operator

The definition of integro-differential operator in the continuous domain is given as:

$$_{\alpha}D_t^r = \begin{cases} d^r/dt^r & \mathbb{R}(r) > 0 \\ 1 & \mathbb{R}(r) = 0 \\ \int_{\alpha}^{t} (dt)^r & \mathbb{R}(r) < 0 \end{cases} \tag{1}$$

where r is the order of integration or differentiation, the order r can be both real and complex number see in Chen et al. (2004). The differ-integral for fractional order systems are given by Grunwald-Letnikov (GL) and Riemann-Liouville (RL) as discussed in [5, 15].

- Grunwald-Letnikov (GL) definition:

$$_{\alpha}D_t^r f(t) = \lim_{h \to 0} h^{-r} \sum_{j=0}^{\left[\frac{t-\alpha}{h}\right]} (-1)^j \binom{r}{j} f(t - jh), \tag{2}$$

where [.] means the integer part.

- Riemann-Liouville (RL) definition:

$$_{\alpha}D_t^r f(t) = \frac{1}{\Gamma(n-r)} \frac{d^n}{dt^n} \int_{\alpha}^{t} \frac{f(\tau)}{(t-\tau)^{r-n+1}} d\tau, \tag{3}$$

where $(n - 1 < r < n)$ and $\Gamma(.)$ is the *Gamma* function.

As we know, the Laplace transform technique is generally used for solving the engineering problems. The Laplace transform procedure for RL fractional derivative (3) is given in [24]:

$$\int_{0}^{\infty} e^{-st} {}_0D_t^r f(t) dt = s^r F(s) - \sum_{k=0}^{n-1} s^k {}_0D_t^{r-k-1} f(t)|_{t=0} \tag{4}$$

The properties of non-integer order calculus motivate the researchers for designing and implementation of fractional order controllers for various systems [17].

2.2 Fractional Order PID Controller

It is the universal form of conventional PID controller and represented as $PI^{\lambda}D^{\mu}$ [6]. The transfer function of the Fractional PID controller can be written as:

$$C_{FOPID} = K_P + \frac{K_I}{s^{\lambda}} + K_D s^{\mu} \quad (\lambda, \mu > 0) \tag{5}$$

where for λ and μ are non-integer order of integral and derivative action respectively. Each classical controller can be realized with a different set of values of λ and μ in FOPID controller which is shown below.

$$\begin{cases} \lambda = 1, \mu = 1; & PID\,controller; & C = K_P + \frac{K_I}{s} + K_D s \\ \lambda = 1, \mu = 0; & PI\,controller; & C = K_P + \frac{K_I}{s} \\ \lambda = 0, \mu = 1; & PD\,controller; & C = K_P + K_D s \end{cases} \tag{6}$$

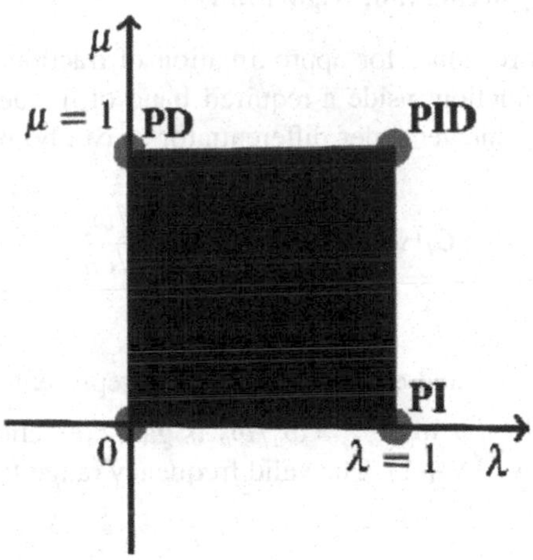

Fig. 1. The plane of FOPID controller

This can also be realized in a two-dimensional plan as given below in Fig. 1.

As it is mentioned earlier, parameters of the FOPI controller $(K_P, K_I\,and\,\lambda)$ are optimized by GWO algorithm. It is a new meta-heuristic algorithm based on Grey wolves of the Canidae family [25]. The interesting thing about the grey wolves is that they share the social hierarchy which claimed by the dominating behavior of the wolf. The apex of the hierarchy is the most dominating level, and the boss of this level is known as alpha (α). The next stage (i.e., Second hierarchy level) is known as beta (β), which assists α in the hunting action. The third level which is denoted as delta (δ), perform as a sub-ordinate. Remaining wolves of the hierarchy are the camp followers and denoted as omega (ω) and have been kept in the bottom most level as shown in Fig. 2. The detail mathematical modeling of hunting process of wolves has been shown in [26–29].

Fractional terms of the FOPI controller is approximated to integer order transfer function. Various approximation techniques have also been developed in the literature [17, 30]. The most proficient Oustaloup's approximation algorithm has been used for this work.

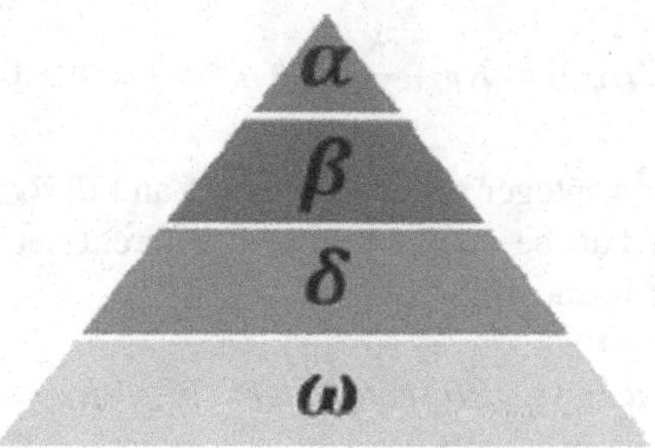

Fig. 2. Hierarchy level of grey wolves

2.3 Oustaloup's Approximation Algorithm

This is a well-known procedure for approximation of fractional power terms into an integer order transfer function inside a required band of frequency [31]. The approximated version of a non-integer order differentiator s^{α} can be written as:

$$G_I(s) = (C_0)^{\alpha} \prod_{k=-N}^{N} \frac{1 + s/\omega'_k}{1 + s/\omega_k} \tag{7}$$

where $\omega'_k = \omega_b \left(\frac{\omega_b}{\omega_u}\right)^{\frac{k+N+\frac{1}{2}+\frac{\alpha}{2}}{2N+1}}$ and $\omega_k = \omega_b \left(\frac{\omega_b}{\omega_u}\right)^{\frac{k+N+\frac{1}{2}-\frac{\alpha}{2}}{2N+1}}$ represents the zeros and poles of rank k respectively and $C_0 = \omega_b/\omega_u = \omega_u/\omega_h$ is gain correction factor. Total sum of zeros or poles is given as $(2N+1)$. The valid frequency range for this approximation is $[\omega_b; \omega_h]$.

3 DC-Buck Regulator System

The DC-buck regulator is the frequently used dc-dc converter topology. It also has vast application area like in microprocessor voltage regulator applications and power management [14]. The DC-buck regulators are a smaller in size and more efficiency compared to the linear regulators. A simplest dc-dc converter circuit i.e. the DC-buck regulator circuit has been chosen for this work.

A DC-buck regulator circuit is a combination of a power stage (i.e., an LC low-pass filter) and a pulse-width modulation (PWM)-based controller [1, 17]. The schematic circuit diagram of the DC-buck converter with voltage controller is shown below in Fig. 3.

The transfer function of DC-buck regulator system can be calculated as the ratio of Laplace transform of the output (regulated voltage) to the Laplace transform of the input (PWM modulator input voltage) and given as:

$$G = \frac{V_{in}(1 + sR_C C)}{V_{OSC}LCs^2 + s(R_C C + \frac{L}{R}) + 1} \tag{8}$$

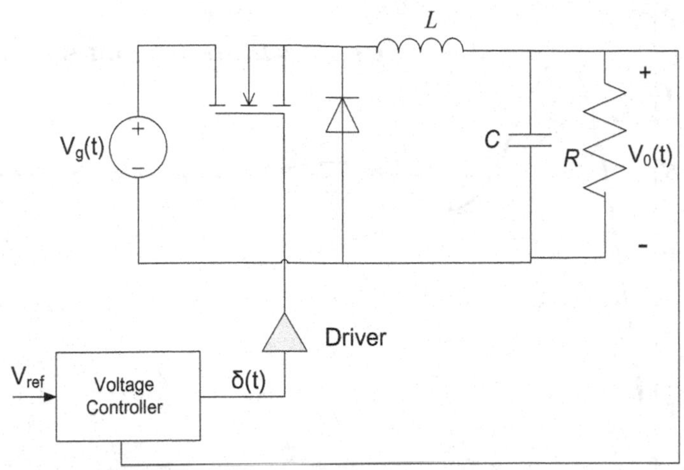

Fig. 3. The circuit diagram of DC-buck converter with a voltage controller.

where C, L, and R represents the output capacitance, output Inductance, and load resistance respectively. R_C is the intrinsic resistance of output capacitor, V_{in} represents the input voltage of power stage and V_{OSC} represents the reference voltage of PWM oscillator. In a particular application of DC-buck regulator taken in [14] with $R_C = 40\,\mathrm{m}\Omega$, the transfer function is given as:

$$G = \frac{4(1 + 1.2 \times 10^{-5}s)}{3 \times 10^{-9}s^2 + 3.6 \times 10^{-5}s + 1} \tag{9}$$

The performance of DC-buck regulator system has been discussed in the next subsection.

4 Simulation Results

4.1 Analysis of DC-Buck Regulator System

The frequency response of the DC-buck regulator is shown in Fig. 4, which clearly shows the non-monotonic phase action of gain and phase both. The closed-loop step response without any controller is also shown in Fig. 5, which shows that the system is under-damped and settled at 0.8 only i.e., the closed-loop system without any controller show at study-error of 0.2. Hence the both the frequency response and step response both encourage use to design a controller for better performance of the system. Here, an optimum FOPI controller designed for this purpose has been discussed in the next subsection.

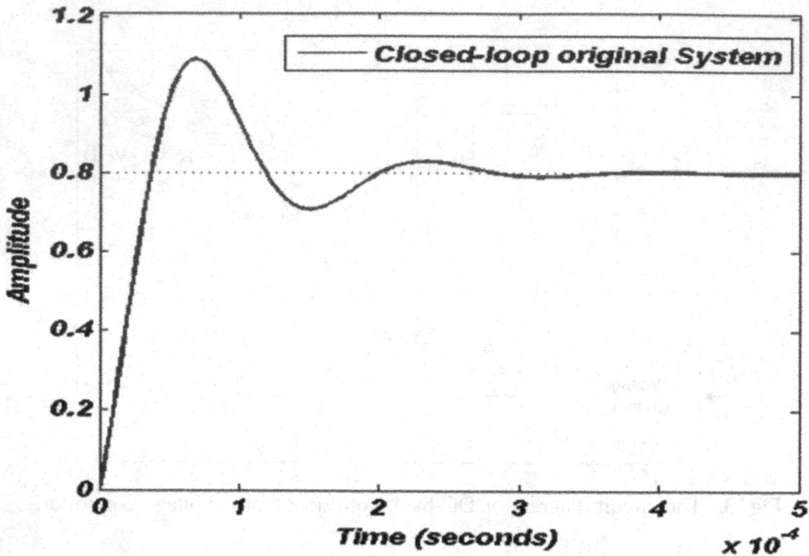

Fig. 4. Step response of closed-loop DC-buck regulator without a controller.

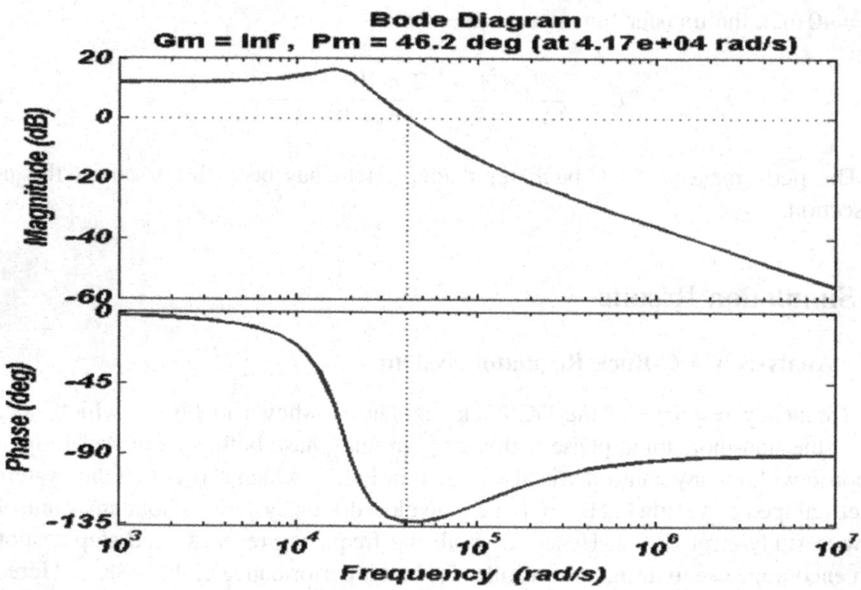

Fig. 5. Bode plot of DC-buck regulator system without a controller.

4.2 Design of Proposed Controllers for DC-Buck Regulator System

In this paper, optimum FOPI, FOPD, and FOPID controllers have been designed to enhance both the time-domain as well as the frequency domain performance of the DC-buck regulator. Values of K_P, K_I, K_D, λ and μ are corresponding to the minimum values of fitness function in GWO algorithm is considered as the best parameters values of the particular controller. The performance of the DC-buck regulator system with all three controllers has been estimated and compared to find the best controller for the system. Fitness function taken for this optimization is discussed in the next subsection.

4.3 Defining the Fitness Function

The performance criterion considered for optimization of the controller parameters is ITSE and defined as:

$$J_{ITSE} = \int_{0}^{\infty} t.e^2(t)dt \tag{10}$$

where e and t are the error and time period respectively.

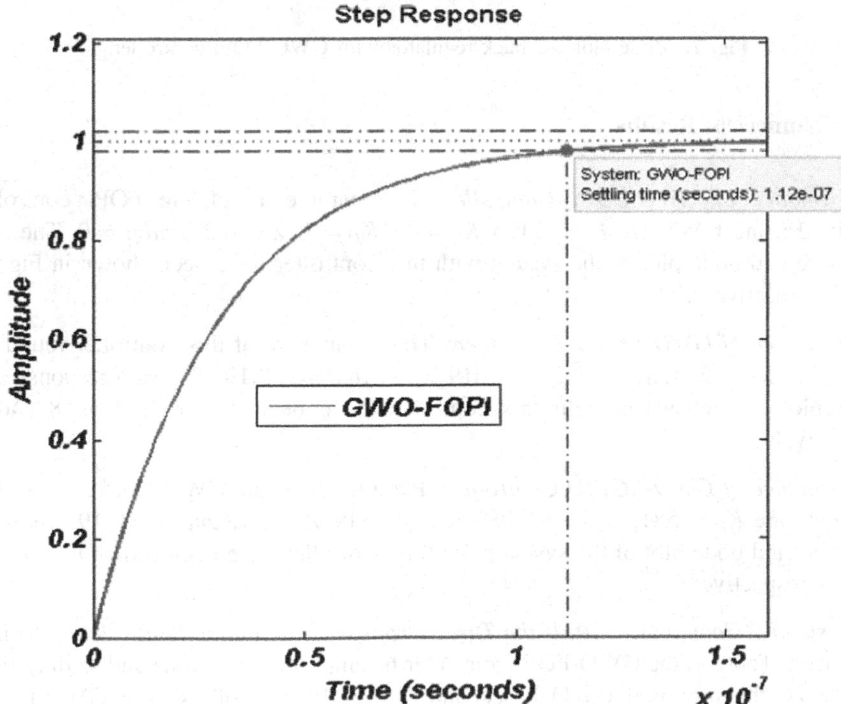

Fig. 6. Step response of closed-loop DC-buck regulator with GWO-FOPI controller.

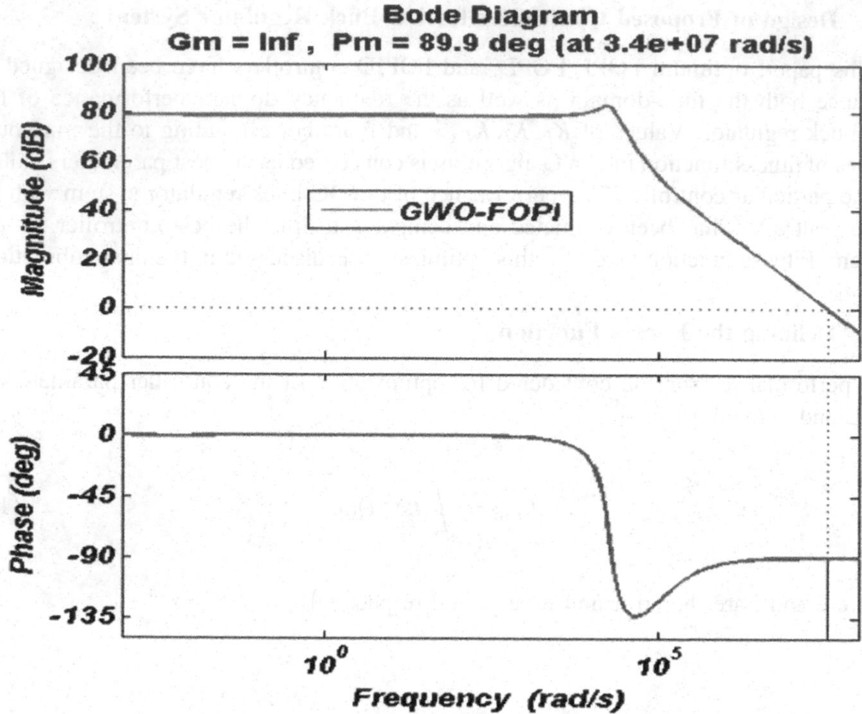

Fig. 7. Bode plot DC-buck regulator with GWO-FOPI controller.

4.4 Numerical Results

Performance of GWO-FOPI Controller: The parameters of the FOPI controller obtained using GWO are $K_P = 2125, K_I = 25, K_D = 0, \lambda = 0.24\, and\, \mu = 0$. The step response and bode plot of the system with this controller have been shown in Figs. 6 and 7 respectively.

Performance of GWO-FOPD Controller: The parameters of this controller found by GWO are $K_P = 341, K_I = 0, K_D = 1.619, \lambda = 0\, and\, \mu = 0.19$. The step response and bode plot of the system with this controller have been shown in Figs. 8 and 9 respectively.

Performance of GWO-FOPID Controller: Parameters of the GWO-FOPID controller achieved are $K_P = 581.35, K_I = 0.089, K_D = 2.619, \lambda = 0.78\, and\, \mu = 0.19$. The step response and bode plot of the system with this controller have been shown in Figs. 10 and 11 respectively.

Analysis and Comparison of All the Three Proposed Fractional Controllers: As it is clear from Table 1, the GWO-FOPI controller has minimum rise-time and settling-time among all the proposed GWO based and NM-FOPI controllers. The GWO-FOPD shows the slowest performance among all. Moreover, in the frequency domain, the

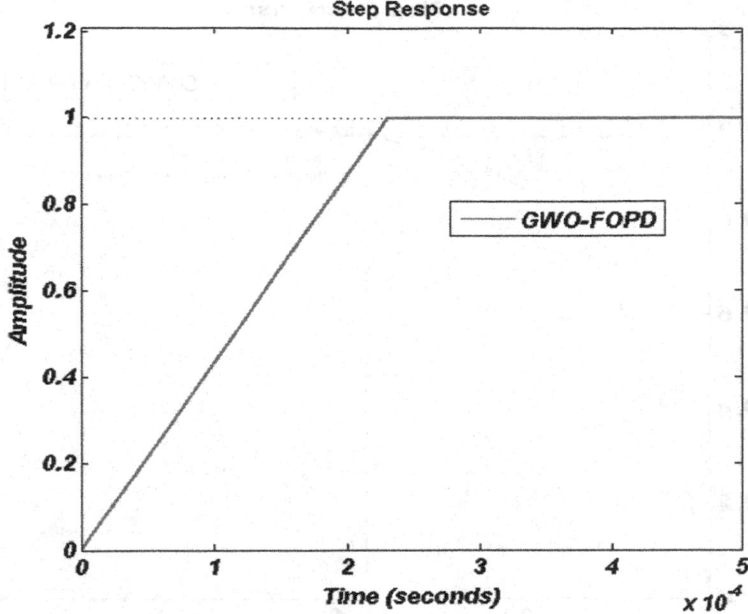

Fig. 8. Step response of closed-loop DC-buck regulator with GWO-FOPD controller.

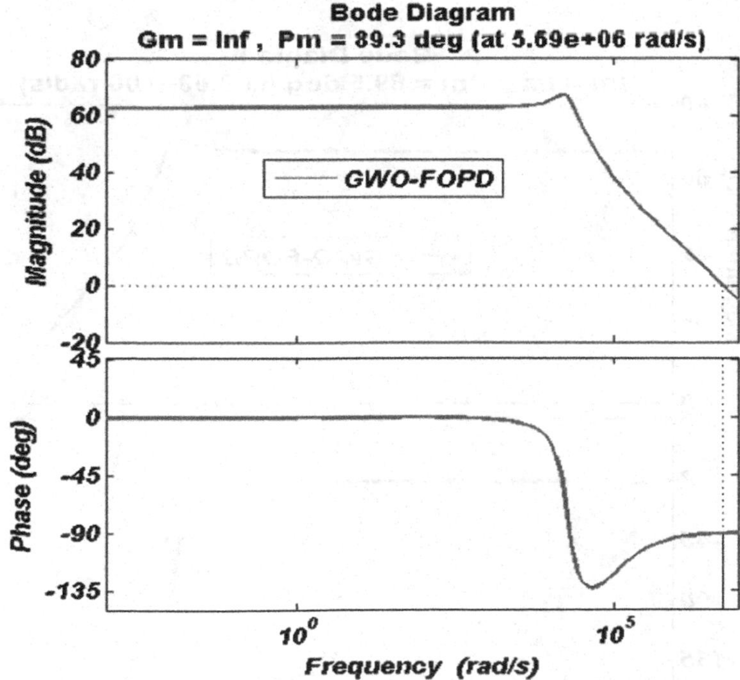

Fig. 9. Bode plot DC-buck regulator with GWO-FOPD controller.

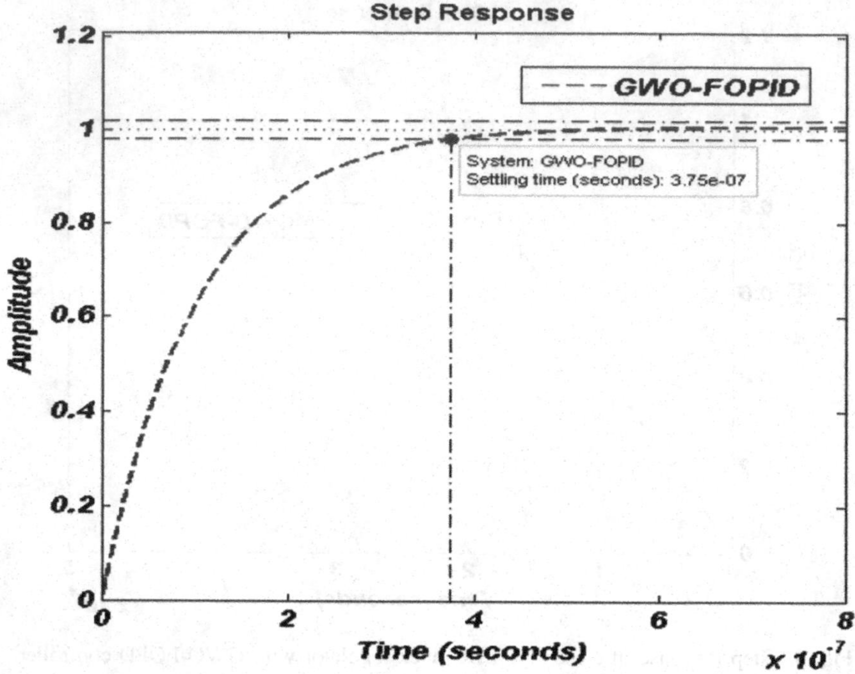

Fig. 10. Step response of closed-loop DC-buck regulator with GWO-FOPID controller.

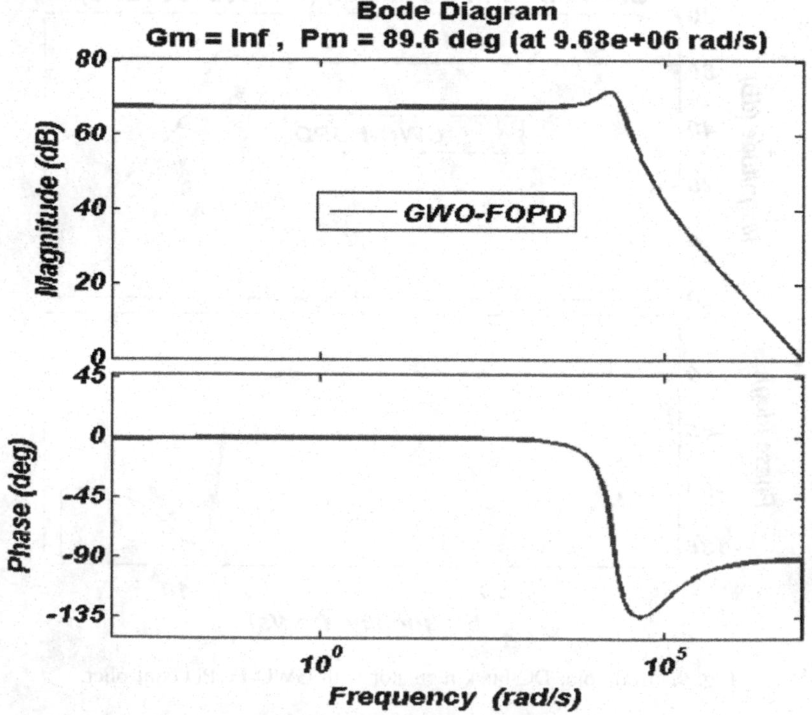

Fig. 11. Bode plot DC-buck regulator with GWO-FOPID controller.

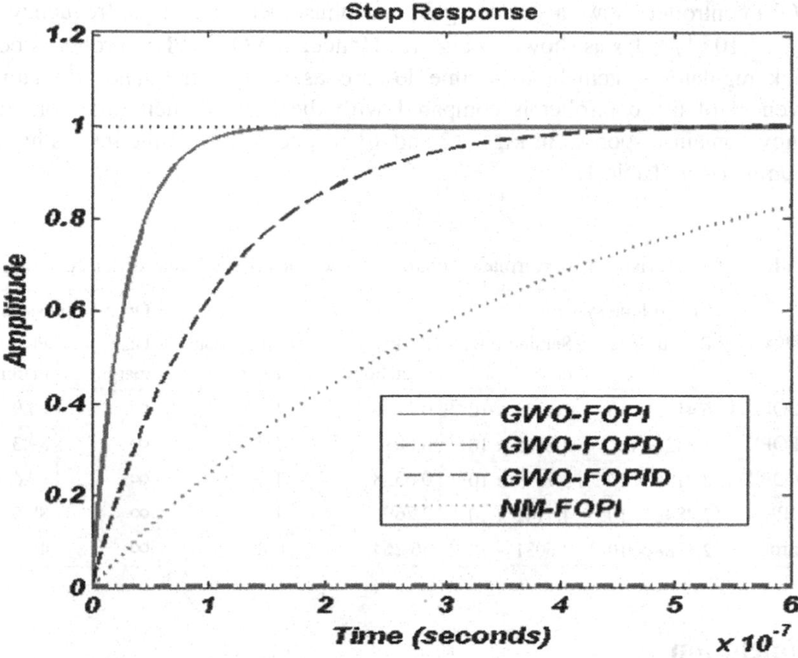

Fig. 12. Step response comparison of DC-buck regulator with each of the proposed controller and NM-FOPI controller

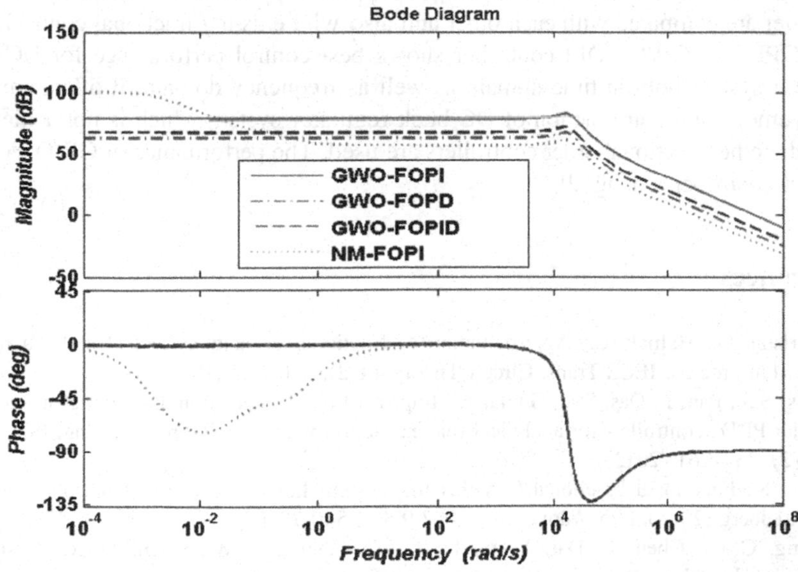

Fig. 13. Bode plots Comparison of the DC-buck regulator with each of the proposed controller and NM-FOPI controller.

NM-FOPI controller shows a variable gain and phase behavior in the frequency range of $(10^{-4} - 10^{+1})$ rad/s as shown in Fig. 13. Hence, GWO-FOPI controller is best for DC-buck regulator system both in time-domain as well as frequency domain. The effectiveness of the controller is compared with the help of their time-domain and frequency domain responses in Figs. 12 and 13 respectively. All the results have also been compared in Table 1.

Table 1. Comparison of performance characteristics of all fractional order controllers

Control techniques	Closed-loop system				Open-loop system	
	Rise time (s)	Settling time (s)	Peak overshoot (%)	Study-state value	Gain margin	Phase margin
GWO-FOPI	6.4142×10^{-8}	1.1221×10^{-7}	0.1136	1	∞	89.9
GWO-FOPD	1.842×10^{-4}	2.2565×10^{-4}	0.0012	1	∞	89.3
GWO-FOPID	2.2196×10^{-7}	3.7459×10^{-7}	0.6338	1	∞	89.6
NM-FOPI	7.2848×10^{-7}	4.4142×10^{-6}	2.2699	1	∞	88.5
No controller	2.8388×10^{-5}	2.6031×10^{-4}	36.2644	0.8	∞	46.2

5 Conclusion

Optimum fractional order controllers are designed to attain the desired output response of the DC-buck regulator system. The controller's parameters are optimized using GWO technique. The Oustaloup's approximation algorithm is practiced for approximation of fractional order terms into integer order. The performances of all GWO based controller are compared with each other and also with existing fractional controller i.e. NM-FOPI. The GWO-FOPI controller shows best control performance for DC-buck regulator system both in time-domain as well as frequency domain. It offers enviable improvements in control action of DC-buck regulator system which is not achievable when the other fractional order controllers are used. The performance of GWO-FOPI is the best controller among all.

References

1. Carlson, G., Halijak, C.: Approximation of fractional capacitors (1/s)^(1/n) by a regular Newton process. IEEE Trans. Circuit Theory **11**(2), 210–213 (1964)
2. Das, S.S., Pan, I., Das, S.S., Gupta, A.: Improved model reduction and tuning of fractional order $PI^{\lambda}D^{\mu}$ controllers for analytical rule extraction with genetic programming. ISA Trans. **51**(2), 237–261 (2012)
3. Das, S.: Functional Fractional Calculus for System Identification and Controls. Springer, Heidelberg (2008). https://doi.org/10.1007/978-3-540-72703-3
4. Zeng, G.-Q., Chen, J., Dai, Y.-X., Li, L.-M., Zheng, C.-W., Chen, M.-R.: Design of fractional order PID controller for automatic regulator voltage system based on multi-objective extremal optimization. Neurocomputing **160**, 173–184 (2015)

5. Podlubny, I.: Fractional-order systems and PI/sup /spl lambda//D/sup /spl mu//-controllers. IEEE Trans. Automat. Contr. **44**(1), 208–214 (1999)
6. Podlubny, I.: Fractional Differential Equations: An Introduction to Fractional Derivatives, Fractional Differential Equations, to Methods of Their Solution and Some of Their Applications. Academic Press, Cambridge (1999)
7. Ramezanian, H., Balochian, S., Zare, A.: Design of optimal fractional-order PID controllers using particle swarm optimization algorithm for automatic voltage regulator (AVR) system. J. Control. Autom. Electr. Syst. **24**(5), 601–611 (2013)
8. Xue, D., Zhao, C., Chen, Y.: Fractional order PID control of a DC-motor with elastic shaft: a case study. In: 2006 American Control Conference, July, pp. 3182–3187 (2006)
9. Verma, S.K., Yadav, S., Nagar, S.K.: Optimized fractional order PID controller for non-minimum phase system with time delay. In: 2016 International Conference on Emerging Trends in Electrical Electronics & Sustainable Energy Systems (ICETEESES), pp. 169–173 (2016)
10. Verma, S.K., Yadav, S., Nagar, S.K.: Optimal fractional order PID controller for magnetic levitation system. In: 2015 39th National Systems Conference (NSC), pp. 1–5 (2015)
11. Verma, S.K., Yadav, S., Nagar, S.K.: Controlling of an automatic voltage regulator using optimum integer and fractional order PID controller. In: 2015 IEEE Workshop on Computational Intelligence: Theories, Applications and Future Directions (WCI), pp. 1–5 (2015)
12. Valério, D., Sá da Costa, J.: Ninteger: a non-integer control toolbox for MatLab. In: Proceedings of the First IFAC Workshop on Fractional Differentiation and its Application, Bordeaux, France, pp. 208–213 (2004)
13. Tepljakov, A., Petlenkov, E., Belikov, J.: FOMCON: fractional-order modeling and control toolbox for MATLAB. In: Proceedings of the 18th International Conference on Mixed Design of Integrated Circuits and Systems (MIXDES), no. 4, pp. 684–689 (2011)
14. De Paula, C.F., Ferreira, L.H.C.: An improved analytical PID controller design for non-monotonic phase LTI systems. IEEE Trans. Control Syst. Technol. **20**(5), 1328–1333 (2012)
15. Monje, C.A., Chen, Y., Vinagre, B.M., Xue, D., Feliu, V.: Fractional-Order Systems and Controls. Springer, London (2010). https://doi.org/10.1007/978-1-84996-335-0
16. Phillips, C.L., Harbor, R.D.: Feedback Control Systems. Prentice Hall, Upper Saddle River (2000)
17. Verma, S.K., Yadav, S., Nagar, S.K.: Fractional order PI controller design for non-monotonic phase systems. IFAC-PapersOnLine **49**(1), 236–240 (2016)
18. Choudhary, S.K.: Stability and performance analysis of fractional order control systems. WSEAS Trans. Syst. Control **9**, 438–444 (2014)
19. Kilbas, A.A., Srivastava, H.M., Trujillo, J.J.: Theory and Applications of Fractional Differential Equations. Elsevier, Amsterdam (2006)
20. Verma, S.K., Yadav, S., Nagar, S.K.: Optimization of fractional order PID controller using grey wolf optimizer. J. Control. Autom. Electr. Syst. **28**(3), 314–322 (2017)
21. Yadav, S., Verma, S.K., Nagar, S.K.: Reduction and controller design for fractional order spherical tank system using GWO. In: 2016 International Conference on Emerging Trends in Electrical Electronics & Sustainable Energy Systems (ICETEESES), pp. 174–178 (2016)
22. Oustaloup, A.: Fractional order sinusoidal oscillators: optimization and their use in highly linear FM modulation. IEEE Trans. Circuits Syst. **28**(10), 1007–1009 (1981)
23. Oustaloup, A.: La commande CRONE : Commande robuste d'ordre non entier. Hermès (1991)
24. Machado, J.A.T., Azenha, A.: Fractional-order hybrid control of robot manipulators. In: Proceedings of the IEEE Conference on Robotics and Automation, pp. 602–607 (1985)

25. Mirjalili, S., Mirjalili, S.M., Lewis, A.: Grey wolf optimizer. Adv. Eng. Softw. **69**, 46–61 (2014)
26. Muro, C., Escobedo, R., Spector, L., Coppinger, R.P.: Wolf-pack (Canis lupus) hunting strategies emerge from simple rules in computational simulations. Behav. Process. **88**(3), 192–197 (2011)
27. Wong, L.I., Sulaiman, M.H., Mohamed, M.R., Hong, M.S.: Grey Wolf Optimizer for solving economic dispatch problems. In: 2014 IEEE International Conference on Power and Energy (PECon), pp. 150–154 (2014)
28. Emary, E., Zawbaa, H.M., Grosan, C., Hassenian, A.E.: Feature subset selection approach by Gray-wolf optimization. In: Abraham, A., Krömer, P., Snasel, V. (eds.) Afro-European Conference for Industrial Advancement. AISC, vol. 334, pp. 1–13. Springer, Cham (2015). https://doi.org/10.1007/978-3-319-13572-4_1
29. Saremi, S., Mirjalili, S.Z., Mirjalili, S.M.: Evolutionary population dynamics and grey wolf optimizer. Neural Comput. Appl. **26**(5), 1257–1263 (2015)
30. Verma, S.K., Nagar, S.K.: Approximation and order reduction of fractional order SISO system. In: 2016 IEEE Annual India Conference (INDICON), pp. 1–6 (2016)
31. Oustaloup, A., Melchior, P., Lanusse, P., Cois, O., Dancla, F.: The CRONE toolbox for Matlab. In: CACSD, Conference Proceedings. IEEE International Symposium on Computer-Aided Control System Design (Cat. No. 00TH8537), pp. 190–195 (2000)

Forecasting Hydrogen Fuel Requirement for Highly Populated Countries Using NARnet

Srikanta Kumar Mohapatra[1], Tripti Swarnkar[2], Sushanta Kumar Kamilla[3(✉)], and Susanta Kumar Mohapatra[4]

[1] Department of Computer Science and Engineering, ITER, Siksha 'O' Anusandhan University, Bhubaneswar 751030, Odisha, India
srikanta.2k7@gmail.com

[2] Department of Computer Application, ITER, Siksha 'O' Anusandhan University, Bhubaneswar 751030, Odisha, India
swarnkar.tripti@gmail.com

[3] Department of Physics, ITER, Siksha 'O' Anusandhan University, Bhubaneswar 751030, Odisha, India
sushantakamilla@soauniversity.ac.in

[4] Apex Resources Inc., 549 Stonegate Dr., Katy, TX 77494, USA
susantk@yahoo.com

Abstract. Petroleum is being consumed at a rapid pace all over world, but the amount of petroleum is constant in earth crust and production to consumption requirement is not up to mark. It is expected that a day may come when this world will witness the crisis of this oil. For this our paper addresses the prediction of petroleum crisis in two most populated country of the world i.e. India and China using novel Artificial Neural Network (ANN) based approach. The set of observation comprising three features like population, petroleum production and petroleum consumption are being considered to design the predictive model. Our work shows that petroleum production over consumption with respect to sharp increase of population, leads to a decisive issue in production of an alternative fuel like Hydrogen fuel. In our analysis, we used the data provided by different government sources over a period of more than 30 years and then simulated by a multistep ahead prediction methodology, i.e. nonlinear autoregressive Network (NARnet) to predict petroleum crisis in near future. The results of present study reveals that for India, the Normalized Mean Square Error (NMSE) values found for population petroleum production and consumption are 0.000046, 0.2233 and 0.0041 respectively. Similarly for China the corresponding values are 0.0011, 0.0126 and 0.0041 respectively, which validates the accuracy of the proposed model. The study forecasts that by 2050 hydrogen fuel may be a suitable replacement for petroleum, and will not only reduce pollution, but also enhance the fuel efficiency at lower cost as compared to that of petroleum.

Keywords: Artificial Neural Network (ANN)
Non Linear Auto Regressive NETwork (NARnet) · Hydrogen fuel
Petroleum production · Petroleum consumption

P. Bhattacharyya et al. (Eds.): NGCT 2017, CCIS 827, pp. 349–362, 2018.
https://doi.org/10.1007/978-981-10-8657-1_27

1 Introduction

The turning point in future is the threat of ‘oil running out’ from the planet. It is a burning issue for all of us i.e. petroleum oil a potential source of energy is being consumed by automobile and other industries in world over at a rapid pace [1]. Technologically advanced countries are exceptional consumers of oil. Globally the use of oil and its derivatives continues to increase except Organization of Petroleum Exporting Countries (OPEC) i.e. oil consumption share is high in comparison to crude oil reserves and petroleum production, which has been reported in transportation energy data book [2]. It is commonly known and also explained that in the modern world, the standard of living is closely associated with energy consumption, particularly in thickly populated countries like India and China [3]. The relationship between the dynamics of population increase and usage of automobiles has played a key factor in consumption of petroleum oil in India and China as well as in the world. According to Transportation energy data book the production of cars and trucks from 2000 to 2013 has increased remarkably. Ever increasing demand of petroleum oil, the reticence on the part of some developed countries like United States and Japan etc. to reduce energy consumption by manufacturing less numbers of vehicles from 2000 to 2015 [2]. Apart from that globally, the automobile industries are looking into the demand for transport by producing more efficient vehicles by supplying alternative fuels. These industries are concerned about both global economy as well as environment. We know that commodity prices always have an upward trend, particularly for petroleum oil production.

India and China are two of the world’s oldest civilizations and have co-existed in peace for millennia and there exists. Cultural and economic relations between these two countries date back to ancient times. Now a day’s China and India are the two countries with developing economy in the world. These two nations have analogous development policies before breaking out of their deliberate insulation from the world economy and the ushering in of market-oriented economic reforms and linearizing [4].

Oil and gas includes 57% of the commercial energy the world consumes, and their combustion accounted for roughly the same proportion of global CO_2 emissions [1]. The increasing population is also a factor of using automobile and other energy consumable related to fossil oil which affects the price of crude oil in near future [5, 6].

As a solution to the above situation or problem may be alternate fuel *i.e.* hydrogen. Lots of research are going on in this field [7, 8]. At the same time the combination of new technology and consistently rising prices in recent decades, is opening new potential for new oil supplies from shale and other low-permeability formations (‘tight oil’), like deep water and pre-salt oil deposits outside the traditional exporting countries, hydrogen fuel being one. The reason for considering hydrogen as an alternate fuel is it’s abundance in the universe [1].

Researchers are trying to develop sustainable hydrogen energy using nanotechnology [9]. Different advance applications are also used by nanotechnology to develop hydrogen fuel [10].

Predicting population and fuel oil requirement in future is a complex mechanism which deals with a number of uncertainties. Still lots of works are required to be done considering various uncertainties to forecast an accurate prediction [11, 12]. Researchers have implemented different forecasting models like RBF neural network for predicting the quantity of tourist visit [13], fuzzy logic to determine future managing water resources, flood control of reservoirs by flow [14] and fisher space within the sea [15] etc. The rapidly adopted research in various forecasting problem solutions like, road traffic management [16], stock index returns [17], population prediction [18] and price prediction of crude oil [5] etc. are solved by neural network with linear method [19]. The approach to estimate the population and amount of registered vehicles in India was reported by our group earlier [30]. The future cannot be projected with any confidence, that's why the present paper is an approach for prediction of solving petroleum crisis in highly populated country like India and China via Artificial Neural Network (ANN) model based on a Non Linear Auto Regressive NETwork (NARnet).

The complete list of comparison of different ANN model is described in Table 1.

Table 1. Different ANN, FUZZY model comparison

Approach	Implementation	Network & algorithm	Data set	Perf. measure	Resources
Fuzzy logic	Flow prediction	Fuzzification & centroid defuzzification	432 months	MSE	[14]
Hybrid neural network-fuzzy mathematical approach	Natural gas price forecasting	MLP, sigmoid transfer function	Year wise data from 1968–2008	MAPE	[20]
Neurofuzzy	Fisher space	Logistic sigmoid, LOLIMOT	Diff. data sets	LLS	[15]
ANN	Oil shale	Sigmoid, back propagation	100	MSE, NMSE	[21]
ANN	Wind speed and power prediction	MLFFN & Levenberg-Marquardt	1yr, 1 h, 24 h, 48 h	RMS	[22]
ANN	Crude oil price	Symmetrical sigmoid function, MLFFN & BP	2705 data points from 1996–2007	MSE, RMSE, MAE	[23]
ANN	Dynamic viscocity of vegetable oils	NN Fitting tool, levenberg-Marquardt back propagation	653 SAMPLES	MSE	[24]
ANN & Fuzzy	Prices prediction of crude oil	MLP, ERNN, RFNN, BP, Sigmoid	January 1, 1990 to April 30, 2005	MSE	[5]
ANN	Price development of crude oil	MLP, BP	2000	MSE	[25]
ANN	Cardiovascular autonomic dysfunction	FF, BP	2092 people	MSE	[26]

(continued)

Table 1. (*continued*)

Approach	Implementation	Network & algorithm	Data set	Perf. measure	Resources
ANN	Prediction of electrical power generated	MLP	35	MAE, MSE, RMSE	[27]
ANN & GA	Forecast crude oil	FNN, BP	Monthly, 1995–07	GA	[28]
ANN	Prediction of solar radiation for Indian stations	MLP, RBF, Levenberg- Marquard (Lm)	12 Indian stations	RMSE, MBE	[29]
ANN	Prediction of tourist quantity	RBF, GAUSSIAN	1988–2088	MSE	[13]

2 Data Sources

Important point to achieve more accuracy in final goal of neural network design is data frequency and data size to forecast. The benchmark data set for population from 1980 to 2016 are taken from United States Census Bureau for population and World[1]. Likewise benchmark data set for Oil production and consumption of India and China from 1980–2016 are taken from United States Energy Information Administration (USEIA)[2,3]. The algorithm with these relevant data as input, predict the population vs. energy scenario in India and China for training, testing and validation. The deviations between the predicted and actual values are used to calculate minimal Normalized Mean Square Error (NMSE).

3 Methodology

3.1 Prediction Using Artificial Neural Network (ANN)

Predicting is making an uncertain opinion referring to forecast often based on information from past and from current state. One can solve any the problem of prediction based upon guess by taking various degrees of information. In technical domain evaluation of predictable information is often expressed by simple equation having different parameters. However, practical purpose due to various parameters, is too

---

[1] Population of India and China. Available at: www.data.worldbank.org/country/india & www.data.worldbank.org/country/china.

[2] India Crude Oil Production and Consumption by Year, Source: United States Energy InformationAdministration. Available at: www.indexmundi.com/energy.aspx?country=in.

[3] China Crude Oil Production and Consumption by Year, Source: United States Energy Information Administration. Available at: www.indexmundi.com/energy.aspx?country=cn&product=oil&graph=production+consumption.

complicated, where some computational technique are required to solve this prediction. Basic criteria for future prediction are based upon either value or trend of a variable with minimized error such as average change. The advantage of ANN for prediction is that, it is done with various level of success by considering the concepts of biological neurons. For predicting future, the network has to train from historical data with the exception that it will be able to consider hidden and significant non-linear dependencies[4].

Comparisons of General Prediction Models

Numerous neural networks can be employed for prediction of future value by input of data from the past. From these Chaotic prediction models, Threshold Autoregressive model (TAR), locally linear prediction etc. are based on linearly output, whereas, Auto-Regressive Moving-Average with Exogenous Input (ARMA), Gaussian Kernel correlation integral, Nonlinear input & output etc. are nonlinearly based prediction models. In the above two cases the prediction is only single step prediction that means if the past data set is a function f(x) = t(1), t(2),…..t(n) then prediction value after successful training, testing and validation is t(n + 1). Where t(1), t(2),…..t(n) are the data from past year while t(n + 1) is the prediction.

Chaotic model is easy to use different combinations of the constants when we do not know which combinations are really appropriate. But it lacks the concept of ANN approach [31].

TAR (Threshold Autoregressive model) [32, 33] is best in dynamic systems but it is not a neural approach. It is conventional linear modelling approach.

$$y_t = \begin{cases} \mu_1 + \phi_1 y_{t-1} + u_{1t} \, if \, s_{t-k} < r \\ \mu_2 + \phi_2 y_{t-1} + u_{2t} \, if \, s_{t-k} < r \end{cases} \tag{1}$$

- Where s_{t-k} is the state determining variable.
- The integer k determines with how many lags does the state-determining variable influences the regime in time t.

Locally linear prediction accuracy for linear system < 5%, but it approximate before prediction and one step prediction[5]. Similarly ARMA model has a unique advantage like most of the time noise shows drifting characteristics and also offset free response. It also tracks both varying and constant future set points. But it is a nonlinear approach and in most of the cases Noise are assumed to be an identically distributed random sequence. It also exerts an excessive control effort and can't be applied to Non-Minimum phased system for a "Minimum variance control"[6].

[4] Obitko, M.: Prediction using Neural networks (1999). http://www.obitko.com/tutorials/neural-network-prediction.

[5] http://www.mpipks-dresden.mpg.de/~tisean/TISEAN_2.1/docs/chaospaper/node20.html.

[6] https://en.wikipedia.org/wiki/Autoregressive%E2%80%93moving-average_model.

$$Y(t) = \varepsilon(t) + \sum_{i=1}^{p} a_i Y_{t-i} + \sum_{i=1}^{Q} b_i \varepsilon_{t-i} \tag{2}$$

Where (p, q), p is autoregressive terms and q moving average terms. Where a_i and b_i are parameters, $Y(t)$ is past data outputs and ε is error.

Gaussian kernel correlation integral method is best in Translation-invariant but it is a non-linear approach[7].

Nonlinear input-output is an efficient computational procedure but predict for only one step [34]. Radial Basic Function (RBF) network have the disadvantage of requiring good coverage of the input space by radial basis functions. RBF centers are determined with reference to the distribution of the input data, but without reference to the prediction task. As a result, representational resources may be wasted on areas of the input space that are irrelevant to the learning task [35].

Most of the prediction models are either linear models or predicts only one step ahead. But our model is based upon both linear and non-linear approach along with multistep ahead prediction capability. Our program shows that if the past data set f (x) = t(1), t(2),…..t(n) then prediction value after successful training, testing and validation is t(n + x) where x is any future interval prediction.

3.2 Model Execution

The NARnet model simulates the current data i.e. known values and dynamically simulates all these for the multistep ahead prediction. By this dynamic method, simulating the present data we can predict any number of future data as desired.

3.3 Predictive Model Flow Control Diagram

The whole processes which are responsible for training the network to get the optimized result can be summarized in 4 steps:

Step a: Selection of data from the larger databases and different data sources.
Step b: Pre-processes the data as required, *i.e.* by keeping the necessary data for the entire calculation from the pool of the collected data.
Step c: Data transformation from the generalized database to Neural network model.
Step d: Selection of neural network and training involving following steps.

(i) inputs are feed forward first
(ii) errors are simulated by back propagation network
(iii) weights are adjusted for future predictions.

[7] www.mpipks-dresden.mpg.de/~tisean/TISEAN_2.1/docs/chaospaper/node32.html.

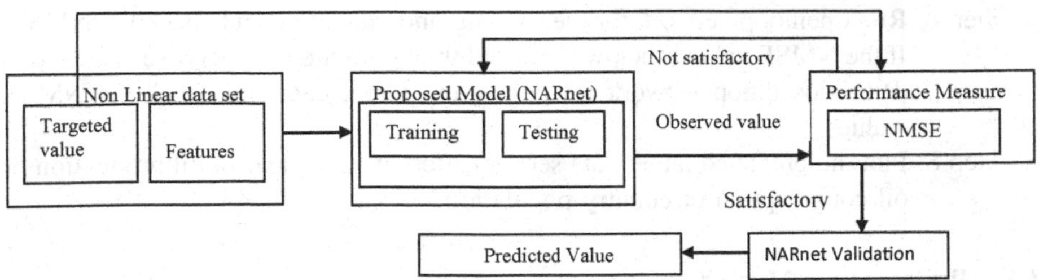

Fig. 1. Block diagram of execution of proposed model

3.4 Predictive Model Neural Diagram and Explanation

Predictive model initiated by loading the trained data, tapped delay lines with two delay then input and output delays are simulated. The predictive model is shown in Fig. 2(a) and (b).

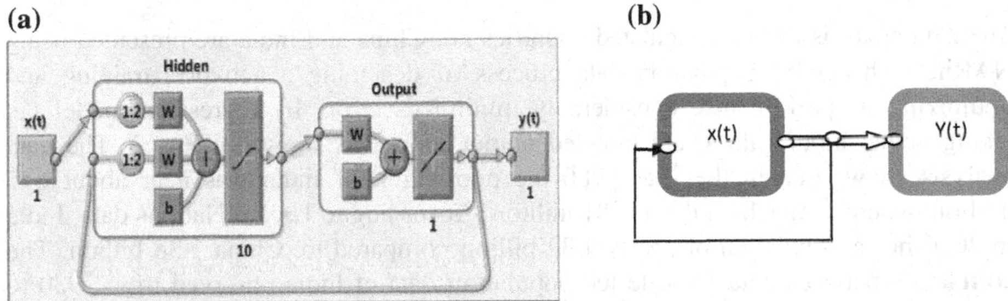

Fig. 2. (a) NARnet model, (b) NARnet input to target

3.5 Principle

NARnet is a dynamic network. It uses two parallel looping architecture functions i.e. open loop and closed loop. Open loop function is used to simulate the training data including validation and testing. The total work-flow network is actually processed by the open loop function and when it is completed, it transfers the link to closed loop for the multistep-ahead prediction. It completely executes from input to prediction by performing open-loop form and closed loop form. Thus the proposed model can be summarised in following 8 steps:

Step 1: Inputs the data set "Y".
Step 2: Set the different parameters viz., InputDelays and number of node in hidden layer for nonlinear autoregressive network.
Step 3: Run the network to simulate the input data to required format.
Step 4: Set target data set as "T".
Step 5: Convert the cell data obtained in step 3 to matrix form and set random number generator to default value.

Step 6: Run openloop network for the training and validation and check the NMSE. If the NMSE value is below threshold then goto Step 2 otherwise else Step 7.
Step 7: Run closedloop network for generating target data and check the NMSE value.
Step 8: Plot the predicted target data set for different years against oil production or oil consumption or country population.

3.6 Performance Measure

To verify the performance of the testing data of the NARnet, it is compared with the actual different set of data. The performance with minimum error confirms the implication of the trained network. The model is targeted to calculate Normalized Mean Square Error [36]. Irrespective of measurement of bias, absolute values *i.e.* the deviations are summed instead of differences. Due to which NMSE is very useful for error calculation in comparison with other models.

4 Outcome Data Analysis

The data analysis of most populated countries i.e. China and India are presented using NARnet. The entire population data process of designing a network, training and optimizing its performance considerably minimizes errors by regression model *i.e.* taking actual input values and targeted output values as shown in Fig. 3. The data analysis shows that in the year 1980 the population of India was near about 697 million, where as in China it was 981 million. According to United Nations data, India in 2016 has a population of nearly 1.32 billion compared to, China 1.38 billion. The correlation between actual and tested population data of India observed from 1980 to 2016 is very high both in training and targeted phase. Moreover, prediction errors for population of India and China are found to be 0.000046 and 0.0011 respectively in both training and test phase from 1980–2016. Apart from that the error trends to zero in test phase. As per our population prediction data using proposed NARnet model, by the year 2025, India's population will exceed that of China's. According to the prediction results, India will have nearly 1.715 billion people by 2045. The population of China, meanwhile, is expected towards stable state until the 2045 s may be because of its population growth control strategies by Govt. The population growth has a major impact on both countries' economy, as there is a linkage between disruption to the economy and petroleum oil limits. Population of China in the year 1980 was very high as compared to India, but current scenario shows the similar growth rate. That means population growth rate of India is much more than that of China. India has modernized its economic policy due to which it is growing faster than that of China. Actually there are different kinds of limits, all leading toward the rising cost of commodity production, which has been caused basically due to very high population relative to resources. Over time, the cost of commodity production tends to rise for several reasons (1) population tends to grow over time; this gives rise to high-priced techniques to fulfil this desalination. (2) Techniques fail to extract the less expensive fuel oil which affects increase in the cost of oil extraction. (3) Least polluting commodity sources are used to substitute for renewable fossil fuels, but these are more expensive. This leads to the higher cost, which has been discussed by Tverberg [37].

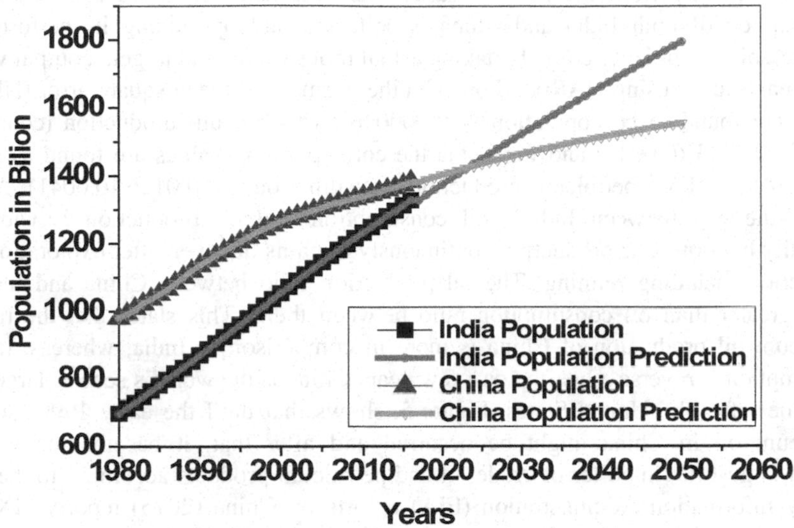

Fig. 3. Prediction of change in population of India and China with increasing year

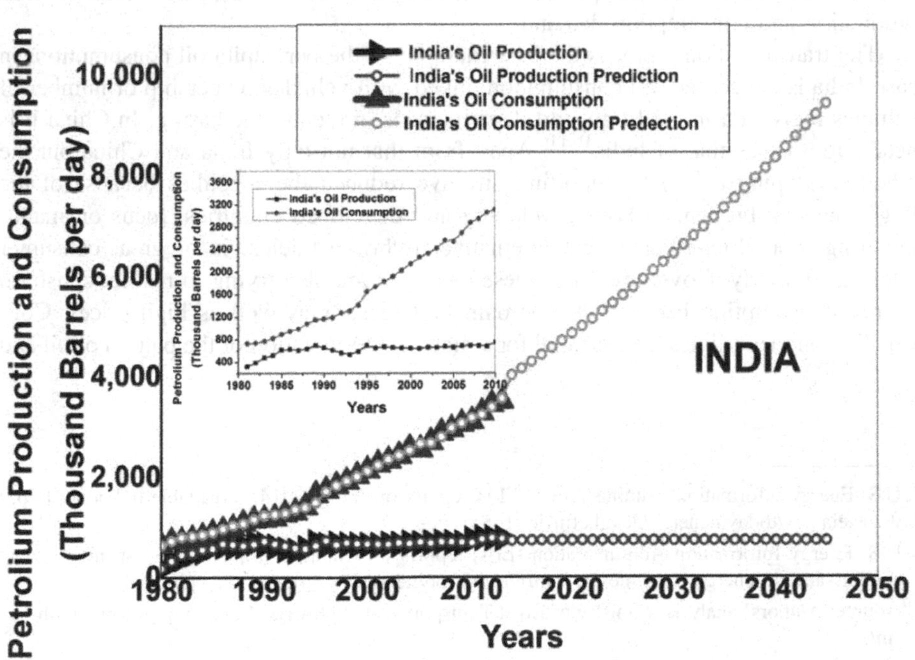

Fig. 4. Prediction of INDIA's oil production and consumption with increasing year

India is the fourth largest consumer of crude oil and petroleum products in the world after the United States, China and Japan and it is also the fourth largest net importer of crude oil and petroleum products. According to U.S. Energy Information Administration (EIA) reports on India (2014) the country depends heavily on imported crude oil, mostly from the Middle East[8]. The data analysis of oil production and consumption of both India and China is collected and optimizing its performance considerably minimizing errors by taking actual input values and targeted output values have analysed by using NARnet. For India the normalised mean square error (NMSE) values are found to be population ~ 0.000046 vs. petroleum production (consumption) ~ 0.2233 (0.0041) and for China the corresponding values are found as population ~ 0.0011 vs. petroleum production (consumption) ~ 0.0126 (0.0041). As per Fig. 4, the gap between India's oil consumption and oil production is widening gradually but domestic production continuously remains flat even after exploration and production including refining. The oil production ratio between China and India is much greater than oil consumption ratio between them. This states that the rate of petroleum oil production of China is more in comparison to India, whereas, rate of consumption is reverse. Over the past few years China is the world's second-largest oil consumer after the United States. Figure 5, shows that until the early 1990s surplus petroleum oil in China might be occurred and after that, it became the world's second-largest net importer of crude oil and petroleum products according to the U.S. Energy Information Administration (EIA) reports on China (2015) reports[9]. Despite China's slower oil consumption growth it predicted that China will surpass the United States in near future as the world's largest net importer of crude oil and petroleum. Both China and India are expected to increase their net oil imports to satisfy their production and consumption demand.

The transportation sector is the best example of the per capita oil consumption. In case India is concerned, oil consumption linked with vehicles ownership or number of vehicles registered in road transport department is gradually increasing. In China it is nearly four times that of India[10,11]. Apart from that not only India and China but the other developing countries importing oil have reduced the subsidies because of the large financial burden. In both developing and developed countries, focus on manufacturing more fuel-efficient and alternative, hybrid vehicles, is of great consumer interest. Similarly, Governments of these countries are also trying to restrict constrain energy consumption because of environmental reasons as well as high prices. Conversely, long lead-times are essential for structural modification of the pattern of oil and

[8] U.S. Energy Information Administration (EIA) reports on India (2014). Available online at: http://www.eia.gov/todayinenergy/detail.cfm?id=17551.

[9] U.S. Energy Information Administration (EIA) reports on China(2015). Available at: http://www.connaissancedesenergies.org/sites/default/files/pdf-ptvue/analysis_report_on_china.pdf.

[10] source: Authors' analysis: Ministry of Road Transport and Highways, India. http://www.morth.nic.in/.

[11] source: Authors' analysis: National Bureau Of Statistics of Chaina. http://www.stats.gov.cn/ENGLISH/Statisticaldata/AnnualData/.

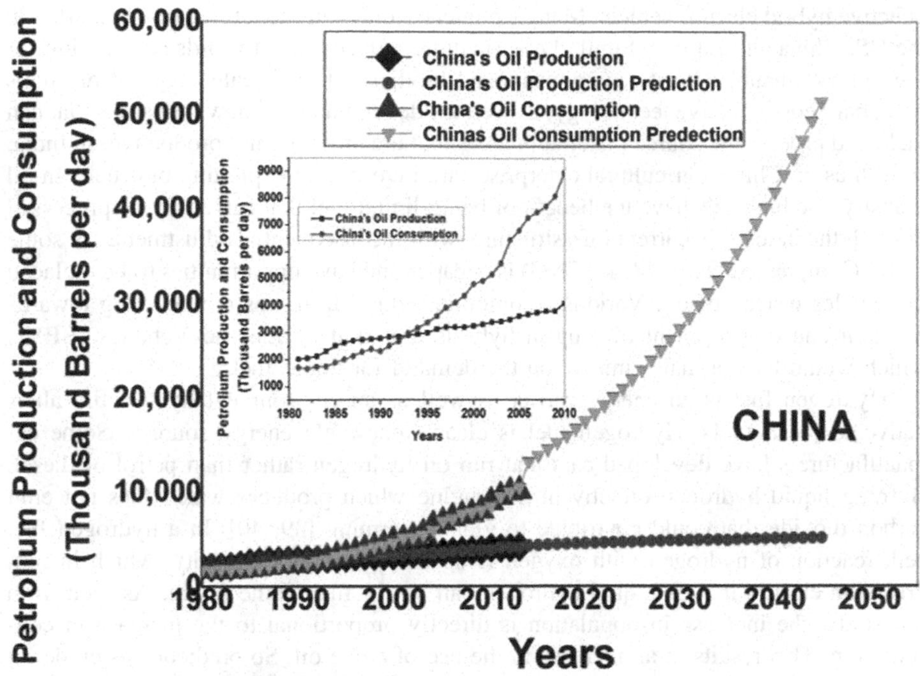

Fig. 5. Prediction of CHINA's oil production and consumption with increasing year

energy demand. In addition, there is an increase of oil demand in developing countries. To solve this issue relatively higher prices are required to significantly restraint global oil demand [38].

Oil reserves comprises of crude oil as well as field condensate and natural gas liquids, this comprehensive method assists in development of uniformity with the fossil oil production. Efforts are being made to come up with a reliable series for reserves found upon a mutual definition. However, in reality different countries use dissimilar strategies and the data have fluctuating levels of reliability. Therefore while attempting detailed assessments between nations or examination of time series, caution needs to be exercised. Reserves-to-production ratio (R/P) of oil signifies the length of time for which those residual reserves will last if production were to continue at a rate equivalent to the previous year. They are calculated by dividing residual reserves at the end of the year by the production in that year[12]. The reserves fossil oil would decline over time as production from the existing reserve base would be exhausted. To overcome these aspects the continual technical improvements have been taken to satisfy the alternate efforts. First of all manufacture of effective vehicles which are capable of attaining the same mileage and performance utilizing lesser fuel, at costs that can be retrieved reasonably quickly at current oil prices. Second, is manufacturing most

[12] http://www.bp.com/en/global/corporate/energy-economics/statistical-review-of-world-energy/oil-review-by-energy-type/oil-reserves.html.

effective hybrid electric vehicle. Many technically different models are on the market in the US, China and Europe. Similarly, agriculture industry step towards substitution for fuel oil by ethanol with its components and biodiesel. Large-scale usage of bio fuels will entail cost-effective technology, as well as, development of new industries that can yield and process the source material in areas that are presently not productive. In India, as well as, in China, agricultural enterprises are investing in exploiting bio-fuels. In oil industry, the bio-fuels have the benefit of being liquid fuel that can easily be processed through the industry's current infrastructure, with inconsequential adjustments. In some cases, Compressed Natural Gas (CNG) is cheaper and have opportunities to be replaced in vehicles instead of oil. Various automobile industrial groups are devoting towards research and development of plug-in hybrids and Battery Electric Vehicles (BEVs) which would have a major impact on the demand for liquid fuels.

Hydrogen fuel is an energy carrier as well as an environmentally friendly alternative to fossil fuels. Hydrogen fuel is clean, renewable energy sources. Some car manufacturers have developed cars that run on hydrogen rather than petrol or diesel. Burning liquid hydrogen directly in the engine which produces water does not emit carbon dioxide that could contribute to global warming [39, 40]. In a hydrogen fuel cell, reaction of hydrogen with oxygen is used to generate electricity, which in turn drives an electric motor. Liquid hydrogen can be the fuel of the future. As seen from our study, the increase in population is directly proportional to the increase in consumption. This results in an increase in the use of crude oil. So prediction is crude oil being a natural resource will be running out and becoming harder to find in future. That is why we propose, liquid hydrogen fuel as an alternate fuel for automobiles in near future around 2040–2050.

5 Conclusion

From the various tests performed on the results of the considered bench mark dataset, it is confirmed that Artificial Neural Network model with Non Linear Auto Regressive NETwork (NARnet) performs better in predicting population growth, and production of petroleum oil and consumption of that oil for two highly populated countries like India and China with more percentage of accuracy and lower MSE. We may conclude by saying that we have no control over population and at the same time over the production of vehicles. The vehicle industry is trying to replace petroleum oil with bio-fuels etc. The reserves fossil oil would tend to decline over time as production depleted the existing reserve base, these are some of the challenges hard to overcome and cannot be practically controlled. Hence, it is proposed that hydrogen fuel is the best alternative solution to the petroleum in future.

References

1. Mitchell, J., Marcel, V., Mitchell, B.: What Next for the Oil and Gas Industry?. Chatham House, London (2012)
2. Davis, S.C., Diegel, S.W., Boundy, R.G.: Transportation Energy Data Book (2016)

3. Yuan, C., Liu, S., Fang, Z.: Comparison of China's primary energy consumption forecasting by using ARIMA (the autoregressive integrated moving average) model and GM (1, 1) model. Energy **100**, 384–390 (2016)
4. Srinivasan, T.N.: China and India: economic performance, competition and cooperation: an update. J. Asian Econ. **15**(4), 613–636 (2004)
5. Hu, J.W.S., Hu, Y.C., Lin, R.R.W.: Applying neural networks to prices prediction of crude oil futures. Math. Probl. Eng. **2012**, 1–13 (2012)
6. Khazem, H., Mazouz, A.: Forecasting the price of crude oil using artificial neural networks. Int. J. Bus. Mark. Decis. Sci. **6**(1), 119–135 (2013)
7. Bossel, U.: The physics of the hydrogen economy. Eur. Fuel Cell News **10**(2), 1–16 (2003)
8. Pillay, P.: Hydrogen economy and alternative fuels. IEEE Emerg. Technol. Portal **2012** (2006)
9. Serrano, E., Rus, G., Garcia-Martinez, J.: Nanotechnology for sustainable energy. Renew. Sustain. Energy Rev. **13**(9), 2373–2384 (2009)
10. Sahaym, U., Norton, M.G.: Advances in the application of nanotechnology in enabling a 'hydrogen economy'. J. Mater. Sci. **43**(16), 5395–5429 (2008)
11. Wali, A.N., Kagoyire, E., Icyingeneye, P.: Mathematical modelling of Uganda population growth. Appl. Math. Sci. **6**(84), 4155–4168 (2012)
12. Armstrong, J.S.: Research needs in forecasting. Int. J. Forecast. **4**(3), 449–465 (1988)
13. Zhang, H., Li, J.: Prediction of tourist quantity based on RBF neural network. JCP **7**(4), 965–970 (2012)
14. Keskin, M.E., Taylan, E.D., Yilmaz, G.: Flow prediction model with fuzzy logic approaches: dim stream. In: International River Basin Management Congress (2007). http://www.dsi.gov.tr/english/congress2007/chapter_4/107.pdf
15. Eftekhari, A., Moghaddam, H.A., Forouzanfar, M., Alirezaie, J.: Incremental local linear fuzzy classifier in fisher space. EURASIP J. Adv. Sig. Process. **2009**, 15 (2009)
16. Yasdi, R.: Prediction of road traffic using a neural network approach. Neural Comput. Appl. **8**(2), 135–142 (1999)
17. Thenmozhi, M.: Forecasting stock index returns using neural networks. Delhi Bus. Rev. **7** (2), 59–69 (2006)
18. Tang, Z., Leung, C.W., Bagchi, K.: Improving population estimation with neural network models. In: Wang, J., Yi, Z., Zurada, J.M., Lu, B.-L., Yin, H. (eds.) ISNN 2006. LNCS, vol. 3973, pp. 1181–1186. Springer, Heidelberg (2006). https://doi.org/10.1007/11760191_172
19. Zhang, G., Patuwo, B.E., Hu, M.Y.: Forecasting with artificial neural networks: the state of the art. Int. J. Forecast. **14**(1), 35–62 (1998)
20. Azadeh, A., Sheikhalishahi, M., Shahmiri, S.: A hybrid neuro-fuzzy simulation approach for improvement of natural gas price forecasting in industrial sectors with vague indicators. Int. J. Adv. Manuf. Technol. **62**(1), 15–33 (2012)
21. Nazzal, J.M., El-Emary, I.M., Najim, S.A.: Investigating Jordan oil shale properties using artificial neural network (ANN). World Appl. Sci. J. **5**, 553–559 (2008)
22. Jayaraj, S., Padmakumari, K., Sreevalsan, E., Arun, P.: Wind speed and power prediction using artificial neural networks. In: European Wind Energy Conference, November 2004
23. Kulkar, S., Haidar, I.: Forecasting model for crude oil price using artificial neural networks and commodity future prices. Int. J. Comput. Sci. Inf. Secur. **2**(1), 81–88 (2009)
24. Aksoy, F., Yabanova, I., Bayrakçeken, H.: Estimation of dynamic viscosities of vegetable oils using artificial neural networks. Indian J. Chem. Technol. **18**, 227–233 (2011)
25. Lackes, R., Börgermann, C., Dirkmorfeld, M.: Forecasting the price development of crude oil with artificial neural networks. In: Omatu, S., Rocha, Miguel P., Bravo, J., Fernández, F., Corchado, E., Bustillo, A., Corchado, Juan M. (eds.) IWANN 2009. LNCS, vol. 5518, pp. 248–255. Springer, Heidelberg (2009). https://doi.org/10.1007/978-3-642-02481-8_36

26. Liu, J., Tang, Z.H., Zeng, F., Li, Z., Zhou, L.: Artificial neural network models for prediction of cardiovascular autonomic dysfunction in general Chinese population. BMC Med. Inform. Decis. Making **13**(1), 80 (2013)
27. Maliki, O.S., Agbo, A.O., Maliki, A.O., Ibeh, L.M., Agwu, C.O.: Comparison of regression model and artificial neural network model for the prediction of electrical power generated in Nigeria. Adv. Appl. Sci. Res. **2**(5), 329–339 (2011)
28. Tehrani, R., Khodayar, F.: A hybrid optimized artificial intelligent model to forecast crude oil using genetic algorithm. Afr. J. Bus. Manag. **5**(34), 13130 (2011)
29. Yadav, A.K., Chandel, S.S.: Artificial neural network based prediction of solar radiation for Indian stations. Int. J. Comput. Appl. **50**(9), 1–4 (2012)
30. Mohapatra, S.K., Kamilla, S.K., Mohapatra, S.K.: A pathway to hydrogen economy: artificial neural network an approach to prediction of population and number of registered vehicles in India. Adv. Sci. Lett. **22**(2), 359–362 (2016)
31. Cui, X., Jiang, M.: Chaotic time series prediction based on binary particle swarm optimization. AASRI Procedia **1**, 377–383 (2012)
32. Gibson, D., Nur, D.: Threshold autoregressive models in finance: a comparative approach. In: Proceedings of the Fourth Annual ASEARC Conference. University of Western Sydney, Paramatta, Australia (2011). http://ro.uow.edu.au/asearc/26
33. Hansen, B.E.: Threshold autoregression in economics. Stat. Interface **4**(2), 123–127 (2011)
34. Chander, P.: The nonlinear input-output model. J. Econ. Theory **30**(2), 219–229 (1983)
35. Markopoulos, A.P., Georgiopoulos, S., Manolakos, D.E.: On the use of back propagation and radial basis function neural networks in surface roughness prediction. J. Ind. Eng. Int. **12**, 389–400 (2016)
36. Poli, A.A., Cirillo, M.C.: On the use of the normalized mean square error in evaluating dispersion model performance. Atmos. Environ. Part A. Gen. Top. **27**(15), 2427–2434 (1993)
37. Tverberg, G.: Oil limits and the end of the debt super-cycle (2016). https://ourfiniteworld.com/2016/01/07/2016-oil-limits-and-the-end-of-the-debt-supercycle
38. Streifel, S.: Impact of China and India on global commodity markets: focus on metals and minerals and petroleum. Development Prospects Group/World Bank, UU World Investment Report (2006)
39. Offer, G.J., Howey, D., Contestabile, M., Clague, R., Brandon, N.P.: Comparative analysis of battery electric, hydrogen fuel cell and hybrid vehicles in a future sustainable road transport system. Energy Policy **38**(1), 24–29 (2010)
40. Cheng, X., Shi, Z., Glass, N., Zhang, L., Zhang, J., Song, D., Liu, L.S., Wang, H., Shen, J.: A review of PEM hydrogen fuel cell contamination: impacts, mechanisms, and mitigation. J. Power Sources **165**(2), 739–756 (2007)

Automatic Diagnosis of Dental Diseases

Punal M. Arabi(✉), T. S. Naveen, N. Vamsha Deepa, and Deepak Samanta

Department of Biomedical Engineering, ACS College of Engineering, Bangalore, India
arabi.punal@gmail.com, naveensanjeevrao@gmail.com, vamshi.deepa@gmail.com, deep.sam316@gmail.com

Abstract. Not taking care of oral health may lead to many health problems, mouth lesions or other oral problems are most often the sign of systemic diseases such as cardiovascular, stroke and pulmonary diseases. The most common oral and dental disease which affects the teeth are dental abscess, dental caries, gingivitis, periodontal disease, pericoronitis, pulpitis, crowding, malocclusion, oral cancer, acid erosion, bad breath, dental plaque. Dental diseases are majorly diagnosed by X-ray imaging. Since the X-rays are harmful as they emit radiation. Exposed levels are not considered safe for adults and children. To eliminate the use of X-ray for imaging modality in dentistry we propose a system which includes digital imaging, thermal imaging and near infrared imaging which are non-invasive, non-harmful, cost effective and ease of use and care. After conducting a clinical study on 47 volunteers and 60 images are obtained on their denture studies reveal their efficiency here image modalities to be used as automatic classification of dental diseases and analyzing the proposed system the results confirm the diseases with greater accuracy of 87.5% hence there is a possibility of replacing X-ray images a hybrid imager which houses a thermal, a near infrared and high resolution imager.

Keywords: Image processing · Dental disease diagnosis · Gingivitis Abscess

1 Introduction

Oral and dental disease are most common in India. Oral bacterial infection is the cause for gum disease. Which if not treated in time might affect other body organs through the blood stream. Dental diseases are often very painful, painful and expensive to treat. But to a great extent preventable and treatable with proper diagnosis and care. Serious systemic illness such as cardiovascular, stroke and pulmonary diseases are found to be closely associated with dental diseases.

1.1 Literature Survey

Shivpuje reviewed a paper on "A Review on Digital Dental Radiographic Images for Disease Identification and Classification" proposed a robust, simple and cost effective, more accurate, interpretation algorithm to identify the types of dental diseases [1].

P. Bhattacharyya et al. (Eds.): NGCT 2017, CCIS 827, pp. 363–375, 2018.
https://doi.org/10.1007/978-981-10-8657-1_28

Price worked on method of Dental Caries Detection Technologies in which various caries detection technologies available to assist the dental professional with this complex task is reviewed. the finding is that deduction of occlusal and smooth surface caries have been focused by most of the researchers [2].

Kells et al. proposed a paper on "Computerized thermographic imaging and pulpal blood flow" proposed a protocol for thermographic imaging of human teeth in thermologically controlled environment [3].

Chandra et al. reviewed on Epidemiology of periodontal diseases in Indian population, estimation of risk factors responsible for periodontal diseases to develop a strategy for the formulation of an effective oral healthcare policy in India [4].

Mostovoy et al. proposed thermographic method to identify asymptotic dental pathology in the paper on "Thermography and Oral Pathology" the areas of suspected inflammation and infection can be easily identified in the thermal image of tooth due to the presence of heat [5].

Zakian et al. proposed a paper on "Occlusal caries detection by using thermal imaging" which explored the deduction and quantification of early tooth decay ad occlusal surfaces by using the thermal changes that are associated with the disease [6].

Nikawa in the paper "Dental Diagnosis and Treatment Using Microwaves" proposed a method to use used microwaves for dental diagnosis and treatment microwave and millimeter wave for dental disease diagnosis and treatment using the heat produced by microwave power [7].

Oprea et al. proposed a method on "Image Processing Techniques used for Dental X-Ray Image Analysis" clearly explains the use of image processing techniques for analysis of X-Ray images to examine and classify caries lesion [8].

Datta et al. proposed a method "Detection of Dental Caries Lesion at Early Stage Based on Image Analysis Technique" describes a technique to filter optical images of teeth, extract caries lesions and later segmented the tooth region. This method can be used to segment each tooth caries lesion and also monitor lesion size [9].

Reddy et al. proposed a method on "Dental X-Ray Image Analysis by Using Image Processing Techniques" proposed a method that can be used in order to apply image processing techniques and thoroughly go through the X-ray images, examine the extent of caries lesion present and classified the type of caries present in the dental radiograph [10].

Since the X-rays are harmful as they emit radiation. Exposed levels are not considered safe for adults and children. To eliminate the use of X-ray for imaging modality in dentistry we propose a system which includes digital imaging, thermal imaging and near infrared imaging which are non-invasive, non-harmful, cost effective and ease of use and care. Studies reveal that thermal imaging and near infrared imaging are safe to use as major modalities. After conducting a clinical study and analyzing the proposed system the results confirms the diseases with greater accuracy so it can be concluded that X-ray imaging can be replaced by the thermal and near infrared imaging upon higher clinical studies and validation.

2 Methodology

The volunteers are identified and are explained about the procedure and consent is sought from them. The volunteers are classified into different disease groups as: 1. Dental Abscess 2. DentalCaries. 3. Gingivitis 4. Periodontitis.

The volunteer is asked to relax on a dental chair and open his mouth and held open of the till the images are taken. The thermal camera is held at a distance from the subject. Thermal images of teeth are captured using the thermal app. Volunteer is asked to remain still and not to make any movements during this. Thermal app is capable of capturing the thermal radiation from mouth. The same procedure is repeated for taking normal and NIR images using smart phone and NIR camera respectively.

Once the images are acquired, the colored image would be converted into gray first. The acquired images are filtered first and then enhanced and these processed images are compared and analyzed by region of interest ROI. ROI is identified in the images first order, second order and GLCM are found and compared. Based on the result obtained a decision rule is formed to categorize various dental diseases (Figs. 1 and 2).

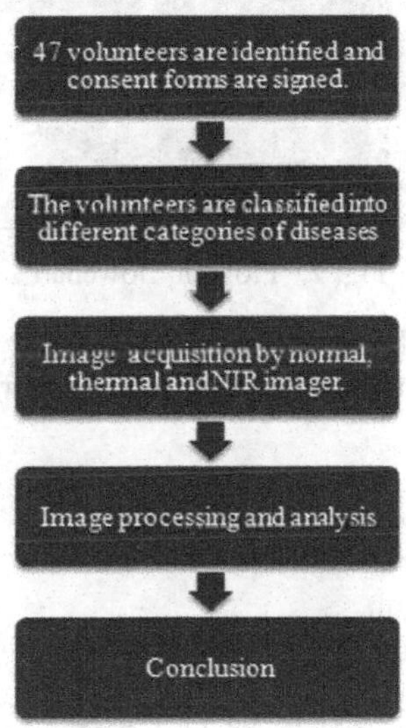

Fig. 1. Steps followed

At first the images are acquired using each modalities i.e. High resolution camera, thermal app and NIR camera and further processing are to be performed. The region of interest is then selected which is an RGB image converted into gray image. For this, four sets of dental diseases i.e. five images for each set consisting of one image of each modality are taken. Illumination correction is done and the first order parameters (i.e. mean, energy, variance, skewness and kurtosis) and the second order parameters (i.e. homogeneity and correlation) values are found by using MATLAB. The obtained parameter values are compared with each other. Then a reference standard value is set for each diseases and the decision is made based on these values. Thermal app is

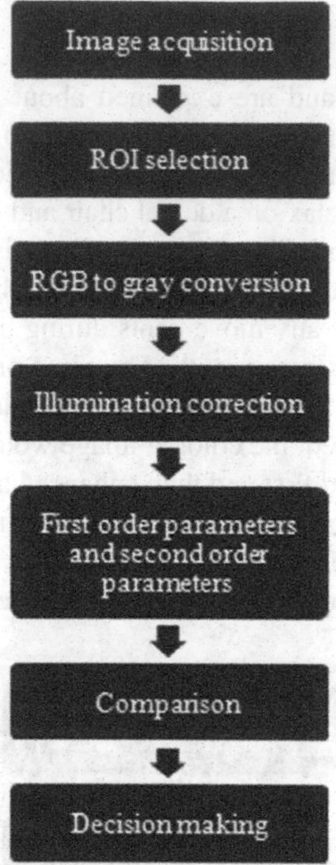

Fig. 2. Program flowchart

available in iOS devices and as well as in android devices transforms iOS or the android smart phones into powerful Android or iOS thermal Camera.

Specifications:

- Resolution: 384 × 288 pixels (>110k pixels).
- Camera type: 8MP Camera.
- Spectrum: LWIR 7.7–14 μm.
- Enhanced version: High-resolution thermal imagery (grayscale day/night version) NETD < 0.07 °C.
- FOV: 19 mm lens (19 × 14). Frame rate: 8.7 Hz
- Operating temperature: −10 to +50 °C (−4° F to +122° F).

Specifications of NIR imager:

- Resolution: 1280 × 960 pixels,
- Camera Type: 1.3 Megapixel,
- Low power consumption,
- Support plug and play, P2P easy installation,
- IR-CUT filter, Support color or black and white mode converting,
- Auto-retrieve function and auto connection network.

A high resolution camera is used to acquire the normal image of the disease affected part of the teeth. This high resolution camera helps to acquire the better clarity images. The specifications of the camera are as follows:

- Camera type: 20 Megapixels
- Resolution: 1080 × 1920 p
- Device: Honor 7.

Images obtained from 47 patients were classified based on the respective diseases.

3 Results

Out of 47 patients, there were 5 patients with dental abscess, 19 with dental caries, 8 with periodontitis, 9 with gingivitis, 3 with crowding, 2 with gingival recession, 3 with periodontitis and 1 with pulpitis. Here we are mainly focusing on 4 most common dental diseases i.e. dental abscess, dental caries, periodontitis and gingivitis.

From the data acquired, five images of each disease consisting 3 images each (1 from all the three modalities i.e. digital, NIR and thermal) are considered for analysis. Then the patients are given serial numbers as P1, P2, and P3 and so on. These images are analyzed, processed and the required parameters are found simultaneously.

The images considered for analysis are shown in the figures below: The images of five patients with dental abscess problem are considered for analysis. The patients are represented by number as P1, P2, P3 and so on (Fig. 3).

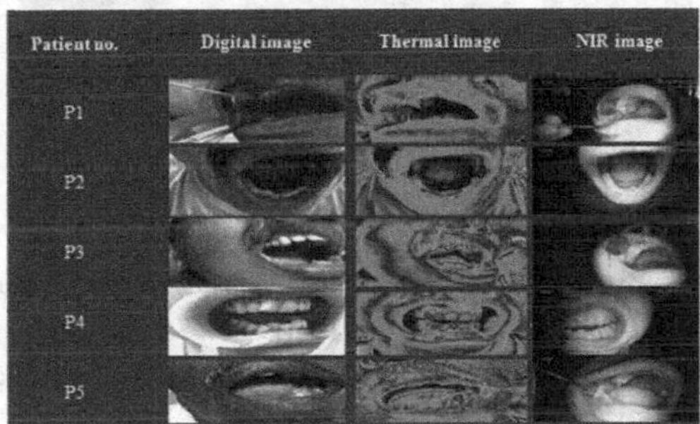

Fig. 3. The images of five patients with dental abscess problem are considered for analysis

The images of five patients with dental caries problem are considered for analysis. The patients are represented by a number as P1, P2, P3 and so on (Fig. 4).

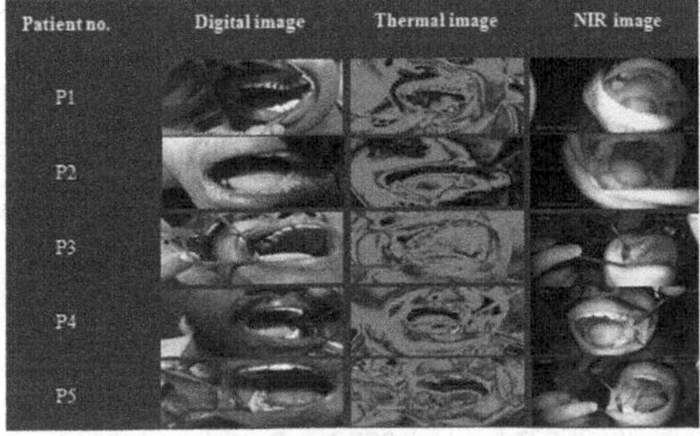

Fig. 4. The images of five patients with dental caries problem are considered for analysis

The images of five patients with periodontitis problem are considered for analysis. The patients are represented by a number as P1, P2, P3 and so on (Fig. 5).

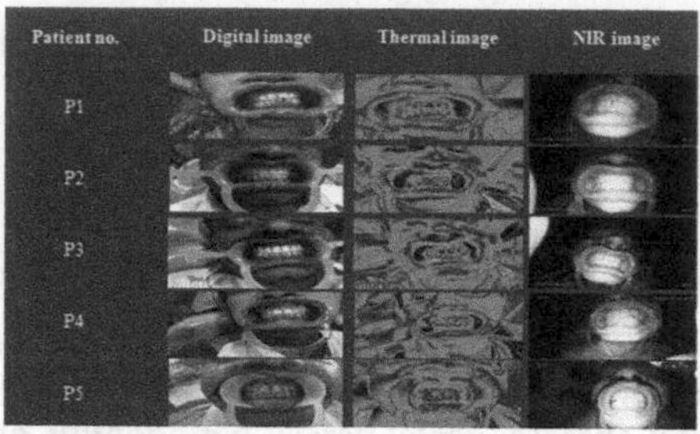

Fig. 5. The images of five patients with periodontitis problem are considered for analysis.

The images of five patients with gingivitis problem are considered for analysis. The patients are given a serial number as P1, P2, P3 and so on (Fig. 6).

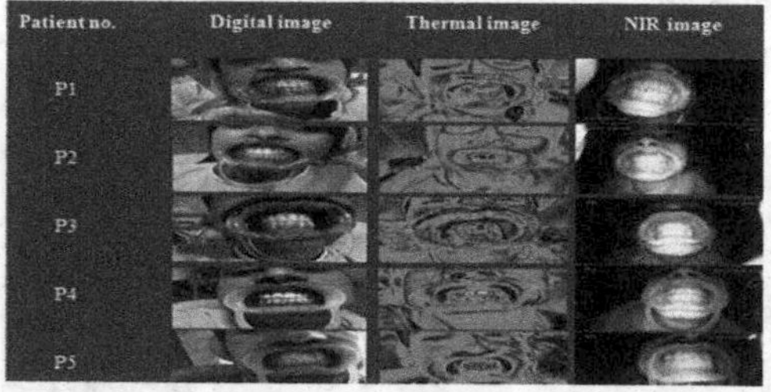

Fig. 6. The images of five patients with gingivitis problem are considered for analysis

Then the parameters- skewness, kurtosis, mean, energy, variance which are of first order and along with the second order parameters-homogeneity and correlation are found using MATLAB 2013a. The parameters values obtained are tabulated as shown in the following tables. These values are compared to each other and a reference unique value is set for each disease for disease diagnosis.

Tables 1, 2, and 3 shows the first order parameters values-mean, variance, skewness and kurtosis along with the second order parameters values-homogeneity and correlation of the digital, NIR and thermal image respectively of dental abscess.

Table 1. First order and second order parameter values of dental abscess using digital

Digital							
Patient	Mean	Energy	Variance	Skewness	Kurtosis	Homogeneity	Correlation
P1	0.4229	0.032	0.0502	0.3008	2.5757	0.5631	0.5616
P2	0.3094	0.0739	0.0389	1.2019	4.8832	0.7231	0.8444
P3	0.5085	0.0486	0.0465	−0.2984	2.878	0.6172	0.6877
P4	0.4876	0.0336	0.052	0.0199	2.4183	0.5944	0.6845
P5	0.5491	0.0396	0.0451	−0.2292	2.8638	0.5919	0.5794

Table 2. First order and second order parameter values of dental caries using NIR imager

NIR							
Patient	Mean	Energy	Variance	Skewness	Kurtosis	Homogeneity	Correlation
P1	0.5599	0.054	0.0585	−0.5908	2.5459	0.6523	0.7637
P2	0.5642	0.058	0.0508	−0.5075	2.7252	0.7209	0.8577
P3	0.5758	0.0276	0.0605	−0.4601	2.4314	0.5466	0.5168
P4	0.4557	0.0333	0.0501	0.1491	2.5494	0.5822	0.6053
P5	0.466	0.0438	0.0487	−0.11	2.6948	0.6465	0.7519

Table 3. First order and second order parameter values of dental abscess using thermal imager.

Thermal							
Patient	Mean	Energy	Variance	Skewness	Kurtosis	Homogeneity	Correlation
P1	0.46	0.0219	0.0647	0.1134	2.0875	0.4905	0.4438
P2	0.4639	0.026	0.0611	0.1889	2.2728	0.5422	0.5845
P3	0.4644	0.0255	0.0619	0.1904	2.2677	0.5361	0.538
P4	0.4549	0.0294	0.0595	0.1824	2.3021	0.5801	0.6687
P5	0.5097	0.0276	0.0589	−0.044	2.1662	0.5729	0.6238

Table 4. First order and second order parameter values of dental caries using digital

Digital							
Patient	Mean	Energy	Variance	Skewness	Kurtosis	Homogeneity	Correlation
P1	0.4893	0.0472	0.0846	0.2551	1.9378	0.6939	0.88
P2	0.5418	0.0532	0.0518	−0.1934	2.4667	0.7339	0.8587
P3	0.4413	0.0426	0.0604	0.1772	2.1491	0.6973	0.85
P4	0.5227	0.039	0.061	−0.1406	2.2282	0.6731	0.8314
P5	0.5849	0.0474	0.05	−0.32	2.6333	0.6893	0.8054

Table 5. First order and second order parameter values of dental caries using NIR imager.

NIR							
Patient	Mean	Energy	Variance	Skewness	Kurtosis	Homogeneity	Correlation
P1	0.5904	0.0448	0.0601	−0.5633	2.5946	0.6367	0.7008
P2	0.4789	0.0631	0.0458	−0.0357	2.5453	0.7734	0.8737
P3	0.6102	0.0646	0.0519	−0.6574	2.8919	0.7445	0.8744
P4	0.4773	0.0485	0.0502	0.1548	2.6499	0.69	0.8123
P5	0.4824	0.0373	0.0559	0.0797	2.2859	0.654	0.7989

Tables 4, 5, and 6 shows the first order parameters values-mean, variance, skewness and kurtosis along with the second order parameters values-homogeneity and correlation of the digital, NIR and thermal image respectively of dental caries.

Tables 7, 8 and 9 shows the first order parameters values-mean, variance, skewness and kurtosis along with the second order parameters values-homogeneity and correlation of the digital, NIR and thermal image respectively of periodontitis.

Table 6. First order and second order parameter values of dental caries using thermal imager.

Thermal							
Patient	Mean	Energy	Variance	Skewness	Kurtosis	Homogeneity	Correlation
P1	0.4745	0.0262	0.066	0.0262	2.0771	0.5556	0.5952
P2	0.5241	0.0409	0.0557	0.0137	2.4019	0.6619	0.7873
P3	0.5116	0.0314	0.063	−0.022	2.1502	0.6218	0.7429
P4	0.5027	0.0224	0.072	−0.0297	1.9667	0.5197	0.5436
P5	0.5282	0.0243	0.0692	−0.1023	2.0272	0.5413	0.6359

Table 7. First order and second order parameter values of periodontitis using digital.

Digital							
Patient	Mean	Energy	Variance	Skewness	Kurtosis	Homogeneity	Correlation
P1	0.5886	0.0668	0,0596	−0.478	2.3037	0.7703	0.8963
P2	0.5298	0.0533	0.0608	−0.116	2.2449	0.7608	0.9077
P3	0.5807	0.0561	0.0704	−0.4399	2.101	0.739	0.8908
P4	0.5556	0.0639	0.0548	−0.366	2.349	0.7707	0.8896
P5	0.5573	0.0579	0.0672	−0.2831	2.0281	0.7783	0.9253

Table 8. First order and second order parameter values of periodontitis using NIR Imager.

NIR							
Patient	Mean	Energy	Variance	Skewness	Kurtosis	Homogeneity	Correlation
P1	0.6381	0.077	0.0543	−0.66	2.8944	0.8104	0.9198
P2	0.7893	0.2805	0.0621	−1.3005	3.8577	0.8986	0.9635
P3	0.6603	0.0965	0.058	−0.8706	2.9239	0.8293	0.9394
P4	0.703	0.1184	0.0533	−1.0913	3.5828	0.8453	0.938
P5	0.707	0.3109	0.063	−0.5174	2.8851	0.9481	0.9767

Table 9. First order and second order parameter values of periodontitis using thermal imager.

Thermal							
Patient	Mean	Energy	Variance	Skewness	Kurtosis	Homogeneity	Correlation
P1	0.5251	0.0335	0.0669	−0.069	2.1006	0.653	0.7314
P2	0.5351	0.0367	0.0707	−0.1415	2.0433	0.6768	0.8464
P3	0.52	0.0275	0.0683	−0.094	2.0687	0.5978	0.6524
P4	0.5522	0.0316	0.07	−0.2751	2.1363	0.6274	0.7051
P5	0.5183	0.0369	0.0793	−0.0706	1.877	0.6698	0.8739

Table 10. First order and second order parameter values of gingivitis using digital imager

Digital							
Patient	Mean	Energy	Variance	Skewness	Kurtosis	Homogeneity	Correlation
P1	0.5351	0.0538	0.0723	−0.216	1.9922	0.7703	0.9123
P2	0.5434	0.0559	0.0633	−0.292	2.176	0.7633	0.9038
P3	0.5509	0.0618	0.0802	−0.2794	1.8729	0.7963	0.9282
P4	0.5313	0.0577	0.0783	−0.1152	1.846	0.7942	0.9361
P5	0.5324	0.0565	0.0666	−0.0603	1.9832	0.7877	0.9272

Table 11. First order and second order parameter values of gingivitis using NIR imager.

NIR							
Patient	Mean	Energy	Variance	Skewness	Kurtosis	Homogeneity	Correlation
P1	0.5803	0.1077	0.0517	−0.2256	2.7059	0.8708	0.9426
P2	0.6297	0.1001	0.0655	−0.5135	2.5449	0.8691	0.9607
P3	0.7234	0.149	0.046	−1.553	4.9511	0.8555	0.9396
P4	0.6545	0.0887	0.0594	−0.8039	2.8145	0.8105	0.9332
P5	0.6242	0.0905	0.0546	−0.6489	2.9284	0.8496	0.9451

Table 12. First order and second order parameter values of gingivitis using thermal imager.

Thermal							
Patient	Mean	Energy	Variance	Skewness	Kurtosis	Homogeneity	Correlation
P1	0.538	0.0348	0.0671	−0.156	2.1539	0.6585	0.7678
P2	0.5268	0.032	0.0698	−0.0816	2.0035	0.6392	0.7693
P3	0.5509	0.0618	0.0802	−0.2794	1.8729	0.7963	0.9282
P4	0.5184	0.0359	0.0697	−0.102	2.1	0.6647	0.748
P5	0.5192	0.0339	0.0748	−0.099	1.9333	0.6515	0.8475

Tables 10, 11 and 12 shows the first order parameters values-mean, variance, skewness and kurtosis along with the second order parameters values-homogeneity and correlation of the digital, NIR and thermal image respectively of gingivitis.

4 Discussion

47 patients with different dental diseases were considered and the patients were grouped based on their diseases. Three different imaging modalities i.e. Digital, thermal and NIR for acquiring images were used. Four common dental diseases were taken for analysis. 5 patients from each dental disease were taken as subject. The acquired images were processed using MATLAB R2013a. The processing involved RGB to gray conversion, preprocessing and then parameters- skewness, kurtosis, mean, energy,

variance which are of first order and second order parameters (i.e. Homogeneity and correlation) of images of all the three modalities (i.e. Digital, thermal and NIR) were calculated. The parameter values were tabulated as shown in Sect. 4.1 and thorough investigation was done. Here all the parameters were compared with each imaging modality of all the four diseases considered. Upon investigation the following decision rule were formed and based on this decision rule, scoring system was developed.

4.1 Decision Rule

In the first rule, the parameter-variance of digital imaging modality and parameter-mean of thermal imaging modality were compared. It is seen that the variance of digital image should be lesser than 0.05 and mean of thermal image should be lesser than 0.5 to classify dental abscess. The scoring system was developed for both the conditions mentioned below (Table 13):

Table 13. The table shows that if both the conditions are satisfied then the disease is dental abscess.

Modality	Parameter	Reference value	Score(S)	Condition	Disease
Digital	Variance	<0.05	1	S = 1 or S = 2 or S ≠ 0	Dental abscess is diagnosed
Thermal	Mean	<0.5	1		

The above table shows that if both the conditions are satisfied then the disease is dental abscess. If only one condition is satisfied then the disease may be dental abscess. If both the conditions are not satisfied then the second rule is framed for other three diseases (i.e. dental caries, periodontitis and gingivitis).

In the second rule, the parameter-correlation of thermal imaging modality and NIR imaging modality were compared. It is seen that the correlation of thermal image should be greater than 0.6 and correlation of NIR image should be lesser than 0.9 to classify dental caries. The scoring system was developed for both the conditions mentioned below (Table 14):

Table 14. The table shows that if both the conditions are satisfied then the disease is dental caries.

Modality	Parameter	Reference value	Score(S)	Condition	Disease
Thermal	Correlation	>0.6	1	S = 2 or S ≠ 0	Dental caries is diagnosed
NIR	Correlation	<0.9	1		

The above table shows that if both the conditions are satisfied then the disease is dental caries. If only one condition is satisfied then the disease may be dental caries. If both the conditions are not satisfied then the third rule is framed for rest two diseases (i.e. periodontitis and gingivitis).

In the third rule, the parameter skewness and kurtosis of digital imaging modality were compared. It is seen that the skewness of digital image should be lesser than −0.3 and kurtosis of digital image should be greater than 2 to classify periodontitis. The scoring rule was developed for both the conditions mentioned below (Table 15):

Table 15. The table shows that if both the conditions are satisfied then the disease is periodontitis.

Modality	Parameter	Reference value	Score(S)	Condition	Disease
Digital	Skewness	<(−0.3)	1	S = 2 or $S \neq 0$	Periodontitis is diagnosed
Digital	Kurtosis	>2	1		

The above table shows that if both the conditions are satisfied then the disease is periodontitis. If only one condition is satisfied then the disease may be periodontitis. If both the conditions are not satisfied then the fourth rule is framed for gingivitis.

In the fourth rule, the parameter correlation of digital imaging modality and mean of NIR imaging modality were compared. It is seen that the correlation of digital image should be greater than 0.9 and mean of NIR image should be lesser than 0.7 to classify gingivitis. The scoring rule was developed for both the conditions mentioned below (Table 16):

Table 16. The table shows that if both the conditions are satisfied then the disease is gingivitis

Modality	Parameter	Reference value	Score (S)	Condition	Disease
Digital	Correlation	>0.9	1	S = 2 or $S \neq 0$	Gingivitis is diagnosed
NIR	Mean	<0.7	1		

The above table shows that if both the conditions are satisfied then the disease is gingivitis. If only one condition is satisfied then the disease may be gingivitis.

To confirm the above decision rule, few images for each dental disease are investigated. The results are obtained as shown:

- **Test Result 1**

Based on the decision rule, here a digital image and a thermal image of a patient with dental abscess problem are taken. It is seen that the variance of the digital image is less than 0.05(<0.05) and mean of the thermal image is less than 0.5(<0.5) which satisfies the decision rule formed and the score is found to be 2, showing 100% accuracy. So it can be concluded that the decision rule 1 formed is satisfied.

- **Test Result 2**

Based on the decision rule, here a thermal image and an NIR image of a patient with dental caries problem are taken. It is seen that the correlation parameter value of the thermal image is greater than 0.6(>0.6) and the correlation parameter value of NIR image is less than 0.9(<0.9) which satisfies the decision rule formed and the score is found to be 2, showing 100% accuracy. So it can be concluded that the decision rule 2 formed is satisfied.

- **Test Result 3**

Based on the decision rule, here a digital image of a patient with periodontitis problem is taken. It is seen that kurtosis parameter value of the digital image is greater than 2.0 (>2.0) which satisfies the second condition of the decision rule 3 formed but the skewness parameter value is varied and the score is found to be 1 resulting in 50% accuracy. So it can be concluded that the more detailed investigation has to be done to satisfy both the conditions of decision rule 3.

- **Test Result 4**

Based on the decision rule, here a digital image and an NIR image of a patient with gingivitis problem is taken. It is seen that correlation parameter value of the digital image is greater than 0.9(>0.9) and the mean parameter value is less than 0.7(<0.7) which satisfies both the conditions of decision rule 4 formed and the score is found to be 2, showing 100% accuracy. So it can be concluded that decision rule 4 is satisfied.

From the above test results it is seen that all the conditions in the decision rule for dental abscess, dental caries, and gingivitis are satisfied but for periodontitis the parameter kurtosis is satisfying and the parameter skewness is not satisfying condition. So for the error metric it can be confirmed that the accuracy of this proposed system is 87.5%.

5 Conclusion

The dental images of diseased patients were acquired using three different imaging modalities i.e. digital, thermal and NIR. The patients were grouped into four common dental disease i.e. Dental abscess, dental caries, periodontitis and gingivitis. Five patients were considered for investigation and images were processed in MATLAB R2013a. parameters- skewness, kurtosis, mean, energy, variance which are of first order and second order parameters (i.e. Homogeneity and correlation) of images of all the three modalities (i.e. Digital, thermal and NIR) were calculated, the values were tabulated and analyzed. Upon analysis Decision rule and scoring system is framed.

Based on the decision rule and scoring system all the four diseases could be classified. It is seen that the accuracy for dental abscess and dental caries and periodontitis is found to be 100% whereas the accuracy gingivitis is found to be 80%. Results are validated using the test images and the accuracy is found to be 100% for dental abscess, dental caries and periodontitis and 80% accuracy for gingivitis.

After validation of the proposed system, it is seen that all the conditions in the decision rule for dental abscess, dental caries, and gingivitis are satisfied but for periodontitis the parameter kurtosis is satisfying and the parameter skewness is not satisfying condition. So for the error metric it can be confirmed that the accuracy of this proposed system is 87.5%. For confirmation more number of patients is to be considered and a detailed clinical study has to be done.

6 Future Work

After the validation, the implementation of "Automatic Diagnosis of Dental Disease" can be performed for the smart screening of the dental diseases by integrating the three imagers i.e. Digital, THERMAL and NIR with the computer so that easy diagnosis of dental disease can be done. As soon as the images are captured, the disease is diagnosed by the computer and the result is displayed in the monitor. For further confirmation a detailed clinical study of different diseases are to be done so that the other different disease can be diagnosed.

Acknowledgement. We thank the doctors of V.S DENTAL COLLEGE & HOSPITAL and MY DENTAL CARE CLINIC for providing us patients to carry on our project. It would not have been possible to do the project in this form without their valuable help, cooperation and guidance.

References

1. Shivpuje, B.V.: A review on digital dental radiographic images for disease identification and classification. Int. J. Eng. Res. Appl. **6**(7) (Part -5), 38–42 (2016). ISSN: 2248-9622, www.ijera.com
2. Price, J.B.: A review of dental caries detection technologies. Academy of General dentistry, Program Approval for Continuing Education, June 2013
3. Kells, B.E., Kennedy, J.G., Biagioni, P.A., Lamey, P.J.: Computerized infrared thermographic imaging and pulpal blood flow: part 1. A protocol for thermal imaging of human teeth. Int. Endod. J. **33**(5), 442–447 (2000). NCBI
4. Chandra, A., Yadav, O.P., Narula, S., Dutta, A.: Epidemiology of periodontal diseases in Indian population since last decade. J. Int. Soc. Prev. Commun. Dent. **6**(2), 91–96 (2016). PMCID: PMC4820580
5. Mostovoy, A., Oprea, Ş., Marinescu, C.: Thermography and oral pathology image analysis, p. 125. IEEE (2008). ISBN 978-1-4244-3974-4/08
6. Zakian, C.M., Taylor, A.M., Ellwood, R.P., Pretty, I.A.: Occlusal caries detection by using thermal imaging. J. Dent. **38**(10), 788–795 (2010)
7. Nikawa, Y.: Dental diagnosis and treatment using microwaves. In: 2004 JEEE MTT Digest. IEEE (2004). ISBN 0-7803-8331-1/04
8. Oprea, Ş., Marinescu, C., Liţă, I., Jurianu, M., Vişan, D.A., Cioc, I.B.: Image processing techniques used for dental X-ray image analysis, p. 125. IEEE (2008). ISBN 978-1-4244-3974-4/08
9. Datta, S., Chaki, N.: Detection of dental caries lesion at early stage based on image analysis technique. In: IEEE International Conference on Computer Graphics, Vision and Information Security (CGVIS). IEEE (2015). ISBN 978-1-4673-7437-8/15
10. Reddy, M.V.B., Sridhar, V., Nagendra, M.: Dental X-ray image analysis by using image processing. IJARCSSE **2**(6), 184–189 (2012)

Ensemble Algorithms for Islanding Detection in Smart Grids

Rubi Pandey and Damanjeet Kaur[(✉)]

Electrical and Electronics Engineering,
UIET, Panjab University, Chandigarh, India
rubypandey92@gmail.com, damaneee@pu.ac.in

Abstract. In this paper, a predictive model for islanding detection in the presence of DG connected in smart grid is presented. In order to predict islanding state, an advanced machine learning approach, has been applied. The data is generated by carrying out simulation for various cases of islanding and non-islanding. The generated data-set for various cases is analyzed with and without dimensionality reduction using Principal Component Analysis. A hybrid classifier is then designed to correctly classify the cases into islanding & non-islanding. A comparison between various learning algorithms in terms of accuracy, precision, recall and F-score is also made.

1 Introduction

The electrical power system complexity is increasing at rapid rate in last few decades. The present day's power system is able to manage electricity demand in a economic, reliable and sustainable manner by employing advanced digital information and communication technologies. With the advancement in technology it is possible to monitor, record, store and process bulk of data generated in a grid. The synchrophasor technology has done this using Phasor measurement unit (PMU). PMU records the data and provide reliability for wide area monitoring system (WAMSs). PMU ensures real-time monitoring, control, adequate situational awareness, secure functioning, and protection of the electrical power system. Apart from this, in order to serve the growing needs of individuals additional power sources (DG) are connected at the distribution end. The inefficiencies and interdependencies associated with distribution & transmission are reduced when power is generated on-site. It is an enhancement of the electric power system and another move towards smart grid.

In fact, there are many utilities across the world which have a significant penetration of DG's in their power system. But there are a few issues to be considered with the DG and one of them is islanding. DG suffers from a series of integration challenges, depending on the strength of the utility power system, and amount of DG connected. The issues include harmonic control, voltage regulation, losses, transient stability, voltage flicker, increased level of short circuits, & injection and islanding control.

Among these challenges, the problem of protection against unintentional islanding [1–3] is intense. Safety can be at danger when DG's feeding a system when primary sources have been opened and not in operation. Islanded system may not be properly grounded by the DG interconnection. The frequency and voltage may not be maintained

P. Bhattacharyya et al. (Eds.): NGCT 2017, CCIS 827, pp. 376–389, 2018.
https://doi.org/10.1007/978-981-10-8657-1_29

within a standard permissible limit. Out of phase reclosing of DG could occur because of instantaneous reclosing. It leads to large mechanical currents and torques that can damage the prime movers or generators. It also results in transients creation, which may damage the customer equipments and the utility. Capacitive switching transients are generated if out of phase reclosing occurs at peak voltage. Also, the crest over-voltage can be three times rated value in a lightly damped system. Various risks leads to degradation and damage of the electric components as a consequence of frequency & voltage drifts.

Due to these reasons, it becomes important to detect the islanding situation accurately & quickly.

The paper is organized as follows. Section 2 presents a brief literature survey in islanding, both using remote and local methods. After that, next section is devoted to problem formulation of islanding detection. Section 3 is dedicated to theoretical basis which includes description of algorithms used and proposed methodology. Also, the SIMULINK model developed to generate various islanding & non-islanding cases is presented. And the classifiers used in this study are discussed. Next section describes approach. In Sect. 6, the SIMULINK model used to generate various islanding & non-islanding cases is presented. Finally results & discussion is carried out in last section followed by conclusion and future scope.

2 Literature Survey

Islanding is a situation in which a portion of grid is disconnected from rest of the distribution system, yet the connected DG keeps it energized. In the early decade, the standards (IEEE-925-1998) have not allowed any kind of intentional or unintentional islanding. But nowadays, only unintentional islanding (IEEE-1547-2003) is not permitted. According to IEEE 1547 standard, the islanding condition should be detected and the island portion should be disconnected within a timeframe of 2 s from the main grid [4]. Unintentional islanding results an unexpected consequences including degradation of the system voltage stability, bad restoration, and also, an increased risk to safety. So the DGs must detect islanding and disconnect from the main grid during islanding condition. Many techniques are available in literature for early detection of an islanding event. Before understanding islanding phenomenon, and techniques of detection, it becomes important to highlight Non Detection Zone (NDZ). NDZ is the range where there is a mismatch between load and DG power and islanding detection scheme could not easily detect it [5]. Also, the type of loads inside an island that can be modelled as a parallel RLC circuit is primarily used for islanding analysis as it makes the worse islanding detection condition by any available techniques. Generally, the islanding techniques do not have much problems with loads with constant power [6] or non-linear loads that produce current harmonics.

A number of approaches are available for islanding detection. Basically islanding detection can be divided into remote and local technique. Local techniques can be further classified into active, passive, hybrid and intelligent techniques. Remote methods are based on communication between utility and DGs. It includes Power line signalling scheme [7], Signal Produced by Disconnect [2], Supervisory control and data acquisition [8], Inter-tripping [9, 10]. The only disadvantage is that they are expensive to implement on a small scale. Passive methods have gained a wide popularity in recent years. Rate of change of output power [11], Rate of change of frequency [12], Rate of change of frequency over power [13], Voltage Unbalance [14, 15], Harmonic Distortion [16, 17], Under/Over Voltage Relay (UVR/OVR) and Under/Over Frequency Relay (UFR/OFR), Phase Jump Detection (PJD) [18, 19] techniques have all attracted widespread attention. But, passive methods face large NDZs. Also, to avoid mal-operation during fault events, the threshold setting must be carefully selected. Active methods on the other hand have a small NDZ. Slip-Mode Frequency Shift (SMFS) [20, 21], Active Frequency Drift (AFD) [22], Current injection [23], High frequency signal injection [24, 25] and other active methods introduce perturbation and disturbance at a regular time intervals, in the system, which affects the power quality. Furthermore, the time taken by active methods is considerably high compared to passive techniques. An online technique [26] was proposed to reduce high dimensionality of synchrophasor data and representing it with their principal components with not much loss of information. Power system islanding detection, identification, classification and state evaluation algorithm [27] was proposed using a decision tree algorithm with its application in Dominion Virginia power system. Another approach based on Decision tree [28] classifier and discrete wavelet transform (DWT) of signals was as a feature extraction technique was proposed. In [29], they used an advanced machine learning technique which takes features extracted by autoregressive signal modelling as input for islanding detection on IEEE 13 bus system. A Naive-Bayes classifier [30], along with a statistical signal-processing algorithm was used to extract new features from the measured voltage and frequency indicators. Another researcher [31], used a random forest (RF) classification technique so as to detect islanding and non-islanding situations with an objective of minimizing the NDZ and avoid unwanted DG tripping during non-islanding conditions using IEEE 34 bus system. A number of Big Data handling techniques are available which can be utilized to tackle huge PMU data. Although the problem has been attempted by many researchers in the recent years, the development in big data handling techniques and the evolution of machine learning motivated to approach the problem in this context to improve reliability and performance. This leads to need for an intelligent technique for Islanding Detection within minimum time. There is a continuous search to look for methods that can minimize Non-Detection Zone.

Also, there are many challenges with the traditional machine learning algorithms which has been used to solve the problem of islanding detection in the past. These challenges includes handling of large PMU data, optimal selection of parameters, performance enhancement of classifiers, etc. which needs to be addressed.

From above discussion, it is clear that there is need of a suitable technique to find islanding conditions for better performance of system.

3 Problem Formulation

This section formulates the problem of islanding detection and defines the objectives of this paper. Islanding is a process in which a part of grid is isolated from rest of the distribution system, yet the DG keeps energizing it. Conventionally, a distribution system does not have any active power generating source in it and it does not get power in case of a fault in transmission line upstream but with DG, this presumption is no longer valid. As per the IEEE 929-1988 [32] standard DG should be disconnected in case of island. Although islanding can be intentional or non-intentional, the scope of this work is not only limited to classification of non-intentional islanding events which are caused by accidental shut down of the grid from those of intentional islanding events. It also aims at developing Ensemble Classifiers with minimum false positives and false negatives so as to give maximum precision and recall.

The problem of present work is to develop a predictive model based on machine learning for islanding detection. The first problem is to simulate a real world bus bar system with PMUs installed at several locations for providing high frequency data. Also, an accurate model of PMU is developed and applied at the buses. The data needs to be stored to a database system which is utilized by the predictive algorithm. The various parameters given by the PMU is selected and utilized by the classifier. The problem is to find the optimal parameters either in their basic form or derivatives of those parameters and analyze them for comparative performance. The next target is the extraction of features which helps in saving otherwise huge computational burden. The extracted features are then fed to the classifier for which model is developed (Fig. 1).

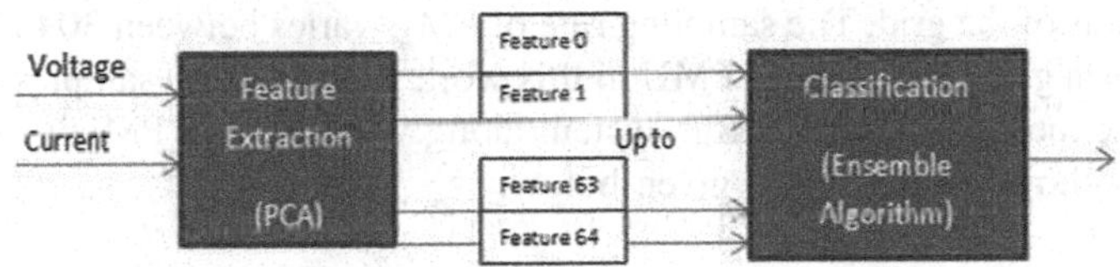

Fig. 1. Proposed technique for islanding detection

4 Proposed Approach

To carry out intensive study, IEEE 13 Bus system is used. The SIMULINK Model of IEEE 13 Bus system is developed for carrying out the study of islanding detection. This circuit model is [33] used to test common features of distribution system analysis, operating at 4.16 kV. It is characterized by a single voltage regulator at the substation, being short, overhead and underground lines, shunt capacitors, relatively highly loaded, an in-line transformer, and importantly unbalanced loading. Complete description of line configuration, line data, transformer data, spot & distributed load data and capacitor data values can be found in reference [33].

A current controlled inverter based DG is then modelled as in [29]. The sampling frequency used in the study is 2.4 kHz. DG used is 5kVA, single phase, 120 V and it is connected through 12/4.16 kV single phase distribution transformer to the distribution system. Presence of DG is a must for islanding scenario to take place. The current controlled inverter based DG is used for the system and is modelled in MATLAB. The parameters of DG system and filter are shown in Table 1.

Table 1. DG-system parameters

S. no	Parameters of the system	
1	Voltage	120 V
2	DG output power	5 kW
3	Switching frequency	8 kHz
4	Input DC voltage	400 V
5	Filter resistance	1 Ω
6	Filter inductance	3 mH
7	Filter capacitance	12 microF

The low-pass filter, with the parameters in Table 1 serves as an interface between inverter and the grid so as to reduce the effect of inverters harmonics. The decoupled current control interface [29] is used in the study. The inverter control is also adjusted in a way that DG always operates at unity power factor as recommended by the IEEE Std. 1547. In this arrangement DG supplies maximum active power while does not provide any reactive power support to the grid.

Next, DG along with the filter and transformer is connected to phase A of node 692 through a single phase circuit breaker. In order to include the concept of wide area monitoring the PMUs are connected at each node. They are responsible to present complete status of the grid. The sampling rate of PMU varies between 30 to 60 which is very high. Data generation rate of PMU in this work is taken as 40 samples per second. The complete model of IEEE 13 Bus system along with DG and PMU's connected at each node is shown in the Fig. 2 given below.

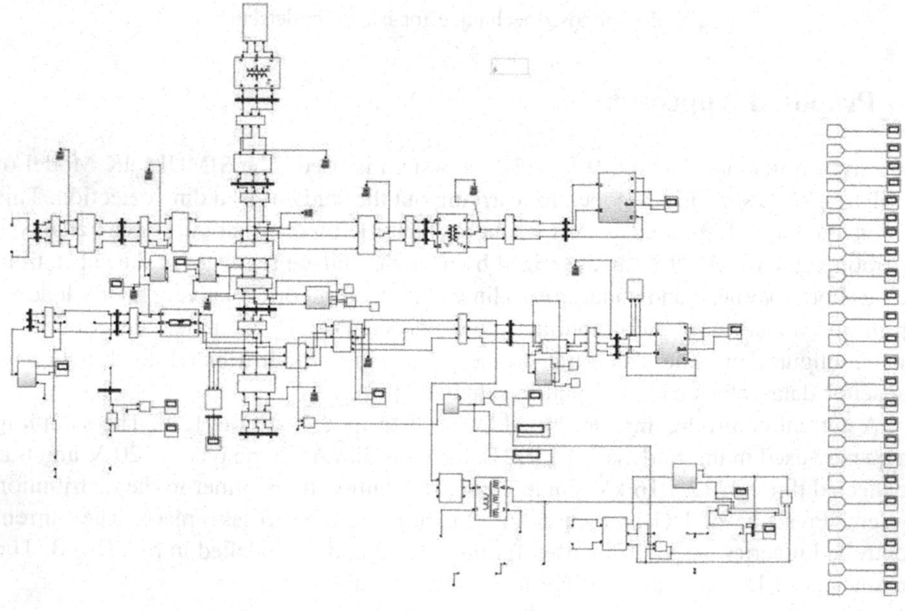

Fig. 2. Proposed model

The Simulink model developed above is used to generate 25 cases of islanding and non-islanding. Islanding occurs when the single phase switch at node 692 is disconnected and a particular section of the grid gets isolated. The set of islanding cases are generated for different combinations of the active and reactive power mismatches. An RLC load is connected in parallel between the grid and DG. A single phase switch is opened up to simulate Islanding conditions. The mismatch power generated by DG and dissipated by the load is varied up to 40% for active and 5% for reactive power. Islanding cases are generated with small and heavy power mismatch between DG and load.

The set of non-islanding cases is generated by switching capacitor banks, switching static loads, applying faults at different locations in the grid & at different points in the system. The line to ground, line to line and 3 faults whose duration & resistance are varied are simulated. The resistance value is changed from 1 Ω to 5 Ω and duration is set as 2 ms, 4 ms, and permanent faults. Both the events are simulated for light system loading conditions up to 40% of the base load. More details about case generation may be found in Table 2.

Table 2. Description of islanding & non-islanding cases

S. no	Cases	No. of events	Description
1	Islanding	6	Various small power mismatches
2	Islanding	5	Various heavy power mismatches
3	Non-islanding	4	Capacitor bank switching
4	Non-islanding	3	Fault level (L-L, L-G,, 3-Phase)
5	Non-islanding	6	Switching static load
6	Non-islanding	1	Switching first DG at node 692

Data Generation. In this paper, continuous monitoring of parameters like Voltage & Current of all phases is done through PMU's and 74 features (V & I) are utilized. A set of non-islanding cases (namely, Capacitor switching, Fault event, Switching of second DG & Static load switching) and islanding cases with small and heavy power mismatches between DG and load are generated. Overall 14 cases of non-islanding and 11 cases of islanding for different conditions are simulated. The PMU model in MATLAB is simulated at 10,000 Hz. But we have assumed a realistic model of PMU with 40 Hz frequency. So, a conversion is made and 160 samples & 74 features for 25 cases are obtained. After combining complete dataset we have got 4000 samples and 74 features.

Feature Extraction. PCA is then applied to extract those features which carry maximum information so as to reduce the high dimensionality and computational time. The generated cases are then classified into islanding or non-islanding using ensemble classifiers. After that a comparison is presented between various algorithms in terms of accuracy, precision and other performance parameters.

After generation of final matrix, dimensionality reduction has been done. Feature extraction has been done with a machine learning algorithm, Principal component analysis (PCA). PCA is a statistical technique which utilizes the variance among data and finds the principal components along which the data contains maximum

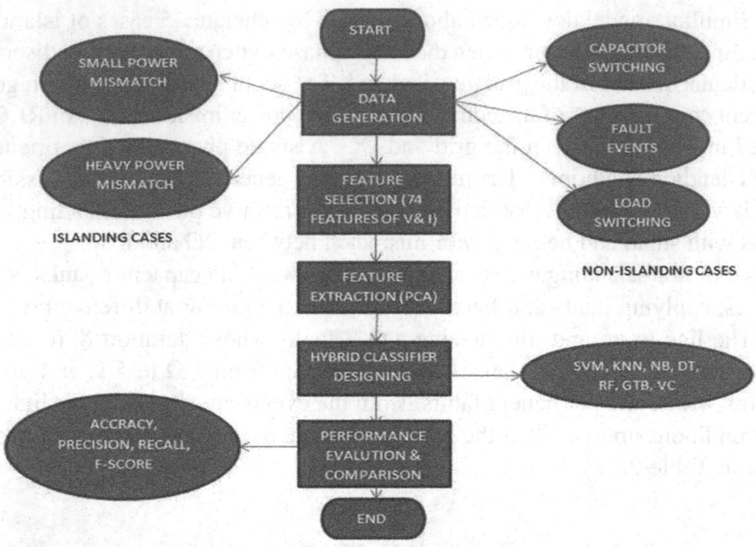

Fig. 3. Flow chart

information. This has helped in improvement in the performance of the classifier and also reduced the time complexity of the algorithm. PCA is applied to reduce the dimensionality of generated data. Using PCA, number of features is reduced from 75 to 24. Finally, advanced machine learning algorithms are applied to make the classification. Ensemble Machine Learning Algorithms use multiple learning algorithms to obtain better prediction than could be obtained from any other constituent learning algorithms. This is a recent advancement in the area of Machine Learning where classifiers are combined to predict resultant class. It helps in building highly accurate models. Basically, there are three categories of ensemble algorithms. They are Bagging, Boosting & Voting classifiers (Fig. 3).

Ensemble Algorithms for Islanding Detection

This paper has utilized all the three categories of ensemble algorithm. Random forest from bagging, Gradient tree boosting from boosting and voting classifier taking votes from K-Nearest Neighbour (KNN), Support Vector Machine (SVM), Naive Bayes (NB) and Decision tree (DT). The results of all classifier are calculated individually and also utilized by voting classifier in classification. They are discussed next.

Gradient Tree Boosting (GTB)

In Boosting algorithms, the predictors learn by sequential learning. First predictor learning is based on the complete data set. The next predictor is based on the training set based on the performance of the previous one. It begins by classifying actual data set & giving equal or same weights to all observation. If class is incorrectly predicted with the first learner, it assigns higher weight to the one which is miss classified. It is an iterative method so adds classifier learner until it approaches a limit in accuracy or the number of models. Hence, we can simply say that boosting algorithms forms a sequence of iterative models that attempt to correct the outputs of the previous models.

Random Forest (RF)
Random forest is a bagging ensemble method where we create random samples of the training data set which are no less than its subsets. And for each subset a classifier is designed and final result is obtained as a combined average or majority voting. Variance error is highly reduced with bagging. In simple terms, Bagging refers to taking multiple samples out of training data-set & training a model for each sample. The training data sets are taken with replacement and trees construction is such that correlation between individual classifiers is reduced. Final output is the averaged sum of all the predictions of sub-models. RF makes use of a number of decision trees so as to improve accuracy and rate of classification.

Voting Classifier (VC)
Ensemble Voting Classifier is a hybrid meta-classifiers that combines various conceptually different or similar machine learning classifiers so as to perform classification through a majority voting. It makes use of soft and hard voting. When the output class is predicted by averaging the probabilities, we call it soft voting. On the other hand, when the predicted output is that class which is mostly predicted by the classification models, we call it hard voting.

5 Results

The SIMULINK model is developed in MATLAB and scripting is done in Python. Also, Sci-kit learn, the machine learning library is used to implement various classifiers. The SIMULINK model developed in above section is utilized to generate various cases related to non-islanding & islanding. Overall 25 cases of both the events are generated with 74 features of voltage & current. The number of features is then reduced from 74 to 25 using PCA. After that various classifiers are tested on it. Results of classifier's performance with constant (74 without PCA and 24 with PCA) and varied set of features are discussed next. Performance of ensemble algorithms remains at the top when features are constant or even varied (Fig. 4).

5.1 Performance Comparison of Classifiers with Constant Features

Random forest has the highest value of accuracy (98% without PCA) in both the cases with and without PCA. Naive Bayes gives better performance with reduced

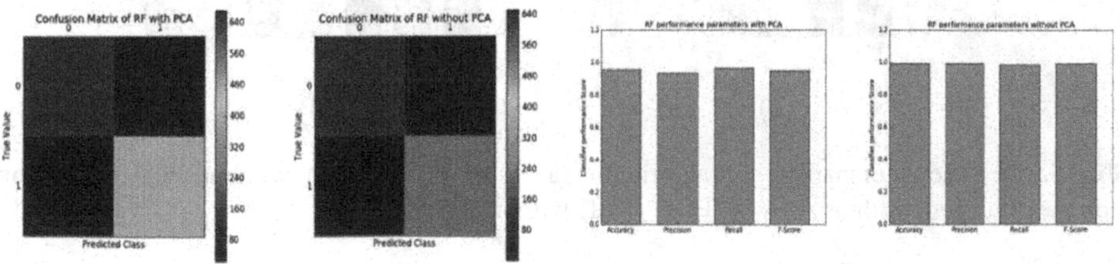

Fig. 4. CM and performance parameters of Random Forest with and without PCA

dimensionality. Accuracy of Voting classifier, Decision tree, KNN and Gradient tree boosting is better than that of SVM. Gradient tree boosting is usually more prone to over fitting problems. Naive Bayes is based upon probabilistic approach. It performs better with a reduced set of features when co-relation among the feature vectors is negligible. Performance of Naive Bayes is better with lower set of features. Naive Bayes has the lowest accuracy equal to 66%. It can be seen that Support vector machine outperforms other classifiers and gives 100% precision. Dimensionality reduction has no significant effect on the performance of SVM in terms of precision. Precision score of Random Forest is 96% followed by Gradient tree boosting, Decision tree and KNN. Naive Bayes has a low precision score. The performance parameters of GTB are good when PCA is not applied. When PCA is applied then the precision is a affected and so F-Score decreases. It can be seen that Random forest and KNN gives the best recall values with PCA. GTB has 99% of recall score without PCA. SVM shows lowest recall score of 49%. Decision tree, Voting classifier and Gradient tree boosting gives a good value of recall score. Naive Bayes has a moderate value of recall score. Random forest has maximum value (98%) of F-score followed by Voting classifier, KNN, Decision tree and Gradient tree boosting. SVM (79%) and Naive Bayes (65%) shows not so good value of F-Score (Fig. 5).

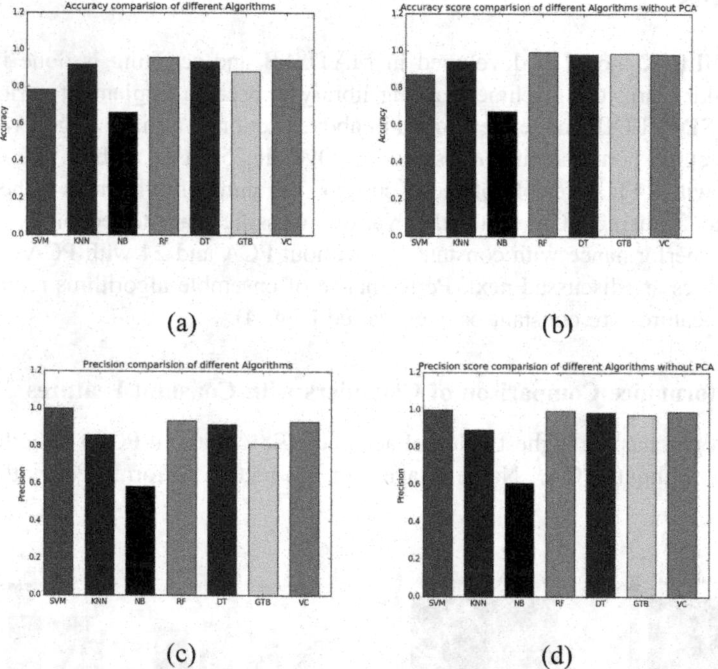

Fig. 5. Accuracy comparison of algorithms (a) with PCA & (b) without PCA. Precision comparison of algorithms (c) with PCA & (d) without PCA.

5.2 Performance Comparison of Classifiers with Variation in Features

It is observed that Random Forest and Voting classifier has maximum accuracy at different features. Naive Bayes, Support vector machine, KNN and Gradient tree boosting gives a constant value of accuracy at different features. Naive Bayes has an accuracy of 66% and that of SVM has 76%. Rest all classifier perform better than NB and SVM. However, Support vector machine outperforms other classifier and gives 100% precision value at any number of features. The graph below gives a relation between precision and variation in features for different classifier. Among all classifiers, KNN gives a constant and maximum value of recall score with variation in features followed by RF. KNN, Decision Tree and Gradient tree boosting gives a constant value of F-Score for any number of features. Random forest and Voting classifier has the highest value of F-Score (Fig. 6).

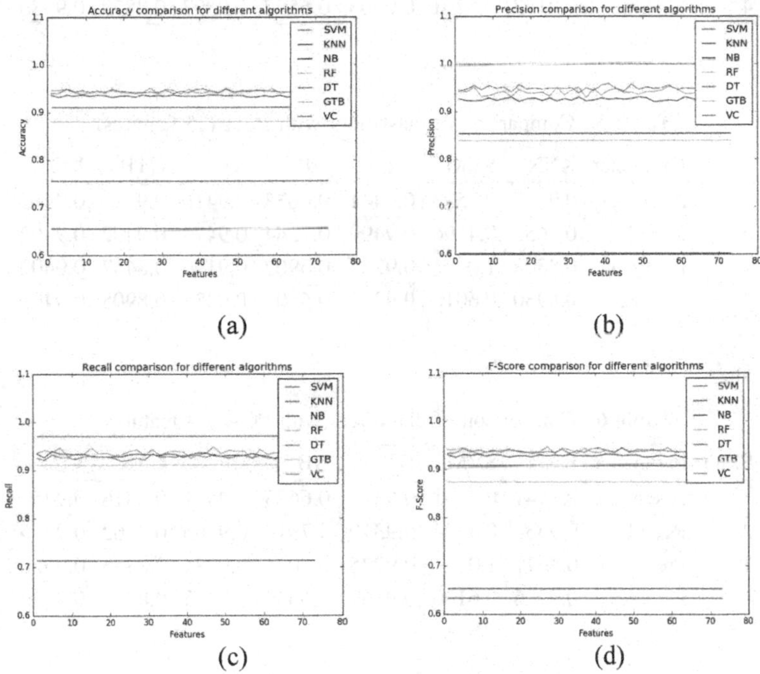

Fig. 6. (a) Accuracy (b) Precision (c) Recall (d) F-score comparison of algorithms with variation in features

Performance parameter of Random Forest, Decision Tree and Voting classifier vary highly with variation in the number of features. So in order to obtain best results an optimal value of features is chosen where classifier performs best. Various classifiers with/without PCA are studied. The features are varied as 3, 25, 53 and 76. The results for the same are tabulated in Tables 1, 2, 3, 4, 5, 6 and 7. On comparison it is found that random forest outperforms the best in less or more number of features.

Table 3. Comparison of classifiers without PCA

S. no	Parameter	KNN	SVM	DT	NB	RF	GTB	VC
1	Accuracy	0.9516	0.8483	0.985	0.6683	0.9883	0.9783	0.9841
2	Recall	0.9759	0.6635	0.9870	0.6913	0.9852	0.9926	0.9685
3	Precision	0.9214	1.0	0.9798	0.6181	0.9888	0.9606	0.9961
4	F-score	0.9479	0.7977	0.9834	0.6527	0.9870	0.9763	0.9821

Table 4. Comparison of classifiers with PCA (3 features)

S. no	Parameter	KNN	SVM	DT	NB	RF	GTB	VC
1	Accuracy	0.9216	0.755	0.9283	0.6733	0.9466	0.89	0.945
2	Recall	0.9775	0.4494	0.9307	0.7116	0.9344	0.9325	0.9363
3	Precision	0.8642	1.0	0.9102	0.6148	0.9450	0.8383	0.9398
4	F-score	0.9173	0.6201	0.9203	0.6597	0.9397	0.8829	0.9380

Table 5. Comparison of classifiers with PCA (25 features)

S. no	Parameter	KNN	SVM	DT	NB	RF	GTB	VC
1	Accuracy	0.9	0.7533	0.9441	0.6633	0.9416	0.9	0.9483
2	Recall	0.9653	0.4296	0.9499	0.7244	0.9479	0.9402	0.9402
3	Precision	0.8308	1.0	0.9232	0.5902	0.9196	0.8457	0.9402
4	F-score	0.8930	0.6010	0.9363	0.6505	0.9335	0.8905	0.9402

Table 6. Comparison of classifiers with PCA (53 features)

S. no	Parameter	KNN	SVM	DT	NB	RF	GTB	VC
1	Accuracy	0.9141	0.7491	0.9341	0.6683	0.9441	0.8816	0.945
2	Recall	0.9534	0.4394	0.9310	0.7318	0.9366	0.9162	0.9236
3	Precision	0.8677	1.0	0.9225	0.6074	0.9384	0.8353	0.9520
4	F-score	0.9086	0.6106	0.9267	0.6638	0.9375	0.8738	0.9376

Table 7. Comparison of classifiers with PCA (76 features)

S. no	Parameter	KNN	SVM	DT	NB	RF	GTB	VC
1	Accuracy	0.9125	0.7541	0.9508	0.65	0.9541	0.9025	0.9566
2	Recall	0.9813	0.4506	0.9459	0.7243	0.9497	0.9553	0.9422
3	Precision	0.8472	1.0	0.9442	0.5885	0.9479	0.8465	0.9601
4	F-score	0.9094	0.6213	0.9451	0.6494	0.9488	0.8976	0.9511

The suggested approach is also compared with other and existing method as mentioned in Table 8. It is clear from Table 8 that RF has highest accuracy among various compared methods.

Table 8. Comparison of classifier accuracy with previous work

S. no	Algorithm	Accuracy
1	SVM [29]	0.9771
2	PNN [34]	0.806
3	RF	0.9883
4	VC	0.9841
5	GTB	0.9783
6	KNN	0.9516
7	DT	0.985
8	NB	0.6683

6 Conclusions and Future Scope

SIMULINK/MATLAB model of IEEE-13 bus system equipped with PMU was prepared along with the DG. Simulation result of IEEE-13 bus system was validated by comparing it with the standard results. Multiple simulations were carried out to obtain data for islanding & non-islanding cases. The discussed problem is solved in two different ways i.e. with and without dimensionality reduction using PCA. Hybrid Ensemble classifier is compared with other learning classifiers.

This study is performed on 13-Bus system. Similar studies can be performed on a large bus system and the methodology can be applied on real data set generated by a PMU. PMU data can be utilized by the machine learning algorithms. Big data handling library spark can find its application in dealing this huge data. It can also be applied on real time scenario for testing purpose. A number of other cases can be included to give more realistic effect. This study can be extended by including the effect of multiple DG's and changing in the system topology. Advanced machine learning techniques can be utilized in a higher bus system.

References

1. Li, C., Cao, C., Cao, Y., Kuang, Y., Zeng, L., Fang, B.: A review of islanding detection methods for microgrid. Renew. Sustain. Energy Rev. **35**, 211–220 (2014)
2. Ahmad, K.N.E.K., Selvaraj, J., Rahim, N.A.: A review of the islanding detection methods in grid-connected PV inverters. Renew. Sustain. Energy Rev. **21**, 756–766 (2013)
3. Lidula, N., Rajapakse, A.: Microgrids research, a review of experimental microgrids and test systems. Renew. Sustain. Energy Rev. **15**, 186–202 (2011)
4. IEEE Standard for Interconnecting Distributed Resources into Electric Power Systems, IEEE Standard 1547TM, June 2003

5. Zeineldin, H.H., El-Saadany Ehab, F., Salama, M.M.A.: Impact of DG interface control on islanding detection and non detection zones. IEEE Trans. Power Deliv **21**(3), 1515–1523 (2006)
6. Bower, W., Ropp, M.: Evaluation of islanding detection methods for photovoltaic utility-interactive power systems. Technical report IEA T5-05, International Energy Agency, Photovoltaic Power Systems, March 2002
7. Xu, W., Zhang, G., Li, C., Wang, W., Wang, G., Kliber, J.: A power line signaling based technique for anti-islanding protection of distributed generators Part I: scheme and analysis. IEEE Trans. Power Deliv. **22**(3), 1758–1766 (2007)
8. Balaguer-Álvarez, I.J., Ortiz-Rivera, E.I.: Survey of distributed generation islanding detection methods. IEEE Lat. Am. Trans. **8**, 565–570 (2010)
9. Chowdhury, S., Chowdhury, S., Crossley, P.: Islanding protection of active distribution networks with renewable distributed generators. Electr. Power Syst. Res. **79**, 984–992 (2009)
10. Ecconnect, Assessment of islanded operation of distribution networks and measures for protection. In: Polymercontents, vol. 18, p. 83077 (2001)
11. Redfern, M.A., Usta, O., Fielding, G.: Protection against loss of utility grid supply for a dispersed storage and generation unit. IEEE Trans. Power Deliv. **8**, 948–954 (1993)
12. Freitas, W., Xu, W., Affonso, C.M., Huang, Z.: Comparative analysis between RO-COF and vector surge relays for distributed generation applications. IEEE Trans. Power Deliv. **20**, 1315–1324 (2005)
13. Pai, F.-S., Huang, S.-J.: A detection algorithm for islanding-prevention of dispersed consumer-owned storage and generating units. IEEE Trans. Energy Convers. **16**, 346–351 (2001)
14. Hashemi, F., Kazemi, A., Soleymani, S.: A new algorithm to detection of anti islanding based on dqo transform. Energy Procedia **14**, 81–86 (2012)
15. Kamyab, E., Sadeh, J.: Islanding detection method for photovoltaic distributed generation based on voltage drifting. IET Gener. Transm. Distrib. **7**, 584–592 (2013)
16. Jang, S., Kim, K.: An islanding detection method for distributed generation algorithm using voltage unbalance and total harmonic distortion of current. IEEE Trans. Power Deliv. **19**(2), 745–752 (2004)
17. Kabayashi, H., Takigawa, K., Hashimato, E.: Method for preventing islanding phenomenon on utility grid with a number of small scale PV systems. In: Proceedings of the Second IEEE Photovoltaic Specialists Conference, vol. 1, pp. 695–700 (1991)
18. Singam, B., Hui, L.Y.: Assessing SMS and PJD schemes of anti-islanding with varying quality factor. In: Proceedings of the IEEE International Power and Energy Conference (PECon), pp. 196–201 (2006)
19. Yin, J., Chang, L., Diduch, C.: A new adaptive logic phase shift algorithm for anti islanding protections in inverter based DG systems. In: Proceedings of the Power Electronics Specialists Conference, pp. 2482–2486 (2005)
20. Liu, F., Kang, Y., Zhang, Y., Duan, S., Lin, X.: Improved SMS islanding detection method for grid-connected converters. IET Renew. Power Gener. **4**, 36–42 (2010)
21. Lopes, L.A.C., Sun, H.: Performance assessment of active frequency drifting islanding detection methods. IEEE Trans. Energy Convers. **21**, 171–180 (2006)
22. Hanif, M., Street, K., Gaughan, K.: A discussion of anti-islanding protection schemes incorporated in a inverter based DG. In: Proceedings of the 10th International Conference on Environment and Electrical Engineering (EEEIC), pp. 1–5 (2011)
23. Hernandez-Gonzalez, G., Iravani, R.: Current injection for active islanding detection of electronically-interfaced distributed resources. IEEE Trans. Power Deliv. **21**, 1698–1705 (2006)

24. Briz, F., Reigosa, D., Blanco, C., Guerrero, J.M.: Coordinated operation of parallel connected inverters for active islanding detection using high frequency signal injection. In: Proceedings of the IEEE Energy Conversion Congress and Exposition, pp. 2296–2303 (2013)
25. Reigosa, D., Briz, F., Blanco, C., Garcia, P., Manuel, G.J.: Active islanding detection for multiple parallel-connected inverter-based distributed generators using high-frequency signal injection. IEEE Trans. Power Electron. **29**, 1192–1199 (2014)
26. Chen, Y., Xie, L., Kumar, P.R.: Dimensionality reduction and early event detection using online synchrophasor data. In: 2013 IEEE Power and Energy Society General Meeting (PES), pp. 1–5. IEEE (2013)
27. Sun, R.: Wide area power system islanding detection, classification and state evaluation algorithm. Doctoral dissertation, Virginia Polytechnic Institute and State University
28. Heidari, M., Seifossadat, G., Razaz, M.: Application of decision tree and discrete wavelet transform for an optimized intelligent-based islanding detection method in distributed systems with distributed generations. Renew. Sustain. Energy Rev. **30**(27), 525–532 (2013)
29. Matic-Cuka, B., Kezunovic, M.: Islanding detection for inverter-based distributed generation using support vector machine method. IEEE Trans. Smart Grid **5**(6), 2676–2686 (2014)
30. Najy, W.K., Zeineldin, H.H., Alaboudy, A.H., Woon, W.L.: A Bayesian passive islanding detection method for inverter-based distributed generation using ESPRIT. IEEE Trans. Power Deliv. **26**(4), 2687–2696 (2011)
31. Faqhruldi, O.N., El-Saadany, E.F., Zeineldin, H.H.: A universal islanding detection technique for distributed generation using pattern recognition. IEEE Trans. Smart Grid **5**(4), 1985–1992 (2014)
32. Recommended Practice for Utility Interconnected Photovoltaic (PV) Systems, IEEE 71 Standard 929-2000 (2000)
33. Kersting, W.H.: Radial distribution test feeders. IEEE Trans. Power Syst. **6**(3), 975–985 (1991)
34. Khamis, A., Shareef, H., Mohamed, A., Bizkevelci, E.: Islanding detection in a distributed generation integrated power system using phase space technique and probabilistic neural network. Neurocomputing **19**(148), 587–599 (2015)

An Analytical Approach for the Determination of Chemotherapeutic Drug Application Trade-Offs in Leukemia

Probir Kumar Dhar[1,2], Tarun Kanti Naskar[2,4], and Durjoy Majumder[3,4(✉)]

[1] ECE Department, BCET, SSB Sarani, Bidhannagar, Durgapur, Burdwan 713212, West Bengal, India
[2] Mechanical Engineering Department, Jadavpur University, 188 RSC Mallick Road, Kolkata 700032, India
[3] Department of Physiology, West Bengal State University, Malikapur, Barasat, Kolkata 700126, India
durjoy@rocketmail.com
[4] Society for Systems Biology & Translational Research, 103, Block – C, Bangur Avenue, Kolkata 700055, India

Abstract. For the treatment of different leukemia different chemotherapies are available. However the success rate of any particular drug scheduling may vary with leukemic condition. In general, low dose of chemotherapy is suggested for chronic leukemia, whereas application of high dose (myeloablative) chemotherapy is applied for acute and vigorous type of leukemia. In present work we have shown that chronic type of leukemia is controlled; however, for controlling vigorously growing leukemia is a challenge due to chemotherapeutic toxicity to the normal cells of the hematopoietic system. Hence for its management, we developed a control analysis model. This model may help to design an optimal chemotherapeutic schedule so that the controlling of the vigorously growing leukemic growth can be possible in one hand with the sustenance of the normal non-leukemic cell population on the other hand. This work shows that for long-term chemotherapeutic success in individual leukemic patients demands a judicious choice of drug dosing strategy that may determine the trade-off between leukemic growth and restoration time of normal cell population of the hematopoietic system.

Keywords: Difference delay equation · Eigen analysis · Optimal drug control Chemotherapy · Leukemia

1 Introduction

Hematopoiesis is a complex process starting from pluripotent hematopoietic stem cell (HSC). These cells have the characteristics of self-renewal and differentiation capacity. Different mature cells like erythrocytes (RBCs), leukocytes (WBCs) and thrombocytes (THBs) (platelets) of the hematopoietic system are generated from these cells through the involvement of different molecular events governed by different humoral factors

P. Bhattacharyya et al. (Eds.): NGCT 2017, CCIS 827, pp. 390–404, 2018.
https://doi.org/10.1007/978-981-10-8657-1_30

[1–3]. Any dysregulation in any of the molecular processes leads to the development of leukemia. Towards the analysis of the process, mathematical modeling has gained importance since 1976 to delineation of the pathophysiological event under the condition of leukemia [4]. In the work, analytical model has constructed for acute myeloid leukemia pathogenesis considering single lineage (neutrophilic) multi-compartment model by using ordinary differential equation (ODE) with delay (DODE). With this model, assessment regarding the effect of chemotherapeutic intervention has been addressed [5]. Later on, considering similar type of model, normal as well as leukemic cell population have included for testing the persistence of leukemic state by varying different kinetic parameters of the considered variables [6]. Further, DODE is used for the development of multi-lineage, multi-compartmental model and parametric influence on the dynamical behavior of the hematopoietic system have been studied [7–11]. Through these models, development of chronic myeloid leukemia (CML) has addressed followed by the effect of application of oral application of low dose of chemotherapy (CHEMO).

Such models are modified further to address the dynamics of CML and different workers have concluded different inferences. It has been established that leukemic HSC is the source of leukemia and analytically the relapse or blast crisis have shown after successful therapy [12]. Other works suggest that successful recovery of CML will depend upon the amount of availability of the functional T-cells [13, 14]. Considering PK-PD (pharmacokinetics and pharmacodynamics), applications of myeloablative (high dose) (MYL) chemotherapeutic drug scheduling have been modeled and applied for AML (acute myeloid leukemia) cases [15, 16]. In a recent work the assessment of spatio-temporal dynamics for CLL (chronic lymphocytic leukemia) is addressed and trajectory of leukemic cell migration to different lymphoid organ is addressed with a two compartmental systems model [17].

There are varied types of leukemia and hence, different types of therapies including different types of therapeutic scheduling are being applied in clinical practice. To address this, a DODE model of hematopoiesis has been developed. This model is further modified for the development of a generalized therapeutic model of leukemia treatment [18–20]. Here an analytical procedure is proposed for the determination of optimal drug dose that govern the successful long-term chemotherapeutic outcome together with restoration of normal (non-leukemic) cell population of the hematopoietic system.

2 Methods

2.1 Model Description

In the recent works, a single model using DODE was developed to test the efficacies of different therapeutic strategies namely low dose chemotherapy (CHEMO) and high dose myeloablative chemotherapy (MYL) along with RBC (T_{RBC}) and platelet ($T_{PLATELET}$) transfusion [18–20]. The developed model considers cells with three states i.e., normal cell (g), drug sensitive cell (s) and dug resistive cell (r). Again each cellular states belong to three lineages i.e., erythrocyte lineage, leukocyte lineage and megakaryocyte lineage. Further, each lineage depending upon maturity has three types of cell i.e., stem cell (*S*), precursor cell (erythroblast, *P1*; leukoblast, *P2* and megakaryoblast, *P3*) and mature cell (RBC, *B1*; WBC, *B2* and platelet, *B3*) population (Table 1).

Table 1. Considered variables in model parameters.

	Stem cell	Progenitor cell compartment			Matured cell compartment		
		Erythroblast	Leukoblast	Megakaryoblast	RBC	WBC	Platelet
Considered cells[†] (Cells/μL)	Sg	$P1g$	$P2g$	$P3g$	$B1g$	$B2g$	$B3g$
	Ss	$P1s$	$P2s$	$P3s$	$B1s$	$B2s$	$B3s$
	Sr	$P1r$	$P2r$	$P3r$	$B1r$	$B2r$	$B3r$
Multiplication rate[†] (Cells/day)	m_{Sg}	m_{P1g}	m_{P2g}	m_{P3g}	m_{B1g}	m_{B2g}	m_{B3g}
	m_{Ss}	m_{P1s}	m_{P2s}	m_{P3s}	m_{B1s}	m_{B2s}	m_{B3s}
	m_{Sr}	m_{P1r}	m_{P2r}	m_{P3r}	m_{B1r}	m_{B2r}	m_{B3r}
Apoptosis rate (Cells/day)	a_{Sg}	a_{P1g}	a_{P2g}	a_{P3g}	a_{B1g}	a_{B2g}	a_{B3g}
	a_{Ss}	a_{P1s}	a_{P2s}	a_{P3s}	a_{B1s}	a_{B2s}	a_{B3s}
	a_{Sr}	a_{P1r}	a_{P2r}	a_{P3r}	a_{B1r}	a_{B2r}	a_{B3r}
Differentiation rate[†] (Cells/day)	$Sgdr$	$P1gdr$	$P2gdr$	$P3gdr$	$B1gdr$	$B2gdr$	$B3gdr$
	$Ssdr$	$P1sdr$	$P2sdr$	$P3sdr$	$B1sdr$	$B2sdr$	$B3sdr$
	$Srdr$	$P1rdr$	$P2rdr$	$P3rdr$	$B1rdr$	$B2rdr$	$B3rdr$
Differentiation delay time[†] (Days)	$Sgdt$	$P1gdt$	$P2gdt$	$P3gdt$	$B1gdt$	$B2gdt$	$B3gdt$
	$Ssdt$	$P1sdt$	$P2sdt$	$P3sdt$	$B1sdt$	$B2sdt$	$B3sdt$
	$Srdt$	$P1rdt$	$P2rdt$	$P3rdt$	$B1rdt$	$B2rdt$	$B3rdt$
Conversion rate[†] (Cells/day)	CS_{gs}	$CP1_{gs}$	$CP2_{gs}$	$CP3_{gs}$	$CB1_{gs}$	$CB2_{gs}$	$CB3_{gs}$
	CS_{gr}	$CP1_{gr}$	$CP2_{gr}$	$CP3_{gr}$	$CB1_{gr}$	$CB2_{gr}$	$CB3_{gr}$
	CS_{sg}	$CP1_{sg}$	$CP2_{sg}$	$CP3_{sg}$	$CB1_{sg}$	$CB2_{sg}$	$CB3_{sg}$
	CS_{sr}	$CP1_{sr}$	$CP2_{sr}$	$CP3_{sr}$	$CB1_{sr}$	$CB2_{sr}$	$CB3_{sr}$
	CS_{rg}	$CP1_{rg}$	$CP2_{rg}$	$CP3_{rg}$	$CB1_{rg}$	$CB2_{rg}$	$CB3_{rg}$
	CS_{rs}	$CP1_{rs}$	$CP2_{rs}$	$CP3_{rs}$	$CB1_{rs}$	$CB2_{rs}$	$CB3_{rs}$

[†]For all parametric values we have followed Dhar & Majumder, 2015 [19].

Different considered variables and their unit in model are shown in Table 1. In the Table 1, rows marked green, blue and grey indicate the considered variables for normal, dug sensitive and drug resistive cell respectively. Algorithmic steps for model development are represented stepwise in Fig. 1. The model is represented by the following DODE [18–20].

$$x(k) = Ax(k-1) + \sum_{m=1}^{4} A_m x(k - dk_m) + RBC_{tf} T_{RBC}(k) + PLATELET_{tf} T_{PLATLET}(k) \tag{1}$$

where $x(k) = [x_1(k); x_2(k); \ldots; x_{21}(k)]$, $x(k-1) = [x_1(k-1); x_2(k-1); \ldots; x_{21}(k-1)]$, $x(k-dk_1) = [x_1(k-dk_1); x_2(k-dk_1); \ldots; x_{21}(k-dk_1)]$, $x(k-dk_2) = [x_1(k-dk_2); x_2(k-dk_2); \ldots; x_{21}(k-dk_2)]$, $x(k-dk_3) = [x_1(k-dk_3); x_2(k-dk_3); \ldots; x_{21}(k-dk_3)]$, $x(k-dk_4) = [x_1(k-dk_4); x_2(k-dk_4); \ldots; x_{21}(k-dk_4)]$. In Eq. 1, matrix A is a $[21 \times 21]$ matrix whose diagonal elements $a_{i,j}$ are represented by $(1 + m_{Nx} - c1 \times Nxdr - a_{Nx} - CN_{xy} - CN_{xz} - C_{myl} \times Myl_{Nx} \times d_{myl}(k))$ where $(i, j) \equiv (1, 1), (2, 2), (3, 3), \ldots, (21, 21)$. In Nx, N denotes the cell type and x denotes the cellular state – normal (g), drug sensitive (s) and drug resistive (r) category.

For example $P1r$ represents erythroblast ($P1$) cell type of drug resistive (r) category. Again m_{Nx}, a_{Nx}, $Nxdr$ represent the multiplication rate, apoptosis rate and differentiation rate of the concerned cell type (Nx). $c1$ represents the ON/OFF switch for cell differentiation. It will become ON on the day of differentiation of the concerned progenitor cell. Conversion rate (C) from concerned cellular state (represented by first subscript) to other cellular state (represented by second subscript) is represented by CN_{xy} and CN_{xz}. For example $CP1_{rs}$ represents conversation rate of erythrocyte cell type from drug resistive to drug sensitive state. Again d_{myl} represents the MYL drug profile in the system. Myl_{Nx} denotes the MYL drug sensitivity of the concerned cell type. C_{myl} represents the ON/OFF switch for MYL drug application. The conversion rates from other cell types are represented by the matrix elements $a(i,j) = CN_{yx} + CN_{zx}$ where $(i,j) \equiv (i-2, j-1), (i-2, j), (i-1, j-2), (i-1, j), (i, j-2), (i, j-1)$ with $i = j = 3, 6, 9, 12, 15, 18, 21$. Again the immunity related killing effect are represented by the matrix elements $a(i,j) = kill_{im} \times kill_{eff} \times CF(k-1)$ where $i = 2, 3, 8, 9, 17, 18, 20, 21$ and for all i, $j = 16$. Genotypic toxicity effect due to malignancy is represented by the matrix element $a(i,j) = -Tox$, where $(i,j) \equiv (1, 2), (1, 3), (4, 5), (4, 6), (10, 11), (10, 12)$. Tox is a fractional number represents the malignancy related toxicity effect on the normal cell population. The high phenotypic cachexia effect due to $P2r$ is represented by the matrix element $a(i,j) = -M_{Tox1}$, where $(i,j) \equiv (1, 9), (4, 9), (7, 9), (10, 9), (13, 9), (16, 9), (19, 9)$. The medium phenotypic cachexia effect due to $P2s$ is represented by the

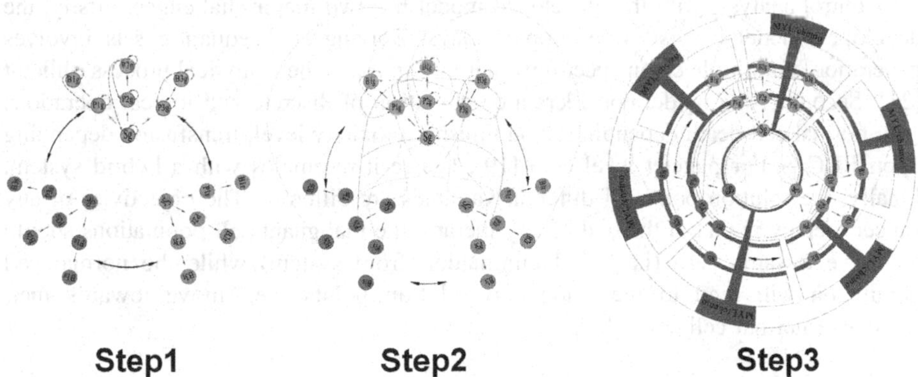

Fig. 1. Gradual development of algorithmic following steps from 1 to 3 for model development. Step1, heterogeneous cell population of the hematopoietic system (green, blue and gray circles representing g-type, s-type and r-type cell populations respectively. The dashed black arrows indicating the feedback signals, solid black straight arrows representing the cell differentiation and curved solid black both side arrows representing the conversions of cells); Step 2 includes the effect of cachexia (it is the detrimental effect produced by the leukemic blast cells on the normal cell population that result in complex symptoms like loss of weight) on g-type cells by the s- and r- type cells (green, blue and black solid arrows represent phenotypic effect of low, medium and high cachexia respectively; whereas solid magenta arrows represent genotypic toxicity effect); Step 3 design of MYL (represented by the red part) within the TCU (Therapeutic Control Unit represented by concentric circular block). (Color figure online)

matrix element $a(i, j) = -M_{Tox2}$, where $(i, j) \equiv (1, 8), (4, 8), (7, 8), (10, 8), (13, 8), (16, 8), (19, 8)$. The low phenotypic cachexia effect due to *B2 s* is represented by the matrix element $a(i, j) = -M_{Tox3}$, where $(i, j) \equiv (1, 17), (4, 17), (7, 17), (10, 17), (13, 17), (16, 17), (19, 17)$. The low phenotypic cachexia effect due to *B2r* is represented by the matrix element $a(i, j) = -M_{Tox3}$, where $(i, j) \equiv (1, 18), (4, 18), (7, 18), (10, 18), (13, 18), (16, 18), (19, 18)$. For the other elements of *A* matrix $a(i, j) = 0$. M_{Tox1}, M_{Tox2} and M_{Tox3} all are fractional numbers represent the cachexia effects by *P2r*, *P2s*, *B2r* and *B2s* on the normal cell population.

In Eq. 1, in matrix A_1, $a_1(i, j) = Sgdr/3$ is represented by $(i,j) = (4, 1), (7, 1), (10, 1)$. Again, $a_1(i, j) \equiv Ssdr/3$ where $(i, j) \equiv (5, 2), (8, 2), (11, 2)$. Again, $a_1(i, j) \equiv Srdr/3$ where $(i, j) \equiv (6, 3), (9, 3), (12, 3)$. In matrix A_2, $a_2(i, j) = P1gdr/3$ where $(i, j) \equiv (13, 4)$, for $a_2(i, j) = P1sdr/3$ where $(i, j) \equiv (14, 5)$ and $a_2(i, j) = P1rdr/3$ where $(i, j) \equiv (15, 6)$. For the other elements of A_2 matrix $a_2(i, j) = 0$. In matrix A_3, $a_3(i, j) = P2gdr/3$ where $(i, j) \equiv (16, 7)$, for $a_3(i, j) = P2sdr/3$ where $(i, j) \equiv (17, 8)$ and for $a_3(i, j) = P2rdr/3$ where $(i, j) \equiv (18, 9)$. For the other elements of A_3 matrix $a_3(i, j) = 0$. In matrix A_4, $a_4(i, j) = P3gdr/3$ where $(i, j) \equiv (19, 10)$, for $a_4(i, j) = P3sdr/3$ where $(i, j) \equiv (20, 11)$ and for $a_4(i, j) = P3rdr/3$ where $(i, j) \equiv (21, 12)$. For the other elements of A_4 matrix $a_4(i, j) = 0$. In RBC_{tf} matrix, $RBC_{tf}(13, 1) = 1$ on the day of RBC transfusion, else = 0, for $RBC_{tf}(i, j) = 0$ where $i \neq 13$ and $j = 1$. In $PLATELET_{tf}$ matrix, $PLATELET_{tf}(19, 1) = 1$ on the day of platelet transfusion, else = 0, for $PLATELET_{tf}(i, j) = 0$ where $i \neq 19$ and $j = 1$.

Control analysis with this developed model has two major challenges. Firstly, the developed model consists of multiple delays. Solving such equation sets involves generation of multiple eigen spectrums that in turn make the analytical process difficult [21]. Secondly, the model considers a combination of discrete and logical operations (e.g. normal cell death depending upon threshold toxicity level, transfusion depending upon RBC and/or platelet level etc.) [19]. Hence it resembles with a hybrid system. Finally, the solution points of different variables are different. The objectivity of any cancer therapy is that at the end of any therapy the malignant cell populations should converge towards zero (i.e., total elimination from system) while the normal cell population will tend to their non-zero solution points (i.e., move towards their respective normal cell count levels).

2.2 Development of Control Analysis Model (CAM)

For the controllability analysis, a [6 × 6] state variable based Control Analysis Model (CAM) has been developed using ordinary difference equations with the most significant variables responsible for leukemia (i.e., the cells of drug sensitive and drug resistive lymphocytic lineages). The model has been developed through the following steps:

1. The differentiation delays in actual model were eliminated using necessary calibration factors. These factors encompass the elimination of the extra cell count that appears earlier in the system output due to elimination of delay time.

2. The transformed non-delay [21 × 21] model was further reduced to a [6 × 6] state variable model selecting the cells of drug sensitive and drug resistive lymphocytic lineages i.e., *Sr*, *Ss*, *P2r*, *P2s*, *B2r* and *B2s*.

The CAM model is represented by following state space relations.

$$x(k+1) = Fx(k) - H\,u(k) \tag{2a}$$

$$y(k) = C\,x(k) \tag{2b}$$

Equation (2b) is the system output. In Eq. (2a), *u*(*k*) is the external forcing function (drug); hence, *u*(*k*) = *K*(*k*)*y*(*k*). Further, with Eq. (2b), (2a) may be updated as:

$$x(k+1) = F\,x(k) - C\,H\,K(k)\,x(k) \tag{3}$$

In Eq. (3), $x(k) = [Ss(k); Sr(k); P2s(k); P2r(k); B2s(k); B2r(k)]$, $F = [f_{11}\ 0\,0\ 0\,0\,0;\ 0 f_{22}\ 0\,0\,0\,0;\ f_{31}\ 0 f_{33}\ 0\,0\,0;\ f_{41}\ 0\,0 f_{44}\ 0\,0;\ f_{51}\ 0\,0\,0 f_{55}\ 0;\ f_{61}\ 0\,0\,0\,0 f_{66}]$, $C = [1\,1\,1\ 1\,1\,1]$. *H*-matrix is a diagonal matrix having diagonal elements: $h_{11}, h_{22}, h_{33}, h_{44}, h_{55}$ and h_{66} elements and *K*-matrix is also a diagonal matrix having the following diagonal matrix elements: $k_{11}, k_{22}, k_{33}, k_{44}, k_{55}$ and k_{66}. In *F* matrix, $f_{11} = (1 + m_{Ss} - a_{Ss} - Ssdr - CS_{sg} - CS_{sr})$, $f_{22} = (1 + m_{Sr} - a_{Sr} - Srdr - CS_{rg} - CS_{rs})$, $f_{33} = (1 + m_{P2s} - a_{P2s} - P2sdr - CP2_{sg} - CP2_{sr})$, $f_{44} = (1 + m_{P2r} - a_{P2r} - P2rdr - CP2_{rg} - CP2_{rs})$, $f_{55} = (1 - a_{B2s} - CB2_{sg} - CB2_{sr})$, $f_{66} = (1 - a_{B2r} - CB2_{rg} - CB2_{rs})$, $f_{31}(k) = 1/3 \times Ssdr$, $f_{41}(k) = 1/3 \times Srdr$, $f_{51}(k) = 1/3 \times P2sdr$, $f_{61}(k) = 1/3 \times P2rdr$. In *H* matrix, $h_{11} = Myl_{Ss}, h_{22} = Myl_{Sr}, h_{33} = Myl_{P2s}, h_{44} = Myl_{P2r}, h_{55} = Myl_{B2s}, h_{66} = Myl_{B2r}$. In *K* matrix, $k_{11} = (C_{myl} \times d_{myl}(k))$, $k_{22} = (C_{myl} \times d_{myl}(k))$, $k_{33} = (C_{myl} \times d_{myl}(k))$, $k_{44} = (C_{myl} \times d_{myl}(k))$, $k_{55} = (C_{myl} \times d_{myl}(k))$, $k_{66} = (C_{myl} \times d_{myl}(k))$. Hence, the closed loop system is represented as:

$$x(k+1) = F_{cl}x(k) \tag{4a}$$

$$y(k) = C\,x(k) \tag{4b}$$

where, $F_{cl} = (F - C\,H\,K(k))$. Eigen value analysis is performed at each time point of the system transfer matrix F_{cl} to find the controllability criteria and the trade-off of different controlling factors of the leukemic system.

3 Results

Rigorous simulation runs of the actual model along with the non-delay model and CAM model were carried out for vigorously growing leukemic condition with the initial parametric conditions as mentioned in Dhar and Majumder, and Dhar et al. [19, 20]. Chronic leukemic condition is considered by changing *Srdr, P2sdr* and *P2rdr* by 1.35 times, 1.55 times and 1.95 times respectively with respect to the vigorously growing condition, other parametric values are kept unchanged. All simulations are carried out in Matlab 6.5. Simulations showed that in case of vigorously growing condition normal stem cell was reduced to zero much earlier than chronic leukemic condition, as leukemic growth in later case was much slower than the previous type.

3.1 Effect of CHEMO and MYL

Simulation was carried out to understand the effect of CHEMO and MYL drug on chronic and vigorous type of leukemia. Both actual and CAM model is applied to both types of leukemic condition and for simulation studies with both the models, we have followed the initial parametric values as mentioned in Dhar and Majumder [19]. Long run simulation shows that in chronic leukemia, leukemic cells converged to zero with low dose CHEMO (daily drug dose = 0.037 for 1500 days) (Fig. 2a). While vigorously growing leukemia, after completion of high dose MYL (dose = 0.7, standard interval between successive day of drug application, t_{myld} was 15 days and considered cycle, n_{myl} was 8) therapy showing unbound nature of leukemic growth in long run (Fig. 2b).

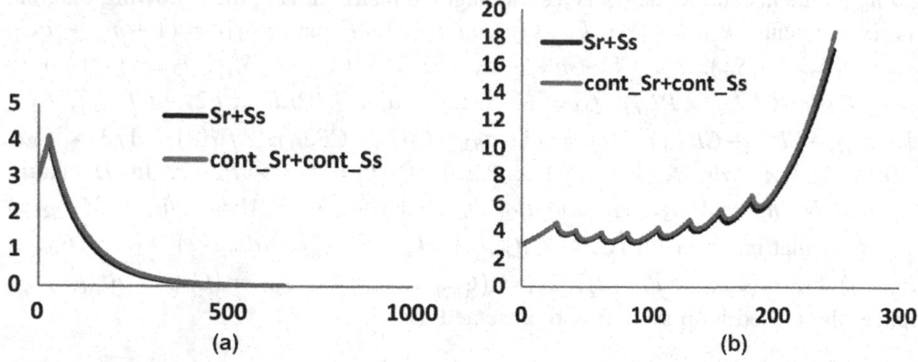

Fig. 2. Comparative growth dynamics of leukemic (drug sensitive and drug resistive) stem cell in actual model (represented by black solid line) and in CAM model (represented by red solid line). Leukemic stem cells' growth dynamics of chronic (treated with CHEMO) and vigorously (treated with MYL) are plotted in (a) and (b) respectively. In both the plots, Y- and X-axis represent cell count (in number) and time (in day) respectively. (Color figure online)

3.2 Change in Drug CR on the Frequency of RBC Transfusion and Its Effect on Leukemic Stem Cell Population

With the change in drug clearance rate (CR), simulation studies reveal that requirement of intermittent RBC transfusion varies; with higher CR, lesser number of intermittent RBC transfusion. With lesser drug CR, there is higher drug retention. This causes drug related toxicity effect on the RBC i.e., $a(13, 13)$ of matrix A through d_{myl} (Fig. 3a).

To maintain the normal physiological condition transfusion is required and here it is operated by transforming $RBC_{tf}(13, 1) = 1$ in RBC_{tf} matrix. However, drug retention causes higher concentration of drug within the system that kills more leukemic cell population. The effect of drug is operated on the malignant leukemic stem cell population through $a(2, 2)$ and $a(3, 3)$ elements of matrix A (Fig. 3b). Similar type of observation is also noted for platelet transfusion.

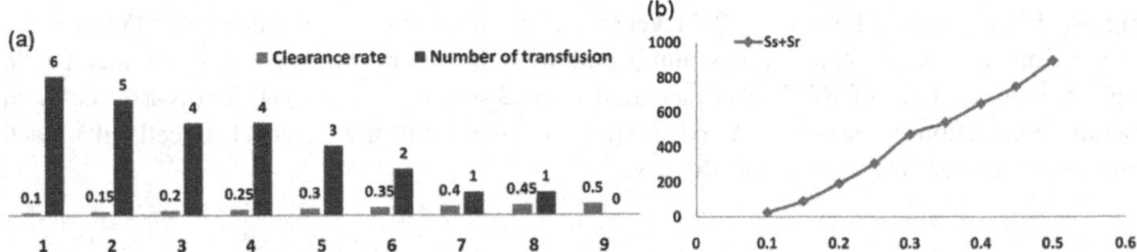

Fig. 3. Effect of drug CR on intermittent transfusion requirement (a) and leukemic cell population (b) when vigorous type leukemia is treated with MYL. In (a) the number on the bar representing the number of transfusion (brown) vis-à-vis CR (blue) during the course of therapeutic regime. Horizontal axis represents number of simulations. In (b) plot shows number of leukemic stem cell population (Y-axis) (after one year from the day of diagnosis) with change in CR (X-axis). (Color figure online)

3.3 Effect of Lower Bound of RBC Level on the Completion of MYL Application

Lower limit of RBC level indicates the physiological variability which may indicate tolerance level of different patients. Considering vigorous type of leukemic condition with MYL drug application (dose = 0.75, CR = 0.2 and standard interval between two consecutive drug applications = 15), simulation runs with the increase of lower limit of RBC reveals that there is increase in transfusion frequency (Fig. 4a). This also makes a shifting in therapy completion, as during RBC transfusion there is a delay in subsequent MYL application (Fig. 4b). Similar type of observation is also noted for the cases of platelet transfusion.

3.4 Eigen Value Assignment

Cancer including leukemic system has been considered as a robust system [22]. Therapy is applied to break this robustness. Low dose CHEMO becomes successful under the considered condition of simulation. However, high dose MYL for vigorously growing leukemia is a challenge due to drug related toxicity within the system. Hence eigenvalue assignment approach has been applied for the assessment of control of leukemic growth with the consideration of MYL related toxicity.

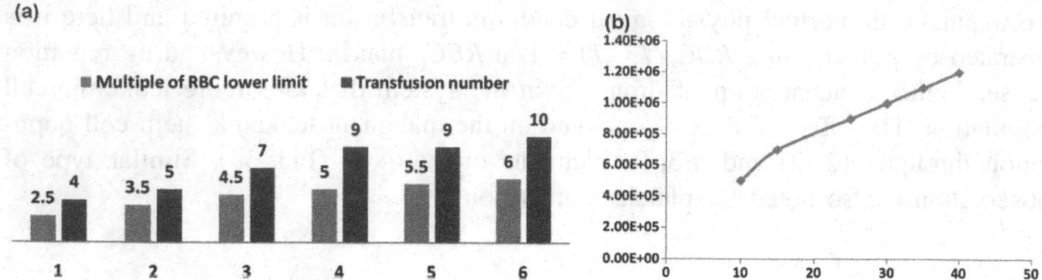

Fig. 4. Effect of lower bound of RBC level on transfusion frequency and delay of MYL therapy completion. In (a), bar chart shows number of transfusions during the course of therapeutic regime as lower limit of RBC level increased from 2×10^5 (cells/μL). In (b) X-axis delay in therapy completion (in days) and Y-axis represents lower limit of RBC level (in cells/μL). Each simulation runs are carried out for 365 days.

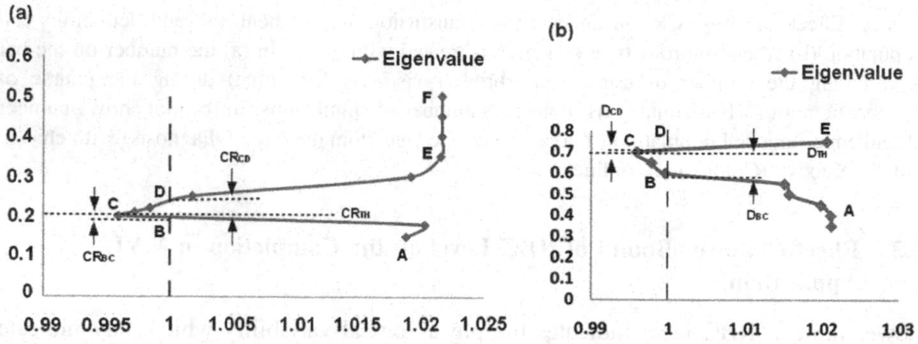

Fig. 5. Movement of rightmost eigenvalues of the system transfer matrix F_{cl} with different drug related parameters in vigorous type of leukemia. Plot (a) shows movement of rightmost eigenvalue (generated on day 158) (X-axis) with CR between 0.1 and 0.5 (Y-axis) (with fixed drug dose) for vigorous type leukemia. Plot (b) shows movement of rightmost eigenvalue (X-axis) with change in drug dose (Y-axis) with fixed CR. Rightmost eigenvalues are indicated in bold in Tables 2 and 3.

System equation is simulated for 365 days considering vigorously growing leukemic cells along with MYL therapy (dose = 0.7, standard interval between successive day of drug application, t_{myld} was 15 days and considered cycle, n_{myl} was 8) [19]. This condition is simulated with different CR and the movement of the rightmost eigenvalue on day 158 is noted (Table 2). This has a nonlinear movement against CR (Fig. 5a). In Fig. 5a point C represents eigenvalue for threshold CR (CR_{TH}). Plot shows that an increase in CR_{TH} up to CR_{CD} whereas a minor decrease up to CR_{BC} are allowed to keep eigenvalue movement in the range <1. Simulation reveals that with other parametric settings unchanged, such variation in CR around CR_{TH}, drug related toxicity may not affect on normal cell population. And hence did not enhance the need of more drug stoppage (for transfusion) and keep system controllable. In the condition when

$CR > CR_{TH} + CR_{CD}$ makes less drug retention in the system allows cachexia related killing of normal cells by the leukemic blast cells. On the other hand, with lower CR (when $CR < CR_{TH} - CR_{BC}$) there is higher amount of drug retention within the system that causes drug related toxicity with simultaneous higher amount of leukemic cell killing (drug related killing). Both the cases necessitate the need of more drug stoppage (for transfusion) and during this time there is an opportunity of leukemic cell growth. These conditions cause failure of therapy control and allow maintenance of the robustness leukemic condition. Plot also indicates that a little bit higher CR is allowable for physiological maintenance, but lower CR is not allowable (poor excretory condition). Under the above leukemic condition with the above-applied dose, for any value of CR, long-run simulation indicates that when drug is totally cleared from the system (on ~365 days), eigen value reaches above 1.

Table 2. Change in eigenvalue with the amount of drug present (that varies with clearance rate, CR) in the system on day 158[†]. Right most eigen values are indicated in bold.

CR	d_{myl}	Eigenvalues
0.15	0.0376	0.9860, 1.0036, 1.0081, 0.9892, 1.0141, **1.0187**
0.2[†]	0.3584	0.8841, 0.9017, 0.9775, 0.9128, 0.9377, **0.9958**
0.21	0.3451	0.8897, 0.9073, 0.9792, 0.9170, 0.9419, **0.9971**
0.22	0.3322	0.8952, 0.9127, 0.9809, 0.9211, 0.9460, **0.9983**
0.25	0.2953	0.9102, 0.9277, 0.9854, 0.9324, 0.9572, **1.0017**
0.3	0.0404	0.9875, 1.0050, 1.0086, 0.9903, 1.0152, **1.0191**
0.35	0.0026	0.9981, 1.0157, 1.0117, 0.9983, 1.0232, **1.0215**
0.4	0.00007	0.9988, 1.0163, 1.0119, 0.9988, 1.0237, **1.0216**

[†]Day 158 is selected as this day is the one week after completion of therapy with amount of drug dose 0.7 and drug present in the system is $\boldsymbol{d_{myl}}$ = 0.3584 with CR = 0.2 of the system [19].

Again, the previously mentioned condition is simulated with different MYL dose and movement of the rightmost eigenvalues are noted on day 164 (fourth day after completion of therapy with MYL dose = 0.75, t_{myld} = 15, CR = 0.2 and cycle (n_{myl}) = 8) (Table 3) (Fig. 5b). System equation is simulated for 365 days considering vigorously growing leukemic cells along with MYL therapy (standard interval between successive day of drug application, $\boldsymbol{t_{myld}}$ = 15 days, cycle n_{myl} = 8 and CR = 0.2). This condition is simulated with different drug dose and the movement of the rightmost eigenvalue on day 30, 164 and 365 are noted (Table 3). This has a nonlinear movement against drug dose (Fig. 5b). In Fig. 5b point C represents eigenvalue for threshold drug dose (D_{TH}). Plot shows that a minor increase in D_{TH} up to D_{CD} whereas a minor decrease up to D_{BC} are allowed to keep eigenvalue movement in the range <1. Simulation reveals that with such variation in drug dose around D_{TH}, drug related toxicity may not affect on normal cell population. And hence did not enhance the need of more drug stoppage (for transfusion) and keep system controllable. In the condition with lower drug dose i.e., $D < D_{TH} - D_{BC}$ results less drug present in the system and allows cachexia related killing of normal cells by the leukemic blast cells. On the other hand, with higher drug dose i.e., when $D > D_{TH} + D_{CD}$ there is higher amount of drug present within the system that causes drug related toxicity with simultaneous higher amount of leukemic cell killing (drug related killing). Both the cases necessitate the need of more drug stoppage (for transfusion) and during this time there is an opportunity of leukemic cell growth. These conditions cause failure of therapy control and allow for maintaining the robustness of leukemic condition. Plot also indicates that a little bit lower D is allowable for physiological maintenance, but higher D is not allowable. Under this condition, for any value of applied dose, long-run simulation ($\sim$365 days) indicates that when drug becomes absent from the system due to physiological clearance rate, eigenvalue becomes >1.

Table 3. Change in eigenvalue and residual drug present within the system for different drug dose application. Right most eigen values are indicated in bold.

Dose	On day 30 (i.e., on the day of 1st dose application)		On day 164 (from the day of diagnosis)	
	d_{myl}	Eigenvalues	d_{myl}	Eigenvalues
0.75	0.75	0.7588, 0.7763, 0.9399, 0.8188, 0.8437, **0.9676**	0.3072	0.9005, 0.9180, 0.9825, 0.9251, 0.9500, **0.9995**
0.7	0.7	0.7748, 0.7923, 0.9447, 0.8308, 0.8557, **0.9712**	0.0940	0.9687, 0.9863, 1.0029, 0.9763, 1.0011, **1.0149**
0.65	0.65	0.7908, 0.8083, 0.9495, 0.8428, 0.8677, **0.9748**	0.0872	0.9709, 0.9884, 1.0036, 0.9779, 1.0028, **1.0153**
0.6	0.6	0.8068, 0.8243, 0.9543, 0.8548, 0.8797, **0.9784**	0.0805	0.9730, 0.9906, 1.0042, 0.9795, 1.0044, **1.0158**
0.55	0.55	0.8228, 0.8403, 0.9591, 0.8668, 0.8917, **0.9820**	0.0242	0.9911, 1.0086, 1.0096, 0.9930, 1.0179, **1.0199**
0.5	0.5	0.8388, 0.8563, 0.9639, 0.8788, 0.9037, **0.9856**	0.0220	0.9918, 1.0093, 1.0098, 0.9935, 1.0184, **1.0200**
0.45	0.45	0.8548, 0.8723, 0.9687, 0.8908, 0.9157, **0.9892**	0.0065	0.9967, 1.0143, 1.0113, 0.9972, 1.0221, **1.0212**
0.4	0.4	0.8708, 0.8883, 0.9735, 0.9028, 0.9277, **0.9928**	0.0019	0.9982, 1.0157, 1.0118, 0.9983, 1.0232, **1.0215**
0.35	0.35	0.8868, 0.9043, 0.9783, 0.9148, 0.9397, **0.9964**	0.0017	0.9983, 1.0158, 1.0118, 0.9984, 1.0233, **1.0215**
0.3	0.3	0.9028, 0.9203, 0.9831, 0.9268, 0.9517, **1.0000**	0.0005	0.9987, 1.0162, 1.0119, 0.9987, 1.0236, **1.0216**

3.5 Effect of MYL Dose on Survival Period of Normal HSC, Presence of Drug Amount, Leukemic Stem Cell Population and Therapy Completion Delay

System was simulated for 600 days in vigorously growing leukemic condition with MYL (dose = 0.75, CR = 0.2 and standard interval between two consecutive drug applications = 15). It was observed that due to drug clearance from the system on day 165, d_{myl} reached below the threshold drug amount 0.3072 (minimum drug level required to keep developed leukemic system controllable) and hence, malignant system became unbounded on day 365 (Table 3). Again with this dose the course of therapeutic regime took longest time to complete because drug related side effect on the normal cell population forced the system for frequent drug stoppage to conduct transfusion.

Keeping other parametric settings unchanged, system was further simulated with stepwise decreasing the drug dose amount and observed the changes in leukemic stem cell population (with respect to freely growing condition), change in therapeutic course completion delay (with respect to drug dose = 0.75) and presence of drug on 164 day after each simulation (Fig. 6). Simulation showed that lower dose reduces the presence of drug amount in the system. Presence of lower amount of drug in the system helped normal HSC to survive (due to lesser amount of drug related toxicity). Hence with lower dose application requirement of frequent drug stoppages (for intermittent transfusion) can be avoided. This favors completion of therapeutic schedule with much less delay time (Fig. 6). However such lower concentration of drug fails to control leukemic population below toxicity level that in turn increased the possibility of normal cell population killing (Fig. 6). Hence in one hand, if drug dose becomes high it causes drug related toxicity (and this is detrimental for the patient) but causes eradication of leukemic cells and delay in therapy completion. On the other hand if drug becomes low that does not impose any drug related toxicity within the physiological system and the completion of therapy would be earlier; but it favors leukemic growth condition which in turn causes cachexia related toxicity in long run (and this is detrimental for patient). Hence, a judicious choice of drug dose optimization becomes important for the chemotherapeutic success.

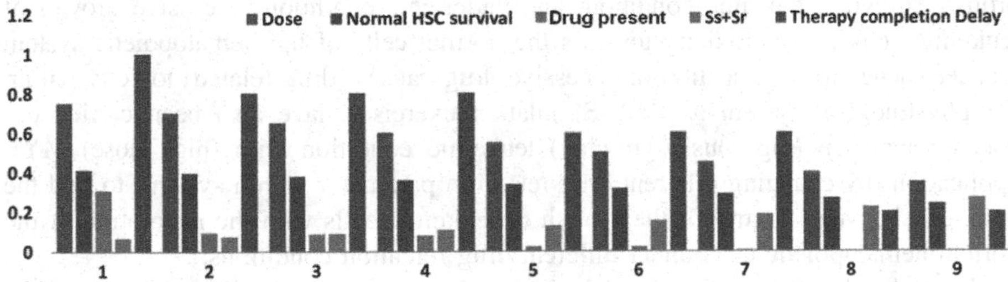

Fig. 6. Effect of drug dose on normal HSC survival span (with respect to free growth), drug presence within the system, leukemic stem cell population (with respect to freely growing condition) and delay in therapy completion (with respect to therapy with dose = 0.75) for vigorous type leukemia treated with MYL. Numbering below the horizontal axis represents number of simulation run (Drug dose is decreased stepwise from 0.75 to 0.35). Vertical axis represents intensity of changes in different variables. Each simulation run is carried out for 365 day.

4 Discussion

The prevalent mindset for the treatment of cancer is to cure the disease by eradicating cancer cells from the body. And to ensure this, high dose chemotherapy is applied in clinical cancer cases. However, this imposes undesirable side effects and toxicity within the physiological system of the concerned cancer patients. Hence, to subdue this side effects and toxicity intermittent gap periods are allowed between two successive chemotherapy applications along with different supportive therapies. In the cases that are beyond cure, this clinical prerogative is changed to extend life with palliative care. However, this is unnecessary and instead of application of conventional treatment regime, the goal could always be control of tumor. And this could be the realistic yardstick for treatment success whether successful eradication of cancer cells is possible or not [23]. With this view, here we have attempted to optimize therapeutic design (e.g., drug dose) under different physiological constraints (e.g., CR) for the controllability of the leukemic system.

However, presence of different delays and feedbacks in the hematopoietic system make the systems equation non-linear; and hence, control analysis and/or optimization of therapeutic dose would be a challenge. To address this, here we developed a linearized control analysis model. With the present parametric settings, the developed control analysis model is calibrated in a way that in freely growing condition its output dynamics will lead to the actual (nonlinear) system and in case of any successful therapeutic control, it lags the dynamics of the actual system. This adjustment will help to make a prior assessment regarding the long term control of future leukemic growth. Such approach is already suggested and applied in the assessment of therapeutic control for the malignancies of solid tumors [24–26].

In the present work, simulation exercises suggest that control of chronic leukemia is possible with low dose chemotherapy application. System is also considered for vigorously growing leukemic condition; and under this condition, excessive growth of leukemic cells causes toxicity towards the normal cells of the hematopoietic system (cancer cachexia). Application of excessive drug causes (drug related) toxicity within the physiological system as well. Simulation exercises have also been carried out considering such (vigorously growing) leukemic condition with (high dose) MYL application (by changing different drug retention parameter within system) to find the trade-offs between control of the growth of leukemic cells with the restoration of the normal hematopoietic cells under different drug retention conditions.

Like all other types of cancers, leukemic cells may exhibit robust behavior [22]. Chemotherapy is applied to break such robustness of cancer cells and to ensure this, high dose of chemotherapy is applied in clinical cancer cases. Simulation studies show that, after application of high dose chemotherapy, absence threshold drug level may help to maintain the robust behavior of the leukemic cells.

The developed model is a generalized model hence it can address any type of leukemia – both acute and chronic types in both myeloid and lymphoid origin. Major objective of leukemia prognosis is to know minimal residual diseases (MDR) in terms of eradication of leukemic stem cells. In clinic, prognostic assessment of leukemia (for any type of leukemia whether it is myeloid or lymphoid origin) is routinely assessed by bone marrow biopsy. Simulation runs may denote the dynamical behavior of the systems future condition and may have the predictive role in the assessment of prognosis in terms of control rather total eradication of leukemic (stem) cells.

Our developed generalized therapeutic model of leukemia can capture the following features:

1. leukemia load in a time dependent manner
2. drug efficacy in terms of cell killing (absorption)
3. delay in drug application (distribution)
4. drug CR (metabolism and excretion).

Simulation runs with the setting of initial parametric values for individual patients followed by matching of prognostic data may be useful in the appreciation of the model. Killing of leukemic cells may indicate bioavailability and efficacy of drug to the target leukemic cells. Considered drug efficacy parameter may indicate the drug absorption. Analysis for the prediction regarding the subsequent drug application or delay is indicative for distribution of drug within the system. Moreover, setting of parametric values for the clearance rate for drug is indicative to the drug metabolism and its excretion. Hence, through this model conventional PK-PD analysis is possible. In the model as cachexia has been addressed and it is a multi-compartmental model (bone marrow and peripheral blood); therefore through this model long-term spatio-temporal therapeutic assessment can also be possible. We hope this model may help in optimization for the designing of chemotherapeutic schedule in leukemia.

References

1. Ogawa, M.: Differentiation and proliferation of hematopoietic stem cells. Blood **81**, 2844–2853 (1993)
2. Orkin, S.H.: Hematopoiesis: how does it happen? Curr. Opin. Cell Biol. **7**, 870–877 (1995)
3. Peschle, C., Botta, R., Muller, R., Valtieri, M., Ziegler, B.: Purification and functional assay of pluripotent haematopoietic stem cells. Rev. Clin. Exp. Hematol. **5**, 3–14 (2001). https://doi.org/10.1046/j.1468-0734.2001.00029.x
4. Rubinow, S.I., Lebowitz, J.L.: A mathematical model of the acute myeloblastic leukemic state in man. Biophys. J. **16**, 897–910 (1976). https://doi.org/10.1016/S0006-3495(76)85740-2
5. Rubinow, S.I., Lebowitz, J.L.: A mathematical model of the chemotherapeutic treatment of acute myeloblastic leukemia. Biophys. J. **16**, 1257–1271 (1976). https://doi.org/10.1016/S0006-3495(76)85772-4
6. Djulbegovic, B., Svetina, S.: Mathematical model of acute myeloblastic leukaemia: an investigation of the relevant kinetic parameters. Cell Prolif. **18**, 307–319 (1985)
7. Colijn, C., Mackey, M.C.: A mathematical model of hematopoiesis—I. Periodic chronic myelogenous leukemia. J. Theoret. Biol. **237**, 117–132 (2005)
8. Colijn, C., Mackey, M.C.: A mathematical model of hematopoiesis: II. Cyclical neutropenia. J. Theoret. Biol. **237**, 133–146 (2005)
9. Colijn, C., Fowler, A.C., Mackey, M.C.: High frequency spikes in long period blood cell oscillations. J. Math. Biol. **53**, 499–519 (2006). https://doi.org/10.1007/s00285-006-0027-9

10. Haurie, C., Dale, D.C., Rudnicki, R., Mackey, M.C.: Modeling complex neutrophil dynamics in the grey collie. J. Theoret. Biol. **204**, 505–519 (2000)
11. Michor, F., Hughes, T.P., Iwasa, Y., Branford, S., Shah, N.P., et al.: Dynamics of chronic myeloid leukemia. Nature **435**, 1267–1270 (2005). https://doi.org/10.1038/nature03669
12. ten Cate, B., de Bruyn, M., Wei, Y., Bremer, E., Helfrich, W.: Targeted elimination of leukemia stem cells: a new therapeutic approach in hemato-oncology. Curr. Drug Targets **11**, 95–110 (2010). https://doi.org/10.2174/138945010790031063
13. Kim, P.S., Lee, P.P., Levy, D.: Dynamics and potential impact to chronic myelogenous leukemia. PLoS Comput. Biol. **4**, e1000095 (2008). https://doi.org/10.1371/journal.pcbi.1000095
14. Peet, M.M., Kim, P.S., Niculescu, S.I., Levy, D.: New computational tools for modeling chronic myelogenous leukemia. Math. Model. Nat. Phenom. **4**, 48–68 (2009). https://doi.org/10.1051/mmnp/20094203
15. Pefani, E., Panoskaltsis, N., Mantalaris, A., Georgiadis, M.C., Pistikopoulos, E.N.: Design of optimal patient-specific chemotherapy protocols for the treatment of acute myeloid leukemia. Comput. Chem. Eng. **57**, 187–195 (2013)
16. Pefani, E., Panoskaltsis, N., Mantalaris, A., Georgiadis, M.C., Pistikopoulos, E.N.: Chemotherapy drug scheduling for the induction treatment of patients with acute myeloid leukemia. IEEE Trans. Biomed. Eng. **61**, 2049–2056 (2014). https://doi.org/10.1109/TBME.2014.2313226
17. Savvopoulos, S., Misener, R., Panoskaltsis, N., Pistikopoulos, E.N., Mantalaris, A.: A personalized framework for dynamic modeling of disease trajectories in chronic lymphocytic leukemia. IEEE Trans. Biomed. Eng. **63**, 2396–2404 (2016). https://doi.org/10.1109/TBME.2016.2533658
18. Dhar, P.K., Mukherjee, A., Majumder, D.: Difference delay equation based analytical model of hematopoiesis. Autom. Control Physiol. State Funct. **1**, 1–11 (2012). https://doi.org/10.4303/acpsf/235488
19. Dhar, P.K., Majumder, D.: Development of the analytical model for the assessment of the efficiencies of different therapeutic modalities in leukaemia. J. Comput. Syst. Biol. **1**, 1–45 (2015). https://doi.org/10.15744/2455-7625.1.104
20. Dhar, P.K., Naskar, T.K., Majumder, D.: Analytical model for the assessment of efficiency of stem cell transplantation with suicidal gene construct for the treatment of leukemia. J. Oncol. Trans. Res. **1**, 1–5 (2015). https://doi.org/10.4172/jotr.1000103
21. Yi, S., Nelson, P.W., Ulsoy, A.G.: Analysis and control of time delayed systems via the Lambert W funtion. In: Proceedings of 17th World Congress, The International Federation of Automatic Control, Seoul, Korea, pp. 13414–13419 (2008)
22. Kitano, H.: Violations of robustness trade-offs. Mol. Syst. Biol. **6**, 1–8 (2010). https://doi.org/10.1038/msb.2010.40
23. Gatenby, R.A.: A change of strategy in the war on cancer. Nature **459**, 508–509 (2009)
24. Mukherjee, A., Majumder, D.: Dynamical model for the assessment of anti-angiogenic therapy of cancer. Mol. BioSyst. **6**, 1047–1055 (2010)
25. Majumder, D., Mukherjee, A.: A passage through systems biology to systems medicine: adoption of middle-out rational approaches towards the understanding of clinical outcome in cancer therapy. Analyst **136**, 663–678 (2011). https://doi.org/10.1039/c0an00746c
26. Majumder, D., Mukherjee, A.: Multi-scale modeling approaches in systems biology towards the assessment of cancer treatment dynamics: adoption of middle-out rationalist approach. Adv. Cancer Res. Treat. **2013**, Article ID 587889 (2013). https://doi.org/10.5171/2013/587889

Term Co-occurrence Based Feature Selection for Sentiment Classification

Sudarshan S. Sonawane[1(✉)] and Satish R. Kolhe[2]

[1] Department of Computer Engineering,
Shri Gulabrao Deokar College of Engineering, Jalgaon, India
sudars2000@gmail.com
[2] School of Computer Sciences, North Maharashtra University, Jalgaon, India
srkolhe2000@gmail.com

Abstract. In this paper, the strategy of feature selection for sentiment classification explored and compared to other significant feature selection strategies found in contemporary literature. The feature selection models performed using the statistical measure of t-score and z-score. SVM, NB and AdaBoost classifiers used for classification and compared. The objective of the paper is to explore and evaluate the scope of statistical measures for identifying the optimal features and its significance to classify the opinion using divergent classifiers. Performance analysis carried out on varied datasets with diverse range like the movie reviews, product reviews and tweets, the experiments carried out on feature selection strategies proposed and other strategies found in literature. From the results of the experimental studies, it is evident that optimal features selected using t-score and z-score are robust and outperformed the other feature selection strategies. In order to assess the significance of the feature selection models proposed, the classification process carried out using three classifiers called SVM, NB and AdaBoost. The classification accuracy about the features obtain by proposed models is much higher that compared to the classification accuracy obtained for the features selected by other contemporary models. Among the three classifiers that used to assess classification accuracy, AdaBoost has outperformed the other two models of SVM and NB.

Keywords: Sentiment classification · Optimal feature selection
t-score · z-score · TF-IDF · IG & GA · SVM · Naïve Bayes · AdaBoost

1 Introduction

Sentiment Analysis is the process of extracting opinions from the set of text documents [1]. The increasing volumes of data over the varied communication platforms facilitates the process of analyzing opinions of the consumers or target audience about the products, services, and events can support to gather the more insights in to the emerging trends, consumer behavior, expectations from the markets, brand perception. Hence, the demand for usage of sentiment analysis is high. The process of sentiment classification is to align a document to various categories like the positive, negative and neutral according to its subjective information. Some of the intrinsic conditions of sentiment classification are in extracting inputs from conglomerate expressions.

P. Bhattacharyya et al. (Eds.): NGCT 2017, CCIS 827, pp. 405–417, 2018.
https://doi.org/10.1007/978-981-10-8657-1_31

For instance, in a movie review, polarity classification is generally the combination of real-facts and the actual data that reviewed.

However, the major challenge of the sentiment analysis is handling negated opinions that envisaged in the process. In comparison to the movie review dataset, product review data sets considerably vary. In product oriented sentiment analysis, reviewers discuss either positively or negatively about the product facets. While some features of the product liked and some features disliked, classifying the overall opinion over the product in to negative or positive opinion is a challenge.

Some kind of specific comments expressed in the product reviews, like "though overall features are good, battery life is a concern" adds more complexity to the analysis. In general, product review dataset usually comprises more comparative sentences than the review of movies and it shall be complex to classify such data [2].

In sentiment classification processes [1] machine learning methods are profoundly adapted. Among the common phenomena used for sentiment classification Bag of Words is the major method adapted as it leverages higher level of dimensionality feature space. Feature selection methods in combination with machine-learning algorithms are implemented, it can support in reducing noisy and irrelevant features and enable managing high-dimensionality feature space in more appropriate conditions [3].

In this paper, emphasis is on the optimizing feature selection process of the opinion mining to achieve the operative analysis of the sentiment related to consumer preferences, reflection of consumer choice over a product is a positive or negative. The term co-occurrence based feature selection is critical objective of the model depicted in this manuscript. Concerning this, the proposed model is using the statistical measures to depict the optimal features those entails to classify the opinions. In addition, the effectiveness of the feature selection strategies over the divergent datasets also analyzed.

2 Related Work

The text comprising inputs of consumer opinions, perceptions and emotions are considered for sentiment analysis, and the process comprise numerous tasks. Four significant tasks that are integral to the sentiment analysis, wherein the most of research effort is focused upon are pre-processing of data, labelling of the class, annotation granularity and identification of target [3].

Review of literature signifies that few of the studies have focused on empirical evaluation of performance from varied classification algorithms adapted for sentiment mining.

The model explored in [3] devised a scale called entropy weighted genetic algorithm for feature selection. This scale is the combination of Information gain and genetic algorithm. Though the experimental study evinced the significant classification accuracy, which is inconsistent, also the computational complexity is maximal, as the GA and IG are expensive since their process complexity is exponential.

In [4] the authors have carried out a comparative study on four classifiers like Decision Trees, NB model, SVM and K-Nearest Neighbors, for evaluating performance in sentiment mining of online product reviews. Vivid sampling methods like the linear sampling, random sampling and bootstrap sampling were adapted to create training examples from vivid product reviews dataset. Results from the study signify that SVM with bootstrap sampling method performs better than the other classifiers and sampling methods for misclassification rate. Unigrams were used for feature space and terms occurrence to populate the classification input. However, the study hasn't provided any information about the influence of input format pertaining to classification results.

Two of the profoundly used sentiment analysis approaches are machine learning approach and lexicon or semantic based approach [5, 6]. There are both pros and cons in both the approaches. In the further sections discusses some related works comprising the previously mentioned approaches.

Lexicon method of sentiment classification proposed in [6] wherein the semantic orientation and machine learning are comprised in to single framework. Emphatically, it evident that the content-specific features and sentiment features with content-free adapted in various existing machine-learning approach.

In [7] unsupervised linguistic method adapted for classifying sentiment of distinct range of product reviews in a sentence levels. Senti Word Net is used for calculating the general sentiment score and upon cumulating the opinion sentiment score for every sentence, either positive review or negative review, process is implemented. The researchers have carried out automatic word classification based on polarity. This work used the data from WSJ (Wall Street Journal) instead of internet-based data, for determination of a word as a positive or a negative element.

In [8], the both the kind of opinions were categorized based on the generated pros and cons from reviews. To evaluate the customer opinion in the context of free text reviews, the classifier trained with data comprising both positive and negative elements, are chosen. Performance of classifiers SVM, NB and ME based on evaluation matrices F1-Measure.

In [9], the study engaged interactive visualization system that targets on analysis of public sentiments for trending topics during the period.

Uncertainty modelling and model-driven adjustments combined in the proposed solution adapts mining for changing sentiment in the public topic scenarios by cataloging and correlating frequent words in the texts.

Statistical method TF-IDF is profoundly applied in text classification for evaluating the significance of a word for a file set. In [10], a contemporary approach wherein the term frequency part of TF-IDF in an unsupervised weighing scheme is assigned to adjusted score for every term. Comparative results of the study signify effective results than the other benchmarking models considered in the experimental study.

There are numerous feature selection techniques depicted in contemporary literature relies on statistical measures. Such strategies depicted in [11] are Hidden Markov Model (HMM) as well as the Latent Dirichlet Allocation (LDA), which aimed to separate entities as features from the subjective expressions in given corpus. Involving the latent topics is critical property of the LDA that enables to explore the documents with unnoticed topics. It is worth pointing out that the feature selection schemes depicted in [11] has shown predominant performance to classify the documents in the context of polarity under class labels depicted by syntactic relations and overlapping of the class labels diffused by using semantic words.

Various researchers like [12, 13] offered the suggestion of new feature reduction methods. A framework depicted in [12] that incorporates the manifold features to reduce the feature count for divergent learning strategies called supervised, unsupervised, as well as semi-supervised technique. The technique of feature reduction depicted in [13] is using the minimization of joint and 1-norms.

The model depicted in [14] is assessing the impact of features using semantic characteristics of the text given in reviews, where the model relied on statistical assessment strategy called Latent Semantic Analysis (LSA) to denote the semantic characteristics. The critical objective of the model is to understand the context of the reviews having voting support and other not entails any voting. This practice helps to depict the scope of the reviews to assess the sentiment scope.

It is also worth pointing out that semantics of electronic WOM content is employed in examining e WOM content analysis in a manner that was Pai et al. [15] proposed. This model intended to detect the sentiment polarity to predict the context of user's decision-making choice that delivers the business intelligence towards improvement and profits.

The opinion mining technique depicted in [16] is mongrelizing the semantic orientation using morpheme-lexical chunking and statistical approach point to mutual information.

At the same time, they assembled the features into matching aspects through the application of semantic techniques. They have used sentence-based SA approach that uses degree of adverbs in each sentence to depict the polarity of every aspect.

3 Problem Statement and Objective

Many of the earlier contributions published in the domain of sentiment analysis have explored varied new techniques. From the review of literature, it is imperative that part of the earlier works have focused on identifying the sentiment orientation of text. These models are considering 1-gram, bi-gram, tri-gram or n-gram term co-occurrence strategy that applied on either sentiment lexicons or bag of words as features. Hence the models limiting their performance to predict the sentiment represented in the form of sarcasm and the diplomatic opinions those reflects the both positive and negative polarity of the sentiment.

Hence, this manuscript argue that the mix of sentiment lexicons and bag of words in term co-occurrence selection process that independent to n-gram, where n in n-gram can be ≥ 1 is effective and significant to depict the sentiment polarity with greater accuracy, which would even in the context of sarcasm and diplomatic presentation of the opinion.

In this regard, the manuscript proposed statistical assessment model that depicts the n-gram term co-occurrence from the mix of sentiment lexicons and bag of words. Moreover, the depicted model prunes the features that are not or less significant to discover the sentiment polarity.

4 Methods and Materials

This section briefs the classifiers used for sentiment classification and the statistical measurements that are adapted for optimal feature selection.

4.1 Pre-processing Phase

Segmenting or Tokenizing. During the phase of pre-processing, tokenization carried out by splitting documents in to list of words. Tokens comprising of words and numbers extracted by scanning the reviews and accordingly the documents are used for further processing.

Eliminating Stop Words. Performance of the feature selection algorithms can be improved upon eliminating Stop words and high frequency words by filtering them from the document. Process of removing the stop words reduces the dimensionality of datasets, and also traces the key words in review corpus using automatic feature extraction techniques. Certain functional words like "about", "me", "is", "the" which do not carry any kind of sentiment information. In the proposed model, the stop words are removed using file index size which do not affecting accuracy levels.

Stemming. In feature extraction models, stemming is profoundly used in pre-processing phase. Stemming transforms words from a text in to stem or to a root form. Stemming as a process is much simple and is faster in extraction process. Porter's stemmer model is widely engaged in stemming process of English language text.

4.2 Machine Learning Classifiers

Identifying and classifying a dataset to appropriate categories (including the subsets) and ensuring right mapping for the new observation is a very significant process in the machine learning and statistic modeling. The success in terms of appropriate identification is dependent on data training set which comprises relevant observations and the category membership of the trained dataset. In the pedagogy of machine learning, supervised learning is termed as classification, while the clustering is the defined term for unsupervised learning process. In the clustering process, grouping of data takes place based on few measures like similarities identified.

Support Vector Machine. SVM [17] shall be a structured supervised machine-learning algorithm chosen for managing the classification and regression related challenges. In the SVM implementation, every data item identified as point in the n-dimensional space, and the value of every coordinate considered as marked value of every feature. Using the hyper-place method, the process of classification is carried out, in which the difference amidst two classes are identified effectively. SVM coordinates the individual observation and can handle the segregation of the classes more effectively.

Naive Bayes. NB techniques predominantly based on assumption related to independence among vivid predictors. The theorem presumes that not every feature in a class may have direct correlation to other features in the class [18]. In the case of an orange fruit, irrespective of its color and diameter, the subject considered as orange fruit, despite of such factors independently contributing towards the probability of that specific fruit being orange. The process of such defining is termed as 'Naïve' Bayes model. The model is very simple and can be very useful in managing high volume datasets. Also, in the other dimension, the performance of NB is profoundly high when compared to vary other classification methods. Usage of predictive and prior probability of a class, estimation of posterior probability can be attained with Bayes theorem.

AdaBoost. Among the [19] is the other resourceful solution for enhancing the deliverable outcome of decision trees, when compared to the other binary classification related issues. It is also vividly used in improving the outcome of varied algorithms related to machine learning, categorically the weak learner kind of algorithms. Decision trees of a specific level and the ones that are more suited for implementation with AdaBoost. Trees are usually considered as decision stumps, as they are short and usually have only one decision for classification.

4.3 Feature Selection Strategies

The bag of words can be obtained from the given training set, which is further filtered to obtain words that are optimal to use as features. The words that are frequently associated to sentiment representative lexicons will be filtered initially as possible features. Further optimal features will be selected based on the covariance between the co-occurrence frequency of positive and negative sentiment lexicons for each feature. The features that are having significant covariance between their co-occurrence frequency with respective positive and negative sentiment lexicons will be considered as optimal features.

In order to estimate the variance of each feature co-occurrence frequency with respective positive and negative sentiment representative lexicons, here in this proposed model we considered t-score and z-score metrics from statistical analysis. This recommendation is adapted with motivation gained from the contributions [20, 21] found in contemporary literature that evinced the significance of these variance assessment strategies. The t-score is adapted to select optimal features respective to each positive and negative words of the sentiment representative lexicons. In contrast to this, the z-score is considered to select optimal features from the positive and negative training sets without considering their association with the sentiment representative lexicons.

t-score. The diversity of the values in two different vectors can be represented by t-score, which is estimated as follows:

$$t\text{-}score = \frac{(M_{v1} - M_{v2})}{\sqrt{\frac{\sum_{i=1}^{|v1|}(x_i - M_{v1})^2}{|v1|-1} + \frac{\sum_{j=1}^{|v2|}(x_j - M_{v2})^2}{|v2|-1}}} \tag{1}$$

Here in the above equation

- M_{v1}, M_{v2} represents the mean of the values observed in respective vectors $v1, v2$
- The notations x_i, x_j represents each element of respective vectors $v1, v2$ of corresponding sizes $|v1|$, $|v2|$

The t-score is the ratio between the mean differences of respective vectors and the square root of sum of mean square distances of the respective vectors. Then find the degree of probability (p-value) [22] in t-table [23] for the t-score obtained. The p-value that is less than the probability threshold $\tau(0 \leq \tau \leq 0.05)$ indicates both vectors are distinct; hence, the feature representing respective vectors is optimal feature.

z-score. In similar passion of assessing t-score that used to calculate the variance of the feature co-occurrence with sentiment representative lexicons, here we use z-score to select optimal features. The z-score explores the status of distribution similarity between the given two vectors, the equation and corresponding notations used to assess the z-score in regard to sentiment analysis are:

Let a be the attribute exists in both positive and negative sets such that r and s are the number of times a exists in positive and negative sets respectively. The notations $\overline{r}$ and $\overline{s}$ represents the number times all attributes other than attribute a occurs in positive and negative sets respectively. The z score $z(a)$ of attribute a is:

$$\begin{aligned} \eta &= \frac{(r+s)}{r+s+\overline{r}+\overline{s}} \\ \gamma &= \sqrt{(r+\overline{r}) * (r+s) * (1-(r+s))} \\ z(a) &= \frac{r-(r+\overline{r}) * \eta}{\gamma} \end{aligned} \tag{2}$$

If the $z(a)$ degree of probability, which can obtain from z-table [24] is comparatively less than the probability threshold $\tau(0 \leq \tau \leq 0.05)$ given, then the 1-gram term a is optimal.

The use of z-score to select optimal features related to sentiment analysis is found in [21], which is notifying optimal sentiment representative lexicons from the given corpus as features. Unlike this, our model is using z-score to identify the optimal terms in bag of words prepared from given corpus as features based on their distinctive associability with negative and positive sentiment representative lexicons.

5 Experimental Study

Comparative analysis of varied machine learning techniques on the pre-processed datasets, input data provided is converted to set of records in a process, where every record is set of words. In the further process, application of t-score and z-score is adapted for finding optimal features from the datasets that are processed. For ensuring that significance of the proposal is assessed appropriately, experiments were carried out TF-IDF [10] feature selection strategies, GA and IG [3]. Results from the process is compared to the results generated using the proposed solution.

Every kind of feature selection techniques can support with unique and reduced set of features. All such a distinctive feature sets are evaluated for accuracy by adapting three distinct classifiers like SVM, NB and AdaBoost. Corroboration of similar kind is performed over the common set of attributes that are generated based on features selections from varied datasets. Validation and analysis is carried out as a final step over minimized feature sets that are performed based on anatomic relevance. The Fig. 1 represents the figurative representation of the process carried out in the experimental study.

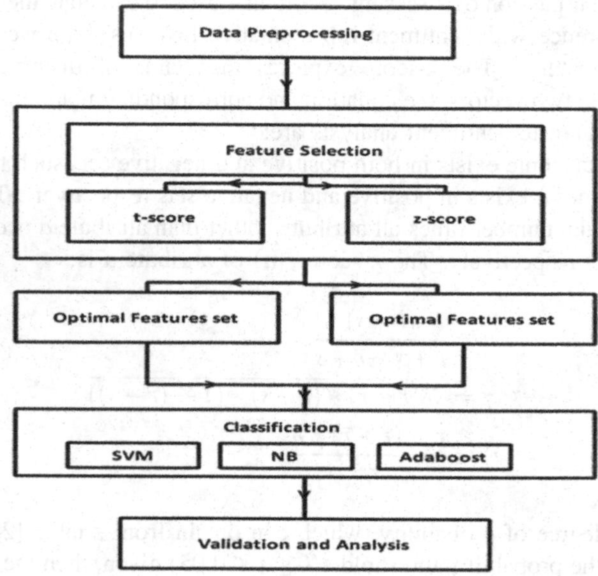

Fig. 1. Schematic diagram of proposed approach

5.1 Experimental Setup

The implementation of proposed model and other contemporary model [25] considered for performance analysis carried out using java 8. The classification accuracy assessment performed by scripts defined in R programming language [26].

5.2 Data Statistics

Product Reviews dataset [27], Movie Reviews Dataset [28], Twitter dataset for Sentiment Analysis [29] were the three datasets that considered for analysis. The movie review dataset is having 27886 reviews, among them, 21933 reviews considered for experiments and rest discarded due to the difficulty noticed at pre-processing step. The original twitter dataset that available at [29] is having tweets labelled as positive and negative. Among them 29700 records retained after pre-processing. The other dataset product reviews of Amazon Instant Video from Amazon product data provided by

JulianMcAuley, UCSD [27] that considered for experiments is having 37126 reviews. Among these 28310 reviews retained after pre-processing. All the datasets were pre-processed and number of instances available for each of the dataset depicted in Table 1.

Table 1. Data statistics for each dataset

Dataset	Total # of records	Number of records used for training	Number of records used for testing	No. # sentiment representative lexicons found in training set
Twitter dataset	29700	20790	8910	39
Movie reviews	21933	15353	6580	37
Product reviews	28310	19817	8493	21

The Movie Reviews and Product Reviews datasets possesses uniform distribution, whereas Twitter dataset skewed.

5.3 Feature Selection and Performance Statistics

Feature selection technique t-score and z-score are chosen and the attributes from the list are reduced. The reduced list of attributes is detailed in Table 2. In the further course, validating of the reduced attributes are performed using three classifiers. Results of the validation is detailed in Fig. 2. Validation of the depicted feature selection by the proposed model carried out in experiments by the metric called classification accuracy that compared against the classification accuracy depicted over other traditional feature selection strategies called TF-IDF [10] and IG-GA [3]. From the tests carried out using the t-score and z-score, it is imperative that features selected by t-score is very much the subset of features chosen in the z-score. Among the performance of the classifiers, NB had little lowered performance than the other classifiers. The results from the experimental study reflects that despite of applying the feature selection techniques, still the improvement of the classifiers performance was a challenge and there is inherent need for targeting the residual features and its importance towards better decision-making.

Table 2. The statistics of the results obtained from feature selection strategy.

Dataset	Actual count of features	Optimal features count			
		t-score	z-score	TF-IDF [10]	IG & GA [3]
Twitter dataset	1857	179	327	417	334
Movie reviews	2235	195	257	355	266
Product reviews	1325	76	132	170	138

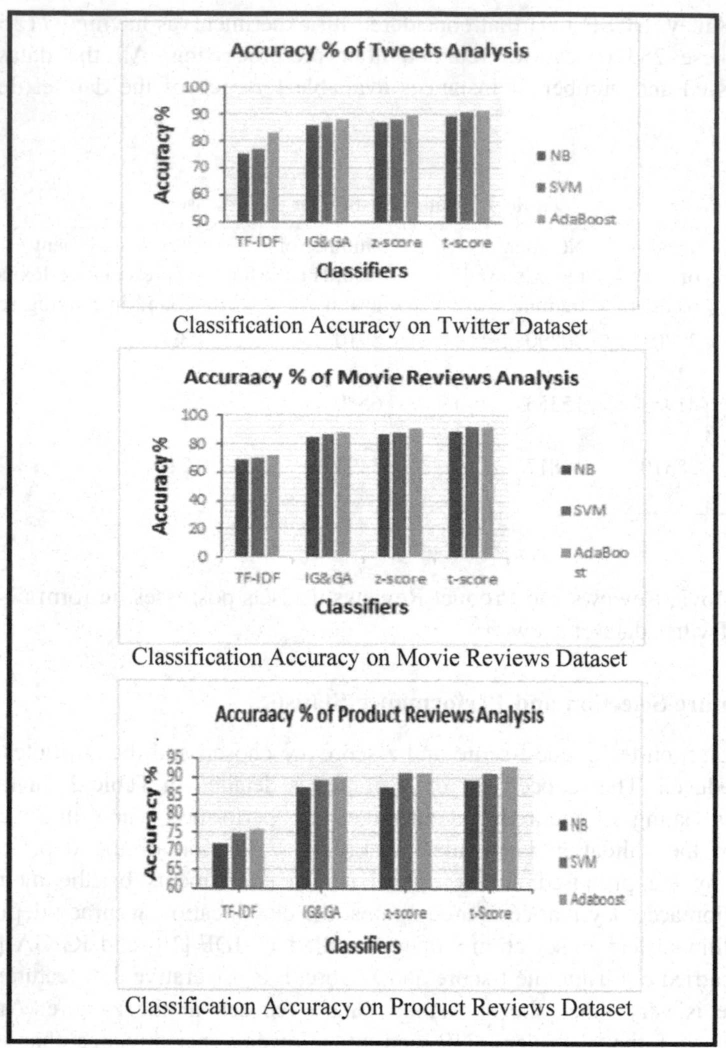

Fig. 2. Classifier performance analysis.

Among the classifiers chosen for the experimental study, AdaBoost classifier was more effective for all the three datasets, with improved accuracy levels of more than 90%, while the other classifiers have shown improvement in its performance than the earlier instances. NB has resulted 86% of accuracy. Performance of the classifiers that are trained by features derived based on t-score and z-score was very effective with 90% accuracy, when compared to the classifiers that are trained based on features sets from TF-IDF, IG &GA, which are 74% and 87% respectively.

The results obtained from this experimental study evincing that the feature selection strategies t-score, z-score defined here in this manuscript are robust and scalable that compared to feature selection by term frequency [10], GA and IG [3]. The number of features obtained from t and z scores is much fewer than the number of features obtained from term frequency. Also, the classification accuracy of the classifiers observed for features selected by t and z scores is much better than that compared to the classification accuracy observed for the features selected term frequency.

6 Conclusion

Sentiment Analysis has become a significant support system for the organizations to understand the market trends, customer expectations and in analyzing the turnkey factors of its business functions that enables better kind of decision making. The way businesses are relying upon advanced analytics, sentiment analysis data mining is gaining prominence and many researches are in progress in the domain. The inadequate structure of the human defined reviews, comments tweets and many other formats those can use as input corpus of the sentiment analysis, identifying the polarity of opinion is daunting task. Concerning to this, text preprocessing and feature selection are critical to perform the opinion mining. Existing models can fall in to two categories, sematic orientation based and feature selection approaches. Among these two features selection and using a classifier that learnt from these features is robust and significant to detect the opinion polarity. The existing feature selection models depends either on bag of words or sentiment lexicons as features. However relying either one of these two strategies limits the classification performance if the opinion expressed with sarcasm or in diplomatic presentation.

In order to limit this, the manuscript projected a novel term co-occurrence based model that selects feature from mix of the both bag of words and sentiment lexicons. The term co-occurrence of the terms from the mix of bag of words and sentiment lexicons is performed using to variance assessment scales called t-score and z-score, which are proven to be best among the other statistical scales to find variance between given two vectors of means. The experimental study aimed to find the fitness of the proposed feature selection strategy in two dimensions and they are applying on divergent datasets and applying on divergent classifiers. The experimental study elevated the significance of the proposed feature selection model that compared to other feature selection models called TF-IDF and IG-GA. Based on the results of the experimental studies, the optimal features selected by the proposed model are low and performs high that compared to other two feature selection strategies. In order to notify the fitness of the proposal, the experiments conducted on divergent datasets like movie reviews, product reviews and twitter corpus also used diversified classifiers like AdaBoost, SVM, and naive bays.

The overall results evincing that the feature selection from the mix of "bag of words" and "sentiment lexicons" that depicted in this manuscript is stable to identify the sentiment polarity with high significance whereas in the other two benchmarking models of feature selection, the quantity of features selected are more as compared to the proposed model at the same time the detection sentiment polarity is significantly low. Despite that the optimal features are discovered based on t-score and z-score are lesser based on optimal features that are discovered using other models like IG & GA and TF-IDF. Currently we are focusing on evolutionary techniques equipped with t-scale and z-scale as fitness metrics for selecting optimal features.

Acknowledgements. The authors are thankful to the University Grants Commission, New Delhi for supporting this research at School of Computer Sciences, North Maharashtra University, Jalgaon under the Special Assistance Programme (SAP) at the level of DRS-II.

References

1. Liu, B.: Sentiment analysis and subjectivity. In: Handbook of Natural Language Processing, 2nd edn, pp. 627–666. CRC Press, Taylor and Francis Group (2010)
2. Verma, S., Bhattacharyya, P.: Incorporating semantic knowledge for sentiment analysis. In: Proceedings of 6th International Conference on Natural Language Processing (2009)
3. Abbasi, A., Chen, H., Salem, A.: Sentiment analysis in multiple languages: feature selection for opinion classification in web forums. ACM Trans. Inf. Syst. (TOIS) **26**(3), 12 (2008). https://doi.org/10.1145/1361684.1361685
4. Vinodhini, G., Chandrasekaran, R.M.: Performance evaluation of machine learning classifiers in sentiment mining. Int. J. Comput. Trends Technol. **4**(6), 1783–1786 (2013)
5. Neviarouskaya, A., Prendinger, H., Ishizuka, M.: SentiFul: a lexicon for sentiment analysis. IEEE Trans. Affect. Comput. **2**(1), 22–36 (2011). https://doi.org/10.1109/T-AFFC.2011.1
6. Dang, Y., Zhang, Y., Chen, H.: A lexicon-enhanced method for sentiment classification: an experiment on online product reviews. IEEE Intell. Syst. **25**(4), 46–53 (2010). https://doi.org/10.1109/mis.2009.105
7. Ghosh, M., Kar, A.: Unsupervised linguistic approach for sentiment classification from online reviews using SentiWordNet 3.0. Int. J. Eng. Res. Technol. **2**(9), 55–60 (2013)
8. Zha, Z.-J., Yu, J., Tang, J., Wang, M., Chua, T.-S.: Product aspect ranking and its applications. IEEE Trans. Knowl. Data Eng. **26**(5), 1211–1224 (2014). https://doi.org/10.1109/tkde.2013.136
9. Wang, C., Xiao, Z., Liu, Y., Xu, Y., Zhou, A., Zhang, K.: SentiView: sentiment analysis and visualization for internet popular topics. IEEE Trans. Hum.-Mach. Syst. **43**(6), 620–630 (2013). https://doi.org/10.1109/thms.2013.2285047
10. Kim, Y., Zhang, O.: Credibility adjusted term frequency: a supervised term weighting scheme for sentiment analysis and text classification. In: Proceedings of 5th Workshop of Computational Approaches to Subjectivity, Sentiment and Social Media Analysis, pp. 79–83 (2014)
11. Duric, A., Song, F.: Feature selection for sentiment analysis based on content and syntax models. Decis. Support Syst. **53**(4), 704–711 (2012). https://doi.org/10.1016/j.dss.2012.05.023
12. Nie, F., Xu, D., Tsang, I.W.-H., Zhang, C.: Flexible manifold embedding: a framework for semi-supervised and unsupervised dimension reduction. IEEE Trans. Image Process. **19**(7), 1921–1932 (2010). https://doi.org/10.1109/TIP.2010.2044958
13. Nie, F., Huang, H., Cai, X., Ding, C.: Efficient and robust feature selection via joint $\ell 2$, 1-norms minimization. In: Proceedings of the 23rd International Conference on Neural Information Processing Systems, pp. 1813–1821 (2010)
14. Cao, Q., Duan, W., Gan, Q.: Exploring determinants of voting for the "helpfulness" of online user reviews: a text mining approach. Decis. Support Syst. **50**(2), 511–521 (2011). https://doi.org/10.1016/j.dss.2010.11.009

15. Pai, M.-Y., Chu, H.-C., Wang, S.-C., Chen, Y.-M.: Electronic word of mouth analysis for service experience. Expert Syst. Appl. **40**(6), 1993–2006 (2013). https://doi.org/10.1016/j.eswa.2012.10.024
16. Zhang, W., Xu, H., Wan, W.: Weakness finder: find product weakness from Chinese reviews by using aspects based sentiment analysis. Expert Syst. Appl. **39**(11), 10283–10291 (2012). https://doi.org/10.1016/j.eswa.2012.02.166
17. Suykens, J.A.K., Vandewalle, J.: Least squares support vector machine classifiers. Neural Process. Lett. **9**(3), 293–300 (1999). https://doi.org/10.1023/A:1018628609742
18. Murphy, K.P.: Naive Bayes Classifiers. University of British Columbia, Vancouver (2006)
19. An, T.-K., Kim, M.-H.: A new diverse AdaBoost classifier. In: Proceedings of International Conference on Artificial Intelligence and Computational Intelligence (AICI), Sanya, China, pp. 359–363 (2010). https://doi.org/10.1109/aici.2010.82
20. Budak, H., Taşabat, S.E.: A modified t-score for feature selection. Anadolu Univ. J. Sci. Technol. A-Appl. Sci. Eng. **17**(5), 845–852 (2016). https://doi.org/10.18038/aubtda.279853
21. Kummer, O., Savoy, J.: Feature selection in sentiment analysis. In: CORIA, Bordeaux, France, pp. 273–284 (2012)
22. Sahoo, P.K., Riedel, T.: Mean Value Theorems and Functional Equations. World Scientific, Singapore (1998)
23. http://www.sjsu.edu/faculty/gerstman/StatPrimer/t-table.pdf. Accessed 18 May 2017
24. http://www.sjsu.edu/faculty/gerstman/StatPrimer/z-table.pdf. Accessed 18 May 2017
25. Tripathy, A., Agrawal, A., Rath, S.K.: Classification of sentiment reviews using n-gram machine learning approach. Expert Syst. Appl. **57**, 117–126 (2016). https://doi.org/10.1016/j.eswa.2016.03.028
26. Ihaka, R., Gentleman, R.: R: a language for data analysis and graphics. J. Comput. Graph. Stat. **5**(3), 299–314 (1996)
27. http://jmcauley.ucsd.edu/data/amazon/. Accessed 18 May 2017
28. http://www.cs.cornell.edu/people/pabo/movie-review-data/. Accessed 18 May 2017
29. http://thinknook.com/wp-content/uploads/2012/09/Sentiment-Analysis-Dataset.zip. Accessed 18 May 2017

A Classification Approach for Monitoring and Locating Leakages in a Smart Water Distribution Framework

Shailesh Porwal[1(✉)], Mahak Vijay[1], S. C. Jain[1], and B. A. Botre[2]

[1] Rajasthan Technical University, Kota, India
shailesh.porrwal@gmail.com, mahakvijay3@gmail.com, scjain@rtu.ac.in
[2] CSIR-Central Electronics Engineering Research Institute, Pilani, India
bhau@ceeri.res.in

Abstract. In a water distribution network, leakages have always remained a problem of significant importance as a large amount of water gets wasted since leakage is localized and repaired for its normal operation. Besides the traditional methods of identifying a leakage which takes a lot of efforts and incurs a huge cost with a low efficiency, the technological advancements has made it possible to develop a smart water distribution system that will capture the real time statistical values of the distribution network through integration of the information and communication technology (ICT) with the physical devices of the water pipeline structure. Further, machine learning techniques can be applied to these statistical parameters to develop a decision model to predict the future. This paper presents the statistical classification framework through support vector machine technique that extracts the pressure and flow values from different locations of the water pipeline network and classifies the features into the leakage or non-leakage condition. The mathematical simulation is done on the EPANET tool and the dataset is deployed on MATLAB for statistical classification.

Keywords: Water distribution network
Leakage identification, classification · SVM · EPANET

1 Introduction

Water is a scarce and limited resource on earth, its efficient utilization is even more important with the growing population. Despite this, water loss due to leakages in water network is one of the major challenges which cause wastage of around 30–40% of the available drinking and usable water in India. Various factors causes leakages in pipelines like iron rust, cracks, incidental harms, unusual pressure conditions, less maintenance, outrageous climate conditions like excessively hot or cold and so on. Consequently, recognizing the leakage condition with its location at an early time stage is very important to prevent any additionally harm in the pipeline structure and also to limit the losses of water with lesser efforts and cost.

P. Bhattacharyya et al. (Eds.): NGCT 2017, CCIS 827, pp. 418–429, 2018.
https://doi.org/10.1007/978-981-10-8657-1_32

Generally, the leakages are detected through visible losses of water, but it becomes difficult to identify when leakages are in underground pipelines. Various traditional methods are used for identification of leakages, these include:

- **Acoustic Methods:** Acoustic signal method [5,7] measures the sound coming out of the crack or leakage in the pipe. But the disadvantage of acoustic method [5] is that the signal may include the noise from the external environment that may disturb the signal. Also, the acoustic signal depends on the pipe material and soil condition which may result in false detection.
- **Non-Acoustic Methods:** Non-acoustic methods incorporates Transient signal analysis method [3], Radio frequency identification method, Analysis of temperature variations due to leakages and other quasi-static analysis. These analyse the output of the sensors located inside the pipe. But these methods require the complex sensors as well as exhaustive knowledge of the hydraulic conditions inside the pipelines, thus not very much suitable for many practical applications.
  A few non-acoustic methods have also been described by injecting some tracing substances in the pipelines that come out of the pipe along with water whenever there is a leakage. But these methods have risk of contamination in the water.

Apart from these, the quasi-static analysis methods determine the system state through measuring the pressure and flow at various point locations in the distribution network. Whenever, there is leakage, there is a change in pressure and flow pattern at that point. The data generated is applied on data mining and machine learning techniques for recognizing the pattern of leakage and non-leakage condition.

In this paper, the SVM classification technique is applied on the dataset of pressure and flow generated from the water distribution network of CSIR-Central Electronics Engineering Research Institute (CEERI), Pilani. Based on the pattern of pressure & flow, SVM technique classifies the leakage and non-leakage points and predicts the location and size of the leakage.

The remaining paper is organized in following style: In Sect. 2, a review over the past research work is reported. In Sect. 3, design and simulation of water distribution network using EAPNET is specified. In Sect. 4 Support vector machine technique is described. Section 5 presents the proposed methodology for leakage localization. Section 6 shows the results and finally, Sect. 7 describes the conclusion and future scope of this research.

2 Literature Review

This section illustrates various research works that had been carried out in the area of leakage detection and localization in the water distribution network.

Apart from the acoustic techniques proposed by Fuchs and Riehle [5] and Khulief et al. [7] and transient methods by Covas et al. [3] for leakage detection in water pipeline network, Caputo and Pelagagge [2] proposed the use of neural networks for monitoring the pipeline systems. Shinozuka et al. [13] utilized the supervisory control and data acquisition for detecting the damage location in water delivery system. Kolczynski et al. [9] in 2010 presented neural network and probabilistic network numerical algorithms to detect fluid leaks in pipe type cable installations. In 2010, Qu et al. [12] proposed a SVM based warning system for leakage through recognizing vibration signals caused by leakages. Zhou et al. in 2009 [17] presented a belief rule-based (BRB) expert system for leak detection. Kim et al. [8] in 2009 introduced a timefrequency analysis for detecting leakages in buried gas pipelines. Zhang et al. [15] proposed to use changes in pressure and flux at the same time to detect leakage of oil-transporting pipeline. Zhang [16] used statistical method for detection and identify location of leakage by measuring the pressure and flow rate at both ends of pipe. Junior et al. [6] presented a black box time series strategy for detection, location and magnitude of leaks in pipeline system. Two time series resources were used as one for detection and the other for location. Yang et al. [14] proposed wavelet analysis for leak localization in the pipelines. Belsito et al. [1] developed artificial neural network method for leak size and its location identification. The system can detect leaks even with 1% of inlet flow rate and having a probability of success greater than 50% for localizing small leaks. Mpesha et al. [11] provided frequency response method for open loop piping system to determine location and leakage rate. Misiunas [10] proposed continuous monitoring technique known as time domain reflectometry (transmission and reflection of pressure waves), for detecting and locating leaks along the pipelines. This method measures the pressure at one location of pipeline and determines the presence of negative pressure wave and accordingly the location of leak by timing of initial and reflected transient wave produced due to leak. Feng et al. [4] utilized fuzzy decision approach and used five features as: inlet pressure, outlet pressure, inlet flow rate, outlet flow rate and difference of inlet to outlet flow rate for leakage detection.

3 Design and Simulation

3.1 Study Area

The study is conducted on the water distribution network of CSIR-CEERI, Pilani. The study area is shown as the Google map image in the Fig. 1:

3.2 EPANET

To distinguish the leakage and non-leakage situations, several patterns of leakages and non-leakages needs to be created in the water pipeline network with different leak sizes which was not feasible in realistic pipeline network of CSIR-CEERI, Pilani, therefore, EPANET tool was used to model the water distribution network of CEERI and simulate the leak cases. EPANET is a simulation tool for water hydraulics and pipeline network given by US Environment Protection Agency. EPANET simulates the water hydraulic behavior of the water

Fig. 1. Map of Study Area.

distribution and pipeline network that can be run over desired time period and generates the hydraulic parameters like pressure and flow at all points for that period of time. Further, leaks of different aperture sizes can also be created in EAPNET and the resultant pressure and flow values can be obtained.

3.3 Simulation in EPANET

For simulation of water distribution and pipeline network of CEERI, the Google map of CEERI campus was uploaded as backdrop in EPANET and various inputs as per the real network of the CEERI campus was applied in EPANET tool such as water head level in reservoir and tanks, the diameter and length of each pipe, the elevation of each node junction and water demand at each of these nodes. The water demand at node junctions was obtained after considering the population of each block. Further, the demand was varied as per the need of water at different time of the day. According the demand pattern was obtained as shown in Fig. 2:

The demand is higher for the daytime hours and lesser for night hours of the day.

The layout of the simulated network of CEERI, Pilani is shown in Fig. 3:

3.4 Leakgae Simulation in EPANET

To simulate the leakages in water network, emitter coefficient property of the junction is to be set in EPANET. Emitter coefficient value usually denotes the sprinklers or fire hydrants, but can also simulate leaks of various sizes by varying its value. The flow through an orifice is given by Torricelli Eq. 1:

$$Flowrate : Q = C * A * P^{P_{exp}} \tag{1}$$

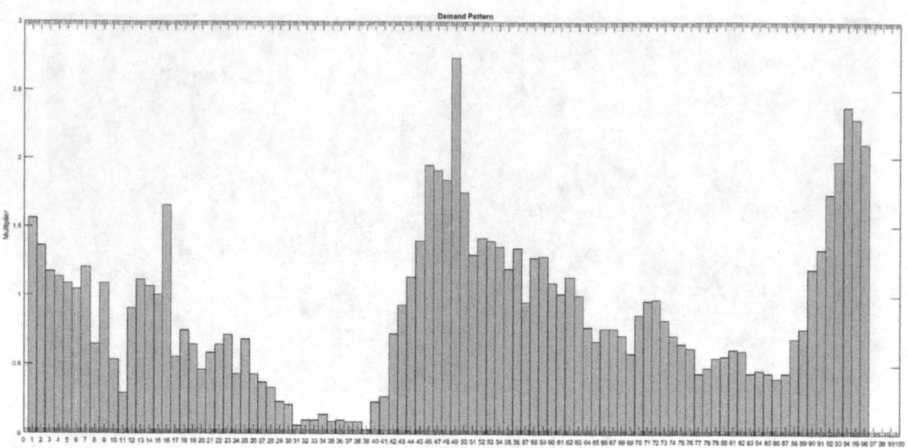

Fig. 2. Demand pattern for the simulated network

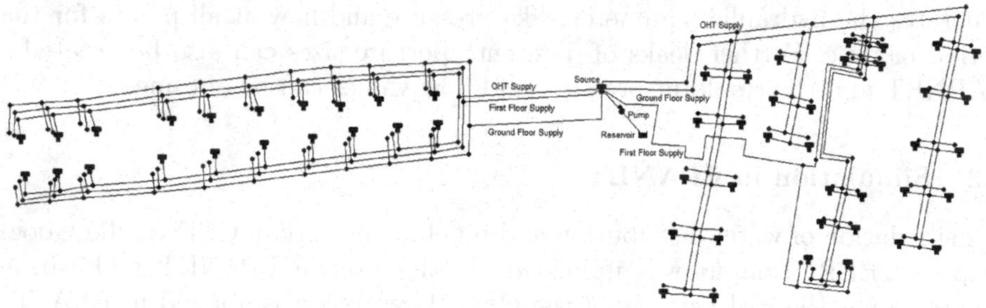

Fig. 3. General layout of the simulated network

where, C denotes coefficient, A is area of orifice aperture, P is pressure and P_{exp} is the pressure exponent usually 0.5 for circular apertures.

Accordingly, EPANET provides the emitter function definition as,

$$EC = Q/P^{P_{exp}} \tag{2}$$

where, EC denotes the emitter coefficient, Q denotes flow rate, P denotes pressure and P_{exp} denotes the pressure exponent. Emitter coefficient units are flow rate per unit pressure, i.e. litres per second per meter of pressure.

The network is run for the period of 6 weeks with the monitoring time steps of 30 min to have an exhaustive dataset of Pressure and flow at all points to train our model for the leakage and non-leakage conditions.

The final simulated network during run denoting pressure at node junctions and flow at pipe is shown in Fig. 4.

Fig. 4. EPANET simulation of CEERI water network

4 Support Vector Machine Technique

Support Vector Machine (SVM) techniques are supervised learning algorithms that uses the learning data sets to train the model and further predict the future values using the trained model.
It assigns the different labels to distinguish among different classes of the learning dataset. SVM try to obtain an optimal separation hyper plane that separates the different classes of learning data vectors to the either sides of the hyper plane.

SVM tries to maximize the margin distance between the support vectors as shown in Fig. 5

The hyper plane divides the D-dimensional feature space into two halves. if any point x_1 lies on the

- Positive side of the hyper plane, then

$$y_1 = W^T * x_1 + b > 0 \tag{3}$$

- Negative side of hyper plane, then

$$y_1 = W^T * x_1 + b < 0 \tag{4}$$

During training, as the targeted label is already known, thus each pair or row of dataset is applied iteratively to the hyper plane equation and value of W^T and b are adjusted in each iteration to obtain the optimal values of them. On completion of the learning, the model is trained with the best optimal hyper

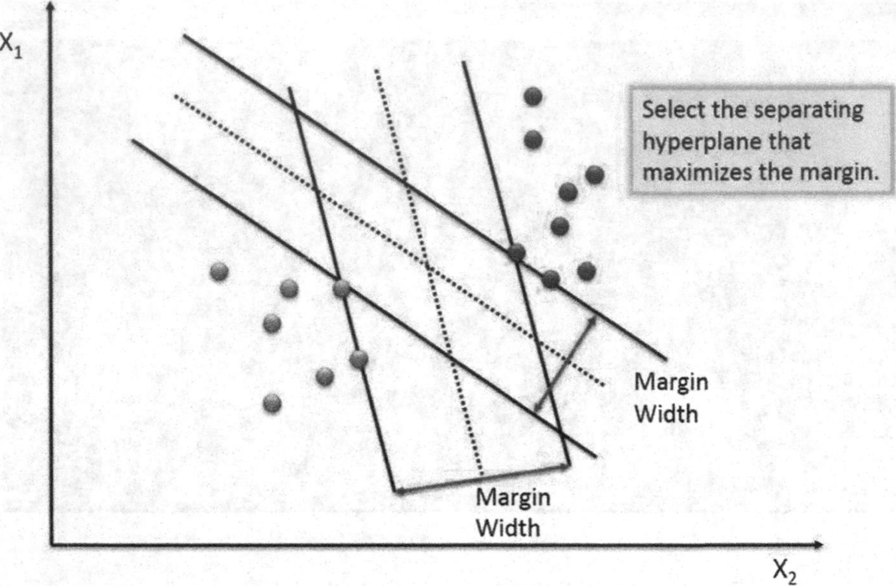

Fig. 5. Support vector machine technique

plane that performs the classification. After that, test data set may be applied to validate the trained model.

5 Proposed Methodology

In most of the earlier approaches, only the reduction in pressure values of the junctions were studied and analyzed to detect the leakage. In order to improve the accuracy and pin point the leakages, this paper proposes to use both the pressure values at junctions and flow values at pipelines to be analyzed through SVM to detect and localize the leakages.

The following key points are performed:

- Learning dataset generation
- Labeling
- Randomization
- Automatic parameter selection
- SVM classification/model training
- Validation

1. **Learning dataset generation:** EPANET tool was used to generate the pressure values at 268 nodes and flow values at 211 pipes in the simulated water network of CEERI for a time period of 6 week running. The values are obtained in the interval of 30 min for closer inspection of any variation in the

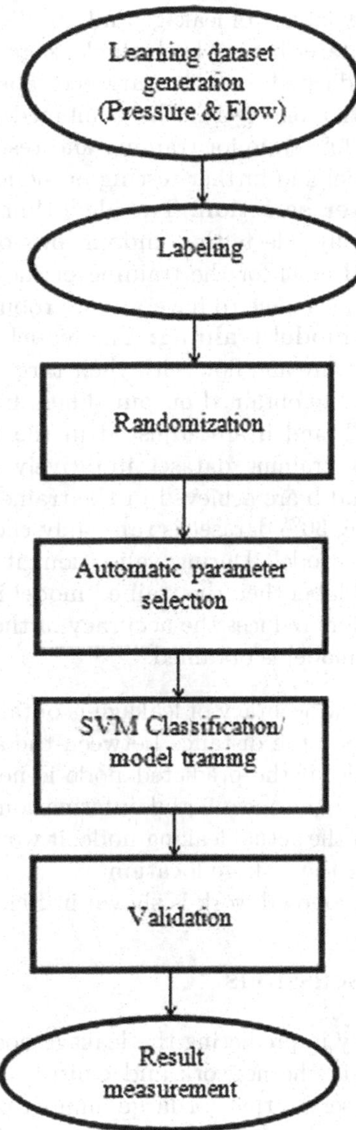

Fig. 6. Flow of proposed work

values of pressure and flow. Leakages are created in random nodes through emitter coefficient and again network is run for 6 weeks of time period to have an exhaustive dataset of leakage and non-leakage condition.

2. **Labeling:** The dataset of non-leakage is labeled with postive one (+1) and the dataset with leakages is labeled with negative one (−1).

3. **Randamization:** The dataset of leakage and non-leakage is randamized and resulted in only one dataset having both the leakage and non-leakage scenarios and each pair is indicated with the targeted labeled value either postive one (+1) or the negative one (−1). The combined random dataset is then divided into 70% and 30% ratio for training and testing dataset respectively for training of the model and further testing of model for validation.
4. **Automatic parameter selection:** The algorithm is structured in such a way that it automatically selects the random rows of pressure and flow values with their targeted label for the training of the model rather than in a sequential manner. This is done to have a more robust trained model.
5. **SVM classification/model training:** The model is trained with the 70% training dataset of pressure and flow with their targeted label output according to Eqs. 3 and 4. If the obtained output differs from the targeted output then the values of WT and b are adjusted in the iteration. The model is trained for all pairs of training dataset iteratively till completion and the refined value of WT and b are achieved in the trained model on completion.
6. **Validation:** Remaining 30% dataset is randomly chosen for testing and validation of the trained model. During validation, if the obtained results is similar to the targeted label then the trained model is working correctly and the values where it differs reduces the accuracy of the trained model. On the basis, accuracy of the model is obtained.

For the points where low accuracy of leakage is obtained, the paper proposes another measure to evaluate the distance between the actual leaking node and the predicted leaking node. If the predicted node is nearby the actual leaking node then also it provides the meaningful information as the leakage can be localized within a range of the actual leaking node, it would not require searching the entire zone for getting the leakage location.

Flow diagram of our proposed work is shown in Fig. 6

6 Results and Discussions

Table 1 shows the accuracy in predicting the leakage nodes when the number of leakage nodes are varied in the network and emitter coefficient value remains constant as 0.005. It is observed that for large number of leakages, the accuracy of prediction is higher than that for the low number of leakages.

Table 2 shows the accuracy in predicting the leakage nodes when the no of leak nodes remain constant as 10 and the value of the emitter coefficient is varied which creates the different size of leakages. It is observed that for large size of leakages, the accuracy of prediction is higher than that for the low size leakages.

Figure 7 shows the distance between the actual leakage nodes and the predicted nodes for the cases where the low accuracy was observed. It shows that the predicted node is nearby in some range of the actual leaking node. Therefore, re-evaluating the accuracy considering the range too for correct prediction, it would not require searching the entire region for locating the leakage, rather only a range would be searched for locating the leakage.

Table 1. Accuracy of prediction v/s Number of leakages

Emitter coefficient (leak size)	Actual leak nodes	Correctly predicted nodes	% Accuracy
0.005	5	2	40%
0.005	8	5	62.50%
0.005	10	7	70%
0.005	15	13	86.60%

Table 2. Accuracy of prediction v/s Size of leakages

Emitter coefficient (leak size)	Actual leak nodes	Correctly predicted nodes	% Accuracy
0.005	10	5	50%
0.010	10	5	50%
0.020	10	6	60%
0.030	10	7	70%
0.040	10	7	70%
0.050	10	8	80%
0.1	10	9	90%

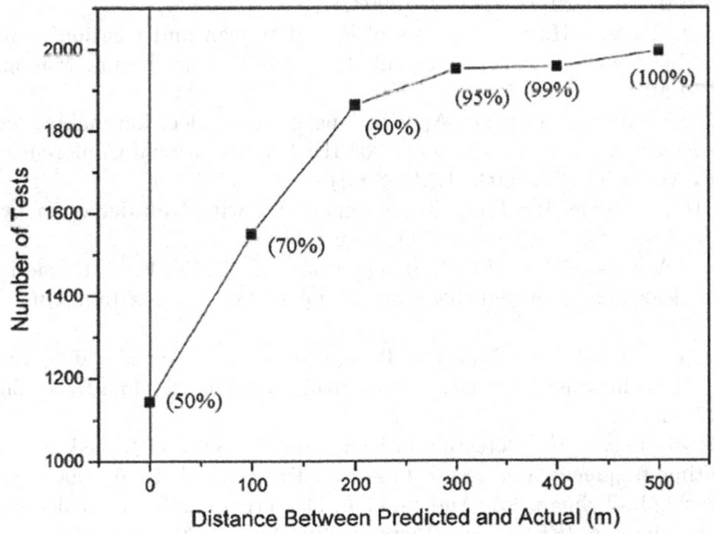

Fig. 7. Graph representing accuracy with respect to distance between actual and predicted leakage node

7 Conclusion

In this paper, support vector machine technique is applied to detect the leakage and predict the location in the water distribution and pipeline network of CSIR-CEERI, Pilani. In order to improve the accuracy and pin point the leakages, both the pressure values at junctions and flow values at pipelines are extracted from the EAPNET tool and used as a feature for analyzing through SVM for identifying the leakages rather than only the pressure value as was done in many previous research works. Finally, the points where low accuracy of leakage was obtained, another measure is used to evaluate the distance between the actual leaking node and the predicted leaking node to localize the leakage within a range of the actual leaking node so that it would not require searching the entire zone for leakage location.

Future work can be done on this model by applying cloud services and try to build a mobile application so that anywhere the water pressure and flow data can be accessed as well as predicted location of leakages.

References

1. Belsito, S., Lombardi, P., Andreussi, P., Banerjee, S.: Leak detection in liquefied gas pipelines by artificial neural networks. AIChE J. **44**(12), 2675–2688 (1998)
2. Caputo, A.C., Pelagagge, P.M.: Using neural networks to monitor piping systems. Process Saf. Prog. **22**(2), 119–127 (2003)
3. Covas, D., Ramos, H.: Case studies of leak detection and location in water pipe systems by inverse transient analysis. J. Water Resour. Plann. Manag. **136**(2), 248–257 (2010)
4. Feng, J., Zhang, H., Liu, D.: Applications of fuzzy decision-making in pipeline leak localization. In: Proceedings of 2004 IEEE International Conference on Fuzzy Systems, vol. 2, pp. 599–603. IEEE (2004)
5. Fuchs, H.V., Riehle, R.: Ten years of experience with leak detection by acoustic signal analysis. Appl. Acoust. **33**(1), 1–19 (1991)
6. Junior, C.A.V., Medeiros, J.L.D., de Queiroz, O., Araújo, F.: ARX modeling approach to leak detection and diagnosis. J. Loss Pre. Process Ind. **23**(3), 462–475 (2010)
7. Khulief, Y.A., Khalifa, A., Mansour, R.B., Habib, M.A.: Acoustic detection of leaks in water pipelines using measurements inside pipe. J. Pipeline Syst. Eng. Pract. **3**(2), 47–54 (2011)
8. Kim, M.-S., Lee, S.-K.: Detection of leak acoustic signal in buried gas pipe based on the time-frequency analysis. J. Loss Pre. Process Ind. **22**(6), 990–994 (2009)
9. Kolczynski, J., Tylman, W., Anders, G.J.: Detecting small fluid leaks in pipe-type cable installations. IEEE Trans. Power Deliv. **25**(1), 279–288 (2010)
10. Misiunas, D.: Monitoring and asset condition assessment in water supply systems. Ph.D. thesis, Lund University, Lund (2005)
11. Mpesha, W., Gassman, S.L., Chaudhry, M.H.: Leak detection in pipes by frequency response method. J. Hydraul. Eng. **127**(2), 134–147 (2001)
12. Qu, Z., Feng, H., Zeng, Z., Zhuge, J., Jin, S.: A SVM-based pipeline leakage detection and pre-warning system. Measurement **43**(4), 513–519 (2010)

13. Shinozuka, M., Liang, J., Feng, M.Q.: Use of supervisory control and data acquisition for damage location of water delivery systems. J. Eng. Mech. **131**(3), 225–230 (2005)
14. Yang, Z., Xiong, Z., Shao, M.: A new method of leak location for the natural gas pipeline based on wavelet analysis. Energy **35**(9), 3814–3820 (2010)
15. Zhang, S.-Q., Jin, S.J., Yang, F.L., Wang, X.Q., Bai, Q.Y.: Crucial technologies of oil-transporting pipe leak detection and location based on wavelet and chaos. Meas. Sci. Technol. **17**(3), 572 (2006)
16. Zhang, X.J.: Statistical methods for detection and localization of leaks in pipelines. In: Proceedings of The International Conference on Offshore Mechanics and Arctic Engineering, pp. 485–485. American Society of Mechanical Engineers (1992)
17. Zhou, Z.-J., Chang-Hua, H., Yang, J.-B., Dong-Ling, X., Zhou, D.-H.: Online updating belief rule based system for pipeline leak detection under expert intervention. Expert Syst. Appl. **36**(4), 7700–7709 (2009)

Chlorine Decay Modelling in Water Distribution System Case Study: CEERI Network

Mahak Vijay[1(✉)], Shailesh Porwal[1], S. C. Jain[1], and B. A. Botre[2]

[1] Rajasthan Technical University, Kota, India
mahakvijay3@gmail.com, shailesh.porrwal@gmail.com, scjain@rtu.ac.in
[2] CSIR-Central Electronics Engineering Research Institute, Pilani, India
bhau@ceeri.res.in

Abstract. In this research paper EPANET and EPANET-MSX software tool is utilized to simulate the water network of CSIR-CEERI, Pilani. System is utilizing a real time contamination event detection algorithm, for detecting a randomly generated event using EPANET-MATLAB Toolkit. According to WHO (World Health Organisation) the required chlorine concentration for maintaining water quality is 0.5 mg/l. So re-chlorination stations are expected to include into network. A fixed detection threshold for chlorine residual is utilized for different sensing areas when chlorine concentration varies from this limit, controller module will adjust the value according to required level. Initial Chlorine, pipe roughness, demand pattern and others parameters of the underlying states of the water supply framework were created by Monte Carlo simulation method. This information of chlorine data is sent over a IOT integrated server. At that point this information is displayed over a user interactive application with the goal that a client intuitive view can be provided. The utilization of the Monte Carlo simulation in blend with heuristic classification have been turned out to be a capable tool to perform chlorine residuals finding and contamination event occurrence in sensors inside the CEERI pressure zone. By utilizing classification module's output the event detection of contamination is done by raising a alert flag. Finally, this information about generated alerts are sent to the user, who is authorised to access and perform possible actions.

Keywords: Monte-Carlo simulation · IOT integrated server EPANET-MSX · EPANET · Water contamination detection

1 Introduction

Giving safe drinking water to individuals, free from pathogenic and other undesirable substances, is the essential objective of all water utilities. Disinfection is an essential angle in accomplishing this objective and in keeping the spread of waterborne infections. Drinking water has been disinfected since the start of

P. Bhattacharyya et al. (Eds.): NGCT 2017, CCIS 827, pp. 430–443, 2018.
https://doi.org/10.1007/978-981-10-8657-1_33

the nineteenth century, when one found that microbiological tainting dangers by water conceived sicknesses, specifically cholera or typhoid fever, diminished radically when disinfectants were utilized. There are a few disinfection techniques which can be connected to high water streams. They can be partitioned into three primary gatherings:

- UV radiation
- Ozone
- Chlorine

The initial two gatherings don't create noteworthy Disinfection By - Products (DBP's) nor associate fundamentally with the water they should purify. In spite of their proficient purifying qualities, they don't ensure a long time disinfection, up until the point that the water supplies the individuals. The most ordinarily utilized disinfectant in water supply frameworks worldwide is chlorine. An appropriately planned chlorine disinfection framework gives a quick destruction of harmful microbes and infections and a defensive residual chlorine amount all through the water supply framework, in this way averting recontamination.

Dosing excessively chlorine has various negative impacts. Expanded chlorine levels additionally raise the danger of framing purification side-effects such as DBPs, which might be harmful to human lives. It is significant that the right measure of chlorine be utilized on the grounds that any abundance may prompt the development of thrihalomethanes, which are suspected cancer-causing agents.

Along these lines, it is critical to accomplish a harmony between the targets of guaranteeing a satisfactory chlorine leftover for microbiological quality and anticipating high chlorine residuals that effect on the characteristics of the drinking water and may likewise posture medical issues.

The target of this research is to build up a model that is fit for keeping up chlorine residuals in a WDS. The contextual analysis considered in this research includes CEERI network for chlorine residuals in a WDS model utilizing model based approach. As an optional goal, various basic issues are likewise tended to, including Contamination detection, generate alerts about any impurity added in water, and available this information about water quality to end users. For achieving these goals model will utilize statistical Monte-Carlo method. This approach offers benefits as opposed to mostly utilize strategies for demonstrating of chlorine decay in drinking water frameworks untill now. The model permits to find out chlorine concentration at sensor nodes of the water supply framework. Then model is embedded with heuristic classification module and a event detection module too, for recognizing the contamination events.

2 Literature Review

This section provides a summary of various research works on chlorine decay modelling and contamination detection.

Water quality can deteriorate due to physical and chemical interaction between distributed water with pipe wall or interaction within bulk water [8]. First order, second order or nth order decay kinetics was accessed for modelling of chlorine decay in water supply framework [10]. The first order equation is as follows (Eq. 1):

$$\frac{dC}{dt} = -KC \tag{1}$$

where dC/dt is the decay of chlorine in mg/l, k is first-order decay coefficient; C is chlorine concentration at time t in mg/l. By integrating Eq. (1) and considering c_0 as initial chlorine concentration, The decay of chlorine is as follows:

$$c = c_0 e^{-Kt} \tag{2}$$

where c_0 is initial residual chlorine concentration(mg/l); c_t is final residual chlorine concentration (mg/l); K = overall decay constant $= K_b + K_w$; K_b= bulk reaction rate coefficient; K_w=overall wall reaction rate coefficient.

Pressure Variations caused by sudden changes in the flow speed, started from water supply framework operations, for example, pump starting and stopping [4] can prompt the external pressure of the pipe, surpassing the internal pressure [8]. In such circumstance, there is a shot of non-potable water entering into the supply framework from the surrounding [4] through faulty links, leakage joints etc [8], giving in this way an open door for contaminants to enter the water supply framework and corrupting the quality of the water [4].

Changes in water demands may cause significant fluctuation in water quality estimations all through the water supply framework, as presented in [14] utilizing Monte Carlo simulations. To oblige instability, a Bayesian Belief Network approach was introduced in [12] as a strategy to infer the probability of contamination. For simulation and contamination event detection numerous chemical reactions dynamics have been utilized by model based methodologies in [5]. In various research program held in past, different methodologies have been proposed for tending to the issue of contamination. One such approach is detecting the contamination event using chlorine measurement [6] and to decrease the rate of development of biofilms [6]. But it is critical to keep up sufficient chlorine leftover so as to maintain the compound and microbial nature of conveyed water [17].

In past research, different methodologies have been proposed for contamination event recognition, utilizing single or multi-type estimations, model-based or model-free methodologies etc. [1]. In light of EEMD and Gaussian fuzzy logic, the contamination identification technique is additionally proposed [9]. Other strategies, for example, control graphs and Kalman filters have likewise been proposed [3]. Time series analysis can be performed in the CANARY tool (for event detection) [3,11], gave by the US Environmental Protection Agency. The EPANET-MSX programming [16] was utilized to simulate the chlorine reaction to the infusion of certain biological species in a water supply framework.

For instance, a bacterial concentration may diminish the amount of free chlorine, diminish the ORP (Oxidation Reduction Potential) and increment the conductivity of the water. Furthermore, in [18], chlorine and contaminant reaction models have been considered in a realistic contamination event detection, identification and warning system, to recognize and classify the contaminant. The utilization of chlorine sensors especially for contamination detection was proposed in [7]. Furthermore, models depicting chlorine responses with contaminants (for example, sodium arsenite and organophosphate) have been proposed. The residual amount of disinfectant at the sensor area may fluctuate due to significant variability in the water demands and in addition the impact of pressure driven and quality control activities [2]. Thusly, the utilization of fixed threshold for chlorine residuals can make the detection of events insensitive to small contamination event.

To figure the estimation errors, the utilization of artificial neural networks for displaying water quality was examined, and by using a sequential Bayesian rule, the contamination event probability was calculated and compared with threshold to recognize an event [15]. An un-supervised approach was also proposed in [13] using minimum-volume ellipsoid.

Rest of the paper is sorted as: In Sect. 3 Design and simulation of network using EPANET and EPANET-MSX and the development of design methodology is reported, in Sect. 4, the results and in Sect. 5 conclusion and future scope of this research is described.

3 Design and Simulation

3.1 Study Area

The study is conducted to assess the performance of water distribution network of CSIR-CEERI, Pilani. The study area is shown as the Google map image in the Fig. 1, the image is taken from Google Earth for digitization of Campus. The campus water network plan with different realistic parameters value and block wise population is utilized by this study.

3.2 Hydraulic Model Using EPANET

1. The base model was taken initially from the General Plan of the 2006 water provided framework of CSIR-CEERI, Pilani.
2. The contextual investigation was done in a division of the drinking water transmission framework that supplies Maitri path and S. K. Mitra marg of CEERI network.
3. A new record INP and NET was made by the Simulator EPANET 2.0 as demonstrated in Fig. 3. The network has one reservoir, 56 tanks, 264 pipes with diameter 12 in. and 211 nodes.
4. Customer demands was allocated in the network nodes and also it was incorporated pump to pump out the water from reservoir to overhead tank of CEERI. The average demand of network is 0.88 ls^{-1} with the demand pattern shown in Fig. 2(a), and the gained system flow plot is shown in Fig. 2(b).

5. Characteristics as the elevation in nodes and tanks, roughness coefficient of pipes, tank parameters and pump with associated pump curve were already in the base model according to realistic CEERI water network.
6. Bulk and wall decay coefficients has the values 0.02 (h^{-1}) and 0.01 (h^{-1}) respectively. For the chlorine levels, the simulation was performed for 1008 h but plotting of residual chlorine is done for 5 days.

Fig. 1. Map of study area

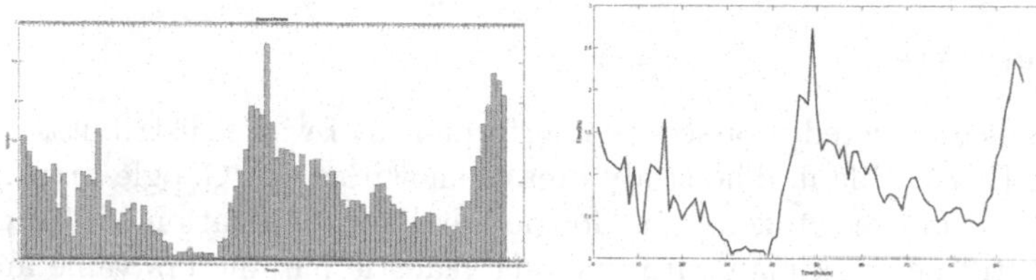

Fig. 2. CEERI water distribution network; (a) Supplied demand pattern for 96 h span, (b) The overall gained system flow plot by distribution network.

3.3 Water Quality Modeling Using EPANET-MSX

This EPANET toolkit together with more desirable characterization and estimation of the bulk and wall decay take into account a more viable and exact modelling of chlorine in water supply frameworks, while exploiting EPANET MSX's improved capacities.

Several notes of explanation require mentioning:

1. The EPANET-MSX utilize a input file for describing the species and reaction system which are being modeled is arranged into segments, where each segment begins with a keyword enclosed in brackets.

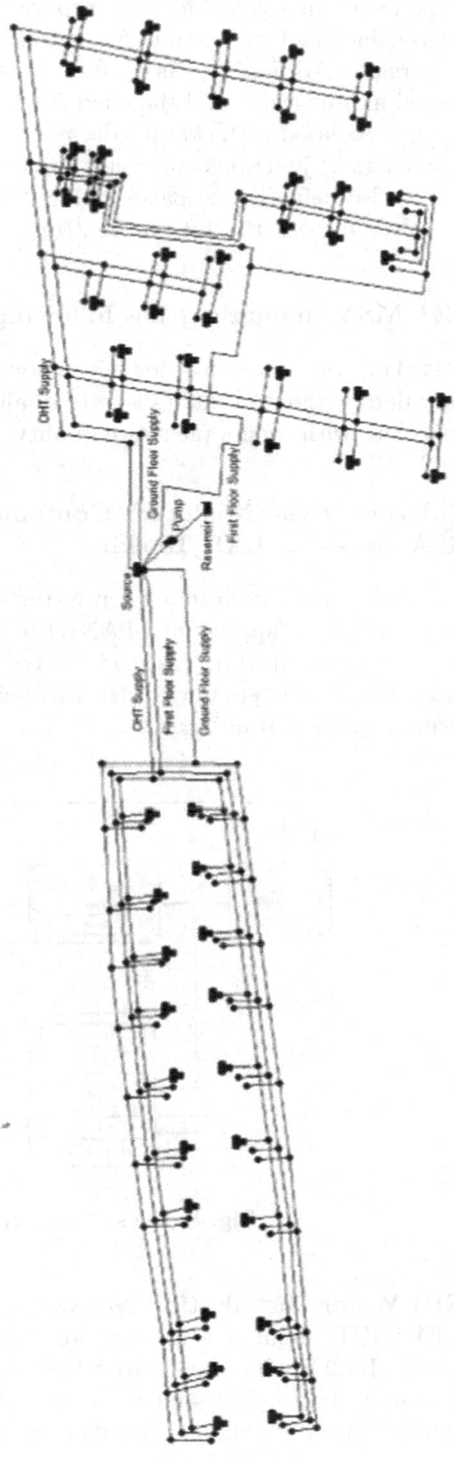

Fig. 3. Simulated input file of CEERI network

2. four species are mensioned for the proposed model: bulk chlorine (CL2), bulk biodegradable dissolved organic Arsenite III (AsIII), bulk biodegradable dissolved organic Arsenite V (AsV), bulk bacterial concentration (Xb). CL2 is measured in milligrams and the bacterial concentrations is in micrograms.
3. Reaction associated with chlorine decay such as bulk and wall decay and with contaminants at junctions and tanks are also defined.
4. MSX file also defines time patterns for different species or substances. The MSX solver utilizes the fifth-order Runge-Kutta strategy with 5 min time step.

EPANET-MSX simulations has following inputs:

1. History data without events, for initial conditions determination.
2. History data without events (generate quality matrix 1).
3. History data with events (generate quality matrix 2).

3.4 Chlorine Decay Model for Contamination Detection Using EPANET-MATLAB Toolkit

To lead a quality simulation in a given water supply framework, one must have a model on which to apply the EPANET quality model. The chosen output parameter to be examined in this model is residual chlorine. For the given case, a few accessible parameters were utilized to build the raw database. The system architecture is presented in Fig. 4.

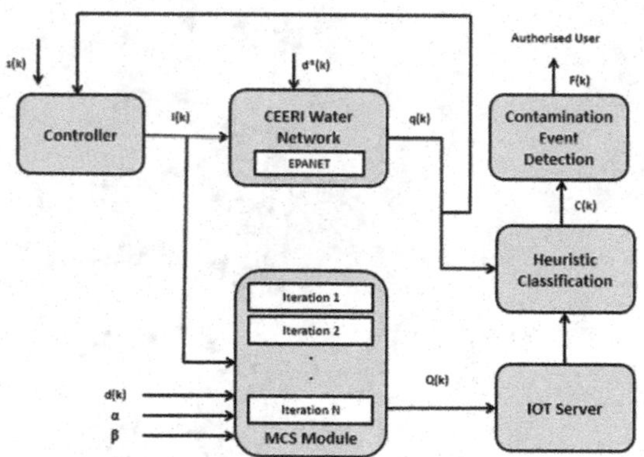

Fig. 4. The system architecture

1. **CEERI Water Distribution Network**
The EPANET simulated network of CEERI is loaded over EPANET-MATLAB Toolkit. Then associated MSX input file is also loaded. The time of simulation duration is set for 5 days. Then fetch the network data such as demand pattern, roughness coefficients and sensor ID. The utilization of

model for assessment of verifiable information and chlorine decay was surveyed in 8 sensor nodes inside the pressure zone of CEERI, Pilani. Since earlier data is accessible about a few parameters, at that point this data was utilized to evaluate chlorine leftover in sensor Nodes 88, 152, 64, 31, 185, 141, 21 and 46. The water demand d(k), where k is discrete time step of 96 h span with 30 min hydraulic time step, where Δt is sampling time is defined for water network. The water demand is randomized with an uncertainty term η_d(k), with the end goal that d*(k) = d(k) + η_d(k).

2. **Controller Module**
The CEERI water network is employed with Controller Module in charge of figuring the input signals I(k)ϵ R^{N_u} for the N_u chlorination actuators. In this work, a controlling algo on the basis of window size of time will be considered, to indicate the setpoint of amount of chlorine at the areas of disinfection. System is set with a threshold value for required amount of residual chlorine, at a certain time interval this chlorine value checked against the measured values from sensors. If the amount of measured chlorine is lesser than the required one then using self-monitored capability of system the chlorine value is adjusted.

3. **Construction of the Input Database using Monte-Carlo Method**
Initial Chlorine, pipe roughness, demand pattern and others parameters of the underlying states of the water supply framework were created by Monte Carlo simulation method that requires the utilization of random number generator. It produces the numbers that follow a uniform and normal distribution depending of the parameter simulated. The topology has reacted precisely to the estimations of the training data set utilizing the MC method. Initial and leftover chlorine, chlorine with and without contamination in these sensors inside the pressure zone were utilized as data set in this model. The MC module keeps running in parallel N randomized simulations. Vector α and β are considered as max uncertainty % for demand pattern and roughness coefficients respectively, for each simulation. The CEERI water network is randomized with d^i(k) = d(k) ± 20%, and r^i(k) = r(k) ± 20%, for i ϵ {1, ...N}. In this research of chlorine decay simulation model, multiple Arsenite and Becterial contamination events of various magnitude occurring at different locations inside 5 days with 5 min sampling time within water distribution network of CEERI is demonstrated. The infused AsIII, AsV and becteria concentration is randomly chosen from a uniform distribution [0, 1] mg/l. Develop dataset from 500 MC Simulations of ordinary operations without contamination and with randomized roughness and demand, and with contamination too. The MC model figures at each time step the matrix Q(k) (e.g. utilizing the EPANET solver), its (i, j)-th component $Q_{(i,j)}$(k) is the evaluated chlorine concentration at j-th sensor, regarding the i-th randomized simulations.

4. **IOT integrated Server**
A user interactive view is provided by proposed model to view the current sensor measurements about the residual chlorine. The activated sensors are displayed at sensing locations. To view the current chlorine measurement

values user should have to click on the sensor button, and its relative information will show through graph and numeric data. For this set up a raspberry pi board is used at server as wi-fi module to receive data from sensors. And to access the information from integrated IOT server a user interactive application is built which is authorized to a selected no of users, who will handle the system.

5. **Heuristic Classification**
The utilization of the Monte Carlo simulation in blend with heuristic classification have been turned out to be a capable tool to perform chlorine residuals finding and contamination event occurrence in sensors inside the CEERI pressure zone. This classification module will take the output of Monte Carlo simulation module as input data Q(k), and distinguish between the chlorine decay occurrence is due to demand pattern or due to the impurities added into the simulated network.
For time window k, and N simulation scenario the chlorine values for with and without contamination event are calculated then find the bound (upper $\overline{Q}_j\,(k)$ and lower $\underline{Q}_j\,(k)$ for j-th sensor) according following Eqs. (3) and (4):

$$\underline{Q}_j\,(k) = min\left\{Q_{(1,\,j)}\,(k)\,,\,\ldots\,,\,Q_{(N,\,j)}\,(k)\right\} \tag{3}$$

$$\overline{Q}_j\,(k) = max\left\{Q_{(1,\,j)}\,(k)\,,\,\ldots\,,\,Q_{(N,\,j)}\,(k)\right\} \tag{4}$$

Then compare the value of chlorine in between with and without contamination event and apply label (label 1 for contamination event and 0 for other cases). When the value is violated from a certain rule, using label we can classify that the variation in chlorine value is due to demand pattern or due to contamination event. The flow graph of classification approach is presented in Fig. 5.

6. **Contamination Event Detection**
For 5 days and 500 simulation scenario the ED module will generate the alert flag F_j(k) for j-th sensor by utilizing classification module's output C(k). Flag generation of the system framework is described below in Eq. 5.

$$F_j(k) = \begin{cases} Alert & \underline{C}_j(k) = 1 \\ & \underline{C}_j(k) = 1 \\ Nothing & \text{otherwise} \end{cases} \tag{5}$$

4 Result and Discussion

The objective is to decide the variables impacting chlorine decay for the contextual investigation in the pressure zone of CEERI, Pilani. These variables depend on nearby estimations of residual chlorine. For deciding elements influencing chlorine decay in WDS, under various parameter conditions, estimations of recorded information are required. Initial Chlorine, Pressure, Flow, Roughness

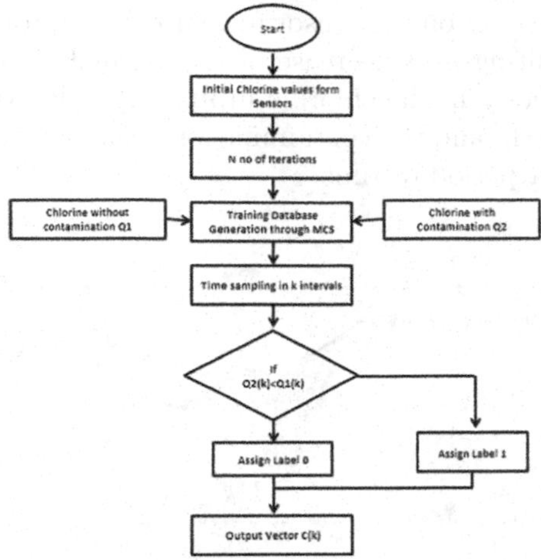

Fig. 5. The flow graph of classification

coefficient, Demands are utilized as a part of this examination as contribution for making sense of chlorine decay in CEERI, Pilani - pressure zone, Case Study. Chlorine decays in system without any contamination due to reaction occurs in bulk and wall phase. So using the controller part of proposed model the system is set to required chlorine concentration by utilizing a fixed threshold strategy. After setting the chlorine concentration according to the required level the value of chlorine measured is in between 0.4–0.5 mg/l (min require chlorine for water quality). In Table 1 the residual chlorine data at one sensor (88) in the time window of 24 h is shown, before and after the chlorine setting by controller module. Same procedure is applied to set chlorine at other sensing areas too.

Table 1. Chlorine concentration before and after chlorination

Node ID	Time (hours)	Chlorine (before chlorination) mg/l	Chlorine (after chlorination) mg/l
88	0 (1st day)	0	0.5
88	24 (2nd day)	0.067522	0.48
88	48 (3rd day)	0.363562	0.43
88	72 (4th day)	0.345692	0.45
88	96 (5th day)	0.326792	0.49

The event of contamination occurrence is also a reason of chlorine decay. A case of how chlorine concentration is influenced because of contamination, is appeared in Fig. 6, when Arsenite III, Arsenite V and Becteria are infused at sensor "88" after Day 1, 2, 3 respectively. The effects of the contamination of these species are appearing on the sensor measurement through peaks in residual chlorine graphs (resulting in a decrease of the normal chlorine concentration). Because of the variability in the chlorine input, the ordinary measured chlorine is between 0.2–0.8 mg/L, and the contamination event causes a violation of these limits for only a short period of time.

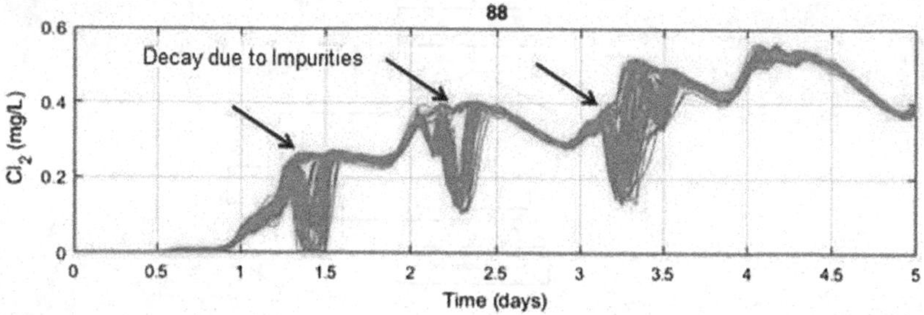

Fig. 6. Residual chlorine concentration at sensor node 88 after contamination of Arsenite III, Arsenite V and Becteria after day 1, 2, 3 respectively (500 simulation scenerio)

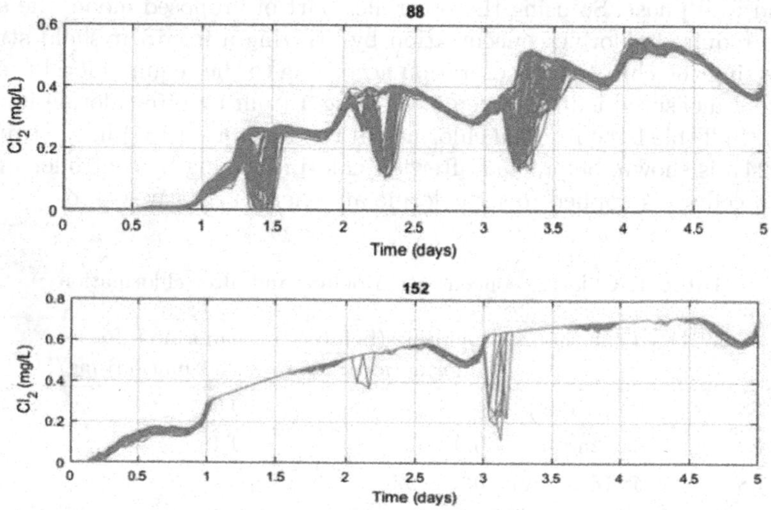

Fig. 7. The evaluated residual chlorine concentration for 500 random simulation scenerio at sensor node 88 and 152

Hence, it won't be conceivable to affirm the contamination based on fixed alarm thresholds. So system will utilize a heuristic classification approach to determine the decay of chlorine is due to demand pattern or due to contamination event without using fixed threshold scheme. Figure 7 depicts the estimated

Fig. 8. Activated water quality sensors at CEERI water network

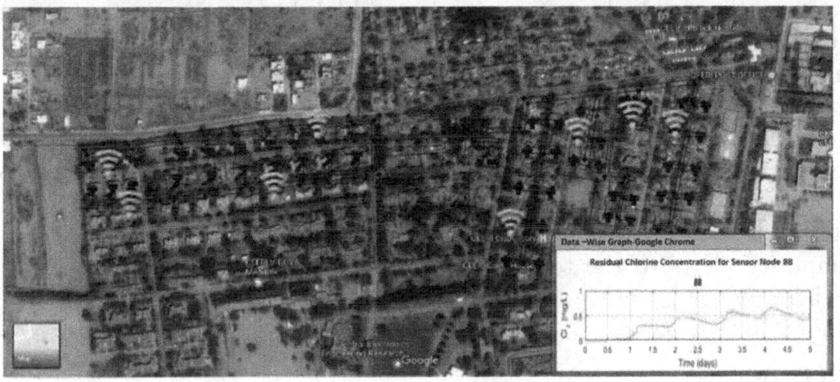

Fig. 9. Graphical representation of sensor data

chlorine concentrations measured at nodes 88 and 152, for 500 randomized simulations.

However, when the results are combined according to the classification rule specified in the methodology then a fair contamination event detection is done by model.

A user interactive view is provided by proposed model to view the current sensor measurements about the residual chlorine. For this set up a raspberry pi board is used at sensor location to send data over IOT server. And to access the information from integrated IOT server a user interactive application is built which is authorized to a selected no of users, who will handle the system. In Fig. 8 the activated sensors are displayed at sensing locations. To view the current chlorine measurement values user should have to click on the sensor button, and its relative information will show through graph (Fig. 9).

When the event detection algorithm is checked against the true event detection alert rates then the system achieve the accuracy of 80.97%. About 20% events are not able to recognize through the proposed methodology.

5 Conclusion and Future Scope

This work depends on the investigation of part of a water supply framework, in CEERI and is simulated by the version 2.0 of the EPANET test system in order to delineate the discovery procedure of impurities and utilizing the water quality model. This paper shows the impacts of contamination event and the initial chlorine concentration have on the chlorine decay in various water tests. It additionally reports the induction of exact formulae of bulk and wall decay which portray these impacts. The data demonstrate that in fresh samples chlorine decays more rapidly and have to perform re-chlorination to set the chlorine concentration about 0.5 mg/l. System is embedded with controller module, which uses a fixed threshold scheme to maintain residual chlorine. Various water quality parameters and contamination event are simulated through a no of simulations using MC method. The information about residual chlorine is send to IOT integrated server, from there using a user interactive application this information is accessed by the users. Model also utilizes the heuristic classification with event detection module. System generates alerts for contamination events and send this information to end users.

In future, development of mobile application can be done for auto generation of Impurity alerts to the technicians of civil department, so they can access anywhere.

References

1. Byer, D., Carlson, K.H.: Expanded summary: real-time detection of intentional chemical contamination in the distribution system. J. (Am. Water Works Assoc.) **97**(7), 130–133 (2005)
2. Eliades, D.G., Polycarpou, M.M.: Contaminant detection in urban water distribution networks using chlorine measurements. In: Hämmerli, B.M., Kalstad Svendsen, N., Lopez, J. (eds.) CRITIS 2012. LNCS, vol. 7722, pp. 203–214. Springer, Heidelberg (2013). https://doi.org/10.1007/978-3-642-41485-5_18
3. Eliades, D.G., Lambrou, T.P., Panayiotou, C.G., Polycarpou, M.M.: Contamination event detection in water distribution systems using a model-based approach. Procedia Eng. **89**, 1089–1096 (2014)
4. Gullick, R.W., LeChevallier, M.W., Svindland, R.C., Friedman, M.J., et al.: Occurrence of transient low and negative pressures in distribution systems. J.-Am. Water Works Assoc. **96**(11), 52–66 (2004)
5. Helbling, D.E., VanBriesen, J.M.: Modeling residual chlorine response to a microbial contamination event in drinking water distribution systems. J. Environ. Eng. **135**(10), 918–927 (2009)
6. Jegatheesan, V., Kastl, G., Fisher, I., Angles, M., Chandy, J.: Modelling biofilm growth and disinfectant decay in drinking water. Water Sci. Technol. **41**(4–5), 339–345 (2000)

7. Jonkergouw, P.M.R., Khu, S.T., Savic, D.: Chlorine: a possible indicator of intentional chemical and biological contamination in a water distribution network. In: Proceedings of IWA Conference on Automation in Water Quality Monitoring (2004)
8. Kirmeyer, G.J., Friedman, M., Martel, K.D., Noran, P.F., Smith, D., et al.: Practical guidelines for maintaining distribution system water quality. J.-Am. Water Works Assoc. **93**(7), 62–73 (2001)
9. Liu, Y., Hou, D., Huang, P., Zhang, G.: Multiscale water quality contamination events detection based on sensitive time scales reconstruction. In: 2013 International Conference on Wavelet Analysis and Pattern Recognition (ICWAPR), pp. 235–240. IEEE (2013)
10. Monteiro, L., Figueiredo, D., Dias, S., Freitas, R., Covas, D., Menaia, J., Coelho, S.T.: Modeling of chlorine decay in drinking water supply systems using epanet MSX. Procedia Eng. **70**, 1192–1200 (2014)
11. Murray, R., Haxton, T., McKenna, S.A., Hart, D.B., Klise, K., Koch, M., Vugrin, E.D., Martin, S., Wilson, M., Cruze, V.A., et al.: Water quality event detection systems for drinking water contamination warning systems: development testing and application of canary. EPAI600IR-IOI036, US (2010)
12. Murray, S., Ghazali, M., McBean, E.A.: Real-time water quality monitoring: assessment of multisensor data using Bayesian belief networks. J. Water Resour. Plann. Manag. **138**(1), 63–70 (2011)
13. Oliker, N., Ostfeld, A.: Minimum volume ellipsoid classification model for contamination event detection in water distribution systems. Environ. Model Softw. **57**, 1–12 (2014)
14. Pasha, M.F.K., Lansey, K.: Effect of parameter uncertainty on water quality predictions in distribution systems-case study. J. Hydroinformatics **12**(1), 1–21 (2010)
15. Perelman, L., Arad, J., Housh, M., Ostfeld, A.: Event detection in water distribution systems from multivariate water quality time series. Environ. Sci. Technol. **46**(15), 8212–8219 (2012)
16. Shang, F., Uber, J.G., Rossman, L.A., et al.: EPANET multi-species extension user's manual. Risk Reduction Engineering Laboratory, US Environmental Protection Agency, Cincinnati, Ohio (2008)
17. Vasconcelos, J.J., Rossman, L.A., Grayman, W.M., Boulos, P.F., Clark, R.M., et al.: Kinetics of chlorine decay. J.-Am. Water Works Assoc. **89**(7), 54–65 (1997)
18. Yang, J.Y., Haught, R.C., Goodrich, J.A.: Real-time contaminant detection and classification in a drinking water pipe using conventional water quality sensors: techniques and experimental results. J. Environ. Manag. **90**(8), 2494–2506 (2009)

Estimation of Link Margin for Performance Analysis of FSO Network

Kappala Vinod Kiran, Vikram Kumar, Ashok Kumar Turuk, and Santos Kumar Das(✉)

National Institute of Technology Rourkela, Rourkela, Odisha, India
dassk@nitrkl.ac.in

Abstract. In a high-speed optical network, the preliminary consideration for a free space optical (FSO) link is the reliability of data communication under various atmospheric conditions, which provides a quality connection to the end user. This paper mainly focuses on the estimation of a quality parameter link margin (LM) in a FSO link. LM is calculated based on the meteorological data obtained at various smart cities under different weather conditions and geometrical attenuation. The availability of FSO link in an optical network is evaluated in terms of LM, which forms to establish a quality based network route for data transmission. The network performance of the proposed scheme is analyzed in terms of blocking probability (BP).

Keywords: FSO · Atmospheric attenuation · Link margin
Blocking probability · Routing and wavelength assignment

1 Introduction

Optical communication without fiber media is termed as FSO. It is an alternative solution to commonly deployed fiber optic and wireless radio-frequency links. FSO is the technology, which is capable of providing high bandwidth communication links between remote sites. It solves the last-mile problem in broadband. The range of frequencies over which it operates makes FSO communication free from licensing [1]. There has been a tremendous increase in digital needs across the globe. In context to developing country like India, there is a need for high-speed data transfer systems. FSO suits the need and provides a viable solution. An FSO system with a clear line of sight (LOS) is workable over distances for several kilometers between the source and the destination [2]. The main limitation to FSO link is the different attenuations created by atmospheric conditions such as rain, fog, snow, and haze. Among all, rain has a significant role that effects the optical power intensity at the receiver. This limits the FSO link availability over a given transmission range. LM is used to determine the availability of an FSO link, the availability of link is considered to be 99.999% for telecommunication (carrier class), and is about 99% for the LAN applications (enterprise class) [3]. In [4], the authors used a cumulative distribution function (CDF) of

P. Bhattacharyya et al. (Eds.): NGCT 2017, CCIS 827, pp. 444–458, 2018.
https://doi.org/10.1007/978-981-10-8657-1_34

meteorological data to estimate the availability of a given link. In [5] the author compares the cumulative distribution of meteorological data and experimental data in a broadband network. If any of the links fails, then there is no provision to provide an alternative connection. Here we estimated the LM based on the statistical analysis of meteorological data of rainfall for different cities over several years to determine the availability of FSO link. This paper emphasizes an intelligent routing technique based on LM for high availability in an FSO network.

This paper has been organized as, following to introduction, Sect. 2 presents the system model for the estimation of LM. In Sect. 3, LM based routing technique is proposed. In Sect. 4, explains the flowchart of routing technique. In Sect. 5, analytical simulation and discussion compares the performance. Finally, Sect. 6, concludes the work.

2 System Model

In FSO link, several effects are considered such as the losses due to atmospheric absorption, scattering, turbulence, microclimate environment, localized effects, link distance and link misalignment. A typical FSO system is as shown in Fig. 1 with transmitter T_{xi} and receiver R_{xj}. It consists of transmitter power, receiver sensitivity, beam divergence angle and atmospheric attenuation due to the atmospheric channel. A key quality parameter in FSO link is the link margin, $LM(i,j)$, which is expressed as [6],

$$LM(i,j) = P_e(i) - S_r(j) - \alpha_{tgeo}(i,j) - \alpha_{atmo}(i,j) - \alpha_{sys}(i,j) \tag{1}$$

where, $P_e(i)$ is the ith transmitter power; $S_r(j)$ is the jth receiver sensitivity; $\alpha_{tgeo}(i,j)$ is geometrical attenuation between link (i,j); $\alpha_{atmo}(i,j)$ is atmospheric attenuation; $\alpha_{sys}(i,j)$ is system losses. These parameters are further explained as follows.

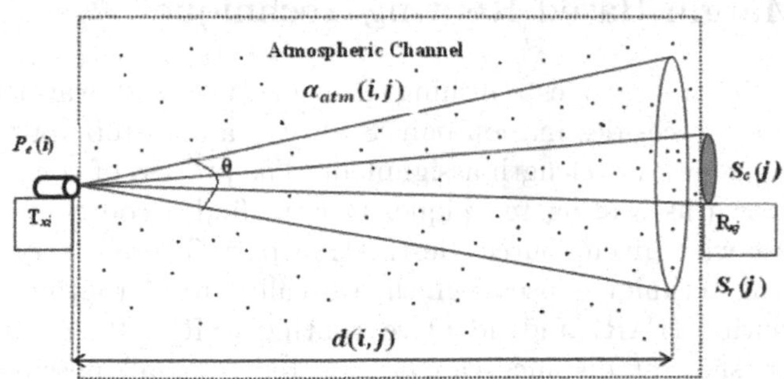

Fig. 1. A typical FSO system

2.1 Geometrical Attenuation

The light beam diverges as it travels a long distance due to small receiver capture area, a very less amount of power is consumed. This problem corresponds to geometrical attenuation (GA), $\alpha_{tgeo}(i,j)$ is expressed as [6],

$$\alpha_{tgeo}(i,j) = \frac{S_t(i)}{S_c(i)} \tag{2}$$

where, $S_t(i) = \frac{\pi}{4}(d(i,j)\theta)^2$ it is the area of illumination; θ is the light beam divergence angle, $d(i,j)$ is the distance from the transmitter (i) to receiver (j) and $S_c(i)$ is the capture area of the receiver.

2.2 Atmospheric Attenuation

There are different types of attenuation occurring due to variation in atmospheric conditions (i.e., rain, fog, snow, haze, and scintillation). Rain is considered to be the major impairment for an FSO link. It has a significant role in determining the LM. Atmospheric attenuation, $\alpha_{atmo}(i,j)$ due to rain is expressed as per unit distance. Using the Carbonneau model [7], it can be expressed as,

$$\alpha_{rain}(i,j) = 1.076 \times R^{0.67} \tag{3}$$

where, R is the precipitation intensity in mm/h. Now, based on (2) and (3), a more precise FSO link margin, $LM(i,j)$ in effect to GA, rain attenuation, and system losses can be expressed as,

$$LM(i,j) = P_t(i) + |S_r(j)| - [10log_{10}\alpha_{tgeo}(i,j)] - [\alpha_{rain}(i,j) \times d(i,j)] - \alpha_{sys}(i,j) \tag{4}$$

where, $\alpha_{atmo}(i,j) = \alpha_{rain}(i,j) \times d(i,j)$.

The next section explains routing technique based on LM.

3 Link Margin Based Routing Technique

RWA refers to the process of establishing the connection with wavelength assignment between a source–destination pair [8,9]. It is a two-step approach such as routing technique and wavelength assignment. The process of connection establishment is known as routing technique. It is to find a route as per the connection request with given source–destination pair. There are typically three types of routing techniques used, which are called fixed routing (FR), fixed-alternative routing (FAR) and adaptive routing (AR) [10–13]. In general, a FAR based on shortest distance can be selected from all possible routes for any source–destination pair (s,d) [14]. In AR, the route can be selected based on the dynamic change of the link quality.

Once the route is selected, a particular wavelength is assigned to it. There are different wavelength assignment (WA) techniques used, which is called first-fit WA, random WA, least-fit WA *etc.* If there is no route or wavelength is available for a (s, d) pair, then the request for connection is to be blocked [15]. BP serves a key role in the evaluation of network performance. This is evaluated by investigating individual node and link in an FSO network [16]. The primary step in the analysis is the computation of all available routes in a given FSO network based on the distance or LM. As proposed in [14], all available routes are computed based on LM is represented by a $n \times n$ matrix, $\mathbf{T}$. The network load in the network is represented as, μ_{net}. The corresponding load matrix $\mathbf{L}$, represents the load carried at each link, that can be expressed as [17],

$$L(i,j) = \frac{\mu_{net}}{\sum_{i=1}^{n}\sum_{j=1}^{n}T(i,j)}\mathbf{T} \tag{5}$$

where, n is the number of nodes; $T(i, j)$ is the no. of supported routes for link (i, j) belongs to $\mathbf{T}$, $L(i, j)$ belongs to $\mathbf{L}$.

The BP matrix, $\boldsymbol{B_p}(i, j)$, for each link with $\mathrm{L}(i, j)$ can be expressed by using the Erlang–B formula as [18],

$$\boldsymbol{B_p}(i,j) = \frac{\frac{L(i,j)^{A(i,j)}}{A(i,j)!}}{\sum_{c=0}^{A(i,j)} L(i,j)^c} \tag{6}$$

where, $A(i, j)$ is the number of wavelengths on link $\mathrm{L}(i, j)$. The overall network BP, $\boldsymbol{B_{pnet}}$, can be expressed as,

$$\boldsymbol{B_{pnet}} = \frac{\sum_{i=1}^{n}\sum_{j=1}^{n} B_p(i,j) \times T(i,j)}{\sum_{i=1}^{n}\sum_{j=1}^{n} T(i,j)} \tag{7}$$

The BP on each node, B_{pnode}, is approximated as follows [17],

$$\boldsymbol{B_{pnode}} = \frac{\sum_{j=1}^{n} B(i,j) \times T(i,j)}{\sum_{j=1}^{n} T(i,j)} \tag{8}$$

4 Flow Chart of LM Based Routing and BP Computation

The flow chart for LM based routing and the evaluation of blocking performance is shown in Fig. 2. Initially, all available paths are estimated with the corresponding LM of each link. The available paths are then sorted in descending order based on the LM. Among the sorted order, paths above the threshold are accepted and form a new all available paths matrix, T. Corresponding blocking probabilities are computed for performance analysis.

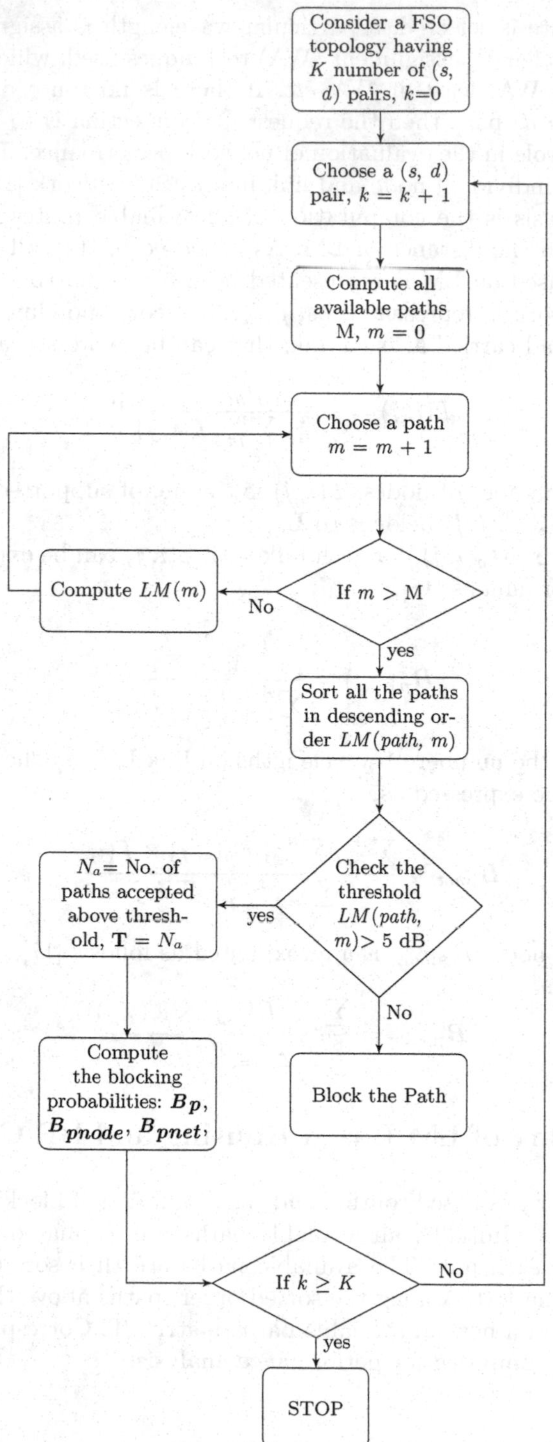

Fig. 2. Flow chart of LM based routing and BP

5 Analytical Simulation and Discussion

Parameters considered for the simulation are shown in Table 1. Simulations are performed using MATLAB and OptiSystem 7.0 [19] software. The performance is analyzed based on link level and FSO network. These are further explained as follows.

Table 1. FSO transceiver

Parameters	FSOA	FSOB
d	1 km	2 km
P_t	14.47 dBm	16.98 dBm
S_r	−34 dBm	−31 dBm
S_c	$0.16\,\mathrm{m}^2$	
θ	2 mrad	
λ	1550 nm	
α_{sys}	10 dB	

5.1 Performance Analysis of FSO Link

The availability of FSO link is evaluated based on GA, rain attenuation, and system losses. Figure 3 shows the GA for different beam divergence angles of light as a function of link distance. It is observed, as the distance increases the attenuation increases considerably. Figure 4 represents the attenuation due to varying precipitation intensity of the rain. Two FSO links (i.e., FSOA and FSOB) of range 1 km and 2 km are considered for the deployment in different parts of India. To analyze the performance of the links, a comprehensive statistical data of rainfall is collected from Indian meteorological department [20] for various smart cities. A period from June–September is focused in our estimation since much of the rainfall is during this session. A case study of the annual distribution of rainfall for 30 days with 4 h/day is considered. Rainfall Rate (RFR) is calculated (i.e for Allahabad, $184.2714/4 \times 30 = 1.53$), which is shown in Table 2. The maximum distance link can operate, and LM (i.e., the minimum received power that is above the receiver sensitivity) of an FSO link can be computed with RFR using (5). Table 3 represents the maximum FSO link distance (LD) and LM. It is observed from the results that, the two transceivers link work properly within a given distances. LM forms an important quality parameter for link status, Figs. 5 and 6 signifies that attenuation due to rain does not have much effect on the FSO link. As the precipitation increased, i.e., for a heavy rainfall of 25 mm/h and using (5), the availability of FSO link for a 2 km is simulated using OptiSystem as shown in Fig. 7, which represents that even for the worst case scenario the link remains stable. An eye diagram is shown in Fig. 8 which signifies that it has very fewer amplitude variations with eye height of 58428e−006 for a 2 km link.

This is not the case if there is a cloud burst or any other atmospheric calamity which drastically leads to a link failure. The following section addresses the problem by using a multi-link network topology with intelligent routing, based on the atmospheric conditions.

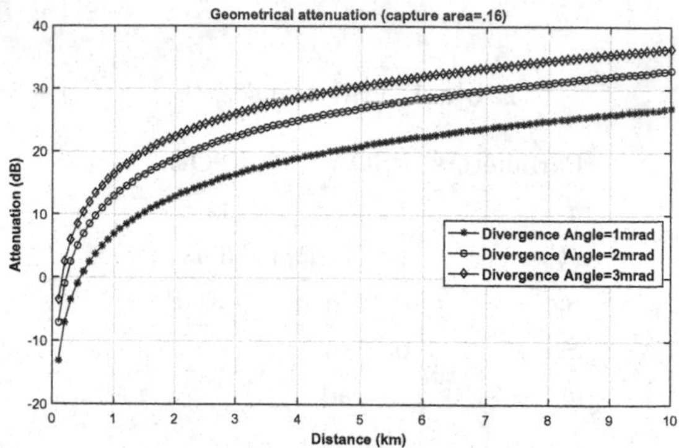

Fig. 3. Geometrical attenuation (dB)

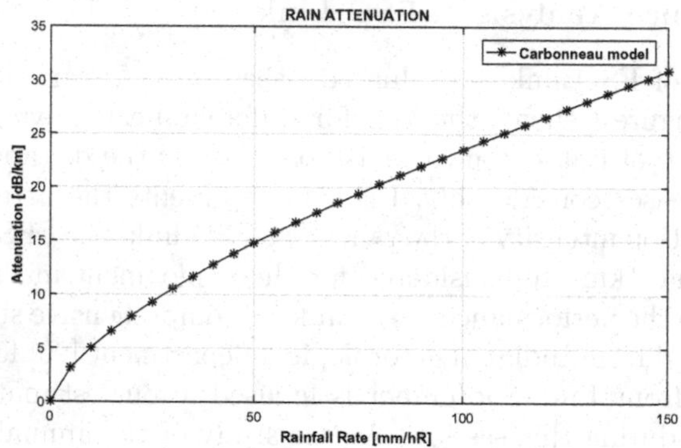

Fig. 4. Rain attenuation (dB/km)

5.2 Performance Analysis Using FSO Network Topology

Consider an FSO network with 10 nodes and 16 links similar to NSFNet topology as shown in Fig. 9. FSO link with 1 span is equal to a transmission distance of 1 km with LM of 5 dB. Initially, all possible paths are computed based on distance and for different LM (i.e, LM > 5 dB and LM > 10 dB) are shown in Figs. 10, 11 and 12. The vertical bar represents a number of possible routes from each source node to the other nodes, i.e., a source–destination pair (2, 3) has 21 paths based on distance, where as 15 paths for LM > 5 dB and 7 paths for LM > 10 dB. It

Table 2. Estimation of rainfall rate (RFR) from average rainfall (ARF) [20]

District	ARF (mm/4 months)	RFR (mm/h)
Delhi	131.275	1.093
Visakhapatnam	165.4375	1.37
Ajmer	103.975	0.866
Chennai	105.5286	0.871
Aurangabad	165.9929	1.37
Goa	760.6179	6.33
Gurgoan	121	1.008
Tumkur	110.9464	0.924
Cuttack	85.964	2.899
Rajkot	204.5286	1.7044
Allahabad	184.2714	1.53
Howrah	297.74	2.481
Coimbatore	85.964	0.716

Table 3. Maximum LM with link distance (LD) for FSOA and FSOB

District	RFR (mm/h)	LD for FSOA	LD for FSOB	LM for FSOA	LM for FSOB
Delhi	1.093	5.84	5.66	20.87	13.22
Visakhapatnam	1.37	5.45	5.3	20.68	12.84
Ajmer	0.866	6.24	6.04	20.68	13.55
Chennai	0.871	6.23	6.03	21.03	13.54
Aurangabad	1.38	5.45	5.28	20.68	12.83
Goa	6.33	3.2	3.13	18.31	8.067
Gurgoan	1.008	5.38	5.79	20.93	13.34
Tumkur	0.924	6.13	5.93	20.99	13.46
Cuttack	2.899	4.27	4.16	19.82	11.11
Rajkot	1.7044	5.1	4.95	20.47	12.43
Allahabad	1.53	5.28	5.12	20.58	12.64
Howrah	2.481	4.51	4.38	20.03	11.55
Coimbatore	0.716	6.57	6.35	21.15	13.78

is observed that as the LM threshold increased the number of supported paths decreased, but this trade-off increases the link reliability. Conventional routing technique such as shortest path algorithm does not include the link status, rather finds the route based on distance. There are situations where the shortest link may suffer from high atmospheric attenuation. The topology is controlled by selecting a path using the current scenario of the network. An intelligent routing algorithm with LM as the quality parameter for routing is explained below.

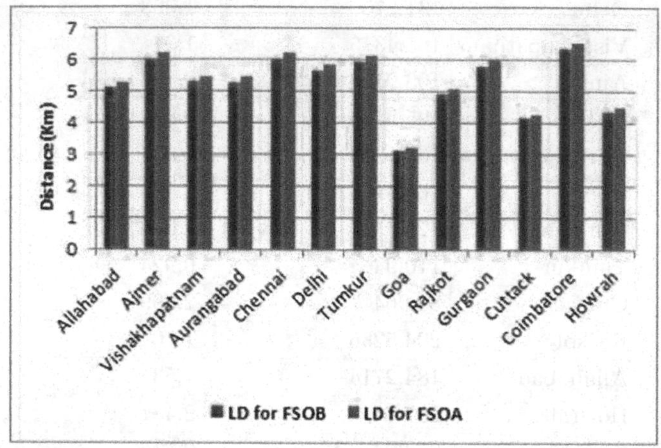

Fig. 5. Maximum operating link distance for FSOA and FSOB

- **Path computation based on LM**
  Following are the steps for path computation based on LM:
  i. Computation of LM for each link of the entire network.
  ii. Compute all available paths with the minimum LM for the connection setup i.e., a source–destination pair (2, 3) has 21 paths for LM > 0 dB as shown in Fig. 13.
  iii. Sort the paths based on highest LM as shown in Fig. 14 for a source–destination pair (2, 3).
  Now, the paths with threshold LM is selected.
- **Analysis of network traffic load**
  The number of supported routes due to LM for the different threshold is shown in Figs. 10, 11 and 12. This result represents that as LM threshold is increased it consequently relates to less number of supported routes, but provides a higher reliable connection. The analysis is performed for LM > 5 dB with network load, μ_{net} and fixed number of wavelengths. Figures 15 and 16 represents the blocking probabilities at each node with different network load, μ_{net} as 50E and 100E. It is observed the least BP is provided by node 5 among all the nodes, which signifies a route with node 5 has less probability of link failure. Figure 17 represents the overall network performance depending on the wavelengths used per link and traffic. It is observed that as the number of wavelengths increased corresponding BP decreases. Figure 18 shows the network blocking performance for distance and LM based algorithms, it is observed as the LM increased the BP has decreased leading to a high availability of the links. Also, the proposed algorithm outperforms the existing distance based algorithm.

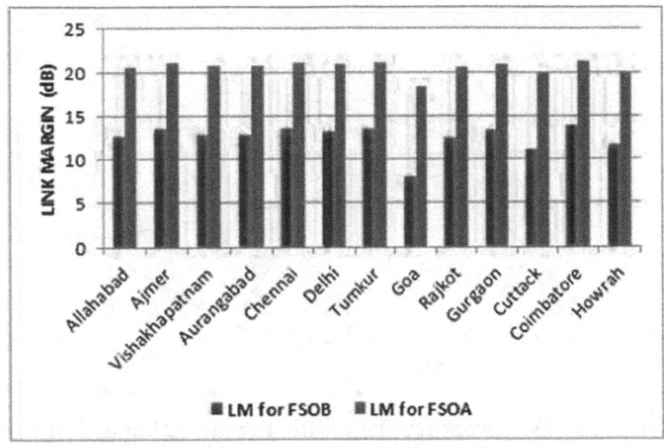

Fig. 6. LM for FSOA and FSOB

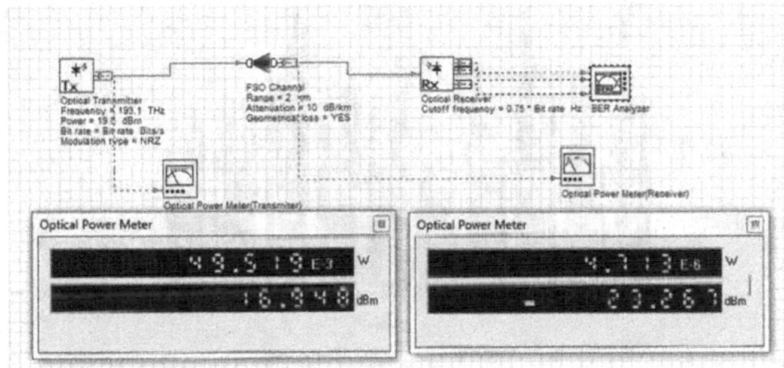

Fig. 7. Simulation for the heaviest rainfall rate of 25 mm/h OptiSystem 7.0

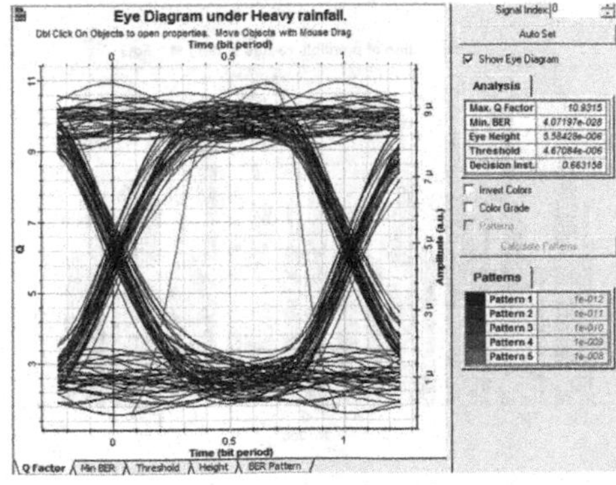

Fig. 8. Eye diagram at 1 Gbps for 2 km FSO link

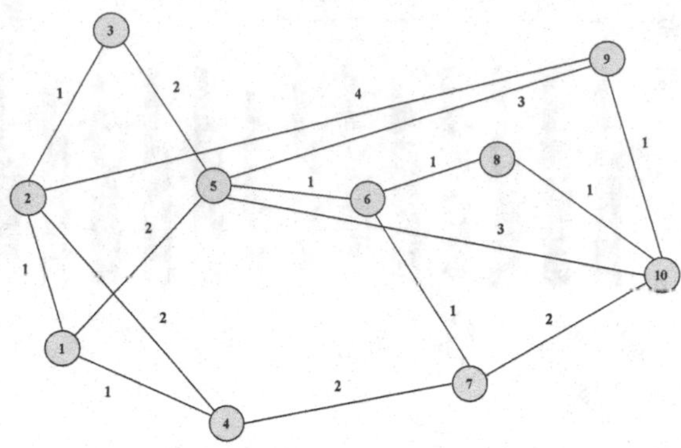

Fig. 9. An FSO network topology with 1 span = 2 km or LM = 5 dB

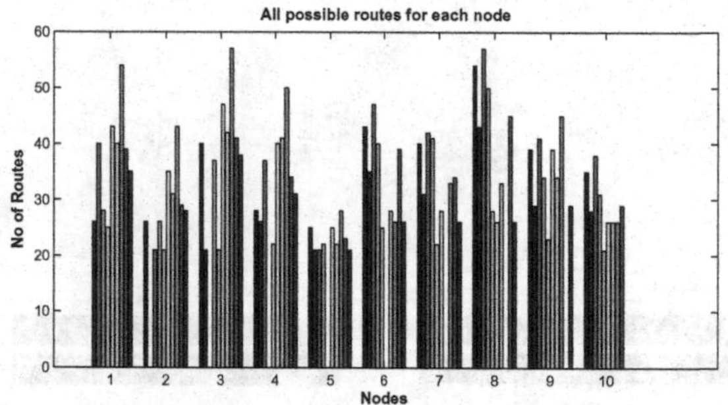

Fig. 10. Computation of all available routes from each node to destination node for LM > 0 dB

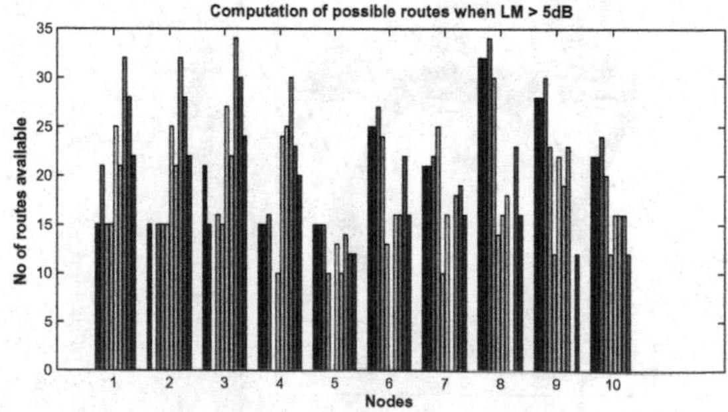

Fig. 11. Computation of available routes, when LM > 5 dB

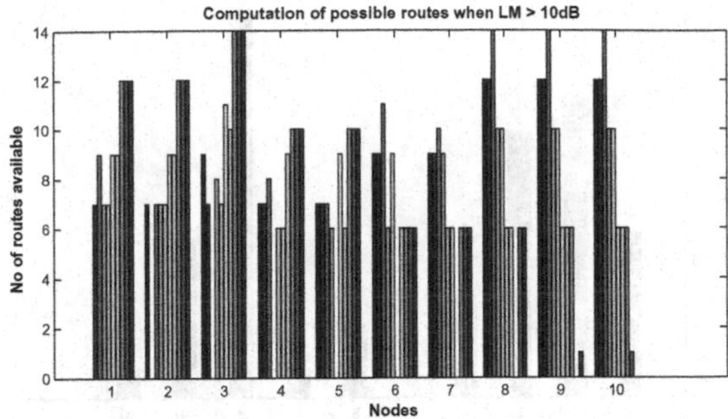

Fig. 12. Computation of available routes, when LM > 10 dB

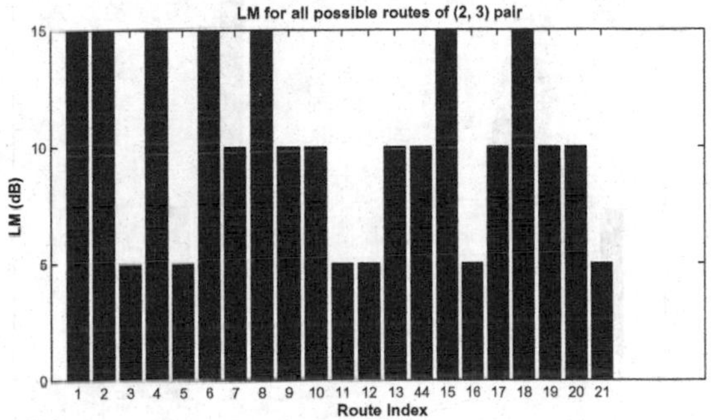

Fig. 13. LM plot for all possible routes of source–destination pair (2, 3)

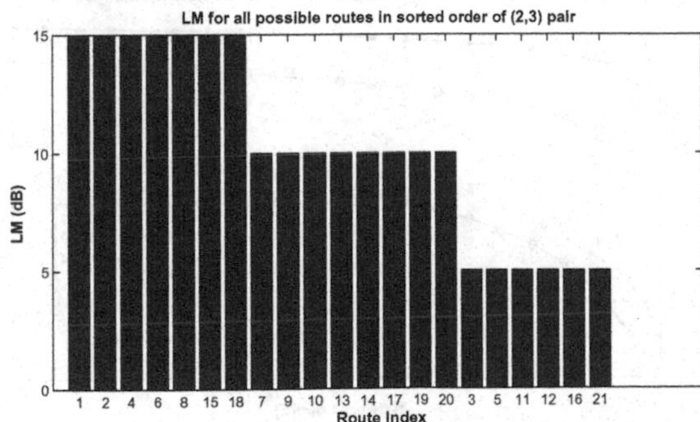

Fig. 14. LM plot for all possible routes of source–destination pair (2, 3) in sorted order

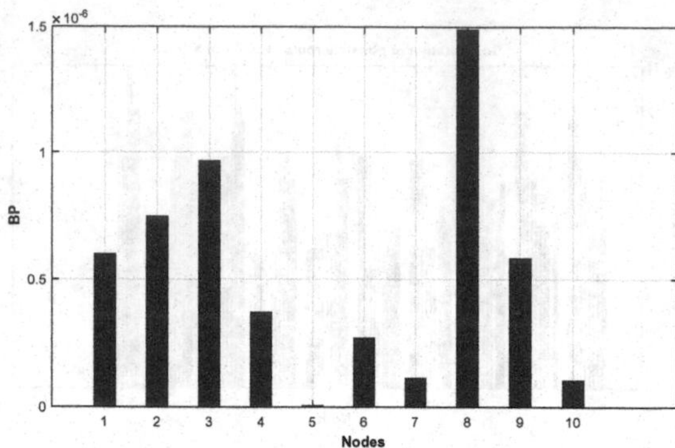

Fig. 15. BP computation for each node with wavelengths = 8 and network traffic = 50E

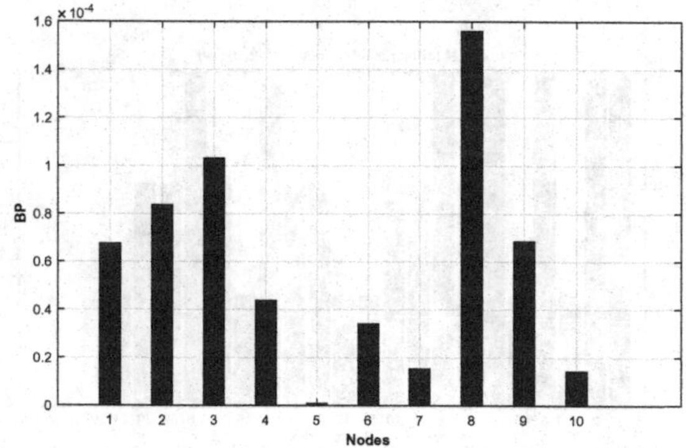

Fig. 16. BP computation for each node with wavelengths = 8 and network traffic = 100E

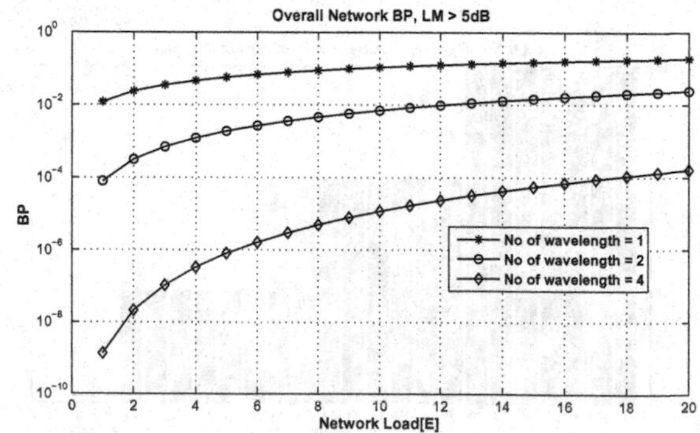

Fig. 17. BP computations of overall network with wavelengths and network traffic (1E to 20E)

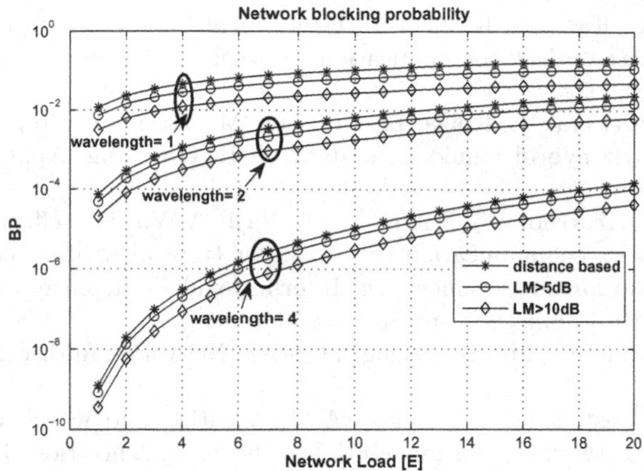

Fig. 18. BP for distance and LM based algorithms

6 Conclusion

The primary goal of this work is to determine the availability of FSO link under rainy weather conditions from the data collected at various smart cities of India. Also, the proposed routing technique for FSO network based on link margin provides a high reliable communication even on adverse conditions. Performance analysis of the network under different traffic conditions and network resources based on LM is done, which comprises the quality in network routing. This work can be extended for different atmospheric attenuation condition, and an optimization based on different factors can give a deeper insight analyzing network quality. This forms a basis for future link design in an FSO network.

Acknowledgments. This work has been supported by Department of Electronics and IT (Deity), Ministry of Communications and IT, Government of India under Visvesvaraya PhD Scheme for Electronics and IT (Grant no: PhD-MLA/4(13)/2015-16).

References

1. Chan, V.W.: Free-space optical communications. J. Lightwave Technol. **24**(12), 4750–4762 (2006)
2. Mustafa, F.H., Supaat, A.S.M., Charde, N.: Effect of rain attenuations on free space optic transmission in Kuala Lumpur. Int. J. Adv. Sci. Eng. Inf. Technol. **1**(4), 337–341 (2011)
3. Kim, I.I., Korevaar, E.J.: Availability of free-space optics (FSO) and hybrid FSO/RF systems. In: ITCom, International Society for Optics and Photonics, pp. 84–95 (2001)
4. Prokes, A., Skorpil, V.: Estimation of free space optics systems availability based on meteorological visibility. In: IEEE Latin-American Conference on Communications, pp. 1–4 (2009)

5. Wakamori, K., Kazaura, K., Oka, I.: Experiment on regional broadband network using free-space-optical communication systems. J. Lightwave Technol. **25**(11), 3265–3273 (2007)
6. Wilfert, O., Kvicera, V., Kolka, Z., Grabner, M., Fiser, O.: Propagation study of 850 nm/58 GHz hybrid municipal system. SPIE Opt. Eng. Appl. **7814**, 781414–781422 (2010)
7. Zabidi, S.A., Khateeb, W., Islam, M.R., Naji, A.W.: The effect of weather on free space optics communication (FSO) under tropical weather conditions and a proposed setup for measurement. In: International Conference on Computer and Communication Engineering, pp. 1–5. IEEE (2010)
8. Stern, T.E., Bala, K.: Multiwavelength Optical Networks. Addison Wesley, Boston (1999)
9. Lezama, F., Castan, G., Sarmiento, A.M.: Routing and wavelength assignment in all optical networks using differential evolution optimization. Photonics Netw. Commun. **26**(2), 103–119 (2013)
10. Zheng, J., Mouftah, H.T.: Routing and wavelength assignment for advance reservation in wavelength-routed WDM optical networks. IEEE Int. Conf. Commun. **5**, 2722–2726 (2002)
11. Ramamurthy, R., Mukherjee, B.: Fixed-alternate routing and wavelength conversion in wavelength-routed optical networks. IEEE/ACM Trans. Netw. **10**(3), 351–367 (2002)
12. Saminadan, V., Meenakshi, M.: In-band crosstalk performance of WDM optical networks under different routing and wavelength assignment algorithms. In: Pal, A., Kshemkalyani, A.D., Kumar, R., Gupta, A. (eds.) IWDC 2005. LNCS, vol. 3741, pp. 159–170. Springer, Heidelberg (2005). https://doi.org/10.1007/11603771_19
13. Poo, G.-S., Ding, A.: Blocking performance analysis on adaptive routing over WDM networks with finite wavelength conversion capability. Photon Netw. Commun. **12**(2), 211–218 (2006)
14. Das, S.K., Kalyan, C.P., Patra, S.K.: Data-path selection mechanism based on physical layer impairments for WDM network. Int. J. Signal Imaging Syst. Eng. **5**(4), 239–245 (2012)
15. Mukherjee, B.: Optical WDM Networks. Springer, New York (2006). https://doi.org/10.1007/0-387-29188-1
16. Ramaswami, R., Sivarajan, K.: Optical Networks: A Practical Perspective. Morgan Kaufmann, Burlington (2009)
17. Bonani, L.H., Fonseca, I.E.: Estimating the blocking probability in wavelength-routed optical networks. Opt. Switch. Netw. **10**(4), 430–438 (2013)
18. Mitra, D., Seery, J.: Comparative evaluations of randomized and dynamic routing strategies for circuit-switched networks. IEEE Trans. Commun. **39**(1), 102–116 (1991)
19. Optiwave Design Software for Photonics. http://www.optiwave.com
20. Indian Meteorological Department. http://www.imd.gov.in

Web Documents Prioritization Using Iterative Improvement

Kamika Chaudhary[1(✉)], Neena Gupta[1], and Santosh Kumar[2]

[1] Department of Computer Science, Gurukula Kangri Vishwavidyalaya, Kanya Gurukula Campus, Dehradun, Uttarakhand, India
kamika.agrohi@gmail.com

[2] Department of Computer Science and Engineering, Krishna Institute of Engineering and Technology, Ghaziabad, Uttar Pradesh, India

Abstract. The amount of information accumulating on World Wide Web is growing in size exponentially. This led to difficulty in accessing the relevant information as it becomes tough for a user to access his required information in minimum amount of time. As a result of single query placed by user in search engine a large number of search results appear in front of him and to dig out the most relevant web link becomes a cumbersome task for user which can lead to decrease in trust for search engine. This paper proposes an approach for web structure and web usage mining by using iterative improvement algorithm. Iterative improvement is a randomized algorithm which is used for solving combinatorial optimization problem. This technique helps in selecting top T web pages and prioritizing them in relevance order. Experimental evaluation has been done which shows significant improvement in performance. The parameters used are access frequency, time duration, no of visitors, hubs and authorities. They cover the area of both web structure and web usage mining.

Keywords: Iterative improvement · Web mining · topT web pages

1 Introduction

The Significantly quick aggregation of information over the internet has resulted into the advancement and development of World Wide Web (WWW) both in size and popularity. As an outcome it has become the largest distributed information space and is considered to be the best source of information. However various properties of web data such as huge size, unstructured contents, heterogeneous and dynamic nature make the utilization and retrieval of information a tedious and cumbersome task for user. Web users mainly come across with the problem of information overload and drowning. Search engines are predominant tools which are mainly concerned with the task of answering the query of user. Though, low precision and recall rate of search engines raises a critical issue how to provide web users with exactly needful information in minimum amount of time. Web mining approach emerges to address this problem. In principle web mining approach utilizes the data mining techniques to actuate and extricate the valuable information from web data and services. Fundamentally web

P. Bhattacharyya et al. (Eds.): NGCT 2017, CCIS 827, pp. 459–473, 2018.
https://doi.org/10.1007/978-981-10-8657-1_35

mining can be arranged into three classifications on the basis of the part of the web which is to be mined: web content mining, web structure mining and web usage mining [17]. Web content mining deals with the real data i.e. the data with which the web pages are made of and tries to retrieve the valuable information from that data. This real data usually consist of text and graphics but do not have any constraints on including various other formats such as image, audio, video and so on. As web content mining is mainly concerned with the textual data therefore sometimes it is also known as text mining. Web structure mining focuses on the link structure of web to discover the analogy and relationship among the web sites. The mutual linkage information is utilised to model the web component called site map which is generated automatically for static web pages on the completion of web site and for dynamic pages the process needs more advanced techniques. Web usage mining works on the log files and tries to uncover and analyze the user access pattern. Unlike web content and web structure mining, web usage mining deals with secondary data and it tries to comprehend the information generated by web surfer's session or behavior. There can be various data sources in which the transactional information of the web user is stored, they may be web server access logs, proxy logs, browser logs, user profiles, cookies, registration forms etc. In the process of web usage mining there are mainly three phases that is pre processing of data, pattern discovery and pattern analysis through which transactional data has to move in order to generate the useful mined information. Generally web users surf the web by clicking on their interesting links or data and this usage pattern can be utilised to improve the web site structure as well as for recommending and personalizing the web site particular to user and his interests.

In the proposed work an effort has been made to address the issue of selecting high quality Top–T web pages in response to a user query by using the randomized optimization heuristics [19]. In randomized algorithm each solution is regarded as state in search space and a cost function is used to compute the cost for each related state. A random walk is performed in search space through a set of moves that resulted in reaching to neighbour of the state. These moves may be uphill move or downhill move and may increase or decrease the cost respectively. In the search of optimal solution, random walk is performed through a set of moves which leads to find local maxima and among those local maxima the one with maximum cost is considered to be global maxima and hence the optimal solution. The proposed algorithm is based on randomized iterative improvement and works towards prioritizing the top web links in the order of their significance to user query. The proposed work has been compared with the algorithm given by Kleinberg in [18] and hereafter referred as K algorithm. He considered hubs and authorities for finding top T document by iterative improvement process and it has been found experimentally that our proposed algorithm is better in performance as compared to K algorithm.

1.1 Related Work

Finding relevant documents and then prioritizing them for user are the most challenging errand for the web search engine. Web page prioritization has an important application potential in web information searches. Practically, a large number of relevant pages are returned for a given query but it has been observed that users mainly go through top 10 or 20 web links. Therefore there is a prerequisite of organizing the web links so that search engine provides best related pages to user in light of their inquiries. This issue of prioritizing the web links has been addressed in [1] by authors. They proposed an algorithm which focuses on both the structural element of the parent page as well as anchor text to make the prediction about pages with highest relevant accuracy. Then for prioritization top down approach has been used for constructing T-graph (Treasure graph) that help in assigning a priority score to the web urls and proposed architecture has been found efficient as it gives precision and recall values close to 50%. Another machine learning technique called reinforcement learning has been used as a powerful tool to develop a novel algorithm called RL_Rank that use link structure of the web pages in order to rank them in the order of their relevance [2]. RL_Rank works by regarding agent as a surfer and web page as a state and then calculate the Rank score as an inverse function of out degree of current page. In addition to RL_Rank authors have also proposed a hybrid algorithm based on content data as well as structure data. Both the algorithms had been evaluated experimentally on benchmark data sets and were found to improve the results. In another approach to prioritize the web links authors in [3] tried to merge a number of content based and connectivity based ranking algorithm by using user click through data. They proposed an algorithm and named it as A3CRank algorithm in which goodness factor of each ranking algorithm such as TF-IDF, BM25, page rank is calculated by using reinforcement learning and then OWA aggregation operator is applied to merge the result. Experimentally algorithm has been implemented and found to outperform previous algorithms in bringing top T pages on top of the result list. Another effort has been put in by authors to improve the relevance of search engines and user experience in [4] by building a novel framework for learning ranking functions by utilizing relative importance judgment. It has been found that it is costly as well as unreliable to use absolute relevance judgment so this problem is dealt by introducing relative relevance judgment by utilizing user click through data and algorithm was named as GBrank which provides more efficient and flexible result even if preference data is not available.

The issue of focusing on most valuable pages with high popularity in order to make web more productive and interesting for web users has been addressed in [5]. As search engine cannot index the entire web therefore a better crawling algorithm based on reinforcement learning called FICA (Fast Intelligent Crawling Algorithm) has been proposed. It models the random user surfing the web and priority of the web page is computed by considering logarithmic distance from the starting url. This algorithm is found to be well versed in performing crawling and ranking altogether. Experimental evaluation of algorithm and its comparison with already established algorithm shows that the FICA is faster and needed less memory for computation. Additionally with respect to search engine it has been found that they lack in demonstrating the perceptual aspects of humans as they rely on keyword based search only [6]. Due to dependency on document index (DI) based search only they become inefficient in providing the desired result of queries in best possible manner so the author introduced the another index called perception index (PI) along with document index. They both will cover the crisp terms as well as fuzzy terms. Experimental evaluation proved that PI based search provides a better way to personalized search and ranking of web pages. Furthermore it has been found that there are websites which tries to cheat the search engine by making the speculations about the ranking algorithm used by search engine and increase their rank by utilizing impersonate means. This kind of act is considered as spam and in an attempt to eliminate spam pages and assigning higher ranks to high quality web pages authors in [7] proposed a link based anti spam ranking algorithm. By using this algorithm punishment of spam pages have been computed on the basis of two parameters reliability and correlativity and experiment and comparison with page rank algorithm have been conducted and proposed algorithm found to be more spam resilient. In [8–10] authors focused on prioritizing the web documents by using evolutionary approach that is genetic algorithm. Several parameters from different web mining such as web content, web usage and web structure mining have been considered in order to develop the tool so that user browsing experience gets improved. Algorithms proposed based on genetic approach uses the selection, crossover and mutation as genetic operators and helps in prioritizing the top k web links and enhances the user experience with the web and reduce his wastage of time in getting the desired information. In an another attempt to find the top k document a simple augmented inverted index structure called block max index have been proposed by authors in [11].

The process of query processing suffers from the problem of length of inverted list index structure that grows in size by storing common terms used in queries which ultimately wastes the time of search engine in processing the user query. So to deal with this problem block max structure that stores maximum impact score have been used that reduces the length of the inverted list and results into the faster retrieval of top k documents. In [12] authors have given another url prioritizing algorithm based on domain specific ontology that changes the less important pages with more important pages in priority queue. The strategy of combining together link analysis along with topic ontology resulted in improving the harvest rate as depicted by experimentation evaluation and outcome has been the efficient discovery of relevant web pages by web crawler. In [13] it has been found that less importance has been given to content quality for ranking of web documents. Link analysis has been on top when we discuss about the ranking of web documents. So the light is focused on content quality of document which is determined by various parameters such as readability, layout ease of navigation etc. and a quality biased ranking method (QSDM) has been proposed which promotes the high quality web pages and hence improves the retrieval performance of the search engine. In further work authors tries to find the solution of "rich get richer" phenomenon which states that popular pages gets on becoming more popular while ignoring the newly added pages. So it becomes problematic for recently added pages to become popular and hence resulted to declare that search engine perform popularity biased ranking [14]. To deal with this problem a framework has been established that define the page quality and term to be quality estimator. Quality estimator predicts the quality of page as the function of probability that user will like the page in first time if he views the page. Experiment has been performed and it evidences that page quality certainly helped in eliminating the "rich get richer" problem. There are a number of algorithms that have been proposed in order to solve NP hard problems. One such algorithm is randomized iterative improvement algorithm used in [15] for university course time tabling problem. In this an attempt is made to use composite neighborhood structure in spite of single neighborhood and the specialty of this algorithm has been that it always accept improved solution and less improved solution acceptance is defined by Monte Carlo acceptability. Experiment evidences show that composite neighborhood structures are better due to different types of search presented by them. In [16] authors discussed that the major reason in the reduction of performance of search engine has been the non matching characteristic of user query with document space. To deal with this problem they proposed an association among queries with the user click through data. This association will work as a metadata of the web pages and an iterative improvement algorithm has been proposed by using same association and experimental data proved to show significant improvement. Furthermore in the quest of searching relevant pages in response to a query Kleinberg in [18] proposed an algorithm which considers the link structure of WWW. The techniques are mainly devised for broad topics which extend towards calculating the authorities and hubs pages on a topic. The result showed that the link topology woks significantly towards its goal and is able to extract better result of a query.

2 The Approach

2.1 Iterative Improvement

Iterative Improvement algorithm is one of the most successful and widely used randomized algorithms for dealing with the combinatorial optimization problem. It is a local optimization technique that works on the basic principle of improving the initial solution by going through a number of iterations. It begins by selecting m random initial states and then n neighbors are generated for each random state. The comparison of the cost of n neighbor state is performed with that of m initial random states and if cost of neighbor succeeds cost of random state then neighbor is selected as the next initial random state.

The process of comparison is continued and random moves are performed that accepts only uphill and a local maxima is achieved. Likewise new initial solutions are randomly produced and their local maxima is computed and after stopping criteria is met global maxima is produced as an output by picking up the solution with maximum cost function from all local maxima of random states. The basic iterative improvement algorithm is shown in Fig. 1 below.

2.1.1 Fitness Evaluation

The fitness of web documents is evaluated by performing the summation of various parameters representing both web usage and structure mining. In general fitness function is used to determine the quality of web documents by calculating the goodness

Algorithm Iterative Improvement
1. Select m (say 5) random states as starting points
2. Generate n (say 60) neighbors of each initial random state
3. If [cost of neighbour] > [cost of initial random state]
   Then neighbour is selected as new initial random state
4. Repeat step 3 for each of the initial random states
5. Repeat step 2 to step 4 until local maximum is reached i.e.
   Perform random series of move and accepts only uphill until it reaches a local maximum.
6. Find the global maximum among all m initial random states.

Fig. 1. Basic iterative improvement algorithm

of the solutions. This function computes the cost of solutions and this cost becomes the most important parameter for determining the good quality web links. A description of various parameters on which fitness function is based on is presented in the next section.

Access Frequency

This is one of the important parameter that describes about the count of visit of a user on a particular web page without considering user id. It has been considered that a web page is visited more frequently if its relevance to the user is more. So the count of access frequency serves as usage related criterion. An access count on different web url irrespective of user id is shown in Table 1.

Table 1. Access frequency count

Web user id	Web_Url	Access frequency
User_Id1	192.168.30.15	34
User_Id2	192.168.30.50	21
User_Id3	10.21.32.14	17
User_Id4	10.0.0.10	43
…	…	…
User_Id N	10.21.60.90	28

Number of Unique Visitor

The significance of a web page can also be depicted by the number of unique web visitor accessed that page. More the number of users visited a web page more acclaimed a web page is. So the number of distinct individual found to be good usage based variable for determining the popularity of a web page. Table 2 shows number of unique user visited a web page.

Table 2. Unique user visited a web page

Unique user id	Web_Url	Unique user
User_Id1	192.168.30.50	121
User_Id2	10.21.40.40	26
User_Id3	192.168.40.15	85
User_Id4	10.0.0.10	48
…	…	…
User_Id N	192.168.30.57	67

Time Duration

The calculation of amount of time user spends on a web page helps in understanding the web user behavior as well as is used to compute the relevance of that web page. If the users spend more time on any particular web page then that web page is considered to be of importance to the user. It is considered that a web user does not stay on a particular page for more amount of time if that page is not of relevance to him. Table 3 shows the duration of time of stay of user with reference to web urls.

Table 3. Time user spent on a web page

Web user id	Web_Url	Stayed time
User_Id1	192.16.30.50	200
User_Id2	10.21.40.40	120
User_Id3	192.168.40.15	65
User_Id4	10.0.0.10	48
…	…	…
User_ID N	192.168.30.57	90

Hubs

The Hubs are set of those important web pages which contains the links to other relevant web pages. They provide a path to reaches to the relevant pages according to user query. Hubs are mainly associated with the topology of the web pages. Hubs pointed to the authority pages that actually contain the user related content. It is considered that a good hub indicates to many good authority pages. Suppose that there n number of hubs represented by HU1, HU2, HU3, …, HUi. Each Hub links to authority page that is HU11, HU12, HU13, … and HU21, HU22, HU23, … and so on.

$$\text{Cost of Hub} = \text{Number of web links pointed by jth hub on ith web page} = \sum_{i=1}^{n} \text{HU}.$$

Authorities

The Authorities are main web pages in relation to a user query. There is a mutual reinforcing relationship exist between hubs and authority web pages. A good authority web page should be indicated by many good hubs pages and a good hub page indicates to many authorities pages. Let there are n number of authorities represented by AT1, AT2, AT3…

$$\text{Cost of authority} = \sum_{i=1}^{n} \text{AT}.$$

Cost Function
The cost of each web is calculated on the basis of above discussed parameters as follows (Fig. 2):

$$\text{Total\_MAX\_COST} = \text{MAX\_ACCESS\_FREQ} + \text{MAX\_VISITOR} + \text{MAX\_DURATION} + \text{MAX\_HUBS} + \text{MAX\_AUTHORITIES}$$

$$\text{Fitness\_Value} = \text{Cost} = \text{c1}.\sum_{i}^{topT} AF_i + \text{c2}.\sum_{i}^{topT} DUR_i + \text{c3}.\sum_{i}^{topT} UNQV_i + \text{c4}.\sum_{i}^{topT} HUB_i + \text{c5}.\sum_{i}^{topT} AUTH_i$$

Where constant c1, c2, c3, c4 and c5 are defined as under:

$$\text{c1} = \frac{Total\_MAX\_COST}{MAX\_ACCESS\_FREQ \times topT}$$

$$\text{c2} = \frac{Total\_MAX\_COST}{MAX\_DURATION \times topT}$$

$$\text{c3} = \frac{Total\_MAX\_COST}{MAX\_VISITOR \times topT}$$

$$\text{c4} = \frac{Total\_MAX\_COST}{MAX\_HUB \times topT}$$

$$\text{c5} = \frac{Total\_MAX\_COST}{MAX\_AUTHORITIES \times topT}$$

Fig. 2. Cost function and used parameters

Proposed Algorithm
See Fig. 3.

Parameter setting:

- List of keywords
- Maximum number of web documents containing result of query, MAX_NO_WEB_DOCS
- Maximum access frequency, MAX_ACCESS_FREQ
- Maximum visitors, MAX_VISITOR
- Maximum duration stayed by visitor on any web document, MAX_DURATION
- Maximum number of links pointed by any document, MAX_HUBS
- Maximum number of links pointed to any document, MAX_AUTHORITIES

Input:

- Number of keywords, n
- Assign ID to each web document(URL)
- Number of top ranked web documents, topT
- Initial population size, Initial_Population_Size
- Number of documents, d (or No_of_Documents)
- Number of initial random states, Intial_Random_State, IRS

Output: Top T Web documents

Cost Function:

$$\text{Fitness\_Value} = \text{Cost} = c1.\sum_{i}^{topT} AF_i + c2.\sum_{i}^{topT} DUR_i + c3.\sum_{i}^{topT} UNQV_i + c4.\sum_{i}^{topT} HUB_i + c5.\sum_{i}^{topT} AUTH_i$$

Method:

I) Initialization

```
1. //Generate frequency of each keyword for each document
        For I=1 to I=No_of_Keywords

        begin
        For J=1 to J=No_of_Documents
        Begin

                //Frequency of I^th keyword in J^th document
                Freq_Keywords[I][J]=random(MAX_FREQUENCY)

        End
        end
```

Fig. 3. Proposed iterative algorithm for calculating topT web documents

```
2. //Generate initial population randomly
        For I=1 to I= Initial_Population_Size
        begin
        For J=1 to J=topT
        begin
        Initial_Population [I][J]=random(MAX_NO_WEB_DOCS)
        end
        end
3. //Generate access frequency of web document
        for I=1 to I= No_of_documents
        begin
                Access_Frequency [I]=random(MAX_ACCESS_FREQ)
        end
4. //Number of unique visitors
        for I=1 to I= No_of_documents
        begin
                unique_visitor [I]=random(MAX_VISITOR)
        end
5. //Duration stayed on each document
        for I=1 to I= No_of_documents
        begin
                //duration stayed by visitor on document I
                duration [I]=random(MAX_DURATION)
                //number of links pointed by documents I
                hubs[I]=random(MAX_HUBS)
                //number of links pointing to documents I
                authorities[I]=random(MAX_AUTHORITIES)
        end
6.      Evaluate all documents in Initial_Population [I][J] using fitness
        function to Fitness_Value[I]
7.      For each Intial_Random_State
        Do
        For Iteration=1 to MAX_ITERATIONS
            o   Generate neighbor and evaluate it
            o   //Improve solution through II
                If Cost_Current_State < Cost_Neighbor then
                        Current_State = Neighboring_State
                        Update Fitness_Value[Current_State]= Fit-
                ness_Value [Neighboring_State]
                end if
    End For
    Enddo
    End For
8. Set of IRS set of Top T web documents and their cost
9. Return Top T web document having minimum cost
```

Fig. 3. *(continued)*

3 An Example

An Experimental simulation has been conducted in order to verify the validity of the proposed algorithm. First an initial random population of 20 web documents has been generated and each web document is designated with a document id. Then frequency of each keyword put up by a user in his query has been calculated for each and every document (Fig. 4).

Keywords	Documents																			
	D1	D2	D3	D4	D5	D6	D7	D8	D9	D10	D11	D12	D13	D14	D15	D16	D17	D18	D19	D20
K1	2	2	2	5	8	9	7	9	4	8	4	9	4	2	7	1	9	6	8	3
K2	1	9	4	9	2	0	2	5	1	7	9	9	4	7	0	9	0	0	1	6
K3	8	6	0	5	9	9	9	5	1	9	0	6	1	0	2	7	8	6	1	2
K4	8	5	9	2	2	3	3	3	1	0	9	0	6	3	9	3	7	2	0	9
K5	2	7	9	4	7	2	9	9	1	9	3	8	9	1	5	0	9	1	5	0
K6	4	2	7	4	8	9	5	9	4	5	4	6	8	7	5	8	1	2	6	2
K7	0	8	3	9	3	1	8	6	8	3	8	4	8	0	7	7	9	0	2	4
K8	0	5	9	6	9	9	5	1	6	3	9	0	2	8	0	9	6	7	1	3
K9	5	9	3	2	0	6	4	8	9	5	0	5	2	7	8	7	8	5	1	7
K10	2	9	2	4	7	1	0	6	6	6	8	2	7	0	6	2	8	6	1	2

Fig. 4. Frequency of each keyword

The values of all the parameters such as access frequency, time duration, unique visitor, hubs and authorities have been calculated and designated in a random fashion (Fig. 5).

	Documents																			
	D1	D2	D3	D4	D5	D6	D7	D8	D9	D10	D11	D12	D13	D14	D15	D16	D17	D18	D19	D20
Document Id	1	2	3	4	5	6	7	8	9	10	11	12	13	14	15	16	17	18	19	20
Access Frequency	57	120	66	148	68	151	118	190	67	4	71	172	73	192	126	62	144	159	189	138
Number of unique visitors	281	327	280	136	89	118	343	302	479	196	336	164	254	408	364	414	327	290	1	321
Duration stayed on page	2997	791	2996	2552	683	2745	752	2199	2270	2629	167	2183	1901	310	856	1754	871	1684	1043	2446
Hubs	0	1	2	3	0	4	0	2	0	3	2	4	1	0	4	1	3	2	1	0
Authorities	3	3	0	0	3	2	0	4	4	0	1	1	0	4	1	3	0	4	2	1

Fig. 5. Parameters and their values for documents

Now two initial random states have been selected and their cost is calculated. Then for the first iteration the neighbors of both the initial random states are computed along with their fitness cost. After that the cost of neighbors are compared with the cost of initial random states and whosoever depicts the more cost is chosen as initial random states for next iteration. In this way the program runs and an example of four iterations shown in the Fig. 6.

	Initial Random States, IRS[i]	Cost(IRS[i])	Neighbors, N[j]	Cost(N[j])	if Cost(IRS[i])< Cost(N[j]) then IRS[i]-> N[j]
Iteration1	IRS[0]=19 5 17 15 11	7480	N[1]=19 5 17 1 11	6480	19 5 17 15 11
			N[2]=19 5 17 15 1	6732	19 5 17 15 11
			N[3]=19 5 14 15 1	6732	19 5 17 15 11
	IRS[1]= 2 10 1 16 11	5236	N[1]=2 14 1 16 11	5438	2 14 1 16 11
			N[2]=14 10 1 16 11	4488	2 10 1 16 11
			N[3]=2 10 8 16 11	5984	2 10 8 16 11
Iteration2	IRS[0]=19 5 17 15 11	7480	N[1]=16 5 17 15 11	6732	19 5 17 15 11
			N[2]=19 5 10 15 11	6732	19 5 17 15 11
			N[3]=19 5 17 15 18	8228	19 5 17 15 18
	IRS[1]=2 10 8 16 11	5984	N[1]=2 10 8 16 6	5236	2 10 8 16 11
			N[2]=2 13 8 16 11	6732	2 13 8 16 11
			N[3]=19 10 8 16 11	5236	2 10 8 16 11
Iteration3	IRS[0]=19 5 17 15 18	8228	N[1]=19 1 17 15 18	7468	19 5 17 15 18
			N[2]=4 5 17 15 18	8976	4 5 17 15 18
			N[3]=19 1 17 15 18	7480	19 5 17 15 18
	IRS[1]=2 13 8 16 11	6732	N[1]=2 13 15 16 11	7480	2 13 15 16 11
			N[2]=2 13 8 16 6	6732	2 13 8 16 6
			N[3]=2 13 8 19 11	6732	2 13 8 19 11
Iteration4	IRS[0]=4 5 17 15 18	8976	N[1]=14 5 17 15 18	8976	14 5 17 15 18
			N[2]=4 5 17 6 18	7480	4 5 17 15 18
			N[3]=4 9 17 15 18	7480	4 5 17 15 18
	IRS[1]=2 13 15 16 11	7480	N[1]=2 13 7 16 11	7480	2 13 7 16 11
			N[2]=3 13 15 16 11	6732	2 13 15 16 11
			N[3]=2 13 14 16 11	6732	2 13 15 16 11

Fig. 6. Cost computation for various iterations and neighbors

4 Experimental Evaluation

An experiment has been conducted by using jdk 1.7 in windows 10 environment and both the algorithms that is proposed iterative algorithm (PIA) and Existing iterative algorithm (EIA) have been implemented and compared for selecting the topT web documents. The experiments were performed for selecting top5 to top10 web pages and in the first set for over 500 iterations and initial random states as 5. The neighbors of each initial random states varies from 30 to 60. The results are analyzed and plotted by using graphs on which x-axis represents top web documents and y axis represents cost or fitness value of web pages. Then in the next set of graphs neighbors are kept as constant which is considered as 10 and number of iteration are varied ranging from 100 to 400 with initial random state value as 5. Both the set of graphs shows variations and in performance resulted better than the existing algorithm (Figs. 7 and 8).

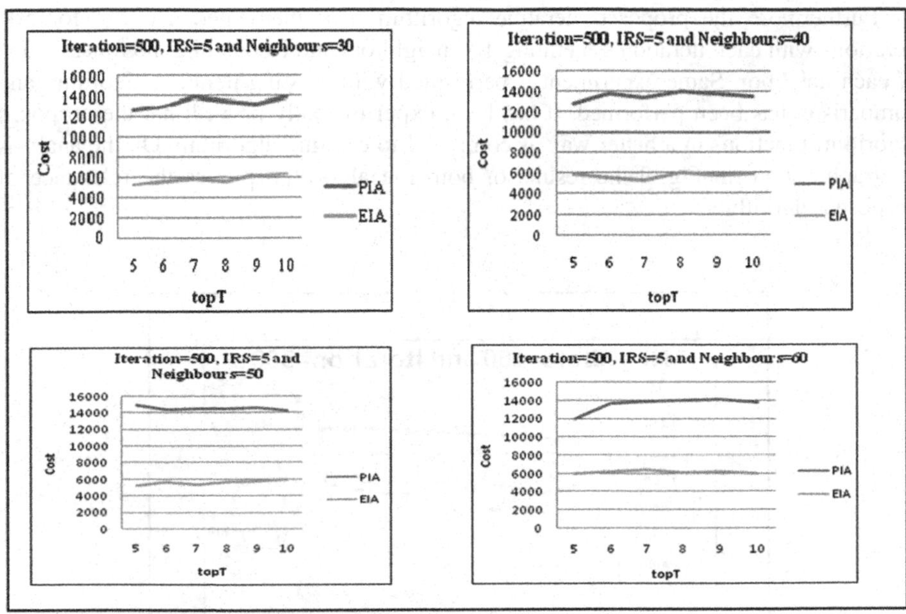

Fig. 7. Graphs with iteration = 500 and neighbors = 30, 40, 50 and 60

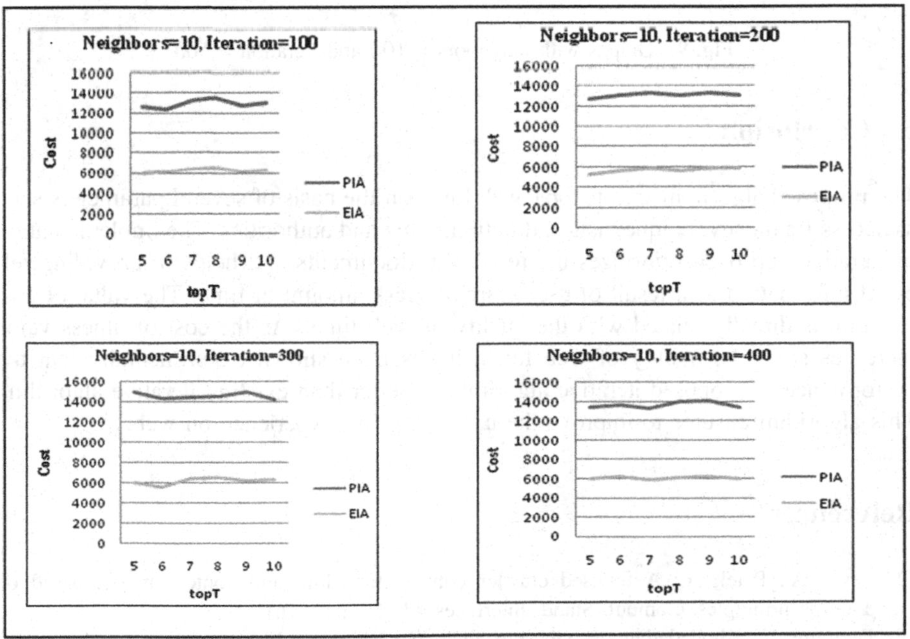

Fig. 8. Graphs with neighbors = 10 and iteration = 100, 200, 300 and 400

Furthermore the proposed iterative algorithm is implemented and run for 500 iterations with each iteration generating 100 neighbors and calculating the fitness value of each neighbor. Same experiment is performed with existing iteration algorithm and comparison has been performed. It has been experimentally proved that the proposed algorithm functions in a better way as compared to existing algorithm. On the analysis of graph shown in Fig. 9 the results of both the algorithm proves the relevance of proposed algorithm.

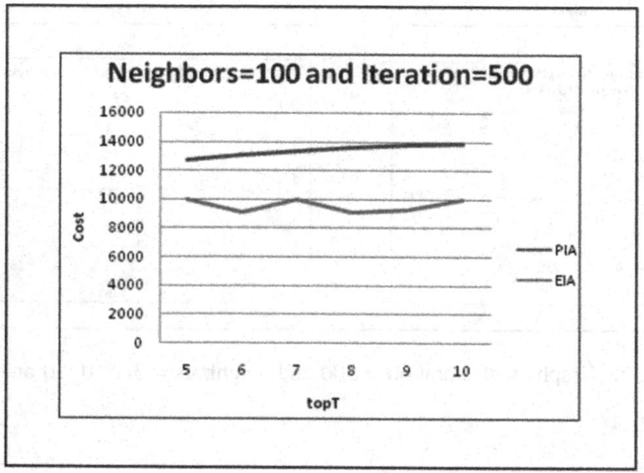

Fig. 9. Graphs with neighbors = 100 and iteration = 500

5 Conclusion

The proposed algorithm selects topT web links on the basis of several parameters such as access frequency, unique visitor, duration, hubs and authorities. The implementation of iterative approach prioritizes the topT web documents and helps in providing relevant information as a result of user search in less amount of time. The value of cost function is directly related with the quality of web links. As the cost of fitness value increases so is the quality of web links. It has been shown experimentally that the performance of proposed iterative algorithm is better than existing iterative algorithm. This algorithm ensures to improve the user browsing experience on web.

References

1. Seyfi, A., Patel, A.: A focused crawler combinatory link and content model based on T-graph principles. Comput. Stand. Interfaces **43**, 1–11 (2016)
2. Derhami, V., Khodadadian, E., Ghasemzadeh, M., Bidoki, A.M.Z.: Applying reinforcement learning for web pages ranking algorithms. Appl. Soft Comput. **13**(4), 1686–1692 (2013)

3. Bidoki, A.M.Z., Ghodsnia, P., Yazdani, N., Oroumchian, F.: A3CRank: an adaptive ranking method based on connectivity, content and click-through data. Inf. Process. Manag. **46**(2), 159–169 (2010)
4. Zheng, Z., Chen, K., Sun, G., Zha, H.: A regression framework for learning ranking functions using relative relevance judgments. In: Proceedings of the 30th Annual International ACM SIGIR Conference on Research and Development in Information Retrieval, pp. 287–294, July 2007
5. Bidoki, A.M.Z., Yazdani, N., Ghodsnia, P.: FICA: a novel intelligent crawling algorithm based on reinforcement learning. Web Intell. Agent Syst.: Int. J. **7**(4), 363–373 (2009)
6. Choi, D.Y.: Enhancing the power of web search engines by means of fuzzy query. Decis. Support Syst. **35**(1), 31–44 (2003)
7. Wang, H., Li, Y., Guo, K.: Countering web spam of link-based ranking based on link analysis. Procedia Eng. **23**, 310–315 (2011)
8. Gupta, S.K., Singh, D., Doegar, A.: Web documents prioritization using genetic algorithm. In: IEEE International Conference on Computing for Sustainable Global Development (INDIACom), pp. 3042–3047 (2016)
9. Chaudhary, K., Gupta, S.K.: Prioritizing web links based on web usage and content data. In: IEEE International Conference on Issues and Challenges in Intelligent Computing Techniques (ICICT), pp. 546–551 (2014)
10. Johnson, F., Kumar, S.: Web content mining using genetic algorithm. In: Unnikrishnan, S., Surve, S., Bhoir, D. (eds.) ICAC3 2013. CCIS, vol. 361, pp. 82–93. Springer, Heidelberg (2013). https://doi.org/10.1007/978-3-642-36321-4_8
11. Ding, S., Suel, T.: Faster top-k document retrieval using block-max indexes. In: Proceedings of the 34th International ACM SIGIR Conference on Research and Development in Information Retrieval, pp. 993–1002 (2011)
12. Koundal, D.: Prioritize the ordering of URL queue in focused crawler. J. AI Data Min. **2**(1), 25–31 (2014)
13. Bendersky, M., Croft, W.B., Diao, Y.: Quality-biased ranking of web documents. In: Proceedings of the Fourth ACM International Conference on Web Search and Data Mining, pp. 95–104 (2011)
14. Cho, J., Roy, S., Adams, R.E.: Page quality: in search of an unbiased web ranking. In: Proceedings of the ACM SIGMOD International Conference on Management of Data, pp. 551–562 (2005)
15. Abdullah, S., Burke, E.K., McCollum, B.: Using a randomised iterative improvement algorithm with composite neighbourhood structures for the university course timetabling problem. In: Doerner, K.F., Gendreau, M., Greistorfer, P., Gutjahr, W., Hartl, R.F., Reimann, M. (eds.) Metaheuristics, pp. 153–169. Springer, Boston (2007). https://doi.org/10.1007/978-0-387-71921-4_8
16. Xue, G.R., Zeng, H.J., Chen, Z., Yu, Y., Ma, W.Y., Xi, W., Fan, W.: Optimizing web search using web click-through data. In: Proceedings of the Thirteenth ACM International Conference on Information and Knowledge Management, pp. 118–126 (2004)
17. Mobasher, B., Cooley, R., Srivastava, J.: Automatic personalization based on web usage mining. Commun. ACM **43**(8), 142–151 (2000)
18. Kleinberg, J.M.: Authoritative sources in a hyperlinked environment. J. ACM (JACM) **46** (5), 604–632 (1999)
19. Narasimhan, H., Satheesh, S.: A randomized iterative improvement algorithm for photomosaic generation. In: Nature & Biologically Inspired Computing World Congress, pp. 777–781 (2009)

On Lagrangian Twin Parametric-Margin Support Vector Machine

Parashjyoti Borah(✉) and Deepak Gupta

Computer Science and Engineering, NIT, Yupia, Arunachal Pradesh, India
parashjyoti@hotmail.com, deepakjnu85@gmail.com

Abstract. A new simple and linearly convergent scheme is proposed in this paper for the dual formulation of twin parametric-margin support vector machine. Here, instead of considering the 1-norm error of slack variables, we have considered 2-norm of the vector of slack variables to make the objective functions strongly convex. Further, the proposed method solves a pair of linearly convergent iterative schemes instead of solving a pair of quadratic programming problems as in case of twin support vector machine and twin parametric-margin support vector machine. The proposed method considers in finding two parametric-margin hyperplanes that makes it less sensitive to heteroscedastic noise structure. Our experiments, performed on synthetic and real-world datasets, conclude that the proposed method has comparable generalization performance and improved learning speed in comparison to twin support vector machine, Lagrangian twin support vector machine and twin parametric-margin support vector machine.

Keywords: Support vector machine · Quadratic programming problem
Twin support vector machine · Lagrangian · Parametric-margin

1 Introduction

Support vector machine (SVM) [20] has been a widely used and very powerful machine learning technique for data classification in the past few decades. SVMs became popular due to its empirical risk as well as structural risk minimization property and high generalization capability. The philosophy of SVM is based on finding a classifying hyperplane by solving a quadratic programming problem (QPP). Since its introduction, SVM has outperformed most other machine learning algorithms in different application fields like text categorization [6], handwritten digit recognition [4], activity detection [8], speech recognition [21], brain-computer interface [14], etc.

Many variants of the classical SVM have been proposed by different researchers since its introduction to the machine learning society. One of them is ν-support vector machine (ν-SVM) [17] which controls the numbers of support vectors and errors by introducing the parameter ν in the formulation of the classical SVM. Based on the ν-SVM, Hao [5] has proposed parametric-margin ν-support vector machine (par-ν-SVM) for heteroscedastic noise structure. Par-ν-SVM uses a parametric margin model of arbitrary shape.

P. Bhattacharyya et al. (Eds.): NGCT 2017, CCIS 827, pp. 474–487, 2018.
https://doi.org/10.1007/978-981-10-8657-1_36

Although, SVM has very high generalization capability, one main disadvantage of SVM is its higher training cost. As its optimization problem is based on solving a large QPP, SVM training becomes a computational overhead for larger datasets. In recent time researchers have proposed different algorithms to overcome this problem which is based on the classical SVM algorithm. Mangasarian and Wild [13] has proposed an algorithm termed as the generalized eigenvalue proximal support vector machine (GEPSVM), which finds two non-parallel hyperplanes instead of one as in case of classical SVM. Jayadeva et al. [7] has proposed another algorithm that also generates two non-parallel hyperplanes which are as close as possible to the data samples of one class and as far as possible from the data samples of the other class. Instead of solving one larger QPP as in case of the classical SVM, TWSVM solves two smaller sized QPPs which make training cost approximately 4 times faster than the classical SVM [7]. Many other variants of TWSVM have also been proposed including least squares twin support vector machine (LS-TWSVM) [10], smooth TWSVM [9], robust energy-based least squares twin support vector machines [19] and twin support vector clustering (TWSVC) [22] to name some. Recently, Peng [15] has proposed a novel twin parametric-margin support vector machine (TPMSVM) which is based on par-ν-SVM and is similar to TWSVM in spirit.

Another way of reducing the training time complexity of the traditional SVM is to substitute the QPP with some other optimization method. Mangasarian and Musicant [12] has proposed an iterative method based on an implicit Lagrangian formulation and named it Lagrangian support vector machine (LSVM). LSVM is much faster than the traditional SVM. Balasundaram et al. [2] proposed an approach for training LSVM via unconstrained convex minimization. Based on LSVM and TWSVM, Balasundaram and Kapil [1] have proposed Lagrangian twin support vector machine (LTWSVM). Tanveer [18] proposed a newton method for implicit LTWSVM. Balasundaram et al. [3] further proposed a new approach for training LTWSVM via unconstrained convex minimization technique.

In this paper, a new simple iterative approach, named as Lagrangian twin parametric-margin support vector machine (LTPMSVM), is proposed which is based on TWSVM and utilizes the benefits of the iterative approach of LSVM for faster training speed and applies the parametric-margin model of TPMSVM to handle heteroscedastic noise. Our method eliminates the computational overhead in solving the QPPs as in TWSVM and TPMSVM by using a linearly convergent iterative scheme. Further, in this paper, we are going to present a performance analysis of TWSVM, LTWSVM and TPMSVM with our proposed method in terms of classification accuracy and training time.

2 Background and Related Work

Let us consider D be the matrix of the training data samples of dimension $m \times n$, where m is the number of training points and n is the number of features present in the dataset. Let us suppose, the matrix X_1 represents the l_1 data samples belonging to class $+1$ and X_2 be the matrix with l_2 data samples of the -1 class and $D = [X_1; X_2]$.

2.1 Twin Support Vector Machine (TWSVM)

TWSVM [7] is a SVM-based classification technique that uses two hyperplanes nearer to one class and is as far as possible from the other class. The non-linear TWSVM maps a data sample x into a higher dimensional feature space by using the mapping function $\varphi(x)$ and finds two non-parallel hyperplanes $K(x^t, D^t)w_1 + b_1 = 0$ and $K(x^t, D^t)w_2 + b_2 = 0$ by solving the following pair of QPPs,

$$\min \frac{1}{2}||K(X_1, D^t)w_1 + e_1 b_1||^2 + C_1 e_2^t \xi$$

subject to,

$$-(K(X_2, D^t)w_1 + e_2 b_1) + \xi \geq e_2, \xi \geq 0 \tag{1}$$

and

$$\min \frac{1}{2}||K(X_2, D^t)w_2 + e_2 b_2||^2 + C_2 e_1^t \eta$$

subject to,

$$(K(X_1, D^t)w_2 + e_1 b_2) + \eta \geq e_1, \eta \geq 0 \tag{2}$$

where C_1 and C_2 are the penalty parameters, ξ and η are the slack variables, $e_1 \in R^{l_1}$ and $e_2 \in R^{l_2}$ are vectors of 1's; w_1, w_2 and b_1, b_2 are hyperplane parameters and $K(x^t, D^t) = (k(x, x_1), \ldots, k(x, x_m))$ is a row vector in R^m, where $k(x, x_i) = \varphi(x)^t . \varphi(x_i) \in R$ for $i = 1, \ldots, m$ is an appropriately chosen kernel. The constraints in Eqs. (1) and (2) subject that the hyperplanes associated with each class is at least unit distance away from the other class.

The Wolfe dual for the above problem can be obtained by introducing Lagrangian function to Eqs. (1) and (2) and by applying Karush-Kuhn-Tucker (KKT) necessary and sufficient conditions as,

$$\max\ e_2^t \alpha_1 - \frac{1}{2}\alpha_1^t S(R^t R)^{-1} S^t \alpha_1$$

subject to,

$$0 \leq \alpha_1 \leq C_1 \tag{3}$$

and

$$\max\ e_1^t \alpha_2 - \frac{1}{2}\alpha_2^t R(S^t S)^{-1} R^t \alpha_2$$

subject to,

$$0 \leq \alpha_2 \leq C_2 \tag{4}$$

where, $R = [K(X_1, D^t) \quad e_1]$, $S = [K(X_2, D^t) \quad e_2]$ and $\alpha_1 \in R^{l_1}$, $\alpha_2 \in R^{l_2}$ are the vectors of Lagrangian multipliers for samples of class $+1$ and class -1 respectively.

After solving the QPPs (3) and (4) for α_1 and α_2, the values of w_1, w_2, b_1 and b_2 can be calculated from the augmented vectors given below,

$$\begin{bmatrix} w_1 \\ b_1 \end{bmatrix} = -(R^t R + \varepsilon I) S^t \alpha_1 \tag{5}$$

and

$$\begin{bmatrix} w_2 \\ b_2 \end{bmatrix} = (S^t S + \varepsilon I) R^t \alpha_2 \tag{6}$$

where, I is an identity matrix of dimension $((n+1) \times (n+1))$ and εI, for $\varepsilon > 0$ is the regularization term [7].

A new data point $x \in R^n$ is assigned to a particular class based on which hyperplane it is closest to, by using the following equation,

$$class\ i = \min|K(x^t, D^t)w_i + b_i|, i = 1, 2 \tag{7}$$

2.2 Twin Parametric-Margin Support Vector Machine (TPMSVM)

TPMSVM [15] is similar to TWSVM in the spirit that defines two non-parallel hyperplanes associated with each class samples. However, the separating hyperplane of TPMSVM is determined through two flexible positive and negative class parametric-margin hyperplanes. The parametric hyperplanes, $\varphi(x)^t w_1 + b_1 = 0$ and $\varphi(x)^t w_2 + b_2 = 0$ for non-liner TPMSVM can be derived from the following formulations,

$$\min \frac{1}{2}||w_1||^2 + \frac{v_1}{l_2} e_2^t(\varphi(X_2)w_1 + e_2 b_1) + \frac{C_1}{l_1} e_1^t \xi$$

subject to,

$$\varphi(X_1)w_1 + e_1 b_1 + \xi \geq 0, \; \xi \geq 0 \tag{8}$$

and

$$\min \frac{1}{2}||w_2||^2 + \frac{v_2}{l_1} e_1^t(\varphi(X_1)w_2 + e_1 b_2) + \frac{C_2}{l_2} e_2^t \eta$$

subject to,

$$\varphi(X_2)w_2 + e_2 b_2 - \eta \leq 0,\ \eta \geq 0 \tag{9}$$

where, $v_1, v_2 > 0$ are regularization parameters for determining the penalty weights. After introducing Lagrangian function to the Eqs. (8) and (9) and then applying KKT necessary and sufficient optimality conditions the dual QPPs of (8) and (9) become

$$\max\ -\frac{1}{2}\alpha_1^t K(X_1, X_1)\alpha_1 + \frac{v_1}{l_2} e_2^t K(X_2, X_1)\alpha_1$$

subject to,

$$0 \leq \alpha_1 \leq \frac{C_1}{l_1} e_1,\ e_1^t \alpha_1 = v_1 \tag{10}$$

and

$$\max\ -\frac{1}{2}\alpha_2^t K(X_2, X_2)\alpha_2 + \frac{v_2}{l_1} e_1^t K(X_1, X_2)\alpha_2$$

subject to,

$$0 \leq \alpha_2 \leq \frac{C_2}{l_2} e_2,\ e_2^t \alpha_2 = v_2 \tag{11}$$

respectively. The vectors w_1, w_2 and the bias terms b_1, b_2 can be calculated as

$$w_1 = \varphi(X_1)^t \alpha_1 - \frac{v_1}{l_2}\varphi(X_2)^t e_2 \text{ and } b_1 = -\frac{1}{|N_1|}\sum_{i \in N_1} \varphi(X_1)^t w_1$$

$$w_2 = -\varphi(X_2)^t \alpha_2 + \frac{v_2}{l_1}\varphi(X_1)^t e_1 \text{ and } b_2 = -\frac{1}{|N_2|}\sum_{i \in N_2} \varphi(X_2)^t w_2$$

where, N_i is the index set of samples satisfying $\alpha_i \in \left(0, \frac{C_i}{l_i}\right)$ for $i = 1, 2$.

The classifier is defined as,

$$class\ i = sign\left(\varphi(x)^t \sum_{i=1,2}\left(\frac{w_i}{||w_i||}\right) + \sum_{i=1,2}\left(\frac{b_i}{||w_i||}\right)\right),\ i = 1, 2 \tag{12}$$

2.3 Lagrangian Twin Support Vector Machines (LTWSVM)

LTWSVM [1] is a TWSVM based classification technique which is inspired by the works of Mangasarian and Musicant [12] and Jayadeva et al. [7], finds two hyperplanes

$K(x^t, D^t)w_1 + b_1 = 0$ and $K(x^t, D^t)w_2 + b_2 = 0$ corresponding respectively to class $+1$ and -1 by solving the following pair of problems,

$$\min \frac{1}{2}||K(X_1, D^t)w_1 + e_1 b_1||^2 + \frac{C_2}{2}\eta^t \eta$$

subject to,

$$-(K(X_2, D^t)w_1 + e_2 b_1) + \eta \geq e_2, \eta \geq 0 \tag{13}$$

and

$$\min \frac{1}{2}||K(X_2, D^t)w_2 + e_2 b_2||^2 + \frac{C_1}{2}\xi^t \xi$$

subject to,

$$(K(X_1, D^t)w_2 + e_1 b_2) + \xi \geq e_1, \xi \geq 0 \tag{14}$$

The corresponding duals of Eqs. (13) and (14) after finding the Lagrangian functions and applying the KKT conditions are obtained as,

$$\min \frac{1}{2}\alpha_1^t Q_1 \alpha_1 - e_1^t \alpha_1 \tag{15}$$

and

$$\min \frac{1}{2}\alpha_2^t Q_2 \alpha_2 - e_2^t \alpha_2 \tag{16}$$

where $Q_1 = \frac{I}{C_1} + R(S^t S)^{-1} R^t$ and $Q_2 = \frac{I}{C_2} + S(R^t R)^{-1} S^t$. The vectors w_1, w_2 and the bias terms b_1, b_2 can be obtained from the following augmented vectors as $\begin{bmatrix} w_1 \\ b_1 \end{bmatrix} = -(R^t R)^{-1} S^t \alpha_2$ and $\begin{bmatrix} w_2 \\ b_2 \end{bmatrix} = (S^t S)^{-1} R^t \alpha_1$.

The dual Eqs. (15) and (16) are in the form $0 \leq \alpha_k \perp (Q_k \alpha_k - e_k) \geq 0$ [11], for $k = 1, 2$ which is equivalent to,

$$(Q_k \alpha_k - e_k) = (Q_k \alpha_k - \beta_k \alpha_k - e_k)_+ \tag{17}$$

for $\alpha_k > 0$, which can be solved by using the following convergent iterative scheme

$$\alpha_k^{i+1} = Q_k^{-1}(e_k + (Q_k \alpha_k^i - \beta_k \alpha_k^i - e_k)_+)$$

where the condition $0 < \beta_k < \frac{2}{C_k}$ for $k = 1, 2$ has to satisfy. After obtaining the hyperplane parameters by solving the dual problems (15) and (16), a new data sample $x \in R^n$ is assigned to its respective class by using classifier given in Eq. (7).

3 Proposed Lagrangian Twin Parametric-Margin Support Vector Machine (LTPMSVM)

Motivated by the works of Peng [15] and Balasundaram and Kapil [1], in this section we propose a Lagrangian twin parametric-margin support vector machine algorithm and its formulations. LTPMSVM is a TWSVM based model, which incorporates the benefits of flexible parametric margin of TPMSVM and faster learning of LTWSVM.

3.1 Linear-Case

LTPMSVM finds the two non-parallel hyperplanes $x^t w_1 + b_1 = 0$ and $x^t w_2 + b_2 = 0$ by solving the following pair of problems

$$\min \frac{1}{2}(w_1^t w_1 + b_1^2) + \frac{v_1}{l_2} e_2^t (X_2 w_1 + e_2 b_1) + \frac{C_1}{2} \xi^t \xi$$

subject to,

$$(X_1 w_1 + e_1 b_1) + \xi \geq 0 \tag{18}$$

and

$$\min \frac{1}{2}(w_2^t w_2 + b_2^2) - \frac{v_2}{l_1} e_1^t (X_1 w_2 + e_1 b_2) + \frac{C_2}{2} \eta^t \eta$$

subject to,

$$-(X_2 w_2 + e_2 b_2) + \eta \geq 0 \tag{19}$$

The Lagrangian equation corresponding to Eqs. (18) and (19) can be formulated as below,

$$L_1 = \frac{1}{2} u_1^t u_1 + \frac{v_1}{l_2} e_2^t H u_1 + \frac{C_1}{2} \xi^t \xi - \alpha_1^t (G u_1 + \xi) \tag{20}$$

and

$$L_2 = \frac{1}{2} u_2^t u_2 - \frac{v_2}{l_1} e_1^t G u_2 + \frac{C_2}{2} \eta^t \eta + \alpha_2^t (H u_2 - \eta) \tag{21}$$

where $G = [X_1 \quad e_1]$, $H = [X_2 \quad e_2]$ and $u_1 = \begin{bmatrix} w_1 \\ b_1 \end{bmatrix}$, $u_2 = \begin{bmatrix} w_2 \\ b_2 \end{bmatrix}$ are the augmented vectors.

By applying KKT necessary and sufficient conditions, the Wolfe dual of Eqs. (18) and (19) can be obtained as,

$$\min_{\alpha_1 \geq 0} \frac{1}{2} \alpha_1^t (\frac{I}{C_1} + GG^t)\alpha_1 + \frac{v_1}{l_2} e_2^t HG^t \alpha_1 \tag{22}$$

and

$$\min_{\alpha_2 \geq 0} \frac{1}{2} \alpha_2^t (\frac{I}{C_2} + HH^t)\alpha_2 + \frac{v_2}{l_1} e_1^t GH^t \alpha_2 \tag{23}$$

The above dual QPPs (22) and (23) are of the form,

$$\min_{\alpha_k \geq 0} \frac{1}{2} \alpha_k^t Q_k \alpha_k + r_k^t \alpha_k \tag{24}$$

for $k = 1, 2$ respectively, where $Q_1 = \left(\frac{I}{C_1} + GG^t\right)$, $Q_2 = \left(\frac{I}{C_2} + HH^t\right)$, $r_1 = \frac{v_1}{l_2} GH^t e_2$ and $r_2 = \frac{v_2}{l_1} HG^t e_1$. Hence, the dual Eqs. (22) and (23) are in the form of the following pair of classical complementary problems [11]:

$$0 \leq \alpha_k \perp (Q_k \alpha_k \quad r_k) \geq 0 \tag{25}$$

for $k = 1, 2$. The Eq. (25) is equivalent to the following form,

$$(Q_k \alpha_k - r_k) = (Q_k \alpha_k - \beta_k \alpha_k - r_k)_+ \tag{26}$$

for $\alpha_k > 0$, which can be solved by using the following iterative scheme

$$\alpha_k^{i+1} = Q_k^{-1}(r_k + (Q_k \alpha_k^i - \beta_k \alpha_k^i - r_k)_+)$$

where the condition $0 < \beta_k < \frac{2}{C_k}$, $k = 1, 2$ has to satisfy. Therefore, the solutions for the Lagrange's multipliers α_1 and α_2 can be found by solving the following pair of iterative schemes that respectively converges to the unique solutions of α_1 and α_2 [12],

$$\alpha_1^{i+1} = \left(\frac{I}{C_1} + GG^t\right)^{-1} \left(r_1 + ((\frac{I}{C_1} + GG^t)\alpha_1^i - r_1 - \beta_1 \alpha_1^i)_+\right) \tag{27}$$

and

$$\alpha_2^{i+1} = \left(\frac{I}{C_2} + HH^t\right)^{-1} \left(r_2 + ((\frac{I}{C_2} + HH^t)\alpha_2^i - r_2 - \beta_2 \alpha_2^i)_+\right) \tag{28}$$

After computing the values of α_1 and α_2 by using Eqs. (27) and (28), the parametric-margin hyperplanes can be found as $[X_1 \quad e_1]u_1 = 0$ and $[\mathrm{X}_2 \quad e_2]u_2 = 0$ respectively, where $u_1 = G^t\alpha_1 - \frac{\nu_1}{l_2}H^te_2$ and $u_2 = -H^t\alpha_2 + \frac{\nu_2}{l_1}G^te_1$.

Finally, a new data sample $x \in R^n$ can be assigned to class ± 1 from the result of the classifier given below,

$$f(x) = sign\left(x^t \sum_{i=1,2}\left(\frac{w_i}{||w_i||}\right) + \sum_{i=1,2}\left(\frac{b_i}{||w_i||}\right)\right) \tag{29}$$

3.2 Non-linear Case

For non-linear case, the parametric-margin hyperplanes for LTPMSVM are derived as $K(x^t, D^t)w_1 + b_1 = 0$ and $K(x^t, D^t)w_2 + b_2 = 0$. The optimization problems are given as,

$$\min \frac{1}{2}(w_1^t w_1 + b_1^2) + \frac{\nu_1}{l_2}e_2^t(\mathrm{K}(\mathrm{X}_2, \mathrm{D}^t)w_1 + e_2 b_1) + \frac{C_1}{2}\xi^t\xi$$

subject to

$$(\mathrm{K}(\mathrm{X}_1, D^t)w_1 + e_1 b_1) + \xi \geq 0 \tag{30}$$

and

$$\min \frac{1}{2}(w_2^t w_2 + b_2^2) - \frac{\nu_2}{l_1}e_1^t(\mathrm{K}(\mathrm{X}_1, D^t)w_2 + e_1 b_2) + \frac{C_2}{2}\eta^t\eta$$

subject to,

$$-(\mathrm{K}(\mathrm{X}_2, D^t)w_2 + e_2 b_2) + \eta \geq 0 \tag{31}$$

After obtaining the Lagrangian equations for Eqs. (30) and (31) and applying KKT necessary and sufficient conditions, the dual equations corresponding to Eqs. (30) and (31) can be formulated as,

$$\min_{\alpha_1 \geq 0} \frac{1}{2}\alpha_1^t(\frac{I}{C_1} + RR^t)\alpha_1 + \frac{\nu_1}{l_2}e_2^t SR^t\alpha_1 \tag{32}$$

and

$$\min_{\alpha_2 \geq 0} \frac{1}{2}\alpha_2^t(\frac{I}{C_2} + SS^t)\alpha_2 + \frac{\nu_2}{l_1}e_1^t RS^t\alpha_2 \tag{33}$$

where $R = [K(X_1, D^t) \quad e_1]$ and $S = [K(X_2, D^t) \quad e_2]$. The values of α_i, for $i = 1, 2$ can be obtained by solving the below iterative schemes,

$$\alpha_1^{i+1} = \left(\frac{I}{C_1} + RR^t\right)^{-1} \left(r_1 + ((\frac{I}{C_1} + RR^t)\alpha_1^i - r_1 - \beta_1\alpha_1^i)_+\right) \tag{34}$$

and

$$\alpha_2^{i+1} = \left(\frac{I}{C_2} + SS^t\right)^{-1} \left(r_2 + ((\frac{I}{C_2} + SS^t)\alpha_2^i - r_2 - \beta_2\alpha_2^i)_+\right) \tag{35}$$

The classifier for the non-linear LTPMSVM is defined as,

$$f(x) = sign\left(K(x^t, D^t)\sum_{i=1,2}\left(\frac{w_i}{||w_i||}\right) + \sum_{i=1,2}\left(\frac{b_i}{||w_i||}\right)\right) \tag{36}$$

4 Experiments

To validate the efficiency of our method, we have conducted experiments on real-world as well as one synthetic datasets, i.e. Ripley's dataset [16] and performed a comparative analysis of our method LTPMSVM with TWSVM, TPMSVM and LTWSVM. The experiments are conducted on a PC with 64 bit, 3.40 GHz Intel© Core™ i7-3770 CPU and 4 GB RAM, running Windows 7 operating system. The software package used is MATLAB R2008a along with MOSEK optimization toolbox for TWSVM and TPMSVM, available at https://www.mosek.com. All the datasets are normalized to the range [0, 1] before experiment is performed on them. In this experiment, we implemented all the methods for linear as well as non-linear case using Gaussian kernel for non-linear case which is given by $K(x_i, x_j) = \exp(-\frac{||x_i - x_j||^2}{2\sigma^2})$.

The optimum value for the kernel parameter σ is obtained from the set $\{2^{-5}, \ldots, 2^5\}$, $C_i (i = 1, 2)$ are also obtained from the set $\{10^{-5}, \ldots, 10^5\}$ and for TPMSVM and LTPMSVM, the optimum values of v_i/C_i $(i = 1, 2)$ are selected from $\{0.1, \ldots, 0.9\}$ by using 10-fold cross-validation of the training data.

The efficiency of all the considered algorithms and the proposed LTPMSVM is evaluated on the basis of average classification accuracy and average training time. To calculate the average accuracy and average training time we have conducted statistical result analysis on 10-folds of the testing data and taken the average accuracy and average training time. Also, along with it we are presenting in this paper the standard deviation of results and the optimum parameter values for all the considered algorithms along with LTPMSVM.

To graphically depict the classifiers of each algorithm we have considered the artificially-generated Ripley's synthetic dataset in R^2 that contains 250 training samples and 1000 data samples for testing. Figure 1(a–d) shows the data points and the classifiers obtained by TWSVM, LTWSVM, TPMSVM and LTPMSVM for Ripley's dataset. In Fig. 1(a–d) each data sample is marked using either '×' or '+' symbol for positive class or negative class respectively. The classifiers are shown using a continuous line and the hyperplanes associated with each class are shown with broken lines. Support vectors are marked using circles around them. The result of each algorithm under consideration along with the proposed LTPMSVM for Ripley's dataset is presented in Table 1.

Table 1. The result of TWSVM, LTWSVM, TPMSVM and LTPMSVM on Ripley's dataset

Dataset (Train size, Test size)	TWSVM $(C_1 = C_2, \mu)$ Time	LTWSVM $(C_1 = C_2, \mu)$ Time	TPMSVM $(C = C_1 = C_2, \mu, \nu/C)$ Time	LTPMSVM $(C = C_1 = C_2, \mu, \nu/C)$ Time
Ripley (250 × 2,1000 × 2)	88.9 $(10^0, 2^{-1})$ 0.124	88 $(10^3, 2^1)$ 0.1170	90 $(10^{-3}, 2^{-3}, 0.4)$ 0.1212	**91** $(10^0, 2^{-3}, 0.7)$ 0.0937

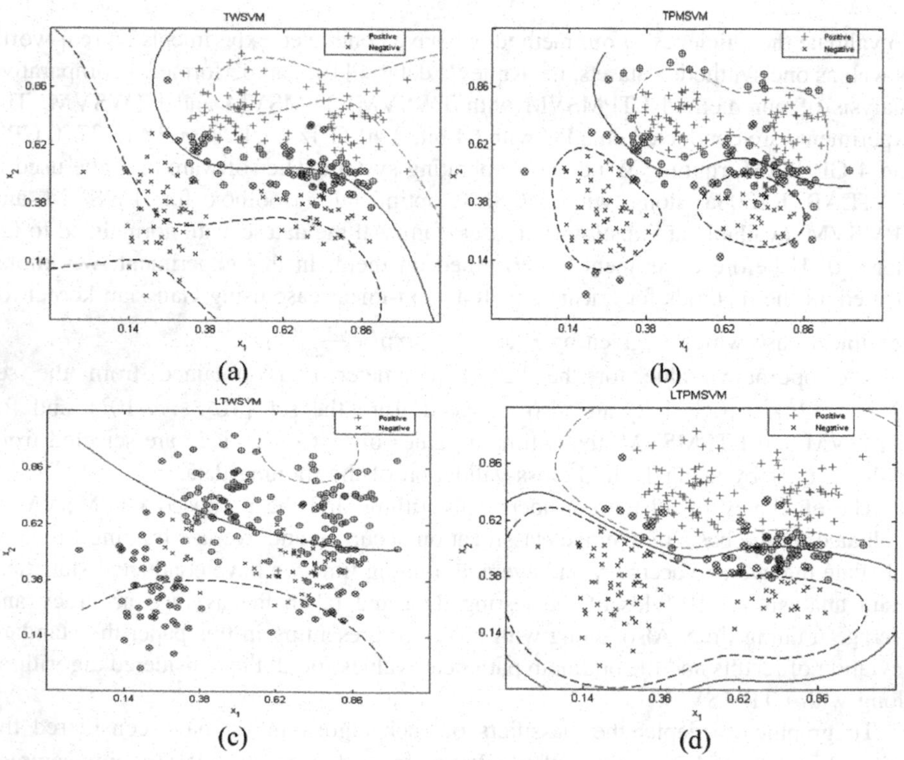

Fig. 1. Discriminant boundaries of (a) TWSVM, (b) TPMSVM, (c) LTWSVM and (d) LTPMSVM on Ripley's dataset using Gaussian kernel.

Table 2. The results of TWSVM, LTWSVM, TPMSVM and LTPMSVM using linear kernel on real-world datasets

Dataset (Train size, Test size)	TWSVM $(C_1 = C_2, \mu)$ Time	LTWSVM $(C_1 = C_2, \mu)$ Time	TPMSVM $(C = C_1 = C_2, \mu, \nu/C)$ Time	LTPMSVM $(C = C_1 = C_2, \mu, \nu/C)$ Time
Breast-cancer (419 × 9, 80 × 9)	97.898 ± 4.167 (10^0) 0.0251	97.5 ± 3.783 (10^0) 0.0864	**98.305** ± 2.567 $(10^{-2}, 0.2)$ 0.0286	73.214 ± 13.389 $(10^{-3}, 0.1)$ 0.0026
BreastTissue (74 × 9, 32 × 9)	73.333 ± 28.54 (10^{-5}) 0.0106	**96.667** ± 10.541 (10^3) 0.0053	70.833 ± 27.003 $(10^{-5}, 0.1)$ 0.0109	80 ± 23.307 $(10^4, 0.5)$ 0.0037
BUPA liver (206 × 6, 139 × 6)	49.983 ± 5.118 (10^0) 0.0111	58.352 ± 20.835 (10^0) 0.0054	56.01 ± 18.534 $(10^4, 0.3)$ 0.013	**62.527** ± 29.787 $(10^{-1}, 0.1)$ 0.0051
German (699 × 24, 301 × 24)	69.992 ± 5.915 (10^{-5}) 0.0222	**74.71** ± 7.315 (10^0) 0.0303	71.973 ± 8.756 $(10^{-3}, 0.4)$ 0.0287	69.462 ± 9.4 $(10^3, 0.6)$ 0.0085
Glass (128 × 9, 86 × 9)	58.351 ± 8.74 (10^{-1}) 0.0073	48.75 ± 18.777 (10^0) 0.0074	50.899 ± 10.72 $(10^{-3}, 0.6)$ 0.0079	**67.222** ± 14.377 $(10^4, 0.4)$ 0.0024
Haberman (183 × 3, 123 × 3)	65.148 ± 18.519 (10^{-5}) 0.0089	75.769 ± 11.609 (10^0) 0.0038	68.868 ± 16.129 $(10^{-1}, 0.6)$ 0.0128	**75.833** ± 11.878 $(10^1, 0.2)$ 0.0013
Iris (59 × 4, 91 × 4)	**100** ± 0 (10^{-5}) 0.0078	**100** ± 0 (10^{-5}) 0.0004	98.661 ± 2.831 $(10^{-5}, 0.1)$ 0.0081	**100** ± 0 $(10^{-3}, 0.1)$ 0.0004
Wdbc (341 × 31, 228 × 31)	94.157 ± 6.804 (10^{-2}) 0.0756	**97.391** ± 3.04 (10^{-1}) 0.0357	96.515 ± 5.858 $(10^{-2}, 0.1)$ 0.6123	84.269 ± 9.168 $(10^2, 0.9)$ 0.362

It is observed form the figures and Table 1 that the proposed method LTPMSVM obtains a better decision classifier as compared to the other reported methods. Further, form Table 1 it can be seen that our proposed method delivers better classification accuracy and provides a lesser training time than the others.

To further validate our results, we considered 8 real-world UCI benchmark datasets, namely Breast-Cancer, Breast Tissue, BUPA liver, German, Glass, Haberman, Iris and Wdbc obtained from the UCI machine learning repository. Some of the considered datasets are non-binary multiclass class datasets which are converted to binary class datasets by considering the majority class as the positive class and taking all the other classes together as the negative class. The classification results and learning time along with the optimum parameter values for all the algorithms are tabulated in Tables 2 and 3 for linear and Gaussian kernel respectively. The proposed method achieved comparative result, if not outperformed the others, in all the cases. However, it can be observed that the proposed LTPMSVM achieved a lower training cost as compared to the other methods.

Table 3. The results of TWSVM, LTWSVM, TPMSVM and LTPMSVM using Gaussian kernel on real-world datasets

Dataset (Train size, test size)	TWSVM ($C_1 = C_2$, μ) Time	LTWSVM ($C_1 = C_2$, μ) Time	TPMSVM ($C = C_1 = C_2, \mu, v/C$) Time	LTPMSVM ($C = C_1 = C_2, \mu, v/C$) Time
Breast-cancer (419 × 9, 280 × 9)	98.214 ± 1.882 (10^{-1}, 2^2) 0.146	98.571 ± 1.844 (10^{-1}, 2^2) 0.1685	98.214 ± 2.525 (10^{-3}, 2^0, 0.2) 0.1254	**98.929** ± 1.725 (10^{-5}, 2^{-1}, 0.1) 0.0952
BreastTissue (74 × 9, 32 × 9)	93.333 ± 21.083 (10^{-2}, 2^1) 0.0121	93.333 ± 21.082 (10^{-2}, 2^1) 0.0075	90 ± 16.101 (10^{-3}, 2^{-2}, 0.2) 0.0131	**94.167** ± 12.454 (10^3, 2^{-2}, 0.1) 0.0049
BUPA liver (206 × 6, 139 × 6)	57.582 ± 24.087 (10^{-1}, 2^{-1}) 0.0386	61.04 ± 16.562 (10^5, 2^{-1}) 0.0486	54.615 ± 16.686 (10^{-1}, 2^1, 0.1) 0.0383	**62.527** ± 29.789 (10^2, 2^3, 0.7) 0.0361
German (699 × 24, 301 × 24)	74.387 ± 7.934 (10^0, 2^2) 0.1645	**74.398** ± 7.268 (10^0, 2^2) 0.1948	71.064 ± 7.13 (10^1, 2^4, 0.2) 0.1304	72.376 ± 10.956 (10^{-5}, 2^3, 0.1) 0.1201
Glass (128 × 9, 86 × 9)	**77.917** ± 8.672 (10^0, 2^{-1}) 0.0205	76.806 ± 9.375 (10^{-2}, 2^{-3}) 0.0191	77.639 ± 9.521 (10^{-2}, 2^{-3}, 0.2) 0.0169	74.306 ± 12.884 (10^2, 2^{-3}, 0.1) 0.0160
Haberman (183 × 3, 123 × 3)	72.5 ± 11.615 (10^{-5}, 2^2) 0.0322	74.936 ± 11.3 (10^0, 2^1) 0.027	69.167 ± 12.875 (10^{-3}, 2^{-5}, 0.5) 0.0256	**77.5** ± 12.875 (10^{-3}, 2^2, 0.1) 0.0218
Iris (59 × 4, 91 × 4)	98.889 ± 3.5136 (10^{-5}, 2^{-3}) 0.0179	98.889 ± 3.514 (10^{-5}, 2^{-3}) 0.0178	**100** ± 0 (10^{-5}, 2^{-2}, 0.1) 0.0173	**100** ± 0 (10^{-5}, 2^{-2}, 0.1) 0.0123
Wdbc (341 × 31, 228 × 31)	97.391 ± 3.04 (10^{-1}, 2^0) 0.0984	**98.261** ± 2.245 (10^0, 2^2) 0.1069	97.826 ± 3.074 (10^{-2}, 2^1, 0.1) 0.0784	95.652 ± 5.020 (10^{-5}, 2^{-1}, 0.1) 0.0679

5 Conclusion

A new linearly convergent iterative approach is proposed in this paper, termed as Lagrangian twin parametric-margin support vector machine (LTPMSVM) where we considered 2-norm of the vector of slack variables instead of 1-norm to make the objective function strongly convex. Instead of solving two QPPs as in case of TWSVM and TPMSVM, the proposed LTPMSVM uses a linearly convergent iterative scheme to solve the dual formulations of the respective optimization problems. However, LTPMSVM is less sensitive towards heteroscedastic error structure unlike in case of TWSVM and LTWSVM. To establish the effectiveness of the proposed method a comparative analysis of the proposed method with three other methods, namely TWSVM, LTWSVM and TPMSVM is presented. Experimental result shows that our proposed method gives comparative or better performance with the other considered algorithms in terms of accuracy. However, our proposed method achieved lower training cost as compared to the other reported methods for all the considered datasets.

References

1. Balasundaram, S., Kapil, N.: Application of Lagrangian twin support vector machines for classification. In: Machine Learning and Computing (ICMLC), pp. 193–197. IEEE (2010)
2. Balasundaram, S., Gupta, D.: Lagrangian support vector regression via unconstrained convex minimization. Neural Netw. **51**, 67–79 (2014)
3. Balasundaram, S., Gupta, D., Prasad, S.C.: A new approach for training Lagrangian twin support vector machine via unconstrained convex minimization. Appl. Intell. **46**(1), 124–134 (2017)
4. Cortes, C., Vapnik, V.: Support-vector networks. Mach. Learn. **20**(3), 273–297 (1995)
5. Hao, P.Y.: New support vector algorithms with parametric insensitive/margin model. Neural Netw. **23**(1), 60–73 (2010)
6. Joachims, T.: Text categorization with support vector machines: learning with many relevant features. Machine Learning: ECML-98, pp. 137–142 (1998)
7. Khemchandani, R., Chandra, S.: Twin support vector machines for pattern classification. IEEE Trans. Pattern Anal. Mach. Intell. **29**(5), 905–910 (2007)
8. Khemchandani, R., Sharma, S.: Robust least squares twin support vector machine for human activity recognition. Appl. Soft Comput. **47**, 33–46 (2016)
9. Kumar, M.A., Gopal, M.: Application of smoothing technique on twin support vector machines. Pattern Recogn. Lett. **29**(13), 1842–1848 (2008)
10. Kumar, M.A., Gopal, M.: Least squares twin support vector machines for pattern classification. Expert Syst. Appl. **36**(4), 7535–7543 (2009)
11. Mangasarian, O.L.: Nonlinear Programming. Society for Industrial and Applied Mathematics. McGraw Hill, New York (1994)
12. Mangasarian, O.L., Musicant, D.R.: Lagrangian support vector machines. J. Mach. Learn. Res. **1**(9), 161–177 (2001)
13. Mangasarian, O.L., Wild, E.W.: Multisurface proximal support vector machine classification via generalized eigenvalues. IEEE Trans. Pattern Anal. Mach. Intell. **27**(12), 1 (2005)
14. Molina, G.N.G., Ebrahimi, T., Vesin, J.M.: Joint time-frequency-space classification of EEG in a brain-computer interface application. EURASIP J. Adv. Sig. Process. **2003**(7), 253269 (2003)
15. Peng, X.: TPMSVM: a novel twin parametric-margin support vector machine for pattern recognition. Pattern Recogn. **44**(10), 2678–2692 (2011)
16. Ripley, B.D.: Pattern Recognition and Neural Networks. Cambridge University Press, Cambridge (2007)
17. Schölkopf, B., Smola, A.J., Williamson, R.C., Bartlett, P.L.: New support vector algorithms. Neural Comput. **12**(5), 1207–1245 (2000)
18. Tanveer, M.: Newton method for implicit Lagrangian twin support vector machines. Int. J. Mach. Learn. Cybern. **6**(6), 1029–1040 (2015)
19. Tanveer, M., Khan, M.A., Ho, S.S.: Robust energy-based least squares twin support vector machines. Appl. Intell. **45**(1), 174–186 (2016)
20. Vapnik, V.N.: Statistical Learning Theory, vol. 1. Wiley, New York (1998)
21. Wan, V., Campbell, W.M.: Support vector machines for speaker verification and identification. In: Proceedings of the 2000 IEEE Signal Processing Society Workshop on Neural Networks for Signal Processing X, vol. 2, pp. 775–784. IEEE (2000)
22. Wang, Z., Shao, Y.H., Bai, L., Deng, N.Y.: Twin support vector machine for clustering. IEEE Trans. Neural Netw. Learn. Syst. **26**(10), 2583–2588 (2015)

Artificial Neural Network and Response Surface Methodology Modelling of Surface Tension of 1-Butyl-3-methylimidazolium Bromide Solution

Divya P. Soman, P. Kalaichelvi(✉), and T. K. Radhakrishnan

Department of Chemical Engineering, National Institute of Technology Tiruchirappalli, Tiruchirappalli, Tamil Nadu, India
kalai@nitt.edu

Abstract. The thermo-physical properties of the ionic liquids are required for engineering and product design applications in many pharmaceutical and food industries. Among the many unique properties of ionic liquids, their surface tension plays an important role for various reasons. In the present study, the aim is to investigate the effect of temperature and concentration on the surface tension of the binary solution of 1-butyl-3-methylimidazolium bromide + water. The concentration of the ionic liquid is varied from 0.1–0.6%w/w and temperature ranges from 302.85–337.45 K. A quadratic mathematical model has been formulated for predicting the surface tension using response surface methodology with central composite rotatable design having a coefficient of determination R^2 as 0.9807. In addition, a two-layered feed forward back propagation neural network 2-4-1 is also modelled which provides a better performance when compared to response surface model. The developed ANN model can predict the surface tension with mean square error, root mean square error and percentage absolute average error equal to 0.156, 0.395 and 0.623, respectively.

Keywords: Surface tension · Artificial neural network
1-butyl-3-methylimidazolium bromide · Response surface methodology

1 Introduction

Ionic liquids are organic salts with a low boiling point below 100 °C. It is entirely composed of organic cations and inorganic anions [1, 2]. Recently, ionic liquids have acquired considerable attention for their applications in wide range of areas viz. catalysis, separation processes as solvents, electrolysis, biosensors, reaction media, polymeric plasticizers, heat transfer fluids and thermal stabilizers [1, 3]. The thermo-physical properties of ionic liquids are solely dependent on the ions of which they are composed [2]. One can tune the properties of the ionic liquid for a given task, which the most remarkable feature of the ionic liquid. This is done by changing the chemical structure of the constituent ions [1]. Some of the interesting properties of the ionic liquids are excellent solubility with organic and inorganic compounds, remarked

P. Bhattacharyya et al. (Eds.): NGCT 2017, CCIS 827, pp. 488–503, 2018.
https://doi.org/10.1007/978-981-10-8657-1_37

catalytic property, high ionic conductivity, low vapor pressure, nonflammability and high thermal stability [1, 4, 5].

Generally, to verify not only the feasibility of using specific ionic liquid structure but also for a better technological design, knowledge of the physiochemical properties is crucial [6]. Surface tension is one such unique thermo-physical property which plays an important role in determining the behavior of the ionic liquid in many circumstances. Surface tension is a measure of cohesive forces between liquid molecules present at the surface and it represents the quantification of force per unit length of free energy per unit area. Hence, the measurement of surface tension of ionic liquids is one of the most effective ways to (indirectly) access the intrinsic energetics that is involved in the interaction between the ions [7]. The experimental data of surface tension property are available in abundance in literature. Tariq et al. [7] had presented a critical review on the surface tension of pure ionic liquids and ionic liquid solutions. They had summarized the works of the other researcher's in the year 2001 and 2010. The most commonly used experimental methods to determine surface tension of ionic liquid are pendant drop (PD), Du Nouy ring (DNR) and capillary rise (CR) techniques. Dynamic light scattering (DLS) is the most sophisticated method used for measuring the surface tension of ionic liquids. Researchers have proposed many models to predict the surface tension of ionic liquids such as correlation methods based on parachors, group contribution methods and state theory approach and molecular modelling methods like molecular dynamic simulation (MDS) [7–9]. Recently, Lashkarbolooki [10] developed a feed forward multilayer perceptron neural network model using mole fraction of ionic liquid, melting point and molecular weight of both ionic liquid and non-ionic liquid as input neuron to predict the surface tension of 32 ionic liquids/non-ionic liquid systems with mean square (MSE) = 6.67×10^{-7} and $R^2 = 0.995$.

Since, thermo-physical property is a basic requirement for most of the heat and mass transfer studies, the task of performing experiments for evaluating these properties at each time is cumbersome [8, 11]. By modelling one can reduce the time of experimentation and use their time effectively. With the aid of multiple experiments performed in this study, we have developed two models for predicting surface tension of ionic liquid. These models may be used in determining the surface tension of solutions were BMImBr is used as additive to water or in pharmaceutical industries, electrochemical or polymeric studies as solvents or electrolytes, where surface tension of BMImBr aqueous solution is a requirement [8]. In all the above reported methods, the accuracy of the prediction can be achieved only for those ionic liquids whose cations and anions fall among the functional groups selected. Response surface methodology (RSM) is a powerful tool to model a mathematical expression relating an independent variable(s) to a dependent variable(s). However, to the best of author's knowledge there is no application of RSM and feed forward back propagation neural network for modelling the surface tension of aqueous ionic liquid as a function of temperature and concentration as presented here, and certainly there is no publication on the surface tension of binary solution of 1-butyl-3-methylimidazolium bromide (BMImBr) and water. Thus, in the present work, we focus on evaluating the surface tension of binary solutions of BMImBr and water at different concentrations (0.1–0.6% w/w) and temperatures (302.85–337.45 K) experimentally using the drop weight method. A new mathematical model has been developed using RSM to calculate the surface tension of BMImBr + water binary solution as a function of concentration and temperature. In addition, feed forward back propagation neural network has also been proposed for prediction of the surface tension of BMImBr and compared with RSM model.

2 Materials and Methods

2.1 Materials

1-butyl-3-methylimidazolium bromide (BMImBr) ionic liquid purchased from Alfa Aesar with 99% purity is used for the experimental study. As the BMImBr is hygroscopic in nature, it is tightly closed and stored in a cool, dry place. A 0.1 L borosil burette and 0.1 L beaker purchased from M/s Royal Scientific Suppliers, Trichy are utilized for the surface tension measurement. The temperature of the samples is measured with digital thermometer having ±0.1 °C precision. The Shimadzu electronic weighing balance with a precision ±0.001 g are employed for weighing the samples.

2.2 Preparation of Solution

A BMImBr sample solution of 0.1 L is prepared on weight by weight basis by mixing the ionic liquid with water to obtain concentration range of 0.1–0.6%w/w. This range is selected in accordance with the conventional values worked in industry. The samples are stirred well with a magnetic stirrer until the ionic liquid completely dissolves in water. The samples are tightly closed while stirring.

2.3 Surface Tension Measurements

Various methods are developed to measure the surface tension of liquids. The drop weight method is employed in our study to evaluate the surface tension of BMImBr solution at different temperatures varying in the range of 302.85–337.45 K. Drop weight method is a popular method that is still widely used owing to its higher accuracy than other methods, simple set up and it is inexpensive.

The principle of the drop weight method is based on Tate's law (Eq. 1). The law approximates the balance between gravitational force pulling the drop down and the surface tension force holding the drop pendant to the tip at the instant of the droplet detachment [12, 13]. The drop of liquid gets released from the tip of burette when the load is greater than the surface tension at the tip of the burette.

$$mg = 2\pi r\sigma \tag{1}$$

where m represents the mass of the drop released from the tip of burette (kg), g is the acceleration due to gravity (ms^{-2}), r is the radius of the burette tip (m) and σ is the surface tension of the liquid (mNm^{-1}). The ratio of surface tension at any temperature and its falling drop weight from any one tip at that same temperature is constant for all liquids [14]. The surface tension of the binary mixture of BMImBr with water is calculated using Eq. 2.

$$\frac{\sigma_{w,T1}}{m_{w,T1}} = \frac{\sigma_{i,T2}}{m_{i,T2}} = \text{Constant} \tag{2}$$

where $\sigma_{w,T1}$ is the surface tension of water at temperature T_1 (mNm^{-1}), $m_{w,T1}$ is the mass of single water drop at temperature T_1 (kg), $\sigma_{i,T2}$ is the surface tension of BMImBr solution at temperature T_2 (mNm^{-1}) and $m_{i,T2}$ is the mass of single BMImBr solution drop at temperature T_2 (kg).

The schematic diagram and the detailed procedure of the experiment are explained elsewhere [12]. The mass of single drop is used for calculating the surface tension using Eq. 2. The same procedure is repeated with all the sample solutions of concentrations 0.1–0.6%w/w at different temperatures ranging from 302.85–337.45 K after cleaning the burette every time.

2.4 Response Surface Methodology

The RSM is a collection of mathematical and statistical techniques that are built on the fitting of the empirical models to the experimental data. Central composite design (CCD) is a popular RSM design that has three groups of design points namely axial points, two-level factorial or fractional factorial design points and center points [15]. Central composite rotatable design (CCRD) with two independent variables coded at four levels between −2 and +2 is enforced to model the surface tension of aqueous solutions of BMImBr. Concentration and temperature of the BMImBr solution are the two independent factors considered for modelling (Table 1). Design Expert 10.0.3.3 software is exploited to model the mathematical equation for the surface tension of the ionic liquid solution. A total of 13 runs is generated for CCRD with two factors in this work.

Table 1. Coded and physical values of independent process variables

Factors	Levels and range				
	Lowest	Low	Center	High	Highest
Temperature (K)	304.01 ± 0.4	308.15 ± 0.4	318.15 ± 0.4	328.15 ± 0.4	332.29 ± 0.4
Concentration (%w/w)	0.02	0.1	0.3	0.5	0.6

The experimental data from the CCRD model for the surface tension of the binary solution of BMImBr and water are fitted to a second order polynomial equation (Eq. 3) and the regression coefficients are obtained.

$$Y = \beta_0 + \sum\nolimits_{j=1}^{k} \beta_j X_j + \sum\nolimits_{j=1}^{k} \beta_{jj} X_j^2 + \sum\nolimits_{j=1}^{k-1} \sum\nolimits_{i=2}^{k} \beta_{ji} X_j X_i + e_i \tag{3}$$

where Y depicts the response variable, Xj and Xi are the independent variables, β_o is the constant or offset term, β_j is the slope or linear effect of the input factors, β_{jj} is the cross product term and e_i is the statistical error [15]. Concentration (C) and Temperature

(T) are the independent variables and surface tension of the ionic liquid solution (σ^{pre}) is the response variable. The response data are obtained from the test work of 13 runs. When the p-value is lower than 0.05, the effects are considered to be statistically significant. The quality of fit of the model equation is conveyed by the value of the correlation coefficients (R^2) and with F-test, the significance is assured [16]. The main aim of RSM modelling is to determine a second order polynomial equation for the surface tension of binary solution of BMImBr + water as a function of concentration and temperature.

2.5 Artificial Neural Network for Predicting Surface Tension

ANN functioning originated from the behavior of biological neurons [17–20]. An ANN is a data processing system constituting a large number of simple highly interconnected processing elements incited by the structure of the cerebral cortex of the brain. ANN possess mapping capabilities, i.e. it can relate input to their associated output with the aid of activation functions and parameters namely weight and bias. In this study, 36 experimental data are randomly divided into three separate groups for training, testing and validation, respectively. Figure 1 depicts the algorithm for the ANN modelling. Out of the total experimental data, 26 data are employed as training and validation sets; and the remaining 10 data (not used for training or validation) for testing. Concentration and temperature are the input variables; and surface tension of BMImBr solutions as the output variable. The ranges of the variables used for ANN are listed in Table 2.

Table 2. Minimum and maximum of the input and output variables in ANN

Set	Variables	Unit	Minimum	Maximum
Input	Concentration (C)	%w/w	0.1	0.6
	Temperature (T)	K	302.85	337.45
Output	Surface tension (σ)	mNm^{-1}	52.99	60.23

The surface tension values of the BMImBr solution for the independent factors within the training set is considered as the target values. Since, the ranges of the input and output variables vary widely, all the target and the input variables are normalized in the range of 0 to 1 using Eq. 4.

$$x^n = \frac{x_{exp} - min(x_{exp})}{max(x_{exp}) - min(x_{exp})} \quad (4)$$

where x^n represents the normalized value of the variable, x_{exp} is the actual experimental value of the x^n, $min(x_{exp})$ is the minimum actual value of x_{exp} and $max(x_{exp})$ is the maximum actual value of x_{exp}.

An ANN with the single hidden layer is efficient enough to correlate any complexities with high accuracy [21]. In the current investigation, a feed forward

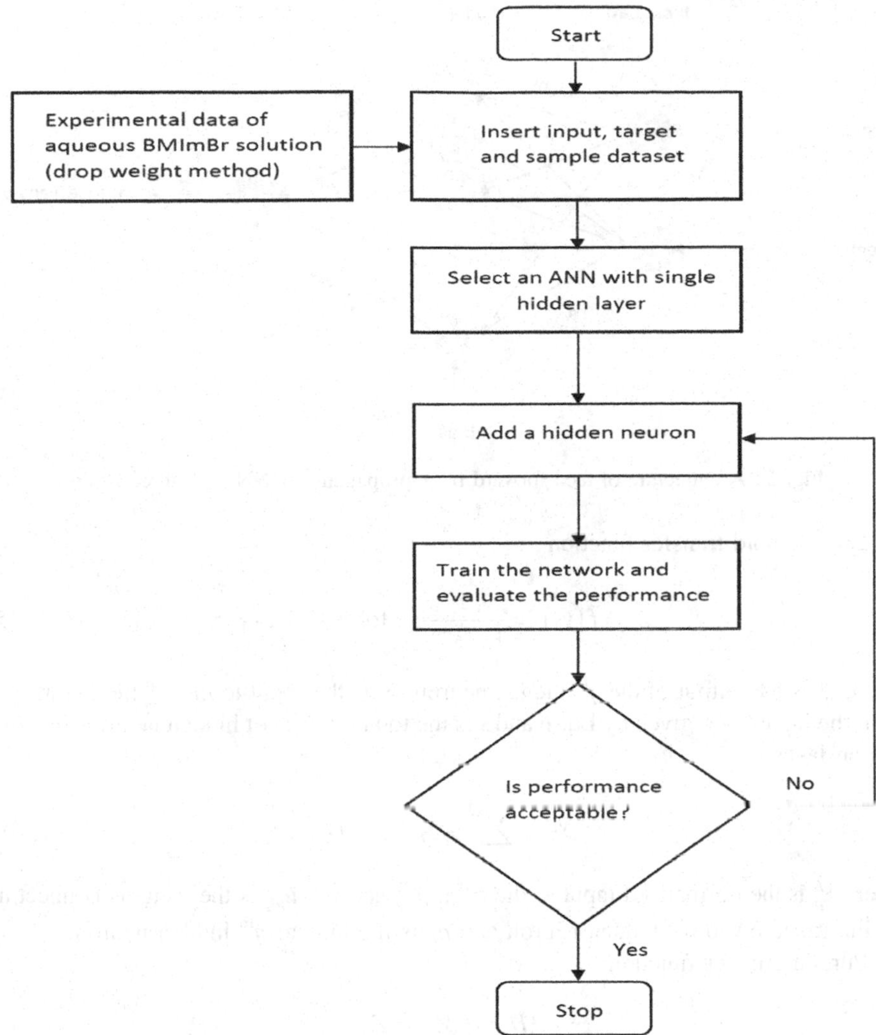

Fig. 1. Algorithm of ANN modelling

back-propagation neural network with the single hidden layer is proposed. The number of neurons or nodes in the hidden layer are varied from 1 to 10 and the structure of the ANN architecture is given in Fig. 2. The solid circle in Fig. 2 denote neuron and *s* denotes the total number of hidden neurons.

The Levenberg-Marquardt training algorithm is used for training the ANN and *MSE* is used as performance function. The log-sigmoid transfer function, an appropriate choice for nonlinear functions [22], is applied as the activation function for input-hidden layers and purelin transfer function for the hidden to the output layer. These functions are defined as follows,

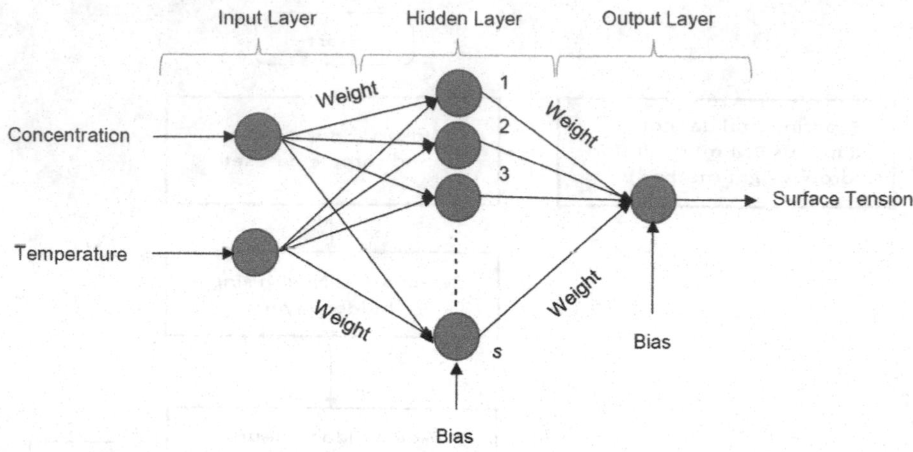

Fig. 2. Architecture of feed forward back-propagation ANN with three layers

Log-sigmoid transfer function

$$z_q = f(y_q) = \frac{1}{1+e^{-y_q}} \quad \text{for } q = 1 \text{ to } s \tag{5}$$

where z_q is the output of the qth hidden neuron, y_q is the input to the qth hidden neuron from the input layer given by Eq. 6 and s is the total number of hidden neurons in a first hidden layer.

$$y_q = \sum\nolimits_{p=1}^{2} x_p^n u_{pq} + a_q \tag{6}$$

where x_p^n is the normalized input to the pth input neuron, u_{pq} is the weights connecting p^{th} input neuron to q^{th} hidden neuron and a_q is the bias to q^{th} hidden neuron.

Purelin transfer function

$$H = f(Z) = Z \tag{7}$$

where H is the output from the output neuron, Z represents input to the output layer given by Eq. 8.

$$Z = \sum\nolimits_{q=1}^{t} z_q v_{q1} + b \tag{8}$$

where z_q depicts the output of the qth hidden neuron in hidden layer, v_{q1} is the weight connecting the qth hidden neuron to the first output neuron and b is the bias to the output neuron.

The optimum network is developed by changing the number of hidden neurons of the hidden layer by trial and error. The network is trained for 1000 epochs and all other parameters are set to defaults as in ANN tool. Generally, during training, the network parameters get adjusted gradually based on the comparison between target and output values; till the number of iterations elapses or when there is no improvement in the error or when the number of validation checks reaches an acceptable level. In this study, as the number of validation check reaches six the training gets terminated. Moreover, the network is tested with testing data (data not included for training or validation) to examine if the developed network reproduce the original data. The optimum ANN model is determined by comparing *MSE* (Eq. 9), percentage average relative error (*PARE*) (Eq. 10) and percentage average absolute error (*PAAE*) (Eq. 11) for different ANN models of the testing data [23].

$$MSE = (\frac{1}{N}) \sum\nolimits_{n=1}^{N} (\sigma_n^{exp} - \sigma_n^{pre})^2 \quad (9)$$

$$PARE = (\frac{1}{N}) \sum\nolimits_{n=1}^{N} \frac{(\sigma_n^{pre} - \sigma_n^{exp})}{\sigma_n^{exp}} \times 100 \quad (10)$$

$$PAAE = (\frac{1}{N}) \sum\nolimits_{n=1}^{N} |\frac{(\sigma_n^{pre} - \sigma_n^{exp})}{\sigma_n^{exp}}| \times 100 \quad (11)$$

In Eqs. 9, 10, 11, *N* represents the total number of testing data, σ_n^{exp} and σ_n^{pre} are experimental and predicted surface tension of the nth data in mNm^{-1}.

3 Results and Discussion

The experimental surface tension of the binary solution is estimated for varying concentrations of BMImBr (0.1–0.6%w/w) at different temperatures (302.85–337.45 K) under ambient pressure and the results are presented as follows.

3.1 Effects of Concentration and Temperature

The effect of temperature and concentration on the surface tension of BMImBr aqueous solutions are shown in Fig. 3. The surface tension varies in the range of 52.99–60.23 mNm^{-1} for 0.1–0.6%w/w in the temperature range of 302.85–337.45 K under ambient pressure. Figure 3 clearly shows that the surface tension of the binary mixture of water and BMImBr decreases with increase in temperature for all the concentrations and increases with increase in concentration. Similar behavior is exhibited by other ionic liquids also [7, 24]. As the temperature of the solution increases the kinetic energy of its molecules also increases, hence there is a weak cohesive force between the molecules of the solution leading to decrease in surface tension with temperature for a particular concentration [12].

The surface tension of the aqueous BMImBr decreases with a decrease in concentration of the BMImBr at a particular temperature. Water accommodates in the ionic liquid structure by virtue of hydrogen bonds with both the cation and anion, thereby leading to decrease in surface tension of the binary solution as the concentration decreases at a particular temperature by means of reduction of the electrostatic attractions between the ions and eventually decreases the overall cohesive energy. The presence of low water content forces the ionic liquid to rearrange into a new different internal order in which more water can be accommodated, till a point where further addition of water leads to a complete solvation of the ions and to the appearance of water molecules, not hydrogen bonded to the ionic liquid and hence, to a new structural rearrangement leading to an increase in the physical properties [24].

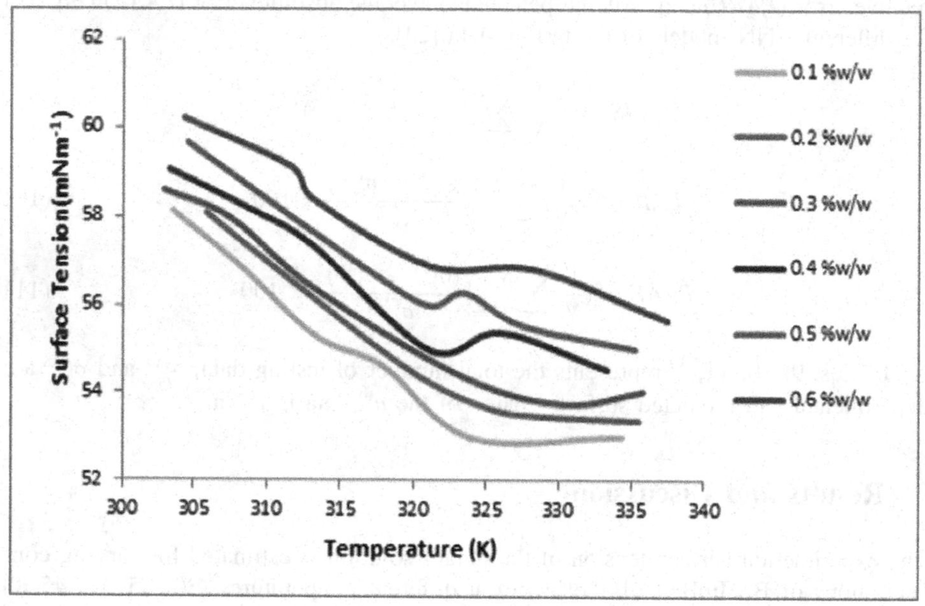

Fig. 3. Effect of concentration and temperature on surface tension of BMImBr solutions

3.2 RSM Analysis

Experimental Design
The experimental results found are utilized to develop a mathematical model equation for the surface tension of BMImBr aqueous solution using CCRD under the RSM, with concentration and temperature as the independent variables.
The final second order quadratic model equation in terms of two actual factors as obtained in RSM is given as Eq. 12,

$$\sigma^{pre} = 89.183 - 0.044\,T - 13.567\,C + 0.056\,TC - 0.0002\,T^2 + 2.32\,C^2 \qquad (12)$$

where σ^{pre} represents the surface tension of BMImBr aqueous solution (mNm^{-1}), T is the temperature (K) and C is the concentration of the BMImBr solution (%w/w).

ANOVA test (Table 3) is used to examine the significant effects of the operating variables such as concentration and temperature. An F value = 1685.67 for the temperature indicates that it is the most significant variable influencing the surface tension of the BMImBr + water binary solution. The source terms with "p value = Prob > F" less than 0.05 are the most significant or influencing factors affecting the response variable. Since the terms with a p value > 0.05 are also considered in the developed model equation (Eq. 12) to minimize the error of the prediction model. The developed mathematical model is validated by comparison with the experimental values and Fig. 4 illustrates that both the experimental values and predicted values are close to the diagonal line. The quality of fit of the quadratic model is assured by the value of the difference between the coefficient of determination R^2 (0.9807) and adjusted R^2 (0.9955), it is less than 0.2 which implies that quality of fit of the model is appreciable. The formulated mathematical equation has predicted the 13 generated runs of CCRD with *MSE* = 0.274, *PARE* = 0.755 and *PAAE* = 0.878.

Table 3. ANOVA table for RSM quadratic model of surface tension

Source	Sum of squares	Degrees of freedom (df)	Mean square	F value	p-value Prob > F	Remarks
Model	31.102	5	6.220	528.418	7.34×10^{-9}	Significant
A-temperature	19.843	1	19.843	1685.67	1.33×10^{-9}	Most significant
B-concentration	11.127	1	11.127	945.2	9.94×10^{-9}	Significant
AB	0.0506	1	0.0506	4.301	0.0768	Significant
A^2	0.0029	1	0.0029	0.246	0.635	Significant
B^2	0.0719	1	0.072	6.11	0.0427	Significant
Residual	0.082	7	0.0117			
Lack of fit	0.082	3	0.027			
Pure error	0	4	0			
Core total	31.184	12				

Combined Effects of Concentration and Temperature on Surface Tension of Ionic Liquid Solutions

The response surface of the surface tension of the BMImBr solution plotted using Eq. 12 is shown in Fig. 5. The response surface plot clearly points the combined effects of temperature and concentration on the surface tension of the ionic liquid solution. The response surface plot depicts good agreement with the experimental results. Figure 5 indicates that as temperature increases from 308.15 to 328.15 K there is a decrease in surface tension of the BMImBr solution for all concentrations and an increase in surface tension with an increase in concentration at a particular temperature. Hence, the effects of both concentration and temperature on the surface tension of ionic liquid solutions are generically studied and can be quantified from the RSM plot.

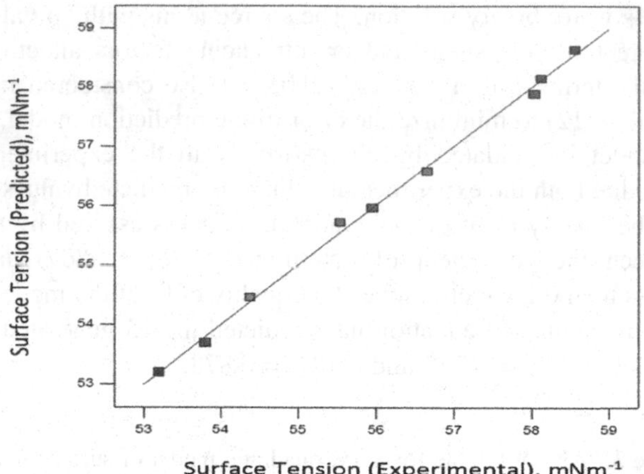

Fig. 4. Comparison between experimental and predicted surface tension of BMImBr solutions

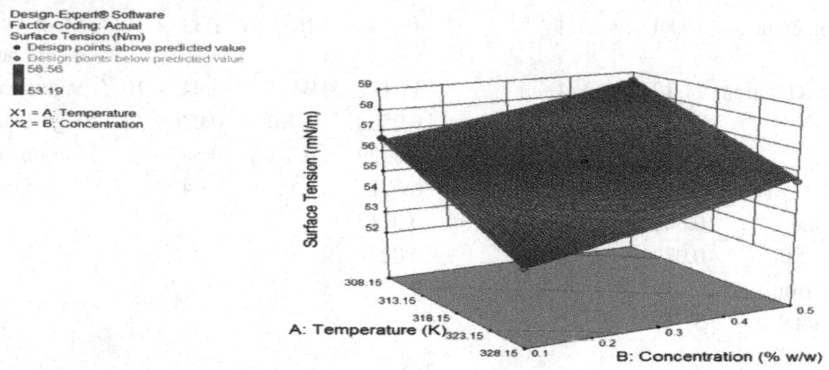

Fig. 5. Response surface plot of surface tension of BMImBr solution

3.3 ANN Analysis

The performance of the ANN models investigated is given in Table 4. It is evident that the predicted responses of the network are affected by amending the number of neurons in the hidden layer. In this investigation, a two layered back propagation neural network with single hidden layer and one input-output layer is considered for modelling as a single hidden layer is capable of predicting many complex problems [21]. The two input neurons are concentration and temperature. The output neuron is surface tension of the BMImBr aqueous solution. The ANN architecture with two input neuron, one hidden layer with four hidden neurons and one neuron in the output layer (2-4-1) with the least *MSE* = 0.156, *PARE* = 0.155 and *PAAE* = 0.623 is chosen as the optimum network (Fig. 6).

The performance and regression plots are generated after training the ANN networks to examine the regression coefficient and *MSE* of training, validation and testing

Table 4. Results of different ANN architecture

ANN Architecture	Transfer function of ANN model: hidden-output	Training dataset R^2	Validation dataset R^2	*MSE* on test dataset	*PARE* on test dataset	*PAAE* on test dataset
2-1-1	logsig-purelin	0.961	0.992	0.162	0.491	0.491
2-2-1	logsig-purelin	0.996	0.962	0.284	0.455	0.585
2-3-1	logsig-purelin	0.990	0.994	0.193	0.322	0.683
2-4-1	logsig-purelin	0.999	0.996	0.156	0.155	0.623
2-5-1	logsig-purelin	0.999	0.961	0.305	−9.45	99.45
2-6-1	logsig-purelin	0.999	0.961	0.277	0.066	0.738
2-7-1	logsig-purelin	0.999	0.967	0.593	1.018	1.277
2-8-1	logsig-purelin	1.000	0.994	0.491	0.420	1.038
2-9-1	logsig-purelin	1.000	0.966	0.304	−0.057	0.814
2-10-1	logsig-purelin	1.000	0.988	0.526	−0.162	0.911

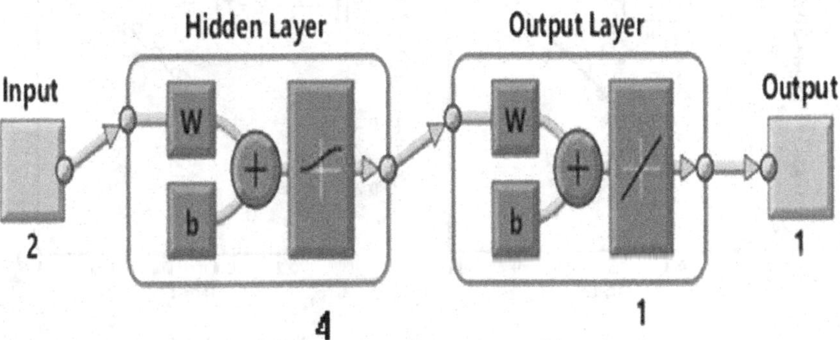

Fig. 6. Optimum neural network model: 2-4-1 architecture

sets. Training is terminated when a fairly good regression coefficient is obtained for all the data sets. Figure 7 illustrates clearly that the cluster line and the fit data line almost coincide with each other with R values as 0.999, 0.996 and 0.972 for training, testing and validation sets, respectively. This indicates that the experimental and model predictions are in excellent agreement. The weight and bias parameters associated with each neuron in the input-hidden and hidden-output layers are updated automatically during each epoch until the number of validation checks became equal to six. The weights and bias of the optimized ANN (2-4-1) are given in Table 5.

3.4 Comparison of RSM and ANN Models

The surface tension of the BMImBr aqueous solution predicted by RSM and ANN models are compared with the experimental surface tension values (data included for modelling is not considered) based on the statistical quality parameters MSE, Root mean square error (RMSE) (Eq. 13) and PAAE (Table 6).

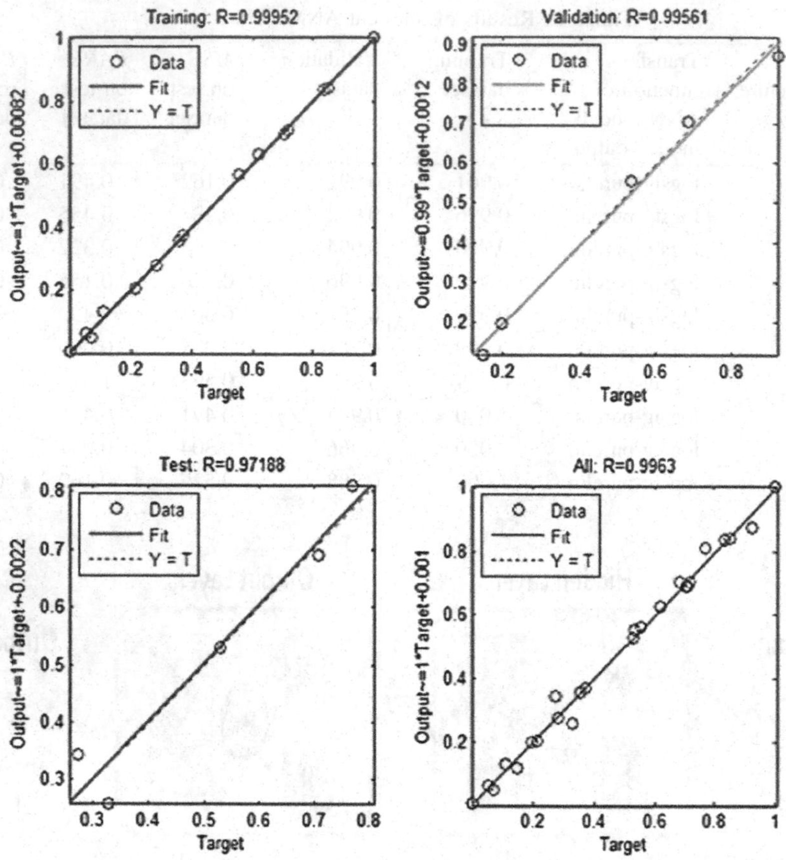

Fig. 7. Regression plots of optimized model: 2-4-1

Table 5. Weight and bias values of the neurons in the optimized 2-4-1 network

Neurons in hidden layer, q	Weights of the input neurons to the hidden layer, u_{pq}		Bias to the hidden layer, a_q	Weight of the hidden neurons to the output layer, v_{q1}	Bias to the output layer, b
	Concentration, u_{1q}	Temperature, u_{2q}			
1	7.3876	−1.6209	−7.1361	0.4131	−1.4402
2	0.46715	3.1259	−1.8025	0.93712	
3	0.7624	−1.9023	0.77588	2.4023	
4	1.9024	5.8913	3.2425	−0.32349	

Table 6. Comparison of RSM and ANN models

S. No.	Concentration (%w/w)	Temperature (K)	Experimental surface tension (mNm^{-1})	Predicted surface tension (mNm^{-1})	
				RSM	ANN
1	0.1	313.35	55.293	56.179	55.6612
2	0.1	317.95	54.613	55.422	54.2634
3	0.2	319.45	54.601	55.675	54.4128
4	0.2	324.95	53.699	54.786	53.5276
5	0.3	313.25	56.353	57.176	56.5863
6	0.4	313.05	57.334	57.765	57.0457
7	0.5	320.85	56.009	57.257	56.3269
8	0.5	323.45	56.2864	56.880	55.9856
9	0.6	313.15	58.3987	59.009	58.8461
10	0.6	321.05	56.8942	57.924	57.7345
			MSE	**0.798**	**0.156**
			RMSE	**0.893**	**0.395**
			PAAE	**1.542**	**0.623**

$$RMSE = \left[\left(\frac{1}{N}\right)\sum\nolimits_{n-1}^{N}\left(\sigma_n^{exp} - \sigma_n^{pre}\right)^2\right]^{1/2} \tag{13}$$

where N is the total number of testing data, σ_n^{exp} and σ_n^{pre} are the actual value of the experimental and predicted surface tension of the nth data.

Based on lower values of $MSE = 0.156$, $RMSE = 0.395$ and $PAAE = 0.623$, it is evident that the ANN model is more robust and accurate in predicting surface tension than the RSM model.

4 Conclusion

The surface tension of BMImBr solutions is evaluated at different temperatures ranging from 302.85–337.45 K and concentrations 0.1–0.6%w/w under ambient pressure. The surface tension is measured using the drop weight method that works on the principle of Tate's law. Based on RSM, from ANOVA analysis it is determined that temperature is the most significant operating variable and its impact is more on surface tension than concentration. A second order quadratic mathematical equation with a coefficient of determination R^2 as 0.9807 is modelled to compute the surface tension of BMImBr solution using RSM. The RSM model can predict the 13 runs of the CCRD with $MSE = 0.274$, $PARE = 0.755$ and $PAAE = 0.878$.

A two-layered feed forward back propagation neural network is also modeled for predicting the surface tension of the BMImBr solution. An ANN architecture with two input neurons, four hidden neurons, and one output neuron is the optimum model designed with *MSE* = 0.156, *PARE* = 0.395 and *PAAE* = 0.623. The statistical values specify that both the models are efficient in the prediction of the experimental surface tension of BMImBr solutions. However, ANN model exhibits better accuracy compared to RSM model due to lower values of the *MSE* = 0.156, *RMSE* = 0.395 and *PAAE* = 0.623. The proposed models are helpful in predicting the surface tension of BMImBr solutions at required temperature and concentration without performing any further experiments. Moreover, the applicability of the proposed models can be enhanced further by expanding the range of temperature and concentration.

References

1. Soman, D.P., Kalaichelvi, P., Radhakrishnan, T.K.: Review on suitability of ionic liquids for heat transfer applications. Emerg. Trends Chem. Eng. **3**, 40–51 (2016)
2. Ghandi, K.: A review of ionic liquids, their limits and applications. Green Sustain. Chem. **4**, 44–53 (2014)
3. Andrade, C.K.Z., Matos, R.A.F., Oliveira, V.B., Duraes, J.A., Sales, M.J.A.: Thermal study and evaluation of new menthol-based ionic liquids as polymeric additives. J. Therm. Anal. Calorim. **99**, 539–543 (2010)
4. Lazzús, J.A.: Estimation of the thermal conductivity λ(T, P) of ionic liquids using a neural network optimized with genetic algorithms. C. R. Chim. **19**, 1–9 (2015)
5. Chen, Y.F., Hu, Y.F., Yang, Z.Y., Qi, J.G., Yin, L.Y., Zhang, H.R., Huang, H.Z., Liu, X.M.: Prediction of density, viscosity, and conductivity of the ternary aqueous solutions of piperidinium-based ionic liquids at different temperatures and atmospheric pressure using the data of their binary subsystems. Fluid Phase Equilib. **383**, 55–71 (2014)
6. Hezave, A.Z., Raeissi, S., Lashkarbolooki, M.: Estimation of thermal conductivity of ionic liquids using a perceptron neural network. Ind. Eng. Chem. Res. **51**, 9886–9893 (2012)
7. Tariq, M., Freire, M.G., Saramago, B., Coutinho, J.A.P., Lopes, J.N.C., Rebelo, L.P.N.: Surface tension of ionic liquids and ionic liquid solutions. Chem. Soc. Rev. **41**, 829–868 (2012)
8. Mousazadeh, M.H., Faramarzi, E.: Corresponding states theory for the prediction of surface tension of ionic liquids. Ionics (Kiel) **17**, 217–222 (2011)
9. Atashrouz, S., Amini, E., Pazuki, G.: Modeling of surface tension for ionic liquids using group method of data handling. Ionics (Kiel) **21**, 1595–1603 (2014)
10. Lashkarbolooki, M.: Artificial neural network modeling for prediction of binary surface tension containing ionic liquid. Sep. Sci. Technol. **52**, 1454–1467 (2017)
11. Valderrama, J.O., Martinez, G., Faúndez, C.A.: Heat capacity of ionic liquids using artificial neural networks and the concept of mass connectivity. Int. J. Thermophys. **32**, 942–956 (2011)
12. Muthamizhi, K., Kalaichelvi, P., Powar, S.T., Jaishree, R.: Investigation and modelling of surface tension of power-law fluids. RSC Adv. **4**, 9771–9776 (2014)
13. Yildirim, O.E., Xu, Q., Basaran, O.A.: Analysis of the drop weight method. Phys. Fluids **17**, 1–13 (2005)
14. Morgan, J.L.R.: The drop weight method for the determination of the surface tension of a liquid. J. Am. Chem. Soc. **37**, 1461–1467 (1915)
15. Biniaz, P., Farsi, M., Rahimpour, M.R.: Demulsification of water in oil emulsion using ionic liquids: statistical modeling and optimization. Fuel **184**, 325–333 (2016)

16. Abdullah, S.B., Man, Z., Bustam, M.: An optimization study via response surface methodology in extracting of Benzothiophene and Xylene from n-C12 using 1-Hexyl-3-Methylimidazolium Tetrafluoroborate ionic liquid. J. Appl. Sci. **14**, 1008–1015 (2014)
17. Najafi-Marghmaleki, A., Khosravi-Nikou, M.R., Barati-Harooni, A.: A new model for prediction of binary mixture of ionic liquids + water density using artificial neural network. J. Mol. Liq. **220**, 232–237 (2016)
18. Hemmat Esfe, M., Ahangar, M.R.H., Toghraie, D., Hajmohammad, M.H., Rostamian, H., Tourang, H.: Designing artificial neural network on thermal conductivity of Al2O3–water–EG (60–40%) nanofluid using experimental data. J. Therm. Anal. Calorim. **126**, 837–843 (2016)
19. Hemmat Esfe, M., Rostamian, H., Toghraie, D., Yan, W.-M.: Using artificial neural network to predict thermal conductivity of ethylene glycol with alumina nanoparticle: effects of temperature and solid volume fraction. J. Therm. Anal. Calorim. **126**, 643–648 (2016)
20. Fazlali, A., Koranian, P., Beigzadeh, R., Rahimi, M.: Application of artificial neural network for vapor liquid equilibrium calculation of ternary system including ionic liquid: water, ethanol and 1-butyl-3-methylimidazolium acetate. Korean J. Chem. Eng. **30**, 1681–1686 (2013)
21. Lashkarbolooki, M., Hezave, A.Z., Babapoor, A.: Correlation of density for binary mixtures of methanol + ionic liquids using back propagation artificial neural network. Korean J. Chem. Eng. **30**, 213–220 (2013)
22. Haghbakhsh, R., Adib, H., Keshavarz, P., Koolivand, M., Keshtkari, S.: Development of an artificial neural network model for the prediction of hydrocarbon density at high-pressure, high-temperature conditions. Thermochim. Acta **551**, 124–130 (2013)
23. Fatehi, M.R., Raeissi, S., Mowla, D.: An artificial neural network to calculate pure ionic liquid densities without the need for any experimental data. J. Supercrit. Fluids **95**, 60–67 (2014)
24. Freire, M.G., Carvalho, P.J., Fernandes, A.M., Marrucho, I.M., Queimada, A.J., Coutinho, J.A.P.: Surface tensions of imidazolium based ionic liquids: anion, cation, temperature and water effect. J. Colloid Interface Sci. **314**, 621–630 (2007)

Optimized Food Recognition System for Diabetic Patients

B. Anusha[1(✉)], S. Sabena[2], and L. Sairamesh[1]

[1] Department of Information Science and Technology, Anna University, CEG Campus, Chennai, Tamil Nadu, India
bsanusharaj@gmail.com, sairamesh.ist@gmail.com
[2] Department of Computer Science and Engineering, Regional Center of Anna University, Tirunelveli, Tamil Nadu, India
sabenazulficker@gmail.com

Abstract. Now a day's, diabetic food recognition for various types of diabetic patients is the challenge proposed by the world medical Association. In order to overcome the challenge and limiting the misclassification rate, the Diabetic calorie measurement system was proposed. This proposed system grants user to acquire a photo of food and to measure calories without human intervention, which offer qualitative nutritional information about foods. Before the classification, Scale Invariant Feature Transform (SIFT) features obtained from different color spaces and texture features extracted by using Histogram Statistics (HS), Gray Level Co-occurrence Matrices (GLCM) and the Fast Fourier Transformation (FFT). By these color and textural features, Support Vector Machine (SVM), Extreme Learning Machine (ELM) and Biogeography Based Classification (BBO) are used for classification of diabetic patient comestible and not comestible foods. Based on the classification results, diabetic patient comestible food image involved in the system to measure their calorie by using GLCM and identify whether the food is comestible by TYPE:1 diabetic patient or TYPE:II diabetic patient. Final experimental results indicated that the performance rate of classification accuracy can be improved for FFT based texture feature compared to other features. The BBO optimizer gives optimized features and enhanced performance for very challenging large food image data set.

Keywords: Feature extraction · Scale Invariant Feature Transform (SIFT) Histogram Statistics (HS) · Gray Level Concurrence Matrix (GLCM) Fast Fourier Transform (FFT) · Food Image Classification Support Vector Machine (SVM) · Extreme Learning Machine (ELM) Biogeography Based Classification (BBO) · Food image recognition Calorie measurement

1 Introduction

Diabetic disease control is the health issue proposed by world health organization. Diabetic is one of the complicated issues for various diseases like cardiovascucardiovascular, neuropathy [1]. It is widely accepted that, diabetic is caused by incorrect diet habits [2]. The world wide series health problem of diabetic is fatness or obesity [3].

P. Bhattacharyya et al. (Eds.): NGCT 2017, CCIS 827, pp. 504–525, 2018.
https://doi.org/10.1007/978-981-10-8657-1_38

Nutrition plays a vital role in health maintenance and it should be guided by the long-term risk of vascular complications, glycemic control for quality life [4]. The suitable diet of carbohydrate restriction in people is used to improve their health and manage obesity problems. The proper medication of diet does not have any side effects. Diabetic metabolism disorder is caused by the limitation of functional beta-cell mass in two ways such as TYPE-I and TYPE:II [3]. TYPE:I is a genetic and chronic disease. Because of insulin resistance and cardiovascular tricky situation cause TYPE:I diabetic in child the diagnosis age for infants was 5 months earlier and he sugar sweetened beverages are taken for their first 12 months of their life. 32% of infant leads to hard risk [4]. The mean age at the diagnosis of TYPE:I diabetes least square predicted means in Table 1 [5].

Table 1. Mean age at the diagnosis of TYPE:I diabetes least square predicted means.

<3 months	3–6 months	7–11 months	>12 months
9.43 ± 0.09	9.43 ± 0.09	9.32 ± 0.1	9.49 ± 0.11
9.42 ± 0.11	9.42 ± 0.11	9.39 ± 0.09	9.47 ± 0.11
9.46 ± 0.08	9.46 ± 0.08	9.34 ± 0.1	9.27 ± 0.16
9.50 ± 0.08	9.50 ± 0.08	9.31 ± 0.1	9.31 ± 0.18
9.36 ± 0.17	9.43 ± 0.08	9.43 ± 0.13	9.38 ± 0.21

TYPE:II is a non communicative disease [6]. Because of lower BMI, C-peptide and cardio vascular tricky situation cause TYPE:II diabetic in old peoples or adults [7, 8]. "There is no healing for diabetic. But public can manage or delay diabetes through exercise, weight control, diet and if essential, medicine" [9]. The majority of people consume fast foods from hotels. Such people extract the calorie content in food image can be measured by using CHO, fat and proteins of food items [5]. Many low carbohydrate food diet plans are proposed. But food consumptions make more confusion.

Rest of the paper is structured as follows. In Sect. 2, we present the background of diabetic food recognition system. In Sect. 3, we discuss about related works. In Sect. 4, gives our proposed diabetic food recognition system. In Sect. 5, give a discussion about food calorie measurement. In Sect. 6, which carry out a discussion about experimental setup and dataset. In Sect. 7, we carry out the implementation analysis. In Sect. 8, that presented a metrics for analyzing performance. In Sect. 9, provide the detailed experimental results. In Sect. 10, we conclude the diabetic food recognition paper and provide a way of doing future works.

2 Background

2.1 Diabetic Food Recognition System

The food recognition system that helps to track health and fitness, which is on the rise, with a myriad of devices and applications available to record everything from blood pressure, to steps walked, to calories consumed or burned. It is a straightforward way to estimate calories in a meal using a camera captured image [10].

3 Related Work

In this section presents some most common food intake different measurement and recognition methods. The aim is to provide the benefit and drawback of existing methods and the need of proposed measurement and recognition methods.

In [11], proposed graph cut segmentation method, which senses the most excellent contour of the object in the input image. During the Graph cut segmentation, the pixels of image are mapped on vertex and its neighboring pixels and are connected by weighted edges for robustness. The goal of this system is to provide the calorie value of intake foods. But it is possible only for smaller datasets.

In [12], author proposed a novel method for calorie measurement. Here the functionality and flexibility of the food image recognition is more and also increasing the number of images in the database the recognition rate can be increased. But the major cause of inconvenience is that the unpredictability of the food objects makes complicated to adapt the techniques and algorithms with real data.

In [13], mobile application based recognition system like a game, which inspires the children to run through healthy food intake habits. It makes an inconvenience of photo color, which varies because of lightening behaviour.

The Recognition system starts with extracting features from image. The color key point extraction from image extract accurate color features. But some diabetic patient comestible and not comestible foods have same color. The food color is also varying because of freeze, dry and so on… So the color information is not sufficient to identify the diabetic patient intake foods.

In [14], the proposed system of spiral pyramid matching approach the features extracted from huge dataset images the classification accuracy is 18%. But for smaller dataset classification accuracy is 86%. So the recognition accuracy for such approach is too low.

In [15], this system the captured images are send to research for performing the feature extraction and analysis. The major drawback of system does not provide adequate information to users in real time. Because of offline processing of images, there is a significant delay for providing the sufficient information.

In [16], proposed a pair wise classification, gain the user's speech as the input for enhancing the recognition process, which is based on maximum response features in a texton histogram model and color neighbourhood. In this method, the feature vector's clustering procedure is omitted. On the other hand, less information is measured, which strength is not sufficient to deal with high visual dictionary of dataset.

To alleviate aforesaid issues, researchers studying the other well-situated user convenient system that take food image as the input and provide the information about food, whether the food is comestible by diabetic patients and also check whether the food is TYPE:I diabetic patient comestible or TYPE:II diabetic patient comestible.

In [17], proposed the base of computer vision problem is feature extraction. SIFT performed at the highest level while testing image. SIFT is slow, but it has high performance. SIFT's matching based on features to be robust to localization errors. By using small number of dimension image provide the significant benefits for both storage space and matching speed.

In [18], after the extraction of features for separation of male genders from female is a challenging task. SVM's high generalization ability offer superior performance while handling this situation. It utilizes kernel trick for handling non linear features.

In our diabetic calorie measurement system, we use food image as an input. But we go one step further in terms of providing the accurate information to patients. By implementing texture feature extraction combine with color feature extraction as a result of improving the recognition accuracy. In addition the processing of huge dataset images and calorie measurement outcome messages will convey to the user instantly. The in depth sketch of the proposed system is discussed in the next section.

4 Proposed Methods Description

In this section we discuss our proposed system in more detail. In particular, we give different feature extraction methods and food image classification methods.

4.1 Architectural Design Overview

In the projected system the automatic color and texture analysis is used to estimate the precise nutritional information from the food images. In automatic diabetic food recognition system, the color visual features are extracted by using color key pointsand the textural visual features are extracted by using HS, GLCM and FFT + GLCM and GLCM for calorie measurement The extracted visual features are quantized by using k-means and fire fly clustering techniques. Finally classifier classifies the image as TYPE:I, TYPE:II diabetic patient comestible or not. The diabetic food recognition system for TYPE:I and TYPE:II diabetic patients are shown in Fig. 1. The Recognition accuracy is achieved by improving the associations between color and textural visual features. Based on the models using ELM and BBO high recognition accuracy can be achieved effectively, where the whole automatic system can be divided into two steps.

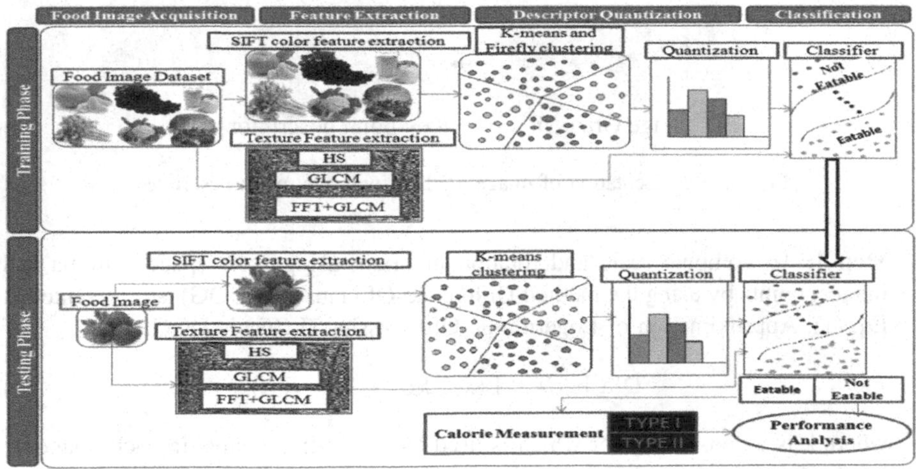

Fig. 1. Block diagram TYPE:I and TYPE:II diabetic food recognition system

(1) Training phase and (2) Testing phase. In First phase, system acquire knowledge by learning visual dictionary set, which is generated based on color and texture visual features extracted from the images. In second phase, checking recognition accuracy for unknown or new images by using acquired knowledge in first phase. Both training and testing phase consists of three basic steps, (a) key point extraction (b) learning visual dictionary and (c) classification.

Key Point Extraction

Key points are the randomly selected points in the image. Each key point as-signs a numerical value to the image area [10]. SIFT key point detector is used for extracting the color key points from image, which compute color histogram in RGB space.

Extracting Image Color Key Point Features

Compared to monochrome images, color image carry more information. Variety of color feature model such as RGB, HSV etc. are extracted from images. In electronic system widely used RGB color model achieve good display result of images [19].

(a) Scale Invariant Feature Transform (SIFT)

SIFT is a feature descriptor is used for performing object identification and classification tasks which extracts key points [21] such as a huge set of local feature vector values from image [20]. Key points are selected extreme points within a selected area of image [24] which are more accurate with less bias in theoretical point [21]. In nature key points are discriminating [22]. SIFT used square image descriptor for extracting features, which remove low contrast pixels. Such SIFT extracted features are less affected by noise [20]. It has strong strength and elevated recognition capability [23].

In Local feature descriptor, once the color key point extraction can be done, a local image descriptor SIFT is applied to a rectangular area around all key points to produce a feature vector by using the following steps, [10, 25]. The image gradient with key point descriptor representation is shown in Fig. 2.

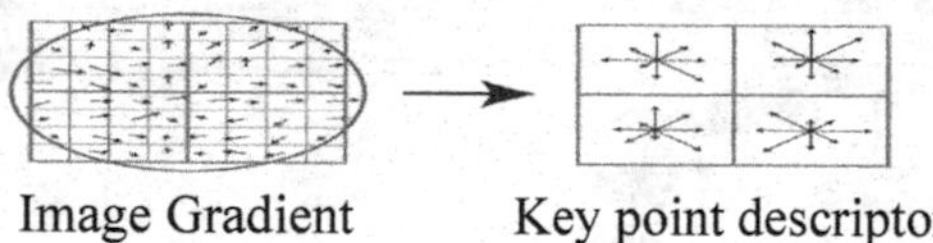

Fig. 2. Representation of image gradient with key point descriptor

Step 1: To compute scale and rotation invariant using scale space extrema and interest points by using the method Difference-Of-Gaussian (DOG) is represented in Eq. (1). Approximation of Logarithmic-Of-Gaussian (LOG) is DOG.

$$D(a, b, \sigma) = L(x, y.k\sigma) - L(x, y, \sigma) \tag{1}$$

where k is a constant factor which is used for separating octave in each image.

Step 2: For each key point, determine scale and location and remove weak key points. The Scaling of descriptor location is represented in Fig. 3. Key point localization can be represented in Eq. (2),

$$KPL_k = (x_k, y_k, \sigma_k) \tag{2}$$

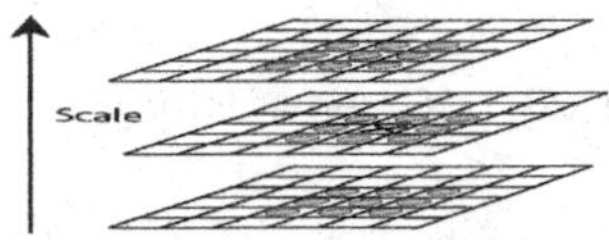

Fig. 3. Scaling of location using descriptor representation

Step 3: Assigning orientation to each key point for handling transformation. Representation of histogram gradient is in Fig. 4. By creating histogram of gradient using Eq. (3),

$$L(x, y, \sigma) = G(x, y, \sigma) * I(x, y) \tag{3}$$

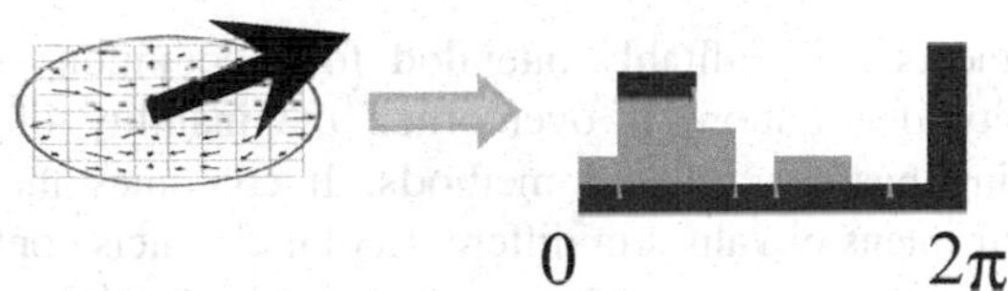

Fig. 4. Representation of histogram gradient

Step 4: To measure local image gradient for handling illumination in image and use at those selected scale. The key point descriptor are created for,

Step 4.1: Create 16 × 16 windows around key point.

Step 4.2: Divide the window into 4 × 4 grids.

Step 4.3: Compute histogram for each cells using local features and color moments.

SIFT descriptorextracts local color features from image. The color features RGB in opponent color space (OCS_1, OCS_2, OCS_3) is extracted by using Eq. (4) [26],

$$\begin{pmatrix} OCS_1 \\ OCS_2 \\ OCS_3 \end{pmatrix} = \begin{pmatrix} a^R[m,n] \\ a^G[m,n] \\ a^B[m,n] \end{pmatrix} = \begin{pmatrix} \frac{Red - Green}{\sqrt{2}} \\ \frac{Red + Green - 2Blue}{\sqrt{6}} \\ \frac{Red + Green + Blue}{\sqrt{3}} \end{pmatrix} \tag{4}$$

where $a^R[m,n], a^G[m,n], a^B[m,n]$ are red, green, blue color values. SIFT extract local color features by using Eqs. (5), (6), (7) and (8),

$$\text{hist}_{\text{RGB}} = \begin{pmatrix} \text{Red} \\ \text{Green} \\ \text{Blue} \end{pmatrix} \tag{5}$$

$$\text{RG}_{\text{normalized channel}} = \begin{pmatrix} \frac{\text{Red}}{\text{Red}+\text{Green}+\text{Blue}} \\ \frac{\text{Green}}{\text{Red}+\text{Green}+\text{Blue}} \end{pmatrix} \tag{6}$$

$$\text{Hue channel} = \text{attan2}\left(\sqrt{3} * (\text{Green} - \text{Blue}), 2 * \text{Red} - \text{Green} - \text{Blue}\right) \tag{7}$$

$$\text{Transformed}_{\text{RGB}} = \begin{pmatrix} \text{Red}_{\text{tran}} \\ \text{Green}_{\text{trans}} \\ \text{Blue}_{\text{trans}} \end{pmatrix} = \begin{pmatrix} \frac{\text{Red}-\alpha_{\text{Red}}}{\sigma_{\text{Red}}} \\ \frac{\text{Green}-\alpha_{\text{Green}}}{\sigma_{\text{Green}}} \\ \frac{\text{Blue}-\alpha_{\text{Blue}}}{\sigma_{\text{Blue}}} \end{pmatrix} \tag{8}$$

Where α and σ represent mean and standard deviation. For the purose of recognition, the minimum of lightness in image can be measured [9] by Eq. (9),

$$\text{Lightness} = \sum\nolimits_{n=0}^{N-1} a^{C}[m, n] \tag{9}$$

The Color moments are profitably intended for recognition purposes, which is based on probability distribution. It overcomes the inability of capturing spatial information by using histogram based methods. It combines the powers of pixel coordinates and their intensity values in different color channels contained in the same integral. The generalized color moments are estimated by the following Eq. (10),

$$\text{Moment}_{ab}^{xyz} = \sum\nolimits_{m}^{W} \sum\nolimits_{n}^{H} d^a e^b R(d, e)^x G(d, e)^y B(d, e)^z \tag{10}$$

Step 5: Generate all local feature values and color moment value as the patches.

Extracting Image Textural Feature
Texture analysis plays a vital role in computer vision [27]. Texture features are measured from image by using Statistical Histogram Statistics (HS) [28, 29], Gray Level co-occurrence matrices (GLCM) [30] and transformation based Fast Fourier Transform (FFT) [31].

(a) Textural feature extraction using Histogram Statistics (HS)

Histogram Statistics is a significant tool in image processing, which gives the first order statistical information of an image. It shows how many pixels of an image have certain intensity values. For measuring smoothness, roughness etc. can be measured by using the histogram based statistical image texture features such as $\text{hist}_{\text{smoothness}}$ [32], $\text{hist}_{\text{roughness}}$, $\text{hist}_{\text{intensity}}$, $\text{hist}_{\text{moment}}$, $\text{hist}_{\text{entropy}}$ are extracted from image [16, 20, 32].

Smoothness (fineness) is the antonym for roughness which is used for measuring gas cells in food. Smoothness can be measured by using the Eq. (11),

$$\mathrm{hist}_{\mathrm{smoothness}} = 1 - \frac{1}{1 + (\text{standard deviation})^2} \tag{11}$$

Roughness is used for identifying oil content in food. So the fried foods are easily recognized. Roughness can be measured by using Eq. (12),

$$\mathrm{hist}_{\mathrm{roughness}} = 1 - \frac{1}{1 + (\mathrm{hist}_{\mathrm{contrast}})^2} \tag{12}$$

Intensity values are used for finding the contrast of the image. It calculated by summing all intensity values with in an image by using Eq. (13),

$$\mathrm{hist}_{\mathrm{intensity}} = \sum_{a=0}^{255} a\ P(a) \tag{13}$$

Contrast is calculated by using intensity value of an image which is related to brightness. It is vary by capturing the image by user. It is calculated by using Eq. (14),

$$\mathrm{hist}_{\mathrm{contrast}} = \left(\sum_{a=0}^{255} \left(a\ \mathrm{hist}_{\mathrm{intensity}}\right)^2 P(a)\right)^2 \tag{14}$$

The moment calculates smoothness in each pixel based on intensity value. It provides first order statistical information of a food image. It is calculated by using Eq. (15),

$$\mathrm{hist}_{\mathrm{moment}} = \sum_{a=0}^{255} \left(a\ \mathrm{hist}_{\mathrm{intensity}}\right)^3 P(a) \tag{15}$$

Entropy provides the quality information of food image. It is calculated by using Eq. (16),

$$\mathrm{hist}_{\mathrm{entropy}} = \sum_{a=0}^{255} P(a)\log_2(P(a)) \tag{16}$$

Where a be a random variable in gray level, P(a) is a statistical histogram of gray level. The gray level varies from 0 to 255.

(b) Textural feature extraction using Gray Level Concurrence Matrix (GLCM)

GLCM provide the second order information about neighboring pixels of an image, which is used for understanding the detail information about image contents [30]. The GLCM are measured by contrast, correlation, energy and homogeneity from image [33]. It is used for identifying whether the food is fresh or frozen. The GLCM are measured by using Eqs. (17), (18), (19) and (20),

$$\text{Contrast} = \sum_{m=0}^{A} \sum_{n=0}^{B} (m\ n)^2 g(m\ n) \tag{17}$$

$$\text{Correlation} = \sum_{m=0}^{A} \sum_{n=0}^{B} \frac{(m\ \alpha_m m)(n\ \alpha_n n) g(m, n)}{\sigma_m \sigma_n} \tag{18}$$

$$\text{Energy} = \sum_{m=0}^{A} \sum_{n=0}^{B} g(m, n) \tag{19}$$

$$\text{Homogeneity} = \sum_{m=0}^{A} \sum_{n=0}^{B} \frac{g(m, n)}{1 + (m\ n)^2} \tag{20}$$

$$\alpha_m = \sum_{m=0}^{A} i \sum_{n=0}^{B} g(i, j) \tag{21}$$

$$\alpha_n = \sum_{m=0}^{A} j \sum_{n=0}^{B} g(i, j) \tag{22}$$

$$\sigma_m = \sqrt{\sum_{m=0}^{A} (i\ \alpha_i)^2 \sum_{n=0}^{B} g(i, j)} \tag{23}$$

$$\sigma_m = \sqrt{\sum_{n=0}^{B} (j\ \alpha_j)^2 \sum_{A=0}^{A} g(i, j)} \tag{24}$$

Where A is the column number and B is the row number of GLCM (g(m, n)) [28, 34].

(c) Textural feature extraction using transformation based Fast Fourier Transform (FFT)

FFT support both real and imaginary feature values of an image which reduce time complexity. In the Fourier domain of the image each and every point in the image is represented as a particular frequency contained in the spatial domain of an image. The output of FFT represents the image in the Fourier as the input image is spatial domain correspondent [31]. The FFT can be calculated by using the Eq. (25),

$$X_a = \sum_{m=0}^{M-1} x_m e^{-2\pi a \frac{m}{M}} \tag{25}$$

Where, M is the number of pixels or points in an image.

Learning Visual Dictionary

After computing the descriptors of each training image patch, the most representative patches are identified which will form the system's visual words. It uses k-means clustering algorithm to create visual dictionary. To overcome the creation ofempty clusters by using fire fly algorithm. Here the centre of visual word represents visual word in the dictionary [10].

K-means Clustering Algorithm

Step 1: In Beginning, for avoiding the problem of forming empty clusters assign the centroid value k. It represents the image is organized into classes.

Step 2: Assign training sample at random.
Step 3: Compute distance from centriod of each cluster such Euclidean distance by using Eq. (26),

$$\text{Euclidean distance} = \sqrt{\sum_{a=1}^{m} (k_a - l_a)^2} \tag{26}$$

Step 4: Repeat 3 until pass through the training sample forming no new assignments of images [35].

Fire Fly Algorithm
Due to its automated grouping ability it is used for clustering. It is appropriate for global optimization associated problems. By the process of bioluminescence firefly produce a flash light which provides the essentials of attraction to opposite sex as well as potential prey? All fireflies are unisex thus attraction is regardless of their sex. The less bright firefly will move towards the brighter firefly which is considered more attractive. The attractiveness decreases as the distance increases. The brightness of a firefly is determined by the landscape of the objective function. If there is no clear and more visible firefly within the range, then each one will move randomly. Distance between two fire fly are calculated by using the Cartesian metric.

Step 1: Create initial features of fire fly by,
F= {f1, f2 ...}
Step 2: Calculate the brightness using objective function
$b_i = f(firefly_i)$
Where $firefly_i$ is an i-th fire fly.
Step 3: Set the light absorption coefficient α
Step 4: a=0
While (a< maximum number of iteration)
For i =1 to m
For j=1 to i
If $(I_i < I_j)$
Moving the firefly i to j by,

$$firefly_i = firefly_i + be^{-\alpha r^2}(firefly_j - firefly_i) + \beta\left(rand - \frac{1}{2}\right)$$

where β is a randomized parameter.
End if
Step 4.1: Measure attractiveness by using equation (27),

$$\alpha_{ij}^{a}(r_{ij}^{a}) = \alpha_{feature} \cdot \frac{1}{1-e^{-\beta.(r_{ij}^{a})^2}} \tag{27}$$

Step 4.2: Evaluate new firefly and update brightness
$b_i = f(firefly_i)$
End for
End for
a=a+1
End while
Step 5: Give ranking to firefly by computing fitness by using distance measurement between features for finding the best fire fly by using equation (28),

$$r_{ij}^{a} = \left\|d_i^a - d_j^a\right\| = \sqrt{\sum_{c=1}^{m}(d_{i,c}^{a} - d_{j,c}^{a})^2} \tag{28}$$

Step 6: Go to step 4 until complete the iteration and identify best firefly grouping.

Descriptor Quantization
Assigning a feature vector value to pre defined visual vocabulary. The visual dictionary is learnt by using k-means and fire fly values are quantized. Such quantized descriptor values complexity depends on the number of visual words in the dictionary [10].

Classification Analysis
For classification analysis Single hidden layer feed forward neural network's Extreme Learning Machine (ELM) [36] and Evolutionary algorithm of Biogeography Based Optimization (BBO) is used. For handling probabilistic situation and theoretical guarantee for fast computation ELM classifier take a place in classification which supports both linear and non linear kernels [37]. Only best solutions are transferred to next iteration without migration, so BBO hold in a place in classification.

ELM Classifier
In ELM he output weights are optimized, and all the weights assigned between the input layer and the hidden layer are assigned random [38]. Due to its fast computational speed and theoretical guarantees this method recently received an active development both theoretically including optimally pruned modification of ELM and in applications. The classification and performance rates of ELM are more. It has the ability to deals with probability and also handles huge data set more effectively [39]. The working ELM is represented in Fig. 5.

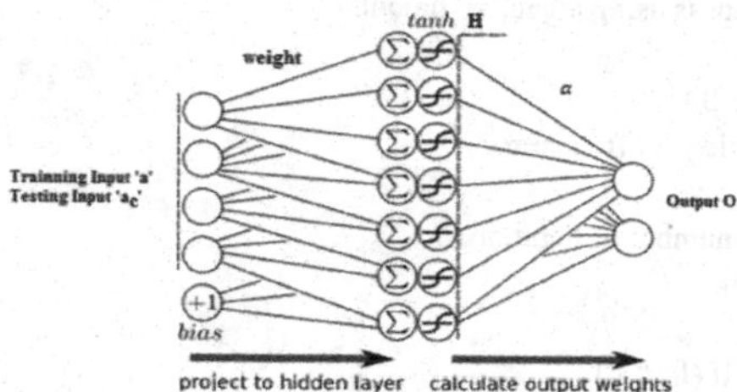

Fig. 5. Representation of working steps of ELM

<u>*ELM algorithm steps*</u>

Step 1: Find ELM by finding N neurons in the hidden layer by using Eq. (29),

$$f(a) - \sum_{c=1}^{N} \alpha_c h(\text{weight}_c.a) \tag{29}$$

Step 2: Selecting optimal number of neurons by using mean square error by Eq. (30),

$$\text{Mean Square Error}_{\text{Leave One Out}}^{\text{Prediction Sum of Squares}} = \frac{1}{M_c}\sum_{m=1}^{M}\sum_{c=1}^{k}\left(\frac{T - HH^{+}T}{[1_M - \text{diag}(HH^{+})]1_k^T}\right)_{ic}^2 \tag{30}$$

Step 3: Use Gaussian mixture model to estimate density of data sample by using Eq. (31),

$$p(a|\theta) - \sum\nolimits_{c=1}^{C} \pi_c N(a|\mu_c, \varepsilon_c) \tag{31}$$

Step 4: By calculating prediction to refine results into more interpretable probabilities using bayer's theorem by using Eq. (32),

$$p(C|O) = p(O|C)\frac{p(C)}{p(O)} \tag{32}$$

Step 5: Refine the training for GMM, to inherit the error of ELM model. It will return weight_c,a, Gaussian Mixture model value, P(C).
Step 6: To test the testing sample a_t and display the conditional probability value $P(C|O_t)$.

In Eqs. (29), (30), (31) and (32) α_c is a vector of c-dimensional, weight_c is a d-dimensional randomly assigned vector, h(.) is a nonlinear activation sigmoid function, H^+ Moore Penrose pseudo Inverse of H, $\theta = \{\pi_c, \mu_c, \varepsilon_c\}$, p(C) is a maximum likelihood estimate, p(O|C) is a conditional distribution, a is a training input, α_c is a testing input.

Biogeography Based Optimization (BBO)
BBO optimizes a function by stochastically or iterativly improving candidate solutions with regard to a given measure of quality, or fitness function [40]. It does not make any assumptions about the problem and can therefore be applied to a wide class of problems [41]. The best solutions are transferred to next iteration withoutmigration procedure [42]. The relation between migrations rates with number of species are shown in Fig. 6.

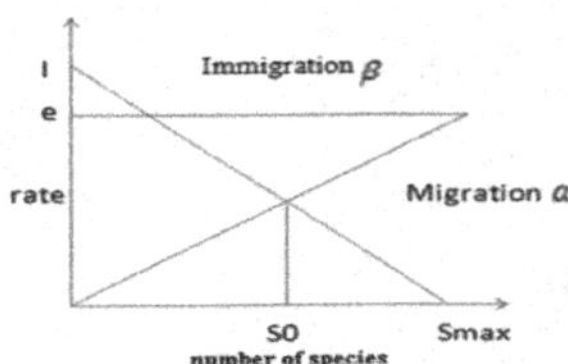

Fig. 6. Schematic representation of relation between migrations rates with number of species

<u>*BBO algorithm*</u>

1. Get the food image.
2. Cluster the image features randomly. Each cluster has images of universal diabetic patient comestible and non comestible food images.
3. Consider other class's type-I, type-II diabetic patient's comestible and not comestible classes having training images as their members.

4. Define class suitability index, A_{max}, immigration rate by using Eq. (33) and emigration rate by using Eq. (34).

$$\alpha_z = \frac{e_z}{m} \tag{33}$$

$$\beta_z = I\left(1 - \frac{z}{m}\right) \tag{34}$$

By combine emigration rate and immigration rate by using Eq. (35),

$$\alpha_z + \beta_z = e \tag{35}$$

Calculate class suitability index of each feature extracted from food image.

5. (i) Select the images from universal food image set and migrate it to one of the class.
   (ii) Recalculate the class suitability index of image features.
6. If the recalculated class suitability index is within threshold value then
   (i) Absorb the images based on image feature and assign to corresponding class.
   (ii) Go to step 8

   else if any unconsidered feature class is left then:
   (i) migrate the image to that feature class.
   (ii) Go to step7.

   else
   (i) use the rough set theory to discretize images and make random cluster which is considered as separate images.
   (ii) Add these new images to universal food image dataset class.

   If no images is left in the universal image data set class then:
   (i) stop the process.
   Else
7. (i) go to step 6.
   End

5 Calorie Measurement

The calorie is a composition of fat, protein so on… If the food has more calories the eaten people are suffer from disease like obesity, Diabetic etc. So calorie measurement places a very important role in food recognition system [11].

Calorie Measurement Using GLCM

Automatic carbohydrate (CHO) counting is used for identifying calorie rich food. It can be done by using GLCM values such as contrast, homogeneity, correlation and energy. If GLCM value exceeds the threshold value the food is a calorie rich food [16].

6 Experimental Set Up

Dataset: Food Image Collection

The food image dataset has collection of variety of food images comestible and not comestible by diabetic patients like fruits, fast foods etc. The web search image database contained 700 general purpose images including 2 concepts such as Diabetic patient's not comestible and diabetic patient's comestible food. Each class contained about 350 images. For classification the database are divided manually into two classes class I and class II. In class I the diabetic patients not comestible food like fry pork meet, ice cream etc.... In class II the diabetic patient's comestible food like apple-pie, Aloe Vera etc.... If the food is diabetic patients comestible check whether the food is comestible by TYPE:I or TYPE:II diabetic patients after measuring the Gray Level Co-occurrence Value (GLCM). The classification of food images are represented as in Table 2.

Table 2. Classification of diabetic and non diabetic food items

Class I: diabetic patients not comestible food	Aloe vera
	Chocolate cake
	Ice creams
Class II: diabetic patients comestible food	Apple-pic
	Bitter guard
	Chapatti

7 Implementations Analysis

Implementation 1: Color feature extraction

Step 1: Input image
Step 2: Key point extraction from input image
Step 3: 16 × 16 descriptor
  Step 3.1 : 16 × 16 descriptor with in food image
  Step 3.2 : 16 × 16 descriptor extract color features from image
  Step 3.3 : calculate the color histogram values from image such as HistRGB, HistOP, HistRGnorm, HistHue, HistRGBtrans
Step 4: Using clustering algorithm to grouping the similar pixel values
Step 5: Classifier

- Classifier is used to train the dataset images. Classify images into Class I and Class II based on color information.
- Identify the input Image belongs to diabetic patients comestible or not comestible.

Step 6: Using GLCM measures calorie by using contrast, correlation, energy and homogeneity. Finally identify the input image belongs to TYPE:I diabetic patients comestible or TYPE:II diabetic patients comestible. Diabetic food classifications based on color features from input food image is represented in Fig. 7.

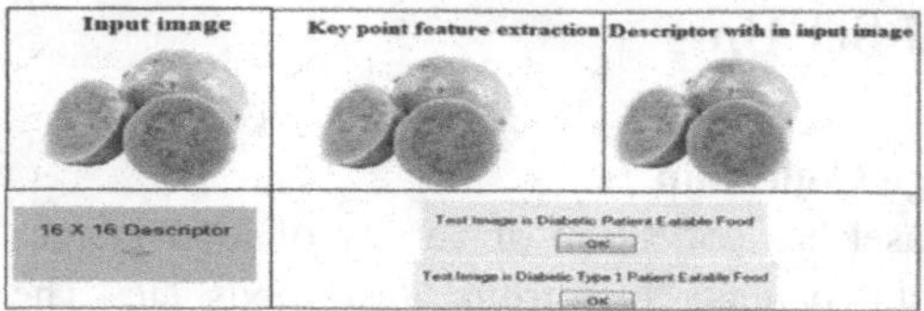

Fig. 7. The color feature extraction results

Implementation 2: Texture feature extraction

- Input image
- Texture feature using GLCM or FFT + GLCM
- Classifier result after texture feature extraction
- Calorie measurement.

Diabetic food classifications based on texture features from input food image is represented in Fig. 8.

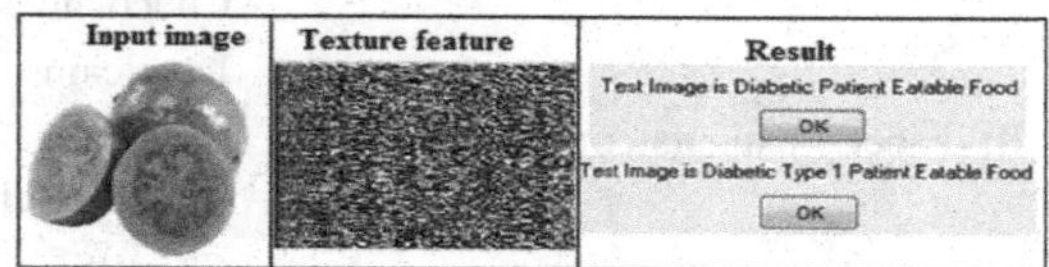

Fig. 8. The texture feature extraction results

8 Performance Analysis Using Metrics

To evaluate the performance for recognition accuracy and significance the following standard metrics are computed [43–45]. The recall refers to the rate of correctly classified foods from the total number of available foods in dataset. The recall value of diabetic food recognition system is evaluated by using the Eq. (36),

$$\mathrm{RE_{call}} = \mathrm{TP_{rate}} = \mathrm{Sensitivity} = \mathrm{R} = \frac{\mathrm{True_{positive}}}{\mathrm{True_{positive}} + \mathrm{False_{negative}}} \tag{36}$$

The precision refers to the rate of relevant foods from the correctly classified foods. The precision of diabetic food recognition system is evaluated by using the Eq. (37),

$$\mathrm{precision} = \mathrm{Positive_{predictive\ value}} = \mathrm{P} = \frac{\mathrm{True_{positive}}}{\mathrm{True_{positive}} + \mathrm{False_{positive}}} \tag{37}$$

Finally, to measure accuracy of diabetic food recognition using both precision and recall, F1 measure is used. The F1 measure of diabetic food recognition system is given in the Eq. (38),

$$F_{measure} = \frac{2PR}{P+R} \tag{38}$$

The Recognition accuracy is a measure of correctly classified images to the total number of images. The recognition accuracy for various classifiers are calculated by using Eq. (39),

$$\text{Recognition accuracy} = \frac{\text{True}_{\text{positive}} + \text{False}_{\text{positive}}}{\text{True}_{\text{positive}} + \text{False}_{\text{positive}} + \text{True}_{\text{negative}} + \text{False}_{\text{negative}}} \tag{39}$$

9 Experimental Results

This section provides a broad report of experimental results as well as the requirement of the proposed optimized TYPE:I and TYPE:II diabetic food recognition system. To assess the performance of the proposed food recognition system for TYPE:I and TYPE: II diabetic patients several experiments are conducted and those results are presented for analysis. For experimentation purpose 6 common foods dataset that are diabetic patient comestible and non comestible. The concepts are fruits, juice, vegetables, snacks, non-veg and mixed foods. The proposed method reveals whether the input food image is TYPE:I or TYPE:II diabetic patient comestible or not comestible.

Experiment 1: Assessment of Color Key Point Extraction and Texture Extraction

In this section of experiment SIFT interest point detector extracts the color key points such as red, green and blue, which use color descriptor. Most of the diabetic patient's comestible and not comestible food has same color. Because of those confusions the color feature values are not sufficient for recognition. So the texture featuresare extracted by using HS, GLCM and FFT + GLCM. Figure 9, shows the sensitivity values for various classifiers with various feature extraction techniques.

The observable depressed performance of SIFT detector, the texture feature extraction helps to generate related features from same group of multiple images. The FFT with GLCM handle transformation as well as the texture feature values. So it gives much better result than other texture features such as HS, GLCM and the SIFT color features. The comparison of color with texture results of classifiers, the texture results are more accurate and reliable compared to color features. The SVM classifier results [10] are low compared to other ELM and BBO classifiers.

Figure 10 discusses some attractive precision results in detail. Classifiers such as SVM, ELM and BBO do not show much difference in precision. But for relative precision ELM is better than SVM. The proposed model BBO reveals that it gives betterresult than the ELM and SVM.

Figure 11 shows the F1 measure for calculating the performance of color and texture features of proposed diabetic food recognition system. It shows the effectiveness of the proposed method with the BBO technique achieves more accuracy.

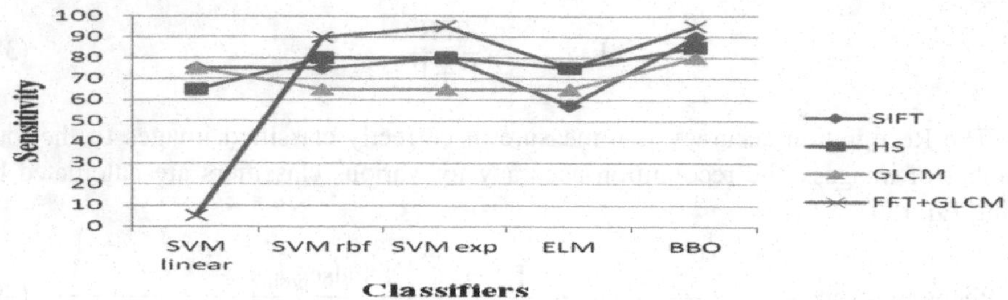

Fig. 9. Sensitivity values for various classifiers with various feature extraction techniques.

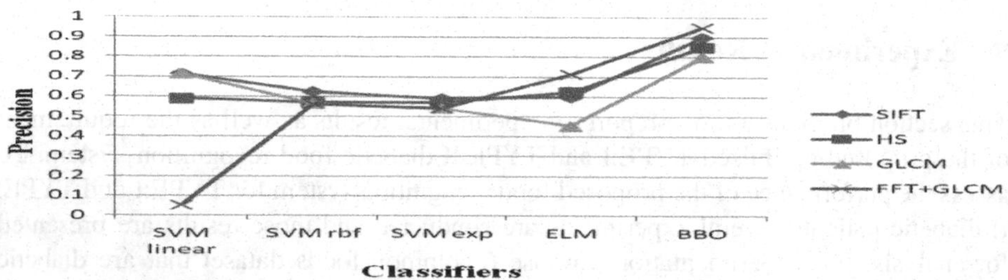

Fig. 10. The precision value various classifiers with various feature extraction methods

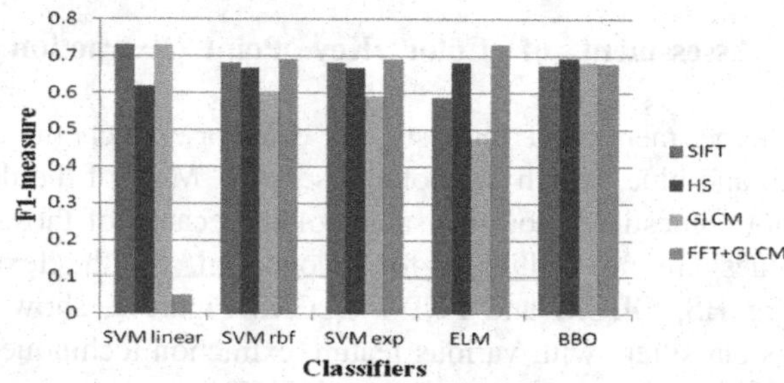

Fig. 11. The F1 measure uses both the precision and recall for calculating performance of color features.

Experiment 2: Comparing Clustering Techniques for Learning the Visual Dictionary
In addition, Table 3 provides a assessment between the three different clustering techniques; k-means, hk-means [10] and Firefly. It is easily observed that Firefly produces more efficient small dictionaries. However, the number of visual words considered to be increases, as same as the hk-means provides equivalent results. At the same time the reduction of computational cost in both training and testing. Table 3 presents the comparison between three clustering techniques. This amazing improvement is suitable to the tree structure of hk-means dictionary. Its results are well-organized and the vector quantization having logarithmic complication with respect to the number of clusters.

Table 3. Comparison between various clustering techniques

Clustering	Computation time	Recognition accuracy
K-means clustering	1.6 s	78%
hk-means clustering	0.03 s	77.6%
Firefly clustering	1.2 s	82%

Experiment 3: Comparing Recognition Accuracy for Various Classifiers

The classifier recognition accuracy can be calculated for various combinations such as Color with Classifier, Texture with Classifier. The Texture FFT feature with Classifier results provides a peak value. Different classes of foods such as Fruits Juice Mixed food non-veg snacks and vegetables with various classifiers accuracy when extracting features using SIFT in color space are shown in Fig. 12. Different classes of foods such as Fruits, Juice, Mixed food, non-veg, snacks and vegetables with various classifiers accuracy while extracting FFT features were shown in Fig. 13. In color the recognition accuracy is 85% for snacks and non-veg. But in texture BBO classifier reach more accuracy for all food items. So the optimization algorithm BBO improves diabetic food classification rate.

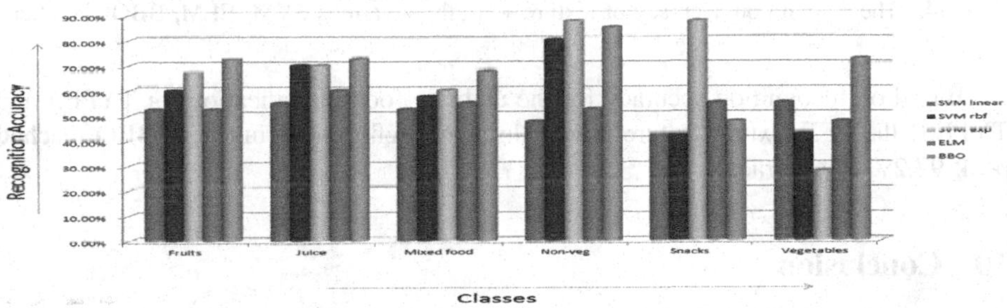

Fig. 12. Different classes of foods such as fruits juice mixed food non-veg snacks and vegetables with various classifiers accuracy when extracting features using SIFT in color space

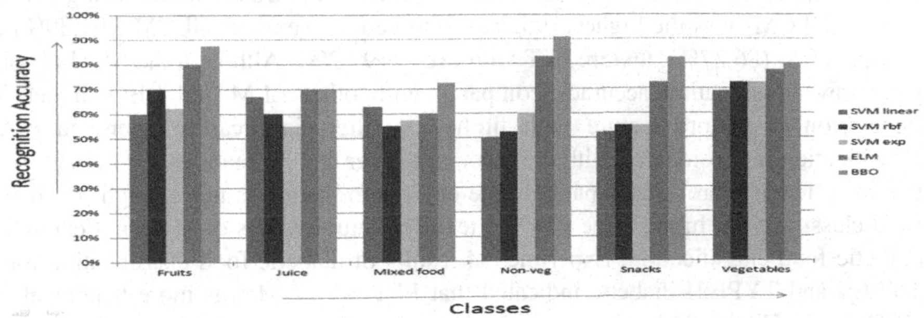

Fig. 13. Different classes of foods such as fruits, juice, mixed food, non-veg, snacks and vegetables with various classifiers

Experiment 4: Optimized Diabetic Food Recognition System for TYPE:I and TYPE:II Diabetic Patients
The recognition accuracy of Texture + Firefly + Various SVM, ELM, BBO Classifiers are shown in Fig. 14.

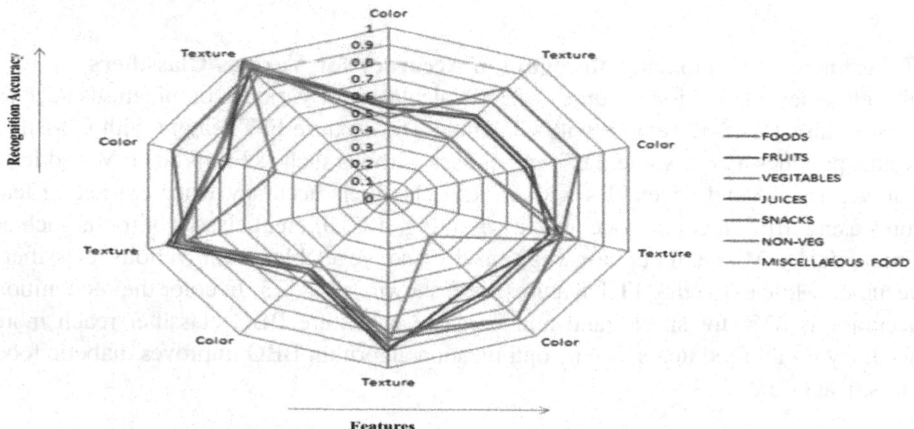

Fig. 14. The recognition accuracy of texture + firefly + various SVM, ELM, BBO classifiers

Based on recognition accuracy for the diabetic food classification for TYPE:I and TYPE:II the FFT texture feature passes through firefly clustering with BBO reached peak 97.2% of accuracy.

10 Conclusion

ELM and BBO were used for classifying the diabetic patient comestible and not comestible foods based on Color (RGB) and Texture. The image color features using SIFT and textural features using HS, GLCM and FFT + GLCM were extracted from food images. The average classification accuracy of BBO model using Texture (FFT + GLCM) was the highest (95.7%) followed by Texture (GLCM) (91.39%) and Texture (HS) (86.37%), texture FFT with firefly (97.2%). Although the SVM classifier gave low classification accuracy compared with other ELM and BBO model. The integration of texture feature with firefly classifier significantly improved correct classification rate compared with the color and other texture features used alone. When the color features are used separately the color information is not enough for diabetic food classification. In the same way the texture feature values only are not enough for diabetic food classification. Experimental results of diabetic food classification for the TYPE:I and TYPE:II diabetic indicated that FFT + GLCM was more beneficial than GLCM and HS used alone in diabetic food classification. In addition, the fusion of textural features had better classification performance than single feature extraction in the classification of diabetic patient's foods. Further studied can be carried out for improving the classification power of this technique at medical fields so that this technique can be used in online and offline evaluation of diabetic patient's food worth.

References

1. Feinman, R.D., et al.: Dietary carbohydrate restriction as the first approach in diabetes management: critical review and evidence base. Nutrition **31**(1), 1–13 (2015)
2. Al-Khalifa, A., et al.: Low carbohydrate ketogenic diet prevents the induction of diabetes using streptozotocin in rats. Exp. Toxicol. Pathol. **63**(7), 663–669 (2011)
3. Westman, E.C., Vernon, M.C.: Has carbohydrate-restriction been forgotten as a treatment for diabetes mellitus? A perspective on the ACCORD study design. Nutr. Metab. **5**(1), 10 (2008)
4. Rizvi, A.A.: Nutritional challenges in the elderly with diabetes. Int. J. Diab. Mellitus **1**(1), 26–31 (2009)
5. Crume, T.L., et al.: Timing of complementary food introduction and age at diagnosis of type 1 diabetes: the search nutrition ancillary study (SNAS). Eur. J. Clin. Nutr. **68**(11), 1258 (2014)
6. Smart, C.E., et al.: Children and adolescents on intensive insulin therapy maintain postprandial glycaemic control without precise carbohydrate counting. Diab. Med. **26**(3), 279–285 (2009)
7. Zhu, F., et al.: The use of mobile devices in aiding dietary assessment and evaluation. IEEE J. Sel. Top. Signal process. **4**(4), 756–766 (2010)
8. Nielsen, J.V., Joensson, E.A.: Low-carbohydrate diet in type 2 diabetes: stable improvement of bodyweight and glycemic control during 44 months follow-up. Nutr. Metab. **5**(1), 14 (2008)
9. Kanchana, M., Bharath, M., Jaffar, K.S.: Automatic food recognition system for diabetic patients. Int. J. Innov. Res. Sci. Technol. **1** (2015)
10. Anthimopoulos, M.M., et al.: A food recognition system for diabetic patients based on an optimized bag-of-features model. IEEE J. Biomed. Health Inf. **18**(4), 1261–1271 (2014)
11. Pouladzadeh, P., Shirmohammadi, S., Yassine, A.: Using graph cut segmentation for food calorie measurement. In: 2014 IEEE International Symposium on Medical Measurements and Applications (MeMeA). IEEE (2014)
12. Pouladzadeh, P., et al.: A novel SVM based food recognition method for calorie measurement applications. In: 2012 IEEE International Conference on Multimedia and Expo Workshops (ICMEW). IEEE (2012)
13. Pollak, J., et al.: It's time to eat! Using mobile games to promote healthy eating. IEEE Pervasive Comput. **9**(3), 21–27 (2010)
14. Konaje, N.K.: Food recognition and calorie extraction using Bag-of-SURF and spatial pyramid matching methods (2013)
15. Martin, C.K., Kaya, S., Gunturk, B.K.: Quantification of food intake using food image analysis. In: Engineering in Medicine and Biology Society 2009, EMBC 2009, Annual International Conference of the IEEE. IEEE (2009)
16. Puri, M., et al.: Recognition and volume estimation of food intake using a mobile device. In: Workshop on Applications of Computer Vision (WACV) 2009. IEEE (2009)
17. El-Gayar, M.M., Soliman, H.: A comparative study of image low level feature extraction algorithms. Egypt. Inf. J. **14**(2), 175–181 (2013)

18. Rahman, M.H., Chowdhury, S., Bashar, M.A.: An automatic face detection and gender classification from color images using support vector machine. J. Emerg. Trends Comput. Inf. Sci. **4**(1), 5–11 (2013)
19. Liu, T., et al.: Extraction of color-intensity feature towards image authentication. J. Shanghai Univ. (Engl. Ed.) **14**(5), 337–342 (2010)
20. Azeem, A., et al.: Hexagonal scale invariant feature transform (H-SIFT) for facial feature extraction. J. Appl. Res. Technol. **13**(3), 402–408 (2015)
21. Zuchun, D.: An effective keypoint selection algorithm in SIFT (2013)
22. Rudinac, M., Lenseigne, B., Jonker, P.: Keypoint extraction and selection for object recognition. In: MVA (2009)
23. Huo, G., Liu, Y., Zhu, X., Wang, H., Yu, L., He, F., Gao, S., Dong, H.: An effective iris recognition method based on scale invariant feature transformation. In: Sun, Z., Shan, S., Sang, H., Zhou, J., Wang, Y., Yuan, W. (eds.) CCBR 2014. LNCS, vol. 8833, pp. 301–310. Springer, Cham (2014). https://doi.org/10.1007/978-3-319-12484-1_34
24. Slot, K., Kim, H.: Keypoints derivation for object class detection with SIFT algorithm. In: Rutkowski, L., Tadeusiewicz, R., Zadeh, L.A., Żurada, J.M. (eds.) ICAISC 2006. LNCS (LNAI), vol. 4029, pp. 850–859. Springer, Heidelberg (2006). https://doi.org/10.1007/11785231_89
25. Lowe, D.G.: Distinctive image features from scale-invariant keypoints. Int. J. Comput. Vis. **60**(2), 91–110 (2004)
26. Barata, C., Marques, J.S., Rozeira, J.: Evaluation of color based keypoints and features for the classification of melanomas using the bag-of-features model. In: Bebis, G., Boyle, R., Parvin, B., Koracin, D., Li, B., Porikli, F., Zordan, V., Klosowski, J., Coquillart, S., Luo, X., Chen, M., Gotz, D. (eds.) ISVC 2013. LNCS, vol. 8033, pp. 40–49. Springer, Heidelberg (2013). https://doi.org/10.1007/978-3-642-41914-0_5
27. Tao, Y., et al.: A texture extraction technique using 2D-DFT and Hamming distance. In: Proceedings of the Fifth International Conference on Computational Intelligence and Multimedia Applications 2003, ICCIMA 2003. IEEE (2003)
28. Pu, H., et al.: Classification of fresh and frozen-thawed pork muscles using visible and near infrared hyperspectral imaging and textural analysis. Meat Sci. **99**, 81–88 (2015)
29. DeCost, B.L., Holm, E.A.: A computer vision approach for automated analysis and classification of microstructural image data. Comput. Mater. Sci. **110**, 126–133 (2015)
30. Bariamis, D.G., et al.: An FPGA-based architecture for real time image feature extraction. In: Proceedings of the 17th International Conference on Pattern Recognition 2004, ICPR 2004, vol. 1. IEEE (2004)
31. Nalamothu, A., Kalluri, H.K.: Texture based palmprint recognition using simple methods. Int. J. Comput. Appl. **50**(4) (2012)
32. Malik, F., Baharudin, B.: The statistical quantized histogram texture features analysis for image retrieval based on median and laplacian filters in the dct domain. IAJIT First Online Publication (2012)
33. Qiao, J., et al.: Predicting mechanical properties of fried chicken nuggets using image processing and neural network techniques. J. Food Eng. **79**(3), 1065–1070 (2007)
34. Guru, D.S., Kumar, Y.S., Manjunath, S.: Textural features in flower classification. Math. Comput. Model. **54**(3), 1030–1036 (2011)
35. Coates, A., Ng, A.Y.: Learning feature representations with k-means. In: Montavon, G., Orr, G.B., Müller, K.-R. (eds.) Neural Networks: Tricks of the Trade. LNCS, vol. 7700, pp. 561–580. Springer, Heidelberg (2012). https://doi.org/10.1007/978-3-642-35289-8_30
36. Tian, H.-X., Mao, Z.-Z.: An ensemble ELM based on modified AdaBoost. RT algorithm for predicting the temperature of molten steel in ladle furnace. IEEE Trans. Autom. Sci. Eng. **7** (1), 73–80 (2010)

37. Zhou, Y., Jiangtao, P., Chen, C.L.P.: Extreme learning machine with composite kernels for hyperspectral image classification. IEEE J. Sel. Topics Appl. Earth Obser. Remote Sens. **8** (6), 2351–2360 (2015)
38. Huang, G.-B., Zhu, Q.-Y., Siew, C.-K.: Extreme learning machine: theory and applications. Neurocomputing **70**(1), 489–501 (2006)
39. López-Fandiño, J., et al.: Efficient ELM-based techniques for the classification of hyperspectral remote sensing images on commodity GPUs. IEEE J. Sel. Topics Appl. Earth Obser. Remote Sens. **8**(6), 2884–2893 (2015)
40. Jain, J., Singh, R.: Biogeographic-based optimization algorithm for load dispatch in power system. Int. J. Emerg. Technol. Adv. Eng. **3**(7), 549–553 (2013)
41. Farswan, P., Bansal, J.C., Deep, K.: A modified biogeography based optimization. In: Kim, J.H., Geem, Z.W. (eds.) Harmony Search Algorithm. AISC, vol. 382, pp. 227–238. Springer, Heidelberg (2016). https://doi.org/10.1007/978-3-662-47926-1_22
42. Zheng, Y.-J., et al.: Localized biogeography-based optimization. Soft. Comput. **18**(11), 2323–2334 (2014)
43. Sumathi, T., Karthik, S., Marikannan, M.: Performance analysis of classification methods for opinion mining. Int. J. Innov. Eng. Technol. (IJIET) **2**(4), 171–177 (2013)
44. Mishra, P., Lotia, P.: Comparative performance analysis of SVM speaker verification system using confusion matrix. Int. J. Sci. Res. (IJSR), **3**(12) (2014)
45. Venkatesan, E., Velmurugan, T.: Perfomance anaysis of decision tree algorithm for brest cancer classification. Indian J. Sci. Technol. **8**(29), 1–8 (2015)

Distributional Semantic Phrase Clustering and Conceptualization Using Probabilistic Knowledgebase

V. S. Anoop[1(✉)] and S. Asharaf[2]

[1] Data Engineering Lab, Indian Institute of Information Technology and Management – Kerala (IIITM-K), Thiruvananthapuram, India
anoop.res15@iiitmk.ac.in
[2] Indian Institute of Information Technology and Management – Kerala (IIITM-K), Thiruvananthapuram, India
asharaf.s@iiitmk.ac.in

Abstract. Distributional Semantics is an active research area in natural language processing (NLP) that develop methods for quantifying semantic similarities between linguistic elements in large samples of data. Short text conceptualization on the other hand is a technique for enriching short texts so that it become more interpretable. This is needed because most text mining tasks including topic modeling and clustering are based on statistical methods and won't consider the semantics of text. This paper proposes a novel framework for combining distributional semantics and short text conceptualization for better interpretability of phrases in text data. Experiments on real-world datasets show that this method can better enrich phrases that are represented in distributional semantic spaces.

Keywords: Distributional semantics · Short text conceptualization
Concept extraction · Phrase2vec · Natural language processing
Text mining

1 Introduction

Most of the text mining algorithms such as clustering, classification and topic modeling are based on statistical methods that will not consider the semantics or meaning of words. For example, the topics which are generated from a traditional topic modeling algorithm such as LDA is always clusters of words which is based on simple probability distribution. Similar to this, many state of the art natural language processing (NLP) algorithms do not consider the relation between words or phrases rather simply treat them as a bag of words. Even though such systems are simple and easy to train and operate, the lack of meaning awareness makes it difficult to interpret the outputs.

One technique in natural language processing that got attention from researchers and practitioners is the distributed representation of natural language elements such as words and phrases in high dimensional vector space. This representation could make use of semantic similarities between those items in that vector space. One seminal approach that explored this idea and developed beyond traditional syntactic or simple

P. Bhattacharyya et al. (Eds.): NGCT 2017, CCIS 827, pp. 526–534, 2018.
https://doi.org/10.1007/978-981-10-8657-1_39

probability based approach was the work introduced by Tomas Mikolov which represented words in high dimensional vector spaces [1]. This paper introduced two strong models – Continuous Bag of Words (CBOW) and Skip-gram. Unlike simple bag-of-words model, CBOW model uses continuous distributed representation of the context. This model could predict the current word based on the context. The second model, skip-gram model tries to maximize classification of a word based on another word in the same sentence [1]. These models were developed to be work with word unigrams initially, but later approaches for distributed representations for phrases [2], sentences, paragraphs and even documents [3] have been introduced.

On the other hand, short text conceptualization has been explored by text mining research community for better interpretation of short texts such as phrases which are leveraged from unstructured text data. As discussed earlier, most of the machine learning tasks such as clustering and topic modeling require bag-of-words as input and as a result the meaning in the text is largely ignored by these algorithms. As the short texts lack enough surroundings from which conclusions can be drawn, it is always challenging and useful to conceptualize short texts for better interpretation.

Contributions of this Paper: The main contributions of this paper are summarized as follows:

1. Proposes a novel framework that combines distributional vector representation of phrases in high dimensional vector space and then do a phrase clustering that retains the semantic relationships between those phrases.
2. Uses a probabilistic knowledge base to conceptualize those distributed representation of phrases so that more interpretable concepts can be leveraged.
3. Experiments conducted on real-world datasets shows that better conceptualization of short texts are possible if a semantics preserving clusters of those phrases can be done prior to the conceptualization.

Organization of this Paper: The remainder of this paper is organized as follows: Sect. 2 discusses some of the very recent approaches in distributed representation of linguistic items and approaches in short text conceptualization. Section 3 outlines the research objective. We define the problem in Sects. 4 and 5 details our proposed framework. Section 6 describes the experimental setup, a detailed evaluation of the results are given in Sects. 7 and 8 gives conclusions and discusses future work.

2 Related Work

In this section, we briefly discusses some recent works in distributed representation of words and phrases and also short text conceptualization, which are very close to our proposed framework. The seminal paper in this dimension that got high attention was the one by Milokov et al. in which the authors proposed a method for efficient estimation of word representations in vector space [1]. The paper proposed two architectures that are Continuous Bag-of-Words (CBOW) model and Skip-gram model, in which the former uses a continuous distributed representation of the context and the latter maximizes the classification of a word based on another word in the same sentence [1]. The CBOW model predicts the current word given a context, and the skip-gram architecture predicts the context given the current word. When compared the results with a traditional bag-of-words, their approach showed significant improvements over BOW approach.

The next paper again by Milokov and team proposed an approach for learning distributed representation of phrases. Their earlier approach was only concerned about the word unigrams and the hypothesis of this new approach was that a large number of phrases have a meaning that cannot be easily obtained by combining the meaning of their individual words [2]. This method first find out words that appear frequently together and very infrequent in other contexts and then trains the Skip-gram model using those n-grams.

Another work which represents sentences and paragraphs in distributed vector space was proposed in 2014 [3]. This paper proposed paragraph vectors that could learn distributed vector representations of pieces of text and the length of the text can be ranging from a sentence to a complete document. One significant advantage of these paragraph vector is that it will be created from unlabeled data thus works well in those situations where not enough labeled data is available. Because of these successful representations ranging from word to paragraph or even documents, the codes published by Google where these ideas were formulated attracted by the text mining and NLP communities. Google's word2vec[1] and phrase2vec are being heavily downloaded and used for creating word and phrase vectors which can be directly used as input for other machine learning and NLP algorithms. In this work we make use of Google's phrase2vec algorithm to create the distributed representation of phrases but using a Python wrapper for the same.

Short text conceptualization is another research area that got attention from text mining communities recently. Most of the text mining tasks such as clustering and topic modeling treat text input as bag-of-words and operate on them using statistical methods to generate the output. During this, the semantics of the text is lost heavily and interpretation of the results are difficult since the contextual information is missing. Song et al. proposed a method for short text conceptualization [4] using a probabilistic knowledgebase. They developed a Bayesian inference based approach for conceptualizing words and short texts. When compared to pure statistical methods, their approach [4] showed significant improvements. Another significant work was proposed by Wu et al. that aimed at constructing a probabilistic knowledge-base called Probase [5]. They presented a universal taxonomy that is probabilistic in nature but much more comprehensive than already existing knowledge-bases. The major attractiveness of their approach is that while traditional taxonomies treat knowledge as black and white, their method could model ambiguous, uncertain and inconsistent information also. Another short text understanding method [6] was proposed by Hua et al. and their method used lexical semantic analysis for conceptualization. This lexical semantic knowledge was provided by a semantic network. The advantage of their method is that they could perform text segmentation, parts-of-speech tagging and concept labeling by inducing semantics into the process.

[1] https://code.google.com/archive/p/word2vec/.

In this proposed work, we also make use of a probabilistic knowledgebase called Probase for conceptualizing phrases that are represented in a distributed high dimensional vector space.

3 Research Objective

The following are our main research objectives:

1. Introduce the task of distributed representation of phrases and short text conceptualization and its relevance in text mining and real-world problems.
2. Propose a framework for combining distributed phrase representation and conceptualization of short texts such as phrases for producing better interpretable phrases.
3. Verify experimentally the effectiveness of the method using real-world unstructured datasets.

4 Problem Definition

Here, we define our problem formally. Given a static unstructured text corpus containing 'n' documents, D = $\{d_1, d_2, \ldots, d_n\}$ our task is to represent the phrases of these documents in a distributional vector space. We then model the similarities between phrases as the cosine distance between those phrase vectors. After that, a meaning aware clustering will be performed on those vectors so that each cluster may contain semantically rich and highly related phrases. We then make use of a probabilistic knowledge-base for enriching those phrases so that better human interpretation will be possible and can create a higher level hierarchy of phrases and concepts.

5 Proposed Framework

In this section, we propose our framework that combines distributed representation of phrases and probabilistic knowledge-base for creating highly human interpretable phrases and concepts. The complete workflow of the proposed approach is shown in Fig. 1. Our proposed framework contain five steps that are ranging from pre-processing of the corpus to the short text conceptualization. A detailed description of each of these steps are given in this section.

5.1 Corpus Pre-processing

As most of the unstructured text data sources contain noises and irrelevant or junk characters, we need to do a thorough pre-processing before proceeding to the actual computation. In this step, we have removed all the stop words such as "a", "and" etc.

and the digits, special characters etc. are also removed. This has been done for each and every documents in the corpus and the cleanses data is written onto new files and made an experiment ready copy of the corpus.

5.2 Phrase Tagging

In this step, we have identified common phrases from each of the document and tagged them. Natural Language Processing rules have been used for the identification of such phrases. Firstly, a Parts-of-Speech (POS) tagging has been done on the pre-processed corps and identified Nouns, Adjective and Verbs tags from the POS tagged list. This is because when we analyze, majority of the phrases are composed of the combinations of these POS tags. For example, the phrase "super computer" is the combination of the word "super" which is tagged as "JJ" (adjective) and "computer" is tagged as "NN" (noun). All such POS tag combinations that we have used for this phase is shown in Table 1. Once we identify the phrases using these POS rules, we tag and combine those word unigrams with an underscore sign (_) in between them. For example, the words "super" and "computer" will be combined as "super_computer" and tagged as a phrase.

Table 1. List of POS rules used for phrase tagging.

Sl. no	Pattern	Sl. no	Pattern
1	JJ + NN	7	NN + VB
2	JJ + NNS	8	NN + VBG
3	JJ + VBG	9	NN + VBN
4	JJR + VBG	10	NNP + NNS
5	NN + NN	11	NNS + VB
6	NN + NNS	12	NNS + VBG

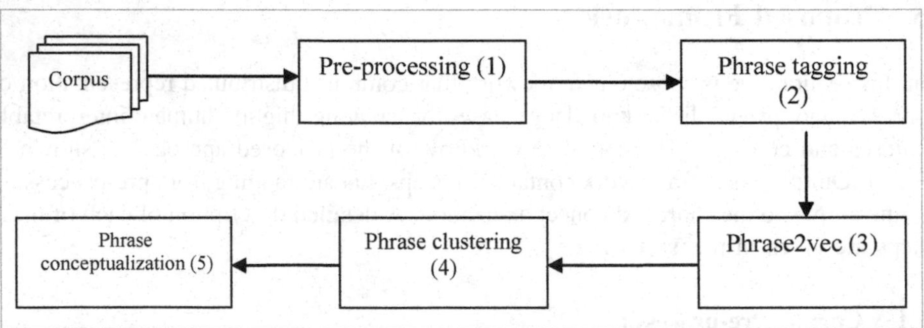

Fig. 1. Proposed framework for distributed representation of phrases and short text conceptualization model.

5.3 Phrase2Vec Training and Phrase Clustering

Once we tag phrases, then we need to train a model using our corpus for representing those tagged phrases in the distributed vector space. We are using the approach discussed in Milokov's paper [2] to create the distributed phrase vectors. The phrases are represented in vector space along with the context so that the similarity between any two phrases can be easily drawn as the cosine angle between those two vectors. Once the model is trained, our next aim is to do a clustering of those vectors so that each cluster may contain a collection of phrases that are very closely related. We apply K-means clustering algorithm on top of these vectors to produce the desired number of clusters. For this experiment, we have used varying values for "K", the number of clusters, ranging from 50 to 100.

5.4 Phrase Conceptualization

In this step, we do short text (phrase) conceptualization for better understanding and interpretation of the phrases. The advantage of the proposed method is that along with the cosine vector similarity of the phrase2vec model, we are able to connect related concepts for a given phrase. For conceptualization, we are using Microsoft's concept tagging or conceptualization model [4] using the probabilistic knowledge base called Probase [5]. Probase is a big graph of concepts and those knowledge are acquired from billions of webpages. Given each phrase, we use Probase [5] to query and find related concepts of each phrase. For example for the phrase "computer network", we may get concepts such as "large network setting", "signal transmission network", "communication system" etc. as the concepts.

Pseudo Code for the Proposed Method

1. Pre-process the corpus (remove stop-words, special characters, digits and url)
2. POS Tagging of documents in the corpus
3. Take all possible combinations of NN + NN, JJ + NN etc. as given in Table 1 and tag those concepts in the corpus
4. Train the corpus using phrase2vec
5. Perform K – means clustering on the resultant vectors
6. For each of these phrase vectors, find semantically similar phrases using cosine similarity
7. Conceptualize each of these phrases using Probase
8. Visualize the phrase graphs.

6 Experimental Setup

This section details the experimental setup we have used for the proposed framework.

6.1 Datasets Used

For this current experiment, we have used two different datasets – the BBC dataset, and much larger Reuters 21578 dataset. The BBC dataset consist of 2225 unstructured text documents extracted directly from their website that corresponds to five different areas such as entertainment, business, politics, sports and technology. These documents were extracted for the period starting from 2004 to 2005. The next dataset Reuters 21578 is a newswire corpus which is popular among text mining communities. The collection was made available for research purposes in 1990.

6.2 Experimental Testbed

All methods discussed in this paper were executed on a server configured with AMD Opteron 6376 @ 2.3 GHz having 16 core processor and 16 GB of main memory. Firstly we have removed all stopwords from the documents and this was implemented using Python NLTK (Natural Language Tool Kit) [10] and used the NLTK provided stopword list [9] for English language. Then POS tagging was performed on those text data. Custom made scripts using Python 2.7 are used for finding out phrases using NLP rules given in Table 1. Once phrases are identified and tagged on the corpus, we used the python wrapper for training phrase2vec using the publicly available repository, https://github.com/zseymour/phrase2vec. Then we perform a K – means clustering [12] on these trained phrase2vec model and scikit.learn machine learning toolkit [11] is used for creating phrase clusters. We randomly choose the value of K and we started with 50 and later the values of K has been increased up to 100. For short text conceptualization, this work makes use of concept graph API provided by Microsoft which can be accessed using the URL - https://concept.research.microsoft.com/Home/API.

7 Results and Evaluation

This section presents result and a detailed evaluation of our proposed framework. Table 2 shows some of the phrases that we have extracted from the corpus using our phrase identification and tagging procedure. For measuring the relatedness of the enriched phrases, we have conducted a crowd-sourcing experiment.

Crowd-sourcing has been applied to tasks such as automated question answering [8] and ontology alignment [9] and proven to be efficient where we need human cognition to validate computer generated output. For this experiment a web based interface has been created that will present the conceptualized phrases along with the connected phrases and entities used for conceptualization. We asked the users to positively reward every conceptualized phrase if they seems to be semantically valid and negative rewards will be given to those invalid phrases. We have used Fleiss Kappa score [7] for the inter-annotator agreement.

Table 3 shows the result of short text conceptualization of some of the phrases that we have identified and extracted using our proposed framework.

Table 2. List of extracted phrases for BBC Technology domain using NLP rules.

Sl. no	Phrase	Sl. no	Phrase
1	Internet_connection	7	Dialup_internet
2	Internet_networks	8	Dialup_phone
3	Broadband_internet	9	Dialup_connection
4	Broadband_networks	10	Web_search
5	Networks_connection	11	Netflix_company
6	Phone_connection	12	Lowcost_mobiles

Table 3. Result of conceptualization using Microsoft Concept Graph API

Sl. no	Phrase	Conceptualized result
1	Internet_connection	Modern communication facility
		Configure computer equipment
		Packet switching application
2	Internet_networks	Static network
		Communication network
		Datum network
3	Broadband_internet	Telecommunication service
		High bandwidth datum communication
		Modern datum service
4	Broadband_networks	Information technology
		Digital medium platform
		Second communication network

8 Conclusions and Future Work

This paper proposed a novel framework that combines distributed semantic representation of phrases in high dimensional vector space and conceptualization of those phrases using probabilistic knowledgebase. In between the vector representation and conceptualization, a K-means clustering has been performed that will create clusters of semantically similar and related phrases. Experiments on large and real-world dataset shows that the proposed method can better conceptualize phrases in a high dimensional vector space and better interpretation of the phrases and context are possible that may increase the accuracy of existing probability based machine learning and natural language processing tasks.

References

1. Mikolov, T., Chen, K., Corrado, G., Dean, J.: Efficient estimation of word representations in vector space. arXiv preprint arXiv:1301.3781 (2013)
2. Mikolov, T., Sutskever, I., Chen, K., Corrado, G.S., Dean, J.: Distributed representations of words and phrases and their compositionality. In: Advances in Neural Information Processing Systems, pp. 3111–3119 (2013)

3. Le, Q., Mikolov, T.: Distributed representations of sentences and documents. In: Proceedings of the 31st International Conference on Machine Learning (ICML-2014), pp. 1188–1196 (2014)
4. Song, Y., Wang, H., Wang, Z., Li, H., Chen, W.: Short text conceptualization using a probabilistic knowledgebase. In: Proceedings of the Twenty-Second International Joint Conference on Artificial Intelligence-Volume, vol. 3, pp. 2330–2336. AAAI Press, July 2011
5. Wu, W., Li, H., Wang, H., Zhu, K.Q.: Probase: a probabilistic taxonomy for text understanding. In: Proceedings of the 2012 ACM SIGMOD International Conference on Management of Data, pp. 481–492. ACM, May 2012
6. Hua, W., Wang, Z., Wang, H., Zheng, K., Zhou, X.: Short text understanding through lexical-semantic analysis. In: 2015 IEEE 31st International Conference on Data Engineering (ICDE), pp. 495–506. IEEE, April 2015
7. Fleiss, J.L., Cohen, J.: The equivalence of weighted kappa and the intraclass correlation coefficient as measures of reliability. Educ. Psychol. Meas. **33**(3), 613–619 (1973)
8. Mrozinski, J., Whittaker, E., Furui, S.: Collecting a why-question corpus for development and evaluation of an automatic QA-system. In: 46th Annual Meeting of the Association of Computational Linguistics: Human Language Technologies, pp. 443–451 (2008)
9. Sarasua, C., Simperl, E., Noy, N.F.: Crowdmap: crowdsourcing ontology alignment with microtasks. In: International Semantic Web Conference, pp. 525–541 (2012)
10. Bird, S.: NLTK: the natural language toolkit. In: Proceedings of the COLING/ACL on Interactive Presentation Sessions, pp. 69–72. Association for Computational Linguistics, July 2006
11. Pedregosa, F., Varoquaux, G., Gramfort, A., Michel, V., Thirion, B., Grisel, O., Blondel, M., et al.: Scikit-learn: machine learning in Python. J. Mach. Learn. Res. **12**, 2825–2830 (2011)
12. Hartigan, J.A., Wong, M.A.: Algorithm AS 136: a k-means clustering algorithm. J. Roy. Stat. Soc. Series C (Appl. Stat.) **28**(1), 100–108 (1979)

Pong Game Optimization Using Policy Gradient Algorithm

Aditya Singh(✉) and Vishal Gupta

BML Munjal University, National Highway 8 67 Km Milestone, Gurgaon 122413, Haryana, India
aditya.deep.singh14@gmail.com, vishal.gupta.14cs@bml.edu.in

Abstract. Pong game was the titanic of the gaming industry in 20th century. Pong is the perfect example of deep reinforcement learning of ATARI game [1]. The game is extremely beneficial to improve concentration and memory capacity. Since the game is played by around 350 million people worldwide at present scenario, hence we saw the opportunity in this interesting game. The project has a great scope in atari game development. We proposed a stochastic reinforcement learning technique of Policy Gradient algorithm to optimize Pong game. The purpose of this study is to improve the algorithms that control the game structure, mechanism and real-time dynamics. We implemented policy gradient algorithm to improve the performance and training which is significantly better than traditional genetic algorithm.

Keywords: Machine learning · Reinforcement learning Policy gradient algorithm · Stochastic policy · Deep Q-Networks Feed forward neural network · Back propagation · Markov decision process Pong game optimization · Efficient training

1 Introduction

The global games market is estimated to cross $130 billion in 2020 with mobile alone taking almost 50%. Pong is the perfect example of deep reinforcement learning and neural network. It is even one of the game which checks the popularity of the game-store i.e. if the pong kind of game is available on a certain platform, then it might be a popular platform. Hence now we certainly agree that the algorithm behind the pong must be improved in order to give better and efficient performance to users. In order to achieve our desired goals, we trained AI bot of pong by implementing Policy Gradient algorithm and neural networks. The algorithm was efficient enough to train the bot in 6–7 h on cloud which is far better than genetic algorithm which take 4–5 weeks.

P. Bhattacharyya et al. (Eds.): NGCT 2017, CCIS 827, pp. 535–548, 2018.
https://doi.org/10.1007/978-981-10-8657-1_40

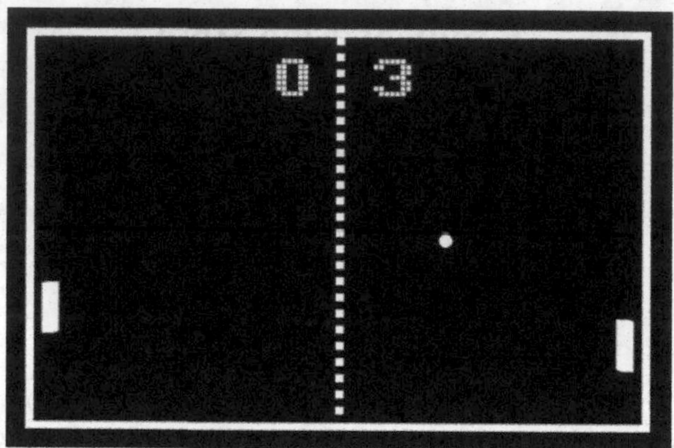

Visual appearance of Pong Game.

2 Pong-the Game

Pong was the first game to earn mass popularity and provided great momentum to video game industry. It was first developed by Atari games in 1972. The motive of the game was to be as a means to practice table tennis in one's free time. The game is very simple. They are two sliding bars on the ends of the screen which can move either vertically or horizontally based on the orientation of the game. One of the slider is controlled by the player and the other one is either controlled by AI driven computer program or another player. The player wins a point if the opponent fails to return the ball to the player. The winning score was meant to be eleven.

Initially the game was played on the special devices (see Fig. 1 below). But as the game started creating huge number of engagements in the market, Atari started giving license to other companies to develop the games on other platforms. Soon, the game was playable in personal televisions at home. After the success of the pong in the market, atari games released several other editions of the game such as home pong chip, super pong etc. These were the dedicated consoles and were used by players at the convenience of being at home. It had 4 different variations of the game compared to the primitive version of the pong. Players used to enjoy for countless hours and it provided amazing gameplay experience to them.

Today pong is available on all major platforms such as: Windows, Android, iPhone, Blackberry etc. The game is vastly played by huge number of people. There are many vendors holding the license of the game. The game is still the favourite of large number of players.

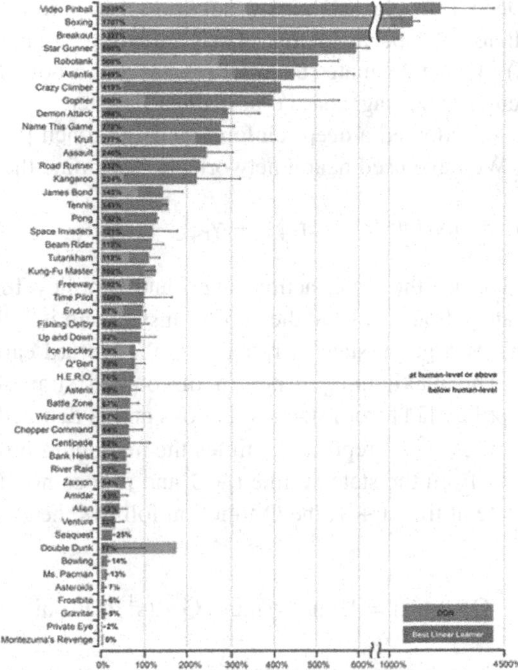

Fig. 1. Atari game market analysis.

3 Research Background

Now let's briefly go through the various methods and techniques involved during the research. We had used stochastic [21] Markov Decision model for our Pong Agent. We need to apply policy gradient algorithm which is a simple Reinforcement learning technique at a broader scale. Since we had two hidden layers in our training model, i.e. required implementing feed forward network and back propagation to produce results. In order to avoid weights being converged or diverged, we also need to apply Xavier initialization for the layers. In our setting of our training model, we have set the hyper parameters and discount reward to generate policies. For the calculation of the dot product of the first layer, we applied ReLU function and for second layer, we converted the numeric values into the appropriate probability by sigmoid [21] functions [22]. In case of the back propagation, we dealt with the derivatives of layers.

3.1 Deep Reinforcement Learning

Machine learning method derived from traditional hit and trial, consigning reward or punishment depending upon the correct hit or error is called reinforcement learning [2]. Just like human beings, the machine bots learn and expand their knowledge-set directly from the level of their measurement such as by vision, sensors and without any hand-engineered features or domain heuristics. This is achieved by deep learning of neural networks. Deep learning and neural networks [3] currently provide the best solution in this field of specialization. The following graph shows the Deep Q-Networks (DQN) [4] that estimates the total reward that a bot can expect to receive after taking a particular action against the best linear learner.

For this project, we adopted a deep reinforcement approach [5, 18] very similar to the one used [3, 4]. We have used neural networks to determine the following function

$$Q*(s, a) = \max \pi E[r_t + \gamma r_{t+1} + \gamma_{t+2} + \ldots | s_t = s, a_t = a, \pi \tag{1}$$

where s_t and a_t and π are the state, action taken and a policy function respectively specifying appropriate action to take at the current instant and is followed at every step from t + 1 onwards. At a given state s_t, r_t and γ is the reward earned and a discount factor respectively. The maximum prospected discounted sum of future rewards is obtained by a fixed policy [11] from states to actions and is denoted by Q function [6]. The term $\gamma r_{t+1} + \gamma^2 r_{t+2} + \ldots$ represent γ times the maximum prospected discounted sum of future rewards from the state at time t + 1 and it does not depend on s, a, or r_t but simply on the state at time t + 1, the Q function follows the Bellman equation and can expressed as:

$$Q*(s, a) = Es'[r + \gamma \max_{a'} Q*(s^1, a')|s, ai] \tag{2}$$

Where s' is the state (or possible states, if the process is nondeterministic) that results from taking action a given state s, and a' is the action taken given state s'.

In order to train the network, Q-learning updates are applied on mini batches of experience, drawn at random from the replay memory. The Q-learning update at iteration i uses the following loss function [6].

$$Li(\theta i) = E(s, a, r, s') \sim U(D)[(r + \gamma \max_{a'} Q(s', a'; \theta - i) - Q(s, a; \theta_i)) \tag{3}$$

Here γ is the discount factor determining the agent's horizon, θi are the parameters of the Q-network at iteration i and θ − i are the network parameters used to compute the target at iteration i. Differentiating the loss function [4, 6] with respect to the network weights gives the following gradient:

$$\nabla \theta i L(\theta i) = Es, a, r, s'[(r + \gamma \max_{a'} Q(s', a'; \theta - i) - Q(s, a; \theta) \nabla \theta_i Q(s, a; \theta_i)] \tag{4}$$

3.2 Policy Gradient Algorithm

Machine learning method derived from traditional hit and trial, consigning reward or punishment depending upon the correct hit or error is called reinforcement learning [2]. Just like human beings, the machine bots learn and expand their knowledge-set directly from the level of their measurement such as by vision, sensors and without any hand-engineered features or domain heuristics. This is achieved by deep learning of neural networks. Deep learning and neural networks [3] currently provide the best solution in this field of specialization. The following graph shows the Deep

Q-Networks (DQN) [4] that estimates the total reward that a bot can expect to receive after taking a particular action against the best linear learner.

Policy gradient algorithm are reinforcement algorithm techniques that depend on enhancing parameterized policies returned by gradient descent. The algorithm has noticeable advantages like it is effective in high dimensional, easily learn stochastic [10, 12] policies and has great convergence properties. Convergence of learning algorithms is not guaranteed for approximate value functions whereas policy gradient methods [5] are well-behaved with function approximation. Value functions can be very complex for large problems and methods run into a lot of problems in partially observable environments. While policy gradient algorithms have a simpler form and methods are "better" behaved even in such scenarios.

Let's now look into the policy optimization formulae. We assume the system in discrete time manner. Let current time be 'k'. Since we must also consider stochasticity [21], it is represented using a probability distribution [5].

$$x_k + 1 \sim p(x_k + 1|x_k, u_k);\ u_k \in RM;\ x_k + 1 \in RN \tag{5}$$

u_k and $x_k + 1$ represents the current and next state respectively. It is understood that policy is parametrized by K/policy parameters where $\theta \in RK$. The sequence of states and actions [25] forms a trajectory [29] denoted by

$$\tau = [x_0 : H, u_0 : H] \tag{6}$$

where H represents horizon which can stretch upto infinite. At any instant of time, the system trains itself by the reward represented by

$$rk = r(x_k, u_k) \in R \tag{7}$$

Basically in reinforcement learning, policy optimization focuses to optimize θ parameters. The expected return [3] is:

$$J(\theta) = E\left\{\sum_{k=0}^{H} a_k r_k\right\}\Big| \tag{8}$$

where a_k represents time-step dependent weighting factors, often set to $a_k = \gamma_k$ for discounted reinforcement learning (where γ is in [0, 1]) or $a_k = 1/H$ for the average reward case [5].

The applications in the real world require smooth parameter changes as sharp changes can manipulate the overall properties of the app. Immediately after a single such update, policy based on dataset which holds domain knowledge will disappear [6]. Hence policy gradient methods giving steepest descent on the expected return update the policy parameterization according to the gradient update rule.

$$\theta_{h+1} = \theta_h + \alpha_h \nabla_\theta J|_{\theta=\theta_h},| \tag{9}$$

where $\alpha_h \in R$ represent learning rate and $h \in \{0, 1, 2, \ldots\}$ the current update number [6].

3.3 Markov Decision Process

Markov decision processes formally describe an environment for reinforcement learning where the environment is fully observable i.e. the current state completely characterizes the process and almost all reinforcement learning(RL) problems can be formalized as MDPs e.g. Optimal control primarily deals with continuous MDPs, Partially observable problems can be converted into MDPs and Bandits [17] are MDPs with one state. We have applied MDP using value iteration algorithm which is applied in case of 2D games [7, 8, 18] to improve the predictions (See Fig. 2).

A Markov Decision Process (MDP) [9] model contains:

- A set of possible world states S
- A set of possible actions A
- A real valued reward function R(s, a)
- A description T of each action's effects in each state.

  $P(s'|s, a)$ denotes the probability that the agent is in state s and does action a.

  $R : S \times A \times S \rightarrow R$, While doing action a and transitioning to state s' from state s, $R(s, a, s')$ gives the expected immediate reward.

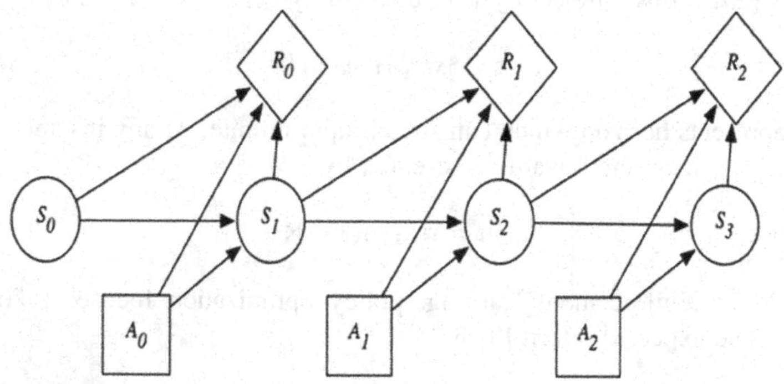

Fig. 2. MDP Representation.

3.4 Feed Forward Neural Network

Feed forward neural networks also often called multilayer perceptrons (MLPs) or Deep feed forward networks are the the quintessential deep learning models. The target of a feedforward network [13] is to estimate some function f*. For example, for a classifier, y = f*(x) [15] maps an input x to a category y. The networks maps y = f(x; θ) and learns the value of the parameters θ that result in the closest [23] estimation.

3.5 Back Propagation Algorithm

Let's understand this with reference to above explained feed forward neural network. Here our motive is to minimize the error (cost) by updating the corresponding model parameters. In order to determine in which direction and how much to update the values, their derivatives w.r.t the error function must be calculated. And this is what backward propagation is used for.

The choice of a error function is always closely related to the specific use case. The details about are implementation are discussed in Game implementation below.

4 Game Implementation

We had implemented Policy Gradient Algorithm and Deep Reinforcement learning on Pong Atari Version. We used OpenAI Gym environment [4] to train our model. We also used feed forward and backward neural network to learn and update the weights derivative of layers. The game theory was applied to make the framework economic and adaptable. The project has a great scope in atari game development. So basically Pong game involve 2 players one is paddle controlled by human and other is decent AI Pong agent which we train using stochastic [24, 29] reinforcement technique.

4.1 Formalizing States and Actions

Pong is a simple game in which 2 paddles on opposite sides of a rectangular map have the goal of preventing a ball from reaching the wall behind them. When a ball hits a paddle, it is sent back in the opposite direction. A player scores a point when the ball hits the opponent's wall. We developed a simple version of the classic game, complete with a hard-coded controller for the opponent paddle. Then, we set hyper parameters, Xavier initialization of layers, learning rate discount rewards, in our Neural Network. Weights and stored them in matrices. The first Layer of our Neural Network is a 200×6400 matrix which represents the weights for our hidden layer. For first layer the element w1_ij that has the weight of neuron i for input pixel j in the first layer.

The Second layer is a 200×1 matrix that has the weights of hidden layer or the final output. The second layer has element w2_i that has the weights which is put on the activation of neuron i in the hidden layer.

We Xavier initialize each layer's weights with random numbers for now.

We takes a single game frame as input and preprocesses before training into the model. We preprocess the $220 \times 161 \times 3$ byte pixel and used the unit frame of 6400 (80×80) 1D float vector.

$$\mathrm{Var}(W) = \frac{1}{n_{\mathrm{in}}} \tag{10}$$

4.2 Hyperparameters

We had 6 hyper parameters to train our model.

- We took number of hidden layer neurons (h = 600).
- Batch size = 10, represents number of rounds to be played before updating the weights of our network.

- Learning rate = 1e − 4 It is for convergence. If the learning rate is too low, it will slowly converge and if it's too high, it will never converge.
- Gamma = 0.99, represents discount factor for reward.
- Decay rate = 0.99, represents decay factor for RMSProp leaky sum of grad^2.
- Resume = False, represents the condition: resume from previous checkpoint.

4.3 Xavier Initialization

Xavier algorithm determines the scale of initialization based on the number of input and output neurons. It randomly returns a sample from the standard normal distribution the algorithm states the scale of initialization on the basis of number of input and output neurons if the weights are initially very close to 0, then the signals either shrink as it goes through each layer until it becomes too tiny to be useful. It also becomes too massive to be useful if the weights are big because the signals grow at each layer by using Xavier initialization, we make sure that the weights are not too small and also not too big to propagate accurately the signals. The weights in our network have a distribution with zero mean and a specific variance, where W is the initialization distribution for the neuron in question, and n_{in} is the number of neurons feeding into it. The distribution used is typically Gaussian or uniform.

4.4 Activation Function

The activation function used are sigmoid function and Relu while learning and updating the weight derivatives of layers. They are used both in Feed Forward neural network and back propagation.

Sigmoid Function
It converts our vector into probabilities called squashing [21] with the help of python numpy library. These functions have domain of all real numbers and has a non-negative derivative [22] at each point.

$$S(x) = \frac{1}{1+e^{-x}} = \frac{e^x}{e^x+1}. \tag{11}$$

Rectified Linear Units (ReLUs)
Instead of sigmoids [21], most recent deep learning networks use rectified linear unit for the hidden layers. ReLU's [13] have output 0 if the input is less than 0, and raw output otherwise. That is, if the input is greater than 0, the output is equal to the input. ReLU's machinery is more like a real neuron in your body.

$$f(x) = x^+ = \max(0, x) \tag{12}$$

4.5 Feed Forward Neural Network

We calculate the hidden state (h) layer of model by taking the dot product of our input pixel(x) and weight matrix [W1] by using feed forward neural network [19].

$$\mathrm{h} = \mathrm{np.dot}([\mathrm{W1}], \mathrm{x}) \tag{13}$$

After getting this value, we squash it with our Relu [13] function to get maximum.

$$\mathrm{h}[\mathrm{h} < \mathrm{o}] = 0, (\text{Relu activation function}) \tag{14}$$

Then we calculate the second state (logp) and take the the dot product of next state of weight matrix(W2) and first hidden state of model (h).

$$\mathrm{logp} = \mathrm{np.dot}([\mathrm{W2}), \mathrm{h})) \tag{15}$$

Then we calculate the probability of (logp) using sigmoid [15, 16] function.

$$\mathrm{p} = \mathrm{sigmoid}(\mathrm{logp}) \tag{16}$$

The sigmoid function gives s probability [22] of paddle going up, down or stay the same. Then we sample that values and use it to get the gradient values by taking the partial derivative [24] with respect to each of their weights as we backpropagate.

4.6 Back Propagation

We take the derivatives of our weights to update their weights. Then we calculate the derivative of weight [w2] by calculating the dot product of transpose of every intermediate state eph.t and epd(logp) (modulate the gradient with advantage).

$$\mathrm{d}[\mathrm{w2}] = \mathrm{np.dot}(\mathrm{eph.t}, \mathrm{epd}(\mathrm{logp})).\mathrm{ravel}() \tag{17}$$

Then we calculate the derivative of hidden state using the model and apply the Relu activation [13, 20] function to it.

$$\text{dh=np.outer(epdlogp,model['w2'])} \tag{18}$$

$$\mathrm{dh} = \mathrm{np}[\mathrm{eph} < = 0] = 0(\text{Relu activation function}) \tag{19}$$

Now we calculate the derivative of weight [w1] by dot product of hidden state [20] transpose(h.t) and input observation (epx) and then we return both the derivatives [20, 21, 29] to update weights.

$$dw1 = np.dot(dh.T, epx) \quad (20)$$

return {'w1' :dw1 , 'w2' :dw2} , program statement.

5 Pong Training and Features

We use an emulator heavily based on the OpenAI Gym library [4], a library for OpenAI Gym is a toolkit for developing and comparing reinforcement learning algorithms. We use it to train our model. OpenAI Gym supports all the libraries such as TensorFlow [27], Theano which is required to train the Pong Agent. The Open AI Gym emulator was used to produce states, actions, and rewards for both training and validation of game bot of Pong (Fig. 3).

```
env = gym.make("Pong-v0")

prev_x = None
xs,hs,dlogps,drs = [],[],[],[]
running_reward = None
reward_sum = 0


while True:

  cur_x = prepro(observation)
  x = cur_x - prev_x if prev_x is not None else np.zeros(D)
  prev_x = cur_x

  aprob, h = policy_forward(x)
  action = 2 if np.random.uniform() < aprob else 3
```

Fig. 3. Code Snippet of Pong Agent Training.

After installing the OpenAI Gym dependencies on local machine for Pong Atari game, it took approximately 2 days to train the game bot using policy gradient which is faster than genetic algorithm.

On using Google Cloud Platform for training of game bot using policy gradient algorithm, it took 6–7 h which is significantly faster.

This is just an implementation of the classic "agent-environment loop". Each timestep, the agent chooses an action, and the environment returns an observation and a reward. Now we calculate the derivative of weight [w1] by dot product of hidden state [20] transpose(h.t) and input observation (epx) and then we return both the derivatives [20, 21, 29] to update weights (Fig. 4).

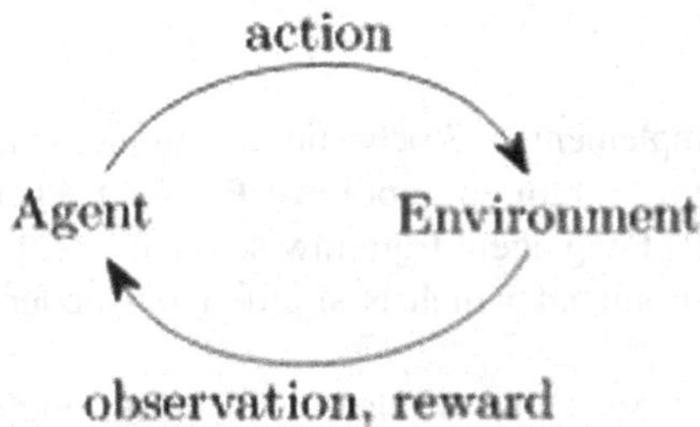

Fig. 4. OpenAI Gym Environment Cycle.

5.1 States and Actions

The state of the game at any time t is simply the pixel array of the game screen at that particular time. We receive an image frame of a 210 × 160 × 3 byte array. It gives pixel value which ranges from integer 0 to 255. We track the state and action of agent using OpenAI Gym dependencies which also give rewards accordingly. We have to decide if we want to move the paddle UP or DOWN. After every single choice the game simulator executes the action. We use OpenAI Gym as our simulator and it gives us a reward: Either a + 1 reward if the ball went past the opponent, a − 1 reward if we missed the ball, or 0 otherwise.

5.2 Discount Rewards

We are optimizing the reward for short term our agent is learning every time the ball passes either one of our player then the game (ball) resets but the score does not resets and we get rewards in array of values and feed into discount reward. We then weigh each of these rewards differently. We weigh the most recent immediate reward higher [28] than the later reward.

$$V = r_1 + \gamma r_2 + \gamma^2 r_3 + \cdots + \gamma^{i-1} r_i + \cdots \tag{21}$$

where γ, the discount factor [14], is a number in the range $0 \leq \gamma < 1$.

If γ was 1, it would be the same as the total reward. When $\gamma = 0$, the agent ignores all the future rewards. If $0 \leq \gamma < 1$ it means that, whenever the rewards are finite, the total value will also be finite

Under this criterion, the future rewards are worth less than the current reward.

We can rewrite the discounted reward [12, 14] as

$$\begin{aligned} V &= \sum_{i=1}^{\infty} \gamma^{i-1} r_i \\ &= r_1 + \gamma r_2 + \gamma^2 r_3 + \cdots + \gamma^{i-1} r_i + \cdots \\ &= r_1 + \gamma(r_2 + \gamma(r_3 + \ldots)). \end{aligned}$$

6 Result

We had successfully implemented Stochastic Reinforcement learning technique of Policy Gradient algorithm to train and optimize Pong AI Agent.

We trained an ATARI Pong agent from raw scratch, in 130 lines of Python and run it on OpenAI Gym environment which is significantly better than genetic algorithm (Fig. 5).

There were many test cases that we had to deal with one of the following are-

Best 100-episode average reward was: 9.43 ± 0.55.
Total runtime: 6–7 h
Training was performed on: 4000 episodes.

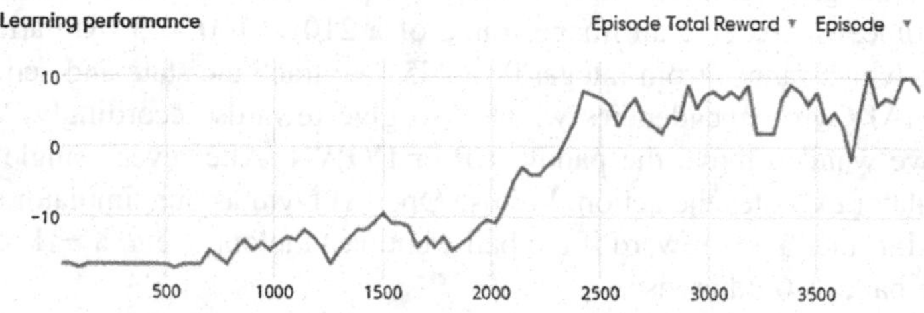

Fig. 5. Pong Agent learning performance curve.

7 Conclusion

Firstly, we examine several critical factors affecting learning quality in this setting, such as the Xavier initialization, hyper parameters, learning rate, average performance of the agent, its variance and the importance of reward discounting in training the model. The experiments show the significant importance of stochastic policy using reinforcement learning for choosing policies and updating the weights. We formulate the problem as a learning one and propose a novel RL technique of policy gradient algorithm capable of generating policies, updating weights and giving discount rewards to the agent.

8 Future Scope

On use in complex robotics settings. The algorithm does not scale naively to settings where huge amounts of exploration are difficult to obtain.

We had implemented Policy Gradient Algorithm and Deep Reinforcement learning on Pong Atari Version. Other approaches can be Asynchronous Methods for Deep Reinforcement Learning which is lightweight framework for deep reinforcement learning that uses asynchronous [26] gradient descent for optimization of deep neural network controllers for different Atari games.

Appendix

ReLU- Rectified linear units,
DQN- Deep Q-Networks
RL- Reinforcement Learning
s_t- State at time t
a_t- Action at time t
r_t- Reward earned
π- Policy function
γ- Discount factor determining the agent's horizon
θ_i- The parameters of the Q-network at iteration i
E- Expected return
i- Iterations
$Li(\theta i)$- Loss function
α_h- Learning rate
h- Current update number [6].
a_k- Time-step dependent weighting factors

References

1. Mnih, V., et al.: Playing atari with deep reinforcement learning, In: NIPS Workshop (2013)
2. Ghory, I.: Reinforcement learning in board games (2013)
3. Mnih, V., Kavukcuoglu, K., Silver, D., Rusu, A.A., Veness, J., Bellemare, M.G., Graves, A., Riedmiller, M., Fidjel, A.K., Ostrovski, G.: Human-level control through deep reinforcement learning (2015)
4. Mnih, V., Kavukcuoglu, K., Silver, D., Graves, A., Antonoglou, I., Wierstra, D., Riedmiller, M.: Playing atari with deep reinforcement learning (2013)
5. Silver, D.: Deterministic policy gradient algorithms. In: ICML (2015)
6. Fu, J., Hsu, I.: Model-Based Reinforcement Learning for Playing Atari games (2014)
7. Hartley, T., Mehdi, Q., Gough, N.: Applying Markov Decision Process to 2-D Real Games (2001)
8. Jaakkola, T., Singh, S.P., Jordan, M.I.: Reinforcement learning algorithms for partially observable Markov decision problems. In: NIPS 7, pp. 345–352. Morgan Kaufman (1995)
9. Marbach, P., Tsitsiklis, J.N.: Simulation-based optimization of Markov reward processes, Technical report LIDS-P-2411, Massachusetts Institute of Technology (1998)
10. Bertsekas, D.P.: Dynamic Programming: Deterministic and Stochastic Models. Prentice-Hall, Englewood Cliffs (1987)
11. Watkins, C.J.C.H., Dayan, P.: Technical note: Q-learning. Mach. Learn. **8**(3/4), 279–292 (1992)
12. Schwartz, A.: A reinforcement learning method for maximizing undiscounted rewards. In: Proceedings of the Tenth International Conference on Machine Learning, pp. 298–305. Amherst (1993)
13. White, D.A., Sofge, D.A.: Neural network based process optimization and control. In: Proceedings of the 29th Conference on Decision and Control, Honolulu, Hawaii, pp. 3270–3276 (1990)

14. Ok, D.: A Comparative Study of Undiscounted and Discounted Reinforcement Learning Methods (1994)
15. Fachantidis, A., Taylor, M.E., Vlahavas, I.: Learning to teach reinforcement learning agents (2017)
16. Kobayashi, M., Zamani, A., Ozawa, S., Abe, S.: Reducing computations in incremental learning for feedforward neural network with long-term memory. In: Proceedings of International Joint Conference on Neural Networks, 1989/1994 (2001)
17. Das, T.K., Gosavi, A., Mahadevan, S., Marchalleck, N.: Solving semi-Markov decision problems using average reward reinforcement learning. Manag. Sci. **45**(4), 560574 (1999)
18. Mannor, S., Tsitsiklis, J.N.: Mean-Variance Optimization in Markov Decision Processes (1998)
19. Wang, J., Li, B., Liu, C.: Research of New Learning Method of Feedforward Neural Network (2003)
20. Seuret, M., Alberti, M., Ingold, R., Liwicki, M.: PCA-Initialized Deep Neural Networks Applied To Document Image Analysis (2007)
21. Saruchi, S.: Adaptive sigmoid function to enhance low contrast images (2016)
22. Minai, A.A., Williams, R.D.: On the derivatives of the sigmoid (2015)
23. Schmidt, W.F., Kraaijveld, M.A., Duin, R.P.W.: Feed forward neural networks with random weight (2016)
24. Tang, Y., Salakhutdinov, R.: Learning stochastic feedforward neural networks (2016)
25. Bottou, L.: Large-scale machine learning with stochastic gradient descent (2012)
26. Stevens, M., Pradhan, S.: Playing Tetris with Deep Reinforcement Learning (2014)
27. Abadi, M., Barham, P.: TensorFlow: a system for large-scale machine learning (2012)
28. Tsitsiklis, J.N., Van Roy, B.: On average versus discounted rewardtemporal-difference learning (2013)
29. Tadepalli, P., Ok, D.: Model-based average reward reinforcement learning (2011)

Forensics Data Analysis for Behavioral Pattern with Cognitive Predictive Task

S. Mahaboob Hussain[1(✉)], Prathyusha Kanakam[2], D. Suryanarayana[1], and Sumit Gupta[1]

[1] Vishnu Institute of Technology, Vishnupur, Bhimavaram, India
mahaboobhussain.smh@gmail.com, dasikasuryanarayana@gmail.com, sumit108@hotmail.com

[2] MVGR College of Engineering (A), Vizianagaram, India
prathyusha.kanakam@gmail.com

Abstract. Web browsing analysis is an emerging task to find the user's behaviour during surfing of Internet. The individual session logs are observed and identified to authenticate and verify the intruders from normal users. While moving from one website to another website, the users will leave the digital footprints used to track the users' interesting information which may assist the stakeholders about online advertising and the users' sentimental analysis. A session log is a source for investigating an individual during a digital crime. Semantic forensics is novel investigation scheme employed to verify a users' behaviour while browsing the Web, as it is a huge repository of information. In this paper, semantic forensics which is a new branch of forensic science is introduced and gives a clear-cut view about how the behavioural pattern of a user influence the semantic forensics. It also analyses the results by considering the sample database related to dark Web communication and explains how a session log can be accessed with the help of various phases in Cognitive Predictive Task (CPT).

Keywords: Forensic · Data analysis · Semantics · Web tracking Cybercrimes

1 Introduction

Tracking the Web over a period of time is a novel scheme to distinguish the intruders from normal Web users. It can also be used to store the data for predictive tasks [1]. The stake holders observe the activities of the Web users for their business purposes (sentiment analysis) to find out the health report of their product in the market. Thus the monitoring of Web is a crucial module in the fields of marketing, sales and product support strategies. As the modern era is full of cybercrimes, investigations need to be employed to preserve the information treasure from the pirates of the Web.

Digital foot prints are the source for Web tracking to identify or verify users' activities during the surfing of internet. This paradigm also monitors about the working condition of a website and it links [2]. The usage of dynamic Web pages has been tremendously increased over the past ten years. So the security issues rise to provide a

P. Bhattacharyya et al. (Eds.): NGCT 2017, CCIS 827, pp. 549–557, 2018.
https://doi.org/10.1007/978-981-10-8657-1_41

safe transaction of a user during online marketing. Security algorithms integration employed in this huge information repository and also training the machine according to the human perception is a difficult task.

Web tracking system (WTs) *: WTs = {Influenced by {n(Pv),t}, {n(Sm),t}, Lb, Db} where Pv is web page visits, Sm is Web Searches made, Lb is location of Web browsing and Db is devices for Web browsing.*

A traditional Web tracking system impacts Web users' activities to target their behavioural pattern are

1. Number of web pages visited – n(Pv) within period of time t
2. Number of searches made by the user within a time interval – n(Sm) within period of time t
3. Location of Web browsing (Lb)
4. The device used for browsing (Db).

The new trend of marketing through this digital media is becoming simple by this behavioural targeting of the WWW users by making them as the group of personal interests [3]. It will happen when anyone uses a search engine or visit a Website, a small cookie file is placed on the device based on the search things without any collection of personal details.

It may watch out the activities of the people closely on the Web. The things one can forget about the past search but the systems may remember. Depending on the interest group, the advertiser may target the group with their advertisements on the website that the user visiting. The statistical studies of 2016 on various network-based attacks reveal that more than 30% vulnerabilities on communication over a network among different peers. In order to investigate these fraudulent crimes, the investigation agencies (enforcement law) should make use of technology which is a crucial part. All the network-based attacks [4] are familiar threats that are launched by a device over a collection of devices and that single device will control the remaining devices in the network. These attacks are subcategories of cyber-crimes that include DOS (Denial of Service) attacks, Probe attacks, Worms, viruses and many others.

2 Preliminaries

When users go online either from a computer or from any mobile devices having Internet access, some of the experts can collect the information about age, location and interested in based upon the search history. This information can be collected from the small database files called cookies but all cookies may not be vulnerable to the users and they help for the better experience of the browsing [5]. Third part or tracking cookies can collect or precise information that will store in a database for analysing of one's searching data. Every digital moment will be stored and watched for the user's prediction. Many tools are there like ghostery [6] to show which advertisers Beacons and analytics and using tracking cookies and to block them. Lou Montulli and John Giannandrea [7] invented an HTTP which is a traditional cookie which helps in ease of browsing. But, nowadays the penetrated cookies by some browsers are harder to notice, and often harder to control.

As per the current scenario of the online social networks like Facebook can record the personal data of an individual and can add the details to the database. As per the survey of Krishna Murthy [8] the Orkut (which does not exist now) among all the existed social networks (authors checked for 12 online social networks) has not leaked any data of the individual.

From the research of the above authors, they expelled various methods that how the third party can obtain the personal data from the social networks with HTTP Referrer header, parameters of URLs and URIs. Request code can be written to store the data like users Facebook Id and also it maintains the login times with the applications.

```
GET /track/?...&fb_sig_time=16261133 &
fb_sig_user=2616&...
Host: adtracker.socialmedia.com
Referer: http://apps.facebook.com/impchu/...
```

3 CPT for Semantic Forensics

The search engine is the part of digital identity which may lead to stealing the precise data of the users. One can easily predict the individuals' Facebook likes, someone's intelligence, political views, happiness, religious views, and studies about the network of connections. Users partially become the part of some programmers on the Web and allowing predicting the actions and the moments. Every individual's browser habits will be recorded using unidentified. Authors in their previous work [9] proposed a novel paradigm, Cognitive Predictive Task (CPT) to identify the user logs and also to predict their future activities which become the base for various applications like sentiment analysis as well as for the investigations to authenticate a normal user with an intruder using the Web. Sometimes, searching amid session is an ambiguous task as the user may not have clear information at the starting and they are unsure of how to explicitly characterize their information need. Let, 'Q' may be a query log of an individual which is the combination of both past and future activities (queries or URL clicks) $\mathrm{Q} = \{\mathrm{P}, \mathrm{F}\}$ where P represents the past activities of the user, $\mathrm{P} = \{\mathrm{Q1}, \mathrm{Q2}, \mathrm{U1}, \mathrm{Q3}, \ldots, \mathrm{Qn}\}$ where each activity either is a URL click or Query and F represents the future activities of the user, $\mathrm{F} = \{\mathrm{U11}, \mathrm{U12}, \mathrm{U13}, \mathrm{U14}, \ldots, \mathrm{U1n}\}$ which contains URLs in a specified table. The principal component score or sentiment score of the user session log leads a way to mine associations in their queries (searching information).

In this work, authors used their CPT scheme and apply three of its phases (parsing, predicting, computing) to monitor the Web sessions of users as shown in Fig. 1. Principal component is calculated as the linear combination of two optimally weighted observed components. The components can be computed as,

$$c_1 = b_{11}(A_1) + b_{12}(A_2) + \ldots + b_{1p}(A_p)$$

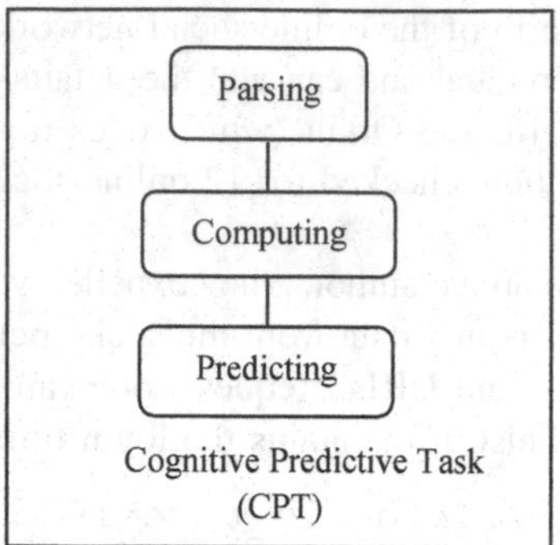

Fig. 1. Phases of Cognitive Predictive Task

Table 1. Words and their frequencies in dark web communication

Words	Frequency
Weapons	918
Terrorists	738
Injured	1008
Violence	1089
Suicide	1148
Death	1214
Bomb	1317
Killing	1589
Militants	1680
Brothers	1692
Fighting	1785

Forensic data analytics or semantic forensic is the combination of data science skills combined with information technology and financial accounting skills to merge together to identify patterns of fact to defend or assert a certain position as well as identify business insight around fraud risk and compliance. Criminals are using computers as weapons against their victims, therefore, it is an emerging challenge for law and enforcement agencies identify the digital evidence and extract essential facts that can be produced. Forensics tools may use to identify the deleted data as well for the evidence.

CPT principle lies in projecting the future prediction of the Web user that helps mostly in online advertisements to increase the sales of the products. Training the machine to understand the human perception is a critical task for behavioural targeting by analysing the past sessions of the users and to identify the root words. In this paper, CPT is applied to find out various communications words and their frequency. As support and confidence are the constructs to compute the sentiment score of each root word observed during distinct sessions of intruders gives the frequency. Thus with the help of oxygen forensics analyst and detective tolls, data from mobile sources and multiple sources are extracted. They can extract data from various devices more than

16000 and easily tract the passwords and encrypted images or files also, it can retrieve deleted data from various devices. From the dark Web communication, depending upon the behavioural targeting some of the words representing cybercrimes along with their computed frequency are represented in Table 1. It represents the words that are used by the frauds to perform an activity. The frequency of crime words has a high impact for "Fighting, Brothers, Militants, Killing, Bomb" from highest to lowest. From these forensics data analytics, cyber security operations can be done in an efficient manner.

4 Semantic Forensics for Behavioral Pattern with CPT

The machine is trained to understand the cognition and also predict the users' behaviour. The behavioural pattern of the user is mined to authenticate each and every individual in order to eradicate cybercrimes up to some extent. Thus the profile of a particular user is estimated by all factors of Web tracking definition. This work possesses the application of CPT in the real-world scenario for investigation purposes of Web users. Sentiment analysis retrieved from semantic forensics data analysis from the communication of frauds of the dark Web. All the phases of CPT grant their discrete functionalities that aids to compute the sentiment score for root words that are parsed in the parsing phase.

Some of the lexicons that are used to develop semantic analysis for cyber security have shown in Table 2 in English and in Arabic in Table 3 along with the seed words, morphological variants and sentiment score [10]. Semantic data (a type of behaviour) related to the Web user is predicted through a threshold value of sentiment score. The sentiment score is a representation of the sentiment polarity and it is compared with that of threshold scale with a verbal representation with positive, neutral, negative. Authors used a logarithmic scale to calculate the sentiment scores for morphological variants in this below Tables 2 & 3. Here, the scores were calculated by considering the most negative value as −10 and the most positive value is +10, where the scores are between −1 and 1. Consider $log(x)* - 1$ for the mandatory multiplier on a negative scale.

Figure 2 shows total 279 seed words of the ansarl dataset and their positive and negative impact (Table 2 shows some seed words among 279). In the selected database, exactly 230 seed words are with negative values ranged from −1 to −0.17. 11 seed words lie at −0.52 sentiment score shows the highest density for the seed words (camp, device, economy, fuel, guard, infidel, Swat, Tank, traffic, victory, Virus). Remaining 148 seed words are with positive sentiment score with 1 neutral seed word. In that 83 words are with 0.08 sentiment score. Some of the words represented here (agent, aircraft, Al Qaeda, army, attempt, Border, checkpoint, Drug, Gunfight, gunman, Jihad, Military, mission, nuclear, Shootout, Worm) considered as high-risk threat words in cyber security perception.

Figure 3 shows total 1019 seed words of the ansarl dataset and their positive and negative impact (Table 3 shows some seed words among 1019). In the selected database, exactly 418 seed words are with negative values ranged from −1.00 to −0.08. 216 seed words lie at −0.67 sentiment score shows the highest density for the seed words. Remaining 579 seed words are with positive sentiment score with 22 neutrals.

Table 2. English root words and their morphological variants

Root words	Morphological variants	Sentiment score
Act	Act, acts, action, actions, acting, acted	0.68
Agent	Agent, agents, agency	0.08
Aircraft	Aircraft, aircrafts, aircraftman, aircraftmen	0.08
Al Qaeda	Al Qaeda, Al-Qaeda, Al Qaida, Al-Qaida, Al Qaeda, AlQaeda	0.08
Blast	Blast, blasts, blasting, blaster, blasted	−0.61
Blow	Blow, blows, blew, blown, blower, blowing, blowy	−0.75
Bomb	Bomb, bombs, bombing, bombings, bomber, bombers, bombed	−0.85
Border	Border, borders, borderer, borderers, bordering, bordered	0.08
Casualty	Casualty, casualties	−0.85
Checkpoint	Checkpoint, checkpoints	0.08
Command	Command, commands, commanding, commanded, commander, commandant, commandment, commanders	0.7
Cyberattack	Cyberattack, Cyberattacks, Cyberattacker, Cyberattackers, Cyberattacked, Cyberattacking	0.08
Cyber terror	Cyperterror, Cyber terrors, Cyberterrorism, Cyberterrorist, Cyberterrorists	0.08
Gunfight	Gunfight, gunfights, gunfought, gunfighter, gunfighters, gunfighty, gunfighting	0.08
Incident	Incident, incidents, incidence, incidences, incidental, incidently	−0.51
Mission	Mission, missions, missioner, missioners	0.08
Powder	Powder, powders, powdered, powderize, powderzed, powderer	0.08
Torture	Torture, tortures, tortured, torturing, torturer, torturers,	−0.75
Violent	Violent, violence, violences, violently	−0.95
Wound	Wound, wounding, wounds, wounded, wounder	−0.81

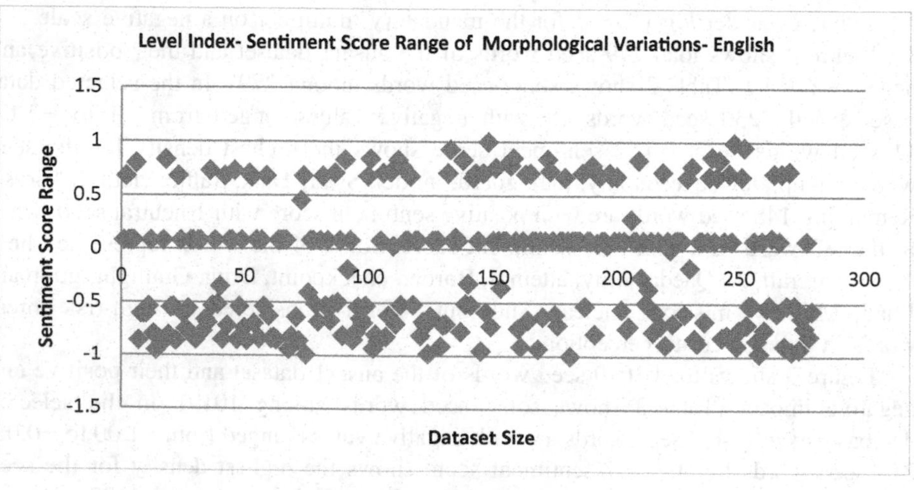

Fig. 2. Distribution of English words' sentiment scores

Table 3. Arabic root words and their morphological variants

Root Words	Morphological Variants	Sentiment Score
بقوة	بقوة, قوى, يقوى, اقوى, تقوى, قوي, قوية	0.65
وإنقاذ	نقذ, ينقذ, انقذ, تنقذ, منقاذ, انقاذ, وإنقاذ, نقذاء	-0.18
راشدة	راشدة, رشد, يرشد, ارشد, راشد, راشدة, ترشد, رشيد, مرشاد, ارشاد, رشدى, رشداء	0.08
استطاعت	استطاعت, طوع, يطوع, اطوع, تطوع, مطوع, مطواع, طوعى, طوعاء	-0.08
والتطرف	والتطرف, طرف, يطرف, اطرف, طارف, طارفة, تطرف, طريف, مطراف, طرفى, طرفاء	-1.00
الظّالِمُونَ	ظلم, يظلم, اظلم, ظالم, ظالمة, تظلالظّالِمُونَ, مظلوم, ظلام, ظلوم, مظلام, اظلام, ظلمى, ظلماء	-1.00
بكاء	بكاء, بكى, يبكي, ابكى, باكي, باكية, تبكي, مبكاء, بكي	-0.67
يضعف	يضعف, ضعف, يضعف, اضعف, تضعف, ضعيف, مضعاف, اضعاف, ضعفاء	-0.25
متفقون	متفقون, ثقف, يثقف, اثقف, ثاقف, ثاقفة, تثقف, ثقيف, مثقاف, ثقفاء	0.65
الجلد	الجلد, جلد, يجلد, اجلد, تجلد, جلود, جليد, مجلاد	-0.67
صريحا	صرح, يصرح, تصرح, صروح, صريح صريحا	0.75
الجمر	الجمر, جمر, يجمر, تجمر	-0.67
الطائفية	الطائفية, طاف, يطوف, طف, طائف, طائفة, تطوف, مطوف, طواف, مطواف	-0.80
الجنس	الجنس, جنس, يجنس, تجنس	-0.67
للجيش	للجيش, جيش, يجيش, تجيش, جيوش	0.00
يخالفه	يخالفه, خلف, يخلف, اخلف, خالف, خالفة, تخلف, مخلوف, خليف	-0.77
الحاد	الحاد, حاد, يحاد, تحاد	0.60
الجنة	الجنة, جنة	0.67
الحبس	الحبس, حبس, يحبس, احبس, حابس, حابسة, تحبس	-0.67
بالإعدام	بالإعدام, عدم, يعدم, اعدم, عادم, عادمة, تعدم, معدوم, عديم, اعدام	-0.97

All the forensic investigations are associated with pattern recognition techniques that are employed in their own system. CPT is a state-of-art mechanism to observe the behavioural pattern of an individual that assist in finding the damagers of society during Web browsing.

Authors previously worked on the query log analysis to predict the users' future queries. Now they have applied the same paradigm to the current scenario problem by

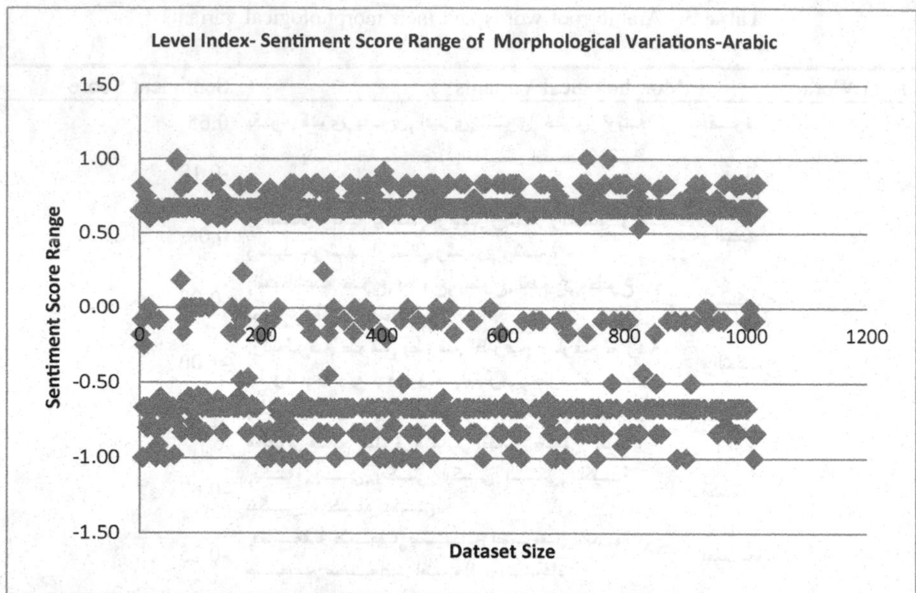

Fig. 3. Distribution of Arabic words' sentiment scores

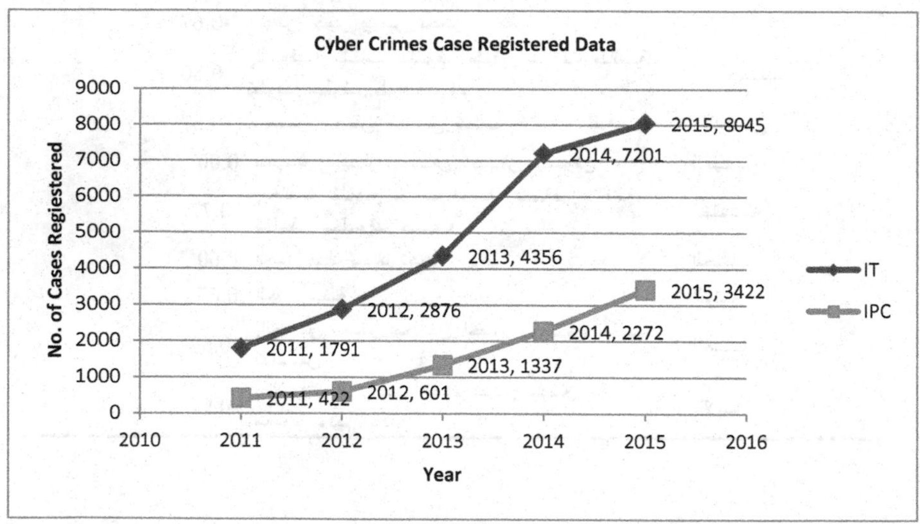

Fig. 4. Cyber-crimes rate over past 5 years

considering the sample dataset. Figure 4 shows the cases registered based upon the IT act and IPC in India in between 2011 and 2015. These actions are undergone with forensic data analysis and proofs.

5 Conclusion

Due to the vast increase in the rate of cybercrimes as well as an increase in a number of cyber attackers, there is a need to investigate and predict the activities of users using the Web. Semantic forensics gives a new path to analyses the huge information repository. While browsing the internet, users leave their digital foot prints when moving from one website to another website and also they provide a lot of clues in their searches. Thus, both these factors can act as sources for crime investigations. The phases in Cognitive Predictive Task furnish an explicit view for these purposes. Sample dataset related to dark Web communication is analysed and experimented with CPT technique especially it focused on phases (parsing and computing) to compute the semantic score for root words derived from that communication and also presented in a graphical format. In extension of this analysis, a tool will be developed based upon this CPT with all the phases and the results for the predictive queries based on the requirements of the crime analysis experts for secure digital India.

References

1. Mayer, J., Mitchell, J.: Third-party web tracking: policy and technology. In: 2012 IEEE Symposium on Security and Privacy (2012)
2. Wexelblat, A., Maes, P.: Footprints. In: Proceedings of the SIGCHI Conference on Human Factors in Computing Systems the CHI is the Limit - CHI 1999 (1999)
3. Rhodes, S.: Collecting behavioural data using the world wide web: considerations for researchers. J. Epidemiol. Commun. Health **57**(1), 68–73 (2003)
4. Subba, B., Biswas, S., Karmakar, S.: A neural network based system for intrusion detection and attack classification. In: 2016 Twenty Second National Conference on Communication (NCC) (2016)
5. Millett, L., Friedman, B., Felten, E.: Cookies and web browser design. In: Proceedings of the SIGCHI Conference on Human Factors in Computing Systems - CHI 2001 (2001)
6. Cranor, L.: Can users control online behavioral advertising effectively? IEEE Secur. Priv. Mag. **10**, 93–96 (2012)
7. Nottingham, M., Mogul, J.: HTTP header field registrations (2005)
8. Liu, Y., Gummadi, K., Krishnamurthy, B., Mislove, A.: Analyzing facebook privacy settings. In: Proceedings of the 2011 ACM SIGCOMM Conference on Internet Measurement Conference - IMC 2011 (2011)
9. Suryanarayana, D.: Cognitive analytic task based on based on search query logs for semantic of semantic identification. IJCTA **9**(21), 273–280 (2016)
10. Al-Rowaily, K., Abulaish, M., Al-Hasan Haldar, N., Al-Rubaian, M.: BiSAL – a bilingual sentiment analysis lexicon to analyze dark web forums for cyber security. Digit. Invest. **14**, 53–62 (2015)

Enhancing Personalized Learning with Interactive Note Taking on Video Lectures–An Analysis of Effective HCI Design on Learning Outcome

Suman Deb[1(✉)] and Paritosh Bhattacharya[2]

[1] Department of CSE, National Institute of Technology Agartala, Jirania, India
sumandeb.cse@nita.ac.in

[2] Department of Mathematics, National Institute of Technology Agartala, Jirania, India

Abstract. E-learning, MOOCS etc. are the present time technology mediated unvoidable pedagogy tools, which along with social media and affordable device inclusion continues to be unabated. Video lectures form a primary as well significantly vital part of MOOC instruction delivery design beyond geogaphical and cultural boundaries. They serve as a gateway to draw students into the course. In going over these videos accumulating knowledge, there is a high occurrence of cases [1] where the learner forgets about some of the concepts taught and focus more on what is the minimum amount needed to carry forward so that the participant can attempt the quizzes, tests and pass required grade. This is a step backward when teaching pedagogy is concerned with giving the student a learning outcome that seems to bridge the gap between what they knew of the course and what level of knowledge upgrades after they have taken the course to completion. To address this issue, we are proposing an interaction model that enables the learner to promptly take notes as and when a learner is viewing a video. This paper contains modeling of UI (User Interaction) issues and discussion of a working prototype as the proposed application **MOOCbook**, aimed at composing personalized notes for MOOC takers. Several world leading MOOC providers content integrated using application program interface (API). Findings of the work and empirical study have revealed encouraging learning outcome with longer retention of MOOC contents.

Keywords: MOOC note · Self pace learning · Personalized Learning MOOCbook · MOOC video interaction · Enhanced learning outcome

1 Introduction

The primary form of information delivery in MOOC format is videos. One of the challenges faced by the online learners of today is the need of an interface

P. Bhattacharyya et al. (Eds.): NGCT 2017, CCIS 827, pp. 558–567, 2018.
https://doi.org/10.1007/978-981-10-8657-1_42

which enables to take notes from the video lectures [2]. Traditional methods used thus far by the student community are time absorbing and cumbersome in terms of organization. This work is an attempt to address the issue enabling the learner to focus more on the curriculum than on how to compile and access the materials later. As MOOC courses being accessed through out world, beyond any geographical region. Inherently it triggers another level of interaction and understanding difficulty due to cultural, linguistic variation. In addition to that human learning variation takes a great role in graceful MOOC acceptance, learning pleasure and learning outcome.

1.1 Learning Variation

Learning difference comes from a diversity of learning styles naturally prevailing with humans. Learning styles can be broadly classified [3] into *three* categories based on sensory impulses perceived by the human brain namely visual, physical and audible. But this can be narrowed down to *seven* subcategories [4] as *Visual, Physical, Aural, Verbal, Logical, Social, Solitary* etc. In all these mentioned categories, there are no clear boundaries of demarcation that apply. People have a mix of these categories in their learning styles and the weightage of each category varies. Also, some topics are better learnt in one learning style or a combination of these. In general, learning content should be created that strives to engage a variety of these styles. Using an online learning approach such as MOOCs that includes most of the media formats such as video, audio, ebooks, forums etc. is undoubtedly one of the best ways of appealing to a learner or in this case, a MOOC taker. It is a way of cumulating multiple styles in an all-inclusive platform. Barrington [5] has argued that the *seven* categories of learning styles as a pedagogy discussed above can and should be applied in the teaching-learning scenario.

1.2 Context of the Visual Style of Learning (VSL)

In the context of MOOCs, the VSL applied to the environment are the most predominant ones employed from the seven categories of learning style. It is a learning approach that is associated with all forms of graphic elements. The visual learning style is also referred to as the spatial learning style [17]. Since persons into VLS, process information better when it is in the form of pictures, images, graphics and charts. Present time technology inclusion in pedagogy enable the possible variation to the conventional study routines and supports individual learning strategies to their learning style. MOOCs' learning curricula include videos, readouts and activities. The major form of information delivery in the MOOCs consist of videos, which can be defined as a recording of visual images accompanied by audio elements, thereby pertaining to audio-visual senses simultaneously. Videos serve as the first interaction with the course content, and is the main method of content delivery [2]. Course content is wrapped into episodic materials which contain various forms of media, but primarily these are full of video lectures. The recent trend is to make the number of videos greater, but keep individual videos length under 2–3 min which may present a single idea in it (micro-lectures).

1.3 Personalized Learning (PL) Record

An individual himself holds the key in identifying what practices help him in succeeding to learn. This is attributed to what he personally feels would help to solve the problem. Personalized Learning (PL) [12] is a way of efficiently connecting instruction to each individual students preferences, interests and needs [6]. Seeing MOOCs through the students eyes [11] is a must if PL needs to be implemented in teaching pedagogy. A very basic example of PL is how a student takes notes from a classroom lecture. Although he may be understanding most of the points being discussed in the classroom, still he is enabling himself to prepare in case when he forgets important parts of the said lecture. The notebook may contain equations, diagrams etc. relevant to the discussion, such that when he returns to the next session of the discussion, he has a fair idea about it. Another thing to note is that when he takes the note, although he may think he will revise them later, there is a certain unconsciousness associated with the activity already, which makes a memory map of what points are being written on the notebook, such that almost readily he is equipped with the knowledge for a future need.

2 Problem Statement

There is a significant concern over what the learners end up learning as compared to what the MOOC instruction designer intended them to do [7]. Many just fall into the trap of knowing just enough to pass the quizzes and course assessments, this neglecting any other concepts that learner may have eventually come across but forgotten about it [8]. For the learners who seem to acknowledge this issue on their own, they tend to view the videos again and again until they feel that they have substantial command over the topic being taught in these videos [6,9]. Now, while this may be a good practice, this takes an awful amount of time. Also, it may happen that the learner takes up a topic, goes through the videos to understand the topic at hand, but after he goes through some other videos in other units of the course, he forgets about the previous videos and at the same time, feels the need to go over them again, knowing that it will take time [10]. Instead, if there was an interface that lets the learner decide on taking essential parts of the video in a form which can enable them to revise the concepts later and on-demand, it would make sense. This work designs an integrated *MOOC takers note book* that makes an integration of various course providers content on a personalized note interface. This enables cross reference, transcript copy, still frame capture and personalize text note.

3 Contents of a Typical MOOC

There has been a surge of MOOC providers over the last couple of years. The variety of subjects taught at these platforms cover almost every topic that one can think of in broad terms. Over this period, there has been numerous changes to MOOC formats but the skeleton of such a framework has not undergone massive changes. Videos remain the most used format for instruction delivery, which serves as a bridge connecting traditional style of instruction delivery using digital media. MOOCs are now pictured as challenges and not mere lectures. So, the videos are made in accordance with the view that they will serve as concept builders. These concept and elementary knowledge gain on a particular topic may get tested later in form of quiz, MCQ etc. All throughout the MOOCs, there is data collected from the user actions which aim at identifying learner practices both unconsciously (keystroke records, mouse movements etc.) and consciously (pre-course and post-course surveys) from the point of view of a user. Other than videos, the key constructs of a MOOC are assignments, quizzes, code editors (for computer science related courses), pdf handouts, links to resources, forums, one-to-one doubt clearing sessions etc. Having such a framework strives to ensure that the learner gets the best of what can be expected over the Internet. The delivery structure of a MOOC goes over weeks. But some of the MOOC providers have a provision that the whole course can be rescheduled to start from another time frame at the wish of the learner, emphasizing the self paced part more [13]. The videos are hosted over a web service available for download by the user for offline viewing [14]. In contrast to the elementary MOOCS frame work of delivering contents, presently subject engagement, course completion and learning outcome are major concern. Each MOOC is different from learner's perspective as how much one reads, watch, discuss and engage is up to any individual and what one wants to get from the MOOC experience is fully user driven.

4 Notes for MOOCs

Note-taking is an indispensable tool when it comes to learning. Notes are kind of a transcript to what a class session teaches. It is like a record of events taking place inside the classroom [15] and has a quantitative description of how short term and long term memory within human brain tend to naturally forget things as they happened. Mueller [16] in his work describes that the brain's hippocampus process declines rapidly, while the neocortex process builds up intensity. In cases of high consolidation rates, which is applicable in active learning scenarios, this may even lead to a temporary increase in total intensity and hence recall probability (see Fig. 1). People tend to forget about things and concepts almost instantly, unless there is a conscious effort not to. Taking notes are a manifestation of that conscious effort. There are several approaches to note taking but a note made by an individual is totally unique when compared to those made by others. Handouts given in class by the instructor are all the same but people seem to remember more when they are actively taking a record of what is happening, on their own. This is also applicable for digital note taking e.g. with the help of a laptop or smartphone. But there is a flipside to the scenario when we are taking about digital note taking. People are more reluctant to take notes verbatim, with every word on the document. There is a trade off when digital notes and conventional notes are discussed. In three experiments presented in [18], students use a classroom setting to take notes and their retention was tested afterwards. Half of the students took digital notes while the other half were instructed to take notes conventionally using pen and paper. The study revealed that those who wrote out their notes by hand had a stronger conceptual understanding and were more successful in applying and integrating the material than those who used took notes with their laptops. But despite these findings, modern day challenges make you aware of how to utilize one's time in the best possible way. When a person takes notes digitally, there is typing involved. This is analogous to a thread of execution of a multi-threaded program running on a human brain, so to say, trying to comprehend and understand the concepts underlying a topic. The other threads at play include assimilating what is taught, keeping the mind open to any announcements made by the instructor, looking up to the white board or a projected screen at regular intervals etc.

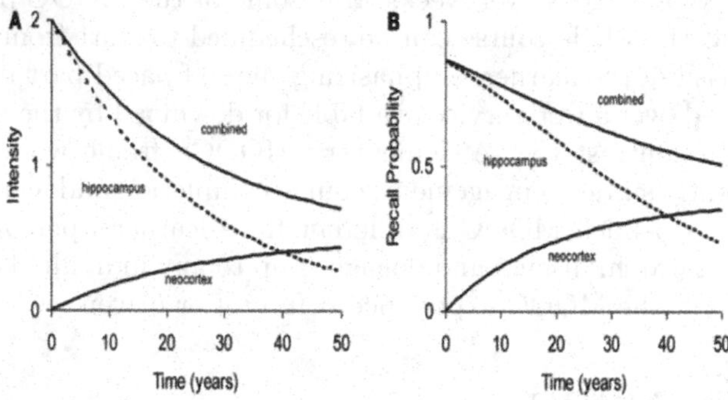

Fig. 1. Example of typical forgetting curve with simulated underlying processes in hippocampal and neocortical stores as described in [15]. (A) Intensity as a function of time. (B) Recall probability as a function of time

5 MOOCbook - A Novel Model

Since videos represent the most significant part of MOOCs, it is a mandate that the note taking process will revolve around them. The length of the videos varies from provider to provider, typically ranging from 2–4 min (micro-lectures) to a maximum of 15 min. As a video progresses, there are certain checkpoints that an instructor breaks a topic into, and these checkpoints serve as the keynotes for the topic at hand. For example, a video about supervised learning of machine learning would typically discuss about the common examples in which it is used, then explain the algorithm employed, plot the points representing the features and interpret it, differentiate with other machine learning algorithms, and finally conclude the scenarios and advantages where the algorithm applies. These checkpoints, although important to the MOOC taker at that instant, seem to fade away when the next video starts. The MOOC taker is reluctant on committing to memory, only those parts which are needed to pass the quizzes, thereby bypassing the concepts which are relevant in learning the topic to have a better learning outcome. This is a step backwards since the MOOC taker often takes a course to supplement the learning he has achieved through his regular curriculum at the institution he has already enrolled into.

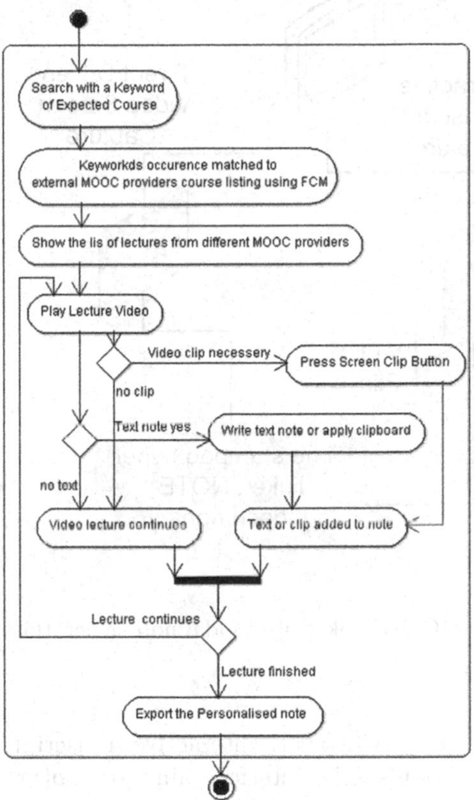

Fig. 2. MOOCbook activity diagram

To address this issue, we propose a novel model whereby the MOOC taker can take notes on the fly when he is taking the course through watching videos. For the MOOC taker, the parts of the course which he intends to take note on happens to be certain points in the video. It is assumed that the video is accompanied by an interactive transcript that scrolls and highlights what the instructor is saying at that moment of the video. During the video, there may happen to be equations, diagrams, graphs and example scenarios that explains the topic from various perspectives. To take the corresponding notes by hand, it would take stopping the video, taking the conventional note book up and writing or drawing what's on the video screen at that instant. This would take up the valuable time that the MOOC taker has invested already. We present a model whereby the digital note taking can be facilitated on the go while the MOOC taker watches the video. We make use of the fact that everything that the learner wants to take note about is present in the video, and these can be extracted by suitable means using client side scripting on the browser that he is currently using to access the materials. The parts of the lecture which catches the attention of the learner are simultaneously displayed in the transcript. So, we grab the transcript and the screen and add the portions to the notebook gets compiled as and when these are added. The learner can save a considerable amount of time which he would otherwise be using for taking the notes conventionally. The user can view the updated note in the browser itself so that it gives a better perspective of what has been learnt already. This plays a role in human brain in instilling a topic repeatedly, as the note document is available to download when the learner needs it. The model MOOCbook is depicted in Fig. 2. The video is the central data source of the note. Associated with the video are two aspects, one being what the screen is presenting at that moment, and the other being what the instructor is speaking, i.e. the transcript. The transcript is assumed to be interactive, meaning that the parts of it will automatically be highlighted. The interactive transcript format is a VTT file.

The VTT file has timestamps and text which is rendered by the browser using javascript code. The model makes use of this and grabs the current sentence, and adds it to the MOOC. Likewise, if anything that the screen is presenting is noteworthy, the model captures the screen, previews it and adds it to the note at the learner's discretion. The outcome of the model is a doc file with all the points captured in the notes (See Fig. 3).

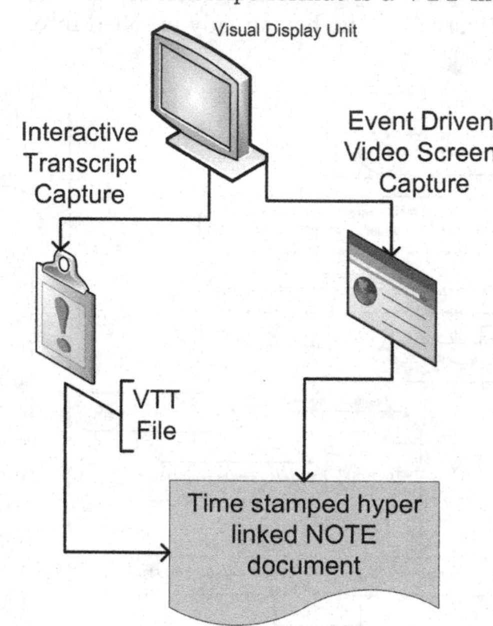

Fig. 3. MOOKBook multi modal note generation

6 Implementation

6.1 Prototype Specifications

The prototype is a web application that hosts a video with interactive transcript, and has buttons to preview and append notes. The interface aims to capture portions of the text of the video content i.e. the transcript along with screen captures, preview them and append to the notebook inside the webpage itself. Finally, the user has the option to download the notebook thus formed. All of this happens using client side scripting, which is relevant since time is of the essence when the user is taking the note as the video plays. This eliminates the load off the servers hosting massive amounts of data in the MOOC servers.

6.2 Prototype Demonstration

A run of the application made will serve as a demo, where the video is one of the those featured in the first week of the Machine Learning course by Professor Andrew Ng of Stanford university, hosted by coursera.org. The instructor goes about explaining "Un-supervised learning" in the course. Figure 4 The

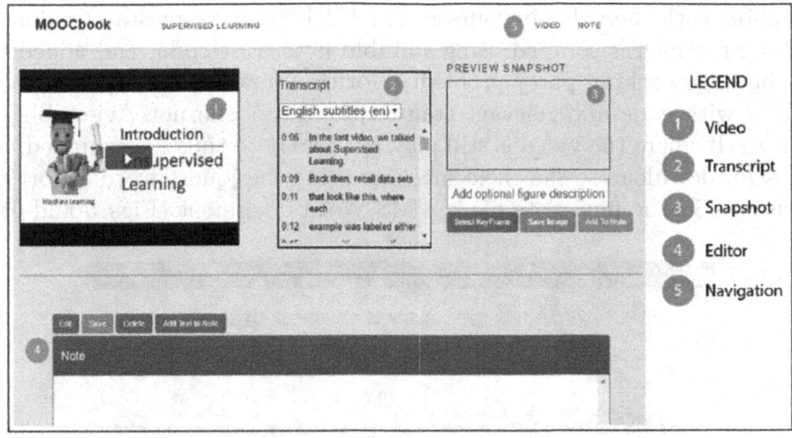

Fig. 4. MOOK Book GUI and interactions

distinguishable parts of the video are listed as under: 1. Difference between unsupervised learning and supervised learning (two graphs). 2. Applications of Supervised Learning (images depicting them). 3. Tackling a problem (cocktail party problem) using unsupervised learning (image depicting the scenario). 4. Cocktail party problem algorithm (code in python). 5. A quiz with options to choose from. These distinguishable parts are of concern to the learner when compiling a digital note about the video. The MOOCbook interface is equipped to take snapshots of these parts and scrape the transcripts of the relevant portions as and when the learner deems it necessary. Figure 4 shows a screen of the video captured for preview. The snapshot is taken using the videojs and videojs interactive transcript JS libraries in tandem. If the preview is deemed good for adding to the note, the user then proceeds accordingly. To capture the lecture discussions relevant to the note being compiled, we have made use of the VTT

Right now

1

active users on site

DESKTOP 100%

Events — Per minute / Per second — Show all: Events

Viewing: Active Users **Events (Last 30 min)**

Metric Total: **21**

	Event Action	Event Label	Events (Last 30 min)	
1.	play	Introduction-UnsupervisedLearning	10	47.62%
2.	pause	Introduction-UnsupervisedLearning	8	38.10%
3.	start	Introduction-UnsupervisedLearning	2	9.52%
4.	end	Introduction-UnsupervisedLearning	1	4.76%

Fig. 5. Analytic dashboard

file available with the video in courser. The VTT file has timestamps along with text content, which is scraped using suitable javascript code, and added to the note. Thus, the cocktail party problem algorithm now has a proposed problem, a solution with code and relevant transcripts, all in one note, viewable in the browser itself where the video is still playing. The note thus far compiled, is now available for download to the client machine using the jquery word export plugin made using JS. The final note file is a MS Word document (Figs. 5 and 6).

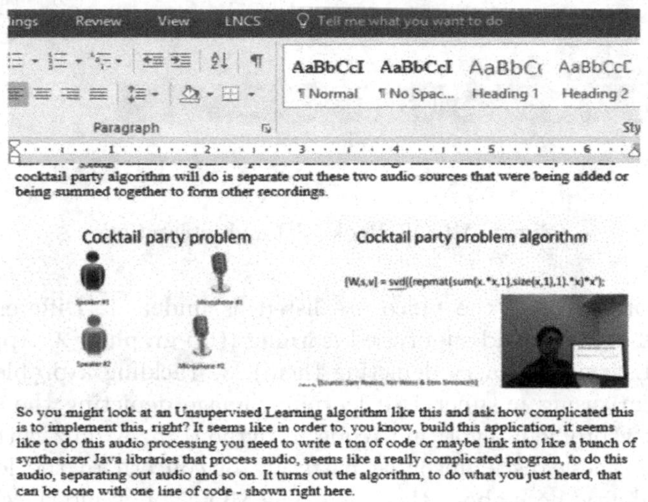

Fig. 6. MOOCBook final note in MS Word

7 Conclusion

The online learners of today face certain challenges when trying to complete MOOCs. These challenges have been studied and a survey for gauging the current status of the MOOC phenomenon has been conducted. The results obtained have provided us with some insights as to what people are looking for in terms of enhancing their learning outcome. One of the major finding was a need of self paced MOOC note. The empirical experiments conducted and anecdotal response have shown significant improvement in engagement to accomplish MOOC course as well enhancement in learning outcome. All the work has been done from a learner's perspective. The inclusion of this tool in MOOC provider platforms will pave the way for enhanced digital learning in the future.

References

1. Barba, N., Gluhanich, L.: 4 Pros and 4 Cons of MOOCs: whether to take study from classroom to online (2014). https://www.geteverwise.com. Accessed 19 June 2017
2. Giannakos, M.N., Jaccheri, L., Krogstie, J.: Looking at MOOCs rapid growth through the lens of video-based learning research. IJET **9**(1), 35–38 (2014)

3. Davis, K., et al.: The theory of multiple intelligence. In: The Cambridge Handbook of Intelligence, pp. 485–503 (2011)
4. Fleming, N., David, B.: Learning styles again: VARKing up the right tree!. Educ. Dev. **7**(4), 4–7 (2006)
5. Barrington, E.: Teaching to student diversity in higher education: how multiple intelligence theory can help. Teach. High. Educ. **9**, 421–434 (2004)
6. Redding, S.: Through the Student's Eyes: A Perspective on Personalized Learning and Practice Guide for Teachers. Center on Innovations in Learning, Temple University (2013)
7. Kop, R., Fournier, H., Mak, J.S.F.: A pedagogy of abundance or a pedagogy to support human beings? Participant support on massive open online courses. Int. Rev. Res. Open Distrib. Learn. **12**(7), 74–93 (2011)
8. Vivian, R., Katrina, F., Nickolas, F.: Addressing the challenges of a new digital technologies curriculum: MOOCs as a scalable solution for teacher professional development. Res. Learn. Technol. **22**(1), 1–19 (2014)
9. Norton, A., Sonnemann, J., McGanno, C.: The online evolution: when technology meets tradition in higher education. Grattan Institute (2013)
10. Kostolnyov, K., Armanov, J.: Use of adaptive study material in education in e-learning environment. Electron. J. e-Learn. **12**(2), 172–182 (2014)
11. Redding, S.: Through the Students Eyes: A Perspective on Personalized Learning and Practice Guide for Teachers. Center on Innovations in Learning, Temple University (2013)
12. Gynther, K.: Design framework for an adaptive MOOC enhanced by blended learning: supplementary training and personalized learning for teacher professional development. Electron. J. e-Learn. **14**(1), 15–30 (2016)
13. IITBombayX: Iitbombayx.in (2017). https://www.iitbombayx.in/dashboard. Accessed 27 June 2017
14. NMEICT: Nmeict.iitkgp.ernet.in (2017). http://www.nmeict.iitkgp.ernet.in/audio.php. Accessed June 2017
15. Rubin, D.C., Wenzel, A.E.: One hundred years of forgetting: a quantitative description of retention. Psychol. Rev. **103**(4), 734 (1996)
16. Murre, J.M.J., Chessa, A.G., Meeter, M.: A mathematical model of forgetting and amnesia. Front. Psychol. **4**, 76 (2013)
17. The Definition of the Visual Learning Style (2017). http://classroom.synonym.com/definition-visual-learning-style-6605691.html
18. Mueller, P.A., Oppenheimer, D.M.: The pen is mightier than the keyboard advantages of longhand over laptop note taking. Psychol. Sci. **25**, 1159–1168 (2014)

Intelligent Data Placement in Heterogeneous Hadoop Cluster

Subhendu Sekhar Paik[1], Rajat Subhra Goswami[2], D. S. Roy[1(✉)], and K. Hemant Reddy[3]

[1] National Institute of Technology, Meghalaya, Laitumkhrah, Shillong 793003, India
diptendu.sr@nitm.ac.in

[2] National Institute of Technology, Arunachal Pradesh, Yupia 791112, India

[3] National Institute of Science and Technology, Berhampur 761008, Odisha, India

Abstract. The MapReduce programming model and Hadoop has become the de facto standard for data-intensive applications. Hadoop tasks are mapped to certain nodes within the Hadoop cluster with data required by tasks. Such a strategy is intuitively appealing for a homogeneous cluster, both in terms of computation and storage capabilities. However most commonplace clusters are indeed heterogeneous, since nodes are added over a prolonged period. This necessitates the use of an intelligent data placement strategy among cluster nodes that accounts for the inherent heterogeneity, which otherwise incurs performance bottleneck. In this paper, we propose to have a performance based clustering of Hadoop nodes and subsequently place data among the nodes. Performance based profiling of nodes can be achieved by running multiple benchmarks in an offline manner and segregating dividing the cluster nodes into two subsets namely low and high performance nodes. Additionally, execution process of Hadoop tasks is monitored using Hadoop's task speculation mechanism and computations are dynamically migrated for slow running tasks based on a prior knowledge of data block regarding the task. Experiments conducted demonstrates that the proposed intelligent data placement improve network utilization and cluster performance.

Keywords: Big data · Hadoop · Heterogeneous cluster performance
MapReduce · Data placement · Job speculation

1 Introduction

MapReduce is a parallel programming model and the implementation of it can best be described by moving computations to data storage with the proliferation of sensors and mobile devices, data sizes required for processing of real-life applications has kept burgeoning. Hadoop and the MapReduce programming paradigm has emerged as the de facto standard for such data-intensive applications. Client logic can be implemented using the predefined map function which processes a key-value pair to generate a set of

P. Bhattacharyya et al. (Eds.): NGCT 2017, CCIS 827, pp. 568–579, 2018.
https://doi.org/10.1007/978-981-10-8657-1_43

intermediate sub results with again several key-value pairs as sub results, and a function known as reducer that merges all intermediate values associated to produce the final result [1].

Data is stored in a Hadoop cluster through the Hadoop Distributed File System (HDFS) write procedure. Hadoop is designed to be fault tolerant, reliable to give uninterrupted availability to data. In order to preserve fault tolerance, data blocks are replicated by the default rack awareness policy, but at the same time Hadoop attempts to achieve Data Locality [2]. Data Locality implies the proximity of the data with map tasks on which the Hadoop MapReduce program will be executed [3]. As per Fig. 1, the white circles are the map tasks and the green circles are the data block, required for the task. It often happens that the data blocks for a map task may not be present in the same local node. This leads the data blocks to be copied from another rack local node or from an off rack node but with a penalty of the time taken to copy the block and additional network bandwidth utilization.

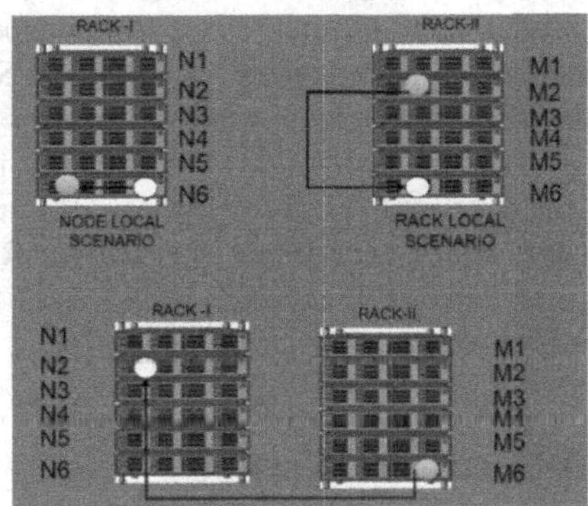

Fig. 1. Hadoop's default replica placement for data locality and rack awareness

Table 1. Estimated data transfer time for different data volumes under varying conditions

Data size	Network type	Delay incurred (d:h:m:s)
500 GB	10 Gib Ethernet	0:00:06:40
1 TB	10 Gib Ethernet	0:00:13:20
10 TB	10 Gib Ethernet	0:02:13:20
20 TB	10 Gib Ethernet	0:04:26:40
30 TB	10 Gib Ethernet	0:06:40:00
50 GB	1 Gib Ethernet	0:01:06:40
1 TB	1 Gib Ethernet	0:02:13:20
10 TB	1 Gib Ethernet	0:22:13:20
20 TB	1 Gib Ethernet	1:20:26:40
30 TB	1 Gib Ethernet	2:18:40:00

This issue arises frequently because Hadoop assumes the cluster to be homogeneous and randomly places data just following the rack awareness approach [4]. When a data local node is overloaded with tasks then the map task is scheduled at an off local node. Since load balancing might slow down map tasks done to heterogeneous cluster scenarios [5] and also run time data transfer. Such delays can incur significant performance bottleneck and Table 1 depicts estimates of such delays for varying network scenarios and data sizes.

This paper proposes a novel data placement algorithm which intelligently places data among different node types and subsequently scheduler tables to nodes, with the option for rescheduling tables by means of Hadoop's task speculation feature as per the two subsets of nodes created by a mathematical function which groups all the DataNodes in a rack into two sets based on their physical capacity of computation i.e. Low Performance Node Group (LPNG) and High Performance Node Group (HPNG). Every data node placed in LPNG will keep its local rack replica in a HPNG and an off rack replica in another HPNG in a different rack. If the cluster built of huge number of nodes, then this approach significantly saves a huge network bandwidth and a big amount of transfer time which is the ultimate goal of this paper.

The remainder of this paper is organized as follows: Sect. 2 presents a brief overview of Hadoop and the MapReduce framework with a summary of related research attempts done previously. Section 3 systematically presents the underlying principles for designing the proposed research. In Sect. 4, implementation details are presented along with a summary of experiments carried out for validating the performance of the proposed methodology. Section 5 summarizes the result and the conclusions are presented in Sect. 6.

2 Background and Literature Review

2.1 Hadoop - A Brief Review

Hadoop is an open source, java built framework, which is implemented to store and process huge amount of data by means of parallel I/O and distributed computing constructs. How every unlike distributed computing paradigm, where data is moved across computers over a network, Hadoop invokes code across different nodes in a network of computer without moving the data and in essence achieving parallel processing and parallel I/O. Figure 2 depicts the basic architecture of Hadoop with its

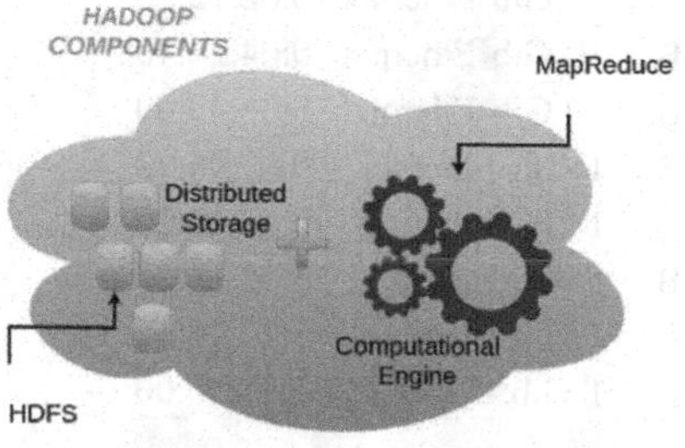

Fig. 2. Hadoop: basic architecture

HDFS distributed storage and distributed computational resources and the MapReduce programming model that enacts the aforesaid functioning.

The MapReduce programming model consists of a map function and a reduce function, that users implement as per their logic. The output of the map function has to be passed to reducer to calculate the final result. Hadoop follows a master slave architecture with one MasterNode and one or more worker nodes. The MasterNode include NameNode, Secondary NameNode and JobTracker whereas the SlaveNode includes DataNode and TaskTracker. Hadoop jobs are distributed in the form of equisized chunks called splits except the last.

These tasks are allocated to TaskTrackers tasks. The TaskTracker allocates a JVM for each task to be executed [7]. In case if a task fails midway then Hadoop collects the status of the task and reallocates the task to another worker node, thus gracefully handling and achieves fault tolerance and hides all underlying details to its users [8].

2.2 Brief Overview of Data Placement Approvals in Hadoop

Adaptive scheduling of computations and load balancing have been studied extensively in distributed computing literature [9–12]. However, Hadoop envision an alternative where only computational tasks are scheduled to nodes having requisite data. Hadoop's default policy of course does not emphasize data placement, which actually randomly places blocks among nodes fulfilling the rack awareness strategy for replica placement.

One of the most fundamental research works on Hadoop's data placement was addressed in [13], which addresses Hadoop's default rack awareness strategy with intuitive reasoning as well as performance ramification of such scheme. However, there has been attempts to place data in Hadoop clusters considering inherent heterogeneity of resources. Most of these attempts have the common strategy of placing data in two phases, one commonly known as the initial placement and the other as dynamic placement. Reference [4] is a case in point where equal sized data fragments are placed among Hadoop nodes initially and in the second phase the algorithm repeatedly relocates file fragments to under-utilized nodes from over-utilized nodes. Similar two phase attempts have also been made for data placement decisions by taking access frequency of data blocks by map tasks and thus creating a 'Heat Map' [14]. In [5], another similar attempt for improved workload management for unbalanced nodes by means of repeatedly adjusting the computing capacity of nodes via a novel Ratio Table. In [15, 17] data aware computational scheduling are proposed, however the emphasis is not so much on heterogeneity of cluster nodes. In [16], a data placement based placement algorithm is proposed. However it does not address issues that may arise due to run-time slow down of jobs. The proposed intelligent data placement in this paper, however address such run-time slowdowns. The following section provides details of our proposed intelligent data placement approach.

Figure 3(a) and (b) depicts these two common phases. However, such data placements are decided using different techniques, such as previous access patterns, inherent dependency among data blocks, dependencies among tasks and data blocks and so forth and different attempts have been made for finding effective schemes.

All these novel methodologies followed two phase algorithms of data placement as shown in Fig. 3(a) and (b) depicting initial placement and runtime placement

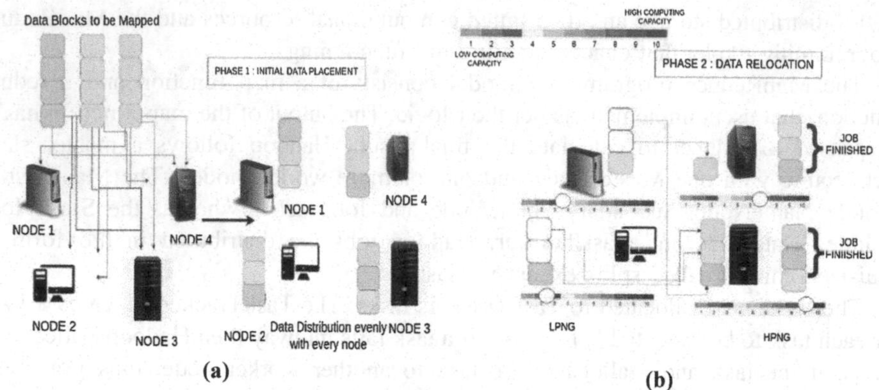

Fig. 3. Two-phase data placement strategy common for addressing heterogeneity

respectively. And this will lead to wastage of network bandwidth and time to transfer, and thus there will be a significant deterioration of the performance. This paper's proposed method will withdraw the chances of any data rearrangement by placing the data intelligently during the initial placement and adding an addon via job speculation of Hadoop.

3 Proposed Intelligent Data Placement

This paper proposes a novel data placement algorithm which intelligently places the data as per data placement algorithm which groups all the DataNodes in a rack into two subsets based on their physical capacity of computation, i.e., Low Performance Node Group (LPNG) and High Performance Node Group (HPNG). Every data block is replicated in Hadoop and Hadoop's default policy supports replication degree of 3. In the proposed schemes first replica is placed randomly to a LPNG. Thereafter the other 2 replicas are placed on two HPNG nodes one on a local rack and the other on an off-rack node. In actual runtime, we proposed to employ task speculation for straggling tasks for running the task on the off-rack HPNG. Such a scheme is motivated to alleviate performance barriers due to costly run-time data movements. In short, the proposed scheme is executed in three phases, namely profiling of the DataNodes in a rack, intelligent data placement, job speculation.

The Fig. 4 depicts that all nodes in a Hadoop cluster are profiled by executing the Hadoop benchmarks individually and collecting the average time of execution. Based on obtained sores, a threshold is set that helps in grouping the available nodes in a rack into two sub sets, namely HPNG and LPNG.

The algorithm in this paper places the data proportionally with the computation power of the nodes as described in the previous subsection, in a way such that the LPNG subset in a rack gets one-third of the data blocks, and then one third is then assigned to HPNG subset in the same rack and the remaining third of the data are assigned to HPNG subset in an another rack. This scenario can be simply explained as

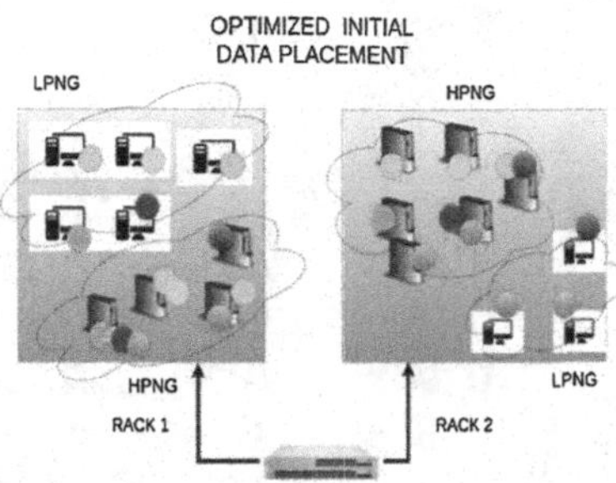

Fig. 4. Overview of data placement in Hadoop cluster with new algorithm

if any DataNode from the subset of LPNG, gets a first replication block, then the algorithm places the rack local replica in a DataNode from the subset of HPNG and the third replica of the data block will be assigned the DataNode from the subset of HPNG from a different local. Figure 5(a) depicts the algorithm for the initial data placement proposed.

Job speculation with the process such that if any LPNG DataNode lags in performance due to any of the physical availability of resource at that moment any DataNode from a HPNG subset will immediately speculate the task and will run parallel by cloning the task but not migrating the data blocks required by task cause two third share of the data already exist in two subsets of HPNG in the same rack and different rack respectively, ultimately which saves a huge time and network bandwidth avoiding unnecessary data transfer between two distant nodes and thus preserving the Rack Awareness algorithm of Hadoop for fault tolerance improving the performance in the heterogeneous cluster. Figure 5(b) captures the step in speculative job execution proposed in this paper.

As per the running connection from the previous sub section, if a simulation is done having two sub groups in each rack of a Heterogeneous Hadoop cluster shown in below figures names as HPNG and LPNG. The incoming data blocks A to G needs to be placed in the rack and this will be done by following a specific algorithm as given in the Fig. 5(a). When the first replica of each block is ready to be stored in the HDFS then this algorithm will check the available rack IDs and randomly will pick one rack and then a DataNode from the previously selected rack and then it will keep a temporary info about the DataNode whether it belongs to the LPNG or HPNG subset and will return location of it. Once the location is available the 1st replica is placed then the second replica will be placed in the same rack but in the opposite subset. As per the diagram the A1 (1st replica of block 'A') is placed in a DataNode belonging to LPNG and hence the A2 (2nd replica of block 'A') will be stored in a DataNode of HPNG. Then algorithm will pick a random rackId again excluding the previous rack and then randomly pick a DataNode from the HPNG subset and A3 will be placed in that DataNode. And similarly following the same steps replicas of each data block will be distributed in the cluster as shown in Fig. 6.

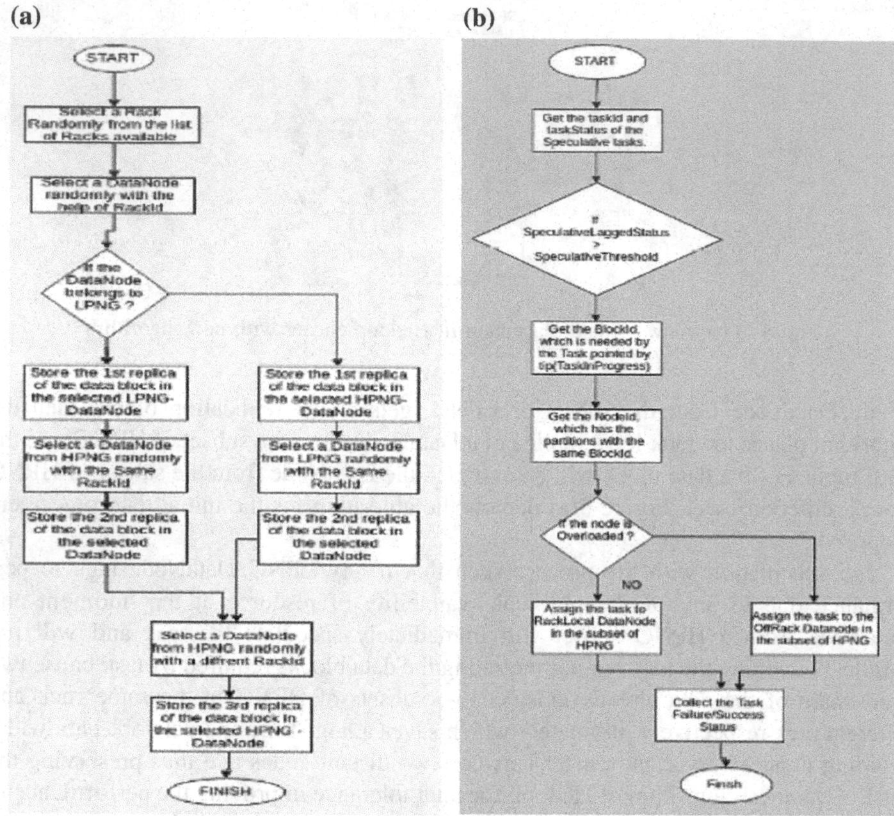

Fig. 5. (a). Algorithm for initial data placement (b). Algorithm for Speculative task execution

Now comes the scenario where the performance will be monitored when the jobs will start executing in the cluster. If it's assumed that a map task scheduled in a DataNode D1 and as it belongs to LPNG, hence there is a higher probability that it may be lagging as compared to the current tasks in the same job. As per the algorithm in Fig. 5(b), an event driven procedure will check the task progress and health of the DataNodes continuously and if any node starts lagging then, immediately it will collect the task ID and the Block IDs on which it's working. Then the next task is to find out the location of the second replication of the same block. Then obviously it will find a node from the subset of HPNG in the same rack and from an another rack. Then it will check the health of the rack local node out of the two. And if it's not critical and its available to accept tasks then it will clone the task from the current DataNode to the DataNode selected.

In this case the task executing on D1 will be cloned to the DataNode containing D2. And in worst case it may clone the task to DataNode in rack 3 containing D3 which is a node in the group of HPNG. But the good news is there is no need to copy the data block 'D'. Thus saving the time to transfer the block and the network bandwidth.

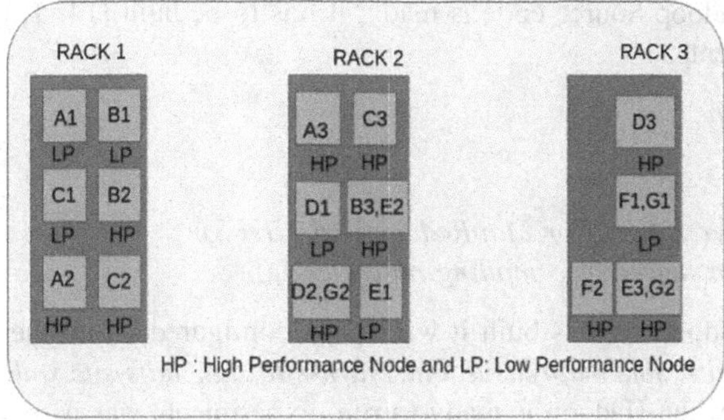

Fig. 6. A Hadoop cluster after classification and initial data placement

4 Implementation and Experimentation

4.1 Implementation

Proposed initial data placement algorithm gives advantage over the speculative execution by keeping a 2/3 share of data blocks in a same rack, and most importantly in a two different groups based on the computational capacity of the nodes i.e. LPNG (Low performance Node Group) and HPNG (High Performance Node Group), such that whenever any LPNG member gives a slower response and acts as a straggler then our job speculative algorithm will clone the job in such a place that there will not be any data clone/transfer to the destination node. So a patch is implanted in existing version of Hadoop to enact the proposed algorithm. Therefore, it is recommended to assess the computational capacities of nodes in a quantitative manner and establish a specific characterization of the newly implemented version of Hadoop through extensive benchmarking.

In order to implement this approach via Hadoop, the source code of Hadoop has been edited to implant piece of source codes in several of files and several of procedures has been modified like:

- *DataOutputStream.java*
- *ApplicationTargetChooser.java*
- *TaskInProgress.java*

and the information needed to clone the task and for decision making are collected from the classes and methods as below:

- *NetworkTopology.java*
- *DatanodeId.java*
- *public List<Node> getDatanodesInRack(String loc)*
- *protected int getWeight(Node reader, Node node)*
- *public boolean isOnSameRack(Node node1, Node node2)*
- *public Node getNode(String loc)*
- *public int getNumOfRacks().*

Once the Hadoop Source code is ready, it has to be built [14, 15] again using the below requirements:

- *Linux Machine*
- *JDK*
- *Maven 3.1.1*
- *ProtocolBuffer 2.4.1+ (for MapReduce and HDFS)*
- *CMake 2.6 or newer (if compiling native code).*

Once the Hadoop code is built it was again configured on all the nodes by modifying the *core-site.xml, mapredsite.xml, yarn-site.xml, hdfs-site.xml, hadoop-env.sh*. And at the end when Hadoop is ready to run, experiments was carried multiple times and their average values were calculated and noted for the performance measurement.

4.2 Test-Bed Set-up

We induced our proposed mechanism by overriding Hadoop's default task speculation. So in order to create the task speculation a temporal delay (thread sleep) was introduced by java code [21] if the node belongs to a LPNG subset. In order to get a real picture of heterogeneous cluster 4 different types of nodes were selected with different families of processor and with different primary memory capacities. 18 nodes of different hardware capacities divided into 3 racks by specifying network location of the nodes with the configuration parameters. Thus there were 3 racks each with 6 nodes with significantly different resources, producing a pragmatic heterogeneous Hadoop cluster. Each node was connected through 1 Gbps network Gigabit network switch. And the final test-bed had the specification as per Table 2.

4.3 Experiments Conducted

In order to profile the nodes into LPNG and HPNG, we executed benchmark prepared by Intel called as HiBench [18]. HiBench is a new versatile, comprehensive, representative benchmark suite for Hadoop performance labeling, that consists of a set of predesigned Hadoop programs containing both analytic micro benchmarks and real-world applications oriented benchmarks [19]. The Micro-benchmarks of HiBench has workloads such as Sort, WordCount, EnhancedDFSIO, TeraSort [20].

Now the performance modulation can only be found out when the cluster executes the Benchmarks. So after configuring the modified version of Hadoop in every node in the cluster, again HiBench benchmark was run and the execution times are collected by varying the job size. Every benchmark has been executed and the corresponding data has been captured as per the figures.

At the beginning benchmarks like WordCount, TeraGen, TeraSort are executed on default Hadoop with default configuration for multiple times with varying job sizes and their average execution times were noted and kept for future references. Then after implementing own source code in Hadoop for decision making, again same bench marks were executed several times with same job sizes and the execution times were recorded to find out average execution time. And finally the average execution times were compared to each other to derive a relation between them.

Table 2. Summary specifications of testbed components

Component	Specification I	Specification II	Specification III	Specification IV
Hard Disk	1 TB SATA	1 TB SATA	1 TB SATA	8 TB
RAM	8 GB DDR3	4 GBDDR3- 2133	2 GB (SODIMM) x1) DDR3 SDRAM	64 GB of SystemMemory (RAM)
Processor	Intel® Core™ i7-4790 CPU @ 3.6 GHz×8 (3 nodes)	Intel Core i3-100T CPU@3.20 GHzx8 (6 nodes)	Intel Core 2 Duo E6750/2.66 GHz (6 nodes)	Intel(R) Xeon(R) CPU E5-2670 v3@ 2.30 GHz (3 nodes)
OS	Ubuntu 16.04 LTS Server edition	Ubuntu 16.04 LTS Server edition	Ubuntu 16.04 LTS Server edition	Ubuntu 16.04 LTS Server edition
Hadoop version	2.6.1	2.6.1	2.6.1	2.6.1
Network	1000 Mbps Gigabit Network Switch	1000 Mbps Gigabit Network Switch	1000 Mbps Gigabit Network Switch	1000 Mbps Gigabit Network Switch

5 Results and Discussion

After multiple times of execution of the benchmarks with the default version of Hadoop and modified version of Hadoop total execution time was collected. At first WordCount benchmark was run and the corresponding values were captured and average execution time was plotted with varying job sizes for both the versions of Hadoop. Figure 7(a) (b) and (c) study the effect of varying job sizes on execution time on default Hadoop and our modified Hadoop with the proposed intelligent data placement for WordCount, TearGen, TeraSort benchmarks respectively.

With the observed values from the execution of WordCount it can be clearly observed that the modified Hadoop version took a lesser time to complete the job as compared to the default version of Hadoop. Performance gains vary from 18% for WordCount and TeraSort, to 7–8% for TeraGen benchmarks on an average. This is quite significant improvements.

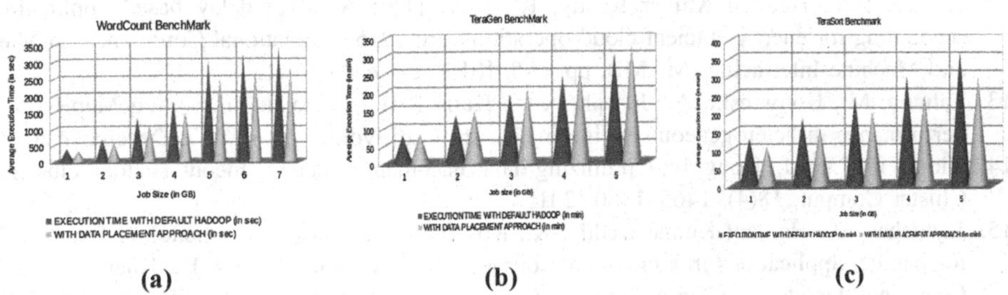

Fig. 7. Effect of increasing job sizes on execution time

6 Conclusion

The default data placement policy in Hadoop is constrained by performance bottleneck owing to its homogeneous treatment of capacity of all its constituent nodes. To this end in this paper we have proposed an intelligent data placement strategy where nodes are segregated on basis of their computing capabilities into subsets of LPNG and HPNG that enables node heterogeneity. Task speculation has been combined to handle straggler tasks. Experiments performed on the prepared strategy shows significant performance improvement ranging from 7 to 18% across different benchmark datasets. In future, we envision to invigilate intelligent reducer placement for performance improvement of Hadoop.

References

1. Dean, J., Ghemawat, S.: MapReduce: simplified data processing on large clusters. Commun. ACM **51**(1), 107–113 (2008)
2. Apache Hadoop Homepage. http://hadoop.apache.org. Accessed 10 Mar 2017
3. Hadoopinrealworld Topic Page. http://hadoopinrealworld.com/data-locality-in-hadoop/. Accessed 25 May 2017
4. Xie, J., Yin, S., Ruan, X., Ding, Z., Tian, Y., Majors, J., Qin, X.: Improving MapReduce performance through data placement in heterogeneous hadoop clusters. In: 2010 IEEE International Symposium on Parallel & Distributed Processing, Workshops and Ph.D Forum (IPDPSW), pp. 1–9. IEEE, April 2010
5. Lee, C.W., Hsieh, K.Y., Hsieh, S.Y., Hsiao, H.C.: A dynamic data placement strategy for hadoop in heterogeneous environments. Big Data Res. **1**, 14–22 (2014)
6. Bardhan, S., Menascé, D.A.: The anatomy of MapReduce jobs, scheduling, and performance challenges. In: International CMG Conference, November 2013
7. Google Hadoop Big Data Webpage. https://cloud.google.com/solutions/hadoop/. Accessed 10 Apr 2017
8. White, T.: Hadoop: The definitive guide. O'Reilly Media Inc, Sebastopol (2012)
9. Hemant Kumar Reddy, K., Patra, M.R., Roy, D.S., Pradhan, B.: An adaptive scheduling mechanism for computational desktop grid using gridgain. Proc. Technol. **4**, 573–578 (2012)
10. Pradhan, B., Nayak, A., Roy, D.S.: An elegant load balancing scheme in grid computing using GridGain. Int. J. Comput. Sci. Appl. **1**(1), 254–257 (2011)
11. Hemant Kumar Reddy, K., Roy, D.S.: A hierarchical load balancing algorithm for efficient job scheduling in a computational grid testbed. In: 2012 1st International Conference on Recent Advances in Information Technology (RAIT), pp. 363–368. IEEE, March 2012
12. Harsha, L.S., Hemant Kumar Reddy, K., Roy, D.S.: A novel delay based application scheduling for energy efficient cloud operations. In: 2015 International Conference on Man and Machine Interfacing (MAMI), pp. 1–5. IEEE, December 2015
13. Zaharia, M., Konwinski, A., Joseph, A.D., Katz, R.H., Stoica, I.: Improving MapReduce performance in heterogeneous environments. In: Osdi, vol. 8, no. 4, p. 7, December 2008
14. Xiong, R., Luo, J., Dong, F.: Optimizing data placement in heterogeneous Hadoop clusters. Cluster Comput. **18**(4), 1465–1480 (2015)
15. Jaykishan, B., Hemant Kumar Reddy, K., Roy, D.S.: A data-aware scheduling framework for parallel applications in a cloud environment. In: Sengupta, S., Das, K., Khan, G. (eds.) Emerging Trends in Computing and Communication. LNEE, vol. 298, pp. 459–463. Springer, New Delhi (2014). https://doi.org/10.1007/978-81-322-1817-3_49

16. Hemant Kumar Reddy, K., Roy, D.S.: DPPACS: a novel data partitioning and placement aware computation scheduling scheme for data-intensive cloud applications. Comput. J. **59** (1), 64–82 (2015)
17. Hemant Kumar Reddy, K., Das, H., Roy, D.S.: A data aware scheme for scheduling big data applications with SAVANNA Hadoop. In: Elkhodr, M., Hassan, Q.F., Shahrestani, S. (eds.) Big Data and the Internet of Things, Part IV. Networks of the Future: Architectures, Technologies, and Implementations. CRC Press, Taylor & Francis Group, LLC, Florida, USA (2017)
18. Huang, S., Huang, J., Liu, Y., Yi, L., Dai, J.: HiBench: a representative and comprehensive hadoop benchmark suite. In: Proceedings ICDE Workshops (2010)
19. Github Repo. https://github.com/intel-hadoop/HiBench. Accessed 10 Apr 2017
20. https://github.com/apache/hadoop. Accessed 03 May 2017
21. https://wiki.apache.org/hadoop/HowToContribute. Accessed 22 Jun 2017
22. https://pravinchavan.wordpress.com/2013/04/14/building-apache-hadoop-from-source/. Accessed 20 Jun 2017

Effective Heuristics for the Bi-objective Euclidean Bounded Diameter Minimum Spanning Tree Problem

V. Prem Prakash[1(✉)], C. Patvardhan[1], and Anand Srivastav[2]

[1] Dayalbagh Educational Institute (Deemed University), Agra 282005, India
vpremprakash@acm.org
[2] Christian-Albrechts-Universitat zu Kiel, Kiel, Germany

Abstract. The Euclidean Bounded Diameter Minimum Spanning Tree (BDMST) Problem aims to find the spanning tree with the lowest cost, or weight, under the constraint that the diameter does not exceed a given integer D, and where the weight of an edge is the Euclidean distance between its two end points (vertices). Several well-known heuristic approaches have been applied to this problem. The bi-objective version of this problem aims to minimize two conflicting objectives, weight (or cost), and diameter. Several heuristics for the BDMST problem have been recast for the bi-objective BDMST problem (or BOMST problem) and their performance studied on the entire range of possible diameter values. While some of the extant heuristics are seen to dominate other heuristics over certain portions of the Pareto front of solutions, no single heuristic performs well over the entire range. This paper presents a hybrid tree construction heuristic that combines a greedy approach with a heuristic strategy for constructing effective tree "backbones". The performance of the proposed heuristic is shown to be consistently superior to the other extant heuristics on a standard benchmark suite of dense Euclidean graphs widely used in the literature.

Keywords: Multi-objective · BOMST · Spanning tree · Bounded diameter

1 Introduction

Given a connected, weighted, undirected graph G and an integer bound D, a bounded-diameter spanning tree (BDST) is a spanning tree on G whose diameter, that is, the maximum number of edges along any path in the tree, does not exceed D. The Bounded Diameter Minimum Spanning Tree (BDMST) Problem aims to find a BDST on G of minimum weight (the weight of a BDST is the sum of its edge weights). The BDMST problem is known to be NP-hard [1] for $4 \leq D < n - 1$. The Euclidean version of the BDMST problem deals with graph instances whose edge weights are the Euclidean distances between the connected vertices.

Applications from several domains map to this problem: routing problems in VLSI often require minimum spanning trees that bound the sink-source delays (diameter bound) and total wire length (minimum cost/weight); large bitmap data structures are often clustered and compressed as MSTs – fast retrieval such structures of such

P. Bhattacharyya et al. (Eds.): NGCT 2017, CCIS 827, pp. 580–589, 2018.
https://doi.org/10.1007/978-981-10-8657-1_44

structures requires the MST to have a low diameter [2]; the work by Raymond [3] presents an application of the BDMST problem for minimizing communication costs while performing distributed mutual exclusion in large scale distributed systems and ad-hoc networks.

The Bi-objective Bounded Diameter Minimum Spanning Tree (BOMST) Problem [4] aims to find BDSTs such that both the diameter and weight of the tree are minimized over the entire range of diameter values. Thus the single-objective BDMST Problem is a special case of the more general BOMST Problem as defined here. The Euclidean BOMST Problem (e-BOMST) restricts the domain to that of Euclidean instances.

Achuthan and Caccetta give two exact algorithms for the BDMST Problem in [5, 6]. Multiple variants of multi-commodity flow (MCF) formulations for the BDMST problem are given by Gouveia and Magnanti [7], which obtain very tight LP bounds. However, these algorithms are only able to solve very small problem instances. This has motivated the search for algorithms that are able to approximate low cost BDSTs well for sufficiently large problem sizes within reasonable time. Several such heuristics abound in the literature of the BDMST problem.

Abdalla and Deo [8] give a construction heuristic based on Prim's algorithm [14] called the *One-time tree construction* (OTTC) heuristic that runs in $O(n^4)$ time and produces low cost BDSTs when the diameter constraint is small. They also give two iterative refinement (IR) algorithms that iteratively decrease the lengths of long paths in an unconstrained MST until the diameter constraint is satisfied. A more effective Prim's-based approach is presented in the *Center-based tree construction* (CBTC) heuristic given by Julstrom [9], which constructs the BDST as a height-restricted tree rooted either at a central vertex, if the diameter limit is even, or a central edge, if it is odd. This heuristic, which takes $O(n^3)$ time, outperforms OTTC both in terms of solution quality and running time. The *Randomized tree construction heuristic* (RTC) [9] builds the BDST by selecting vertices in a random order and appending each vertex to the tree at the lowest cost possible. This heuristic also requires $O(n^3)$ computation time. The *Center-based Least Sum-of-Costs* (CBLSoC) heuristic given by Patvardhan and Prakash [10] builds a low cost BDST in $O(n^3)$ time by repeatedly appending the non-tree vertex with the lowest mean cost to all the remaining non-tree vertices in the graph. Parallel versions of the CBTC, RTC and CBLSoC heuristics are given in [16] and their performance studied on several benchmark problems. A recursive, clustering-based heuristic called *Center-based Recursive Clustering* heuristic (CBRC) is given for the problem by Nghia and Binh [11].

Kumar and Saha [4, 12] adapt several extant BDMST heuristics for the bi-objective MST formulation of the problem and compare their performance on standard problem instances. The results obtained are further improved using a bi-objective meta-heuristic algorithm seeded with different heuristic solutions.

This paper presents a comprehensive comparison of some well known extant heuristics with a hybrid heuristic that is adapted to the Euclidean version of the BOMST problem. The performance of all the heuristics is obtained on much larger problem instances than in earlier work on the BOMST problem, and the proposed heuristic is shown to give superior performance on a benchmark suite comprised of several dense Euclidean graph instances used widely in the literature.

The rest of the paper is organized as follows. Section 2 describes two extant heuristics that were shown to obtain superior Pareto fronts on Euclidean graphs in an earlier work [4], and another well known heuristic for the BDMST problem which is recast for the bi-objective version of the problem. Section 3 presents a hybrid heuristic that computes low cost BDSTs across the diameter range in $O(n^3)$ time. The performance of the heuristics on the benchmark suite is presented and discussed in Sect. 4, and concluding remarks made in Sect. 5.

2 Three Extant Heuristics

Several heuristics have been developed in the literature for the BDMST problem, some of which were recast for the BOMST problem in [4, 12]. Of these, the Center-based Tree Construction (CBTC) and Randomized Tree Construction (RTC) were found to generally obtain superior results on Euclidean instances over different ranges of the Pareto front [12]. Therefore both of these are taken as baselines for comparing the performance of the heuristics presented in this work with. The CBLSoC heuristic has also been shown to perform well on Euclidean instances [15], and has been adapted here for the eBOMST Problem. Following is a brief description of each of these heuristics.

2.1 Center-Based Tree Construction (CBTC)

In a tree with diameter D, no vertex is more than D/2 hops or edges from the root vertex of the tree [13]. The Center-Based Tree Construction (CBTC) heuristic [9] uses this idea to build a BDST starting with an arbitrary graph vertex as the center of the tree, and repeatedly appending to the BDST, the graph vertex with the lowest cost edge to the partial tree. The heuristic dynamically maintains the depth information of each tree node and ensures that the depth of any leaf node of the tree is at most D/2. The center of the tree comprises of a single vertex if D is even, and one edge if D is odd. The algorithm repeatedly appends to the growing BDST, the edge with the lowest-cost/weight that adds a new vertex to the tree, while not violating the diameter bound. In order to obtain a low cost BDST, this process is repeated n times, taking a different graph vertex as the root node in each iteration.

Lemma 1. The running time of Center-based Tree Construction heuristic is $O(n^3)$.

Proof. The heuristic builds a BDST from its center, keeping track of the depth of each incoming vertex and ensuring that node depth is strictly less than D/2. By using an O(n) space data structure to dynamically keep track of the tree node of depth $\leq$ D/2 closest to each graph vertex, the computational cost of appending each incoming node to the growing BDST becomes a linear time operation. Appending $n - 1$ vertices (or $n - 2$ vertices to the BDST if D is odd) results in $O(n^2)$ time for building one BDST. As the heuristic repeats this process for each vertex, the total computation time required is $O(n^3)$.

2.2 Randomized Tree Construction (RTC)

The Randomized Tree Construction (RTC) heuristic sets a randomly chosen vertex (or edge, depending on whether D is even or odd, respectively) as the root of the BDST. All subsequent vertices are chosen at random and appended to the tree via the lowest cost edge that does not violate the diameter bound D. As with the CBTC, this process is repeated n times, and the lowest cost BDST is returned.

Lemma 2. The running time of Randomized Tree Construction heuristic is $O(n^3)$.

Proof. If a partially constructed BDST has k nodes (represented by the set T), then there are $n - k$ graph vertices (represented as the set U) that are not part of the BDST. Choosing a vertex u at random from U and appending it greedily to the vertex $v \in T$ such that cost (u, v) is minimal would require O(n) time. Appending $n - 1$ vertices in this manner to complete the BDST would therefore require $O(n^2)$ time. Repeating this process n times and returning the best BDST would thus need a total of $O(n^3)$ time.

2.3 Center-Based Least Sum-of-Costs (CBLSoC) Heuristic

The CBLSoC heuristic tries to construct the BDST in a relatively "less greedy" manner by repeatedly appending to the partial tree, the graph vertex with the lowest average cost to all other graph vertices, via the edge with smallest cost that does not violate the diameter bound. This process is repeated starting from each graph vertex, and the lowest cost BDST obtained is returned by thc algorithm.

Lemma 3. The running time of the CBLSoC heuristic is $O(n^3)$.

Proof. For each vertex u, the sum of costs (and hence the mean cost) to all other $n - 1$ vertices in the graph G can be computed in O(n) time. Hence the time to compute the sum-of-costs for all vertices in the graph would take $O(n^2)$ time. The BDST is initially empty, i.e., $T = \varphi$. Starting with a center based approach, identifying the graph vertex u with lowest mean cost to all other vertices in G would require O(n) time. Appending u to vertex $v \in T$ such that cost (u, v) is minimal would also take O(n) time. As explained in the proofs of Lemmas 1 and 2, appending $n - 1$ vertices in this manner to complete the BDST would require $O(n^2)$ time; repeating this process n times and returning the best BDST would therefore result in a total of $O(n^3)$ time.

3 Hybrid Tree Construction (Hyb-TC) Heuristic

The CBTC heuristic loses out to other heuristics (notably the RTC heuristic) for small values of D, but its performance improves quickly as the diameter bound is relaxed (cf. Table 1). This is because the greediness inherent in the CBTC heuristic constrains it to always choose the vertex that can be appended to the tree at the lowest cost possible. In Euclidean BDSTs, this often results in backbones comprised of a small number of low-depth vertices that are very close to each other, forcing the remaining vertices to be appended to these vertices via higher cost edges and thereby returning BDSTs with high total cost, or weight. As the diameter bound is gradually increased, the BDST returned by CBTC tends to shape up like an unconstrained MST, resulting in lower cost BDSTs. Another fast heuristic strategy that proves very effective on small D in Euclidean instances is the greedy Quadrant-centers based Heuristic (gQCH) [15], which empirically breaks up the Euclidean space of graph vertices into different numbers of equal sized sub-spaces, or quadrants, and tries to build a backbone of tree vertices that can in turn form the roots for low cost sub-trees obtained by greedily appending the remaining graph vertices to the BDST. In each quadrant, the vertex with the lowest average cost to all other vertices (in that quadrant) is set as a backbone node. When the number of quadrants is 1, this heuristic "collapses" into a single run of the CBTC heuristic with the root node(s) set as the vertex (if the diameter limit is even) or pair of vertices (if the diameter limit is odd) with the lowest mean cost to all other graph vertices.

The proposed Hybrid Tree Construction (Hyb-TC) heuristic combines these two strategies in order to obtain better results over the entire range of diameter bounds. The heuristic starts in the same manner as the CBTC does, and builds n BDSTs starting once each from each vertex/vertex pair. Thereafter, it tries to quickly build effective BDST backbones using a subset of the vertex set to which the remaining vertices may be appended greedily at a lower cost on average, thereby leading to lower tree costs. With this objective, the heuristic chooses the graph vertex/vertices with the lowest mean cost(s) to all other graph nodes as the central, or root vertex/vertices (depending respectively on whether D is even or odd), and segregates the remaining graph vertices into the "quadrants" of a uniform $K \times K$ matrix in the two dimensional Euclidean plane, for $2 \leq K \leq \sqrt{n}$. Within each quadrant, the vertex with the lowest mean cost to all other vertices within the same quadrant is set as a tree backbone node of depth 1. Once the backbone has been constructed in this manner, the remaining vertices are appended to the tree greedily, as in CBTC. Another $\sqrt{n} - 1$ BDSTs are constructed in this manner, and the algorithm returns the lowest cost tree from amongst the $n + \sqrt{n} - 1$ BDSTs thus constructed.

Lemma 4. The running time of the Hyb-TC heuristic is $O(n^3)$.

Proof. In order to build the backbone, the heuristic computes the mean cost of each vertex to every other vertex within its designated quadrant. Computing the mean cost of each vertex v over K^2 quadrants comprising a total of n vertices would require at most O (n^2) time. Over $\sqrt{n-1}$ iterations, this would require a total of $O(n^2\sqrt{n})$ time. In each iteration, the remaining vertices are then appended greedily to the partial BDST – if the backbone consists of m vertices, then n – m graph vertices need to be appended to the tree – this operation would take another $O(n^2)$ time. Thus the total computation time to compute the $\sqrt{n-1}$ BDSTs would be $O(n^2\sqrt{n})$ time. The remaining n BDSTs are generated using a greedy approach starting from each vertex. As shown in the proof for Lemma 1, constructing each BDST would require an additional $O(n^2)$ time, and repeating this process for n vertices would take $O(n^3)$ time. Thus the total computation time of the heuristic is the sum of these two components: $O(n^3)$ time for finding the lowest cost BDST starting once from each vertex, and $O(n^2\sqrt{n})$ for computing $\sqrt{n} - 1$ BDSTs using the backbone construction heuristic, thus resulting in a total computation time of $O(n^3)$.

4 Experiments

The benchmark graphs used in this work were taken from the Euclidean Steiner Problem data sets given in Beasley's OR-Library [17]. These data sets contain fifteen instances each of completely connected graphs with 50, 100, 250, 500 and 1000 vertices, working out to a total of seventy five graphs. The x- and y- co-ordinates of random points in the unit square form the vertices of the graph, and the Euclidean distance between these vertices their edge weights. These instances have been used in the literature for benchmarking heuristics and algorithms for the BOMST Problem.

The heuristics presented in this paper were tested on the first five instances of 50, 100, 250 and 500 vertex dense graphs of the Euclidean Steiner data sets, a total of twenty problem instances, and the BDST costs returned by the heuristics were obtained for diameter D, $2 \leq D \leq D_{max}$, where the upper limit for the D values, D_{max} was chosen as the diameter of an unconstrained MST on each graph instance. Pareto fronts were obtained for the heuristics in this paper on each test instance, and plots of the Pareto fronts obtained for the first instance of each size (50, 100, 250 and 500) of benchmark graph are shown in Figs. 1, 2, 3 and 4 respectively. All the heuristics were implemented in C on a Dell Precision T5500 workstation with 12 Xeon (2.4-GHz) processor cores and 11 GB of RAM running RHEL 6. The BDST costs obtained by

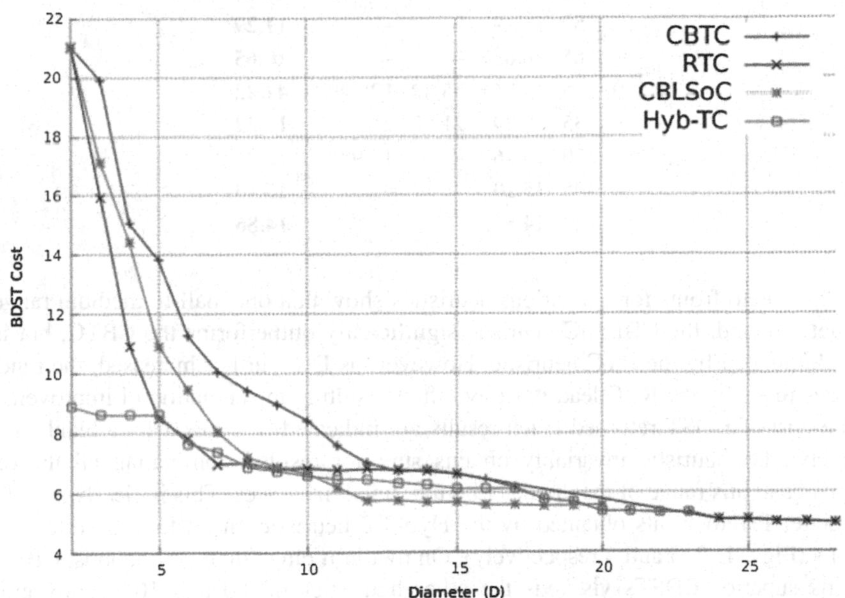

Fig. 1. Pareto fronts obtained over the entire diameter range for the first 50 vertex dense Euclidean graph for the CBTC, RTC, CBLSoC and Hyb-TC heuristics, up to D = 28.

each heuristic for five selected diameter limits on the first instance of each of the 50, 100, 250 and 500 vertex benchmark graphs are given in Table 1.

Table 1. BDST costs obtained for selected values of diameter bound on dense graphs of 50, 100, 250 and 500 vertices

n	D	BDST cost/weight			
		CBTC	RTC	CBLSoC	Hyb-TC
50	5	13.04	8.53	10.94	**8.63**
	10	8.44	6.84	6.66	**6.59**
	15	6.64	6.63	**5.68**	6.14
	20	**5.35**	–	5.56	**5.35**
	25	**5.08**	–	–	**5.08**
100	5	27.12	15.13	23.16	**12.97**
	15	11.41	8.80	8.39	**8.33**
	25	7.07	–	**7.03**	7.07
	35	**6.79**	–	–	**6.79**
	45	**6.61**	–	–	**6.61**
250	5	75.68	32.34	60.58	**25.63**
	20	26.74	15.11	17.70	**13.55**
	35	14.35	–	12.17	**11.71**
	50	**11.29**	–	–	**11.29**
	65	**10.65**	–	–	**10.65**
500	5	153.44	65.42	128.40	**42.22**
	35	39.89	21.50	24.00	**17.29**
	70	16.46	–	15.98	**15.92**
	105	**15.10**	–	–	**15.10**
	140	**14.86**	–	–	**14.86**

The Pareto fronts for the various heuristics show that on small-to-medium range of diameter bound, the CBLSoC heuristic significantly outperforms the CBTC, but is in turn dominated by the RTC heuristic. However, as D is further increased, the random choices made by the RTC lead it astray, often resulting in stagnation of improvements in the cost of BDST returned (such results are indicated in Table 1 by a blank entry). The Hyb-TC heuristic invariably obtains superior results, dominating all the other heuristics in this range of the diameter bound, on all instances. This is clearly seen from the better Pareto fronts obtained by the Hyb-TC heuristic on up to 500 vertex dense graphs (Figs. 1, 2, 3 and 4 respectively). On medium range diameter bounds, CBLSoC returns superior BDSTs vis-à-vis the other heuristics on 50 and 100 vertex graphs (Figs. 1 and 2 respectively), and remains competitive on larger instances. However, CBLSoC fails to obtain further improvements in the best trees returned when the diameter bound is large. With the exception of a few cases on 50 and 100 vertex graphs where the CBTC heuristic obtains better trees, the Hyb-TC heuristic outperforms all the other heuristics over the medium range of diameter bound. As the diameter bound becomes large, the low cost BDST returned by the Hyb-TC heuristic tends towards an

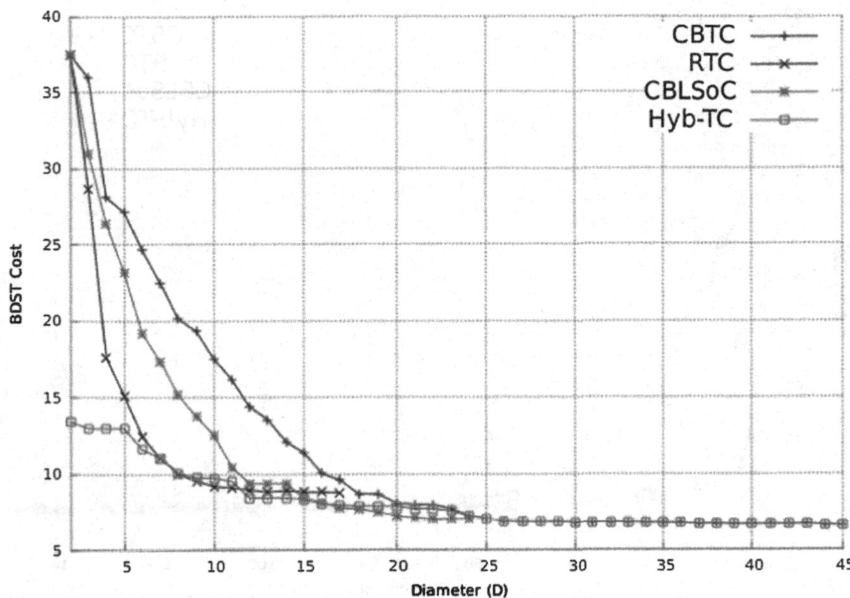

Fig. 2. Pareto fronts obtained over the entire diameter range for the first 100 vertex Euclidean benchmark instance for the CBTC, RTC, CBLSoC and Hyb-TC heuristics, up to D = 45.

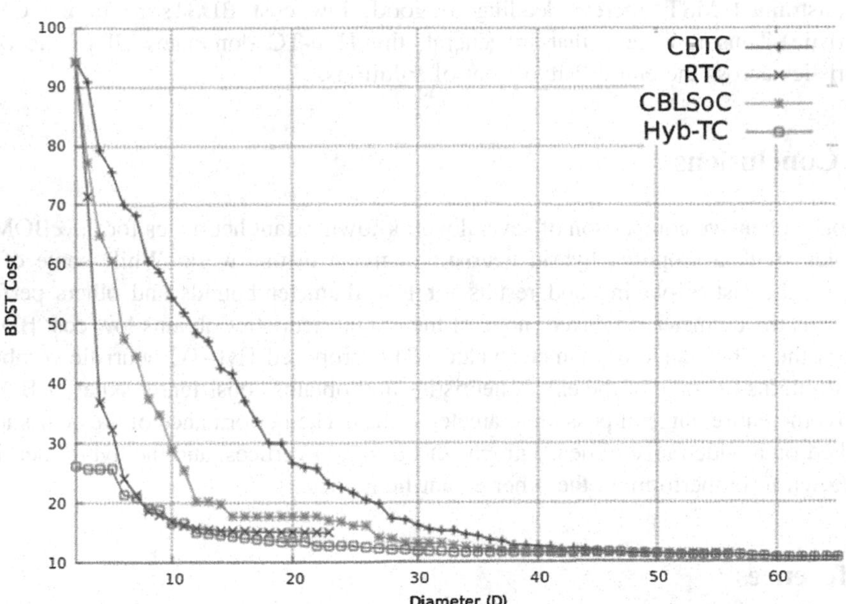

Fig. 3. Pareto fronts obtained over the entire diameter range for the first 250 vertex Euclidean benchmark graph for the CBTC, RTC, CBLSoC and Hyb-TC heuristics, up to D = 65.

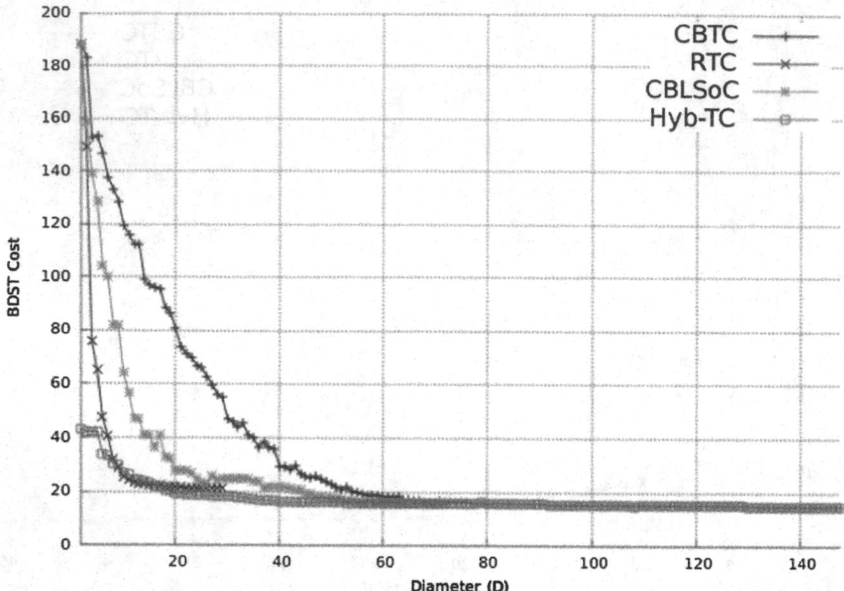

Fig. 4. Pareto fronts obtained over the entire diameter range for the first 500 vertex Euclidean benchmark graph for the CBTC, RTC, CBLSoC and Hyb-TC heuristics, up to D = 145.

unconstrained MST, thereby leading to good, low cost BDSTs as in the CBTC heuristic. Thus it is seen that in general, the Hyb-TC dominates all of the other heuristics across the entire Pareto front of solutions.

5 Conclusions

A comprehensive comparison of several well known extant heuristics for the eBOMST problem with a proposed hybrid heuristic is made in this work. While some of the existing heuristics obtain good results for low diameter bounds and others perform better as the diameter is relaxed, none of the extant heuristics obtains low cost BDSTs across the entire range of diameter values. The proposed Hyb-TC heuristic combines the strengths of some of the extant heuristics and obtains consistently superior BDSTs across the entire range of possible diameter values. The performance of the heuristics is studied on a wide range of dense graphs of up to 500 vertices, and the hybrid heuristic is shown to outperform all the other extant heuristics.

References

1. Garey, M.R., Johnson, D.S.: Computers and Intractability: A Guide to the Theory of NP Completeness. Freeman, New York, W.H (1979)
2. Bookstein, A., Klein, S.T.: Compression of correlated bit-vectors. Inf. Syst. **16**(4), 110–118 (1996)

3. Raymond, K.: A tree-based algorithm for distributed mutual exclusion. ACM Trans. Comput. Syst. **7**(1), 61–77 (1989)
4. Saha, S., Aslam, M., Kumar, R.: Assessing the performance of bi-objective MST for Euclidean and non-Euclidean instances. In: Ranka, S., Banerjee, A., Biswas, K.K., Dua, S., Mishra, P., Moona, R., Poon, S.-H., Wang, C.-L. (eds.) IC3 2010. CCIS, vol. 94, pp. 229–240. Springer, Heidelberg (2010). https://doi.org/10.1007/978-3-642-14834-7_22
5. Achuthan, N.R., Caccetta, L.: Minimum weight spanning trees with bounded diameter. Australas. J. Comb. Univ. Queensland Press **5**, 261–276 (1992)
6. Achuthan, N.R., Caccetta, L., Caccetta, P., Geelen, J.F.: Computational methods for the diameter restricted minimum weight spanning tree problem. Australas. J. Comb. Univ. Queensland Press **10**, 51–71 (1994)
7. Gouveia, L., Magnanti, T.L.: Network flow models for designing diameter constrained minimum spanning and Steiner trees. Netw. **41**(3), 159–173 (2003)
8. Deo, N., Abdalla, A.: Computing a diameter-constrained minimum spanning tree in parallel. In: Bongiovanni, G., Petreschi, R., Gambosi, G. (eds.) CIAC 2000. LNCS, vol. 1767, pp. 17–31. Springer, Heidelberg (2000). https://doi.org/10.1007/3-540-46521-9_2
9. Julstrom, B.A.: Greedy heuristics for the bounded diameter minimum spanning tree problem. J. Exp. Algorithmics **14**(1), 1–14 (2009)
10. Patvardhan, C., Prakash, V.P.: Novel deterministic heuristics for building minimum spanning trees with constrained diameter. In: Chaudhury, S., Mitra, S., Murthy, C.A., Sastry, P.S., Pal, Sankar K. (eds.) PReMI 2009. LNCS, vol. 5909, pp. 68–73. Springer, Heidelberg (2009). https://doi.org/10.1007/978-3-642-11164-8_12
11. Binh, H., Nghia, N.: New multi-parent recombination in genetic algorithm for solving bounded diameter minimum spanning tree problem. In: First Asian Conference on Intelligent Information and Database Systems, pp. 283–288 (2009)
12. Saha, S., Kumar, R.: Bounded-diameter MST instances with hybridization of multi-objective EA. Int. J. Comput. Appl. **18**(4), 17–25 (2011). (0975 – 8887)
13. Handler, G.Y.: Minimax location of a facility in an undirected graph. Transp. Sci. **7**, 287–293 (1978)
14. Prim, R.C.: Shortest connection networks and some generalizations. Bell Syst. Tech. J. **36**, 1389–1401 (1957)
15. Patvardhan, C., Prakash, V.P., Srivastav, A.: Fast heuristics for large instances of the Euclidean bounded diameter minimum spanning tree problem. Informatica **39**(2015), 281–292 (2015)
16. Patvardhan, C., Prakash, V.P., Srivastav, A.: Parallel heuristics for the bounded diameter minimum spanning tree problem. In: India Conference (INDICON), 2014 Annual IEEE, 11–13 December 2014, pp. 1–5. IEEE Press (2014)
17. Beasley's OR Library, Department of Mathematical Sciences, Brunel University, UK. http://people.brunel.ac.uk/mastjjb/orlib/files. Accessed 21 Jan 2017

Analysis of Least Mean Square and Recursive Least Squared Adaptive Filter Algorithm for Speech Enhancement Application

Mrinal Bachute[1,2(✉)] and R. D. Kharadkar[1,2]

[1] Savitribai Phule University, Pune, Maharashtra, India
mrinalbachute@gmail.com
[2] G.H. Raisoni Institute of Engineering and Technology, Wagholi, Pune, Maharashtra, India
mrinal.bachute@raisoni.net

Abstract. Speech enhancement is a vital area of research, the performance of speech based human machine applications such as automatic speech recognition system, in car communication depends on the quality of speech communicated. Different methodologies have been used by various researchers to improve the quality of speech signal. In this paper an attempt is made to analyze the performance of Least Mean Square (LMS) and Recursive Least Squared (RLS) adaptive filter algorithm for speech enhancement application. The performance indices used for the evaluations is Mean Square Error (MSE), Signal to Noise Ration (SNR) and execution time. The detail analysis is done and experimentally the results are validated and certain modifications are suggested in the algorithm. The experimentation revels that LMS have fast convergence than RLS. The computational complexity of RLS is very high as compared to LMS.

Keywords: LMS · RLS · Convergence · Learning curve

1 Introduction

An adaptive noise cancelation system estimates signal corrupted by additive noise as described by Widrow et al. [1]. The primary input consists of the corrupted signal and the reference input contains noise correlated with the primary noise signal. The signal estimate is obtained after iterative comparison of reference input signal adaptively filtered and subtracted from the primary input. Adaptive noise cancellation is a method of optimal filtering that can be applied with a suitable reference input signal. The advantage of the method is adaptive capability, low output noise and its low signal distortion. The adaptive capability processes the inputs signal even when properties are unknown and non stationary. It leads to a stable system that automatically turns itself off when no improvement in Signal to Noise Ratio (SNR) can be achieved. Output noise and signal distortion are generally lower than can be achieved with conventional Filter Setup.

P. Bhattacharyya et al. (Eds.): NGCT 2017, CCIS 827, pp. 590–604, 2018.
https://doi.org/10.1007/978-981-10-8657-1_45

The experimentation is carried out to study the existing adaptive filter algorithms and their application for speech enhancement. This paper describes and analyzes the performance of Least Mean Square (LMS) algorithm and Recursive Least Square (RLS).

2 The Adaptive Filter Structure

Adaptive filter is computational device that attempts to model the relationship between two signals in iterative manner [2]. Adaptive filters are realized as a set of program instructions running on arithmetical processing device. Adaptive filter is defined by four aspects (i) The signal being processed by the filter. (ii) The structure that defines how the output signal of the filter is computed from its input signal. (iii) The parameters within this structure that can be iteratively changed to alter the filter input output relationship. The adaptive algorithm that describes how the parameters are adjusted in every iteration. By choosing a particular adaptive filter structure, it specifies the number and types of parameters that can be adjusted. The adaptive algorithm is used to update the filter weight values of the system to optimize mean square error (Fig. 1).

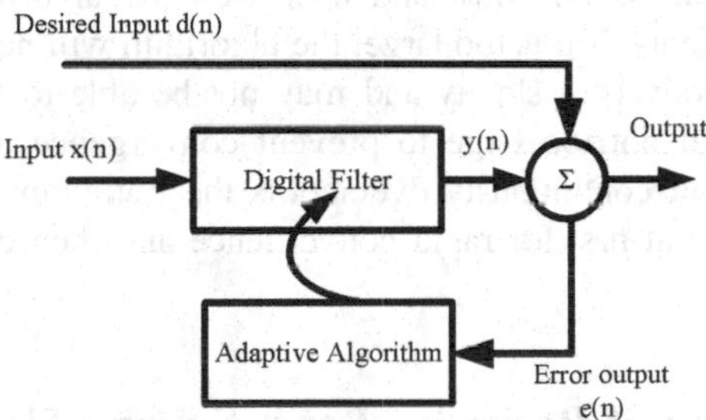

Fig. 1. Basic adaptive filter structures

An adaptive algorithm is a procedure for adjusting the parameters of an adaptive filter to minimize a cost function chosen for a task at hand. In practice quantity of interest is not always d[n]. There are situations in which d[n] is not available at all times, in such cases adaptation occurs only when d[n] is available. When d[n] is unavailable, the most recent parameter estimates are used to compute y[n]. There are real world situations in which d[n] is never available then, a hypothetical d[n] is predicted in applications like blind adaptive algorithm. The relation between x[n] and d [n] varies with time in such situations adaptive filter attempts to alter its parameters to follow the changes in this relationship as encoded by x[n] and d[n] this behavior is called tracking. Over the last decade there has been significant research directed towards development of adaptive algorithms. There are basic two algorithms, the Least Mean Square (LMS) algorithm, which is based on a gradient optimization for determining the coefficients and the class of recursive least squares algorithms, which includes both direct form FIR and lattice realization [2].

3 Implementation of Least Mean Square Algorithm

An adaptive filter with tapped delay line FIR structure, the LMS update algorithm is simple. After each sample, the coefficients of the FIR filter are adjusted with respect to weight update equation. The algorithm here does not require the input values to have any particular relationship and it can be used to adapt a linear FIR filter. The update equation is as:

$$w(n+1) = w(n) + \mu e(n)w(n) \tag{1}$$

Where μ is the convergence parameter (i.e. step-size),
$e(n) = d(n) - w^T(n)x(n)$ is the output error, d(n) is the desired signal and x(n) is the input signal.

The effects of the LMS algorithm make a small change in weight. The objective of the change is to decrease the error. The magnitude of the change in each weight depends on μ, the associated input value and the error at time n. The weights making the largest contribution to the output are changed the most. If the error is zero, there should be is no change in the weights. If the associated value of inputs to algorithm is zero, then changing the weight makes no difference, so weight is not changed. Convergence factor μ controls how fast and how well the algorithm converges to the optimum filter coefficients. If μ is too large, the algorithm will not converge. If μ is too small the algorithm converges slowly and may not be able to track changing conditions. If μ is large but not too large to prevent convergence, the algorithm reaches steady state rapidly but continuously overshoots the optimum weight vector. Sometimes, μ is made large at first for rapid convergence and then decreased to minimize overshoot.

4 Implementation of Recursive Least Square Algorithm (RLS)

Recursive Least Square is an algorithm that searches filter coefficients so as to minimize weighted linear square cost function related to input signal, whereas LMS aims to reduce mean square error. In derivation form RLS is deterministic, whereas LMS & other algorithms are stochastic (i.e. non-deterministic/random in nature). The RLS algorithm depends on forgetting factor λ (lambda). The smaller λ, indicates smaller contribution of previous values. So filter becomes more sensitive to recent samples hence more fluctuations in filter coefficients. λ is hence taken between 0.98 & 1. That is it indicates how quickly filter forgets past sample value. When λ is close to 1, algorithm achieves low misadjustment & good stability, but tracking capabilities are reduced. When λ is smaller, it improves tracking but increase misadjustment & affects stability of algorithm. By the use of this algorithm equation a recursive loop have been introduced as defined in Eq. (2). Thus set certain predefined constant values, and then the equation can be updated. The algorithm equations are adjusted by initially considering a higher value and then taking its inverse. For that purpose forgetting factor is used. Forgetting factor will control the step size as well as convergence speed of the AF.

The weight update equation for RLS algorithm is given by,

$$z(n) = w(n-1) \cdot y^T(n) \tag{2}$$

$$e(n) = d(n) - z(n) \tag{3}$$

$$k(n) = \frac{P(n-1) \cdot z(n)}{\lambda + z^H(n) \cdot P(n-1) \cdot z(n)} \tag{4}$$

$$P(n) = \frac{P(n-1) - P(n-1) \cdot z^H(n) \cdot k(n)}{\lambda} \tag{5}$$

$$w(n) = w(n-1) + e(n) \cdot k(n) \tag{6}$$

5 Comparison Between Least Mean Square and Recursive Least Square

In the LMS algorithm, the correction that is applied in updating the old estimate of the coefficient vector is based on the instantaneous sample value of the tap-input vector and the error signal. On the other hand, in the RLS algorithm the computation of this correction utilizes all the past available information. The LMS algorithm requires approximately 20M iterations to converge in mean square, where M is the number of tap coefficients contained in the tapped-delay-line filter. On the other band, the RLS algorithm converges in mean square within less than 2M iterations. The rate of convergence of the RLS algorithm is therefore, in general, faster than that of the LMS algorithm by an order of magnitude. Unlike the LMS algorithm, there are no approximations made in the derivation of the RLS algorithm. Accordingly, as the number of iterations approaches infinity, the least squares estimate of the coefficient vector approaches the optimum Wiener value, and correspondingly, the mean square error approaches the minimum value possible. In other words, the RLS algorithm, in theory, exhibits zero misadjustment. On the other hand, the LMS algorithm always exhibits a nonzero maladjustment; however, this misadjustment may be made arbitrarily small by using a sufficiently small step-size parameter μ. A great deal of research efforts have been used up characterizing the role that μ(n) plays in the performance of adaptive filter in terms of statistical or frequency characteristics of the input and desired response signal. Often success or failure of an adaptive filtering application depends on how the value of μ(n) is chosen or calculated to obtain the best performance from the adaptive filer. The issue of choosing μ(n) for both stable and accurate convergence of LMS is very important. LMS incorporates an iterative formula that makes successive corrections to the weight vector in the direction of the negative of the gradient vector which finally leads to the minimum mean square error. Compared to other algorithms LMS algorithm is relatively simple; it does not require correlation function calculation nor does it require matrix inversions.

Parameters : M = number of taps (filter length)

μ = step size parameter 0 < μ

The Normalized LMS (NLMS) introduces a variable adaptation rate. It improves the convergence speed in a non-static environment. In another version, the Newton LMS, the weight update equation includes whitening in order to achieve a single mode of convergence. For long adaptation processes the Block LMS (BLMS) is used to make the LMS faster. In Block LMS (BLMS), the input signal is divided into blocks and weights are updated block wise. A simple version of LMS is called the Sign LMS (SLMS). It uses the sign of the error to update the weights. Also, LMS is not a blind algorithm i.e. it requires a priori information for the reference signal.

Parameters : M = number of taps (filter length)

$[D(n)]/E\left[|e(n)|^2\right]$

Where,
$E[|e(n)|^2]$ = error signal power
$E[|u(n)|^2]$ = input signal power
D (n) = mean square division.
Initialization:
If prior knowledge about the tap-weight vector w(n) is available, use the knowledge to select an appropriate value for $\hat{w}(0)$. Otherwise set $\hat{w}(0) = 0$.
Data Given:
u(n) = M-by-1tap input vector at time n.
d(n) = desired response at time step n. To be computed: $\hat{w}(n + 1)$ = estimate of tap-weight vector at time step n + 1.
Computation:
For n = 0, 1, 2, ………compute $e(n) = d(n) - \hat{w}(n)u(n)\ \hat{w}(n + 1)$.

5.1 Convergence Performance

Least Mean Square (LMS) adaptive filter is the most popular algorithm and d(n) widely used adaptive system, appearing in numerous commercial and scientific applications.

The LMS adaptive filter is described by the mathematical equation as

$$W(n+1) = W(n) + \mu e(n)X(n) \tag{7}$$

$$e(n) = d(n) - W^T(n)X(n) \tag{8}$$

Where
$W(n) = [w_0(n)w_1(n)\ldots\ldots\ldots w_{L-1}(n)]^T$ is the coefficient vector
$X(n) = [x(n)x(n-1)\ldots.x(n-L+1)]^T$ is the input signal vector
$d(n)$ is the desired signal
$e(n)$ is the error signal

$\mu(n)$ is the step size.

The three main reasons for the popularity of LMS adaptive filter. First, it is relatively easy to implement in software and hardware due to its computational simplicity and efficient use of memory. Secondly, it performs robustly in the presence of numerical errors caused by finite-precision arithmetic. Third, its behavior has been analytically characterized up to such appoint that user can setup system to obtain adequate performance with only limited knowledge about the input and the desired response.

5.2 Characterizing the Performance of Adaptive Filter

The two practical methods for characterize the behavior of an adaptive filter are discussed. The simplest method is simulation, a set of input and desired response signals are either collected from a physical environment or are generated from mathematical or statistical model of physical environment. These signals are further processed by applying trial-and error based important design parameters like step size and filter length L, are selected on observed behavior of the system when operated on the signal. The straight forward simulation has two drawbacks. First is selecting design parameters via simulation alone is an iterative and time consuming process and the best combination of design parameter is daunting. Secondly, the amount of data needed to accurately characterize the behavior of the adaptive filter for all cases of interest may be large. If real world signals are used it may become costly to store large amount data and processing this huge data becomes time consuming. For these reason, we are motivated to develop an analysis of adaptive filter. In such analysis, the input and desired response signal $X(n)$ and $d(n)$ are characterized by certain properties t at govern the forms of these signals for the application of interest. These properties are statistical in nature like means of the signal or the correlation between the two signals at different time instances. Analytical approach is then developed that is based on theses signal properties, based on this analytical description selection of the parameters are done followed by experimentation.

The Fig. (2) shows the analysis approach for parameter selection. Usually both analysis and simulation are employed to select the design parameters for adaptive filter; simulation provides the accuracy check of the signal model.

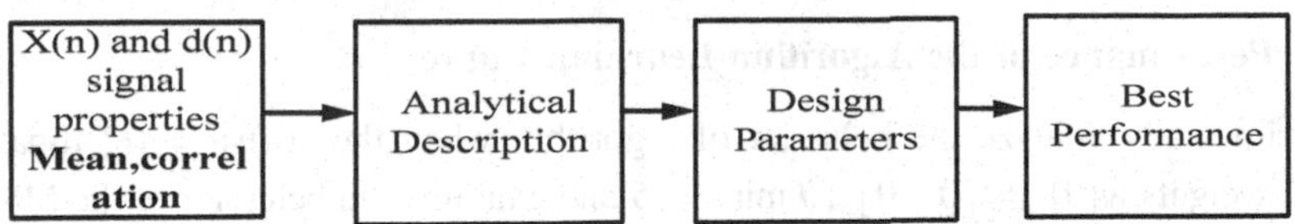

Fig. 2. Analytical approach for characterizing the performance of adaptive filter

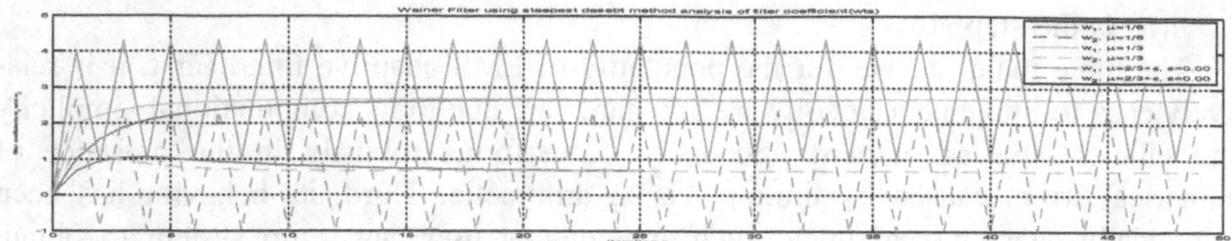

Fig. 3. Analysis for filter coefficient update of wiener filter using steepest decent

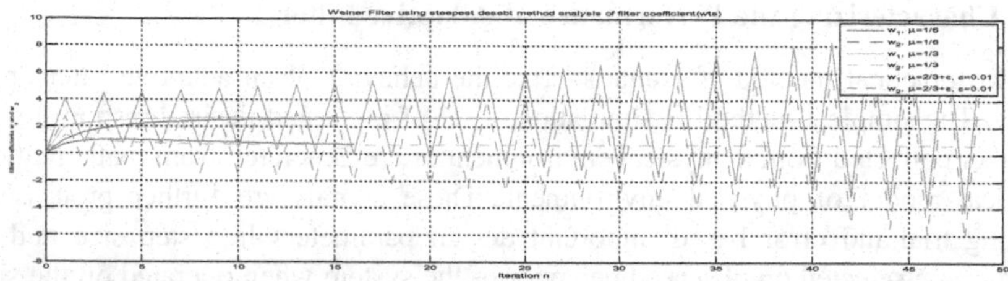

Fig. 4. Weiner filter weight updation when μ = 1/6 μ = 1/3 μ = 2/3 + ε ε = 0.01

5.3 Experimentation for Convergence Analysis of Steepest Decent Method

Investigate the (steepest descent) filter coefficient approaches to the optimum $W_0 = R^{-1}P$ different step size $\mu = \frac{2}{\lambda_{\max}}$, $\mu > \frac{2}{\lambda_{\max}}$. The experimentation is performed with initial value of w(0) and different step-size. The Fig. 3 show the experimental result for filter coefficient update of wiener filter using steepest descent method.

Figures 3, 4 and 5 shows the effect of change of μ on convergence. The step size is varied and its effects on filter coefficients are analyzed. Initially step size μ = 1/6, 1/3 and 2/3 are considered. When μ = 1/6 filter smoothly converges as seen in the Figs. 3, 4 and 5, When μ = 1/3 filter converges as shown in the Fig. 4.5, 4.6 and 4.7, but when the value of μ is again increased further by setting μ = 2/3 the filter weights change abruptly. Choice of μ is very important, a small μ value gives slow convergence and large μ value constitutes a risk for divergence.

5.4 Performance of the Algorithm Learning Curve

Experimentally analyze the behavior of algorithm when the J(n) μ = 1/2 μmax, set initial weights $w(0) = [0 \quad 0]^T$, $J\min = 5$ and examine the behavior of the MSE for first few iterations. Calculated by $J(n) = J\min + 2\left(\frac{4}{9}\right)^n$.

Time constant τk analysis and the effect of step size on the time constant τk determined by inspection of the curve $\tau_k = \frac{-1}{\ln(1-\mu\lambda_k)}$ & Observe the behavior at μ = 1/6, 1/3 (Figs. 6, 7, 8 and 10).

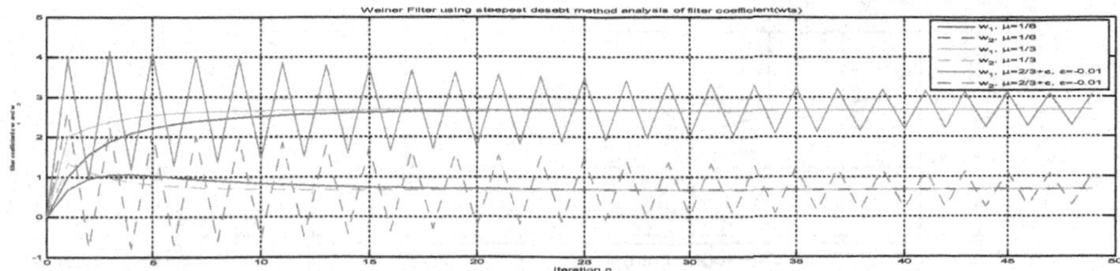

Fig. 5. Weiner filter weight off updation μ = 1/6 μ = 1/3 μ = 2/3 −E on the filter coefficients

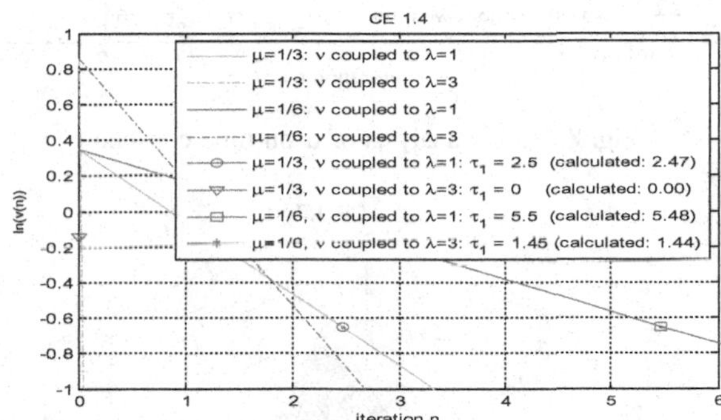

Fig. 6. Time contant analysis with μ = 1/3 & μ = 1/6 with λ = 1, λ = 3 τ1 = 2.5, 5.5 1.45

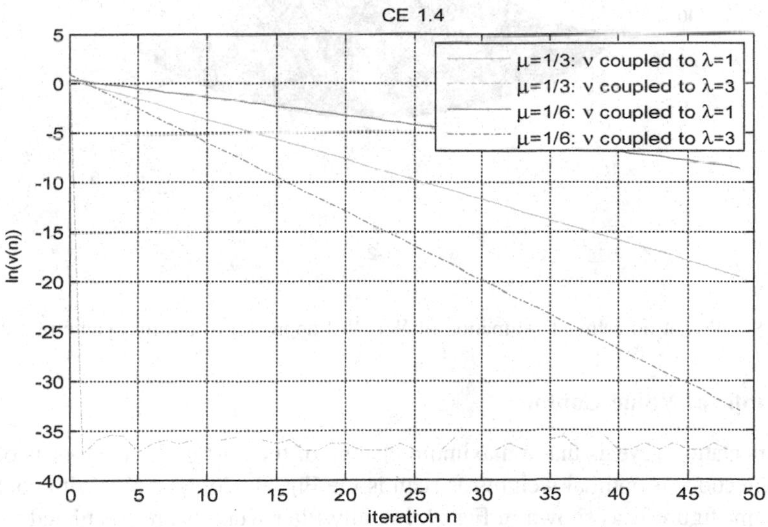

Fig. 7. Time constant analysis with μ = 1/3, μ = 1/6 and λ = 1 λ = 3

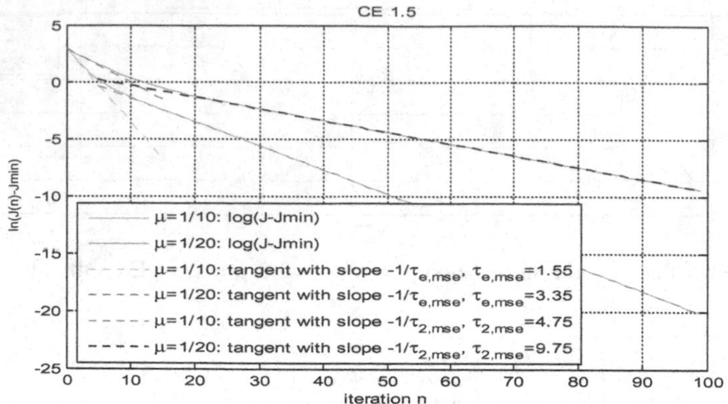

Fig. 8. Effect analysis of μ on time constant

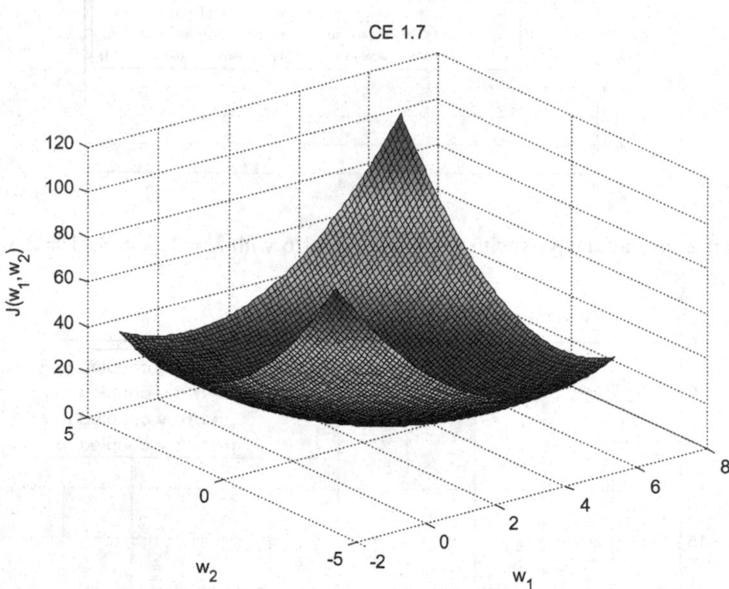

Fig. 9. Weight adjustment estimation of W1, W2 approach to optimal value of weights

5.5 Optimal Value Contour

Experimentation reveals that a maximum change of the cost in the contour is observed in the direction of optimal weights as seen is the Fig. 9. Contour plot with coefficients in the same figure is as shown in Fig. 9. Initially filter weights are calculated. Examine the weights approaching to optimal value; the iterations are marked with x (cross). It is observed that each timestamp is normal to contour curve and in the direction of gradient. The analysis is carried out with different step size μ. Observations show that, if μ is small then it converges fast to optimal value and if μ is too large it diverges (Fig. 11).

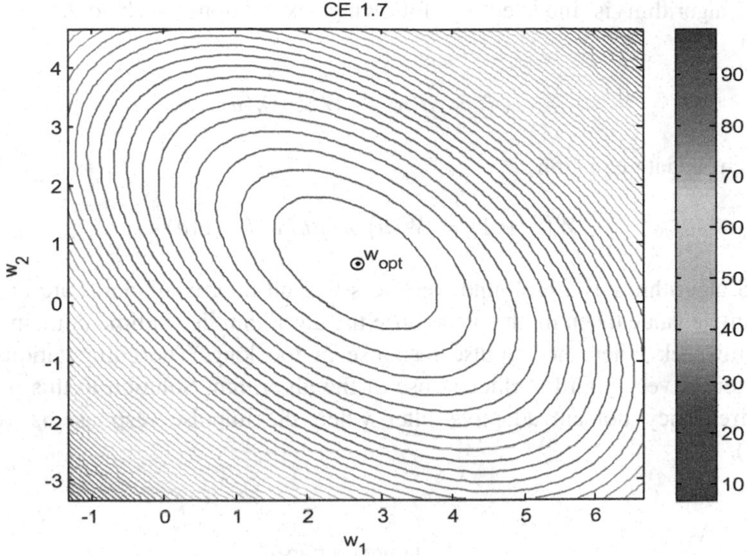

Fig. 10. Optimal weight adjustment of adaptive filter algorithm

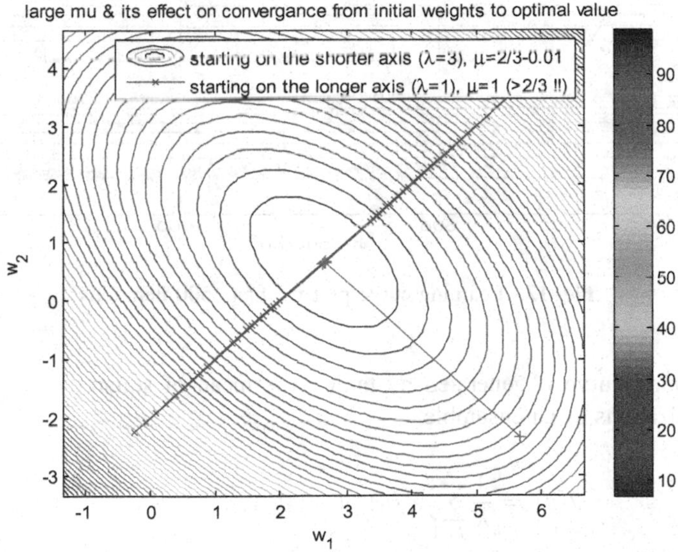

Fig. 11. Effect of step size μ on the weight adjustment and approach to optimal value of weight

This algorithm is modeled by following expressions as below, error update equation

$$e(n) = d(n) - W^T(n)X(n) \tag{9}$$

Weight update equation

$$W(n+1) = W(n) + \mu LMSX(n)e(n) \tag{10}$$

LMS algorithm has a profound weakness that all filter coefficients are updated for every sample value taken in, this is because the algorithm lies in time domain and have major drawback when the impulse response in too long. The computational power requirement is very high for efficient use of the algorithm. Solution to this problem is use of frequency domain adaptive filter when the impulse response is very long (Fig. 12).

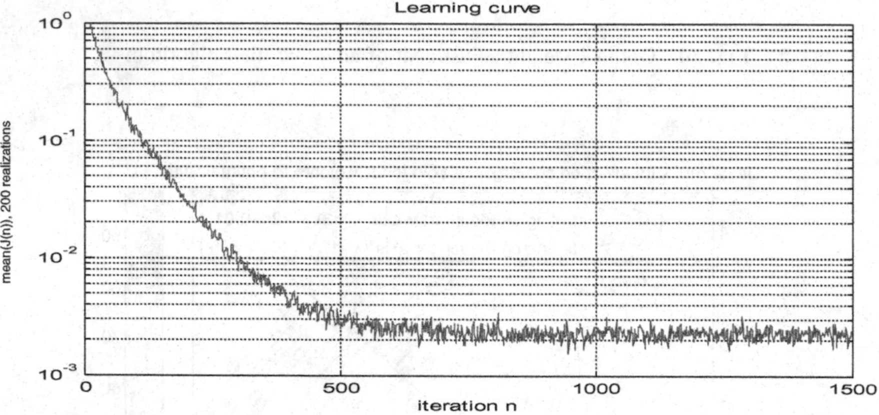

Fig. 12. Learning curve plot for first 1500 iterations

A Learning curve is generated by taking the mean of squared error e_2 (n) over several realizations of an ensemble

$$J(n) = \frac{1}{K}\sum_{k=1}^{K} e_k^2(n), \text{ n} = 0, 1, 1, \ldots \text{N} - 1 \tag{11}$$

Where, ek = estimation error at time instance n for kth iteration
K = number of iterations.

Observe the effect of change in step size on learning curve and Jmin. Small value of μ converges fast and have a small value of Jmin as seen in the plot. When the value of μ is increased the convergence takes place fast as compared to previous case but the

Jmin value is little higher then the previous case. If we experiment with $\mu = 0.750$ then the LMS algorithm converges fast as seen in the plot but the value of Jmin also increases (Fig. 13).

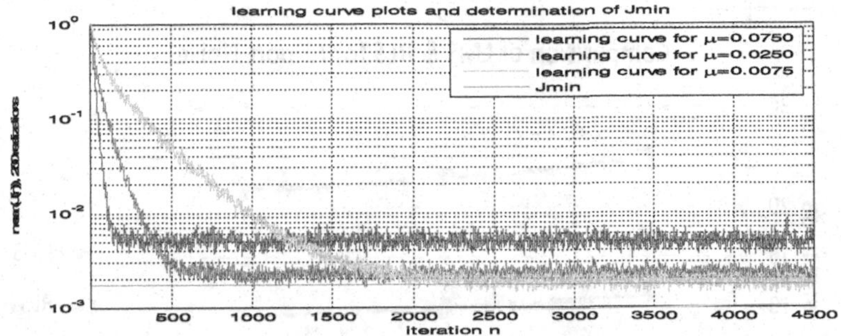

Fig. 13. Learning curve with varying value of μ

6 Performance Comparison of Least Mean Square and Normalized LMS

The experimentation were carried out for LMS algorithm in airport noise with different level of noise 0 dB, 5 dB and 10 dB Table 1 show the detail results of the same. The Performance comparison of speech enhancement using NLMS algorithm in presence of airport noise is shown in Table 2.

Table 1. Performance comparison of speech enhancement using LMS algorithm in presence of airport noise

Algorithm/method: LMS			
Noise type: airport			
Noise level	SNR	MSE	TIME
0 dB	11.1708	0.000218	2.39115
5 dB	9.9084	0.000193	0.24389
10 dB	9.1533	0.000186	0.24631

Table 2. Results for RLS algorithm

Algorithm method: RLS			
Type of noise: airport noise			
Noise level	SNR	MSE	TIME
0 dB	24.7705	1.14E−05	0.39084
5 dB	22.6959	1.27E−05	0.34427
10 dB	21.6435	1.35E−05	0.34369

The Tables 1 and 2 lists the results of LMS algorithms and RLS algorithm. It is observed that the range of SNR is 9.15 to 11.17 dB with MSE 0.000186 to 0.000218. The execution time is 0.24 to 2.3 s. The RLS provide much better SNR ranging from 21.6 to 24.77 dB with better MSE in range of 1.14E−05 to 1.35E−05 with slightly more execution time.

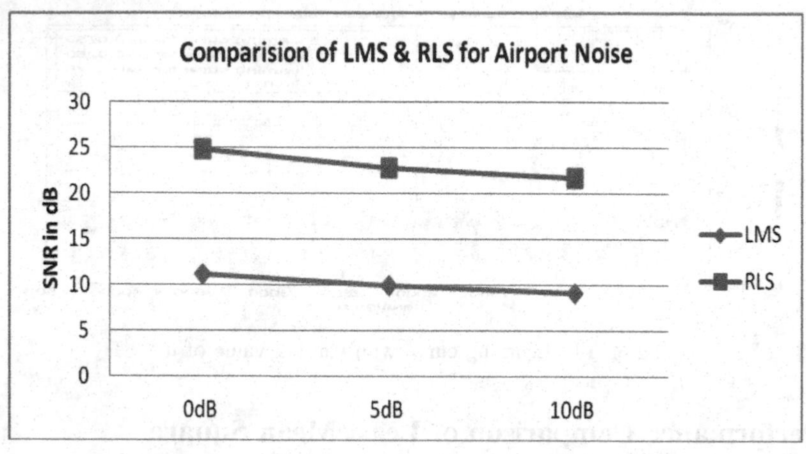

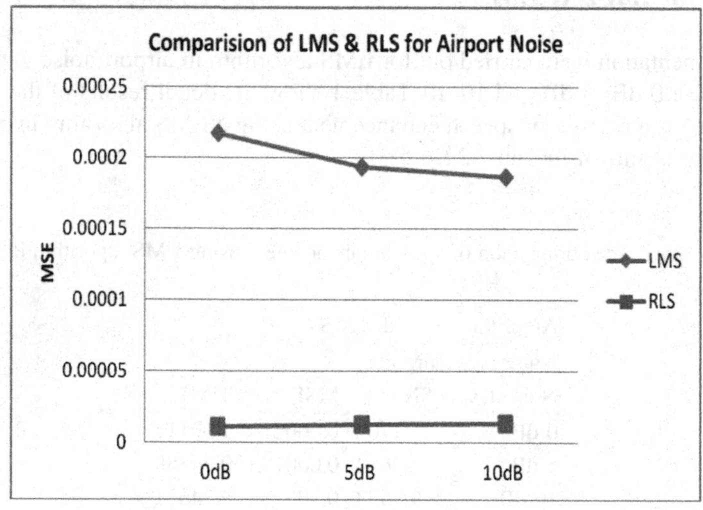

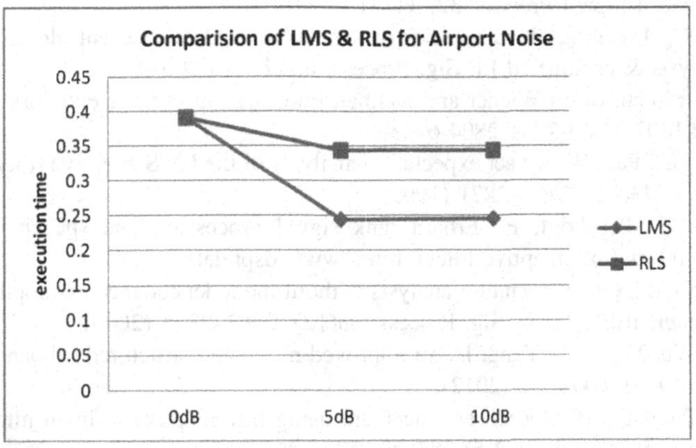

7 Conclusion

This paper discussed the implementation of Least Mean Square and Recursive Least Square adaptive filter algorithms. Researchers have made certain modification in LMS which leads to evolution of Leaky LMS, CLMS, SLMS and SLMS. The performances of the algorithms are compared on the basis of the performance indices like signal to noise ratio, MSE and Convergence speed. The experimentation revels that LMS have fast convergence than RLS. The computational complexity of RLS is very high as compared to LMS. After comparison there is a scope for performance improvement of the algorithms

References

1. Jie, Y., Zhenli, W.: On the application of variable-step adaptive noise cancelling for improving the robustness of speech recognition. In: ISECS International Colloquium on Computing, Communication, Control, and Management 2009 CCCM 2009, vol. 2, pp. 419–422. IEEE (2009)
2. Pandey, A., Malviya, L.D., Sharma, V.: Comparative study of LMS and NLMS algorithms in adaptive equalizer. Int. J. Eng. Res. Appl. (IJERA) **2**(3), 1584–1587 (2012)
3. Douglas, S.C., Pan, W.: Exact expectation analysis of the LMS adaptive filter. IEEE Trans. Signal Process. **43**(12), 2863–2871 (1995)
4. Chu, H.S., An, C.K.: Design of the adaptive noise canceler using neural network with backpropagation algorithm. In: Proceedings the Third Russian-Korean International Symposium on Science and Technology, 1999, KORUS 1999, vol. 2, pp. 762–764. IEEE (1999)
5. Hu, Y., Loizou, P.C.: Subjective comparison and evaluation of speech enhancement algorithms. Speech Commun. J. SPCOM Sci. Direct **49**, 588–601 (2006)

6. Caraiscos, C., Liu, B.: A round of error analysis of LMS adaptive algorithm. IEEE Trans. Acoust. Speech Signal Process. **32**, 34–41 (2000)
7. Gardner, W.: Learning characteristics of scholastic gradient descent algorithms: a general study analysis & critique. IEEE Sig. Process. **6**, 113–133 (2010)
8. Kailath, T.: Lectures on Wiener and Kalman Filtering. Springer, New York (1981). https://doi.org/10.1007/978-3-7091-2804-6
9. Douglas, S.C., Pan, W.: Exact expectation analysis of the LMS adaptive filter'. IEEE Trans. Sig. Process. **43**(12), 2863–2871 (1995)
10. Feldbauer, C., Pernkopf, F.: Erhard rank signal processing and speech communication laboratory tutorial on adaptive filters. http://www.dsprelated.com
11. Douglas, S.C.: Exact expectation analysis without the independence assumption of the LMS adaptive filter. IEEE Trans. Sig. Process. **43**(12), 2863–2871 (2000)
12. Yang, F., Wu, M., Ji, P., Yang, J.: An improved multiband-structured subband adaptive filter algorithm. **19**(10) 647–650 (2012)
13. Sami, S., Padmaja, P.: Speech enhancement using fast adaptive Kalman filtering algorithm along with weighting filter. **2**(5) 387–390 (2013)
14. Ravi, B., Kumar, T.K.: Speech enhancement using kernel and normalized kernel affine projection. **4**(4), 129–138 (2013)
15. Widrow, B., Stearns, S.D.: Adaptive Signal Processing, 4th edn. Cliff, Prentice Hall, Upper Saddle River (2009)
16. Haykin, S.: Adaptive Filter Theory. Pearson Education, London (2011)
17. Farhang Boroujeny, B.: Adaptive Filters: Theory and Applications. Wiley Publications, Hoboken (2006)
18. Hayes, M.H.: Statistical Digital Signal Processing and Modeling. Wiley, Hoboken, pp. 493–552 (1996)
19. Haykin, S.: Adaptive Filter Theory. Prentice-Hall Inc, Upper Saddle River (1996)
20. Bachute, M.: Performance Evaluation of PSO based Speech Enhancement Technique for Speech Communication System Technical Journal of Institution of Engineers (India) Pune Local Center, India, October 2013. ISBN 978-81-924990-1-7
21. Bachute, M.R., Kharadkar, R.D.: Performance analysis and comparison of complex LMS, sign LMS and RLS algorithms for speech enhancement application. IJCSN Int. J. Comput. Sci. Netw. **4**(5) (2002)
22. Bachute, M.R., Kharadkar, R.D.: Performance analysis and comparison of complex LMS, sign LMS and RLS algorithms for speech enhancement application
23. Bachute, M., Kharadkar, R.D.: Analysis and implementation of time-varying least mean square algorithm and modified Time-Varying LMS for speech enhancement. Int. J. Sci. Res. (IJSR). ISSN (Online) 2319-7064, Index Copernicus Value (2013): 6.14, Impact Factor (2013)

A Novel Statistical Pre-processing Based Spatial Anomaly Detection Model on Cyclone Dataset

Lakshmi Prasanthi Malyala[1(✉)] and Nandam Sambasiva Rao[2]

[1] Department of Information Technology, BVRITH College of Engineering for Women, Hyderabad, India
prasanthi.malyala@gmail.com

[2] Department of Computer Science and Engineering, Vardhaman College of Engineering, Hyderabad, India
snandam@gmail.com

Abstract. Anomaly detection in heterogeneous severity feature space is a challenging issue for which only a few models have been designed and developed. Detection of spatial objects and its patterns helps to find essential spatial decision patterns from large spatial datasets. Traditional spatial anomaly detection techniques are failed to process and detect anomalies due to noise, sparsity and imbalance problems. Also, most of the traditional statistical anomaly detection models consider the homogeneous type of objects for outlier detection and ignore the effect of heterogeneous objects. In this proposed model, a novel statistical pre-processing based spatial anomaly detection model was proposed to find the anomalies on cyclone dataset. Experimental results proved that the proposed model has high computational detection rate with less mean error rate compared to the traditional anomaly detection models.

Keywords: Cyclone spatial mining · Anomaly detection · Imbalanced data

1 Introduction

Data mining can be defined as a knowledge discovery tool, which is generally implemented in the process of pattern discovery, modeling relationships and identifying hidden patterns in huge databases [1]. Among the spatial data mining tasks, identification of outlier is an essential research topic for pattern analysis. Outlier identification is considered as an important research problem in the domain of statistics, data η Control factor. In some research works, it is termed as anomaly identification [2]. The process of outlier detection is quite complex when implemented in real world applications using the traditional spatial methods. Hence, a profile of normal behavior of data is created and the degree of deviation is evaluated by computing the given dataset in the profile. The resulted instances are extracted out of the profile data and labeled as outliers [3]. Most of the traditional spatial approaches are dependent on pre-labeled training data, which are more complex to detect outliers. Let us consider an example including a data stream with huge amount of data and these data are generated

P. Bhattacharyya et al. (Eds.): NGCT 2017, CCIS 827, pp. 605–616, 2018.
https://doi.org/10.1007/978-981-10-8657-1_46

with respect to time. Therefore, a standard model which is constructed at a particular time can become invalid due to variation in data objects and its bound values.

Figure 1a, illustrates the geographical map with shaded and non-shaded cyclone regions. Here non-shaded regions specify cyclone affected regions and a shaded region specifies the non-cyclone affected regions. Figure 1b, represents the distance computation between the cyclone affected regions and the non-cyclone affected regions. Figure 1c, illustrates the classification of cyclone affected regions to the non-cyclone affected regions without outlier detection.

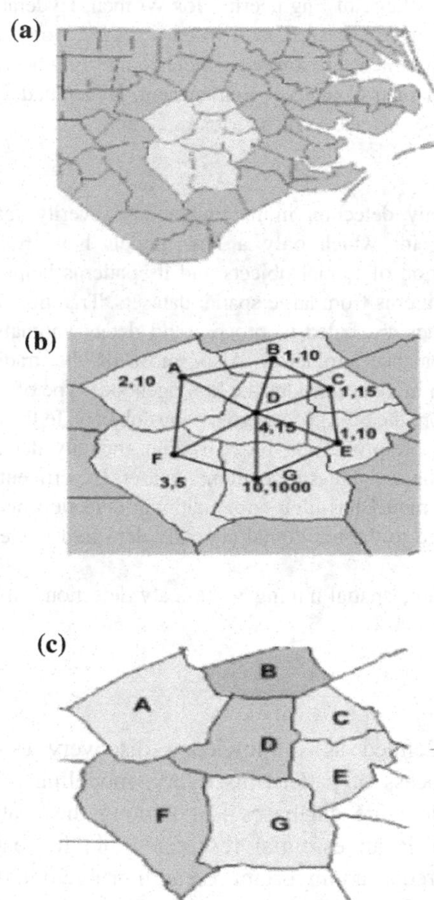

Fig. 1. (a) Non shading region specifies the cyclone affected regions, (b) Finding nearest neighbor region patterns, (c) Clustering affected and non-affected regions using distance measure

1. Types of Outlier Detection Models

A. Statistical Approach Outlier Detection: Statistical approach is an efficient outlier detection approach in spatial analysis. It is mostly implemented in large scale data analysis systems. It considers the given dataset as statistical model like normal distribution. It is also responsible for detection of outliers related to the model through statistical tests. These approaches are comparatively easy with time complexity of O(logn).

B. Distance-based Approach: Distance-based technique [7] is applicable, if data does not fit into any standard distribution model. The approach is capable of identifying outliers efficiently in multiple dimensions. Also, these methods only identify outliers which are far from their neighborhood, the approach can't be applicable on datasets having non-dense neighborhood.

C. Density-based Approach: Density based approach presents a new outlier representation i.e., local outlier. Local outlier can be defined as the degree of an object in order to become an outlier with respect to its local neighborhood. It is also known as local outlier factor (LOF) which is assigned to each and every object. One major issue of distance-based technique is, it can't handle data points having different densities. Hence, density-based method is developed to manage such types of data points. In this scheme, the evaluation of standard deviation is very costly [8]. Three mostly implemented density-based techniques are:- LOF, influenced outlier and local outlier correlation integral.

Almost all outlier elimination approaches are one-pass means the outliers are eliminated through a single step. The technique has two limitations, those are:-

1. The outliers depend upon descriptor space and several spaces can generate numbers of different outliers.
2. In case of multiple outliers, one outlier masks other outliers and vice versa.

The spatial outlier detection approach is applicable for various applications like:-

(i) Detection of anomalous sensors.
(ii) Detection of a place with abnormal number of attack cases.
(iii) Detection of anomalous spatial weather patterns.
(iv) Detection of anomaly objects in spatial datasets.

Outliers are treated as noise and influence the outcomes of clustering. It follows the basic concept of clustering which is:- the objects present in same cluster have similar properties and objects of different clusters have dissimilar properties. Most of the Commercial ETL tools result very poor data cleaning capability on spatial datasets. Vast amount of data are extracted and stored in different databases such as financial data, web log data, censored data and spatial data. There are numbers of applications which utilize these data effectively. As these datasets are not always pre-processed, the quality of data is degraded which is a major concern in data mining models. Efforts have been carried out in order to filter the data uniquely, consistently and accurately [9]. Duplicate records are not always relational with each other, but they always have a higher degree of similarity among features. Some approaches have been developed in order to discard these duplicate records which are mentioned below:-

According to [10], a new method is developed which manages the consistency and accuracy labels of data by using minimum change method. All the previously developed approaches have both advantages as well as disadvantages. Some of the major disadvantages are mentioned below:

- When these approaches are implemented in real world scenarios, pre-processing techniques failed to find the outliers in most of imbalanced classes.
- Additionally, such type of manual cleaning process are more time consuming and impractical in nature. For example, users' assignment of weight. This happens because of large size of database and complexity of the data.
- The available data streams are ubiquitous in nature. Such approaches have vast application in the fields of online spatial data.
- The data sets are static in nature in case of conventional methods.
- As data streams have huge size, so it is quite impossible to store them in memory and to perform multiple scans throughout the process. In case of conventional techniques
- Time is an important variant in case of outlier detection techniques. The outcomes of data stream approaches usually changes time to time which is not possible for the conventional schemes.

Hence, there is an essential requirement of optimized data mining approaches for spatial streaming data. In this work, a novel anomaly detection and pattern mining model are used to find the spatial anomaly objects and spatial anomaly patterns on the cyclone dataset.

2 Related Work

The main issues arise in case of spatial data analysis are, detecting and controlling the anomaly objects. In data streams, both outlier and normal object can behave differently in different cases. Here, outlier can behave like normal object and vice versa according to the change of data.

Anomaly Detection Using Clustering Cluster based outlier detection techniques cannot find the problems of high dimensionality. The issue arises due to the sparsity of the data in the high dimensional feature space. Here, all pairs of points are almost equally placed from each other.

DenStream [7] is basically a density-based clustering approach which also involves the ideas of DBSCAN [1]. In this algorithm, the traditional DBSCAN technique is modified and extended. Further it includes micro-cluster mechanism in order to store a particular representation of the data points. The whole process of DenStream algorithm completes in two steps, those are:-

1. The initial step is an online phase which is responsible for management of micro-cluster structure.
2. The second step is represented by an offline procedure which ultimately produces final clusters out of a set of online micro- clusters. This process is carried out through implementing DBSCAN approach. This step can manage outliers.

DenStream approach is developed in order to result clustering techniques depends on streaming data. In this approach, the traditional DenStream technique is included and modified thoroughly to enhance the accuracy rate. Hence, it can be recommended to develop a proper data cleaning system in order to enhance the overall accuracy rate. This data cleansing system can also be named as E-Clean system, data cleansing or scrubbing system. A proper data cleaning system must satisfy the following criteria:-

- Initially, each model must determine and discard all vital data noise and inconsistent data.
- Additionally, traditional data pre-processing models usually involves a mapping function as well as merging function. Several other data sources and query processing techniques re-use the mapping function more efficiently for filtering. The implementation of merging function includes combining two different features by means of some common attributes present in both the training and test datasets.In [8–10] a comparative analysis of novelty detection approaches are implemented for outlier detection. The proposed model depends upon statistical as well as neural network technique. They have considered traditional outlier detection methods, but ignore the classification of outlier detection methods involving different types of datasets, Analyzed different outlier detection approaches in terms of three types of measures which are statistics, neural networks and machine learning. Such types of approaches are not applicable on complex data sets like high-dimensional, mixed attributes and spatio-temporal datasets. A new approach which is capable to handle complex outlier detection methods. Further, it can be also mentioned that, a lot of pre-existing outlier detection approaches are unable to process and handle huge data. In the recent era, the prime concern is how to handle huge volume of data efficiently and instantly. In order to resolve the above issue, some researchers presented various big data processing platforms like:- Hadoop and Spark.

All the previously developed techniques are divided into five different categories, those are:- statistics model-based, distance-based, depth-based, cluster-based and density-based [4, 5]. Statistics model-based outlier detection technique considers that the dataset is bound to support a specific distribution [2]. This model has a limitation of detecting or constructing the appropriate model. The reason behind this limitation is the unknown distribution of dataset. Apart from this limitation, another issue exists in the field of dimension [3]. It can be concluded that when an object does not satisfy the criteria of statistical model, the object is considered as an outlier. According to distance-based outlier detection method, the object is identified as outlier when it is far apart from rest of the objects.

KNN approach can determine whether an object is far apart from rest of all objects. KNN technique is more basic and simple method as compared to the previously mentioned statistical techniques. They presented a new approach which is based on distance. Their approach completely depends upon pruning mechanism and its complexity is assumed to be close enough to linear approaches.

Cluster-based outlier detection techniques are responsible for formation of clusters by using the given datasets. The objects which can't be included in any clusters are considered to be outlier. The major disadvantage of the above approach is that:- it focuses on forming clusters, rather than detecting the outliers. In case of density-based outlier detection techniques, the objects present in the lower-density regions are selected as outliers in most of the cases. Besides the above techniques, relative density-based outlier identification scheme provides quantitative measurement for outliers. The above proposed technique can also handle data distributed through numbers of density regions. The parameters of the proposed technique are quite challenging to evaluate.

close to another objects and exhibit anomalous behavior is the key research area in large number of applications. Spatial outlier analysis is essential for many domain applications such as (a) Detection of unusual disease patterns in geospatial locations, (b) detection of sensor objects in traffic, environment and radiological datasets (c) detection of weather spatial objects such as cyclones, earthquakes, tornadoes etc.

Limitations in Traditional Spatial Outlier Detection Models. Traditional data mining models failed to process the spatial objects for anomaly detection due to the fact that the behavior of the large number of spatial objects and its feature space. Spatial patterns and objects are correlated with both spatial and non-spatial feature space. Traditional spatial outlier detection models first define a nearest neighbor distance and then compute the outlier patterns. The main limitations of the traditional spatial outlier detection models are:

(a) First, these models always consider the homogeneous type of objects for outlier detection and ignore the effect of heterogeneous objects.
(b) Second, these models ignore the mixed type of attributes for spatial outlier or anomaly detection.
(c) Third, most of the spatial outlier detection models consider the deviation of a single attribute and multiple attributes are not considered for distance computation.

3 Proposed Model

In this proposed approach a statistical control chart algorithm is used in order to find the anomalies in different continuous datasets. We proposed a dynamic three sigma based n-SPC (n-dimensional statistical process control) to detect anomaly objects in the dataset [ftp://eclipse.ncdc.noaa.gov/pub/ibtracs/v03r06/wmo/csv].

The main objectives/advantages of this work:

- Provided an efficient feature based bound checking for anomaly objects.
- Spatial anomaly objects are analyzed on cyclone data.
- Spatial anomaly patterns are analyzed using k-cyclone patterns.
- As the size of cyclone objects are increasing, this model detects spatial anomaly objects and patterns efficiently in terms of runtime and complexity are concerned.

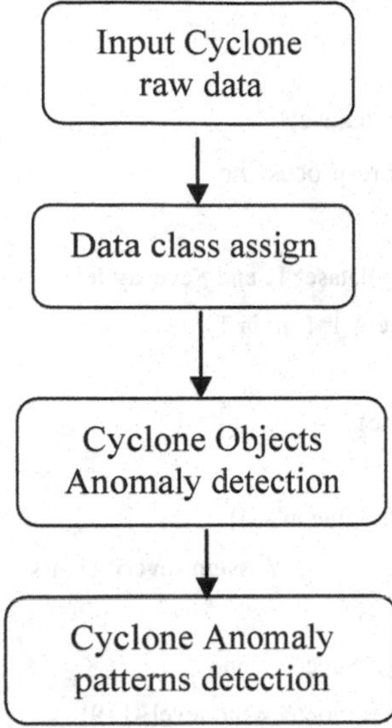

Fig. 2. Proposed system

The basic flowchart of the proposed model is shown in Fig. 2. Initially, raw data is processed for class label assignment. Each object in the cyclone raw data is compared with the corresponding wind range to find its severity level. In the next step, cyclone objects are processed for anomaly detection. In the final step, cyclone anomaly objects are analyzed using training data and testing instances.

Table 1. Sustained wind range and it class label for cyclone anomaly detection.

Severity level	Sustained wind range
Super cyclonic storm	$\geq$ 120 kt
Extremely severe cyclonic storm	90–119 kt
Very severe cyclonic storm	64–89 kt
Severe cyclonic storm	48–63 kt
Cyclonic storm	34–47 kt
Deep depression	28–33 kt
Depression	17–27 kt

Table 1 illustrates the different levels of cyclone severity classes and its wind ranges for anomaly detection. Each instance in the cyclone raw data is processed to find its severity class according to the wind range. These severity class labels are used to find the anomaly points and patterns in the proposed model.

Algorithm 1:

Input: Cyclone dataset

Output: Data pre-processing.

Procedure:

```
Initialize training dataset Tr and Severity levels S.
For each attribute A(i=1,,n) in Tr
Do
 If(A[i] is numeric)
Then
For each attribute value in A[i]
Do                          // assign severity class labels
if(Wind level>120)
          S[0]="Supercyclone";
 else if(Wind level>90&&Wind level<119)
          S[1]="ExtremeSeverecyclone";
else if(Wind level>48&Wind level<63)
          S[2]="Severecyclone";
else if(Wind level>34&&Wind level<47)
          S[3]="VerySeverecyclone";
  else if(Wind level>28&&Wind level<33)
          S[4]="Deepdepression";
else if(Wind level>17&&Wind level<27)
          S[5]="Depression";
else
          S[6]="VerySeverecyclone";
If(A[j]!=null)
```

$\text{SNormalize}(A[j]) = |A[j] - \mu_{A[j]}| / (\text{Max}\{\mu_{A[j],S[m]}\} - \text{Min}\{\mu_{A[j],S[m]}\})$ Else

$\text{MissVal}(A[j]) = |A[k] - \mu_{A[k]}| / (\text{Max}\{\mu_{A[k],S[m]}\} - \text{Min}\{\mu_{A[k],S[m]}\});$ End if

where $j \neq k$

If(A[j] is nominal and A[j]==null)

Then

$\text{NominalVal}(A[j]) = \sum \text{Prob}(A[j]/S_m / (\text{Max}\{\mu_{A[j],S[m]}\} - \text{Min}\{\mu_{A[j],S[m]}\})$

Where S_m represents the m –severity classes

$\mu_{A[j],S[m]}$ represents the mean of the each cyclone severity level.

End if

Done

Algorithm 2: Spatial anomaly points and pattern detection algorithm

Input : Spatial Cyclone Data T_r, Severity Levels S[m], η Control factor.

Output: Normalized Preprocessed Data.

Procedure:

```
Initialize Preprocessed dataset D and Severity levels S.
For each attribute A(i=1,,n) in D
 Do
 If(D[i] is numeric)
Then
For each attribute value in A[m] ;// m severity level
do
Compute lower bound on each severity level as
Lower Cyclone Bound limit: L[m] = μ_A[m] − ησ_A[m] --(1)
Compute control bound on each severity level as
Control Limit: C[m] = μ_A[m] ----(2)
Compute upper bound on each severity level as
Upper Control Limit: U[m] = μ_A[m] + ησ_A[m] ---(2)
Done
End if
End for
L=Min{ L[m] } ,C=Min{ C[m] }, U=Min{ U[m] }
For each value in D[]
Do
If(D[i] <L)
Then
Remove D[i] from dataset
Else if(D[i]>U)
Then
Remove D[i] from dataset
Else if(L<=D[i]<=U)
Add to DS[]
End if
End for
For each cyclone severity class m
Do
    For each object O_i in DS[]
 Do
   For each object O_j  in DS[] // where i!=j
 Compute distance N_m^k using Manhattan distance.
   Done
N_m^k []=Find Top K- nearest objects from Sorted list of Dist;        //Neighbor k-points in each severity level
        Assign a class to p' based on majority vote: c'=argmaxy∑(xi,ci) belonging to S, I(y=ci)
          Done
```

In the Algorithm 1, each data object is processed for severity level assignment and data pre-processing. Each value in the attribute is pre-processed according to its numerical and nominal features. Each non-empty numerical spatial object is normalized and empty numerical spatial object is predicted using the proposed measures.

In the Algorithm 2, initially lower bound, upper bound and control bound are computed on the given cyclone dataset. Each spatial feature and its values are checked against the bound limits using the n-dimensional statistical process control measures. The objects which are above the lower bound and below the upper bound are labeled as non-anomaly objects. Similarly, the objects which are above the upper bound and below the lower bound are labeled as anomaly objects. Finally, spatial anomaly patterns are computed using the k-nearest distance metric and the majority voting of the proposed model.

4 Experimental Results

In this section, experimental results are evaluated on cyclone dataset using the proposed anomaly detection model. In the experimental results, training data and testing data are used for cross-fold validation. The sample cyclone dataset is summarized in Table 2 (Figs. 3, 4 and 5).

Table 2. Sample cyclone dataset.

cyclone.cyclonedata: 3,697 rows total (approximately), limited to 1,000

f1	f2	f3	f4	f5	f6	f7	cls
1990	8.5	87	16	1006	0.543	1.386	VerySeverecyclone
1990	8.5	87	25	1002	1.88	14.665	Depression
1990	9.5	87	25	1000	1.88	27.021	Depression
1990	9.5	86	25	1002	1.88	14.665	Depression
1990	10	85.5	30	998	19.507	39.117	Deepdepression
1990	10	85	35	999	37.678	38.568	VerySeverecyclone
1990	10.1	84.7	45	994	60.401	59.988	VerySeverecyclone
1990	10.3	83.9	55	991	73.058	73.297	Severecyclone
1990	10.3	83.3	55	991	73.058	73.297	Severecyclone
1990	10	83.2	77	976	89.933	92.841	VerySeverecyclone
1990	10.2	82.9	77	976	89.933	92.841	VerySeverecyclone
1990	10.3	82.5	77	976	89.933	92.841	VerySeverecyclone
1990	11.3	82.3	90	964	93.066	98.612	VerySeverecyclone
1990	11.3	81.8	115	940	97.953	98.701	ExtremeSeverecyclone
1990	11.4	81.7	115	938	97.953	99.163	ExtremeSeverecyclone
1990	12.3	81.8	102	950	96.157	97.777	ExtremeSeverecyclone
1990	13.3	81.8	127	924	99.373	99.567	Supercyclone
1990	13.6	81.4	127	924	99.373	99.567	Supercyclone
1990	13.9	81.1	127	920	99.373	99.654	Supercyclone
1990	14.5	80.8	102	950	96.157	97.777	ExtremeSeverecyclone
1990	15.1	81	90	960	93.066	96.594	VerySeverecyclone
1990	15.4	80.9	90	960	93.066	96.594	VerySeverecyclone
1990	15.9	81	90	954	93.066	97.055	VerySeverecyclone
1990	16	80.5	65	0	83.751	-100	VerySeverecyclone
1990	16.5	80	65	0	83.751	-100	VerySeverecyclone
1990	16.5	79.5	48	0	72.431	-100	VerySeverecyclone

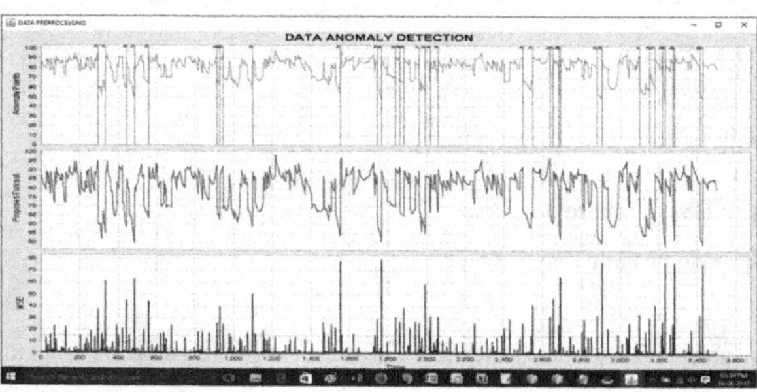

Fig. 3. Anomaly points detection using bound limits

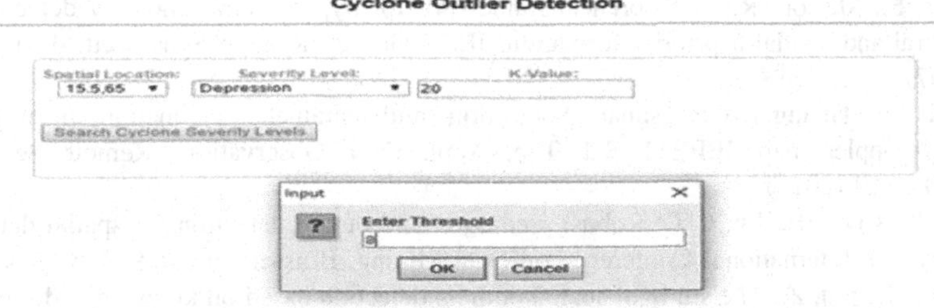

Fig. 4. Cyclone anomaly patterns detection.

Location 15.5,65 K-val 20

Lat	Lon	Wind	Pressure	Severity Level	Spatial Closest Distance
16.4	65.5	25	1000	Depression	1.0295630140986987
15	66	25	1000	Depression	1.118033988749895
16	64	25	998	Depression	1.118033988749895
16	64	25	1000	Depression	1.118033988749895
16	66	25	1000	Depression	1.118033988749895
16.5	65.5	25	1000	Depression	1.118033988749895
15	64	25	1001	Depression	1.118033988749895
17	65	25	1000	Depression	1.5
15.5	63.5	25	1001	Depression	1.5
15.5	63.5	25	999	Depression	1.5
15	63.5	25	1004	Depression	1.5811388300841898
15	66.5	25	1002	Depression	1.5811388300841898
16	66.5	25	[illegible]	Depression	[illegible]
[illegible]	[illegible]	[illegible]	[illegible]	Depression	[illegible]
[illegible]	[illegible]	25	1000	Depression	[illegible]
[illegible]	[illegible]	[illegible]	[illegible]	[illegible]	[illegible]
[illegible]	[illegible]	[illegible]	[illegible]	Depression	[illegible]
[illegible]	[illegible]	[illegible]	[illegible]	[illegible]	[illegible]

Fig. 5. Cyclone anomaly patterns in red mark.

5 Conclusion

In this paper, we discussed spatial anomaly detection model using statistical pre-processing based pattern mining model. Traditional spatial anomaly detection techniques are failed to process and detect anomalies due to noise, sparsity and imbalance problems. Also, most of the traditional statistical anomaly detection models consider the homogeneous type of objects for outlier detection and ignore the effect of heterogeneous objects. In this proposed model, spatial objects and patterns are detected from the cyclone dataset. Experimental results proved that the proposed model has high computational accuracy and less error rate compared to traditional anomaly detection models.

References

1. Agarwal, D., McGregor, A., Phillips, J.M., Venkatasubramanian, S., Zhu, Z.: Spatial scan statistics: approximations and performance study. In: Proceedings of the 12th ACM SIGKDD International Conference on Knowledge Discovery and Data Mining, KDD 2006 (Philadelphia, PA, USA, 20–23 August 2006), pp 24–33. ACM, New York (2006)
2. Izakian, H., Pedrycz, W.: Anomaly detection and characterization in spatial time series data: a cluster-centric approach. IEEE Trans. Fuzzy Syst. **22**(6), 1612–1624 (2014)

3. Yver, B., Marion, R.: A theoretical framework for hyperspectral anomaly detection using spectral and spatial a priori information. IEEE Geosci. Remote Sens. Lett. **4**(3), 436–440 (2007)
4. Yan, Q., Huang, W.: Tsunami detection and parameter estimation from GNSS-R delay-doppler map. IEEE J. Sel. Top. Appl. Earth Observations Remote Sens. **9**(10), 4650–4659 (2016)
5. Liu, X., Chen, F., Lu, C.T.: Robust prediction and outlier detection for spatial datasets. In: IEEE 12th International Conference on Data Mining, Brussels. pp. 469–478 (2012)
6. Zhang, L., Qu, Z.: The study of spatial outliers detection based on knowledge discovery and data mining. In: Sixth International Conference on Fuzzy Systems and Knowledge Discovery, Tianjin, pp. 539–541 (2009)
7. Chen, Y., Dang, X., Peng, H., Bart Jr., H.L.: Outlier detection with the kernelized spatial depth function. IEEE Trans. Pattern Anal. Mach. Intell. **31**(2), 288–305 (2009)
8. Shuyu, Z., Zhongying, Z.: Detection of outliers in spatial data by using local difference. In: International Conference on Intelligent Mechatronics and Automation, pp. 400–405 (2004)
9. Altmann, Y., McLaughlin, S., Hero, A.: Robust linear spectral unmixing using anomaly detection. IEEE Trans. Comput. Imaging **1**(2), 74–85 (2015)
10. Estivill-Castro, V., Lee, I.: Clustering with obstacles for geographical data mining. ISPRS J. Photogrammetry Remote Sens. **59**(1–2), 21–34 (2004)

Mathematical Modeling of Economic Order Quantity in a Fuzzy Inventory Problem Under Shortages

P. K. De[1(✉)], A. C. Paul[2], and Mitali Debnath[2]

[1] Department of Mathematics, National Institute of Technology, Silchar 788010, India
pijusde@gmail.com

[2] Department of Mechanical Engineering, National Institute of Technology, Silchar 788010, India
paul_arunratan@yahoo.com, mdebnath.18@gmail.com

Abstract. The purpose of this article is to develop an EOQ model to find the optimal order quantity of inventory items where shortages are allowed. Here shortages are uncertain and characterized by triangular fuzzy number and all other parameters like carrying costs, ordering cost, demand and time are considered as crisp numbers. For defuzzification sign distance ranking method has been employed. Total cost in fuzzy environment has been calculated and then by applying sign distance method corresponding crisp values have been calculated. The results have been compared and discussed with sensitivity analysis. To demonstrate the efficiency and feasibility of the proposed approach, one numerical example [2] has been solved with the existing method.

Keywords: EOQ · Triangular fuzzy number · Sign distance ranking

1 Introduction

Today's human life is not simple rather it is very much complex in nature. It is observed that a system become more complex when the information that characterized the system involves more imprecise or ambiguous parameters in it. The term inventory means stock of goods in physical form. inventory may be of different types - raw materials inventory and finished product inventory. In real life inventory is a day to day problem and it is involve with suppliers, whole sellers, retailers and customers.

Here attention has been made to the study of some inventory model under fuzzy environment. Raw materials inventory is considered and an EOQ model is studied where shortages are allowed. These shortages are considered in elastic form by which we can estimate the total cost which can be beneficial for a firm in the overall production process.

De and Rawat [1] used fuzzy approach in their inventory model. They considered the cost parameters like carrying cost and ordering cost as triangular fuzzy numbers. For defuzzification purpose they have used sign distance ranking method.

P. Bhattacharyya et al. (Eds.): NGCT 2017, CCIS 827, pp. 617–622, 2018.
https://doi.org/10.1007/978-981-10-8657-1_47

Chang et al. [2] designed one inventory model to obtain economic order quantity and total cost in fuzzy environment where shortages are allowed. They have applied sign distance ranking method for getting defuzzification of fuzzy numbers. Yao and Chiang. [4] studied one inventory problem and obtained total cost in fuzzy environment where shortages were not allowed. To characterize the fuzzy parameters they have used trapezoidal fuzzy number and then defuzzified by applying centroid method and sign distance ranking method.

Yao and Su [5], Kao and Hsu [6] considered backorder inventory models in fuzzy environment. Chen and Wang [7] discussed an fuzzy inventory model where backorder is permitted and consider the inventory parameters like demand, ordering cost and backorder cost as fuzzy number. They used function principle instead of extension principle, to calculate the total inventory cost in fuzzy environment.

De and Rawat [8, 9], optimizes fuzzy inventory model under fuzzy demand and fuzzy lead time using exponential fuzzy number. They also obtained optimal order quantity of an EOQ model by using expected value of a fuzzy function.

In the present paper shortage cost is considered as fuzzy quantity and it is characterized by triangular fuzzy number [3]. The other inventory parameters like odering cost, carrying cost, demand etc. are assumed as crisp numbers. Fuzzy total cost is obtained and it is defuzzyfied by using sign distance ranking method.

2 Definition and Preliminaries

Definition 1 Triangular fuzzy number
The characteristic function of a triangular fuzzy number $\tilde{P} = (p_1, p_2, p_3)$ is given by:

$$\mu_{\tilde{P}}(x) = \begin{cases} 0, & x < p_1 \\ \mu_{\tilde{P}} l(x) = \frac{x-p_1}{p_2-p_1}, & p_1 \le x \le p_2 \\ \mu_{\tilde{P}} r(x) = \frac{p_3-x}{p_3-p_2}, & p_2 \le x \le p_3 \\ 0, & x > p_3 \end{cases}$$

The graphical representation of triangular fuzzy number is shown in the following Fig. 1:

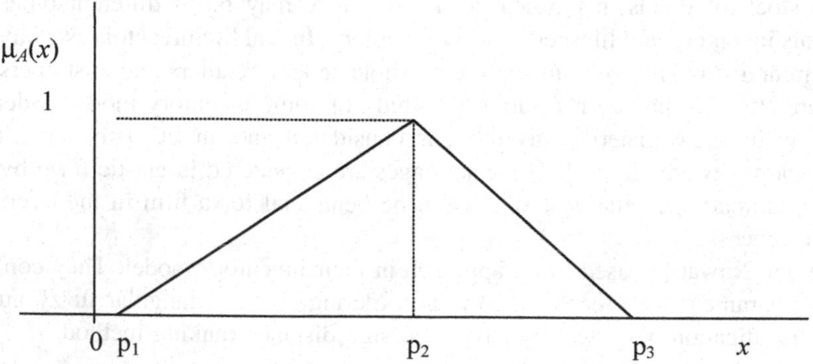

Fig. 1. Interpretation triangular fuzzy number

Properties of triangular fuzzy number and sign distance ranking method are discussed by De and Rawat [1]. Ranking of TFN $\tilde{P} = (p_1, p_2, p_3)$ with respect to the origin O is given by

$$\mathrm{d}(\tilde{P}, \tilde{O}) = \frac{1}{4}(p_1 + p_2 + p_3)$$

3 Deterministic Model of EOQ with Shortages

Here the discussion is been done with the EOQ Model with shortages [2]. Following parameters and notations we use for the present model:

T: Total time of the plan
c: Carrying cost for one unit per day.
c_s: Backorder cost for one unit per day.
o: Setup cost/ordering cost per order.
D: Total demand over the planning time period [0, *T*].
t_q: Length of a cycle.
q: Order quantity per cycle.
s: Shortage quantity per cycle.

According to the Fig. 2 of the model we have

$$\frac{q - s}{t_1} = \frac{q}{t_q} = \frac{s}{t_2} = \frac{D}{T}$$

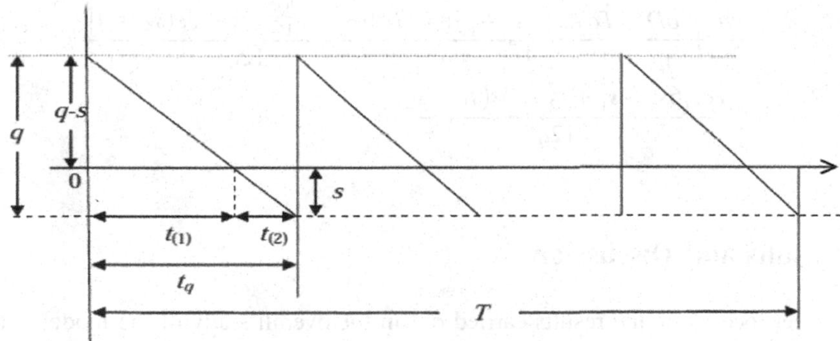

Fig. 2. Inventory model with backorder

During the planning period [0, *T*] the total inventory cost is obtained as

$$\begin{aligned} \mathrm{F}(q, s) &= [ct_1 \frac{q - s}{2} + c_s t_2 \frac{s}{2} + o]\frac{D}{q} \\ &= \frac{c(q - s)^2 T}{2q} + \frac{c_s s^2 T}{2q} + \frac{oD}{q} \end{aligned}$$

The optimal solutions of the model under crisp environment are obtained as follows:

Economic order quantity $q^* = \sqrt{\frac{2(c+c_s)oD}{cc_sT}}$

Economic backorder quantity $s^* = \sqrt{\frac{2coD}{c_s(c+c_s)T}}$

TC = Minimal total cost $F(q^*, s^*) = \sqrt{\frac{2cc_soDT}{c+c_s}}$

4 Fuzzy Inventory Model with Shortages

It is very difficult to take managerial decision to assume the crisp values of the inventory parameters as stated earlier. These inventory parameters are mostly uncertain and in practical situation it may fluctuate a little. Here in the present model the shortages quantity (q) is characterized by fuzzy number and it is represented as $\hat{s} = (s - s_1, s, s + s_2)$ and the rest parameters are considered as fuzzy points.

Finally, if we fuzzify s then the fuzzy total cost is obtained as.

$$\mathrm{TC}(q, \tilde{s}) = T\frac{cq}{2} - Tc\tilde{s} + T\frac{c\tilde{s}^2}{2q} + T\frac{c_s\tilde{s}^2}{2q} + \frac{oD}{q}$$

Applying defuzzification the fuzzy total cost as stated above become crisp value as below

$$\begin{aligned} &\mathrm{FTC}\ (q,\ s - s_1,\ s + s_2) = \\ &\frac{Tcq}{2} + \frac{oD}{q} - \frac{Tc[4s - s_1 + s_2]}{4} + \frac{Tc\left[6s^2 + s_1^2 + s_2^2 - 3s(s_{1-}s_2)\right]}{12q} \\ &+ \frac{Tc_s\left[6s^2 + s_1^2 + s_2^2 - 3s(s_1 - s_2)\right]}{12q} \end{aligned}$$

5 Results and Discussion

This paper focuses on the results carried out in the overall study of the model both in the crisp and the fuzzy environments and finally the sensitivity analysis has been done in the first case. Whereas in the second case the comparative study is performed on stochastic modeling based on the data collected from the respective organizations.

The problem shown in the following is studied from the reference of [2] where, carrying cost (c) = 10; backorder cost (c_s) = 20; ordering cost (o) = 200; Demand (D) = 2000; T = 12.

The optimal solution for q and s and minimum total cost F (q, s) as obtained in crisp environment are as follows:

$$q = 100,\ s = 33.33 \text{ and the minimal total cost } F(q, s) = 8000$$

The Table 1 shows the results performed in fuzzy environment where the shortage quantity ($\hat{s}$) is defuzzified by using sign distance ranking method and the sensitivity analysis is shown with respect to the fuzzy parameter $\hat{s} = (s - s_1,\ s,\ s + s_2)$ in the following.

Table 1. Considering shortage quantity ($\hat{s}$) as fuzzy number

Shortage quantity fuzzy number			Shortage quantity		Total cost	
s	s_1	s_2	s_d	%age error	FTC	%age error
33.33	0.83	1.09	33.3950	0.1950	8000.60	0.0070
33.34	0.74	1.09	33.4275	0.2624	8000.50	0.0065
33.35	0.65	1.09	33.4600	0.3298	8000.50	0.0061
33.36	0.56	1.09	33.4925	0.3972	8000.50	0.0058
33.37	0.47	1.09	33.5250	0.4645	8000.40	0.0056
32.5	0.6	1.7	32.7750	0.8462	8001.40	0.0175
32.6	0.8	1.7	32.8250	0.6902	8001.40	0.0179
32.7	1.0	1.7	32.8750	0.5352	8001.50	0.0185
32.8	1.2	1.7	32.9250	0.3811	8001.60	0.0196
32.9	1.4	1.7	32.9750	0.2280	8001.70	0.2100
34.5	1.0	1.0	34.5250	0.0725	8003.20	0.0402
34.6	1.1	1.1	34.6000	0.0000	8003.60	0.0452
34.7	1.2	1.2	34.6750	0.0720	8004.00	0.0504
34.8	1.3	1.3	34.7500	0.1437	8004.50	0.0560
34.9	1.4	1.05	34.8125	0.2507	8004.80	0.0605
31.5	1.25	1.82	31.6425	0.4524	8006.60	0.0821
31.6	1.34	1.72	31.6950	0.3006	8006.20	0.0780
31.7	1.43	1.62	31.7475	0.1498	8005.90	0.0740
31.8	1.52	1.52	31.8000	0.1117	8005.60	0.0702
31.9	1.61	1.42	31.8525	0.1489	8005.30	0.0666
35.01	1.1	1.5	35.1100	0.2856	8006.70	0.0838
35.02	1.1	1.5	35.1200	0.2856	8006.80	0.0846
35.03	1.1	1.5	35.1300	0.2855	8006.80	0.0854
35.04	1.1	1.5	35.1400	0.2854	8006.90	0.0862
35.05	1.1	1.5	35.1500	0.2853	8007.00	0.0870

6 Conclusion

Observations obtained from the above model with shortage are given below. Signed distance ranking method has been used to defuzzify the fuzzy total cost. So, the case study is done in order to estimate the relative changes of the total cost in both crisp and fuzzy environments. Numerical example shows that the results are very close to the crisp case. Our presented result shows an analytical approach to solve deterministic inventory model transformed from fuzzy inventory model.

References

1. De, P.K., Rawat, A.: A fuzzy inventory model without shortages usingtriangular fuzzy number. Fuzzy Inf. Eng. **1**, 59–68 (2011)
2. Chiang, J., Yao, J., Lee, H.M.: Fuzzy inventory with backorder defuzzifica-tion by signed distance method. J. Inf. Sci. Eng. **21**, 673–694 (2005)
3. Zimmermann, H.J.: Fuzzy Set Theory and its Applications, pp. 1–16. Kluwer Academic Publishers, Dordrecht (2010)
4. Yao, J.S., Chiang, J.: Inventory without backorder with fuzzy total cost & fuzzy storing cost defuzzified by centroid and signed-distance. Eur. J. Oper. Res. **148**, 401–409 (2003)
5. Yao, J.S., Su, J.S.: Fuzzy total demand and maximum inventory with backorder based on signed distance method. Int. J. Innov. Comput. Inf. Control **4**(9), 2249–2261 (2008). p. 9
6. Kao, C., Hsu, W.K.: Lot size- reorder point inventory model with fuzzy demands. Comput. Math Appl. **43**, 1291–1302 (2002)
7. Chen, S., Wang, C.: Backorder fuzzy inventory model under function principle. Inf. Sci. **95**, 71–79 (1996)
8. De, P.K., Rawat, A.: Optimization of fuzzy inventory model under fuzzy demand and fuzzy lead time using Exponential fuzzy number. In: International Conference on IEEE FSKD 2012, 978-1-4673-0024-7/10/$26.00 ©2012, pp. 465–467. IEEE (2012)
9. De, P.K., Rawat, A.: Optimal order quantity of an EOQ model using expected value of a fuzzy function. In: International Conference on IEEE Fuzzy System (2013). https://doi.org/10.1109/fuzz-ieee.2013.6622534

Dynamic Processing and Analysis of Continuous Streaming Stock Market Data Using MBCQ Tree Approach

M. Ananthi[1(✉)] and M. R. Sumalatha[2]

[1] Department of Information Technology, Sri Sairam Engineering College, Chennai, Tamil Nadu, India
ananthi.it@sairam.edu.in

[2] Department of Information Technology, Anna University, Chennai, India
sumalatha.ramachandran@gmail.com

Abstract. The most challenging facet in today's analysis is dealing with real time dynamic data that has characteristic of changing in time, hence results in a continuous flow of data, often signified as streaming data. A distinct database has been assimilated to store the continuous data and designed in a way to query for the gushing data at that point rather than working on snapshot data. Consequently querying of these dynamic data have various confronts in the areas of data distribution, retrieving resultant set in an optimized way and query processing. To overcome the issues on querying the continuous data, a new idea Multilevel with Balanced Continuous Query tree (MBCQ) indexing technique have been commenced to handle querying of continuous data efficiently. The proposed system is applied in the Stock market analysis, which addresses these issues of obtaining the business data for stock market by implementing dynamic timestamp-based sliding window that controls incoming data and filters it with the necessary data to be viewed. These are used to make valuable stock decisions that help the analyst in winning a stock deal. This also validates for memory handler and index maintenance cost to that of existing technique and observed that the proposed system outperforms in a better way.

Keywords: Data streams · Stream management · Query processing Indexing · Timestamp · Sliding window

1 Introduction

As the information era rules the world in nanoseconds, instant processing is the major hitch in today's world that involves data streaming. Data Stream Management System (DSMS) can be applied in various areas such as sensor based applications, network traffic analysis to monitor streams of network packet flows, telephone call records in web servers, online financial applications i.e. streams of stock trade where the data flow is based on the timestamp. Real-time analysis of data streams and data stream mining are important for business and financial applications. These applications entail on-line monitoring and dynamic answering of user queries which helps the analytic users and the information seekers in making successful business deals. It may impose

P. Bhattacharyya et al. (Eds.): NGCT 2017, CCIS 827, pp. 623–640, 2018.
https://doi.org/10.1007/978-981-10-8657-1_48

response-time constraints, i.e. the time it takes to produce an up-to-date result of a continuous query upon request by the users. The system should be time and space efficient to execute continuous queries and to process incoming data streams.

In DSMS, queries are processed by incremental operators with respect to the incoming arrival rate of streaming tuples. Query plans require buffers, queues and scheduling techniques throughout the lifetime of a query. Complex queries such as joins and range aggregations are much more difficult to process than simple queries. For each incoming data stream tuple, the system needs to identify the continuous queries that are affected by the incoming records without scanning each item. Periodic query execution of streaming data is an expensive operation and continuous query optimization is still an open issue. Scalability is an another issue in indexing queries on large dynamic streaming data. Indexing is a challenging task where high volume of incoming streaming data is to be filtered. An adaptive query plan is required to minimize the processing cost of real-time streaming data rather than minimizing the number of disk accesses as in traditional DBMS. Hence, adaptive query execution plans are required based on the streaming arrival rate, query load and memory availability. Adaptive indexing of streaming data and continuous queries with competent query optimization is proposed to reduce the execution time and improve the accuracy of streaming data. This helps the stock market users to obtain the instantaneous results on the live data through the user queries.

2 Related Work

A new indexing approach CKDB-tree [2] was proposed with general purpose graphics processing unit (GP-GPU) to reduce the storage cost and to handle dynamic continuous queries over streaming data. Here, queries were split into cells and KDB-tree was constructed by repeatedly partitioning of particular cell that lead to space overhead and reduces the efficient retrieval. Declarative crowd sourcing [4] was designed to hide the complexities and relieve the user from the burden of dealing with the crowd. The best optimal plan to execute a given query was selected by the optimizer based on the cost factor. Dynamic, complex queries were not considered and not optimized in this work. A complete simulator [7] implemented that entailed fragments of data distributor, data processor and data storage resulted in consuming high outfit cost. The entire raw data considered which increases the processing cost and the making it available in the local memory augmented the high storage. The Multilayer Inverted List (MIL) [5] proposed to work with the tweets by the upper bound pruning. The clusters updated only with the new tweets and the fresh one was replaced by the surviving tweets. Thus, frequent changes in clusters results that in turn bring difficulty in query processing and searching would be chaotic. E-Tree (Ensemble-tree) technique [8] implemented that the index-tables were updated fairly on the prediction and patterns that were prevailed by the user's search. The index would be populated if the pattern of quest changes to adopt larger node traversal for rarely searched words. CHive query processing technique [3] with a parameter RQP (Reference Query Plan) would be effective only if the same kind of query plan has already been executed. The selectivity [1] stored the particular sliding window samples and records it for a predefined window size of 200 which is highly impossible to determine the window size in streaming data.

An adaptive stream query processor engine [16] was developed to execute streaming data in which feed rates are higher in real-time streaming applications and not scalable when the number of tasks increases. Efficient query processing could be achieved by using structural clustering and optimizing using steepest gradient method using the feedback rate control method [20]. Structural clustering was done using k-means clustering algorithm, identification of nearest neighbour and feedback from previous clusters would reduce the system efficiency and the analysis was done for plain-text based data, not for time related data. Bitmap indexing method was implemented in ArQSS [19] for fast archiving and querying sensor data streams. Queries stored in sections where a summary of the sections maintained in separate arrays. Three index structures were used with additional tuning parameters for extra-bit allocation and expiration of attributes which reduces the system performance. A persistent query agent (PQA) for real-time application [12] implemented and network performance feedback to clients and applications was to improve the ability by adding new kinds of monitoring sources dynamically and coming up with measurement ontology to describe and discover new metrics. k-EGA and A-SEGO methods [11] implemented to monitor a set of sub plans simultaneously. Each scheme also employed a user-defined, cost-bound parameter for controlling the number of monitoring sub plans. A more optimized global plan might be generated by using a more highly configured cost-bound parameter. Outlier data using multi-objective genetic algorithm [13] was used to find unsupervised learning and subspaces were used to spot the expected outliers. Incremental k-means clustering algorithm was implemented and previous results were repeatedly applied to find the outliers which made the system inefficient. Two clustering algorithms CURE with k-means and CLARANS were proposed [14] to detect outliers in data streams to find the closest pair of representatives for each cluster that lead an additional overhead in data stream processing. ClusTree [9] proposed to cluster multiple data streams concurrently. Maintaining summary statistics of each data object lead to more workload. New Structure index proposed [15] for handling structured and semi structured RDF to retrieve queries and number of join procedures employed to execute incomplete or unavailable RDF schema. The BFS recursive algorithm used in this method takes more time for processing both structure-level and data-level operations.

Queries were indexed using a nearest neighbour algorithm [18], doubly linked-list was used to represent skyline queries. Doubly linked-list and pointer usage take more memory and computation. Gaussian distribution based on heuristic rules [10] was developed on continuous attributes for classifying data streams. Rules were determined based on batch processing. An analysis of the prevailing systems on spatial keyword search [6] was done by indexing keywords on the particular geological locations that befall primarily based on the *top-K* searches. The indexing structure was not supporting any fresh words/keywords, and outmoded method is also adopted to obtain results. The DINER and MINER system [17] proposed had an effective query processing technique for the static data that resided in the memory. It is less suggestible in case of streaming data from memory could not hold the entire streaming data till the query is being processed.

From the existing work, it is observed that the adaptive indexing structure is required to efficiently store incoming data readings so that it can be accessed quickly by user queries. Another challenge is processing of multiple queries concurrently to produce accurate results which need to consider the optimal query plan cost when there is a change in the flow of the incoming stream.

3 Dynamic Data Stream Processor

The adaptive stream processing algorithm is designed to analyze and act on real time streaming data that are controlled by buffer windows. The working principle of stream processor is shown in Fig. 1. Online stock market data have been given as streaming data input. Continuous streams of data, obtains through online financial trading as a web interface that is embedded with timestamp. The timestamp is affixed as one of the attribute in the tuples that produces easy retrieval and execution of temporal, complex and multi queries. The variation in stock values with current timestamp use as a threshold to filter and control boundless vibrant data which is implemented through dynamic sliding window technique that is covered in the next section.

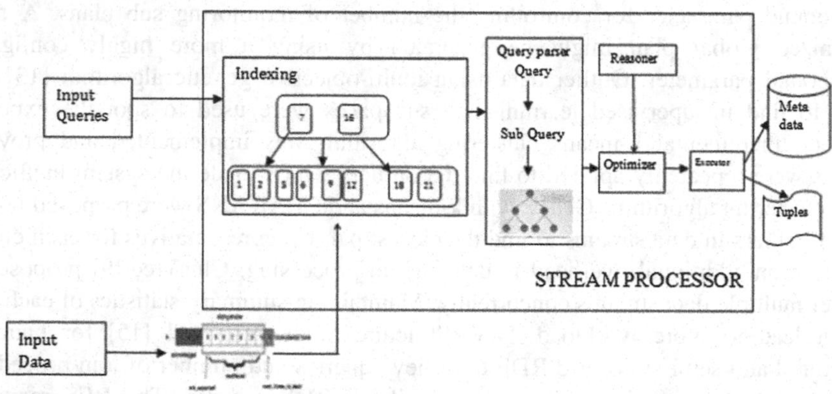

Fig. 1. Stream processor

3.1 Dynamic Time-Based Sliding Window

Dynamic time-based sliding window replaces the existing data with the new incoming data that are changed over time by filtering through sliding window. The size of the sliding window changes dynamically based on the flow rate of incoming data that depends on the variation in time. It accepts windows with either fixed starting time t_s or within the specified time range between t_1 and t_2. The notations used in dynamic time-based sliding window are represented in the Table 1.

A dynamic sliding window with a timestamp is represented in Fig. 2. Whenever a new tuple arrives, window over data streams are measured in terms of timestamp defined as time units. $\mathcal{W}$ signifies a consistent time-based extent of the dynamic sliding window.

Table 1. Notations used in dynamic time-based sliding window

Notation	Description
S	Data streams
t_s	Start time
T	Current timestamp
t_1, t_2	Time interval between previous and forthcoming timestamp
ω	Consistent temporal extent of the window
γ	Progression step
δ	Delay
$\aleph$	Variation in price value
$wl(S, t_s, T)$	Sliding window entries between starting time and current timestamp
$W(S, ts, T, \omega, \gamma, \delta, \aleph)$	Dynamic sliding window
A^t, A^{t-1}	Stock current price value, previous price value
$\Delta(A^t)$	Modulo of $(A^t - A^{t-1})$

Window slides with initial starting time t_s and current timestamp is represented as T. The overlapping window contains some delay δ based on the current timestamp to measure the change in the timestamp and data value. Progression step γ is set with small time units based on the speed of incoming tuples for the smooth arrival of streams. Unit values of w, δ, γ are taken as 1, 0, and 1 as on time-based sliding window for the successive retrieval of tuples with current timestamp.

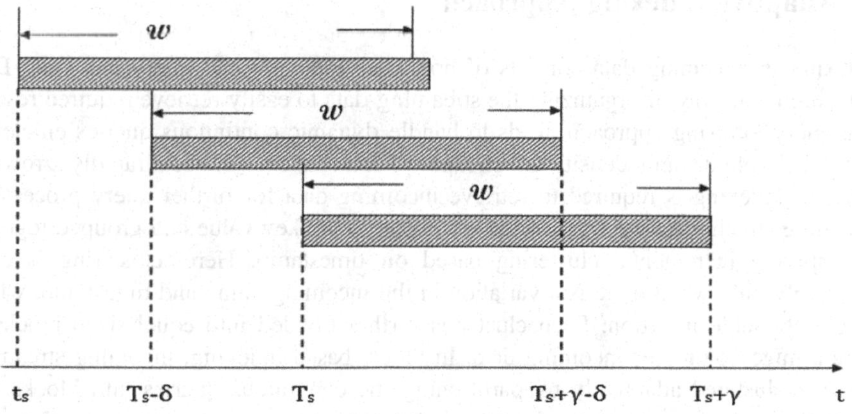

Fig. 2. Dynamic sliding window based on time-based sliding window. Continuous state of sliding window at time instant T_s and $T_s + \gamma$.

Dynamic time-based sliding window is specified in (1) and (2). Whenever a new tuple arrives, window over data streams are measured in terms of timestamp defined as time units. W represents the size of the dynamic time-based sliding window which consists of initial starting time t_s, adaptable temporal extent of the sliding window ω, current timestamp T, delay δ, arrival of incoming streaming tuples varies progressively with progression step γ.

$$\mathrm{W(S, t_S, T, \omega, \gamma, \delta, N) = w1(S, t_S, T), T \geq t_S\ and\ N \leftarrow \Delta(A^\wedge t)} \tag{1}$$

$$\mathrm{w1(S, t_1, t_2)} = \begin{cases} \mathrm{S(T), t_1 \leq T \leq t_2\ and\ mod((T - t_1), \gamma) = 0} \\ \mathrm{0, T < t_s} \end{cases} \tag{2}$$

Where $\Delta(A^t) = 0$ and $\Delta(A^t) = mod(A^t - A^{t-1})$

Continuous query execution flow is controlled using this dynamic sliding window and a new parameter ℵ is added along with existing time-based sliding window. Variations in both timestamp and incoming price value are checked to adopt the changes in streaming data. This is to eliminate redundant and unchanged values which are not required for further processing to reduce space cost and speed up the retrieval time. The overlapping window contains some delay δ based on current timestamp. Delay includes measuring the change in timestamp and data value. Progression step is set with smaller time units based on the speed of incoming tuples for the smooth arrival of streams. Unit values of W, δ, γ are taken as 1, 0, and 1 as on time-based sliding window for the successive retrieval of tuples with current timestamp. The dynamic incoming data has been filtered using dynamic sliding window and adaptive clustering based indexing method is used for query processing that is described in the next section.

4 Adaptive Indexing Approach

Indexing in streaming data consists of both data indexing and query indexing. Data indexing is the way of organizing the streaming data to easily retrieve required results. The query indexing approach needs to handle dynamic continuous queries efficiently since the volume and density of streaming data have also been rapidly growing. Efficient indexing is required to retrieve incoming data for further query processing. Incoming stream data are fragmented according to the key value and grouped together by applying incremental clustering based on timestamp. Here, clustering is done adaptively only when there is a variation in the incoming value and timestamp, which ensures scalable insertion. Each cluster is further divided into equal sized blocks to store a huge volume of incoming data. In block–based indexing, incoming streaming data are clustered adaptively by partitioning the continuous queries into blocks that keeps the top k list of queries, i.e. the most frequently enquired queries by the users which are considered as registered queries. Dynamic query processor executes these indexed queries further to fetch the result in a particular point of time that helps the user make decision at once. The indexer will construct index to the newly received query whenever the new query arrives. Then processor will first look at the index stored in the main memory for processing and exact result set is retrieved. The query indexing approach is mandatory to access the query results during continuous query processing and to avoid lavish operations in index maintenance.

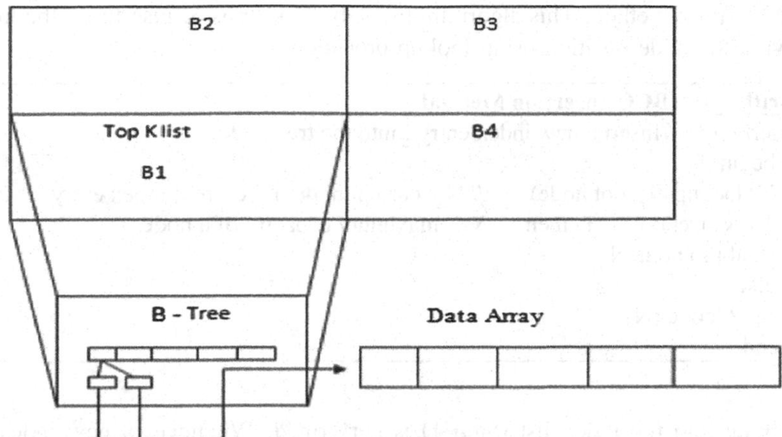

Fig. 3. MBCQ structure

4.1 MBCQ Approach

Multilevel index with a balanced structure referred as MBCQ-tree (Multilevel with Balanced Continuous Query tree) is constructed and shown in Fig. 3. This index structure helps in obtaining appropriate results for the queries issued by the user. When a stream query is generated, the incoming symbols are processed and the matching query-string from the index structure is found. Moreover, the user query is continuously compared with the incoming data streams to find whether the matched results exist. Therefore, in order to efficiently find the matched data, all the queries should be indexed and the corresponding query processing mechanism should be designed. For the incoming data streams, each symbol is used to traverse the index structure and the query is identified by matching the index.

In the MBCQ-tree, continuous queries are grouped into blocks, i.e. B1, B2, B3 and so on and each block contains top-k list and B-tree structure. The queries are split into sub queries and are not overlapped in more than one cell. Unlike existing systems, top-k list maintains only registered queries. If any new query executes repeatedly by number of users, then that is considered as a top-k query and updated in the registered query list. So, query retrieval, searches either in top-k list or tree list based on the incoming query that speeds up query processing and avoids more comparisons and search.

4.2 MBCQ Insertion Method

The MBCQ insertion method describes how continuous queries are indexed into blocks. Block range is bounded by fixing an upper bound limit. During insert, upper bound condition is initially tested and the queries can be inserted into the same block if it falls within the limit, otherwise these blocks will be divided into sub-blocks. The same partitioning is repeated recursively until none of them has value greater than the upper bound limit. Each block is then converted into a tree. Algorithm 1 describes a

MBCQ insertion method. This algorithm has sub algorithms to insert into the tree and identifying the node position using lookup procedure.

Algorithm 1 MBCQ Insertion Method

```
Insertion(I) //Insert a new index entry I into the tree node
1: begin
2: N=lookups(I, root node)      // N – current node, I – current index entry
3: If (N.size()<=M+1) then  // M – maximum capacity of a node
4: Add I to node N
5: else
6: Split_node (N)
7: end
```

Looking into the index list (Step 1) is performed. Whenever a new index entry arrives, the first step is to find a node N in leaf for inserting the new entry (Step 2). If N satisfies the upper boundary condition $(2 \le U_b \le M + 1)$ then the current node is enumerated with a new entry (steps 3–4) otherwise SplitNode(N) algorithm is invoked (step 6). SplitNode method is described in Algorithm 3. If maximum capacity M reaches, then the new node created and data inserted into new node (steps 2–4). Otherwise, data inserted into existing node itself (Steps 5–6). New parent is created in case of leaf nodes overflow (Steps 7–10).

Algorithm 2 lookup (Node leafentry, root)

```
1: begin
2: TP ← null                              // TP-Target Pair
3: If Child.size = 0 then
4:      reach the target leaf block
5:      TP ←leafentry                     // current node
6:      return TP
7: else
8:      search leafentry(A_L,N)           //A_L-ArrayList
9:      TP ←get_min(A_L)
10:     Insertion(leafentry)
10:     return TP
11: end
```

Algorithm 2 describes search procedure for selecting a leaf node N to place the new index entry I. Initially child node size is calculated. If the size of the children is 0 then, current node N is returned (steps 3–6). Again the upper bound condition of the node N is tested for inserting new index entry I, otherwise leaf node is selected from min (pair). If the target pair in min (pair) satisfies $(2 \le U_b \le M + 1)$ the following condition then insert the new entry I in N otherwise split the node (steps 8–10).

Algorithm 3 SplitNode(N)

```
begin
If (leafentries.size()==M+1) /*the node overflows*/
        Ns ϵ {N,N1}               // copy the live entries of node N into new node N1
        insert(N1,Pn)
        If Pn≠M+1 then                     // parent node underflow
            Merge (N, N1)
        else
            Create a new index node as the new parent Pn1
        insert(N1,Pn1)
        end if
end if
end
```

4.3 Dynamic Query Processor

A Stream query processor is designed to achieve fast retrieval of streaming data by processing continuous queries efficiently. Queries are executed based on the adaptive plan. Reduction of multiple self-joins are required to optimize the query that can help to improve the efficiency. Storing intermediate results and materialized approach becomes time and cost consuming. Intermediate results are reduced by pipelining the query processing and dynamic optimization of query cost. Dividing queries into sub queries and executing them in parallel using pipelined approach that leads to time efficiency and increases the execution speed. In DSMS, queries are one time queries which execute continuously and it is difficult to choose an optimal plan for continuous queries. So, adaptive query optimizer is required to process continuous queries and streaming data. Adaptive query optimization is implemented using dynamic heuristic optimization algorithm and dynamic query plan is chosen adaptively. Figure 4 illustrates the overall flow diagram of the dynamic query processor. The user enters their desired queries regarding stock market its analysis. Meanwhile the web interface will also be receiving the streaming and static data of stock exchange.

Queries are continuously received from users and query execution process consists of three phases such as (i) Query Fragmentor (ii) Query Plan (iii) Query Merger. The incoming rate of flow of push based queries is controlled by query indexing method and dynamic sliding window. These queries are categorized as registered and unregistered queries which make them easy for fast retrieval of query results. Queries which are continuously accessed by users are considered as registered queries. Some unpredictable queries that can be asked by users rarely or for historical analysis are considered as unregistered queries. For a given query set $Q \in \{q_1, q_2, q_3, \ldots, q_n\}$, query executor initially analyzes the incoming query and classifies whether the query is already registered or not. If it is a registered, it will be processed by the processor, otherwise the new query has to be registered and then the processing of query is carried out. After registering the query, query processor starts executing the incoming query in

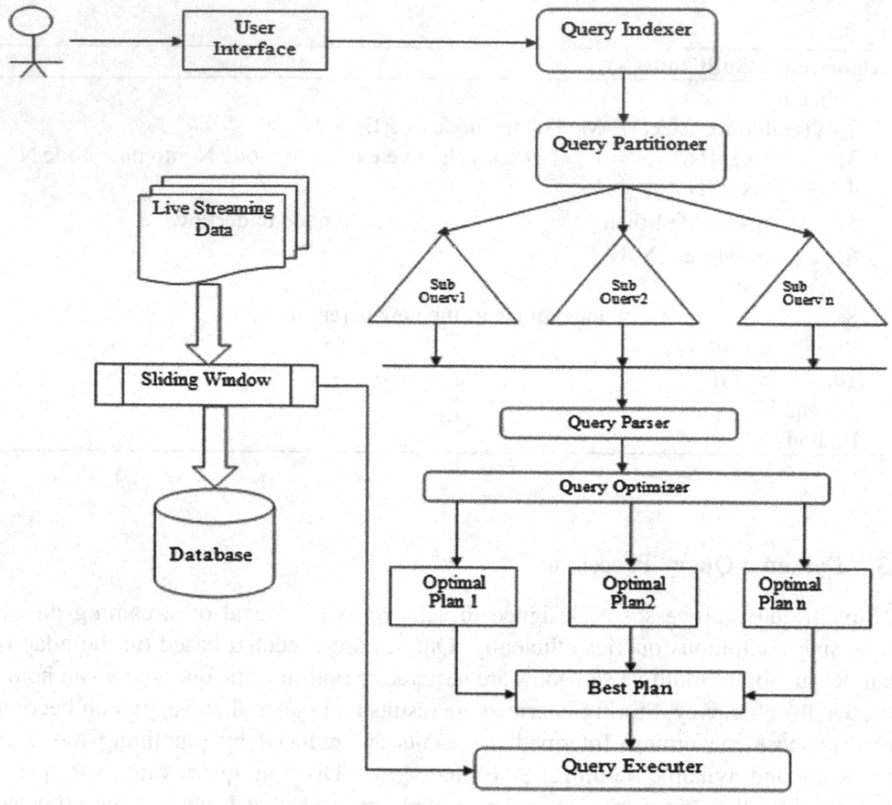

Fig. 4. Dynamic query processing flow

a pipelined manner. Query Fragmentor splits the query into sub queries to simplify the processing task.

Complex query is divided into sub queries here. Query partition is represented as in Eqs. 3 and 4. Q_n is a collection of all queries where each query is represented as Q_i. Each query Q_i is divided into sub queries as $q_{i1}, q_{i2} \ldots q_{in}$.

$$Q_i = q_{i1} \cup q_{i2} \cup q_{i3} \ldots \cup q_{in} \tag{3}$$

$$Q_n = \sum_{i=1}^{n} Q_i \tag{4}$$

Each sub query is processed in parallel and the results are collected from each sub query. Query plan performs the parser task to check the validity of the query and determine the possible path for processing the query. The dynamic optimal plan is chosen for each sub query using dynamic heuristic optimization approach. Then, each sub optimal plan executes and the results are combined to get query result. Resultant query set Q_{RS} is represented by combining sub query results sq_{ij} as shown in Eq. 5.

$$Q_{RS} = \bigcup_{i=1}^{n} (sq_{i1} \bowtie sq_{i2} \bowtie sq_{i3} \ldots \bowtie sq_{in}) \quad (5)$$

In this work, the logical query plan is parallelized into sub queries using a query splitter to increase the execution speed. The query plan is constructed dynamically and sub queries are executed in parallel. The query optimizer converts the logical query plan to physical query plan tree i.e. query execution plan. Input to process the query has been fetched as tuples either statically or dynamically based on the query requirement. Sub query results are merged together using query merger. Finally, it produces the query results in terms of tuples.

5 Experimental Analysis of MBCQ Evaluation

The Experiments are carried out in an Intel® Core i5 M480 2.67 GHz CPU machine that has 4 GB RAM with x64-based processor. Stock market application has been taken as a real-time streaming application for carrying out the experiment. The http://money.rediff.com website is used to obtain livestock values. A TrayApp application has been developed to receive the stock values of NSE and BSE of various companies and continuously update the current stock values of each company which is the key interest areas of all the users. The update will be carried out every time whenever a small change is observed in the live values. The updates of stock values are carried out every 30 s, which will be facilitating the users in knowing the latest stock data and helps in analyzing the progress of the stock market based on their investment. The proposed MBCQ tree has analyzed for effectiveness of the algorithm proposed. This analysis is based on the incoming data stream tuples over time to calculate the overall response time and the amount of memory consumed by using the adaptive clustered approach. The actual number of entries retrieved from stock website compared with entries taken using adaptive index approach.

Parameter setting for index tree is mentioned in Table 2. Number of tuples vary depending on the current market trends. So, average range of the number of tuples that are received within 60 s is measured and is set at 100 to 1000. Receiving entries are updated for every 30 s and this unit is set by calculating average variation in input streams. The maximum number of entries allowed in each node is up to eight entries. Node underflow and overflow status contain weak version and strong version as in the existing CKDB tree. At least two minimal entries are required for each node to be considered as weak version underflow. But, the minimal underflow condition is three entries per node that is to be maintained for making balanced tree. So, strong version condition underflow signifies three entries. A node split occurs during overflow condition which contains/the limit 7 entries per node. Readings from 232 companies are taken for experimentation. On average more than 40000 entries are retrieved per hour in traditional existing system and more than 2 lakhs entries are received per day. The proposed method is compared with the existing method described by Deng et al. [2].

Table 2. Index parameter settings

Parameter	Value
# data tuple	[100, 1000]
Update period	30 s
Max # of entries in a node	8
Weak version condition	2
Strong version condition underflow	3
Strong version condition Overflow	7

5.1 Computation of Update Cost and Response Time

Update cost is calculated based on the number of times the data will be updated. In MBCQ, all entries i.e non changing price values that are considered as duplicate entries are eliminated by filtering incoming data using adaptive incremental clustering based approach. Only change in stock price and timestamp is considered for validating and depicted as valid input data. Though it consumes quite a lot processing time, it saves 90% of memory and processing time. Accuracy in results are maintained as only the exact information is retrieved as input. The update cost U_c is calculated as shown in (6).

$$U_c = k + h \times N_i \tag{6}$$

Where k is the capacity of top k list, h is the height of the tree and N_i is the number of leaf nodes.

Response time is calculated as the minimal elapsed time between receiving incoming data and retrieving query result with some delay for calculation. Delay is very minimal that it does not affect the accuracy of output. Response time calculation is compared with traditional approach and represented as in Eq. 7.

$$R_t = \frac{(R_s - N_E)}{unittime} + \delta \tag{7}$$

R_t – Response time, N_E – Number of incoming entries after updation, R_s – Result set, δ – Minimal delay.

5.2 Computation of Memory Consumption

The proposed MBCQ approach is compared with the existing cell-tree indexing approach CKDB tree in which the queries are split into cells and KDB-tree was constructed. The same query is fragmented into two cells, so referring that query requires the comparison of more than one cell in CKDB tree. The query retrieval must compare both the top-k list and the KDB tree, which requires additional space and more processing time in the existing system. The graph drawn below in Fig. 5 shows the amount of memory (in MB) consumed by MBCQ approach and existing CKDB tree. Storage cost S_c is measured based on three factors, (1) Total available memory space for block array – S_b, (2) space occupied by the data item – S_d and (3) space occupied by update transaction S_{ut} It is formulated as in Eq. 8.

$$S_c = \frac{(S_d + S_{ut})}{S_b} \tag{8}$$

The amount of memory consumed by proposed MBCQ tree is compared with existing CKDB tree by varying the number of queries as shown in Fig. 5. The memory consumed by MBCQ tree is reduced by 44% compared with CKDB tree since repeated use of queries are considered as registered queries and kept on the top-k list. So, query retrieval, searches only in the top-k list, which speed up query processing and registered queries need not be stored in cells once again, which reduces memory consumption whereas CKDB-tree had more number of cell-split leads to more memory usage.

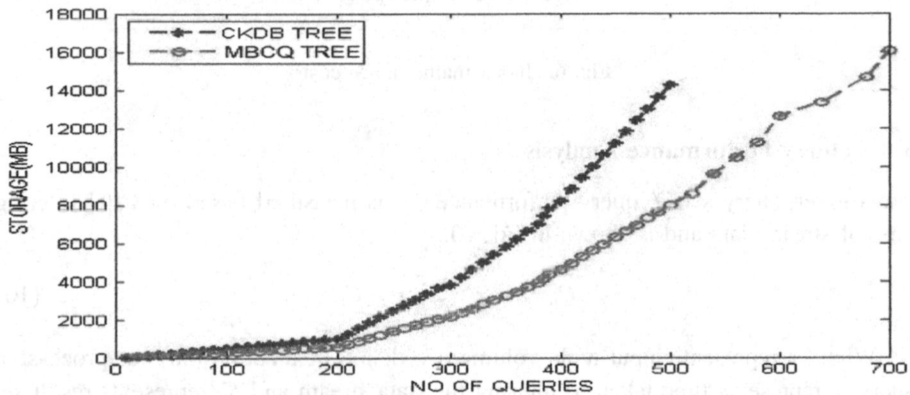

Fig. 5. Memory consumption of MBCQ tree and existing CKDB tree

5.3 Index Maintenance Cost Analysis

The index maintenance cost is measured based on the updation of a number of entries in each index node. It is calculated as the percentage of incoming streams from the number of the incoming entries with incremental updation and filtering time. The index maintenance cost calculation is shown in Eq. 9.

$$IMC = \frac{(nk \times s)}{E} \tag{9}$$

Where *nk* is the number of incoming data entries after incremental updation of k actual entries, *s* is the CPU filtering time for query set Q and *E* represents the actual amount of data stream entries.

Figure 6 shows the maintenance cost of index compared with KDB, CKDB and proposed indexing structure. Due to the unique index structure of MBCQ approach, average update transaction cost is reduced by 15% when compared with CKDB-tree and 200% more than KDB tree.

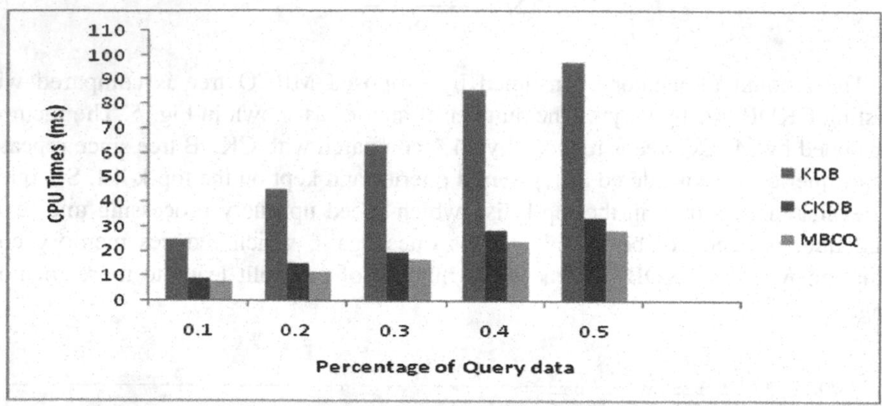

Fig. 6. Index maintenance cost

5.4 Query Performance Analysis

For a given query set Q, query performance Q_p is measured based on CPU filtering time of stream data and is shown in Eq. 10.

$$Q_p = n \times C_p + s \times C_i \tag{10}$$

Where n represents input tuple volume, C_p denotes execution time for processing query, s represents time taken to filtering the data stream and C_i represents result set retrieval time. Query performance is analyzed by varying the distribution of number of queries such as uniform, skewed and hyper-skewed. Uniform arrival of incoming data is considered as uniform distribution, whereas the variation in the speed of incoming tuples is considered as skewed and hyper-skewed. The query performance is compared with existing approach CKDB tree and the results are shown in Fig. 7. MBCQ tree improved by 36% than CKDB-tree in uniform distribution, 37% in skewed distribution and 10% improvement in hyper-skewed distribution. The X-axis represents the number of data tuple and y-axis represents the execution time for query set Q where data tuple n is proportional to query execution time and is shown in Eq. 11.

$$n \alpha E_t \tag{11}$$

When data tuple size increases, processing time of query will also increases.

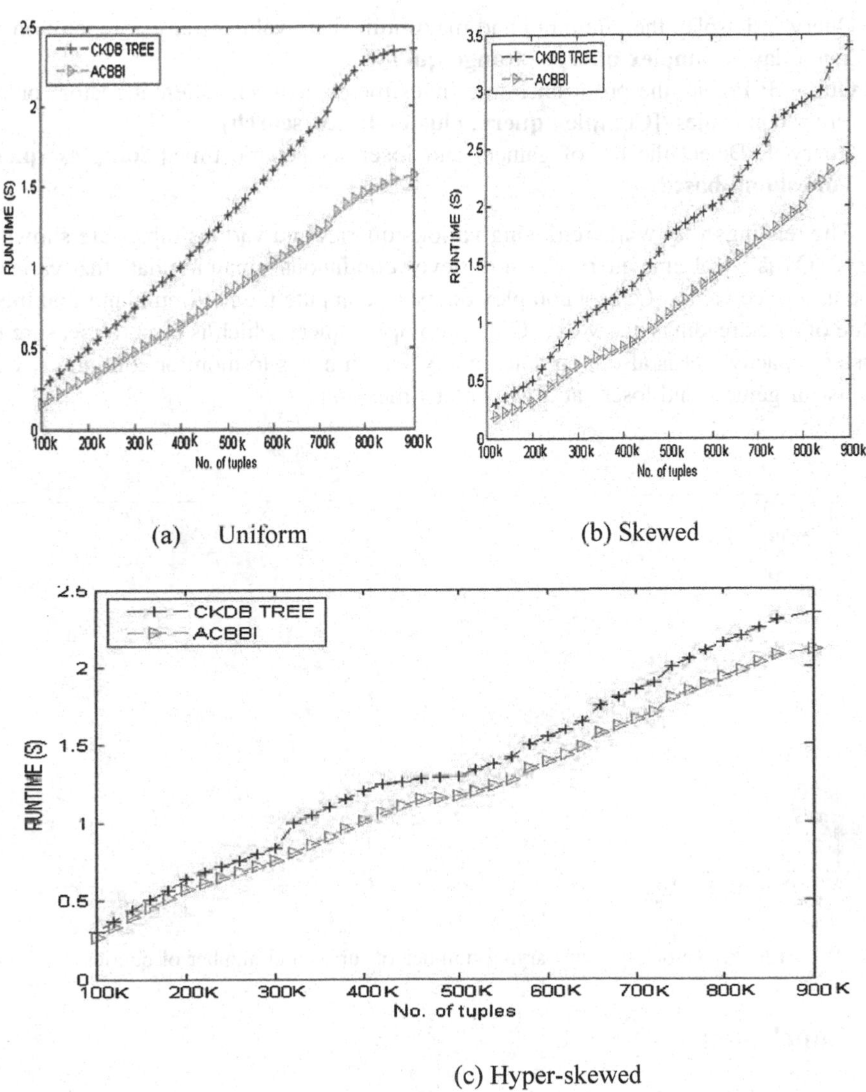

(a) Uniform (b) Skewed

(c) Hyper-skewed

Fig. 7. Query performance with uniform, skewed and hyper-skewed distribution

5.5 Throughput Analysis

Throughput of MBCQ approach is analyzed by varying number of tuples and number of queries by executing various queries. The set of queries tested for experimentation includes

- Query 1: Retrieve the stock values observed once in 30 s. **[Dynamic query – continuous, Timestamp-based]**

- Query 2: Display the minimum and maximum share value of any company on the given day. **[Complex query – Range query]**
- Query 3: Predict the profit on future investments between different sectors or different companies. **[Complex query, cluster-based search]**
- Query 4: Detect the list of gainers and losers at generic time.**[Complex query, Timestamp-based]**

The readings vary while retrieving various queries and various tuples are shown in Fig. 8. Q1 is a real time query which retrieves continuous streaming data that varies in time and price values. Q2 is a complex query to compute the minimum and maximum value of stock readings every day. Q3 is a complex query which is used to measure the cluster capacity, Q4 is also a complex query which needs to monitor continuously for the list of gainers and losers at a particular timestamp.

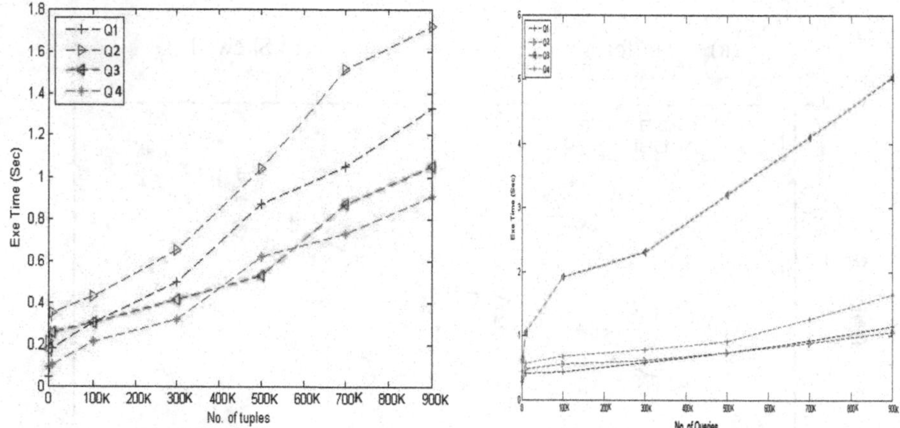

Fig. 8. Throughput by varying number of tuples and number of queries

6 Conclusion

Dynamic query processor with multi-level balanced continuous query tree indexing approach is implemented for processing continuous queries. Dynamic timestamp-based sliding window is used for controlling the incoming flow rate, which filters the excess data that is provided to the users. This technique results in consumption of only 8% of memory, thus enhancing the performance beyond 30% and could observe no backlog in performance resulting is the better functioning of the proposed system. This system helps in providing the significant information to the analytical users who will seek the data to win a business deal. This proposed system also enables the stake holders in knowing the trends in the stock market through the top-k queries and helps in retrieving point in time data using indexing. This multi-level based continuous query processing can be used in big data and internet of things in the future.

References

1. Xie, Q., Zhang, X., Li, Z., Zhou, X.: Optimizing cost of continuous overlapping queries over data streams by filter adaption. IEEE Trans. Knowl. Data Eng. **28**(5), 1258–1271 (2016)
2. Deng, Z., Wu, X., Wang, L., Chen, X., Ranjan, R., Zomaya, A., Chen, D.: Parallel processing of dynamic continuous queries over streaming data flows. IEEE Trans. Parallel Distrib. Syst. **26**(3), 834–845 (2015)
3. Theeten, B., Janssens, N.: CHive: bandwidth optimized continuous querying in distributed clouds. IEEE Trans. Cloud Comput. **3**(2), 219–232 (2015)
4. Fan, J., Zhang, M., Kok, S., Lu, M., Ooi, B.C.: CrowdOp: optimization for declarative crowd sourcing systems. IEEE Trans. Knowl. Data Eng. **27**(8), 2078–2092 (2015)
5. Cai, H., Huang, Z., Srivastava, D., Zhang, Q.: Indexing evolving events from tweet streams. IEEE Trans. Knowl. Data Eng. **27**(11), 3001–3015 (2015)
6. Chen, L., Cong, G., et al.: Temporal spatial-keyword top-k publish/subscribe. In: ICDE Conference, pp. 255–266 (2015)
7. Maske, M.M., Prasad, P.: A real time processing and streaming of wireless network data using Storm. In: International Conference on Computation of Power, Energy Information and Communication (ICCPEIC), pp. 0244–0249 (2015)
8. Zhang, P., Zhou, C., et al.: E-tree: an efficient indexing structure for ensemble models on data streams. IEEE Trans. Knowl. Data Eng. **27**(2), 461–474 (2015)
9. Hesabi, Z.R., Sellis, T., Zhang, X.: Anytime concurrent clustering of multiple streams with an indexing tree. In: JMLR: Workshop and Conference Proceedings, vol. 41, pp. 19–32 (2015)
10. Le, T., Stahl, F., Gomes, J.B., Gaber, M.M., Fatta, G.D.: Computationally efficient rule-based classification for continuous streaming data. In: Bramer, M., Petridis, M. (eds.) Research and Development in Intelligent Systems XXXI, pp. 21–34. Springer, Cham (2014). https://doi.org/10.1007/978-3-319-12069-0_2
11. Lee, H.-H., Park, H.-K., Park, J.-C., Lee, W.-S., Joo, K.-H.: Adaptive run-time overhead adjustments for optimizing multiple continuous query processing. Int. J. Softw. Eng. Appl. **8** (11), 183–196 (2014)
12. Mandal, A., Baldin, I., Xin, Y., Ruth, P., Heermann, C.: Enabling persistent queries for cross-aggregate performance monitoring. IEEE Commun. Mag. **52**, 157–164 (2014)
13. Koupaie, H.M., Ibrahim, S., Hosseinkhani, J.: Outlier detection in stream data by clustering method. Int. J. Adv. Comput. Sci. Inf. Technol. **2**(3), 25–34 (2013). ISSN 2296-1739
14. Vijayarani, S., Jothi, P.: Detecting outliers in data streams using clustering algorithms. Int. J. Innov. Res. Comput. Commun. Eng. **1**(8), 1749–1759 (2013)
15. Tran, T., Ladwig, G., Rudolph, S.: Managing structured and semi structured RDF data using structure indexes. IEEE Trans. Knowl. Data Eng. **25**(9), 2076–2089 (2013)
16. Le-Phuoc, D., Dao-Tran, M., Xavier Parreira, J., Hauswirth, M.: A native and adaptive approach for unified processing of linked streams and linked data. In: Aroyo, L., Welty, C., Alani, H., Taylor, J., Bernstein, A., Kagal, L., Noy, N., Blomqvist, E. (eds.) ISWC 2011. LNCS, vol. 7031, pp. 370–388. Springer, Heidelberg (2011). https://doi.org/10.1007/978-3-642-25073-6_24
17. Bornea, M.A., Vassalos, V., Kotidis, Y., Deligiannakis, A.: Adaptive join operators for result rate optimization on streaming inputs. IEEE Trans. Knowl. Data Eng. **22**(8), 1110–1125 (2010)
18. Bohm, C., Ooi, B.C., Plant, C., Yan, Y.: Efficiently processing continuous k-NN queries on data streams. In: IEEE 23rd International Conference on Data Engineering, ICDE (2007)

19. Pu, K.Q., Zhu, Y.: Fast archiving and querying of heterogeneous sensor data streams. In: Second International Conference on Digital Telecommunications, ICDT 2007, pp. 28–33 (2007)
20. Pu, K.Q., Zhu, Y.: Efficient indexing of heterogeneous data streams with automatic performance configurations. In: Proceedings of the 19th International Conference on Scientific and Statistical Database Management, p. 34 (2007)

Energy Consumption Forecast Using Demographic Data Approach with Canaanland as Case Study

Oluwaseun Aderemi[1], Sanjay Misra[1(✉)], and Ravin Ahuja[2]

[1] Covenant University, Ota, Ogun, Nigeria
oluwaseunaderemi@yahoo.com,
sanjay.misra@covenantuniversity.edu.ng
[2] University of Delhi, New Delhi, India

Abstract. Various methods or models of forecasting energy have been addressed in the past, but it has been observed from exhaustive research that these methods are highly complex and usually require past or historical data of load consumption in its analysis. Hence, a new model that is simple and only makes use of readily available demographic user data such as the Energy consumption in KWh per capita of the country in view, population and land mass area of the urban community under study (Canaanland in this case) was expatiated here. This paper reiterates this model in a clearer, more explicit and applicable way; developing a flow chart that shows a step by step process of forecasting the energy consumption and a matlab code which does the actually computation in KVAh for each forecast year. Results obtained in this case showed that though the forecast values seemed a bit lower than the actual peak consumption for past years covered in the forecast, it still gives an average estimate of the future energy needs for any community without previous information on consumption, which would be very useful in planning.

Keywords: Kilowatt hour per capita · Energy consumption · Forecast Model · Demographic

1 Introduction

Over the years especially in countries where generated capacity of electric power per hour meets or is in excess of the energy consumption, there has been a growing need to have an idea of what quantity of power is actually being consumed per hour so as to curb energy wastage and hence reduce spending in the power sector by producing about just what is needed. This practice has also been found to be useful even in countries where consumption exceeds the generation, as it aids the efficient distribution of the limited generated power. This practice is what is known as load or energy consumption forecast; and a forecast is an estimate of the value of a variable (or set of variables) at a future point in time [1].

Accurate forecast of energy consumption in general results in both commercial and environmental benefits such as reduction in electricity use, peak load demands and greenhouse gas emissions. It is also indispensable in power system planning,

P. Bhattacharyya et al. (Eds.): NGCT 2017, CCIS 827, pp. 641–652, 2018.
https://doi.org/10.1007/978-981-10-8657-1_49

evaluating the cost effectiveness of investing in new techniques and strategy for effective delivery of power [2–4] and power companies use it for operation and planning the future demands of their customers [5, 6]. It reveals the shortfalls in generated power and hence gives a clue as to extra power that needs to be generated to satisfy the current demand and future demands. Researchers have over the years developed various models or methods of forecasting energy consumption or demand. The most widely used of these models includes: Fourier series, neuronal networks (NN), Gaussian process, autoregressive, fuzzy logic, wavelets, multiple regression, linear, non-linear, parametric and non-parametric. Certain factors that determine which model will be used include: the duration of the forecast period i.e. short or long term, seasonal changes in each year, daily peak and off peak periods.

But one common pitfall noticed in these methods is that they all require past consumption data. Hence the need for a model that will be useful in communities that lacks or has inaccurate data. A typical example of such a method will be that using demographic data which are readily available [25]. This paper reiterates the unique benefits of this method, develops a flow chart model which contains more explicit steps to be taken, and a matlab code which takes the year being forecasted and energy consumption per capita as inputs and returns the average energy consumption of the area in view. It is structured using the standard paper format such that after this introduction is the literature review, methodology, results, conclusion and lastly references.

The structure of this paper is as follows: Sect. 2 contains the literature review, Sect. 3: The Methodology used in this paper for forecasting energy, Sect. 4: Results obtained, presented in both pictorial and tabular forms and finally Sect. 5: Conclusion pointing out the benefits and shortfalls of the proposed method.

2 Literature Review

Several professionals have written exhaustively on the subject of load or energy forecast in reputable journals. In [7] we see that as at 2009, Nigeria had a total of 14 generating plants, with an installed capacity of 7,876 MW and available capacity of less than 4,000 MW. Hence the major challenge in the Nigerian power sector was shown to be in the area of power generation because with a population of about 170 million people, the available capacity is overwhelmed by the energy demand due to inadequate supply and of course the inefficient distribution of the insufficient generated power. But the later can only be achieved when the power demand of the various localities is known and this is possible via efficient load forecasting. In the study talked about earlier on [7], the General Auto-regressive Conditional Heteroscedasicity (GARCH) model [8–10] was employed to study the changing volatility of demand and supply in the Nigerian electric market over a period of 36 years while the Harvey logistic model [11, 12] was used to predict the demand and supply of electricity in Nigeria from 2005 to 2026. Data analysed was obtained from the Nigerian Bureau of Statistics' yearly generation and consumption of electricity in Nigeria.

In this same study, a class of stochastic process denoted by Autoregressive Moving Average ARMA (p, q) which is a combination of autoregressive process of order p and a moving average of order q was used to obtain an Autoregressive Integrated Moving Average ARIMA (p, d, q) series. These two models were used to generate a wide range of time series models, when the ARIMA model reduces to an ARMA model and when, it becomes a pure white noise called the error term, used in computing the GARCH model. Also different transformation was performed on the annual data series (1970–2005) used in the study and obtained from the National Bureau of Statistics to make it stationary as no inference procedure can be applied to non-stationary series since they do not produce reliable estimates of parameters.

MATLAB was then used to estimate the parameters of the GARCH model, from which the market volatility was obtained; the ordinary least square method of regression was used to calibrate the Harvey model and analysis was done using the SPSS software.

Results obtained from the prediction showed that the demand for electricity in Nigeria is continuously increasing and clearly outweighed the supply. An estimate from the National Electric Regulation of Nigeria suggests that the minimum requirement of electricity in Nigeria is about 50,000 MW. Hence, with the current available capacity at a maximum of 4,000 MW, and cost of a kilowatt of electricity in Nigeria per hour at about #23.6, [13] profit to be made if the shortfall of 46,000 MW were supplied by new independent power stations stands at #1.0856 billion per hour, revealing a great window of opportunity in Nigeria for investors in the power sector. The benefit of the methods used in the forecast of energy demand and supply in the study is that it can be used to determine the electric power requirement and hence exact capacity of power plants needed to meet the load demand in any community.

In [14], statistical modelling techniques of forecasting energy demand (i.e. obtaining an expression for energy demand) were classified in the following ways:

- Based on the nature of the equation, the techniques were classified as: linear and non-linear, discrete and continuous, while
- Based on the adjustment methods used, we have the parametric and non-parametric types.

Another paper classified the models in seven categories: Fourier series, neuronal networks (NN), Gaussian process, autoregressive, fuzzy logic, wavelets, and multiple regression [15]. While in [16, 17] the modelling techniques are classified based on the class of data, amount and type of variables to be used in the modelling process, leading to two main classification: bottom-up and top-down models which are further sub-divided to deterministic, statistic, engineering etc.

Though it is important we note that the various classification for the energy demand forecast models stated above is not standard and it exclusively depends on the point of view from which the different techniques are seen [15–17].

But it has been observed from the literature in [14] that some new hybrid methods based on stochastic differential equations (SDE) have not been considered in previous reviews. Hence the paper goes on to compare this non-tested SDE method with four of the common linear parametric techniques: multi linear, harmonic regression, Seasonal Autoregressive Integrated Moving Average with Exogenous Variables model (SARIMAX) and time series analysis thereby contributing to the energy demand forecasting models using an average energy consumption data in KW obtained from a residential distribution feeder in Santiago a Chilean city over a period of 135 days (from 1st August - 13th December 2013) [14].

From the paper, results obtained showed that after comparing the four methods by the mean percentage error (MPE), the multi linear regression model was found to be the best to describe and to predict demand followed by SARIMAX time series model, and harmonic regression. But in the case of long time projection, the harmonic regression method would be the best since its MPE measure showed considerable improvements. From the study, the SDE did not enhance forecasting energy demand, but it would be advantageous when the resolution of real measure available data has a bigger interval time than the desired forecast resolution.

In yet another study, [18], we see that of all the methods that have been developed in forecasting electricity load in commercial buildings, the regression models is most commonly used because it is simple to develop, use and interpret when compared with other models (such as thermal, auto regressive, and machine learning models). This study goes on to review regression models and highlights different applications where this model can be used successfully. What the regression model does is it relates energy consumption with external weather and internal building parameters. The model is of two types: the type developed using real historical load data or the other type where no accurate past load data is available and hence simulated load data is used.

The model is a statistical method that estimates the relationship between an output and the variables that have influence on it (also known as influence parameters). Influence parameters in load forecasting include Ambient Dry Bulb Temperature (DBT), Humidity, Solar gain, Scheduling (weekdays/weekends/holidays), and Time resolution.

Regression models are also of the single and multi linear/multi variate (i.e. variable) types. The multi linear regression models are more accurate than the single variable type because they model HVAC energy use in commercial buildings because it has been observed that the consumption in large commercial buildings is not always simple, but can be a complex function of climatic conditions, building characteristics and HVAC systems [19].

For proper analysis, hourly energy consumption and weather data of a university campus (that consists of various lecture theatres, tutorial rooms, academic and administration offices, laboratories, restaurants, shops, and a fitness & aquatic centre) and a 5 storey building called the Tyree Energy Technologies Building (TETB) in the university campus was analysed using the models stated above. The hourly electricity load data and minute interval weather data including DBT and relative humidity (RH) was obtained from the Campus and TETB electricity meters and a local weather station respectively. The data analysis was carried out using Matlab_R2015b and the associated Statistical and Neural Network toolboxes and LibSVM [20]. The results showed that in contrast to what was stated earlier on in the study's literature; most of the machine learning models used showed a better forecast performance than the multi linear regression (MLR) models. But the MLR analysis enabled greater user engagement and control over the forecast analysis which is a major advantage of regression models over machine learning models.

In [17], we see again that there are several methods or models of forecasting electricity load or energy consumption. But here it is indicated that electric loads as well as the corresponding mechanisms for forecasting them are not the same for different seasons, and we need different models to describe such different mechanisms. This is because theoretical and systematic discrepancies between the models imply that a model usually prevails in some proper conditions than other. Hence, choosing the best model from all others for each condition is key. This is done by carefully examining recent electric loads, temporal and meteorological factors, and other exogenous data, before deciding the final choice based on the feature of a model.

Finally, in [21], we see that the techniques of load forecasting accumulated from other studies includes conventional methods such as linear regression, time series, exponential smoothing, stochastic processes, the ARMA model, data mining models, and artificial intelligence methods such as fuzzy logic and artificial neural network (ANN) [1, 22, 23]. Of all these techniques, the paper states that artificial intelligence method is widely used as it provides greater efficiency when compared with the others. However, fuzzy logic seems to take the lead over ANN because of its distinct characteristics [24] (e.g. when a reasonable fluctuation between weather parameters and load occur, fuzzy logic handles it with less forecast error). In the study, a fuzzy logic model was developed (based on the weather parameters - temperature and humidity and the historical load data for the town of Mubi in Adamawa state) to forecast a year - ahead load. Result obtained showed the forecast had an MAPE of 6.9% and efficiency of 93.1%.

From the various papers reviewed, it can be easily seen that while there are actually various methods of forecasting load, the authors do not agree on a specific methods as standard models of forecasting loads, while some models are mentioned or used repeatedly in several papers, some are considered in only a few. Also some are best for short term load forecasting, while others are more suitable for long term forecasts and still others work best at certain seasons of the year and mostly require past data except the new less complex model using readily available demographic user data [25]. This paper gives a clearer, more explicit and applicable way of using this model; developing a flow chart that shows a step by step process of forecasting the energy consumption and a matlab code which does the actually computation. Also results obtained here proved how viable this method is in obtaining an average estimate of energy consumption for places without or with inaccurate past information on consumption.

3 Methodology

The urban community whose load is being forecasted in this paper is Canaanland Km 10 Idiroko road, Ota, Ogun State. The method used in this paper for the forecast as said earlier on does not require past energy consumption data. It only uses demographic data that are readily available such as:

- The energy consumption in Kwh per capita for Nigeria from the base year 2006 to 2015 obtained from the world development indicators [26].
- The population of the local government area where Canaanland is located (i.e. Ado Ota L.G.A) which was 234647 as at 26th November, 1991 and 527242 by 21st March, 2006 [27].

- The land mass of Canaanland in square Km which is about 20 km square [27].
- The land mass of Ado Odo Ota L.G.A in square Km which is about 878 km square [27].

Power factor was assumed to be 0.8 [28]. Figure 1 below shows a step by step procedure to be taken towards forecasting the energy consumption.

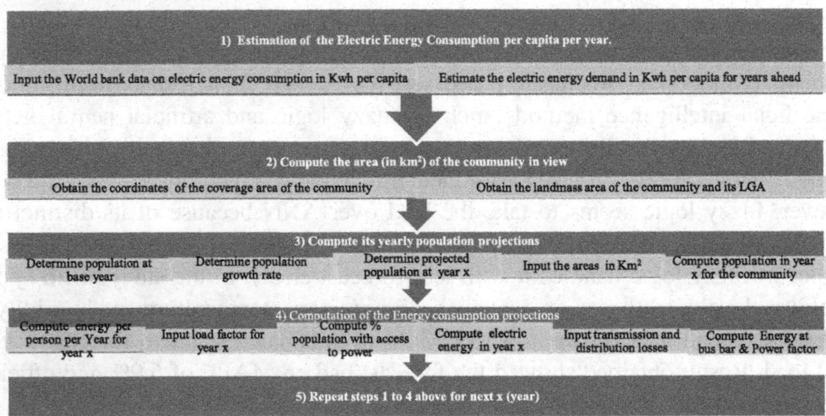

Fig. 1. Flow chart showing step by step procedure to be taken towards arriving at the energy consumption

Figures 2 and 3 shows a matlab code that estimates future energy consumption in Kwh per capita for 2016 to 2025 and results obtained. Inputs used in the estimation are the already available values for previous years [26] and that of 2025 which has already been predicted in literature to be 433 KWh [29].

```
% Code to estimate the Electric energy consumption in Kwh per capita for
% Nigeria from 2016 to 2025
n = input ('Enter the number of years covered in the estimate : ');
i = 0.1111; % Projected electric energy consumption in Kwh per capita growth rate
E1 = 151; % Electric energy consumption in Kwh per capita at base or start year
equ = @(m) ((i + 1)^(m)) * E1; % The equation
for m = 0:n
    str = num2str(m+2015);
    E = equ(m);
    disp(['the Electric energy consumption in Kwh per capita for ',str,' is'])
        disp(E)
end
```

Fig. 2. A matlab code that estimates future energy consumption in Kwh per capita for 2016 to 2025

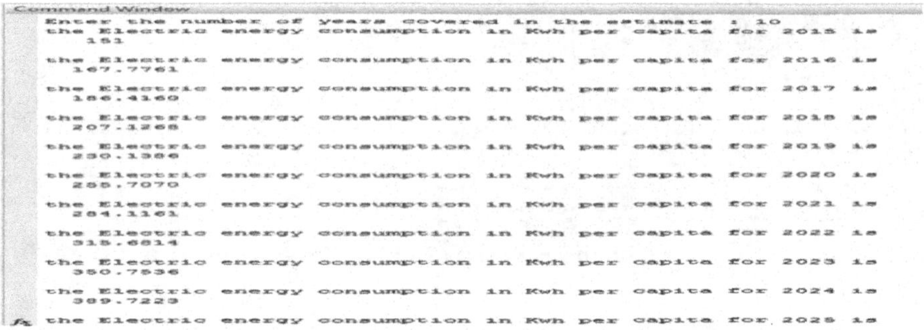

```
Command Window
Enter the number of years covered in the estimate : 10
the Electric energy consumption in Kwh per capita for 2015 is
   151

the Electric energy consumption in Kwh per capita for 2016 is
   167.7761

the Electric energy consumption in Kwh per capita for 2017 is
   186.4160

the Electric energy consumption in Kwh per capita for 2018 is
   207.1268

the Electric energy consumption in Kwh per capita for 2019 is
   230.1386

the Electric energy consumption in Kwh per capita for 2020 is
   255.7070

the Electric energy consumption in Kwh per capita for 2021 is
   284.1161

the Electric energy consumption in Kwh per capita for 2022 is
   315.6814

the Electric energy consumption in Kwh per capita for 2023 is
   350.7536

the Electric energy consumption in Kwh per capita for 2024 is
   389.7223

fx the Electric energy consumption in Kwh per capita for 2025 is
```

Fig. 3. Kwh per capita values obtained for 2016 to 2025

For clarity, the energy consumption in kwh per capita extracted from literature alongside that calculated and displayed in Fig. 3 is also presented in Table 1. Instead of carrying out manual step by step calculations as guided by the flow chart, Fig. 4 shows another matlab code that accepts inputs and gives back the final values of the energy consumption for each year being forecasted.

Table 1. Complete electric energy consumption in Kwh per capita used as inputs for the average energy consumption forecast of Canaanland.

Year	Electric energy consumption in Kwh per capita
2006	111.1
2007	138.1
2008	126.5
2009	119.9
2010	135.6
2011	149.3
2012	155.9
2013	141.9
2014	144
2015	151
2016	167.8
2017	186.4
2018	207.1
2019	230.1
2020	255.7
2021	284.1
2022	315.7
2023	350.8
2024	389.7
2025	433

```
% Code to Estimate the yearly energy demand in KVA per hr for
% canaanland
a = 234647; % Population of Ado-Odo LGA in 26/11/1991
b = 527242; % Population of Ado-Odo LGA in 21/03/2006
n1 = 14.33; % Number of years between population of 1991 and that of 2006
i = ((b/a)^(1/n1))-1; % Population growth rate
y = input ('Enter the year being forecasted : ');
E1 = input ('Enter Electric energy consumption in kwh per capita of the country for the year being forecasted : ');
A1 = 20; % Area of cannanland in square km
A2 = 878; % Area of Ado-Odo Ota LGA in square km
P3 = 1; % Estimate of percentage of population in canaanland with access to electricity
PF = 0.8; % Power factor
LF = P3; % Yearly load factor assumed to be same as percentage of the population with access to electricity
L1 = 0.1; % Transmission and distribution losses in year estimated to be 10%
equ = @(m)((A1/A2)*(b*(i+1)^m)*P3*E1)*(1+L1)*(1/PF)*(LF)*(1/(24*365));
for m = y - 2005; % Number of years from the base year (2006)
    str = num2str (y);
    E3 = equ(m);
    disp(['the Estimated energy consumption in KVA per hr of canaanland for ',str,' is'])
        disp(E3)
end
```

Fig. 4. Matlab code that accepts inputs and gives back the final values of the average energy consumption for each year being forecasted for Canaanland

4 Results

Figures 5, 6 and 7 below shows the results obtained after running the code.

```
Command Window
Enter the year being forecasted : 2006
Enter Electric energy consumption in kwh per capita of the country for the year being forecasted : 111.1
the Estimated energy consumption in KVA per hr of canaanland for 2006 is
  221.6122

Enter the year being forecasted : 2007
Enter Electric energy consumption in kwh per capita of the country for the year being forecasted : 138.1
the Estimated energy consumption in KVA per hr of canaanland for 2007 is
  291.4801

Enter the year being forecasted : 2008
Enter Electric energy consumption in kwh per capita of the country for the year being forecasted : 126.5
the Estimated energy consumption in KVA per hr of canaanland for 2008 is
  282.5149

Enter the year being forecasted : 2009
Enter Electric energy consumption in kwh per capita of the country for the year being forecasted : 119.9
the Estimated energy consumption in KVA per hr of canaanland for 2009 is
  283.3385

Enter the year being forecasted : 2010
Enter Electric energy consumption in kwh per capita of the country for the year being forecasted : 135.6
the Estimated energy consumption in KVA per hr of canaanland for 2010 is
  339.0640

Enter the year being forecasted : 2011
Enter Electric energy consumption in kwh per capita of the country for the year being forecasted : 149.3
the Estimated energy consumption in KVA per hr of canaanland for 2011 is
  395.0185

Enter the year being forecasted : 2012
fx Enter Electric energy consumption in kwh per capita of the country for the year being forecasted : 155.9
```

Fig. 5. Results obtained after running the code

From the command prompt, the required inputs (i.e. the year being forecasted and the energy consumption per capita for that year) were entered one at a time from 2006 to 2012. The results obtained which is the estimated energy consumption in KVAh of Canaanland for years 2006 to 2011 is as shown in Fig. 5 above.

Figure 6 above is a continuation of Fig. 5 and displays estimated energy consumption in KVAh of Canaanland for years 2012 to 2018.

```
the Estimated energy consumption in KVA per hr of canaanland for 2012 is
  436.4548

Enter the year being forecasted : 2013
Enter Electric energy consumption in kwh per capita of the country for the year being forecasted : 141.9
the Estimated energy consumption in KVA per hr of canaanland for 2013 is
  420.3501

Enter the year being forecasted : 2014
Enter Electric energy consumption in kwh per capita of the country for the year being forecasted : 144
the Estimated energy consumption in KVA per hr of canaanland for 2014 is
  451.3639

Enter the year being forecasted : 2015
Enter Electric energy consumption in kwh per capita of the country for the year being forecasted : 151
the Estimated energy consumption in KVA per hr of canaanland for 2015 is
  500.8145

Enter the year being forecasted : 2016
Enter Electric energy consumption in kwh per capita of the country for the year being forecasted : 167.7761
the Estimated energy consumption in KVA per hr of canaanland for 2016 is
  588.7971

Enter the year being forecasted : 2017
Enter Electric energy consumption in kwh per capita of the country for the year being forecasted : 186.4160
the Estimated energy consumption in KVA per hr of canaanland for 2017 is
  692.2362

Enter the year being forecasted : 2018
Enter Electric energy consumption in kwh per capita of the country for the year being forecasted : 207.1268
the Estimated energy consumption in KVA per hr of canaanland for 2018 is
fx  813.8475
```

Fig. 6. Results obtained after running the code

```
Enter the year being forecasted : 2019
Enter Electric energy consumption in kwh per capita of the country for the year being forecasted : 230.1386
the Estimated energy consumption in KVA per hr of canaanland for 2019 is
  956.8234

Enter the year being forecasted : 2020
Enter Electric energy consumption in kwh per capita of the country for the year being forecasted : 255.707
the Estimated energy consumption in KVA per hr of canaanland for 2020 is
  1.1249e+003

Enter the year being forecasted : 2021
Enter Electric energy consumption in kwh per capita of the country for the year being forecasted : 284.1161
the Estimated energy consumption in KVA per hr of canaanland for 2021 is
  1.3225e+003

Enter the year being forecasted : 2022
Enter Electric energy consumption in kwh per capita of the country for the year being forecasted : 315.6814
the Estimated energy consumption in KVA per hr of canaanland for 2022 is
  1.5549e+003

Enter the year being forecasted : 2023
Enter Electric energy consumption in kwh per capita of the country for the year being forecasted : 350.7536
the Estimated energy consumption in KVA per hr of canaanland for 2023 is
  1.8280e+003

Enter the year being forecasted : 2024
Enter Electric energy consumption in kwh per capita of the country for the year being forecasted : 389.7223
the Estimated energy consumption in KVA per hr of canaanland for 2024 is
  2.1492e+003

Enter the year being forecasted : 2025
Enter Electric energy consumption in kwh per capita of the country for the year being forecasted : 433.0205
the Estimated energy consumption in KVA per hr of canaanland for 2025 is
  2.5268e+003

fx >>
```

Fig. 7. Results obtained after running the code

Finally Fig. 7 above shows the estimated energy consumption in KVAh of Canaanland for years 2019 to 2025.

For clarity, the entire results obtained in Figs. 5, 6 and 7 are summarised and displayed in Table 2 above. It should be noted however that the energy consumption forecast is expressed in MVAh here.

Table 2. Forecast of average electric energy consumption in MVAh for Canaanland from 2006 to 2025

Year	Forecast of average electric energy consumption in MVAh for Canaanland
2006	0.2216
2007	0.2915
2008	0.2825
2009	0.2833
2010	0.3391
2011	0.3950
2012	0.4365
2013	0.4204
2014	0.4514
2015	0.5008
2016	0.5888
2017	0.6922
2018	0.8138
2019	0.9568
2020	1.1249
2021	1.3225
2022	1.5549
2023	1.8280
2024	2.1492
2025	2.5268

Even though we could not determine the accuracy of the results obtained above (Figs. 5, 6 and 7 and Table 1) by comparing the actual energy consumption of Canaanland with values obtained in the earlier years of the forecast, it seems obvious that the results obtained above will be a bit lower than the actual energy consumption of Canaanland. This is so because the primary data used (i.e. Nigeria's Electric energy consumption per capita, which is the average electric energy a person in a country consumes expressed in Kwh) does not account for consumption disparities between individuals in the country which is high for a wealthy class of individuals or low for a poor class of individuals within the population. It is also a measure of the general electric power generation distributed across the entire population evenly; but in reality this power is not evenly distributed. While a densely populated community may have to share a considerably small amount of power supply; a comparably smaller population of people in another area might have a larger share of the generated power.

5 Conclusion

As stated earlier, the advantage of this method of energy consumption forecast over other methods found in literature is that it requires no previous data of the power consumption of the community under study. Hence, it can be used to provide a rough estimate of future load demand in areas where no previous data of consumption exists; thereby making it possible to plan for future expansion of the power generating or supply capacity to the area with some degree of accuracy. But as seen from the results, this method of energy consumption forecast equally has its shortfalls. The primary data used which is Nigeria's Electric energy consumption per capita, does not account for consumption disparities between individuals and unbalanced distribution formula in the cumulative generated power. Hence, the results obtained using this method could be considerably lower than the actual peak consumption for some communities (as in this study) and higher than that of others. This method also doesn't account for the varieties in consumption rate at yearly and daily peak periods or off peak periods. The best energy consumption forecast model possible will thus be that which will account for the differences in daily and seasonal energy consumption and also the unique consumption of each individual (which varies based on each user's need and financial status).

We recommend that to achieve a perfect energy consumption forecast, we need to do either of the following:

- DISCOs (Power distribution companies in Nigeria) should develop applications which allow users to enter their daily consumption themselves for a whole year. This will capture their power usage at both daily peak or off peak periods and at various seasons of the year.
- All users must have smart meters or be disconnected. The meters should be made smarter by making it able to log and store hourly power consumption (of the household) which should be remotely accessible by the DISCOs via wireless internet connection.

References

1. Filik, U.B., Gerek, O.N., Kurban, M.: Hourly forecasting of long electrical energy demand using novel mathematical models and neural networks. Int. J. Innov. Comput. Inf. Control **7** (6), 3545–3557 (2011)
2. Parth, P., Shah, A.P.: Fuzzy logic methodology for short term load forecasting. Int. J. Res. Eng. Technol. **3**, 322–327 (2014)
3. Nguyen, T., Liao, Y.: Short term load forecasting on adaptive neuro-fuzzy inference system. J. Comput. **6**, 2267–2271 (2011)
4. Pal, S., Sharma, K.: Short term load forecasting using adaptive neural fuzzy inference system (ANFIS). Int. J. Nov. Res. Electr. Mech. Eng. **2**, 65–71 (2015)
5. Jagadish, H., Puja, S.: Fuzzy ideology based long term load forecasting. Int. J. Comput. Electr. Autom. Control Inf. Eng. **4**(4), 790–795 (2010)
6. Dogra, S., Sidu, S.D., Kaur, D.: Long term load forecasting using fuzzy logic methodology. Int. J. Adv. Res. Electr. Electron. Instrum. Eng. **4**(6), 5578–5585 (2015)
7. Oyelami, B.O., Adewumi, A.A.: Models for forecasting the demand and supply of electricity in Nigeria. Am. J. Model. Optim. **2**(1), 25–33 (2014)
8. Bodger, P.S., Tay, H.S.: Logistic and energy substitution models for electricity forecasting: a comparison using New Zealand consumption data. Technol. Forecast. Soc. Chang. **31**, 27–48 (1987)

9. Dahl, C.A.: A Survey of Energy Demand Elasticities in Support of Development of the NEMS. US Department of Energy (1993)
10. North America Electric Reliability Council: Electricity Supply and Demand for 1990–1999, Princeton, New Jersey (1990)
11. Dilaver, Z., Hunt, L.C.: Industrial electricity for Turkey: a structural time series analysis. Energy Econ. **33**, 426–436 (2011)
12. Harvey, A., Koopmans, S.J.: Forecasting hourly electricity demands using time-varying splines. J. Am. Stat. Assoc. **88**, 1228–1237 (1993)
13. http://venturesafrica.com/is-the-new-electricity-tariff-justifiabe/
14. Verdejo, H., Awerkin, A., Becker, C., Olguin, G.: Statistic linear parametric techniques for residential electric energy demand forecasting, a review and an implementation to Chile. Renew. Sustain. Energy Rev. **74**, 512–521 (2017)
15. Fintan, M., Aidan, D., Michael, C.: Evaluation of time series techniques to characterise domestic electricity demand. Energy **50**(1), 20–30 (2013)
16. Swan, L.G., Ismet, U.V.: Modeling of end-use energy consumption in the residential sector: a review of modeling techniques. Renew. Sustain. Energy Rev. **13**(8), 1819–1835 (2009)
17. Duan, Q., Liu, J., Zhao, D.: A Short term electric load forecasting using an automated system of model choice. Electr. Power Energy Syst. **91**, 92–100 (2017)
18. Yildiz, B., Bilbao, J.I., Sproul, A.B.: A review and analysis of regression and machine learning models on commercial building electricity load forecasting. Renew. Sustain. Energy Rev. **73**, 1104–1122 (2017)
19. Katipamula, S., Reddy, T., Claridge, D.E.: Multivariate regression modelling. J. Solar Energy Eng., 120—177 (1998). http://dx.doi.org/10.1115/1.2888067
20. Hsu, C.-W., Chang, C.-C., Lin, C.-J.: LIBSVM: a library for support vector machines. ACM Trans. Intell. Syst. Technol. **2**, 1–27 (2011). https://doi.org/10.1177/02632760022050997
21. Ali, D., Yohanna, M., Puwu, M.I., Garkida, B.M.: Long-term load forecast modelling using a fuzzy logic approach. Pac. Sci. Rev. Natural Sci. Eng. **18**, 123–127 (2016)
22. Swaroop, R., Ali, A.H.: Load forecasting for power system planning using fuzzy-neural networks. In: Proceedings of the World Congress on Engineering and Computer Science, vol. 1, San Francisco, USA, 24–26 October 2012
23. Gohil, P., Gupta, M.: Short term load forecasting using fuzzy logic. Int. J. Eng. Dev. Res. (IJDRC) (2014). National Conference (RTEECE-2014)
24. Karwade, S.B., Ali, M.S.: Review paper on load forecasting using neuro fuzzy system. J. Electr. Electron. Eng. **10**(3), 38–42 (2015). Ver. II
25. Mfonobong, A., Nseobong, U., Okpura, I., Markson, I.: Rural electrification peak load demand forecast model based on end user demographic data. Math. Softw. Eng. **3**(1), 87–98 (2017)
26. World Development Indicators: Electric power consumption (Kwh per capita) (2015). http://data.un.org/Data.aspx?d=WDI&f=Indicator_Code%3AEG.USE.ELEC.KH.PC
27. Ogun State Government Nigeria Projected Population Figures. http://www.ogunstate.gov.ng/population-figures
28. Power factor correction: a guide for the plant engineer, August 2014. http://www.eaton.com/ecm/groups/public/@pub/@electrical/documents/content/sa02607001e.pdf
29. Calculated with available information of projects in the pipeline.BMI Research Data, 18th February 2016. http://www.bmiresearch.com/nigeria

A Cloud-Based Intelligent Toll Collection System for Smart Cities

Segun I. Popoola[1(✉)], Oluwafunso A. Popoola[1,2], Adeniran I. Oluwaranti[2], Aderemi A. Atayero[1], Joke A. Badejo[1], and Sanjay Misra[1]

[1] Department of Electrical and Information Engineering, Covenant University, Ota, Nigeria
segun.popoola@covenantuniversity.edu.ng
[2] Department of Computer Science and Engineering, Obafemi Awolowo University, Ile-Ife, Nigeria

Abstract. Electronic Toll Collection (ETC) systems may be adopted by city managers to combat the problems of long vehicular queues, fuel wastage, high accident risks, and environmental pollution that come with the use of traditional or manual toll collection systems. In this paper, an intelligent system is developed to eliminate long vehicular queues, fuel wastage, high accident risks, and environmental pollution in a smart city based on seamless interconnections of Wireless Sensor Networks (WSNs), and web and mobile applications that run on an Internet of Things (IoT)-Enabled cloud platform. A ZigBee WSN is designed and implemented using an Arduino UNO, XBee S2 radios, an XBee Shield, and a Seeduino GPRS Shield. For vehicle owners to make toll payments, view toll historical data, and get toll news feeds, a web application and a mobile application are designed and implemented based on Hyper Text Mark-up Language (HTML), Cascading Style Sheets (CSS), Javascript and Hyper Text Pre-processor (PHP). The mobile application is deployed using an Android platform. A cloud platform was also developed to provide business logic functionalities by using PHP as a scripting language, and MySQL as the database engine driver. Deployment of the developed ETC system in smart and connected communities will drastically minimize the challenges of long vehicular queues, fuel wastage, high accident risks, and environmental pollution in urban centers.

Keywords: Smart city · Electronic Toll Collection · Internet of Things
Mobile application · Cloud computing

1 Introduction

Applications of Intelligent Transportation System (ITS) technologies is highly encouraged in emerging smart cities to handle the current challenges of the continuous growth in the number of vehicles that ply the highways in urban centers [1]. Electronic Toll Collection (ETC) systems may be adopted by city managers to combat the problems of long vehicular queues, fuel wastage, high accident risks, and environmental pollution that come with the use of traditional/manual toll collection systems [2].

P. Bhattacharyya et al. (Eds.): NGCT 2017, CCIS 827, pp. 653–663, 2018.
https://doi.org/10.1007/978-981-10-8657-1_50

Electronic mode of payment is an integral part of ETC systems and it has been widely adopted in toll collection across the globe. The core operations in traditional toll plazas or booths are automated with the combined use of embedded systems and mobile communication technologies to minimize the need for human intervention, reduce latency, and increase system efficiency [3–8]. In short, the introduction of ETC in smart cities is aimed at achieving efficient toll operations with minimal constraints.

Among other advantages, deploying ETC on ever-busy city highways will drastically reduce unnecessary long queues of vehicles, curb fuel wastage, and save the environment from adverse carbon emission. Different techniques and technologies proposed in [9–15] may be useful for different automation processes required for successful and efficient implementation of ETC systems in smart and connected communities. Chattoraj *et al.* [16] designed a more reliable payment and surveillance methods for ETC systems using strain gauge load cell, Arduino Mega 2560, smart card reader, and Optical Character Recognition (OCR) system. Each category of vehicle is levied based on its weight as detected by the strain gauge load cell. This information is communicated to the payment platform through the interconnection of the Arduino device and smart card reader. All vehicles are uniquely identified by capturing the license number plate using the OCR system. In a related work, Gupta *et al.* [17] addressed the issues of illegal toll collection, system failure, and insecure connections in ETC systems. The authors employed Radio Frequency Identification (RFID), Global System for Mobile Communication (GSM) and ZigBee technologies to reduce fuel consumption, traffic jams, and car theft. The system peripherals include RFID readers and tags, and ZigBee transmitter and receiver. Inserra *et al.* [18] designed an RFID reader that can handle a minimum of three coverage sectors in real-life scenario where the size of the antenna array is limited.

In order to minimize the occurrence of accidents on highways where ETC systems are in use, Chung *et al.* [19] proposed some useful guidelines that are relevant to both ETC and manual toll collection systems. The proposed methods were designed to address the challenges of speed variations and lane crossing by computing the minimum allowable distance to handle the risks. Abuzwidah and Abdel-Aty [20] measured the safety contribution of the adopting a complete ETC in lieu of the conventional toll plaza. Based on empirical evidences, the authors reported that the introduction of the electronic form of toll collection has widely reduced accident risks of different forms on the highways. Regarding security and environmental friendliness, a novel ETC system was proposed in [21] to reduce the probability of failures in the detection of violations and address security and privacy related issues.

Regarding Dedicated Short-Range Communications (DSRC) ETC systems, the lifetime of On-Board Unit (OBU) is determined by the capacity of the in-built cell and the strength of the received radio signal. The experimental results reported in [22] showed that the performance of the OBU can be optimized by incorporating an upper and lower parasitic element in the antenna design parameters since their relationship is already established. The OBU proposed by [23] employs microcontroller unit and it was found to be more suitable for ETC applications with minimum energy requirements. "Open-Road" ETC has been successfully implemented to accommodate "mileage-based charge" in Intelligent Transportation System (ITS) [1].

Research advances reported in [20] revealed that toll collection can be performed without necessarily having the vehicles to stop over at a toll booth. These new developments allow free flow of traffic on highways and open up another form of use case in multi-lane highways.

In this paper, an intelligent system is developed to eliminate long vehicular queues, fuel wastage, high accident risks, and environmental pollution in a smart city based on seamless interconnections of Wireless Sensor Networks (WSNs), and web and mobile applications that run on an Internet of Things (IoT)-Enabled cloud platform. ZigBee transceivers are used as sensor nodes because of their simultaneous wireless transmission and reception capabilities. They were considered preferable because of the low power consumption, cost effectiveness, and network security. The automated toll collection system is designed to identify vehicle encroachment and charge a pre-determined toll, working solely by pre- and post-paid subscriptions. An enhanced user interface was developed on the Android platform for vehicle owners. The Android-based mobile application also has an administrative end for system regulations. This work is limited to the automation of toll collection from owners of registered vehicles using the existing vehicle identification system. The enforcement of toll payment, and the handling of toll debtors, is left to the appropriate parties or agencies.

The remainder of this paper is organized as follows: in the next section of describe the methodology used in the design and implementation of the automated toll collection system. Section 3 provides details regarding the system implementation details, and presents the main results obtained, with appropriate discussion. Finally, in Sect. 4 we present the main conclusions of this work.

2 Materials and Method

This section focuses on the methodology used in the design and implementation of the automated toll collection system. It provides detailed information about the components, modules, and units of the system. It also explains the procedure, techniques, and the working principle of the system.

First, relevant data were collected to properly understand the problem domain, and to avoid wrong assumptions that could crumble the supposed solution. The hardware and software requirements of the system were identified based on the data collected. The main hardware devices are the Arduino Uno board and two ZigBee devices. Other hardware components include: SparkFun XBee shield; SparkFun USB explorer; 9-volt batteries; and connecting wires.

The program codes were written in the Java programming language using the Arduino Integrated Development Environment (IDE), which is open source. PHP was used in the implementation of the backend that provides services for logging monitored data. Database content was created, accessed, and managed using MySQL, an open source Relational Database Management System (RDBMS) that uses Structured Query Language (SQL). It is most noted for its quick processing, proven reliability, ease of use and flexibility. The web dashboard was designed using HTML. An object-oriented computer programming language, JavaScript, was used to add more user-interactivity to the web dashboard for toll administrators. Presentation value was added to the web

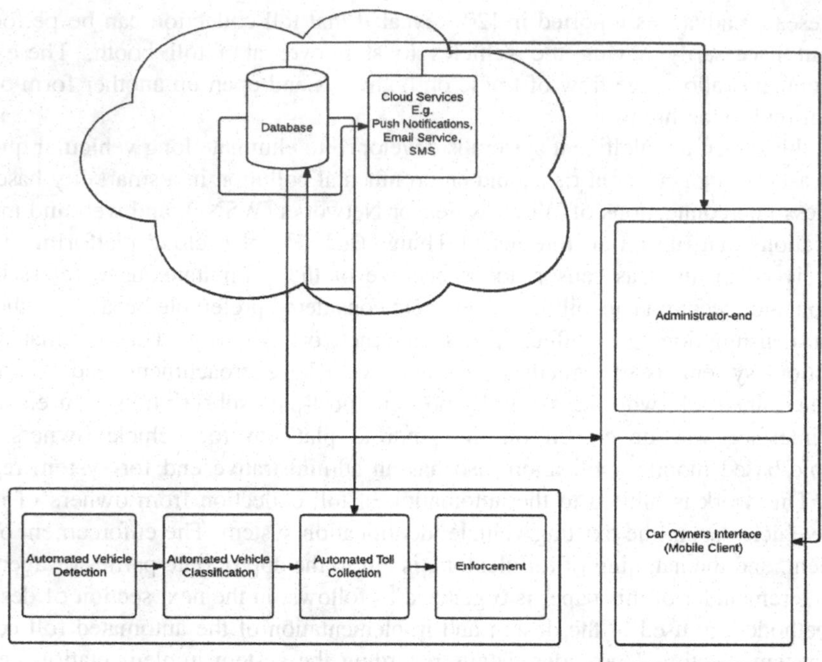

Fig. 1. Architecture of automated toll collection system

dashboard using CSS. PhpStorm IDE, a commercial cross-platform for PHP, provided an editor for PHP, HTML and JavaScript with on-the-fly code analysis, error prevention and automated refactoring for PHP and JavaScript code. The mobile application for toll subscription and tracking was developed in Android Studio IDE.

Figure 1 shows the major components of the proposed architecture. The ZigBee device at the toll plaza (being the Controller) and the in-Vehicle unit form a network of wireless sensor nodes. By so doing, the identity of the vehicle can be easily verified for appropriate toll fee deduction for the subscription of the vehicle owner. The central database was hosted and operated as cloud-based service. A similar operational method was designed for the web server. This cloud platform allows easy and efficient communication between the ETC and the highway users by providing the facility to view the history of transactions performed with real-time notification options. One of the major advantages of the cloud platform is in its ability to offer on-demand self-service. It also provides location-independent resource pool. In addition, it allows users to pay per use, and it offers required elasticity.

In the developed ETC system, data transmission between the ZigBee and the central processing unit was achieved through the web application that was hosted on the cloud platform. Vehicle owners can easily interact with the ETC system by using a mobile application designed for that purpose. This Internet-enabled facility allows road users to conveniently renew their subscriptions and receive prompt notifications on transactions in real-time. Toll payment history can equally be tracked on the mobile application. The mobile application of the ETC system was implemented on an

Android platform to exploit its popularity, simplicity, cost-effectiveness, and user-friendliness. An enhanced web application was designed for city managers to effectively maintain, manage, and control toll evasion in a bid to uphold strict compliance. This platform also provides a good means for electronic audit of the toll fees collected over a particular period of time, in a particular area.

3 System Implementation

The toll plaza is equipped with a ZigBee device to control the operations of the WSNs. Each vehicle is uniquely identified with the use of a ZigBee device, which is built into the internal electrical circuitry of the automobile. All vehicles are pre-registered with active accounts with the city managers in charge of the administration of the ETC system. This is aimed at facilitating toll subscription, toll payment, and electronic receipt issuance. Toll activities are monitored and managed in real-time through the user-friendly dashboard of the developed web application. The overall system was designed to grant access to registered vehicle owners only. ZigBee devices on different vehicles are uniquely identified and verified based on their respective Media Access Control (MAC) address. The remote detection of a pre-registered ZigBee device was programmed to deduct appropriate toll charge from the subscription of the vehicle owner. Upon toll fee payment and corresponding deduction from user's account, a push notification is sent to the mobile dashboard of the user to acknowledgement successful transactions.

Figure 2 shows the use-case activity diagrams of the developed ETC system. The figure illustrates possible lines of activities of a typical ETC system user. The vehicle owners interact with the mobile application while the toll administrators manage the web application. The following assumptions were made to handle uncontrollable factors in the automation process of the ETC system: (1) first, the Internet access is ubiquitous and reliable; (2) strict vehicle registration policy is actively in place to ensure maximum compliance; and (3) lastly, an efficient legal provision is in force to handle cases of toll fee evasions and outright violation of traffic laws.

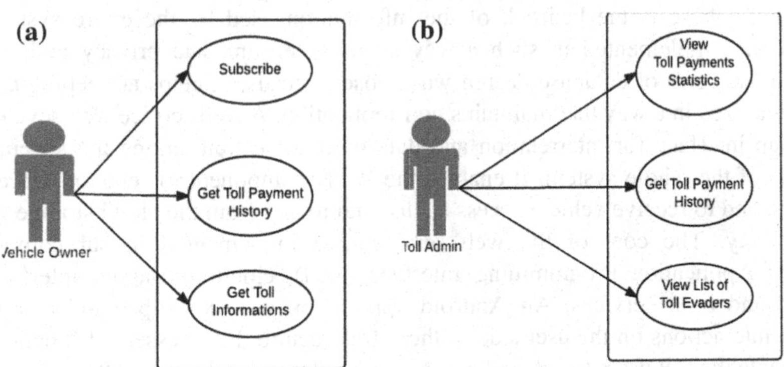

Fig. 2. Use case diagram for (a) Vehicle owners (b) Toll administrators [7]

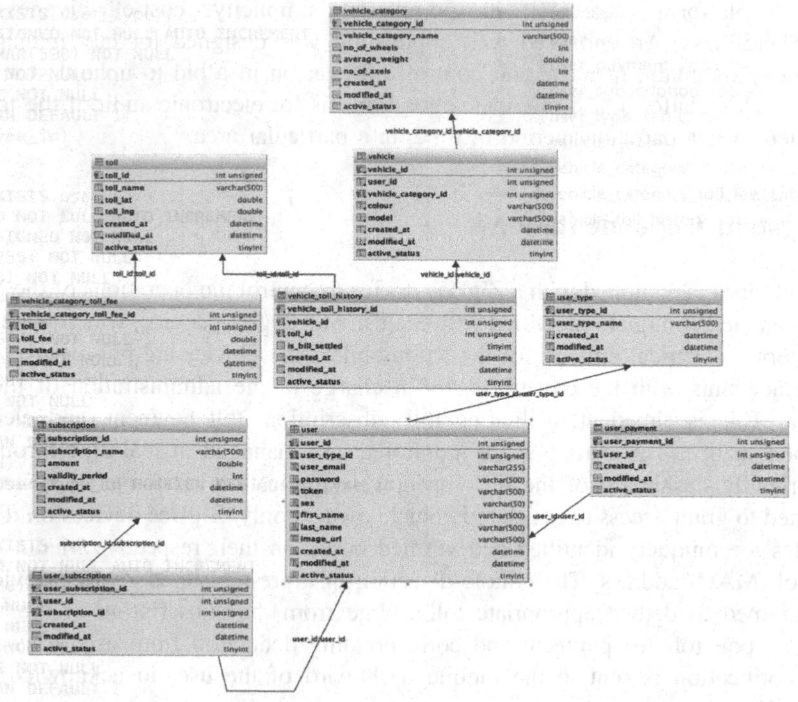

Fig. 3. Entity-relations diagram.

The system design was implemented in five modules: (i) database design; (ii) web service (cloud component); (iii) Android application (mobile client); (iv) administrative web application (web client); and (v) XBee-driven WSN component. All these sub-components were integrated together in the following sequence: the XBee radio was mounted on the XBee Shield; the GPRS Shield was mounted on to the Arduino board; the XBee Shield was mounted on the GPRS Shield; finally, the Arduino code was uploaded to the board. The entity relationship diagram is illustrated in Fig. 3.

The database is the bedrock of the information used by the entire system. The design was implemented in such a way so as to ensure data privacy and security. A relational form of database design was chosen because it helps at keeping complex data organized in a way that maintains non-replication. A web service was developed to act as an interface for interrelation and data communication among the several components of the whole system. It enables the WSN component to send an XBee MAC address, and to receive vehicle access status data to and from the cloud storage facility, respectively. The core of the web service was implemented in sub-components, namely: Application Programming Interface (API), cloud messaging interface, and background *cron* services. An Android application was developed to cater for the system interactions on the user side of the infrastructure. It has essential functionalities that enable the toll users to subscribe to payment plans of different tariffs and durations. It also supports the notification of toll transactions, and provides toll users access to

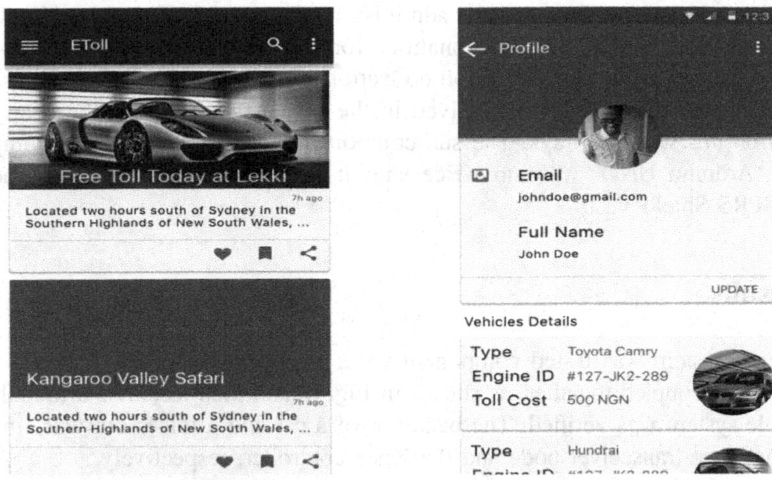

Fig. 4. Android user interface for toll feeds and profile details.

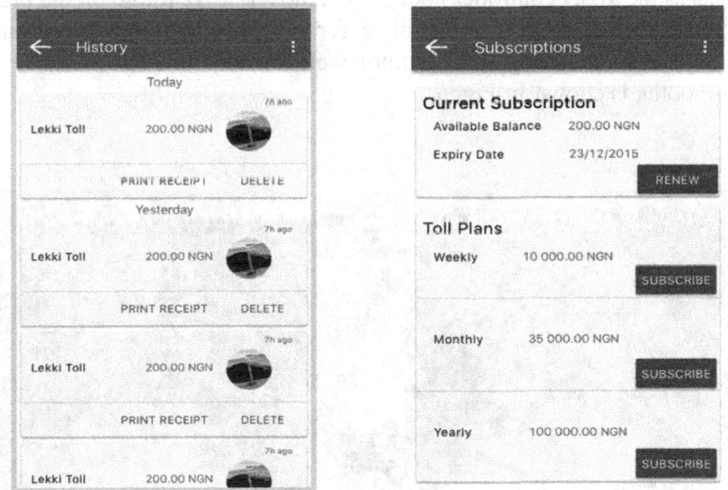

Fig. 5. Android user interface for user toll history and subscriptions.

their toll history. As a spin-off, the user feed was included to display information related to toll gates, fees and other user-related management decisions. The Android interface was filled with dummy/placeholder data before connecting to the cloud services for data population, as shown in Figs. 4 and 5.

The administrative web application mainly developed to provide a suitable administration of the toll collection system. It was equipped with monitoring facilities that allow a quick toll data visualization, as well as the management of the configurable entities of the automated toll collection system. The design and development phases are the following: user interface design; administrative control logic; and major Create-Read-Update-Delete (CRUD) functionalities for all major entities. The XBee-driven WSN component of the automated toll collection system constitutes the trigger for all other automated events that are involved in the system. In fact, it is the heart of the automation this work portrays. The sub-components under this particular component include: Arduino UNO; Arduino XBee shield; XBee Series 2 S2 Radio; and Seeduino GPRS Shield V2.0.

4 Results

The whole system was tested component-wise, one after the other. All tested components were coupled together, as shown in Fig. 6, and then tested as a module until the whole system was verified. The behavior of a car and a toll-booth was simulated using the Xbee transceiver node and the Xbee controller, respectively.

The two of them were noted to be out of wireless connection and communication until they got into each other's range of communication. The operational Xbee-controlled WSN coupling is shown in Fig. 6. The XBee attached to the Arduino XBee explorer acts as the WSN controller node, while the XBee S2 Radio on the bread-board acts as the transceiver node in the vehicle for proper vehicle identification and toll collection. The corresponding administrator web interface for basic CRUD operation on the toll booths is shown in Fig. 7.

Fig. 6. Integration of the XBee WSN component

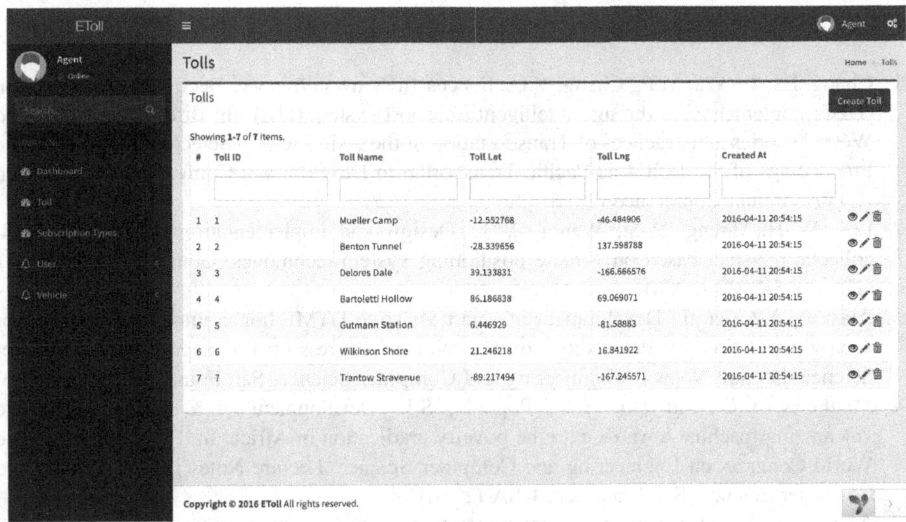

Fig. 7. Toll CRUD dashboard page on the admin web-end

5 Conclusion

This paper detailed the framework, design, and implementation of an automated toll collection system that uses Wireless Sensor Networks (WSNs), web and mobile applications, and a cloud platform. A ZigBee-based WSN was designed and implemented using an Arduino UNO, XBee S2 radios, an XBee Shield and a Seeduino GPRS Shield. Web and mobile applications were developed, using Hyper Text Mark-up Language (HTML), Cascading Style Sheets (CSS), Javascript and Hyper Text Pre-processor (PHP), for vehicle owners to make toll payments, view toll histories, and get toll news feeds. The mobile application was implemented in Java on the Android platform. A cloud platform was developed for business logic functionalities using PHP as a scripting language, and MySQL as the database engine driver. Simulation results show that the system implementation significantly improved toll collection efficiency in terms of speed and flexibility.

This prototype was developed as a unit that can fit into the whole electronic toll system. It was also developed in a greatly controlled environment which is a wide gap from the real toll environment. Deployment of the developed ETC system in smart and connected communities will drastically minimize the challenges of long vehicular queues, fuel wastage, high accident risks, and environmental pollution in urban centers.

Acknowledgement. The authors wish to appreciate the Center for Research, Innovation, and Discovery (CU-CRID) of Covenant University, Ota, Nigeria, for partly funding this research.

References

1. Chang, E.C.P., Wu, M.F., Chang, Y.C.: Successful Taiwan freeway electronic toll collection (ETC) implementation through intelligent transport system (ITS). In: Bridging the East and West: Theories and Practices of Transportation in the Asia Pacific - Selected Papers from the Proceedings of the 11th Asia Pacific Transportation Development Conference and the 29th ICTPA Annual Conference (2016)
2. Lee, W.-H., Tseng, S.-S., Wang, C.-H.: Design and implementation of electronic toll collection system based on vehicle positioning system techniques. Comput. Commun. **31** (12), 2925–2933 (2008)
3. Atayero, A.A., et al.: Development of smart assistive DTMF home automation system for ageing population. In: Proceedings of The World Congress on Engineering and Computer Science. Lecture Notes in Engineering and Computer Science, San Francisco, USA (2016)
4. Matthews, V.O., Atayero, A.A., Popoola, S.I.: Development of a solar photovoltaic vulcanizing machine towards extreme poverty eradication in Africa. In: Proceedings of The World Congress on Engineering and Computer Science. Lecture Notes in Engineering and Computer Science, San Francisco, USA (2016)
5. Adoghe, A.U., et al.: Free energy generation using neodymium magnets: an off-grid sustainable energy solution for sub-saharan Africa. In: 2017 Proceedings of The World Congress on Engineering. Lecture Notes in Engineering and Computer Science, London, U.K. (2017)
6. Matthews, V.O., et al.: Solar photovoltaic automobile recognition system for smart-green access control using RFID and LoRa LPWAN technologies. J. Eng. Appl. Sci. **12**(4), 913–919 (2017)
7. Popoola, S.I., et al.: A framework for electronic toll collection in smart and connected communities. In: Proceedings of The World Congress on Engineering and Computer Science (2017)
8. Atayero, A.A., et al.: Occupancy controlled lighting system for smart buildings. In: 2017 Proceedings of The World Congress on Engineering and Computer Science, San Francisco, USA. Lecture Notes in Engineering and Computer Science (2017)
9. Kim, J., et al.: Using electronic toll collection data to understand traffic demand. J. Intell. Transp. Syst. **18**(2), 190–203 (2014)
10. Nagothu, S.K.: Automated toll collection system using GPS and GPRS. In: 2016 International Conference on Communication and Signal Processing (Iccsp), vol. 1, pp. 651–653 (2016)
11. Tan, J.Y., et al.: GPS-based highway toll collection system: Novel design and operation. Cogent Eng. **4**(1) (2017)
12. Vats, S., et al.: Selection of optimal electronic toll collection system for india: a subjective-fuzzy decision making approach. Appl. Soft Comput. **21**, 444–452 (2014)
13. Lu, S.J., He, T.J., Gao, Z.H.: Design of electronic toll collection system based on global positioning system technique. In: 2009 Isecs International Colloquium on Computing, Communication, Control, and Management, vol. I, pp. 350–353 (2009)
14. Ren, Z.G., Gao, Y.B.: Design of electronic toll collection system in expressway based on RFID. In: Proceedings of the 2009 International Conference on Environmental Science and Information Application Technology, Vol. III, pp. 779–782 (2009)
15. Lee, W.H., Tseng, S.S., Wang, C.H.: Design and implementation of electronic toll collection system based on vehicle positioning system techniques. Comput. Commun. **31**(12), 2925–2933 (2008)

16. Chattoraj, S., et al.: Design and implementation of low cost electronic toll collection system in India. In: Proceedings of the 2017 2nd IEEE International Conference on Electrical, Computer and Communication Technologies, ICECCT (2017)
17. Gupta, S., et al.: Electronic toll collection system using zigbee and RFID. Int. J. Civil Eng. Technol. **8**(4), 1714–1719 (2017)
18. Inserra, D., Hu, W., Wen, G.: Planar antenna array design considerations for RFID electronic toll collection system. In: 2016 IEEE MTT-S International Wireless Symposium, IWS (2016)
19. Chung, Y., Choi, Y.H., Yoon, B.J.: Safe operation guidelines for electronic toll collection systems: a case study in Korea. Int. J. Civil Eng. **16**(3), 281–288 (2018)
20. Noor, N.M., et al.: RFID-based electronic fare toll collection system for multi-lane free flow - a case study towards Malaysia toll system improvement. J. Telecommun. Electron. Comput. Eng. **8**(4), 71–76 (2016)
21. Jardí-Cedó, R., Castellà-Roca, J., Viejo, A.: Privacy-preserving electronic toll system with dynamic pricing for low emission zones. In: Garcia-Alfaro, J., Herrera-Joancomartí, J., Lupu, E., Posegga, J., Aldini, A., Martinelli, F., Suri, N. (eds.) DPM/QASA/SETOP -2014. LNCS, vol. 8872, pp. 327–334. Springer, Cham (2015). https://doi.org/10.1007/978-3-319-17016-9_22
22. Homsup, N., et al.: Simulation and analysis of an antenna in a transponder for the electronic toll collection system of expressway in Thailand. In: 2016 13th International Conference on Electrical Engineering/Electronics, Computer, Telecommunications and Information Technology, ECTI-CON 2016 (2016)
23. Yang, C., et al.: Specific MCU design of on board unit in electronic toll collection system. In: Proceedings - 2014 IEEE 12th International Conference on Solid-State and Integrated Circuit Technology, ICSICT 2014 (2014)

An Announcer Based Bully Election Leader Algorithm in Distributed Environment

Minhaj Khan(✉), Neha Agarwal, Saurabh Jaiswal, and Jeeshan Ahmad Khan

Shri Ramswaroop Memorial University, Lucknow, Uttar Pradesh, India
minhajkhan7786@gmail.com, lko.neha@gmail.com, saurabhjaiswalcs@gmail.com, jeeshan.jak@gmail.com

Abstract. In distributed system, a job is divided into sub jobs and distributed among the active nodes in the network; communication happens between these nodes via messages passing. For better performance and consistency, we need a leader node or coordinator node. There is no compulsion that leader node should be same all the time because of out of services, crashed failure etc. Over past years, tremendous algorithms have been introduced to select a new leader when leader is dead or crashed. Bully algorithm is a well known traditional method for the same when leader or coordinator becomes crashed. In this algorithm the highest Id node is selected as a leader, but this algorithm has some drawbacks such as message passing complexity, heavy network traffic, redundancy etc. To overcome this problem, we are introducing an announcer based Bully election leader algorithm which is the modified version of original algorithm to overcome the above mentioned shortcomings. In our proposed algorithm we use an announcer who will decide the next leader or coordinator after current leader failure. Our analytical comparison presents that our proposed algorithm uses less messages passing with respect to the existing algorithms.

Keywords: Distributed systems · Bully algorithm · Announcer Message passing

1 Introduction

In distributed computing various nodes connected to one another via a network to solve a common problem without having any concern who performed it. In a network each node communicates with each other to make an acceptable decision but problem arises when consistency needed among the active nodes. To determine consistency, a node is selected as a leader and act as a centralized controller node for that decentralized distributed system to achieve some specific goals like synchronization, time scheduling, load balancing, mutual exclusion etc. [10]. Several algorithms have been presented to select a leader or coordinator in a distributed system like bully algorithm, ring algorithm, LCR algorithm which use some specific topology such as spanning tree, fully connected graph, ring topology etc. [1, 14]. So here we got a chance to select any topology for designing the distributed system which reduces time and message passing during the leader selection [14].

P. Bhattacharyya et al. (Eds.): NGCT 2017, CCIS 827, pp. 664–674, 2018.
https://doi.org/10.1007/978-981-10-8657-1_51

Here we are presenting a new approach which uses the fully connected topology and extended version of bully algorithm by which we can reduce message passing, network traffic, redundancy as well as time to select a leader. This approach is based on below basic assumptions:

a. A synchronous timeout based system is in use.
b. Each node contains only information about its owned unique node id and announcer id as well as leader id.
c. During election, the highest id node will be the announcer.
d. Whoever will have noticed that leader is down, it will become a new leader and same information will broadcast by the announcer.
e. There are N nodes in the network and N^{th} node is announcer by default. If it will crash, then $(N - 1)^{th}$ node will be the new announcer.
f. If message will come from new announcer, then node will have to validate the announcer id and update its table accordingly.
g. After recovery, failed node can again join the system again.

The layout of the paper is organized as follows. This paper is separated into 6 sections. Section 1 is describing the basics of distributed system. Section 2 is introducing literature survey regarding leader selection in distributed system with its limitations. Section 3 presents the proposed algorithm and is briefly explained with an example. In Sect. 4 we have figured out the performance analysis of the proposed modified algorithm. In Sect. 5 there is a comparison between proposed and other existing algorithms. Section 6 concludes the paper along with future work.

2 Literature Survey

For electing a leader in distributed system, various algorithms have been proposed. In this section we are going to describe two notable leader election algorithm i.e. original bully algorithm which is one of the basic election algorithm [1], and second is modified bully election algorithm [4].

2.1 Original Bully Algorithm

Bully algorithm was proposed by Garcia Molina in 1982. In this algorithm, the node having the highest Id works as a leader [4, 8, 9]. If any node observes that the coordinator is not responding i.e. the coordinator failed then detector node will start an election and sending election message to all nodes which are having higher Ids than its own Id. If detector node doesn't receive any response from the receivers within certain time duration, then it elects itself as a leader and send leader message to all nodes in the network but if the detector node receive responses from the receivers, it means these nodes are alive and will take over the election. Afterwards all nodes give up except one node that means the last one node who wins is now work as a current leader and broadcast leader message to all nodes that have lower Id [12].

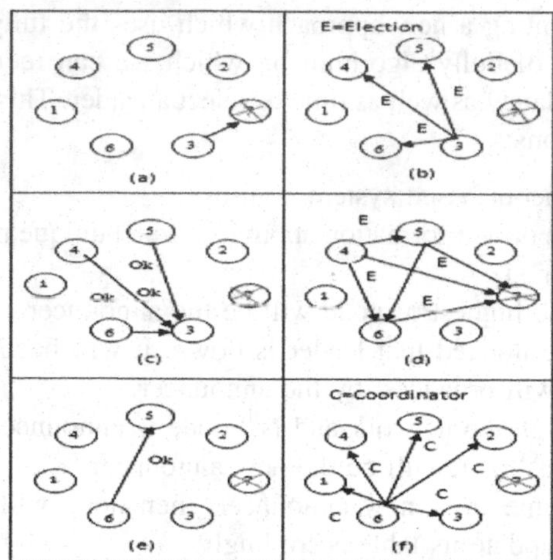

Fig. 1. Traditional Bully algorithm steps for electing a coordinator

In Fig. 1 node 7 has biggest Id and work as a coordinator.

a. Node 3 observes the coordinator is failed.
b. After observing coordinator is failed, node 3 send election message to their biggest Id nodes i.e. nodes 4, 5 and 6.
c. Node 3 received Ok messages from nodes 4, 5 and 6 that means these nodes now will take over the election.
d. After sending ok message to node 3, nodes 4, 5 and 6 will send election message to their biggest Id nodes.
e. Nodes 5, 6 send ok message to node 4 and node 6 send ok message to node 5.
f. Node 6 wins the election and elects as a new coordinator and send coordinator message to all nodes.

2.1.1 Limitations

a. This algorithm needs high number of messages passing for electing a new coordinator when current coordinator is failed and due to this heavy network traffic generates in the system.
b. At a time two nodes may broadcast as a coordinator if they are next biggest IDs nodes.
c. When N nodes observe that the coordinator is failed then accordingly number of nodes, election message will be started which will impose heavy network traffic.
d. There is no confirmation that the coordinator is exactly failed or not.

2.2 Modified Bully Algorithm Presented by M. S. Kordafshari et al.

M. S. Kordafshari et al. proposed a new algorithm which is the enhanced version of original Bully algorithm. This algorithm basically focuses on reducing message passing and network traffic and ensured that only one leader remains in the system at a time. In this algorithm, when any node finds that the leader is crashed then it will send election message to its highest process number. If it will not receive any response messages from the receivers, then it elects itself as a leader and send coordinator message to all alive nodes. If it will receive response message from them, then it will send GRANT message to highest process number between them [4, 11]. After receiving the GRANT message, the highest process number will have to send coordinator message to all alive nodes [4, 11, 13].

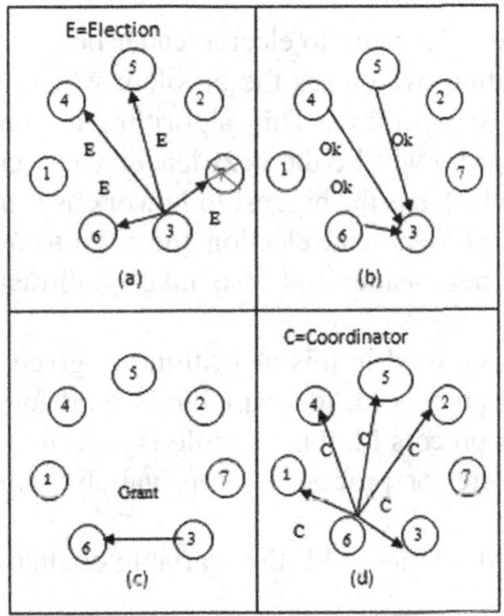

Fig. 2. Modified bully algorithm steps for selecting a coordinator

In Fig. 2, node 7 is working as a leader because it has highest process number.

a. Node 3 observes the coordinator is failed then send election message to their biggest Id nodes i.e. nodes 4, 5 and 6. If node 3 doesn't receive any responses from these nodes, then it will select itself as a leader and send coordinator message to all alive nodes.
b. After receiving the election message these nodes send responses (ok) to node 3.
c. After receiving the responses from these nodes, node 3 compares the Ids of these nodes and send grant message to biggest Id node. Here node 6 is biggest Id node.
d. After receiving GRANT message from node 3, node 6 will elect as a new coordinator and node 6 send coordinator message to all nodes.

2.2.1 Limitations

a. If a node failed after sending election message to biggest Id nodes or failed after getting priority of biggest Id nodes, the biggest Id nodes will wait for 3D time D is average propagation delay time) for coordinator message [11],if they don't get any coordinator message, they will start election again [4].

b. After getting the GRANT message if that node crashed (which send Grant message) then detector will have to start election again and send the GRANT message again to the biggest Id nodes between the remaining ones and this will create redundancy
c. Each redundant election consumes resources and generates more messages passing and network traffic.
d. There is no such guarantee of coordinator is exactly failed or not.

3 Proposed Algorithm

This paper proposes a new algorithm to elect a leader between nodes in the distributed environment. This algorithm overcomes the problem which is revealed in bully algorithm and modified bully algorithm. This algorithm is announcer based algorithm where announcer decide who will be the next leader when current leader is failed. In this algorithm the node which has the biggest Id is work as a announcer and if any node notices the leader is failed then send election message to announcer, the announcer decide who will be the next leader and also take confirmation of the old leader is exactly crashed or not.

The variables which are used in this algorithm are given below:

anp_id -> announcer process Id, this variable is used for announcer
slp_id -> store leader process Id, this variable is used to store the leader process Id
mcp_id -> message creator process Id, this variable create the message creator process Id
clp_id -> crashed leader process Id, this variable contains recently crashed leader process Id.

3.1 Algorithm

Here we are going to describe the algorithm which is used for leader node election (Figs. 3, 4 and 5).

```
int anp_id, slp_id, mcp_id, clp_id
//when any node N detect the leader is crashed, initiate an election
Create message msg (mcp_id, clp_id) and send to announcer
Start timer
//upon receiving message by announcer
If (slp_id = = clp_id)
{
        If (leader is failed)
         slp_id = mcp_id
broadcast leader msg (anp_id, mcp_id, clp_id)
else
broadcast  message msg (anp_id, slp_id, null)
}
else
discard the received message msg (mcp_id, clp_id)
}
```

Fig. 3. Pseudo code when any node finds that the leader is crashed

```
//when nodes N1,N2,N3.....Nn detect the leader is crashed, initiate an election
Create message msg (mcp_id, clp_id) and send to announcer
 Start timer
//upon receiving messages from N1,N2,N3.....Nn for i=1 to n
Find the node Ni whose mcp_id is highest and discard the messages transmitted by other
nodes If (slp_id = = clp_id) \\clp_id taken from node Ni {

   If (leader is failed)
        slp_id = mcp_id
broadcast leader msg (anp_id, mcp_id, clp_id)
else
broadcast message msg (anp_id, slp_id, null)
}
else
discard the received message msg (mcp_id, clp_id)
```

Fig. 4. Pseudo code when two or more nodes find the crash of the leader

```
//when announcer and leader both are crashed and any node X detect the leader is
crashed Initiate an election
Create message msg (mcp_id, clp_id) and send to announcer
Start timer
If (sender not receives any responses from announcer)
Send message to N-1 node \\N-1 node is the next highest Id node
//after receiving message by N-1 node Check (anp_id is crashed
or not)
If (anp_id is crashed)
anp_id(N) = anp_id(N-1)
Check (leader is failed or not)
If (leader is failed)
broadcast leader message (anp_id, mcp_id, clp_id)
else
broadcast message msg (anp_id, slp_id, null)
}
else
discard the received message msg (mcp_id, clp_id)
```

Fig. 5. Pseudo code when any node find announcer and leader both are crashed

Case1: When any node found that leader is crashed and it needs a leader then immediately it will start election by sending election message [(msg <mcp_id, clp_id>)] to the announcer. Announcer will check the slp_id with clp_id and if it matched then it will check whether stored leader is really crashed or not. If it is crashed then announcer will store the mcp_id as a leader and broadcast this message [(msg <anp_id, mcp_id, clp_id>)] to remaining nodes in the network to inform others about the new leader.

After getting message from the announcer, nodes will update their table and replace old leader id with new one.

In the example (shown in Fig. 6), node 4 founds that the current leader (node 5) is crashed, so node 4 create a message (msg <4, 5>) and send to announcer (node 7). After receiving the message (msg <4, 5>), announcer compare its store leader process

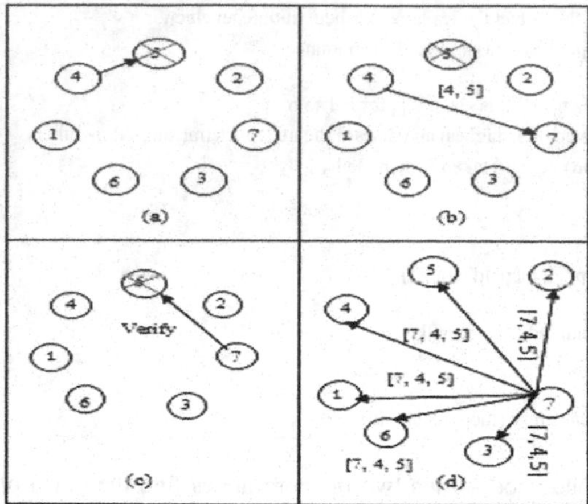

Fig. 6. Steps when one node detect leader is failed

id (slp_id) with the second field of the received message (clp_id). Here slp_id (5) = clp_id(5). According to our algorithm the announcer (anp_id) verify the leader is exactly crashed or not. If leader is crashed then it store mcp_id(4) as a new leader and broadcast this message (msg <7, 4, 5>) to remaining nodes in the network to inform others about the new leader. After getting message from the announcer, nodes will update their table and store mcp_id(4) as a slp_id(4).

Case2: If simultaneously two or more nodes noticed that leader is down, they will send message to the announcer. Now announcer have to elect leader between them based on whose node id is bigger.

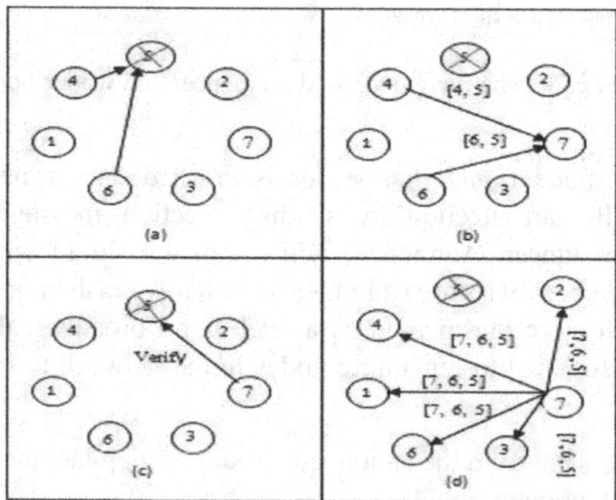

Fig. 7. Steps when two nodes detect leader is failed

In the example (shown in Fig. 7) when at a time node 4 and node 6 detect the leader is down or crashed. In this case node 4 create the message <4, 5> and node 6 create the message <6, 5> and send to announcer (node7). After getting message the announcer compare the message creator process id (mcp_id) of both nodes. Here mcp_id (6) > mcp_id(4). So announcer will discard the message <4, 5> and select the message <6, 5> . After that the announcer compares slp_id and clp_id. Here slp_id (5) = clp_id(5), so announcer check the slp_id is exactly crashed or not if crashed then it store mcp_id(6) as a slp_id and broadcast message <7, 6, 5> to all active nodes in the network to inform about the new leader. After receiving message the nodes update their table and store mcp_id(6) as a slp_id.

Case3: If leader and announcer both were crashed and any node notices it then it will send this message (msg < mcp_id, clp_id >) to $(N - 1)^{th}$ node considering it a new announcer. After receiving the message, $(N - 1)^{th}$ node will have to validate it and broadcast message (msg <anp_id, mcp_id, clp_id>) to the network.

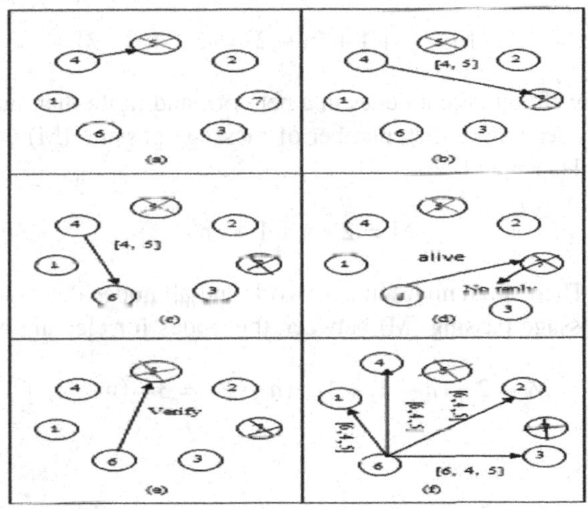

Fig. 8. When any node detect announcer and leader both are crashed

Here in example (shown in Fig. 8) node 4 detect that the leader 5 is crashed then it immediately create a message <4, 5> and send to announcer (node 7). After a certain period of time if node 4 not received any responses from the announcer. Then it sends the message <4, 5> to node 6. According to our algorithm after receiving the message node 6 will check the announcer (node 7) is exactly down or not if node 7 is down then node 6 updates their table and store as new anp_id. After that it compares slp_id and clp_id. Here slp_id(5) = clp_id(5). So node 6 store mcp_id(4) as a new slp_id and broadcast to all active nodes. After receiving message the nodes update their table and store the anp_id(6) as a new announcer and mcp_id(4) as new store leader process slp_id.

4 Performance Analysis

In Bully algorithm [11] for choosing a leader we need of huge number of messages passing and time. The message complexity of this algorithm in worst case is O(n2) and message complexity of modified Bully algorithm is O(n) in worst case. It is more efficient than Bully algorithm but it also require more messages to choose a leader but our proposed algorithm more efficient and better performance in comparison to these algorithm because it require less message passing for choosing a leader in distributed system which is shown in Table 1. The message complexity of our proposed algorithm is O(n) and mathematical analysis of this algorithm is shown in Sect. 4.1.

4.1 Mathematical Analysis

Best Case: If there are n nodes in a network and only one node observes leader failure then number of message passing (M) between the nodes for electing a leader will be

$$M = 2 + 1 + (n - 2) = 3 + (n - 2)$$

Average Case: If there are n nodes in a network and more than one node (assumed x) observes leader failure then number of message passing (M) between the nodes for electing a leader will be

$$M = 2 * x + 1 + (n - 2)$$

Worst Case: There are n nodes in a network and all nodes detect leader failure then number of message passing (M) between the nodes for electing a leader will be

$$M = 2 * (n - 2) + 1 + (n - 2) = 3 * (n - 2) + 1$$

5 Comparison with Other Algorithms

In this section, we compare our proposed algorithms with respect to the existing algorithms based on their message passing complexity. Table 1 shows the number of message passing to select a leader in worst case. Figure 9 shows a comparison graph in our proposed algorithm, Bully Algorithm and modified Bully Algorithm. Graph shows comparison where number of nodes denoted by horizontal axis and number of message denoted by vertical axis.

Table 1. Comparison among bully algorithm, modified bully algorithm and our proposed algorithm

No of nodes in a network	Leader election algorithms		
	Bully algorithm	Modified bully algorithm	Proposed algorithm
5	24	14	10
10	99	29	25
15	224	44	40
20	399	59	55
25	624	74	70

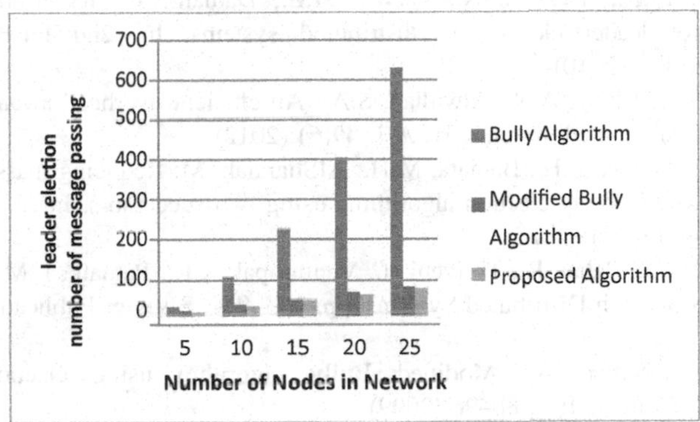

Fig. 9. Comparison among proposed algorithm, bully algorithm and modified bully algorithm

6 Conclusion and Future Works

After analysis of Bully algorithm and modified Bully algorithm, we propose a new algorithm for selection of a leader that gives overall less message passing during the selection of a leader. The main idea of over proposed algorithm is that it uses highest ID as an announcer node who will decide which one is the next leader in case of leader failed or crashed. And by analytical simulation, we have shown that in our propose algorithm the number of message passing for selecting a leader is less than with respect to entire leader election algorithm.

As a future work, we will study to overcome the problem of message complexity in worst case that will never affect the performance of our proposed algorithm.

References

1. Garcia-Molina, H.: Elections in a distributed computing system. IEEE Trans. Comput. **31**, 48–59 (1982)
2. Mirakhorli, M., Sharifloo, A.A., Abbaspour, M.: A novel method for leader election algorithm. In: The 7th IEEE International Conference on Computer and Information Technology (CIT 2007), pp. 452–456, October 2007
3. Kordafshari, M.S., Gholipour, M., Jahanshahi, M., Haghighat, A.T.: Modified bully election algorithm in distributed systems. In: WSEAS Conference (2005)
4. Park, S.H., Hwang, Y.K.: An efficient algorithm for leader-election in synchronous distributed systems. IEEE Trans. Comput. **43**(7), 1991–1994 (1999)
5. Gholipur, M., Kordafshri, M.S., Jahanshani, M., Rahmani, A.M.: A new approach for election algorithm in distributed systems. In: International Conference on Computer and Information Technology (2009)
6. Effat Parvar, M.R., Yazdani, N., Parvar, M.E., Dadlani, A., Khonsari, A.: Improved algorithms for leader election in distributed systems. In: 2nd International (IEEE) conference, vol. 2 (2010)
7. Yassein, M.B., Alslaity, A.N., Alwidian, S.A.: An efficient overhead-aware leader election algorithm for distributed systems. IJCA J. **49**(6) (2012)
8. Alhadidi, B., Baniata, L.H., Baniata, M.H.: AlSharaiah, M: Reducing massage passing and time complexity in bully election algorithms using two successors. Int. J. Electron. Electr. Eng. **1**(1), 1–4 (2013)
9. Soundarabai, P.B., Sahai, R., Thriveni, J., Venugopal, K.R., Patnaik, L.M.: Efficient Bully Election Algorithm in Distributed Systems, pp. 243–251. Elsevier Publications, Amsterdam (2013)
10. Rahman, M., Nahar, A.: Modified Bully algorithm using election commission. MASAUM J. Compu. **1**(3), 88–96 (2009)
11. Chhabra, S., Tyagi, G., Mundra, A., Rakesh, N.: Location based coordinator election algorithm in distributed environment. In: International Conference on Computer and Computational Sciences (2015)
12. Kordafshari, M.S., Gholipour, M., Jahanshahi, M., Haghighat, A.T.: Two novel algorithms for electing coordinator in distributed systems based on bully algorithm. In: 4th WSEAS International Conference (2005)
13. Biswas, A., Dutta, A.: A timer based leader election algorithm. IEEE (2016)
14. Yadav, D.K., Sharma, V.K.: Optimal distributed leader election algorithm. Int. J. Adv. Res. Comput. Sci. Technol. (IJARCST), **2** (2014)
15. Gawali, D.P.: Leader election problem in distributed algorithm. Int. J. Comput. Sci. Technol. (IJCT), **3** (2012)
16. Beaulah Soundarabai, P., Thriveni, J., Venugopal, K.R., Patnaik, L.M.: An improved leader election algorithm for distributed systems. Int. J. Next Gener. Netw. **5**, 21 (2013)
17. Gajre, V.P.: Comparison of bully election algorithms in distributed system. Int. J. Sci. Res. Publ. **3** (2013)
18. Katwala, H., Shah, S.: Study on election algorithm in distributed system. IOSR J. Comput. Eng. **7**, 34–39 (2012)
19. Shirali, M., Toroghi, A.H., Vojdani, M.: Leader election algorithms: history and novel schemes. IEEE Computer Society (2008)
20. Sathesh, B.M.: Optimized bully algorithm. Int. J. Comput. Appl. **121** (2015)
21. Mamun, Q.E., Moham, S.: Modified bully algorithm for electing coordinator in distributed systems. In: WSEAS International Conference on Software Engineering, Parallel and Distributed Systems, pp. 22–28

Deep Learning Based Adaptive Linear Collaborative Discriminant Regression Classification for Face Recognition

K. Shailaja[1(✉)] and B. Anuradha[2]

[1] Computer Science Engineering, Anurag Group of Institutions, Ghatkesar, (M) Ranga Reddy (Dist.), Venkatapur, Hyderabad 501301, Telangana, India
shailaja_kalvagadda@yahoo.com

[2] Computer Science Engineering, Abhinav Hi-Tech College of Engineering, Chilkur Balaji Temple Rd, Himayat Nagar, Hyderabad 501301, Telangana, India
anuradhabs@yahoo.co.in

Abstract. Face recognition is a popular research problem in the domain of image analysis. The steps involved in face recognition are mainly face verification and face classification. Face verification algorithms have been well-defined in recent years, but face classification researchers are still facing problems. In this regard we propose face recognition using Adaptive Linear Collaborative Discriminant Regression Classification (ALCDRC) with Deep Learning (DL) algorithm by considering different sets of the training images. In particular, ALCDRC makes utilization of various weights to describe different training sets and uses such weighting data to compute between-class and with-in-class reconstruction errors and after that ALCDRC endeavors to locate an ideal projection matrix which maximize the ratio of Between-Class Reconstruction Error (BCRE) over With-in-Class-Reconstruction Error (WCRE). Experimentation was done on two challenging face databases called ORL and YALE-B and prominent results are obtained.

Keywords: Deep learning
Linear collaborative discriminant regression classification · Penalty function
Reconstruction error

1 Introduction

From past few years face recognition research is achieving a great success in the fields of pattern recognition [1]. Face recognition is a difficult task, because true face images are influenced by various conditions, for example, lighting changes and expression [2]. In a face recognition system, feature extraction and classification are important key steps [3]. To develop a robust face recognition system, some of the issues need to be resolved, especially on classification and feature extraction [4]. While classifying, the individual face images are transformed into a vector, which is very high dimensional in nature. It is essential to convert a higher dimensional image space into lower dimensional image space [5]. Generally, a lot of dimensionality reduction systems are there in

P. Bhattacharyya et al. (Eds.): NGCT 2017, CCIS 827, pp. 675–686, 2018.
https://doi.org/10.1007/978-981-10-8657-1_52

face recognition, to reduce "curse of dimensionality" such as Principle Component Analysis (PCA), Linear Discriminant Analysis (LDA), Discrete Cosine Transform (DCT), Independent Component Analysis are familiar methods [6, 7].

Performance of the face recognition methods is highly affected by the number of images of a person in the training set [8, 9]. Particularly, when the number of images per person is low, then the learned sub-space projection might be deficient [10]. In order to overcome this issue, an effective collaborative classification method is implemented named as Adaptive Linear Collaborative Discriminant Regression Classification (ALCDRC) along with DL algorithm which considers the Collaborative-Between Class Reconstruction Error (C-BCRE) instead of BCRE. The C-BCRE representation utilizes a cross-class training face that represents an input face. The large class-specific BCRE domination problem can be reduced by considering CBCRE as a lower bound of all the class-specific BCRE. The CBCRE mainly obtained by those small class-specific BCRE. Then maximizing the CBCRE gives a better separation of WCRE and small class-specific BCRE than BCRE.

In the following section we summarize recent survey on face recognition, description of our proposed ALCDRC-DL method and presents experimentation results to show effectiveness of the proposed algorithm.

2 Literature Review

Huang et al. [11] have evaluated an Adaptive-Linear Discriminant Regression Classification (A-LDRC) method by considering different contributions of the training samples. The A-LDRC is an extension of LDRC which determines discriminate subspace for LDRC by considering the different contribution of training images to construct between-class and with-in-class reconstruction errors that improves the performance of the proposed method. The disadvantage of A-LDRC method was more complex to find the projection of free space where Free space can able to provide better discriminant ability in the feature extraction phase of face recognition.

Qu et al. [12] have presented a face recognition method that improves LDRC algorithm. In this scenario, author uses collaborative representation in the place of class-specific representation for better BCRE measurement, which can be regarded as the lower bound of all the class-specific BCRE. Therefore, maximization of the collaborative BCRE maximizes each class-specific between-class reconstruction and emphasizes the small class-specific BCRE, which was beneficial for the following Linear Regression Classification (LRC). Experiments were conduct and performance of the proposed method was verified. In LDRC algorithm, there was a need to identify Eigen values and Eigen vector that leads to time consumption.

Zhou et al. [13] proposed a new method for face recognition which uses PCA and logistic regression. In this literature, PCA extracts features from face images and also reduce the dimensions of the input images. Then, the author designed a classifier called logistic regression for face recognition. Experimentation was done on challenging face databases and the result presented shows the efficacy the proposed method. Though, the PCA was highly influenced by the number of samples per person in the training set. So, when the number of samples was low that affects the recognition rate.

Gao et al. [14] presents a method for both data representation and each occlusion-induced error image simultaneously. In order to learn more discriminative low-rank representations, the author formulated an objective such that the learned representations are optimal for classification by the available supervised information and close to an ideal-code regularization term. The Robust-Discriminative Low-Rank Representation (R-DLRR) works well on face recognition problems especially when face images are corrupted by severe occlusions. The author designed a simple linear classifier that outperformed several other face recognition methods on databases with a variety of face variations. In large dataset, R-DLRR failed to achieve better recognition by means of accuracy.

Li et al. [15] presents a new approach for face recognition which retrieves discriminant information from each individual person by considering the dynamic subspace of images. Then, the author uses this information to represent the characteristic of discriminative components. The experiments performed on publicly available databases (AR, Extended Yale B, and ORL) and achieved high recognition rate compared to other popular approaches. In this literature, the inter-personal and intra-personal variations were high due expression and facial hair of individual person.

To overcome the above - mentioned drawbacks, a penalty function is included in LCDRC along with DL algorithm, which enhances the process acclimated in our anticipated approach.

3 The Proposed Method

The proposed method shows how the large class-specific BCRE and WCRE problems are diminished by the collaborative representation idea. A brief discussion about LDRC, LCDRC, and adaptive-LCDRC are detailed below along with deep learning algorithm.

3.1 Linear Discriminant Regression Classification (LDRC)

LDRC is aims to acquire Discriminant information in the LRC that guarantees for separation of face images. It utilizes labeled training information to build a more productive subspace on which effective Discriminant regression classification can be applied. The LDRC approach is summarized as follows. To get a more effective discriminant subspace for LRC, LDRC looks to find a projection by maximizing the ratio of BCRE over WCRE. In this scenario, the training face images of the ith class are stated as $X_i \in \Re^{S \times n_i}$, each column X_i is S dimensional to the face images of class i. In which, the training images n_i are exemplified in vector as $i = 0, 1, 2, \ldots c.$, where, c is the no. of classes. Considering, the probe face images Y, which is denoted by employing X_i,

$$Y = X_i \beta_i, i = 0, 1, 2 \ldots c \tag{1}$$

Where, $\beta_i \in \Re^{n_i \times 1}$ stated as regression parameter, β_i is determined by applying the least square estimation, which is symbolized as,

$$\hat{\beta}_i = \left(X_i^T X_i\right)^{-1} X_i^T Y, i = 0, 1, 2, \ldots c \tag{2}$$

Projected vector of parameters $\hat{\beta}_i$ with the predictor X_i is applied to calculate the response vector of each class i, by equating the Eqs. (2) and (1),

$$\hat{Y}_i = X_i \hat{\beta}_i = X_i \left(X_i^T X_i\right)^{-1} X_i^T Y = H_i Y, i = 0, 1, 2, \ldots c \tag{3}$$

Where, H_i is stated as hat matrix, which plots P into $\hat{P}_i$. Finally, reconstruction error of each class is determined and then LRC allocates the class P with lowest reconstruction error.

$$e_i = \left\| Y - \hat{Y}_i \right\|_2^2, i = 0, 1, 2, \ldots c \tag{4}$$

We know LDRC implements discriminant analysis in the LRC to provide effective discrimination, by employing labeled training data. Assuming, all the facial images from the matrix are denoted as $X = [X_1, \ldots\ldots X_i, \ldots, X_n] \in \Re^{S \times n}$.

Where, n is characterized as the number of images and S denotes the dimension of images. Hence, the class label of X_i is declared as $l(X_i) \in \{0, 1, 2, \ldots c\}$. Considering, the sub-space projection matrix $U \in \Re^{S \times n}$ and each face images can be projected into the sub-space as,

$$U^* = \max_U \frac{tr(U^T BCREU)}{tr(U^T (WCRE + \in l)U)} \tag{5}$$

Where, $\in$ is symbolized as a positive number, l is an identity matrix and $tr(.)$ represents a trace operator,

In case $n < S$, the label of Y_i is similar to label of X_i and it is characterized as $l(Y_i) \in l(X_i)$. The sub-space of projection matrix U is determined by increasing BCRE and decreasing WCRE at the same time, WCRE and BCRE are mathematically expressed as follows,

$$WCRE = \frac{1}{n} \sum_{i=1}^{n} (X_i - X_i^{\text{intra}})(X_i - X_i^{\text{intra}})^T \tag{6}$$

$$BCRE = \frac{1}{n(c-1)} \sum_{i=1}^{n} \sum_{j=1\, j \neq l(X_i)}^{c} (X_i - X_{ij}^{\text{inter}})(X_i - X_{ij}^{\text{inter}})^T \tag{7}$$

Where, X_{ij}^{inter} is denoted as the reconstruction error of X_i and $l(X_i) \neq j$, X_i^{intra} is characterized as the reconstruction error of X_i.

3.2 Linear Collaborative Discriminant Regression Classification (LCDRC)

In LCDRC, the with-in class features are compared with the total number of classes' c features. While comparing, the ratio of distance between the classes are extremely maximized and also significantly reduce the distance of with-in class features. In WCRE, the individual features of the class are compensating with the c number of class features. Finally, the association between the WCRE and CBCRE can be denoted as,

$$WCRE = \sum_{i=1}^{c}\sum_{j=1}^{n}\left\| U^T X_{ij} - U^T X_{ij}^{intra} \beta_{ij}^{intra} \right\|_2^2 \tag{8}$$

$$CBCRE = \sum_{i=1}^{c}\sum_{j=1}^{n}\left\| U^T X_{ij} - U^T X_{ij}^{inter} \beta_{ij}^{inter} \right\|_2^2 \tag{9}$$

3.3 Deep Learning Algorithm

Deep Learning is used in the experimental analysis which modifies U projection matrix as a memory matrix that expressively decreases the sematic gap between reference and training images. In LCDRC, memory matrix diminish the error occurred in the system, also improves the LCDRC performance. In addition, back propagation weight is applied utilizing stochastic gradient descent as stated in the following equation,

$$U^{T*} = U^T + \omega \frac{\partial f}{\partial U} \tag{10}$$

Where, η is specified as learning rate, $\omega \frac{\partial f}{\partial U}$ illustrates the whole learning function and f is the cost function.

Training images X_i from the class i are learned by employing deep learning algorithm and the projection matrix forms the linear discrimination function which can be mentioned as,

$$Y_i = U^{T*} X_i \in \Im^{S \times n} \tag{11}$$

In order to determine an optimum solution of DL-LCDRC algorithm, it is necessary to maximize the ratio of BCRE over WCRE. Substitute Eq. (11) in Eq. (4). Then BCRE and WCRE are exemplified in inter-class and intra-class variances of the training samples that are represented in Eqs. (12) and (13).

$$BCRE = \frac{1}{n}\sum_{i=1}^{c}\sum_{j=1}^{n}\left\| Y_i - \overset{\Lambda r}{Y}_{ij} \right\|_2^2 \tag{12}$$

$$WCRE = \frac{1}{n}\sum_{j=1}^{n}\left\| Y_i - \overset{\Lambda^a}{Y_{ij}} \right\|_2^2 \tag{13}$$

Where, inter and intra- classes are determined by $\overset{\Lambda^r}{Y_{ij}} = Y_{ij}^r\beta_{ij}^r$ and $\overset{\Lambda^a}{Y_{ij}} = Y_{ij}^r\beta_{ij}^r$. Value Y_{ij}^r indicates Y with Y_i eliminated and the value Y_{ij}^a describes Y_i with Y_{ij} eliminated.

Whereas, Value β is unknown until the projection matrix is accomplished. The value of β_{ij}^r and β_{ij}^a is attained from $\hat{\beta}_i = \left(X_i^T X_i\right)^{-1} X_i^T Y, i = 0, 1, 2, \ldots c$. For improving the recognition rate, the modified deep learned $\hat{\beta}_i$ value is included in the Eqs. (8) and (9).

The respective Eqs. (8) and (9) can be further re-written as follows,

$$WCRE = \sum_{i=1}^{c}\sum_{j=1}^{n}\left(X_{ij} - X_{ij}^{\text{intra}}\beta_{ij}^{\text{intra}}\right)^T UU^T\left(X_{ij} - X_{ij}^{\text{intra}}\beta_{ij}^{\text{intra}}\right)^T \tag{14}$$

$$CBCRE = \sum_{i=1}^{c}\sum_{j=1}^{n}\left(X_{ij} - X_{ij}^{\text{inter}}\beta_{ij}^{\text{inter}}\right)^T UU^T\left(X_{ij} - X_{ij}^{\text{inter}}\beta_{ij}^{\text{inter}}\right)^T \tag{15}$$

In CBCRE and WCRE equations we have a factor $1/n$. So there is a need to remove this factor from both equations without affecting the value of CBCRE over WCRE. By using some algebraic logic, CBCRE and WCRE are denoted as follows:

$$WCRE = \sum_{i=1}^{c}\sum_{j=1}^{n} tr\left(U^T\left(X_{ij} - X_{ij}^{\text{intra}}\beta_{ij}^{\text{intra}}\right)\left(X_{ij} - X_{ij}^{\text{intra}}\beta_{ij}^{\text{intra}}\right)^T U\right) \tag{16}$$

$$CBCRE = \sum_{i=1}^{c}\sum_{j=1}^{n} tr\left(U^T\left(X_{ij} - X_{ij}^{\text{inter}}\beta_{ij}^{\text{inter}}\right)\left(X_{ij} - X_{ij}^{\text{inter}}\beta_{ij}^{\text{inter}}\right)^T U\right) \tag{17}$$

Where $tr(\cdot)$ is represented as the trace operator, eventually the following WCRE and BCRE can be denoted as follows,

$$WCRE = \frac{1}{n}\sum_{i=1}^{c}\sum_{j=1}^{n}\left(X_{ij} - X_{ij}^{\text{intra}}\beta_{ij}^{\text{intra}}\right)\left(X_{ij} - X_{ij}^{\text{intra}}\beta_{ij}^{\text{intra}}\right)^T \tag{18}$$

$$CBCRE = \frac{1}{n}\sum_{i=1}^{c}\sum_{j=1}^{n}\left(X_{ij} - X_{ij}^{\text{inter}}\beta_{ij}^{\text{inter}}\right)\left(X_{ij} - X_{ij}^{\text{inter}}\beta_{ij}^{\text{inter}}\right)^T \tag{19}$$

3.4 Adaptive-LCDRC (A-LCDRC)

In this section, data samples are exploited in a significant manner. In order to demonstrate the contribution of samples X_i to its individual class, by employing a penalty function. Generally, samples from the similar class have high intra-class reconstruction error, so, to limit the reconstruction error, a penalty F(i) should be enforced. In mathematically, the penalty is determined as,

$$F(i) = \left\|X_i - X_i^{intra}\right\|^{-t_1} \tag{20}$$

Where, $X_i - X_i^{intra}$ is represented as the Euclidean distance between X_i and its intra-class reconstruction error, $t_1 > 0$ represented as a tuning parameter.

In this scenario, penalty function F(i) is a monotone increasing function which depends on the distance between X_i and its intra-class reconstruction error vector. Likewise, for the inter-class reconstruction error, a penalty function G(i,j) is enforced, to determine the importance of X to $j - th$ inter-class data samples ($j \neq l(X_i)$).

It specifies that G(i,j) is a monotone decreasing function and it depends on the distance between X_i and $j - th$ inter-class data samples. In mathematically, G(i,j) is stated as,

$$G(i,j) = \left\|X_i - X_{ij}^{inter}\right\|^{-t_2} \tag{21}$$

Where, $t_2 > 0$ is represented as a tuning parameter, $X_i - X_{ij}^{inter}$ denoted as the Euclidean distance between X_i and inter-class reconstruction error vector. Substitute, the two penalty functions in the respective Eqs. (18) and (19),

$$WCRE = \frac{1}{n}\sum_{i=1}^{c}\sum_{j=1}^{n} F(i)\left(X_{ij} - X_{ij}^{intra}\beta_{ij}^{intra}\right)\left(X_{ij} - X_{ij}^{intra}\beta_{ij}^{intra}\right)^T \tag{22}$$

$$CBCRE = \frac{1}{n}\sum_{i=1}^{c}\sum_{j=1}^{n} G(i,j)\left(X_{ij} - X_{ij}^{inter}\beta_{ij}^{inter}\right)\left(X_{ij} - X_{ij}^{inter}\beta_{ij}^{inter}\right)^T \tag{23}$$

The objective function of the A-LCDRC is obtained, by substituting WCRE and BCRE in the Eq. (5),

$$U_{ALCDRC} = \max_U \frac{tr(U^T\,\overline{CBCRE}U)}{tr(U^T(\overline{WCRE} + \in l)U)} \tag{24}$$

To obtain the optimal matrix of $U_{ALCDRC} = (U_1, U_2, \ldots\ldots\ldots\ldots U_d)$, by solving the respective comprehensive Eigen value concern,

$$\overline{CBCRE}\,U_K = \gamma(\overline{WCRE} + \in l)U_K, K = 1, 2, \ldots c \tag{25}$$

Where, $\gamma_1 \geq \ldots.\gamma_K\ldots.\gamma_c$.

4 Experimentation Results

Experimentation was implemented in PC with 1.8 GHz Pentium IV processor using MATLAB. To validate the efficiency of proposed algorithm, the performance of ALCDRC-DL was compared with LCDRC on the reputed face databases like ORL and YALE B. In this experiment, all the facial images are scaled to 32×32.

4.1 Results for ORL Dataset

The ORL face dataset holds 400 face images with 40 persons where each person contains 10 face images respectively. Here, face images are considered under numerous facial expressions and altered lightening conditions. The sample face images of ORL database is given below in Fig. 1.

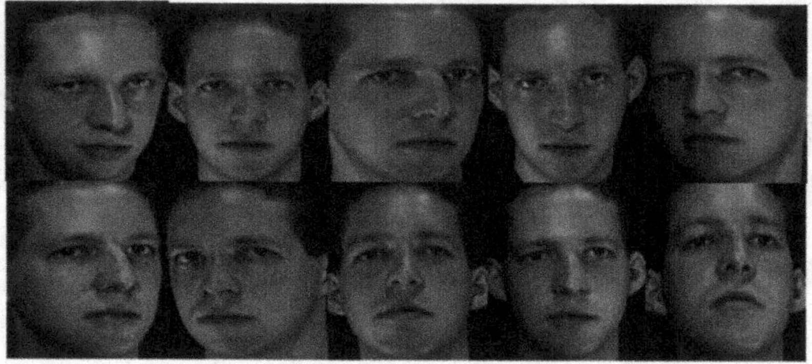

Fig. 1. The ORL face dataset

The performance of LCDRC and the proposed ALCDRC-DL in the ORL database is determined and compared by referring the following Figs. 2 and 3. In Fig. 3, the

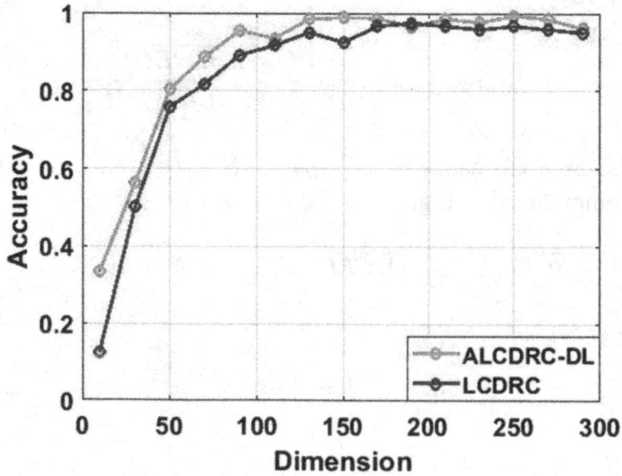

Fig. 2. The seven train (dimension vs accuracy)

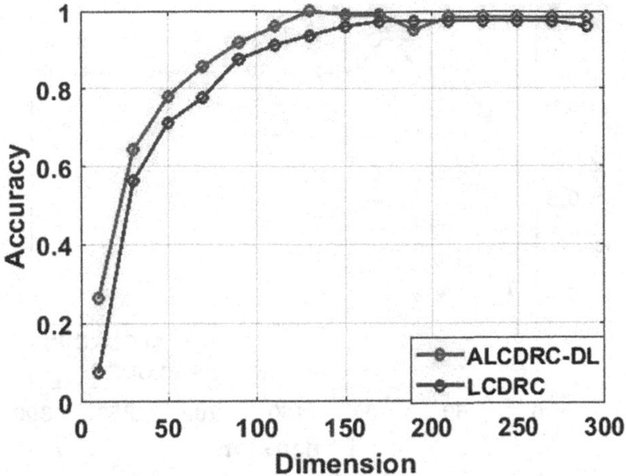

Fig. 3. The eight train (dimension vs accuracy)

high dimensional recognition rate was almost achieved 100% outcome in proposed method for ORL dataset. And the respective, training class confirms that the proposed scheme is very effective in nature.

4.2 Results for YALE B Dataset

Normally, the YALE B face database contains 15 persons, with 165 face images where each person holds 11. The face images have different expression and configuration such as center-light, with-glasses, happy, sad, etc. The sample face images of the YALE B database is mentioned in Fig. 4.

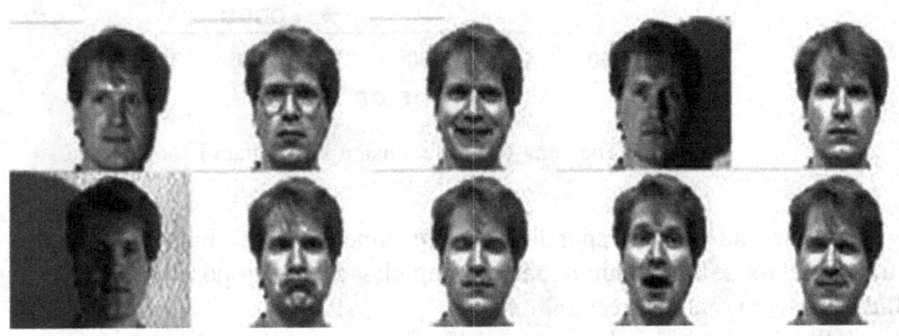

Fig. 4. The YALE-B dataset

The performance of LCDRC and the proposed approach ALCDRC-DL in YALE B database is evaluated and compared by referring the Figs. 5 and 6. In these figures,

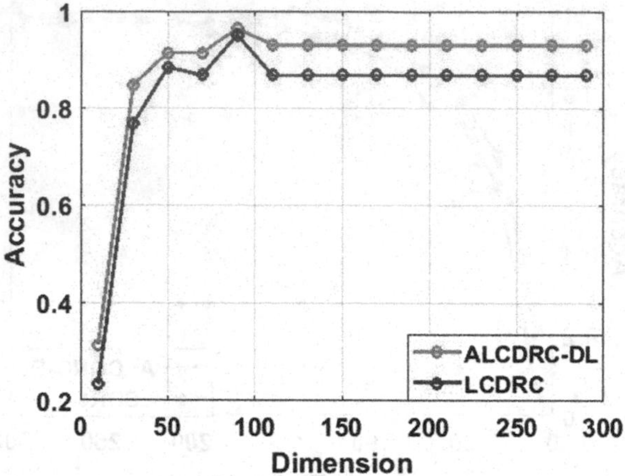

Fig. 5. The seven train (dimension vs accuracy)

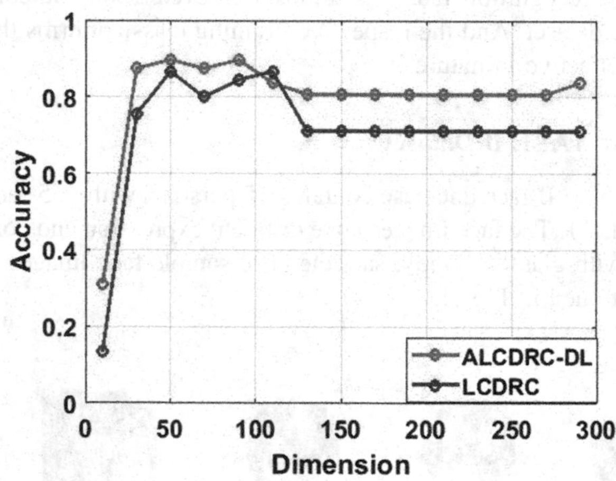

Fig. 6. The eight train (dimension vs accuracy)

recognition rate and the corresponding feature dimensions are mentioned in two various training classes. By examining the training classes, the proposed approach shows a significant outcome in face recognition.

The following Table 1 indicates the performance analysis of the proposed approach over LCDRC for two different datasets. Here, the maximum value of each train is mentioned in this table.

Table 1. The performance evaluation table for ORL and YALE B database

Facial database	Methods	Two training accuracy	Three training accuracy	Four training accuracy	Five training accuracy	Six training accuracy	Seven training accuracy	Eight training accuracy
ORL	LCDRC [12]	83	83.64	84.5	90.8	93.23	98.32	98.23
	Proposed	89	86.4	89.2	92.6	94.5	99.33	100
YALE B	LCDRC [12]	78	87.5	88.10	86.77	89.7	91.98	86.78
	Proposed	87.9	89.1	89.05	91.67	94.84	94.32	90.34

5 Conclusion

A new Discriminant approach named as ALCDRC-DL that is employed for extracting the features and classification. In this scenario, the proposed ALCDRC-DL approach is an improved version of LCDRC and traditional LDRC that helps to maximize the value of BCRE and minimize the value of WCRE, which result in an optimal projection matrix. The experiments done on publicly available databases like ORL and YALE-B, which shows a superiority of the proposed approach. The recognition rate on the sub-space is more significant in ALCDRC-DL than the previous methods.

References

1. Cao, F., Feng, X., Zhao, J.: Sparse representation for robust face recognition by dictionary decomposition. J. Vis. Commun. Image Represent. **46**, 260–268 (2017)
2. Li, H., Shen, F., Shen, C., Yang, Y., Gao, Y.: Face recognition using linear representation ensembles. Pattern Recogn. **59**, 72–87 (2016)
3. Su, Y., Gao, X., Yin, X.C.: Fast alignment for sparse representation based face recognition. Pattern Recogn. **68**, 211–212 (2017)
4. Leng, B., Yu, K., Jingyan, Q.I.N.: Data augmentation for unbalanced face recognition training sets. Neurocomputing **235**, 10–14 (2017)
5. Dong, X., Zhang, H., Sun, J., Wan, W.: A two-stage learning approach to face recognition. J. Vis. Commun. Image Represent. **43**, 21–29 (2017)
6. Xu, C., Liu, Q., Ye, M.: Age invariant face recognition and retrieval by coupled auto-encoder networks. Neurocomputing. **222**, 62–71 (2017)
7. Tu, X., Gao, J., Xie, M., Qi, J., Ma, Z.: Illumination normalization based on correction of large-scale components for face recognition. Neurocomputing **266**, 1–12 (2017)
8. Liu, S., Peng, Y., Ben, X., Yang, W., Qiu, G.: A novel label learning algorithm for face recognition. Signal Process. **124**, 141–146 (2016)
9. Sukhija, P., Behal, S., Singh, P.: Face recognition system using genetic algorithm. Proc. Comput. Sci. **85**, 410–417 (2011)
10. Yang, W., Wang, Z., Zhang, B.: Face recognition using adaptive local ternary patterns method. Neurocomputing **213**, 183–190 (2016)
11. Huang, P., Lai, Z., Gao, G., Yang, G., Yang, Z.: Adaptive linear discriminant regression classification for face recognition. Digit. Signal Process. **55**, 78–84 (2016)

12. Qu, X., Kim, S., Cui, R., Kim, H.J.: Linear collaborative discriminant regression classification for face recognition. J. Vis. Commun. Image Represent. **31**, 312–319 (2015)
13. Zhou, C., Wang, L., Zhang, Q., Wei, X.: Face recognition based on PCA and logistic regression analysis. Opt. Int. J. Light Electron Opt. **125**, 5916–5919 (2014)
14. Gao, G., Yang, J., Jing, X.Y., Shen, F., Yang, W., Yue, D.: Learning robust and discriminative low-rank representations for face recognition with occlusion. Pattern Recogn. **66**, 129–143 (2017)
15. Li, H., Suen, C.Y.: Robust face recognition based on dynamic rank representation. Pattern Recogn. **60**, 13–24 (2016)

A Novel Clustering Algorithm for Leveraging Data Quality in Wireless Sensor Network

B. Prathiba[1(✉)], K. Jaya Sankar[2(✉)], and V. Sumalatha[1(✉)]

[1] Department of Electronics and Communication Engineering, Jawaharlal Nehru Technological University, Anantapur, India
balireddyprathibha@gmail.com, sumaatp@yahoo.com

[2] Department of Electronics and Communication Engineering, Vasavi College of Engineering, Hyderabad, India
kottareddyjs@gmail.com

Abstract. Till date, the research work in Wireless Sensor Network is mainly inclined towards rectifying the problem associated with the nodes and protocol associated with it, e.g., energy problems, clustering issue, security loopholes, uncertain traffic, etc. However, there is less emphasis towards the user's demand, i.e., data quality. As wireless nodes undergo various forms of adverse wireless condition in order to carry out data aggregation, it is quite inevitable that an aggregated data forwarded may not have a good data quality. Therefore, we present a novel clustering technique that concentrates on achieving the lowest possible error. With an aid of analytical modeling, a novel clustering technique is formulated using probability theory that targets the node with higher retention of redundant information so that it can be mitigated effectively. The study outcome shows better data quality of the proposed system.

Keywords: Wireless Sensor Network · Clustering techniques
Data quality · Error minimization · Sensor nodes

1 Introduction

A Wireless Sensor Network (WSN) is a collection of highly interconnected sensor nodes that are spread across the area that is required to be monitored. All the sensor nodes collect environmental data and forward it to its leader node that is finally forwarded to either base station or next leader node. In this entire process, proper organizations of the sensor nodes are highly essential to confirm a required communication for a specific application in WSN. The clustering mechanism in Wireless Sensor Network (WSN) plays an essential role in grouping the senor nodes that are spread in the monitoring area either in grid manner or in random manner [1, 2]. Inspite of effective clustering process, there are situations when a similar event is captured by nodes residing on different clusters [3]. This phenomenon gives rise to an increase in redundant information that affects the data quality when the aggregated data reaches the base station [4]. This problem takes a critical shape especially in large scale deployment of sensor nodes with high node density [5]. At present, the existing clustering techniques have mainly focused on addressing energy problems at the cost of data

P. Bhattacharyya et al. (Eds.): NGCT 2017, CCIS 827, pp. 687–694, 2018.
https://doi.org/10.1007/978-981-10-8657-1_53

quality [6, 7]. It was also noticed that a majority of the clustering techniques mainly emphasize on selection process of a leader node as a means of energy efficiency. The importance of data quality is quite high in certain applications of WSN, e.g., healthcare-based, nuclear plant monitoring, oil-rigs monitoring system, cargo surveillance system, etc. [8, 9]. Therefore, the proposed system introduces a novel clustering mechanism that solely focuses on ensuring that the aggregated data should have as much lowest error as possible to ensure peak data quality. Section 2 discusses the existing research work followed by problem identification in Sect. 3. Section 4 discuss about proposed methodology followed by an elaborate discussion of algorithm implementation in Sect. 5. Comparative analysis of the accomplished result is discussed under Sect. 6 followed by conclusion in Sect. 7.

2 Related Work

This section discusses the work being carried in clustering technique in WSN as a continuation of our prior review work [10]. Chidean et al. [11] have presented a clustering mechanism along with network processing methodologies for addressing energy problems in WSN. Addressing energy problems using clustering technique is also seen in the work of Hong et al. [12] where a tree topology has been used to achieve prediction of energy. Currently many researchers are working in the area of Weight based Clustering. The work carried out by Belabed and Bouallegue [13, 14] have presented a clustering mechanism where the sole focus was to select cluster head. The authors have integrated the use of fountain code as well as clustering approach for this purpose. Usage of weighted clustering reported in the work carried out by Kumrawat and Dhawan [15] have presented an optimization technique to enhance network lifetime. Weighted clustering technique is also found integrated with hierarchical approach for solving issues. Studies in that direction have been carried out by Jingxia et al. [16] where the conventional hierarchical routing protocol was found to be integrated with weighted clustering technique. Tripathy and Chinara [17] have carried out investigation of different forms of clustering techniques in WSN. Wang et al. [18] have presented a clustering technique on the basis of received signal strength indicator as well as link quality indicator in WSN. Individual usage of hierarchical clustering mechanism is researched by Liu et al. [19] that performs grouping of the nodes with equivalent characteristics in multihop network. Literatures have also reported usage of multihop clustering as a means for saving the energy dissipation in WSN. Study of Ebadi [20] has presented one such approach that focuses on selection of cluster-head on the basis of residual energy and node degree. The work carried out by Zhang et al. [21] has presented an uneven clustering technique for concentrating on energy problems in heterogeneous nodes. The analysis of the clustering process is carried out by Zeb [22] for designing certain performance metric. It can be seen that there are various types of work being carried out towards clustering techniques where majority of the techniques have only focused on energy problems and very less on data quality. The next section briefly outlines the problem identification of existing system.

3 Problem Description

In order to crisply monitor the data, there are many techniques that use the sensor nodes deployed in the highest number. It also means that increase of node density can offer more data to be aggregated, which will be later on analyzed. Majority of the applications, e.g., habitat monitoring system, forest fire detection, natural calamities detection, etc., use dense network. The biggest issue in such deployment is generation of redundant data owing to overlapping of sensing ranges of the densely populated sensor nodes. Hence, the problems generated that significantly degrade the data quality are as follows:

- Generation of massive redundant data in the network.
- Unwanted consumption of energy to process redundant data leading to faster node death.

4 Proposed Methodology

The proposed system in this stage will implement an algorithm that uses statistical approach to measure the relationship factor among the various forms of node densities (Fig. 1).

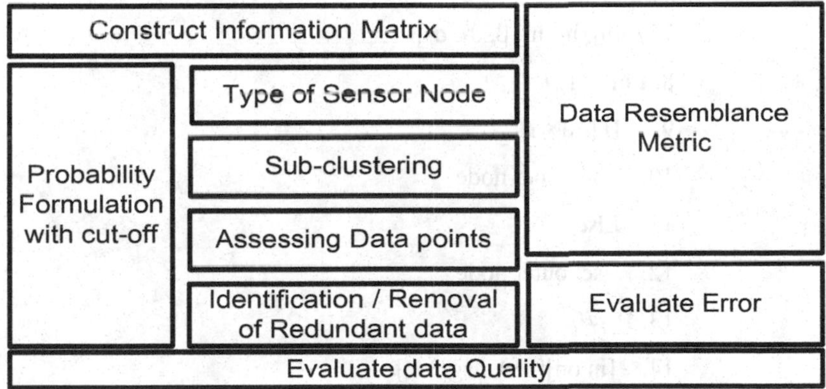

Fig. 1. Tentative schema of statistical approach for DQ enhancement

This paper discusses a novel clustering method, which is mainly responsible for evaluating the type of the sensor node as well as designing the local and global clustering process. The proposed system uses graph theory and probabilistic approach. Unlike the concept of Cluster Head in conventional clustering mechanism, the proposed system will consider selection of a new type of sensor node called as target node. The prime responsibility of the target node is to carry out statistical computation over the node density and forward the information to the base station. The clustering is allowed to be iterated and data quality is checked for each clustering process. The data quality is checked using an error percentage that should represent the relative errors for the aggregated data.

5 Algorithm Implementation

The proposed algorithm mainly targets at introducing a novel clustering technique for the purpose of emphasizing data quality as the consequence of the clustering in WSN. The significant steps of the algorithm are as follows:

Algorithm for Data Quality Resembles Factor

Input: n, r, α, β, S_a, I_{mat}, A, γ

Output:cl

Start

1. init*n*, *r*, α, β

2. $S_a \leftarrow$ rand(x,y)

3. $I_{mat} \rightarrow$ [I-0.5.arb(I)]/max(I)

4. **For** i=1:*n*

5. A=find($d \leq r$)

6. **End**

7. γ=[h_1, h_2, h_3, β, d_1, d_2]

8. **For** j=1:*A*

9. **If** $|\Delta d| \leq \alpha$

10. set inner node

11. **Else**

12. set outer node

13. **If** $\gamma \neq 0$

14. [in on][$n_i \rightarrow$ msg $\rightarrow n_j$]

15. obtain cl $\rightarrow$ unique (in)

16. **End**

End

The above-mentioned algorithm takes the input of *n* (number of nodes), *r* (communication radius), α (cut-off value of data), β (minimum number of sensor node), and S_a (Simulation Area) [Line-1] which after processing yields an output of *cl* (cluster) (Line-15). All the nodes are randomly deployed over the simulation area (Line-2) with a base station positioned at a far distance. The proposed algorithm also introduces *Information Matrix I* for better visualization of the data points in the monitoring area

(Line-3). The next part of the algorithm is to consider all the adjacent nodes that resides within the transmission range R (Line-5). The algorithm introduces a new parameter Data Resemblance Metric DRM γ (Line-7) that is empirically formed as follows:

$$\gamma = o \tag{1}$$

$$\gamma = h_1.\phi + h_2.\phi + h_3.\delta \tag{2}$$

Basically, the formulation of DRM depends on certain quality coefficients h_1, h_2, and h_3 considering the probability theory in which the summation results to maximum value of 1. Similarly, the variable ϕ, φ, and δ correspond to empirical normalization of two different cut-off points α and β. The formulation of DRM also depends on two distance factors d_1 and d_2. These represent Euclidean distance between two data points and mean distance between data possessed by adjacent nodes and matrix respositing aggregated data respectively. The next part of the algorithm performs assessing target and non-target nodes. The target node will mean a node that bears some sort of data that resembles its own neighboring data. The method checks whether the absolute value of distance Δd is less than the cut-off value of α for all the adjacent nodes and similarly it also checks if the nearest value of the similarity matches with the second cut-off value of β (Line-9). Any nodes that are compliant of this condition is considered to be part of a new cluster, i.e., inner nodes (Line-10) and outer nodes are considered to be discarded (Line-12). The outer nodes are then converted to inner node by same clustering process until it covers all the nodes in simulation area. If the DRM value is a non-zero number (Line-13) then all the sensor nodes initiate an intra-cluster communication followed by inter-cluster communication (Line-14). Finally, the system forms a cluster *cl* as the outcome (Line-15). Basically, the algorithm initially computes DRM value which gives a near indication of redundant data for a large scale dense network in WSN. Computation of DRM for a node assists in extracting the information of a node if it carries a lot of redundant information during the clustering process as the value of DRM will increase that of the adjacent node and there will be decrease in d_2, i.e., distance from data matrix to the centroid of data points. DRM will also increase as the value of d minimizes, i.e., mean distance between d_2 and the entire data matrix that is found to reside in the adjacent d_2 matrix. The proposed algorithm also formulates a cut-off value β that also represents minimum number of nodes that are assumed to have represented some of the target nodes. The proposed clustering initially assesses the characteristics of target/non-target nodes and computes DRM. It then formulates sub-clusters based on the outcome of prior steps of DRM calculation. Finally, the algorithm integrates all the sub-clusters in its prior steps to find the node with highest quantity of DRM information retained. This process leads to generation of the clusters with highly reduced number of errors whenever the clustering is carried out. It identifies the resembles factor of data and reformulates it to reduce the value of such similarity of data. The outcome of this algorithm essentially ensures that at any positioning of cluster formation, all the cluster nodes will only forward non-redundant information to the base station by prior interaction with each other (intra-clustering). The complete clustering is carried out using probability theory in order to ensure better inference the outcome.

6 Results Discussion

The implementation of the proposed clustering algorithm is carried out in Matlab considering the simulation area of $1100 \times 1200\ \text{m}^2$ with 100–1000 nodes of 6 m of communication range. The complete analysis is carried out using α value of 0.31 and β value of 2. The proposed algorithm mainly emphasizes achieving superior data quality. Therefore, the study outcome is assessed using error percentage on increased iteration. In order to scale the effectivity of the outcome of study, we compare the study outcome with most frequently used weight-based clustering and hierarchical clustering. For this purpose, we implement the general theoretical concept of this existing algorithm in our designed simulation test-bed retaining similar parameters to carry out comparative analysis. The study outcome is shown in Fig. 2.

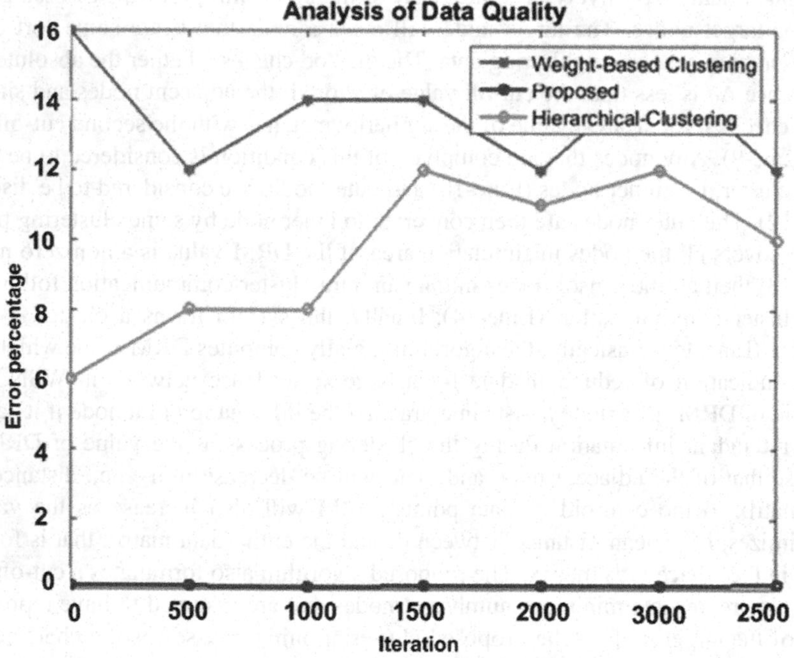

Fig. 2. Comparative analysis of error percentage

From the study outcome, it can be observed that the proposed system offers a significant minimization of the error percentage in redundant data transmission during the data aggregation process. This is the direct outcome of the proposed clustering technique which ensures the minimization of redundant data packet. The weight-based clustering technique fine tunes the clustering process to achieve an overall resource utilization among the sensor nodes. During this process, such algorithm using summation of all the weights are directly dependent on multiple parameters, e.g., distance, mobility, time, energy, etc., in highly iterative manner. This operation causes such algorithm to maintain higher resource utilization but at the cost of overlooking the redundant data information. Therefore, implementing the weight-based protocols in present simulation environment offers highest error percentage, i.e., lower data quality. However, hierarchical routing algorithm offers a good balance between the clustering operation as well as energy efficiency. Majority of the existing variants of the hierarchical clustering protocol offers a different mechanism of selection of cluster-head in such a way that routing performed by this offers energy conservation. Unfortunately, hierarchical routing protocol does not offer indepth-check for presence of redundant data for which the data quality is lowered. Therefore, we put forward a justification that in existing system there are various forms of clustering algorithms. However, a majority of them have not focused on enhancing data quality. The second reason for superior performance of data quality of the proposed system is that the proposed algorithm offers a capability to the sensor node for furnishing enough information about the amount of redundant information it carries within itself using DRM than relative error between the data from DRM matrix. Data from sensor node will be comparatively low compared to any existing clustering protocol in WSN. The third reason behind the highly enhanced data quality of proposed clustering is also the usage of probability theory that allows a node to furnish maximum information pertaining to all forms of data (raw data for member node and fused data for cluster head). The algorithm offers a flexible mechanism to identify the node with increased error percentage and re-establishes the clusters while not affecting the ongoing data communication from other clusters. At the same time, we also find that the proposed system takes approximately 0.654421 s on core-i7 system where the average algorithm processing time of existing clustering approach is found to be 4.3386 s for 3000 iterations.

7 Conclusion

The target of this modeling is to establish a fact that it is feasible to enhance data quality using clustering algorithm as normally clustering techniques are seen as a source to control energy dissipation in sensor nodes. The proposed system uses a probability theory in order to formulate better control over the error minimization problem. Requirement of increased data quality is highly essential for a different range of application in WSN, and hence, a faster response time is also a demand. It is also observed that the proposed system offers comparatively faster algorithm processing time with reduced computational complexity.

References

1. Ibnkahla, M.: Wireless Sensor Networks: A Cognitive Perspective. CRC Press, Boca Raton (2016)
2. Ray, N.K., Turuk, A.K.: Handbook of Research on Advanced Wireless Sensor Network Applications, Protocols. And Architectures. IGI Global, Hershey (2016)
3. Forster, A.: Introduction to Wireless Sensor Networks. Wiley, Hoboken (2016)

4. Khan, S., Pathan, A.S.K., Alraje, N.A.: Wireless Sensor Networks: Current Status and Future Trends. CRC Press, Boca Raton (2016)
5. Ilyas, M., Mahgoub, I.: Smart Dust: Sensor Network Applications. Architecture and Design. CRC Press, Boca Raton (2016)
6. Dobre, C., Xhafa, F.: Pervasive Computing: Next Generation Platforms for Intelligent Data Collection. Morgan Kaufmann, Burlington (2016)
7. Cao, J., Liu, X.: Wireless Sensor Networks For Structural Health Monitoring. Springer, Heidelberg (2016). https://doi.org/10.1007/978-3-319-29034-8
8. Akyildiz, I.F., Vuran, M.C.: Wireless Sensor Networks. Wiley, Hoboken (2010)
9. EL Emary, I.M.M., Ramakrishnan, S.: Wireless Sensor Networks: From Theory to Applications. CRC Press, Boca Raton (2013)
10. Prathiba, B., Sankar, K.J., Sumalatha, V.: Enhancing the data quality in wireless sensor networks — a review. In: 2016 International Conference on Automatic Control and Dynamic Optimization Techniques (ICACDOT), Pune, pp. 448–454 (2016)
11. Chidean, M.I., Morgado, E., Sanromán-Junquera, M., Ramiro-Bargueño, J., Ramos, J., Caamaño, A.J.: Energy efficiency and quality of data reconstruction through data-coupled clustering for self-organized large-scale WSNs. IEEE Sens. J. **16**(12), 5010–5020 (2016)
12. Hong, Z., Wang, R., Li, X.: A clustering-tree topology control based on the energy forecast for heterogeneous wireless sensor networks. IEEE/CAA J. Automatica Sinica. **3**(1), 68–77 (2016)
13. Belabed, F., Bouallegue, R.: Performance evaluation of the optimized weighted clustering algorithm in wireless sensor networks. In: IEEE - 31st International Conference on Advanced Information Networking and Applications Workshops (2017)
14. Belabed, F., Bouallegue, R.: An optimized weight-based clustering algorithm in wireless sensor networks. In: 2016 International Wireless Communications and Mobile Computing Conference (IWCMC), Paphos, pp. 757–762 (2016)
15. Kumrawat, M., Dhawan, M.: Optimizing energy consumption in wireless sensor network through distributed weighted clustering algorithm. In: IEEE International Conference on Computer, Communication and Control (2015)
16. Jingxia, Z., Junjie, C., Xu, Z., Liu, Y.: LEACH-WM: weighted and intra-cluster multi-hop energy-efficient algorithm for wireless sensor networks. In: IEEE - Proceedings of the 35th Chinese Control Conference (2016)
17. Tripathy, A.K., Chinara, S.: Comparison of residual energy-based clustering algorithms for wireless sensor network. Hindawi – Int. Sch. Res. Netw. (2012)
18. Wang, Y., Guardiola, I.G., Wu, X.: RSSI and LQI data clustering techniques to determine the number of nodes in wireless sensor networks. Int. J. Distrib. Sens. Netw. **10**, 380526 (2014)
19. Liu, Z., Xing, W., Wang, Y., Lu, D.: Hierarchical spatial clustering in multihop wireless sensor networks. Int. J. Distrib. Sens. Netw. **9**(11), 528980 (2013)
20. Ebadi, S.: A multihop clustering algorithm for energy saving in wireless sensor networks. Int. Sch. Res. Netw. ISRN Sens. Netw. **2012** (2012)
21. Zhang, Y., Xiong, W., Han, D., Chen, W., Wang, J.: Routing algorithm with uneven clustering for energy heterogeneous wireless sensor networks. J. Sens. **2016** (2016)
22. Zeb, A., Islam, A.K.M.M., Zareei, M.: Clustering analysis in wireless sensor networks: the ambit of performance metrics and schemes taxonomy. Int. J. Distrib. Sens. Netw. **12**(7), 4979142 (2016)

Smart and Innovative Trends in Natural Language Processing

Development of a Micro Hindi Opinion WordNet and Aligning with Hown Ontology for Automatic Recognition of Opinion Words from Hindi Documents

D. Teja Santosh[1], Vikram Sunil Bajaj[2(✉)], and Varun Sunil Bajaj[3]

[1] GITAM (Deemed to be University), Hyderabad, Telangana 502329, India
tejasantoshd@gmail.com

[2] New York University, Brooklyn, NY 11201, USA
vikrambajaj@nyu.edu

[3] Rochester Institute of Technology, Rochester, NY 14623, USA
vsb6444@rit.edu

Abstract. The Indian languages are deprived in terms of accessibility of natural language tools. Especially, the tools for carrying out the particular opinion mining task: opinion word orientation in native language is not available. Reasoning about such natural language words requires a semantically rich lexical resource. When the ontology is aligned with a lexical resource like WordNet, a rich knowledge base is created which can be useful for various information retrieval and natural language processing applications. In order to do this, a micro level Hindi Opinion WordNet is developed and is aligned with the Hindi Opinion WordNet Ontology (HOWN). The opinion lexicon (both Hindi positive and negative words) for 700 Hindi adjectives is also developed. The synset ID values of Hindi opinion synsets are mapped with the synset ID values of corresponding English opinion WordNet synsets. A front end query interface is designed to query the HOWN ontology for opinion word details. This query is transformed into SPARQL format. This task is for automatic recognition of opinionated terms from Hindi documents by the machine.

Keywords: Semantic web · Ontology · Hindi · WordNet · Opinion words SPARQL

1 Introduction

Majority of the data on the World Wide Web is inscribed as natural language text anticipated for humans but complicated for machines to comprehend. Amid the tremendous growth of Internet during the latest years, huge proportions of amorphous texts in many languages and forms are supplemented to the data storehouses on a diurnal way. Through the introduction of Unicode, the indicated trend is pragmatic for texts in Indian languages like Bengali, Hindi and Telugu in the recent years [1]. In general, the aforementioned languages are meagre with reference to accessibility of

P. Bhattacharyya et al. (Eds.): NGCT 2017, CCIS 827, pp. 697–708, 2018.
https://doi.org/10.1007/978-981-10-8657-1_54

absolute corpus, natural language processing tools, and so forth. This has turned out to be a significant area of research in the Indian community.

Over the last two decades, the world is witnessing tremendous growth in Web content of Indian languages. This made people feel comfortable with their native language. Especially, for the last few years there has been an enormous growth in the Hindi content on the web. Hindi is the 4th biggest spoken language in the world. It has 490 million speakers across the world in which the majority of them are from India [2].

In order to process the content in native language towards meaningful information retrieval, the language specific WordNet is required. WordNet [3] has emerged as a great resource for the Natural Language Processing applications for English documents. Following English WordNet, WordNets are built for many languages of the world. Hindi WordNet [4] is the first WordNet built for an Indian language.

Opinionated data in Hindi is essential to be analysed for the use of industries and governments. Automatic reasoning about such natural language documents by the machine requires the support of Hindi WordNet. When such lexical resource is integrated with the concepts of ontology, the automatic identification of opinionated words from Hindi documents happens easily.

This paper is structured as follows: literature survey is described in Sect. 2 and the proposed approach is explained in Sect. 3, the observations from the proposed method is discussed in Sect. 4 and in the end the conclusions and the scope for future work are presented in Sect. 5.

2 Literature Survey

A good amount of research has happened on determining orientations of the opinion words in Hindi language. The development of lexical resources for both traditional information retrieval and Opinion Mining tasks is the first step in this research.

To start with, Chakrabarti et al., developed [4] Hindi WordNet for intelligent information retrieval. This is the first WordNet developed for the Indian language. Inspired from the Vossen work [5], WordNets for other 16 indian languages were built by the same set of researchers from Hindi WordNet.

Das and Bandopadhya developed [6] SentiWordNet for Bengali language. 35,805 Bengali entries were reported from their experiment. Joshi et al., developed [7] Hindi-SentiWordNet (H-SWN) by using English SentiWordNet and English-Hindi WordNet mappings. Bakliwal et al., created [8] Hindi subjective lexicon for Hindi content polarity classification. They developed this lexicon with Hindi adjectives and adverbs and their polarity scores. Mittal et al., improved [9] the H-SWN by adding the missed and inflected Hindi adjectives and adverbs.

The research work on linking of WordNet with ontology is inspired from the motivation of automated reasoning about natural language resources. The benefits of linking WordNet with ontology are multifold [10]. These are: (i) The formal specifications of the ontology are possible to be used with WordNet, (ii) WordNet concepts, when required, be refined and restructured using ontology, (iii) The formal axioms of ontology are possible to be applied with natural language text. This kind of linking must lead to theoretically more precise, cognitively clear and professionally utilizable WordNet in several applications.

Gangemi et al., introduced [11] DOLCE upper-level ontology that orients with the semantic interpretation of WordNet taxonomy. The researchers aligned WordNet's upper level with DOLCE concepts to make WordNet ontologically agreeable. Niles and Pease aligned [12] WordNet with Suggested Upper Merged Ontology (SUMO) to answer the important question of automatically using the ontology by those applications that process natural language text. Bhatt and Bhattacharyya linked [10] IndoWordNet [13], a multilingual WordNet developed on 17 Indian languages by the second researcher of the work with SUMO ontology.

In the above works, the native WordNets are developed for all the four major word categories namely Noun, Adjective, Verb and Adverb. To the best of author's knowledge, these works never concentrated on developing a micro wordnet for interpreting exclusively the Hindi opinion words from the electronic documents as these opinion words express the information regarding the like and dislike of a user on various target entities. Continuous monitoring of likes and dislikes information from the ever updating electronic documents are very useful to the governments in particular for making better governmental decisions. This must occur in an automatic manner as and when the application senses the incoming documents. This is possible to carry out when the WordNet is aligned with the corresponding ontology.

A separate ontology is required to align with the constructs of micro Hindi opinion wordnet as opposed to standard DOLCE and SUMO ontologies. This is because the query execution time is high [14] when these ontologies are used in the alignment process. Also, no sophisticated tools are available for extracting sub ontology [15] from upper merged ontology like SUMO which specifically concentrates on natural language processing tasks. An application that supports querying the knowledge base for uniquely identifying the opinionated terms from the Hindi documents is required.

The main contributions of this work are: developing a micro Hindi opinion wordnet, developing the Hindi opinion lexicon of adjectives using micro Hindi opinion wordnet, developing HOWN ontology, linking micro Hindi opinion wordnet with HOWN ontology and finally querying the HOWN ontology to retrieve the opinion word related details.

3 Development of Micro Hindi Opinion WordNet and Aligning with Hown Ontology

The principal objective of linking micro Hindi opinion wordnet with HOWN ontology is to make the machine automatically recognize the opinion words from the Hindi documents. In order to achieve this goal, a framework is presented in Fig. 1 below.

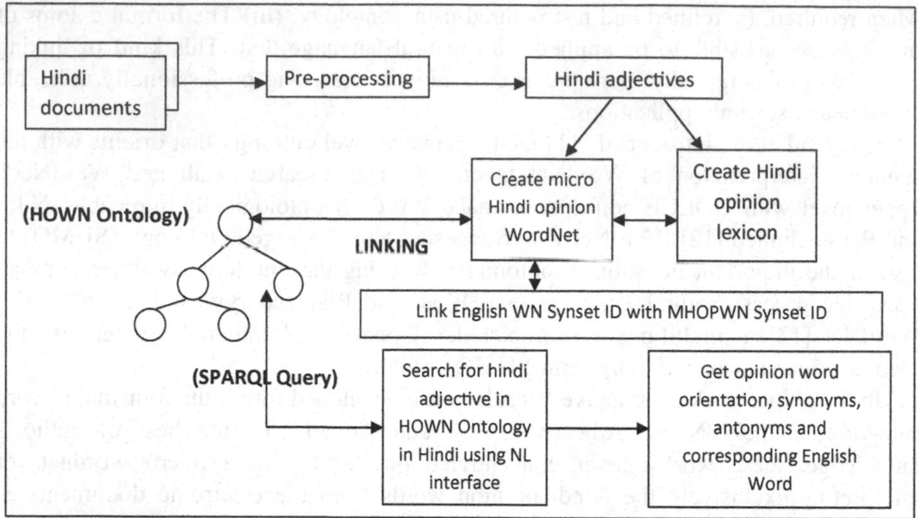

Fig. 1. Micro Hindi opinion WN and HOWN ontology linking and querying

3.1 Description of Dataset

The quality of the HOWN-ed micro Hindi opinion wordnet is understood by the type of dataset which largely impacts the performance of the NLP applications. Hence the accessibility of the datasets when it is not available creation of suitable lexicons is vital for the current work. Preferably for text processing tasks, a lexicon represents real-world data and contains secondary data that allows mining relevant language specific semantic information to create understandable descriptions. Additionally the dataset should be easily accessible for the rationale of performing experiments with nominal human efforts.

As a general rule, a news story is clear and specific and tries to be independent of argot. In general, journalists do not make use of lengthy words where short ones preserve the meaning. They attempt to avoid recurrence of words for the same passage. They use subject-verb-object structure for sentences writing. Words selected by the journalists are normally based on the subject with the aim of stressing important pieces of the news article. News writing joins vocabulary and sentence structure in such a manner that the editorials in the newspaper present the information in terms of relative importance of the anticipated audience.

Abundant online news providers namely BBC Hindi, Dainik Bhaskar, NDTV Khabar and so on furnish Hindi news articles from a wide extent of categories such as politics, business, entertainment, sports, science and technology, etc. The domestic dataset is collected from the BBC Hindi news website [16]. The dataset consists of 900 news articles. The details of the BBC Hindi news dataset is presented in Table 4 under Sect. 4.

3.2 Pre-processing

At the pre-processing stage of the dataset, the document collection is segregated into independent documents at first. Then every document is assayed into consecutive file of words. Then the punctuations, special characters and numbers are removed.

Next, the stop-words are separated from the documents as they rarely assume any meaning. This elimination is based on the stop-word list as furnished by the University of Neuchatel [17]. Further the redundant occurrences from the remaining word set are removed leaving only unique words.

Finally, Part-of-Speech (PoS) tagging is carried out on the stop-words removed words from the document collection. This PoS tagger used to tag the Hindi words is Knowledge Based Computer Systems (KBCS) Hindi Postagger [18]. Only adjectives are considered for building micro Hindi opinion wordnet.

3.3 Creation of Micro Hindi Opinion WordNet (MHOPWN)

The wordNets that are developed for native languages almost follow the design concepts of Princeton WordNet for English although paying particular attention to language specific cases whenever they are surfaced.

The work of creating micro Hindi opinion wordnet is easy as only Hindi adjectives for which both synonyms and antonyms are added. The principles of minimality, coverage and replaceability [13] must and should govern the creation of synsets.

(i) Minimality: The minimum set of associated words that distinctively identifies the meaning is first used to create the synset. For example, in the synset {अच्छा, उत्तम} for the word भला, अच्छा itself is not enough to exclusively denote the concept Good. The inclusion of उत्तम to synset brings out this meaning uniquely.

(ii) Coverage: Next, the synset should contain all the words indicating a particular meaning. The words are written down in the decreasing frequency of their occurrence in the corpus. For example for the word Good, the synset is {अच्छा, उत्तम, ठीक}..

(iii) Replaceability: The words forming the synset should be mutually replaceable in a specific context. For example in the following sentences, अच्छा परिणाम and सुभ परिणाम, अच्छा and सुभ can replace each other.

The synsets for synonyms and antonyms are developed in this manner. Every synset is assigned with a unique synset ID in the alphabetical, ascending order. The purpose of this ID is to uniquely identify a common word classified under different PoS categories. English WordNet version 1.7 has 18,523 synsets [19] under adjective category. The synset IDs of considered 100 synsets (300 positive adjective words, 400 negative adjective words) for the creation of micro Hindi opinion wordnet are mapped with the corresponding English WordNet synset IDs. This mapping helps the people to understand the English equivalent word for the searched Hindi word.

3.4 Hindi Opinion Lexicon of Adjectives Creation Using Micro Hindi Opinion WordNet

The considered positive and negative adjective synset words are arranged in Hindi language dictionary order. The size of the opinion lexicon increases as and when the size of the micro Hindi opinion wordnet increases.

3.5 Development of Hindi Opinion WordNet (HOWN) Ontology

Ontology defines a set of representational basics that are used to model a domain of knowledge or discourse. The representational primitives are usually classes, properties, and relationships among the classes. The definitions of these primitives include information about their meaning and constraints on their logical application [20]. Ontology with a set of individuals of classes constitutes a knowledge base.

The Hindi Opinion WordNet ontology is created for Hindi opinion words, each having a positive or negative opinion. A web interface is built to query the ontology, to return the opinion, synonyms, antonyms and corresponding English word for a given Hindi opinion word.

The HOWN ontology is created using Protege [21], a popular open-source ontology editor. It was created in the OWL syntax. Figure 2 depicts the structure of HOWN ontology in the form of a semantic network. A semantic network is a graph, where the vertices represent classes and the edges represent the relations between these classes. This visualization was created using WebVOWL (Web-based Visualization of Ontologies), a web application for the interactive visualization of ontologies.

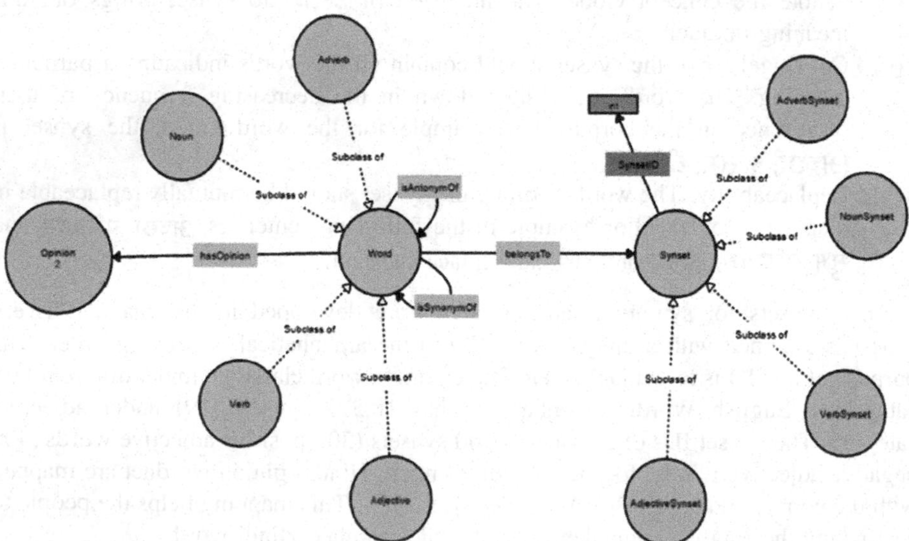

Fig. 2. Semantic network for the Hindi opinion WordNet ontology

Table 1 lists the classes and subclasses present in our ontology, as depicted in Fig. 2. Also shown in Fig. 2 are the object properties and the data properties present in our ontology. These have been listed in Tables 2 and 3 respectively. An object property relates individuals (i.e. instances) of one class to individuals of the same class or to those of another class. A data property, on the other hand, relates individuals of a class to literals (constant values).

Table 1. Classes and subclasses in HOWN ontology

S. No.	HOWN concept	Description
1	Word	Superclass for Adjective, Adverb, Noun and Verb classes
2	Adjective	Subclass of Word; for opinion words that are adjectives
3	Adverb	Subclass of Word; for opinion words that are adverbs
4	Noun	Subclass of Word; for opinion words that are nouns
5	Verb	Subclass of Word; for opinion words that are verbs
6	Synset	Superclass for AdjectiveSynset, AdverbSynset, NounSynset and VerbSynset classes; a synset is a collection of words having the same/similar meaning
7	AdjectiveSynset	Subclass of Synset; for adjective opinion words having the same meaning
8	AdverbSynset	Subclass of Synset; for adverb opinion words having the same meaning
9	NounSynset	Subclass of Synset; for noun opinion words having the same meaning
10	VerbSynset	Subclass of Synset; for verb opinion words having the same meaning
11	Opinion	The opinion of a word; has 2 instances: Positive and Negative

Table 2. Object properties in HOWN ontology

S. No.	Object property	Domain	Range
1	belongsTo	Word	Synset
2	hasOpinion	Word	Opinion
3	isSynonymOf	Word	Word
4	isAntonymOf	Word	Word
5	isEquivalentTo	Word	Word

Table 3. Data properties in HOWN ontology

S. No.	Data property	Domain	Range
1	SynsetID	Synset	Int

3.6 Linking Micro Hindi Opinion WordNet with HOWN Ontology

The linking of micro Hindi opinion wordnet with HOWN ontology occurs by the following way.

(i) getHindiSynsetID: This process returns the synset ID of the searched Hindi opinion word from micro Hindi opinion wordnet.

(ii) mapEnglishSynsetID: This process returns the mapping set of Hindi synset ID and English WordNet synset ID. This provides the English variant of the Hindi opinion word from English WordNet.

(iii) alignHOWNConcept: All the adjectives obtained after PoS tagging are annotated with the HOWN Adjective concept as the instances. Also, the corresponding opinion orientation, synonyms, antonyms and the English Word of the searched Hindi opinion word are also linked with the concept as instances. This overcomes the confusion between concept and instance.

3.7 Querying HOWN Ontology to Retrieve the Opinion Word Related Details

An interface is developed for carrying out the search process on ontology by using PHP library called ARC2. This API supports transforming the end user inputted opinion word in Natural Language into SPARQL query and searches under Adjective concept of HOWN. All the details that are present under the Adjective concept are retrieved and are shown as result. The following SPARQL query is used to extract all the details that are present under the Adjective concept (Fig. 3).

```
SELECT DISTINCT ?hasOpinion ?isSynonymOf ?isAntonymOf ?belongsTo

WHERE  {  {<http://www.vikrambajaj.me/hown/HindiOpinionWordNet.owl#अच्छा>  :hasOpinion ?hasOpinion}

{<http://www.vikrambajaj.me/hown/HindiOpinionWordNet.owl#अच्छा>  :isSynonymOf ?isSynonymOf}

{<http://www.vikrambajaj.me/hown/HindiOpinionWordNet.owl#अच्छा>  :isAntonymOf ?isAntonymOf}

{<http://www.vikrambajaj.me/hown/HindiOpinionWordNet.owl#अच्छा> :belongsTo ?belongsTo}

}
```

Results

hasOpinion	isSynonymOf	isAntonymOf	belongsTo
Positive	भला	बुरा	Good
Positive	भला	ख़राब	Good
Positive	भला	गंदा	Good
Positive	भला	अयोग्य	Good
Positive	ठीक	बुरा	Good
Positive	ठीक	ख़राब	Good

Fig. 3. SPARQL result

Following are the details obtained from HOWN ontology:

(i) getOpinionOrientation: This process returns the opinion word orientation (positive or negative).
(ii) getWordSynonyms: This process returns three synonyms of the searched Hindi opinion word.
(iii) getWordAntonyms: This process returns four antonyms of the searched Hindi opinion word.
(iv) getEnglishWord: This process returns the corresponding English opinion word.

The query interface (http://vikrambajaj.me/hown/) with the end user queried Hindi opinion word and the corresponding details from HOWN are shown in Figs. 4. and 5 below.

Enter a word:

अच्छा

Results:

Opinion: Positive
Synonyms: उत्तम, ठीक, भला
Antonyms: अयोग्य, गंदा, बुरा, ख़राब
Corresponding English Word: Good

Fig. 4. Querying interface upon HOWN ontology - positive opinion word

Enter a word:

बुरा

Results:

Opinion: Negative
Synonyms: अयोग्य, गंदा, ख़राब
Antonyms: अच्छा, उत्तम, ठीक, भला
Corresponding English Word: Bad

Fig. 5. Querying interface upon HOWN ontology - negative opinion word

4 Results and Observations

The Hindi documents obtained from BBC Hindi News website were used for this experiment. Three categories of documents were considered. Table 4 presents the details of the dataset.

Table 4. Hindi documents dataset details

Document features	Values
Number of documents in the corpus	900
Number of categories	3
Number of documents per category	300

Once all the special characters and stop words which does not play any role in the information processing, the words in the document collection are PoS tagged. The sample output of PoS tagged Hindi words is displayed in Fig. 6 below.

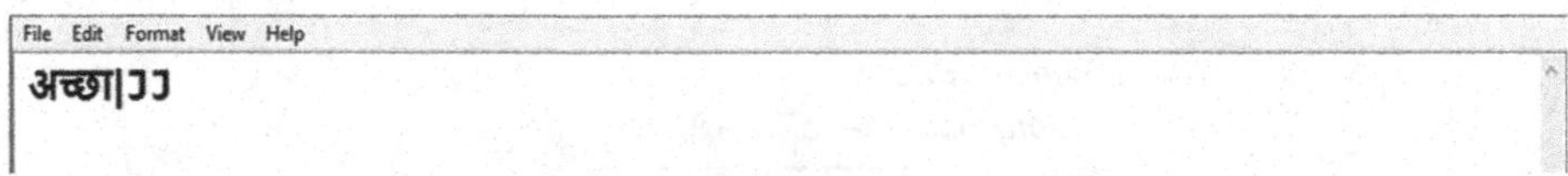

Fig. 6. PoS tagging of the word **"अच्छा"** using knowledge based computer systems Hindi PosTagger

The Hindi opinion lexicon is created with both 300 Positive and 400 Negative adjective words. The sample Hindi opinion lexicon with 16 positive adjective words (http://vikrambajaj.me/hown/positive_words.txt) and 16 negative adjective words (http://vikrambajaj.me/hown/negative_words.txt) are made available. The Micro Hindi Opinion WordNet is created with all the adjectives. Currently, 100 Hindi synsets are linked with their corresponding English synsets and HOWN.

4.1 Inferencing Using SWRL Rues on HOWN

Formal semantics of SUMO can be used for inferencing on natural language text using WordNet. For example, for the two annotated words,

X: "ठीक" and Z: "शुभ" where Z is a new adjective which is searched.

then using WordNet there is no easy way to infer Z from X, as ठीक and शुभ are not related through hypernymy-hyponymy relation. It requires processing gloss or to measure semantic distance to relate these two concepts. However in HOWN, ठीक is related to शुभ by direct objectproperty relation. The relation is word ***isEquivalentTo*** word. The New Adjective is asked to relate with the any one of the relevant instances from HOWN. So inferring Z from X becomes easier. The corresponding SWRL rules that support this inferencing are (Fig. 7);

NewAdjective is belongsTo(?z, ?y) → Adjective(?z)
EquivalentWord is belongsTo(?x, ?y) ∧ Adjective(?z) ∧ belongsTo(?z, ?y) → isEquivalentTo(?x, ?z)

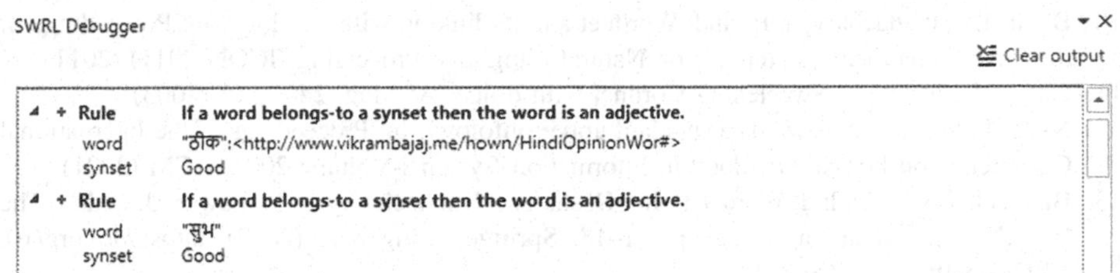

Fig. 7. Inferencing the word PoS category based on its synset

5 Conclusions and Future Work

The linking of Micro Hindi Opinion WordNet with HOWN creates a useful resource for natural language processing applications targeted at Hindi language. The formalism of HOWN ontology can be used with WordNet for various text processing applications. The system is made available through HOWN ontology querying interface that provides WordNet browsing in a more formally agreeable manner. This system can be useful for concept and relation extraction from Hindi language documents.

Future aim is to include nouns, verbs and adverbs words and various lexical relations in and among them with adjectives to create a Micro Hindi WordNet so that the subjective words identified around their targets and the targets themselves are evaluated efficiently.

References

1. Krishnamurthi, K., Panuganti, V.R., Bulusu, V.V.: Understanding document semantics from summaries: a case study on Hindi texts. ACM Trans. Asian Low-Resour. Lang. Inf. Process. (TALLIP) **16**(1), 7 (2016)
2. Sharma, R., Nigam, S., Jain, R.: Opinion mining in Hindi language: a survey. arXiv preprint arXiv:1404.4935 (2014)
3. Fellbaum, C. (ed.): WordNet: An Electronic Lexical Database. MIT Press, Cambridge (1998)
4. Chakrabarty, D., Pande, P., Narayan, D., Bhattacharyya, P.: An experience in building the indowordnet - a wordnet for Hindi. In: International Conference on Global WordNet (GWC02), Mysore, India (2002)
5. Vossen, P.: A Multilingual Database with Lexical Semantic Networks. Kluwer Academic Publishers, Dordrecht (1998)
6. Das, A., Bandyopadhyay, S.: Sentiwordnet for bangla. Knowl. Shar. Event-4: Task **2** (2010)
7. Joshi, A., Balamurali, A.R., Bhattacharyya, P.: A fall-back strategy for sentiment analysis in Hindi: a case study. In: Proceedings of the 8th ICON (2010)

8. Bakliwal, A., Arora, P., Varma, V.: Hindi subjective lexicon: a lexical resource for Hindi polarity classification. In: Proceedings of the Eight International Conference on Language Resources and Evaluation (LREC) (2012)
9. Mittal, N., et al.: Sentiment analysis of Hindi review based on negation and discourse relation. In: Proceedings of International Joint Conference on Natural Language Processing (2013)
10. Bhatt, B., Bhattacharyya, P.: IndoWordnet and its linking with ontology. In: Proceedings of the 9th International Conference on Natural Language Processing (ICON 2011) (2011)
11. Gangemi, A., et al.: Sweetening wordnet with dolce. AI Mag. **24**(3), 13 (2003)
12. Niles, I., Pease, A.: Towards a standard upper ontology. In: Proceedings of the International Conference on Formal Ontology in Information Systems-Volume 2001. ACM (2001)
13. Bhattacharyya, P.: IndoWordNet. In: Dash, N., Bhattacharyya, P., Pawar, J. (eds.) The WordNet in Indian Languages, pp. 1–18. Springer, Singapore (2017). https://doi.org/10.1007/978-981-10-1909-8_1
14. Álvez, J., Lucio, P., Rigau, G.: Improving the competency of first-order ontologies. In: Proceedings of the 8th International Conference on Knowledge Capture. ACM (2015)
15. Xu, B., Kang, D., Lu, J.: A framework of extracting sub-ontology. In: Chi, C.-H., Lam, K.-Y. (eds.) AWCC 2004. LNCS, vol. 3309, pp. 493–498. Springer, Heidelberg (2004). https://doi.org/10.1007/978-3-540-30483-8_61
16. http://www.bbc.co.uk/hindi/
17. http://members.unine.ch/jacques.savoy/clef/hindiST.txt
18. http://kbcs.in/tools.php
19. Baek, S., Cho, M., Kim, P.: Matching colors with KANSEI vocabulary using similarity measure based on WordNet. In: Gervasi, O., Gavrilova, M.L., Kumar, V., Laganà, A., Lee, H.P., Mun, Y., Taniar, D., Tan, C.J.K. (eds.) ICCSA 2005. LNCS, vol. 3480, pp. 37–45. Springer, Heidelberg (2005). https://doi.org/10.1007/11424758_5
20. Gruber, T.R.: Toward principles for the design of ontologies used for knowledge sharing? Int. J. Hum.-Comput. Stud. **43**(5-6), 907–928 (1995)
21. Alani, H., et al.: Using protege for automatic ontology instantiation (2004)

Evaluation and Analysis of Word Embedding Vectors of English Text Using Deep Learning Technique

Jaspreet Singh[1(✉)], Gurvinder Singh[2], Rajinder Singh[1], and Prithvipal Singh[1]

[1] Department of Computer Science, Guru Nanak Dev University, Amritsar, Punjab, India
profjaspreetbatth@gmail.com, prithvipalsingh89@gmail.com, tovirk@yahoo.com

[2] Faculty of Engineering and Technology, Department of Computer Science, Guru Nanak Dev University, Amritsar, Punjab, India
gurvinder4371@gmail.com

Abstract. Word embedding is a process of mapping words into real number vectors. The representation of a word as vector maps uniquely each word to exclusive vector in the vector space of word corpus. The word embedding in natural language processing is gaining popularity these days due to its capability to exploit real world tasks such as syntactic and semantic entailment of text. Syntactic text entailment comprises of tasks like Parts of Speech (POS) tagging, chunking and tokenization whereas semantic text entailment contains tasks such as Named Entity Recognition (NER), Complex Word Identification (CWI), Sentiment classification, community question answering, word analogies and Natural Language Inferences (NLI). This study has explored eight word embedding models used for aforementioned real world tasks and proposed a novice word embedding using deep learning neural networks. The experimentation performed on two freely available datasets of English Wikipedia dump corpus of April, 2017 and pre-processed Wikipedia text8 corpus. The performance of proposed word embedding is validated against the baseline of four traditional word embedding techniques evaluated on the same corpus. The average result of 10 epochs shows the better performance of proposed technique than other word embedding techniques.

Keywords: Word embedding's · Singular Value Decomposition
Skip Gram · Continuous Bag of Words · Global Vector Representation
Deep neural networks

1 Introduction to Word Embeddings

Word embedding is benefiting many Natural Language Processing (NLP) real world tasks these days. The burgeoning field of deep learning is quite remarkable in efficient word representations through vector space modeling. The traditional word embedding techniques include Singular Value Decomposition (SVD), Skip Gram (SG),

P. Bhattacharyya et al. (Eds.): NGCT 2017, CCIS 827, pp. 709–722, 2018.
https://doi.org/10.1007/978-981-10-8657-1_55

Continuous Bag of Words (CBOW), Global Vector representation (GloVe), negative sampling, Log Bilinear Language model (LBL) and Long Short Term Memory (LSTM). These techniques are modeled by Mikolov et al. in 2013 [14] under his project word2vec for vector space modeling of NLP. The motivations of word embedding's from traditional models have pushed researchers to develop fast, easy and low dimensional vector representation of words into vector space model. The contribution of neural networks in word embedding is significant when efficient modeling is in need. The deep learning neural networks are beating state-of-the-art performances with their extreme computational strengths. The mandatory insights needed to be explored from traditional word embedding techniques. The discussion of key aspects of word embedding techniques is described with their brief mathematical modeling in the following sections of this paper.

1.1 Singular Value Decomposition Model (SVD)

SVD is a mathematical technique of decomposing matrix into three sub-matrices. The corpus of words converted into co-occurrence matrix is taken for SVD feed as *an input. Consider a corpus of* 'd'-documents and vocabulary-'v' of words. The SVD maintains a matrix 'M' of corpus of size 'v × d' where C[i, j] introduces association between word 'i' and document 'j'. SVD splits C into three matrices as:

$$M = U\Delta V \tag{1}$$

Where U is 'v × v' matrix, Δ is a diagonal matrix of size 'v × d' and V is 'd × d' matrix. Each row of M determines a word and each column corresponds to a document. Here the diagonal matrix contains singular values corresponding to corpus matrix M in descending order. SVD at its best can be used in word analogy task of NLP through cosine similarity of vectors.

$$Word\_Analogy <x, y> \; = \frac{<x \cdot y>}{|x||y|} \tag{2}$$

Where '*x*' and '*y*' are word vectors.

1.2 Skip Gram (SG)

The SG model is used to predict surrounding words of the context word. Given a context word '*x*' SG model predicts its word vectors of left and right contexts. Consider '*x*' as one-hot vector representation of input word. The embedding word vector for target word of '*x*' will be $v_x = Vx \in \boldsymbol{R}^n$. Where $V \in R^{n\times|V|}$ be an input word matrix. The conditional probability $P(v_x|v;\theta)$ of word v_x from vocabulary v falls under the context θ is found using SG model as softmax function.

$$P(v_x|v;\theta) = \frac{e^{v_x \cdot v}}{\sum_{c\in C} e^{v_x \cdot v}} \tag{3}$$

Where v_x and v are embedding vectors for context and target words and C is the set of all available contexts of word v_x and vocabulary set v with hyper-parameter θ aims to maximize the corpus probability as:

$$\arg\max_\theta \prod\nolimits_{(v_x,v)\in d} P(v_x|v;\theta) \tag{4}$$

Taking logarithm of this product term will switch it to summation; again summation term's goal is to make selection of hyper-parameter θ which further pushes the corpus probability to maximum. i.e.

$$\arg\max_\theta \sum\nolimits_{(v_x,v)\in d} \log P(v_x|v) = \sum\nolimits_{(v_x,v)\in d} \log e^{v_x.v} - \log \sum\nolimits_c e^{v_x.v} \tag{5}$$

1.3 Continuous Bag of Words Model (CBOW)

Another method used for word embedding is CBOW which it takes as an input the left and right contexts of a target word and outputs the target word. CBOW model takes one-hot vectors of input context as $(x_{-m},\ldots\ldots,x_{-1},x_1,\ldots\ldots,x_m)$ of size 'm' of context and each $x_i \in \boldsymbol{R^M}$. Where V is input word matrix. The embedding word vectors for context $v_i = Vx_i$ where $i \in (-m,\ldots\ldots,-1,1,\ldots\ldots,m)$

The general notion of this model is the dot product of similar word vectors as given in Eq. (2) which pushes similar words close to each other in order to maximize the performance of the model. The average of all word embedding vectors is taken to generate the output score vector as $Z = U\hat{v}$ where U is the output word matrix and $\hat{v}$ is the average of 'm' context vectors of target word. The output of CBOW model is word vector $\widehat{y}$ for the target word obtained from softmax function.

$$\widehat{y} = \frac{e^{\widehat{y}}}{\sum_{k=1}^{|V|} e^{\widehat{y_k}}} \tag{6}$$

The classification of target word from left and right context words makes this model for CWI task. The softmax classifier in Eq. (6) determines the appropriate class of target word followed by comparison of target word with output word vector on the basis of loss or distance. The loss or distance measure of output word vector $\widehat{y}$ and y is given by cross entropy. Here $\widehat{y}$ is derived from softmax classifier and y is one-hot word vector embedding of output word vector. The cross entropy is given as:

$$H(\widehat{y},y) = -\sum\nolimits_{j=1}^{|V|} y_i \log(\widehat{y}_i) \tag{7}$$

1.4 Global Vector Representation Based Model (GloVe)

The next effective method for word embedding is GloVe that takes global word-word co-occurrence counts to produce unique word embedding's. Consider X as word-word co-occurrence matrix and X_{ij} gives number of time's word 'j' occurs in the context of word 'i'. Let $X_i = \sum X_{ik}$ represents number of time's word 'k' appears in the context of word 'i'. Then P_{ij} gives probability of word 'j' to occur in the context of word 'i' is:

$$P_{ij} = \frac{X_{ij}}{X_i} \tag{8}$$

The softmax function as given in Eq. (6) is used to compute the probability of occurrence of word v_x in context of word v as given in the SG model:

$$Q_{ij}(v_x|v, \theta) = \frac{e^{v_{xi} \cdot v_j}}{\sum_{c \in C} e^{v_{ci} \cdot v_j}} \tag{9}$$

The global cross entropy loss for this probability distribution is given by:

$$J = -\sum\nolimits_{i \in corpus} \sum\nolimits_{j \in context} X_{ij} \log Q_{ij} \tag{10}$$

The probability values taken from Eqs. (8) and (9) give context word representation in the given corpus. Frequency based word context and word context from softmax classifier need normalization in the corpus. The normalized cross entropy loss found by GloVe using least square objective function of probability distribution P_{ij} and softmax Q_{ij} is:

$$J = \sum\nolimits_{i \in corpus} \sum\nolimits_{j \in context} X_{ij} (\mathrm{P_{ij}} - Q_{ij})^2 \tag{11}$$

1.5 Word to Vector Model (word2vec)

Mikolov et al. in 2013 [14] proposed a new embedding model known as word2vec. This is a neural network based model that produces vector representation of words after learning word embedding's from corpus. The simple architecture of neural networks contains one input layer, one hidden layer to reduce vector dimensions and an output layer to generate word vector representation for surrounding words. The training of each word vector is carried out using neighboring word vectors in the corpus. The goal of this model is to maximize the logarithm of probability for given sequence of words $(v_1, v_2, \ldots\ldots\ldots, v_3)$ is:

$$\frac{1}{N} \sum\nolimits_{i=1}^{N} \sum\nolimits_{j \in nhd(i)} \log P\left(v_j | v_i\right) \tag{12}$$

Where nhd(i) represents the set of neighboring words of word v_i and $P\left(v_j | v_i\right)$ is the standard softmax classifier of word vectors v_i and v_j.

1.6 Long Short Term Memory Based Model (LSTM)

The LSTM is another famous model introduced by Hochreiter and Schmidhuber in 1997 [32]. This model is used to generate word embeddings as it can process word vectors on a time step and filtration of words. LSTM decides the hidden state of word vector using two general functions:

$$h_t = q_\theta(x_t, M_{t-1}) \quad (13)$$

$$= f_\emptyset(g_\theta(x_t M_{t-1}) M_{t-1}) \quad (14)$$

Where $\emptyset$ and θ are parameters of state machine and M_{t-1} represents memory cell at previous time step (t − 1) i.e. $M_{t-1} = h_{t-1}$, q_θ determines present state of word vector while g_θ computes map of previous hidden state and currently encountered word vector. Recently in [10] LSTM model is utilized on simple Recurrent Neural Network (RNN) where hidden state is given by:

$$h(t) = \emptyset(Vh_{t-1} + Wx_t + b + h_{t-1}) \quad (15)$$

where $\emptyset$ is identity function as $\emptyset(x) = x$, x_t is input word vector at time t, V and W are weight matrices initialized with small weights, h_{t-1} is previous hidden state, b is bias vector and h_t represents current hidden state of word vector in LSTM modeling.

1.7 Log Bilinear Language Model (LBL)

Another most scalable language model is LBL model that can be trained on large datasets of vocabulary. Only word vectors are utilized in LBL instead of word matrices, thus reducing the cost of matrix multiplication. LBL uses two vector embedding's like other models, one embedding vector for target word and one for context word. The prediction function f(n) for target word is computed by taking linear combination of context vectors as:

$$f(n) = \sum\nolimits_{i=1}^{n} c_i . v_{xi} \quad (16)$$

For given sequence of context words $cw = x_1, x_2, \ldots\ldots\ldots\ldots, x_n$. Where x_i is the weight vector of ith context word and '.' denotes linear multiplication of corresponding vectors (context word vector and weight vector). The similarity between predicted word embedding's for word x_i can be calculated using the score function:

$$S_\theta(x, cw) = f(n)^T v_{xi} + b_{xi} \quad (17)$$

Where b_{xi} is the bias vector of ith context word vector x_i.

1.8 Negative Sampling (NS)

Another SG based word embedding model is Negative Sampling that describes its objective function with two probability distributions. One probability function finds maximum chances of occurrence of word and its context being present in corpus and other function gives chances of non-occurrence of word and its context. i.e.

$$\theta = arg\max_{\theta} \prod\nolimits_{(v_{x_i},c)\in D} P(D=1/v_x,c,\theta).\prod\nolimits_{(v_{x_i},c)\in \bar{D}} P(D=0/v_x,c,\theta) \quad (18)$$

Using sigmoid activation function and taking logarithm will turn product terms into summation terms:

$$\theta = arg\max_{\theta} \sum\nolimits_{(v_{x_i},c)\in D} \log\frac{1}{1+e^{-v_x^T v_c}}.\sum\nolimits_{(v_{x_i},c)\in \bar{D}} \log\frac{1}{1+e^{v_x^T v_c}} \quad (19)$$

Here D is the set of documents and $\bar{D}$ is the negative corpus containing un-natural sentences like "Horse music fish stock is eating table hamburger". These un-natural sentences have got low probability of words occurring in them. The negative corpus $\bar{D}$ can be generated through randomly sampling negative from main corpus of words.

2 Related Work

Existing work carries out evaluation of word embedding's in natural language processing from scratch by Collobert et al. in 2011 [1, 6, 8, 11]. Nayak et al. in 2016 [1] have used word embedding's for six real world tasks as POS, Chunking, NER, Sentiment Analysis, Question Answering and NLI. They have used SVD as a baseline word embedding and the evaluation metrics taken were accuracy and F1 score. The observed improvement of aggregation of all six tasks was reported as 1% on the baseline word embedding.

Word embedding was widely used for lexical substitution and distribution of word similarities by Levy et al. in 2015 [1, 2, 12–15, 17, 19]. They have utilized SG model for context substitution in lexical entailment of text and word2vec model for word similarity task proposed by Levy et al. in 2016. The representation of words into vectors as word2vec tool was introduced by Mikolov et al. in 2013 [1, 2, 5–8, 14]. The improvement in results from state-of-the-art was found significant by Levy et al. in 2016. They have derived Mikolov et al.'s SG and Negative Sampling models from word2vec word embedding method [3, 18, 20, 21] in 2014. Yoav Goldberg has analyzed vector space modeling of SVD model and introduced the Eckart Young's Theorem in mathematical modeling of SVD in 2014 [4]. Kusner et al. in 2015 introduced document distance concept by proposing a new parameter of word mover's distance by taking the inspiration from vector space modeling of word embedding [5, 22]. They have utilized traditional Bag of Words (BOW) and Term Frequency inverse Document Frequency (TFIDF) methods for representing sentences as documents [11, 12].

Stratos et al. in 2016 demonstrated Canonical Correlation Analysis (CCA) on count Metrics to perform model based word embedding [6]. They have exploited word2vec, SVD and GloVe word embedding's with CCA [13]. The work including CCA has also been extended in NER task of NLP in [6, 11]. Another latest word embedding technique using LBL model was proposed by Mnih et al. from Deep-Mind technologies in

2014. They have performed noise contrastive estimation on word embedding's and compared the accuracy obtained from LBL with standard SG and CBOW embedding models [7, 14]. Levy and Goldberg in 2015 have generalized SG and Negative Sampling word embedding's by introducing dependency based context vectors [16]. They have proposed dependency based modeling of word-context pairs by exploiting CBOW approach [3, 8, 21, 24–26]. The proposed word2vec model with dependency based contexts are tested on two windows sizes (k = 3 and k = 5). Their results showed similar recall-precision curves as that of state-of-the-art embedding's. Another work on word embedding's includes the latest contribution of Rao and Spasojevic in 2017. They have configured neural networks with LSTM and applied it on a word embedding tasks [9, 23]. The contribution of this work was taken and evaluated by Erik Cambria for real world task of Sentiment Analysis of social media [27]. They have proposed a new metric of actionability to classify social media messages as they are actionable or not for the product owners and companies to lift up their quality standards. Introduction and fusion of LSTM, deep learning and neural networks has significantly changed the computational power of word embedding's [28–31].

Recently Ororbia et al. 2017 tested CBOW and LSTM models on deep learning neural network with differential state framework for word embedding's [10, 32–35]. They have tested the proposed model using Penn Treebank and IMDB datasets. The proposed Delta-RNN showed similar or better performance in terms of accuracy than complex-RNN models for word embedding's.

In this paper, the four traditional word embedding techniques (SVD, SG, CBOW and GloVe) have been duplicated and proposed another word embedding using deep learning neural network. The next sections will enlist datasets, architecture of proposed model, pseudo code and experimental results. The final section will conclude this work along with the future direction.

3 Architecture of Proposed Model

The architecture of proposed model for deep learning neural network is designed for evaluation and validation of word embedding's as shown in Fig. 1 below. The pre-processed dataset after splitting is being provided to the traditional embedding methods and generation of baseline accuracy scores is collected. Deep neural network containing one input layer, one hidden, one max pooling layer and an output layer is configured in a Python 3.5 using tensorflow, scipy, bs4, keras, theano, sklearn, pandas and nltk libraries [13]. The Deep Neural Network (DNN) is trained with the pre-processed training set. The input of proposed DNN based model is processed document D with word sequence w1, w2,……… wn. The output of this model gives sentiment class of document.

Let us define $CL(w_i)$ be the left context and $CR(w_i)$ be right context around word (w_i). The left context matrix and right context matrix of word w_i is calculated as:

$$CL(w_i) = f\left(W^{(l)} CL(w_{i-1}) + W^{(sl)} e(w_{i-1})\right) \tag{20}$$

$$CR(w_i) = f\left(W^{(r)} CR(w_{i+1}) + W^{(sr)} e(w_{i+1})\right) \tag{21}$$

Where $e(w_{i-1})$ and $e(w_{i+1})$ are word embeddings of previous words on the left and right side of the target word wi respectively. W(l) and W(r) are the matrices mappings of contextual hidden layer to the next hidden layer in convolution neural networks respectively. W(sl) and W(sr) are matrices used to compute semantics of target word with words on the respective left and right contexts. DNN finds all $CL(w_i)$'s in forward pass and all $CR(w_i)$'s in the backward pass of text scan. So the fixed window of word embeddings is given by vector xi for the word w_i.

$$x_i = [CL(w_i) : e(w_i) : CR(w_i)] \tag{22}$$

DNN uses tanh activation function to this vector x_i followed by linear transformation of neural networks to pass the result to the next hidden layer in DNN.

$$y_i^{(2)} = \tanh\left(W^{(2)} x_i + b^{(2)}\right) \tag{23}$$

$y_i^{(2)}$ is calculated for the whole set of word vectors inputted to the input layer of DNN. It gives semantic vector representation of text. In feature representation layer i.e. max pooling layer, the max of $y_i^{(2)}$'s is taken as:

$$y^{(3)} = \max_{1 \le i \le n} y_i^{(2)} \tag{24}$$

Finally the output layer of proposed architecture computes the linear transformation again to obtain the final latent semantic representation vector of text.

$$y^{(4)} = W^{(4)} y^{(3)} + b^{(4)} \tag{25}$$

The validation of word embedding vectors is done using cosine similarity function given in Eq. (2) above in Sect. 1. In the last stage the softmax probabilities are used for validation of class of text.

$$P_i = \frac{\exp(y_i^{(4)})}{\sum_{k=1}^{n} \exp(y_k^{(4)})} \tag{26}$$

In our case the value of k = 3. This softmax function with higher probability for a class k is taken and corresponding text is classified in the respective class.

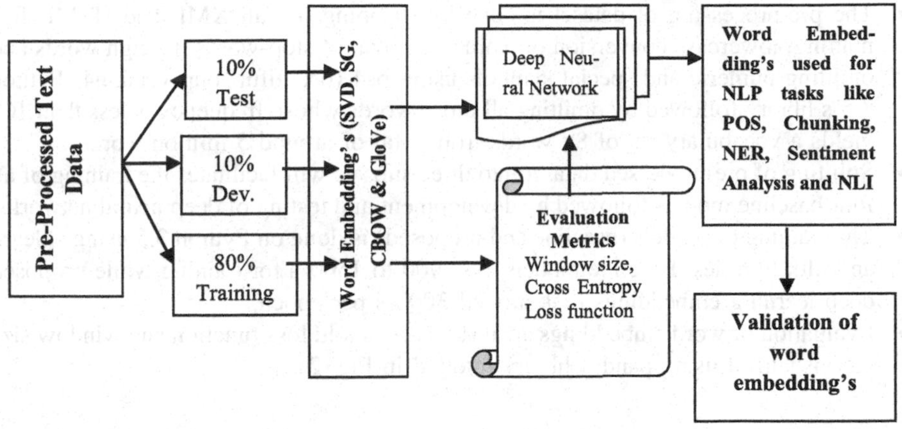

Fig. 1. Architecture of word embedding's evaluated using Deep Learning

4 Pseudo Code of Proposed Model

1. Pre-process raw web text using bs4 library of python to extract a vocabulary set.
2. Split dataset into three subsets in the ratio 80:10:10 as (Training: Dev.: Test) sets.
3. Train a model using training subset with SVD, SG, CBOW and GloVe for baseline results and with deep learning neural network based model for validation.
4. Evaluate the word embedding's on Dev. subset and obtain the loss function given in Eq. (7) above.
5. Evaluate and test word embedding's against the threshold loss $H(\widehat{y}, y) \leq 4.605$. If the value exceeds then go to Step3 for retraining using increased window size by value 2.
6. Stop when $H(\widehat{y}, y) \leq 4.605$ *or* Window-size = 10

The complexity of proposed model depends on four main factors including size of raw web text, size of vocabulary set, window size and cross entropy function given in Eq. (7). The processing time of proposed model shows the rising trend with an increase in window size. The complexity function of proposed model is taken as: O(size of input pickle file + size of vocabulary set + window size + cross entropy loss function)

5 Experimental Setup and Datasets

We have utilized two freely available datasets for the experimentation work. One is April 2017 dump of English Wikipedia[1] and second is Text8[2] containing compressed Wikipedia text. Text8 is already preprocessed and compressed from 100 MB to 29 MB text file whereas the first dataset is in raw text form and needs to be pre-processed.

---

[1] The dataset is freely available at https://dumps.wikimedia.org/enwiki/20170401/.

[2] The cleaned, truncated and compressed version of file9 of Wikipedia text using 25 compressors is available at http://mattmahoney.net/dc/text8.zip.

- The pre-processing of dataset is done by stripping out all XML and HTML formatting, lowercase conversion of words, removal of stop-words, foreign words and omitting numeric and special symbols using bs4 (beautiful-soup version4) Python 3.5's library followed by omitting all those words whose frequency is less than 100 yields a vocabulary set of 8k words from total of around 5 million words.
- Splitting of pre-processed dataset into three subsets will facilitates the training of all four baseline models followed by development and testing of deep neural networks.
- The training of models (baseline and proposed) is done on Python 3.5 using sklearn and nltk libraries. Baseline models took 900 to 1500 s for training while proposed deep learning embeddings took around 3000 s per epoch.
- Evaluation of word embeddings against the threshold loss function and window size are visualized using pandas library (plotted in Fig. 2).

6 Results and Discussions

The training of word embedding models is done first followed by the storage of pickle files on local machine to evaluate models on dev. and testing subsets. The average result of accuracies of 10 epochs of SVD, SG, CBOW, GloVe and DNN models are obtained in the Table 1 below. It is observed that with the increase in window size, the accuracy of word embedding rises. The proposed model with DNN also shows significant hike over state-of-the-art accuracies of other four models under investigation. The results clearly indicates that the rise of accuracy from GloVe to Proposed DNN is nearly 13% when window size ws = 3 as well as for ws = 5.

Table 1. Accuracies of models with different window sizes (ws = 3, 5, 7 & 10). Size of pickle files are obtained after training five word embedding models.

Model	Size of pickle file (in KB)	Accuracy (%age) for ws = 3	Accuracy (%age) for ws = 5	Accuracy (%age) for ws = 7	Accuracy (%age) for ws = 10
English Wikipedia April 2017's test Set					
SVD	3.42	40.24	56.92	67.43	79.42
SG	4.18	45.38	56.95	68.71	80.90
CBOW	4.22	46.42	57.64	67.60	82.29
GloVe	6.38	53.04	57.17	61.60	83.26
Proposed DNN	7.76	66.78	70.01	71.51	88.31
Text8's Test Set					
SVD	53.67	46.23	50.41	62.81	72.20
SG	56.43	55.86	65.47	67.30	66.86
CBOW	57.12	59.69	64.52	68.24	68.87
GloVe	60.32	52.92	55.78	59.44	78.12
Proposed DNN	64.78	62.75	63.46	70.38	84.28

The ANOVA of results produced from five models is performed and the average mean value of proposed model is found at significant level of 0.05. Further post hoc Scheffe test of multiple comparisons is applied on it, which depicts that proposed DNN model is significant at ws = 5. SVD, CBOW and GloVe are found similar for at

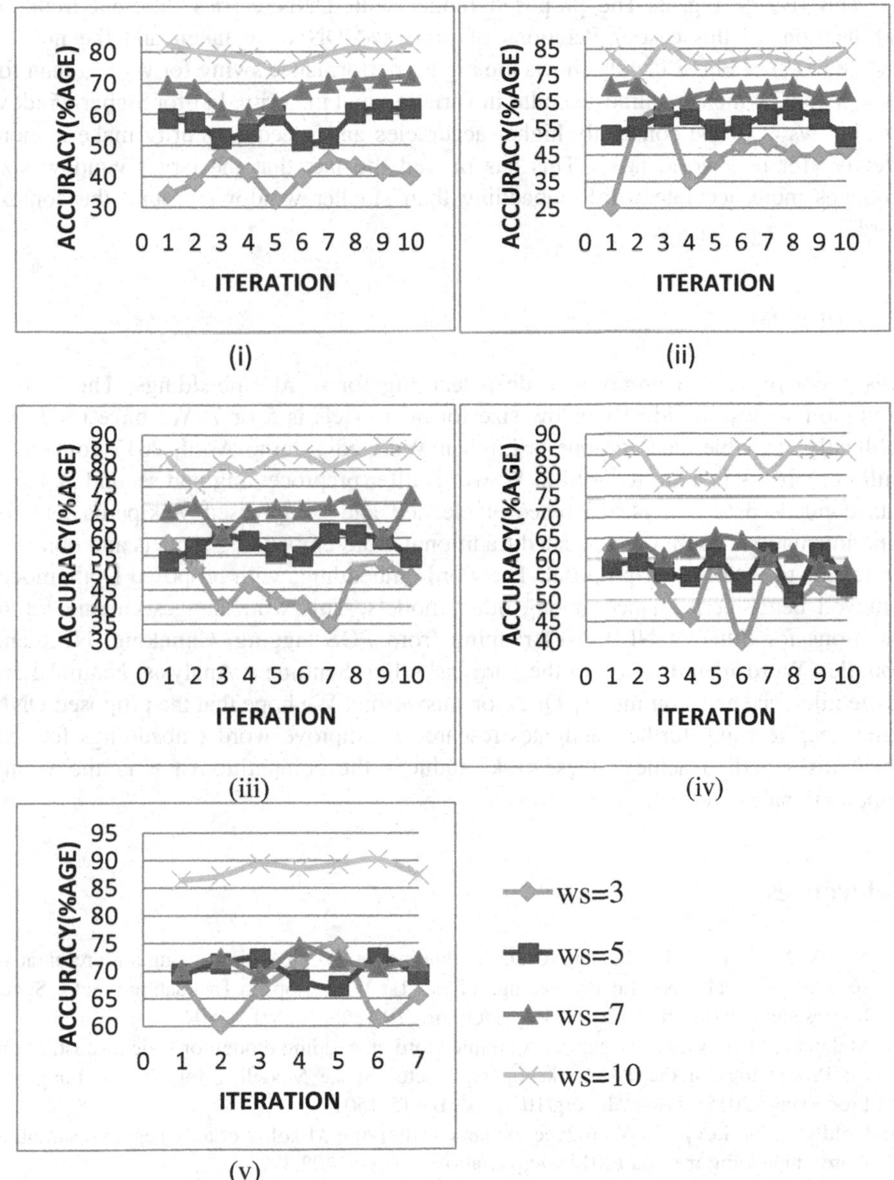

Fig. 2. Results of 10 epochs with accuracies (i)-SVD, (ii)-SG, (iii)-CBOW, (iv)-GloVe and (v)-Proposed DNN

window size 3 while Proposed DNN and SG seems to be equivalent in performance for higher window sizes ws = 7 and 10. The comparison of accuracies with number of epochs shows that SVD and SG models have lower performances in the initial runs and training stabilizes after 7 epochs (as shown in (i) and (ii) of figure-2 below) whereas in CBOW and GloVe the initial iterations shows remarkably good accuracies, after a dip during first 7 iterations and models stabilize to nearly average performance levels in (iii) and (iv) of Fig. 2. The proposed model with DNN carries different trend of stabilization. In this case 7 iterations of proposed DNN are taken and the noticed change in (v) of Fig. 2 clearly shows the higher performance swing for ws = 3 than for ws = 5 and 7 which are almost similar in variation and maturity, but for higher window size i.e. ws = 10 the constantly higher accuracies and speedy maturity make it more effective for real world tasks. This has proved the fact that the larger window size produces more accurate word embedding than smaller windows around the context word.

7 Conclusion

This paper presents a proposal of deep learning for word embeddings. The experimentation shows that ideal window size for all models is 5 or 7. We have used two publically available datasets; one is English Wikipedia dump April, 2017 contains 5 million words which are reduced to 8k words after preprocessing and second is Text8 data condensed to 31,344,016 bytes of cleaned and compressed Wikipedia text for experimentation. We have duplicated traditional word embedding models and obtained the results to validate our proposal. The word embeddings with proposed DNN model achieved better performance among other models. This work suggests many future directions for different NLP tasks ranging from POS tagging, Chunking, NER and Complex Word Identification to the hard tasks like Sentiment Analysis, Natural Language inference and Community Question answering. We hope that the proposed DNN using deep learning further facilitates research to improve word embeddings for real world tasks and to achieve these tasks induces the competition among the young computational linguists.

References

1. Nayak, N., Angeli, G., Manning, C.D.: Evaluating word embeddings using a representative suite of practical tasks. In: Proceedings of the 1st Workshop on Evaluating Vector-Space Representations for NLP (2016). https://doi.org/10.18653/v1/w16-2504
2. Melamud, O., Levy, O., Dagan, I.: A simple word embedding model for lexical substitution. In: Proceedings of the 1st Workshop on Vector Space Modeling for Natural Language Processing (2015). https://doi.org/10.3115/v1/w15-1501
3. Goldberg, Y., Levy, O.: Word2vec explained: deriving Mikolov et al.'s negative sampling word embedding method (2014). https://arxiv.org/abs/1402.3722
4. Goldberg, Y.: A Note on Latent Semantic Analysis (2014)

5. Kusner, M.J., Sun, Y., Kolkin, N.I., Weinberger, K.: From word embeddings to document distances. In: Proceedings of the 32nd International Conference on International Conference on Machine Learning, ICML 2015, vol. 37, pp. 957–966 (2015). http://dl.acm.org/citation.cfm?id=3045221
6. Stratos, K., Collins, M., Hsu, D.: Model-based word embeddings from decompositions of count matrices. In: Proceedings of the 53rd Annual Meeting of the Association for Computational Linguistics and the 7th International Joint Conference on Natural Language Processing, vol. 1 (2015). https://doi.org/10.3115/v1/p15-1124
7. Mnih, A., Kavukcuoglu, K.: Learning word embeddings efficiently with noise-contrastive estimation. In: Burges, C.J.C., Bottou, L., Welling, M., Ghahramani, Z., Weinberger, K.Q. (eds.) Proceedings of the 26th International Conference on Neural Information Processing Systems (NIPS 2013), pp. 2265–2273. Curran Associates Inc. (2013)
8. Levy, O., Goldberg, Y.: Dependency-based word embeddings. In: Proceedings of the 52nd Annual Meeting of the Association for Computational Linguistics, vol. 2 (2014). https://doi.org/10.3115/v1/p14-2050
9. Spasojevic, N., Rao, A.: Identifying actionable messages on social media. In: IEEE International Conference on Big Data (2015). https://doi.org/10.1109/bigdata.2015.7364016
10. Ororbia II, A.G., Mikolov, T., Reitter, D.: Learning simpler language models with the differential state framework (2017). https://arxiv.org/abs/1703.08864
11. Collobert, R., Weston, J., Bottou, L., Karlen, M., Kavukcuoglu, K., Kuksa, P.: Natural language processing (almost) from scratch (2011). https://arxiv.org/abs/1103.0398
12. Levy, O., Goldberg, Y., Dagan, I.: Improving distributional similarity with lessons learned from word embeddings. TACL Trans. Assoc. Comput. Linguist. **3**, 211–225 (2015)
13. Manning, C.D., Surdeanu, M., Bauer, J., Finkel, J., Bethard, S.J., McClosky, D.: The Stanford Core NLP Natural Language Processing Toolkit (2014). https://nlp.stanford.edu/pubs/StanfordCoreNlp2014.pdf
14. Mikolov, T., Chen, K., Corrado, G., Dean, J.: Efficient estimation of word representations in vector space (2013). https://arxiv.org/abs/1301.3781
15. Huang, E.H., Socher, R., Manning, C.D., Ng, A.Y.: Improving word representations via global context and multiple word prototypes. In: ACL 2012 Proceedings of the 50th Annual Meeting of the Association for Computational Linguistics: Long Papers, vol. 1, pp. 873–882 (2012)
16. Levy, O., Goldberg, Y.: Dependency-based word embeddings. In: Proceedings of the 52nd Annual Meeting of the Association for Computational Linguistics, pp. 302–308 (2014)
17. Thater, S., Furstenau, H., Pinkal, M.: Word meaning in context: a simple and effective vector model. In: Proceedings of the 5th International Joint Conference on Natural Language Processing, pp. 1134–1143 (2011)
18. Petterson, J., Smola, A., Caetano, T., Buntine, W., Narayanamurthy, S.: Word Features for Latent Dirichlet Allocation (2010)
19. Parker, R., Graff, D., Kong, J., Chen, K., Maeda, K.: English Gigaword Fifth Edition (2011). ISBN 1-58563-581-2
20. Sanders, N.J.: Twitter Sentiment Corpus, Sanders Analytics LLC (2011). http://www.sananalytics.com/lab/twitter-sentiment/
21. Ratinov, L., Bengio, Y., Turian, J.: Word representations: a simple and general method for semi-supervised learning. In: Proceedings of the 48th Annual Meeting of the Association for Computational Linguistics, pp. 384–394 (2010)
22. Le, Q., Mikolov, T.: Distributed representations of sentences and documents. In: Proceedings of the 31st International Conference on Machine Learning (2014)
23. Levy, O., Goldberg, Y.: Neural word embedding as implicit matrix factorization. In: Advances in Neural Information Processing Systems 27 (2014)

24. Bullinaria, J.A., Levy, J.P.: Extracting semantic representations from word co-occurrence statistics: a computational study. Behav. Res. Methods **39**(3), 510–526 (2007)
25. Ritter, A., Etzioni, M.O.: A latent dirichlet allocation method for selectional preferences. In: Proceedings of the 48th Annual Meeting of the Association for Computational Linguistics, pp. 424–434 (2010)
26. Turney, P.D., Pantel, P.: From frequency to meaning: vector space models of semantics. J. Artif. Intell. Res. (2010). https://arxiv.org/abs/1003.1141
27. Cambria, E.: Affective computing and sentiment analysis. IEEE Intell. Syst. **31**(2), 102–107 (2016). https://doi.org/10.1109/mis.2016.31
28. Glorot, X., Bordes, A., Bengio, Y.: Domain adaptation for large-scale sentiment classification: a deep learning approach. In: Proceedings of the 28th International Conference on Machine Learning, Bellevue, WA, USA (2011)
29. Hochreiter, S.: Long short-term memory. Neural Comput. **9**(8), 1735–1780 (1997)
30. Kim, Y.: Convolutional neural networks for sentence classification. In: Proceedings of the 2014 Conference on Empirical Methods in Natural Language Processing (EMNLP), pp. 1746–1751. Association for Computational Linguistics (2014)
31. Zhang, X., LeCun, Y.: Text Understanding from Scratch (2015). https://arxiv.org/abs/1502.01710
32. Hochreiter, S., Schmidhuber, J.: LSTM Can Solve Hard Log Time Lag Problems (1997)
33. Jernite, Y., Grave, E., Joulin, A., Mikolov, T.: Variable Computation in Recurrent Neural Networks (2016). https://arxiv.org/abs/1611.06188
34. Maas, A.L., Daly, R.E., Pham, P.T., Huang, D., Ng, A.Y.: Learning word vectors for sentiment analysis. In: Proceeding HLT 2011 Proceedings of the 49th Annual Meeting of the Association for Computational Linguistics: Human Language Technologies, vol. 1, pp. 142–150 (2011). ISBN 978-1-932432-87-9
35. Turian, J., Bergstra, J., Bengio, Y.: Quadratic features and deep architectures for chunking. In: Proceedings of NAACL HLT 2009, pp. 245–248, Boulder, Colorado, June 2009

POS Tagging of Hindi Language Using Hybrid Approach

Nidhi Mishra and Simpal Jain(✉)

Poornima University, Jaipur, India
simplejain.4@gmail.com

Abstract. Natural language processing (NLP) is the process of extracting meaningful information from natural language. Part of speech (POS) tagging is considered as the one of the important tool for Natural language processing. Part of speech is a process of assigning a tag to every word in the sentences as a particular part of speech such as Noun, pronoun, adjective, verb, adverb, preposition, conjunction etc. Hindi is a natural language so there is a need to perform natural language processing on Hindi sentence. So this paper present pos tagging of Hindi Language using Hybrid Approach. First we tagged the Hindi words with the help of WordNet dictionary which consists of around 1 lakh unique class category of words like Noun, verb, adjective, and adverb. But still, many words are not tagged so we used Rule-based approach to assign a tag to untagged words. We use HMM model as a statistical approach to remove ambiguity. We evaluated our system over a corpus of 1000 sentences and 15000 words with 7 different standard part of speech tags for Hindi We achieved an accuracy of 92%.

Keywords: Hidden Markov model · POS tagging · Hindi WordNet NLP · Rules · Hybrid

1 Introduction

Natural language processing is a broad area of computer science and artificial intelligence. Part of speech is a very important application for NLP. A sentence is made of words which play their different part in the framework of the sentence. Words can broadly be classified on the basis of the part they play or work they do in a sentence. These are called the Parts of Speech (POS) which are a noun, conjunction, adjective, adverb, preposition, pronoun, verb, etc. Ambiguity across POS categories is a big challenge in Part of Speech where a word has got multiple tags in the pos categories. For example "आम" can be treated as noun or adjective. Hindi POST is the process of identifying the lexical category of the Hindi word existing in a sentence [3]. Part of Speech tagging can be done using many techniques i.e. Rule-based, stochastic (or Statistical) and Hybrid.

P. Bhattacharyya et al. (Eds.): NGCT 2017, CCIS 827, pp. 723–735, 2018.
https://doi.org/10.1007/978-981-10-8657-1_56

Natural Languages are ambiguous in nature. At a different level of Natural language processing (NLP) task ambiguity appears. Multiple parts of speech tags are taken by many words. The correct Tag depends on the context [4].

For Example:

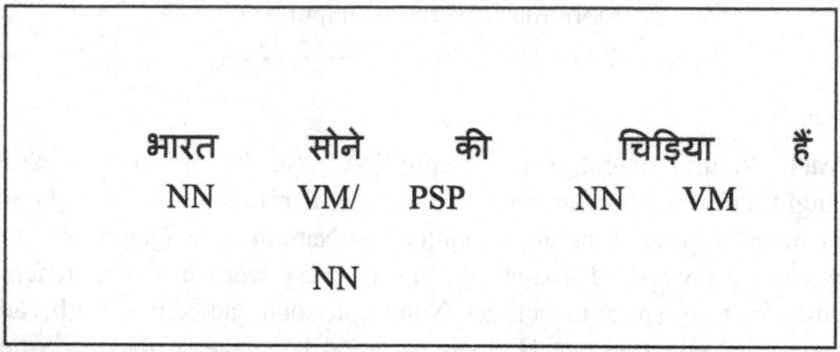

Fig. 1. POS ambiguity of a Hindi sentence with seven basic tags

In Fig. 1 the word "सोने" can be a verb or can be a Noun. So we used HMM as statistical approach to remove Ambiguity. In this paper we present POS tagging of Hindi language. First we browse Hindi corpus and split them into sentences using delimiter (?, |, !). We have selected one sentence then tokenize that sentence into words using space delimiter. We have used Hindi WordNet dictionary to tag the each word. After that we applied rule base approach to tag untagged words. We have also applied statistical approach to remove ambiguity.

The rest of the paper is organized as follows: Sect. 2 presents the literature review of the proposed work. Section 3 includes the architecture of the proposed work. Section 4 describes the methodology which is used for the proposed work. Section 5 describes the flow graph and algorithm of the proposed work. In Sect. 6 we evaluate the result. Section 7 concludes the proposed work.

2 Literature Survey

Many types of research are carried out in POS tagging for Hindi languages. There have many implementations using Rule-Based approach, Statistical approach and Hybrid Approach. Hybrid approach provides higher accuracy compared to rule-based and statistical. Mishra and Mishra developed a POS tagger tool that can assign a tag to every Hindi word occurring in the Hindi sentence as a particular part of speech such as Noun, Pronoun, Verb, Adjective etc. The system implemented a Hindi corpus of 4 lines, 7 sentences, and 68 words. It splits the corpus into the sentences a/c to the delimiter. It displays the tag structure and corresponding sentence in a grid according to tag pattern [1]. Rathod and Govilkar discussed different POS tagging Techniques for Indian regional language. They discussed Rule-based, statistical and hybrid approach [2]. Mohnot et al. proposed a Hybrid approach for Part Of Speech tagger for the Hindi language which enters a Hindi input text and tokenizes Hindi corpus. It uses Hindi WorldNet dictionary and assigns a tag to every word occurring in the sentences. If there is a word which is not tagged using Hindi WordNet then it applied the rule-based approach to tag all words. It also handles ambiguity problem using hybrid approach The accuracy achieved by the system was 89.9% [3]. Joshi et al. developed a Part Of speech tagger based on hidden Markov model and also used IL Pos tag set. It disambiguated correct word tag combination using contextual information available in the text. The accuracy achieved by the system was 92.13% [4]. Garg et al. developed a rule-based Hindi part of speech tagger.It assigns a tag to a word a/c to the corresponding tag and applied different rules to tag unknown words and display the tagged data. The accuracy achieved by the system was 87.55 [5]. Dwivedi and Malakar proposed a hybrid approach based POS tagger for Hindi language. It has collected 500 Hindi sentences and analysis them [7]. Sinha et al. proposed POS tagging for Nepali language. In this Author used Nepali corpus which contains 15430 words. The achieved accuracy was 93.15% [6]. Antony et al. discussed different POS tagging Approaches for Indian Language. This paper discussed various developments of POS tagger. It also presented a review of POS tag set for Indian language. This paper concludes that almost all existing POS tagger for Indian language are based on statistical approach and hybrid approach [8]. Mall and Jaiswal the paper proposed four different algorithms. Author Implement 300 Hindi sentences. First is tokenize algorithm the Hindi paragraph and apply some rules. Accuracy label is 92.4%. Second algorithm is conversion algorithm translated the Hindi word into English transliteration word. Accuracy label is 95.7%. Third algorithm is for POS Tagging. Accuracy label is 95.5%. Forth algorithm is translation algorithm convert the grammatical tag word into English Tagging. Accuracy label is 95.5%. Forth algorithm is translation algorithm convert the grammatical tag word into English translation by using with Hindi to English dictionary. Accuracy label is 96.7% [9]. Gupta et al. developed an Urdu POS tagger. Author have used two stochastic approaches CRF and HMM to tag Urdu sentences. The author has used Urdu POS tagset, designed by TDIL. Author has used a corpus of 70,000 sentences. The system has achieved 83.37% accuracy for CRF approach and 81.07% accuracy for HMM model [10]. Yuan proposed Hidden family model which is a statistical approach and is an improvement over the Hidden Markov model. Hidden family model increased performance compared to HMM model i.e. The precision increased from 94.642% to 96.214% [11].

3 Architecture of Proposed POS Tagger

See Fig. 2.

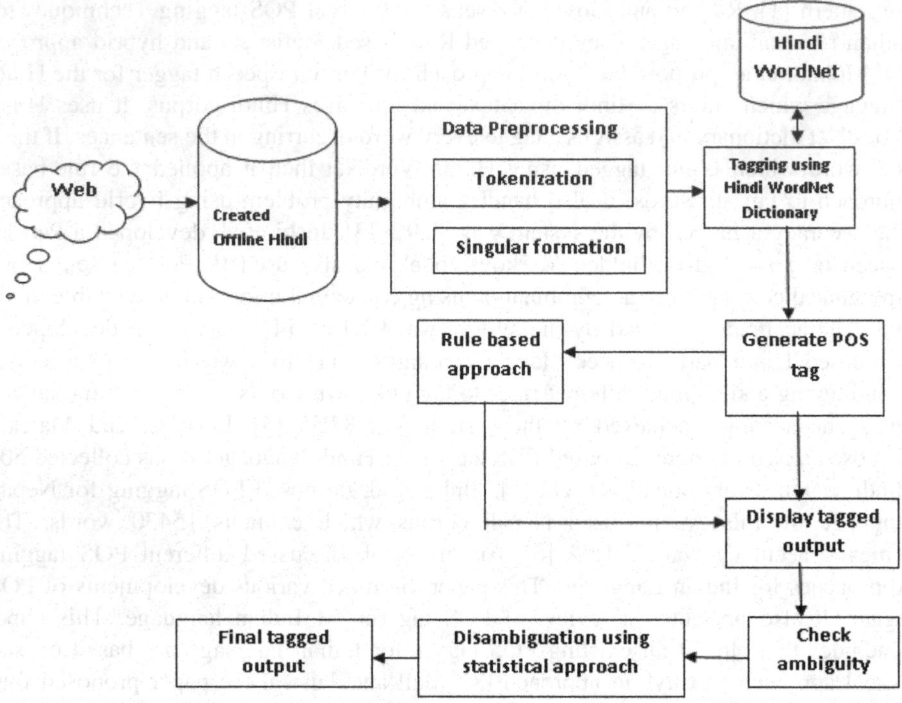

Fig. 2. Architecture of the proposed POS tagging system

4 Methodology

In the proposed work we have taken Hindi sentences in a text file. And the each sentence of the text file is tokenized into words and the whole sentence is tagged. We have created a GUI (Graphical User Interface) in which the Hindi data set is selected and tokenized into sentences. After this, the selected sentence is tokenized into words and then tagged using a hybrid approach. In this process following steps are performed as:

4.1 Offline Corpus Creation

We collect 1000 sentences, 15000 words from the social media and create a Hindi corpus. These are related to short stories, history, news, and essay.

4.2 Data Preprocessing

After collecting the Hindi sentences, pre-processing is done before POS tagging like tokenization, the singular formation is done.

4.2.1 Tokenization

Tokenization is done at two levels:

- **Sentence level tokenization:** First we browse Hindi corpus then we tokenize the corpus into sentences using delimiter like |, ?, !.
- **Word level tokenization:** After sentence level tokenization we tokenize the sentence into words using space delimiter (" ").

4.2.2 Singular Formation

If any Hindi word is in plural form then we convert them into a singular form. Following rules are applied for plural to singular formation (Table 1):

Table 1. Rules for singular formation

Singular formation Rules	Input	Output
Rule 1: If current word ends with "एं" then we convert them to "अ" to make the word singular	आइऐ जानते है दलिली में हुऐ इस उलटफेर की कुछ वजहें ।	आइऐ जानते है दलिली में हुऐ इस उलटफेर की कुछ वजह ।
Rule 2: If current word ends with "ओं" then we convert them to "अ" to make the word singular	आमलोगों का गुस्सा केंद्रसरकार के खलिाफ शीला सरकार को झेलना पडा	आमलोग का गुस्सा केंद्रसरकार के खलिाफ शीला सरकार को झेलना पडा
Rule 3: If a current word ends with "एँ" then we remove" एँ" from the Hindi word to make the word singular	वस्तुएँ इधर उधर नहीं रखनी चाहिए ।	वस्तु इधर उधर नहीं रखनी चाहिए ।

4.3 Tagging with the Help of Hindi WordNet Dictionary

The Hindi WordNet contains the following category of words- Noun, Verb, Adjective and Adverb. In proposed work, we tag the Hindi words with the help of Hindi WordNet dictionary.

4.4 Rule-Based Approach

Hindi WordNet dictionary tagged all words but there is some word for which Hindi WordNet dictionary does not assign any tag. So for tagging other words, we used Rule-based approach. Rule-based pos tagger applies a set of Handwritten rules to resolve the tag Ambiguity. Rules are written on the basis of next and previous tags. It also uses contextual information to assign tags to words in rule-based tagging. It needs expressive rules and requires a good knowledge of grammar-related rules. We used six rules in our proposed work which are shown in below Table 2:

Table 2. Handwritten Rules for Hindi POS tagging

Handwritten rules	Input	Output
Rule 1: If the present word is Postposition (PSP) then there will be a high probability that next word is Noun (NN)	अंकेश ने खाना खाया |	अंकेश**<NN>** ने**<PSP>** खाना<VM> खाया<VM> | <PUNC>
Rule 2: If the present word is an adjective (Adj) Then there will be a high probability that next word is Noun (NN)	सीता को कच्चा आम पसंद हैं |	सीता<NN> को **<PSP>**कच्चा**<ADJ>** आम **<NN>**पसंद <VM>हैं<VM> | <PUNC>
Rule 3: If a current word ends with तर (tar), तम (tam) postfix then the token is tagged as an adjective	हाथी वशिालतम जानवर है |	हाथी<elephant>वशिालतम**<Adj>**जानवर < Noun >है<Verb> | <punc>
Rule 4: If the current token is not tagged and next token tagged as an auxiliary verb, then there is a high probability that current token will be the main verb	मै और आप एक ही घर में रहते है |	मै <pron>और <conj>आप <pron>एक <Adj>ही <Noun>घर <Noun>में <ppp>रहते है **<verb>** | **<punc>**
Rule 5: If the current word is मैं, आप, इसका, इसकी, यह, वह, etc then we tagged them as a pronoun	मै और आप एक ही घर में रहते है |	मै **<pron>**और <conj>आप **<pron>**एक <Adj>ही <Noun>घर <Noun>में <ppp>रहते है <verb> | <punc>
Rule 6: if the current word is और, तथा, क्यूकिं, बल्कि etc. then we tagged them as a conjunction	मै और आप एक ही घर में रहते है |	मै <pron>और **<conj>**आप <pron>एक <Adj>ही <Noun>घर <Noun>में <ppp>रहते है <verb> | <punc>

4.5 Disambiguation Using Statistical Approach as HMM

A word can have more than one grammatical POS categories based on the context where it is used. So disambiguation is necessary to resolve the ambiguity. Disambiguation selects a possible sequence of lexemes by the use of Hidden Markov Model. Natural Languages are ambiguous in nature. At a different level of Natural language processing (NLP) task ambiguity appears multiple parts of speech tags are taken by many words. The correct Tag depends on the context. For example (Table 3):

Table 3. Sample of ambiguity

Input	Tagged output
भारत सोने की चड़िया है	भारत <Noun> सोने **<verb>** सोने **<Noun>** की <Postpos> चड़िया <Noun> है <verb>

In above table "सोने" can be a noun or verb. So we developed a POS tagger for Hindi using Hidden Markov Model (HMM) to remove ambiguity.

4.5.1 Hidden Markov Model

A POS tagger based on HMM assigns the best tag to a word by calculating the forward and backward probabilities of tags along with the sequence provided as an input.

4.5.2 Steps for HMM Model

Step 1: Input the tagged sentence which has tagged using Hindi WordNet dictionary and a rule-based approach.
Step 2: Check if any word in the tagged sentence has multiple categories or not. If two POS are assigned to a single word then remove ambiguity using step 3 to 5.
Step 2.1. Else go to step 6.
Step 3: Select the first POS tag for that ambiguous word and find out the transition probability which is estimated based on previous tags and future tags. We used following equation:

$$\mathbf{P(ti/wi) = P(ti/ti - 1) \cdot P(ti + ti/1) \cdot P(wi/ti)} \tag{1}$$

where P(ti/ti − 1) is the probability of current tag given the previous tag. P(ti + 1/ti) is the probability of future tag given current tag. P(wi/ti) is the probability of a word given current tag.

$$\mathbf{P(ti/ti - 1)} = \frac{\boldsymbol{freq(ti - 1, ti)}}{\boldsymbol{freq(ti - 1)}} \tag{2}$$

$$\mathbf{P(ti + ti/1)} = \frac{\boldsymbol{freq(ti, ti + 1)}}{\boldsymbol{freq(ti)}} \tag{3}$$

$$\mathbf{P(wi/ti)} = \frac{\boldsymbol{freq(ti, wi)}}{\boldsymbol{freq(ti)}} \tag{4}$$

Step 4: Now consider the second tag for that word and find out the transition probability with respect to the second tag using the Eq 1 to 4.
Step 5: Compare the transition probability of both tag.
Step 5.1. If first tag transition probability is greater than second tag transition probability then the first tag is assigned to word and go to step 6.
Step 5.2. Else the second tag is assigned to word and go to step 6.
Step 6: Display tagged sentence with the appropriate tag.

4.5.3 Working of HMM

HMM is used to remove ambiguity. Working of HMM can be understood with the help of example which is shown as in below table:

Calculation:

Case 1: When VM assigned to "सोने"

Case 2: NN assigned to "सोने"

So from the Figs. 3 and 4, we conclude that the computation p2 (ti/wi) > p1 (ti/wi) so "सोने" will be Noun.

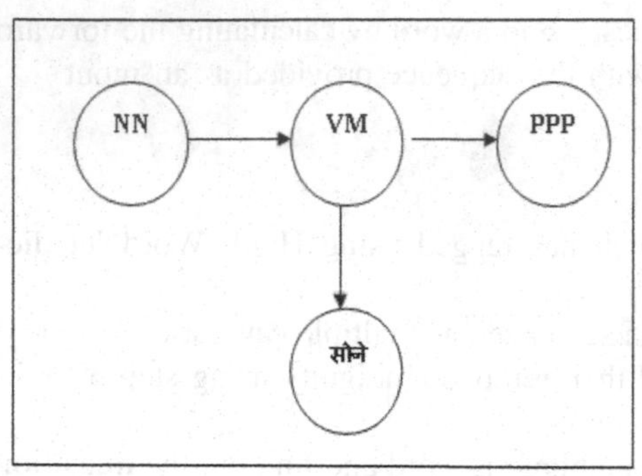

$$P\,(ti/ti\text{-}1) = \frac{freq(ti-1,ti)}{freq(ti-1)}$$

So P (VM/NN) = 2/2 =1

P (ti+1/ti) = ½

P (wi/ti) = ½

P1(ti/wi) = 1*1/2*1/2 = .25

Fig. 3. Transition probability of "सोने" with Verb as a Tag

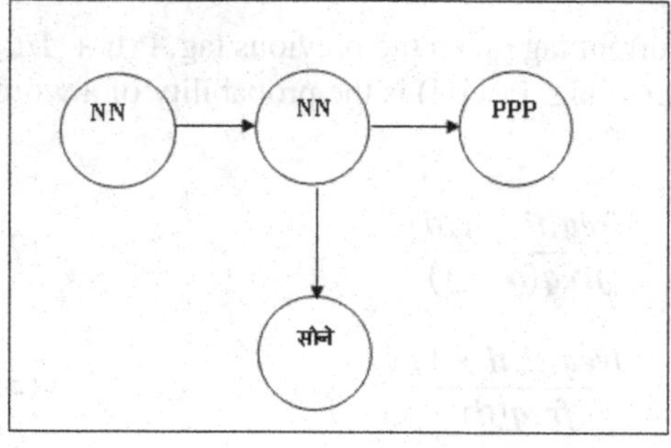

$$P\,(ti/ti\text{-}1) = \frac{freq(ti-1,ti)}{freq(ti-1)}$$

So P (VM/NN) = 1/3 =.6666

P (ti+1/ti) = 1/3 =.6666

P (wi/ti) = 1/3=.66666

So p2 (ti/wi) = .30076

Fig. 4. Transition probability of "सोने" with Noun as tag

4.6 Tag Generation

This is the final phase of the POS tagger. Tag generator generates the appropriate tag based on tokenization. In Figs. 3 and 4 transition probability of "सोने" with Verb as a Tag is less then transition probability of "सोने" with noun as a Tag. So "सोने" will be Noun which is shown in below table (Table 4).

Table 4. Tagged sentence after removing ambiguity using HMM

Input	Tagged output
भारत सोने की चड़िया है	भारत <Noun> सोने **<Noun>** की <Postpos> चड़िया <Noun> है <verb>

5 Flowchart for the POS Tagging of Hindi Corpus Using Hybrid Approach

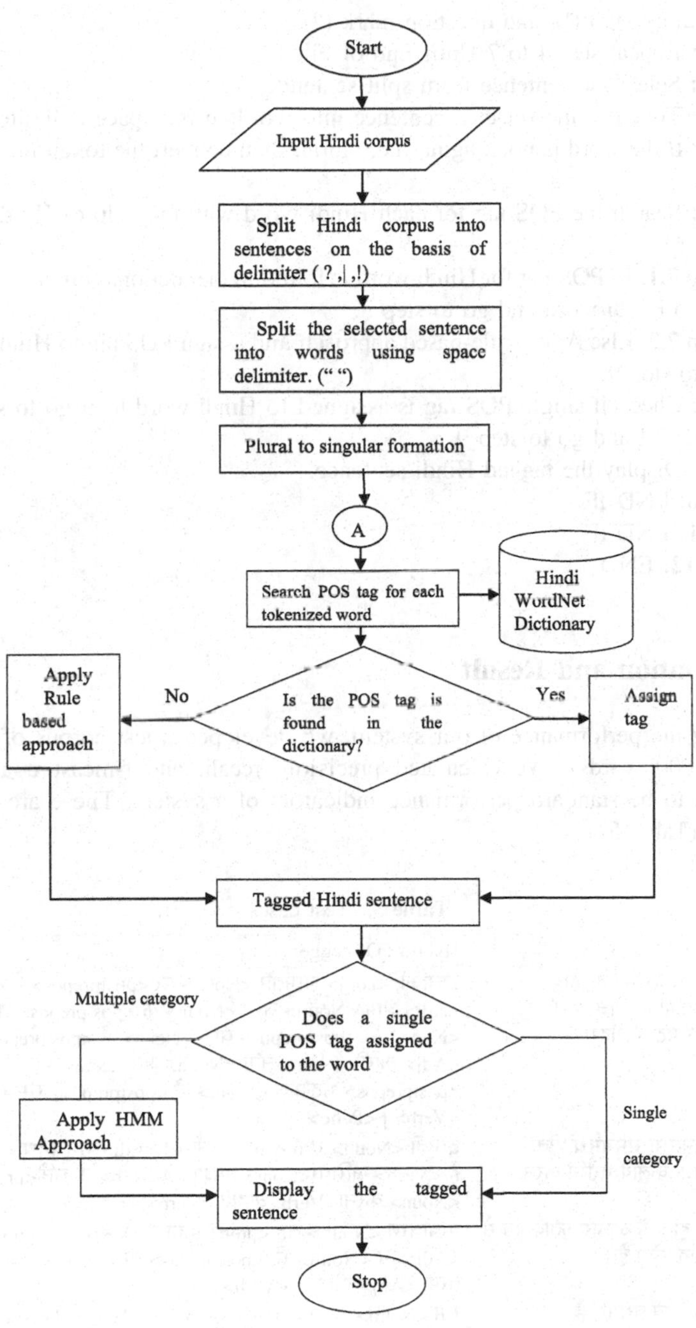

Algorithm:

Step 1: Input Hindi corpus.
Step 2: Split the Hindi corpus into Hindi sentences using delimiter like full stop (|), exclamatory sign (!), and question mark (?).
Step 3: Repeat step 4 to 7 Until End of File.
Step 4: Select the sentence from split sentences.
Step 5: Tokenize the selected sentence into words using space delimiter (" ").
Step 6: If the word is not singular i.e. plural, then convert the token into a singular form.
Step 7: Search the POS tag for each Hindi word with the help of Hindi WordNet dictionary.
  Step 7.1. IF POS tag for Hindi word is found in the dictionary then assign a POS tag to Hindi word and go to step 8.
  Step 7.2. Else Apply rule-based approach and assign POS tag to Hindi word and go to step 9.
Step 8: Check if single POS tag is assigned to Hindi word then go to step 9, else apply HMM and go to step 9.
Step 9: Display the tagged Hindi sentence.
Step 10: END IF
Step 11: END IF
STEP 12: END

6 Evaluation and Result

For testing the performance of our system, we developed a test corpus of 1000 sentences (15000 words). We calculated precision, recall, and f-measure as they are considered to be standard performance indicators of a system. These are defined as following (Table 5):-

Table 5. Test cases

Sentences	Hybrid POS tagger
हालांकि, आमतौर पर ये एक आयु वर्ग के व्यक्तियों के बीच में बिना किसी लिंग और पद के भेदभाव के संभव है |	हालांकि, <conj> आमतौर <Noun> पर <postprepos> ये <pron> एक <Adj> आयु <Noun> वर्ग <Noun> के <postprepos> व्यक्तियों <Noun> के <postprepos> बीच <Noun> में <postprepos> बिना <Adj> किसी <Noun>लिंग <Noun> और <conj> पद <Noun> के <postprepos> भेदभाव <Noun> के <postprepos> संभव है <Verb> | <Punc>
दोस्ती एक अन्तरंग सम्बन्ध होता है जिसपर हमेशा केलिये भरोसा करना चाहिए |	दोस्ती <Noun> एक <Adj> अन्तरंग <Adj> सम्बन्ध <Noun> होता है <Verb> जिसपर<Conj> हमेशा <Adverb> के लिये<prepos >भरोसा <Noun> करना<Verb>चाहिए <Verb> | <Punc>
पर्यावरण वह होता है जो प्राकृतिक रूप से, हमारे चारों तरफ होता है |	पर्यावरण <Noun> वह <pron> होता है <Verb> जो<pron> प्राकृतिक <Adj> रूप <Noun> से, <postprepos> हमारे <pron> चारों <Noun> तरफ <Adj> होता है <Verb>
राम को कच्चा सेब पसन्द है |	राम <Noun> को <postprepos> कच्चा <Adj> सेब <Noun> पसन्द है <Verb> | <Punc>

Precision: precision is defined as the ratio of a number of correct tags assigned to the total number of a tag assigned.

$$\text{Precision} = \frac{\text{Number of correct tags assigned}}{\text{total number of tag assigned}}$$

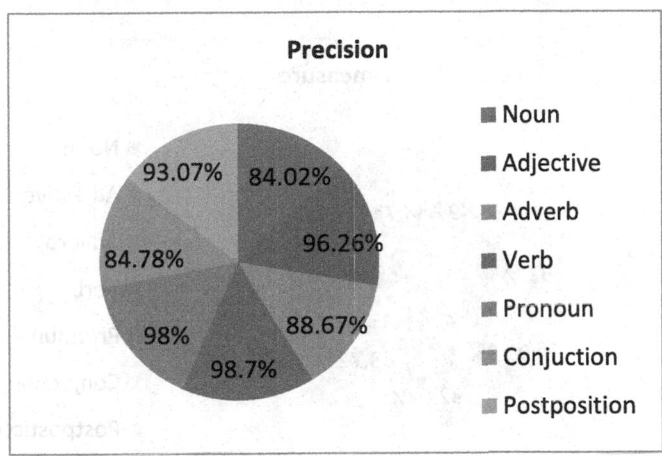

Recall: recall is defined as the ratio of a number of a correct tag assigned to the total number of tag in the annotated test corpus.

$$\text{Recall} = \frac{\text{Number of correct tags assigned}}{\text{total number of tag in the annotated test corpus}}$$

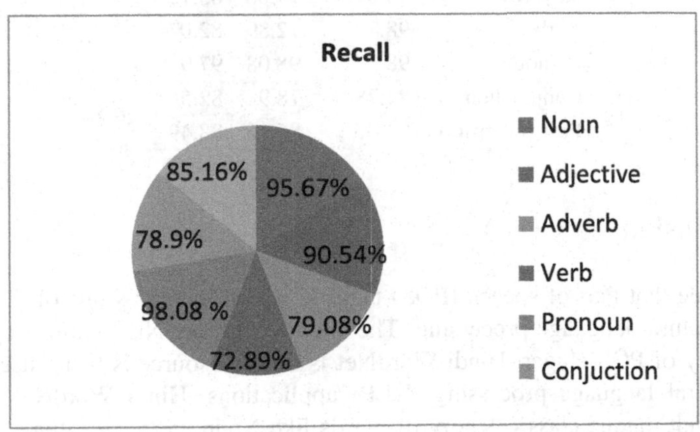

F-measure: F-measure is calculated as a weighted average of precision and Recall. It combines Precision and recall by calculating harmonic mean of precision and recall (Table 6).

$$\text{F-measure} = \frac{2RP}{R+P}$$

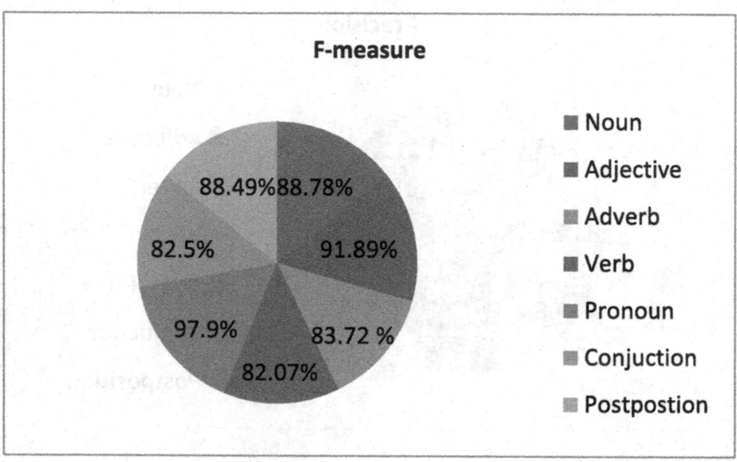

Table 6. Precision, recall and f-measure of each POS tag

Tags	Precision	Recall	F-measure
Noun	84.02	95.67	88.78
Adjective	96.26	90.54	91.89
Adverb	88.67	79.08	83.72
Verb	98.7	72.89	82.07
Pronoun	98	98.08	97.9
Conjunction	84.78	78.9	82.5
Post preposition	93.07	85.16	88.49

7 Conclusion

We conclude that Part of speech (POS) tagging is considered as one of the important tools for Natural language processing. The accuracy of any NLP tool is dependent on the accuracy of POS tagger. Hindi WordNet is a rich resource is being used by many Hindi Natural language processing (NLP) applications. Hindi WordNet consists of around 1 lakh unique class category of words like Noun, verb, adjective, and adverb. But still, many words are not tagged so we use Rule-based approach to assign a tag to all words and use context rules to disambiguate stochastic based approach assigns the most likely tag to a word based on then-set values frequency in a corpus. Hybrid based tagging is a combination of the two approaches. We presented a POS tagger of Hindi Language using a hybrid approach. We evaluated our system over a corpus of 1000 sentences and 15000 words with 7 different standard part of speech tags for Hindi We achieved an accuracy of 92%.

References

1. Mishra, N., Mishra, A.: Part of speech tagging for Hindi corpus. In: International Conference on Communication Systems and Network Technologies, Katra, Jammu, pp. 554–558 (2011)
2. Rathod, S., Govilkar, S.: Survey of various POS tagging techniques for Indian regional languages. Int. J. Comput. Sci. Inf. Technol. **34**(8) (2015)
3. Mohnot, K., Bansal, N., Singh, S.P., Kumar, A.: Hybrid approach for part of speech tagger for the Hindi language. Int. J. Comput. Technol. Electron. Eng. (IJCTEE), **4**(1) (2014)
4. Joshi, N., Darbari, H., Mathur, I.: HMM-based POS tagger for Hindi. In: Proceedings of International Conference Artificial Intelligence, Soft Computing, CS & IT Proceedings, vol. 3, no. 6 (2013)
5. Garg, N., Goyal, V., Preet, S.: Rule based Hindi part of speech tagger. In: Proceedings of Coling, Mumbai, India, pp. 163–174 (2012)
6. Sinha, P., Veyie, N.M., Purkayastha, B.S.: Enhancing the performance of part of Speech tagging of Nepali language through hybrid approach. Int. J. Emerg. Technol. Adv. Eng. **5**(5) (2015)
7. Dwivedi, P.K., Malakar, P.K.: Hybrid approach based POS tagger for Hindi language. Int. J. Emerg. Technol. Adv. Eng. 63–68 (2015)
8. Antony, P.J., Soman, K.P.: Parts of speech tagging for Indian languages: a literature survey (0975 – 8887). Int. J. Comput. Appl. **34**(8), 22–29 (2011)
9. Mall, S., Jaiswal, U.C.: Innovative algorithms for parts of speech tagging in Hindi-English machine translation language. In: 2015 International Conference on Green Computing and Internet of Things (ICGCIoT), Noida, pp. 709–714 (2015)
10. Gupta, V., Joshi, N., Mathur, I.: POS tagger for Urdu using Stochastic approaches. In: International Conference on Information and Communication Technology for Competitive Strategies (2016)
11. Yuan, L.C.: Improvement for the automatic part-of-speech tagging based on hidden Markov model. In: Proceedings of 2nd International Conference on Signal Processing Systems (ICSPS 2010), pp. 744–747 (2010)

Prosody Detection from Text Using Aggregative Linguistic Features

Vaibhavi Rajendran(✉) and G. Bharadwaja Kumar

Vellore Institute of Technology, Chennai, Tamilnadu, India
vvaibavi@gmail.com

Abstract. With the advent of digital revolution and new technologies the demand for commodious interfaces has increased. A speech interface in a person's native/first language gives an epitome of ease in accessing information. Tamil Text-To-Speech synthesis is one such speech interface and this paper is focused on developing a prosody prediction model for enhancing the naturalness of the synthesized speech. The proposed prosody prediction model for multifarious Tamil text is developed to classify the text into three classes of high, mid and low using the generated aggregative linguistic feature score. The proposed prosody prediction model resulted in a f-measure of 0.84 when tested against multifarious text and the performance of this model is certainly encouraging to explore further in this direction.

Keywords: Tamil · Prosody · Text To Speech · Sentiment analysis Text processing

1 Introduction

Communication plays a key role in exchanging information, the digital revolution has made the communication between man and the machine essential to acquire and spread information to all realms of people. The key factor of a good communication interface between man and a machine is 'ease-of-use'. A speech interface provides a much more naturalistic way of communication when compared to any graphical interface. Further, a speech interface in one's own native/first language makes a person to communicate comfortably and helps the person to access and dispense information without any inhibitions. Speech synthesis enables the artificial production of human-like speech and hence a Text-To-Speech (TTS) interface can increase the ease-of-use of any system.

A TTS synthesizer can function as a speaking aid to people who are vocally challenged and concurrently it can also function as a complacent interface to people who are visually challenged by helping them acquire access to digital data. The global communicating language, English was the prime locus of researches on speech technology from 1980's but in the recent years, research on several languages around the globe has begin to advance. Although, researchers have conquered many challenges in the development of such speech synthesis interfaces,

P. Bhattacharyya et al. (Eds.): NGCT 2017, CCIS 827, pp. 736–749, 2018.
https://doi.org/10.1007/978-981-10-8657-1_57

'naturalness' is one factor which is still difficult to procure. This paper is fixated on the development of a prosody model from Tamil text to foster a more naturally sounding speech synthesis interface. People in TamilNadu, Pondicherry, Andaman & Nicobar in India, Srilanka, Singapore and Malaysia speak Tamil as an official language. Hence, a Tamil TTS synthesizer empowers people who speak in Tamil language to gain access to computers and thus bridges the gap in accessing digital data to even people who cannot speak English language.

The next section briefs on why naturalness is essential in a speech synthesizer and also provides insights on the existing work. Section 3 explains how sentiment analysis can be incorporated for increasing the naturalness in a speech synthesizer, Section 4 gives the details about the proposed model and it's working, Sect. 5 exemplifies the performance of the proposed model and finally the last section holds the conclusion and future work.

2 Encompassing Naturalness in a TTS Synthesizer

Naturalness can be viewed as a measure which states how close the synthesized speech is to human speech. Naturalness in human speech can be attributed to the way a person articulates and co-articulates along with a variance of loudness, duration and fundamental frequency of utterance. The loudness/intensity, duration (utterances and pauses) and the fundamental frequency of utterance (intonation) are inturn a result of the speaker's state of mind. A speaker's state of mind varies in accordance to his/her emotions. Hence, finding the speaker's state of emotion will help us understand how to induce the naturalness artificially into a speech synthesizer. Emotion plays a key role in realizing the variance in pitch generation, loudness level and differences in placing pauses. We can map this variance in pitch, loudness and pause to intonation, intensity and duration paramaters in prosody.

A TTS generally has two modules namely a Natural Language Processing (NLP) module and a Digital Signal Processing (DSP) module. A NLP module comprises of a Text Normalizer, Letter-To-Sound (LTS) converter and a prosody predictor; a DSP module comprises of an appropriate unit selector, prosody generator and a speech waveform generator. To improve the naturalness in synthesized speech we need to first understand the connection between the text and the possible interpretation from the writer's point. Determining the intention of a writer is very difficult when compared to finding the intention of a speaker and is the biggest challenge here.

Related Work. A prosody model is inclined at modeling duration, intonation and intensity patterns which are the three main prosodic parameters in speech [23]. Some popular generic prosody models are ToBI (Tones Breaks and Indices) [9], Tilt [29,30] INSTINT [7], Fujisaki [8], Klatt [3] and Tones. A prosody model focussed on duration, varies the duration patterns of speech unit utterances to provide naturalness in speech. A rule based duration model for Hindi, a Classification and Regression Tree (CART) based duration model for Hindi & Telugu and a Neural Network based duration model for Hindi, Telugu & Tamil are the most significant developments seen in the literature for Indian languages [19,20].

A prosody model which focusses on modeling the fundamental frequency is known as an intonation model [21]. Fundamental frequency can be determined by the rate at which the vocal folds vibrate when a person produces speech. Fundamental frequency is denoted using F0 and it is the perceptual equivalent to pitch [19]. Both rule based and statistical intonation models have been experimented for few Indian languages like Hindi, Telugu and Tamil [13,21]. A prosody model to address only the intensity parameter specific to Indian language is still evolving [23]. Generic intensity models have been into experimentation for a long time, but it's adaptability for Indian Languages is yet to be explored.

Apart from these three parameters, prosody analysis can be looked with four different perspectives: linguistic, articulatory, acoustic and perceptual perspective [19]. The linguistic perspective of prosody emphasizes on the presence of certain linguistic elements (syllables/words/phrases) in the text in order to imply prosodic parameters into text. The tongue, lips, jaws and vocal folds are termed as the articulatory organs as they play a vital role in the production of different sounds. Understanding and emulating these articulatory movements according to the sound unit requirement in the text also helps in increasing the naturalness of the synthesized speech. The acoustic/auditory realizations of sound units helps us to analyse the three prosodic parameters in speech signals. After observing these sound wave forms, researchers try to generate acoustically similar sound waveforms to ensure the naturalness of the synthesized speech. The perceptual perspective of prosody is based on what a person observes from a spoken sound unit, it is mostly subjective to the listener, it can be expressed in terms of melody, loudness and pause or stress. Most of the existing prosody models discussed in the literature [19–23] are developed with acoustic and articulatory perspectives of prosody. Development of multimodal prosody models [13] for Indian languages and as well as many other languages is still unexplored.

Linguistic level of prosody prediction or generation has not been speculated much. Since a TTS synthesizer takes in text as input and prosody needs to be predicted from text, a linguistic perspective to prosody prediction and generation can be conducive. In this paper, we have experimented with some of the possible linguistic features which can help us predict the prosody from text.

3 Incorporating Sentiment Analysis for Prosody Prediction

Sentiment analysis is a task of determining the valence or polarity of a given text into positive, negative or neutral. It can also be used to determine the affectual category of a given text such as joy, anger, sadness, etc [10]. Determining the polarity/valence or the affectual category (emotion) of the speaker is always easy as we listen to their voice. A speaker's high pitch, high tone and a faster rate of speech could mean he/she is excited, happy or surprised while a low pitch, low tone, slower speech utterance could mean he/she is bored, sad or depressed. Valence/polarity and affect based sentiment analysis can both be linked together as certain emotions always tend to produce a positive valence while others produce a negative valence. For example the sentence, 'I won the first prize, am so happy' is a statement which clearly shows a 'happy' emotion being conveyed and it is a statement of positive valence/polarity. However the biggest challenge here is determining the state of mind of a person from text.

Developing a system which can categorize all the emotions a person experiences would actually be impractical. Hence, researchers have tried to delineate to a few basic emotions for working with affectual sentiment analysis. A set of 6 basic emotions such as joy, sadness, anger, fear, disgust and surprise are mostly followed [5,6], an additional pair of emotions such as trust and anticipation are sometimes added on to these basic set of six emotions [15,16]. For the experimentation of sentiment analysis on text, firstly the size of input text segment is to be decided and secondly, the development of appropriate linguistic resource is to be carried out.

Sentiment analysis can be carried out on: a full document with a number of pages (document level), sentence (sentence level), or on a word (word level). Since our intention is to incorporate sentiment analysis for prosody prediction in a Tamil TTS synthesizer we chose to work at sentence level. Sentence level prosody would be more natural and would help in conveying the varied emotions or valence present in the text and would reduce the monotonous synthesis of speech.

Another general requirement for experimenting on sentiment analysis would be the development of appropriate linguistic resources like a valence based or affect based word lexicon. The availability of such lexicons are tenuous since Tamil is a low resource language [11].

Although a twitter specific corpora (SAIL-Sentiment Analysis in Indian Languages) [12,14] is available for Tamil, a properly annotated sentiment analysis corpora for multifarious Tamil Text is not available [24]. Some of the significant work that has been done for Tamil sentiment analysis include: Tamil movie review classification using word frequency as a feature [2]; valence based classification of tweets using embedded scores for each word [4] and Tamil tweet classification using SVM with the help of word sense disambiguation and path length similarity between similar words [25,31]. The only work where sentiment analysis has been mapped to a TTS is discussed in [28], four affect categories such as anger, sadness, joy and disgust are dealt in the system for a restricted domain. This annotated data is trained using Hidden-Semi Markov Model (HSMM) and used for improving the prosody generation acoustically.

Hence, sentiment analysis on constrained/restricted domain has been experimented and fair results have been achieved using Support Vector Machines [24,25]. However, sentiment analysis for multifarious Tamil text has not been explored much owing to low resources [11]. The prosody model developed by us in Sect. 4 is an attempt to experiment the valence and affect level feature unification for prosody prediction at sentence level.

Generally a prosody generation model is applied in the DSP module to achieve naturally sounding speech waveform but our work is fixed on developing a prosody prediction model from linguistic perspective in text (in NLP module) and annotating certain prosodic values to the words. This annotated values can then be used to generate prosody in the later stage of TTS (DSP module). An illustration of the components of a TTS synthesizer which incorporates the proposed prosody prediction model is given in Fig. 1.

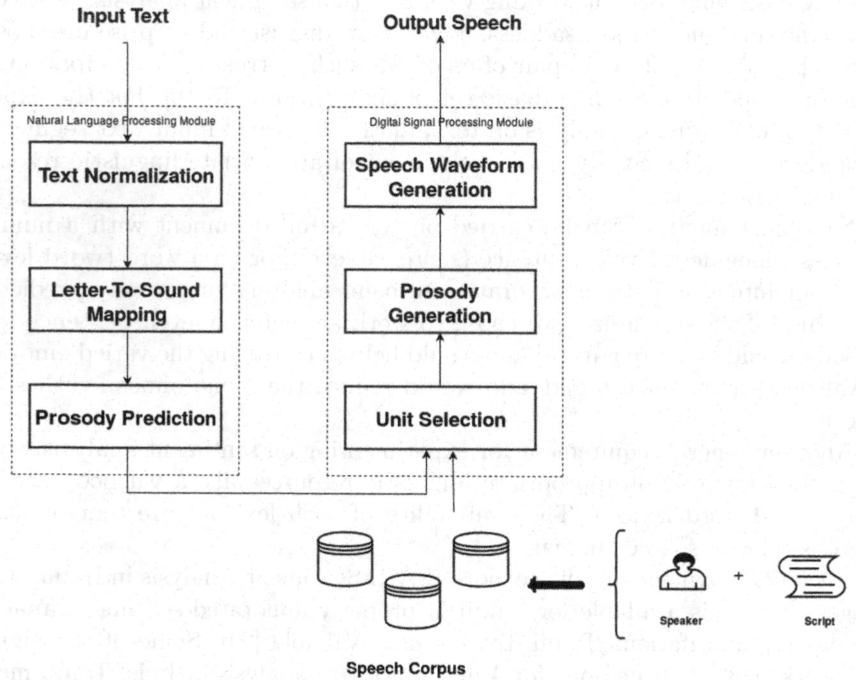

Fig. 1. Components of a TTS

4 Prosody Prediction Model Using Aggregative Linguistic Features

In this paper, we have proposed a prosody prediction model for a multifarious Tamil Text-To-Speech synthesizer using linguistic feature aggregation at sentence level and the components of this model are depicted in Fig. 2. The model will classify the sentences into high, mid or low level prosodic sentences based on the aggregate score calculated after applying some consecutive linguistic feature extraction process. For a sentence level sentiment analysis task, generally the features lie within phrases or words. We have chosen to work with words as our features. The possible linguistic feature extraction which we can apply to a word are POS (Part-Of-Speech) tags, word frequencies, word n-grams, word polarity/valence scores, word affect tags from affect adverb/adjective list and SynSets. Word frequency list is a general option considered by many researchers for sentiment analysis on restricted domains. But a word frequency list which follows a bag of words approach cannot be very effective for an unrestricted domain. The bag of words approach can be really useful when we deal with topic classification, event detection and other related tasks. Next, an affect adverb/adjective list [27] is not available for Tamil language, similarly subjectivity wordlist [32] and wordnet affect list [27] are also not available for Tamil. Hence, we stick onto the usage of the available linguistic resources such as SentiWordnet [1], POS tagger [26] and Stemmer [17] to develop our prosody model.

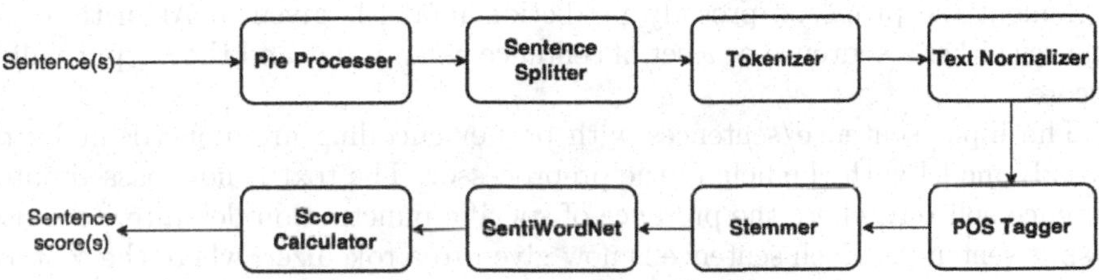

Fig. 2. Components of the prosody prediction model

The classes of 'high, mid and low' have been chosen after considering the 6 basic emotions 'joy, sadness, anger, fear, disgust and surprise' [5,6] usually taken for sentiment analysis into account. Out of these 6 emotions a general notion is that when a person is happy (joy), excited (surprised) or angry (anger), the person will tend to speak in a high tone and high pitch. On the controrary, a person will tend to speak in a low pitch and low tone when he/she is sad (sadness), afraid (fear) or disgusted. A person uses a normal (mid) pitch and tone during all other times. This classification is based on assumptions on how generally human beings portary their emotions and this might as well vary from person to person. Moreover, we are dealing with text and not speech as the input. Given a speech segment we might draw out several pitches and tones, we can expand into several classes as we hear what a person speaks. But, when we look into prosody detection from the context of a text segment alone as an input it is very difficult to deal the categorization. For our experimentation, we decided to go with the majorly accepted emotion-to-pitch/tone correspondence and we have considered the basic three classes (high, mid, low) for our prosody detection task. Moreover, the intent of this prosody model is to bring in some variance in the synthesized speech by a text-to-speech synthesizer and hence, three classes would suffice this requirement. The classification can further be expanded into additional classes if required.

4.1 Working of the Prosody Model

The proposed prosody prediction model for Tamil text developed by encompassing sentiment analysis requires a POS (Part-Of-Speech) tagger, a stemmer and a SentiWordNet list for Tamil. A POS tagger reads in the text from a specific language and assigns a tag to each word in the text according to the part of speech category followed by the syntax of the language. A stemmer outputs the root word or stem form of a word by removing the inflections present in the input word. Generally, a WordNet serves as a basic requirement for developing most of the other lexical resources in any language as it contains the list of words along with it's definition, example usage of the word and it's relation to other words. SentiWordNet is a lexical resource formulated from a WordNet and each item in the SentiWordNet is associated with a value/valence denoting the polarity of the word into positive, negative or neutral. The POS tagger given in [26], the stemmer in [17] and the SentiWordnet in [1] has been used. The algorithm to implement the proposed prosody prediction model is given in Algorithm 1, it requires either a sentence or a set of sentence as an input and the output will be a score.

The input sentence/sentences with proper encoding are alone dealt by the prosody model with the help of the preprocessor. The text is now passed onto a sentence splitter, where the presence of specific punctuation delimiters are used to split sentences. Each sentence is now given to a tokenizer, where the sentence is split into tokens (words) using the space delimiter. Next, each token is given to a Text Normalizer to check for the presence of any Non Standard Word (NSW) and if present are converted into a Standard Word (SW). The possible set of NSW are numbers, acronyms, abbreviations and special characters, a set of 8 NSW to SW conversion was addressed by us in [18], we have used this text normalizer to increase the verbalization of the sentences. This increase in verbalization may attribute to chances of increase in the sentence score. Once all the tokens are available as standard words, the sentence is fed to a POS tagger to find out the part of speech tag of each word. The POS tagger has been developed using Conditional Random Fields, it has a total of 42 POS tags and we have split them into 3 levels for scoring purpose (for details about the POS categories refer [26]). The adjectives, adverbs and verbs are given the highest scoring level, nouns are given the second highest level and all the other POS are placed at the lowest level. The rationale behind using POS as a feature and categorizing the POS into different levels is due to the fact that predominantly the polarity and affect state of a sentence depends highly on certain POS like verb, adverb and adjectives. The other POS categories also contribute to the polarity and affect portrayal in a sentence, but the accentuation level is low. According to the priority level, discrete values have been set as POS score to each of them. Now each word is annotated with a discrete POS score with respect to it's POS tag and is then given to a stemmer to obtain the root word of each token. Generally, the linguistic resources contain the root form of the words in a language hence it is essential to remove the inflections of a word and provide only the root form of the word to process it. A stemmer has been used for this purpose, the stemmer follows a rule based iterative affix removal strategy given in [17]. The root word of each token is now checked with the SentiWordNet which has four lists: positive, negative, ambiguous and neutral. This SentiWordNet has been developed by combining the polarity based SynSet in a WordNet along with a POS tagged subjectivity wordlist. If the word is present in the SentiWordNet a valence score according to the category of list is provided. Discrete values have been used for each list such that a significant difference is induced into the sentence score for determining the polarity of the sentence. Once both a POS score and a valence score is obtained for all the words in the sentence, the final sentence score is generated by aggrandizing both the POS and valence score of every word in the sentence.

Algorithm 1. Prosody prediction algorithm

```
for input do
    Preprocess the input to resolve encoding issues
    Perform sentence splitting
    Perform text normalization on each sentence
    for each sentence do
        Apply POS tagger
        for each word do
            Store POS of each word
            Match POS of each wordwith the POS_score_list and obtain a score
            Apply stemmer to obtain the root word
            for each root word do
                Check the SentiWordNet list and retrieve appropriate valence score
            end for
            Store the valence score in a wordwise manner
            Calculate the wordscore by aggrandizing the valence and POS score
        end for
    end for
    Calculate the sentence score by aggregating each word's score in the sentence
end for
```

5 Results and Discussion

The effectiveness of the proposed prosody prediction model was evaluated using a set of 308 sentences, out of which around 100 are sentiment-bearing sentences. These 308 sentences were randomly picked from various sources of Tamil text like news websites, blogs and magazines. A considerable amount of randomness in the text source is ensured to determine the ability of this prosody prediction model in processing multifarious Tamil text. The 308 sentences were pre-categorized into three categories of high, mid and low manually by a few Tamil native speakers before subjecting them to the prosody prediction model. This pre-categorization is referred as the 'actual' categorization, here 'High' represents sentences with a positive polarity or sentences with a affect state which requires the generation of a high intonation and high intensity. 'Mid' represents sentences with a medium polarity or sentences with an affect state of neither high nor low but a medium level of intonation and intensity generation. 'Low' represents the set of sentences with a negative polarity or sentences with an affect state of low intonation and intensity. The categorization which is performed using the generated score by the proposed prosody prediction model is referred as 'predicted' categorization. The scores were analysed to set a range for each category, based on the range the sentences have been categorized into high, mid and low classes. The maximum, minimum and average score generated were analysed and an interval drift of around 'n' values downwards from the maximum score was taken to be the range for 'high' class. Similarly, an interval drift of 'n' upwards from the minimum score was taken to be the range for 'low' class. Subsequently, the intermediate range fell into the 'mid' category. The value of 'n' for the interval was chosen by estimating an equitable coverage of the score from the average score of the sentences and hence is empirical. Example categorization based on the generated aggregative score by the proposed prosody model for a few sentences is given in Fig. 3.

Sentence	Score	Class
இதனால் நரம்பு மண்டலத்துக்கும் களைப்பு ஏற்படுகிறது. (idhanAl Narambu maNdalaththukkum kaLaippu ERpadugiRadhu .)	-19	Low
சுற்றுலா துறையின் முக்கியத்துவம் மற்றும் வளர்ச்சியை கருத்தில் கொண்டு விசா நடைமுறையை அரசு எளிமையாக்கி உள்ளது. (sutRula thuRaiyin mukkiyaththuvam matRum vaLarchchiyai karuththil koNdu visa nadaimuRaiyai arasu eLimaiyakki uLLadhu.)	53	Mid
தமிழகத்தில் ஜல்லிக்கட்டு மீண்டும் நடப்பதற்க்கு உதவியதற்காக பிரதமர் மோடிக்கு முதல்வர் பன்னீர் செல்வம் நன்றி தெரிவித்து கடிதம் எழுதியுள்ளார். (thamizagaththil Jallikkattu mINdum NadappadhaRkku udaviyadhaRkaga piradhamar modikku mudhalvar pannIr selvam Nandri theriviththu kadidham ezudhiyuLLAr.)	96	High

Fig. 3. Example categorization of the sentences

The actual number of sentences in the 'low' category is 58. Out of these 58 sentences, 52 have been classified correctly into the 'low' category. The classification is dependent on the scores generated for the aggregative linguistic features prevalent in each sentence. To obtain the score for these linguistic features a set of NLP tools as discussed in Sect. 4.1 has been used. The accuracy of the classifier is inturn dependent on the accuracy of these NLP tools. Hence, there will exist a variation in actual and predicted sentences in all the three classes.

The actual and the predicted categorization of sentences are used to construct a confusion matrix for further evaluation. The confusion matrix given in Table 1 provides us a clear indication of how many sentences have been correctly classified into the respective classes. The actual number of sentences in each category are given as Actual High, Actual Mid and Actual Low (underlined values in the last row of the confusion matrix). The sentences categorized based on the generated score are given as Predicted High, Predicted Mid and Predicted Low. It is to be noted that the predictions include correct and as well incorrect classifications, the correct classifications which is popularly known as the True Positive of each category can be found in the left to right diagonal of the confusion matrix (the values are 19, 208, 52). The correct and incorrect classifications of each class constitutes to the Total Predicted value of each category. The formulae for calculating the precision and recall values for a multi-class classification using the confusion matrix is given in Eqs. 1 and 2. The precision and recall values of the 3 classes are tabulated in Table 2. A final precision and recall value for a multi-class classification is usually obtained by taking a mean of the precision and recall values of each class. The F-measure for a multi-class classification can be calculated using the formula in Eq. 3 and the value is 0.8439. The comparison between the actual and predicted categorization are depicted in the graph given in Fig. 4. Apart from the 'high' categorization of sentences the prediction of the other two classes have been comparatively better and is evident from the graph in Fig. 4. The predicted (208 sentences) and the actual (209 sentences) categorization of the 'mid' class is almost equal and hence the deviation is almost null (illustrated in Fig. 4). Although, the generated score is associated with 3 categories, the analysis of the sentence scores indicates that the scores can be directly applied to vary the intonation (pitch) and intensity (loudness) of sentences during speech synthesis to induce naturalness.

Table 1. Confusion matrix of prosody prediction results

	Actual High	Actual Mid	Actual Low	Total Predicted
Predicted High	19	0	0	19
Predicted Mid	11	208	6	225
Predicted Low	11	1	52	64
Total Actual	<u>41</u>	<u>209</u>	<u>58</u>	308

Table 2. Precision and recall values-prediction

Class	Precision	Recall
High	1.0000	0.4634
Mid	0.9244	0.9952
Low	0.8125	0.8966
Final	**0.9123**	**0.7851**

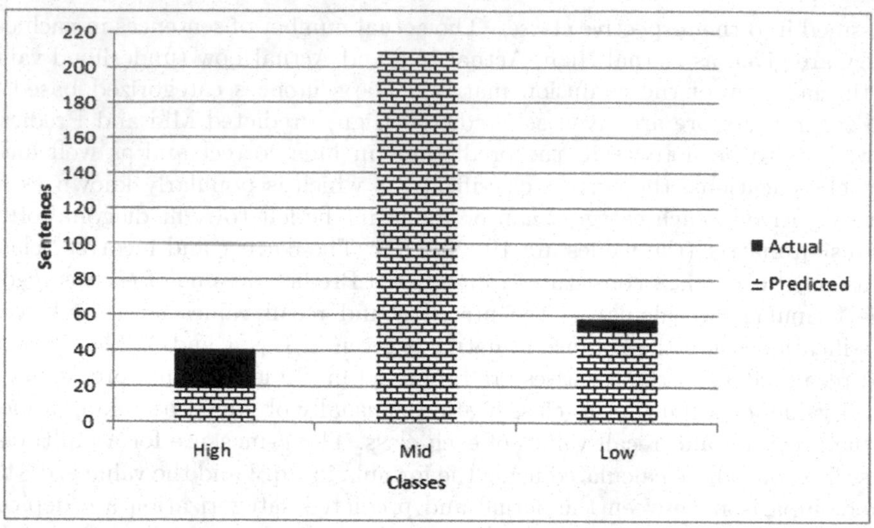

Fig. 4. Actual vs Predicted categorization

$$Precision_{class} = \frac{(True\_Positive_{class})}{(Total\_Predicted_{class})} \tag{1}$$

$$Recall_{class} = \frac{(True\_Positive_{class})}{(Total\_Actual_{class})} \tag{2}$$

$$F - measure = \frac{(2 * Precision * Recall)}{(Precision + Recall)} \tag{3}$$

As an additional evaluation to analyse the credibility of this prosody prediction model, videos of Tamil native speaker's spontaneous speech were taken from Youtube (a popular video sharing source, the links of the videos are given in the reference section). To analyse the performance of the prosody prediction model, videos portraying three different intonation and intensity levels were chosen [33–35]. The video sources depict varied emotional state of the speaker such as anger, sorrow and pride. Despite the usage of vernacular language in the sentences, the prosody prediction model was able to perform well and the classification results of some sentences (along with the transliteration) from the video sources are given in Fig. 5. In Fig. 5, the first column holds the sentences from the video sources, the second column holds the score generated by the prosody prediction model, the third column holds the actual classification of the sentence based on the speakers state of mind in the video and the last column holds the classification by the prosody prediction model. The sentences have been classified correctly into high, mid and low classes representing the need for a respective intonation and intensity generation during speech synthesis. An extensive analysis of such sentences can further help in modeling the intonation and intensity parameters for natural speech synthesis.

Sentence	Score	Video	Predicted
சென்னை மெரினால தொடங்கி கன்னியாகுமரி கடலோரம் வரைக்கும் எல்லா இடங்கள்லயும் உணர்வோடையும் , புரிதலோடையும் ஜல்லிகட்ட மீட்டெடுக்கனும் ஏறுதழுவுதல் எங்களுடைய உரிமை இது எங்கள் வாழ்வியல் ஆதாராத்தோட தொடர்புடையது அப்டிங்கிற புரிதலோடும் சேர்த்து களம்கண்டு இருக்கக்கூடிய இளைஞர்கள் எல்லோருக்கும் என்னுடைய வணக்கங்களும் வாழ்த்துக்களும். (chennai merinAla thodaN;gi kanniyAkumari kadalOram varaikkum ella idaN;gaLlayum uNarvOdaiyum, puridhalOdaiyum Jallikatta mIttedukkanum Eruthazuvudhal eN;gaLudaiya urimai idhu eN;gal vAzviyal AdharAththoda thodarbudaiyadhu apdiN;giR puridhalOdum serththu kaLamkaNdu irukkakkUdiya iLaiN:argaL ellOrukkum ennudaiya vaNakkaN;gaLum vazththukkaLum.)	99	High	High
இதுல எவ்ளோ விஷயங்கள் அடங்கியிருக்கிறது அப்டிங்கிறத இளைஞர்கள் மிகத் தெளிவாகவே தெரிஞ்சி வச்சிருக்குறாங்க. (idhula evlO vishayaN;gaL adaN;giyirukkiRadhu apdiN;giRadha iLaiN:argaL migath thelivAgve theriN:ji vachchirukkuRAN:ga.)	33	Mid	Mid
தமிழகத்தினுடைய முதலமைச்சர் மாண்புமிகு அம்மையார் ஜெயலலிதா அவர்களுடைய மறைவு பெரும் அதிர்ச்சியை வேதனையை அனைவருக்கும் ஆளாக்கி இருக்கிறது. (thamizgaththinudaiya mudhalamaichchar mANbumigu ammaiyAr Jeyalalidha avargaLudaiya maRaivu perum adhirchchiyai vedhanaiyai anaivarukkum ALAkki irukkiRadhu.)	0	Low	Low

Fig. 5. Performance analysis of sentences from video sources

The comparison of results is mostly not possible in sentiment analysis task due to the unavailability of a common training and testing data [12,14]. Moreover, the existing sentiment analysis models for Tamil in the literature has been developed for a restricted domain and thus comparing our results with those models will be inapt.

6 Conclusion and Future Work

The performance of the prosody prediction model built using linguistic aggregative features (linguistic perspective) is clearly encouraging and a few enhancements can further increase the prediction accuracy. The reasons for the deviation in prediction can be contoured to three factors. First, all types of punctuations are placed in one POS scoring level and equal priority is given to all punctuators. Varying the scoring of the punctuators in the POS score with respect to type and number of occurrences can enhance the aggregative score. Second, the number of words in the SentiWordNet is quiet low in comparison to the actual possible words in Tamil language and hence retrieving a valence score for every word in the language is confined. Third, the absence of word based linguistic resources for Tamil language hinders the experimentation of other word based features into the model. Addressing these factors will expeditiously increase the prediction performance of the proposed prosody prediction model.

Acknowledgements. We would like to thank the Tamil native speakers who helped us in the construction of the test set by categorizing the text into appropriate classes required for our work.

References

1. Amitava: SentiWordNet for Tamil (2012). http://amitavadas.com/sentiwordnet.php. Accessed Jan 2017
2. Arun, S., Kumar, M., Soman, K.: Sentiment analysis of Tamil movie reviews via feature frequency count. In: Innovations in Information, Embedded and Communication Systems (2015)
3. Bailly, G., Holm, B.: SFC: a trainable prosodic model. Speech Commun. **46**(3), 348–364 (2005)
4. E, N., Sanjay, S., Kumar, M.A., Soman, K.: Unsupervised word embedding based polarity detection for Tamil tweets. Int. J. Control Theor. Appl. 4631–4638 (2016)
5. Ekman, P.: Are there basic emotions? (1992)
6. Ekman, P.: An argument for basic emotions. Cogn. Emot. **6**(3–4), 169–200 (1992)
7. Louw, J., Barnard, E.: Automatic intonation modeling with INTSINT. In: Proceedings of the Pattern Recognition Association of South Africa, pp. 107–111 (2004)
8. Mixdorff, H.: A novel approach to the fully automatic extraction of Fujisaki model parameters. In: Proceedings of 2000 IEEE International Conference on Acoustics, Speech, and Signal Processing, ICASSP 2000, vol. 3, pp. 1281–1284. IEEE (2000)
9. Mixdorff, H.: Speech technology, ToBI, and making sense of prosody. In: International Conference on Speech Prosody (2002)
10. Mohammad, S.M.: Sentiment analysis: detecting valence, emotions, and other affectual states from text. In: Emotion Measurement, pp. 201–238 (2015)
11. Parlikar, A., Sitaram, S., Wilkinson, A., Black, A.W.: The festvox indic frontend for grapheme to phoneme conversion. In: WILDRE: Workshop on Indian Language Data-Resources and Evaluation (2016)
12. Patra, B.G., Das, D., Das, A., Prasath, R.: Shared task on sentiment analysis in Indian languages (SAIL) tweets - an overview. In: Prasath, R., Vuppala, A.K., Kathirvalavakumar, T. (eds.) MIKE 2015. LNCS (LNAI), vol. 9468, pp. 650–655. Springer, Cham (2015). https://doi.org/10.1007/978-3-319-26832-3_61
13. Pérez-Rosas, V., Mihalcea, R., Morency, L.P.: Utterance-level multimodal sentiment analysis. ACL **1**, 973–982 (2013)
14. Phani, S., Lahiri, S., Biswas, A.: Sentiment analysis of tweets in three Indian languages. In: WSSANLP 2016, vol. 1001, p. 83 (2016). IIEST Shibpur
15. Plutchik, R.: A general psychoevolutionary theory of emotion. Theor. Emot. **1**(3–31), 4 (1980)
16. Plutchik, R.: The Emotions. University Press of America, Lanham (1991)
17. Rajalingam, D.: An Affix Stripping Iterative Stemming Algorithm for Tamil (2013). https://github.com/rdamodharan/tamil-stemmer. Accessed Jan 2017
18. Rajendran, V., Kumar, G.B.: Text processing for developing unrestricted Tamil text to speech synthesis system. Indian J. Sci. Technol. **8**(29) (2015)

19. Rao, K.S., Koolagudi, S.G.: Selection of suitable features for modeling the durations of syllables. J. Softw. Eng. Appl. **3**(12), 1107 (2010)
20. Rao, K.S., Yegnanarayana, B.: Modeling durations of syllables using neural networks. Comput. Speech Lang. **21**(2), 282–295 (2007)
21. Rao, K.S., Yegnanarayana, B.: Intonation modeling for Indian languages. Comput. Speech Lang. **23**(2), 240–256 (2009)
22. Reddy, V.R., Rao, K.S.: Two-stage intonation modeling using feedforward neural networks for syllable based text-to-speech synthesis. Comput. Speech Lang. **27**(5), 1105–1126 (2013)
23. Reddy, V.R., Rao, K.S.: Prosody modeling for syllable based text-to-speech synthesis using feedforward neural networks. Neurocomputing **171**, 1323–1334 (2016)
24. Se, S., Vinayakumar, R., Kumar, M.A., Soman, K.: Predicting the sentimental reviews in Tamil movie using machine learning algorithms. Indian J. Sci. Technol. **9**(45) (2016)
25. Seshadri, S., Madasamy, A.K., Padannayil, S.K.: Analyzing sentiment in Indian languages micro text using recurrent neural network, 313–318 (2016)
26. Sobha Lalitha Devi, P.R.R., Ram, R.V.S.: Tamil POS tagger. AUKBC Tamil Part-of-Speech Tagger (AUKBC-TamilPOSTagger2016v1). Web Download. Computational Linguistics Research Group, AU-KBC Research Centre, Chennai, India (2016). Accessed Jan 2017
27. Strapparava, C., Valitutti, A., et al.: Wordnet affect: an affective extension of wordnet. LREC **4**, 1083–1086 (2004)
28. Sudhakar, B., Bensraj, R.: Enhanced evaluation of sentiment analysis for Tamil text-to-speech synthesis using hidden semi-Markov model. Communications **3**, 13–16 (2015)
29. Taylor, P.: The tilt intonation model (1998)
30. Taylor, P.: Analysis and synthesis of intonation using the tilt model. J. Acoust. Soc. Am. **107**(3), 1697–1714 (2000)
31. Uma, V.: Sentiment analysis of English and Tamil tweets using path length similarity based word sense disambiguation. IOSR J. (IOSR J. Comput. Eng.) **18**, 82–89 (2016)
32. Wilson, T., Hoffmann, P., Somasundaran, S., Kessler, J., Wiebe, J., Choi, Y., Cardie, C., Riloff, E., Patwardhan, S.: Opinionfinder: a system for subjectivity analysis. In: Proceedings of HLT/EMNLP on Interactive Demonstrations, pp. 34–35. Association for Computational Linguistics (2005)
33. Youtube: Newsglitz-video-source (2016). https://www.youtube.com/watch?v=oDlUjAJEQjU. Accessed Feb 2017
34. Youtube: Newsglitz-video-source (2016). https://www.youtube.com/watch?v=tsBJUReSt7w. Accessed Feb 2017
35. Youtube: Newsglitz-video-source (2016). https://www.youtube.com/watch?v=NYtPf7PEKNM. Accessed Feb 2017

Deep Neural Network Based Recognition and Classification of Bengali Phonemes: A Case Study of Bengali Unconstrained Speech

Tanmay Bhowmik[1(✉)], Amitava Choudhury[1], and Shyamal Kumar Das Mandal[2]

[1] SoCSE, University of Petroleum and Energy Studies, Dehradun, India
tanmay.bhowmik@gmail.com, a.choudhury2013@gmail.com

[2] CET, Indian Institute of Technology, Kharagpur, Kharagpur, India
sdasmandal@cet.iitkgp.ernet.ac.in

Abstract. This paper proposed a phoneme recognition and classification model for Bengali continuous speech. A Deep Neural Network based model has been developed for the recognition and classification task where the Stacked Denoising Autoencoder is used to generatively pre-train the deep network. Autoencoders are stacked to form the deep-structured network. Mel-frequency cepstral coefficients are used as input data vector. In hidden layer, 200 numbers of hidden units have been utilized. The number of hidden layers of the deep network is kept as three. The phoneme posterior probability has been derived in the output layer. This proposed model has been trained and tested using unconstrained Bengali continuous speech data collected from the different sources (TV, Radio, and normal conversation in a laboratory). In recognition phase, the Phoneme Error Rate is reported for the deep-structured model as 24.62% and 26.37% respectively for the training and testing while in the classification task this model achieves 86.7% average phoneme classification accuracy in training and 82.53% in the testing phase.

Keywords: Bengali phoneme recognition
Bengali phoneme classification · Deep Neural Network
Stacked Denoising Autoencoder · Phoneme confusion matrix

1 Introduction

Speech recognition community witnessed great success and a lot of advancements in the Automatic Speech Recognition (ASR) area during last few decades. Hidden Markov Model (HMM) is used in state-of-the-art speech recognition system to model the sequential structure of speech signal with local spectral variability [23]. HMM-based speech recognition systems use a pattern matching framework to decode the speech signal into the possible sequence of words and achieve high

P. Bhattacharyya et al. (Eds.): NGCT 2017, CCIS 827, pp. 750–760, 2018.
https://doi.org/10.1007/978-981-10-8657-1_58

recognition accuracy for well-formed utterances of a variety of languages. However, recognition of spoken item from real-time, continuously spoken speech data is one of the most challenging tasks in the field of the phoneme or word recognition as the recognition error rates are still very high in case of unconstrained speech. Sometimes the acoustic resemblance between many of the phonemes creates a lot of phonetic confusions at the time of recognition. So the system needs to perform the fine phonetic classification.

There are some factors behind the intention of phoneme recognition. Low phone error rate (PER) leads to lower word error rate (WER), and the ability of accurate recognition of Bengali phoneme from unconstrained Bengali speech will provide the basis of an accurate Bengali word recognizer. Most popular and successful approach to phone recognition is the statistical learning approach where hidden Markov model (HMM) is the most successful technique. HMM has been successfully applied to a variety of constrained tasks, such as speaker dependent phone recognition, isolated word recognition [1], continuous speech recognition [3], and speaker-independent, isolated, small-vocabulary word recognition [22], speaker-independent phone recognition [13]. Along with the HMM technique, many experiments are also performed with the Multilayer Perceptron (MLP) approach also for isolated phoneme recognition [28], and isolated word recognition [21].

English and Bengali are two languages which have connections as well as variations in their phonemic systems. This paper states phoneme recognition and classification from Bengali unconstrained speech. Some efforts are made to recognize Bengali phoneme [11], isolated and continuous Bengali speech [10], and to study on Bengali voicing vowels [4]. Recognition of Bengali phoneme by Artificial Neural Network is done in [20,24], and a brief overview of recognition and synthesis of Bengali speech is also found in [18]. In continuous Bengali speech, sometimes consecutive phonemes contain almost same co-articulatory information, so it becomes difficult to pronounce them separately and distinguish from each other [5]. Regarding this problem, the classification of phonemes are performed in this study and the phoneme confusion matrix (PCM) is generated. Phoneme confusion is not only found in ASR, but it is very regular in Human also. Meyer et al. studies about phoneme confusion in Human speech recognition (HSR) and ASR [17].

Most of the research effort to recognize Bengali speech is prepared with conventional HMM or ANN approach. In this study, the recent advancement of neural network approach, the Deep Neural Network (DNN) has been applied to Bengali continuous speech to recognize and classify the phonemes. We used Stacked Denoising Autoencoder (SDAE) pre-training approach to complete this DNN based study.

An Autoencoder (AE) is a particular type of DNN for unsupervised learning where training is done to reproduce the input at the output layer [2], so the output has the same dimension as the input. AE acts in a non-linear fashion without using any class labels [7]. Speech recognition is difficult in case of real time input data which may be noisy and corrupted. Denoising Autoencoder

(DAE) is a solution of this type of problems as it recovers undistorted data from the noisy and corrupted input signal during the pre-training phase of DNN based model. The DAE is a stochastic version of an Autoencoder (AE) [27].

In this experiment, three Denoising Autoencoders are stacked together to form a Stacked Denoising Autoencoders (SDAE). This deep-structured model is applied to the Bengali speech data which is collected from various sources like TV, Radio, and regular laboratory conversation. The deep-structured model is also applied on the English speech corpus TIMIT [8] to validate the performance. The proposed model achieved better performance in comparison to the baseline systems.

2 Deep Neural Network

A DNN is a feed-forward, artificial neural network consists of more than one layer of hidden units between its input and output. In general, each hidden unit uses a logistic function to map its entire input to output layer [12].

$$y_j = logistic(x_j) = \frac{1}{1+e^{-x_j}} \tag{1}$$

where

$$x_j = b_j + \sum_i y_i w_{ij} \tag{2}$$

In the above equations, b_j is the bias of unit j, i is the index of input layer, and w_{ij} is the weight of the connection from unit i to unit j. In our experiment we are about to recognize multiple phonemes. For multi-class classification, the total input x_j of unit j is converted into a class probability p_j in the output layer with the use of softmax nonlinearity [12].

$$p_j = \frac{exp(x_j)}{\sum_k exp(x_k)} \tag{3}$$

Here k is an index of all classes.

Discriminative training is found in the case of DNN with backpropagation of derivatives of the cost function which measure the deviation of actual output from the target output for each training case [26]. At the time of softmax normalization, the natural cost function C acts like the cross entropy between target probability and softmax output.

$$C = -\sum_j d_j \log p_j \tag{4}$$

where d, the target probability usually takes the value of one or zero, and this is the supervised information used to train the DNN classifier. The softmax output is denoted by p. Usually, for the large training sets, computation of derivatives on a small, random minibatch of training cases is more efficient than the whole training set before the updating of weights in gradient scale [12]. The biases are updated by considering them as the weights on connections coming from units with a state of one. DNNs with numbers of hidden layers are difficult to optimize. The initial weights of a fully connected DNN are given small random values to prevent from having the exactly same gradient to all the hidden units in a layer. Glorot and Bengio state that gradient descent from a starting point which is very close to the origin is not the best way to find a better set of weights, and to obtain that initial scales of weights are deliberately chosen [9]. Due to the presence of large numbers of hidden layers and hidden units, the DNNs are a very adjustable model with huge numbers of parameters. That is why DNNs are capable to model complex and non-linear relations between inputs and outputs. This ability is crucial in better acoustic modeling [12]. The deep model needs generative pre-training to ensure effective training of the complex and non-linear relationship.

3 Experimental Setup

3.1 Speech Corpus

The unconstrained Bengali speech data is collected from different sources. They are recorded from TV programs, Radio News, and regular Laboratory conversation. The total corpus has been distributed for training, validation and testing. The distribution of these data is given in Table 1. Sampling frequency is kept as 16000 Hz. To validate the proposed model, all the experiments were gone through a subset of TIMIT corpus. The TIMIT subset contains particularly chosen 500 sentences of all the types that exist in the corpus [8]. Those sentences are spoken by 50 speakers, including 25 male speakers and 25 female speakers of different age group vary from 20 to 50 years. Due to some computational constraint, it was not possible to use the whole TIMIT dataset.

3.2 Baseline Systems

Two phoneme recognition systems based on HMM and MLP respectively were built as baseline systems. The HMM-based system uses triphone model.

Table 1. Distribution of unconstrained Bengali speech data

Total duration of collected speech from different sources: 2 h 10 min				
Sources	Duration of the recordings in minutes			
	Collected speech	Training	Validation	Testing
TV	55	40	5	10
Radio	35	25	5	5
Lab-conversation	40	25	5	10

Table 2. Detail information for MFCC extraction

Sampling frequency (f_s)	16000 Hz
Window type	Hamming
Analysis frame duration	25 ms
Analysis frame shift	10 ms
Pre-emphasis	Yes
Number of filters in filterbank	floor($3 \times \log(f_s)$) = 12
Number of cepstral coefficients	13

The second baseline system is an MLP based system with 200 hidden units in the hidden layer and the posterior probability for every phoneme was derived in the output layer.

3.3 Input Features

The Mel Frequency Cepstral Coefficient (MFCC) features has been used as input features for this study. 12 MFCC features plus the 0th cepstral coefficient is computed for each frame. 13 numbers of Δ and $\Delta\Delta$ coefficients are also computed as $\Delta(n) = [x(n+1) - x(n-1)]$ and $\Delta\Delta(n) = [0.5x(n+1) - 2x(n) + 0.5x(n-1)]$ respectively to get a complete 39 dimensional input dataset. A contextual representation of seven frames per context has been taken to prevent data loss; three frames in the back and three frames ahead. In the absence of a speech frame, zero is appended to complete the context. Due to this, input data dimension becomes $39 \times 7 = 273$. The input feature detail is described in Table 2. Here pre-emphasis is executed to flatten the magnitude spectrum and balance the high and low frequency components. In general, it is a first-order, high-pass filter with the time-domain equation $y[n] = x[n] - \alpha x[n-1]$ where $y[n]$ is the output, $x[n]$ is the input, and $0.9 \leqslant \alpha \leqslant 1.0$. Default values are kept for other parameters. The matlab toolkit 'voicebox' is utilized to use the 'melcepst()' function [16] for MFCC feature extraction.

3.4 Softwares

The HMM-based phoneme recognition system was built using the HTK speech toolkit [29]. For the MLP based system the Matlab Neural Network toolkit [6] has been used. A deep learning toolkit [19] has been used for phoneme recognition using the Stacked Denoising Autoencoder.

3.5 Hardware System

A DELL Precision T3600 workstation is used for this experiment. This workstation is a six-core computer with a CPU clock speed of 3.2 GHz, 12 MB of L3 cache memory and 64 GB DDR3 RAM and a NVIDIA Quadro 4000 General Purpose Graphical Processing Unit (GPGPU).

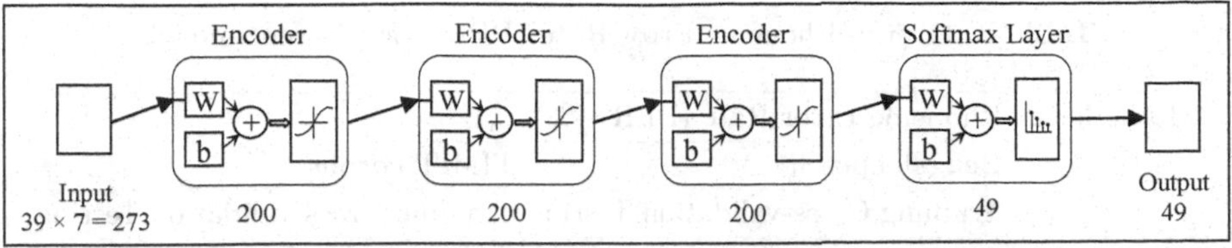

Fig. 1. Deep Neural Network based phoneme recognition and classification model

3.6 Proposed Model

To execute the phoneme recognition process on Bengali continuous speech, a recognition model has been designed using DNN. A functional block diagram of this DNN-based model is given in Fig. 1. While considering the deep architecture, during pre-training, denoising autoencoders are trained. In this experiment, three autoencoders are stacked to form the deep architecture. For each autoencoder, the Rectified Linear Unit (ReLU) function has been used as the non-linear activation function. 200 hidden units are used in each hidden layer. In output layer, classification has been done between 49 phonetic classes. In continuous Bengali speech there is almost no difference in pronunciation between the phoneme 'ɽ' and 'ɽ^h'. That is why these two phonemes have been considered as a single class in this experiment. Apart from this, we considered 'silence' as another class as each continuously spoken sentence possesses some silent regions in the initial and final position of the sentence. Continuous spoken sentences also may have some small pauses in between utterances. This is considered as another class named 'short pause'. There exist diphthongs in Bengali. A diphthong is a vowel-vowel combination. Two of them are found in the selected sentences of the Bengali speech corpus [14]. So in the output layer, there are total 49 nodes have been considered. The learning rate is kept as one, and the minibatch size is fixed at 120. The input zero masked fraction value is taken as 0.5. In input and output layer, there are the MFCC features and the posterior probabilities respectively. A deep learning toolbox has been used for this recognition model [19].

4 Results and Discussion

The overall phoneme error rate and the overall classification accuracy for the deep-structured model are reported in Tables 3 and 4 respectively. PER and phoneme classification accuracy for the HMM and MLP based baseline models are also reported. The HMM-based recognition system performs under the monophone labeling.

To validate this result, the same experiment was carried out with a subset of TIMIT speech corpus. The DNN based model performed better in comparison to HMM and MLP based model for both the Bengali and English speech datasets.

From the overall classification results which are obtained through the DNN based model, the overall Phoneme Confusion Matrix (PCM) of dimension 49×49,

Table 3. Overall Phoneme Error Rate (PER) for different models

Methodology	Phoneme Error Rate (PER) (%)					
	Bengali speech			TIMIT corpus		
	Training	Cross-validation	Testing	Training	Cross-validation	Testing
DNN	24.62	26.14	26.37	19.17	20.79	21.46
HMM	27.08	27.31	28.86	20.97	21.33	22.39
MLP	27.86	28.16	28.78	21.53	22.87	23.28

Table 4. Overall phoneme classification accuracy for different models

Methodology	Phoneme classification accuracy (%)					
	Bengali speech			TIMIT Corpus		
	Training	Cross-validation	Testing	Training	Cross-validation	Testing
DNN	86.70	85.16	82.53	85.31	84.57	83.42
HMM	76.52	76.17	73.86	79.23	77.84	76.82
MLP	75.81	74.36	74.12	78.64	78.23	76.26

GR1	ক /k/	খ /kʰ/	ট /ʈ/	ঠ /ʈʰ/	ত /t̪/	থ /t̪ʰ/	প /p/	ফ /pʰ/	Precision (%)
ক /k/	**7209**	262	184	23	280	21	186	46	83.3
খ /kʰ/	88	**1844**	14	37	11	22	5	43	84.5
ট /ʈ/	128	14	**1342**	46	81	3	29	1	75.5
ঠ /ʈʰ/	11	12	42	**623**	6	16	7	6	79.9
ত /t̪/	338	11	148	7	**7694**	163	149	19	85.5
থ /t̪ʰ/	11	22	1	25	77	**607**	1	15	70.3
প /p/	220	1	70	7	190	5	**4468**	17	83.5
ফ /pʰ/	11	15	0	1	15	14	2	**115**	53.7
Recall (%)	85.0	79.6	66.5	72	86.8	61.3	85.2	34.1	

(a)

GR2	গ /g/	ঘ /gʰ/	ড /ɖ/	ঢ /ɖʰ/	দ /d̪/	ধ /d̪ʰ/	ব /b/	ভ /bʰ/	Precision (%)
গ /g/	**734**	3	6	1	51	3	67	4	72.6
ঘ /gʰ/	3	**212**	0	5	0	11	0	18	64.2
ড /ɖ/	3	0	**153**	7	9	3	7	1	70.8
ঢ /ɖʰ/	0	6	1	**36**	2	10	0	1	40.0
দ /d̪/	79	0	54	1	**2921**	32	100	2	82.3
ধ /d̪ʰ/	1	9	0	30	38	**1092**	0	33	78.2
ব /b/	149	2	15	0	99	5	**4912**	39	88.3
ভ /bʰ/	1	19	0	12	5	40	9	**968**	80.1
Recall (%)	57.8	46.5	46.2	23.8	83.0	77.5	90.8	75.1	

(b)

GR3	য় /e̯/	/w/	উ /u/	ও /o/	অ /ɔ/	আ /a/	অ্যা /æ/	এ /e/	ই /i/	Precision (%)
য় /e̯/	**3221**	16	0	23	5	92	56	216	51	86.9
/w/	21	**254**	1	18	3	28	3	2	1	77.2
উ /u/	0	0	**1654**	279	10	0	0	28	34	76.8
ও /o/	35	23	379	**15090**	573	152	15	120	3	88.2
অ /ɔ/	5	1	11	477	**8047**	408	0	5	0	89.7
আ /a/	105	14	1	195	359	**19844**	239	135	2	93.7
অ্যা /æ/	46	0	0	9	0	108	**1918**	64	11	87.0
এ /e/	440	2	23	121	20	161	125	**19614**	1217	88.5
ই /i/	105	2	26	12	0	0	14	947	**13160**	90.3
Recall (%)	80.3	78.4	72.8	91.6	88.8	94.9	79.5	91.5	89.4	

(c)

GR4	চ /ʧ/	ছ /ʧʰ/	জ /ʤ/	ঝ /ʤʰ/	Precision (%)
চ /ʧ/	**1797**	218	71	13	80.3
ছ /ʧʰ/	265	**4382**	44	37	90.3
জ /ʤ/	48	49	**3908**	54	90.5
ঝ /ʤʰ/	1	4	12	**9**	26.5
Recall (%)	78.4	91.9	91.3	6.0	

(d)

GR5	ল /l/	র /r/	ড় /ɽ/	Precision (%)
ল /l/	**3416**	52	1	90.3
র /r/	77	**7345**	80	86.1
ড় /ɽ/	9	39	**376**	79.2
Recall %)	86.9	88.9	70.9	

(e)

GR6	শ /ʃ/	স /s/	হ /h/	Precision (%)
শ /ʃ/	**9826**	26	3	98.2
স /s/	29	**2937**	0	94.8
হ /h/	5	0	**2793**	88.9
Recall %)	98.6	96.3	90.4	

(f)

GR7	ম /m/	ন /n/	ঙ /ŋ/	Precision (%)
ম /m/	**3439**	199	63	88.1
ন /n/	327	**9027**	102	88.3
ঙ /ŋ/	47	52	**996**	86.0
Recall %)	86.8	92.0	81.2	

(g)

Fig. 2. Confusion matrices of different phonemes using DNN based classification model

has been generated. Some sections of the whole confusion matrix is represented in Fig. 2. In Fig. 2(a) the confusion matrix of unvoiced stop consonants has been provided followed by the confusion between voiced stop consonants, vowels and semivowels, affricates, trill and lateral, fricatives, and nasal phonemes in Fig. 2(b), (c), (d), (e), (f) and (g) respectively. From the confusion matrices, it is found that all the unvoiced stop consonants have high degree of confusion in continuous speech. This is because each of them contains an occlusion period which is a silence due to the blockage of nasal and air passage of mouth [15]. The spectrogram of the unvoiced phonemes k, ʈ, t̪, p in Fig. 3 shows that the occlusion period spans along a significant portion of the total duration of each unvoiced phoneme. The occlusion is nothing but silence. The difference between these phonemes are observed only in the transitory part which comes after the occlusion period, and it spans along a very little duration. As a result, sometimes it becomes difficult for a classifier to found differences between them in continuous speech. Same thing is observed in case of voiced stop consonants. Instead of the occlusion period, a voiced segment is spanned over a significant duration in every voiced phoneme.

From the confusion matrices of Fig. 2(a) and (b) it can be observed that almost each unaspirated consonant has confusion with the aspirated one whether they are voiced or unvoiced. This is because in Bengali continuous speech sometimes it becomes quite difficult to separate the unaspirated and aspirated stop consonants as the duration of glottal aspiration is very less for continuous speech data. For example, in continuous speech, it is very common to pronounce the Bengali word 'bag^h' (The Tiger) as 'bag'. Similarly, 'ʃhank^h' (SHELL), 'mɔʈ^h' (MONASTERY) becomes 'ʃhank' and 'mɔʈ' respectively. Most of these types of confusions occur when the corresponding phonemes are placed at a utterance-final position that is, they act as a stop consonant.

The affricates have confusion in between the phoneme of their own class and not so much with other phonemes. However from the phoneme confusion matrix

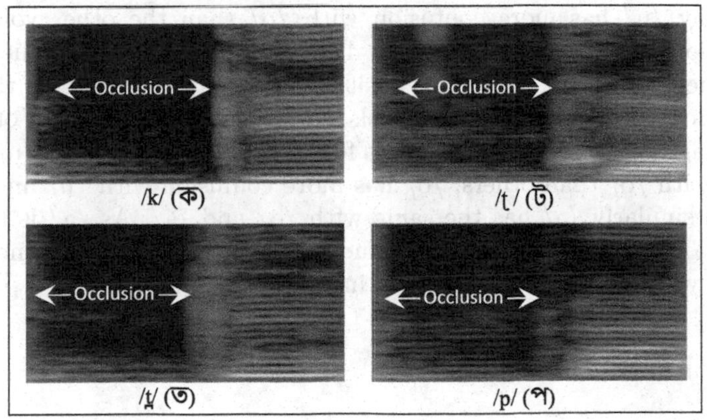

Fig. 3. Spectrogram for unvoiced phoneme /k/, /ʈ/, /t̪/, /p/

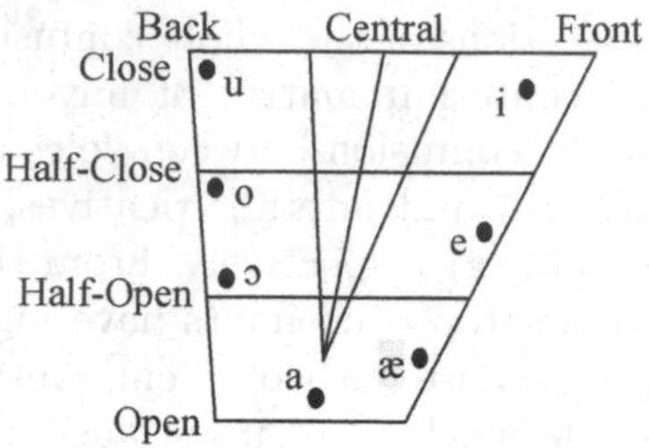

Fig. 4. Cardinal diagram of Bengali vowels [25]

it is observed that sometimes the affricate /ʧ/ is confused with /ʃ/. This is because the sound of phoneme /ʧ/ is very close to /ʃ/ with the common place of articulation as the post-alveolar and unvoiced manner of articulation. /ʧ/ starts with a complete stoppage of airflow at the post-alveolar point of articulation. From the IPA notation it might be thought that /ʧ/ has pronunciation similarity with /t̪/ on that stoppage segment. But /ʧ/ is pronounced more at post-alveolar point of articulation. As it is also unvoiced phoneme, so it also has an occlusion periods. Sometimes phoneme recognizers treat this occlusion section as a silence and rest of the section as /ʃ/ and results a confusion between /ʧ/ and /ʃ/ in Bengali continuous speech.

In continuous Bengali speech it is hard to pronounce separately trill /r/ and the flap/tap consonants /ɽ/, /$ɽ^h$/. That is why the phoneme 'ɽ' has confusion with 'r'. Moreover the lateral phoneme /l/ and the trill /r/ has confusion between them. So /l/, /r/ and /ɽ/ are grouped together.

Semivowel /e̯/ and /w/ have confusion with the vowels which is shown in Fig. 2(c). So they are clustered in a group. From the confusion matrix of 2(c) it is observed that the vowel /u/ holds maximum confusion with the vowel /o/ compared to other vowels. According to the Bengali vowel-cardinal diagram [25], shown in Fig. 4, it is observed that vowel /u/ and /o/ are consecutive vowels. That is why /u/ has more confusion with /o/ than the other vowels. From the confusion matrix of Figs. 2(c) and 4 it is also observed that the confusion between the vowels depend on the position of vowels according to the Bengali vowel cardinal diagram. More the vowels are situated closer to each other in the cardinal diagram, more the confusion is found between them. Like /u/ has more confusion with /o/ than others, /o/ has more confusion with /u/ and /ɔ/ than others and similarly /ɔ/ has the same with /o/ and /a/. As /a/ is the central vowel so /a/ has confusion with /ɔ/ and /æ/ and also with /o/ and /e/. The rest of the vowels also have confusions in similar manner.

5 Conclusion

In this paper, Bengali phonemes are recognized and classified from Bengali continuous and unconstrained speech. Low PER and good phoneme classification accuracy increase the phoneme boundary information. Phonemes are classified with reasonably good overall classification accuracy using DNN-based approach. Almost all the phonemes are classified with high precision, recall and f-score value.

In Bengali continuous speech sometimes the pronunciation of /r/ is omitted. As example, the words like ḓurgapuʤo, parbon is pronounced as ḓuggapuʤo and pabbon respectively in continuous spoken Bengali speech. Due to this type of deletion error, it is tough to identify the word sequence by the language model. Incorporation of some knowledge based information can resolve this kind of issues.

In this paper, a DNN based phoneme recognition and classification model are presented where almost 12–20% average improvement over the baseline systems is observed. Some works are going on other Indian regional languages to ensure the robustness of the scheme.

References

1. Averbuch, A., Bahl, L., Bakis, R., Brown, P., Daggett, G., Das, S., Davies, K., De Gennaro, S., De Souza, P., Epstein, E., et al.: Experiments with the TANGORA 20,000 word speech recognizer. In: Acoustics, Speech, and Signal Processing, IEEE International Conference on ICASSP 1987, vol. 12, pp. 701–704. IEEE (1987)
2. Bengio, Y.: Learning deep architectures for AI. Found. Trends® Mach. Learn. **2**(1), 1–127 (2009)
3. Chow, Y., Dunham, M., Kimball, O., Krasner, M., Kubala, G., Makhoul, J., Price, P., Roucos, S., Schwartz, R.: BYBLOS: the BBN continuous speech recognition system. In: IEEE International Conference on Acoustics, Speech, and Signal Processing, ICASSP 1887, vol. 12, pp. 89–92. IEEE (1987)
4. Das, B., Mandal, S., Mitra, P., Basu, A.: Effect of aging on speech features and phoneme recognition: a study on Bengali voicing vowels. Int. J. Speech Technol. **16**(1), 19–31 (2013)
5. Das Mandal, S.: Role of Shape Parameters in Speech Recognition: A Study on Standard Colloquial Bengali (SCB). Ph.D. thesis (2007)
6. Demuth, H., Beale, M.: Neural Network Toolbox: For Use with MATLAB: User's Guide (1993)
7. Deng, L., Yu, D.: Deep learning for signal and information processing. Microsoft Res. Monogr. (2013)
8. Garofolo, J., Consortium, L.D., et al.: TIMIT: Acoustic-Phonetic Continuous Speech Corpus. Linguistic Data Consortium, Philadelphia (1993)
9. Glorot, X., Bengio, Y.: Understanding the difficulty of training deep feedforward neural networks. In: AISTATS, vol. 9, pp. 249–256 (2010)
10. Hasnat, M.A., Mowla, J., Khan, M., et al.: Isolated and continuous Bangla speech recognition: implementation, performance and application perspective (2007)
11. Hassan, M.R., Nath, B., Bhuiyan, M.A.: Bengali phoneme recognition: a new approach. In: Proceedings of 6th International Conference on Computer and Information Technology (ICCIT 2003) (2003)
12. Hinton, G., Deng, L., Yu, D., Dahl, G., Mohamed, A.R., Jaitly, N., et al.: Deep neural networks for acoustic modeling in speech recognition: the shared views of four research groups. IEEE Signal Process. Mag. **29**(6), 82–97 (2012)

13. Lee, K.F., Hon, H.W.: Speaker-independent phone recognition using hidden markov models. IEEE Trans. Acoust. Speech Signal Process. **37**(11), 1641–1648 (1989)
14. Mandal, S.D., Saha, A., Datta, A.: Annotated speech corpora development in Indian languages. Vishwa Bharat **6**, 49–64 (2005)
15. Mandal, S., Chandra, S., Lata, S., Datta, A.: Places and manner of articulation of Bangla consonants: an EPG based study. In: INTERSPEECH, Florence, Italy, pp. 3149–3152 (2011)
16. MATLAB: MATLAB version 8.5.0.197613 (R2015b). The Mathworks Inc., Natick, Massachusetts (2015)
17. Meyer, B.T., Wächter, M., Brand, T., Kollmeier, B.: Phoneme confusions in human and automatic speech recognition. In: INTERSPEECH, pp. 1485–1488 (2007)
18. Mukherjee, S., Mandal, S.: A Bengali hmm based speech synthesis system. arXiv preprint arXiv:1406.3915 (2014)
19. Palm, R.B.: Prediction as a candidate for learning deep hierarchical models of data. Master's thesis (2012)
20. Paul, A.K., Das, D., Kamal, M.M.: Bangla speech recognition system using LPC and ANN. In: Seventh International Conference on Advances in Pattern Recognition, ICAPR 2009, pp. 171–174. IEEE (2009)
21. Peeling, S., Moore, R.: Isolated digit recognition experiments using the multi-layer perceptron. Speech Commun. **7**(4), 403–409 (1988)
22. Rabiner, L.R., Juang, B.H., Levinson, S., Sondhi, M.: Recognition of isolated digits using hidden Markov models with continuous mixture densities. AT&T Tech. J. **64**(6), 1211–1234 (1985)
23. Rabiner, L.: A tutorial on hidden Markov models and selected applications in speech recognition. Proc. IEEE **77**(2), 257–286 (1989)
24. Rahman, K., Hossain, M., Das, D., Islam, T., Ali, M.: Continuous Bangla speech recognition system. In: Proceedings of 6th International Conference on Computer and Information Technology (ICCIT 2003) (2003)
25. Roach, P.: English Phonetics and Phonology Fourth Edition: A Practical Course. Ernst Klett Sprachen, Stuttgart (2010)
26. Rumelhart, D., Hinton, G., Williams, R.: Learning representations by back-propagating errors. Nature **323**, 533–536 (1986)
27. Vincent, P., Larochelle, H., Lajoie, I., Bengio, Y., Manzagol, P.A.: Stacked denoising autoencoders: learning useful representations in a deep network with a local denoising criterion. J. Mach. Learn. Res. **11**, 3371–3408 (2010)
28. Waibel, A., Hanazawa, T., Hinton, G., Shikano, K., Lang, K.: Phoneme recognition: neural networks vs. hidden Markov models vs. hidden Markov models. In: 1988 International Conference on Acoustics, Speech, and Signal Processing, ICASSP-1988, pp. 107–110. IEEE (1988)
29. Young, S., Evermann, G., Gales, M., Hain, T., Kershaw, D., Liu, X., Moore, G., Odell, J., Ollason, D., Povey, D., et al.: The HTK Book, vol. 2. Entropic Cambridge Research Laboratory, Cambridge (1997)

Do Heavy and Superheavy Syllables Always Bear Prominence in Hindi?

Somnath Roy(✉) and Bimrisha Mali

Centre for Linguistics, Jawaharlal Nehru University, New Delhi, India
somnathroy86@gmail.com, bimrishal23mali@gmail.com

Abstract. Lexical stress in Hindi is not distinctive in nature. Past studies on Hindi stress system have an agreement that syllable weight is the most influencing feature for stress. In this paper, we investigate the change in the duration of syllable nucleus as an acoustic correlate of syllable weight. The duration is captured in four contexts—(i) vowel identity (ii) voiced/voiceless coda in closed syllables and (iii) word uttered after a stressed and an unstressed syllable. It is found that heavy syllables are prominent in limited context only. The prominence pattern of a heavy syllable is largely affected by aforementioned contexts. Moreover, it is also found that superheavy syllables are independent of these contexts and are always prominent.

Keywords: Syllable weight · Duration · Prominence · Stress

1 Introduction

The phonological account of lexical stress in Hindi is explored by [1–3]. These studies have partial agreement for stress placement rule but fully agree to the fact that lexical stress in Hindi can be predicted by the syllable weight. Hindi is a quantity sensitive language. Syllables in Hindi are categorized as light, heavy and superheavy based on moraic weight count. The syllable having one, two and three moras are called light, heavy and superheavy respectively. The moraic weight count in Hindi syllables follows simple rule as stated below.

- Assign one mora to short vowel and one mora to each coda consonant.
- Assign two moras to long vowel.

Acoustic correlates of lexical stress in Hindi are investigated by [4–7]. A production-perception based experiment conducted in [4] for ascertaining the phonetic correlates of lexical stress in Hindi. The experiment measured the duration of vowel and coda in stressed and unstressed syllables. The study reports no significant difference between the duration in these units between stressed and unstressed counterparts. The role of pitch is investigated in [5] for lexical stress categorization. The study was carried for word in isolation and also when spoken with a carrier sentence. The analysis of the study reveals that there is no particular pitch pattern for lexical stress in Hindi. Therefore, [4, 5] concludes that Hindi does not have lexical stress but can bear pragmatic stress. The possible causes of ambiguity in the result of [4, 5] is explained in [6]. They report that the study by [4, 5] used the word pair mətlab /Meaning/ and prətje:k /

P. Bhattacharyya et al. (Eds.): NGCT 2017, CCIS 827, pp. 761–768, 2018.
https://doi.org/10.1007/978-981-10-8657-1_59

Every/, which contains /t l/ and /t j/ pairs. The /t j/ pair geminates thus its duration cannot be compared with /t l/ pair as described in [2]. [6] also claims that Hindi bears lexical stress. They extracted the vowel duration and formant frequencies (F1 and F2 only) in stressed and unstressed syllables. The recording is carried out by inserting words in two carrier sentences. The sentences were (i) / kəha:—a:pne:/ (said—you) (ii) bo:la:—a:pne: (spoke—you). The first carrier sentence contains the stressed syllable and second carrier sentence contains unstressed syllable before the word to be inserted. Their analysis reports that the formants are a weak indicator of lexical stress but duration is an important acoustic cue for this purpose. That is, the duration is a useful acoustic cue for stress in Hindi. The study of [7] reports that lexical stress in Hindi can be realized in the form of varying prominence pattern among constituent syllables of a word. He found that pitch contour (LH) and duration are the significant acoustic cues associated with lexical stress in Hindi. The motivation for this work lies in the following three points.

- There exist a handful studies on acoustic correlates of lexical stress in Hindi. Moreover, there does not exist an study on acoustic correlates of syllable weight in Hindi.
- The identification of prominent syllable in citation speech or in continuous speech are of utmost importance for building a dictionary or lexicon for Text-to-Speech (TTS) system and Automatic speech recognition (ASR) system.
- The present study uses only duration of syllable nucleus as an acoustic correlate of syllable weight in Hindi. The acoustic cue is captured by the taking the context of (i) vowel identity (i.e., the type of vowel used as syllable nucleus), (ii) syllable uttered after stressed or unstressed syllable and (iii) the type of coda con sonant in case of closed syllables.

The present study differs from the past studies based on following novel contributions.

- Syllable weight is considered as the most influencing factor for stress placement in Hindi. However, past studies have only decreed this claim based on their intuition based analysis. The present study investigate duration of syllable nucleus as an acoustic correlate of syllable weight in Hindi.
- Based on duration as a cue, current study also investigate the context in which heavy and superheavy syllables are prominent.

2 Experimental Details

This section describes the linguistic data collected and process of speech recording. It also describes the acoustic cues extracted for the analysis.

2.1 Linguistic Data

Monosyllabic and bisyllabic words having only oral vowels for syllable nucleus are used for the recording. These words are recorded using the carrier sentence presented in [6].

The carrier sentences are—(i) kə**ha:**—a:pne: /Said—You/. (ii) **bo:**la:—a:pne: /Spoke—You/. The bold syllables shown in these sentences are stressed one. The words inserted in the first sentence are uttered followed by an stressed syllable and in second sentence words are uttered after an unstressed syllable. Speech data are recorded from ten male speakers in normal tempo. The speakers[1] were either Delhite (born and brought up in Delhi) or one who has been studying in Delhi for the last 10 years. Speakers are asked to take a short break between two sentences. The description of the word types and its contextual features are summarized in Table 1. The acronym SP denotes position of a syllable in a word. The acronym F means the final or last syllable in a word and NF means non-final syllables.

Table 1. Summary of word type and the its feature in terms of syllable position (SP) syllable weight (SW), close or open (C/O) and vowel identity (VI)

Word type	SP	SW	C/O	VI	#Words
Monsyllabic	F	Heavy	C	Lax	20
Monsyllabic	F	Heavy	O	Tense	20
Monsyllabic	F	Superheavy	C	Tense	20
Bisyllabic	NF and F	Heavy	O	Tense	20
Bisyllabic	F	Superheavy	C	Tense	20

The acronym SW means syllable weight—(i) weak (ii) heavy and (iii) superheavy. The acronym C/O represents C for close syllable and O for open syllable. The acronym VI represents vowel identity. Close syllables used in this study contains 10 different coda consonants—p, t, k, s, tʃ, ʃ, b, d, g, dʒ.

2.2 Syllable Boundary and Syllable Nucleus Boundary Marking

The present study follows the syllabification rules proposed in [2, 3]. Words are sliced from the carrier sentences. A praat script [8] is written for automatic syllable boundary and vowel boundary marking in the sliced words. The syllable boundaries thus obtained in the form of Textgrid are manually verified and corrected by the first author (see Fig. 1).

2.3 Acoustic Cues

Duration is the most important acoustic cues for the categorization of syllable weight or stressed vs. unstressed syllable in many languages including Hindi [6, 7]. The present study extracts duration of syllable nucleus in all four the contexts described above.

[1] Each speaker were recorded on his/her consent and there is no ethical issue involved.

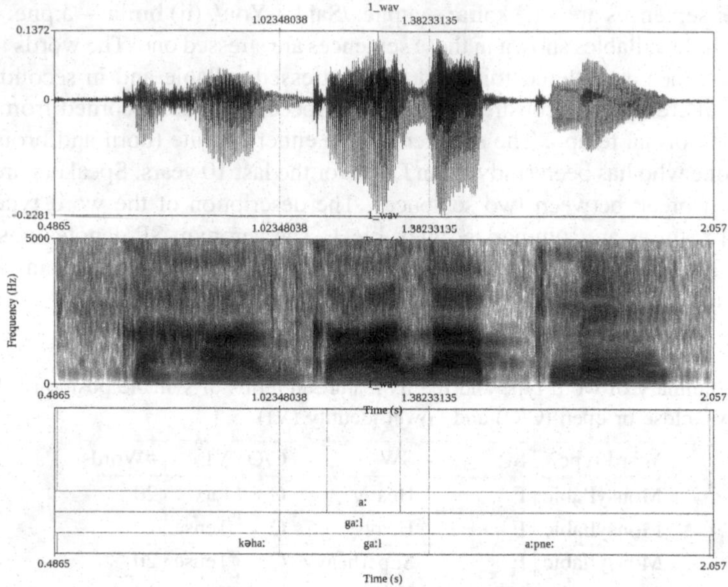

Fig. 1. The wav file, spectrogram and textgrid for a sample sentence kəha: ga:l a:pne: /Said cheek you/. The top textgrid shows the vowel boundary of the word ga:l, the second textgrid shows the syllable boundary of the word ga:l, and the third textgrid shows the whole sentence.

3 Subjective Analysis of Vowel Duration for Prominence

Sixty monosyllabic and fourty bisyllabic words as described in Table 1 are recorded in a noise proof sound recording studio. These words are recorded at a sampling rate of 16 kHz and stored as 16 bit PCM data. A Praat MFC-based production perception experiment is designed to determine the prominent syllables in a word. Five subjects participated in this experiment and manually annotated the syllables as prominent or non-prominent based on the listening test. The subjects have formal training in phonetics and are native Hindi speakers. The vowel duration of prominent and non-prominent syllables are extracted from the annotated syllables for prominent and non-prominent. The summary of average vowel duration and corresponding standard deviation in prominent and non-prominent syllables are descried in Table 1.

The values described in the Table 2 can be stated as the following.

a. A syllable having lax vowel of duration less than 98 ms are not prominent.
b. A syllable having lax vowel of duration more than 105 ms are prominent.
c. A syllable having tense vowel of duration less than 153 ms are not prominent.
d. A syllable having tense vowel of duration more than 162 ms are prominent.

The following sections use the above four points as a basic generalization for classifying prominent and non-prominent syllables.

Table 2. Summary of average duration and its standard deviation for identifying prominent (P) and non-prominent (NP) syllables

VI	Average duration (ms)	Standard deviation (ms)	P/NP
Lax	95.20	2.10	NP
Lax	105.10	10.32	P
Tense	146.70	5.74	NP
Tense	162	15.57	P

4 Prominence Pattern

This section describes the prominence pattern for heavy and superheavy syllables uttered after stressed and unstressed syllable. Heavy syllables in Hindi are either closed or open. The closed heavy syllables have lax vowel and open heavy syllables have tense vowel e.g., मन /soul/ (closed heavy) and गा /sing/ (open heavy). The superheavy syllables in Hindi are always closed e.g., गाल /cheek/. The vowel duration of these syllables are extracted for classifying it as prominent and non-prominent. The classification decision using vowel duration is based on the four points rule described in Sect. 3.

4.1 Closed Heavy and Superheavy Syllables with Voiceless Coda

This section describes the prominence pattern in closed heavy and superheavy syllables with voiceless coda. These syllables are uttered after stressed and unstressed syllable. The extracted vowel duration is shown below in Fig. 2. The data suggests the following points.

i. The heavy syllables with nucleus as schwa (mid-central vowel) and /u/(back vowel) are not prominent. The average duration for these vowels are less than 100 ms. The vowel duration has slightly increased when uttered after an unstressed syllable but the value is not enough to become prominent. However, the heavy syllables with front vowel /i/as nucleus is found prominent irrespective of the context in which it is spoken.
ii. All superheavy syllables are prominent because all the tense vowels have crossed 162 ms mark.
iii. The context of speaking i.e., speaking a word after stressed syllable and unstressed syllable has no role in making a syllable prominent in this case.

4.2 Closed Heavy and Superheavy Syllables with Voiceless Coda

This section describes the prominence pattern in closed heavy and superheavy syllables with voiced coda. These syllables are uttered after stressed and unstressed syllable. The extracted vowel duration is shown below in Fig. 3. The data suggests the following points.

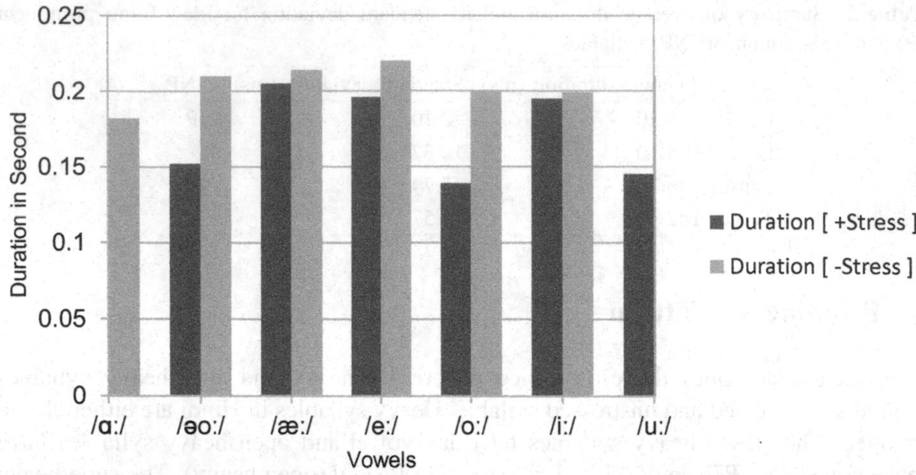

Fig. 2. Vowel duration of closed and heavy monosyllabic words with voiceless coda uttered after stressed syllable (duration [+stress −voice]) and unstressed syllable (duration [−stress −voice]). b

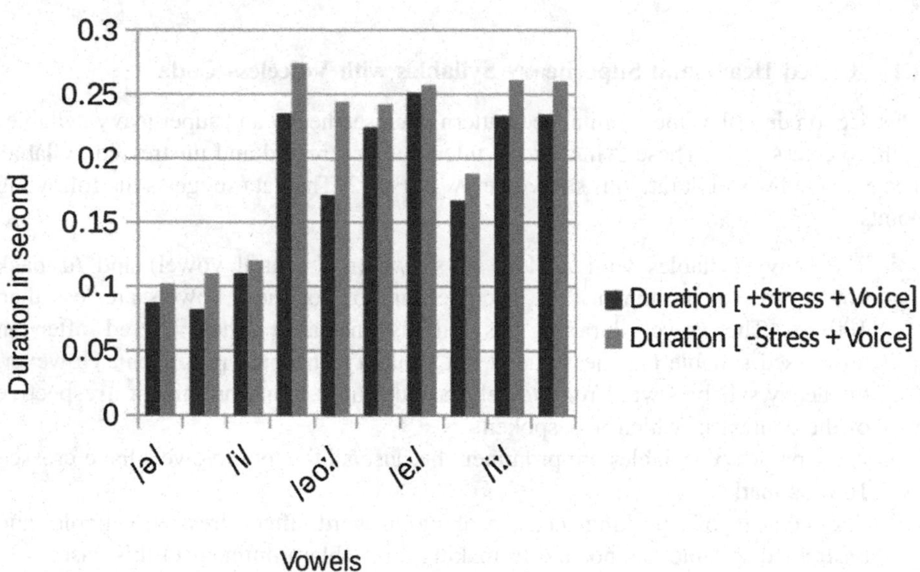

Fig. 3. Vowel duration of closed and heavy monosyllabic words with voiced coda uttered after stressed syllable (duration [+stress −voice]) and unstressed syllable (duration [−stress −voice]).

i. All closed heavy syllables with lax vowels as nucleus are prominent if uttered after an unstressed syllable. Here the voiced coda constant clearly increasing the duration of nucleus which can be observed by comparing the Figs. 2 and 3.
ii. The closed heavy syllables with lax vowels as nucleus are not prominent if uttered after a stressed syllable.

iii. All superheavy syllables are stressed.
iv. If we compare the Figs. 2 and 3, it can be clearly observed that the nucleus vowel duration increases with voiced coda consonant.

4.3 Open and Heavy Syllables

A heavy syllable with no coda constant always has tense vowel as nucleus. The data for such words is shown below in Fig. 4. The analysis of these data suggests the following points.

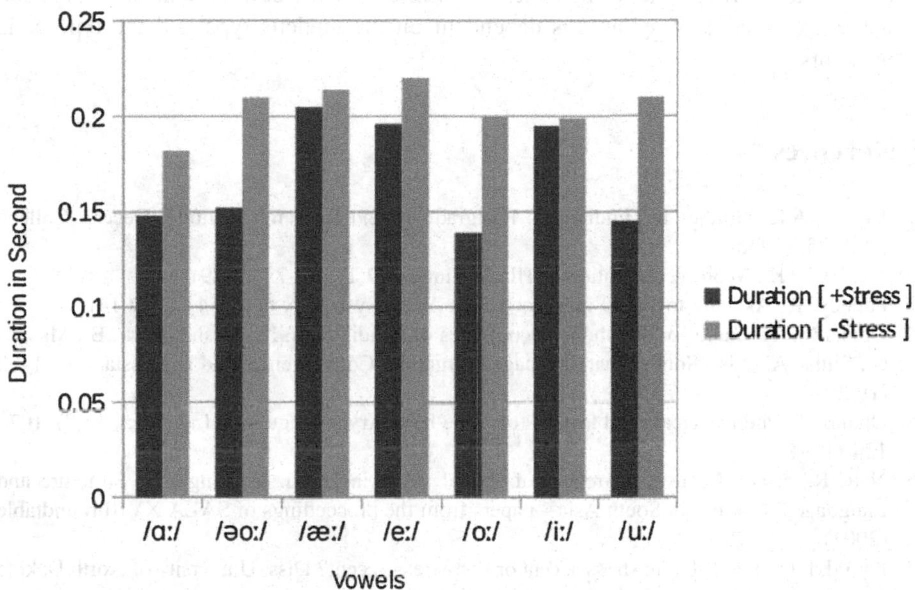

Fig. 4. Vowel duration of open heavy monosyllabic words uttered after stressed syllable (duration [+stress]) and unstressed syllable (duration [−stress]).

i. The open heavy syllables with back vowel as nucleus are not prominent.
ii. All other syllables are prominent and these syllables are independent of the context of uttering a syllable after a stressed or unstressed syllable for prominence.

5 Conclusion

We have found that the closed heavy syllables having voiceless consonants and schwa (i.e., mid-central vowel) or back vowel /u/as nucleus are not prominent. Such syllables are independent of the context of uttering a syllable after a stressed or unstressed one for prominence. Moreover, these types of syllables are found to be stressed if it contains the front vowel /i/ as nucleus. The closed heavy syllables having voiced consonants are largely affected by the context of uttering a syllable after stressed or an unstressed one. All such syllables are prominent if uttered after an unstressed syllable. The open heavy syllables are also independent of the context of uttering a syllable after a stressed or unstressed syllable for prominence. Moreover these syllables are not all prominent if it contains back vowels as nucleus.

It is also found that superheavy syllables are independent of all such contexts and are always prominent in Hindi. These analyses suggest that there is a need of revision of the existing notion that the heavy syllables are always stressed if followed by an unstressed syllable. The intuition based analyses proposed in [2, 3] need to be revised because it suggests that if there is a pattern like weak syllable followed by a heavy syllable and so on then heavy syllable is prominent. In the current analysis it is found that the prominence of syllable is dependent on the nucleus type and the type coda consonants.

References

1. Kelkar, A.R.: Studies in Hindi-Urdu. Postgraduate and Research Institute, Deccan College (Vol. 35) (1968)
2. Pandey, P.K.: Word accentuation in Hindi. Lingua **77**(1), 37–73 (1989)
3. Pandey, P.: Akshara-to-sound rules for Hindi. Writ. Syst. Res. **6**(1), 54–72 (2014)
4. Ohala, M.: A search for the phonetic correlates of Hindi stress. In: Krishnamurti, B., Masica, C., Sinha, A. (eds.) South Asian languages: structure, Convergence, and Diglossia, pp. 81–92 (1986)
5. Ohala, M.: Phonological areal features of some Indo-Aryan languages. Lang. Sci. **13**(2), 107–124 (1991)
6. Nair, R., et al.: Acoustic correlates of lexical stress in Hindi. In: Linguistic Structure and Language Dynamics in South Asia—papers from the proceedings of SALA XVIII roundtable (2001)
7. Dyrud, L.O.: Hindi-Urdu: stress accent or non-stress accent? Diss. University of North Dakota (2001)
8. Boersma, P., Weenink, D.: Praat-a system for doing phonetics by computer [computer software]. Institute of Phonetic Sciences, University of Amsterdam, The Netherlands (2003)

Design and Development of a Dictionary Based Stemmer for Marathi Language

Harshali B. Patil(✉), Neelima T. Mhaske, and Ajay S. Patil

School of Computer Sciences, North Maharashtra University, Jalgaon, Maharashtra, India
patilharshalib@gmail.com, neelimamhaske@gmail.com, aspatil@nmu.ac.in

Abstract. Stemming is one of the term conflation techniques used to reduce morphological variations of the term into a unique term called as "stem". Stemming is one of the significant pre-processing steps performed in various applications of natural language processing (NLP) and information retrieval (IR): like machine translation, named entity recognition, automated document processing, etc. In this paper, we focus on the development of automated stemmer for the Marathi language. We have adopted the dictionary lookup technique for this task. The experiment is tested on news articles in the Marathi language consists of 4500 words. The proposed stemmer achieved a maximum accuracy of 80.6% when tested on nine different runs. The over-stemming error rate is low. The satisfactory result of proposed stemmer encourages us to use this stemmer for the information retrieval task.

Keywords: Stemming · Marathi · Dictionary lookup · NLP

1 Introduction

The profusion of words appearing in various morphological forms due to inflection or derivation adversely affects on the effectiveness of IR systems. One of the common methods to reduce this adverse effect of morphological variations of the terms, is to use normalized representation of the inflected words. Stemming is one of such approach that transform morphological variations of terms to their common stem, for instance, "भारतच, भारतही, भारताचा, भारतामधून, भारतामध्ये", etc. are transformed into "भारत". The use of stemmers in IR improves the performance and decreases the index size. Several techniques of stemmer development have been proposed by researchers for different languages. Popular approaches include rule-based, dictionary/table lookup, statistical and hybrid. The rule-based technique uses a set of rules based on linguistic analysis for stripping the suffixes while table lookup stemmers simply look up the words in the lookup table and assigns stem to them. Statistical stemmers are developed by using corpus statistics in the form of measures like n-gram, HMM, etc. Each of these approaches has their own pros and cons; so some hybrid stemmers are developed by combining some of these techniques to overcome the drawbacks of individual approach.

P. Bhattacharyya et al. (Eds.): NGCT 2017, CCIS 827, pp. 769–777, 2018.
https://doi.org/10.1007/978-981-10-8657-1_60

In this digital era, a large amount of digital content is available on the web in regional languages, and Marathi is not the exception for this. The huge amount of Marathi digital data like government records, news, books, etc. are available on the web. To access and process this data NLP tools are required, and stemmer is one such important pre-processing tool used in most of the NLP systems. In this work, we propose dictionary based stemmer for the Marathi language. Marathi is one of the 22 official languages of India. It is the official language of Maharashtra and the co-official language of Goa.

The rest of the paper is organized as follows: Sect. 2 presents the related work. The proposed stemmer is discussed in Sect. 3 followed by the results in Sect. 4. Section 5 concludes the paper and discusses the future work.

2 Related Work

As a research area stemming has been explored since late 60 s. Lovins developed one of the earliest stemmers for English language using context sensitive longest match basis [1]. The early work related to stemmer development was focused on English language, some most notable stemmers for English language were developed by Dawson and Porter [2, 3] and a comparison of various English stemmers have been reported in [4, 5]. As there is a spectacular growth in the digital data available in non-English languages on a world wide web, a need has been emerged for research and development of basic language processing tools like stemmer and morphological analyzers related to these languages. Some non-English stemmers are developed like Arabic [6], Portuguese [7], Persian [8], etc.

Dictionaries are incorporated in stemming to reduce the over-stemming errors. Brute-force based stemmer for Punjabi language is developed by Kumar et al. where the author used 28000 words lookup table along with some suffix removal rules and reported an average accuracy of 80.73% and concluded that the similar type of approach can be used for development of stemmer for other Indic languages [9]. Mishra et al. reported MAULIK: an effective stemmer for Hindi language which is a hybrid stemmer based on brute force and suffix removal approach [10]. Joshi et al. hybridized a stemmer based on lookup table algorithm and rule-based algorithm for Punjabi language and tested it on 250 words [11]. The detailed analysis of stemming algorithms available for Indic languages is done by Patil et al. [12]. Many Stemmers are available for Indic languages but the work for Marathi stemmer development has been started recently. The currently available stemmers for Marathi language include the stemmer developed by Almeida et al. that uses n-gram technique [13]. They obtained the mean average precision (MAP) of 35.79% against baseline MAP of 23.94%. Majgaonkar reported their efforts for Marathi stemmer development. They used rule-based and unsupervised techniques, and concluded that with statistical suffix stripping approach they obtained maximum accuracy for a test dataset of 1500 unique words [14]. Another Marathi rule-based stemmer has been proposed in reference [15]. Dolamic et al. developed light and aggressive stemmers for Marathi and obtained a change in MAP of 41.6% with aggressive stemmer and 13.9% with light stemmer [16]. Husain used an unsupervised approach for stemmer development using frequency based method and length based method. The author tested this stemmer for Urdu and Marathi language and found that length based method works better as compared to frequency based method when tested on 1200 words [17]. It would be interesting to investigate the performance of a stemmer for Marathi that hybridizes rule-based approach with other stemming techniques. To begin with, we propose a dictionary based stemmer for the Marathi language as explained in the following sections.

3 Proposed Stemmer

Dictionary lookup stemmers employ a dictionary, sometimes called as a lookup table, which contains inflected forms of words along with their stems. To obtain the stem for an inflected word the table is queried to find a matching inflection. If a matching inflection is found then the associated stem is returned otherwise the same inflected word is returned as a stem.

3.1 Preparation of Dictionary

Dictionary is the imperative component in this type of stemmers. Dictionary development process is carried out by various phases like document cleaning, tokenization, etc. The logical view of dictionary development is as given in Fig. 1.

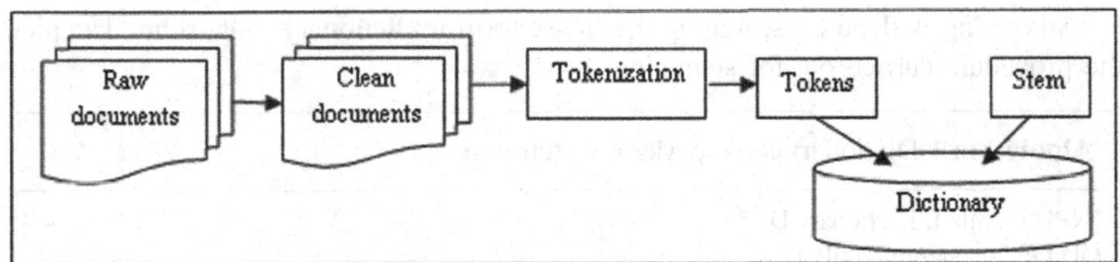

Fig. 1. Dictionary development

Large vocabulary is required for development of dictionary, therefore we used some documents of FIRE[1] corpus. FIRE (Forum for Information Retrieval Evaluation) offers the large corpus and queries along with some resources for research purpose. Table 1 summarizes the detailed statistics of FIRE Marathi collection. The corpora consist of newspaper articles from Maharashtra Times and Daily Sakal spanning the period of April 2004 - September 2007.

Each document is in textual format and having 2 fields, DOCNO and TEXT. DOCNO is a unique identifier assigned to each document. TEXT field contains entire news article in plain text. The encoding system used is UTF-8. We extracted 7,82,922 words from

[1] http://www.isical.ac.in/fire/.

Table 1. FIRE Marathi corpus statistics

Factor	Data size
Documents	99275
Size	485 MB
Unique terms	855980

3000 documents of FIRE corpus. Among these words after removing numbers and duplicate entries 1,02,638 unique words are used for developing the dictionary. The corresponding stems are added manually with the words and thus the word-stem dictionary is prepared. The statistical information related to dictionary is summarized in Table 2. The number of Unicode characters represents the length of the word.

Table 2. Dictionary statistics

Factor	Data size
Documents	3000
Words	782922
Unique words	102638
Maximum length of word	17
Minimum length of word	2
Mean word length	5.57

Stemming is done by searching the index term in dictionary. Algorithm 1 depicts the procedure carried out for stemming.

Algorithm 1 Dictionary lookup Marathi stemmer

```
INPUT : File f, Dictionary D.
OUTPUT : Stemmed file f'
Begin
Read the file f to be stemmed
Tokenize the file f and populate token vector TV
for Each token t in TV do
   if t is present in D then
      add corresponding stem s from D in stem vector sv
   else
      add t in stem vector sv // t may not be the correct stem.
   end if
end for
Write sv in output file f'
return f'
End
```

4 Results

For evaluation purpose of the proposed dictionary based stemmer, various parameters like its percentage accuracy, strength, over-stemming and under-stemming errors are used. The following section discusses the results produced by the proposed dictionary based stemmer.

4.1 Testing Data

Unavailability of standard test data for this application motivated us to create testing data. We used 50 documents consisting of 11,193 tokens from the FIRE corpus which are not used while dictionary creation. After omitting numbers and duplicate terms, total 4500 unique terms were selected and their stems were added manually in the key file (test data statistics is given in Table 3). Then the results produced by proposed dictionary based stemmer are compared with the manually prepared key file and presented in the following subsections.

Table 3. Test data statistics

Factor	Data size
Documents	50
Words	11193
Unique words	4800
Testing terms	4500

4.2 Stemming Accuracy

The accuracy of the stemmer define the fraction of words stemmed correctly and it is calculated based on the formula 1 as mentioned in reference [17].

$$Accuracy = \frac{Number\ of\ correct\ stems\ of\ words}{Total\ number\ of\ terms\ submitted\ for\ stemming} \times 100 \tag{1}$$

To perform the evaluation of the proposed stemmer, the test data is equally distributed in nine runs including 500 unique terms. Table 4 depicts the % accuracy obtained and the stemming errors made by the proposed stemmer.

4.3 Stemmer Strength

The strength of stemmer denotes the degree to which a stemmer changes the words that it stems. According to Frakes and Fox it is important because, it can be predictive of recall and precision and of index compression. Some ways suggested by the author to measure stemmer strength includes: the mean number of words per conflation class

Table 4. Stemmer accuracy and errors

Run No.	Accuracy (%)	Under-stemming errors (%)	Over-stemming errors (%)
1	79.2	27.2	0.6
2	80.6	28.8	0.4
3	72.4	24.2	1.2
4	68.6	34.4	0.4
5	76.8	19.8	2.8
6	78.2	16.6	0.0
7	76.0	26.8	2.4
8	75.0	21.6	0.4
9	75.0	22.6	1.0

(MWC), index compression factor (ICF), word change factor, the mean number of characters removed (MNCR) in forming stems [18]. The mean number of words per conflation class (MWC) is computed by Eq. 2.

$$MWC = \frac{N}{S} \tag{2}$$

Where N denotes the number of unique words before stemming and S denotes the number of unique stems after stemming. The index compression factor (ICF) is calculated by formula 3.

$$ICF = \frac{(N - S)}{S} \tag{3}$$

where N and S are same as above. The word change factor indicates the proportion of the words in a sample that have been changed in any way by the stemming process. The mean number of characters removed (MNCR) is the average number of characters removed when a stemmer is applied to a text collection. It is calculated based on formula 4.

$$MNCR = \frac{\sum Characters\ removed\ from\ each\ term}{Total\ number\ of\ terms} \tag{4}$$

The various factors suggested by Frakes and Fox have also been considered for evaluating the proposed stemmer and Table 5 summarizes the results. From this table it is observed that 0.55 words i.e. 55% has been changed while stemming. The mean number of characters removed shows that near about 1.74 characters are removed from each word.

Table 5. Stemmer strength

Factor	Data size
Mean number of words per conflation class	1.55
Index compression factor	0.35
Word change factor	0.55
Mean number of characters removed	1.74

4.4 Stemming Errors

According to Paice two types of errors are generated by the stemming process, i.e. under-stemming errors and over-stemming errors [19]. Under-stemming errors refer to the words that should be grouped together by stemming, but that are not grouped. Over-stemming errors refer to the words that should not be grouped together by stemming but they are grouped. The errors made by the proposed stemmer in each run is as mentioned in Table 4.

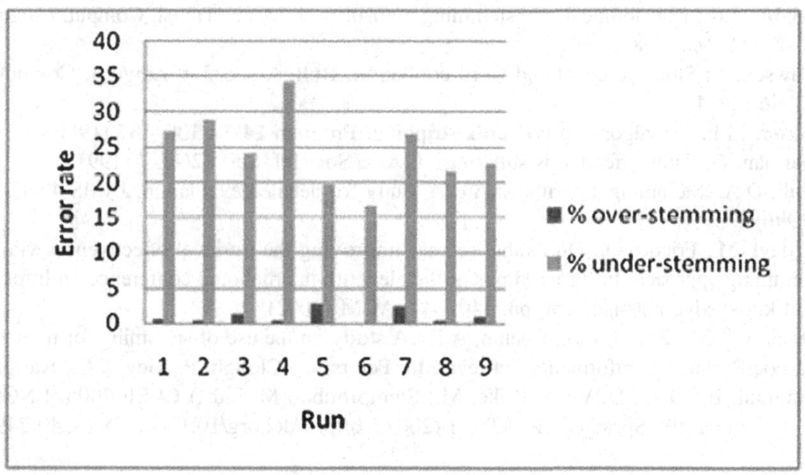

Fig. 2. Stemming errors

From Fig. 2 it is observed that the average number of over-stemming errors are less but many number of under-stemming errors are generated due to the fact that if the inflected word is not available in the dictionary it cannot be stemmed properly.

5 Conclusion

Stemming is one of the important pre-processing steps in several NLP applications. With present work, we intend to construct efficient stemmer for Marathi. The proposed stemmer based on dictionary lookup technique provides the average accuracy of

75.75% when tested in 9 different runs which includes 4500 unique terms extracted from 50 documents of FIRE corpus. With this approach, the terms from the queries and documents are stemmed very fast but the accuracy of this type of stemmers depends upon the size of the dictionary. The over-stemming error rate is low but many under-stemming errors are generated due to the fact that if the word is not present in the dictionary the stemmer is unable to stem it correctly. The major challenge with this technique is the unavailability of standard dictionaries. Manual development of this type of data requires lots of time. In future, the authors plan to develop a hybrid stemmer for the Marathi language by combining this dictionary with existing rule-based stemmer.

Acknowledgments. The authors are very much thankful to the Forum for Information Retrieval Evaluation for providing the Marathi corpus. The work presented in this paper is supported by SAP DRS-II research grant of UGC, New Delhi.

References

1. Lovins, J.B.: Development of a stemming algorithm. J. Mech. Transl. Comput. Linguist. **11** (1–2), 22–31 (1968)
2. Dawson, J.: Suffix removal and word conflation. Bull. Assoc. Lit. Linguist. Comput. **2**(3), 33–46 (1974)
3. Porter, M.F.: An algorithm for suffix stripping. Program **14**(3), 130–137 (1980)
4. Harman, D.: How effective is suffixing? J. Am. Soc. Inf. Sci. **42**(1), 7 (1991)
5. Hull, D.A.: Stemming algorithms: A case study for detailed evaluation. JASIS **47**(1), 70–84 (1996)
6. Aljlayl, M., Frieder O.: On Arabic search: improving the retrieval effectiveness via a light stemming approach. In: Proceedings of the eleventh international conference on Information and knowledge management, pp. 340–347. ACM (2002)
7. Orengo, V.M., Buriol, L.S., Coelho, A.R.: A study on the use of stemming for monolingual ad-hoc Portuguese information retrieval. In: Peters, C., Clough, P., Gey, F.C., Karlgren, J., Magnini, B., Oard, D.W., de Rijke, M., Stempfhuber, M. (eds.) CLEF 2006. LNCS, vol. 4730, pp. 91–98. Springer, Heidelberg (2007). https://doi.org/10.1007/978-3-540-74999-8_12
8. Taghva, K., Beckley, R., Sadeh, M.: A stemming algorithm for the Farsi language. In: International Conference on in Information Technology: Coding and Computing, vol. 1, pp. 158–162 (2005)
9. Kumar, D., Rana, P.: Design and development of a stemmer for Punjabi. Int. J. Comput. Appl. **11**(12), 18–23 (2010)
10. Mishra, U., Prakash, C.: MAULIK: an effective stemmer for Hindi language. Int. J. Comput. Sci. Eng. **4**(5), 711–717 (2012)
11. Joshi, G., Garg, K.D.: Enhanced version of Punjabi stemmer using synset. Int. J. Comput. Sci. Eng. **4**(5), 1060–1065 (2014)
12. Patil, H.B., Pawar, B.V., Patil, A.S.: A comprehensive analysis of stemmers available for Indic languages. Int. J. Nat. Lang. Comput. **05**(1), 45–55 (2016)
13. Almeida, A., Bhattacharyya, P.: Experiments in N-gram based indexing and retrieval in Marathi. FIRE Working Note (2010)

14. Majgaonker, M.M.: Discovering suffixes: a case study for Marathi language. Int. J. Comput. Sci. Eng. **02**(08), 2716–2720 (2010)
15. Patil, H.B., Patil, A.S.: MarS: a rule based stemmer for morphologically rich language Marathi. In: IEEE International Conference on Computer, Communications and Electronics (COMPTELIX 2017), Manipal University Jaipur, 1st-2nd July 2017 (2017)
16. Dolamic, L., Savoy, J.: Comparative study of indexing and search strategies for the Hindi, Marathi and Bengali languages. ACM Trans. Asian Lang. Inf. Process. (TALIP) **9**(3), 11 (2010). Article no. 11
17. Husain, M.S.: An unsupervised approach to develop stemmer. Int. J. Nat. Lang. Comput. (IJNLC) **1**(2), 15–23 (2012)
18. Frakes, W.B., Fox, C.J.: Strength and similarity of affix removal stemming algorithms. ACM SIGIR Forum **37**(01), 26–30 (2003)
19. Paice, C.D.: Method for evaluation of stemming algorithms based on error counting. JASIS **47**(08), 632–649 (1996)

Deep Convolutional Neural Network for Handwritten Tamil Character Recognition Using Principal Component Analysis

M. Sornam(✉) and C. Vishnu Priya

University of Madras, Chepauk, Chennai 600005, Tamil Nadu, India
madasamy.sornam@gmail.com

Abstract. Offline handwritten character recognition is one of the most challenging researches in the field of pattern recognition. This challenge is due to unique writing style for different users. Many techniques were presented for recognition of handwritten English, Bangla, Gurmukhi, Chinese, Devanagari, etc. Due to the complexity of Tamil characters, recognition of Tamil character is a challenging task in the field of machine learning. To overcome this complexity, a new approach called deep learning had entered into the field of machine learning. Convolutional neural network is the special kind of network that comes under deep learning used to work with images. Therefore the main idea behind this research is to develop a novel method by combining principal component analysis (PCA) and convolutional neural network for feature extraction, to recognize the Tamil characters in a superior way.

Keywords: Deep learning · Pattern recognition · Tamil characters
PCA · Convolutional neural network

1 Introduction

Machine learning is a field of computer science which focuses in choosing a network model, which trains a machine in a best manner, so that it performs like a human-being. Besides choosing a network model, feature extraction is the great challenge faced in the traditional neural networks. This brings a great challenge for developer in complex problems like object recognition and handwritten character recognition. Therefore the developer must choose the reliable feature information for the above complex problems such that it helps machine to take effective decision.

Deep learning is a state-of-art in machine learning technique which overcomes this problem and reduces the burden of a programmer. The model used in deep learning is capable of extracting right features by themselves with the little guidance from the programmer. So this idea of deep learning had taken machine learning to a new era. With this advantage it has placed its footprints in various real-time applications namely face book's Deep face, Apple's SIRI, Microsoft Cortana and Google's DeepMind. This made deep learning as an energetic research area where researchers mainly focus in utilizing these models in effective way and progress artificial intelligence to human-level. Deep learning includes various networks namely Convolutional neural networks, Recurrent neural network, Deep belief network, Deep Boltzman, Auto encoders.

P. Bhattacharyya et al. (Eds.): NGCT 2017, CCIS 827, pp. 778–787, 2018.
https://doi.org/10.1007/978-981-10-8657-1_61

Among these networks, convolutional neural network (CNN) is mostly used for classification of images and for pattern recognizing. So the author focuses on convolutional neural networks for handwritten Tamil character recognition. Convolutional neural network architecture consists of convolution layer, pooling layer followed by a fully connected layer (see Fig. 1). In detail the input holds the raw pixel of an image and then it is passed to convolutional layer which applies the specific number of convolution filters to the image. And then the output is passed to an RELU activation function. After that the output is downsampled in pooling layer to reduce the dimensionality of the feature map. Finally the output is passed to fully connected layer for classification.

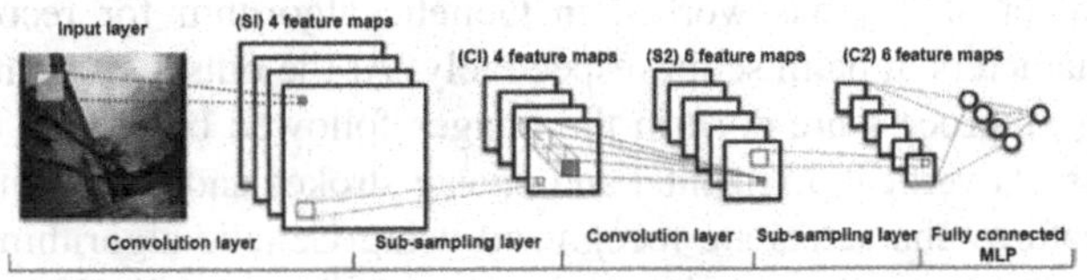

Fig. 1. A sample convolutional neural network.

Handwritten character recognition is one of the most important areas in machine learning. In many situations a pen with a paper is more convenient than a keyboard. But the recognition of this handwritten character is a most difficult task because it varies from person to person and it also varies due to different mood of the same person [10]. But this automation in character recognition would be more useful for blind people to read the texts, for automatic classification of postal letters, cheque, bank notes, license plate detection etc. [4, 5, 14] and for many mobile applications. So this character recognition has created its own marks in the field of pattern recognition. Though many techniques have been emerged for character recognition but still it has its own position in research area.

Tamil language is one of the oldest South Indian languages in the world. Tamil character is written in Tamil Nadu, Sri Lanka and some parts of Malaysia. So Tamil language is most widely spoken language by millions of people. Tamil alphabets have 30 basic characters which includes 12 vowels and 18 consonants. It also has one ayudha ezhuthu and 6 Grantham characters as shown in Fig. 1. The combination of vowels and consonants obtains 216 alphabets. So the total number of characters in Tamil language is 247 except 6 Grantham characters as (see Fig. 2).

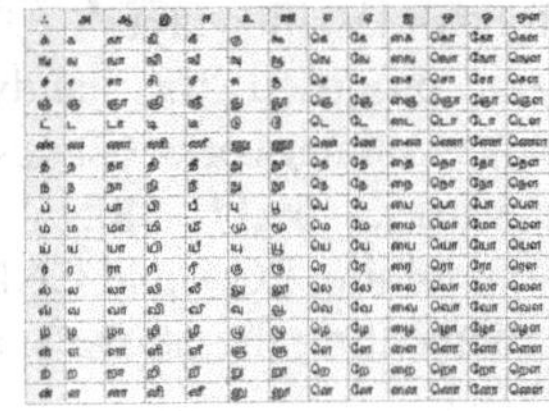

Fig. 2. Tamil characters without Grantham character.

Remaining part of this paper is organized as follows. Existing work of the Tamil characters recognition is discussed in Sect. 2. Section 3 explains the proposed work. Experimental results are discussed in Sect. 4, followed by conclusion and future work in Sect. 5.

2 Existing Methods on Tamil Characters

Siromoney et al. [1] developed a method for machine printed Tamil character recognition. The procedure includes converting each character into binary matrix and the features are extracted by row and column wise scanning. And these features are encoded to recognize the characters.

Vellingiriraj et al. [2] has worked in Genetic algorithm for recognizing Tamil handwritten characters in palm script respectively. At the outset cropping, binarization and thickening preprocess are done in the images followed by feature extraction process which extracts vertical, horizontal and zigzag strokes and loops detection is done. Using these features characters are recognized using Genetic algorithm.

Sundar et al. [8] proposed printed character recognition in Tamil script using Histogram of Oriented Gradients features. These features are classified using back propagation classifier followed by the Fisher linear discriminant analysis (FLDA) classifier to overcome the misclassification done by back propagation classifier.

Aparna et al. [19] recognized Tamil characters in the printed documents. At first the images are skew corrected and segmented into individual characters using horizontal and vertical projections the feature from the each character are extracted and then the images are classified in three levels. At first level it is classified based on height and the second level classifies based on extensions and final level performs recognition based on Euclidian distance and K-Nearest neighbour respectively.

Niu et al. [7] has brought a successful idea in combining CNN and Support vector machine (SVM) classifier for recognizing the MNIST dataset digits. Here the CNN architecture is used to extract the features and these features are classified using SVM with radial basis kernel by replacing the last layer in the CNN with SVM.

Subbuthai et al. [17] has proposed the method for recognizing the digits and English alphabets, by extracting the features using PCA and classifying it by using Euclidean distance.

Vijayaraghavan et al. [20] had proposed CNN architecture for Tamil character recognition using IWFHR-10 dataset. Here the traditional convolutional neural network architecture is improved with spatial pooling and local contrast normalization. The training is done using stochastic gradient descent with an adaptive learning rate and the classification is done using Softmax classifier layer.

Many techniques have been proposed for handwritten character recognition [12, 13, 15]. Using convolutional neural networks Chinese, Arabic, English, Numerical digits are classified in efficient way [3, 6, 11, 18]. Yet now there was no effort in recognizing Tamil character by combining PCA and CNN on this particular dataset. So this paper totally focuses on implementing the above said idea and to get the result in an efficient way.

3 Proposed Work

3.1 Dataset

The dataset contains Tamil characters written by different Tamil native writers which include school children, university graduates, and adults from the cities of Bangalore, Karnataka, India and Salem, Tamil Nadu, India. These data was collected in standard UNIPEN format using HP TabletPCs. It includes both offline and online version. The offline version of the data is in the form of bi-level TIFF images. This dataset were used for the IWFHR 2006 Tamil Character Recognition Competition. Among large number of samples only 47,160 samples [21] were used as an input for the network. Since the images were in different size, they were brought to standard size of 100 × 100 pixels.

3.2 Principal Component Analysis

Principal Component Analysis is a statistical method that simplifies the explanation to input by extracting good feature of it. These features highlight the similarities and differences in the input image which is significant for classifying the images [17]. This also used in dimensionality reduction by ignoring the insignificant features of the image. The most significant features of PCA are the first p eigenvectors of the n eigenvalues and eigenvectors obtained from the covariance matrix of the n dimensional data. Since the p eigenvector of the covariance matrix points to the direction of maximum variance and so on, these p eigenvectors acts as a feature vector of the data.

PCA algorithm:

Let X be a gray scale image with n dimensions.

Step1: The image is flattened as a set of n x 1 vectors as shown in Eq. 1

$$Xi = \begin{bmatrix} x_{i1} \\ x_{i2} \\ x_{i3} \\ \vdots \\ x_{in} \end{bmatrix} \quad for\, i = 1, 2 \ldots n \tag{1}$$

Step 2: The mean of the image is calculated using Eq. 2.

$$X_{avg} = \frac{1}{n} \sum\nolimits_{i=1}^{n} \begin{bmatrix} x_{i1} \\ x_{i2} \\ x_{i3} \\ \vdots \\ x_{in} \end{bmatrix} \tag{2}$$

Step 3: Translate the flattened image *Xi* to column vector and standardize the image by subtracting X_{avg} from x_i. So that it creates a zero mean image using the Eq. 3.

$$X = \left[x_1 - X_{avg}\ x_2 - X_{avg} \ldots x_n - X_{avg}\right] \tag{3}$$

Step 4: The covariance matrix Q is calculated using Eq. 4

$$Q = XX^T = \left[x_1 - X_{avg}\ x_2 - X_{avg} \ldots x_n - X_{avg}\right] \begin{bmatrix} \left(x_1 - X_{avg}\right)^T \\ \left(x_2 - X_{avg}\right)^T \\ \vdots \\ \left(x_n - X_{avg}\right)^T \end{bmatrix} \tag{4}$$

Step 5: Calculate the eigenvalues (λ_1 to λ_m) and eigenvectors (X_1 to X_m) by solving Eq. 5. Eigen vectors are ordered according to the corresponding eigenvalues from high to low.

$$[Q - \lambda I]X = 0 \tag{5}$$

Step 6: Convert the p eigenvectors into matrix and construct the eigenimage using the p eigenvectors.

With the above algorithm, eigen features for Tamil character recognition are extracted from the input image of size 100 × 100. Since the image reconstructed with top 40 eigenvectors has reasonable noise as shown in Table 1, it is used as input for the convolutional neural networks.

Table 1. Eigenvector values and corresponding images.

Images	Eigenvector value
	Original image
	Image formed using top 10 eigenvector
	Image formed using top 20 eigenvector
	Image formed using top 30 eigenvector
	Image formed using top 40 eigenvector

3.3 Feature Extraction and Training

Feature extraction is the greatest problem in handwritten Tamil character recognition. The feature quality is directly proportional to the decision of the computer. The best features will make computer to take accurate decision. So to overcome this complication, feature extraction process is done automatically by the convolutional neural networks [9, 20].

The network uses 37728 samples for training, 9432 samples for validation and 1000 samples for testing respectively. There are totally nine layer which includes two convolutional layer, two maxpooling layer, three fully connected layer and one input and output layer. The PCA features extracted Tamil character image dataset was resized into 40 × 40. The resized images are normalized to [−1, 1] and passed as an input to the stack of different kind of layers in the architecture. The first layer is a convolution layer obtains 20 feature maps of 5 × 5 filters. And then it is passed to RELU activation function. The output from the previous layer is downsampled by MaxPooling with 2 × 2 filters. 32 feature maps are extracted from the next convolution layer with 3 × 3 filters. And the output is downsampled by maxpooling layer using 2 × 2 filters. Atlast the downsampled images are passed to fully connected layers and then the extracted features are classified in the output layer of 8 neurons for 146 classes. The model summary is shown in Table 2.

The model is trained using backpropagation with the learning rate of 0.001 with batch size 5 and the training, validation loss are calculated using categorical crossentropy. The model was trained upto 50 epochs and got maximum validation accuracy of 88.86%.

Table 2. Model summary.

Layer	Type	Input	Filter size	Stride	Num filters	Activation	Output
Layer 1	Conv	40 × 40 × 1	5 × 5	1	20	ReLu	36 × 36 × 20
Layer 2	Pool (max)	36 × 36 × 20	2 × 2	1	–	–	18 × 18 × 20
Layer 3	Conv	18 × 18 × 20	3 × 3	1	32	ReLu	16 × 16 × 32
Layer 4	Pool (max)	16 × 16 × 32	2 × 2	1	–	–	8 × 8 × 32
Layer 5	FC	8 × 8 × 32	–	–	–	Tanh	(None, 2048)
Layer 6	FC	(None, 2048)	–	–	–	Tanh	(None, 146)
Layer 7	FC	(None, 146)	–	–	–	Sigmoid	(None, 146)

4 Experimental Results

The model is trained for 50 epochs and it got converged into 88% approximately in the 27th epoch. The training accuracy curve shows the increase of accuracy for 50 epochs (see Fig. 3). The gradual decrease of training and validation loss is represented using graph (see Fig. 4).

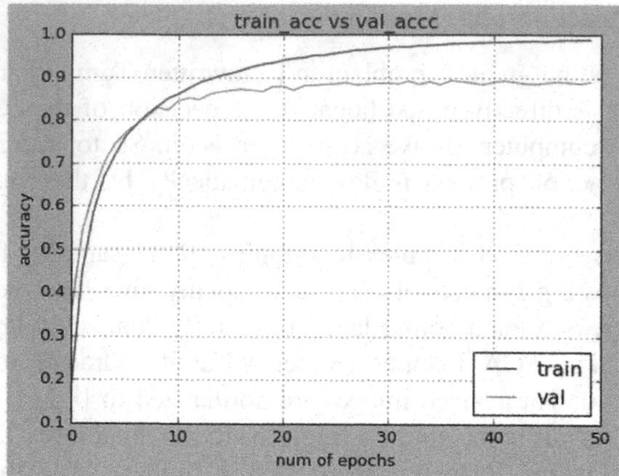

Fig. 3. Training and validation accuracy curve.

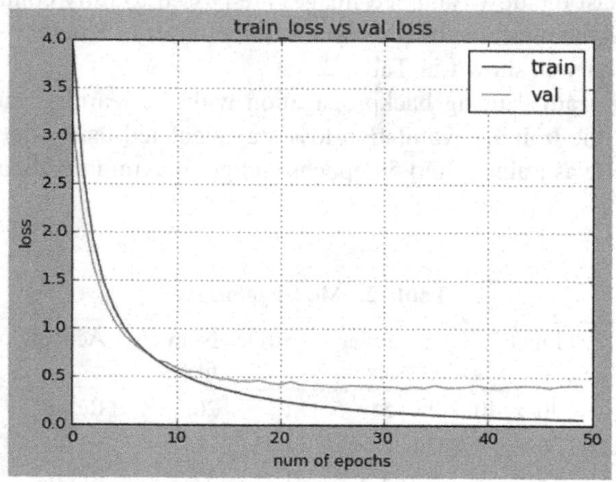

Fig. 4. Training and validation loss curve

	Predicted class		
Actual Class		Class = Yes	Class = No
	Class = Yes	True Positive	False Negative
	Class = No	False Positive	True Negative

Fig. 5. True positive, true negative, false positive, false negative. (Color figure online)

The green colour of true positive and true negative indicates that the value of actual class is equal to the predicted class. Likewise the red colour indicates that the values are not equal (see Fig. 5). Using these true positive, true negative, false positive, false negative the precision, accuracy, recall, F1score values are calculated.

Accuracy: Accuracy is the ratio of correctly predicted observations to the total number of observations.

$$Accuracy = \frac{(TP + TN)}{(TP + FP + FN + TN)}$$

Precision: Precision is the ratio of rightly predicted positive observations to the total predicted positive observations.

$$Precision = \frac{TP}{(TP + FP)}$$

Recall: Recall is ratio of correctly predicted positive observations to all the actual class observations.

$$Recall = \frac{TP}{(TP + FN)}$$

F1 score: Weighted average of precision and recall is F1 score. This score includes both false positive and false negative.

$$F1Score = \frac{(2 * (Recall * Precision))}{(Recall + Precision)}$$

Using these values the performance of the model was calculated and the average results for 146 classes in Table 3 shows that the performance of model with PCA is better than model without PCA.

Table 3. Performance measures

Metrics	Without PCA (%)	With PCA (%)
Accuracy	85.05	88.86
Precision	85	89
Recall	85	89
F1 score	85	89

5 Conclusions and Future Work

We presented a Tamil character recognition system by hybrid combination of PCA and Convolutional neural networks with good performance in the offline IWFHR-10 dataset from the HP Labs website. The classification of dataset was reasonable by this hybrid combination and the performance measures was promising for a system with 2 GB ram and processor Intel(R) Pentium(R) CPU B950 @ 2.10 GHz. So this work can be further extended by recognizing the slogans in the images with the use of GPU.

References

1. Siromoney, G., Chandrasekaran, R., Chandrasekaran, M.: Computer recognition of printed tamil characters. Pattern Recogn. **10**, 243–247 (1978)
2. Vellingiriraj, E.K., Balasubramanie, P.: Recognition of ancient tamil handwritten characters in palm manuscripts using genetic algorithm. IJSET **2**(5), 342–346 (2013)
3. Ciresan, D., Meier, U.: Multi-column deep neural networks for offline hamdwritten chinese character classification, pp. 2161–4407. IEEE (2015)
4. Thadchanamoorthy, S., Kodikara, N.D., Premaretne, H.L., Pal, U., Kimura, F.: Tamil handwritten city name database development and recognition for postal automation. In: IEEE-ICDAR, pp. 793–797 (2013)
5. Feng, B., Ren, M., Zhang, X., Suen, C.: Automatic recognition of serial numbers in bank notes. Sci. J. Pattern Recogn. **47**, 2621–2634 (2014)
6. Ahranjany, S., Razzazi, F., Ghassemian, M.: A very high accuracy handwritten character recognition system for Farsi/Arabic digits using convolutional neural networks, pp. 1585–1592. IEEE (2010)
7. Niu, X., Suen, C.: A novel hybrid CNN-SVM classifier for recognizing handwritten digits. Sci. J. Pattern Recogn. **45**, 1318–1325 (2012)
8. Sundar, K.A., John, M.: A High precision printed character recognition method for tamil script. IEEE (2013)
9. Alwzwazy, H.A., Albehadili, H.M., Alwan, Y.S., Islam, N.E.: Handwritten digit recognition using convolutional neural networks. IJIRCCE **4**(2), 1101–1106 (2016)
10. Sundaram, S., Ramakrishnan, A.G.: An improved online tamil character recognition engine using post-processing methods. In: ICDAR-IEEE, pp. 1216–1220 (2009)
11. George, C., Podhumani, S., Monish, K.R., Pavithra, T.: Survey on handwritten character recognition using artificial neural network. IJETA **10**(2), 287–290 (2016)
12. Kussul, E., Baidyk, T.: Improved method of handwritten digit recognition tested on MNIST database. Sci. J. Image Vis. Comput. **22**, 971–981 (2004)
13. Sornam, M., Vishnupriya, C.: A comparison of deep learning neural networks for image processing applications. IJETA **4**(2), 60–64 (2017)
14. Sornam, M., Kavitha, M.S., Devi, P.: An efficient morlet function based adaptive method for faster backpropagation for handwritten character recognition. In: ICACA-IEEE, pp. 135–139 (2016)
15. Sornam, M., Manimozhi, S.: License plate detection and character recognition system. In: ICCCMIT, pp. 28–31 (2014)
16. Subavathi, S.J., Kathirvalavakumar, T.: Adaptive modified backpropagation algorithm based on differential errors. IJCSEA **1**(5), 21–34 (2011)
17. Subbuthai, P., Periasamy, A., Muruganand, S.: Identifying the character by applying PCA method. IJCA **60**(1), 8–11 (2012)
18. Kannan, R.J., Subramanian, S.: An adaptive approach of tamil character recognition using deep learning with big data-a survey. In: Satapathy, S., Govardhan, A., Raju, K., Mandal, J. (eds.) Emerging ICT for Bridging the Future - Proceedings of the 49th Annual Convention of the Computer Society of India (CSI) Volume 1, vol. 337, pp. 557–567. Springer, Cham (2015). https://doi.org/10.1007/978-3-319-13728-5_63

19. Aparna, K.G., Ramakrishnan, A.G.: A complete tamil optical character recognition system. In: Lopresti, D., Hu, J., Kashi, R. (eds.) DAS 2002. LNCS, vol. 2423, pp. 53–57. Springer, Heidelberg (2002). https://doi.org/10.1007/3-540-45869-7_6
20. Vijayaraghavan, P., Sra, U.: Handwritten tamil recognition using a convolutional neural network. MIT Media Lab. https://web.media.mit.edu/~sra/tamil_cnn.pdf
21. HPLabs isolated handwritten tamil character dataset. http://shiftleft.com/mirrors/www.hpl.hp.com/india/research/penhw-resources/tamil-iso-char.html. Accessed 28 Jan 2010

Neural Machine Translation System for Indic Languages Using Deep Neural Architecture

Parth Shah(✉), Vishvajit Bakarola, and Supriya Pati

Chhotubhai Gopalbhai Patel Institute of Technology, Bardoli, India
parthpunita@yahoo.in, {vishvajit.bakrola,supriya.pati}@utu.ac.in

Abstract. Translating into an Indic language is a challenging task. Indic languages are based on Sanskrit and have rich and diverse grammar. Due to its vast grammar, it requires very large number of complex rules for creating traditional rule based machine translation system. In this work, we have created an Indic machine translation system that utilize recent advancement in the area of machine translation using deep neural architectures. Results presented in this article shows that using neural machine translation we can achieve more natural translation for indic languages such as Hindi that was previously not efficiently possible with rule based or phrase based translation systems.

Keywords: Deep learning · Deep neural network · Indic translation
Machine translation · Natural language processing (NLP)
Hindi neural machine translation

1 Introduction

Humans have several different ways to communicate with each other. Spoken and written languages are among the most preferred communication ways. Amongst various such languages only English is accepted as standard language for communication globally. While online content is dominated by English, only 20% of the world population speaks English. This disconnects the availability and consumption of online contents. In order to bridge this gap of language we need to convert these contents to regional language. This process is also called as translation process. Process of translation is very complex task for which we require complete grammatical knowledge of both source and target language. Another challenge in this process are exceptions that required to handle while translating. Most accurate way to perform translation is to be performed by human expert. However, it is complex and slow process. Human expert may also not be available every time. If we are able to perform this translation tasks by machine we can greatly increase speed of translation. Although efficiency of machine translation system is increased in recent years, translating to and from an Indian language is still a challenging task.

P. Bhattacharyya et al. (Eds.): NGCT 2017, CCIS 827, pp. 788–795, 2018.
https://doi.org/10.1007/978-981-10-8657-1_62

In this paper, we have studied different approaches to perform the task of machine translation (MT) and presented advantages and disadvantages of them. In addition to that, we have implemented sequence to sequence model for neural machine translation for indic languages.

2 Related Work

Machine translation is a technique that is used to translate between pair of human language by use of machine. The language from which we want to translate is called source language and language into which we want to translate is called target language. So we can formally define machine translation as conversion of sequence of source language words into target language words.

First ever work on machine translation began in 1950's in United States of America at IBM research laboratory. At that time researchers had very optimistic approach on Machine Translation task. It was mainly involved with English to Russian translation and vice-a-versa. In 1956, Georgetown University and IBM had successfully demonstrated Machine Translation system with limited set of vocabulary and grammar [1]. This attracted lot of new research projects and huge amount of funding for machine translation projects. But soon it was discovered that scalability was the major problem in machine translation system. Automatic Language Processing Advisory Committee in their report suggested that Machine Translation was not possible and practical in any time soon. Most of research on Machine Translation is halted in US due to this report. Research of Machine Translation came much later into main stream in 1979 from very different approach. It was domain specific translation of weather bulletin from English to French [2]. Due to its limited domain specific nature it had produced very good results. This lead to domain specific machine translation research from other countries like Japan and Europe [3].

Only after 1990's a purely statistical general purpose machine translation research had started. Also these new research projects were aimed for practical purposes instead of just research applications. Huge growth in machine translation research was seen till the end of 90's. At the same time research in indic machine translation had also started in India. IITK and University of Hyderabad had started building system called "Anusaaraka" which was the foundational work on Indic machine translation. After "Anusaaraka" several indic machine translation system were developed for English to Hindi machine translation like NCST, SHIVA - CMU, IISC-B, LTRC IIIT, SHAKTI - LTRC IIIT, etc.

3 Machine Translation

French researcher Vauquois [4] had explained the process of machine translation using simple triangle representation given in Fig. 1. This process contains three parts. First part represent characteristics of source language while last part represent target language. Middle part represents conversion process. So in Fig. 1, first arrow represent analysis of source language sentence which is given as an

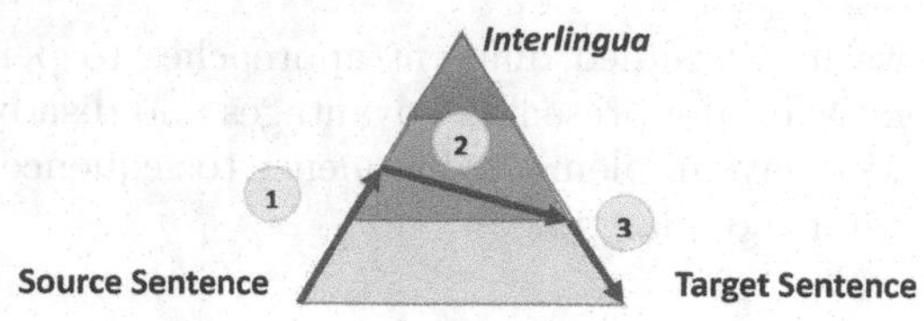

Fig. 1. Architecture of machine translation [4]

input. Once analysis is completed that knowledge is converted into language independent representation also known as Interlingua. Third arrow represents the conversion of interlingua knowledge into target language sentence using preciously known information about target language.

There are many different approaches derived for the task of machine translation. In this paper, we have described three different widely popular machine translation techniques as Rule Based Machine Translation, Phrase Based Machine Translation and Neural Machine Translation.

3.1 Rule-Based Machine Translation

Rule-Based Machine Translation is one of the earliest approach to the task of machine translation. It uses large set of predefined rules that represent language. In this technique different level of analysis is done like Part of Speech (POS) Tagging, Monographical Analysis, Semantic Analysis, Constituent Analysis, Dependency analysis. Indic machine translation system "Sakti" was based on this rule based approach [5].

3.2 Phrase-Based Machine Translation

It is one of the most simple and widely used machine translation method. It is part of the Statistical Machine Translation family. This method does not involve steps like analysis or generation like previous Rule-Based approach. Instead it generates multiple translated sentences for same source sentences and based on some statical parameters it will select best suitable result as an output. This approach is mainly based on three resources. A phrase table which contains phrases of source languages and its translated version with probability of both in source as well as in target language. A re-ordering table which has information like how source sentence should be reordered when it is translated to target sentence. In addition to that it contains language model that predicts the probability of each predicted word given the source language sentences. Indic machine translation system "Shiva" was based on this phrase-based or statistical machine translation system [5].

3.3 Neural Machine Translation

Neural machine translation is significantly different approach compared to previous approaches of machine translation. It leads to remarkable improvements in terms of human evaluation, compared to rule-based or statistical machine translation systems [6]. Process of neural machine translation is mainly divided in two phases. In first phase, process called as Encoder is used. Encoder converts the input source language in sequence of vectors. In the second phase, process called as decoder is used. Decoder decodes this sequence of vector and directly converts into target language sentence as show in Fig. 2. There were several different neural machine translation systems developed in past. Most of them were closed source propriety implementations from industries like Google, Microsoft, Baidu, etc. One of the most widely used model for neural machine translation was sequence to sequence model. It was originally proposed by Ilya Sutskever et al. [7] from Google Research.

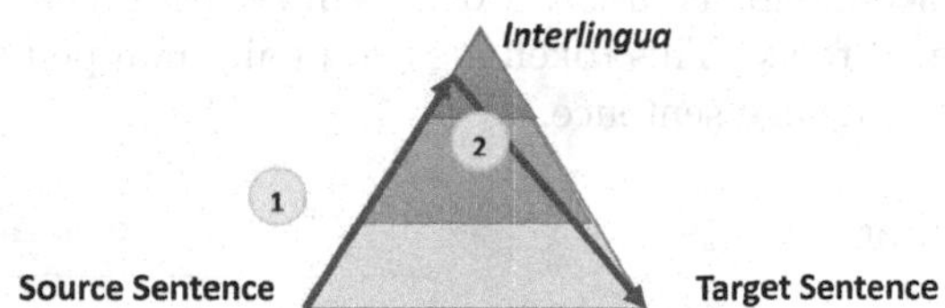

Fig. 2. Architecture of neural machine translation [4]

It uses multi-layered Long Short Term Memory (LSTM) for the purpose of encoding. This encoder takes sequence of words as input and converts into high dimensional word embedding. In order to generate the target language sentences this model utilize beam search method. Which will decode the word embedding into target language sentence. Basic architecture of Sequence to Sequence model is described in Fig. 3.

In addition to standard vocabulary, three additional tokens are added to vocabulary (start symbol, stop symbol and unknown symbol). In order to produce each word in targeted language sentence, full source sentence and generated translated sentence till now will be provided into sequence to sequence model. Based on that it will produce the next translated word. For training this sequence to sequence model, large corpus containing source and target language sentence pair is required. As vocabulary is created during training phase using these sentences it can only output words that are present in training set.

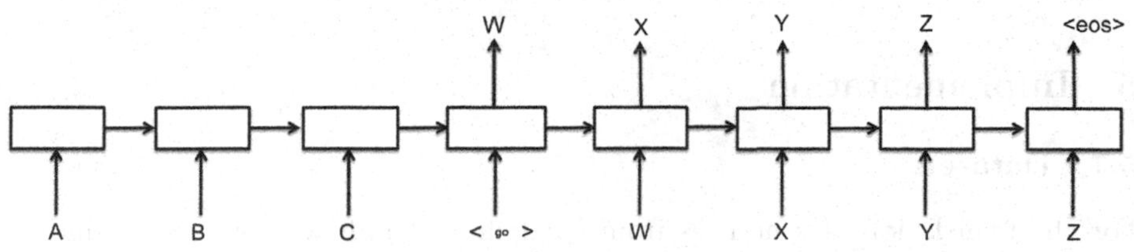

Fig. 3. Architecture of sequence to sequence model [7]

4 Proposed System

Proposed system utilize sequence to sequence model for translating text from source language (in our case of English) to target language (in our case of Hindi). In first step we will tokenize the source and destination language pair using space and special characters as separator. As number of words in each sentence varies from sentence to sentence, we divided sentences into fix sized bucket. If sentence length is less then nearest bucket limit it will add padding of null word to make it of bucket size. We provide these tokenize input and output into sequence to sequence model which internally maps source language and destination language tokens to higher dimensional word embedding vectors as explained in Sect. 3.3. At the time of inferencing we have provided source language sentence into trained sequence to sequence model as input. Model will return token ids corresponding to target language sentence. This token ids are finally mapped to original tokens to generate target language sentence.

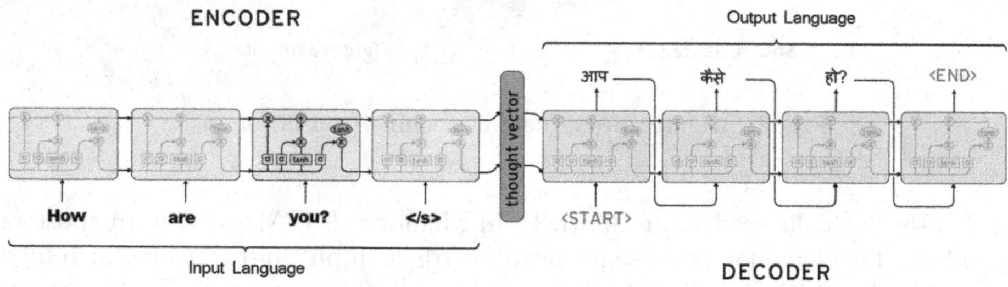

Fig. 4. Working of proposed system using sequence to sequence model

In our case we have taken dataset of English and Hindi sentences where English is source language and Hindi is target language. Each sentence pair of our dataset is tokenized and provided as training data into sequence to sequence model. Sequence to sequence model will map this token pair into word embedding vector. At the time of inferencing, model will automatically map provided input string tokens to target language tokens. By combining these tokens we generate target language sentence. For example "how are you" is tokenized into "how", "are" and "you". When this string is provided as input into sequence to sequence model it will be mapped into "आप ", "केसे ", "हो " as shown in Fig. 4. Some of the generated sentences using this approach is shown in Fig. 5.

5 Implementation

5.1 Datasets

For the translation of sentences from English to Hindi we have used HindEnCorp corpus from Institute of Formal and Applied Linguistics, Charles University, Czech Republic [8]. It is a parallel corpus of around 274k sentences. It was composed of multiple different sources like Tides, Commentaries by Daniel Pipes, EMILLE, The Indic multi-parallel corpus, Launchpad.net, TED talks, Intercorp and other small datasets. It was also used as standard benchmark dataset for WMT translation challenge. Original dataset is converted from single XML format containing both English and Hindi sentences into multiple plain text files in different languages that are mapped line by line.

5.2 Implementation Tool and Experiment Setup

For the implementation of this experiment we have used machine with Intel Xeon E3 processor with 12 cores and 32 GB RAM running CentOS 7. TensorFlow library is used for creating and training deep neural networks. TensorFlow is a deep learning library developed by Google [9]. It provides heterogeneous platform for execution of algorithms so that it can be run on low power devices like mobile as well as large scale distributed system containing thousands of GPUs. In order to define structure of our neural network, TensorFlow uses graph definition. Once graph is defined it can be executed on any supported devices.

6 Results and Discussion

6.1 Results

For the task of neural machine translation we have implemented sequence to sequence model for English to Hindi translation. The specific version of sequence

```
t compiled to use AVX instructions, but these
could speed up CPU computations.
Reading model parameters from /cgpit/enhi/trar
> Can you imagine saying that?
क्या आप ये कल्पना कर सकते है
> What's going on?
" क्या हो रहा है ?
> That is the final lesson of the story .
यह इस कहानी का अंतिम सबक है .
> Not only that,
और वही नहीं ,
> People get new clothes stitched.
लोग नए-नए वस्त्र पहनते हैं।
> Show all topics
सारे टॉपिक दिखायें ( w )
> I am talking
मैं बात कर रहा हैं
> He is talking
वह बात कर रहा है
> Where am I?
मैं कहाँ हैं ?
> it was an elite concept.
यह एक विशिष्ट अवधारणा थी .
> History of Rajasthan
राजस्थान का इतिहास
> At least she got it close.
कम से कम वह इसके करीब है।
> It could benefit
इसे फायदा हो सकता है
> The chest should be broad and deep .
छाती चौडी और गहरी होनी चाहिए .
> If ture, I am here .
translate : python
```

Fig. 5. Result of sequence to sequence model for English to Hindi translation

to sequence model used for our English to Hindi translation uses 3 layers of LSTM cells and each layer consist of 1024 LSTM cells.

As seen in Fig. 5, our model produces comparable result with human translator in most of the cases.

6.2 Evaluation Matrices

In order to measure the performance of proposed Indic Machine Translation system using Sequence to Sequence architecture, we have used Perplexity as performance measure. It is considered as standard evaluation matrix by NIST [10]. Perplexity is defined as the inverse probability of the test set, normalized by the number of words:

$$PP_T(PM) = \frac{1}{\left(\prod_{i=1}^{t} PM\left(w_i \mid w_1 \cdots w_{i-1}\right)\right)^{\frac{1}{2}}} \tag{1}$$

In Eq. 1, $PP(PM)$ represent the perplexity of a language model $PM(next\ word\ w \mid history\ h)$.

```
global step 100000 learning rate 0.1964 step-time 6.13 perplexity 1.13
  eval: bucket 0 perplexity 1.11
  eval: bucket 1 perplexity 1.06
  eval: bucket 2 perplexity 1.09
  eval: bucket 3 perplexity 1.42
```

Fig. 6. Perplexity of sequence to sequence model for English to Hindi translation

For our model we get perplexity of average 1.13 on our test dataset after training of 100000 epoch as shown in Fig. 6.

7 Conclusion

Traditional machine translation methods like rule based or phrase based MT are unable to provide human like fluent or natural translation for Indic languages due to their vast grammar. Solution for this problem can be achieved by applying deep neural architectures for machine translation. Sequence to sequence model will prototype the behaviour of source as well as target languages using concept of word-embedding technique, which results in better accuracy in machine translation for Indic languages.

Acknowledgments. We would like to thank Department of Computer Engineering, C. G. Patel Institute of Technology for providing us computer resources as and when needed for training and implementing models presented in this paper.

References

1. Sheridan, P.: Research in language translation on the IBM type 701. IBM Tech. Newslett. **9**, 5–24 (1955)
2. Lawson, V. (ed.): Practical Experience of Machine Translation. North-Holland Publishing Company, Amsterdam (1982)
3. Durand, J., Bennett, P., Allegranza, V., van Eynde, F., Humphreys, L., Schmidt, P., Steiner, E.: The Eurotra linguistic specifications: an overview. Mach. Transl. **6**(2), 103–147 (1991). https://doi.org/10.1007/BF00417680
4. Vauquois, B.: A survey of formal grammars and algorithms for recognition and transformation in mechanical translation. In: IFIP Congress (2), pp. 1114–1122 (1968). http://dblp.uni-trier.de/db/conf/ifip/ifip1968-2.html
5. Naskar, S., Bandyopadhyay, S.: Use of machine translation in India: current status. In: Proceedings of MT SUMMIT X, Phuket, Thailand, pp. 13–15 (2005)
6. Wu, Y., Schuster, M., Chen, Z., Le, Q.V., Norouzi, M., Macherey, W., Krikun, M., Cao, Y., Gao, Q., Macherey, K., Klingner, J., Shah, A., Johnson, M., Liu, X., Kaiser, L., Gouws, S., Kato, Y., Kudo, T., Kazawa, H., Stevens, K., Kurian, G., Patil, N., Wang, W., Young, C., Smith, J., Riesa, J., Rudnick, A., Vinyals, O., Corrado, G., Hughes, M., Dean, J.: Google's neural machine translation system: bridging the gap between human and machine translation. CoRR abs/1609.08144 (2016). http://arxiv.org/abs/1609.08144
7. Sutskever, I., Vinyals, O., Le, Q.V.: Sequence to sequence learning with neural networks. In: Ghahramani, Z., Welling, M., Cortes, C., Lawrence, N.D., Weinberger, K.Q. (eds.) Advances in Neural Information Processing Systems, vol. 27, pp. 3104–3112. Curran Associates, Inc. (2014). http://papers.nips.cc/paper/5346-sequence-to-sequence-learning-with-neural-networks.pdf
8. Bojar, O., Diatka, V., Rychlý, P., Straňák, P., Suchomel, V., Tamchyna, A., Zeman, D.: HindEnCorp-Hindi-English and Hindi-only corpus for machine translation. In: Chair, N.C.C., Choukri, K., Declerck, T., Loftsson, H., Maegaard, B., Mariani, J., Moreno, A., Odijk, J., Piperidis, S. (eds.) Proceedings of the Ninth International Conference on Language Resources and Evaluation (LREC 2014). European Language Resources Association (ELRA), Reykjavik (2014)
9. Abadi, M., Agarwal, A., Barham, P., Brevdo, E., Chen, Z., Citro, C., Corrado, G.S., Davis, A., Dean, J., Devin, M., et al.: TensorFlow: large-scale machine learning on heterogeneous distributed systems. arXiv preprint (2016). arXiv:1603.04467
10. Chen, S., Beeferman, D., Rosenfeld, R.: Evaluation metrics for language models. In: DARPA Broadcast News Transcription and Understanding Workshop, pp. 275–280 (1998)

Author Index

Abbas, S. Q. II-956
Acharya, Bibhudendra II-396
Aderemi, Oluwaseun I-641
Agarwal, Neha I-664
Agarwal, Rashmi I-246
Ahmad, Manzoor II-577
Ahuja, Laxmi I-199
Ahuja, Ravin I-641
Ainapure, Bharati S. II-361
Ananthi, M. I-623
Anoop, V. S. I-526
Anuradha, B. I-675
Anusha, B. I-504
Arabi, Punal M. I-363, II-835, II-887
Asharaf, S. I-526
Atayero, Aderemi A. I-653

Baby Chellam, Manjith II-381
Bachute, Mrinal I-590
Badejo, Joke A. I-653
Baggam, Durga Shankar II-488
Bagirathi, S. II-513
Bajaj, Varun Sunil I-697
Bajaj, Vikram Sunil I-697
Bajoria, Vinayak II-168
Bajpai, Abhishek II-371
Bakarola, Vishvajit I-788
Balasubramanian, Yagnesh II-488
Banerjee, Ayushi II-396
Bangroo, Rashika I-75
Bansal, Rakesh Kumar II-278
Bansal, Savina II-278
Basharat, Shifaa II-577
Bhagat, Amit II-246, II-263
Bharti, Jyoti II-752
Bhat, Nagaraj II-677
Bhat, Tejaswi II-835
Bhatt, Ashutosh I-66, I-190
Bhattacharjee, Debotosh II-704
Bhattacharya, Paritosh I-558
Bhattacharya, Sudeepto I-97
Bhattacharya, Ujjwal II-870
Bhavsar, Moxanki A. II-771
Bhingarkar, Sukhada II-440
Bhowmik, Tanmay I-750
Bhutiani, Rakesh I-190
Bisht, Anil Kumar I-190
Biswas, K. K. II-908
Borah, Parashjyoti I-474
Botre, B. A. I-418, I-430

Chakraborty, Rupak II-761
Chandak, Rishabh I-3
Chandra, Prakash II-419
Chaudhary, Kamika I-459
Chauhan, Aarti II-25
Chauhan, Rahul I-88
Chaurasiya, Sandip K. II-138
Chhabra, Bharti I-47
Chinnabhandar, Varini II-835
Chithra, P. L. II-918
Choudhary, Ravi Raj II-824
Choudhary, Sachi II-238
Choudhury, Amitava I-750
Chowdhury, Sanjoy II-870
Christalin Nelson, S. II-198
Chugh, Mitali I-310

Damahe, Lalit B. II-612, II-628
Das Mandal, Shyamal Kumar I-750
Das, Santos Kumar I-444
De, P. K. I-617
Deb, Suman I-558
Debnath, Mitali I-617
Deepika Malar, N. II-805
Desai, Mitali I-122
Devalla, Vindhya II-238
Dhakad, Saurav II-752
Dhanoriya, Sachin II-246
Dhar, Probir Kumar I-390
Dhingra, Sunita I-110
Dhiviya Rose, J. II-198
Dobre, Octavia A. II-99
Dubey, Sipi II-733, II-790

Eranna, U. II-677
Eswaran, M. II-805

Ganesan, P. II-854
Gangrade, Jayesh II-752
Garg, M. L. II-761
Geetha, R. II-601
Geetha, S. II-601
Gehlot, Anita II-419
Ghosh, Mridul II-704
Goel, Diksha II-502
Goswami, Rajat Subhra I-568
Gour, Abhisek II-640
Gowrishankar II-146
Gupta, Ashish I-263
Gupta, Deepak I-474
Gupta, Neena I-459
Gupta, Priya I-3
Gupta, Sumit I-549
Gupta, Vishal I-535

Harigovindan, V. P. II-227
Hemalatha, R. J. II-862
Hemanth Kumar, G. II-899
Husain, Arshad II-692
Hussain, S. Mahaboob I-549

Jain, Ankit Kumar II-502
Jain, S. C. I-418, I-430
Jain, Simpal I-723
Jain, Subhi I-88
Jain, Sweta II-70
Jaiswal, Saurabh I-664
Jayasheela, C. S. II-146
Jeya Mala, D. II-805
Joshi, Amit M. II-944
Joshi, Gayatri II-835
Joshi, Maulin II-771

Kalaichelvi, P. I-488
Kalist, V. II-854
Kamilla, Sushanta Kumar I-349
Kanakam, Prathyusha I-549
Katal, Avita II-168
Kathuria, Kriti I-3
Kathuria, Mamta I-19
Katiyar, Shivangi II-305
Kaur, Amanpreet I-30
Kaur, Bikrampal I-30
Kaur, Damanjeet I-376
Kaur, Jaspreet II-944
Kaur, Jasvir II-722
Kaushik, Praveen II-459
Khan, Jeeshan Ahmad I-664
Khan, Minhaj I-664
Kharadkar, R. D. I-590
Khulbe, Manisha II-88
Kiran, Kappala Vinod I-444
Kokila, J. II-381, II-430
Kolhe, Satish R. I-405
Komalan, Nitya II-25
Krishna, Nanditha II-899
Kumar, Abhishek II-40
Kumar, G. Bharadwaja I-736
Kumar, Hareesh II-291
Kumar, Krishan II-469
Kumar, Manoj I-75, II-663
Kumar, Neetesh I-75
Kumar, Rajendra II-543
Kumar, Rajesh II-651
Kumar, S. Phani I-286
Kumar, Santosh I-459
Kumar, Sumit II-138
Kumar, Vikram I-444
Kumar, Vinod II-543
Kumari, Meena II-526

Leo Joseph, L. M. I. II-854
Li, Cheng II-99

Mahesh, Miriyala II-227
Majumder, Durjoy I-390
Mali, Bimrisha I-761
Malyala, Lakshmi Prasanthi I-605
Manjith, B. C. II-430
Mathur, Aradhya Neeraj I-3
Meena, Gaurav II-824
Meghanathan, Natarajan I-176
Mehta, Mayuri A. I-122
Mhaske, Neelima T. I-769
Mishra, Atul II-347
Mishra, Nidhi I-723
Mishra, Piyush I-139
Misra, Sanjay I-641, I-653
Mittal, Mamta II-419
Mittal, Namita II-651
Mittal, Parul I-139
Mohapatra, Srikanta Kumar I-349
Mohapatra, Susanta Kumar I-349
Mohideen Sameer, P. M. I-323
Mondal, Amit Kumar II-238

Mourya, Diwaker I-66
Mukherjee, Parthasarathi II-870
Munjani, Jayesh H. II-771
Murali Das, Arjun II-381

Nagar, Shyam Krishna I-334
Nagra, Baljeet Kaur I-47
Narain Ponraj, D. II-932
Narendrababu Reddy, G. I-286
Narwal, Abhikriti I-110
Naskar, Tarun Kanti I-390
Natarajan, Ramasubramanian II-430
Nath, Rajender II-526
Naveen, T. S. I-363
Nayyar, Anand II-3
Negi, Sarita II-124
Negi, Surbhi I-88
Nigam, Shivangi II-371
Nigudgi, Surekha II-887
Nirmala, Y. N. II-291
Nitin I-310

Oluwaranti, Adeniran I. I-653

Padhy, Jagana Bihari II-155
Paik, Subhendu Sekhar I-568
Pancholi, Sidharth II-944
Pandey, Manish II-246, II-263
Pandey, Rubi I-376
Pandey, S. K. II-543
Panwar, Neelam II-124
Parthasarathy, Harish II-88
Patel, Arushi II-183
Patel, Vivek I-139
Pati, Supriya I-788
Patil, Ajay S. I-769
Patil, Harshali B. I-769
Patnaik, Bijayananda II-155
Patni, J. C. I-139
Patro, K. Abhimanyu Kumar II-396
Patvardhan, C. I-580
Paul, A. C. I-617
Popoola, Oluwafunso A. I-653
Popoola, Segun I. I-653
Porwal, Shailesh I-418, I-430
Prajith, R. II-844
Prakash, Chandra II-651
Prakash, V. Prem I-580
Prasad, Devendra II-305
Prashanthi, B. II-918
Prathiba, B. I-687
Prathibha, T. P. II-887

Radhakrishnan, T. K. I-488
Raj, Shaji N. II-335
Rajawat, Ankita I-228
Rajendran, P. Selvi II-112
Rajendran, Vaibhavi I-736
Ramasubramanian, N. II-381
Ramaswamy, V. II-488
Ramesh, Dharavath II-450
Rao, A. Ananda II-361
Rao, Nandam Sambasiva I-605
Rauthan, Man Mohan Singh II-124
Reddy, K. Hemant I-568
Revathi, S. II-536
Roy, D. S. I-568
Roy, Somnath I-761

Sabena, S. I-504
Sabrol, Hiteshwari II-790
Sahla Habeeba, M. A. II-844
Sahoo, Sarat Kumar II-56
Saini, Bhawana II-40
Sairamesh, L. I-504
Sairamya, N. J. II-932
Samanta, Deepak I-363
Samkaria, Rohit II-419
Sandhya II-513
Sangal, Satyam I-3
Sankar, K. Jaya I-687
Sankar, Sharmila II-513
Sankaranarayanan, Suresh II-212
Santosh, Thakur II-450
Sarin, Sachin Kumar II-183
Sarkar, Bikash Kanti I-263
Sathish, B. S. II-854
Sehgal, Priti II-555
Sen, Supriya II-183
Shafique, Muhammad Nouman I-162
Shah, Deven II-361, II-440
Shah, Parth I-788
Shailaja, K. I-675
Shanu, Saurabh I-97
Sharma, Harish I-228, I-246
Sharma, Mugdha I-199
Sharma, Nirmala I-228, I-246
Sharma, Rashmi II-238

Sharma, Reya I-75
Sharma, Ruchi D. II-628
Sharma, Savita II-824
Sharma, Sukhwinder II-278
Shelly I-19
Shendre, Akshata V. II-612
Sherly, Elizabeth II-335
Simon, Philomina II-844
Singh, Aditya I-535
Singh, Devendra II-419
Singh, Dheerendra I-30
Singh, Gurvinder I-709
Singh, Harvinder II-183
Singh, Jaspreet I-709
Singh, Kh. Manglem II-663
Singh, Manisha I-298
Singh, Manoj Kumar II-677
Singh, Prerna II-555
Singh, Prithvipal I-709
Singh, Rajesh II-419
Singh, Rajeshwar II-3
Singh, Rajinder I-709
Singh, Ravendra I-190
Singh, Sanjay Kumar II-956
Singh, Shrish Kumar II-323
Singh, Thipendra Pal I-298
Smithamol, M. B. I-211
Soman, Divya P. I-488
Somani, Antriksha II-752
Sonawane, Sudarshan S. I-405
Sornam, M. I-778
Sreerangaraju, M. N. II-291
Sridhar, Rajeswari I-211
Srivastav, Anand I-580
Srivastava, Awadhesh Kumar II-908
Srivastava, Meenakshi II-956
Subathra, M. S. P. II-932
Sumalatha, M. R. I-623
Sumalatha, V. I-687
Suryanarayana, D. I-549
Sushil, Rama II-761
Suvitha, D. I-323
Swarnkar, Tripti I-349

Takhar, Gourav II-651
Tarar, Sandhya II-323
Tayde, Varsha Dipak II-459
Teja Santosh, D. I-697
Tembhurne, Jitendra V. I-276
Thakur, Nileshsingh V. II-612, II-628
Thomas George, S. II-932
Tom, Rijo Jackson II-212
Tomar, Anurag Singh II-138
Tripathy, Malay Ranjan II-88
Turuk, Ashok Kumar I-444

Vaishya, R. C. II-692
Vamsha Deepa, N. I-363, II-899
Vats, Isha II-722
Venkatesan, Ramachandran II-99
Venkatraman, Swaminathan II-488
Verma, Amit I-47, II-722
Verma, Arunima I-148
Verma, Santosh Kumar I-334
Verma, Toran II-733, II-790
Vijay, Mahak I-418, I-430
Vijayabaskar, V. II-862
Vijayalakshmi, M. I-323
Vikram, K. II-56
Vishnu Priya, C. I-778
Vishwakarma, Lalit Kumar II-263

Walia, Savita II-469
Wani, Azka II-536

Yadav, Deepti I-148
Yadav, Pavan II-70

Zaidi, Subiya II-323
Zhang, Yi II-99

Printed in the United States
By Bookmasters